THE
ENCYCLOPEDIA
OF
PROTESTANTISM

THE ENCYCLOPEDIA

OF

PROTESTANTISM

VOLUME 2
D–K

HANS J. HILLERBRAND

EDITOR

Routledge
New York   London

Published in 2004 by

Routledge
29 West 35th Street
New York, NY 10001-2299
www.routledge-ny.com

Published in Great Britain by
Routledge
11 New Fetter Lane
London EC4P 4EE
www.routledge.co.uk

Routledge is an imprint of Taylor & Francis Books, Inc.

10   9   8   7   6   5   4   3   2   1

Printed on acid-free, 250-year-life paper
Manufactured in the United States of America

Library of Congress Cataloging-in-Publication Data

Encyclopedia of Protestantism / Hans J. Hillerbrand, editor.
    p. cm.
Includes bibliographical references and index.
    ISBN 0-415-92472-3 (set)
    1. Protestantism—Encyclopedias. I. Hillerbrand, Hans Joachim.
BX4811.3.E53 2003
280′.4′03—dc21

2003011582

Contents

DALE, ROBERT WILLIAM (1829–1895)

English Congregationalist. Dale, born December 1, 1829, was a minister and theologian and was also known as a leader of social Christianity in ENGLAND. A pastor at Carr's Lane Chapel in Birmingham (1853–1895) he was an early advocate of bringing the KINGDOM OF GOD on earth through individual Christians doing the will of God. From the 1860s on he served on local civic committees, the city council, and school board. Dale died March 13, 1895.

A "gospel of civic betterment," formulated with his copastor John Angell James, remained central to his later argument that the obligation of Christians to participate in civic and political life was a law of Christ. His approach to social problems like the sacredness of property and relations between employers and employees was grounded in an incarnational theology.

Dale expected the new EVANGELICALISM to lead to a new Christian theory of the social and political organization of the state. Distancing himself from an absolute separation of CHURCH AND STATE, he urged Christians to participate in local politics and social reform. This moved him closer to a historic Reformed position on church and state at a time when most English evangelicals avoided all political and state matters.

Dale was in polemic against both the older Calvinist ORTHODOXY and the new liberalism. His views on original sin and ATONEMENT led to HERESY charges. Yet the earnest, practical Christian morality of his theology and PREACHING was deeply admired by Congregationalists in England and the UNITED STATES. He was the LYMAN BEECHER lecturer in preaching at Yale in 1877– 1878 and was elected president of the first International Congregational Council in 1891. Most of his eighteen books were collections of sermons and public lectures.

See also Calvinism; Congregationalism; Liberal Protestantism & Liberalism; Socialism, Christian; Social Gospel

References and Further Reading

Dale, R. W. *Laws of Christ For Common Life.* 2nd edition. London: Hodder and Stoughton, 1899.

JANET F. FISHBURN

DARBY, JOHN NELSON (1800–1882)

English church leader. John Nelson Darby is the most prominent of the early leaders of the PLYMOUTH BRETHREN denomination, and its most prolific writer. He is generally credited with being the father of dispensational premillennialism (see DISPENSATIONALISM; MILLENARIANS AND MILLENNIALISM). His extensive travels throughout Western Europe, the West Indies, NEW ZEALAND, and North America helped spread his theological influence throughout the fundamentalist and evangelical traditions of Protestant Christianity.

Life and Ministry

Darby was born in London on November 18, 1800 into a prominent Irish family. His father was a well-to-do landowner and merchant. Darby's uncle, Admiral Sir Henry Darby, was a friend of Admiral Lord Horatio Nelson, the young Darby's sponsor and namesake. His mother seems to have been estranged from the family when Darby was young, an absence which he felt strongly.

Darby was educated at Trinity College in Dublin, IRELAND, from which he graduated with a B.A. as a Gold Medalist in 1819. He then began the study of law and was called to the Irish Bar in 1822, although he seems to have practiced only for a short time. He was ordained by Archbishop Magee as a deacon in the Church of Ireland, which had been united with the CHURCH OF ENGLAND by the Act of Union (1801), on August 7, 1825. He was ordained as a priest on February 19, 1826. He was appointed to a poor parish in County Wicklow. Throughout his life, Darby taught and modeled CHARITY for the poor and had little tolerance for those who placed too much emphasis on material possessions and social position. In his parish ministry, Darby was particularly noted for his CONVERSION of Roman Catholics to Protestantism.

A turning point in Darby's life occurred in late 1826. He was injured in a riding accident and returned to Dublin for several months of convalescence. This period of reflection and BIBLE study seems to have crystallized some of his convictions and laid the foundation for his theological system. When he returned to his parish, he learned that Archbishop Magee was requiring all new converts to take an oath of allegiance to the crown. In protest of what he perceived to be Erastianism and clericalism, Darby resigned from his parish and left the established church.

By the late 1820s, Darby was meeting with a group of like-minded believers in Dublin, the beginning of the Brethren movement. Due to the prominence of the assembly at Plymouth, ENGLAND, this fellowship of churches is commonly designated as the "Plymouth Brethren." Although not the founder of this movement, John Nelson Darby quickly became its most effective and important leader.

Beginning in the 1850s, Darby made at least six trips to the UNITED STATES and CANADA. He founded several Brethren assemblies and taught his dispensational interpretation of Scripture. A lifelong bachelor, Darby remained active in ministry until his death on April 29, 1882.

Darby's Theological Influence

At the center of Darby's THEOLOGY was his conviction that the Scriptures, interpreted literally, must have supreme AUTHORITY, not the CHURCH. He had a lifelong suspicion of ecclesiastical hierarchy. Second, Darby's view of spirituality was individualistic and personal, focusing on the believer's position in Christ. Third, Darby perceived that the CHURCH in the New Testament era was pure and unadulterated, and that the institutional church of his day was apostate. In his view, the established church was in ruins and was likely beyond reform. This led to a strict separatism in belief and practice. Finally, Darby's literal hermeneutic resulted in the expectation that biblical prophecy will be fulfilled literally. One result of this hermeneutic was that Darby saw a clear distinction between Israel and the church, a strict dichotomy between two peoples of God. Thus prophecies related to Israel, an earthly/material/this-worldly people, must be fulfilled literally on this earth. Prophecies to the church, a Gentile/heavenly/spiritual/other-worldly people, cannot be fulfilled on this earth. This separation of the two peoples of God is an eternal one. Israel's destiny is the earth while the church's is heaven.

The Brethren had a futurist premillennial ESCHATOLOGY, believing that the Apocalypse should be interpreted as prophecy, describing unfulfilled future events. They expected the return of Christ at any time, to be followed by the establishment of an earthly 1,000-year kingdom. Darby's major innovation is the DOCTRINE of the secret RAPTURE of the church. This teaching divides the second coming of Christ into two stages. In the first stage, Christ will come to earth before a seven-year period of tribulation (cf. Daniel 9:26–27) to take believers to be with him. Then, after the tribulation, Christ will come in judgment of his enemies and establish the millennium. Darby was not the first to hold this view, although the direct influence of others on his view of the rapture is difficult to ascertain. The rapture position seems to be consistent with Darby's theological development. His view of the apostate church ("the church in ruins") led to his eschatology (a pessimistic form of premillennialism), and his view of "two peoples of God" seemed to require the removal of the spiritual/heavenly people for God to judge and then to bless the material/earthly people, Israel. But Darby would also point to 1 Thessalonians 4:13–18 for scriptural support of the rapture.

With the publication of the SCOFIELD REFERENCE BIBLE (1909) and the growth of the Bible Conference Movement, Darby's dispensationalism spread widely among American fundamentalist and evangelical Protestants. Nonetheless, Darby remains largely unknown and his works unstudied outside of Plymouth Brethren circles.

See also Apocalypticism; Evangelicalism; Fundamentalism

References and Further Reading

Primary Sources:

Darby, John Nelson. *The Collected Writings of John Nelson Darby.* Edited by William Kelly. 34 vols. Reprint, Sunbury, PA: Believers Bookshelf, 1971.
———. *Letters of John Nelson Darby.* 3 vols. Reprint, Sunbury, PA: Believers Bookshelf, 1971.
———. *Synopsis of the Books of the Bible.* 5 vols. Reprint, Sunbury, PA: Believers Bookshelf, 1992.

Secondary Sources:

Crutchfield, Larry V. *The Origins of Dispensationalism: The Darby Factor*. Lanham, MD: University Press of America, 1992.

Kelly, William. *John Nelson Darby As I Knew Him*. Belfast: Words of Truth, 1986.

Turner, W. G. *John Nelson Darby: A Biography*. London: C. A. Hammond, 1926.

Weremchuk, Max S. *John Nelson Darby*. Neptune, NJ: Loizeaux Brothers, 1992.

DALLAS KREIDER

DARWINISM

This term is commonly identified with theories of biological evolution, and in particular the theory that organic life evolved from earlier forms through a process of natural selection. Darwin's discovery of this evolutionary mechanism was based on a vast body of observations and inspired by the insights of such thinkers as Charles Lyell, Thomas Malthus, and WILLIAM PALEY. While there continue to be scientific debates and discussions about the exact mechanisms and pathways of evolution, Darwin's theory of natural selection has become the central theoretical model for the study of life, uniting fields as diverse as biogeography, ecology, paleontology, animal behavior, physiology, and neuroscience. Darwinism implies that the designs of all organisms are the result of contingent, natural processes. This apparently conflicts with traditional Christian views of the relationship between God and the creation, and of the place of humans in it. Since 1859 there have been diverse Protestant responses to Darwinism. This broad spectrum of responses reflects diverging schools of Protestant theology, changes in popular impressions of Darwinism and evolution, and different political uses of science in particular contexts. This article describes the discovery and evolution of Darwinism, gives a brief history of some Protestant reactions, and examines in more detail two issues that remain controversial: the status of humans and the place of the argument from design.

The Genesis of Darwin's Theory

Charles Darwin (1809–1882) had an early love of natural history that he pursued in university to the detriment of his official studies (first, medicine at Edinburgh; later, classics at Cambridge). However, Darwin's extracurricular immersion in natural history rapidly paid dividends. He published an article on invertebrate marine biology under the guidance of a professor who embraced the evolutionary theories of French biologist Jean Baptiste Lamarck; he went on botanical and geological expeditions with the clerical science professors at Cambridge; and he read William Paley's *Natural Theology* (1802) with great enthusiasm and attention. By the time Darwin earned his B.A. at Cambridge, he considered himself well qualified to settle down as an Anglican parson naturalist in a country parish, despite some religious doubts about being ordained.

It was at this point that Darwin was offered an unpaid position as a naturalist on a naval vessel, the HMS Beagle, which would be mapping the South American coast and continuing on around the world. With the encouragement of his Cambridge professors and the grudging consent (and financial support) of his father, Darwin began his voyage of discovery in 1831. His collections and studies were wide ranging, and his letters to his professors were read to scientific societies and published in their journals. During the voyage he read Charles Lyell's *Principles of Geology* (1831–1835), a work that sought to explain vast geological changes in terms of the gradual, uniform action of normal geological processes. Darwin's theory of coral reef formation used Lyell's gradualist approach; as islands subsided corals grew upwards, eventually accumulating as circular reefs surrounding a central lagoon. The idea that small natural changes can be accumulated over vast stretches of time to create significant effects would later be applied to another mystery on which Darwin started to reflect during the voyage: What was the origin of species, and how did they come to exist where they did?

On his return in 1836, Darwin settled in London and began a series of remarkable notebooks addressing these questions. Although he was familiar with Lamarck's view that organisms inherited characteristics that their parents acquired, he felt that this theory failed to explain the origin of adaptations in NATURE. The manifold adaptations of biological structure to function had been used by Paley (and many others) to argue for the existence of a benevolent Creator. The challenge for an evolutionary theory was to explain how such a design might have arisen naturally. Darwin knew that all organisms varied somewhat from their parents, and that their progeny could inherit such variations. However, he found a key insight in Thomas Malthus's *Essay on the Principle of Population* (1798). Malthus had argued that humans reproduce too rapidly for growth in food supply to keep up. In nature, where no moral restraint held back reproduction, and many organisms produced hundreds or thousands of seeds or offspring every year, Darwin saw that Malthus's principle operated with "manifold force." Organisms reproduce so quickly that only a fraction of each generation can possibly survive. The struggle for existence that ensued favored those with advantageous variations and so these became more common in successive generations. When this process is repeated over many generations, favorable variations gradually accumulate to form new adaptations and ultimately new species.

Although Darwin arrived at this insight in 1838, there remained many unanswered questions about the process, particularly about hybridism and speciation. He began a series of studies to investigate these questions and sketched out various versions of his theory, which he shared with a very small circle of scientific friends. He published *The Origin of Species* in 1859, after another naturalist, Alfred Russel Wallace, wrote to him with a very similar theory in 1858. The *Origin* is an abstract of a much longer work on which Darwin was working, but it nonetheless contains a very complete defense of the theory of common descent and clearly describes both natural and sexual selection.

The theory as it appears in the *Origin* bears traces of the influence of Paley's natural theology. In a passage that parallels one of Paley's, Darwin compares natural selection to an imaginary being constantly scrutinizing variations and selecting those best fitted to the environment. Some of Darwin's passages on the superiority of natural adaptations to human contrivances read like rewritings of the psalms that glorify God's handiwork. As Darwin later wrote in his *Autobiography,* "... my former belief... that each species had been purposely created... led to my tacit assumption that every detail of structure... was of some special, though unrecognized, service."

Despite the influence of natural theology on the metaphor of natural selection, the theory itself did not require God to explain the origin of species or adaptations, and Darwin came to reject the view of his friend, the American botanist Asa Gray, which suggested that God directed variation and evolution. By 1859 Darwin had drifted into agnosticism, in large part because he found certain Christian doctrines (such as that of Hell) morally repugnant. Darwin guarded his religious opinions as part of his private life, although he put forward a model for the natural evolution of religion in his *Descent of Man* (1871). In successive editions of the *Origin,* Darwin admitted the possibility of other mechanisms of evolution, although he maintained that natural selection was the most important. Darwin died an agnostic in 1882, and was buried in Westminster Abbey. Some evangelicals claimed much later that he had renounced evolution and embraced Jesus Christ on his deathbed, and this anecdote remains popular in some circles to this day. James Moore traces the history of this rumor in his book, *The Darwin Legend* (1994).

The Evolution of Darwinism

The term "Darwinism" was rapidly adopted in the 1860s to denote any evolutionary theory of common descent. It was only in the 1880s that many of Darwin's followers, lead by Alfred Wallace, began to focus on the evolutionary mechanism of natural selection as the defining criterion of Darwinism. However, by the early twentieth century, partial insights gained from studies of heredity and paleontology led to alternative mechanisms for evolutionary change. Mutationists held that species changed by sudden and large genetic alterations. Neo-Lamarckists claimed that organisms inherited characteristics acquired by their parents. Orthogenists claimed that there were indwelling tendencies for certain organisms to follow directional evolutionary trends. Darwinism was also eclipsed at this time by optimistic philosophical recastings of evolution, such as Henri Bergson's *Creative Evolution* (1907)

By the 1930s and 40s, however, researchers from GERMANY, the Soviet Union, America, and Britain had developed the "new synthesis," which brought together evidence from genetics, palaeontology, statistical biology, ecology, and systematics to show the superiority of Darwin's key theoretical insight that natural selection was the most important evolutionary mechanism. Since then, Darwinism has been strongly identified with evolution by natural selection. The current Darwinian paradigm has produced much fruitful research in a wide range of fields. Through the late twentieth century, most biologists agreed that natural selection plays a very important role in evolution, although some controversy remains over the role of other factors, such as the rate of evolutionary change, the physiological constraints in variation, and the gradual genetic drift of characters without the influence of selective pressure.

Darwinism, then, has had diverse meanings within the scientific community, but there are close parallels between the situation in the late nineteenth and late twentieth centuries, when natural selection was the primary focus. Because of this, we will pay particular attention to Protestant responses to Darwinism from these periods.

Nineteenth-Century Protestant Responses

In the nineteenth century, biologists disagreed on the metaphysical implications of Darwinism. For example, Wallace did not believe that natural selection could explain the development of the human mind, although most others, including Darwin, held that the natural evolution of human consciousness was one of the most exciting insights of Darwinism. Other scientists, such as Darwin's American champion Asa Gray, believed that Darwinism was compatible with a view that God directed evolution, although they were strongly challenged by George Romanes, who held that there was no actual evidence of this. Darwin's German popularizer, Ernst Haeckel, used Darwinism as a foil for the "teleological" worldview of traditional religion; he claimed that Darwin had shown that design in nature was imperfect, or "dysteleological." Haeckel used "Darwinismus" as the foundation of his antitheological monistic philosophy. Some held that Darwinism could explain the evolution of human morality, but Thomas Huxley, Darwin's great early defender, later argued that moral behavior had to oppose the demands of Nature. Given that Darwinism had different implications in different contexts, it is not surprising that it gave rise to diverse Protestant responses.

Among the most famous of these responses is that of the Anglican bishop SAMUEL WILBERFORCE, who spoke against Darwin at an 1860 meeting of the British Association for the Advancement of Science. He argued that Darwin's theory fell down on several points, and stipulated that he was rejecting it because of its poor scientific merit, not because of its religious implications. However, he also jokingly asked whether Huxley, who was present, had descended from an ape on his grandmother's or his grandfather's side. Huxley implied that he would rather have an ape for an ancestor than an obfuscating cleric. Later reports of this encounter, written by Huxley and other Darwinists, magnified its importance and exaggerated its effect on the audience. Neither Huxley nor Wilberforce entirely won over the crowd.

The myth of the Huxley–Wilberforce "debate" still flourishes as an archetype of Protestant hostility to Darwinism, glossing over the substantive arguments of the participants and focusing on the dramatic exchange of punchlines. The popular imagination is still entertained by similarly dramatized struggles of critics and proponents of Darwinism. However, there were and are more subtle and influential Protestant responses.

At the same 1860 Oxford meeting at which Huxley and Wilberforce traded barbs, the BROAD CHURCH Anglican FREDERICK TEMPLE gave a sermon embracing the idea that God can act through natural laws. Temple, later archbishop of Canterbury, continued to defend the compatibility of evolutionary thought and orthodox belief through the nineteenth century (see ORTHODOXY). Although there was much variation in detail, this approach was common to mainstream clergy and theologians in Europe and North America through the late nineteenth century, particularly those who were moderate liberal Protestants. Some held that a God who could design a natural process that would result in designed organisms was an even grander conception than Paley's God, who merely designed the organisms themselves. Others, afraid that this position bordered on DEISM, insisted that Darwinism showed that God was immanent in nature and was constantly involved in the ongoing process of creation. In Germany, Rudolf Schmid argued that intelligent design could be seen in the gradual evolution of nature, and that natural order was an expression of God's presence in it. A few Protestants, influenced by MODERNISM, attempted to recast their THEOLOGY in terms of evolution. Lyman Abbott, for instance, in his *Theology of an Evolutionist* (1897), reframed the concept of SIN as a reversion to a lower, animal behavior.

Scientists who were Protestants also came to accept evolutionary theory through the late nineteenth century. The first naturalist to publicly endorse the theory of natural selection was an evangelical Anglican clergyman (see EVANGELICALISM). In 1859 Henry Tristram applied natural selection to explain the camouflaging coloration of Saharan birds. He later opposed materialistic readings of evolution, and agreed with Wallace that humans could not have evolved by natural selection alone. Tristram's openness to evolution was mirrored in the work of other late nineteenth-century Protestant biologists, such as the microscopist and Methodist William Dallinger and the evolutionary theorist and Congregationalist missionary John Gulick. The most influential Protestant evolutionist was Asa Gray, who battled against the anti-Darwinian biologist Louis Agassiz and promoted a theistic version of evolution.

Some older Protestant theologians and scientists were more hesitant about evolutionary theory, and they continued to publish their warnings into the 1890s. All maintained that evolutionary theory was not proven and that the Darwinian model of natural selection was particularly weak. The former OXFORD MOVEMENT leader EDWARD PUSEY denounced Darwinism applied to humans as "unscience." The Princeton Presbyterian CHARLES HODGE claimed that because Darwinism denied the existence of a designing God, it was necessarily atheistical; however, he did not rule out the possibility of evolution guided by God. A wide range of conservative theologians took up similar stances. Otto Zöckler opposed fellow German Ernst Haeckel with a similar argument. The Scottish-Canadian geologist John Dawson outlined this position in a series of books that warned against Darwinism even as they gradually warmed to the possibility of theistic evolution. Calvinist minister ABRAHAM KUYPER lectured on evolution in Holland and America, accepting a process of divine "election" while rejecting the possibility of a natural "selection." All of these powerful conservative Protestants accepted, at least in theory, the possibility of some kind of divinely guided, gradual evolution.

Whereas Protestant responses to Darwin are often divided into "for" and "against" camps, the differences between them were largely matters of emphasis. Those concerned that some Darwinians were attempting to undermine religion distanced themselves from "Darwinism" as such. Others, anxious to show that religion did not conflict with science, as some scientists were claiming, accepted "Darwinism." Still others, seeking to show that theology could gain from the increasing prestige of science, revised theological doctrines along evolutionary lines. However, all of these responses ultimately depended on (or at least allowed) a version of evolution that was somehow progressive and governed or directed by God.

The Twentieth Century: The Great Divide

Through the early twentieth century, the acceptance of some kind of evolution was common among mainstream Protestants and remained a particular feature of LIBERAL PROTESTANTISM. A providential, progressive vision of evolution was easy to maintain in light of the "eclipse of Darwinism" in the scientific community. Many alternative versions of evolutionary theory at the time left room for providential guidance and a pattern of cosmic progress (see above). In the 1920s, the process philosophy of Alfred North Whitehead inspired Protestant versions of PROCESS THEOLOGIES, which ultimately depended on an evolutionary worldview. These views were later informed by the progressive religioscientific evolutionary model of Catholic philosopher Teilhard de Chardin. However, by the end of the century, few of these schemes seemed reconcilable with a popular neo-Darwinian view of evolution that emphasized natural, random processes and challenged the idea of upward progress. If there were any advancement in this kind of Darwinism, it was more like an undirected arms race than a gradual ascent to higher levels of being.

Such claims did not directly strike at the faith of the many Protestants influenced by the liberal theology of FRIEDRICH SCHLEIERMACHER and ALBRECHT RITSCHL, who put religious experience at the center of belief. This school played down the importance of scientific explanation in Christian apologetics. From a very different perspective, the neo-orthodox theologian KARL BARTH also discounted the possibility that science had much meaning for faith. Revelation comes through divine initiative, he argued, whereas science is simply a human endeavor that cannot bridge the gap between God and man. The strength of these positions allowed many Protestants to stop paying attention to developments in Darwinism as something important to their belief (see SCIENCE).

Nonetheless, some American Protestants did remain concerned about science. As part of their response to the SECULARIZATION of American society, some early fundamentalists identified evolution as a dangerous doctrine, used by enemies of the faith to undermine the beliefs of the young (see FUNDAMENTALISM). This movement gathered political support, and many states banned the teaching of evolution in public schools. The matter reached a head in the famous 1925 show trial of biology teacher John Scopes in Tennessee. Scopes intentionally broke the law by teaching evolution, and in the subsequent media circus surrounding the trial, Clarence Darrow mocked the anti-evolutionary views of evangelical WILLIAM JENNINGS BRYAN for the benefit of an increasingly liberal and secular America. The bad publicity and mockery served only to fuel hostility to Darwinism among fundamentalists. Until about 1920, there had been only a handful of creationists arguing that God had literally created the earth and its creatures over seven 24-hour days a few thousand years ago. However, this movement grew rapidly in an anti-Darwinian atmosphere to become the powerful CREATION SCIENCE movement by the 1970s (see ELLEN GOULD WHITE, SEVENTH DAY ADVENTISTS).

By the late twentieth century, the popularity of creationism with the CHRISTIAN RIGHT in America was matched by the rise of a popular and aggressively secular version of Darwinism, defined in books written by such leading neo-Darwinists as Richard Dawkins, Edward O. Wilson, and Daniel Dennett. These authors challenged both creationism and theistic evolution by contending that natural selection necessarily has materialistic implications. The result has been a popular feeling that Darwinism and Protestant belief are incompatible, although some eminent scientists, theologians, and philosophers have challenged this view. The subsequent discussions have mirrored nineteenth-century dialogues and debates, and the fundamental issues of a century ago—the status of humans and the question of design—remain matters of controversy.

Darwinism and Human Uniqueness

Human uniqueness is essential to traditional Christian doctrines of Creation, Incarnation, ATONEMENT, and SALVATION, and is particularly important to branches of Protestantism that emphasize the supremacy of the BIBLE and the personal relationship between God and humans. Much of the initial post-Darwinian controversy centered on the question of "ape ancestry." If humans evolved from animals, then how could Christ's death atone for the sins of Adam ("the first man")? What basis was there for morality? If there was continuity between apes and humans, then why were humans alone given divine dispensation?

Some of these questions remain intractable for certain Protestants. Others find them easier to answer because they read the first chapters of Genesis as an allegory of God's relationship with humans. Others, particularly in the nineteenth century, developed theories of pre-Adamite humanity that allowed them to accept some version of human evolution. However, Darwinism is difficult to reconcile with the notion of a literal "first pair" of humans, because this would be a genetic bottleneck normally fatal to populations of complex animals.

Late twentieth-century Darwinists have offered explanations of the natural evolution of altruism, consciousness, and religion, following Darwin's program in *The Descent of Man*. Proponents of sociobiology and evolutionary psychology explain various human and animal behaviors in terms of natural selection. A central tenet of sociobiology is that humans love one another because this kind of behavior provides, and provided in the past, an advantage for the survival of human social groups.

Many Protestants simply reject this position, just as many rejected Darwin's claims about humans in the late nineteenth century. Sociobiologists are accused of making up "just so" stories to reduce virtue to mere selfishness and of importing metaphysical assumptions into their science. However, some have argued that even if sociobiology is a true explanation of the evolution of social behaviors, those behaviors may be moral nonetheless. It may make evolutionary sense for a mother to love her children, but that does not make the love any less valuable or real. God may have worked through natural law to create in us a consciousness of right and wrong.

The question of continuity between humans and animals has been dealt with in various ways (see ECOLOGY). Some, like Wallace, argued for some kind of supernatural intervention in the creation of human consciousness. Similarly, others have claimed that the soul was breathed into a population of beings that had naturally evolved to be physically human. These approaches have been criticized as being too dualistic, because they imply that mind and body have little to do with one another. Michael Ruse has suggested that there is an affinity between the Darwinian model of mind as contained by the structure of the brain and the Aristotelian Christian notions of the soul as a formative principle that activates the body. Protestants who emphasize divine immanence in matter might well have less difficulty conceptualizing the evolution of a soul.

Although a wide range of arguments on this subject have been written in theological journals, many ordinary believers either do not think about the difficulties of reconciling Darwinian and Christian conceptions of humanity, or hold these positions to be, at some level, incompatible.

Darwinism and Design

If Darwinism destroys the argument from design, many Protestants and atheists feel that it is necessarily destructive of Christian belief. The argument from design has an ancient pedigree and is central to much natural theology. Its classic formulation is in Paley's *Natural Theology* (1802), where the author reflects on coming across a watch on a heath. Because the parts of the watch are well adapted to their functions, an intelligent cause, or watchmaker, must have made it. For the watch, substitute any organism packed with still more exquisite adaptations, and the intelligent cause implied must be God. Paley wrote in part to answer DAVID HUME's skeptical *Dialogues on Natural Religion* (1779), which claims that although we might compare nature to a watch, it might as easily be compared to a spider web. Although we might imagine nature to have been designed by a beneficent Creator, it is quite as probable that every organism has a separate creator, or that the creators are at war, or that this is just one of a series of botched creations. By focusing on beautiful organic adaptations, Paley sought to blunt the strength of Hume's argument.

Darwin, on the other hand, offered a suggestive mechanism explaining how nature selects without intelligence and so brings about marvelous adaptations over many generations. In various writings, Darwin stressed that adaptations are not perfect, that they are made up of organs and parts that previously had other uses, and that they resemble the work of a dogged tinkerer rather than an omniscient Creator. In an effort to salvage the design argument, Darwin's friend Asa Gray suggested that God directed variations along beneficial and adaptive paths. Here Gray was taking advantage of a lack of knowledge about the causes of variation. A similar move has been proposed more recently by those who hold that because variations ultimately depend on atomic changes at the quantum level, God can intervene in variation at the level of quantum indeterminacy without violating natural law. Both moves have been criticized as attempting to locate God in the gaps of human knowledge.

Darwin responded to Gray with what has come to be known as the "stone house" argument. Imagine, he wrote, an architect building a structure from stones that have fallen from a cliff. The stones have gained their shapes from natural laws of erosion. Given an architect who could select the stones best fitted to the structure's demands, it would be unnecessary to claim that the shape of the stones or the laws of erosion had been providentially arranged to aid the architect. Natural selection presents an analogous case, Darwin claimed. Variations are the stones, the organism is the stone house, and natural selection is the architect. Variations may be determined by natural laws, but they are essentially random when it comes to the needs of the organism. Natural selection selects those best fitted to the organism, just as the architect selects the best building stones from a pile of scree.

Darwin's argument made it difficult to prove that God directs evolution. Those who wish to prove this have followed several paths. Some have simply rejected natural selection as the mechanism of evolution, or discounted Darwin's interpretation of variation. A few Protestant theologians have suggested that God might well act through a contingent and seemingly random process. This position, however, seems to magnify the problem of pain in nature. Why do animals suffer, and why are there so many apparently cruel and painful interactions between organisms in nature? It is one thing to explain pain as the result of the Fall, or some imperfection in the world, and another to claim that it is an inevitable part of the process by which God creates. However, it has always been difficult to "justify the ways of God to man," and some theologians have claimed that Darwinism at least gives pain and suffering a purpose. Without pain, natural selection would not work, and so humans would never have come into being and the creation would never have developed.

Some Protestants have backed away from the claim that it is possible to find evidence of design in nature. The Anglo-Catholic Aubrey Moore (1848–1890) claimed that the regular action of natural law seen in natural selection could be taken as a confirmation of the Christian doctrine of the divine immanence of the Logos. However, he admitted that this was merely a confirmation of, not evidence for, belief. In doing this, he sharply reduced the apologetic value of nature to Christian theology, but suggested a way in which Christians could accept a law-like, but apparently undirected and random, process of evolution.

The 1990s brought a concerted attempt to revive Paley's argument from design by demonstrating the inadequacy of Darwinism to explain the existence of irreducibly complex adaptations. American intelligent design theorists claim that certain adaptations, such as the Krebs cycle in cellular metabolism, are too complex to have developed gradually. Alter any part of the process and it simply does not work. Although intelligent design has gained a certain popularity among a segment of American Protestants, it has met with strong criticism from many scientists and some theologians. Darwinists claim that they are constantly finding explanations for the evolution of supposedly irreducibly complex adaptations, and that these typically involve pre-existing parts changing their function. Theologians suggest that it is unwise to locate God in the gaps of human knowledge, because such gaps have a tendency to get filled in. These arguments mirror those that raged in the 1860s and 70s.

It may be asked whether the argument from design is necessary to Christian belief. After all, Paley's argument draws an analogy between God and a human watchmaker. Some Protestant critics of natural theology have claimed that this is an unjustifiable comparison, and that we cannot know how God and the Creation are related. The argument from design has proven a powerful analogy, however, and it continues to play an important role in some American Protestants' arguments about evolution.

Future Prospects

There are diverse Protestant approaches to Darwinism, only a few of which have been touched on here. Through the 1990s numerous attempts were made to create forums for constructive dialogue, which are supported in several countries by the Templeton Foundation. In the UNITED STATES, the loudest discussion seems to be between those who believe that Darwinism is in effect a secular religion that promotes metaphysical naturalism and those who claim that it may be compatible with Protestant religion. In the United States, at least, Darwinism has been thoroughly politicized, with the Christian Right and the secular establishment taking opposing stands on its validity and its right to dominate the science classroom in the public schools. There have been repeated claims that Darwinism is "just a theory" or that it has become a secular religion. However, these claims have been persuasively rebutted by many commentators and have not been accepted by the courts or legislatures.

There are some difficulties in reconciling Darwinism with Protestant beliefs, but these difficulties alone do not explain why the most popular perception of their relationship is one of necessary conflict. This conflict is in part a product of the political chemistry of religion and CULTURE, particularly in the United States. It also may be attributed to our human love of the inherent drama of combat. Most of us learn about the world through MASS MEDIA narratives that favor entertaining dramatic struggles as the chief relationship between worldviews. As long as this is true, for most people Darwinism and Protestantism will remain locked in battle.

References and Further Reading

Primary Source:

Darwin, Charles. *The Origin of Species.* London: Murray, 1859.

Secondary Sources:

Bowler, Peter. *Evolution: The History of an Idea.* Berkeley, CA: University of California Press, 1989.

Durant, John, ed. *Darwinism and Divinity: Essays on Evolution and Religious Belief.* Oxford, UK: Blackwell, 1985.

Livingstone, David. *Darwin's Forgotten Defenders: The Encounter between Evangelical Theology and Evolutionary Thought.* Grand Rapids, MI: William B. Eerdmans, 1987.

Moore, James. *The Post-Darwinian Controversies: A Study of the Protestant Struggle to come to terms with Darwin in Great Britain and America, 1870–1900.* Cambridge: Cambridge University Press, 1979.

———. *The Darwin Legend.* Grand Rapids, MI: Baker, 1994.

Numbers, Ronald. *Darwinism Comes to America.* Cambridge, MA: Harvard University Press, 1998.

Roberts, Jonathan. *Darwinism and the Divine in America: Protestant Intellectuals and Organic Evolution, 1859–1900.* Madison, WI: University of Wisconsin Press, 1988.

Ruse, Michael. *Can a Darwinian be a Christian? The Relationship Between Science and Religion.* Cambridge: Cambridge University Press, 2001.

RICHARD ENGLAND

DÁVID, FRANCIS (FERENC) (1510–1579)

Hungarian theologian. Dávid studied at the University of Wittenberg, was appointed school principal, and converted to LUTHERANISM. In 1556 he became superintendent of the evangelical church in Transylvania. Initially a Catholic, then an ardent Lutheran, he gradually shifted his allegiance to CALVINISM. Still, until 1558 he was one of the leading Lutheran figures in Transylvania. One year later he had turned Calvinist-Reformed, and when Calvinist churches obtained legal status, Dávid served as the first superintendent of the Calvinist churches in Transylvania (1564).

The increasing influence of Socinian–Unitarian notions prompted Dávid to reevaluate his christological beliefs. This embroiled him, beginning in 1566, in bitter controversy with Calvinist theologians. When in 1568 a Unitarian church was formally established in Transylvania, Dávid became its first superintendent.

In 1571 Dávid triggered the "adorantist" controversy in the Unitarian church. The controversy had to do with the question of whether Jesus was to be adored in prayer, a question that split the Unitarian church. In 1579 Dávid and his supporters succeeded in obtaining synodical concurrence for the principle of nonadoration. Dávid's chief antagonist, Georgio Blandrata, obtained governmental suppression of

Dávid's views. That same year, Dávid debated the issue at a SYNOD meeting with the result that he was condemned as a theological innovator and blasphemer and sentenced to life imprisonment at the fortress of Deva, where he died. Dávid's significance lies in the fact that he delineated, with striking consistency, a thoroughgoing Unitarian CHRISTOLOGY. Dávid also warrants recognition for the fact that he is the only sixteenth-century reformer who divorced his wife.

See also Anti-Trinitarianism; Christology; Lutheranism; Socinianism; Unitarian Universalist Association

References and Further Reading

Primary Source:

David, Francis. "Theses de non invocando Jesu Christo in precibus." In *Defensio Francisci Dávidis.* [Krakow: 1581]. Leiden: 1983.

Secondary Source:

Robert, Dan, and Antal Pirnat, eds. *Antitrinitarianism in the Second Half of the Sixteenth Century.* Leiden: 1982.

HANS J. HILLERBRAND

DAVIDSON, RANDALL THOMAS (1848–1930)

Archbishop of Canterbury. Born in Edinburgh in 1848, Davidson's studies for ministry, in the precincts of the English Law Courts, readied him for realistic witness to civil officials. He served a brief assistant curacy, and became chaplain (secretary) to ARCHIBALD CAMPBELL TAIT, archbishop of Canterbury (1877–1883). As dean of Windsor (1883–1891), Davidson cared for the Royal Family and became a trusted adviser to Queen Victoria. He was consecrated bishop of Rochester in 1891, and transferred to Winchester (1985), then to Canterbury (1903), retiring in 1928. Davidson died in London in 1930.

Davidson's primacy was a time of great change in CHURCH-STATE relations, in Anglican identity, and in world affairs. The Welsh Church was disestablished. Parliament allowed the CHURCH OF ENGLAND a large measure of self-regulation (1919), but crushingly rejected its proposed Prayer Book revision in 1927 and 1928. State and churches fought over public education, over matrimonial law, over labor relations, and over war policies.

Davidson led the churches in fights for persecuted Jews and Orthodox clergy in Russia, for Abyssinian and Armenian Christians, and for abused Chinese laborers in AFRICA. He encouraged the foundation of the Save the Children Fund. He worked for national unity during the constitutional crisis over the Lords and the emergence of the Republic of Ireland, and during the General Strike.

He led cautiously in new relationships across the ecumenical spectrum. Within his church, Davidson sought moderation and mediation between Anglo-Catholics and Evangelicals. He was prepared to ordain men with creedal doubts (including a future archbishop, WILLIAM TEMPLE). A theological student (A. R. Vidler) saw him "as a very great, tactful, cautious statesman: a great pilot in these troublous times."

See also Anglicanism; Anglo-Catholicism; Ecumenism; Evangelicalism; Judaism; Orthodoxy, Eastern

References and Further Reading

Bell, George K. A. *Randall Davidson, Archbishop of Canterbury.* 3rd ed., 1 vol. London: Oxford University Press, 1954.

DAVID H. TRIPP

DAVIES, SAMUEL (1723–1761)

American clergy. Virtually forgotten in the long shadows of such towering eighteenth-century figures as GEORGE WHITEFIELD, JONATHAN EDWARDS, and JOHN WESLEY, Samuel Davies sowed seeds of revolutionary change in colonial America. As Presbyterian pastor and leader of the Great Awakening in Virginia, published poet, America's first composer of hymns, educator of slaves, successful advocate for religious TOLERATION, and the fourth president of the College of New Jersey (now Princeton University), he helped shape much of the religious landscape that developed in nineteenth-century America.

Call to Ministry

Born November 3, 1723 to David and Martha Davies in New Castle County, Delaware, his mother named him after the Old Testament prophet Samuel in response to answered prayer for a son, and similarly dedicated him to the service of the Lord. He studied for the ministry in Samuel Blair's famed "log college" at Fagg's Manor, Pennsylvania. Davies appeared before the New Light Presbytery of New Castle and received his ordination in 1747.

Davies settled in Hanover County in May, 1748 to pastor four meetinghouses of Presbyterian dissenters (see DISSENT). Willing to work within the ecclesiastical system of the CHURCH OF ENGLAND, the established church of Virginia, Davies sought and obtained a license to preach from the colonial governor. Unlike many New Light preachers, the temperate Davies took care to cultivate warm relations with those who belonged to the established church and colonial government. He did not openly evangelize their members,

nor did he disparage the Anglican ministers. Indeed, on October 4, 1748 he married Jane Holt, the daughter of a prominent family from Williamsburg and a member of the Church of England. As a result, even those who disagreed with him found no grounds to criticize his character or actions.

Great Awakening in Virginia

The Great Awakening (see AWAKENINGS) solidified its hold in Virginia under the ministry of Davies. Soon the number of Presbyterian congregations was spreading beyond Hanover County. Davies found a ready audience for the gospel when he arrived in the colony. New Light evangelists before him had brought many people into the faith and prepared many for the evangelical message. Davies's own revival success was not predicated on the great emotional outbursts or physical manifestations common elsewhere during the Great Awakening (see REVIVALS). His moderate disposition and his audience's Anglican background served to restrain such behavior. For his part Davies neither encouraged nor discouraged excess emotionalism, although he did consider it to be a valid expression of the salvific experience.

The fine oratorical ability and humble demeanor of Davies received favorable responses wherever he preached. He focused the content of his sermons on the harsh reality of frontier life, especially the imminence of death. Because of his own weak physical constitution he carried the conviction that his life had been spared from premature death so that he could preach to the people of Virginia (see DEATH AND DYING). Consequently he considered his own PREACHING to be "as a dying man to dying men" (Pilcher 1971:65). He balanced such dire preaching, however, with sermons on the enjoyment and pleasure to be derived from the justified life. His sermons, which were collected and published as *Sermons on Important Subjects,* were still being read on both sides of the Atlantic a century after his death.

Preaching did not exhaust the means that Davies used to reach Hanover with the gospel. He also wrote poetry to explicate further the divine truths gathered from his sermon preparations and to express his own devotional feelings toward God. They appeared in the local *Virginia Gazette* and were collected for the private libraries of a number of Anglican planters. In 1752 over fifty of his poems were published under the title *Miscellaneous Poems.* He was, as well, the first colonial American to write and publish hymns, many of which he wrote to accompany his sermons and to prepare his parishioners for the LORD'S SUPPER. His "Communion Hymns" were still being used into the twentieth century.

Davies, himself a slave owner, made the evangelistic outreach to the slave population a significant priority of his ministry (see SLAVERY). By 1755 nearly three hundred slaves attended his church services. With the help of friends in ENGLAND, JOHN and CHARLES WESLEY numbered among them, Davies provided spelling books, catechetical material, and the hymnals of ISAAC WATTS for the slaves (see HYMNS AND HYMNALS). The slaves especially valued Watts's hymnals. Davies recounted that at times the "sundry of them were lodged all night in my kitchen; and sometimes, when I have awaked about two or three a-clock in the morning, a torrent of sacred harmony poured into my chamber and carried my mind away to heaven" (Pilcher 1971:112).

Advocate and Educator

Davies's revivalistic success brought him into frequent conflict with the colonial government. Davies pressed the officials in Williamsburg to recognize the Act of Toleration passed in ENGLAND in 1689 as having force in the British colonies. Not until his trip to England (1753–1755) did he successfully secure a declaration from the royal government that the Act of Toleration extended to the dissenters in Virginia. With the commencement of the French and Indian War, the government of Virginia found it expedient to ignore remaining restrictions on the Presbyterians to ensure their loyalty to the Crown. Davies's fight for the toleration of dissenters is recognized as laying the groundwork for the separation of CHURCH AND STATE in the United States.

In 1758 Samuel Davies became the fourth president of the College of New Jersey. He had earlier visited England with GILBERT TENNENT to raise money for the fledgling college. The funds procured on the trip built Nassau Hall and helped to put the college on sound economic footing. During his brief two years as president he raised the standard for both entrance and graduation and planned to expand the library. His untimely death came on February 4, 1761, at the age of thirty-seven.

References and Further Reading

Primary Sources:

Davies, Samuel. *Letters from the Rev. Samuel Davies, &c., Shewing the State of Religion Particularly Among the Negroes.* London: R. Pardon, 1757.
———. *The Duty of Masters to Their Servants in a Sermon.* Lynchburg, VA: William W. Gray, 1809.
———. *The Godly Family.* Morgan, PA: Soli Deo Gloria Publications, 1993.

Davies, Samuel and George William Pilcher. *The Reverend Samuel Davies Abroad.* Urbana: University of Illinois Press, 1967.
Davies, Samuel and Thomas Gibbons. *Sermons.* Philadelphia, PA: Presbyterian Board of Publication, 1864.

Secondary Sources:

Alley, Robert S. "The Reverend Mr. Samuel Davies: A Study In Religion and Politics, 1747–1759." Ph.D. dissertation, Princeton University, 1962.
Bost, George H. "Samuel Davies: Colonial Revivalist and Champion of Religious Toleration." Ph.D. dissertation, University of Chicago, 1959.
Larson, Barbara Ann. "A Rhetorical Study of the Preaching of the Reverend Samuel Davies in the Colony of Virginia from 1747 to 1759." Ph.D. dissertation, University of Minnesota, 1969.
Pilcher, George W. *Samuel Davies: Apostle of Dissent in Colonial Virginia.* Knoxville: University of Tennessee Press, 1971.

JOSEPH L. THOMAS

DEACONESS, DEACON

The terms "deaconess" and "deacon" refer to a present-day office of service in the church that dates back to the first century. The terms themselves are derived from the Greek verb, *diakonein,* and its cognate nouns *diakonos* and *diakonia. Diakonein* meant to serve or to minister. The noun *diakonos*, or deacon, meant servant or minister.

The Early and the Medieval Church

The early church created the deacon out of a need to administer CHARITY. The tradition of the church held the first deacons to have been the "seven men of good repute" chosen by the apostles of Jesus Christ to serve tables and to help with the daily distribution, recorded in the Acts of the Apostles 6:1–4. These seven men included the first martyr, Stephen, considered by the church father Irenaeus (c. 135–200) as the first deacon, but nowhere does the New Testament name these seven men as deacons. The first reference to deacons as officeholders in the New Testament is in the salutation of Paul in the first verse of his letter to the Philippians. They appear also in his first letter to Timothy 3:8–13, where their expected attributes are described. In Paul's letter to the Romans 16:1–2, he speaks of a woman, Phoebe, as a *diakonos* of the church of Cenchreae.

Deacons began in the first century with little if any obvious place in the liturgy and a large role with the poor. The elders or presbyters (later priests) existed alongside deacons and were not initially necessarily above them. Deacons worked closely with bishops, helping them with financial administration and with charity. The role of the deacons in the Christian congregations brought them into close proximity with other Christians. Deacons visited the sick and prepared the dead for burial. Deacons were called the eyes and ears of the bishops, conveying messages and reporting problems.

Apparently some WOMEN were deacons in the earliest Church. As the church hierarchy evolved, women were moved out of the office of deacon and, at least by the second or third century, into an office of their own as deaconesses. The deaconesses did for women what deacons did for men. This office evolved on the eastern end of the Mediterranean Sea to fulfill diaconal roles among women that were thought inappropriate for men, such as anointing the naked bodies of women before BAPTISM. Deaconesses existed alongside the widows of the church who lived from the church's charity, were supposed to have been married once, and were to be over a minimum age. In the western end of the Mediterranean, widows could fulfill the deacon's functions among women.

Gradually, as assistants to the bishops, the deacons and the widows and deaconesses assumed some importance in the liturgy alongside their role in social welfare. The deacons were given functions that varied over time but included reading the Gospel and later the epistle, reciting certain prayers, and serving the wine and sometimes the bread in Communion (see LORD'S SUPPER). The deacons and deaconesses were doorkeepers and ushers during services and instructed new Christians before and after baptism. Some deacons presided over the Eucharist, particularly in churches over which the bishop had given them charge, notably with the expansion of the church in the third century. Deacons conducted catechism classes, and they sometimes preached.

Some churches, such as the Church of Rome, limited the number of their deacons to seven because of the precedent in Acts (chapter 6), but allowed the number of presbyters to expand. Churches appointed subdeacons to aid the deacons. By the third century, some churches had, as well, acolytes, readers, exorcists, and doorkeepers in an evolving expansion of church office. Among deacons, there was often a senior or principal deacon, called "archdeacon."

As the bishop's right-hand helpers, some deacons succeeded to the office of bishop directly without becoming presbyters. This practice continued right down at least to Hildebrand (Gregory VII, pope, 1073–1085), who was an archdeacon in diaconal orders when chosen pope. There was disagreement in the church in the third and fourth centuries as to the role of deacons in relation to presbyters, especially with regard to who was higher in church hierarchy, who could preside at the Eucharist, and who could preach. Although the

diaconate eventually became a stepping stone to becoming a priest, this was not a foregone conclusion in these early centuries.

As Christianity became legal in the Roman Empire, however, deacons became subordinate to presbyters, deaconesses to deacons, and widows to deaconesses. The emperors Constantine and Licinius announced official toleration of Christians in the Roman Empire in 313, and in 380–382 the emperor Theodosius required the people of the empire to practice orthodox Christianity. This meant enormous change for the church. The church could now own property. Worship moved from house churches into large basilicas, and worship leaders adopted liturgical dress. Deacons served as bishops' representatives to church councils and meetings. Deacons judged with other clerics over assemblies, adjudicating quarrels among Christians. Church offices and liturgical roles developed. The role of the church in social welfare expanded. Christian emperors relied heavily on the bishops to administer relief of the poor, care for orphans, run hospitals, and oversee prison conditions.

Church office became a full-time occupation for many bishops, presbyters, and deacons, who came to depend on ecclesiastical revenues for support rather than on their own incomes, but with financial support came demands, such as CELIBACY. Just like monks in the newly forming monastic communities, bishops, presbyters (priests), and deacons in the western end of the Mediterranean were asked to be celibate. That priests and deacons not marry took a long time to make official, and longer still to enforce. It was not until the Second Lateran Council of the church in 1139 that marriages of subdeacons, deacons, and priests were invalid.

Just as the legalization of Christianity had enormous ramifications for the church, so too did the fall of the Western Roman Empire in 476. Deacons retained a role in social welfare and property management at least into the fourth and the fifth centuries, but they lost it by the seventh century, when parishes were taking responsibility for their own poor rather than relying on the bishops whose assistants the deacons had been.

As deacons lost their social welfare functions, the church emphasized their liturgical roles. By the time of Gregory the Great (pope, 590–604), deacons had become renowned for their singing in the liturgy. By the early sixth century or before, deacons blessed the paschal candle at the Easter Vigil, but monasteries helped the needy, as did religious orders as they emerged. The male diaconate became an office one occupied on the way to the priesthood.

Deaconesses and widows formed female religious communities that sometimes included dedicated virgins. From these female living situations emerged religious orders (see MONASTICISM). The deaconesses and the widows were absorbed into the emerging religious orders.

Some functions of the deacons continued in the hands of the archdeacons, who retained important responsibilities in the financial, judicial, and charitable work of the church. Medieval archdeacons were legal representatives of bishops and exercised jurisdiction over priests. By the twelfth century archdeacons were themselves generally also priests in the West.

By that time, governments were also taking more of a role in social welfare, and in the fourteenth and fifteenth centuries, confraternities or lay brotherhoods and sisterhoods began to assume these responsibilities. By the fifteenth century the deacon's role was almost exclusively liturgical, and the diaconate prepared men for the priesthood.

From the Reformation to the Nineteenth Century

The reformers of the Protestant REFORMATION of the sixteenth century found the diaconate ripe for a reform along biblical lines. The model that they advocated was that of the early church when deacons had had responsibilities for the poor. This was practical as well, for in areas that became Protestant, Roman Catholic religious orders and confraternities were abolished or gradually dissolved, leaving communities bereft of the social welfare and education services they had performed.

City councils took over the Catholic Church's endowments and properties and also the responsibility for social welfare and education. Reformers such as MARTIN LUTHER, MARTIN BUCER, and JOHN CALVIN wanted those who cared for the poor to be called deacons, but, of these three, only Calvin was able to impose the title of deacon onto those who were responsible for social welfare. Deacon was one of the four church offices in the plural ministry of the ecclesiastical ordinances of Geneva (1541) that Calvin was instrumental in writing: (1) deacons served alongside (2) pastors, (3) doctors (teachers), and (4) elders.

As for the diaconate, Calvin envisioned a "double diaconate" based on his reading of Romans 12:6–8. He interpreted these verses to imply a difference between (1) those who "serve the church in administering the affairs of the poor" (the procurators, or trustees, of the city hospital) and (2) those who care "for the poor themselves" (those who ran the hospital on a day-to-day basis). The title of deacon seems to have been seldom used in Geneva for these officials, however, at least in the city's documents. "Deacon" more commonly referred to the administrators of the pri-

vately endowed funds for Protestant refugees to Geneva that sprang up in the city in the sixteenth century: the French Fund, the Italian fund, and the German fund. There were no female deacons in Geneva, although Calvin supported the restoration of the ancient office of widow for women in the church.

The actual organization of city welfare did not differ greatly in Protestant cities such as Geneva, Wittenberg, and Strasbourg, however. Those responsible for social welfare tended, whatever their title, to be officials as much of local government as of the church, even in Reformed churches in Switzerland. HULDRYCH ZWINGLI's Reformed Church of Zurich did not call deacons those who worked with the poor, for instance.

There were some Lutheran regions where those responsible for poor relief were called deacons (see LUTHERANISM). JOHANNES BUGENHAGEN (1485–1558), Luther's pastor and minister of the city church in Wittenberg, used the title of deacon for those responsible for social welfare in the church orders that he wrote or edited for Lutheran churches in north Germany and Denmark. Still, some Lutherans of the sixteenth century called those ordained clergy who were serving as assistants to parish pastors "deacons." By the seventeenth century, among Lutherans the title *deacon* generally referred to assistant pastors.

This was not the case in Reformed churches that emerged from the Genevan model. Of the four offices of the church that Calvin identified, it was "doctor" rather than deacon that tended to get dropped as Reformed churches organized elsewhere. Thus the organizational manual of the CHURCH OF SCOTLAND, its *Book of Discipline* of 1561, included deacons. Deacons were found in Reformed churches of FRANCE, the Germanies (see GERMANY), the Low Countries (modern-day Belgium and the Netherlands), and even among the refugees from the Continent of Europe to ENGLAND, and deacons were actively involved in poor relief. The Reformed churches of Wessel on the Rhine allowed women as deacons of the sort who cared for the sick.

The Anabaptists (see ANABAPTISM) who came out of the Protestant Reformation appeared to more freely allow women service that involved a title than did Lutheran or Reformed Churches. Mennonite Anabaptists (see MENNONITES) allowed for both deacons and deaconesses in their Confession of Dordrecht or Dort (April 21, 1632).

The Church of England retained the transitional diaconate of the medieval era, however, even though those Englishmen who had lived on the Continent in Reformed cities during the Marian exile (1553–1558), or who were Puritans (see PURITANISM), preferred the Reformed model of deacons as serving the poor.

When the spiritual descendants of some of these people migrated to the New World as Separatists or Puritans in the seventeenth century, they retained the office of deacon in their churches, but gradually that term was telescoped with that of elder or trustee. The Boards of Deacons became governing boards of many Congregational or Baptist churches (see CONGREGATIONALISM, BAPTISTS). Meanwhile, in the eighteenth century back in England, Methodists (see METHODISM) emerging from within the Church of England naturally retained the transitional deacon of that church.

There were, then, broadly, two models for deacons in the denominations that emerged from the Reformation and the early-modern era up to the nineteenth century: (1) The transitional diaconate in which the office of deacon was held by a clergyman on his way to becoming a priest or pastor. This was true in the Catholic Church, the Church of England, and the Methodist Church. (2) The deacon as social worker and financial officer. These deacons were chosen from the congregation and had no intention of becoming pastors. They usually worked part time at their diaconal tasks. This model was found in Reformed churches modeled on Switzerland or churches that adopted that model. Lutherans, as they came to the new world and founded congregations, used the term "deacon" in both senses. There were "congregational deacons" in some synods of Lutheranism. "Deacon" was also used to refer to men on their way to becoming Lutheran pastors.

The Nineteenth Century

The next major development in the diaconate, after the Protestant Reformation, occurred in the nineteenth century and originated in the Germanies. The Napoleonic Wars, which ended in 1815, left families disrupted, women widowed, and children orphaned. The industrial revolution, arriving later in Europe than in England, brought with it the problems of urbanization.

Germany made a unique contribution to urban work in the form of the Inner Mission, a program of social action and evangelism that began with rescue houses for children who were neglected or abandoned during the wars. In 1833, in Hamburg, Johannes Wichern founded a home for vagrant boys, educating them and training them, gathering them into groups of twelve to fourteen boys with an "older brother," a new type of deacon. In 1839 Wichern founded a brother house and trained deacons for work in jails, slums, and places where many pastors would not go. As the movement spread in the Germanies and beyond, deacons were trained in other places, too, sometimes in conjunction with their female counterparts, deacon-

esses. The Inner Mission included institutions such as seamen's missions, hostels, hospices, halfway houses, and homes to rescue women from PROSTITUTION and work such as visitation of prisons, distribution of literature, and youth work. Deacons would also work in hospitals.

The deaconess movement in the Germanies owes its origins to Theodore Fliedner (1800–1864), a parish pastor at Kaiserswerth on the Rhine River just below Düsseldorf, who was inspired by trips to England where he visited ELIZABETH FRY, the prison reformer, and to the NETHERLANDS where he became aware of Mennonite deaconesses. Fliedner established at Kaiserswerth a halfway house for women prisoners in 1833 and a kindergarten and a school for nurses in 1836, an orphanage in 1842, and a mental hospital in 1852. To staff these institutions he educated women to be nurses, teachers, and social workers, and called them deaconesses.

The Napoleonic Wars had left many women without men. Single women of rural or artisan families came to Kaiserswerth to be educated. Many became deaconesses, living together in mother houses, dressed in the blue dress and white bonnet of the Kaiserswerth deaconess, committing themselves for five years at a time, receiving no salary except pocket money and a promise that they would be cared for in their old age. From Kaiserswerth they were sent out to other parts of Germany and abroad. They founded the nursing movement in the Germanies, some of them heading up the hospitals in which they served.

The movement grew enormously both in numbers of deaconesses and of mother houses. In 1861 Fliedner organized a General Conference of deaconess mother houses. Besides Fliedner, others founded mother houses, among whom was WILHELM LÖHE of Neuendettelsau, Bavaria (1854). Some mother houses, such as Bielefeld in Westphalia (1869), built clusters of institutions for the sick, mentally ill, and elderly. Later, under Adolf Hitler, German deaconesses took heroic measures to protect these disadvantaged.

The deaconess movement spread beyond Germany to France, Switzerland, the Netherlands, Scandinavia, RUSSIA, Austria-Hungary, and Britain. In 1862 the first deaconess of the Church of England, Elizabeth Ferard, was set apart by the Bishop of London. Her movement continues today in the deaconesses of St. Andrew's House, London. However, the OXFORD MOVEMENT in England and its religious sisterhoods interfered with the attraction of the deaconess movement, as did the fact that nursing in England developed along secular lines, Florence Nightingale having stayed at Kaiserswerth but never having become a deaconess. British deaconesses were less involved in nursing than their Continental counterparts.

Methodists and Baptists in England also had deaconesses, and Methodism would play a prominent role when deaconesses spread to the New World, although the deaconess movement in America owes its foundation to William Passavant, a Lutheran pastor, who, after a visit to Kaiserswerth, consecrated his first deaconesses in America on May 28, 1850.

The Lutheran deaconesses movement in the New World followed the mother-house model of the Old World with centers in areas where Germans and Scandinavians settled: Milwaukee, Philadelphia, Minneapolis, St. Paul, Brooklyn, and Omaha, for instance. In some centers there was training for deacons, too, in Colorado and Nebraska. Philanthropists and trustees founded deaconess homes and hospitals, but in the case of the Norwegians, a deaconess from Norway, Elizabeth Fedde, brought the movement to Brooklyn and Minneapolis. Lutheran deaconesses often spoke the language of the mother country to each other and in the mother house.

Although the deaconesses movement never became as large in the United States as it had been in Europe, there were deaconesses from many Protestant denominations: Reformed, Baptist, Episcopal, Congregational, Presbyterian, Mennonite, and Methodist. There were also interdenominational deaconess associations. Women of German descent were well represented, and sometimes mother houses in Europe, such as Bielefeld and Neuendettelsau, sent deaconesses to the United States. Deaconesses founded or staffed hospitals that dot the country today, some still with "Deaconess" in their titles, but it was not so much nursing that caught on among American deaconesses as the inner-city work of the Methodists.

Among Methodists in America, deaconesses got a later start than among Lutherans. Prominent Methodist women agitated for the deaconess cause, including the well-educated sisters, Jane and Henrietta Bancroft, deans of the women's colleges at Northwestern University and the University of Southern California. The General Conference of the Methodist Church recognized deaconess work as an institution of the church in 1888, and the Chicago Training School for City and Home and Foreign Missions (1885) became the first school for deaconesses in the Methodist Church, although it was not limited to deaconesses. By 1915 Methodists had founded sixty such schools across the country in cities such as Boston, New York, San Francisco, and Grand Rapids.

Methodist deaconesses were particularly active in work in the inner city, especially among immigrants. They met women arriving at train stations and found them safe housing, helped people find work, opened clubs for young people, sponsored mother's circles, and established kindergartens and nurseries. Aware of society's problems, they opposed child labor (see CHILDHOOD) and were active in the TEMPERANCE movement.

The Twentieth Century

The deaconess movement and the deacons on the inner mission model thrived into the twentieth century. In some regions, such as Europe, growth continued until after World War II, but by the 1950s the movement appeared to have peaked, although some groups modernized and fared better, switching from pocket money to salaries, making deaconess "garb" optional or modernizing it, educating deaconesses in colleges and universities, and allowing deaconesses to marry or to work part time. As more denominations accepted women pastors, deaconesses had problems with recruitment, although some DENOMINATIONS, especially if they did not ordain women pastors, had ongoing success with their deaconess movements. This was true of the LUTHERAN CHURCH-MISSOURI SYNOD, which did not have deaconesses until the twentieth century, but which now has deaconesses in the Concordia Deaconess Program, founded in 1980, and from the older Lutheran Deaconess Association at Valparaiso University. The Valparaiso deaconess has members in several Lutheran synods, including some who are ordained pastors.

Deacons and deaconesses organized on a worldwide basis. After World War II, the World Federation of Deaconess Associations became the precursor to DIAKONIA, an organization intended to further ecumenical relationship among diaconal associations of various countries. There are also five regional organizations including DOTAC (Diakonia of the Americas and the Caribbean). These have regular conferences.

Denominational affiliation could create obstacles for deaconess associations, and in the case of Norwegian Lutheran Deaconess, it may be what rushed them out of existence. Denominations could mandate that women be either pastors or deaconesses but not both at the same time, for instance, as is the case for the Deaconess Community of the Evangelical Lutheran Church in America (see LUTHERAN CHURCH IN AMERICA) headquartered at Gladwyne, Pennsylvania. Deaconesses who became pastors were removed from the deaconess roster, although they might have preferred to continue to participate in the deaconess community. The Gladwyne Community suffered from a five-year hiatus in new deaconess consecrations from 1988 to 1993 imposed by the church when the denomination was studying ministry.

The modern tendency is for deacons and deaconesses to be subsumed under one name, usually "deacon" but sometimes diaconal minister. In some denominations the title of deaconess has been dropped, or deaconesses have been allowed to keep their title but admit no new deaconesses. That is the case with the Church of England. Most Church of England deaconesses became deacons after 1987 when they were allowed to do so. Those who stayed deaconesses could keep the title, but there were to be no new deaconesses. Some female deacons went on to become ordained priests in the 1990s when it was allowed, if they had had the appropriate education. Some continued to live in community.

The UNITED METHODIST CHURCH IN AMERICA has allowed Methodist deaconesses to remain and recruit, although the denomination, at its 1996 General Conference, approved the "Deacon in Full Connection," or permanent deacon. These are men or women, with the appropriate theological and professional education, ordained as deacons. Methodist deacons can preach, but not preside at the LORD'S SUPPER. The transitional diaconate was eliminated as a stepping stone to becoming an elder (pastor) within the Methodist Church, although a probationary period was not eliminated. Diaconal ministers already in office in Methodism were given the opportunity to join the order of deacon. In the year 2000 there were 1,000 permanent deacons among United Methodists and 35,000 elders.

Long before the Methodists, the AMERICAN EPISCOPAL CHURCH affirmed the permanent deacon in 1952 by adding a provision for *perpetual deacons* who were not transitional to the priesthood but who served permanently, after appropriate education, as deacons. An exciting development in the acknowledgment of a permanent diaconate was that of the Roman Catholic Church. In the Second Vatican Council in 1967 it restored the permanent diaconate and allowed men thirty-five years of age or older to serve in that ordained capacity even though they were married. Catholic Permanent Deacons have liturgical roles and can preach and serve the community in various ways. However, because they cannot preside over the Mass, they have not made up for the widespread shortage of priests.

The existence of the threefold ministry of bishops, pastors, and deacons has added a dynamic to ecumenical dialogue (see ECUMENISM) that is not easily resolved among church bodies that have a more unitary concept of the ministry as embodied in the pastor. On the other hand, church bodies with a unitary concept of ministry sometimes have a proliferation of "lay ministers" or workers, performing various tasks, many of which are appropriate to a deacon. The solution of the WORLD COUNCIL OF CHURCHES, described in its *Baptism, Eucharist, and Ministry* of 1982, was to encourage, for the sake of unity and because of his-

torical precedent, consideration of the threefold ministry by denominations that did not have it.

In addition to permanent deacons, there are still, of course, congregationally elected deacons in some denominations or deacons who serve as governing boards of churches, and there are programs to train them in diaconal service such as the Order of St. Stephen, Deacon.

See also Clergy; Women Clergy

References and Further Reading

Baptism, Eucharist & Ministry. Faith and Order Paper no. 111. Geneva: World Council of Churches, 1982.

Barnett, James M. *The Diaconate: A Full and Equal Order.* New York: Harper and Row, 1981.

Echlin, Edward P. *The Deacon in the Church, Past and Future.* Staten Island, NY: Alba House, Society of St. Paul, 1971.

Lauterer, Heide-Marie. *Liebestätigkeit für die Volksgemeinschaft Der Kaiserswerther Verband deutscher Diakonissenmutterhäuser in den ersten Jahren des NS-Regimes.* Göttingen: Vandenhoeck & Ruprecht, 1994.

Martimort, Aimé. *Deaconesses: An Historical Study.* Translated by K. D. Whitehead. San Francisco: Ignatius Press, 1986.

McKee, Elsie. *Diakonia in the Classical Reformed Tradition and Today.* Grand Rapids, MI: Wm. B. Eerdmans, 1989.

———. *John Calvin on the Diaconate and Liturgical Almsgiving.* Geneva: Librairie Droz, 1984.

Olson, Jeannine. *Calvin and Social Welfare: Deacons and the Bourse française.* Cranbury, NJ: Susquehanna University Press; London and Toronto: Associated University Presses, 1989.

———. *Deacons and Deaconesses through the Centuries: One Ministry, Many Roles.* St. Louis: Concordia Publishing House, 1992.

Plater, Ormonde. *Many Servants: An Introduction to Deacons.* Cambridge, MA: Cowley Publications, 1991.

JEANNINE E. OLSON

DEATH AND DYING

Christianity does not deny death. Jesus, it attests, "was crucified, dead and buried." However, in Christian perspective "death" has many faces. It is "natural," established by the Creator. It limits the time of human existence and thus makes it important, and points it beyond itself to the eternal God. Natural death is penultimate; it is death unto God, who alone is ultimate. Death is also unnatural. In this fallen, sinful world, death pretends to be ultimate, the last word, an absolute nothingness that threatens the meaning of existence and in the end would separate the individual from the world, from others, and finally from God.

As the power that separates existence from God, death is indeed the power of SIN. As a true human being Jesus suffered this sinful death; as the Messiah he did so for the SALVATION of humankind. His death was a martyr's death—the natural and expected outcome of the life he led. The cross was also a sinful "no" to the intrusion of God into this death-defined world. On the other hand, it is the overriding divine "no" of God's judgment on the "no" of a sinful world. In Jesus's death God, not death, has the last word, the word of forgiveness and reconciliation unto God.

With the loss of this perspective in the early decades of the twentieth century, discourse on death was silenced. However, in the 1970s following the publication of Elisabeth Kubler-Ross's *On Death and Dying,* Americans realized that after all death and dying are universal, "natural" phenomena subject to rational reflection and control. Consequently there appeared a plethora of excellent books and school courses on "death and dying," exploring all facets of the phenomena. These have helped the church understand just "what" this phenomenon of death is, but leave questions of meaning generally unexplored.

See also Heaven and Hell

References and Further Reading

Braaten, Carl E., and Robert W. Jenson, eds. *Sin, Death and the Devil.* Grand Rapids, MI: Wm. B. Eerdmans, 2000.

Fulton, Gere B., and Eileen K. Metress. *Perspectives on Death and Dying.* Boston: Jones and Bartlett, 1995.

Kubler-Ross, Elisabeth. *On Death and Dying.* New York: Macmillan, 1969.

Thielicke, Helmut. *Death and Life.* Philadelphia, PA: Fortress Press, 1970.

ROBERT T. OSBORN

DEATH OF GOD

For theology, the concept of the death of God is associated with a movement in radical theology in the United States in the 1960s. Behind the phrase lie two philosophical traditions: that of G. W. F. HEGEL (1770–1831) and FRIEDRICH NIETZSCHE (1844–1900). The death of God refers not to the death of God but to the experience of the absence of God or to the absence of the experience of God. Both of these have been features of Western culture since the 1950s, and the analyses of Hegel and Nietzsche have been revived to address these twin crises. The death of God has been, in turn, the critique of modernity and the foundation of postmodernity. The theology of the death of God is associated with the vivid imagery of Nietzsche's Madman, who proclaims the death of God, but the more suggestive and profound meaning of the movement derives from the writings of Hegel.

G. W. F. Hegel

The death of God might well be taken as the starting point of Hegel's philosophical system. During the early days in Jena, as he began to develop his own position, it was the dramatic, even nostalgic device by which he distinguished his own speculative philosophy from the alternatives of the day. The phrase appeared in *The Journal of Critical Philosophy* in an essay entitled "Faith and Knowledge" (1802). He had been critical of philosophy since the writings of Rene Descartes (1596–1650) with its dualism, which separates thinking and being. This tradition was exacerbated by the scepticism of philosopher IMMANUEL KANT's (1724–1804) *Critique of Pure Reason.* The consequence was that God became a hypothesis, beyond the limits of the knowable. God could well be dead. The outcome was not necessarily atheism, for the loss of God was experienced as "infinite grief." The Absolute had not been rejected, but the relationship of the finite and the infinite was broken, not simply in fact but as an idea. Hegel later described the process in *The Phenomenology of Spirit.* In absolute subjectivity the Unhappy Consciousness succumbs to the tragic fate of becoming itself absolute and self-sufficient, finally losing even this certainty of self. It is "the bitter pain which finds expression in the cruel words, 'God is dead'."

Hegel, as a good Lutheran, accepted the truth of Christianity as a religion, but sought to supersede it in his philosophy. Even the phrase "death of God" he took from a seventeenth-century Lutheran hymn. In Christian piety it refers to the death of Christ, the incarnation of God. The death of God in this sense was a historical event, cruel but not tragic, because beyond death at Golgotha lies the resurrection. In fact, the phrase Hegel borrows is "Gott *selbst* ist tot." "God himself is dead" is a philosophical, not a theological utterance. For Hegel the truth of Christianity lies in its exemplification of the universal in the particular, the idea in the event. The death of God refers not now to the death of Christ, but to the loss of the Absolute in a culture informed by ENLIGHTENMENT duality. Hegel's entire philosophical project therefore began from this analysis. His system of Absolute Idealism was intended to lead not back to religion but on to a new identification of thinking and being. The historical Good Friday points to the Speculative Good Friday.

Dietrich Bonhoeffer

The phrase "death of God," therefore, refers not to a historical event but to a cultural milieu of the nineteenth century that resulted not in atheism but in "infinite grief." When this cultural milieu was replicated in the middle of the twentieth century, Hegel's use of the phrase was revived. The milieu itself was first described by the German theologian DIETRICH BONHOEFFER (1906–1945), who was arrested and executed by the Gestapo for his part in plotting against Adolf Hitler (1889–1945). In spite of the fact that his fragmentary writings in prison were tentative, incomplete, and at times enigmatic, indeed precisely because they were not developed, they became the starting point for several post–World War II theological movements, each of which he would no doubt have disowned. In these *Letters and Papers from Prison* he claims that we are moving toward a time of no religion at all: people as they are now simply cannot be religious any more. God is no longer present to the believer, yet belief remains. How is this absence of God to be interpreted? God is teaching us that we must live as people who can get along very well without him. "The God who is with us is the God who forsakes us (Mark 15:34)." At Gethsemane the disciples of Jesus are called to watch. Christians are challenged to participate in the sufferings of God at the hands of a godless world. Bonhoeffer expresses the infinite grief of absence and the hope of finding an appropriate way not back but forward. It was left to others to revive the Hegelian theme of the death of God.

William Hamilton

Gabriel Vahanian was the first to announce the death of God (1961), but the two main exponents of the theology of the death of God were William Hamilton American and Theologian Thomas Altizer (1927–). Hamilton offered not logic but biography, not metaphysics but personal experience. In describing his own religious history he invites others to identify with it. Earlier in his life there was experience of God, a God to be enjoyed, celebrated, and obeyed. Now that experience has gone. Argument has played no part, least of all argument designed to disprove the existence of God. There is now a sense of loss, comparable to the death of a loved one. There is a particular kind of grieving endured when the body of the loved one is not found, so Hamilton experiences the death of God, and yet there is part of him that waits for the return of God. Clearly Hamilton is not influenced by Hegel, but themes from Bonhoeffer appear. One is "secret discipline": paradoxically, he prays for the return of the God who apparently is dead. But it must be the return of the God who is revealed in Christ. Another is the concentration of the person of Jesus. Christians waiting for God must adopt the life-style of the "man for others." It is in this that the true humanity of Jesus is revealed, and that true divinity is revealed. Hamilton might be better described as a secular theologian. He uses the phrase "death of God," but does not develop it theologically.

Thomas Altizer

Thomas Altizer's work is much more sophisticated and ambitious. If Hamilton explores his personal experience of the unhappy consciousness, Altizer launches himself into a theological reinterpretation of the doctrine of incarnation that is thoroughly dialectical. In the secular culture of the 1960s there was a widespread acknowledgement that God was absent: but only Christians knew that God was dead. The absence might be assumed to be the work of man: the death of God was the work of God himself. According to Altizer, Christians should not hold back, but should will the death of God. At the beginning and end of the period of the "death of God" theology, Altizer published on American novelist Mircea Eliade (1907–1986) in 1963 and on English poet William Blake (1757–1827) in 1967. He proposed an alternative reading to that of Eliade. It is God himself who, by the incarnation, has brought an end of the sacred in its primordial form. For Christians there is no going back. The sacred can be regained only by a dialectical negation of the profane, but it must be a sacred understood now in the light of the death of God. Nor is it simply the pre-Christian God who has died. As early as World War I KARL BARTH (1886–1968) declared that such a God is dead. Altizer pursues his dialectic in a more Hegelian vein through the doctrine of *kenosis,* the self-emptying of God (Philippians 2:6–11). The kenotic movement of the Incarnation sees Spirit becoming flesh, eternity becoming time, and the sacred becoming profane. Christians must not look romantically or nostalgically to the beginning, but rather with hopeful anticipation to the end. The death of God marks the epiphany of the eschatological Christ. Altizer describes this as the gospel of Christian atheism. It was not received as good news in the churches, and unlike Hamilton he did not recommend radical Christians participate in the traditional religious life. However, by pursuing his profane destiny he still hoped to find a way "to return to the God who is all in all."

The death of God theology was short-lived, but sufficiently lively that writers in other fields of radical theology felt it necessary to relate their own movement to it. Thus feminist theology welcomed the death of the divine patriarch, while liberation theology rejected the theme as distracting from the real issue, the death of men [sic!]. But these movements were calling for a new understanding of God the liberator and did not extend the theology of the death of God.

Friedrich Nietzsche

It was assumed in the 1960s that it was Nietzsche whose influence lay behind the theology of the death of God. As we have seen, the more fruitful influences were Hegel and even Bonhoeffer. The contemporary revival of interest in Nietzsche relates not to modernity but to postmodernity. He is influential on theology, but the outcome is not a revival of the movement of the 1960s.

Even more so than for Hegel, the death of God is the starting point of Nietzsche's philosophy. But unlike Hegel, he does not appropriate it from theology, nor does he attempt to develop it in such a way as to correct or complete a theological project. The intense religious faith of his youth gave way to a loss of religious beliefs in his student days. The reasons for this are not clear and apparently do not matter. Nietzsche claims that religious faith does not come about by rational argument, nor does argument lead to the loss of belief. It is as if the possibility of belief is relative to the culture in which we live. In some epochs everyone believes in God: in other periods few share such beliefs. In this sense God has a history. In the emerging secular culture the possibility of believing in God dies out. For Nietzsche it is irrelevant to protest whether this should be so or not. As a prophet of the coming age he proclaims that God is dead. For atheism this would be the end of the story; for Nietzsche it is only the beginning. For atheism the death of God would be a conclusion; for Nietzsche it is a premise: he wishes to explore the consequences.

Throughout his works Nietzsche refers frequently to the death of God, but there are two passages in *The Gay Science* in which he describes the event and its consequences in some detail. In the first passage, "The Meaning of Our Cheerfulness," he describes the death of God as if it were a cosmic event that had already taken place at the edge of the universe, not caused or planned here on earth; an event that nevertheless will eventually engulf this world. He foresees a period of destruction and desolation. The whole of Western culture was based upon religious premises. The death of God means the loss of the foundations of truth, morality, and aesthetics. Some are unaware of what has happened, others choose to ignore, but a few like Nietzsche experience "this monstrous logic of terror." The abyss of nihilism opens up. Why then cheerfulness? Because those who are brave enough to accept the death of God, who are steadfast enough to accept their fate, discover that with the end of the old world, a new world beckons. Nietzsche frequently uses the metaphor of putting out to sea. Previously men set the course of their lives by looking to the heavens. Now the old religious framework has been dismantled, but instead of being tossed about in a hostile flood, the free spirits discover that they can take responsibility for the ship, for the course, indeed can declare it to be "our sea." Some of the same themes appear in the more famous passage, "The Madman." Now the death of God is not an event that takes place out of sight of mankind. All those who have participated in the creation of the secular culture have had a hand on the assassin's knife that killed God. They knew not what they did. At a stroke they wiped out the horizon by which to steer a course, loosed the earth from the sun so that judgments such as higher and lower have no meaning. There is only one thing for it: they will have to become gods. They will have to take responsibility for discovering a new foundation for life, the life of meaning and significance, the truly human life.

For Nietzsche the death of God is a metaphor for the loss of the old religious foundations of life. It is the preface to his criticism of religion, particularly the Christian religion as a religion of decadence and *ressentiment*. Bonhoeffer was influenced by these themes in Nietzsche, as for example when he condemned the "religious premise," the presentation of mankind as weak, incompetent, and dependent on God. However, the current revival of interest in Nietzsche relates to postmodernism. Writers on this subject begin with the dissolution of the Enlightenment project, with the loss of consensus on the conditions of truth and universal moral and aesthetic values. The death of God in this context means the end of the religious basis of modernity. Those who wish to continue theology under the condition of postmodernity must do so *post mortem dei*.

References and Further Reading

Anderson, Deland S. *Hegel's Speculative Good Friday.* Atlanta: Scholars Press, 1996.

Altizer, Thomas J. J. *The Gospel of Christian Atheism.* London: Collins, 1967.

Altizer, Thomas J. J., and William Hamilton, eds. *Radical Theology and the Death of God.* New York: Bobbs-Merrill Co., 1966.

Cobb, John Jr. *The Theology of Altizer: Critique and Response.* Philadelphia: The Westminster Press, 1970.

Haynes, Stephen R., and John K. Roth. *Death-of-God Movement and the Holocaust.* Westport, CT: Greenwood Press, 1999.

Kee, Alistair. *The Way of Transcendence.* London: Penguin Books, 1971.

———. *Nietzsche Against the Crucified.* London: S.C.M. Press Ltd., 1999.

Murchland, B., ed. *The Meaning of the Death of God.* New York: Vintage Books, 1967.

Ogletree, Thomas W. *The Death of God Controversy.* New York: Abingdon Press, 1966.

Schiffers, Norbert, "Analysing Nietzsche's 'God is Dead,'" In C. Geffré, and Jean-Pierre Jossua, eds. *Nietzsche and Christianity,* Concilium 145, 1981.

Schindler, David L. "On the Meaning and the Death of God in the Academy." *Communio* 17 (1990): 192–206.

ALISTAIR KEE

DEISM

Deism was a current of thought originating in seventeenth-century ENGLAND that formed the basis for eighteenth-century ENLIGHTENMENT attitudes toward religion, reason, and nature in FRANCE, GERMANY, and beyond. Deists typically challenged the notion of revelation from God in a BIBLE and proposed the alternative of commonsense reason as a guide to religion and morality.

Definition

It is difficult to define "deism" because some who have been called "deists" rejected the label, and even those who accepted the term disagreed on its meaning. Two of the best-known English deists, CHARLES BLOUNT and JOHN TOLAND, for example, claimed to be fighting deism, and a third, ANTHONY COLLINS, never confessed to being a deist. No doubt this was because "deist" was something of a dirty word, which polemicists in the seventeenth and eighteenth centuries used as a weapon against their opponents. The word was coined by Pierre Viret in 1564 to designate anything that fell between atheism and Christianity, and was used with similar imprecision in the early eighteenth century. Most of those given the name accepted God's creation of the world and rejected the notion of special revelation in the Bible, while disagreeing on the existence of an immortal soul, future retribution, freedom of the will, human nature, and the possibility of divine intervention in the world.

Generally, however, these thinkers agreed that one can start with abstract reason and then proceed from an abstract ("self-evident") principle to conclusions about goodness, justice, and God. All rejected a simple appeal to AUTHORITY (religious or political) because their understanding of what is reasonable—and on this they differed—was their criterion for truth. The location of a DOCTRINE in the Bible was not enough for it to be thought divine—it had to meet the approval of what their understanding of reason considered acceptable. In a sense, this was a development of MARTIN LUTHER's Protestant principle that the locus of authority is not an ecclesiastical institution but a particular construal of the Bible. However, although Luther debated not the truth of the Bible but its interpretation, deists judged Scripture's veracity by its coherence with what they determined to be reason's dictates.

Origins

The first impulses of deist thinking emerged as an attempt to protect French Protestants against persecution by Catholics. EDWARD LORD HERBERT OF CHERBURY (1583–1648), widely regarded as a progenitor of deism, proposed his five "common notions" (the existence of God, that God ought to be worshipped, the necessity of moral virtue and piety, sin's expiation by repentance, rewards and punishment after death) in the hope that they would help end the wars of religion. Herbert and his successors believed that appeals to religious authority, which emphasized differences rather than similarities among religions, were responsible for the intellectual and political violence of the seventeenth century. They were determined to rely on evidence from nature and reason, which all were thought to share, rather than TRADITION, which tended to divide.

The rise of deism also involved a battle for political control. Deists insisted on persons' fundamental right to understand truth for themselves—an indirect result of Protestantism's emphasis on the FAITH of the individual. Most English deists were Anglicans (see ANGLICANISM) fearful that without autonomy people would be susceptible to political control by Roman Catholics using implicit faith and papal infallibility, and by enthusiasts claiming immediate inspiration.

A third factor was the seventeenth century's burgeoning faith in the power of reason. Progress in physics (Sir ISAAC NEWTON), law (SAMUEL PUFENDORF and Baron de Montesquieu), and biblical criticism (Richard Simon) offered hope that reason could bring life and society under control. The CAMBRIDGE PLATONISTS (Ralph Cudworth, Benjamin Whichcote, and HENRY MORE) appeared to demonstrate that reason could recognize and appropriate divine truth as well. They also brought morality to the fore, linking it to religion by making moral disposition a prerequisite to true spiritual experience.

Fourth, some deists were reacting against the scandal of particularity—the notion that God revealed himself to particular peoples at particular times rather than to all humans from the beginning. The orthodox Christian God who sent people to hell (see HEAVEN AND HELL) without giving them a chance to respond to the gospel seemed to be a monster, unworthy of a rational person's devotion. This reaction was strengthened by reports from voyages to the New World and East of millions of non-Christian but religious souls who often seemed more moral than their European contemporaries.

Other factors included a sense of ecclesiastical corruption, pluralism, moral turpitude in the established church, and political and theological wrangling by the CLERGY—all of which seemed to justify deists' rejection of religious authority.

Basic Themes of English Deism

Although French and German deists further developed the early thinking of the English deists, it was the latter who established the basic outlines of deist reasoning that persisted through the eighteenth century. A number of important themes originated with English thinkers in the late seventeenth and early eighteenth centuries.

Epistemological Optimism Based on Common Sense. The English deists believed that reason was perfectly capable of discerning between good and evil, and truth and error, by appeal to what is intuitively obvious—or as deists put it, common sense. By this they meant not knowledge from everyday experience so much as abstract principles divorced from experience and traditions grounded in religious experience. For example, they thought Christ's resurrection unlikely because of the abstract principle that the course of NATURE is never altered. Confucius knew better how to treat enemies because reason shows intuitively that Jesus's command to love enemies is improper. These things can be known with a certainty akin to that produced by mathematical reasoning because truth is a set of clear propositions that can be proven, whereas traditional religion relies on authority and mystery. Therefore the rational person can determine what is true in religion by comparing religious claims to what is thought to be intuitively clear. As Toland asserted, nothing could be true of God that exceeded the limits of his understanding.

Elitism and Hostility to "Priestcraft." Truth can be understood in its full clarity only by the educated who can follow rational argument; the uneducated masses comprehend only fables and religious allegories. Like Benjamin Franklin, they thought Christianity useful for teaching the untutored hordes for the purpose of social control. Collins said he sent his domestics to church so they would learn not to rob him or cut his throat. As Tindal remarked, citing a Greek proverb, "Miracles for fools and reasons for wise men." He and other deists believed the masses were kept ignorant of "natural religion" by a conspiracy of priests who for the sake of selfish gain distorted or destroyed the original knowledge given by reason and intuition to all human beings. In a Golden Age at the beginning of creation, the first generations practiced a simple and clear religion of nature that institutional religion had subsequently suppressed.

Religion as Moralism. For deists the essence of religion is morality. According to WILLIAM WOLLASTON, "By religion I mean nothing else but our obligation to do (under which I comprehend acts both of body and mind. I say to *do*) what ought not to be omitted, and to *forbear* what ought not to be done." These moral obligations are known a priori, before and without revelation. In fact, intuition showed deists that much of what passes for revelation in the Bible is in fact immoral.

Ahistorical Religion. God and true religion were thought by deists to be absolutely invariable since the beginning of history. Because they had decided a priori that revelation must have always been available equally to all human beings from the very beginning of history, and that to admit anything otherwise would be to conceive an unjust and malevolent God, they insisted on the unchanging character of both true religion and its deity. Hence all positive religions connected to history were necessarily suspect—products of an arbitrary god who is not God.

Sincerity as the Heart of True Religion. Because no religious doctrine has been known universally, sincerity is all that matters for divine acceptance. Theological differences are insignificant, and all religions are relative expressions of divine sanctions for morality. Hence none is better than another at reconciling the individual to the divine, and each demonstrates the importance of character, not belief.

Rejection of Christian Theology. Christian doctrines were particularly noteworthy for being superfluous and downright pernicious. For example, the satisfaction theory of the ATONEMENT smacked of ancient heathen sacrifices appeasing a bloodthirsty god. Why cannot God simply forgive? asked the deists. Besides, if God requires satisfaction, he can be hurt, which implies weakness and imperfection. The person of Jesus was also controversial. He could not be central in true religion because he was a latecomer to the history of humanity and therefore inaccessible to many. To accept his central role would be to accept ORTHODOXY's claim that some times and places were privileged over others, which in turn would make God an arbitrary god.

Hostility to Judaism. For this reason JUDAISM was execrable to most deists, who were leaders of the Enlightenment's reevaluation of Judaism. The notion of a chosen people, they felt, implies divine favoritism, and the religion as a whole is full of human ceremonialism and priestly imposture. In a way, the deists' strictures of the Old Testament were those of the New Testament, and those of the Jewish religion were those of the Christian religion. As far as the deists were concerned, "priests" had perverted the original purity of the natural religion in both instances. While the English deists left no doubt that they favored the legal emancipation of Jews in England, their disparagement of the "legalism" of the Jewish religion could easily be used to label the Jewish religion as morally and religiously inferior, especially when their analogous denunciation of the Christian religion were ignored.

The English Deists

LORD HERBERT of Cherbury published his five common notions, which he claimed were known a priori by intuition, *in De Veritate, Prout Distinguitur a Revelatione, a Verisimile, a Possibili, et a Falso,* first in Paris in 1624, then in London in 1633 and 1645. In *Antient Religion of the Gentiles* (1663) he cited heathen who had lived "innocent and commendable lives" as illustrations of why the Fathers of the church had been "too rigid and severe" to sentence the majority of humanity to damnation because they did not know Christ. He learned from Vossius's *De Origine ac Progressu Idololatriae* (1641) that all the wise Gentiles were monotheists.

Charles Blount (1654–1693), a disciple of Herbert, used the Jesuit travelogues from CHINA to rail against "particular religions" and stipulate that "revealed religion" cannot be true because it is not known by all. Only that which is universal is true. In *Summary Account of the Deist's Religion* (1693), Blount argues that reason is the first revelation of God and by the nature of things makes moral truths self-evident. It also reveals that there was no divine mediator, and that morality is far more important than any supposed mystery. Blount often attacked classical religion in his writings, but the astute reader can discern between the lines a critique of Christian orthodoxy that has been veiled for fear of legal action.

JOHN TOLAND (1670–1722) was a learned philosopher whose many writings made deism accessible to a broad audience. His most famous work, *Christianity Not Mysterious: Or a treatise Shewing That there is nothing in the Gospel Contrary to Reason, Nor above it: And that no Christian Doctrine can be properly call'd a Mystery* (1696), charged that truth is always clear and true religion always reasonable and intelligible. Original Christianity therefore was free of mystery, which came only with the admixture of Platonic and Aristotelian thought imported by the Fathers. Other superstitions came through gentile additions of mysteries and ceremonies from pagan religions. The clergy's greatest crime was to prevent people from thinking for themselves because self-determination is the greatest gift. Ironically, Toland, who was a materialist and pantheist, both decried mystery in Chris-

tianity and tried to rehabilitate Druidism and continental Freemasonry. Toland admired some classical authors for their elegance and disdain for superstition, but denounced Plato for his "incomprehensible" mysteries, and Epicurus, Aristotle, and Plato for their repugnant morals.

MATTHEW TINDAL (1657–1733) was the most learned of the British deists. His *Christianity as Old as the Creation* (1730) was not called "the Deists' Bible" without reason: it elicited more than 150 published replies. Despite having sat at Locke's feet as an admiring disciple, Tindal, like most deists, believed in a priori knowledge. His basic argument in *Christianity* began with the assumption that rational religion is clear, accessible, and perfect. If perfect, it cannot be made clearer. Any claim to make it clearer is therefore false. Because traditional Christianity makes that claim, it is false. Hence any pretenses to external (outside the human mind and heart) revelation owe to enthusiasm or imposture. To be governed by such revelation is to renounce reason and replace understanding with implicit faith. In the second half of *Christianity,* which Tindal wrote when he was seventy-five years old, the Oxford fellow systematically attacked the Bible by impugning the character of biblical heroes and the intelligence of the apostles, questioning the reliability of the prophecies and miracle stories, and challenging the limits of the biblical canon. Much of the New Testament, he declared, was hyperbolic and parabolic, so its words must be interpreted in a contrary sense to make common sense. In contrast to the confusion elicited by the Bible, the light of nature clearly shows us the way to God by repentance and moral amendment.

THOMAS CHUBB (1679–1746), a Salisbury tallow chandler and glovemaker who confessed he knew no languages but his own, was the least educated of all the deists. He began as a disciple of the Arians WILLIAM WHISTON and Samuel Clarke, then became a deist. He was able to express the currents of his age in a vigorous and accessible fashion; more than anyone else, Chubb took deism to the common people. Chubb's basic rule of thinking was that reason is or ought to be a sufficient guide in matters of religion. He taught that all persons have the divine law in their hearts, so they can easily determine whether something purporting to be divine is truly so. Religion is valuable only as it serves human morality; far from central, life after death is at best uncertain and prayer is unnecessary.

The aristocratic ANTHONY COLLINS (1676–1729) was the best educated and most sophisticated of the English deists. A friend of Locke, he argued in his *Discourse of Free-Thinking* (1713) for the right to think and publish freely, and charged that enthusiasm and superstition are worse than atheism. A necessitarian who argued against free will, Collins is particularly known for his criticisms of supposed New Testament fulfillments of Old Testament prophecies. Other English deists include WILLIAM WOLLASTON, THOMAS WOOLSTON, Thomas Morgan, Lord Henry St John Bolingbroke, and Peter Annet.

Attacks on Deism from England and America

The early eighteenth century was flooded with pamphlets and treatises written by orthodox divines attacking deist claims. Yet many of these attacks shared the rationalistic premises of the deists and so were not particularly effective. Bishop JOSEPH BUTLER's *Analogy of Religion* (1736), however, dealt English deism a crippling blow. Butler contended that nature is just as mysterious as revelation. The deist description of nature as clear and indubitable, he argued, was more fanciful than accurate. Nature is neither uniform nor transparent in intelligibility. Furthermore, deists have no good reason to presume that the grand system of being, much of which is beyond human ken, is anything like the empirical realities that we know. So if revealed religion seems irrational at points, natural religion is not without its own dark enigmas.

Others had made similar but less compelling arguments. Philosopher and bishop GEORGE BERKELEY had asserted that some mathematical axioms are as puzzling as the Christian mysteries (*The Analyst*, 1734), whereas in *The Case of Reason* (1731) WILLIAM LAW denied the use of abstract reason in morality and religion, arguing that religion is best validated by historical evidence and implicit faith. Later in that century JOHN WESLEY proposed that inner conversion is the best argument.

The American philosopher-theologian JONATHAN EDWARDS (1703–1758) made the most pointed criticisms of the deist project without at the same time denying a role for reason in apprehending religious truth. In his notebooks and treatises he charged that the deist bar of common sense fails to admit truths of life even deists affirm. For life, like religion, abounds with mystery and paradox. The deist restriction of truth to propositions that can be understood comprehensively presumes a one-dimensional view of the human person. Propositions are functions of the affections, which in turn are grounded in aspects of the person that transcend thinking. Hence religious claims are borne not of mere rational perception but a complex blend of passion, interest, and ratiocination. Reason is also the product of complex forces; it is not neutral but interested. So although it can and must determine the possibility of revelation, it is no wonder that unregenerate reason cannot comprehend regener-

ate arguments for revelation. Edwards also challenged deist views of nature and the religions. He portrayed the world not as a giant machine but as a living organism, sustained not by laws of nature but by immediate re-creation from moment to throbbing moment. Like the deists, Edwards took other religions seriously, acknowledged their providential role in world history, and made room for the Holy Spirit in the work of pagan philosophers in China, Greece, and Rome. However, he denied a common substratum at the heart of all religions. Finally, Edwards resisted the move of deists (and a surprising number of "orthodox" thinkers) to make true religion synonymous with moral virtue. Edwards insisted instead that true religion always issues from aesthetic vision (see AESTHETICS). Hence moral sincerity is not enough, unless it is the appeal of true virtue. Unlike the deists, Edwards was more interested in internal states and sensibilities than external works.

DAVID HUME (1711–1776) had even less confidence in abstract reason. In "Of Miracles," "Of a Particular Providence and of a Future State" (1748), *The Natural History of Religion* (1757), and *Dialogues Concerning Natural Religion* (1779), he proposed that reason is impotent to either establish or falsify religious beliefs. His criticism of mechanism—that the idea of causation corresponds to actual fact—was devastating to the model of the universe as machine. It denied that reality was as transparent as deists claimed.

Deism on the Continent

Although deism in England dissipated by mid-century, it took on new life across the English Channel. François Marie Arouet (Voltaire was his adopted name) (1694–1778) was less a philosopher than a satirist who popularized deism in France by clear and crisp wit. After the suppression of the *Encyclopédie* and the execution of Huguenot Jean Calas in 1762, Voltaire raised his battle cry, "Ecrasez l'infâme" ("Crush the infamous thing."). By this he meant orthodox, institutional Christianity, whose mysterious doctrines inspired persecuting fanaticism. Influenced by the English deists, Voltaire decried the "immorality" of Old Testament heroes such as David, and found the gospels self-contradictory: God could not have been born of a girl or died on a gibbet. Voltaire was nevertheless a theist who was convinced by the argument from design and taught a religion of praise, adoration, and moral virtue.

Deist thinking in Germany led to a new emphasis on biblical criticism. JOHANN SALOMO SEMLER (1725–1791), professor of theology at HALLE and often called the father of historical criticism of the Bible, followed Tindal in saying that the essence of biblical religion was the moral teachings of Christ. Readers should consider as revelation only what is reasonable and agrees with one's moral experience. HERMANN SAMUEL REIMARUS (1694–1768), professor of oriental languages at Hamburg, was the most famous German deist. In his 4,000-page *An Apology for the Rational Worshippers of God* (published in portions by GOTTHOLD EPHRAIM LESSING), Reimarus declared that Christianity was not only unnecessary but fraudulent: there are contradictions in the stories of both the Exodus and Jesus's resurrection, and evidence that Jesus's disciples stole his body and created a religion foreign to his intentions when it became clear that Jesus's prophecy of the imminent kingdom had failed.

Lessing (1729–1781) took a more nuanced approach to Christianity, but accentuated deism's skepticism toward the Bible's historical claims. In "On the Proof of the Spirit and of Power," Lessing pronounced that although reason delivers truths that are a priori and therefore certain, historical claims are dependent on human testimony and therefore uncertain. Miracle stories are particularly unreliable because we no longer have experience to compare them with. Hence "accidental truths of history can never become the proof of necessary truths of reason." The teachings of Christ teach an inward truth that existed long before the Bible, and this inward truth can be known only by "spirit and power" or personal experience. In *The Education of the Human Race* (1777), Lessing departed from the English deist view of religious history by suggesting progressive revelation in which historical religions are superseded by a more sublime eternal gospel—deism. In another departure, Lessing insisted that historical revelation can tell us things reason cannot, and that reason in fact develops under the tutelage of positive revelation. Thus the infinite manifests itself only through the finite, the eternal through the temporal process of becoming. The terminus of this development is moral autonomy in which one does right not for rewards but because it is right.

Deism in America

Near the end of the eighteenth century, deism borrowed from the American Revolution a passion it had previously lacked and enjoyed considerable popularity among the cultural elite. The majority of students at Yale, Dartmouth, and Princeton were said to have become skeptics under its influence. Franklin, THOMAS JEFFERSON, and other leaders of the new republic were proponents of this Enlightenment religion.

By the age of seventeen, Benjamin Franklin (1706–1790) was convinced of deism after reading Collins and Tindal. He never reconciled his deist belief in comprehensive natural laws with his faith in divine intervention, but maintained throughout his life a near-obsession with the idea of moral perfection through good works. Convinced of divine benevolence by nature's benefits, Franklin was skeptical of orthodox Christian beliefs. Shortly before his death he said he believed that Jesus was the best moral teacher ever but doubted his divinity. He affirmed immortality and retribution, and fought fervently for religious tolerance.

Dismissed by his political archrival Alexander Hamilton as an "atheist and fanatic," THOMAS JEFFERSON (1743–1826) believed that apparent design in the universe points to a First Cause. Jefferson adopted deist insistence that ideas must be distinct before reason can act on them, and decided that the Incarnation, Jesus's resurrection, revelation, biblical miracles, and the Trinity are indistinct if not murky. Jesus taught a rational religion of three propositions: one perfect God, reward and punishment in the future, and love for God and neighbor. Like Toland, Jefferson dismissed Christianity as hopelessly corrupted by "Platonic absurdities." Calvinism contained the worst of these: "If I were to found a new religion, [my fundamental principle] would be the reverse of Calvin's, that we are saved by our good works which are within our power, and not by the faith which is not within our power." True religion, he wrote, is essentially social morality, which the man Jesus taught better than anyone. Though not a philosopher, he was the most capable proponent of deism in early America.

Ethan Allen (1737–1789), leader of the Green Mountain Boys during the Revolution, wrote America's first systematic treatise on deism, *Reason the Only Oracle of Man,* in 1784. The least gifted of American deists, Allen contributed no innovations, but went to great lengths to deny the divinity of Jesus and to accuse the biblical deity of immorality and arbitrariness. Thomas Paine's *Age of Reason* (1794–1795), America's best-known deist treatise, was a response to the dogmatic atheism of the French Revolution. It opened with the words, "My own mind is my own church." America's leading polemicist, Paine attacked written revelation as hearsay, and miracles as portraying a deity who performed tricks to amuse.

Elihu Palmer (1764–1806), America's most sophisticated deist, was blinded by a yellow fever epidemic in 1793. In his *Principles of Nature* (1801) he developed a natural ethics based on "reciprocal justice" and "universal benevolence." It is utilitarian in method, appealing to whatever maximizes pleasure and minimizes pain. Palmer taught that rational investigation of the laws of nature reveals both ethics and religion, and condemns the subjugation of WOMEN, people of color, and coercion of conscience. It also points up the immorality and absurdity of Christian doctrine: eternal damnation punishes finite sins with infinite pain; original sin suggests that vice and virtue can be transferred; and the atonement is savage retaliation of evil for evil. Palmer's deist newspaper, *The Temple of Reason,* attacked both church and state as twin obstacles to progress.

The Corrosion of Deism

While deism was capturing the minds of many in the American cultural elite, two original minds in Europe were launching devastating salvos against a religion of reason. JEAN-JACQUES ROUSSEAU (1712–1778), an intellectual bridge between deism and Romanticism, held to deist beliefs about God and morality but rejected deist isolation of reason from feeling and willing. His 1762 "Profession of Faith of the Savoyard Vicar" in *Emile* suggests that although nature (not the Bible) teaches religious truth, the way to nature's truth is through "feeling" and "conscience." The Bible is unreliable because it is founded on human testimony, and abstract reasoning is equally unable to find God. Certainty and the divine are found only at the intersection of rational evidence, religious intuition, and moral conviction. Innate sentiments of justice and virtue are the only true guides to divine truth. In a move not unlike Edwards's, Rousseau located reason in the maelstrom of human experience, and denied empirical reason's access to the divine.

IMMANUEL KANT (1724–1804), in *The Critique of Pure Reason* (1781), agreed with Rousseau that faith is not a product of empirical knowledge, but insisted on the rationality of faith in *The Critique of Practical Reason* (1788) by arguing that moral reason demands a *summum bonum* that is possible only with a Supreme Being. Faith is moral faith, or a recognition of our moral duty as divine command. Kant agreed with deists that theology is essentially morality and moral knowledge is a priori, but disagreed on the capacity of abstract reason to prove God's existence, and suggested that moral knowledge is more certain than scientific knowledge. He rejected deists' optimism about human nature, hinting that divine assistance is necessary to break the power of an innate propensity to evil.

The Legacy of Deism

In the next two centuries after Kant there were few serious attempts to construct a religious system using abstract or empirical reason. Most concluded that the deist portrait of humanity and nature had been shallow and alienating. Humans seemed little more than animated bodies conforming to nature's laws, and the mechanistic universe of deism appeared cold and deterministic. God seemed to have been an absentee landlord, far removed from the quotidian struggles of existence. Terrifying divinity had been transmuted into an enlightened English squire. The depths of experience were flattened and the mysteries of life replaced by a bland and regular simplicity.

Yet deism's influence has been far-reaching nevertheless. The grand Enlightenment project, which has been the intellectual foundation for MODERNITY, largely stems from deist rejection of authority (both political and religious) and its stubborn devotion to the claims of empirical and abstract reason. Politically, deism played a role in the development of religious tolerance, which was expressed institutionally in the First Amendment of the United States Constitution. Theology was never the same after deism. Now it would search for God in human experience rather than the Bible or ecclesiastical institution. In response to Kant's response to deism, FRIEDRICH SCHLEIERMACHER (1768–1834) and his liberal Protestant successors found truth outside the Bible and the church, and then reconstructed God, humanity, and church accordingly. Theology could no longer ignore biblical criticism or the sciences, and in most of the next two centuries the universal was to be preferred to the historically particular. Academic study of the Bible was dominated by historicism, which was inspired by deist challenges to historical narratives in the Bible. The larger cultures of Europe and America came to adopt the deist view that religion's essence and purpose is morality. Protestantism in general has come to be increasingly marked by the deist approach to authority as located in the individual conscience. Conservative Protestants claim the authority of reason to start new churches in the name of differing interpretations of the Bible. Mainline and liberal Protestants reject parts or all of traditional doctrine because of perceived conflicts with reason. Both tendencies pay tribute to the rationalistic legacy of deism.

See also: Ethics

References and Further Reading

Byrne, Peter. *Natural Religion and the Nature of Religion: The Legacy of Deism.* London: Routledge, 1989.

Champion, J. A. I. *The Pillars of Priestcraft Shaken: The Church of England and Its Enemies, 1660–1730.* Cambridge: Cambridge University Press, 1992.

Cragg, Gerald R. *Reason and Authority in the Eighteenth Century.* Cambridge: Cambridge University Press, 1964.

Gay, Peter. *Deism: An Anthology.* Princeton, NJ: Van Nostrand, 1968.

Harrison, Peter. *Religion and the Religions in the English Enlightenment.* Cambridge: Cambridge University Press, 1990.

Leland, John. *A View of the Principal Deistical Writers.* Original edition, 1755–1757. New York: Garland Publishing, 1978.

McDermott, Gerald R. *Jonathan Edwards Confronts the Gods: Christian Theology, Enlightenment Religion, and Non-Christian Faiths.* New York: Oxford University Press, 2000.

Mossner, Ernest Campbell. *Bishop Butler and the Age of Reason: A Study in the History of Thought.* New York: Macmillan, 1936.

Stephen, Leslie. *English Thought in the Eighteenth Century,* vol. I. New York: G. P. Putnam's Sons, 1927.

Sullivan, Robert E. *John Toland and the Deist Controversy.* Cambridge, MA: Harvard University Press, 1982.

Torrey, Norman L. *Voltaire and the English Deists.* New Haven: Yale University Press, 1930.

Walters, Kerry S. *The American Deists: Voices of Reason and Dissent in the Early Republic.* Lawrence: University Press of Kansas, 1992.

———. *Benjamin Franklin and His Gods.* Urbana and Chicago: University of Illinois Press, 1999.

GERALD R. MCDERMOTT

DELANY, MARTIN (1812–1885)

American black nationalist and civil rights activist. Born of a free mother and enslaved father in western Virginia, Martin Delany spent most of his early life in Pennsylvania. He worked as a physician's assistant, and even attended a semester at Harvard Medical School before the protests of white students led to his dismissal. In 1848, FREDERICK DOUGLASS hired Delany as a co-editor of the abolitionist newspaper, *The North Star.* Delany toured the North in an anti-slavery campaign promoting moral suasion—the idea that moral and material improvement of blacks would negate the proslavery presumptions of black inferiority. Despite his membership in the AFRICAN METHODIST EPISCOPAL (AME) church, Delany drew little support from black churches, which rejected the materialist aspects of his message in favor of a more otherworldly focused Christianity.

Delany's mission changed dramatically with the passage of the 1850 Fugitive Slave Law, which he saw as the first step toward nationalization of SLAVERY and continued degradation of free blacks. Although he vigorously opposed the AMERICAN COLONIZATION SOCIETY, Delany now believed that the future for blacks lay outside the UNITED STATES. In *The Condition, Elevation, Emigration, and Destiny of the Colored People of the United States, Politically Considered* (1852), Delany argued that forming a new nation remained the only way that blacks could gain full economic and political freedom. Delany's appeal combined the biblical language of the Exodus with missionary zeal to redeem AFRICA with Christian civ-

ilization. Delany secured West African land for a colony, but his plans changed again with the outbreak of the CIVIL WAR. Delany recruited for the Union Army, served as major of a regiment of black troops in the South, and, after the war's close, worked for the Freedmen's Bureau.

See also Slavery, Abolition of

References and Further Reading

Adeleke, Tunde. "Religion in Martin Delany's Liberation Thought." *Religious Humanism* 27 (Spring 1993): 80–92.

STEPHEN R. BERRY

DEMOCRACY

At its core, *democracy* means "rule" (*kratein*) by the "people" (*demos*). More fully conceived, democracy is a blend of distinct social, political, and legal ideas and institutions. Democracy embraces the ideals of liberty, equality, and fraternity, pluralism, toleration, and privacy. It insists on a limited government that is accessible and accountable to the people. It typically features a constitution and a charter of civil and political freedoms, a system of popular representation and political checks and balances, a guarantee of procedural rights in civil and criminal cases, and a commitment to majoritarian rule and minority protection, to regular popular political elections, to state-sponsored education and social welfare programs, to protection and promotion of private property and market economies, among others. Democracy, however, has no paradigmatic form. The four dozen national democracies around the world today have cast these basic ideas and institutions into widely variant forms.

Democratic ideas and institutions have an ancient pedigree. Classical Greek and Roman writers, notably Aristotle and Cicero, described democracy, alongside monarchy and aristocracy, and these discussions were echoed and elaborated by dozens of medieval and early modern Catholic writers. Small communities like the Greek polis, the medieval cloister, and the colonial township practiced various forms of direct democracy. Legal documents from the Edict of Milan (313) to the Magna Carta (1215) to the Petition of Right (1628) spoke of liberties, rights, privileges, and religious TOLERATION. Before the seventeenth century, however, these instances of democracy remained incidental and isolated. Monarchical and aristocratic theories and forms of government dominated the Western state and church. Democracy emerged as a formal theory and form of civil government and social organization only in early modern times.

Protestant Support

Protestantism helped to shape the modern rise of democracy. Although none of the leading Protestant reformers of the sixteenth century taught democracy per se, their theology was filled with democratic implications. Following MARTIN LUTHER and JOHN CALVIN, many early Protestants taught that a person is at once saint and sinner. On the other hand, each person is created in the image of God and has equal access to God. Each person is called by God to a distinct vocation, which stands equal in dignity to all others. Each is a prophet, priest, and king and responsible to exhort, minister, and rule in the community. Each is thus vested with a natural liberty to live, to believe, and to serve God and neighbor; each is entitled to the vernacular Scripture, to education, to work in a vocation. On the other hand, all persons are inherently sinful. They need the restraint of the moral and civil law to deter them from vice and drive them to virtue. They need the association of others to exhort, minister, and rule them with law and with love. Persons are thus by nature communal creatures and belong to families, churches, schools, and other associations. Such associations, which are ordained by God and instituted by human covenants, are essential for the individual to flourish and for the state to function.

In the later sixteenth and seventeenth centuries, various Protestant groups in Europe began to derive democratic theory from this early Protestant theology. The Protestant theology of the *person* was cast into democratic social theory. Because all persons stand equal before God, they must stand equal before God's political agents in the state. Because God has vested all persons with natural liberties of life and belief, the state must assure them of similar civil liberties. Because God has called all persons to be prophets, priests, and kings, the state must protect their freedoms to speak, to worship, and to rule in the community. Because God has created people as social creatures, the state must promote and protect a plurality of social institutions, particularly the church, the school, and the family. The Protestant theology of COVENANTS (see also COVENANT THEOLOGY) was cast into democratic constitutional theory. Societies and states must be created by voluntary written covenants, compacts, or constitutions, to which parties swear their mutual allegiance before God and each other in the form of oaths. These founding documents describe the community's ideals and values, delineate the citizen's rights and responsibilities, and define the officials' powers and prerogatives. The Protestant theology of SIN was cast into democratic political theory. The political office must be protected against the inherent sinfulness of the political official. Power must be distributed among self-checking executive, legislative, and judicial branches. Officials must be elected to limited terms of office. Laws must be clearly codified, and discretion and equity closely guarded. If officials abuse their office, they must be disobeyed; if they persist in their abuse, they must be removed, even if by force of arms.

Democracy and Protestant Movements

These Protestant democratic ideas were among the driving ideological forces of the revolts of the French HUGUENOTS, Dutch pietists (see PIETISM), and Scottish Presbyterians (see PRESBYTERIANISM) against their monarchical oppressors in the later sixteenth and seventeenth centuries. They inspired Anglo-Puritans in the English civil wars of 1640–1688 that truncated royal prerogatives, augmented parliamentary power and popular representation, and ultimately yielded the famous 1689 BILL OF RIGHTS and Toleration Act and their many eighteenth-century constitutional progeny. These ideas remained a perennial source of inspiration and instruction for various neo-Lutheran and neo-Calvinist political movements in Europe in the eighteenth and nineteenth centuries. They also had a modest place, alongside more dominant Catholic views, in the establishment of the Christian Democracy Party at the end of the nineteenth century.

These Protestant democratic ideas also helped to inspire the creation of several democratic church polities in Europe and America. Anabaptist churches (see ANABAPTISM), notably the AMISH and MENNONITES, separated themselves from secular society into small democratic communities, which featured popular election of church officers, public participation in church governance, and intensely egalitarian organizations and activities. Calvinist churches were often created as democratic polities. Church congregations were formed by ecclesiastical constitutions. Church power was separated among pastors, elders, and deacons, each of whom was elected to a limited term of office and held a measure of authority over the others. CHURCH LAW was codified and administered through a variety of public or representative bodies. Church members convened periodic popular meetings to assess the performance of church officers and to deliberate changes in doctrine, liturgy, or government.

Puritan writers in New England drew ready political lessons from this democratic understanding of the church, and these lessons were reflected in several of the new American state constitutions in the eighteenth and nineteenth centuries. Methodists (see METHODISM), BAPTISTS, and various other smaller religious groups born of the First and Second Great Awakening (see AWAKENINGS) in America eventually made democratization a centerpiece of their political theologies and ecclesiologies—a feature that such nineteenth-century European observers as ALEXIS DE TOCQUEVILLE, Lord Acton, and ABRAHAM KUYPER both celebrated and advocated among their coreligionists in Europe.

In eighteenth- and nineteenth-century America, many Anglicans (see ANGLICANISM), Baptists, Congregationalists (see CONGREGATIONALISM), Lutherans, Methodists, and other Protestants joined with Catholics, Jews (see JUDAISM), and ENLIGHTENMENT exponents to establish the core constitutional forms of federalism and separation of powers and to secure the constitutional guarantees of freedom of religion, speech, assembly, and press, due process, and equal protection under the law. Many of these same Protestants later also worked to abolish SLAVERY (see also SLAVERY, ABOLITION OF), to establish public schools, to reform laws of MARRIAGE and FAMILY life, to institute prohibition, TEMPERANCE and other moral reforms, and to broaden the political franchise—although these reform movements permanently splintered Presbyterian, Lutheran, Baptist, and other denominations among more conservative and progressive factions. Some of these Protestant democratic reform efforts found new life in the SOCIAL GOSPEL movement led by WALTER RAUSCHENBUSCH and his allies on both sides of the Atlantic in the early twentieth century. Protestant democratic theory found later theological champions in such luminaries as H. RICHARD and REINHOLD NIEBUHR in America and KARL BARTH and DIETRICH BONHOEFFER in Europe, and enjoyed intense rejuvenation and reformation in the immediate aftermaths of both World War I and World War II.

Today, most mainline Protestant churches in Europe have only a negligible effect on mainstream democratic politics, although Lutheran churches continue to have moral influence on public policy in GERMANY and Scandinavia, and several Anglican and Evangelical intellectuals have come to public and political prominence in ENGLAND and SCOTLAND. American Protestant influence on and in democracy is also somewhat diffuse and diluted, although pockets of intense intellectual and institutional strength remain in black churches, in various Reformed and Evangelical academic, human rights, and public policy groups, and in such political movements as the Christian Coalition.

Although the political influence of mainline Protestantism waned in much of North America and Western Europe in the later twentieth century, it waxed in Latin America, AFRICA, and Eastern Europe as well as in SOUTH KOREA, JAPAN, and scattered pockets of the Indian subcontinent. Particularly in Africa, Latin America, and Eastern Europe, Protestant mission churches had for decades served as zones of liberty during the harsh reigns of fascist, socialist, or colonial authorities. These churches were organized democratically like their American and European counterparts. They served as centers of poor relief, education, health care, and social welfare in the community. They catalyzed the formation of voluntary associations, and provided a sanctuary for political dissidents and a sanction for movements of democratic reform and renewal. They also leveled indigenous social hierarchies with their insistence on vernacularizing the BIBLE, on educating all persons for a vocation, and on relativizing all political authority to the authority of God. Protestant churches thereby provided models of democracy and bulwarks against autocracy in these long-trammeled societies, and have emerged as key leaders of the democratic movements now breaking out in these regions.

See also Church and State, Overview

References and Further Reading

Dahl, R. A. *A Preface to Democratic Theory.* Chicago and London: University of Chicago Press, 1956.

Hatch, Nathan O. *The Democratization of American Christianity.* New Haven, CT: Yale University Press, 1989.

Huber, Wolfgang, ed. *Protestanten in der Demokratie.* Munich: Kaiser, 1990.

Kingdon, Robert M., and Robert D. Linder, eds. *Calvin and Calvinism: Sources of Democracy?* Lexington, MA: D. C. Heath, 1970.

Klaassen, Walter. *Anabaptism in Outline: Selected Primary Sources.* Scottdale, PA: Herald Press, 1981.

Nichols, J. H. *Democracy and the Churches.* Philadelphia: Westminster Press, 1951.

Niebuhr, H. Richard. *The Kingdom of God in America.* New York: Harper and Brothers, 1959.

Noll, Mark A. *One Nation Under God? Christian Faith and Political Action in America.* New York: HarperCollins, 1988.

Niebuhr, Reinhold. *The Children of Light and the Children of Darkness: A Vindication of Democracy and a Critique of its Traditonal Defense.* New York: Scribner's Sons, 1960.

Schumpeter, Joseph, *Capitalism, Socialism, and Democracy.* 3rd ed. New York: Harper & Row, 1962.

Walzer, Michael. *The Revolution of the Saints: A Study in the Origins of Radical Politics.* Cambridge: Harvard University Press, 1965.

Witte, John, Jr. *Christianity and Democracy in Global Context.* Boulder, CO: Westview Press, 1993.

———. *Religion and the American Constitutional Experiment.* Boulder/New York/Oxford: Westview Press, 2000.

JOHN WITTE, JR.

DEMOGRAPHY

See Statistics

DENMARK

When discussing Protestantism in Denmark, the history of the Lutheran Church is the most important. Because members of other Protestant religious communities constitute less than half a percent of the population, this article focuses on the history, theology, mission, and ecumenical relations within the Lutheran Church. Other Protestant groups are discussed at the end of the article.

History of the Lutheran Church in Denmark

In the 1520s the Carmelite provincial Poul Helgesen (Paulus Helie) was at the forefront of a humanistic Catholic MODERNISM, which was inspired by Erasmus of Rotterdam. Some of his students converted to the evangelical movement, which grew in all large towns, even though it was illegal (see EVANGELICALISM). After a civil war, King Christian III removed and jailed each and every Catholic bishop, and confiscated the bishop's estate (see BISHOPS AND EPISCOPACY). He started an evangelical REFORMATION (1536–1537) conducted in close cooperation with MARTIN LUTHER and other reformers in Wittenberg. The fundamental law of the church, the Church Ordinance, was created on the basis of JOHANNES BUGENHAGEN's German organization of the church and with Bugenhagen's help.

The University of Wittenberg became the model for the reestablished University of Copenhagen, and the leaders within the church and within the education system were trained in Wittenberg. The LITURGY was based on Luther's suggestions, and the first Danish translation of the BIBLE (1550) was based on Luther's Bible from 1545. The king became the actual leader of the church. The state continued to control the church following the ORTHODOXY of the seventeenth century, which included forced confessions, unification, control of the CLERGY and the LAITY, as well as persecution of reformed Christians and other non-Lutheran Protestants. During the royal absolute rule, emphasis was placed on ties to the early Christian church as well as to the Lutheran Reformation from Wittenberg. As the basis for CONFESSION, the connection was emphasized (1683) by using the Bible, the Apostle's Creed, the Nicaean and the Athanasian confession of faith, Luther's shorter CATECHISM, and the unchanged AUGSBURG CONFESSION of 1530. Jews and reformed Protestants were given a certain amount of freedom of religion because of dynastic and trade politics.

A movement of PIETISM from GERMANY that was critical of the church gained ground in Copenhagen at the beginning of the eighteenth century, but both orthodox theologians and the government fought against it. Using legal means, the government forced on the public a Pietism that belonged to the established

Church. A mission in the Danish colony of Trankebar in INDIA was established, and during this process there was close contact with the theologians from HALLE. It was the first mission in the Lutheran world and was followed by another mission in Greenland. Confirmation was also established, and compulsory mass was conducted for Jews in Copenhagen. A Royal Ordinance (1741) was characteristically put in place to promote private spiritual development, but at the same time the priests oversaw these meetings. During the Age of ENLIGHTENMENT (c. 1760–1800), a number of reforms were put in place within social and educational spheres, as well as within the church. The Moravians were allowed to establish a colony in the south of Denmark, which had religious and financial freedom. Once censorship was removed, a group of men gave voice to their opinions. They were strongly influenced by foreign philosophers critical of the church. They fiercely criticized the Protestant form of Christianity, and called instead for a "religion of reason," inspired by the ideas of the FRENCH REVOLUTION. Some theologians, who were also influenced by the ideas of the Enlightenment, did try to produce a defense against the criticism, and the government once again limited freedom of the press.

Several popular religious revival movements came about at the beginning of the nineteenth century. They were inspired by German Pietism, the MORAVIAN CHURCH, and changes within the society. These revival movements branched out into different ecclesiastical factions. In general terms one can say that the LAITY came of age, became independent, and that the people insisted on self-determination in religious and political matters. The revival movements grew out of societal changes to a certain extent, but the movements themselves also contributed to these changes. During this period, both N. F. S. GRUNDTVIG (1783–1872) and SØREN KIERKEGAARD (1813–1855) had a great influence on Protestantism both within Denmark's borders and abroad. At first the authorities tried to limit the laity's insistence on evaluating the priests' preaching, their illegal private gatherings, and their rejection of textbooks, which were produced during the Enlightenment. With the creation of the modern *Danish Constitution* (Grundloven) in 1849, many issues were resolved.

The Danish Constitution of 1849 (and slightly revised in 1953) maintains that the Lutheran Church is The Danish People's Church (Folkekirke). The basis for CONFESSION is the same as during the absolute monarchy. Because freedom of religion had been established, people from other religious communities were free to practice the Protestant faith, although that did not mean that equality of religion was established. Church and state were separated, but not completely.

The ruling king or queen is obligated to belong to the Lutheran Church, and it was decided that The Danish People's Church would be the only church in Denmark to be supported by the state. The state underwrites two theological faculties, graduates from which are employed as priests in The Danish People's Church. It also collects a church tax, and maintains a curriculum in religion in the schools, which is based on Lutheran THEOLOGY. Weddings and christenings belong to the realm of civil law. The state also gives the church a direct annual financial contribution. A common department has never controlled the internal conduct of the church within a SYNOD or a bishop's department because a planned synod constitution has never been realized. Every bishop is the leader of the church in his diocese, but there is no legal bishop's department with the AUTHORITY to speak of the behalf of the entire church.

The state's Ministry of Ecclesiastical Affairs administers The Danish People's Church, and all church-related laws are passed in the Danish parliament (Folketinget), which is religiously neutral. The church minister is politically announced and does not have to be a member of The Danish People's Church. Of a population of 5.2 million, 86 percent are members of The Danish People's Church, and around 84 percent have their children baptized within the church. Both percentages have been declining in the past few years. The yearly budget of The Danish People's Church is around five billion Danish crowns, 80 percent of which comes from church taxes paid by its members. The direct financial contribution from the state is around 11 percent.

Debates about the privileges of The Danish People's Church in relation to other Protestant religious communities and confessions have taken place in recent years within both church and political spheres. Other topics that have been discussed are the lack of common religious administration, the relationship between CHURCH AND STATE, and the finances of the church.

Theology and Church Life

The government, which introduced the Protestant Reformation in 1536–1537, decided that the theological basis for Danish Protestantism was to be a combination of the theology of Luther and PHILIPP MELANCHTHON. A few theologians held opinions about religious education that were close to those of CALVINISM, whereas other Protestant opinions were prohibited. The government came down firmly, also dismissing the traditional Lutheran Formula of Concord (Konkordieformel) of 1574 because it feared internal religious upheaval and worried about foreign policy issues. During the orthodoxy of the seventeenth century a penitential movement spread, and a CHURCH DISCIPLINE inspired by Calvinism was introduced.

Jesper Brochmand presented the theological basis for this movement in his dogmatic handbook *Systema Universæ Theologiæ* (1633), which was partly the Lutheran theology based on the aforementioned confession writings and partly a ferocious attack on all other Protestant beliefs as well as on Catholicism. Johann Gerhard was a particularly great influence when the book was written, and English devotional writings were also translated into Danish at that time. A huge number of hymns written by Thomas Kingo reflected Lutheran orthodoxy, and these hymns are still frequently sung (see HYMNS AND HYMNALS). Conditions in Germany and the pietistic movement influenced Danish theological development. Bishop H. A. Brorson wrote poetic hymns, which people still sing and appreciate, concerning the need for repentance, CONVERSION, and becoming a believer. The theologians of the Enlightenment, such as N. E. Balle and Fr. Münter, who were both bishops, were also very influenced by the German spiritual movements of the time.

A major turning point came at the beginning of the nineteenth century, with the first popular revival movements based on both the Lutheran doctrine and Pietism from HALLE. The *Ecclesiastical Association of the Home Mission in Denmark* (*Kirkelig Forening for den Indre Mission i Danmark*) pursued this, becoming a tightly knit organization, which ran a number of schools and social institutions and whose members gathered in hundreds of mission houses. Emphasis was placed on personal conversion and a pious life, where one distanced oneself from worldly pleasures and emphasized the gap between believer and disbeliever. A number of priests joined this movement, and so it became ecclesiastical and sacramental. The organization is still very active. The influence of the American and English revival and conversion movements around the end of the nineteenth century also led to a significant religious activism, especially among the laity.

The theologian Nicolaj Frederick Grundtvig inspired the other large religious movement (*Grundtvigianismen*) in Denmark. Grundtvig had moved from rationalism to biblical Christianity, which again was replaced by a critical stand toward the Bible and the conviction that one found the true core of Christianity through the profession of faith and by BAPTISM. This "Living Word" existed before the Bible and was orally handed down in the congregations up until the present. Grundtvig also added a new dimension to Protestantism in Denmark when it came to the relationship between church and state. He was of the opinion that all points of view should be represented within the framework of the official church, that priests should be able to preach freely and freely conduct their rituals, and that the laity should freely be able to choose the priest they preferred. The last point of view was the only one that was realized and remains in effect. Furthermore, it was important to sharply distinguish between Christian belief and social upbringing, which was the domain of the school. Grundtvig became one of the founding fathers of hundreds of folk high schools that were established, some of which still exist. As a composer of hymns, Grundtvig was unsurpassed. His hymns make up about one third of the current Danish book of hymns. Grundtvig's movement, which is still very active, is much more open toward contemporary art, literary CULTURE, and politics than the Home Mission (Indre Mission).

Søren Kierkegaard was the other great philosopher and theologian who in the nineteenth century added a new dimension to Protestantism in Denmark and elsewhere. In his early writing he described how humans were presented with possibilities in life. He dissociated himself from philosophers such as GEORG W. F. HEGEL from Germany and H. L. Martensen from Denmark, who thought that the truth of Christianity could be proved objectively. For Kierkegaard, Christianity existed once the individual passionately embraced the "paradox" of faith. God was not a feeling within a human being, but came from the outside through Jesus, who encouraged either faith or indignation. Kierkegaard challenged people to follow Christ's imitation in suffering. Using very acerbic language he fought the official church during the last months of his life because he believed that it had abandoned the ideal of the New Testament. Few listened to him, and except for a few pious and anticlerical groups, nobody paid much attention to him at the time, although he became one of the founding philosophical fathers of existentialism and was behind the renewal of Protestant theology in the twentieth century.

H. L. Martensen (1808–1854), a professor who later became bishop, was very influential at the end of the nineteenth century. He in turn was influenced by Hegel's holistic view of the world, and Martensen was a great inspiration for what became the third influential ecclesiastical faction, *Kirkeligt Centrum,* which still exists. This ecclesiastical faction fell between the Indre Mission and Grundtvig's movement. It has a certain shared spiritual community with Indre Mission, and yet by being critically open to art and culture, it also resembles the school of thought that Grundtvig established.

Protestantism was in a deep crisis at the end of the nineteenth century. Philosophers launched heavy attacks on Martensen's harmonious way of thinking. At the same time the followers of Grundtvig launched

serious accusations against the theological faculty because it did not hire their people. The fundamentalist members of Indre Mission rejected the criticism of the Bible, which the faculty taught. Georg Brandes, a man of letters, and other atheists and free thinkers mercilessly rejected the entire Christian faith and notion of culture. They demanded that the country be purged of all religion, which would be replaced by secular humanism. A few theologians from the university did try to defend Christianity by using a theology based on experience, which came from Germany. Another form of Protestant activism unfolded within the realm of a Christian-social movement, which was based on English CHRISTIAN SOCIALISM. That, however, was dissolved again in 1948.

At the beginning of the twentieth century a liberal theology became popular, which was also influenced by the situation in Germany. Liberal theologians respected Bible criticism but were of the opinion that the Christian faith should be a personal experience. Jesus was to serve as the model for imitation and as a Christian, one should live morally and without straying. The American and English youth organizations were a great influence, and extensive work was initiated among Christian young people, which generated a great following. In the 1930s another movement, the Oxford Group Movement, also became popular among the previously mentioned groups. However, a group of theologians who were connected to the magazine *Tidehverv* launched fierce and personal attacks on so-called religious idealism. Using Luther, Kierkegaard, KARL BARTH, and RUDOLF BULTMANN as their basis, they emphasized the great distance between God and human, who in himself/herself has nothing on which to base his/her life. Humans are solely subject to the mercy of God. Any Christian morality and all forms of Christian activism were rejected. The movement, which is modest in size, has recently attacked the view of human nature, which it feels is the basis for the welfare state and it has emphasized a close connection between the national sentiment and the Christian sentiment.

K. E. Løgstrup (1905–1981) has had a tremendous influence through his writing, which is focused on philosophy and cultural criticism. However, one cannot point out any common denominators in his work and the current Protestant theology. One can be of the opinion that a form of Barthianism takes a leading place, apart from the fact that the research of Søren Kierkegaard is also very significant.

Mission and Ecumenism

The Danish People's Church cannot operate foreign MISSIONS because of a special clause in the guidelines of the church. However, a large number of private corporations, which are financed solely by private fund-raisers, help run the foreign mission. The largest is *Danmission,* which recently has absorbed several smaller corporations. During the past several years, the mission's purpose and goals have been discussed and work within Denmark's borders has been conducted.

Until recently The Danish People's Church was not able to participate officially in ecumenical work, but after a trial period, a board was established, *Det mellemkirkelige Råd,* in 1994. The minister of ecclesiastical affairs and the dioceses choose its members. This board initiates contact with the WORLD COUNCIL OF CHURCHES, the LUTHERAN WORLD FEDERATION, and the Conference of European Churches. The board also reaches out to other Danish Protestant organizations and to the Catholic Church in Denmark.

When the bishops of The Danish People's Church refused to join a formalized agreement with the Anglican Church and with Protestant churches in SWEDEN, NORWAY, and the Baltics (the so-called Porvoo Declaration [1995]), it was a source of tension between these churches. Denmark also refused to sign The Joint Declaration of Justification, which states that Catholics and Lutherans have a shared theological position on that topic. The theological reason for the refusals came after an agitated discussion among the clergy and the laity.

Other Protestant Religious Communities

In 1667 King Christian V married Charlotte Amalie from the principality Hessen-Kassel in Germany. She was a Calvinist, and as queen she was allowed to keep her faith. A few years later, the HUGUENOTS, Calvinist refugees from FRANCE, were allowed a certain degree of freedom of religion. Today Copenhagen has German, French, and Korean Reformed congregations, and in Frederica in Jutland there is a Danish congregation. The church has about 750 members.

In 1839 Julius Købner (1806–1884) founded a Baptist congregation in Copenhagen. He had become a Baptist while in Hamburg, Germany. The revival movements strongly emphasized personal conversion to religion, and a number of people went a step further and became BAPTISTS. However, they were persecuted by the government, which among other things forced them to baptize their infants. After freedom of religion had been introduced in 1849, a Danish-German Baptist congregation was organized, but from 1888 the members attached themselves to the congregation in the UNITED STATES, where a number of Danish emigrants had become Baptists. The church has operated a theological seminary since 1918. The Baptist community is internationally linked to the BAPTIST WORLD ALLIANCE. Currently it has 5,800 members, forty-seven congregations, and fifty-five pastors.

The Pentecostal movement, Pinsevaekkelsen, gained ground after a number of meetings conducted in 1907 by the Norwegian Methodist T. B. Barratts. Today it has about 5,000 members, forty-six congregations, and forty ministers, and the movement is represented in most of the joint institutions of the church. One part branched out and created the Church of the Apostles (Den apostolske kirke), which was influenced by Evan Roberts's awakening in WALES. It counts about 2,300 baptized members, forty-one congregations, and forty-four pastors. Christian Willerup, educated and ordained in the United States, founded the Methodist Church (Metodistkirken) in Denmark in 1859. It is part of the United Methodist Church, and its ministers are educated at the church's Nordic Theological Seminary (Nordiske Teologiske Seminarium) in Sweden. It has twenty-one local churches, twenty ordained clergy, and forty lay preachers. Also to be mentioned are the Moravians, the SALVATION ARMY, and the Danish Society for Mission, part of the International Federation of Free Evangelical Churches, all of which are smaller Protestant church congregations with fewer than 2,000 members.

References and Further Reading

Allchin, Arthur Macdonald. *N. F. S. Grundtvig: An Introduction to his Life and Work with an Afterword by Nicholas Lossky.* Århus, Denmark: Aarhus University Press, 1997.

Brohed, Ingmar, ed. "Church and People in Britain and Scandinavia." In *Bibliotheca Historico-Ecclesiastica Lundensis.* Vol. 36. Lund, Sweden: University Press, 1996.

Grell, Ole Peter, ed. *The Scandinavian Reformation. From Evangelical Movement to Institutionalisation of Reform.* Cambridge: Cambridge University Press, 1995.

Hope, Nicolas. "German and Scandinavian Protestantism 1700–1918." In *Oxford History of the Christian Church,* edited by Henry and Owen Chadwick. Oxford, UK: Clarendon Press, 1995.

Lausten, Martin Schwarz. *A Church History of Denmark.* Translated by Frederick Cryer. Aldershot, UK: Ashgate, 2002.

Malantschuk, Gregor. *Kierkegaard's Thought.* Princeton, NJ: Princeton University Press, 1971.

MARTIN SCHWARZ LAUSTEN

DENOMINATION

A denomination is a religious organization (historically Protestant) that emphasizes the voluntaristic and inclusive nature of ecclesial bodies. Emerging in Europe and North America during the early modern era, the denomination has been historically the preeminent ecclesial understanding of religious bodies in the UNITED STATES. Scholars disagree as to the usefulness of the term outside of the specific American context. Students of American religion see denominationalism as largely peculiar to the religious world of the United States (although they accept its use in other cases where both ecclesiastical bodies and the larger society bear parallels with the American experience). Sociologists have been on the whole more willing to use the term in a less specific usage.

All agree that denominations stand over against the historic categories of church and sect. In the typology established by MAX WEBER and ERNST TROELTSCH, a CHURCH was understood as being coterminous with its society and inclusive in membership. A sect, in turn, was seen as a voluntary religious community at odds with the larger society and imposing strict requirements on its followers. In contrast to both, a denomination is a voluntary community, formally separate from the state, but more inclusive in its membership requirements than a sect and less antagonistic to its host society. Likewise, denominationalism presupposes a certain social parity or equality among religious communities vis-à-vis the larger society. Whereas the church/sect division historically emerged out of a milieu of established state religion, in which churches were part of the established order and sects were outsiders, denominationalism has flourished best in the absence of a state church. Finally, in contrast with both churches and sects, a denomination does not normally posit an absolute or exclusive claim to truth. A distinctive mark of denominations is that although they are competitive with each other vis-à-vis membership, they nonetheless can cooperate with one another for broader purposes. Indeed, some have argued that the very term "denomination" suggested the implicit recognition that particular religious communities are in some senses but members of a larger group "denominated" by a particular name.

Historical Origins

The idea of the religious denomination has its roots not in America but in the Puritan phase of the REFORMATION in ENGLAND, particularly during the period of the Puritan Commonwealth (1649–1660). As divisions emerged within the Puritan party over ecclesiastical polity—particularly between Presbyterians and Independents (i.e., Congregationalists)—some Independents, reacting to claims of Presbyterian exclusivism, began to suggest that divisions over POLITY were not actually schismatic divisions within the church. Communities who agreed on the fundamental doctrines of the Christian message could still see themselves as being united even though they differed concerning church order. The belief that ecclesial differences did not necessarily lead to sectarian conflict but could allow for cooperation can be seen as the beginning of the denominational principle.

The Commonwealth period ended with the reestablishment of the CHURCH OF ENGLAND, and with the reassertion of an established church, discussion of denominationalism largely faded away. But in the Toleration Act of 1689, which granted legal status to most non-Anglican Protestants, some elements of denominationalism reemerged (although many political proscriptions continued to be enforced on Nonconformists). The concept of denomination became important in the late seventeenth- and eighteenth-century movements of PIETISM and EVANGELICALISM. The emphasis on subjective religious experience and practical Christian living allowed Pietists to de-emphasize many traditional Christian divisions. Religious experience and practical morality marked the true Christian, and accordingly true Christianity could be found in religious communities with differing understandings of polity and particular theological formulas. The same attitude was reflected by JOHN WESLEY, who claimed that he refused to distinguish between professing believers by any category except the common principles of Christianity.

It was in eighteenth-century America that the denominational understanding began to firmly take root. The openness of the American colonial environment to differing religious communities, and the absence of any established church in many of the colonies (and the weak establishments in colonies outside of New England), set American church life in a voluntary direction and led to a spirit of comparative tolerance (see TOLERATION). Scholars have argued that denominationalism emerged out of this milieu as a fact in American life before it was worked out as a theory. The denominational impulse was particularly strong in the middle colonies (New York, Pennsylvania, New Jersey, and Delaware). Church life developed here along the pattern of voluntary, independent communities supported by committed individuals. The free environment of these colonies proved conducive to groups like the BAPTISTS (who were ideologically committed to voluntarism), as well as to those, such as Presbyterians and Anglicans, who in Europe were established churches but in America relied on voluntary support.

In the development of the American denominational pattern, the middle years of the eighteenth century proved crucial. The great religious excitement of the mid-century (usually referred to as the Great Awakening) severely undermined the Anglican religious establishment in the southern colonies (Virginia, Maryland, North Carolina, South Carolina, and Georgia) and also weakened the established churches of New England (see AWAKENINGS). The new emphasis on an active, conversion-centered piety made many individuals both impatient with established churches and interested in a new vision of Christian unity. The American Revolution also contributed to the triumph of denominationalism. British policy between 1763 and 1776 had been to bring the colonial practices more completely into line with British models. Historians have referred to this as a policy of "anglicization." Because of the link between the crown and the established church and the importance of the church in contemporary English legal theory, this policy of anglicization had religious as well as political implications. The campaign to establish an American-Anglican episcopate during these years can be seen as an attempt to extend a more formal recognition of the place of the Church of England in the colonies. The triumph of the revolutionary forces in the Revolution of 1776 not only stymied this plan politically, but also allowed for the triumph of denominationalism. The Virginia Act for Establishing Religious Freedom (1785), which firmly rejected the idea of any religious establishment, became the model for the First Amendment to the United States Constitution and its vision of the separation of CHURCH AND STATE. By law, churches became understood as voluntary associations.

Denominationalism and the Early American Republic

During the years immediately following 1783, as the new American nation began to address the question of political organization, the colonial denominations likewise began to take on formal structure. Episcopalians (i.e., Anglicans) organized themselves nationally between 1785 and 1789. Methodists established a national organization in 1784. Presbyterians did the same in 1788, and the (historically Dutch) Reformed Church organized itself in 1792.

The situation in America during the early national period gave still a further set of characteristics to denominationalism. As organizations, these denominational bodies emphasized purposefulness, instrumentality, and nationality—all of which were key elements for survival during this period. In contrast with many forms of sectarianism that taught that the proper religious response to the social order was withdrawal, denominations were socially active in orientation and involved in their cultures. Indeed, denominational organization was often for the purpose of action. Typically it was because of the need to become involved in such tasks as home MISSIONS that denominational organization emerged. The emphasis on purposefulness also gave to denominations a self-perception of instrumentality. Church structures were tools or instruments for a higher good and not ends in

themselves. Finally, no higher good was more pressing than the extension of Christian organization and influence across the new nation. As the nation poured out into the trans-Appalachian west, the churches, it was argued, needed to follow. Only through organization and cooperation could this great national need be met.

The emphasis on denominations as instruments for a purpose greater than themselves can perhaps best be seen in the celebrated Plan of Union of 1801 that united Presbyterians and Congregationalists. Both of these bodies had emerged out of the Puritan protest of the Elizabethan settlement. They differed, however, concerning the basis of church order. Congregationalists believed that the fundamental Christian unity was the individual congregation and were wary of overarching ecclesial structures. Presbyterians believed that ordained ministers and lay elders should be associated in session meetings above the congregational level and be involved with oversight. This issue of polity had divided Presbyterians and Congregationalists (see PRESBYTERIANISM AND CONGREGATIONALISM) since the middle of the seventeenth century. But the combination of a perceived need for mission, coupled with a sense of evangelical camaraderie flowing from the Great Awakening, convinced both bodies that cooperation was possible. Hence the Plan of Union, while recognizing ecclesial diversity, set forth a plan of cooperation between the two bodies for missionizing the west.

With the collapse of the Standing Order of Connecticut (which had established the Congregational church in that state) in 1818, the last major colonial religious establishment came to an end, and denominationalism became the dominant motif in American Protestantism. Denominational Protestantism was marked during these years by two attributes, both tied to the dynamics of denominationalism. The first of these was a vigorous emphasis on institution-building that included evangelization, church planting, large-scale PUBLISHING, and the creation of institutions of learning. In the religious marketplace of antebellum America, denominations competed for persons and resources. The vigor and activity of this competition, and its effect on the larger society, impressed foreign observers. The German church historian PHILIP SCHAFF, in his work America (1854), famously contrasted the number, size, and strength of the independent churches of the city of New York with that of his native Berlin, where church and state were still united. A second characteristic was that, despite the competition, there was a degree of cooperation between the religious communities. In one of the earliest accounts of the state of American Protestantism, Robert Baird, in Religion in America (1843), argued that this cooperation stemmed from the fact that all of the "evangelical denominations" (by which he excluded Roman Catholics, Unitarians, Jews, Mormons, and others) were on the same social footing and were united in maintaining the religious health of the nation. This common task engendered a spirit of unity. The unwritten compact of cooperation by Protestant denominations to strengthen the role of religion in the society, joined with full sympathy for the separation between the state and any individual religious community, has sometimes been called the "voluntary establishment."

During the nineteenth century, the denominational idea of ecclesial differences, coupled with cooperation, found an international voice in the Evangelical Alliance, an association of European and American Protestant churches. Founded in 1845, the Evangelical Alliance was the first pan-Protestant cooperative organization. As early as 1867, it sponsored prayer for Christian unity. The Evangelical Alliance was concerned primarily with cooperation. As one spokesperson at an early meeting explained, "Alliance is a well-chosen term. It solves the question immediately by force of definition. It expresses all union expedient or possible among Christians who conscientiously differ in forms of administration; while it admits full liberty of individual opinions, within a range agreed upon" (Bedell 1874:151).

The Second Denominational Arrangement

The paradox of the antebellum denominational model—vigorous activity by individual religious communities (often in direct competition with other groups) and at the same time a sense of shared cooperation in the larger task of maintaining the religious and moral health of the nation—flowed from the very idea of denomination. Denominational organizations, although independent, nonetheless shared some "common denominator" with other religious groups that allowed for compromise. In the antebellum period, this common denominator was evangelical (Protestant) Christianity. By the end of the nineteenth century, the denominational spirit, while alive and well, was transformed by the growing complexity of American society. The large-scale growth of Roman Catholics, Jews, and other religious bodies, who Robert Baird had earlier dismissed as being simply "non-evangelical" bodies, undermined the unifying principle of evangelical Christianity. By the early twentieth century, the category of denomination became refitted with a far broader unifying principle. Denominations (now including Catholics and Jews) were seen as being committed to defending certain general religious and moral values—a "Judeo-Christian ethic"

—or the values of Western culture. This trend was captured by the sociologist Will Herberg in *Protestant, Catholic, Jew* (1955), which depicted each of these historic religious faiths as functioning in a quasi-denominational fellowship, united in maintaining the "American way of life." Some historians have referred to this reconfiguration of denominationalism as the second denominational arrangement.

The victory of denominationalism was not total, however. The period of the second denominational arrangement also saw a growing theological critique of the idea of denominationalism among Protestants themselves. H. RICHARD NIEBUHR in *The Social Sources of Denominationalism* (1929), condemned existing denominational divisions as reflective of the "moral failure" of the church. For Niebuhr, the panoply of denominations reflected social, racial, ethnic, and economic distinctions rather than any meaningful theological issues. Hence the source of denominationalism was *social* and not theological. Likewise, the emergence of an ecumenical spirit within Protestantism (usually dated from the international WORLD MISSIONARY CONFERENCE OF EDINBURGH of 1910) began to challenge the principle of denominationalism. The twentieth-century ecumenical movement rejected the alliance model of church cooperation favored in the nineteenth century (which assumed the perpetuity of denominational existence and called simply for cooperation between denominations), and lifted up a vision of a church united in faith and order as well as life and work (see ECUMENISM). A true and visible church unity was the goal now, not simply interdenominational cooperation. From this perspective, continuing denominational divisions were seen as a scandal in the Christian life.

Recent Developments

The great social, religious, and cultural revolutions of the 1960s may be seen as largely disrupting the second denominational arrangement. Much of this affected denominationalism on the social level. During the 1960s, the unifying social appeal of a "Judeo-Christian ethic" began to receive criticism by advocates of secularist understanding of the separation of church and state, who believed that the government should be far more neutral concerning religious values than it had been in earlier eras. Another set of criticisms came from multiculturalists, who felt that the waves of new immigration from AFRICA and Asia (flowing as a result of changes in immigration law in the mid-1960s), made the old denominational compromise of "Protestant, Catholic, Jew" far too constraining. The presence of Muslims, Buddhists, Hindus, and others called for a new understanding of the place of religion in American life. The complex new religious make-up of the nation challenged all of the earlier models of denominationalism and raised anew the question of what was to be the nature of the common denominator.

If the social basis of denominationalism was being questioned, so too was the category's continuing religious usefulness. Particularly because of the crisis in membership and identity among the older "main line" or "old line" denominations beginning in the late 1960s, critics began to claim that denominational identity was both too "high" and too "low" to describe usefully the state of American religious (and particularly Protestant) identity. Loyalty and identity, it was argued, were now more firmly entrenched in both the local community or congregation (in contrast to the large national denomination), and at the same time in broad transdenominational categories of identification. As the importance of personal identity through race, GENDER, sexual orientation, ideology, and so forth grew, denominational identification waned. A conservative evangelical Presbyterian (to use one example) displayed more loyalty to conservative and evangelical principles than to Presbyterian ones. To some, denominations are a relic of the past. The future of the idea of the denomination as it emerged in eighteenth-century America, and as it flourished for well over a century, remains unclear.

Denominations sociologically conceived as voluntary inclusive religious communities are also be found in other societies where there is no established church and freedom of religion is practiced. The degree to which these communities fit the American denominational system in all its permutations is still a matter of debate.

References and Further Reading

Bedell, George T. "Spiritual Unity Not Organic Unity," in *The History of the Sixth General Conference of the Evangelical Alliance. . . .*, ed. by Philip Schaff and S. Irenaeus Prime. New York, 1874.

Butler, Jon. *Power, Authority, and the Origins of American Denominational Order: The English Churches in the Delaware Valley, 1580–1730.* Philadelphia, PA: The American Philosophical Society, 1978.

Greeley, Andrew. *The Denominational Society: A Sociological Approach to Religious America.* Glenview, IL: Scot, Foresman, 1972.

Martin, David A. ""The Denomination." *The British Journal of Sociology* 13 no. 1 (1962): 1–14.

Moberg, David O. *The Church as a Social Institution: The Sociology of American Religion.* 2nd ed. Grand Rapids, MI: Baker Book House, 1984.

Mullin, Robert Bruce, and Russell E. Richey, eds. *Reimagining Denominationalism: Interpretive Essays.* Oxford, UK: Oxford University Press, 1994.

Newman, William M., and Peter L. Halvorson. *Atlas of American Religion: The Denominational Era, 1776–1990.* Walnut Creek, CA: Rowman and Littlefield, 2000.

Niebuhr, H. Richard. *The Social Sources of Denominationalism.* New York: Henry Holt, 1929.

Richey, Russell E., ed. *Denominationalism.* Nashville, TN: Abingdon, 1977.

Scherer, Ross, P. *American Denominational Organization: A Sociological View.* Pasadena, CA: William Carey Library, 1980.

Swatos, William H., Jr. *Into Denominationalism: The Anglican Metamorphosis.* Storrs, CT: Society for the Scientific Study of Religion, 1979.

Wuthnow, Robert. *The Restructuring of American Religion: Society and Faith Since World War II.* Princeton, NJ: Princeton University Press, 1988.

ROBERT BRUCE MULLIN

THE DEVIL

The leaders of the sixteenth-century Protestant REFORMATION derived their concept of the Devil from the BIBLE and from early Christian writers, especially Augustine of Hippo (354–420), but current Protestant concepts range from the view that the Devil does not exist at all through the view that he exists as a metaphor of human evil to the view that he is a real being with enormous powers to tempt and disrupt humans, nations, and the whole earth. Traditional Protestant concepts of the Devil also borrowed from, and added to, concepts of evil in AFRICA, Asia, and elsewhere.

Origins

The word "Devil" derives from Greek *diabolos* (adversary or slanderer) and the Greek translation of Old Testament (OT) Hebrew *satan* (obstructor). In the OT, the word "satan" is either a common or a proper noun meaning different things in different contexts—sometimes a great angel as in the Book of Job, sometimes simply as "something in the way." Two key passages often cited by Christians as references to the Devil—Genesis 3 and Isaiah 14—do not mention Satan at all, though many if not most commentators have taken "the serpent" in the first and "the bright morning star" in the second to refer to him. The first clear appearance of the Devil as the powerful leader of all the forces of evil is in the intertestamental (pseudepigraphical) literature of the second century B.C. to the first century A.D.

In the New Testament (NT), the Devil and the spiritual powers of darkness at his command are at constant war against God and the good, and the victory of Christ over evil is perhaps the main theme of the whole NT. In the Gospels, Christ frequently encounters and defeats Satan and his demons. In the Epistles, Paul warns against the Devil and other spiritual powers of darkness. A variety of names exist for the Devil in biblical literature; Satan is only the most common. The NT presents the Devil as an angel created by God who falls by rebelling against the divine will. His purpose and that of his followers—angelic and human—is to obstruct the coming of the Kingdom of God. God grants the Devil power for a time over "this world," a common theme in John and Paul, but God never eases his control over him, so that although Satan roams the world seeking the ruin of souls, Christ's Passion and Resurrection have shaken his power. Toward the end of time, a human ruler, the Antichrist, will rise up under Satan's command and make one last effort to block the kingdom, but Christ will be victorious and will destroy Satan and his Antichrist forever.

Fifteenth through Seventeenth Centuries

Conservative Protestant Reformers such as MARTIN LUTHER (1483–1546) and JOHN CALVIN (1509–1564) drew deeply from Augustine as well as the Bible, adopting his view that God creates the world, including angels and humans, for the purpose of extending his goodness. But if God forced his creatures to be good, they would be only puppets lacking moral choice and, therefore, goodness. So God creates angels and humans with free will, knowing in all eternity that some will choose good and others evil. The great choice between good and evil was first offered to the angels: some chose eternally to love and serve their maker; others, through pride, eternally chose to deny his will. The angels who fell, led by Satan, were cast out of HEAVEN into hell. God allows them to roam on earth and tempt humans. God created human beings in the image of Adam and Eve, completely good yet also completely free to make their own choice to love God or to prefer their own will instead. Satan could not force them, but he was permitted to tempt them, and they yielded, falling into sin through free choice. Because all humanity is present in Adam and Eve, all humanity fell with their original sin. Original sin bent humans so much that their inclination is to evil, and no human has enough power to break that inclination by himself or herself. After original sin, humanity was under Satan's power. In strict justice, God could have left humanity in this wretched state forever, but in God's mercy and love God comes to us as Christ. Christ, being completely God himself, has the strength to break Satan's power, and, being completely human, Christ can represent humanity in atonement with God.

The Reformers readily accepted these ideas because they, like other Christians, needed the Devil as a partial answer to the classical problem of evil: God is all-powerful and all-good; how, then, can there be evil in the world that he creates and maintains? One of the many strategies designed to cope with this problem involves the Devil as a powerful principle of evil in stark and powerful (though ultimately vain) opposition to God's will. Luther's and Calvin's strong belief in predestination shaped their view of the Devil. Luther argued that a corollary of the absolute omnipotence of God was God's predestination of humans to either heaven or hell: predestination could not be denied without blasphemously limiting God's sovereignty over all times and all places, and God chooses those whom he saves and those he does not. Thus free will is an illusion, and every man and woman is either under God's complete power and protection, or under Satan's.

God has direct, immediate control over every creature, including humans, angels, and the Devil, and Luther unflinchingly accepted the corollary that God causes the Devil's activity. God wills evil but uses it for the good; on another level God both wills evil and wills us to resist and oppose it. Luther's emphasis on the Devil's power derived from this idea of God's twofold will. God does not do evil himself but uses the Devil to do evil. The Devil is God's tool, like a hoe that he uses to cultivate his garden. The hoe takes its own pleasure in destroying the weeds, but it can never move out of God's hands, never weed where God does not wish, never thwart his purpose of making a beautiful garden. Christ's Incarnation, Passion, and Resurrection have broken Satan's power.

Calvin expressed similar views with his own characteristic logical precision, which led him to teach double predestination. God predestines some to be saved and others to be damned, and he does so not only because he knows that they are damned but also because he wills them to be damned. As a result of original sin, human nature is completely deformed as to both reason and will, incapable of finding truth without faith and the illumination of the Bible. The Bible declares the Devil's existence, but Calvin grasped that it has little to say about it, so he focused on the central concept of the Devil: evil. Like Luther, Calvin believed that no creature, even a great angel, can act against God's will. God carries out his justice through Satan. Such beliefs had destructive consequences, especially in the religious wars and the trials for witchcraft, where all sides in the sixteenth and seventeenth centuries viewed their opponents as tools of Satan.

The radical Reformers of the sixteenth-century Reformation, in their efforts to return to Biblical Christianity, tended to pay less theological attention to the Devil than the conservative Reformers. They were less interested in theory than in practice, concentrating more on reforming themselves and their own communities than on spreading their own doctrines. Such radicals as the Anabaptists, the Unitarians, and the followers of THOMAS MÜNTZER (1489–1525), JAKOB HUTTER (d. 1536), MENNO SIMONS (1496–1561), and, later, GEORGE FOX (1624–1691) lacked the power, and usually the will, to repress their opponents. They believed that the world was under the power of the Devil and that Christians had no business with worldly affairs. Muntzer viewed Christ as a moral model rather than as Redeemer, thus removing the cosmic struggle of Christ against Satan from center stage, where the conservatives had kept it. Some radicals believed in universalism: the view that every creature—even Satan—would eventually return to the Kingdom of Heaven; a few Anabaptists even denied the existence of the Devil altogether. After reaching its peak in the early seventeenth century, Protestant belief in the Devil declined toward the end of the century at the same time that prosecutions for witchcraft were declining. Protestant scholars finally discovered that there was no biblical basis for belief in diabolical witchcraft. Still, few of the seventeenth-century skeptics who denied that Satan worked through witches expressed doubt as to his existence.

Eighteenth Century and Beyond

That changed in the eighteenth century as part of a broader cultural movement characterized by the ENLIGHTENMENT. The old theological worldview shared by all Christians was challenged by the rise of natural science. Causation seemed to be mechanical, leaving no place for divine intervention or human free will, let alone the Devil. Even though logically such a view disallowed human freedom, liberal Christians and secularists increasingly insisted on human effort as opposed to divine decree, and predestinarian views, along with belief in original sin, slowly withered. Gradual moral progressivism slowly took the place of stark moral choice, and the dichotomy between good and evil—God and the Devil—closed. Deists, while denying original sin, still took the human propensity to evil seriously.

Material progressivism, which increasingly dominated thought in the eighteenth, nineteenth, and twentieth centuries, treated the past, and therefore both tradition and the Bible, as a positive evil to be cast off in order to establish a new order of the ages. Not only the Devil but also God became symbols of ancient repression and despotic kingship. The profoundly influential arguments of the Scottish philosopher DAVID HUME (1711–1776) against Christianity undermined its theological foundations; the rise of democracy undermined ideas of hierarchy, even those of heaven and hell. Popular revolutionary and antireligious writers such as Thomas Paine (1737–1809) derided Christian beliefs and scorned the idea of Satan as absurd. On the other hand, the Marquis de Sade (1740–1814) proved both in his writings and in his life that if there is no objective standard for evil, then there is no way of judging torturing children as worse than eating peach pie. Without a foundation for belief in good and evil, Sade demonstrated, there is no basis for rational moral judgment. Satan, in other words, is as good as Christ.

In the nineteenth century, the mechanistic theories of the previous century were made real by industrialization, with its hell-like factories and its depletion of the rural villages where the sense of Christian community had been stable for hundreds of years. From its beginning, Christianity had been communitarian; now the uprooted were forced to bear the brunt of the individualistic entrepreneurial theories of their masters. Having to confront the Devil alone, without the support of community, in hellish labor conditions, caused many impoverished Christians to abandon their faith altogether. Meanwhile, many Protestant leaders retreated from the old worldview centered on Christ's sacrifice as saving humanity from sin. Abandoning the independent epistemological bases of Christianity in experience, revelation, and tradition, they began trying to fit Christianity into the empirical, scientific framework that had begun to dominate intellectual circles, a task achieved only by gradually amputating theological limbs and eventually excising spiritual vital organs. Liberal Christians staggered back before agnostic sarcasm about the grotesque absurdity of Satan even more quickly than they did before direct philosophical attacks. As they abandoned traditional and biblical beliefs, the Devil was usually first to go as an encumbrance in their effort to make Christianity easy and optimistic in a world where secular progress was in vogue. FRIEDRICH SCHLEIERMACHER (1768–1834), a pastor of the Reformed (Calvinist) Church, argued that it was obvious that evil existed but that displacing its origins from humanity onto Satan did nothing to explain it. Conservatives argued in response that without the Devil, the purpose of Christ's mission was lost. A third, middle persuasion, a sort of practical mysticism (for example, original METHODISM), abandoned traditional theological certainties yet affirmed the authority of the Bible and therefore the existence of the Devil.

During the nineteenth and twentieth centuries, Christian beliefs were further undermined by reductionism (the belief that everything can be explained in materialist terms alone). Most weakening was biblical criticism, which sapped the authority of the Bible and the credibility of tradition. One nineteenth- and twentieth-century Christian reaction to this criticism was to dismiss it and to affirm the words of the Bible "literally"; a second was to adopt mystical and metaphorical interpretations; a third was to reject the reliability of the Bible. Modern psychology revealed the power of evil in negative projection (assigning the destructive impulses within ourselves to outsiders whom we choose as scapegoats). Disbelief in the Devil did not prevent Protestants (or others) from demonizing people. In the third view, biblical mentions of the Devil and demons in the Bible were considered the product of the primitive first-century worldview of Jesus and the NT writers. Scripture and tradition were abandoned in favor of the shifting arguments of the latest historians.

By 1800, liberal intellectual Protestants in Western civilization had abandoned the core of Christian beliefs; by 1900 more and more educated Christians had done so; by 2000, most Christians—in the West but not among newly converted peoples—had done so. The Devil had become a comic figure or a childish bogey. One result has been a peculiar defenselessness against the problem of evil. Against the flood of de-sacralization, a generation of theologians bred in the experience of World War II—KARL BARTH (1886–1968), PAUL TILLICH (1886–1965), and REINHOLD NIEBUHR (1892–1971)—tried to reverse the dilution of Christianity by reaffirming neo-orthodox values, expressing ancient truths in opposition to materialist reductionism, but in ways understandable to their culture. The obscene horrors of the world wars, they argued, demonstrated that radical evil (if not the Devil as a personality) was real. For a while, their ideas caught, but in Western culture they were swept away by the socially popular view that evil does not exist and that accident, fate, circumstance, genetics, and environment are all to blame for other people's actions. The term "evil" has been replaced by "disturbed," "sick," "inappropriate," or "mean-spirited" (while hatred, rage, and incivility have actually increased).

By the end of the twentieth century identifiably Protestant concepts of the Devil had become rare except among the Evangelicals. The contemporary worldview among leading intellectuals, including clergymen as well as professors and journalists, is irony. Use of terms such as "evil," "truth," "sin," "beauty," "God" (and most of all "the Devil"), have become social blunders unless set in the ironic quotation marks that let contemporaries know that we do not take them seriously. In a world where irony elides into cynicism, when any behavior is simply a matter of personal choice, when any idea is as good as any other, there are no standards by which Hitler is worse than Lincoln. In such a world, the Devil is no longer even a joke or a scary story; he simply has no place at all.

The Protestant self has been replaced by the post-modern self, a random collection of feelings, impulses, desires, and functions, a self that has no moral being at its center—indeed, no center—but only fluctuating identities that sway with cultural fashion. In such a society, Protestantism has had a variety of responses to the concept of the Devil and of radical evil. Three main strands can be traced in current Protestantism: a conservative, traditional, view; a liberal, skeptical view; and a so-called "literalist" biblical view typical of Evangelicals. The tension between liberal and conservative forces within Protestantism continues into the twenty-first century, but in broad societal terms the liberals have been successful in persuading most of the Western world (though not less devolved cultures) to disbelieve in both the Devil and hell. To many contemporary Christians the Devil seems old-fashioned and absurd in the context of the dominant materialist worldview of the time, which in fact has no room for any sort of Christianity at all, demythologized or not. What remains to be seen is whether Protestantism has the resources to give society the ability to suspend irony in the face of real suffering—in the face of the Devil.

References and Further Reading

Delbanco, Andrew. *Satan: How Americans Have Lost the Sense of Evil.* New York: Farrar, Straus, & Giroux, 1995.
Forsyth, Neil. *The Old Enemy: Satan and the Combat Myth.* Princeton, NJ: Princeton University Press, 1987.
Pagels, Elaine. *The Origin of Satan.* New York: Random House, 1995.
Russell, Jeffrey Burton. *The Devil.* Ithaca, NY: Cornell University Press, 1977.
———. *Satan.* Ithaca, NY: Cornell University Press, 1982.
———. *Lucifer.* Ithaca, NY: Cornell University Press, 1984.
———. *Mephistopheles.* Ithaca, NY: Cornell University Press, 1986.
———. *The Prince of Darkness.* Ithaca, NY: Cornell University Press, 1988.

JEFFREY BURTON RUSSELL

DEVOTIONAL LITERATURE

See Publishing, Media

DE VRIES, PETER (1910–1993)

American writer. The author of twenty-three novels, De Vries narrated the consequences of social mobility and cultural change for religious identity and community.

Life and Works

Born on the south side of Chicago of Dutch immigrant parents February 27, 1910, De Vries was raised in the CHRISTIAN REFORMED CHURCH (Calvinist), educated in its schools, reared in an ethos that judged movie attendance, dancing, card playing, and shopping or sports on Sunday as "worldly," and graduated from

Calvin College, a denominational institution, in 1931. He lived in Chicago until 1944, where he published stories in *Story* and *Esquire,* joined the editorial staff of *Poetry* in 1938, and published his first novel (1940). With the encouragement of writer James Thurber (1894–1961), he joined the staff of *The New Yorker.* He lived in Westport, Connecticut with his wife, nee Katinka Loeser (1913–1991), whom he married in 1943. They had four children, one of whom, Emily, died in 1960.

The Blood of the Lamb (1962), which narrates the protagonist's upward mobility and the death of his daughter, is typical of De Vries's work. It juxtaposes Midwestern and Eastern settings, religious/ethnic and secular/mobile cultures, and experiences of pain and loss with rollicking comedy. De Vries's achievement of posing and mutually illuminating these and other contraries in his narratives and securing, at the same time, the integrity, generosity, and modesty of his main characters and/or narrators is noteworthy.

De Vries clarifies the distinction between traditional, ethnic Protestant beliefs and behaviors and those of a religiously vague or diverse American culture. He also records the tension between Reformed doctrines, particularly divine sovereignty and human depravity, and experience, particularly personal suffering and human friendship. His comedy does not ridicule, but encourages those who encounter and negotiate religious, cultural, and personal conflicts, and it affirms that experience, for better and worse, challenges expectations. De Vries died September 2, 1993, in Connecticut.

WESLEY A. KORT

DIALECTICAL THEOLOGY

See Neo-Orthodoxy

DIALOGUE, INTERCONFESSIONAL

Interconfessional dialogue designates a process aimed at settling historically and theologically divisive differences among communities that all claim to be in some sense "Christian" and "church." Although the procedure may go back to the sixteenth century (the "colloquies" between the Saxon and the Swiss Reformers at MARBURG in 1529, between Roman Catholics and Protestants at Ratisbon/REGENSBURG in 1541, or between Lutherans and Reformed at Montbéliard in 1586), or even to the fifteenth century (as in the attempted reconciliation between Western Catholics and Eastern Orthodox around the council of Ferrara-Florence), it was in the ecumenical movement of the twentieth century that the practice of such dialogue flourished, albeit with variations of pace and perhaps with different visions of the final goal. Conversations

between two parties became known as bilateral dialogues, whereas several parties are said to engage in multilateral dialogue. Dialogues have taken place at national, regional, and universal levels. Particular dialogues have stretched over years and even decades.

The most comprehensive dialogues have been those characteristic of the Faith and Order movement, which dates from 1920 and has since 1948 taken institutional form as the Faith and Order commission of the WORLD COUNCIL OF CHURCHES. At first, the participants were Protestant (including Anglicans in prominent roles) and Orthodox, but since 1968 the 120-member commission has also included twelve official Roman Catholic members. World Conferences on Faith and Order—Lausanne (1927), Edinburgh (1938), Lund (1952), Montreal (1963), and Santiago de Compostela (1993)—were staging posts along a way of continuous study and conversation on such topics as the nature and structure of the CHURCH, its WORSHIP, and its sources and agencies of AUTHORITY. In particular the statement achieved at Montreal on "Scripture, Tradition and Traditions" provided a framework for progress toward agreement on particular issues. The most widely produced and received document was that issuing from the meeting of the commission at Lima, Peru, in 1982, under the title *Baptism, Eucharist and Ministry*; it stated a convergence and developing consensus on those three themes. The Lima text had been fifty-five years in the making before being considered mature enough for presentation to the sponsoring churches with the request for an official response as to "the extent to which your church can recognize in this text the faith of the Church through the ages," "the consequences your church can draw from this text for its relations and dialogues with other churches," and "the guidance your church can take from this text for its worship, educational, ethical, and spiritual life and witness." Although the churches were not invited to formally adopt the Lima text, its influence in all the mentioned areas has been quite considerable. Ongoing projects in Faith and Order include "the common expression of the apostolic faith today" (study document *Confessing the One Faith,* 1991) and *The Nature and Identity of the Church* (interim statement, 1998).

Although some transconfessional unions of a structural or organic kind have been achieved at the national or regional level (as between Anglicans, Methodists, and Reformed in South India since 1947; or between Methodists, Presbyterians, and Congregationalists in CANADA since 1925 and in AUSTRALIA since 1977), it is more by the bilateral route that new or restored relationships have been sought and formalized between what were for a while called "world confessional families" and more recently "Christian world communions." Dialogue between Anglicans and Old Catholics resulted in the Bonn Agreement of 1931, whereby the two communions enjoy full mutual recognition and sacramental sharing. Dialogue between Lutherans and Reformed in Europe led to the establishment of a similar mutual relationship by the Leuenberg Agreement of 1973, which has either been directly extended or had repercussions in other parts of the world, and has more recently allowed for some Methodist churches also to be brought into the Leuenberg Church Fellowship.

A global Anglican–Lutheran dialogue has provided at least a framework for the establishment of new relationships of various kinds between some Lutheran and Anglican churches at the regional or national level, as between the CHURCH OF ENGLAND and the Evangelical Church in GERMANY (by the Meissen Declaration, signed in 1991), or between churches in the British Isles and in the Nordic countries (by the Porvoo Declaration, signed in 1996), or in the United States between the EPISCOPAL CHURCH and the EVANGELICAL LUTHERAN CHURCH ("Called to Common Mission," effective 2001). The dialogue between the LUTHERAN WORLD FEDERATION and the WORLD METHODIST COUNCIL, with its report on "The Church—Community of Grace" (1984), supplied a context for the "fellowship of word and sacrament" subsequently established between Lutheran and Methodist churches in Germany, Austria, SWEDEN, and NORWAY. A dialogue between the World Methodist Council and the WORLD ALLIANCE OF REFORMED CHURCHES concluded in its report "Together in God's Grace" (1987) that there was "sufficient agreement in doctrine and practice" to justify existing unions between denominations of the two traditions and to encourage further fellowship, cooperation, and even unions elsewhere.

Although some of these dialogues began earlier, it was the official entrance of the Roman Catholic Church on the ecumenical scene with the Second Vatican Council (1962–1965) that made bilateral dialogues the most prominent instrument of sustained doctrinal conversation and negotiation at the universal level. Having its own self-understanding as a universal ecclesial body composed of episcopally governed particular churches that are in a mutual communion, the touchstone of which is their respective communion with the church and bishop of Rome, the Roman Catholic Church has successfully invited into dialogue with itself a number of partners whose self-understandings and implied ecclesiologies vary among themselves. These include the Eastern Orthodox Churches, which look to Constantinople as the Ecumenical Patriarchate (see ORTHODOX, EASTERN); the various Oriental Orthodox Churches, which never accepted the council of Chalcedon 451; the Anglican

Communion; the Lutheran World Federation; the World Alliance of Reformed Churches; the World Methodist Council; the BAPTIST WORLD ALLIANCE; the DISCIPLES OF CHRIST; the Mennonite World Conference (see MENNONITES); and several harder-to-pinpoint groups of Pentecostals and Evangelicals. By far the largest body of Christians in the world, the Roman Catholic Church, appears to have met with the agreement of the other communities to treat in distinct dialogues the issues that were controversial and divisive between Rome and each of them. On the Roman side the dialogues have been conducted under the aegis of the Secretariat (later Pontifical Council) for Promoting Christian Unity.

Among post–Vatican II dialogues between Protestant bodies and the Roman Catholic Church, it was probably the work of the Anglican–Roman Catholic International Commission (ARCIC) that made the early program. The first ARCIC produced "agreed statements" on "Eucharistic Doctrine" (Windsor 1971), "Ministry and Ordination" (Canterbury 1973), and "Authority in the Church" (Venice 1976), and these were incorporated—together with "elucidations" and a further statement on Authority—into a "Final Report" (1981). Although the worldwide Anglican bishops at the LAMBETH CONFERENCE of 1988 found the texts on eucharist and on ministry "a sufficient basis for taking the next step toward the reconciliation of our Churches grounded in agreement in faith," the response from the Vatican in 1991 considered the welcome "progress" made in the dialogue as yet insufficient to permit the affirmation of "substantial agreement" in some "essential matters" in those two areas, let alone in the areas of magisterial and pastoral authority. Nevertheless a second ARCIC pursued the dialogue and issued statements on "Salvation and the Church" (Llandaff 1986), "Church as Communion" (Dublin 1990), "Life in Christ—Morals, Communion and the Church" (1993), and "The Gift of Authority" (Palazzola 1998). It is insisted that the statements of the Commission are not "authoritative declarations" by the sponsoring bodies but are published for the sake of allowing wide discussion before authoritative evaluations are made.

Contemporaneously the dialogue between the Lutheran World Federation and Rome had proceeded by way of a study commission's work on "The Gospel and the Church" (Malta 1972) and then reports of a Joint Roman Catholic–Lutheran Commission on "Eucharist" (1978) and "Ministry in the Church" (1981) as well as texts produced around the time of the 450th anniversary of the Diet of Augsburg on "Ways to Community" and "All Under One Christ" (both 1980), themes that were pursued around the time of the 500th anniversary of MARTIN LUTHER's birth in "Martin

Luther—Witness to Jesus Christ" (1983) and "Facing Unity—Models, Forms and Phases of Catholic–Lutheran Church Fellowship" (1984). It was, however, the sharpening of the focus on the recurrent topic that Lutherans have always considered central to the REFORMATION—that is, the doctrine of JUSTIFICATION—that eventually allowed what is perhaps the most significant achievement so far of any dialogue between a Protestant body and the Roman Catholic Church. The Joint Commission's lengthy report "Church and Justification" was completed in 1993 and stands—together with work done in national dialogues in Germany and in the UNITED STATES—as the backdrop for the Joint Declaration on the Doctrine of Justification (JDDJ) that was solemnly signed on behalf of the Lutheran World Federation and the Roman Catholic Church at Augsburg on October 31, 1999. The attainment of "consensus on basic truths of the doctrine of justification"—allowing for "differing explications" of detail—meant that the mutual doctrinal condemnations of the sixteenth century "do not apply to today's partner" as the common and respective teachings are set forth in the JDDJ. It is expected that the JDDJ will provide "a solid basis" for "further clarification" on such topics as "the relationship between the word of God and church DOCTRINE, ECCLESIOLOGY, ecclesial authority, church unity, ministry, the SACRAMENTS, and the relation between justification and social ETHICS" and thus more generally "bear fruit in the life and teaching of the churches." The JDDJ is not yet viewed as making possible eucharistic communion between Lutherans and Roman Catholics. In 2001 explorations began with a view to finding ways in which Methodist and Reformed bodies could become associated with the Lutheran–Roman Catholic agreement on justification.

Both the World Methodist Council and the World Alliance of Reformed Churches engaged in their own dialogues with the Roman Catholic Church in the final third of the twentieth century. The Joint Commission between the Roman Catholic Church and the World Methodist Council treated eucharist and ministry among a plethora of themes in its reports of 1971 and 1976, but began to achieve more systematic focus with documents on the Holy Spirit (1981) and the Church (1986) before developing a series of statements in fundamental THEOLOGY that were intended to "set out theological perspectives within which more specific questions may be viewed": "The Apostolic Tradition" (1991), "The Word of Life: A Statement on Revelation and Faith" (1996), "Speaking the Truth in Love: Teaching Authority among Roman Catholics and Methodists" (2001). The sponsoring bodies have encouraged the continuing work of the Joint Commission without yet coming to a formal evaluation of its

results. The commitment to a "goal of full communion in faith, mission and sacramental life" has been repeatedly affirmed. The dialogues between representatives of the World Alliance of Reformed Churches and the Roman Catholic Church have emphasized the location and role of the church in the world: thus "The Presence of Christ in Church and World" (1970–1977), "Towards a Common Understanding of the Church" (1984–1990, with the important theme of "a reconciliation of memories"), and "Church as Community of Common Witness to the Kingdom of God" (since 1998)—an approach found also in the Reformed dialogue with Anglicans that produced "God's Reign and Our Unity" (1984).

In addition to these dialogues dealing with the inherited divisions in Western Christendom, not only the Roman Catholic Church but also several Protestant bodies have engaged at various levels in dialogue with the Eastern Orthodox churches and even, in some cases, with the Oriental Orthodox.

The highly complex pattern of bilateral dialogues raises the question of consistency between positions expressed and results achieved by the various participant bodies in relation to different partners. Thus the multilateral dimension cannot be ignored. Since Vatican II, a Joint Working Group has existed between the Roman Catholic Church and the World Council of Churches, and the WCC Faith and Order Commission has facilitated periodic forums to trace the progress of the various bilateral dialogues. From a positive point of view, the mutual influences and borrowings between the bilateral dialogues must be recorded.

The complexity of the ecumenical scene is compounded by the question of what a final resolution of inherited divisions would entail. The dominance of "world confessional families" or "Christian world communions" in the latter part of the twentieth century has tended to favor a goal of "reconciled diversity" or a "communion of communions" in which the diverse traditions would continue to bear a certain ecclesiological significance. Cardinal Jan Willebrands, president of the Secretariat/Council for Promoting Christian Unity (1969–1989), launched the notion of ecclesial "typoi," which would each maintain certain theological, liturgical, spiritual, and disciplinary characteristics of their own, even while agreeing in fundamental doctrine and sharing some kind of pastoral and governmental structure. Precisely the last is the likely sticking point insofar as it involves the question of overlapping jurisdictions. In ancient, medieval, and even early-modern times, ecclesial unity has been thought to carry a certain geographical quality, whether in the primitive picture of one bishop in one church in one place reflected in the letters of Ignatius of Antioch, or in the sees and dioceses of the

Constantinian era, or even in the post-Reformation settlement of *cuius regio eius religio*. A communion of spatially coinciding communions would presumably require some form of collegial or corporate oversight in each of an agreed and perhaps mobile set of units.

This is the developing landscape that has seen the reemergence of the question of a universal ministry of unity. Pope John Paul II took the matter up in his 1995 encyclical affirming the "irrevocable" commitment of the Roman Catholic Church to ECUMENISM. For the pope, dialogue is the appropriate, "personalist" modality in the search for full communion among Christians and their communities, involving not only an "exchange of ideas" but always an "exchange of gifts." Mindful of "the grave obstacle which the lack of unity represents for the proclamation of the Gospel," John Paul II in "Ut Unum Sint" invited "church leaders and their theologians to engage with [him] in a patient and fraternal dialogue" toward finding a way of exercising the primacy claimed and offered by the see of Rome in the service of truth and love that, "while in no way renouncing what is essential to its mission," would nonetheless be "open to a new situation."

See also Anglicanism; Catholic Reactions to Protestantism; Catholicism, Protestant Reactions; Congregationalism; Lutheranism; Methodism; Presbyterianism

References and Further Reading

Baptism, Eucharist and Ministry 1982–1990: Report on the Process and Responses. Geneva, Switerland: WCC, 1990.

Burgess, Joseph A., and Jeffrey Gros, eds. *Building Unity: Ecumenical Dialogues with Roman Catholic Participation in the United States.* Mahwah, NJ: Paulist Press, 1989.

Gassmann, Günther. "Nature and Function of Bilateral and Multilateral Dialogues and Their Inter-relation." *Mid-Stream* 25 (1986): 299–308.

Gros, Jeffrey, Harding Meyer, and William G. Rusch, eds. *Growth in Agreement II: Reports and Agreed Statements of Ecumenical Conversations on a World Level, 1982–1998.* Geneva, Switerland: WCC; Grand Rapids, MI: Wm. B. Eerdmans, 2000.

Hill, Christopher, and Edward Yarnold. *Anglicans and Roman Catholics: The Search for Unity. The ARCIC Documents and Their Reception.* London: SPCK/CTS, 1994.

Meyer, Harding, and Lukas Vischer, eds. *Growth in Agreement: Reports and Agreed Statements of Ecumenical Conversations on a World Level.* Geneva, Switerland: WCC; Ramsey, NJ: Paulist Press, 1984.

Storman, E. J., ed. *Towards the Healing of Schism: The Sees of Rome and Constantinople. Public Statements and Correspondence between the Holy See and the Ecumenical Patriarchate 1958–1984.* Mahwah, NJ: Paulist Press, 1987.

GEOFFREY WAINWRIGHT

DIBELIUS, FRIEDRICH KARL OTTO (1880–1967)

German Lutheran bishop. Dibelius was born in Berlin on May 15, 1880, the second of three sons of a high-ranking postal administrator. He died on January 31, 1967, also in Berlin where he had become an honorary citizen in 1958. He studied theology in Berlin with the church historian ADOLF VON HARNACK being the primary influence on him. After the presentation of his philological dissertation at the University of Gießen and completion of the first theological exam, Dibelius attended the seminary in Wittenberg (1904–1906), the place where the future leaders of the Prussian state church were educated. He received his Ph.D. there and a licentiate (doctor) of theology in 1906. This stage of his studies took him to SCOTLAND on a church-financed month-long trip, where he was especially impressed by the devoutness practiced in the CHURCH there.

After brief stints in several provinces (in Crossen/Brandenburg, Danzig, Lauenburg/Pommerania, 1907–1915) Dibelius became a pastor in the German capital Berlin. He understood World War I to be a just and defensive war for GERMANY; the abolition of the monarchy at the end of the war upset him, but initially it did not threaten his nationalist mentality. His position at the Evangelical Consistory in Berlin hung in the balance with the dissolution of the royal church regiment, but the representatives of an advisory council set up to lead the church under these new conditions named him chairman. At the same time Dibelius published prolifically both on the church policy pursued by the political left and against those in the church who sought to reform a governmentally organized Evangelical Church in Prussia.

Subsequently Dibelius's career advanced quickly. In 1921 he was put in charge of the Evangelical Consistory concerned with social issues and the evangelical schools, but also with evangelical minorities abroad. In 1925 he became superintendent of the church in the Kurmark, roughly the area near Berlin. He tackled work issues with fervent energy. He bought a car to be able to visit all the pastors in his district, held regional church meetings, supported the church press, and intensely debated public issues. He developed his broader program in a book, *Das Jahrhundert der Kirche* (*The Century of the Church,* 1926, 1928). In this best-seller, he called on German Christians to use the separation of CHURCH AND STATE that had been forcibly introduced in 1919, to hold on to an evangelical-Christian and nationalist-conservative culture and morality vis-à-vis a secular Weimar Republic, and to expand and defend that culture comprehensively and forcefully. The ecumenical conference on "Life and Work" in Stockholm (1925) had influenced this concept. Two additional books by Dibelius showed the extension of his historical compass and the degradation of his nationalism: *Kirche und Völkerbund* (*Church and the League of Nations*, 1927) as well as *Friede auf Erden* (*Peace on Earth*, 1930), the former a book that examined the subject of militarism prevalent in the church, the latter advocating the individual's right to refuse military service for reasons of conscience.

Initially Dibelius was not at all critical of National Socialism, but sought to fend off its intervention in church matters. Subsequently, in June 1933 he was dismissed from his post of superintendent. He joined the CONFESSING CHURCH, where he participated loyally and consistently, although in a secondary position. In the sometimes divisive battles of the Confessing Church, he opted neither for the direction advocated by MARTIN NIEMÖLLER, nor for the Lutheran confessionalists who gathered around Bishop Hanns Meiser of Bavaria. Rather, Dibelius strongly supported the "Church Unity Project" of Bishop Theophil Wurm in Württemberg, who after 1941 sought to build a coalition of those with a neutral position and those who had taken a specific position within the Confessing Church. In 1945 this "Unity Project" provided the foundation for the Evangelical Church in Germany (EKD).

In 1945 he was elected bishop of the Evangelical Church in Berlin-Brandenburg—a position he held until 1966—where he contributed substantially to the integration of the evangelical churches within the EKD. His sober and pragmatic style, always geared toward the essential, never lost sight of the goal to integrate the divergent personalities and groups. It characterized his tenure as EKD council chairman; this was not a time without tension, but he was always sustained by the majority. He drew the wrath of the powers in the German Democratic Republic, however, because he refused to recognize that state and because he often drew comparisons between their policies, especially vis-à-vis the church, and the Nazi policy toward the church. Dibelius was fervent and uncompromising in this regard. Over the years, however, his position met opposition among those church groups that sought a more flexible policy in the interest of a coherence of churches and congregations in East and West; until 1968 the EKD was an all-German entity. The disagreement escalated in 1959 when Dibelius claimed in a publication entitled "Obrigkeit?" ("Authorities?") that the government of the GDR should not be recognized as an authority ordained by God. Hence, in the eyes of many evangelical Christians in both parts of Germany, he came to be seen as a reactionary personality. Yet within the ecumenical movement, the attitude toward him was partly different. Dibelius, who was consistently active in that movement, was elected one of the six presidents of the WORLD COUNCIL OF CHURCHES during the plenary at the 1954 Evanston meeting—against the forceful resistance of some German delegates. He held that office until 1961.

Along with sometimes vociferous antagonism, Dibelius also met with worldwide approval and recognition during his lifetime. The concept he advocated, that of a church and society modeled after a national church that reflects morally religious grandeur toward society, but is also partially inflected by an antisecular, antisocialist, and, partially, anti-Semitic sense, was seen in the outlook of ADOLF STOECKER, a man Dibelius admired. It was also combined with other traits, however, especially in connection with his experiences with ECUMENISM. The evangelical theologian and bishop is one of the most important representatives of the evangelical church in Germany in the twentieth century.

See also German Christians

References and Further Reading

Primary Source:

Dibelius, Otto. *Ein Christ ist immer im Dienst*. Stuttgart, Germany: Kreuz-Verlag, 1961.

Secondary Source:

Stupperich, Robert. *Otto Dibelius*. Göttingen, Germany: Vandenhoeck & Ruprecht, 1989. [Includes bibliography with publications by Dibelius.]

MARTIN GRESCHAT

DIBELIUS, MARTIN (1883–1947)

German New Testament scholar. Born in Dresden, GERMANY, Dibelius studied THEOLOGY in Neuchatel, Leipzig, Tuebingen, and Berlin. He passed his first theological exam and received his Doctor of Philosophy in 1905. After receiving his license in theology (1908) and completing his habilitation in the New Testament (1910), he became a professor at Heidelberg (1915), and remained there until his death.

The history of religions school influenced his methodology; this was evident in his early commentaries on the Pauline epistles and the Pastoral epistles. His work in form criticism was pathbreaking. See *Die Formgeschichte des Evangeliums* (1919, *From Tradition to Gospel*, tr. 1934). Dibelius understood the gospels as collections of smaller units originally transmitted orally; he traced the development of these units, classified them, and sought to discern their original function and context. He saw PREACHING as the key to understanding the formation of Christian TRADITION. He also applied form-critical principles to Acts, the canonical epistles, and other early Christian literature. Dibelius was interested in the gospel's relationship to the world, both in early Christianity and in his own time. His commentary on James (1921), one of the most influential in the twentieth century, presented James as an exhortation to live the Christian life.

Dibelius believed it the Christian's duty to be involved in public matters. He was politically involved in democratic causes from his student days. The Nazi regime curtailed his scholarly and political activities, but did not remove him from his position. After the end of World War II, the Americans sought his help in reopening and reconfiguring Heidelberg University.

See also Bultmann, Rudolf

References and Further Reading

Epp, Eldon Jay, and George W. MacRae. *The New Testament and Its Modern Interpreters.* Philadelphia, PA: Fortress and Atlanta: Scholars Press, 1989
Geiser, Stefan. *Verantwortung und Schuld: Studien zu Martin Dibelius.* Hamburg, Germany: LIT, 2001

MARY JANE HAEMIG

DICKINSON, EMILY (1830–1886)

American poet. Dickinson was born December 10, 1830, and spent her entire life in the New England village of Amherst, Massachusetts. Her parents, Edward and Emily Norcross Dickinson, were members of the nineteenth century's rising professional class, and the family's life centered around Amherst College, which her grandfather founded and where her father and brother both served in various capacities.

The oldest of three children, Emily grew up in an environment that was Whiggish in its politics and modified Calvinist in its theology (see CALVINISM). Her training emphasized the benefits of prudence more than the ecstasies of the spirit and the virtues of benevolence more than the terrors of hell. Dickinson attended church regularly with her family through her twenties, but never joined the congregation and, by the age of thirty, no longer took part in its services.

Dickinson's adult years were occupied with the writing of poetry and letters and, with the help of her sister Lavinia, the managing of her family's home. Emily entertained seriously the thought of marriage only once, and that was when she was past fifty. Increasingly reclusive, she left the grounds of her family's home but once in the last two decades of her life.

Dickinson began to write poetry in her late twenties, and by the age of thirty-five had written over a thousand poems. Although her pace slackened in later years, she continued to compose works and left behind at her death almost 1,800 poems. The first edition of her poetry was published four years after her death and proved an instant success. Her reputation was quickly established, and she is now regarded as one of the finest lyric poets in the English language.

Taking the metrical patterns of the Protestant hymnal as her guide (see HYMNS AND HYMNALS), Dickinson fashioned a brilliantly eccentric poetic style, which she employed to explore the great religious themes of suffering, belief, personal identity, and the existence of God. Scientifically articulate and philosophically astute, Dickinson confronted in her poetry the crucial issues that prompted doubts about the Christian faith in the nineteenth century. To the end, she remained troubled about God the Father, who exists "Somewhere—in Silence," but found comfort in Jesus the Son, the "Tender Pioneer" who has gone before us in the way of suffering and death.

While living the most intensely focused inward life of any major figure in American history, Dickinson produced a body of work that made her the greatest of all American poets and one of the most creatively enigmatic religious thinkers American culture has ever produced.

References and Further Reading

Eberwein, Jane Donahue. *Dickinson: Strategies of Limitation.* Amherst: University of Massachusetts Press, 1985.
Franklin, R. W., ed. *The Poems of Emily Dickinson.* Cambridge: The Belknap Press of Harvard University Press, 1999.
Lundin, Roger. *Emily Dickinson and the Art of Belief.* Grand Rapids, MI: Wm. B. Eerdmans, 1998.

ROGER LUNDIN

DISCIPLES OF CHRIST

The religious reform movement, originating in America and Great Britain at the turn of the nineteenth century, was also known as the Christian or Restoration Movement, although it was increasingly labeled the Stone–Campbell Movement in the late twentieth century after its founding leaders, BARTON W. STONE and Thomas and Alexander Campbell (see CAMPBELL FAMILY). The original impulse was to restore the primitive New Testament church as a means to effect Christian unity. The American movement suffered two divisions in the twentieth century, resulting in three church bodies: the Churches of Christ, the undenominational fellowship of CHRISTIAN CHURCHES and CHURCHES OF CHRIST—often known as independent Christian Churches—and the Christian Church (Disciples of Christ). Congregations with roots in this movement exist in over 160 countries.

American Origins

The movement's earliest American origins are found in the work of Barton W. Stone (1772–1844). Baptized Anglican at birth (see ANGLICANISM), Stone experienced CONVERSION in 1791 under the preaching of Presbyterian revivalists James McGready (1760–1817) and William Hodge (see PRESBYTERIANISM). He became pastor for two Presbyterian congregations near Paris, Kentucky in 1796. In spring 1801 he witnessed events of the Great Western Revival led by McGready in Logan County, Kentucky, connected with annual sacramental services (see REVIVALS). Stone organized such a gathering for his church at Cane Ridge, August 7–12, 1801. The Cane Ridge CAMP MEETING was one of the largest and most spectacular of the era in its emotional fervor and interdenominational cooperation.

Stemming partially from events at Cane Ridge, the antirevival Synod of Kentucky moved against Stone's colleague, Richard McNemar (1770–1839). At the 1803 synod meeting, Stone, McNemar, and three other ministers withdrew to form the Springfield Presbytery. In "An Apology for Renouncing the Jurisdiction of the Synod of Kentucky" (1804), the ministers stated that although they still considered themselves in communion with the Presbyterian Church, they were compelled to separate to avoid constant conflict over issues of theology and polity.

Within a year, however, the leaders of the Springfield Presbytery dissolved the body. In "The Last Will and Testament of the Springfield Presbytery" (1804) they wrote, "We will that this body die, be dissolved, and sink into union with the body of Christ at large; for there is but one Body, and one Spirit. . . ." In an attempt to avoid distinguishing themselves from other followers of Christ, they called themselves simply Christians and their churches Christian Churches, taking their cue from the Christian groups led by James O'Kelly (1757–1826) in North Carolina, and by Elias Smith (1769–1846) and Abner Jones (1772–1841) in New England. Stone became the acknowledged leader of the movement that by the late 1820s had over 12,000 members in at least ten states.

Campbell Movement

The second part of the Stone–Campbell Movement originated in Northern Ireland in the ministry of Thomas Campbell (1763–1854). Campbell was part of the Old Light, Anti-Burgher division of the Secession Church, known as the Associate Synod, itself a schism from the CHURCH OF SCOTLAND. He spent years trying to heal the divisions in IRELAND to no avail. When Campbell became ill under the stress, he was advised to remove himself from the situation or face continued deteriorating health, so he immigrated to the United States.

Upon arrival in Philadelphia in 1807, Campbell presented himself to the meeting of the Associate Synod—already organized in America—and received a preaching appointment in western Pennsylvania between Pittsburgh and Washington. His proclivity for unity led him to allow Presbyterians who were not members of his group to participate in the communion service. A fellow minister traveling with Campbell reported him to the Presbytery of Chartiers on their return to Pittsburgh, beginning a nearly two-year procession of accusations and trials that ended in 1809 with Campbell's withdrawal from the Associate Synod.

Friends in western Pennsylvania continued to support Campbell's ministry. They formed a society for the promotion of unity and evangelical Christianity named the Christian Association, and designated Campbell to write an explanation of its nature and aims. In "The Declaration and Address of the Christian Association of Washington, Pennsylvania" (1809) he described the mechanism he believed would bring about Christian unity. True Christians should abandon allegiance to denominational creeds and structures as terms of communion and recognize each other as Christians based solely on adherence to the clear teachings of scripture. Such Christians should come together in every locality to form a church of Christ, in communion with every other such body worldwide.

Thomas Campbell's son Alexander provided substance to his father's proposals. Alexander Campbell (1788–1866) and the rest of Thomas's family arrived in America in 1809 in the midst of Thomas's religious changes. The younger Campbell threw himself into the reform work his father had begun and within a few years took the lead. In 1811 the Christian Association organized itself into the Brush Run Church and ordained Alexander to the ministry the following year.

The issue of BAPTISM became crucial at the birth of Alexander Campbell's first child in 1812. Both Campbells knew of the controversies over baptism among Scottish independents, especially the division among followers of John Glas that produced the Scotch Baptists. Alexander studied the matter for some time, concluding that infant baptism was not scriptural. This led to his decision to seek immersion at the hands of a Baptist minister, Matthias Luce (1764–1831). Several others in the Brush Run Church, including his mother and father, joined Campbell, and soon the congregation was one of baptized believers.

This stance on baptism led many to view the Campbells as BAPTISTS, prompting the Redstone Baptist Association to invite their church to join. Although the Campbells made it clear they could not accept the Baptists' Philadelphia Confession of Faith, the Brush Run Church was admitted into the Redstone Association in 1815, and the Campbells did their reform work as Baptists until around 1830. From 1823 to 1830 Alexander Campbell published a religious journal named *The Christian Baptist*. Campbell also gained considerable fame through his debates on baptism with Presbyterians John Walker (1820), William Maccalla (1823), and Nathan Rice (1843).

Joining Forces

By the 1820s the Campbell and Stone Movements experienced increasing contact. The two groups shared anticreed, antisectarian, prounity, and Bible-only stances, although they differed in significant ways. Stone focused on the power of scripture to transform lives, whereas Alexander Campbell emphasized the importance of discerning New Testament facts concerning belief and practice. In 1825 Campbell began a series of articles in the *Christian Baptist* titled "A Restoration of the Ancient Order of Things," describing beliefs and practices of the early church he believed had been lost or corrupted. These included immersion of believers, weekly observance of the Lord's Supper, congregational polity with governance by local elders, and simple worship with songs reflecting scriptural concepts, all of which became central tenets of the movement.

Although the Stone churches taught immersion of believers, they often practiced "open membership," accepting those who had been baptized as infants. The Campbell churches generally insisted on immersion as a prerequisite for membership, though not denying there were unimmersed Christians. The Stone movement preferred the name Christian; Alexander Campbell preferred disciples, partly to avoid confusion of his movement with the Smith–Jones Movement Christians who were unitarian. Stone held a premillennial eschatology and a negative view of human nature. Campbell was postmillennial and optimistic about the ability of Christians to restore the primitive church, bring Christian unity, and the conversion of the world (see MILLENARIANS AND MILLENNIALISM). The two leaders differed as well in their understanding of the nature of Christ, the ATONEMENT, and the role of the Holy Spirit in conversion.

Despite the differences, beginning in the early 1830s many Stone and Campbell congregations in Kentucky and surrounding states united. Individual congregations used the names Christian Church, Church of Christ, and Disciples of Christ interchangeably. By 1860 the movement in the United States claimed over 200,000 members in about 2,000 congregations. Initial evangelistic success was attributed largely to the work of Walter Scott, who developed a simple Christocentric method of teaching. Instead of a Calvinist appeal to wait for the Holy Spirit, Scott taught that anyone could hear and believe the gospel, repent of past sins, submit to baptism (immersion), and receive the gift of the Holy Spirit and eternal life (see CALVINISM). This was often referred to as the "five finger exercise" because its five points could be taught using the fingers of one hand.

Scotch Baptists who immigrated to eastern Canada in the early 1800s formed the nucleus of the movement in that country. David Oliphant Sr., James Black (1797–1886), and John McKellar were among the earliest leaders. Early contact with both the Stone and Campbell Movements in the United States led many of these Baptist congregations to affiliate with the Stone–Campbell Movement in the 1830s and following. These churches tended to be narrow and legalistic and did not experience the growth of the movement in the United States. By 1867 there were about seventy churches, with an estimated membership of 4,000.

The early movement in Great Britain had similar contours. Independent congregations practicing immersion and designated Church of Christ existed in SCOTLAND and Ireland in the late 1700s and early 1800s. Scotch Baptist minister William Jones (1762–1846) began in 1835 republishing material from Alexander Campbell's journal the *Millennial Harbinger* (1830–1870), although he later repudiated Campbell's ideas. James Wallis, also a Scotch Baptist, broke with that group in 1836 and began publishing *The Christian Messenger and Reformer*, which became a major force among Churches of Christ in Great Britain. By 1847 these churches numbered eighty, with about 2,300 members. British members took the movement to New Zealand in 1843, and in 1845 Thomas Magarey brought it from New Zealand to Australia.

In October 1849 the first General Convention, held in Cincinnati, Ohio, created the American Christian Missionary Society (ACMS). Alexander Campbell was elected President (in absentia), a post he held until his death in 1866. Although some opposed the society as an unscriptural organization, the issue did not become divisive until the CIVIL WAR. Many leaders in both North and South were pacifists (see PACIFISM). When the war broke out, however, the Society, now a de facto northern institution, felt pressure to make a statement of loyalty to the Union. In 1861 and 1863 the ACMS passed resolutions supporting the northern cause. Southern leaders like Tolbert Fanning (1810–1874) concluded that they could not endorse the society until it repented of this evil.

Division

The circumstances of the first division of the movement in the late nineteenth and early twentieth centuries were not merely sectional. Economic and sociological factors stemming from the war played a part in the rejection by many southern churches of the missionary society and instruments in worship. Yet theological objections had been raised early, and many northern churches also rejected the "innovations." In the U.S. religious census of 1906, many of the conservative churches were listed separately as Churches of Christ, with the others listed as Disciples of Christ.

The second division reflected issues of the fundamentalist–modernist controversy, including higher criticism of scripture and the controversy over evolution (see FUNDAMENTALISM, MODERNITY). The most divisive early issue, however, was that of "open membership" on the mission field. The United Christian Missionary Society (UCMS), formed in 1920 by a merger of Disciples agencies, investigated the charges and cleared the missionaries involved despite evidence it was being practiced. Congregations that stopped support of the UCMS and organized independent mission work became known as independent Christian Churches. Members of these churches began meeting in a North American Christian Convention in 1927, though not at first as a rival to the International Convention of Disciples of Christ. From 1934 to 1948 the Commission on Restudy of the Disciples of Christ attempted to work through the problems with little success. The Panel of Scholars (1957–1963), the Study Committee on Brotherhood Restructure (1958–1960), and the Commission on Restructure (1962–1966) culminated in the adoption of the Provisional Design for Restructure of the Christian Church (Disciples of Christ) in 1968. The restructuring led many independent Christian Churches to final separation.

British Churches of Christ underwent similar divisions surrounding issues of cooperation and public worship. Many congregations organized themselves for cooperative work as early as 1842, but an "Old Paths" group resisted the organization and by 1945 was regarded as a completely separate body. In 1981 many of the churches in the "Co-Operation," then known as the Association of Churches of Christ, joined the United Reformed Church. Those that rejected the union continued as the Fellowship of Churches of Christ. Churches in Australia and New Zealand reflected comparable tensions.

Contemporary Organization

In the United States, the largest of the three bodies at the beginning of the twenty-first century was Churches of Christ, with approximately 1.25 million members in 13,000 congregations. Extensive twentieth-century mission work, especially in AFRICA, resulted in a membership outside the United States of over one million. This stream of the Stone–Campbell Movement experienced internal tensions over issues such as worship practices and exclusivist attitudes beginning in the 1970s. Informal structures such as annual lectureships and periodicals that helped provide a coherent identity for Churches of Christ in the past have come to serve as rallying points for differing positions. A number of colleges, universities, and seminaries are affiliated with Churches of Christ in the United States, including Pepperdine University (California), Abilene Christian University (Texas), and Lipscomb University (Tennessee).

The 1968 Restructure of the Christian Church (Disciples of Christ) focused on three manifestations of the church: local, regional, and general. At the General level a new office of general minister and president was created, and multifaceted ministries of the denomination were coordinated into units. The national offices for the denomination in the United States are in Indianapolis, Indiana. A General Assembly meets in uneven years. The Christian Church (Disciples of Christ) suffered membership losses similar to those suffered by other mainstream Protestant denominations in the late twentieth century. A small group of dissident members formed Disciple Renewal in 1985 to protest what they saw as a move away by leadership from a historic focus on Christ and biblical teaching. Disciples began the new millennium with approximately 800,000 members in 3,800 congregations in the United States and Canada. New church planting and theological discernment initiatives signaled efforts both to grow and strengthen the body in the twenty-first century.

Independent Christian Churches numbered over one million in the United States in 2000. These churches, although experiencing tensions like the other streams, have enjoyed significant growth in the early twenty-first century through church plantings by local evangelistic associations and parachurch organizations like the Christian Missionary Fellowship. The annual North American Christian Convention, although without any delegated authority over the churches, provides a forum for networking, reports from ministries, inspiration, and fellowship that provides a sense of identity for many in these churches.

Churches historically related to the Stone–Campbell Movement exist in over 160 countries. The World

Convention of Churches of Christ (WCCC), established in 1930 by Jesse M. Bader and meeting roughly every four years, serves as a forum to maintain contact between all parts of the movement in a context of Bible study and worship. In addition, yearly meetings between members of Churches of Christ and independent Christian Churches, known as Restoration Forums, were begun in 1984; and a more formal Stone–Campbell Dialogue with representatives from the three major streams in the United States began in 1999.

References and Further Reading

Chapman, Graeme. *One Lord, One Faith, One Baptism: A History of Churches of Christ in Australia.* 2nd ed. Glen Iris, Victoria: Vital Publications, 1989.

Cox, Claude E., ed. *The Campbell–Stone Movement in Ontario: Christian Church (Disciples of Christ, Churches of Christ, Independent Christian Churches/Churches of Christ).* New York: Edwin Mellen Press, 1995.

Foster, Douglas A. *Will the Cycle Be Unbroken? Churches of Christ Face the Twenty-First Century.* Abilene, TX: ACU Press, 1994.

Garrett, Leroy. *The Stone–Campbell Movement.* Rev. ed. Joplin, MO: College Press Publishing Company, 1995.

Hughes, Richard T. *Reviving the Ancient Faith: The Story of Churches of Christ in America.* Grand Rapids, MI: Wm. B. Eerdmans, 1996.

McAllister, Lester G., and William E. Tucker. *Journey in Faith: A History of the Christian Church (Disciples of Christ).* St. Louis: The Bethany Press, 1975.

North, James. *Union in Truth: An Interpretive History of the Restoration Movement.* Cincinnati: Standard Publishing Company, 1994.

Richardson, Robert. *Memoirs of Alexander Campbell: Embracing a View of the Origin, Progress and Principles of the Religious Reformation Which He Advocated.* Philadelphia, J. B. Lippincott & Co., 1868–1870; reprint edition, Indianapolis: Religious Book Service, 1980.

Thompson, David Michael. *Let Sects and Parties Fall: A Short History of the Association of Churches of Christ in Great Britain and Ireland.* Birmingham, UK: Berean Press, 1980.

Toulouse, Mark G. *Joined in Discipleship: The Shaping of Contemporary Disciples Identity,* rev. ed. St. Louis: Chalice Press, 1997.

Webb, Henry. *In Search of Christian Unity: A History of the Restoration Movement.* Revised edition. Abilene, TX: ACU Press, 2003.

West, Earl I. *The Search for the Ancient Order: A History of the Restoration Movement.* 4 vols. Nashville, TN: Gospel Advocate Company, 1949ff.

Williams, D. Newell. *Barton Stone: A Spiritual Biography.* St. Louis: Chalice Press, 2000.

DOUGLAS A. FOSTER

DISPENSATIONALISM

Dispensationalism is a tradition within American evangelical ORTHODOXY. Thus, it has much in common with other traditions within the extended family of Evangelicalism, both in thought and practice. The movement has consistently affirmed the inspiration, inerrancy, and AUTHORITY of Scripture (see BIBLICAL INERRANCY). Dispensationalists argue that the BIBLE, when interpreted according to a historical–grammatical–literary–theological method, results in the conclusion that God's purpose in history is to bring glory to himself. Further, God's work in history is seen to occur in clearly distinguishable periods of time, or dispensations. The number of dispensations is not as essential to the TRADITION as the recognition that there are discontinuities in the historical administration of God's plan. This tradition has a strong ecclesiastical emphasis, believing that the CHURCH is the primary means by which God carries out God's purposes in this age. Dispensationalists have emphasized both the universal, transdenominational identity of the church and its localized form in gathered communities of faith. Believing that apocalyptic and prophetic Scriptures have relevance for the present as well as the future, dispensationalists have strongly affirmed the imminent (at any time) return of Christ and a political future for Israel in God's plan (see APOCALYPTICISM). Dispensationalism is futurist premillennial in its ESCHATOLOGY and most of its proponents have believed in the doctrine of the RAPTURE of the church before the bodily return of Christ, although there are adherents of both the mid- and post-tribulation rapture positions in this tradition.

Dispensationalists generally agree that these distinguishable periods of time include different responsibilities for humans as they relate to God. A dispensation ends in the failure of humans to fulfill their obligations to God, which brings a resulting judgment on their SIN. A new dispensation, with a different administrative relationship, replaces the former one. Some critics of dispensationalism have caricatured the system as holding the unorthodox view that these rules and regulations are differing ways of SALVATION. Dispensationalists have always emphatically denied this charge, affirming with evangelical orthodoxy that salvation is always by GRACE through FAITH. In every dispensation, salvation is a gracious gift of God. What changes in the administrative discontinuity is the content of faith and the responsibilities God places on humanity. In response to the charge that dispensationalism is Antinomian (see ANTINOMIANISM), the tradition has consistently affirmed that there is law in every dispensation, although the content of that law may be different in each period of time. None of the legal requirements God places on humans was ever intended to produce salvation; rather, they were the means by which redeemed people maintain fellowship with their God.

Biblical Defense

Critics sometimes charge that dispensationalism is an interpretive grid imposed on the Scriptures. In response, dispensationalists point to the biblical usage of the Greek *oikonomia* in support of their view of history. In short they claim that dispensationalism is taught in Scripture, that the biblical writers use the word essentially in the same way that dispensationalists do. The basic meaning of *oikonomia,* which in its various forms appears about twenty times in the Greek New Testament, is "to manage, regulate, administer, and plan the affairs of a household." The word is rendered in various translations as "dispensation, economy, stewardship, arrangement, plan, administration." The word appears in a nontheological sense in the parable of Jesus in Luke 16:1–13. The household steward is accountable to his master for his handling of the affairs of the household. His failure to carry out his responsibilities to the satisfaction of his master results in a change of administration. This steward or manager is relieved of his duties and, presumably, a new *oikonomos* will be hired. Thus, the dispensation of the former steward ends and is replaced by another.

Theologically, the Apostle Paul uses *oikonomia* to define the responsibility that God has given to him (Ephesians 3:2–10). This dispensation is based on the work of Christ in his DEATH and resurrection (Ephesians 3:10; cf. Ephesians 2:13–18). This text seems to indicate that a dispensation preceded the Christ event, which was then replaced by one based on the work of the Messiah in his first coming. Further, Paul anticipates a future period of time, the "dispensation of the fulness of times" (Ephesians 1:10; KJV), when all things in HEAVEN and earth will be gathered together in Christ. Although some evangelicals see this as a reference to the present age, dispensationalists affirm that it is the eschatological Messianic age that is in view. Thus, dispensationalists claim, their reading of redemptive history is consistent with that of the Apostle Paul, whose writings provide biblical support for at least three dispensations.

Origins of Dispensationalism

Dispensationalism originated in the nineteenth century in the teaching of the Anglican JOHN NELSON DARBY (1800–1882) (see ANGLICANISM). Darby rejected the organized church as apostate, leading him to become part of a separatist group that later became known as the PLYMOUTH BRETHREN. Darby adopted a futurist premillennial eschatology, rejecting the historicist approach popular among British millennialists (see MILLENARIANS AND MILLENNIALISM) of his era. Central to Darby's hermeneutics was an anthropological dualism. In his view the true church is a heavenly people, an invisible group with heavenly citizenship, promises, and prophecies. Israel, on the other hand, is God's earthly people. All of the biblical prophecies to Israel will be fulfilled on the earth in the millennium and the eternal state. The church inherits spiritual blessings and her eternal destiny is in heaven. These two peoples never commingle. A strict separation of these two peoples of God must be maintained when interpreting promises and prophecies in Scripture. The future eschatological plan of God has both an earthly and a heavenly component.

Darby developed two distinctive doctrines related to this heavenly people. He proposed that the church age was a parenthesis between the sixty-ninth and seventieth weeks of Daniel 9:25–27. This period of time was a mystery, not revealed in Scripture before the coming of the Messiah. The seventieth week of Daniel, the Great Tribulation, was prophesied for God's earthly people (Israel), and has not yet been fulfilled. Because the wrath of God will be poured out on the earth during this time, God's heavenly people will be taken away, or raptured, before this seven-year period. Darby based his doctrine of the RAPTURE of the church before this period of tribulation on I Thessalonians 4:15–18. With the heavenly people removed from the earth, God's judgment is then unleashed on Israel and unbelieving Gentiles (see Revelation 6–19).

In Darby's view, God's promises to his earthly people, Israel, would then be fulfilled in a millennial kingdom. Although they had rejected their Messiah in his first coming, Israel would turn to him in faith during the Great Tribulation. The Messiah will destroy all of his enemies and rule over the world from the Davidic throne in Jerusalem for one thousand years (Revelation 20:1–6). After one last rebellion is quashed, a new heaven and earth are created, the former the eternal home of the church and the latter the realm of Israel.

Dispensationalism spread to North America through a series of Bible and prophecy conferences in the late nineteenth century. The most prominent of these was the Niagara Conference (1883–1897). Darby himself made several trips to America to speak at these gatherings. Through the teaching of J. H. Brookes, A. J. Gordon, and C. I. Scofield, this teaching took on a distinctive American flair. American dispensationalists generally rejected Darby's view of the organized church as apostate and focused on purifying or reviving their denominations.

This period of dispensationalism's history has been designated by historians of the tradition as the classic stage. These dispensationalists maintained Darby's anthropological dualism and his futurist ESCHATOLOGY. The failure of WILLIAM MILLER's date-setting

(1844) clearly demonstrated to them the danger of historicism. Further, dispensationalists claimed that their theology was based on a literal interpretation of the Bible. Fundamentalist in their theology, representatives of many denominations were found in their ranks, including Presbyterians and Congregationalists (see FUNDAMENTALISM; PRESBYTERIANISM, CONGREGATIONALISM). Later, BAPTISTS and nondenominational churches were represented as well.

The major teachings of this classic stage of American dispensationalism were systematized in the SCOFIELD REFERENCE BIBLE. C. I. Scofield, a prominent spokesman in the tradition, published a King James Version of the Bible (Oxford University Press) with copious notes explaining his interpretation of much of the biblical text in successive editions in 1909 and 1917 (see BIBLE, KING JAMES VERSION). Although not all dispensationalists agreed with every one of his interpretations, Scofield's system became the major articulation of the tradition. The influence of the *Scofield Reference Bible* is so pervasive that in popular understanding, his sevenfold scheme of history is often assumed to be the essential statement of dispensationalism.

Scofield's disciple, L. S. Chafer, founded the Evangelical Theological College in Dallas, Texas in 1924. This institution was renamed Dallas Theological Seminary in 1936 and Chafer served as its president until his death in 1952. Chafer's eight-volume *Systematic Theology* (1948) is the most developed articulation of classic dispensationalism.

A Dynamic Tradition

The next generation of dispensational scholars continued to develop their own understanding of Scripture within the framework of this hermeneutical tradition. J. F. Walvoord, J. D. Pentecost, and C. C. Ryrie, all students of Chafer, each introduced modifications to classic dispensationalism. These modifications are perhaps most visible in the *Revised Scofield Reference Bible* (1967), in which many notes were changed and others added. This period of the tradition's history is differentiated from the previous one with the label "revised," based on the "revision" of the original *Scofield Reference Bible*.

In the mid-1960s, Charles Ryrie wrote an apologetic for the movement, which was intended to coincide with the revision of Scofield's study Bible. *Dispensationalism Today* (1965) provides one of the clearest articulations of revised dispensationalism and quickly achieved textbook status. Ryrie defended and explained the systematization and development in the movement. Gone is the strict anthropological dualism of the classic stage, although the futurist eschatology

and the strong biblical emphasis remain. Ryrie defined the essence of dispensationalism in terms of three sine qua non: the consistent use of literal hermeneutics, which results in a distinction between Israel and the church, and the conviction that God's purpose in all that he does is to glorify himself.

During the latter decades of the twentieth century, dispensational scholars proposed additional modifications of this tradition. These modifications grew out of a renewed interest in studying the history of the tradition and a fresh look at biblical revelation, as well as an evaluation of the sina qua non approach to definition. There were proposals for each of the three as *the* essence of dispensationalism. Eventually some of these dispensationalists concluded that perhaps the attempt to articulate the essence of dispensationalism, in contrast to other orthodox traditions, was an inadequate approach to the question of definition. Some concluded that a better approach might be to focus on the major themes and emphases of the tradition. The tradition has always claimed to be committed to the task of biblical hermeneutics, and here is an illustration of how deep that commitment was.

At the heart of these modifications in dispensational thought seems to be an emphasis on more continuity or progression in the plan of God. Thus, these progressive dispensationalists stress the present inauguration of God's eschatological blessings, which will culminate in their fullness in the eternal state. The distinction between Israel and the church remains, although it is defended not on the basis of an anthropological dualism or a modified "two people of God" approach, but rather as part of the historical fulfillment of God's COVENANT program. The church, although not revealed explicitly in the Old Testament, is an integral part of God's plan for history, not simply a parenthesis within God's historical scheme. There remains a future for political Israel, not simply in the millennium but in eternity as well. In the eschatological Messianic kingdom, all redeemed humanity will exist eternally on a re-created earth. In its progressive form, dispensationalism remains futurist premillennial in its eschatology, usually including a pretribulation rapture of the church, and continues to emphasize the authority of Scripture as support for its view. C. A. Blaising, D. L. Bock, and R. L. Saucy are the most prominent representatives of progressive dispensationalism.

Impact of Dispensationalism

Because of the consistent emphasis within this tradition on the authority of Scripture, dispensationalism has provided numerous contributions to Protestantism. First, the tradition has had a strong MISSIONS emphasis, which is reflected in the founding of faith mission agencies and other parachurch organizations. C. I. Scofield founded Central American Mission (now CAM International). Dispensationalists have been active in Africa Inland Mission (now AIM International), Sudan Interior Mission (now SIM), Campus Crusade for Christ, INTERVARSITY CHRISTIAN FELLOWSHIP, the Navigators, YOUTH FOR CHRIST, Young Life, and numerous other nondenominational missions agencies. In addition, dispensationalists serve in many capacities in denominational missions organizations (see MISSIONARY ORGANIZATIONS). Through this missionary emphasis, the teachings of dispensationalism have spread throughout the world, resulting in a global presence of the movement. Second, dispensationalists have always been active in social work, including Rescue Missions, orphanages, ministry to the poor, and other service agencies. Third, dispensationalists have written biblical commentaries, usually with a particular emphasis on the practical implications of the text for life and ministry. Fourth, many have launched radio and television ministries (see TELEVANGELISM; PUBLISHING MEDIA). Charles Fuller's "Old Time Gospel Hour," M. R. DeHaan and Richard DeHann on "Radio Bible Class," J. Vernon McGee's "Through the Bible," JERRY FALWELL'S "Old Time Gospel Hour," Theodore Epp and Warren Wiersbe on "Back to the Bible," and Chuck Swindoll's "Insight for Living" are all examples of the national and worldwide influence of this tradition. Fifth, dispensationalists were involved in founding BIBLE COLLEGES and SEMINARIES. In addition to Dallas Theological Seminary, several other institutions have their roots in dispensationalism, such as MOODY BIBLE INSTITUTE, Philadelphia College of the Bible, Lancaster Bible College, Grace Theological Seminary, Biola University and Talbot Seminary, and Multnomah Bible College/Seminary. In addition, dispensationalists serve on the faculties of many other Protestant educational institutions. Sixth, dispensationalists serve the church in pastoral and lay leadership capacities in many Protestant denominational and independent churches.

Dispensationalism is a dynamic tradition, developing as its adherents dialogue with other Christians around the biblical text. Although the study of its history demonstrates unmistakable paradigmatic stages in dispensational thought, this does not mean that every dispensationalist in each period was in total agreement on the understanding of Scripture. Rather, the strength of this tradition is its unity amidst diversity. Further, under the umbrella of the label dispensationalism, one today finds representatives of the various stages in its historical development. Throughout its history, dispensationalism has consistently had a strong ministry focus, serving the church and the world with the gospel in word and deed.

References and Further Reading

Bass, C. *Backgrounds to Dispensationalism.* Grand Rapids, MI: Wm. B. Eerdmans, 1960; reprint, 1977.
Blaising, C., and D. Bock. *Progressive Dispensationalism.* Grand Rapids, MI: Baker Book House, 1993.
———, eds. *Dispensationalism, Israel, and the Church.* Grand Rapids, MI: Zondervan Publishing House, 1992.
Crutchfield, L. V. *The Origins of Dispensationalism.* Lanham, MD: University Press,1992.
Kraus, C. N. *Dispensationalism in America.* Richmond, VA: John Knox Press, 1958.
Marsden, G. *Fundamentalism and American Culture.* New York: Oxford University Press, 1980.
Poythress, V. S. *Understanding Dispensationalism,* 2nd ed. Phillipsburg, NJ: Presbyterian and Reformed, 1994.
Ryrie, C. C. *Dispensationalism Today.* Chicago: Moody Press, 1965.
———. *Dispensationalism.* Rev. ed. Chicago: Moody Press, 1995.
Sandeen, E. *The Roots of Fundamentalism, British and American Millenarianism, 1800–1930.* Chicago: University of Chicago Press, 1970.
Saucy, R. *The Case for Progressive Dispensationalism.* Grand Rapids, MI: Zondervan Publishing House, 1994.
Weber, T. *Living in the Shadow of the Second Coming.* New York: Oxford University Press, 1979.

G. R. KREIDER

DISSENT

The dissenting tradition of ENGLAND and WALES began with the late medieval Lollards and then the separatists who left the CHURCH OF ENGLAND under ELIZABETH I (1533–1603). The dissenters grew in the mid-seventeenth century but were persecuted between 1662 and 1689. Enjoying toleration in the eighteenth century, they polarized into rational Dissenters and Evangelicals, whose numbers were hugely expanded by the creation of METHODISM. They played a large part in Victorian public affairs, but declined in the twentieth century.

Origins

The Dissenters, or Nonconformists, were those in England and Wales who worshipped outside the established Church of England. Similar groups existed in Ireland, and for a while the term "dissent" was used for those Presbyterians who seceded from the CHURCH OF SCOTLAND. Theoretically applicable to Roman Catholics, the description was normally confined to Protestants. Dissent goes back to the Lollards of the late fourteenth and fifteenth centuries who criticized clerical and papal abuses, appealing to the text of the English scriptures translated by their founder, English theologian John Wyclif (1330–1384). Putting down roots in parts of southeastern England such as Buckinghamshire, they persisted into the sixteenth century and probably into the seventeenth. Following the settlement of the Church of England under Elizabeth I, some of those Puritans who wanted further reformation began to worship separately. The early separatist leaders ROBERT BROWNE and Robert Harrison left the country for the NETHERLANDS in order to escape persecution, but Henry Barrow and John Greenwood, who both wrote in defense of separatism, were hanged in 1593. Fifteen years later a group of separatists escaped to the Netherlands under THOMAS ROBINSON, and in 1620 some of his followers crossed the Atlantic to settle as the PILGRIM FATHERS. Another group, under John Smyth, also fled in 1608 to Amsterdam, where their leader baptized himself and so began the Baptist tradition. A small number of churches followed Smyth in holding an Arminian theology of general redemption and so were called General Baptists. Other Baptists who emerged in the 1630s were known as Particular Baptists because, like the great majority of separatists, they upheld the Calvinist doctrine of particular redemption.

Development

The upheavals of the CIVIL WAR and interregnum in the 1640s and 1650s allowed an upsurge of dissent. The separatists who practiced infant baptism, now called the Independents, flourished, together with the Baptists. The SOCIETY OF FRIENDS, repudiating Calvinism in favor of guidance by the inner light, was founded by English religious leader George Fox (1624–1691) and soon earned the nickname of the Quakers. Smaller sects holding radical views—the Ranters, Diggers, Muggletonians, and others—briefly came into existence in this disturbed period. The restoration of the monarchy in 1660 was followed two years later by the "Great Ejection," the expulsion from their parishes on St. Bartholomew's Day of about 1,000 clergy, mostly Presbyterians, who would not agree to accept the exclusive use of the prayer book. Dissenters were subject to the penalties of the Clarendon Code of legislation that excluded them from public office, and after 1664 prohibited more than five people from meeting for non-Anglican worship. Despite a short respite between 1672 and 1673, the reigns of Charles II (1630–1685) and James II (1633–1701) were marked by serious persecution, which was terminated only by the Glorious Revolution of 1688 and the consequent passing of the Toleration Act of 1689. Henceforth dissenters were allowed to worship freely so long as their meetings were licensed.

During the eighteenth century, dissent broadened theologically under the influence of the intellectual currents of the times. Most Presbyterians and General Baptists gradually turned toward Arian beliefs and became known as rational Dissenters; most Independents and Particular Baptists retained their Trinitarian orthodoxy. By the end of the century the nominal Presbyterians, often well educated and prosperous, were increasingly Unitarian in theology. The century also witnessed, however, the transformation of dissent by the Evangelical Revival. JOHN WESLEY (1703–1791) created METHODISM as vigorous societies within the Church of England, but even before his death in 1791 it was tending to function as a separate denomination. Its status was always unclear: although technically dissenting, it did not identify with the dissenting tradition. A similar form of evangelical religion gradually transformed the Independents and Baptists into rapidly growing bodies, which, like Methodism, appealed to the poor as well as the middle classes. By the middle of the nineteenth century almost half the churchgoing population was Nonconformist.

In 1828 the repeal of the Test and Corporation Acts meant that Nonconformists were no longer treated as second-class citizens. They subsequently organized campaigns demanding the removal of the remaining marks of discrimination and pressed unsuccessfully for disestablishment. The "Nonconformist conscience" around the end of the century called for the enactment of what was considered moral legislation, such as the prohibition of alcohol. Growth petered out in the middle years of the century, and from the 1880s Nonconformity went into long-term decline. The explanation has been much debated, but must include competition from new forms of recreation and a weakening of former doctrinal convictions in the chapels. Nevertheless fresh denominations were created, notably the SALVATION ARMY (1878) and the Pentecostalists (from 1907). In the twentieth century, Nonconformists preferred to call themselves the FREE CHURCHES and increasingly cooperated in ecumenical activities. Although the older Free Churches went into accelerated decline from the 1960s, in the same decade new black-led denominations were organized to serve the immigrant community and charismatic "house churches," subsequently styled the "New Churches," started their rapid growth. Hence by the end of the twentieth century the non-Anglican Protestant bodies attracted more worshippers than either the Church of England or the Roman Catholic Church.

References and Further Reading

Payne, Ernest A. *The Free Church Tradition in the Life of England.* London: SCM Press, 1944.

Sell, Alan P. F. *Dissenting Thought and the Life of the Churches: Studies in an English Tradition.* Lewiston, NY: Mellen University Press, 1990.

Watts, Michael R. *The Dissenters: From the Reformation to the French Revolution.* Oxford: Clarendon Press, 1978.

———. *The Dissenters: The Expansion of Evangelical Nonconformity, 1791–1859.* Oxford: Clarendon Press, 1995.

D. W. BEBBINGTON

DISTLER, HUGO (1908–1942)

German composer. Distler. One of Germany's foremost composers of sacred music in the twentieth century, was born in Nuremberg on June 24, 1908. He was brought up by his maternal grandparents, graduated from the famous Melanchthon Gymnasium in Nuremberg, and subsequently studied at the Leipzig conservatory. At the age of twenty-two he was appointed organist at the St. Jakobi Church in Lübeck. In 1937 he joined the faculty of the Württembergische Musikhochschule (Conservatory) in Stuttgart. Three years later, in May 1940, he was promoted to professor and in the same year received an appointment to the Conservatory of Music in Berlin. Early in 1942 he was also appointed conductor of the Berlin Opera and Cathedral choirs. The increasing Allied air raids on Berlin had triggered the evacuation of his family to a rural area on the Baltic Sea. Thus, alone in Berlin, Distler committed suicide on November 1, 1942.

Distler's opus consists of motets, organ preludes, and cantatas; in fact, most of his compositions are church music. Because his style combined adherence to classical forms of compositions with modern tonality, the Nazis decried his music as "degenerate," a fact that undoubtedly contributed to his youthful suicide.

References and Further Reading

Grabner, Hermann. *Hugo Distler.* Tutzing, Germany: H. Schneider, 1990.

Palmer, Larry. *Hugo Distler and his Church Music.* St. Louis, MO: Concordia, 1967.

HANS HILLERBRAND

DIVORCE

During the sixteenth century, a majority of Protestant authors formulated theological perspectives on divorce that reacted against the Roman Catholic doctrine of the indissolubility of consummated marriages and the accompanying prohibition against remarriage by reinterpreting the biblical testimony and texts from Christian antiquity on the subject. Divorce might be possible, but only on "scriptural grounds." Protestant writings and ecclesiastical legislation of subsequent generations drew on the work of the reformers, but also took into account the social and political contexts of their own time, thereby gradually moving further away from the Catholic position (see CATHOLICISM, PROTESTANT REACTIONS). Because of the increasing secularization of divorce in the West from the seventeenth century onward, ecclesiastical opinions on divorce came to have less of a direct influence on civil laws and practices than in previous years. By the twenty-first century, most Protestant denominations acknowledged divorce to be a regrettable social reality as well as a sign of human fallibility, but nevertheless encouraged full acceptance of the divorced within the Christian community and permitted remarriage within church walls.

Early Protestant Perspectives

Because Protestant writers of the sixteenth century affirmed that MARRIAGE was a divinely ordained institution (although not a sacrament), many were reluctant to take up the topic of divorce and did so only when pressed by pastoral need. Although some Protestants held to the indissolubility of marriage, the greater number rejected the Catholic position, later set down at the Council of Trent, that a validly celebrated and consummated Christian marriage could be dissolved only by the death of a spouse. Among Protestant "dissolubilists" there were two camps: those who interpreted Matthew 5:32 and 19:9 (the "Matthean exception") to permit divorce only for adultery, and those who allowed for other causes defensible by scripture. Protestants were also critical of the methods that Catholics used for circumventing the indissolubility of marriage by allowing for dispensations and annulments granted by ecclesiastical authorities. Annulment could be obtained, for example, in cases of marriage with an unbeliever by citing the so-called "Pauline privilege" (*privilegium Pauli*) of 1 Corinthians 7:15, and in marriages in which diriment (nullifying) impediments could be identified, such as a union falling within certain degrees of consanguinity or affinity, marriage by coercion, impotence, or a previous marriage or espousal. Protestants to varying degrees acknowledged that certain impediments could warrant divorce, but limited them to those with "scriptural" precedent.

The term "divorce" (*divortium*) was used in a variety of senses during the sixteenth century. It could refer to the legal dissolution of the marriage bond (*a vinculo matrimonii*) that could enable a former spouse or spouses to contract a new—and legally valid—marriage. Temporary or permanent restrictions, such as a delay of at least nine months for a woman to ensure there was no pregnancy, might be imposed on those wishing to remarry. The term could mean judicial separation literally from "bed and board" (*a mensa et thoro)*, by which a couple legally might live apart physically although they were still married by law. Numerous Protestant commentators who were persuaded that cohabitation was essential to any definition of marriage challenged this practice. "Divorce" was applied to annulments, though the granting of an annulment assumed that the marriage never existed legally in the first place. For example, the severing of the relationship between KING HENRY VIII and Catherine of Aragon was technically an annulment because of a preexisting impediment of affinity, though the term "divorce" is sometimes used in the historic documents.

In *The Babylonian Captivity of the Church* (1520), MARTIN LUTHER directed his comments toward divorce *a vinculo matrimonii*. So concerned was he to uphold the scriptural mandate that what God had joined was not to be broken apart (Matthew 19:6) that he stated he preferred bigamy to divorce, and indeed he counseled such for Henry VIII and PHILIP OF HESSE. Unscriptural impediments were no justification for annulling marriages, and those who allowed them were guilty of treason against God. Yet Luther conceded that annulments might be possible in cases of impotence, a previously contracted marriage, and a vow of CELIBACY. Despite his belief that couples ought to make every effort to be reconciled and remain together, Luther recognized that Christ himself had permitted divorce in cases of adultery (Matthew 5:32, 19:9) and that St. Paul had compelled no one, particularly the innocent person in a divorce, to remain unmarried lest that one burn (cf. 1 Corinthians 7:9). He also claimed, hesitatingly, and in reference to the Pauline privilege, that the spouse abandoned by a believer ought to be able to remarry, because the deserter was little more than an unbeliever. Two years later, in his sermon on the "Estate of Marriage," Luther argued from the basis of Deuteronomy 22:22–24 that the innocent party of a scriptural divorce could remarry because it was as if the adulterer had died (cf. Romans 7:2–3). He also added two more grounds for divorce and remarriage: bodily or natural deficiencies, and refusal to fulfill conjugal duties (cf. 1 Corinthians 7:5). However, when the issue was unreconcilable incompatibility, Luther would allow for divorce but not remarriage.

PHILIPP MELANCHTHON followed his teacher Luther in upholding the sanctity of marriage ("an eternal, inseparable fellowship of one husband and one wife"; *Loci Communes*, 1555), and in permitting divorce for adultery and for desertion. He relied on Genesis 2:24 (cf. 1 Corinthians 6:16) and an interpretation of sexual chastity to bolster his argument for divorce as a consequence of adultery, and argued that the innocent party should be permitted to remarry. Following the "evidence" of Leviticus 18:29 and 1 Corinthians 6:9–10, the guilty ought to be condemned to death or banished. Justified by the Pauline privilege, he linked desertion with adultery, because those who strayed from home were usually perceived as adulterers. Disease (e.g., leprosy), however, was not a ground for divorce, but rather was to be dealt with by compassion and faithfulness.

HULDRYCH ZWINGLI, on the other hand, did consider contagious diseases to be grounds for the dissolution of the marriage bond. He viewed adultery, following Christ's words in Matthew's Gospel, as the benchmark for permitting divorce, and identified what he perceived as equally or more serious conditions, including disease, impotence, desertion, marriage with an unbeliever, and serious crime, to be sufficient causes as well. Zwingli's views were codified in a 1525 marriage law for Zurich that imposed penalties on those proven of adultery: physical punishment, excommunication, confiscation of property, and, in serious or repeat cases, even death. The marriage tribunal *(Ehegericht)* of Zurich investigated and considered cases individually, and if attempts at reconciliation failed, reluctantly granted the divorce and allowed the possibility of remarriage. Both the innocent and guilty (but reformed in behavior, as judged by the tribunal) parties were allowed to remarry within certain restrictions. The policy established in Zurich influenced other city-state policies in SWITZERLAND, including Basel's *Ehegerichtsordnung* of 1533.

Sixteenth-century civil divorce laws in Protestant GERMANY and in Nordic countries were formulated on the basis of Luther's views, although in practice they tended to be more conservative. Even if divorce and remarriage were approved on scriptural grounds, church leaders typically denied a public celebration of a new union in the church building. Adultery and abandonment were justifiable causes for divorce in Württemberg, Nuremberg, and in the Swedish church's 1572 Church Ordinance, which drew on the ordinances of Württemberg as mediated by the laws of Pfalz-Neuberg. The 1572 ordinances, which remained in effect until 1686, permitted divorce only after all avenues for reconciliation had been exhausted, and then granted that both parties could remarry; after 1686, other circumstances, including marital incompatibility, might lead to divorce. In the Kingdom of DENMARK (which in the sixteenth century included NORWAY and Iceland), the 1582 Articles of Marriage recognized under certain conditions adultery and desertion as legitimate grounds, but allowed only the innocent party of adultery to remarry, and then with restrictions. Impotence and disease, if proven to have existed and to have been concealed at the time of the wedding, might effectively nullify the marriage union.

The views on divorce proffered by JOHN CALVIN in his scripture commentaries influenced legislation in Geneva, SCOTLAND, and other Calvinist centers in Europe. In principle, Calvin held to the indissolubility of marriage because of his belief that God ties couples in an unbreakable bond. Yet, drawing on Old and New Testament texts, he made a singular exception when either party violated the union by adultery, and permitted divorce as a substitute for the old COVENANT's penalty of death. According to Calvin's exegesis of 1 Corinthians 7, divorce might also be possible in situations where an unbelieving spouse deserted the believer by presuming that the deserter was engaged in an adulterous relationship. Other so-called "causes," such as disease or impotence, Calvin found indefensible. Calvin's successor in Geneva, THEODORE BEZA, built on Calvin's position in his *Tractatio de repudiis et divortiis* (1569). Beza upheld the two scripturally sanctioned grounds for divorce and no other: adultery (where he allowed both the guilty and innocent parties to remarry after meeting certain conditions, with the former receiving some type of punishment); and desertion (which he expanded to include situations where both parties are believers and other than religious reasons). The Genevan *Ordonnances ecclésiastiques* (1561) anticipated Beza's broader understanding of desertion, but made a distinction between willful and unintentional abandonment; different processes were advised depending on the GENDER of the deserting spouse. Adultery could dissolve the marriage (but only when one party was truly innocent), but in practice, punishment was meted out more often than divorce. In Scotland, where JOHN KNOX built on Calvin's teachings, adultery was the sole ground for divorce during the 1560s, but by 1573 willful desertion of four or more years was added as a cause; with both conditions, divorce was granted only after lengthy procedures and with reluctance. Until the 1930s, adultery and desertion remained the only legal grounds for divorce in Scotland.

The radical reformers in general allowed only adultery and a strict reading of the Pauline privilege as causes for divorce. Some Anabaptists (inspired by Ezra 10:11ff) stressed the supremacy of the Christian's union with Christ over any human covenant to the extent that believers were expected to break marriages with non-Anabaptist spouses who hindered religious practices (see ANABAPTISM). Regarding such mixed marriages, the fifth article of the Wismar resolutions (1554) advised that the nonbeliever should initiate any divorce for reasons of faith. The believer could not contract a second marriage until such a time as the former spouse remarried or committed adultery, and only then after consultation with the elders of the congregation. A much more liberal view was taken up by Strasburg Reformer MARTIN BUCER, who added to these two grounds other causes as a consequence of his view that mutual benevolence and companionship were primary in marriage. If these characteristics were absent, then claimed Bucer, there was no marriage—even before the formality of divorce. Continual cohabitation was therefore essential to marriage, unless a calling of God could be discerned. In the section on divorce in *De Regno Christi* (translated in 1644 by JOHN MILTON as *The Judgement of Martin Bucer, Concerning Divorce*), Bucer contended that a marriage in which the two were no longer one flesh on account of crime, impotence, mental or physical illness, and emotional or physical abandonment could be severed by mutual consent or by repudiation. Divorce was deemed a remedy instituted by God, and as such, equal opportunity for divorce was to be given to wives and husbands. Nevertheless, the breakdown of a marriage was a serious matter; punishments of varying degrees were given to violators, although remarriage could occur later. Bucer advised church leaders to admonish all parishioners to cultivate their marriages according to godly precepts to stave off discord.

Although Bucer influenced the REFORMATION in ENGLAND, his permissive policy on divorce was not formally taken up there. Indeed, the CHURCH OF ENGLAND officially adhered to the indissolubility of marriage and would not recognize divorce *(a vinculo)* legislation until the mid-nineteenth century, although from the 1670s a private Act of Parliament could be granted in individual cases that dissolved the marriage bond and allowed remarriage. Despite the church's legal stance, certain English theologians, among them WILLIAM TYNDALE, Thomas Becon, and John Hooper, argued from the Matthean exception that adultery could justify dissolution of the marriage, though each interpreted the conditions and consequences required differently; Tyndale also cited the Pauline privilege (coupled with 1 Timothy 5:8) for desertion. The *Reformatio Legum Ecclesiasticarum*, drafted by commission in 1552 with the first printed edition in 1571, provided for divorce *a vinculo* in cases of adultery, desertion, hostility, and ill-treatment, and condemned as unscriptural and confusing the practice of separation *a mensa et thoro*. Never ratified, the *Reformatio Legum* nonetheless articulated the opinions of numerous bishops and divines during the sixteenth and seventeenth centuries. Even so, the approved Canons of 1604 concerning divorce did not permit divorce *a vinculo* or remarriage, but did recognize judicial separation. By the end of the seventeenth century, separation *a mensa et thoro* granted by the ecclesiastical court was usually expected before further proceedings that could lead to dissolution by Parliamentary action.

By the end of the sixteenth century, most Protestant countries had legalized divorce for specified conditions, with adultery and abandonment most often the grounds identified. Fornication and desertion remained the only causes for divorce *a vinculo* until well into the eighteenth century in some locations, whereas in others civil legislation expanded the list of causes. Such was not the case in England, where the Church of England maintained its stance on the indissolubility of marriage. Lively debates continued at length throughout the seventeenth century as some theologians by tract and treatise reinforced the indissolubilist position, whereas others took the Continental dissolubilist approach that adultery alone or with desertion stood as legitimate scriptural grounds. Within the Puritan wing of ANGLICANISM, this range of opinions was evident. Robert Cleaver claimed that besides death, only adultery could sever the marriage bond, because it broke the covenant that God had witnessed. WILLIAM PERKINS added desertion, because a spouse who abandoned another was to his mind no Christian. William Whately, who in a 1617 sermon admitted the possibility for divorce on account of adultery, unchastity, and the unwillingness to perform certain marital duties, seven years later reversed his opinion and denied any grounds for divorce. John Milton published three treatises on divorce between 1643 and 1645 in addition to Bucer's text. Not surprisingly, Milton expressed views similar to Bucer, although he was not as egalitarian along the lines of gender as was the older theologian. Milton's liberal position never found legal expression in his own day. In fact, during the periods of the English CIVIL WAR and the interregnum, no legislation regarding divorce was enacted by Cromwell's government save for the 1650 Adultery Act, which made fornication a capital offense. Across the Atlantic, however, Puritans in New England legalized divorce through civil courts from the 1620s (see PURITANISM).

The Secularization of Divorce

Starting in the seventeenth century, church courts, many of which had been established during the Reformation to deal with matrimonial matters in Protestant countries and states, began to become more limited in their dealings or to be eliminated entirely. Secular civil governments and their courts increasingly determined the principles that would procure divorces for the population. In some contexts, churches and denominations were able to continue to exert an influence on legislation and policy, particularly where CLERGY were members of the legislative bodies, lay legislators brought their church's teachings to bear in civic matters, or civil governments found it politic to be attentive to churchly opinion. In other situations, no such partnership or toleration existed, or it persisted for only a short duration. Many German states in the 1870s, for example, followed the Prussian divorce code that went well beyond Luther's conditions for divorce and included such causes as incurable madness, defamation of the spouse's character, conviction for a felony, drunkenness, and extravagance.

In tandem with this shift away from ecclesiastical pressure on civil law, or perhaps as a result of it, writings on divorce relied less on the teachings of scripture and the arguments of past generations of Protestant theologians and more on interpretations of contract theory and natural law as well as on social expediency. Discourse and debate on divorce was taken up predominantly outside of the church by writers who might give a cursory nod to the biblical witness or to the prevailing theological stance of the region. Notable and influential secular authors on divorce included SAMUEL PUFENDORF and CHRISTIAN THOMASIUS in Germany and JOHN LOCKE, DAVID HUME, Daniel Defoe, and Caleb Fleming in England. Protestant theological writings on marriage and divorce continued to be produced, though in much lesser quantity than in the sixteenth century. The exception was in England, where throughout the seventeenth century writers persisted in debates. Thereafter the number of theological treatises published declined significantly, and sometimes they were included within wider discussions on canon law and on the THEOLOGY and practices of the ancient church.

Discussions regarding divorce continued in England during the late eighteenth and early nineteenth centuries as the Church of England dealt with the reality that Parliament was granting divorces *a vinculo*—especially for the wealthy—in ever-increasing numbers. With successful petitions for divorce came a sense of threat to the sanctity of marriage as well as the prospect of requests for remarriages solemnized by church officiants. Dissolubilist and indissolubilist opinions by Anglicans and Dissenters (and by Catholics) circulated in essays and printed sermons as a succession of divorce-related bills were introduced to the House of Lords and House of Commons. In 1857, Parliament decreed that divorce could be obtained through a secular court of divorce for reason of adultery in the case of a wife and for adultery with aggravating circumstances (e.g., incest, bigamy, cruelty, or desertion) by the husband; no involvement in an ecclesiastical court was expected in the process. It was also determined that although an incumbent could object to solemnizing the remarriage of the guilty party of a divorce (and in such a case he should allow a willing clergyman to officiate in his stead), he could not oppose the remarriage of the innocent spouse. Not surprisingly, this decree drew mixed reactions. Numerous theologians, bishops, and clergy welcomed the Matrimonial Causes Act, among them FREDERICK DENISON MAURICE, Christopher Wordsworth, and William Bright. Others raised objections to the new civil policy, including Tractarian JOHN KEBLE, who posited that distinctions existed between churchly and secular marriages (the former, as "blessed in heaven," was indissoluble). Although most English Protestant writers approved of divorce within the bounds of the Matthean exception, the indissolubilist position was still championed, especially by Anglo-Catholics (see ANGLO-CATHOLICISM).

At the end of the nineteenth century and the beginning of the twentieth century, the indissolubilist interpretation was strengthened by developments in biblical criticism that gave historical and literary precedence to the Gospel of Mark. Neither Mark (10:11–12) nor Luke (16:18) identifies adultery as a cause for divorce; this cause is found only in the Matthean exception, which some scholars came to consider a secondary gloss on the original text and hence a corruption of what was said by the Lord himself. Questions about biblical interpretation generated the publication of books and articles on the subject of divorce (and marriage) at a time that was also marked by an accelerating divorce rate that became of great concern in both ecclesiastical and civil ranks. Even into the twenty-first century, theologians and church leaders within the Church of England have continued the debate on what were (if any) legitimate grounds for divorce, and what the church's ministry should be to the divorced and to those who seek the church's blessing on a second marriage.

Ecclesiastical Perspectives and Practices

No Protestant DENOMINATION takes delight at the dissolution of a marriage. However, different responses to marital breakdown are registered among the denominations, and even within a single ecclesiastical communion. Historical and current theological reflection affect a denomination's understanding of divorce, as do contemporary approaches to biblical exegesis and interpretation. Social contexts and pressures, civil laws, and customs also have an influence, whether the denomination chooses to accommodate to them or to be countercultural.

The ASSEMBLIES OF GOD ("Divorce and Remarriage," 1973) discourages divorce because of their belief that God hates divorce (cf. Malachi 2:16) and that nothing should separate those joined in matrimony (Matthew 19:6). When both spouses are professing Christians, divorce is not an option (1 Corinthians 7:10–11). However, when one spouse is an unbeliever, divorce is possible in situations in which the unbeliever is guilty of adultery or abandonment, although reconciliation is considered the better course. Under these circumstances, the divorced believer may remarry, but only with a Christian.

Because God instituted marriage and abhors divorce, the Lutheran Church of Australia ("Marriage, Divorce, and Re-Marriage," 2001) recognizes that divorce may be possible, but only in cases of unchastity and willful separation. If a divorced person made an attempt toward reconciliation in the previous marriage, repented of his or her part in its failure, and now expresses the desire to begin a new marriage on a Christian foundation, then a pastor may officiate at the second wedding. The EVANGELICAL LUTHERAN CHURCH IN AMERICA ("A Message on Sexuality," 1996) holds to the permanence of marriage and acknowledges divorce to be the result of human sinfulness, though without specifying particular grounds. The divorced are to be cared for compassionately and given the opportunity for a new relationship by remarriage after counsel by the pastor or other professionals.

Although permanency in marriage is demanded of Christ's disciples, the CHRISTIAN REFORMED CHURCH IN NORTH AMERICA ("Divorce," 2002) recognizes that persistent SIN may rend the union asunder. Because marital breakdown is the result of sin, the church's ministry must be one of reconciliation and, when necessary, of discipline (see CHURCH DISCIPLINE). In addition, the church is called on to care for the divorced and their children. The church's stance on remarriage is situational: "The church should neither issue a clear prohibition against remarriage nor attempt to list with legal precision the circumstances under which remarriage does not conflict with biblical teaching. The church must apply biblical principles to concrete situations in the light of its best understanding of what happened in a particular divorce and what is being planned for a particular remarriage." A minister of the CHURCH OF SCOTLAND, at his or her discretion, may conduct the marriage of a divorced person whose former spouse still lives.

Within the Anglican community, the Church of the Province of New Zealand in 1970 permitted the remarriage of a divorced person in the church whose former spouse was still living. The General Synod of the Church of England in 2002 allowed the same but only in "exceptional circumstances," and left the decision whether or not to solemnize the new union to the individual ministers. Despite this option, marriage was still affirmed as a "solemn, public and lifelong covenant"—indissoluble, in the sense that unconditional promises are made for life.

In recognition of the need for pastoral care at the time of divorce, some denominations have proposed rituals that include one or both spouses. The UNITED METHODIST CHURCH published an experimental "Rituals with the Divorced" in 1976 that drew a largely negative response from members and nonmembers alike. However, convinced that some resource was needed, the denomination included in its 1992 *Book of Worship* a prayer (". . . grant forgiveness for what is past and growth in all that makes for new life") and selected scripture lessons in a section on healing services. Other Protestant denominations have similarly included prayers or blessings for those with marital difficulties or for the divorced in service books published since the 1990s.

References and Further Reading

Eells, Hastings. *The Attitude of Martin Bucer Toward the Bigamy of Philip of Hesse.* New Haven, CT: Yale University Press, 1924; London: Oxford University Press, 1924.

Ellingsen, Mark. *The Cutting Edge: How Churches Speak on Social Issues.* Geneva, Switzerland: WCC Publications and Grand Rapids, MI: Eerdmans, for the Institute for Ecumenical Research, Strasbourg, France, 1993, esp. pp. 80–86.

Guerry, Edward B. *The Historic Principle of the Indissolubility of Marriage: According to the Doctrine and Discipline of the Anglican Communion.* Sewanee, TN: University Press, University of the South, 1953.

Johnson, James Turner. *A Society Ordained by God: English Puritan Marriage Doctrine in the First Half of the Seventeenth Century.* New York: Abingdon Press, 1970.

Kingdon, Robert M. *Adultery and Divorce in Calvin's Geneva.* Cambridge, MA: Harvard University Press, 1995.

Phillips, Roderick. *Putting Asunder: A History of Divorce in Western Society.* Cambridge: Cambridge University Press, 1988.

Safley, Thomas Max. *Let No Man Put Asunder: The Control of Marriage in the German Southwest. A Comparative Study, 1550–1600.* Kirksville, MO: Sixteenth Century Journal Publishers, 1984.

Winnett, Arthur Robert. *Divorce and Remarriage in Anglicanism.* London: Macmillan, 1958.

See also doctrinal statements posted on denominational websites.

KAREN B. WESTERFIELD TUCKER

DOCTRINE

Doctrine, meaning teaching, is an elastic term: its range of use extends from the most solemn determination of ecumenical councils concerning indispensable dogma ("the doctrine of the Trinity") through a body of tenets and beliefs characteristic of one ecclesiastical community ("reformed doctrine") to the views of a single theologian on a particular topic ("Pannenberg's doctrine of the last things").

The sixteenth-century reformers sought to purify the Western Church from inherited accretions and distortions, and to concentrate, correctively and positively, on the essentials of the Gospel. In the face of tradition their formal principle of doctrine was Scripture, even though "*sola Scriptura*" as a formula may belong to later generations of Protestant ORTHODOXY. In the face of SALVATION as human achievement, the Reformers' material principle of doctrine was salvation as divine gift, solely on the merits of Christ (*propter Christum solum*), sheerly by GRACE (*sola gratia*), received through FAITH alone (*sola fide*); these are the "exclusive particles" of which the Lutheran Formula of Concord (1580) speaks in connection with "the righteousness of faith before God" (Epitome, III.7; Solid Declaration, III).

Scripture as Formal Principle of Doctrine

In the Formula of Concord, Holy Scripture is affirmed as the sole judge (*iudex, Richter*), rule (*regula, Regel*), plumb-line (*Richtschnur*), and touchstone (*Probierstein*) by which "all doctrines should and must be known and judged as good or evil, right or wrong" (Epitome, 3): "We believe, teach, and confess that the prophetic and apostolic writings of the Old and New Testaments are the only norm according to which all doctrines and teachers alike must be measured and judged, as it is written, 'Thy word is a lamp to my feet and a light to my path' (Psalm 119:105); and St. Paul says, 'Even if an angel from heaven came and preached any other gospel, let him be accursed' (Galatians 1:8)" (Epitome, 1). Confessions in the Reformed ("Calvinist") line typically insist on the divine inspiration of Scripture: "We believe and confess the canonical Scriptures of the holy prophets and apostles of both Testaments to be the true Word of God, and to have sufficient authority of themselves, not of men. For God himself spoke to the fathers, prophets, and apostles, and still speaks to us through the Holy Scriptures" (Second HELVETIC CONFESSION, 1566, ch. 1).

The degree to which beliefs and practices must be explicitly revealed and authorized in Scripture has sometimes been controversial. Regarding the law of WORSHIP: whereas MARTIN LUTHER allowed hymns "of human composition," Calvinists for long sang only biblical psalms and canticles, and the English Puritans in their "Admonition to the Parliament" of 1572 even objected to antiphonal recitation as "tossing the psalms like tennis balls." Regarding the law of belief: JOHN CALVIN could wish that the terms "Trinity" and "person" were buried, provided that those who objected to them—as absent from Scripture and "fashioned by the human mind"—agreed on "the faith that Father, Son, and Spirit are one God, yet the Son is not the Father, nor the Spirit the Son, but that they are differentiated by their particular characteristics"; but in fact, in the face of HERESY, these terms could and should be used as "explaining nothing else than what is attested and sealed by Scripture" (*Institutes* I.13.3–5). JOHN WESLEY, in his sermon "On the Trinity," declared that he "dare not insist" on others' using those terms, although he used them himself "without scruple" and looked in substance for a fully trinitarian faith. On the whole, classical Protestantism has been content with the primacy or supremacy of Scripture, allowing for variety in "indifferent" matters (ADIAPHORA) and for the reflective deduction of doctrines from a scriptural basis, especially where these encapsulate in summary form the complex biblical witness or are necessary to avert its misapprehension.

All Protestants assert the "sufficiency" of Scripture, in the sense that it "containeth all things necessary to salvation, so that whatsoever is not read therein, nor may be proved thereby, is not to be required of any man, that is should be believed as an article of the Faith, or be thought requisite or necessary to salvation" (Church of England, Article VI).

When read in the same Spirit as they were written, the Scriptures are considered to be in principle "perspicuous." Nevertheless, MATTHIAS FLACIUS (Illyricus), in his *Clavis Sacrae Scripturae* (1567), acknowledges the difficulties that sometimes occur in the understanding of Scripture: the presence of foreign idioms and literary conventions; the occasional character of the writings; some seeming contradictions in them; the fact that in this life we see God and his mysteries only "*in aenigmate*." The central clue to understanding Scripture resides in knowing "our sickness and Christ as our physician." Crucial is the relation and distinction that Scripture itself establishes between law and gospel: the law drives us to Christ as the way to the eternal life that the law could only promise but never, because of our SIN, deliver. Flacius points to the many pieces of procedural advice that the Scriptures themselves offer for their own understanding. Nor does the Holy Spirit disdain the use of exegetical rules for the sake of clarity; and, following a notion and practice that goes back at least to St. Augustine, Johann Gerhard of Jena (1582–1637), in the first volume of his *Loci Theologici* (1610), sets out in technical form quite a list of them in the course of 229 paragraphs "on the interpretation of Scripture." The main points are: Scripture should be understood from within itself; all interpretation should be governed by "the rule of faith," which consists in the Apostles' Creed, as itself an excellent summary of sacred doctrine drawn from Scripture, and in the Decalogue, which together compose "the form of sound words in the faith and love of Christ" (cf. II Timothy 1:13); the less clear texts are to be illuminated on the basis of the clearer, on the assumption that there will be no contradiction between them; a knowledge of grammar, rhetoric, argument, and the original languages is called for; attention must be paid to the larger context and the particular circumstances of a passage as well as its aim; dogmas and requisites for salvation can be established only from the clearer passages and their proper and primary sense. Both Flacius and Gerhard insist that a fruitful reading of the Scriptures requires PRAYER, assiduous study, and spiritual discipline. Scholars have the responsibility of providing good translations and faithful interpretations for the benefit of those who lack learning (see BIBLE TRANSLATION).

So vital is the Scripture principle for self-conscious Reformation Protestants that Gerhard Ebeling, for example, could define "church history as the history of the exegesis of Holy Scripture" (1946; in idem, *Wort Gottes und Tradition: Studien zu einer Hermeneutik der Konfessionen*, Göttingen: Vandenhoeck & Ruprecht 1964:9–27). Doctrinal history is a story neither of continuous decline nor of continuous development but rather of the decisions of the church in ever renewed attempts to understand and expound Holy Scripture (W. Schneemelcher). Dogma, according to KARL BARTH, is properly "the agreement of the Church's proclamation with the revelation to which Holy Scripture testifies" (*Kirchliche Dogmatik* I/1: 280; *Church Dogmatics* I/1: 304).

Subsidiary Standards

The Protestant Reformers acknowledged the utility of subsidiary standards of doctrine—"normae normatae," themselves governed by Scripture—to safeguard the scriptural message and faith, especially on controversial points.

> Thus the Formula of Concord: "Immediately after the time of the apostles, indeed already during their lifetime, false teachers and heretics arose. Against these the primitive Church composed symbols, i.e. brief and explicit confessions, which were accepted as the unanimous, catholic, Christian faith and the confession of the orthodox and true Church, namely, the Apostles' Creed, the Nicene Creed, and the Athanasian Creed. We publicly pledge ourselves to these, and we hereby reject all heresies and all teachings that have ever been introduced into the Church contrary to them" (Epitome, 2).

Similarly, in regard to contemporary controversies, the AUGSBURG CONFESSION of 1530 and the SMALKALD ARTICLES of 1537 are affirmed as "the unanimous consensus and exposition of our Christian faith" (ibid., 3). Because these matters affected "the laity and the salvation of their souls," the signatories of the BOOK OF CONCORD also endorsed Luther's Small and Large Catechisms, interestingly characterized as "the Laypeople's Bible," in which "is briefly comprehended everything that is treated at greater length in Holy Scripture and which a Christian must know for his eternal salvation" (ibid.). Among Lutheran churches the Augsburg Confession has enjoyed a more widespread recognition that any other of the sixteenth-century documents, equaled perhaps only by the Small Catechism.

On the Reformed side also, subsidiary standards took shape as CONFESSIONS and CATECHISMS, each bearing strong family resemblances, even though locally formulated. The Second Helvetic Confession of 1566 may be taken as representative also of others that included the First Helvetic (1536), the GALLICAN (1559), the BELGIC (1561), the Scots (1560), and the WESTMINSTER CONFESSION (1647). Whereas the confessions used technical language, the catechisms were more pastorally oriented. Thus the first two items in the HEIDELBERG CATECHISM of 1563:

Q. What is thy only comfort in life and in death?
A. That I, with body and soul, both in life and in death, am not my own, but belong to my faithful Savior Jesus Christ, who with his precious blood has fully satisfied for all my sins, and redeemed me from all the power of the devil; and so preserves me that without the will of my Father in heaven not a hair can fall from my head; yea, that all things must work together for my salvation. Wherefore, by his Holy Spirit, he also assures me of eternal life, and makes me heartily willing and ready henceforth to live unto him.
Q. How many things are necessary for thee to know, that thou in this comfort mayest live and die happily?
A. Three things: First, the greatness of my sin and misery; second, how I am redeemed from all my sins and misery; third, how I am to be thankful to God for such redemption.

The CHURCH OF ENGLAND included catechisms in the successive versions of its BOOK OF COMMON PRAYER (1549, 1552, 1559, 1604, 1662), and considerable doctrinal AUTHORITY was vested in the Prayer Book itself as providing "an Order for Prayer, and for the reading of the holy Scripture, much agreeable to the mind and purpose of the old Fathers," such that "nothing is ordained to be read but the very pure Word of God, the holy Scriptures, or that which is agreeable to the same" ("Concerning the Service of the Church"). The English Articles of Religion (1571) mention the two Books of Homilies of 1547 and 1571 as containing "a godly and wholesome Doctrine, and necessary for these times" (Article 35); and Article 11 declares "justification by faith alone" to be "a most wholesome Doctrine, and very full of comfort, as is more largely expressed in the Homily of Justification [no. 3 in the First Book]."

John Wesley abridged the Anglican Articles of Religion for the Methodists in North America, and his version retains its constitutional authority in the UNITED METHODIST CHURCH. The most widespread subsidiary standards in worldwide METHODISM, however, are Wesley's *Explanatory Notes upon the New Testament* (1755) and the first four volumes of his *Sermons* (1746–1770), which the 1932 constitution of the Methodist Church of Great Britain states "are not intended to impose a system of formal or speculative theology on Methodist Preachers, but to set up standards of preaching and belief which should secure loyalty to the fundamental truths of the Gospel of Redemption and ensure the continued witness of the Church to the realities of the Christian experience of salvation" (Deed of Union, clause 30). In practice Methodism, perhaps more than any other church, has treated hymnody as an informal instrument of doctrine. In his preface to *A Collection of Hymns for the Use of the People Called Methodists* (1780), Wesley claimed that the hymnal contained "all the most important truths of our most holy religion, whether speculative or practical," "a distinct and full account of scriptural Christianity (see HYMNS AND HYMNALS)."

Justification as Material Principle of Doctrine

The classical reformers all took for granted—as undisputed with Rome and as evidence of their own apostolicity and catholicity—the trinitarian and christological determinations of the ecumenical councils of Nicea, Constantinople, Ephesus, and Chalcedon, as enshrined in the early creeds and definitions (thus the Augsburg Confession, 1 and 3; Second Helvetic Confession, 3 and 11; Anglican Articles 1–2, 5, and 8). It was over the understanding of salvation—its nature, its mediation, and its location—that the crunch came with the papal church.

The Augsburg Confession, in its article 4 on justification, declares that "we cannot obtain forgiveness of sin and righteousness before God by our own merits, works or satisfactions, but we receive forgiveness of sin and become righteous before God by grace, for Christ's sake, through faith, when we believe that Christ suffered for us and that for his sake our sin is forgiven and righteousness and eternal life are given to us, for God will regard and reckon this faith as righteousness, as St. Paul says in Romans 3 and 4." In the Anglicanic Articles concerning "the office and work of Christ, or our redemption," similar teaching on JUSTIFICATION is called "the first and chief article," in which "nothing can be given up or compromised, even if heaven and earth and things temporal should be destroyed," for "on this article rests all that we teach and practice against the pope, the devil, and the world." Luther himself called justification "the lord, ruler, and judge of every kind of doctrine, which preserves and governs all Christian teaching" (WA 39/I:205), and "when this article stands, the Church stands; when it falls, the Church falls" (WA 40/III: 352). Calvin considered a proper doctrine of justification "the principal article of the Christian religion," and he stated its importance existentially: "Unless you first of all grasp what your relationship to God is, and the nature of his judgment concerning you, you have neither a foundation on which to establish your salvation nor one on which to build piety toward God" (*Institutes* III.11.1).

Although none perhaps has insisted on it with such single-mindedness as the Lutherans, other Protestant churches also teach justification by grace alone through faith alone, as in chapter 15 of the Second Helvetic Confession and article 11 of the English Articles of Religion. For Lutherans, Reformed, and Anglicans alike, these articles are accompanied by teaching on original and actual sin (which call for a redemption that human beings can in no way achieve for themselves) and on the good works that are the proper fruit of justification, but never its meritorious cause (Augsburg Confession, 2 and 6, then 18–19 and 20; Second Helvetic Confession, 8–9 and 16; Anglican Articles, 9–10 and 12–14). The Second Helvetic Confession (10) and the Anglican Articles (17) also teach in this connection "predestination to life" and "election of the saints."

Soteriology is intrinsically connected with ecclesiology. The Augsburg Confession speaks first of the ministerial function of the church: "To bring about such faith [as to receive justification], God has instituted the office of preaching [*Predigtamt*; *ministerium ecclesiasticum*], to teach the Gospel and to provide the Sacraments. For through the Word and the Sacraments, as by instruments, God gives the Holy Spirit, who works faith, where and when he pleases, in those who hear the Gospel" (article 5). Only then is "the one holy Church, which will endure for ever" defined as "the gathering [*congregatio*; *Versammlung*] of saints [*sanctorum*] or all believers [*aller Gläubigen*]," in which—precisely—"the Gospel is purely taught [*docetur*] or preached [*gepredigt*] and the Sacraments are administered rightly [*recte*] or according to the Gospel [*lauts des Evangelii*]" (article 7). Similarly, Anglican Article 19 defines "the visible Church of Christ" as "a congregation of faithful men, in the which the pure Word of God is preached, and the sacraments be duly ministered according to Christ's ordinance in all those things that of necessity are requisite to the same." The Second Helvetic Confession begins its description of the church thus: "Forasmuch as God from the beginning would have men to be saved, and come to the knowledge of the truth [1 Timothy 2:4], it is necessary

that there always should have been, and should be at this day, and to the end of the world, a Church—that is, a company of the faithful called and gathered out of the world; a communion of all saints, that is, of them who truly know and rightly worship and serve the true God, in Jesus Christ the Savior, by the word of the Holy Spirit, and who by faith are partakers of all those good graces which are freely offered through Christ" (17).

According to the Augsburg Confession, "it is sufficient for the true unity of the Christian Church that the Gospel be preached according to a pure understanding of it and that the sacraments be administered in accordance with the divine Word [so the German; the Latin has: it is enough to agree (*consentire*) concerning the preaching of the Gospel and the administration of the sacraments]. It is not necessary for the true unity of the Christian Church that [Latin: traditions or rites or] ceremonies, instituted by men, should be observed uniformly in all places" (7). The English (Article 34) and the Swiss agree that uniformity of rites and ceremonies is not necessary: "The truth and unity of the Church consists . . . not in outward rites and ceremonies, but rather in the truth and unity of the catholic faith. This catholic faith is not taught us by the ordinances or laws of men, but by the holy Scriptures, a compendious and short sum whereof is the Apostles' Creed. . . . The true unity of the Church consists in several points of doctrine, in the true and uniform preaching of the Gospel, and in such rites as the Lord himself has expressly set down" (Second Helvetic, 17). It is this last principle that leads the Reformers to include in their subsidiary standards teaching on the dominical sacraments of baptism and the Lord's Supper (Augsburg Confession, 9–13, 22, 24; Second Helvetic, 19–21; Anglican Articles, 25–31).

Doctrine and Community

FRIEDRICH SCHLEIERMACHER, in *The Christian Faith* (2nd edition, 1830–1831), famously defined "dogmatic theology" as "the science which systematizes the doctrine prevalent in a Christian church at a given time" (section 19). That definition prompts the questions of the senses in which doctrine itself may be descriptive or prescriptive or both, and of whether doctrine, even in a particular community, may shift over time.

The question of description or prescription obliges us to examine who, in the living church, are the bearers of the faith that intends conformity to the documents regarded as authoritative, both Scripture and subsidiary texts, whether these are functioning as sources or as criteria. Because the Holy Spirit is the final instance of Christian teaching (John 14:26; 16:13–15), there is a strong scriptural case to be made for all who have been anointed with the Spirit of truth (I Corinthians 2:4–16; I John 2:20f., 27). From New Testament times, however, there have also been "pastors and teachers" (Ephesians 4:11) with special responsibilities within the believing community (for "teachers," cf. also I Corinthians 12:28f.; I Timothy 2:7; II Timothy 1:11; James 3:1), as well as "bishops (*episkopoi*)" (Philippians 1:1), who should be "apt teachers" (I Timothy 3:1f; cf. Titus 1:7–14), and "elders (*presbyteroi*)" who "oversee the flock and feed the church of God" (Acts 20:17–28) and "labor in the word and doctrine" (I Timothy 5:17).

The CONFESSION OF AUGSBURG declares that "nobody should publicly teach or preach or administer the sacraments in the church without a regular call" (14); but Lutheran churches have, on the whole, placed less constitutional significance on particular structures of ecclesiastical governance and ministry than either Anglicans or the Reformed have invested in the episcopal or presbyterian patterns they have respectively found in the New Testament. All Protestant churches in practice agree that some human instances are needed to arouse and sustain faith in the congregations, to guide their fellow believers in Christian truth, and to correct those who err. Protestant bodies have tended to synodical organization for units wider than the local congregation. Concomitant with the rise and spread of modern democracy, lay persons have increasingly participated in various ways with the ordained in the pastoral and doctrinal government of the Protestant churches, so that the sharper distinctions between the teachers and the taught have yielded in varying degrees to an interaction in which all may from the start both learn and instruct.

Although anything like "professional theologians" can scarcely be found in the earliest church, Protestantism from its beginnings inherited this medieval development from the universities and schools. Protestant churches recognize a vocation to intellectual theological work as a principal occupation, usually carried out in conjunction with teaching future pastors. Theologians are concerned for the fidelity and internal consistency of doctrine as well as the faith's communicability. WOLFHART PANNENBERG, perhaps the most considerable Protestant theologian in the generations since Karl Barth, reckons the perennial task of systematic theology to be the critical construction of coherent models of reality that at least render plausible—without yet fully and finally proving its truth—the Christian confession of the Triune God as the creator, sustainer, redeemer, and final savior of the world. Theologians vary in the weight and roles they allow, in the interactive task, to the scriptural and ecclesiastical givens (the "message") and to the ambient culture (the "addressees"). Tensions may occur between the intellectual freedom claimed by academic theologians as necessary to their work and the concern of the church's pastoral governance for the stability of communal belief systems; but in principle all seek to subserve the veracity of the Christian faith and the authenticity of its proclamation. The sense of human fallibility affecting any particular instance of teaching is countered by confidence in the abiding power of God's Word to strike home.

Protestant churches have solemnly rejected what they consider false teachings, from the sixteenth-century anathemas to the "*Verwerfungen*" of the BARMEN DECLARATION of 1934 against the positions of the so-called GERMAN CHRISTIANS. They have sometimes deposed their own pastors and teachers for heresy, when stubbornly persisted in. Very rarely are laypeople excommunicated for mistaken beliefs. Moral discipline is seldom exercised today in the larger churches, although some smaller communities such as the MENNONITES still practice fraternal admonition and suspension from privileges.

Historical Shifts?

Suspicious of what he called "cognitive propositionalism," George Lindbeck, in his much noticed book *The Nature of Doctrine* (1984), put less emphasis on the substantive content of doctrines than on their function as "rules of speech" within an ecclesial community (a "cultural-linguistic" approach); he considered "dogmas" to be irreversible as long as the conditions of their original formulation obtained. History does, however, bring changes in social, cultural, intellectual, and ecclesiastical conditions, and Protestantism has certainly experienced shifts at least in theological fashion, whose effects on the interpretation of formal doctrine have been considerable, even where the official primary and subsidiary standards have remained in place.

The Protestant centuries have seen the development of certain elements that may have been present in the REFORMATION but were later joined by other factors to produce shifts in emphasis and in the overall configuration of the faith. Like the concomitant Renaissance, the Reformation may be understood in part as the contestation of inherited authorities. Thus the attention to the subjective "faith by which one believes" could turn toward INDIVIDUALISM, such that, on the ENLIGHTENMENT front, GOTTFRIED E. WILHELM LESSING could view the right to private judgment as an outworking of Luther's concerns, especially when supported by confidence in universal "reason" (Luther's attacks on reason would have really been directed only against late medieval scholasticism); and on the PIETISM front, the "religion of the heart" could elevate "personal experience" over a "dead orthodoxy" and lead, ecclesiologically, to the self-grouping of "real Christians" somehow distinct from the nominal. The rejection of "the authority of the past" found intellectual expression in historicism, whereby previous achievements were subjected to criticism on the basis of "modern" criteria. The "historical conditioning" of both Scripture and tradition was highlighted in such a way as to make their deconstruction possible and their reconstruction necessary: thus the rejection of "miracle" and much else in the biblical texts, and a program such as that of RUDOLF BULTMANN in favor of "demythologization" and an "existential" restatement of the Gospel; or a reading of "the history of dogma" like ADOLF VON HARNACK'S, which evaluated negatively the early "hellenization" of the Gospel and prompted attempts to "de-metaphysicalize" Christianity. Viewing these moves as reductionistic, some Protestants have swung to an extreme reaction in the form of "FUNDAMENTALISM," reminiscent in some ways of "Scripture alone," but now characterized by a "literalistic" reading that often fails to acknowledge the complexity of the Bible, its multiplicity of literary and rhetorical genres, and its traditionally proven openness to constructive interpretation in different senses that do not derogate from its authority and salvific functioning.

Not all developments in Protestant doctrine have stood in such problematic relation to the efforts made in the sixteenth century to reform the (Western) Church. Various movements have sought to rejoin the magisterial reformers in the advocacy of a scriptural Christianity that does not forfeit the catholicity embodied in authentic tradition. Among Anglicans, in particular, a steady stream of patristic scholarship has helped maintain continuity with early Christian doctrine. The twentieth century saw "Luther revivals" of various kinds (KARL HOLL and G. Ebeling in the first and second halves of the century in GERMANY; T. Mannermaa toward its end in FINLAND). Karl Barth, and such pupils as T. F. Torrance, revitalized the classic Reformed tradition, and Barth's influence in particular extended through wider swathes of Protestantism and even beyond. Attention to Wesley as theologian on the part of such scholars as G. C. Cell, A. C. Outler, and C. W. Williams gave some credibility to the Methodists' claim of him as their guide to "plain old Christianity." A doxological approach to doctrine (E. Schlink; J.-J. von Allmen), taken in conjunction with liturgical reform and renewal, has encouraged both Protestants and Roman Catholics to find common ground in worship that is both nourished by the BIBLE and shaped according to patristic patterns. Ecumenical concerns have in fact assumed increasing prominence in Protestantism over the past several generations as part of the broader search for unity in a historically divided Christendom.

Ecumenical Dialogues

In the twentieth century ecumenically minded Protestants engaged energetically in "doctrinal dialogues (*Lehrgespräche*)" (see DIALOGUE, INTERCONFESSIONAL ECUMENICAL AGREEMENTS). In Europe, the most significant intra-Protestant case focused on the LORD'S SUPPER, a contentious issue since the MARBURG COLLOQUY between Luther and HULDRYCH ZWINGLI in 1529: the agreement between German Lutherans and Reformed on the Arnoldshain Theses of 1957 was consolidated over a broader range of topics and on a wider geographical basis in the Leuenberg Concordat of 1973, and the Leuenberg Church Fellowship has more recently included Methodist churches also. British Anglican churches have produced in doctrinal dialogue with the Evangelical Church in Germany the Meissen Agreement (1988–1991), and with Scandinavian and Baltic churches the Porvoo Agreement (1992–1996), the latter of which was considered sufficient for the establishment of full communion. In North America doctrinal dialogues have achieved sufficient agreement for Lutherans to enter into official communion with both Reformed and Anglicans. The principal Protestant families of churches have, in many countries and globally, engaged in doctrinal dialogue with the Orthodox churches (see ORTHODOXY, EASTERN) and especially, in view of Western history, with the Roman Catholic Church. In this last case, the most dramatic result was the Joint Declaration on the Doctrine of Justification (1998–1999), officially signed between the Roman Catholic Church and the churches of the LUTHERAN WORLD FEDERATION: it formally states that the mutual condemnations of the sixteenth century do not touch the common and respective teachings of the two parties as they are now formulated in the document itself; and the consequences of this settlement regarding a key doctrine are awaited for other doctrinal and ecclesiological matters that have been controversial, and even divisive, between Protestants and Roman Catholics (see CATHOLIC REACTIONS TO PROTESTANTISM; CATHOLICISM, PROTESTANT REACTIONS). In multilateral ECUMENISM, Protestant churches have engaged energetically in the Faith and Order movement, whose principal achievement was the "convergence text" on *Baptism, Eucharist and Ministry* issuing from the WORLD COUNCIL OF CHURCHES' commission at Lima, Peru, in 1982.

References and Further Reading

Andresen, Carl, ed. *Handbuch der Dogmen- und Theologiegeschichte.* Göttingen, Germany: Vandenhoeck & Ruprecht, 1982 [Especially vol. 2 ("Die Lehrentwicklung im Rahmen der Konfessionalität")].

Barth, Karl. *Kirchliche Dogmatik I/1–IV/4.* Munich, Germany: Kaiser; Zurich, Switzerland: EVZ, 1932–1967.

———. *Church Dogmatics.* Edinburgh: T. & T. Clark, 1936–1969.

———. *Die Bekenntnisschriften der Evangelisch-Lutherischen Kirche.* Göttingen, Germany: Vandenhoeck & Ruprecht, 1930.

Calvin, John. *Institutes of the Christian Religion.* Edited by John T. McNeill and translated by Ford Lewis Battles. 2 vols. Philadelphia, PA: Westminster, 1960.

Lindbeck, George A. *The Nature of Doctrine: Religion and Theology in a Postliberal Age.* Philadelphia, PA: Westminster, 1984.

McGrath, Alister E. *The Genesis of Doctrine.* Oxford, UK: Blackwell, 1990.

Pannenberg, Wolfhart. *Systematische Theologie.* 3 vols. Göttingen: Vandenhoeck & Ruprecht, 1988–1993.

———. *Systematic Theology.* 3 vols. Grand Rapids, MI: Wm. B. Eerdmans, 1991–1998.

Pelikan, Jaroslav, ed. *Creeds and Confessions of Faith in the Christian Tradition.* 5 vols. New Haven, CT: Yale University Press, 2003 [with an accompanying "historical and theological guide" by Pelikan entitled *Credo*].

Schaff, Philip. *The Creeds of Christendom with a History and Critical Notes.* 3 vols. New York: Harper & Row, 1931 [Especially vol. 3. ("The Evangelical Protestant Churches")].

Schneemelcher, W. "Das Problem der Dogmengeschichte." *Zeitschrift für Theologie und Kirche* 48 (1951): 63–89.

Tappert, Theodore G., ed. and trans. *The Book of Concord: The Confessions of the Evangelical Lutheran Church.* Philadelphia, PA: Fortress, 1959.

Wainwright, Geoffrey. *Doxology: The Praise of God in Worship, Doctrine and Life.* London: Epworth; New York: Oxford University Press, 1980.

———. *Is the Reformation Over? Catholics and Protestants at the Turn of the Millennia.* Milwaukee, WI: Marquette University Press, 2000.

Wiles, Maurice F. *The Making of Christian Doctrine.* Cambridge: Cambridge University Press, 1967.

———. *The Remaking of Christian Doctrine.* London: SCM, 1974.

GEOFFREY WAINWRIGHT

DONNE, JOHN (1572–1631)

Anglican theologian, religious author. John Donne was brought up a Roman Catholic (it was rumored that two of his uncles on his mother's side of the family shared between them a relic from the Catholic martyr or English traitor, Sir Thomas More, Donne's great-great uncle) and remained keenly conscious of his Catholic heritage. His early years were spent as a student at Oxford and Cambridge, as well as Lincoln's Inn, where he seemed headed for a career as a witty young gallant and a sensual, cynical poet. He traveled broadly in FRANCE and ITALY; was a gentleman adventurer in two of the Earl of Essex's naval expeditions

against Spain; worked as secretary for Sir Thomas Egerton, the Lord Keeper; and, after his romantic marriage to Ann More and subsequent disgrace, did backwork for various patrons before finally becoming ordained in 1615. In 1621 Donne was nominated Dean of St. Paul's Cathedral by King James, eventually becoming, along with Launcelot Andrewes, one of the most widely acclaimed preachers of James's reign.

Donne's religious writings fall into three general groups: The first group includes religious lyrics and satires, mostly written during the first decade or so of the seventeenth century. The most famous of these are the "Holy Sonnets," dramatic and intensely personal expressions of anguished guilt and appeals for divine grace and mercy. The second group is a series of occasional prose tracts: *Biathanatos* (1608), an apologia for suicide; *Pseudo-Martyr* (1610), a defense of the oath of allegiance; and *Ignatius his Conclave* (1611), a satire on the Jesuits. The third group includes sermons and other devotional writing. *Devotions upon Emergent Occasions* (1624), a series of meditations Donne wrote while dangerously ill, reveals the primary characteristics of all Donne's later religious writings: an intense and very material preoccupation with physical and spiritual sickness; an acute analysis of the often paradoxical psychological urgencies of a mind in turn dejected, turbulent, or exalted. Some 160 of Donne's sermons survive, thirty-four of them written on the *Psalms.* Like his *Devotions,* Donne's sermons are unique in the intensity of their portrait of personal religious experience, and in the consistency of their focus on sickness and sin as the defining condition of human existence.

References and Further Reading

Carey, John. *John Donne: Life, Mind, and Art.* New York: Oxford University Press, 1981.

Donne, John. *The Sermons of John Donne.* 10 vols. Edited by George Potter and Evelyn Simpson. Berkeley: University of California Press, 1953–1962.

Shuger, Debora Kuller. *Habits of Thought in the English Renaissance.* Toronto: University of Toronto Press, 1997.

A. LEIGH DeNEEF

DORT, CANONS OF

The Canons of Dort are an early and important doctrinal statement of the Reformed Church of the Netherlands. The some one hundred delegates to the Synod of Dort drafted and approved the Canons during their 180 sessions at the town of Dordrecht (English Dort) between November 1618 and May 1619. Also known as the Five Articles against the Remonstrants (see REMONSTRANTS), they were prepared in response to the theological challenge posed by the followers of JACOB

ARMINIUS (1559–1609). The controversy focused above all on the question of PREDESTINATION. Yet it soon encompassed other doctrinal issues, including the character and extent of ATONEMENT, human corruption and depravity, the nature of divine GRACE, and the possibility of a total fall from grace. The dispute, which had smoldered within the Dutch Reformed community for some time, erupted in 1604. The Canons themselves were a vigorous, point-by-point refutation and response to a subsequent 1610 declaration formulated by the Arminians (see ARMINIANISM). Together with the BELGIC CONFESSION OF FAITH (1561) and the HEIDELBERG CATECHISM (1563), the Canons formed a precise doctrinal standard of Dutch Reformed belief during the decisive initial period of the REFORMATION.

The gathering at Dordrecht was, strictly speaking, a national SYNOD of the Reformed Church of the Netherlands. The official deputies—pastors, elders, and theological experts—were by and large firm Calvinists. Thirteen Remonstrant theologians were also present, but their discussions with the delegates were shrill, if not acrimonious. The Remonstrants were eventually deemed obstructionists and expelled. Finally, attendance by twenty-six representatives from eight foreign countries, principally the German principalities, Swiss city-states, and British Isles, lent the synod a decidedly international flavor with concomitant significance. Altogether, the Canons enjoyed wide circulation and were the subject of extensive discussion long after their formulation.

Arminius had been a pastor at Amsterdam and later professor of theology at the University of Leiden. Although he had studied at Geneva with THEODORE BEZA, Arminius eventually broke with Calvinist ORTHODOXY on the doctrine of predestination, moderating in particular the Calvinist stance on predestination of the reprobate (see CALVINISM). His followers formalized these views in an official Remonstrance, which they presented to the Estates of Holland and West Friesland in 1610, several months after his death. In light of this petition, they were dubbed "Remonstrants." Their Remonstrance called for a national synod to revise the Belgic Confession and the Heidelberg Catechism. More specifically, it asserted five articles of faith that the petitioners deemed a necessary revision of prevailing Calvinist understanding. Briefly, these theological views, as elaborated in the Remonstrance and elsewhere, were that (1) God has from eternity elected those who believe in Christ and persevere in their faith; (2) Christ atoned for all humanity, but only believers will be saved; (3) regeneration and CONVERSION are dependant on the gift of the Holy Spirit; (4) all good works are the result of the operation of grace in the believer, but this grace is not irresistible; and (5) all such believers will be aided in their faith, although Scripture must be examined closely to determine whether they may fall from grace.

The nature of the Remonstance indelibly colored and shaped the character of the Canons, whose authors insisted on that which they considered proper Reformed doctrine, all the while explicitly rejecting the views contained in the Remonstrance. The structure of the Canons reflects their purpose. Drafted in Latin and replete with strong biblical language, they are divided into chapters, or Heads of Doctrine, which reply in turn to each of the five articles of the 1610 Remonstrance. But the Canons have only four chapters, having collapsed Heads of Doctrine Three and Four into one, because no controversy existed over point three of the Remonstrance. Each head provides a lengthy exposition of what its authors regarded as the correct theological position on the subject. The explanations are followed by specific repudiations of the alleged errors of the Arminians.

The first, crucial Head of Doctrine maintains divine predestination. It affirms unconditional ELECTION—the belief that election was not founded on foreseen faith or any human disposition. In addition, God has not elected all persons; some have been passed over in the eternal election. A long list of rejected errors is attached. The second head deals with Christ's DEATH and human redemption. The essential theological point is an avowal of particular or limited atonement, as opposed to what its authors regarded as the Remonstrance's position of universal atonement. The third and fourth heads are combined, and consider human corruption and conversion to God. As such, they underscore the total incapacity of humanity. Divine grace, moreover, ultimately cannot be resisted. Again, the Canons reject what the delegates to the synod took to be the Remonstrants' belief in humanity's partial depravity and the possibility of resisting God's grace. The fifth and final head discusses the perseverance of the SAINTS, ruling out any possibility of their lapse from grace, an error attributed to the Remonstrants. The Canons' concluding remarks reiterate the Synod's affirmation of orthodox DOCTRINE and vigorous rejection of Remonstrant errors.

The Canons of Dort mark a critical consensus among the resolute Calvinist ecclesiastical authorities in the NETHERLANDS. They worked jointly to draw up the Canons and affixed their signatures on completion. During the decades that followed the Synod, the Canons became the basis for an imposed unity and uniformity among the Dutch Reformed churches. Some 200 nonconforming pastors were dismissed, and the Remonstrants found themselves generally persecuted. Several were forced into exile. The result of this intense struggle was the dominance of a strict Calvinist orthodoxy within the DUTCH REFORMED CHURCH.

References and Further Reading

Primary Sources:

Acta Synodi nationalis. . . Dordrechti habitae anno [M][D]CXVII et [M][D]CXIX. Dordrecht, 1620. "Canones Synodi Dordrechtanae" (with partial English translation), in *The Creeds of Christendom*, 6th ed., edited by Philip Schaff, vol. 3, 550–597. Grand Rapids, MI: Baker, 1990.

Secondary Sources:

van Deursen, Arie Theodorus. *Bavianen en Slijkgeuzen: Kerk en kerkvolk ten tijde and Maurits en Oldenbarnvelt.* Franeker, Netherlands: Van Wijnen, 1998.
van't Spijker, Willem et al. *De Synode van Dordrecht in 1618 en 1619.* Houten, Netherlands: Hertog, 1987.

RAYMOND A. MENTZER

DOUGLASS, FREDERICK (1818–1895)

American slave, freedman, abolitionist, and author. Frederick Douglass embodied African-American engagement with evangelical Protestantism. He received religious instruction from enslaved blacks and free whites. He joined a Baltimore church around 1830 and, as a runaway, was licensed in Massachusetts in 1839 to preach in the AFRICAN METHODIST EPISCOPAL ZION CHURCH. He criticized American churches for tolerating SLAVERY, but his criticisms were not faithless. Central Protestant theological issues, such as the relationship between human activity and divine providence, remained important to him, and he published some important writings in evangelical periodicals.

Douglass made two significant contributions to Protestantism—culminations of trends commencing in black religion around 1770. First, Douglass articulated a standard of CONVERSION relevant to a society marred by slaveholding and racial inequity. The slaveholders' standard was manumission of their slaves; the slaves' standard was the determination to be free. African American religion by 1845 had resolved two problems in conversion in the pietistic tradition—the converts' self-centeredness and the conversion narratives' focus on the self even while recommending self-abnegation. The slaves' desire to be free, articulated in the slave narrative, could never be understood as selfish. Second, Douglass racialized the spiritual autobiography that by 1800 had become a staple of popular Protestantism. He sacralized blacks' yearning for liberation. Of global significance in religious history, Douglass confirmed the evangelical Protestantism of most black North Americans. Neither animism, Islam, nor Roman Catholicism, all known in West Africa, promoted individual freedom as vibrantly as evangelical Protestantism could or offered blacks a tradition of popular autobiographies that could justify both individual freedom and opposition to slavery.

See also Evangelicalism; Slavery, Abolition of

References and Further Reading

Primary Sources:

Douglass, Frederick. *Narrative of the Life of Frederick Douglass.* New York: St. Martin's, 1993.
———. *My Bondage and My Freedom.* Urbana, IL: University of Illinois Press, 1987.
———. *The Life and Times of Frederick Douglass.* New York: Crowell-Collier, 1962.

Secondary Sources:

Blight, David W. *Frederick Douglass and Abraham Lincoln: a Relationship in Language, Politics, and Memory.* Milwaukee, WI: Marquette University Press, c2001.
Chesnutt, Charles Waddell, 1858–1932. *Frederick Douglass, edited by Ernestine W. Pickens; introduction by William L. Andrews.* Atlanta, GA: Clark Atlanta University Press, 2001.
Stauffer, John. *The Black Hearts of Men: Radical Abolitionists and the Transformation of Race.* Cambridge, MA: Harvard University Press, 2002, 2001.
Williamson, Scott C. *The Narrative life: the Moral and Religious Thought of Frederick Douglass.* Macon, GA: Mercer University Press, 2002.

JOHN SAILLANT

DRUMMOND, HENRY (1851–1897)

Scottish professor and writer. The most enduring work of Henry Drummond is his study of 1 Corinthians 13, *The Greatest Thing in the World*. It was first published in 1887 and has never been out of print.

Born in Stirling, SCOTLAND, August 17, 1851, to a financially comfortable, religious family, Drummond entered the University of Edinburgh at age fifteen and proceeded to New College (theological). In the fall of 1873, he interrupted his studies for two years, assisting DWIGHT L. MOODY's first mission to Britain in the inquiry room and speaking at follow-up meetings. Later, Moody said of his friend Drummond, "He is the most Christ-like man I ever knew."

In 1877, Drummond was made Lecturer, later Professor, of Natural Science at Free Church College, Glasgow. His effort to reconcile evolution with Christian thought, published as *Natural Law in the Spiritual World* (1883), and released just before he left on a ten-month exploration of central AFRICA, became a best seller and made him famous. *Tropical Africa* (1888) detailed his experience. Other essays circulated widely and were collected posthumously in a volume titled *The Ideal Life* (1897). A dapper dresser who never married, Drummond worked in the Boys Brigade movement and pioneered university student Christian work from 1884 until his final illness.

Drummond's first visit to America was an 1879 geological expedition to the Rocky Mountains. He returned in 1887 to speak at colleges, at Moody's summer conference at Northfield, Massachusetts, and to receive his only degree, an honorary doctorate, from Amherst. In America and CANADA in 1893, he lectured at Lowell Institute (*The Ascent of Man*, 1894), Harvard, and Chicago and visited friends.

The first stages of a debilitating disease, perhaps bone cancer, began in the spring of 1894, and Drummond died at Tunbridge Wells, March 11, 1897. He is buried in Stirling.

See also Darwinism; Nature; Creation Science

References and Further Reading

Primary Sources:

Drummond, Henry. *Natural Law in the Spiritual World*, 1883.
——. *The Greatest Thing in the World*, 1887.
——. *Tropical Africa*, 1888.
——. *The Ascent of Man*, 1894.
——. *The Ideal Life and Other Unpublished Addresses with Memorial Sketches by Ian Maclaren [pseud] and W. Robertson Nicoll*, 1897.
——. *The New Evangelism and Other Papers*, 1899.
——. *Stones Rolled Away and Other Addresses to Young Men Delivered in America*, 1899.
——. *The Evolution of Bible Study*, edited by A. Fleming. 1901.
Christmas Booklets:
——. *The Greatest Thing in the World,* Christmas, 1889.
——. *Pax Vobiscum*, Christmas, 1890.
——. *The Programme of Christianity*, Christmas, 1891.
——. *The City without a Church*, Christmas, 1892.
——. *The Changed Life*, Christmas, 1893.
Henry Drummond Papers, National Library of Scotland.

Secondary Sources:

Corts, Thomas E., ed. *Henry Drummond: A Perpetual Benediction*. Edinburgh: T & T Clark, 1999.
Kennedy, James W. *Henry Drummond: An Anthology*. New York: Harper, 1953.
Lennox, Cuthbert (J. H. Napier). *Henry Drummond: A Biographical Sketch*. London: Andrew Melrose, 1901.
Simpson, James Y. *Henry Drummond*. Edinburgh: Oliphant, Anderson, & Ferrier, 1901.
Smith, George Adam. *The Life of Henry Drummond*. London: Hodder and Stoughton, 1899.

THOMAS E. CORTS

DU PLESSIS, DAVID JOHANNES (1905–1987)

South African pentecostal leader. David Johannes du Plessis, a descendant of French HUGUENOTS and father of the charismatic or neopentecostal movement, was born in SOUTH AFRICA in 1905. There in the 1930s he was the General Secretary of the Apostolic Faith Mission, a pentecostal organization. According to du Plessis, in 1936 Smith Wigglesworth, a British pentecostal evangelist, prophesied to him that he would become a world leader in causing the pentecostal doctrine of the baptism in the Holy Spirit, evidenced by speaking in TONGUES and other supernatural gifts, to be recognized by the mainline churches.

Du Plessis was one the architects of the Pentecostal World Conference launched in 1947, and in 1949 became its first General Secretary. He believed that PENTECOSTALISM—considered an offshoot of Protestantism—was for all Christians regardless of DENOMINATION. He maintained that the work of the Holy Spirit overrode ecclesiastical boundaries and took this message to leading American universities and SEMINARIES, including Princeton and Yale.

Du Plessis became a pentecostal ambassador to the WORLD COUNCIL OF CHURCHES and also to the Roman Catholic Church. He was a Protestant operating within Catholic circles, and in 1964 was an official observer at the Second Vatican Council.

David du Plessis's work has occasioned admiration and condemnation; regarded by some as a champion of Christian unity helping to bring Catholicism and also Protestantism with its evangelicals and pentecostals all together; but considered by others as having undermined the REFORMATION. The David J. du Plessis Center at Fuller Theological Seminary, Pasadena, California houses his archives.

See also Catholic Reactions to Protestantism; Catholicism, Protestant Reactions; Evangelicalism

References and Further Reading

Primary Sources:

Du Plessis, David J. *A Man called Mr. Pentecost*. Plainfield, NJ: Logos, 1977.
———. *The Spirit Bade Me Go*. Plainfield, NJ: Logos, 1970.

Secondary Source:

Durasoff, Steve. *Bright Wind of the Spirit: Pentecostalism Today*. Plainfield, NJ: Logos, 1972.

THOMAS A. WELCH

DUBOIS, WILLIAM EDWARD BURGHARDT (1868–1963)

Author, editor and educator, civil rights leader. DuBois was a towering figure among twentieth-century black leaders with a keen sense of mission to free black America. He was born in Great Barrington, Massachusetts. He had a Christian upbringing and was a devoted Christian in his youthful days, accompanying his mother to a nearby Congregational Church at Great Barrington. He studied at Fisk (Nashville), Harvard, and Berlin and subsequently taught at Wilberforce and Pennsylvania universities. He also served as director of publications for the National Association for the Advancement of Colored People (NAACP), as editor of *Crisis Magazine* (1910–1932), as editor of *Atlanta University Studies* (1897–1911), and as editor of *Phylon Quarterly Review* (1940–1944).

DuBois became secretary of the NAACP, but in 1948 he left the association. He advocated total elimination of discrimination and equality of all races. He was a major speaker at the All African Conference held in Accra, Ghana in 1958 where he advocated socialism over capitalism (see SOCIALISM, CHRISTIAN). Three years later, at the age of ninety-three, he joined the Communist party. He was invited to Ghana by the first prime minister of the country, Dr. Kwame Nkrumah. Consequently he returned to Ghana in 1961 as a voluntary exile where he died two years later as a citizen of Ghana.

Apart from his background in the Congregational Church, his major significance for Protestantism lies in the fact that he influenced and worked in close association with the AFRICAN METHODIST EPISCOPAL ZION CHURCH (A.M.E. Zion), which became strongest in North Carolina in 1820. The A.M.E. Zion Church was a religious/Christian variant of the black consciousness movement. DuBois collaborated with Bishop Alexander Walters, bishop of the A.M.E. Zion Church in the African Association in London, which held a conference in July 1900. Sylvester Williams who founded the association was the general secretary; Walters was the president while DuBois served as chairman of the Committee on Address.

See also Civil Rights Movement; Slavery, Abolition of

References and Further Reading

Primary Sources:

DuBois, W. E. B. *The Suppression of the African Slave Trade.* Cambridge: Harvard University Press, 1896.
———. *The Philadelphia Negro.* New York: Lippencott, 1899.
———. *The Souls of Black Folk.* Chicago: AC McClurg & Co., 1903.
———. *Negro Church.* Atlanta, GA: University of Atlanta Press, 1903.
———. *The Negro.* New York: Henry Holt, 1915.
———. *The Gift of Black Folk.* Boston: Stratford, 1924.
———. *Black Reconstruction.* New York: Harcourt Brace, 1935.
———. *Black Folk: Then and Now.* New York: Henry Holt, 1939.
———. *Color and Democracy.* New York: Harcourt Brace, 1945.
———. *The World and Africa.* New York: International Publishers, 1946.

Secondary Sources:

Logan, Rayford, ed. *W. E. B. DuBois: Profile.* New York: Hill and Wang, 1971.
Partington, Paul G. *W. E. B. DuBois: A Bibliography of His Published Writings.* Whittier, CA: Partington, 1977.

CEPHAS N. OMENYO

DUKE UNIVERSITY

Deeply rooted in North Carolina METHODISM, Duke University has always maintained meaningful and friendly relations with the Methodist church. The university traces its origins to a primitive, one-room school that the Methodists and Quakers (see FRIENDS, SOCIETY OF) of Randolph County, North Carolina, jointly organized in 1838. The following year Brantley York, the school's principal and a Methodist preacher, converted the school into Union Institute.

Moving on to other work in 1842, York was succeeded by his young assistant, Braxton Craven, also a Methodist preacher, and for the next forty years Craven was to be the chief sustainer of the school. Hoping, in vain as it turned out, to gain monetary support from the state, Craven arranged in 1849 for the school to be incorporated as Normal College, with the primary mission of training young men to become school teachers. Disappointed by his inability to gain financial support for Normal College from the state, Craven turned to the North Carolina Conference of the Methodist Episcopal Church, South, and offered to give preministerial training to aspiring preachers. The church conference responded warmly to the proposal and in 1856 adopted the college as its own. Accordingly, in 1859 the school became Trinity College and sought to grow as a Methodist liberal arts institution.

Although Trinity College, unlike many similar schools, managed to survive the CIVIL WAR, it was desperately poor. Only Craven's determination and sacrifices allowed the school to survive, although gradually there developed a small body of alumni who cherished the institution. When Craven died in 1882 Trinity faced a crisis: its financial situation was so bleak that there was talk of closing the college and selling the property (which was not much). Three trustees, however, all Methodist laymen and prominent businessmen, stepped into the breach to save Trinity. They not only did that but also hired a twenty-nine year-old Pennsylvanian and Yale graduate, John F. Crowell, to become Trinity's president.

Among many revitalizing ideas that Crowell introduced, the most important was his conviction that if

Trinity was serious about its ambitions, then it would have to move from its rural, isolated location in Randolph County to one of North Carolina's livelier, more prosperous manufacturing towns in the Piedmont region. Therefore, in 1892, in response to generous offers of money and land from two Methodist laymen in Durham—Washington Duke and Julian S. Carr—Trinity opened its doors there. Whereas the economic depression of 1893 only made a bad situation worse in North Carolina, Trinity had the good fortune in 1894 to name as Crowell's successor a spellbinding Methodist preacher from South Carolina, John C. Kilgo.

Responding quickly to Kilgo's charismatic leadership and impassioned preaching, Washington Duke, the patriarch of the Durham family that was growing rich in tobacco and textiles, offered Trinity $100,000 in 1896 if it would admit women on "an equal footing" with men. The college promptly agreed and Trinity became coeducational long before most of its peers. Other significant gifts to the college continued to come from Duke and two of his sons, Benjamin N. and James B. Duke. The problem of financial support that had so haunted Craven was finally solved through the generosity of the Duke family.

Long before Kilgo became a Methodist bishop in 1910 and was succeeded as president by Methodist layman William P. Few, Trinity had begun to move cautiously toward university status. Benjamin and James Duke underwrote a small but high-quality law school in 1904; there was also talk of a medical school, and the department of religion grew steadily with help from the Methodists.

In 1921 President Few conceived the idea of organizing a major research university around Trinity College and gradually sold the plan, with constant help from Ben Duke, to the wealthiest member of the family, James Duke. The dream became a reality in December 1924 when Duke University was born. The institution's ties with the Methodist church, however, continued exactly as they had been earlier—friendly and steady, but not constricting. That is, both Kilgo and Few felt deeply that, although it was important to maintain certain formal ties with the Methodist church, it was equally important that there should be a certain arm's-length aspect to the relationship. Committed church bodies, like state legislatures, sometimes responded to popular, fleeting passions and could cause serious trouble for educational institutions.

In practice this meant that first Trinity and then Duke had a self-perpetuating board of thirty-six trustees who nominated their own successors. The charter provided that the older North Carolina Conference of the Methodist church should "elect" (actually "ratify") one-third of the trustees, the newer Western North Carolina Conference another third, and the alumni the final third. Aside from some financial support to Duke's ecumenical divinity school from the Methodist conferences and a wide variety of cooperative ventures, the charter's provision about the trustees remains the historic symbol of Duke University's relationship with Methodism.

References and Further Reading

Chaffin, Nora C. *Trinity College, 1839–1892: The Beginnings of Duke University.* Durham, NC: Duke University Press, 1950.

Durden, Robert F. *The Launching of Duke University, 1924–1949.* Durham, NC: Duke University Press, 1993.

Porter, Earl W. *Trinity and Duke, 1892–1924: Foundation of Duke University.* Durham, NC: Duke University Press, 1964.

ROBERT F. DURDEN

DUTCH PROTESTANTS IN AMERICA

Dutch Protestants in America are products of JOHN CALVIN'S (1509–1564) Genevan reformation, which spread to FRANCE, ENGLAND, the German Palatinate, and the Low Countries. Under Prince William of Orange, Dutch patriots rallied around the Calvinist (Reformed) faith to throw off Catholic Spanish rule and establish the Dutch Republic, with the *Nederlands Gereformeerde* (later *Hervormde*) *Kerk* (Netherlands Reformed Church) as the established church. This body defined its THEOLOGY and POLITY in the historic national Synod of Dort (1618–1619) (see DORT, CANONS OF). Roman Catholics held their ground in the provinces below the Rhine River, but the nine provinces north of the Rhine became overwhelmingly Protestant. In 1815, the population comprised 60 percent Reformed, 38 percent Roman Catholics, and 2 percent Jews, Mennonites, and other Protestants. In 1834, the Netherlands Reformed Church suffered a schism when a conservative minority, despite severe persecution, formed a free church, the Christian Seceded Church.

Immigration

Dutch immigrants brought this religious history as part of their cultural baggage. In the nineteenth century, 80 percent were Reformed and less than 20 percent Catholic. Of the Reformed immigrants, 20 percent belonged to the Seceded Church. In the UNITED STATES a second schism occurred in 1857, which divided the Dutch Reformed Church into two rival denominations.

The Dutch immigrated to America in three waves: the Dutch West India Company colony of New Netherland beginning in the 1620s; the nineteenth-century free migration to the Midwest; and the planned migration after the Second World War, when the Dutch government encouraged its dispirited citizens to emigrate overseas to relieve overcrowding and widespread deprivation.

The colonial migration brought 7,000 Dutch to the New World in the forty years before the English seized New Netherlands in 1664. This number increased to 100,000 by 1790, when the Dutch comprised one-sixth of the populace within a fifty-mile radius of New York City. From 1820 to 1920, 250,000 Dutch came; most congregated within fifty miles of Lake Michigan, led by the flagship colony of Holland, Michigan. The pioneer colony of Pella, Iowa was the nest for colonies in upper Midwest, especially Orange City. In 1945–1965, another 80,000 Dutch came, many with one-way steamship tickets paid by their government. The Dutch Reformed Church in America is a direct offshoot of these immigration waves, and church life and theological debates bear the stamp of Netherlandic origins.

Founding the Dutch Reformed Church

One of the oldest American denominations, the Reformed Protestant Dutch Church (after 1867, the Dutch Reformed Church in America) was founded in 1628 in New Amsterdam (later New York City), under the auspices of the Classis of Amsterdam of the Netherlands Reformed Church, by Jonas Michaëlius (1577–1646), the first ordained minister in New Netherlands. Director Peter Minuit, who purchased Manhattan Island from the Indians for $24, began Reformed worship in his home. He and his successors permitted "no other services than those of the true Reformed Religion." Leading clerics in New Netherlands were Everardus Bogardus (1607–1647) in New Amsterdam, from 1633 to 1647; Johannes Megapolensis (1601–1670) in Rensselaerwyck (later Albany) from 1642 to 1649 and in New Amsterdam from 1647 to 1670; Samuel Drisius in New Amsterdam from 1652 to 1673; and Gideon Shaats in Beverwyck (later Albany), from 1652 to 1694.

Although only the Reformed faith was publicly funded, private WORSHIP was allowed to other Protestants and even to Catholics. However, when twenty-three Dutch Jews from Brazil came seeking refuge in 1654, Governor Peter Stuyvesant and the Reverend Megapolensis wanted to throw the "godless rascals" out. This "deceitful race," the governor declared, "must not be allowed to infect and trouble this new colony." But the West India Company's board of directors in Amsterdam overruled the governor and, much to his chagrin, ordered him to "connive," that is,

to allow the Jews to remain, provided that they cared for their own poor, as all non-Reformed colonists were required to do. Profit took precedence over profession.

The English government, after seizing the colony in 1664, guaranteed freedom of religion to the Dutch Reformed Church (see TOLERATION). Fresh immigration ceased and government monies were cut off, but the Dutch Reformed Church remained the dominant religion and culture. Filling the pulpits was the major challenge; only six clerics were available to serve twenty-three congregations in 1700. Aspiring colonial clerics had to cross the ocean to take seminary training and ordination in the NETHERLANDS. In 1776, the Dutch Reformed Church counted more than 100 congregations, centered in New York and New Jersey.

The Dutch language was used in worship services and catechetical instruction until 1762, when English services began. Sunday worship included Genevan psalm singing and prayers, but the focal point was the sermon, which was often doctrinal and always lengthy. One sermon each Sunday expounded on the HEIDELBERG CATECHISM, one of the three Dutch Reformed confessions, called the "Three Forms of Unity." Dutch CALVINISM was shaped theologically by its stress on the sovereignty of God and God's COVENANT with believers (see COVENANT THEOLOGY). Culturally, the Reformed stressed vocation as a "calling," which led to a strong work ethic and directing every task to the "glory of God."

Americanization

The First and Second Great Awakenings and the American Revolution greatly impacted the Dutch Reformed Church (see AWAKENINGS). Its leaders generally frowned on the New Measures, as employed by GEORGE WHITEFIELD (1714–1770) in the 1740s and CHARLES G. FINNEY (1792–1875) in the 1820s, for giving too much credence to "free will" over God's sovereign decree. But both Whitefield and Finney were quasi-Calvinists by upbringing and profession, and many Dutch Reformed Church members embraced their revivalist methods (see REVIVALS). One result was factionalism—"Old Side/New Side" factions in the eighteenth century, and "Old School/New School" parties in the nineteenth century. The Reverend Theodore Jacobus Frelinghuysen (1692–c. 1747), who from 1720 served Dutch Reformed congregations in central New Jersey for twenty years, was the leading preacher of the New Birth. American revivalism thus modified traditional Dutch Reformed theology and polity as formulated in the Canons and Church Order of Dort.

Dutch Reformed teachings about human nature, covenants, and the nexus between freedom and virtue helped inspire the Whiggish American Revolution and the Constitution. (The Netherlands was the first government to recognize the new American nation in 1782.) Most Dutch Reformed Church members supported the Patriot cause, although more than one-third of the CLERGY were Tories. Internal tensions were exacerbated by depredations of the British armies, who viewed the Dutch as enemies and occupied many of their churches.

The war had a further fallout; it brought to a head a lengthy debate over whether or not the American church should remain under the Classis of Amsterdam. The progressive, pro-American party, called the "Coetus" (pronounced "seetus"), strongly demanded the right to train and ordain its own ministers in America, and they established Queens (later Rutgers) College in 1766 to do so. The traditional, pro-Dutch party, called the "Conferentie," favored the status quo under Amsterdam's control. The deeper issue was the pace of Americanization. In 1771, the Reverend Dr. John Henry Livingston managed to bring the factions together in a Union Convention, and in 1784, he helped found New Brunswick Seminary, the oldest in the nation.

In 1792, Livingston led the CHURCH to break with Amsterdam and form an American, "voluntary-membership denomination" with its own LITURGY, polity, and constitution. The document, in an echo of the First Amendment's disestablishment clause, allowed for freedom of conscience for every member, which was a weakening of the Reformed creedal basis and a sharp departure from the Dort church order. The new church constitution gave clerics greater latitude to reinterpret cardinal Reformed doctrines, such as ELECTION and limited ATONEMENT, in favor of the rising spirit of ARMINIANISM that came to full fruition in the Second Great Awakening. Weekly sermons from the Heidelberg Catechism also fell away in many churches. In 1822, under the leadership of theology professor Solomon Froeligh (1750–1827), a number of New Jersey churches seceded from the Reformed Protestant Dutch Church—the name adopted in 1819 to distinguish it from the German Reformed and other Reformed bodies—and formed the True Reformed Dutch Church.

The Reformed Protestant Dutch Church did not fare well in the new democratic religious age, with its popular revolt against Calvinist doctrines and an educated clergy. Like other denominations with Calvinist roots—Anglican, Presbyterian, and Congregational—the Dutch fed on internal growth but gained few converts on the frontier, in comparison to the "upstart" Methodists and BAPTISTS with their evange-listic efforts. "Marrying Dutch" (i.e., within the denomination) was so common as to be a cliche, and almost every Dutch Reformed cleric had a close relative in the profession. All five sons of Frelinghuysen, for example, were ordained.

True (Christian) Reformed Church

New immigration from the Netherlands, beginning in the mid-1840s, saved the day for the Reformed Protestant Dutch Church and boosted its mission efforts on the midwestern frontier. The first major accession was in 1850, when the Reverend Albertus C. Van Raalte, leader of the Holland (Michigan) Colony, founded in 1847, arranged for the nine congregations in the Classis of Holland to affiliate. Some families refused to go along, however, believing that the Reformed Church of the East was so Americanized as to have left the orthodox way in faith and practice. Some 10 percent of the member families of the Classis of Holland seceded in 1857 and formed the "True" Dutch Reformed Church (later the CHRISTIAN REFORMED CHURCH IN NORTH AMERICA). That year, the Noon Day Prayer Meeting at the Fulton Street Dutch Reformed Church in New York City sparked a religious revival that spread nationwide.

The two Dutch Reformed churches competed for members and their church buildings often stood within eyesight of one another. The True denomination, with its old Dutch ways, received most of the new immigrants and grew rapidly, eventually gaining parity with the senior denomination. But the Reformed Church also attracted its share of immigrants, especially in the Midwest, which created a cultural division between the old American Eastern wing and the young Western wing. The immigrant churches were more conservative theologically and culturally; they slowed the process of change and blocked merger movements with German Reformed and Presbyterian bodies that Eastern leaders orchestrated.

Two new Dutch Reformed denominations emerged in the twentieth century, both largely the result of conservative secessions from the Christian Reformed Church. These are the Protestant Reformed Church (in 1922) and the United Reformed Church (in 1995). Several smaller Reformed groups also exist. Since about 1950, a growing number of Dutch have joined Baptist, Pentecostal, nondenominational, and independent churches, some of which also espouse Reformed theology. Upwardly mobile Dutch increasingly affiliate with mainline Protestant denominations, especially Presbyterian bodies.

A significant factor in the growth of the Christian Reformed Church was its staunch refusal to accept Freemasons. The Reformed Church had long permitted such members. This prompted a second schism in the 1880s, which led several thousand Reformed Church members (10 percent), mainly in the Midwestern congregations, to switch to the Christian Reformed Church. Furthermore, the mother church in the Netherlands, which viewed FREEMASONRY through the lens of the anti-Christian French ENLIGHTENMENT, in 1882 began strongly advising its immigrating families to affiliate with the Christian Reformed Church. This decision, which coincided with the increasing immigration from the northern Netherlands in the 1880s due to a severe agricultural depression, brought thousands of devout families into the junior denomination.

Starting after 1900, the Christian Reformed Church developed a national system of Christian day schools (K–12), to raise up biblically and doctrinally literate church members. These parent-controlled schools became the feeders of the church, and led to intermarriage within the covenant community. They were modeled after Netherlandic schools that gained full public funding under Dr. ABRAHAM KUYPER, the foremost Calvinist leader in the Netherlands from 1880 to 1920. Until the 1970s, over 80 percent of Christian Reformed families enrolled their children in *onze* (our) schools, which are conjoined in Christian Schools International, which today includes 300 schools with 60,000 students in the United States.

In contrast, the Reformed Church in America supported public schools. The 1892 General Synod declared that the "Common School is vitally essential to the fusing of the heterogeneous elements of our population into one nation." This resolution reflects the denomination's three centuries of assimilation. Their youths would be "salt and light" in public schools.

Reformed Dutch liberal arts colleges include Hope (1866), Central (est. 1853, became Reformed in 1916), Calvin (1876), Northwestern (1882), Dordt (1955), and Trinity Christian (1959). Theological seminaries, in addition to New Brunswick, are Western (1866), Calvin (1876), and Mid-America (1982). Lay missionaries train at Reformed Bible College (1937) (see CHRISTIAN COLLEGES; BIBLE COLLEGES AND INSTITUTIONS; SEMINARIES).

Today the two largest Dutch Reformed denominations number about 280,000 each. The Reformed Church remains headquartered in New York City; the Christian Reformed "Zion" is in Grand Rapids, Michigan. Both bodies include Canadian congregations. Post-1945 immigrants to CANADA compose 28 percent of Christian Reformed Church membership, which strengthened its flagging "Dutchness." The more "Americanized" Reformed Church is affiliated with the NATIONAL COUNCIL OF CHURCHES and WORLD COUNCIL OF CHURCHES. Grand Rapids is also the national center of Christian book PUBLISHING, with four

firms—William B. Eerdmans, Zondervan, Kregel, and Baker Book House—all founded by interrelated Christian Reformed immigrants.

Dutch Reformed Church groups share a common "world and life view," rooted in a strong diaconal tradition, which has led them to establish human service institutions—"Holland homes" for the elderly, mental health hospitals (Pine Rest in Grand Rapids, Michigan; Bethesda in Denver; and Goffle Hill in Paterson, New Jersey), homes for special needs children and adults, institutions for troubled youth and women in transition, day care centers, an international child welfare and adoption agency (Bethany Christian Services), and world relief organizations.

Notables

Dutch Protestants claim three U.S. presidents: Martin Van Buren, Theodore Roosevelt, and Franklin D. Roosevelt. Theodore Roosevelt cherished his Reformed Church heritage.

The Reformed Church pioneered in foreign MISSIONS in Asia and the Middle East, under Samuel Zwemer (1867–1952), missionary to Arabia and Egypt, and Ida Scudder (1870–1959), medical missionary in INDIA. NORMAN VINCENT PEALE (1898–1993), though non-Dutch, pastored New York City's seminal Marble Collegiate Church for more than fifty years (1932–1984). In 1955, Robert H. Schuller (b. 1926) founded the Crystal Cathedral in southern California.

Leading Christian Reformed theologians include Gerhardus Vos (1862–1949) of Princeton Seminary, Louis Berkhof (1874–1957) of Calvin Seminary, Cornelius Van Til (1895–1987) of Westminster Seminary (Philadelphia), and Peter Eldersveld (1911–65), radio minister of the denominational "Back to God Hour" program. Christian ETHICS professors include Henry Stob (1908–2000) of Calvin College and Lewis Smedes (b. 1921) of Calvin and Fuller Seminaries. Scholars in Reformed philosophy include Alvin Plantinga (b. 1932) of the University of Notre Dame and Nicholas Wolterdorff (b. 1932) of Yale University.

Dutch Reformed denominations today stand with at least fifteen other Reformed bodies, but the combined Dutch membership of 750,000 (one-third of whom are Canadian), pales in comparison with the total six million Reformed in America members. Dutch Reformed presses, periodicals, books, and academic and social institutions play a large role in the evangelical community (see EVANGELICALISM). In the defense of biblical AUTHORITY and commitment to cultural transformation, the Dutch Reformed Church has made a mark on American Protestantism far out of proportion to its numbers.

References and Further Reading

Bratt, James D. *Dutch Calvinism in Modern America: A History of a Conservative Subculture.* Grand Rapids, MI: Eerdmans, 1984.

Corwin, Charles E. *A Manual of the Reformed Church in America, 1628-1922.* New York: Reformed Church of America, 1922.

De Jong, Gerald F. *The Dutch Reformed Church in the American Colonies.* Grand Rapids, MI: Eerdmans, 1978.

Fabend, Firth Haring. *Zion on the Hudson: Dutch New York and New Jersey in the Age of Revivals.* Albany, NY: University of New York Press, 2000.

Kromminga, John. *The Christian Reformed Church: A Study in Orthodoxy,* Grand Rapids, MI: Baker Book House, 1949.

Schaap, James C. *Our Family Album: The Unfinished Story of the Christian Reformed Church.* Grand Rapids, MI: CRC Publications, 1998.

Swierenga, Robert P., and Elton J. Bruins. *Family Quarrels in the Dutch Reformed Churches in the Nineteenth Century.* Grand Rapids, MI: Eerdmans, 1999.

ROBERT P. SWIERENGA

DUTCH REFORMED CHURCH (GEREFORMEERDE KERK)

The Dutch Reformed Church (DRC) had its beginning in the sixteenth century and became the established church in the Protestant Dutch Republic, although Roman Catholics and Protestant dissenters enjoyed a considerable amount of freedom (see DISSENT). The DRC was Calvinist in doctrine and survived serious doctrinal conflicts. In the eighteenth and nineteenth centuries the DRC became a pluralistic church. The NETHERLANDS lost its typical Protestant stamp after the French Revolution, and the influence of the DRC on society waned. Several schisms hampered the DRC, and the secularization of the twentieth century caused a great loss in membership. In reaction, the DRC showed a new missionary and ecumenical zeal after World War II.

Founding of the DRC

The organization and the doctrine of the *Gereformeerde Kerk* or Dutch Reformed Church evolved gradually during the persecution of the REFORMATION by the Spanish government and its suppression by the Roman Catholic Church. Reformed groups arose in the southern provinces of the Low Countries in the 1550s, when numerous groups from inside and outside the country had already paved the way for new religious ideas. The Reformation movement was marked by several influences, including sacramentalism, ANABAPTISM, CALVINISM, the Modern Devotion, and biblical humanism. From the start of the reign of the Spanish King Philip II in 1559, the situation deteriorated for the Dutch Reformation movement. In an attempt to explain its intentions to the government, the Reformed pastor Guido de Bres, following the French example, formulated the BELGIC CONFESSION in 1561, which was immediately given confessional status by the DRC. From 1566 Reformed people fled persecution in the Netherlands, and congregations were formed in ENGLAND and GERMANY while the Netherlands rebelled against Spain. At the Convent of Wezel (1568) and the Synod of Emden (1571), these congregations agreed on unification and certain ecclesiastical standards. The HEIDELBERG CATECHISM (1563) was adopted along with the Belgic Confession. From 1572 the DRC reappeared as a predominantly Calvinist church in the liberated parts of the Netherlands, and the first national synod was held in Dordrecht in 1578.

Established Church

The DRC became the established church in the Dutch Republic, although the government tolerated the Catholic church and other dominations, like the Lutherans (see LUTHERANISM) and the Anabaptists. A minority of the Dutch adhered to the Reformed faith and only part of this minority were confessing members of the DRC. Nevertheless, the DRC was dominant in society, especially because EDUCATION was part of its task. It was not just its confession but also its Calvinistic piety and life- and worldview that permeated Dutch society. Public offices could be held only by members of the DRC.

The first serious test for this partnership was the struggle over ARMINIANISM in the early 1600s. Arminius held the eternal election as a fruit of FAITH, whereas according to the Calvinist doctrine faith is a fruit of ELECTION. This disagreement led to serious tensions in both church and state. The matter was settled at the international synod of Dordrecht (1618/19), which formulated the CANONS OF DORT, rejecting the Arminian viewpoints and stressing the Calvinistic character of the DRC's doctrine. Together with the Heidelberg Catechism and the Belgic Confession, these canons were adopted as the doctrinal basis of the church, the so-called Three Forms of Unity. This synod also accepted a democratic church order, which functioned for almost two centuries. Maurits, prince of Orange and the informal head of the state, settled the dispute all over the country, replacing unwilling magistrates with loyal ones. State and church preserved unity, a unity that was fostered by the synod's decision to issue a new Dutch translation of the BIBLE, financed by the States-General of the Republic, the so-called *Statenbijbel* (1637). This translation exerted a unifying force with unsurpassed influence on Dutch language and culture and was replaced by a new translation only in 1951. This feat could not hide that tensions in the relationship had surfaced during the

Arminian dispute. The state guarded its interests with zeal, and never again during the Dutch Republic was the DRC (see CHURCH AND STATE, OVERVIEW) allowed to convene a national synod. The influence of the state included the governor's right to attend synodical meetings, the right of the local magistrates to accept or reject a minister, but also the obligation to pay him and to defend and uphold the DRC. Concord in society was the aim of the magistrates. For this reason the dominant position of the DRC included a tolerant attitude toward dissenters, Jews, and Roman Catholics and dismissal of overly strict ministers. The Republic was renowned for its freedom of conscience. Most books published in the seventeenth century were printed there, and persecuted Christians, like the French HUGUENOTS, often fled to the Republic for the sake of freedom.

The economic success of the early Dutch Republic was based on the development of Amsterdam as a stable market for international trade, organized and regulated by trade companies. At the trading posts founded in INDIA, AFRICA, and America the DRC also established congregations. The best known is the DRC founded in New Amsterdam (New York) in 1628. A full-grown American denomination developed out of this church. Known today as the REFORMED CHURCH IN AMERICA, its congregations are located mainly in New York, New Jersey, and Michigan. Until they became independent in 1792, these churches were part of the classis of Amsterdam. In 1867 the church deleted the word "Dutch" in its name, although the Dutch language and hymns were still present in services at certain occasions until about 1900. Its constitution is still in accordance with that of the DRC and consists of the Three Forms of Unity.

New Religious Trends

Despite the prolonged dominant position of the DRC, the reformation of Dutch society was not as successful as might have been expected. Some groups argued that the Reformation in the Netherlands had stalled halfway. An international movement for ongoing reformation of personal life and society gained influence in the Netherlands as *Nadere Reformatie* (Further Reformation). This movement played a substantial role in the church, thanks to theologians like Voetius, the founder of the university of Utrecht (1636). These groups engaged in long-running disputes on issues like the observance of the Lord's day with theologians like JOHANNES COCCEJUS (1603–1669), who defended a more historical interpretation of Scripture. Concern for CONVERSION, personal piety, and SALVATION took precedence over concern for social reform and the Christian life.

This emphasis on personal religion coincided with the stressing of personal convictions over authoritative opinions, as promulgated by ENLIGHTENMENT philosophers. They emphasized the need for religious tolerance. This was already practiced in the Republic, but the DRC was still the predominant public church. This historical privilege was at odds with the Enlightened theory of the equality of all people and the ideal of tolerance (see TOLERATION). In the eighteenth century, the influence of the *Nadere Reformatie* became entangled with the Enlightenment movement among both the Reformed and dissenters. In Enlightened fashion, theologians tried to synthesize reason and revelation. Classic Reformed theological positions were adapted to the spirit of the times: God was an impersonal *primus movens,* the Christian life was a matter of virtues, and Christians were rewarded for their virtues in an afterlife. Reformed theology became thin in these years and just clung to the old standards, although the DRC continued to be an important institution, mainly because its preaching upheld prudent civil behavior. The idea of the fatherland became the cohesive factor in society instead of the confession of the divine guidance of Dutch history.

After the French Revolution

In 1795 the Dutch Republic was occupied by the French and finally collapsed. A Batavian Republic was founded in which the ties between church and state were severed, according to the principles of the French Revolution. All existing churches received equal protection, and state offices were open to all. When the United Kingdom of the Netherlands was created in 1813, King William I of Orange adopted the Napoleonic idea of a uniform state supported by a uniform DRC—to which 55 percent of the Dutch people at that time belonged. The DRC—now called *Nederlandse Hervormde Kerk*—accepted the king's control, which meant a fixation of the theological status quo and a loss of self-governance by the provincial and local bodies. This was the low ebb in the history of religious freedom in the Netherlands. Meanwhile, a countermovement to deistic rationalism and rigid ORTHODOXY had arisen in eighteenth-century Europe in the form of the Methodists (see METHODISM) and the MORAVIANS and of ROMANTICISM in general. The REVEIL movement gained importance within Christian circles in the Netherlands from the 1820s, whereas quite a few Reformed people gathered in CONVENTICLES on weekdays because the Sunday services did not match their doctrinal and liturgical standards. Protests of the Reformed against the new hierarchy and Enlightenment theology led to the Secession of 1834. Several ministers were excommunicated for disobedience to the church order and the small groups that left the DRC thereupon were fined and imprisoned whenever they gathered. With the new constitution of 1848, the Seceders received the right to organize their *Christelijke Gereformeerde Kerk* (Christian Reformed Church) freely. The DRC synod regained its freedom in church matters, but the DRC kept its link with the state, though in a less prominent way than was the case before 1795.

A Divided Church

The synod governed the DRC but did not decide theological disputes when several theological schools gained ground in the nineteenth century, from MODERNISM, with its rejection of the supernatural, to a neo-Calvinistic theology, which advocated a return to the confessional standards and to the decentralized governmental structure of the seventeenth century. Famous theologians like J. H. Scholten, P. Hofstede de Groot, and ABRAHAM KUYPER (1837–1920) tried to adapt the DRC to modern times. Their differing opinions led to serious disputes and controversies within the DRC and resulted, on the one hand, in a church without a distinct character, irreligiousness among the elite, and a massive loss of laborers to the Socialist movement and, on the other, to a rapid growth of nonestablished churches, like the REMONSTRANTS and the Reformed. In the year 1886 and following, about 10 percent of the members of the DRC left. These so-called *Dolerenden* (Lamenters), led by Kuyper, merged in 1892 with a majority of the *Christelijke Gereformeerde Kerk* and founded the *Gereformeerde Kerken in Nederland* (Reformed Churches). Less than half the Dutch population now belonged to the DRC. Still claiming to be the church of the fatherland, it entered the twentieth century in a state of confusion and dismay, whereas the smaller but cohesive Reformed Churches dominated the Protestant scene for about half a century. Within the DRC, several groups organized to alter the character of the church: the Confessionals, who, inspired by Ph. J. Hoedemaker, tried to restore the church; their more outspoken Reformed allies, the Ethicals; and the Liberals. This period of confusion lasted until the 1920s, when the rise of the theology of KARL BARTH (1886–1968) and the emergence of gifted theologians like K. H. Miskotte and O. Noordmans gave a new impulse to the DRC and its theology. Under the influence of Barth's struggle against German National Socialism, the DRC looked beyond its sixteenth- and seventeenth-century standards to confess her belief anew in the face of the challenges of the twentieth century.

In the meantime, membership of the DRC had dwindled down to one third of the Dutch population in the 1930s; the percentage of Dutch nonbelievers had grown to fourteen percent in the 1930s. In these dramatic circumstances, a movement took hold in the 1920s and 1930s in the DRC for reorganization of its governmental structure and for return to its basics. This movement seemed to fail until the war and the German occupation of the Netherlands accelerated this process. Nazi terror and the spiritual and material needs of the Dutch forced the DRC to speak out for its confession and made her relevant within Dutch society as a whole. This new confidence combined with the urge to reorganize, resulting in a general synod—the first since 1619—that accepted a new church order, which was implemented in 1951. Although not a return to the Dordrecht order, several elements were retained: congregations were represented in the governmental bodies again, and a formula was agreed upon regarding the function and status of the Three Forms of Unity: "confessing in community with our forefathers." The influence of Barth was dominant in the new church order; liberals were criticized for relying on the concept of the human being as a religious being, and the orthodox were criticized for relying on their knowledge of God's will.

New Self-Consciousness

The DRC presented itself as a church that confessed Christ for the Dutch people as a whole. This meant that, according to its understanding of the structure of the divine covenant, the DRC also included those who had not expressly left the church. This self-understanding also implied that it should have a missionary, apostolic attitude. By assuming this role, the DRC claimed a responsibility for Dutch society, not only in concord with the state, as in former days, but in its own right, over against the state, if need be. In the 1950s and 1960s the DRC formulated its opinion on social issues on a regular basis. In the 1960s the ordination of WOMEN (see also WOMEN CLERGY) was accepted, although parts of the DRC never acquiesced to this decision. When Dutch society polarized in the 1960s, polarization got hold of the church as well. The DRC lost many members as a result of growing secularization and became marginalized in Dutch society. The secularization and the internal tensions tempered the pretensions of the DRC and led to new contacts with the *Gereformeerde Kerken*. These churches had experienced two schisms since its formation in 1892 and had also had difficulties in coping with secularization. From the 1960s on, both churches began talking together about a possible merger, a process called *Samen op Weg* (Together on the Way), joined by the small Lutheran Church in 1986. Since that year the churches have been in a "state of reunion." The strong

Reformed minority of the DRC has serious concerns about the union, although the merger of the three churches will be effectuated in 2004. The new church will be called the *Protestantse Kerk in Nederland* (Protestant Church in the Netherlands).

References and Further Reading

Primary Source:

Bakhuizen van den Brink, J. N., ed. *Documenta reformatoria: Teksten uit de geschiedenis van kerk en theologie sedert de hervorming.* 2 vols. Kampen: Kok, 1960–1962.

Secondary Sources:

Aalders, M. J., and C. Augustijn, eds. *Reformatorica: Teksten uit de geschiedenis van het Nederlandse protestantisme.* Zoetermeer: Meinema, 1996.

Augustijn, C., and E. Honée. *Vervreemding en verzoening: De relatie tussen katholieken en protestanten in Nederland, 1550–2000.* Nijmegen: Valkhof Pers, 1998.

Bakhuizen van den Brink, J. N., ed. *De Nederlandse belijdenisgeschriften.* Rev. ed. Amsterdam: Bolland, 1976.

Frijhoff, Willem. *Embodied Belief: Ten Essays on Religious Culture in Dutch History.* Hilversum: Verloren, 2002.

Jong, O. J. de. *Nederlandse kerkgeschiedenis.* Nijkerk: Callenbach, 1985.

Po-Chia Hsia, R., and F. K. van Nierop Henk, eds. *Calvinism and Religious Tolerance in the Dutch Golden Age.* Cambridge: Cambridge University Press, 2002.

Rasker, A. J. *De Nederlandse Hervormde Kerk vanaf 1795: Geschiedenis, theologische ontwikkelingen en de verhouding tot haar zusterkerken in de negentiende en twintigste eeuw.* Kampen: Kok, 1986.

Rooden, Peter Van. *Religieuze regimes: Over godsdienst en maatschappij in Nederland, 1570–1990.* Amsterdam: Bakker, 1996.

GEORGE HARINCK

DUTCH REFORMED CHURCH IN AFRICA

The Dutch Reformed Church, or Nederduitse Gereformeerde Kerk (NGK), is the dominant Afrikaner church in SOUTH AFRICA. Founded in 1652, when the first Dutch settlers came to South Africa, the NGK has been the church of the Afrikaner establishment and was closely linked with the racist policies of apartheid from 1948 to 1994.

Theologically the Calvinist NGK stresses God's sovereignty, human sinfulness in a fallen world, and the redemptive work of Christ, not only in saving human souls but also transforming culture, through the work of the Holy Spirit in the Christian community.

Their stress on transforming human culture led the NGK to work on shaping a "New Jerusalem" in South Africa. The Afrikaners saw strong parallels between themselves as the people of God, and the biblical nation of Israel, which led them to focus on the Old Testament rather than the New.

In the early years the NGK was an interracial church in which whites and blacks worshipped together. Some white Afrikaners came to object to drinking out of the same cup as black Christians during the LORD'S SUPPER. The Synod (annual general meeting) of 1857 proposed that "as a concession to the prejudice and weakness of a few, it is recommended that the church serve one or more tables to the European members after the non-white members have been served." This recommendation came in spite of the church's recognition that the BIBLE taught that all Christians ought to worship together. In addition the Synod recommended that "if the weakness of some requires that the groups be separated, the congregation from the heathen should enjoy its privilege in a separate building and a separate institution." This concession soon grew into a policy of separating white and non-white churches, and eventually led to formation of separate mission churches for non-whites in South Africa.

In 1948 the NGK minister, Daniel Malan, became Prime Minister of South Africa and established apartheid, in which not only the churches but the entire society was segregated by race. The NGK supported and defended Malan's policies on theological grounds.

The NGK gradually found itself ostracized by virtually the entire Christian community, to the point that in 1986, the WORLD ALLIANCE OF REFORMED CHURCHES declared apartheid to be HERESY, and broke off fellowship with the NGK.

The Afrikaner community responded with a feeling that it was an embattled minority struggling to be obedient to God while faced with hostile forces all around trying to prevent it from doing so. This sense of threat—from the black majority and from the powerful English supported by liberal world opinion—led the Afrikaner churches to entrench themselves in their racist and exclusivistic ideology.

The church and South African society as a whole took an abrupt about-face in the early 1990s, when South Africa abolished apartheid and developed a multiracial government and society. The NGK has supported these developments wholeheartedly and has gradually been welcomed back into the worldwide community of Christian Churches.

References and Further Reading

Davenport, T. R. H. *The Afrikaner Bond: The History of a South African Political Party.* Cape Town, London, New York: OUP, 1966.

Elphick, Richard, and Rodney Davenport, eds. *Christianity in South Africa.* Berkeley and Los Angeles: University of California Press, 1997.

Isichei, Elizabeth. *A History of Christianity in Africa from Antiquity to the Present.* London: SPCK, 1995.

Mitchener, James. *The Covenant.* New York: Random House, 1980.

Moodie, T. Dunbar. *The Rise of Afrikanerdom: Power, Apartheid, and the Afrikaner Civil Religion.* Berkeley, Los Angeles, and London: University of California Press, 1975.

NEIL LETTINGA

DWIGHT, TIMOTHY (1752–1817)

New England theologian. Dwight was born in Northampton, Massachusetts, May 14, 1752, the son of Timothy (Major) Dwight and Mary Edwards, oldest daughter of distinguished Puritan divine, JONATHAN EDWARDS. In 1777 he married Mary Woolsey, with whom he had seven sons. In 1795 he became president, chaplain, and professor of THEOLOGY at Yale College, where he died January 11, 1817.

Like his grandfather, Dwight entered Yale at the age of twelve, and there he studied JOHN LOCKE's philosophy, rhetoric, poetry, and the arts. When in 1771 he was appointed a tutor by the college, he worked with several colleagues, the most prominent of whom was Joel Barlow, to seek an authentic American literary style. Dwight's experiments with poetry, such as *The Conquest of Canaan* (1785) and *Greenfield Hill* (1794), fell short of his literary aspirations but communicated Dwight's feelings about America's destiny. In 1774 Dwight joined the College Church as a professing member and rededicated himself to serving God, and in 1777 he was licensed to preach by the Congregational church. That same year he became a chaplain to the Continental Army.

Accepting the invitation to Greenfield Hill in 1783 marked the beginning of Dwight's life work, advancing the cause of evangelical Christianity in the nation. He published the first of many arguments, an anonymous poem *The Triumph of Infidelity,* against the "infidels," whom he believed threatened the Protestant establishment of New England. These perceived enemies of Christianity were as varied as Deists, Universalists, or President THOMAS JEFFERSON. He also began the series of sermons that would be his theological statement, *Theology Explained and Defended.* The return to Yale gave him a pulpit to address not only New England, but also the nation. Claiming the mantle of the Edwardian TRADITION, he constructed a Christianity informed by empirical rationalism and pragmatism that was the foundation for the PREACHING of the Second Great Awakening (see AWAKENINGS). Through his students, among whom were LYMAN BEECHER and NATHANIEL TAYLOR, he declared that the Christian religion and New England CULTURE mutually supported each other and could create the KINGDOM OF GOD in America. The Protestant crusade of the nineteenth century proceeded on the basis of this claim.

See also Deism; Unitarian Universalist Association; Universalism

References and Further Reading

Primary Source:

Dwight, Timothy. *Travels in New-England and New York.* 4 vols. London: William Baynes and Son, 1823.

Secondary Sources:

Cunningham, Charles. *Timothy Dwight 1752–1817, A Biography.* New York: Macmillan, 1942.

Howard, Leon. *The Connecticut Wits.* Chicago, IL: University of Chicago Press, 1943.

Wenzke, Annabelle. *Timothy Dwight and the Beginning of the American Evangelical Tradition.* Lewiston, NY: The Edwin Mellen Press, 1989.

ANNABELLE S. WENZKE

E

ECCLESIASTICAL ORDINANCES

When it became clear that the earliest Protestants were not going to be able to secure the reforms they wanted within the structure of the Roman Catholic Church, they began creating new ecclesiastical institutions. To give these institutions shape, they drafted new laws or ordinances, which in effect became constitutions for reformed churches. These ecclesiastical ordinances were normally first drafted by a clergyman for a city, and then adopted, usually with a few revisions and amendments, by the city's government. Many of these ordinances were later revised and extended to cover broader areas, an entire province, even a kingdom.

Perhaps the first complete set of ecclesiastical ordinances was drafted for the Hanseatic city of Stralsund by the Lutheran theologian Johannes Aepinus (1499–1553) in 1525. It provided for the selection of clergymen whose primary function would be to preach, thus providing a significant break with Catholic parish priests whose primary function had been to administer the sacraments. It provided for schools to teach children basic skills and Scripture, with additional provision of Latin schools to prepare students for professions. It also provided for the care of the poor through the creation of a common chest. The Stralsund Council added the provision that one of the preachers would have general charge of the entire establishment, becoming its superintendent.

This pattern was duplicated again and again by clergymen all over Europe. There were some who became particularly well known for the ecclesiastical ordinances they drafted and often then implemented. One of these was Johannes Brenz (1499–1570), who drafted an ordinance for the city of Hall and the surrounding territory in 1526, and then went on to become one of the leading creators and leaders of new ecclesiastical institutions in the principality of Würt-

temberg. Another was Johannes Bugenhagen (1485–1558). He drafted ordinances for a number of leading cities in north Germany, including Braunschweig in 1528, Hamburg in 1529, and Lübeck in 1531. He also assisted in creating ordinances for wider territories, including Pomerania in 1535, Denmark between 1537 and 1539, and Schleswig-Holstein in 1542. The ordinances drafted by Bugenhagen followed the same basic pattern as those of Aepinus and Brenz. They typically created an office of superintendent and provided for the selection and supervision of preaching clergy, the establishment of schools (both elementary and advanced), and a common chest to finance the church and assist the poor. They also, however, added a good deal. Bugenhagen began the practice of adding details on the rituals to be practiced by clergymen that became an ever more important feature of later Lutheran ecclesiastical ordinances. They often became liturgical manuals as much as constitutions, sometimes even appending an entire catechism or confession of faith.

A significantly different pattern was devised by John Calvin (1509–1564) for the city of Geneva in 1541. Unlike the Lutheran ecclesiastical ordinances, it made no provision for a superintendent. It did include provision for selecting a first order of ministers called pastors, on the basis of their willingness to accept received theology, their skills as preachers, and their willingness to live according to strict moral precepts. The second order of ministers, called doctors, taught in schools, both on elementary and advanced levels. The fourth order of ministers, called deacons, gathered and administered assets for the relief of the poor. Its most important innovation, however, was a third order of ministers called elders. Their function was to gather with the pastors once a week in a new institution called the Consistory, to supervise the behavior of everyone in the community and to see to it that Genevans not only accepted correct belief but also behaved in a truly Christian manner—in short, to exercise discipline. The only powers they could use in enforcing their judgments were admonition and excommunication, and it took some time before their right to excommunicate was generally accepted. Once it was, however, they shaped the Genevan community in powerful ways and made it a model either feared or respected throughout Europe.

This Genevan pattern proved enormously influential. It was was extended and imitated throughout those parts of Europe that turned Reformed or Calvinist rather than Lutheran and was revised to fit entire nations in books of discipline, notably one adopted for the Protestants of FRANCE in 1559 and for SCOTLAND in 1560.

Ecclesiastical ordinances thus served throughout Europe to consolidate the Protestant REFORMATION, and to give it an important ongoing structure.

References and Further Reading

Richter, Aemilius Ludwig, ed. *Die evangelischen Kirchenordungen des sechzehnten. Jahrhunderts.* Nieuwkoop: B. de Graaf 1846, reprinted 1967. (Complete set of ecclesiastical ordinances of the period.)

Sehling, Emil, et al. *Die evangelischen Kirchenordnungen des XVI. Jahrhunderts.* Leipzig: O.R. Reisland 1902–.

Rivoire, Emile, and Victor van Berchem. *Les sources du droit du canton de Genève.* Arau: Sauerländer, Vol. II. 1930, 377–390.

ROBERT M. KINGDON

ECCLESIOLOGY

Ecclesiology is the theological study of the nature and characteristics of the church. It is concerned primarily with the theological identity of the one, holy, catholic, and apostolic church of Jesus Christ and secondarily in a derivative sense with the identities of particular churches (denominations). This article focuses on programmatic and formal aspects of ecclesiology rather than on the biblical material, the substantive issues, and the seminal theologians.

The Scope of Ecclesiology

Ecclesiology has undergone a renaissance since the 1960s, thanks to the impetus of the significantly titled *Church Dogmatics* of KARL BARTH, the revolution in Roman Catholic attitudes to other churches at the Second Vatican Council (1962–1965), and the ecumenical movement and its stimulus to theological dialogue on the nature of the church. Ecclesiology is one of the most creative areas of theological activity today.

The term "ecclesiology" derives from Latinized forms of the Greek *ekklesia* (church, assembly, congregation) and *logos* (reasoned discourse). As a major department of the theological enterprise ecclesiology stands alongside such traditional theological disciplines as fundamental THEOLOGY (the methods, norms, and sources of theology), anthropology (the theological study of human nature), soteriology (the theological exploration of salvation), and ESCHATOLOGY (theological reflection on the last things and the fulfilment of God's purposes in history).

Ecclesiology embraces a wide range of subdisciplines. It may take the form of objective study of the church as an institution, an enduring, structured organization, and will then need to draw on nontheological academic approaches, such as those of sociology and statistics. Theological work on the ministry, the SACRAMENTS and LITURGY, and the forms of oversight and structures of governance in the church also fall under the purview of ecclesiology.

Ecclesiology and Missiology

The relationship between ecclesiology and MISSIOLOGY is particularly interesting. There is a sense in which missiology is a subdivision of ecclesiology, for it is the church that is mandated to mission and it is the lay and ordained members of the church who engage in it. Mission is not the act of freelance individuals who bear no relation to the church, but is an activity of the church. Mission is, therefore, an ecclesial matter. On the other hand, mission is greater than the church, taking its rise in the *missio dei* that springs from God's eternal being and purpose. The church plays its God-given part as an instrument of a purpose that transcends it.

Missiology, the study of the principles and practice of Christian mission (including EVANGELISM/evangelization) is therefore a major theological discipline in its own right. However, ecclesiology and missiology should always go hand in hand. A study of the church that is not orientated to mission will tend to be inward-looking and uncritical. Reflection on mission that is not geared to the WORSHIP, ministry, and oversight of the church is likely to be rather freewheeling, individualistic, and unaccountable. An ecclesiology for our time, an age of pluralism of faiths and consumerist materialism—as well as of spiritual searching and New Age syncretism—will be infused with mission concerns and insights. Now that the momentum of Barthianism, Vatican II, and ECUMENISM has slackened, it seems likely that ecclesiology will take its direction from missiology in the immediate future and so find fresh energy.

The fact that ecclesiology today is conducted in the context of a pluralism of world religions and secular worldviews lends it an "apologetic" dimension; it will always have one eye on the claims of alternative positions. It will need to show why the Christian vision of divine community is valid and can be justified in the face of criticism and indifference. Ecclesiology needs to be persuasive, to engage in advocacy, and to set out its credentials. It will strive to bring to light the Christian understanding of the church as the body of Christ, to lead the enquirer beyond the institutional face of the church (and of the churches), and to reveal its mystical nature.

The Ecumenical Context

Ecclesiology today also needs to take the ecumenical context seriously. On the basis of gradual growth in mutual understanding and respect through virtually a century of the ecumenical movement, the churches now stand in an unprecedented relationship to each other. Through their association in the WORLD COUNCIL OF CHURCHES (WCC) and national councils of churches (or equivalents) and through theological dialogue, they recognize, implicitly or explicitly and to one degree or another, the one church of Jesus Christ in each other. The churches stand in a relation of mutual reception (drawing from each other's life and theology) and mutual accountability. That is to say, they are in various degrees of communion (*koinonia*) with each other.

Because ecclesiology in an ecumenical age is compelled to recognize the degree of communion that exists between churches, it cannot be merely confessional. In confessional ecclesiology we tend to define our own church over against other churches, as though they were not also and equally church. Ecclesiology must be pursued in a explicitly ecumenical manner, so that different ecclesial voices are invited to participate in the discussion, and conclusions are formulated in a way that is sensitive and respectful to ecumenical partners. The fullest expression of this approach is found in the work of the World Council of Churches Faith and Order Commission, and its most fruitful outcome so far is the report *Baptism, Eucharist and Ministry* (1982).

A Viable Ecclesiology

A good deal of ecclesiology in the second half of the twentieth century reflected the culture of modernity (see MODERNISM). It was optimistic, expansive, and even grandiose. Self-criticism and humility were not its most obvious characteristics. Ecumenical ecclesiology has often been conducted in the stratosphere,

drawing up ideal models of a united church, without sufficiently reflecting on the ambiguities of the concept of unity itself or the intractable difficulties of implementing a strong organizational concept of unity. It has not been sufficiently grounded in practical realities, including the hard-won convictions and well-winnowed practices that help to form the identities of particular churches. As modernity gives way to postmodernity, a somewhat chastened ecclesiology—one that is pursued in a more tentative, exploratory, piecemeal, and down-to-earth way—is appropriate. It needs to find a voice that is practical and realistic and can point to incremental ways forward to greater unity in mission.

A Feminist Ecclesiology?

FEMINIST THEOLOGY has not been drawn to ecclesiology. Christian feminists tend to be ambivalent about ordination. The dominantly androcentric, patriarchal, and sexist character of historic Christianity provokes alienation from the institutional church. Feminist ecclesiology often espouses a radically alternative vision of church, one shaped by women for women. However, feminist theologians who have remained within the historic churches point out that the church has given women much as well as denying them much. Feminist ecclesiology wants to reshape the church's self-understanding and to transform its practice. This involves a critique of CHRISTOLOGY that emphasizes that it was human nature, created in the image of God, not merely the nature of the human male, that was united with the Word in the Incarnation. Feminist ecclesiology goes on to deconstruct the biblical and traditional images of the church as the body or bride of Christ, before setting about reconstructing ecclesial imagery along androgynous lines, stressing the mutuality of women and men.

Strength and Weakness

The Protestant traditions of ecclesiology are marked by a critical principle: The gospel is more important than the institution, spirit is superior to structure. Catholic ecclesiology, on the other hand, stresses that structure is necessary for the spirit to work and that the institution is the essential vehicle of the gospel. It is Protestant shorthand to say that the gospel—and only the gospel—constitutes the church. What this slogan means is that Christ constitutes the church as his mystical body through the power of the gospel, which is tangibly embodied in word and sacrament. These two concrete expressions of the gospel make Christ present in the community. Thus, Protestant ecclesiology has centered around the twin foci of Word and

Sacrament. In this sense, the gospel is the radical critical principle of Protestant ecclesiology and relativizes every institutional structure of ministry and oversight.

The weakness of Protestant ecclesiology has been the tendency to equate the spiritual with the invisible and the worldly with the visible. MARTIN LUTHER and PHILIPP MELANCHTHON had to defend themselves against the charge that they were postulating a purely Platonic church, one removed from concrete reality. KARL BARTH and FRIEDRICH SCHLEIERMACHER played off the unchanging inward essence of the church against the changing outward form. To this extent Protestant ecclesiology veers toward docetism and gnosticism, whereas Catholic ecclesiology is typically in danger of idolizing the institutional expression of the church. However, institutional structures of ministry and oversight are needed in every properly constituted church. The tension between the authenticating power of the Gospel and the structures that are necessary to facilitate its work generates much of the creative energy of ecclesiology.

Of course, anyone, Christian or not, may take up ecclesiology or any other aspect of theology, but it makes a difference if one loves the church as such—and one's own church, too. Christians often need to be given permission to love the church. Then ecclesiology becomes a joy and a privilege. However, theologians, like other Christians, sometimes have a love–hate relationship with the Church/church, which can result in destructive elements creeping into ecclesiology. Ecclesiology should be constructive and conducted in an irenic, ecumenical spirit as far as possible, but without being bland and the ecclesiastical equivalent of politically correct. Only occasionally, and where necessary to maintain a lively dialogue, should it be fiercely polemical, in the spirit of the Reformers and their antagonists alike.

See also Church

References and Further Reading

Avis, P. "Church," in *Christianity: A Complete Guide.* Edited by J. Bowden. London and New York: Continuum, 2004.
———. "Ecclesiology," in *The Blackwell Encyclopedia of Modern Christian Thought.* Edited by A. E. McGrath, 127–134. Oxford, UK and Cambridge, MA: Blackwell, 1993.
———. *Christians in Communion.* London: Geoffrey Chapman Mowbray; Minneapolis, MN: Liturgical Press, 1990.
———. *Ecumenical Theology*, London: SPCK, 1986.
———. *Truth Beyond Words.* Cambridge, MA: Cowley Press, 1986.
Bosch, D. *Transforming Mission*, Maryknoll, NY: Orbis, 1992.
Fiorenza, E. S. *In Memory of Her: A Feminist Reconstruction of Christian Origins*, 2nd ed. London: SCM Press, 1993.
Healy, N. M. *Church, World and the Christian Life: Practical-Prophetic Ecclesiology*, Cambridge: Cambridge University Press, 2000.
Holze, H., ed.*The Church as Communion: Lutheran Contributions to Ecclesiology.* Geneva, Switzerland: Lutheran World Federation, 1997.
Ward, K. *Religion and Community*, Oxford, UK: Clarendon Press, 2000.
Watson, N. K. *Introducing Feminist Ecclesiology.* London and New York: Continuum/Sheffield Academic Press, 2002.
Zizioulas, J. D. *Being as Communion: Studies in Personhood and the Church.* London: Darton, Longman & Todd; New York: St. Vladimir Seminary Press, 1985.

PAUL AVIS

ECOLOGY

"Ecology" etymologically derives from the Greek *oikos* + *logos*, or "study of the household." Herein lies a clue to its modern usage: both the branch of scientific study called ecology and the popular movement regarding the proper treatment of the natural environment accent living things in relation, depending as in a household on one another.

As a recognizable social and moral movement, ecology arose in the late 1960s following the CIVIL RIGHTS MOVEMENT in the UNITED STATES. Many early writings of the ecology (or "green") movement were secular, even antagonistic to Christianity, alleging it encouraged humankind to view the nonhuman, natural world entirely instrumentally. Development of this critique issued in the charge of "anthropocentrism" or human-centeredness. In response, the great chorus of Christian theological writing on ecology or environmental ethics in the final quarter of the twentieth century opened on a defensive note. Some theologians, drawing on PROCESS THEOLOGY or FEMINIST THEOLOGY, have pressed for a radical reform of Christianity based on the new ecological consciousness. Yet others, accenting common biblical ideas such as creation stewardship, have maintained that Christianity is inherently ecological, even if this requires rediscovery.

Historical Protestant Thought

Protestantism can claim a history of ecological concern. In prayers published in 1910, WALTER RAUSCHENBUSCH confessed that "in the past we have exercised the high dominion of man with ruthless cruelty, so that the voice of the Earth, which should have gone up to thee in song, has been a groan of travail" (Rauschenbusch 1984:223). Further back, the typical pattern of classical Protestant systematic THEOLOGY opened with an exposition of "God the creator" of all things. So JOHN CALVIN speaks of the "excellence of divine art" apparent in the "whole workmanship of the universe." Hence, ecology as the study of relations in the natural *oikos* is contained within the DOCTRINE of creation. Intriguingly, KARL BARTH places ETHICS there also; it concerns human work, formed on the creative work of God. For Barth, Sabbath rest locates the meaning of human and divine work in creation and redemption, because the Sabbath celebrates the completed work of God. Creation, consequently, cannot be for mere use; rather, we glory in its dizzying variety and, as in Genesis, properly steward it as *gift*. Indeed, the strength of the concept of stewardship preserves classical REFORMATION Theologies like Calvin's from maintaining that creation is solely for human benefit, as secular critics allege. Earthly things are "entrusted to us, and we must one day render account of them" (Calvin 1559:III,X,5).

Contemporary Ecology and the Bible

One strand of contemporary Protestant ecological thinking has continued to emphasize creation and stewardship. American evangelical Christians have favored stewardship language with its clear biblical roots. Paul Santmire has accented this biblical and Reformation legacy, attempting an "ecological reading of biblical faith." Acknowledging Christianity's ambiguous ecological record, Santmire maintains Christianity is inherently ecological and resists the radical reorganization of Christian thought according to recent trends. The ecological challenge has no quick answer—the BIBLE teaches that life's struggles are complicated and hard—but Christians can respond from within their TRADITION with thoughtfulness and care.

Biblical emphasis among Protestant fundamentalists on environmental issues has led to controversy. American Secretary of the Interior (1980–1983) and ASSEMBLY OF GOD church member James Watt publically noted that "the Lord may come soon" when speaking of ecological policy; to some this implied the environment need not be protected. Bible reading, many LIBERAL PROTESTANTS contend, can therefore hardly be sufficient; instead, theology must be radically transformed by ecology.

New Ecotheologies

Searching for "deep ecology" in theology, while yet accenting creation, thinkers such as Matthew Fox and Thomas Berry have attempted to reconstruct a "universe story" that depends on evolutionary theory but sees all created things as deeply interconnected. On both thinkers' admission, the Christian tradition, although providing insight, is inadequate to the ecological reorientation required by current knowledge about the interdependency and fluidity of the universe.

In a related reorientation, citing Alfred North Whitehead's view that the universe was a process, open-ended in its ultimate destination, process theologians such as John Cobb have advanced a speculative view of God and nature unfolding together. Such theology hopefully can empower Christians and others to live as activate participants in the rich variety of interwoven and evolving communities that make up the unfolding world.

A third set of thinkers, "ecofeminists," have linked hierarchical models of AUTHORITY to the domination and destruction of the natural environment wrought by Western cultures. An earthier, embodied feminist theology can result in revolutionized understandings of how humankind and nature relate. Catholic feminist Rosemary Ruether has directed this critique toward ENLIGHTENMENT philosophies that develop sharp distinctions between humans and NATURE. Because these philosophies sustain liberal Protestantism, ecological rethinking may need also to transcend it. Indeed, the pervasive intellectual instability of POSTMODERNISM introduces unclarity about where the radical ecological critique will lead. Perhaps fittingly, ecotheology is in flux, and likely will be for some time.

Practical Outcomes

Despite differences, the various ecological theologies agree on increased need for "green" sensitivity and on policies that protect the environment. Indeed, predominantly Protestant bodies have issued practical recommendations, such as the NATIONAL COUNCIL OF CHURCHES' *101 Ways to Help Save the Earth*. Theology cannot reduce to policy and recommendations, for at the heart of Christianity lies a vision of interdependencies in the *oikos* between human beings, God, and creation. Because Protestantism inspired the rise of capitalist modernity (as MAX WEBER maintained), it may indeed be implicated in the human abuse of creation rooted in the denial of these dependencies (see MODERNISM). However, the pragmatic orientation of Protestant thought and its commitment to reexamine cultural practices in the light of the biblical witness suggest both a deep theological/ecological reexamination and practical ecologically sensitive behavioral changes are both within its future reach.

References and Further Reading

Calvin, John. *Institutes of the Christian Religion,* 1559. Translated by Ford Lewis Battles. Philadelphia, PA: Westminster Press, 1960.

Cobb, John B. *Is It Too Late? A Theology of Ecology.* Berkeley, CA: Bruce, 1972.

Fowler, Robert Booth. *The Greening of Protestant Thought.* Chapel Hill, NC: University of North Carolina Press, 1995.

Fox, Matthew. *Creation Spirituality: Liberating Gifts for the Peoples of the Earth.* San Francisco: Harper, 1991.

———. *101 Ways to Help Save the Earth.* New York: Eco-Justice Working Group of the National Council of Churches, 1990.

Rauschenbusch, Walter. *Walter Rauschenbusch: Selected Writings.* Edited by Winthrop S. Hudson. New York: Paulist Press, 1984.

Ruether, Rosemary Radford. *Gaia and God: An Ecofeminist Theology of Earth Healing.* New York: HarperCollins, 1992.

Santmire, H. Paul. *The Travail of Nature: The Ambiguous Ecological Promise of Christian Theology.* Philadelphia, PA: Fortress, 1985.

CHARLES R. PINCHES

ECONOMICS

Protestant theology has been a fertile source of reflection on economics. Many Protestant theologians contributed to the development of the discipline and the entrepreneurial lifestyle of many Protestant church members encouraged economic growth in their societies. In the twentieth century Protestant churches engaged in dialogue about economic development worldwide, whereas in recent decades there has been great interest in the economic potential of Pentecostal congregations in the developing world.

The two great Reformation theologians who wrote on economic life were MARTIN LUTHER and JOHN CALVIN. Luther developed an account of VOCATION (*Beruf*), although there is no single work in which he reflects on the meaning of employment. He argued that love of neighbor is fulfilled through daily work, which becomes a divine ordinance. The four orders of creation where God expresses God's will are the FAMILY, the state, employment, and the CHURCH. Any form of work can express a vocation by which we serve God and enable society to be preserved. Such an understanding of society means that vocation applies to all people and the governance of this ordering is by law and not gospel. This teaching enabled late medieval society to break free of an ethic where only religious employment was of value. In medieval teaching, praecepta were ethical maxims for all Christians but consilia were for the minority who were ordained or in religious orders. Luther swept this distinction away.

However, Calvin was to take Luther's teaching considerably further. Calvin argued that the proof of ELECTION was demonstrated by the fruits of daily life, especially in employment and one's calling. The three ethical maxims that Calvin enjoined were diligence in lawful callings, ASCETICISM in regard to consumption, and the constructive use of time. All this led to what was later called the Protestant work ethic. Calvin put it well when he wrote: "We know that people were created for the express purpose of being employed in labour of various kinds, and that no sacrifice is more pleasing to God than when everyone applies diligently to one's own calling, and endeavours to live in such a manner as to contribute to the general advantage." The Calvinist interest in stewardship created a new workforce that responded to the discipline of work. Protestant beliefs encouraged a moral and ascetic workforce.

Calvin also provided an exegesis of Deuteronomy 23:20, which enabled the restrictions on usury to be put aside. He claimed that this restriction applied only to the Hebrews. Usury should be regulated but it could be allowed. Calvin fixed the maximum rate of interest for the parishes of Geneva at 5 percent, prohibited exacting interest from the poor, and allowed ministers to invest for interest. Calvin transformed scriptural exegesis by arguing that money could be used to create wealth in the same way as land. This was not entirely a free market, however. The new technology in Calvin's day was printing and Calvin regulated the industry carefully.

In the centuries succeeding the REFORMATION the teaching of Protestantism was consistent on the nature of work. Some Protestant theologians also contributed to the study of economics, especially the nineteenth-century Scottish minister THOMAS CHALMERS.

Chalmers argued for a free market alongside a campaign of charitable giving that would replace state welfare (see CHARITY). He was deeply influential among business leaders in nineteenth-century SCOTLAND. However, it was to be the American WALTER RAUSCHENBUSCH who next contributed to an analysis of the market economy. He was a Baptist pastor in New York in the 1890s who challenged both society and the churches to engage with "men out of work, out of clothes, out of shoes, out of hope." Rauschenbusch launched the SOCIAL GOSPEL movement, which argued that the moral dimension of economics must always be considered by Christians. Shortly after this, MAX WEBER wrote his famous study in 1904 in GERMANY on "The Protestant Ethic and the Spirit of Capitalism," in which he claimed that economic development occurred in cultures that had a strong Protestant ethic to encourage entrepreneurial behavior. These two dimensions of the moral response to economics, and the contribution Protestant values and beliefs make to economics, have shaped the debate ever since.

Contemporary debates on economics divide on the ethics of the free market and whether this is a "status confessionis" for Christians. Those who argue this include Ulrich Duchrow, a German theologian, who has published many books through the WORLD COUNCIL OF CHURCHES (WCC). He has argued for radical church protest against the involvement of the Western Protestant churches in the capitalist economy. He believes contemporary capitalism is demonic; he was a major influence at the 1983 Vancouver Assembly and the 1991 Canberra Assembly of the WCC. Another German Protestant theologian committed to socialist economics is JÜRGEN MOLTMANN, although his views differ slightly from those of Duchrow. Moltmann argues for "economic co-determination and control of economic power by the producers."

There are many Protestant theologians and churches that would disagree with any adoption of socialist, or Marxist, economic beliefs. Among the critics of this approach would be the English Anglican theologians Ronald Preston and John Atherton. In the UNITED STATES, Lutheran Robert Benne and Methodist J. P. Wogaman would have a similar debate about the free market. Lord Griffiths in England is a Protestant banker who espoused the neoclassical economics of the Conservative Government of Prime Minister Margaret Thatcher. His books argue for the need to adopt free market economics.

Finally many Pentecostal churches in AFRICA, Asia, and Latin America, as well as in the Western world, have become agents of economic renewal in impoverished societies.

References and Further Reading

Atherton, J. *Christianity and the Market.* London: SPCK, 1992.

Hilton, B. *The Age of Atonement: The Influence of Evangelicalism on Social and Economic Thought 1785–1865.* Oxford, UK: Clarendon Press, 1988.

Stackhouse, M. *Public Theology and Political Economy.* Grand Rapids, MI: Wm. B. Eerdmans, 1987.

Weber, M. *The Protestant Ethic and the Spirit of Capitalism.* London: Allen and Unwin, 1985.

PETER SEDGWICK

ECUMENICAL AGREEMENTS

The twentieth century has been the era of ecumenism, the effort, both formal and informal, both domestic and international, to bridge the chasms that have divided not only the various Protestant churches but Protestant churches and the Roman Catholic and Orthodox churches as well. The goals of these ecumenical efforts has ranged from organizing common local activities, such as ecumenical Thanksgiving Day services in the United States, to "altar and pulpit fellowship," where the churches involved allow exchange of clergy both for preaching and celebrating the Lord's Supper. An important aspect of the twentieth century ecumenical momentum has been the organizational merger of different denominations, such as the merger of the Congregational Christian Churches and the Evangelical and Reformed Church into the United Church of Christ or the formation of the United Methodist Church. In countries such as Nigeria, Canada, or India, the ecumenical momentum has entailed the formation of "united" or "uniting" churches.

Perhaps the most important, albeit not widely known, phenomenon in this connection has been a number of ecumenical agreements reached in Europe by various churches. The Leuenberg Agreement of 1973 instituted church fellowship or "full mutual recognition" among some 85 Lutheran, Reformed, and United (Lutheran and Reformed) churches all over Europe even including five churches in Argentina and Uruguay. In 1988, agreement was reached in Meissen, Germany, between the CHURCH OF ENGLAND and the 24 Lutheran, Reformed, and United churches in Germany that comprise the Evangelical Church of Germany (EKD) with regard to pulpit and altar fellowship. The *Meissen Common Statement*'s six paragraphs identify ten agreements in matters of theology but acknowledge the unresolved difference over the historic episcopal succession. This latter point of unresolved disagreement prevented the mutual recognition of ministries in the Meissen Statement.

The Archbishops of Canterbury and York and the Chairmen of the EKD Council and the Church Leaders' Conference of the Federation (Bishops Kruse and Demke) solemnly signed the Meissen *Common Statement* in Westminster Abbey in January 1991. A second signing of the *Statement* took place in February 1991 in Berlin. The two parties declared their intention to "take all possible steps to closer fellowship in as many areas of Christian life and witness as possible, so that all our members together may advance on the way to full, visible unity."

In 1993, a similar agreement to enter into fellowship was reached at Porvoo, Finland, between the Church of England, the Church of Ireland, the Church of Wales on the one side and the Scandinavian Lutheran Churches, together with the Lutheran Churches of Iceland, Estonia and Lithuania, on the other. The agreement is named Porvoo after the city in which it was signed.

The agreement covers important points of agreement under six headings. It acknowledges all signatory churches as belonging to the one holy, catholic, and apostolic church. The agreement also acknowledges that in the signatory churches the Word of God is authentically preached, and the sacraments of baptism and the Eucharist are properly administered; that the signatory churches share the common confession of the apostolic faith; that oversight (episcope) is exercised in the signatory churches in various ways in order to express continuity of apostolic life, mission, and ministry; that the episcopal office is valued in the signatory churches as a visible sign of expressing and serving the unity of the church and its continuity in apostolic life, mission, and ministry; that persons episcopally ordained in any of the churches to the office of bishop, priest, or deacon are welcome to serve, by invitation, in the same ministry in the receiving church without reordination; and that bishops from another signatory church normally be invited to participate in the laying on of hands at the ordination of new bishops as a sign of the unity and continuity of the church.

A Lutheran–Roman Catholic *Joint Declaration on the Doctrine of Justification* evoked considerable controversy at its public presentation, especially in Germany, where virtually all Lutheran professors of theology signed a letter of opposition. Nonetheless, it was signed by representatives of the Vatican and the LUTHERAN WORLD FEDERATION on October 31, 1998. It summarized the sixteenth century controversies over this issue as essentially disagreements over language.

In the United States, the agreement of 2001 between the EVANGELICAL LUTHERAN CHURCH IN AMERICA and the EPISCOPAL CHURCH, USA, entitled *Called to Common Mission*, stipulated that in return for the Episcopal recognition of the legitimacy of current Lutheran ELCA ministry, the ELCA would henceforth ordain candidates for the ministry with a bishop present, and candidates for the office of bishop with an Episcopal bishop present. A temporary Episcopal concession was here matched by a permanent ELCA concession. The Call to Common Mission statement at first did not receive the necessary majority vote by the church-wide assembly of the ELCA. The document had to be submitted to a second vote, where it was approved. The document gave rise to an opposition movement within the ELCA, the Word Alone Network, and it continues to threaten a split in the ELCA.

All in all, these ecumenical initiatives appear to have excited mainly church officials and rarely had significant or meaningful impact on the local congregational level. The explanation may well lie in the reality that on the local, personal level traditional religious antagonisms have long given way to mutual understanding and acceptance, despite continuing theological or ecclesial differences. Moreover, the various agreements have essentially involved only churches of the Lutheran, Reformed, and Anglican traditions. Thus, large denominations, such as the Baptists, have not been involved.

See also Dialogue, Interconfessional

References and Further Reading

Best, Thomas F., ed. *Survey of Church Union Negotiations, 1988–1991.* Geneva, Switzerland: World Council of Churches, 1992.
Best, Thomas F., ed. *Survey of Church Union Negotiations, 1996–1999.* Geneva, Switzerland: World Council of Churches, 2000.
Bouteneff, Peter C., ed. *Episkopé and Episcopacy and the Quest for Visible Unity: Two Consultations.* Geneva: WCC Publications, 1999.
Hüffmeier, Wilhelm, and Podmore, Colin, eds. *Leuenberg, Meissen and Porvoo: Consultation Between the Churches of the Leuenberg Church Fellowship and the Churches Involved in the Meissen Agreement and the Porvoo Agreement.* Frankfurt am Main: O. Lembeck, 1996.
Making Unity More Visible: the Report of the Meissen Commission, 1997–2001. London: Church House Publishing, 2002.
Nigeria Church Union Committee. *Scheme of Church Union, Including Basis of Union, Constitution of the Church of Nigeria, and Inauguration and Interim Arrangements.* Lagos, 1963.

HANS J. HILLERBRAND

ECUMENISM

Ecumenism is a relatively recent term for an ancient Christian commitment to both unity and mission "to the whole inhabited earth." It was not widely embraced as a major religious imperative in Protestantism until the twentieth century, despite earlier foreshadowings. Although it seems like a simple concept, ecumenism is beset with ambiguities and tensions regarding the nature of the unity that Protestants seek.

Terminology

Ecumenism, conceived as the task of knitting together the divisions within Christianity on behalf of the entire world, may extend as far back as New Testament times and the debate concerning Gentile missions at the Jerusalem Conference. However, the term "ecumenism" is itself modern, unlike its more ancient cognate "ecumenical," and reflects an intentionality and sense of urgency coordinate with an era of religious freedom, pluralism, and globalism.

According to a 1997 study by the WORLD COUNCIL OF CHURCHES (WCC), "there is no authoritative definition of the term, and it is in fact used to characterize a wide range of activities, ideas and organizational arrangements" ("TCUV," p. 4). Part of the terminological difficulty is that an old wineskin is being made to hold new wine. The terms "ecumenism" and "ecumenical" both derive from the Greek *oikoumene,* which referred to a geographical—not theological or ecclesiological—reality, that is: "the whole inhabited world." This is the usage in scripture. During the patristic era "ecumenical" assumed a more ecclesiological connotation meaning the whole church. From the first, therefore, ecumenism was dual: concern for all humanity; concern for the unity of Christians.

The term "ecumenical" was seldom used until the nineteenth century, although a few European Protestant leaders, like the Swiss founder of the Red Cross, Henri Dunant, began speaking of an "ecumenical spirit," apparently referring to the promotion of cooperation and unity among Christians. The specific nature of that unity was unclear.

This usage was also complicated by the fact that the task of promoting Christian unity was never conceived as an end in itself but linked to a grander mission—to witness and serve the whole world (the *oikoumene*). Thus the actual corporate "reunion" of divided churches expresses only a small part of what is generally meant by ecumenism.

As these terms became increasingly common in twentieth-century Protestantism—and Christianity generally—different ecumenical orientations materialized: ecclesial ecumenism, theological ecumenism, mission-driven ecumenism, and even interfaith ecumenism, which broadens the term beyond its specifically Christian content. Although useful to evaluate differences in emphasis and orientation, these orientations overlap in practice. What unites all forms of ecumenism is the divine imperative to reconnect Christians to each other and to the presence of God in the world.

History of Protestant Ecumenism before 1900

The first Protestant reformers did not intend to divide Western Christianity but to make the gospel the basis for Christian unity. JOHN CALVIN, PHILIPP MELANCHTHON, MARTIN BUCER, and THOMAS CRANMER, among others, sought to reconcile their own theological differences and even explored rapprochement with Roman Catholic authorities, especially at the Colloquy of Regensburg in 1541 (see REGENSBURG, COLLOQUY). Unfortunately the hardening of doctrinal divisions and the emergent national and territorial Protestant church systems dashed such hopes. However, isolated Protestant voices—such as JAN LASKI, JOHN COMENIUS, GEORGE CALIXT, Hugh Grotius, John Dury, and many others—continued to keep alive the irenic ideal of a theologically and spiritually unified Christendom.

The roots of modern Protestant ecumenism, however, do not lie primarily in past schemes for reunion but with the Pietist and the Evangelical movements of the eighteenth and nineteenth centuries. These built a sense of international Christian fellowship and sympathy across the Northern European and trans-Atlantic communities. By focusing on personal experience rather than DOCTRINE or liturgical conformity, they promoted a form of Protestantism that transcended its divisions. JOHN WESLEY's phrase, "if thy heart is as mine, give me thy hand," exemplified this spirit.

Equally important, these movements expected a coming universal church based on a union of hearts and prayers. There was an undercurrent of apostolic and eschatological fervor in this anticipation of a global "Age of the Spirit," and a missionary zeal. In ENGLAND the Wesleys and GEORGE WHITEFIELD, in America COTTON and INCREASE MATHER and JONATHAN EDWARDS, and in GERMANY the MORAVIAN CHURCH and Count NIKOLAUS LUDWIG VON ZINZENDORF were all drawn to mission frontiers. In Pennsylvania Zinzendorf tried in vain to unite Quakers (see FRIENDS, SOCIETY OF) and other Christians in a "Church of the Spirit." In Massachusetts Edwards issued a "Humble Plea" for a worldwide concert of PRAYER for the arrival of the KINGDOM OF GOD on earth. In 1793 New Divinity preacher SAMUEL HOPKINS described a future world united by Christianity in global peace, justice, goodwill, racial harmony, and enlightenment.

The nineteenth century witnessed countless examples of practical interdenominational cooperation. These included reform and service agencies, like the AMERICAN BIBLE SOCIETY, the American Anti-Slavery Society, the Inner Mission in Germany, and international agencies like the YMCA/YWCA, the EVANGELICAL ALLIANCE, the Student Volunteer Movement, and the World's Student Christian Federation (WSCF). The latter provided the leaders of the twentieth-century ecumenical movement: JOHN R. MOTT, NATHAN SÖDERBLOM, WILLEM ADOLF VISSER'T HOOFT, J. H. Oldham, WILLIAM TEMPLE, and others.

Proposals for church unions proliferated. The PRUSSIAN UNION (1817) set the stage for later efforts to reunify the continental Reformation churches. Proposals for a united Protestant Church came from a variety of corners: the CAMPBELL FAMILY (DISCIPLES OF CHRIST), SAMUEL SCHMUCKER (LUTHERANISM), PHILIP SCHAFF (Reformed), William Augustus Muhlenberg and William Reed Huntingdon (Episcopal), and Henry Lunn (British METHODISM). In the 1890s the Grindelwald Conferences held in SWITZERLAND brought Protestants together to explore differences and pray for unity. The LAMBETH QUADRILATERAL adopted by Anglicans (see CHURCH OF ENGLAND) in 1888 proposed using the historic apostolic episcopacy and the faith of the first Christian communities as a basis for a unity that would not only build bridge Protestantism but reach out to Eastern Orthodoxy and Roman Catholicism (see ORTHODOXY, EASTERN; CATHOLICISM, PROTESTANT REACTIONS).

Even the new theological trends of the nineteenth century contributed. The nascent liberalism of FRIEDRICH SCHLEIERMACHER in Germany, FREDERICK DENISON MAURICE in England, and HORACE BUSHNELL in America created an impatience with doctrinaire theological divisions and argumentation. TRANSCENDENTALISM generated an impatience with institutions; and theological ROMANTICISM and ANGLO-CATHOLICISM yearned for the experience of sacramental unity.

Within a brief span of time transnational confessional associations were formed: the LAMBETH CONFERENCE (1867), the WORLD ALLIANCE OF REFORMED CHURCHES (1875), the WORLD METHODIST COUNCIL (1881), the International Congregational Council (1891), the BAPTIST WORLD ALLIANCE (1905), and the LUTHERAN WORLD FEDERATION (1923). These created a structure that facilitated later ecumenical dialogue and cooperation.

Modern Protestant Ecumenism

By 1900 the stage was set for a worldwide ecumenical movement. Modern ecumenism was to have both a churchward and a worldward direction, consistently linking unity in matters of faith and fellowship to shared mission, witness, and service to the world at large. Many diverse strands of thought and activity fed this enterprise. Until the 1960s the overriding motivation was to stall the seeming erosion of the Christian West and revitalize the Christian presence in the world in the wake of modernization and the impact of religious freedom. This apparent convergence of interests, however, was more apparent than real, and it began to be challenged in the 1960s. By the end of the century the notion that Christian diversity and pluralism might be better signs of ecumenical health than like-mindedness was espoused openly, requiring rethinking of the nature of ecumenical unity.

In 1900 the large Ecumenical Missionary Conference, which was organized in New York City by WSCF leaders, called for a unified Protestant missionary effort. Their hopes came to fruition at the WORLD MISSIONARY CONFERENCE of 1910 in Edinburgh, in which representatives of international Protestant missionary agencies around the world spoke of unity as the key to successful global evangelization. Meanwhile major Protestant denominations in the United States—concerned about home missions, urbanization, and industrialization—collaborated in 1908 to form the Federal Council of Churches of Christ in America (the predecessor of the NATIONAL COUNCIL OF CHURCHES). Several American denominations also called for new initiatives at theological and ecclesial unification.

World War I disrupted all such plans. Rather than quenching enthusiasm, however, the war spurred it on. Protestant leaders dealt with the collapse of "Christendom" in Europe and the new realities of international politics, economics, and social thought by taking advantage of the molten situation. Three major strands of ecumenical activity emerged in the 1920s: the Faith and Order movement, the Life and Work movement, and the International Missionary Conference. All three eventually merged to form the WCC.

The Faith and Order movement, which was begun in 1927 at Lausanne, Switzerland, by American Episcopal bishop CHARLES BRENT, promoted a theological brand of ecumenism. Its immediate goal was not to construct church merger schemes but to pursue theological dialogue to clarify confessional differences and misunderstandings and prepare a path for full sacramental reconciliation and ministerial mutuality among the churches. The Ecumenical Institute at Bossy, Switzerland was particularly instrumental in promoting comparative ecclesiological studies.

In 1948 the Commission on Faith and Order of the new WCC took over this task. With the addition of Eastern Orthodox members in 1961 and official Roman Catholic members after Vatican II, Faith and Order envisioned the possibility of theological rapprochement among all the major branches of Christianity, based on common creedal principles and a core consensus on sacramental fellowship and ministerial orders. The result was the release in 1982 of the notable ecumenical document on *Baptism, Eucharist, and Ministry,* which described the theological opportunities and obstacles to this goal.

The apparent confluence of these theological streams, however, was soon interrupted by demands to give the voices of people of color, the poor, WOMEN, and the Third World a powerful hearing. The new mandate pursued ecumenical theology pluralistically, with an eye for cultural context and nontheological factors. By the 1990s the coexistence of older and new visions of theological ecumenism in the Faith and Order movement had produced creative tensions that crisscrossed traditional confessional lines.

Mission-driven ecumenism found a home within the International Missionary Conference (IMC), the immediate successor to the 1910 Edinburgh Conference. Formed in 1921 at Lake Mohonk, New York, by Mott and Oldham, it repudiated the traditional notion of simply "exporting" Western Christianity. Rather than replicating the divisions of the West, it tried to create indigenous Christian churches that would be responsive to local cultures and local needs and flexible in worship and ministry. It shared Western resources and encouraged programs "to help unite the Christian forces of the world in seeking justice in international and inter-racial relations." At its 1938 world conference at Tambaram, INDIA over 50 percent of the delegates were non-Western.

Ironically this ecumenical embrace of indigenous cultures and regional diversity generated more actual ecclesial unions than the Faith and Order movement. One of its successes was the formation of the CHURCH OF SOUTH INDIA, the first union church in which the barriers between Episcopal and non-Episcopal ministerial orders were overcome. The united churches in

Northern India (see CHURCH OF NORTH INDIA) and Sri Lanka were similarly notable. In addition the IMC helped to set up many of the important local, regional, and national councils of churches throughout the mission world.

When the IMC formally merged with the WCC in 1961 as the Division (now Commission) on World Mission and Evangelism (CWME), the process of de-Westernizing Protestant ecumenism was accelerated. Over the next several decades the CWME zeroed in on the global fight against racism and apartheid, poverty and economic exploitation, restrictions on women, environmental exploitation, the dangers of globalization, and the eradication of local traditions. Such thinking created a new ecumenical agenda that situated theological and ecclesial reflection within specific cultural contexts and needs, including the need for dialogue with indigenous religious traditions. In 1976 the CWME assembled the Ecumenical Association of Third World Theologians and in 1982 released the important document "Mission and Evangelism—An Ecumenical Affirmation."

A third major ecumenical player was the Life and Work movement, founded at Stockholm in 1925 under the leadership of Swedish archbishop Nathan Soderblom. It reflected Western social idealism in its urgent desire to bring a prophetic Christian moral witness to bear on the forces of modernity and secularity. In many ways Life and Work initially sought to recreate a unified Western Christian culture—to act, as Soderblom said, "on behalf of Christendom." This bias showed up at its Second World Conference at Oxford in 1937 when only thirty delegates of 425 were from non-Western regions.

Adopting a neo-Reformation theological stance in the late 1930s, which claimed to be able to disentangle Christ from CULTURE, Life and Work recognized the benefits of mating with the Faith and Order movement. Out of this marriage came the WCC, whose vision would be "a whole church speaking the whole gospel to the whole world." Not posing as a "superchurch" nor brokering corporate mergers, the WCC created a forum, or "space," that might function as a symbol of "visible union" by nurturing ecumenical fellowship, theological dialogue, and "mission through witness and service."

The sense of cohesion was soon tempered, however, by calls for renewal and change coming out of the West. Starting with the 1969 "Programme to Combat Racism" and continuing through the 1974 Berlin conference on "Sexism in Church and Society," ecumenical programs received sharp scrutiny. The "Ecumenical Decade of Churches in Solidarity with Women, 1988–1998" mandated a renewed ecumenical vision built on "solidarity" across racial, GENDER,

class, and cultural divides. The WCC added SCIENCE, technology, nuclear development, bioethics, and ECOLOGY to its list of ecumenical concerns, climaxing with a program on Justice, Peace, and the Integrity of Creation.

This complicated situation was not so abnormal as it may have seemed to observers. It developed from the perennial duality of Protestant ecumenism that balanced unity and mission, witness and service, church and world. No wonder that fifty years after its founding, the WCC was still struggling with the meaning of ecumenism but now thinking in terms of pluralism, mutuality, forbearance, and "reconciling diversity."

Additional Manifestations of Modern Ecumenism

The work of the WCC hardly exhausts the reality of ecumenism, even within Protestantism. In addition to the ecumenical work of many local, regional, and national councils of churches, formal mergers or covenant agreements between specific denominational communities were important. Between 1906 and 1968 at least twenty-six church unions took place in the UNITED STATES. Examples elsewhere were the UNITED CHURCH OF CANADA, the Evangelical Church in Germany, the Federation of Swiss Protestant Churches, Church of South India, Church of North India, Church of Sri Lanka, United Church of Zambia, Uniting Reformed Church in Southern Africa, United Church in Jamaica and the Cayman Islands, and the UNITING CHURCH in Australia. According to the 1995 Consultation of United and Uniting Churches, such unions continue to provide the benchmarks for "modeling diversity within unity in communities of increasing pluralism."

Nonetheless the fate of the CONSULTATION ON CHURCH UNION, begun in America in 1960 by EUGENE CARSON BLAKE, reveals a growing denominational disinterest in corporate mergers. The failure of its initial proposals for the full union of nine Protestant denominations in 1970 and later in 1988 for a "covenant communion" led to a more modest 2002 cooperative proposal, called "Churches Uniting in Christ." The "Ecumenical Partnership" agreement of 1989 between the UNITED CHURCH OF CHRIST and the DISCIPLES OF CHRIST is another such cooperative scheme, as is the "Concordat of Agreement" of the EPISCOPAL CHURCH and the EVANGELICAL LUTHERAN CHURCH IN AMERICA, which became effective in 2001.

In Central Europe since 1973 over 100 "Reformation" churches have formed the Leuenberg Church Fellowship, agreeing to full sacramental and pulpit fellowship with each other and "common witness and service." Such agreements established what they termed a "communion of communions," in which, according to the Leuenberg Agreement, "the lively plurality in styles of preaching, ways of worship, church order, and in diaconal and social action" that characterizes particular communions are preserved. As "A Protestant Understanding of Ecclesial Communion," adopted in 2000 by the Evangelical Church of Germany, insists, "it is not the diversity that needs to be overcome, but the separation."

The entrance of Eastern Othodoxy and Roman Catholicism into the ecumenical arena with Protestantism has also shaped the course of Protestant ecumenism. The Orthodox have brought a deep commitment to unity based on conciliar traditions and the AUTHORITY of ancient precedents. After the Second Vatican Council, Roman Catholic (RC) delegates became official members of the Commission on Faith and Order, although not full members of the WCC. The RC Church and the WCC also formed a Joint Working Group that has worked for the "restoration of the unity of all Christians" in "real and full communion." By the 1990s nearly all programmatic units of the WCC included Catholic representation. In addition, RC delegates are full members of 35 national councils of churches and ecumenical organizations worldwide.

The bilateral dialogues between Catholics and a wide variety of Protestant faiths have been equally significant. These have removed much misunderstanding and mistrust on both sides. Especially noteworthy was the 1997 Joint Declaration on the Doctrine of Justification, in which Catholic and Lutheran theologians reached a "common understanding" of the doctrine of JUSTIFICATION by FAITH.

Although many Protestant evangelicals today avoid terms like ecumenical or ecumenism, they tend to continue the nineteenth-century tradition of associational cooperation. In the United States the NATIONAL ASSOCIATION OF EVANGELICALS was created in 1942; in CANADA, the Evangelical Fellowship of Canada in 1964. In 1951 evangelicals formed the World Evangelical Fellowship (now the World Evangelical Alliance), which resurrected the Evangelical Alliance's tradition of uniting evangelicals in global prayer.

In 1974 the LAUSANNE COMMITTEE FOR WORLD EVANGELIZATION, an international gathering from over 150 nations, approved "The Lausanne Covenant," affirming that God seeks "the Church's visible unity" through "fellowship, work, and witness." "Evangelism summons us to unity," they said, echoing the 1910 Edinburgh Missionary Conference. Although rejecting liberal utopianism, the covenant signers affirmed that the gospel witness must not be separated from human welfare everywhere. EVANGELISM requires

a "concern for justice and reconciliation throughout human society" and the "liberation of men and women from every kind of oppression." In a phrase strikingly reminiscent of the founding statement of the WCC, though nuanced differently, Lausanne declared that "world evangelization requires the whole Church to take the whole gospel to the whole world." Evangelicals reaffirmed this covenant fifteen years later in "The Manila Manifesto" (1989). An increased discomfort with ecumenicity, however, was apparent in its emphasis on the work of local churches and its warning that cooperation with nonevangelicals is appropriate only when biblical truths were not comprised.

Conclusion

The question remains if the past century of ecumenical enterprise would have exhilarated or disappointed its founders. Support for ecumenism continues to ebb and flow, especially within local congregations, which often prove resistant to ecumenical enthusiasms. Nonetheless global communications, technology, and cultural pluralism have all forced Christians to think and act in less parochial ways. Whether that will continue to produce an ecumenism of visible unity, as sought by the WCC, or merely one of mutual influence and cross-fertilization remains unclear. What can be said is that ecumenism has become something more complex, diverse, interactive, and organic than the simple word "unity" suggests. It is based as much on a commitment to the task of togetherness as on like-mindedness, and that has not always been characteristic of Protestant history.

See also Dialogue, Interconfessional

References and Further Reading

Brown, Robert McAfee. *The Ecumenical Revolution*. Garden City, NY: Doubleday, 1967.

Cavert, Samuel McCrea. *Church Cooperation and Unity in America: A Historical Review: 1900–1970*. New York: Association Press, 1970.

Gros, Jeffrey. *Introduction to Ecumenism*. New York: Paulist Press, 1998.

Irwin, Dale. *Hearing Many Voices: Dialogue and Diversity in the Ecumenical Movement*. Lanham, MD: University Press of America, 1994.

Kinnamon, Michael. *Ecumenical Movement: An Anthology of Texts and Voices*. Geneva, Switzerland: WCC Publications, 1997.

Lossky, Nicholas, et al. *Dictionary of the Ecumenical Movement*. Grand Rapids, MI: Wm. B. Eerdmans, 1991.

Raiser, Konrad. *Ecumenism in Transition*. English edition. Geneva, Switzerland: WCC Publications, 1991.

Rouse, Ruth, et al. *A History of the Ecumenical Movement, 1517–1968*. 4th edition. Geneva, Switzerland: WCC Publications, 1993.

Wainwright, Geoffrey. *The Ecumenical Movement: Crisis and Opportunity for the Church.* Grand Rapids, MI: Wm. B. Eerdmans, 1983.

World Council of Churches. Towards a Common Understanding and Vision of the World Council of Churches. Geneva: World Council of Churches, 1997.

WILLIAM M. KING

EDDY, MARY BAKER (1821–1910)

Founder of the Church of Christ, Scientist. Mary Baker was born July 16, 1821, in Bow, New Hampshire. The daughter of Mark and Abigail Baker, both descendants of New England Puritan families, Mary Baker grew up amidst the Protestant revivals, reform movements, and utopian experiments known as the Second Great Awakening. The religious idealism of the awakening exerted a lasting influence on her thought, as did the awakening's emphasis on the transformational power of religious experience. With regard to more specific elements of her theology, a nearby community of Shakers probably inspired her concept of a mother church as well as her belief that God was the mother as well as father of life.

Physical Problems

In 1843 Mary Baker entered into a short marriage with George W. Glover, who died in 1844. Chronic back pain and other maladies, many of which she had suffered since childhood, prevented her from caring for their son George, born after his father's death. She experimented with homeopathy and, in 1853, married Daniel Patterson, an itinerant dentist who shared her interest in alternative medicine but failed to help prevent her invalidism. In a state of desperation, she appealed for help to Phineas P. Quimby (1802–1866), a clockmaker, daguerreotypist, and healer in Portland, Maine, who used mental influence to treat disease.

Quimby had successfully treated hundreds of patients using a technique he developed out of his study of mesmerism, a practical philosophy named after the eighteenth-century Austrian physician Franz Anton Mesmer (1734–1815), who posited the existence of an intangible magnetic fluid permeating human bodies and their surroundings. Mesmer and his followers believed that this magnetic fluid could convey positive, therapeutic influence from an operator to a subject. Through his own experiments, Quimby discovered that ideas themselves could trigger feelings of recovery and well-being. This discovery led Quimby to dispense with belief in the existence of a ubiquitous magnetic fluid and marked an important development in the understanding of hypnosis, and of human psychology more generally.

Mary Baker Patterson recovered her health under Quimby's care and stayed on to study mental healing with him. As Quimby's student, she believed that he had discovered the scientific explanation for Jesus's power as a healer as well as the essential teaching of the New Testament. Later on, she downplayed Quimby's influence, maintaining that he practiced a form of materialistic "animal magnetism" and never grasped the true idealism of Christian Science.

Turning Point

Shortly after Quimby's death in 1866, she took a serious fall on the ice and lapsed into a hopeless state, unable to move from bed. Three days later, while reading the New Testament stories of Jesus's healing, she experienced the healing power of Christ and rose from her bed, completely cured. In 1870 she began teaching her own version of mental healing. In 1873 she divorced Daniel Patterson, from whom she had long been estranged, and married Gilbert Eddy, one of her students.

In 1875 Mary Baker Eddy published the first edition of *Science and Health,* her most famous writing. The fourth and final edition, published in 1906, remains the centerpiece of Christian Science life, along with the New Testament. Rejecting literal interpretations of Christian doctrine, *Science and Health* explains the apparent existence of disease and other forms of material reality as consequences of erroneous belief. The suffering caused by erroneous belief in material reality could be eradicated, Eddy argued, through belief in the omnipotent power of Divine Love. Ignorance of Divine Love, and the suffering entailed by this ignorance, defined mortality. Conversely, identification with the loving presence of Christ through prayer and meditation offered perfect happiness and immortality.

Eddy's Place in Protestantism

Eddy founded the Massachusetts Metaphysical College in Boston, where she taught short courses in Christian Science to hundreds of students from 1881 until 1889, when disputes with students led her to close the college. In an effort to control the interpretation of Christian Science and consolidate her own authority, Eddy established the Church of Christ, Scientist. This religious institution grew rapidly during the last decades of the nineteenth century and first decades of the twentieth. By 1906, 682 branches of the church existed across the United States, and a new mother church was erected in Boston to replace the smaller mother church built in 1884. After Eddy's death in Chestnut Hill, outside of Boston, on December 3, 1910, the church continued to grow under the guidance of a board of directors, which Eddy had assembled to conduct church business and disseminate her teachings. As a result of the effective institutionalization of her principles, no other church leader emerged to inherit the mantle of her authority.

Eddy's importance in the history of American Protestantism goes beyond her role as the founder of a denominational church. She represents the historical connection between the enthusiasm for religious experience characteristic of evangelical Protestantism in the early nineteenth century and the emergence of popular metaphysical movements in the later nineteenth and twentieth centuries. Like other advocates of metaphysical religion, Eddy focused on bridging the gap between religion and science and, more specifically, on offering experimental proof for the existence and influence of unseen spiritual forces. While other advocates of metaphysical religion looked to Hinduism, Buddhism, and other non-Christian religions to help them in their efforts to understand the power of mind over matter, Eddy stayed within Protestant Christianity and found the power of mind over matter solely within Christ.

In certain respects, Eddy's understanding of Christian Science was similar to ideas about the power of Jesus's characteristic faith healing in African-American traditions, which led to the emergence of PENTECOSTALISM in the early twentieth century. Eddy was more concerned with justifying Christian healing scientifically, while faith healers and Pentecostals have been far more straightforward in acknowledging the reality of bodily suffering, but both traditions share strong belief in the healing power of religious faith and experience. In this regard, Eddy represents the important but often overlooked connection between the rich tradition of religious experience and experimentation flowing out of nineteenth-century Protestant EVANGELICALISM and the religious approach to science characteristic of the New Age movement and other forms of metaphysical religion.

References and Further Reading

Primary Sources:

Eddy, Mary Baker. *Science and Health with Key to the Scriptures.* Boston: First Church of Christ, Scientist, 1971; orig. 1875.
———. *Prose Works Other Than Science and Health with Key to the Scriptures.* Boston: First Church of Christ, Scientist, 1925.

Secondary Sources:

Gottschalk, Stephen. *The Emergence of Christian Science in American Religious Life.* Berkeley: University of California Press, 1973.

Peel, Robert. *Mary Baker Eddy: The Years of Discovery.* New York: Holt, Rinehart and Winston, 1966.
———. *Mary Baker Eddy: The Years of Trial.* Boston: Christian Science Publishing Society, 1971.
———. *Mary Baker Eddy: The Years of Authority.* New York: Holt, Rinehart and Winston, 1977.

AMANDA PORTERFIELD

EDINBURG MISSIONARY CONFERENCE OF 1910
See World Missionary Conference

EDUCATION, EUROPE

In its original sense education contains two slightly different meanings: the action of a parent or teacher to educate children or students, and the development of knowledge, rationality, and cognitive ability by certain authorities. Although in the first understanding a certain knowledge can be examined, the development of erudition turns the created being into a human being in the image and likeness of God. Thus education means in the widest sense any developing impact on human beings toward personality, knowledge, and rationality through other people or institutions, nature, and experience. In the second, more specific sense, education can be understood as the reflected rational children toward a moral/ethical understanding and responsibility. Shaping of education depends on the historical context and the contemporary impacts of mentality, social order, society, culture, and so on. Thus the understanding of the term cannot be used in the sense of a *nomen universale*. Education as part of the theoretical reflection within theology has its place in anthropology, doctrine of creation, sin and redemption, in Christology and eschatology. Education thus becomes the focus of the (self-)understanding of the human being and therefore has to be developed in the tension of sin/nature and grace—in the Protestant tradition within the tension of law and gospel.

Education in the Early Church

Ever since the establishment of the church as part of the state in the fourth century, tensions between secular-pagan education and Christian teaching have dominated the history of Western schooling. The responsibility for education swung like a pendulum between ecclesiastical and secular authorities. Although early medieval schools derived from classical Roman institutions, they became increasingly "Christianized"—not so much in terms of teaching methods, but certainly in subject matter. The sixth century proved an important turning point: in response to the missionary challenge posed by the pagan Germanic environment, the educational emphasis shifted toward the sacramental and liturgical life of the church. CONVERSION to Christianity, at the time, was not merely a change of religion, but a more wide-ranging *conversio* of lifestyle, CULTURE, and manners of speech. From this perspective it is clear that a fundamental reorientation was needed to develop a Christian educational system.

"Palace" or "court schools" (*scholae palatinae*) catered to the leading nobility, but their curriculum was limited to the acquisition of basic administrative skills, primarily written and spoken Latin. It was important, therefore, to supplement this level with more sophisticated clerical education. The Irish-Scottish mission tackled the task in Central Europe and a new ideal of the ministry emerged wherever British monks established their foundations. Boniface (d. 755) followed this tradition and erected schools for clerical novices in the Benedictine monasteries. This type of education, of course, was intended exclusively for members of the order (and the occasional aristocratic patron). Chrodegang of Metz (d. 766) filled the emerging gap in the education of the secular clergy through the foundation of cathedral schools.

Both school forms found their legal financial basis in the Germanic church system (*Eigenkirchenwesen*). Local lords not only took physical possession of churches and monasteries in their territories, but also exercised extensive spiritual supervision. It was inevitable that princes and emperors gradually extended these powers to ecclesiastical schools, and clerical education, only recently emancipated from secular influence, soon returned under worldly control. The *Admonitio generalis* of Charlemagne (789) ordered that every monastery and every diocese should teach psalms, musical notes, chants, the *computus* (i.e., calendar calculation), and grammar. In addition every school had to be in possession of dogmatically sound Catholic books, and the emperor recommended careful examination of candidates for the priesthood at annual meetings of the diocesan clergy.

Even traces of compulsory popular education can be detected. With reference to Caesarius of Arles (470/1–543) and the Synode of Baison (529), the emperor and bishops called for the establishment of parish schools. These schools were to teach reading, writing, and ecclesiastical LITURGY alongside the Creed and the Lord's Prayer (to be expounded in the vernacular).

Charlemagne's system, developed under the influence of Alcuin (735–804), was equally open to secular concerns. Apart from other topics, the reading of profane texts was introduced, and liberal arts were taught as preparation for studies on Holy Scripture. Ludwig the Pious, however, advised by Benedict of Aniane, refocused his educational policy on the training of clergymen. The Imperial Diet of Aachen (817) closed monastic schools to outsiders. Henceforth monasteries ceased to provide public education and limited their teaching to their own needs. At the same time the boarding school system enhanced the unity of clerical upbringing and training, a principle resuscitated in the sixteenth century by reformers of all confessional persuasions. In short the church claimed full and exclusive responsibility for education.

At the same time the level of education in kings and rulers declined so much so that cultured rulers such as Friedrich II (1194–1250) or Alfons X (1221–1284) were regarded as exceptional by their contemporaries. From the thirteenth century a growing number of observers complained about the deplorable educational standards of political leaders and about the unprecedented increase in the power of peasants and other commoners who were eager to learn.

Twelfth to Fourteenth Centuries

In a fresh educational offensive starting in the twelfth century, imperial and papal legislators began to regulate the fast expanding range of new methods of teaching and study and eventually helped to establish corporate bodies of masters and scholars in *universitates magistrorum et scholarium* under central control. On the secular side the *Authentica habita,* issued by Fredric Barbarossa (1122–1190) around 1158, provided for the safety and protection of scholars while traveling to and staying at the place of study, prohibited their arrest for crimes committed by fellow countrymen, and guaranteed them a free choice of court.

On the ecclesiastical side, a new wave of legislation, beginning with the Lateran Councils of 1123, endeavored to expand papal jurisdiction and to consolidate the church's hold over education. The main elements were (1) a commitment to the education and training of priests; (2) financial safeguards for teachers (salaries, benefices) and students (new foundations, scholarships, dispensations from residence requirements); (3) privileges of jurisdiction (universities and their members to enjoy immunity from local courts); (4) teaching licenses; (5) institutionalization of courses and curricula (limited to certain social groups); and (6) protection of scholarly communities from local authorities. This blueprint for a centrally (in fact, papal) controlled dissemination of knowledge, however, soon fell victim to the dynamics of European state development. National or princely prestige, as well as ambitions of the academic communities themselves, ensured that university expansion failed to adhere to papal planning. Eventually all institutions were allowed to offer the full range of faculties (art, medicine, law, theology) and to award their own doctorates.

The growth of the educational system from the thirteenth century, evident above all in the spread of the ability to read and write Latin beyond the clerical estate, cannot be explained by purely socioeconomic or purely religious reasons, but depended on a whole range of interconnected factors: the establishment of universities; the foundation of mendicant orders; the increasing number of towns as centers of educational institutions; the emergence of an ambitious "middle class" engaged in commerce, trade, economy, and arts; the growing need for administrative and especially legal expertise in the nascent territorial and city states; and the rising demand for educational and edifying literature among the LAITY, to name but a few. All of these tendencies combined to destroy the basic assumption that "clerici" were "litterati" and "laici" were "illitterati," albeit without revolutionizing the social order. From the fourteenth century, princes started to found universities in Central Europe, and—alongside the pope—the emperor became one of the main patrons of learning. With ever-greater frequency, universities approached them for improved charters and privileges.

Elementary schools, too, had been revived by the papal reform legislation in the twelfth century. As a result of the increasing economic and cultural importance of towns, however, magistrates started to intervene in the running of Latin schools, and to promote the establishment of German institutions.

Fifteenth and Sixteenth Centuries

After the thirteenth century a certain stream of intellectuals emphasized the main sources of the ancient world. This way back to the sources (*ad fontes*) was a diverse movement, which later on was subordinated under the label "Humanism." As modern research has developed, this label has come into question, even though we can find some common understanding of education founded in a common anthropology focusing on the understanding of the image of God in the creation of man, *homines non nascuntur, sed finguntur* (Erasmus 1529). During the process of education the human being can grow and develop in the image of God. Thus education has its goal in the image and likeness of individuals to their creator.

This attempt of education became very influential. In the northern parts of Europe, Erasmus of Rotterdam (1466–1536) became the core of a large movement, which related back through the philosophers of the Renaissance to the understanding of education in Rome and Athens. Erasmus became influential not only for transferring this understanding over the Alps

but also for a certain merger of Christian and pagan thoughts subordinated to an elaborated interpretation of Scripture based on the old languages. His theological focus came to the fore when he used Christ as the basis for his interpretation of the image of god. Nevertheless it is not clear how much Erasmus's understanding of Christology had an impact on his anthropology or the other way around. Christ becomes the true model for pious behavior and the prototype of ethical orientation. In Christ, human beings find their model of true humanity and the image of God that they bear within their souls. Thus the discussion of piety and the way to SALVATION becomes more and more a discussion of true human behavior and orientation of life. Erasmus matches human activity—education, knowledge, and the struggle for more and better knowledge—with God's GRACE and eternal mercy.

The Reformation

Even though MARTIN LUTHER (1483–1546) feared a certain kind of semipelagianism in this attempt, the later educational reform ideas of the Wittenberg professor and his followers take root in this development. Against the background of the Western church's traditional knowledge of the first centuries, the Wittenberg reformer saw the Roman (i.e., papal) limitation of the church system, as well as the scholastic educational reform, as apostasy from the original norm. Because of that he feared another ecclesiastical reform, which would spoil the system of education, schooling, and teaching even further.

Thus, with his reform program Luther referred to scriptural authority as the last and ultimate AUTHORITY. It determines the critique on the scholastic but also the humanistic education and school reforms, as well as the emphasis of the future reformed teaching plan. Luther pointed out three theological arguments for a new, enforced commitment for teaching the youth: first, fighting Satan, who strives to destroy God's good creation; second, turning to God's mercy, which only the Germans received in this century, but will not keep forever. Third, simple obedience to God's commandment and the natural order of creation binds church and its representatives to youth education. Even though Luther makes school education part of worldly considerations and the responsibility of secular authorities, the biblical theological argumentation of this idea must still be taken into consideration. Juvenile education, school, and training are not only matters of natural reason, but part of theological contemplation. Luther closely combines this unity of ecclesiastical and worldly responsibility for education and training with medieval reform concepts on the one hand; on the other hand he clearly splits it from early modern educational endeavors of the secular authorities.

Other reformers—especially PHILIPP MELANCHTHON (1497–1560) and JOHANNES BUGENHAGEN (1485–1558) who worked out the merely practical matters of the reformed concept of teaching and schooling in church ordinances, handbooks, textbooks, catechisms and other helpful and quite successful materials—followed Luther in his theological grounding of school reform and in their efforts to deal with this problem as a consequence of their REFORMATION insights. They are basically concerned with the general education of youth, which has to be realized in *omnibus civitatibus, oppidis et pagis* (in all societies, towns, and villages).

Main elements of school ordinances in Wittenberg, Zurich, or other stem cells of the Reformation include the following items: the knowledge of languages (mainly Latin), a certain knowledge of science and arts (*orbis litterarum*), the classical *artes liberales,* and finally a biblically grounded knowledge of ETHICS and piety. Any content of the school ordinances influenced by Reformation thought was related and focused on a better understanding of Scripture as the revelation of God, God's love and mercy, and God's will to redeem the sinner. Thus the knowledge of God's revelation implies certain knowledge of God's will and God's orders for humankind.

Of course Luther and others refer to the education of an academic elite when they recommend special furthering of the "prodigy." Although Luther did not concentrate on that in his early years, his reform attempts after the visitation of churches and schools in rural Saxony of 1527 more and more accentuated the education of future evangelical CLERGY and a biblically founded knowledge for the ruling elites. Improved education was seen as a tool in the apocalyptic battle between God and Satan: the study of the past as much as other disciplines would alert people to God's omniscience and help them to understand the Scriptures and the fate of the world. It thus obtained an important place in school and university education, even though profane—and especially classical—historians were to be studied in strict subordination to the overall authority of the Bible.

Even though Luther did not explicitly mention religious education, the requirement for special lessons on the Holy Book can be found in almost all school regulations and school foundations. Probably as a helpful handbook or model of biblical lessons in school or at home Luther worked out in several steps his CATECHISMS: first the Great catechism for pastors and trained clergy and later on the Small catechism for the house father (*pater familias*). One can hardly overestimate the influence and importance of Luther's catechisms for the history of evangelical theological

education. Even though several other handbooks for elementary education in faith and piety had been written, none of them ever became as important as Luther's two books (later included in the Book of Concord and other collections of main sources of the evangelical faith).

Whereas Luther separated the Erasmian synthesis of Christianity and Humanism by the secularization of the medieval performance of education by the church on the one hand and a strong focus on its Christian grounding, referring to a certain mystical understanding of education on the other, Melanchthon strongly accentuated the humanistic ideal. Although Luther denied a human activity to rebuild the human being after God's image and likeness, Melanchthon and JOHN CALVIN (1509–1564) supported an academic education if not for the salvation of humankind then for the teaching of human beings in the will of God. Melanchthon went back to humanistic ideals as *eloquentia* and other virtues as described in the antique books. This concept is strengthened through his accentuation of natural law. It contains the *testimonium* of God's eternal justice and preforms future ethical behavior of humankind. Nevertheless Melanchthon does not understand education as a way to heaven. True Christian education develops the *iustitia civilis* but not *iustitia christiana.*

Even more, the humanistic heritage comes into the fore in the pedagogical concepts of John Sturm (1507–1589) in Strasbourg and Calvin in Geneva. The latter stressed the doctrinal character of an ecclesiastical education and focused on the training of future clergy and an ecclesiastical elite. Schools became places in which children get trained in a certain orientation of life and a biblically grounded ethical doctrine. At this point Calvin continued the pedagogical reform attempts of HULDRYCH ZWINGLI (1484–1531) as he had performed them in Zurich and as were continued by HEINRICH BULLINGER (1504–1575). Within this reformed concept, education became part of God's pedagogy. SIN was understood in the meaning of not knowing. As much as ignorance leads to hell, the true knowledge of God as revealed in Scripture becomes the exclusive way to heaven.

The humanistic heritage was continued in the Lutheran and the Reformed tradition but also within a large educational reform movement initiated by the Jesuits in Catholicism, where again Christian Humanism came to the fore. In their schools, Jesuits taught future soldiers of Christ, instruments of the will of God, and servants of a catholic reform, which would protect the unity of the church. Although Erasmus tried to work out the personality of human beings after the image of God, the Jesuits accentuated the giving up of personal interests and a pure obedience to the will of God represented in the orders of the superior.

Seventeenth to Twentieth Centuries

In the age of CONFESSIONALIZATION up to the Napoleonic Age, the tension between a more or less secular education and an ecclesiastically dominated teaching of the youth continued. Even though the Reformation radically secularized the question of responsibility for education, at the same time the reformers on both sides of the confessional border focused on its deeper foundation within theology and its goal to understand Scripture and to improve personal or collective piety. After the "golden age" of a confessional reform of schools and university documented in hundreds of church and school ordinances in the end of the sixteenth century, a certain kind of skepticism arose. Michel de Montaigne (1533–1592) skeptically described the human ability of cognition and knowledge. Increasingly, the educational concept focuses pragmatically on the ability for ethical decision and a more general orientation of life. The humanistic emphasis on (re-)building human beings in the image and likeness of God fades.

JOHN AMOS COMENIUS (1533–1592), the Bohemian theologian, pedagogue, and pansophical philosopher, developed a holistic understanding of education. Deeply rooted in his theological understanding of creation, Comenius understood his pedagogical responsibility as cooperation of human beings in God's preservation of God's creation. Because of the analogy of cosmic order (nature) and individual development (human nature) Comenius's concept of education improves the human ability to continue and work out God's plans. Within a holistic concept he accentuates the teaching in native languages and natural science (realia), and the development of didactic methods.

Although Comenius's educational concept is related to his heterodox pansophic theological tradition, Wolfgang Ratke (1571–1635) developed his pedagogy from within his Lutheran setting: "Schooling and education can be justified by its meaning for salvation of souls only." Again a certain theological focus becomes important. Methods and contents of schooling following Ratke develop an ability to teach the human mind all reasonable things. This understanding is founded on the conviction of an evident analogy between nature and language (harmony of creation).

A fresh impulse came through the Pietist movement (see PIETISM); in particular AUGUST HERMANN FRANCKE (1663–1723) developed a concept of Christian education in relation to the reform of church and

piety: "Change of the world by changing the humans." The center of the concept is Francke's understanding of rebirth and renewal. God's grace pours faith into the soul of a human being. This effects a total change of life and behavior that should be obvious to people from outside. Thus education focuses on the knowledge of God through certain knowledge of Scripture, practical (craftworks) and social abilities for the improvement of taking over responsibilities for church and society. Godliness, erudition, good and pious behavior to honor God and serve one's neighbors are the main topics of the Pietist tradition of HALLE impacting the Prussian General-Landschul-Reglement of 1763.

Parallel to the Pietist movement, pedagogical concepts related to the philosophy of ENLIGHTENMENT were developed. JEAN-JACQUES ROUSSEAU (1712–1778) concentrated on the development of human beings as a process starting with CHILDHOOD. Even though some reformers had seen the need for an appropriate educational approach to children, the individual attempt was worked out a century later. Rousseau merges experience of world and self into a holistic concept of learning. Stressing his anthropological conviction that human beings are as good as God had created them, his educational theory accentuates developing moral and ethical competence toward perfection. Next to the individual education of human beings Rousseau focuses on the education of citizens. Later his concept became part of a mainstream pedagogy, which combines educational, economic, political, and legalistic efforts.

The tension between a merely secular education of citizens and a theological education of pious children of God continued even though the history of education concentrated more and more on the development of three main humanistic tendencies.

First, JOHANN GOTTFRIED HERDER (1744–1803) understood humanity in terms of historical development. Thus the idea of progress had a deep impact on his pedagogical thought: education develops progressively the humanity of humans. Herder's understanding of humanity was in agreement with humanistic and biblical ideas. Humanity is the goal of any human development. Because young people are tempted and endangered by negative forces, the pedagogue trusts in God's mercy and grace to fulfill his duty in educating them.

After Wilhelm von Humboldt (1767–1835) the individualistic approach became a critical note. Although Rousseau and his followers focused on an education to develop human ability in relation to the objective and evident needs of nature, society, and culture, Humboldt and—from another perspective—Johann Heinrich Pestalozzi (1746–1827) argued that individual abilities should be improved to develop an individual performance of humanity without regard to heteronomistic orders and needs or transcendental principles. Thus the new humanistic movement stressed a critical distance from society, culture, economy, and state.

Second, the German classic education, on the contrary, tried to open its educational concept to the needs of culture and society on the one hand and to preserve and accept nature and individuality on the other. So JOHANN WOLFGANG VON GOETHE (1749–1832) understood education as a lifelong process of conscious and experienced life, as an individual performance of the development of humankind within the progress of history. The neo-humanistic movement related its ideal of humanity back to ancient traditions and the heroes of the Greek and Latin legends. Finally the Kant scholar Johann Gottlieb Fichte (1762–1814) focused his understanding of education on an "axiom, it is unrelated trust in the creative and self-reflected power of the human spirit." Although GEORG FRIEDRICH WILHELM HEGEL (1770–1831) worked out the dialectic-idealistic reconciliation of individual and society, nature and culture, rationality and self-consciousness, the term emancipation comes into the fore: Hegel stresses the need for a productive and creative distance of the human individual from collective developments. Positively this process builds the self—negatively it distorts an effective development of self-consciousness and mind (*Entfremdung*). Karl Marx (1818–1883) turned this idealistic concept into practical advice: Because the socioeconomic surroundings force human beings into a distorted process of non–self-determined life (*Entfremdung*) the historical process has to be corrected. Education has to change the socioeconomic impact into a productive support of the development of humanity and freedom.

The third tendency has its main figures in FRIEDRICH ERNST SCHLEIERMACHER (1768–1834) and Wihelm Dilthey (1833–1911). Even though their pedagogical concepts reflect a strong relation between society and education, they do not see this relation as static as, for instance, did Karl Marx and others. Schleiermacher understands the sociocultural context as the sum of individual developments and experiences that affect each other. Education needs to improve the reflection of these individual experiences and to work out the ability to take over responsibility and innovative power for the future.

In the nineteenth century the impact of greater philosophical or theological systems on the concepts of education declined. Since then, pedagogy was secularized completely and theological principles cannot be found in its theoretical setting. Even though some reform attempts had been made, it seems that for the theological reflection of education, pedagogy was not needed. The later development of totalitarian educational reform shows that this theological reluctance was extremely dangerous and a mistake.

Within the debate for educational reform in the twentieth century, theological arguments were suspected to be doctrinal or, even worse, ideological. After World Wars I and II, totalitarian pedagogy needed to be radically corrected and its consequences avoided. Even though ideological systems still continued with their diverse types of right, Hegelian principles made their impact on indoctrination. Because these concepts showed clearly the negative side of the complete and radical secularization of education and its theory, theological reform worked out its answer focusing on the crisis of theology as a consequence of the crisis of occidental culture and society (Karl Spranger), and its critique. Educational theory performed as critique of ideology and any kind of "-ism." Theologians still struggled with the problem of defining education as a genuine theologically reflected part of ecclesiastical work within the world. Although some Protestant educational concepts influenced by KARL BARTH (1886–1968) and his followers refused and denied any influence of secular thought and disciplines within theological discourse, other ideas related to the liberal theology of the beginning twentieth century seem to be more open to pedagogical, sociological, and psychological questions, answers, and methods (see LIBERAL PROTESTANTISM AND LIBERALISM). Reform pedagogy after World War II primarily was oriented to a practical reform. The methods and ideas that seemed to be main parts of totalitarian and indoctrinating political or cultural systems were to be avoided. Whereas this critique after World War I focused on the distinction of law and gospel and accentuated pedagogy under the law, Karl Barth's influence after World War II forced theologians to reflect education more in the light of God's promise and the gospel. Even though the Protestant church of GERMANY, for example, still claims its responsibility for education, schooling, and teaching in universities and schools for applied sciences (synod of 1958 in Berlin, 1971 in Frankfurt/Main, and 1978 in Bethel) the dialogue with pedagogy, sociology, psychology, and other disciplines about pedagogical reform does not reflect any genuine theological contributions and ideas.

It seems that education newly becomes a challenge for theological reflection. Four main dimensions or circles of questions have to be reflected before a new concept of evangelical education can be sketched out: (1) the question of life orientation, change of virtues (*Wertewandel*), and an increasing discontinuity between the generations; (2) globalization or internalization of cultural change and its impacts; (3) cultural diversity and multiversity within national societies; and (4) radical and complete secularization of previously religious spheres and rooms. These problems provoke new answers to the old question of a Christian, Scripture-based, and theologically reflected education in the beginning of the twenty-first century.

References and Further Reading

Primary Sources:

Barth, Karl. *Evangelium und Bildung.* Zollikon b. Zürich: 1947.

Garin, Eugenio. *Geschichte und Dokumente der abendländischen Pädagogik.* Starnberg: 1971.

Hartfelder, Karl. *Philipp Melanchthon als Praeceptor Germaniae.* Berlin: Hofmann, 1897.

Schleiermacher, Daniel Friedrich Ernst. *Pädagogische Schriften.* 2 vols. Düsseldorf/Munich: 1966.

Vormbaum, Reinhold. *Die evangelischen Schulordnungen des 16. Jahrhunderts.* Gütersloh: Bertelsmann, 1860.

Secondary Sources:

Asheim, Ivar. *Glaube und Erziehung bei Luther.* Heidelberg: 1967.

Breen, Quirinius. *Christianity and Humanism.* Grand Rapids: Eerdmans, 1968.

Catto, J. I., ed. *The History of the University of Oxford I.* 97–150. Oxford: Clarendon Press, 1984.

———. *Università e società nei secoli XII–XVI. Atti del nono convegno internazionale di studio tenuto a Pistoia nei giorni 20–25 settembre 1979.* Pistoia: 1982.

Dagron, Gilbert, Pierre Riché, and André Vauchez, eds. *Histoire du christianisme des origines à nos jours IV: Évêques, moines et empereurs (642–1054).* Paris: Desclée-Fayard, 1993.

Dienst, Karl. *Die lehrbare Religion.* Gütersloh: 1978.

Fraas, Hans-Jürgen. *Katechismustradition. Luthers kleiner Katechismus in Kirche und Schule.* Göttingen: Vandenhoeck and Ruprecht, 1971.

Garin, Eugenio. *L'éducation de l'homme moderne. La pédagogie de la Renaissance.* Paris: Fayard, 1968.

Grendler, Paul. *Schooling in Renaissance Italy: Literacy and Learning, 1300–1600.* Baltimore: Johns Hopkins University Press, 1989.

———. *Books and Schools in the Italian Renaissance.* Aldershot: Ashgate, 2002.

———. *The Universities of the Italian Renaissance.* Baltimore: Johns Hopkins, 2002.

Grethlein, Christian, Georg Zenkert, Henriette Harich-Schwarzbauer, Michael V. Fox, Hans Josef Klauck, Eckhard Reichert, Ulrich Köpf, and E. Brooks Holifeld. "Erziehung." In *Religion in Geschichte und Gegenwart,* edited by Hans Dieter Betz et al., 4th edition, vol. 2, 1505–1519. Tübingen: Mohr-Siebeck, 1999.

Hahn, Friedrich. *Die evangelische Unterweisung in den Schulen des 16. Jahrhunderts.* Heidelberg: 1957.

Harran, Marilyn J. *Martin Luther. Learning for Life.* St. Louis, Mo.: Concordia Publishing House, 1997.

Hedtke, Reinhold. *Erziehung durch die Kirche bei Calvin.* Heidelberg: Quelle und Meyer 1969.

Kittelson, James M., and Pamela J. Transue, eds. *Rebirth, Reform and Resilience. Universities in Transition 1300–1700.* Columbus: Ohio State University Press, 1984.

Lennert, Rudolf, Pierre Riché, Ivar Asheim, Karl Dienst, and Robert Leuenberger. "Bildung I.IV–VII." In *Theologische Realenzyklopädie,* edited by Gerhard Krause and Gerhard Müller. vol. VI, 568–635. Berlin: de Gruyter, 1980.

Merz, Georg. *Das Schulwesen der Reformation im 16. Jahrhundert.* Heidelberg: 1902.

Nipkow, Karl Ernst. "Erziehung." In *Theologische Realenzyklopädie,* edited by Gerhard Krause and Gerhard Müller. vol. X, 232–254. Berlin: 1982.

Padberg, Rudolf. *Das Billdungsverständnis des Erasmus von Rotterdam und seine Bedeutung für die Gegenwart.* Paderborn: Schöningh,1964.

Rüegg, Walter, ed. *Geschichte der Universität.* Munich: 1993ff.

Schurr, Johannes. *Schleiermachers Theorie der Erziehung.* Düsseldorf: Schwann, 1975.

Steffen, Hans. *Bildung und Gesellschaft. Zum Bildungsbegriff von Humboldt bis zur Gegenwart.* Göttingen: Vandenhoeck and Ruprecht, 1972.

Stichweh, Rudolf. *Der frühmoderne Staat und die europäische Universität.* Frankfurt/Main: Suhrkamp, 1991.

Woodward, William Harrison. *Desiderius Erasmus concerning the Aim and Method of Education.* Cambridge: 1904.

Zenkert, Georg, Reiner Preul, Friedrich Schweitzer, and Achim Leschinsky. "Bildung." In *Religion in Geschichte und Gegenwart,* edited by Hans Dieter Betz et al., 4th edition, vol. 1, 1577–1587. Tübingen: Mohr-Siebeck, 1998.

MARKUS WRIEDT

EDUCATION, OVERVIEW

The Protestant REFORMATION cannot be understood apart from its relationship to education. The point of the Reformation, for many of its leaders, was to rejuvenate the piety and faith of the people by replacing popular belief with a purer and simpler presentation of the Gospel. MARTIN LUTHER, during his early, optimistic years, raised the expectation that most people could break through moribund TRADITION to religious transformation. It has been popular among some recent historians, however, to emphasize the extent to which this project failed in its objectives. These historians have argued that the impact of the Protestant Reformation was limited to representatives of elite CULTURE, while leaving popular culture largely unaffected. They point to the persistence of popular superstitions among the largely illiterate peasantry as evidence that the Protestant Reformation failed to penetrate and transform all levels of society.

The historical debate about the extent of religious change in the sixteenth century is difficult to resolve. Nevertheless, the question of Protestantism's ability to achieve its goals remains a viable and pressing topic of debate. If the Protestant Reformation set out to inculcate a Christian way of life grounded in claims about the proper knowledge of God, then its impact on education will be one measure not only of its practical success, but also of its historical significance and continued theological vitality.

Relationship to the New Learning

The Protestant Reformation is commonly thought to have given rise to widespread literacy among the LAITY due to its emphasis on reading the BIBLE in the vernacular. Recently, however, historians have been complicating this view by pointing to trends of increased schooling and literacy that began in the late medieval period. The call for ecclesiastical reformation, which frequently included proposals for improving education for both CLERGY and laity, long preceded the Protestant movement. Moreover, expanding opportunities in administrative and governmental careers fueled the demand for higher rates of literacy. Luther is an example of this trend: he had just begun the study of law after earning his baccalaureate and master's degrees when a storm sent him to a monastery instead.

In Luther's day, primary education typically began with vernacular lessons focused on devotional works, with some attention to Latin scripture and the Latin psalter. Boys who went on to Latin grammar school encountered a curriculum shaped by the rise of humanism. The "new learning" was first developed in the fifteenth century in northern ITALY, but it soon spread throughout Europe. The humanists emphasized the study of classic texts—the Latin poets, playwrights, historians, and especially Cicero, with his emphasis on rhetoric—as models of good speaking and writing. The *studia humanitatis* dominated Western education up to the nineteenth century. Its most basic pedagogic tool was imitation, in the forms of recitation and memorization. Its goal was to cultivate moral character and promote civic responsibility.

For the study of scripture and the preparation of pastors, the Protestant reformers found the humanist emphasis on the rhetorical arts more helpful than the scholastic reliance on syllogistic logic and abstruse metaphysics. But the reformers also shaped the new learning in significant ways. Their commitment to the liberation of the Word of God led to an affirmation of the vernacular in the LITURGY and in translations of the Bible. They also took advantage of the advent of printing to mount an ambitious program for lay literacy. The publication of countless pamphlets and an enthusiasm for sermons is witness to the often-repeated observation that piety shifted from the visual and sacramental to the verbal and pedagogic. The emphasis on sermons gave many people their first opportunity to hear learned orations from men trained in university theology faculties. In contrast with these advances, Protestantism brought about the dissolution of the monasteries and the schools that they housed. Another system of education was needed to fill this void.

State-Sponsored Education and the Role of the Catechism

Early in his career, Luther defended an unlimited and voluntary access to the Bible, and he saw the FAMILY as the natural place for such instruction. Events soon made him change his mind. The Peasants' War, the rise of ANABAPTISM, and the popularity of spiritualists who rejected formal education convinced him that religious instruction needed to be in the hands of the secular authority. Luther came to think that children are a gift from God and that parents have an obligation to send them to school, regardless of the parents' own economic interests (see CHILDHOOD).

Many parents who did not intend their children to pursue one of the professions—medicine, law, or THEOLOGY—resisted Luther's call for state-sponsored education. When Luther grew impatient with the lack of progress in educating the laity, he turned to the ancient tradition of catechesis to rectify the situation. Baptismal catechesis was essential to the early church—a necessary means of instructing pagan adults, at the time of their CONVERSION, in the mysteries of the faith. Luther revived this practice by creating a new genre, the CATECHISM, which, like medieval primers, brought together the basics of the Christian faith in a question-and-answer format.

Luther's idea of the PRIESTHOOD OF ALL BELIEVERS, coupled with his emphasis on each individual's particular vocation in the world, required that the laity be properly educated. The Small Catechism of 1529 illustrates these twin objectives. It includes discussions of the Ten Commandments, the creed, and the Lord's Prayer, as well as instruction about saying grace before meals. It also contains passages of scripture that outline the duties associated with various social roles. This influential text (and its equivalents in the Reformed tradition) was taught by schoolmasters, parents, and pastors and became the basis for religious education throughout Protestant GERMANY.

Luther's success in making religious DOCTRINE an essential part of the curriculum produced the first Protestant school system. Nevertheless, his training in nominalism, as well as his two-kingdom theology, made him pessimistic about the possibility, so fervently pursued by the scholastics, of integrating faith and learning. With his emphasis on the sovereignty of God, JOHN CALVIN had a more positive approach to the unity of all knowledge. All knowledge, Calvin insisted, should be for the purpose of glorifying God. Calvin founded the Geneva Academy in 1558 because he believed that the liberal arts are a gift of God and that all people are born with a desire for learning. He also organized the city of Geneva along the lines of a school that educates its citizens in a wise and eloquent piety, on the assumption that all of culture should be animated by religion.

The Teaching Task of the Ministry

The reformers were distinguished by their insistence on the teaching task of the ministry. The authority of the pastor is not given by his office, nor is it the product of personal charisma. Instead, it is to be demonstrated by his teaching abilities. The content of this teaching is to be the Gospel as it is disclosed in the Scriptures.

The role of teaching in the CHURCH was not limited to the pastor. Calvin argued that while every pastor is a teacher, not every teacher is a pastor. Teachers correspond to the ancient role of the prophets, while pastors correspond to the apostles. The task of the teacher is to instruct people in a godly way of life.

The Protestant idea that Scripture is clear and accessible to all meant that there was no need for a single AUTHORITY on its interpretation. Consequently, the reformers envisioned a pluralistic and nonauthoritarian approach to Christian education. Both Luther and Calvin, for example, accepted the teaching authority of church councils, even though they held them to be fallible and subject to the Gospel. Both also recognized the need for theological scholarship as a source of teaching authority. Finally, both acknowledged the responsibility of the congregation to check the authority of pastors, teachers, and theologians.

Modern Education

The beginning of modern education can be connected to the decline of the humanist curriculum and the catechism in religious instruction. Several factors were involved in this transformation. First, the EN-LIGHTENMENT defined rationality as objectivity, which contributed to the separation of the sciences from the humanities and the subsequent fragmentation of knowledge. Consequently, the classics no longer served as the foundation for education. Moreover, the Enlightenment equated religious authority with unwarranted dogmatism and the arbitrary restriction of individual freedom. This made catechization look like rote memorization of formulaic statements.

Second, the Industrial Revolution pressured education to become more practical and functional. Under the increasing demands of complex and dynamic economies, education lost much of its coherence. The differentiation and rationalization of social systems made the religious justification of learning superfluous. As nation-states became increasingly pluralistic and secular, religion was relegated to a marginal or private role, and state-sponsored education was stripped of its moral and religious character.

Third, the growth of national literatures in the eighteenth century displaced the Latin and Greek classics. The modern version of the humanities, organized around the study of national literatures, provided a substitute for religion with aesthetic and literary ideals. This reconfiguration of the humanities gave modern education some badly needed unity as well as token spiritual values, although it is doubtful today whether the humanities, riven as they are by ideological disputes, can still provide this service.

Beginning as early as JEAN-JACQUES ROUSSEAU's work in the eighteenth century and climaxing with John Dewey's work in the twentieth century, modern education gives priority to the process of learning, rather than the content. Active participation thus eclipses the pedagogy of imitation. The purpose of schools is to provide the proper environment for the natural development of student potential. Perhaps it was inevitable that psychological theories that focus on childhood development would emphasize the nurturing of personal growth in opposition to the traditional goal of internalizing the style and content of the classics. What might be surprising is that much of the impetus for modern innovations in education came from within Protestantism itself.

The background to much of this pedagogic shift is the Protestant emphasis on subjectivity, which was formulated most clearly by the German theologian FRIEDRICH SCHLEIERMACHER. A decline in the reformers' understanding of original sin also contributed to modern views of education. JOHN AMOS COMENIUS, a minister of the MORAVIAN CHURCH who is often called the "father of modern education," systematized and expanded Protestant ideas by advocating a free and universal system of education that adapts the curriculum to student needs and capacities. In the United States, HORACE BUSHNELL defended the growing SUNDAY SCHOOL movement by arguing that parents and churches should work together in nurturing the natural piety of children. He rejected the revivalist idea that children are mired in SIN until their conversion.

Liberal Protestantism and secularism thus cooperated in the privatization of religious faith. The result has been a growing dissatisfaction with state-sponsored education. While the United States is an extreme example (much of Europe still permits religious education in government schools), it nonetheless is a test case of Protestantism's ability to preserve its distinctive identity. When state-sponsored education emerged in the United States in the early nineteenth century, Protestantism served as the basis for cultural and social unity. The most popular elementary school reading texts, MCGUFFEY READERS, were a kind of American catechism, using illustrated stories to teach millions of children biblical principles. By the 1960s, it was clear that American society was too pluralistic to warrant Protestant control of state-sponsored education. The dismantling of the Protestant establishment has led to an increase in HOMESCHOOLING and private schools, as well as legal battles over governmental regulation of public schools.

The Problem of Globalism

Perhaps the most pressing question for Christian education today concerns the relationship between the twin goals of educating for faithfulness and educating for citizenship. There are legitimate goals of education that are universal, namely preparation for citizenship and the acquisition of basic skills. But it is becoming increasingly difficult for educational systems to express the collective identity of a nation when globalism blurs the boundaries that give nations character. When religious traditions are commodified as alternative means of satisfying basic human needs, religious education becomes a matter of appreciating the relative truths and universal values of all religious traditions, rather than the particularities of any single faith.

Must socialization in the skills of tolerance and inclusivity, required by a global economy, be taught at the expense of commitments and traditions that are particular and local (see TOLERATION)? Given the consumerism that drives globalism, it is reasonable to assume that moral instruction will increasingly be dependent on participation in well-defined communities whose educational agendas will not necessarily coincide with the needs of nation-states. Providing schools with more local authority over educational policy is not a sufficient solution because, even within a particular geographical area, multiple moral communities will be the norm. The hard question concerns how these moral communities can be given institutional expression.

Clearly, Christian communities will have to become more active in helping to reinvent state sponsored education. Minimally, nation-states should continue to support a wide variety of educational options. Instead of thinking of public and private, state-sponsored and home-based, and secular and religious schooling as separate and opposing entities, one should see them as alternatives that can coexist in complementary and mutually reinforcing ways. Pluralism should be encouraged within schools, as well as among them. State-sponsored schools can go a long way toward promoting diverse approaches to moral education, rather than imposing a single model of moral development on all students. In a time of increasing moral complacency and the widespread assumption of moral relativism, the strong ties that bind students to their religious communities need to be protected and nurtured, in the context of weaker and yet still essential ties to the public good.

Can Education Be Christian?

What is so Christian about education? Schools today face a legitimation crisis as the lofty goals of higher education give way to the pressing demands of rapid technological transformation. Not surprisingly, then, there are a number of proposals for restoring education to its religious roots.

One set of proposals concerns the need to reintegrate education and morality. Character education has become a popular topic of reform for those worried about the ability of fragmented families to raise children in a moral tradition. Character education, however, decontextualizes moral values by disconnecting them from the religious traditions that give them meaning. The problems of moral relativism and corrosive INDIVIDUALISM are only exacerbated when students are encouraged to exercise their personal preference by selecting moral principles from a menu of options. If character is to be about belief and not just behavior, it will have to be an expression of a life-long commitment to habits of living rooted in a theological understanding of good and evil.

More significant are calls to ground education in the objective morality of the NATURAL LAW tradition. Appeals to the natural law in Protestantism are usually not as explicit or systematic as in Roman Catholicism. Nonetheless, the natural law has the advantage of being rooted in Christianity but theoretically accessible to everyone. Reason alone, some theologians argue, can illuminate the natural constraints to human behavior that promote human flourishing and the public good. The definition of NATURE, however, has never been so contentious as it is today. Moreover, Protestant theology traditionally insists that nature cannot be a source of truth beside the one revelation of Jesus Christ, so that the proper understanding of nature is, in the end, theological and not philosophical.

Another set of proposals concerns the content of education rather than its purpose. Some Protestants are among the most vocal supporters of a return to the classical texts of the humanist curriculum. While it might seem ironic that Christian schools would be at the forefront of defending the study of ancient pagan thinkers, there is a long tradition in the church of enjoying and using the liberal arts for the glory of God. Others argue for a greater role for religious texts and religious ideas in state-sponsored instruction. Still others want teachers and students alike to have more freedom to approach their material from a religious perspective.

In sum, education is not one concern among many for the Protestant churches. From birth to death, the church immerses the believer in religious formation. Christian education is thus not one kind of education, as if education is an object whose nature is well understood and "Christian" is a modifier that specifies a certain variation of that object. Christians do not use education for a specific ideological purpose. Instead, Christianity is a system of education. This means, in part, that no single institution can carry the full weight of Christian education. The church, family, and school must work together to ensure the vitality of Protestantism.

Two questions seem paramount: (1) How far can state-sponsored education be stretched to accommodate religious communities and their need to pass on their traditions to new generations; and (2) how far can Christians go in reclaiming education as a Christian enterprise while still recognizing the largely secular needs of nation-states to use the socializing effects of education for national purposes? At the point where those questions meet lies the future of Christian education.

See also Education, Theology: Asia, Europe, and United States

References and Further Reading

Osmer, Richard R. "The Case for Catechism. *Christian Century* 114 (1997): 408-412.
Pazmiño, Robert W. *God Our Teacher: Theological Basics in Christian Education*. Grand Rapids, MI: Baker Academic, 2001.
Reed, James E., and Ronnie Prevost. *A History of Christian Education*. Nashville, TN: Broadman & Holman, 1993.
Strauss, Gerald. *Luther's House of Learning: Indoctrination of the Young in the German Reformation*. Baltimore, MD: Johns Hopkins University Press, 1978.
Webb, Stephen H. *Taking Religion to School: Christian Theology and Secular Education*. Grand Rapids, MI: Brazos Press, 2000.
Williamson, Clark M., and Ronald J. Allen. *The Teaching Minister*. Louisville, KY: Westminster/John Knox Press, 1991.

STEPHEN H. WEBB

EDUCATION, THEOLOGY: UNITED STATES

Broadly defined, theological education in the Protestant tradition, as in that of the Catholic and the Eastern Orthodox traditions, took place in a variety of venues: the home, catechetical programs, public worship, SUNDAY SCHOOLS, denominational and BIBLE COLLEGES, ministerial apprenticeships, and in SEMINARIES and divinity schools. Although a dizzying diversity in loci and aims characterized theological education within American Protestantism from the early seventeenth to the end of the twentieth century, the primary aim of all formal theological education was to integrate learning and piety in preparation for the ministry. Protestants, though, did not always agree among themselves on what the terms learning and piety meant, and how the relationship between the two was to be understood. Protestant theological educators, particularly in the twentieth century, also promoted an empirical approach to the study of religion in state colleges and universities that gradually separated piety and learning (see HIGHER EDUCATION).

The first generation of Massachusetts Bay Puritans, the dominant religious tradition in the American colonies during the seventeenth century, built Harvard College in 1636, six years after the settlement of Boston, to provide the colony not only with an educated pulpit but also an educated pew, demonstrating the high priority they placed on theological education. A Harvard education, the primary source of formal theological education in the seventeenth century, aimed to bring intelligence, critical organization, and study into communion with genuine piety. In 1701 some CLERGY in Connecticut, believing that the theological education at Harvard suffered from the influence of rationalism and ARMINIANISM, obtained a colonial charter for the establishment of Yale College. The professors of the new school, also educated at Harvard, wanted to restore to ministerial preparation the old connection between Calvinist piety and learning.

Other attacks on formal ministerial education arose in the midst of the First Great Awakening (see AWAKENINGS) when GILBERT TENNENT, Presbyterian pastor in New Brunswick, New Jersey, preached on "The Danger of an Unconverted Ministry" (1740). That sermon sounded an alarm about the "Pharisee-teachers" who were "letter-learned" but unconverted, and called for a new kind of ministerial education that gave due emphasis to religious conversion as a necessary prerequisite for ministerial training. That new education, he asserted, could be had at his father William Tennent's Log College (the future Princeton College). The revivalist emphasis on CONVERSION was not greeted with universal approval. Many at Harvard criticized the new emphasis on conversion because they perceived it as an escape from an enlightened examination of the Christian tradition. Spiritual enthusiasm without the guidance of reason, even revivalist supporters like JONATHAN EDWARDS argued, brought heat without light. A ministry, Edwards maintained, needed a spiritually formed reason, one that was guided by the biblical criteria. Other supporters of the Great Awakening, those on the radical edge, saw formal education of any kind as a hindrance to the movements of the spirit and sought to make the conversion experience itself the sole criterion for admittance into the ministry. Such a view of ministerial preparation was not widespread in the eighteenth century, but it became an increasing emphasis among the emerging evangelical Baptist and Methodist traditions in late eighteenth and early nineteenth-century America.

Not all theological education in the colonies took place in the confines of Harvard, Yale, Princeton, William and Mary (established in 1694 by Anglicans), or Brown (established in 1764 by the BAPTISTS). Nor did evangelical conversion become the sole criterion for ministry among large numbers of the old Puritan denominations or the new evangelical traditions in the eighteenth century (see EVANGELICALISM). Much theological education for the ministry took place in parsonages or on Methodist circuits where young men were apprenticed to mature pastors or seasoned itinerant preachers. In the parsonages or on the circuits young men read THEOLOGY with senior pastors and learned the art of PREACHING and pastoring by following their example. Such apprenticeship programs developed throughout the seventeenth and eighteenth centuries and into the first decades of the nineteenth century within a number of Protestant traditions, from PRESBYTERIANISM to UNIVERSALISM. Such theological preparations, though, were not universally reliable forms of education and in the nineteenth century the old Puritan traditions as well as some among the new evangelical traditions increasingly turned to colleges for theological education.

Throughout the nineteenth century the colleges became a significant locus for theological preparation for the ministry. In the antebellum period numerous new denominational colleges arose, many of them the creations of the graduates from Yale and Princeton, and a good number the result of efforts by Baptist and especially Methodist ministers. Many of these colleges were established in part to encourage vocations to the ministry. However, for Baptists and Methodists, the two largest Protestant denominations by 1830, the colleges were by no means the primary loci for theological education of the ministry. Less than half of the Baptist and Methodist ministers in the nineteenth and first half of the twentieth century had college degrees or were trained in theological schools. The antebellum Methodist Conferences, however, had prescribed a course of study for all their ministers. That course of study could be achieved through apprenticeship programs and did not have to be delivered through formal schooling.

In the early nineteenth century the seminary or divinity school became a new locus of theological education for the ministry. The seminaries arose from a variety of motivations: a desire to provide a more systematic and formal theological education than was provided in apprenticeship programs; an emerging sense of the ministry as a professional career comparable to that of other professional careers (physicians and lawyers) that needed formal education and training; and a need to preserve denominational or confessional identity in a religiously pluralistic society. The emergence of the Protestant seminary system was the result of the Unitarian takeover of Harvard University in 1805 when the liberal Henry Ware, a Unitarian, was appointed to Harvard's Hollis chair of divinity, succeeding the Old Calvinist theologian David Tappan. That appointment angered the Old Calvinists and the New Divinity Men who, realizing that they had lost control of Harvard, joined together in 1808 to establish the first American freestanding Protestant divinity school, the Andover Theological Seminary. Soon thereafter other seminaries were established, many of them associated with the major universities.

Princeton Theological Seminary (1812) was the first among the universities to create a school specifically separated from the rest of the university and dedicated solely to the theological education of the Presbyterian ministry. Harvard, too, responded to this trend by founding the Society for the Promotion of Theological Education in 1816, a society that eventually created Harvard Divinity School (1826), the training ground for over fifty years for the Unitarian ministry. Yale followed suit in 1822 when it created its own Divinity School, which became a potent theological force in the nineteenth century, developing, under the initiative of NATHANIEL WILLIAM TAYLOR, what became known as the New Haven theology. These seminaries and a number of others that were established as either freestanding or university-affiliated institutions focused on preparing a learned and pious ministry.

Although the seminaries and divinity schools fostered a relationship between piety and reason, they did not all understand or emphasize that relationship in the same way and by the 1840s and 1850s an incipient rift developed between the two. Learning could mean different things at various times: for the early seventeenth-century Puritans, learning meant following Peter Ramus and his philosophy; for some during the Great Awakening and thereafter it meant following JOHN LOCKE and ISAAC NEWTON; for Unitarians as well as Presbyterians at the end of the eighteenth and beginning of the nineteenth century it meant the Scottish ENLIGHTENMENT; for others in the early to midnineteenth century it meant ROMANTICISM and/or German critical scholarship. Protestants, too, saw learning either as an instrumental means of promoting piety or as a critical discipline that was independent of piety. That division in the Protestant understanding of the relationship between spiritual and academic education would become increasingly evident in the late nineteenth and early twentieth centuries.

Theological education in the divinity schools affiliated with major universities changed significantly in the 1880s with the rise of the modern research university. Between 1880 and 1930 those divinity schools particularly developed a theological scholarship that many considered freed from dogma and in keeping with the scientific methods of the age. The liberal evangelicals in the divinity schools saw education itself (not revivalism) as the primary means of winning Americans to the truth of Protestantism and as the chief way of enlarging Protestant influence in the country. The university divinity schools understood their roles as national agents or promoters of Christian truth, piety, and religious values in a scientific and bureaucratic age.

The development of specialized studies in the universities and in the divinity schools led to a certain fragmentation in the theological discipline as divinity school programs incorporated critical scholarship in biblical, historical, and systematic studies, and added specialties in the new sciences of sociology, psychology, and education to serve the needs of changing, multipurpose "social congregations" in urban America. Piety and religious practice continued to provide a unifying element in the divinity schools, but the demands of new doctoral and master's level degree programs left little time for spiritual development.

Throughout the late nineteenth century and well into the twentieth century conservative evangelicals, members of the HOLINESS MOVEMENT, and fundamentalists suspected all forms of critical learning (understood as learning without faith) in the divinity schools because they believed it threatened piety and the received faith of the churches. Many conservative Protestants, therefore, developed new forms of theological education that emphasized piety and in many cases subordinated learning to piety.

The new form of learning that emerged among conservative evangelical Protestants during the last two decades of the nineteenth century and well into the middle of the twentieth century was the Bible institute and Bible colleges. These new institutions promoted inductive biblical studies over critical methods, and practical over systematic theology in the preparation of ministerial candidates. These new schools, moreover, placed little or no focus on the traditional liberal arts curriculum as a preparation for theological education. Gradually after World War II many Bible institutes and colleges emerged from their almost exclusive emphasis on Bible studies and developed into accredited colleges with a liberal arts curriculum. Seminaries, too, for conservative evangelicals and fundamentalists emerged before and after the war, developing, as was the case with Fuller Theological Seminary, into degree-granting institutions of higher learning where critical thought and conservative evangelical piety entered into dialogue. However, the split in Protestantism between critical and precritical theological education for the ministry continued throughout the twentieth century.

Although liberal Protestant theological educators were primarily interested in ministerial education, they gave increasing attention in the twentieth century to the study of religion at the undergraduate level. Throughout the nineteenth and well into the twentieth century the theological education of undergraduates was perceived as part of the Christian ministerial mission, and the divinity schools as well as freestanding seminaries prepared ministers and minister-professors for the denominational college religion programs. In 1911 Charles Foster Kent of Yale Divinity School lamented the sorry state of undergraduate religion at the denominational colleges and universities, where, in his estimation, the programs were catechetical and not focused on primary texts or the acquisition of foreign languages. In 1922 he helped found the National Council on Religion in Higher Education, a society that was devoted throughout much of the twentieth century to the improvement of the academic study of religion in undergraduate programs. By the 1940s and 1950s, undergraduate and graduate programs in religion began to develop in the state colleges and universities as well as in the denominational schools, and by the 1960s the growth of religious studies programs in these institutions forced a clear separation between teaching religion as a ministerial mission and teaching about religion from the perspective of a variety of empirical disciplines as well as from a theological perspective. The growth of these new programs also brought into existence in 1964 the American Academy of Religion to serve as a national professional organization for academic specialists in the study of religion. The impetus behind these movements to improve the study of religion came primarily from the divinity schools. The need to fill academic positions in the new religious studies programs, moreover, transformed Protestant theological education to some extent by emphasizing the academic or empirical study of religion, a study that was divorced from spiritual formation.

By the late twentieth century a number of scholars in both the liberal and conservative Protestant evangelical traditions began to call attention to the historical developments that led to an increasing split between piety and learning in Protestant theological education and called for a reexamination of the relationship. The separation of the two was not by intention because by intention many of the divinity schools and seminaries continued to speak of FAITH seeking understanding as a goal of Protestant theological education. That relationship, however, was by no means evident in the time and energy given to WORSHIP and spiritual development in the large university-affiliated divinity schools, nor was it evident in the conservative evangelical institutions that had subordinated or made learning instrumental to piety.

See also Arminianism; Calvinism; Fundamentalism; Liberal Protestantism and Liberalism; Methodism; Puritanism; Revivals; Unitarian Universalist Association

References and Further Reading

Brereton, Virginia Lieson. *Training God's Army: The American Bible School Movement, 1880–1940.* Bloomington, IN: Indiana University Press, 1990.

Cherry, Conrad. *Hurrying Toward Zion: Universities, Divinity Schools, and American Protestantism.* Bloomington, IN: Indiana University Press, 1995.

Farley, Edward. *Theologia: The Fragmentation and Unity of Theological Education.* Philadelphia, PA: Fortress Press, 1983.

Hart, D. G., and R. Albert Mohler Jr. *Theological Education in the Evangelical Tradition.* Grand Rapids, MI: Baker Books, 1996.

Kelsey, David. *Between Athens and Berlin: The Theological Education Debate.* Grand Rapids, MI: Wm. B. Eerdmans, 1993.

Marsden, George. *Reforming Fundamentalism: Fuller Seminary and the New Evangelicalism.* Grand Rapids, MI: Wm. B. Eerdmans, 1987.

Miller, Glenn T. *Piety and Intellect: The Aims and Purposes of Ante-Bellum Theological Education.* Atlanta, GA: Scholars Press, 1990.

Noll, Mark. *The Princeton Theology: Scripture, Science, and Theological Method from Archibald Alexander to Benjamin Warfield.* Grand Rapids, MI: Baker Book House, 1983.

PATRICK W. CAREY

EDWARDS, JONATHAN (1703–1758)

Colonial American theologian. Jonathan Edwards was known in his own era as a Congregationalist pastor, a proponent of Reformed THEOLOGY, a prolific biblical exegete, a theologian adept in philosophy, a proponent of Protestant missions, and a defender of revivalism. He elaborated an aesthetic vision of theology—and a conception of divine beauty—that has continued to attract the attention of historians and theologians (see AESTHETICISM).

The Divine Beauty and Revivalist Piety

Born in East Windsor, Connecticut, on October 5, 1703, Edwards was the only son of the Congregationalist pastor Timothy Edwards and Esther Stoddard Edwards. A precocious child, he entered Yale College in 1716, graduating four years later and earning a master's degree in 1722. While a graduate student, he began his essay "Of Being," in which he drew on a philosophical idealism to contend that the world could not exist apart from an omniscient consciousness. A two-year pastorate at a Presbyterian Church in New York City allowed him to begin his notes on "The Mind," in which he explained human judgments about excellence and beauty as reflections of the mind's intuitive grasp of being as a vast set of relations and proportions, which Edwards believed to be manifestations of God's own excellence or beauty. During the same period, he began his lifelong habit of puzzling over ESCHATOLOGY, attempting in his "Notes on the Apocalypse" to decipher biblical clues about the beginning of a millennial age and the timing of the final judgment. In 1724 he moved to New Haven, Connecticut to teach as a tutor at Yale, where he continued his reflections on natural and spiritual beauty.

After receiving his M.A. degree, Edwards became an assistant to his grandfather, Solomon Stoddard, at the Congregational Church in Northampton, Massachusetts. There he began "The Images of Divine Things," which proposed that the harmony of being entailed a resemblance between physical facts and spiritual truths. When Stoddard died in 1729, Edwards became the sole pastor, quickly gaining a reputation as a preacher and lecturer who combined a talent for philosophy with a Calvinist piety and theology. In 1734, his sermons sparked a revival of religion in his church and the surrounding region. After a second wave of AWAKENINGS in 1740, Edwards defended the REVIVALS against critics who found them disruptive and divisive. His *Treatise Concerning Religious Affections* (1746) argued that genuine CONVERSION produced a love for the divine beauty and a selfless concern for one's neighbor. The book suggested that despite their excesses, the New England revivals displayed the presence of the Holy Spirit, and later published defenses of the revivals helped confirm generations of English-speaking Protestants in the belief that an experience of rebirth would be a mark of true faith. In 1747, Edwards published *A Humble Attempt* to stimulate a concert of PRAYER among Protestants throughout the world, and his correspondence with other Protestant CLERGY in America and the British Isles brought him into union with advocates of an international awakening.

Missions and Metaphysics

Edwards's zeal for converts led him to support MIS-
SIONS to the Native Americans, and his 1749 account
of the missionary DAVID BRAINERD would inspire later
Protestant mission efforts. A dispute with his Northampton congregation over his desire for stricter membership standards led to his dismissal in 1751, but it
also generated a discussion of the nature of the church
that would continue for the next century. After his
dismissal, Edwards became the pastor and missionary
to the Housatonics and Mohawks in the outpost of
Stockbridge, Massachusetts, and he also found time to
enter more deeply into European philosophical and
theological discussions. His treatise on *The Freedom
of the Will* (1754) attempted to refute Arminian ideas
of self-determination, while his closely argued *Original Sin* (1758) attempted to undercut Arminian efforts
to define sinfulness as a matter of human acts rather
than innate dispositions (see ARMINIANISM). His *Nature of True Virtue* (1765) resumed his longstanding
ethical interests by arguing, in contrast to British ethicists, that only a special divine GRACE could produce
a truly virtuous "love to being in general." His *Concerning the End for Which God Created the World*
(1765) used both biblical and philosophical argument
to contend that the end of creation was, as Calvinists
had long maintained, the Glory of God. In 1758 Edwards became the president of the College of New
Jersey (in Princeton), but he died as a result of a
smallpox inoculation within three months.

Edwards had a long-enduring influence on Protestantism in America and Britain. His disciples in the
Edwardean tradition—especially SAMUEL HOPKINS
(1721–1803), Joseph Bellamy (1719–1790), and
Nathaniel Emmons (1745–1840)—kept alive Edwards's demand for stricter church membership and
his revivalist fervor while also popularizing his distinction between natural inability, or constraint external to the will, and moral inability, or the will's
inability to choose against its own inclinations, for
which human agents bore responsibility. The distinction reappeared in Congregationalist and Presbyterian
revivalism and in English and American Baptist mission movements, but it also intensified tensions among
English-speaking Protestants. Some nineteenth-century Old School Presbyterians and Calvinistic BAP-
TISTS distrusted Edwards as a fount of HERESY; British
and American Methodists liked his revivalist piety but
deplored his CALVINISM; nineteenth-century liberals
relegated him to a forgotten past (see LIBERAL; PROT-
ESTANTISM AND LIBERALISM). Even many of Edwards's
critics in America, however, from the Yale theologian
NATHANIEL TAYLOR (1786–1858) to the Oberlin revivalist CHARLES G. FINNEY (1792–1875), bore residues of
an Edwardean theological culture. HARRIET BEECHER
STOWE (1811–1896), an admiring critic, used more
than one of her novels to draw a broader Protestant
public into the intricacies of Edwards's heritage. By
the 1920s, Edwards served for progressives as a symbol of America's unfortunate Calvinist heritage, but
two world wars and an economic depression, along
with the rise of a neo-orthodox Protestant theology,
helped spark a reassessment of a thinker who combined a sober reading of human nature with a hopeful
glimpse of transcendent beauty.

See also Congregationalism; Neo-Orthodoxy; Presbyterianism

References and Further Reading

Edwards, Jonathan. *Freedom of the Will*. Edited by Paul Ram-
sey. New Haven, CT: Yale University Press, 1957.
——. *Religious Affections*. Edited by John Smith. New Ha-
ven, CT: Yale University Press, 1959.
——. *Ecclesiastical Writings*. Edited by David D. Hall. New
Haven, CT: Yale University Press, 1994.
——. *Notes on Scripture*. Edited by Stephen S. Stein. New
Haven, CT: Yale University Press, 1998.

E. BROOKS HOLIFIELD

ELECTION

Although often identified with the REFORMATION, the
doctrine of election (and its associated idea of PRE-
DESTINATION) had a long and somewhat uneasy history
in the Christian church well before the Reformation.
The uneasiness of this doctrine derives from the fact
that it inevitably raises the question of God's justness
in choosing some and not others. As traditionally
defined, the doctrine of election is the sovereign act of
God in eternity past in choosing or electing some
persons to be saved or rescued from the consequences
of their sins and therefore being destined for eternal
life. Of course, theologians have recognized that election logically raises the difficult question of the eternal
destiny of those God did not elect. This nonelection is
called reprobation and may be conceived passively as
passing over or actively as willful rejection.

Historically the DOCTRINE of election was not a
theological conviction that necessarily distinguished
Protestants from Catholics. From the time of Augustine this doctrine had been part of the theological
lexicon of Christian thought. Augustine forged his
understanding of election in large part through the
polemics of the Pelagian controversy. For him divine
election begins, not with abstract speculations about
God in eternity, but with fallen man who exists in a
mass of perdition (*massa perditionis*). This miserable
fact governed his understanding of this doctrine.
God's rescue of some from the mass of fallen human-

ity lies at the heart of Augustine's conception of divine election. In Augustine's vocabulary, election and predestination are synonymous and both are employed exclusively as the positive expression of the divine will to save a specific number of sinners (*pradestinaio ad vitiam*). God elects "not because He foreknew that we should be such, but in order that we would be such by the election of His grace" (*De praedestinatione sanctorum,* 19.38). According to Augustine election is an exercise of sovereign free will without any regard to what man does or does not do in the future. He occasionally referred to reprobation as a corollary to election, but it was a topic he preferred to avoid.

Although the Pelagian controversy wreaked havoc in the early church, Augustine's doctrine of election received approval at the Second Council of Orange (529). To be sure not all actually agreed with Augustine, but it represented the standard view of the medieval CHURCH. There were those who felt Augustine's avoidance of reprobation was unwarranted and thus turned it into a doctrine of double predestination (*gemina pradestinatio*)—the idea that in eternity past God decreed the election of some to SALVATION and reprobated others to damnation. Gottschalk of Orbais articulated this view in the seventh century and suffered imprisonment, but in the fourteenth century, the general of the Augustinian Hermits, Gregory of Rimini, and Thomas Bradwardine, the archbishop of Canterbury, advocated much the same view with impunity. Some have pointed to the existence of a late medieval school of thought (*Schola Augustiniana moderna*) that descended from Rimini and served as a theological resource for MARTIN LUTHER and the Protestants.

The Protestant Development of the Doctrine of Election

Reformation theologians evidence a broad acquaintance with all of the major fathers, both Greek and Latin, but it was Augustine who occupied first place in the pantheon of fathers. Although not infallible, he was the preeminently judicious and wise mentor on most theological questions, not the least of which was the doctrine of predestination. Because Protestants saw themselves as drawing on this heritage, they self-consciously appropriated an Augustinian doctrine of election.

All the major first-generation reformers (Luther, JOHN CALVIN, HULDRYCH ZWINGLI), following Augustine, affirmed unconditional election and were unafraid to go the extra step and embrace a doctrine of double predestination. Although the doctrine of election is most often identified with the Reformed branch of Protestantism, it was a vital part of early LUTHERANISM as well. Luther was no systematic theologian and never articulated a fully developed doctrine of election. However, it is abundantly clear from his work against Erasmus, *De servo arbitrio* (The Bondage of the Will), that he embraced a full-orbed doctrine of unconditional election and one can occasionally glimpse an underlying double predestination. For the most part Luther identified election with predestination and highlighted its pastoral benefit. It was a fundamental theological presupposition for Luther that everything flows from God's eternal decree in accordance with his sovereign will.

There is, however, a certain theological tension between Luther's emphasis on the overarching divine causality and his recognition that God desires the salvation of all. He solved this riddle by appealing to the distinction between the *Deus absconditus* (hidden God) and the *Deus revelatus* (revealed God). According to Luther the revealed will of God in the scriptures must be distinguished from the secret will of God who decrees all things including election to salvation and rejection unto damnation. In all of this Luther insists that God's ways are inscrutable and Christians must not pry into the mysteries of heaven.

Even before Luther's death in 1546 some followers of Luther began to retreat from his bold doctrine of double predestination. Leading the way was Luther's closest associate, PHILIPP MELANCHTHON, who gradually moved in a synergistic direction. In the first edition (1521) of his *Loci Communes,* Melanchthon had been a staunch defender of Luther's rigorous doctrine of election and predestination, although over time his Erasmian humanistic tendencies surfaced, leading to a significant modification of Luther's doctrine. The 1535 revision of the *Loci Communes* marked a turning point in Melanchthon's understanding of election. His insistence that God is not the author of SIN became an overriding concern in his thought. Although retaining his conviction that election depends entirely on the mercy of God, he maintained at the same time that human beings retain some ability to accept or reject FAITH. Melanchthon famously concludes "the cause must be in man that Saul is cast away and David is accepted." Whatever else one can say about election, Melanchthon insisted that humans must cooperate with God to bring about salvation, although such cooperation must not be viewed as meritorious.

Melanchthon's synergistic view of election and reprobation eventually prevailed in Lutheran confessional statements. Article 11 of the *Formula of Concord* (1577) acknowledges election, but all speculation about the reprobate is dismissed as "inspired by Satan." Melanchthonian synergism exercised determinative influence on later Lutheranism in two ways. First, it led to the ultimate rejection of Luther's more rigorous doctrine of double predestination. Second, it led inevitably to what would become a constitutive difference between the Lutheran and Reformed communities and a source of much hostility.

From a distance Calvin may appear to tower over other Reformed theologians, but the intervening centuries have had a way of distorting the historical reality. In recent years it has been increasingly recognized that the origins of Reformed theology do not derive exclusively from Calvin, but rather from a coterie of theologians who were associated with Swiss reform, including besides Calvin, Zwingli, HEINRICH BULLINGER, Peter Martyr Vermigli, and Wolfgang Musculus. Although each embraced the doctrine of election, they had varying emphases, and none of them made predestination the central dogma of their theological system.

Zwingli was a first-generation magisterial reformer and the inaugurator of Swiss reform. He did not give a lot of attention to the topic of predestination until his meeting with Luther at the COLLOQUY OF MARBURG in 1529. There Zwingli preached a sermon on providence and predestination to an audience that included Luther himself. This sermon was later expanded and published as *De providentia* (On Providence). There can be little doubt that of all the major Protestant reformers, Zwingli articulated the most extreme doctrine of predestination. Zwingli's *De providentia* reveals his strongly philosophical cast of mind. Most obviously his philosophical orientation is signaled by the constant parade of ancient philosophers across the pages of this work. Concerning the ancients Zwingli reserved his greatest praise for the last great representative of Roman Stoicism, Lucius Annaeus Seneca. The most significant impact from Seneca is found in Zwingli's all-encompassing doctrine of providence, of which predestination is a subcategory. Following Seneca he insists there is no secondary causality: "Nothing," he writes, "is done or achieved which is not done and achieved by the immediate care and power of the Deity." Indeed providence looms so large that there appears to be no room for human will or human responsibility. What is more, Zwingli's understanding of predestination as indistinguishable from providence logically inclined him to the conclusion that God is the cause of human sin. Although God is absolved of any personal culpability, yet Zwingli can assert that God is the "author, mover and instigator of human sin." At the core of Zwingli's thought about election and reprobation is the notion that both issue directly from the divine will. Zwingli attributed both to the divine will in the same way, constructing an absolutely *symmetrical* doctrine of double predestination. The cause

and means of both election and reprobation are precisely the same. For Zwingli God is the exclusive and immediate cause of all things.

More than any other, Calvin is identified with the doctrine of predestination, in large part because he was called on to defend it repeatedly during his tenure in Geneva. However, the first signs of his predestinarian views became evident during the years in Strasbourg with MARTIN BUCER (1538–1541), first in his 1539 edition of the INSTITUTES OF THE CHRISTIAN RELIGION and then his commentary on *Romans* (1540). His debates with Albert Pighuis (1543) and Jerome Bolsec (1550) prompted further refinement, resulting in his *De aeterna praedestinatione* (On Eternal Predestination) in 1552 and reached its final expression in the 1559 edition of the *Institutes*. For Calvin election was most often regarded as a subcomponent of the broader category of predestination—a rubric under which the positive aspect of election is distinguished from the negative aspect of reprobation. His conception of election is part of a "double predestination" in that God willed from eternity to elect some to eternal life for his own glory and reprobated others to eternal death to display his justice. He defines predestination as "God's eternal decree by which he compacted with himself what he wills to become of each man. For all are not created in equal condition; rather eternal life is foreordained for some, eternal damnation for others" (*Institutes*, III.21.5). His doctrine of predestination was asymmetrical (contra Zwingli) in that he identified a different cause for eternal life than for eternal damnation. The cause of the former was the will of God in election, but the cause of the latter was identified as the sins of the reprobate. In Calvin the salvation of the elect reveals the depth of God's mercy, and the condemnation of the reprobate displays the severity of his justice. He acknowledges that election and predestination are an inscrutable mystery, but he insists that an inability to understand does not give one the right to reject a doctrine so clearly revealed in scripture.

Calvin's view more or less prevailed in Reformed confessions of the sixteenth and seventeenth centuries, although even in the Reformed branch there were various refinements. Peter Martyr Vermigli affirmed a doctrine of double predestination like Calvin. However, unlike Calvin, Vermigli tended toward a passive understanding of reprobation as a passing over, whereas Calvin seemed to conceive of reprobation as active. There were also theologians of the Reformed tradition who demurred about a full-fledged doctrine of double predestination. Bullinger of Zurich refused to accept reprobation as a necessary corollary to election, and his colleague at Zurich, Theodore Bibliander, openly opposed the rigorous predestinarianism of

Peter Martyr Vermigli. So, despite the general consensus, there was some soteriological divergence.

In seventeenth-century Holland within the Reformed church, opposition to the Calvinistic teaching on predestination arose in the teaching of JACOBUS ARMINIUS. In his *Declaration of Sentiments* (1608) Arminius objected not only to double predestination, but also to the *supralapsarian* (as well as *infralapsarian*) conception of election. Although never normative for Reformed Protestantism, there were those whose doctrine of predestination inclined them to a *supralapsarian* order of the divine decrees—that is, in eternity, God's decree of election (and reprobation) was logically before the decree to permit the fall. In effect this made the fall a means by which the decree of election and reprobation could be implemented, The majority tended to a more historic view of *infralapsarianism*— that is, in eternity, God decreed to permit the fall logically before God's decree of election (and reprobation). According to this line of thinking, election was seen as a rescue of sinners. Debate over this speculative aspect of predestination sparked intense controversy in the Dutch Protestant church between the Arminians and the Reformed (see ARMINIANISM).

Along with his rejection of the *supralapsarian* conception of predestination, Arminius also concluded that divine election is conditioned upon foreseen faith. The theological debate became a national controversy that was resolved at the Synod of Dordrecht (1618–1619). This national SYNOD, which included representatives from various Reformed Protestant churches throughout Europe, upheld the traditional Reformed belief in unconditional election along with the other so-called four main points of CALVINISM (total depravity, limited ATONEMENT, irresistible GRACE, and perseverance of the SAINTS). The Canons of Dordrecht (or Dort; see DORT, CANONS OF) clearly favored an infralapsarian conception of predestination, although without condemning supralapsarianism. This became normative for the Reformed ORTHODOXY.

Under the influence of the continental Reformed theologians, the THIRTY-NINE ARTICLES of Religion of the CHURCH OF ENGLAND also embraced unconditional election (article 17). There was a good deal of resistance but never enough to excise the article. The Puritan movement within the Anglican Church continued generally to uphold unconditional election and double predestination (see PURITANISM). For many Puritans the doctrine of election took on added significance by establishing a link to the doctrine of assurance. Scholars have often noted that among English and American Puritans the doctrine of election seems to provoke a certain anxiety over the assurance of one's election. In other words, Puritans came to increasingly ask the question: "How can I be assured that I am one of God's elect?" Early reformers tended to answer this question by pointing the anxious Christian exclusively to the promises of Christ. However, later Protestants and especially the Puritans, although acknowledging the viability of the earlier Reformed answer, wanted something more tangible and began to answer the question by pointing to certain signs (*signa posteriora*) of spiritual fruit in the individual's life, such as regular attendance at church, partaking of the SACRAMENTS, reading the BIBLE, and PRAYER. These signs became concrete evidences of one's election and thus, it was argued, relieved the anxiety. This kind of spiritual logic became known as the *practical syllogism* and, following a standard pattern of spiritual argument, was based on the theological principle that the elect necessarily exhibit certain observable signs of their election. If the individual exhibits those signs, then they are among the elect. The *practical syllogism,* in varying forms, was manifested in the teachings of the Synod of Dordrecht as well as in the thought of the American Puritan JONATHAN EDWARDS.

One of the most public controversies among leading Protestants in the eighteenth-century centered on the doctrine of predestination. The two founders of the Methodist movement, GEORGE WHITEFIELD and JOHN WESLEY, were bitterly divided over this theological issue. In 1740 when Whitefield was preaching in the American colonies during the Great Awakening (see AWAKENINGS), Wesley preached and published his sermon entitled "On Free Grace," in which he labeled the doctrine of election "blasphemy." The Wesleyan Methodists followed Arminius's view that election was based on foreseen faith, whereas the Calvinist Methodists and Whitefield upheld traditional Reformed doctrine of unconditional election. This controversy led to an irreversible breach between Wesley and Whitefield as well as their followers.

Modern Developments of the Doctrine of Election

Generally the doctrine of election continued to be advocated by Presbyterians and Evangelical Anglicans, denied by Methodists and Baptists, and ridiculed by secularists during the ENLIGHTENMENT of the eighteenth and nineteenth centuries. It was not until KARL BARTH that the doctrine of election received a new and revolutionary interpretation. For the Swiss theologian the doctrine of election was "the sum of the gospel." In essence Barth turned the whole of theology into CHRISTOLOGY. While looking to the reformers for theological inspiration, he developed his understanding of election in a vastly different way. Where the Reformers tended to advocate a double predestination—election of some to salvation and reprobation to condemnation for others—Barth identified Christ with both the elect and the reprobate. According to his view divine predestination is properly described as a double predestination, which he understood as God making the double decision to elect all mankind to salvation in Christ as well as the decision to reprobate Christ himself in place of sinful humanity. Christ is at once the elect for all and the reprobate for all. Although Barth was unwilling to acknowledge a doctrine of *apokatastasis* (universal salvation), this seems to be the necessary conclusion to his unique understanding of double predestination. Thus Barth's understanding of election is the victory over reprobation or, as he said, it is the "triumph of grace." Barth's distinctive approach has indeed removed the long-standing uneasiness of this doctrine, but in so doing has divorced the doctrine from its Augustinian origins.

References and Further Reading

Berkouwer, G. C. *The Triumph of Grace in the Theology of Karl Barth*. Translated by Harry R. Boer. Grand Rapids, MI: Eerdmans, 1956.

Bloesch, Donald G. *Jesus is Victor! Karl Barth's Doctrine of Salvation*. Nashville, TN: Abingdon, 1976.

Bray, John S. *Theodore Beza's Doctrine of Predestination*. Nieuwkoop: B. DeGraaf, 1975.

Jacobs, Paul. *Prädestination und Verantwortlichkeit bei Calvin*. Reprint. Darmstadt, 1968.

James, Frank A. *Peter Martyr Vermigli and Predestination: The Augustinian Inheritance of an Italian Reformer*. Oxford, UK: Clarendon Press, 1998.

Klooster, Fred H. *Calvin's Doctrine of Predestination*. 2d edition. Grand Rapids, MI: Baker Book House, 1977.

McSorley, Harry J. *Luther Right or Wrong?* New York: Newman Press, 1969.

Muller, Richard A. *Christ and the Decree: Christology and Predestination in Reformed Theology from Calvin to Perkins*. Grand Rapids, MI: Baker Book House, 1988.

Steinmetz, David C. *Luther and Staupitz: And Essay in the Intellectual Origins of the Protestant Reformation*. Durham, NC: Duke University Press, 1980.

Walser, Peter. *Die Prädestination bei Heinrich Bullinger im Zusammenhang mit seiner Gotteslehre*. Zurich, Switzerland, 1957.

FRANK A. JAMES III

ELIOT, GEORGE (1819–1880)

English writer. Under the pseudonym George Eliot, Mary Ann (Marian) Evans wrote eight novels that all implicitly or explicitly explore religious themes. She explored religion throughout her own life as well.

Eliot was born November 22, 1819, in Warwickshire, ENGLAND. Early in life she experienced an evangelical CONVERSION, prompted by interaction with a boarding school teacher. After a family move in 1841, she came into contact with a circle of Unitarians. She left EVANGELICALISM and began to immerse herself in the ideas of DAVID FRIEDRICH STRAUSS (whose *Life of Jesus* she translated), LUDWIG FEUERBACH, Auguste Comte, GEORG WILHELM FRIEDRICH HEGEL, and Baruch Spinoza. In 1854 she entered a relationship with George Henry Lewes, whom she would have married if his wife had granted him a divorce. His death in 1878 devastated her, but she did fall in love again and marry an old friend, John Walter Cross, shortly before her death on December 22, 1880.

Some scholars have concluded that Eliot abandoned Christianity entirely, but her writing suggests otherwise. Eliot's first two works, *Scenes of Clerical Life* (1858) and *Adam Bede* (1859), feature protagonists engaged in Christian ministry, including, in the latter, a female Methodist preacher. Eliot's best novel, *Middlemarch* (1872), centers on Dorothea Brooke, an autobiographical character who engages in religious scholarship and social justice work. Eliot's last novel, *Daniel Deronda* (1876), interweaves JUDAISM, Christianity, and elements of Comte's "religion of humanity." This blend reflects the views of the author, who wrote in an 1873 letter, "Every community met to worship the highest Good (which is understood to be expressed by God) carries me along in its main current."

See also Jesus, Lives of; Unitarian Universalist Association

References and Further Reading

Dodd, Valerie A. *George Eliot: An Intellectual Life*. London: Macmillan, 1990.

Hodgson, Peter C. *The Mystery Beneath the Real: Theology in the Fiction of George Eliot*. Minneapolis, MN: Fortress Press, 2000.

ELESHA COFFMAN

ELIOT, JOHN (1604–1690)

New England Puritan. John Eliot was a longtime minister in Roxbury, Massachusetts, and a missionary to American Indian peoples of southern New England. He was born in Widford, Hertfordshire, ENGLAND. A graduate of Jesus College, Cambridge in 1622, he was likely converted under Puritan pastor THOMAS HOOKER in 1629. Eliot emigrated to Massachusetts Bay in 1631 to enjoy worship services characterized by New Testament purity rather than by the "human additions and novelties" that he believed plagued an insufficiently reformed CHURCH OF ENGLAND. The following year the Roxbury congregation ordained him a teaching elder, and he remained there for fifty-five years.

Eliot embraced mostly mainstream Puritan positions, although two of his works, *The Christian Commonwealth* (1659) and *The Communion of Churches* (1665), expressed unconventional political, eschatological, and ecclesiological views that he later largely abandoned (see ESCHATOLOGY, ECCLESIOLOGY). He helped translate the *Bay Psalm Book* (1640), a metrical Psalter that was the first book printed in New England. Eliot sought to make the Puritan church inclusive, as illustrated by his support for the Halfway Covenant and, more dramatically, his outreach to the Indians. He first preached to natives in 1646, gathered early converts into their own settlement at Natick by 1651, and published his first work in the Indians' own Massachusett language in 1654. Eliot went on to found fourteen Indian "praying towns" and to translate the BIBLE and several Puritan devotional works into Massachusett. Such efforts earned him the title "Apostle to the Indians." Although Eliot sought to transform the natives' religion and much of their CULTURE, his long-term interaction with Indians in turn transformed him into a great respecter of their humanity and a great sympathizer with Indian problems. Eliot died on May 21, 1690.

See also Puritanism; Bible Translation

References and Further Reading

Cogley, Richard W. *John Eliot's Mission to the Indians Before King Philip's War.* Cambridge, MA: Harvard University Press, 1999.
_____. "John Eliot's Puritan Ministry." *Fides et Historia* 31 (Winter/Spring 1999): 1–18.
Winslow, Ola E. *John Eliot.* Boston: Houghton Mifflin, 1968.
RICHARD W. POINTER

ELIOT, T. S. (1888–1965)

English poet. Because he once described himself as "a classicist in literature, a conservative in politics, and a catholic in religion," it would seem paradoxical to include T.S. Eliot in an *Encyclopedia of Protestantism.* However, Eliot's final ANGLO-CATHOLICISM was as self-conscious a personal construction as his writing and politics—the outcome of a long and complex journey, mirroring his career pilgrimage from patrician Bostonian (albeit born in St. Louis, Missouri) to *enfant terrible* of modernist poetry, to London publisher and arbiter of English critical taste.

Critical opinion has always been sharply divided over Eliot's poetical and religious evolution. For some the change from the disillusioned and agnostic radical of *Prufrock* (1917), the early poems, and *The Waste Land* (1922), to the Christian poet of *Ash Wednesday* (1930) and the *Four Quartets* (1943), was a retreat as unforgivable aesthetically and philosophically as his taking of British citizenship (1927) and his subsequent conservatism was politically. Yet with hindsight, early poems like *The Hippopotamus* are visibly more Christian than agnostic, and essays like *Tradition and the Individual Talent* (1919) presented an argument about the necessity of change as applicable to THEOLOGY as to its ostensible AESTHETICS.

More important, the later self-advertised "conservatism" conceals only thinly a continued poetic and theological radicalism. The apparent mysticism of *Ash Wednesday* distracted many readers from the fact that Eliot's style was even more elliptical and fragmented than *The Waste Land*; the *Quartets*—together with the four verse plays, beginning with *Murder in the Cathedral* (1933)—continued to break new ground aesthetically. It was, moreover, typical of Eliot to advocate adherence to the traditions of the past at the very time that he was at his most theologically innovative. For him the great Christian "tradition" of European poetry and philosophy did not involve imitation of the past, but *changing* it—and seeing each new work as implying a radical reappraisal of all that had gone before. Proclaimed as an aesthetic and critical creed, it was less noticed that this was *also* a theological principle. Eliot's critical veneration for Dante and the Metaphysical poets, JOHN DONNE, GEORGE HERBERT, Vaughan, and Marvell, stemmed also from a desire to write poetry that would change not merely readers' understanding of the present, but of the past—a move that reached its fullest expression in his meditations on Britain at war in *Little Gidding.* Similarly for his new-found ANGLICANISM to survive, it was essential that it could answer JOHN HENRY NEWMAN's criticism that it lacked self-awareness—and part of the answer lay in changing our understanding of the tradition to which the Catholic Newman had appealed. Essays such as *Notes Towards a Definition of Culture* and *The Idea of a Christian Society,* controversial as they were to prove, were part of the same attempt to see his faith in social as much as aesthetic terms.

His encouragement of new poetic talent as a publisher, his Nobel Prize (1948), and his service in liturgical and educational developments made him a leading English public figure after World War II.

References and Further Reading

Primary Sources:

Eliot, T. S. *Complete Poems and Plays.* London: Faber, 1969.
_____. *Notes Towards a Definition of Culture.* London: Faber, 1947.
_____. *Selected Essays,* Third edition. London: Faber, 1951.
_____. *The Idea of a Christian Society.* London: Faber, 1940.

Secondary Source:

Ackroyd, Peter. *T. S. Eliot: a Life.* New York: Simon & Schuster, 1984.
STEPHEN PRICKETT

ELIZABETH I (ELIZABETH TUDOR) (1533–1603)

Elizabeth I was the savior of Protestantism in England, establishing it permanently as the state religion, ANGLICANISM, with the conservative Elizabethan Settlement of Religion in 1559. But Elizabeth's reluctance to permit any further religious change created the Puritan movement within Anglicanism and spawned a number of separatist churches. Elizabeth created the religious foundation for English-speaking Protestantism.

Her birth precipitated a schism between ENGLAND and Rome, and Elizabeth was educated by evangelical tutors. Spending some of her formative years in the household of Queen Katherine Parr of England, she learned the attitudes of Erasmian humanism and Protestant reform. As a youth she also learned the political necessity of cautious dissembling, appearing to be a Henrician Catholic under her father, HENRY VIII, an obedient Edwardian Protestant under her half-brother Edward VI, and a dutiful attendee of Catholic masses under her half-sister Mary.

After she took the throne on November 17, 1558, Elizabeth indicated her clear rejection of Catholicism. She repudiated TRANSUBSTANTIATION, refusing to allow the elevation of the host in her chapel services and at her coronation. By Easter 1559 her chaplain celebrated at a table rather than an ALTAR, and she received both the bread and the wine—sure signs of Protestantism. Elizabeth prudently refused to explain her personal theology, but her behaviors and writings demonstrate her to have been Erasmian, evangelical, and Lutheran in her preferences. Despite her certain Protestantism, Elizabeth was very cautious about religious change, irritating and infuriating Protestants who hoped that she would create a better disciplined, preaching church.

The Elizabethan Settlement of Religion created the Anglican Church with its prayer book LITURGY and its continued Episcopal structure of governance. Though Protestant in THEOLOGY, the church looked Catholic in structure. Its form may well have reflected Elizabeth's personal tastes in Protestantism. It certainly reflected the necessity of compromise with powerful Catholic forces in the nation. The queen, a Nicodemite keeping her religious conviction concealed, wanted political stability more than she wanted to please a jealous God, so the Act of Uniformity required all her subjects to use the BOOK OF COMMON PRAYER (1552), slightly amended, and left the bishops in charge. By the Act of Supremacy, Elizabeth became Supreme Governor of the CHURCH OF ENGLAND.

As Supreme Governor, Elizabeth would not allow any infringement of her right to control religion. In 1562/3, when it was still expected that she would complete the reforms, the Convocation of CANTERBURY, representing the CLERGY, proposed to Parliament a set of disciplinary reforms and a statement of belief that became the THIRTY-NINE ARTICLES. Elizabeth exploded, making it clear that decisions about religion were not to be made without her permission. It was not until 1571 that the Thirty-Nine Articles became law, leaving the English church in a theological limbo for the first dozen years of her reign. Moreover, Elizabeth never permitted a reform of the discipline, so the church administered discipline according to the canon law (see CHURCH DISCIPLINE).

As events in the 1560s made it clear that Elizabeth was not going to allow further reformation of her church, those committed to it began to agitate for change. These "Puritans" were, in many ways, Elizabeth's direct creation, because she refused to respond to their concerns. One result was a Presbyterian movement that sought to strip the English church of its "evil" bishops and give power to congregations, but Elizabeth was not interested in sharing power with anyone. The 1570s and 1580s were dominated by the struggle between those who wanted a church more like Calvinist churches and those who defended the queen's prayer book religion and her bishops.

This caught her bishops between their queen and their consciences. In 1576, commenting that England already had enough preachers, Elizabeth ordered Edmund Grindal, archbishop of Canterbury, to suppress "prophesyings," educational exercises that encouraged PREACHING. Grindal refused, reminding Elizabeth that she was a mortal creature and would be judged by God for hindering the duties of the bishops. She suspended him as archbishop, further encouraging the belief that PRESBYTERIANISM, or even separation from the established church, was the only way for the godly to complete the REFORMATION. When Grindal died in 1583, he was replaced by JOHN WHITGIFT. Called her "little black husband" by Elizabeth, Whitgift accepted the job of forcing the Puritans into obedience to their sovereign.

Elizabeth's commitment to religious stability meant that she was unwilling to allow persecution on religious grounds, but she did practice political persecution. She demanded obedience to her law, not ideological purity. Consequently, she did not punish Catholics for their faith, but for their allegiance to a foreign power, the Pope. After the Catholic Revolt of the Northern Earls in 1569 and her excommunication by the Pope in 1570, her government squeezed Catholics harder and harder, insisting they attend church and take communion or pay heavy fines. But they were not burned for heresy. On the other hand, Catholic missionary priests working in England were frequently executed for treason against the queen. By the 1590s, Elizabeth, feeling embattled on both sides, accepted harsher and harsher measures against anyone, Catholic or Protestant, who refused to participate in the religion established by law.

Elizabeth's intransigence was her most important contribution to English-speaking Protestantism. Her religious settlement created a national church with Protestant theology and Catholic structures. Across her long reign, supporters and detractors of that settlement hardened into forerunners of recognizable denominations. If Elizabeth had been less stubborn, the religious history of the English-speaking world might have been very different.

See also Bishop and Episcopacy; Catholicism, Protestant Reactions; Evangelicalism; Lutheranism; Puritanism

References and Further Reading

Collinson, Patrick. "Windows in a Woman's Soul: Questions About the Religion of Queen Elizabeth I," *Elizabethan Essays*.

Doran, Susan. *Elizabeth I and Religion*. London: Routledge, 1994.

———. "Elizabeth I's Religion: Clues from Her Letters," *Journal of Ecclesiastical History* 51 (2000), 699–720.

Haigh, Christopher. *Elizabeth I*. London: Longman Group, 1988.

Haugaard, William P. "Elizabeth Tudor's *Book of Devotions*: A Neglected Clue to the Queen's Life and Character," *Sixteenth Century Journal* XII (1981), 99–106.

Jones, Norman. *The Birth of the Elizabethan Age. England in the 1560s*. Oxford, UK: Blackwell, 1993.

MacCaffrey, Wallace, *Elizabeth I*. London: Edward Arnold, 1993.

NORMAN L. JONES

EMERSON, RALPH WALDO (1803–1882)

Essayist, philospher, and poet. Emerson was a guiding light in the movement of religious reform known as American transcendentalism. His essays also figured importantly in the emergence of a distinctively American literary tradition and the development of religious liberalism and romantic religion in the United States.

Early Years

Born May 25, 1803, in what was once the staunchly Puritan town of Boston, Emerson was the second of four surviving sons of Ruth Haskins Emerson and William Emerson (1769–1811), minister to Boston's First Church. The Emersons descended from a long line of New England clerics, but in contrast to the Calvinist faith of his Puritan forebears, Emerson's father aligned himself with the liberal *Unitarian* wing of the the Congregational churches. After his father died in 1811, Emerson and his brothers were raised primarily by their mother and a charismatic aunt, Mary Moody Emerson (1774–1863) who was for years her nephew's chief religious confidante and mentor.

At the age of fourteen Emerson entered Harvard College, where he was trained in the standard curriculum of the classics, rhetoric, history, English, and theology. Though only a middling student, he demonstrated some flair as an aspiring poet and essayist. It was in college, however, that he first began keeping the voluminous journal that served throughout his life as a rich resource for his essays, lectures, and addresses. Here he was also introduced to the new German school of biblical scholarship—the HIGHER CRITICISM—from the popular lecturer Edward Everett (1794–1865).

In 1825, after much indecision, Emerson resolved to enter the ministry, whereupon he began formal study at Harvard's Divinity School. Licensed to preach the following year, he served as a supply preacher for congregations in eastern Massachusetts until his ordination in 1829 at Boston's historic Second Church. Having meanwhile married a beautiful young heiress named Ellen Tucker, Emerson now seemed launched on a happy and prosperous career, but after a mere sixteen months of marriage, Ellen succumbed to tuberculosis, leaving her husband adrift and disconsolate. The next year, in protest over his church's insistence on the traditional administration of the COMMUNION rite, Emerson resigned his pastorate and embarked on his first extended journey abroad.

In the wake of Ellen's death in 1831, Emerson underwent a kind of religious transformation, of which the first fruit was the publication in 1836 of his book, *Nature*. Part sermon, part prose-poem, *Nature* was Emerson's earliest attempt to put his new romantic religious and philosophical vision into words. In the weeks following the appearance of *Nature*, Emerson began meeting informally with several of his friends, mostly Unitarian clergymen, to discuss recent views on art, religion, and science. The meetings soon attracted the attention of a wider association that formed the nucleus of the transcendentalist movement.

Emerson's Views Develop

Two addresses delivered in the decade of renewal following Ellen's death serve as the best gauges of Emerson's mature views on Unitarian religion and Christianity in general. The first of these, "The Lord's Supper," he presented to his parishioners in the fall of

1832 to explain his reasons for stepping down. Reviewing the history of the communion rite in Western churches and the gospel evidence concerning its origins, he concluded that Jesus never intended to establish a rite of perpetual observance and that it was not appropriate to celebrate the rite as the church was then doing. Emerson's critique of the communion rite reflected the influence of German historical methods, but was fueled by his growing dissatisfaction with the church's general adherence to what he termed "formal religion"—religion in which the outer forms of religious observance are thought to overwhelm its inner spirit.

The famous address Emerson delivered at the commencement ceremonies of Harvard's Divinity School in 1838 set out his considered theological positions even more defiantly. Here he argued that traditional Christianity had committed two grave errors: first, it had become unduly preoccupied with the person of Jesus of Nazareth, and second, it no longer gave sufficient heed to the true source of revelation—the soul itself, stronghold of the "moral nature"—what Emerson variously referred to as the Self, the Oversoul, or the God within. Here he made his Christological views explicit: Jesus was the "true man," the greatest moral exemplar and teacher in the history of the world, but he was not the son of God in any exclusive sense. Emerson's address triggered an avalanche of protest from Unitarian authorities, including Harvard's professor of biblical literature, Andrews Norton (1786–1853), who condemned Emerson's address as the "latest form of infidelity."

Following the controversy triggered by the Divinity School address, Emerson withdrew from religious polemics to dedicate his energies to various writing projects. Besides his involvement with *The Dial* (1840–1844), the first transcendentalist literary magazine, he worked assiduously to complete two collections of essays upon which his subsequent reputation was built: *Essays: First Series* (1841) and *Essays: Second Series*, published three years later. "Self-Reliance," perhaps America's most famous and controversial essay, appeared for the first time in the collection of 1841. Emerson's ruminations on the universal immanence of the moral law had convinced him that the human soul was itself grounded in divinity, a concept for which he found corroboration in the Quaker doctrine of the inner light, and later in his reading of the Bhagavad Gita and the Upanishads.

While continuities may be seen between Emersonian self-reliance and Quaker piety, and even with older patterns of New England faith, Emerson's theological views represented a striking departure from tradition. Quick to affirm his belief in the divinity of man and nature, he also voiced doubt about doctrines ascribing personality to God. The "Self" or divine principle in Emersonian thought was impersonal and monistic, not theistic. Also distinctive of Emersonian thought was its emphasis on process and transformation. Thus, Emersonian thought exhibited marked suspicion of traditional metaphysical or theological formulations. Good flowed from the soul's outward expansions; evil was its mere privation.

Emerson's Writings

The publication of Emerson's first two books of essays was followed in 1850 by *Representative Men*, and by *English Traits* in 1856. Before his death in 1882, several more collections followed, including *The Conduct of Life* (1860) and *Society and Solitude* (1870). By mid-century, Emerson had acquired the status of an American cultural icon. Through the popularization of his poems and essays, "the Sage of Concord" had become America's representative philosopher. Emerson died on April 27, 1882.

Although Emerson did not participate actively in the affairs of the Unitarian church after the controversies of the 1830s, by the end of the century the views of the transcendentalist ministers had become part of a normative Unitarian outlook. On the other hand, mainline Protestant denominations have tended to ignore Emerson because of his abandonment of traditional theological forms, his preference for the languages of science and philosophy, and his conception of Jesus primarily as a moral exemplar. Nevertheless, his legacy fundamentally altered the cultural landscape within which American churches have developed.

See also Romanticism; Unitarian-Universalist Churches

References and Further Reading

Primary Sources:

Emerson, E. W., ed. *The Complete Works of Ralph Waldo Emerson*. Centenary Ed., Boston: Houghton Mifflin, 1903–1904.

Ferguson, Alfred R., et al., ed. *The Collected Works of Ralph Waldo Emerson*. Cambridge: Harvard University Press, 1971–.

Gilman, William H., et al., ed. *The Journals and Miscellaneous Notebooks of Ralph Waldo Emerson*. Cambridge: Harvard University Press, 1960–1982.

Secondary Sources:

Hutchison, William R. *The Transcendentalist Ministers: Church Reform in the New England Renaissance*. New Haven and London: Yale University Press, 1959.

Richardson, Robert D., Jr. *Emerson: The Mind on Fire*. Berkeley: University of California Press, 1995.

Robinson, David. *Apostle of Culture: Emerson as Preacher and Lecturer.* Philadelphia: University of Pennsylvania Press, 1982.

Rusk, Ralph L., and Eleanor Tilton, eds. *The Letters of Ralph Waldo Emerson.* New York: Columbia University Press, 1939–.

von Frank, Albert J., ed. *The Complete Sermons of Ralph Waldo Emerson.* Columbia: University of Missouri Press, 1989–.

ALAN D. HODDER

EMPIRICAL THEOLOGY

How is one to know what is religiously true? Dissatisfaction with poor answers to this question has led religious thinkers to examine critically their religious knowledge. Among those who have done this are empirical theologians.

In their efforts to justify their claims to truth, empirical theologians have based their religious knowledge on religious experience. Unlike most other religious thinkers, empirical theologians have understood religious experience to be a form of perception. Also, for the empirical theologians this perception refers to concrete and natural evidence rather than to supernatural events.

Empirical theologians are often called "liberals," because they assume that people must decide for themselves whether their evidence is religiously persuasive (see LIBERAL; PROTESTANTISM AND LIBERALISM). Many other theologians have disagreed with them, particularly neo-Reformation theologians, who have followed in the line of thought extending from St. Augustine (354–430), to MARTIN LUTHER (1483–1546), to KARL BARTH (1886–1968). The neo-Reformation theologians argued that people are so misled by their sin and natural limitations that their evaluation of evidence is unreliable, so that God must intervene and lead them to the truth (see NEO-ORTHODOXY).

Philosophical Origins of Empirical Theology

To introduce empirical theology historically, the story of its philosophical origins will be interpreted with the bias of an empirical theologian. Empirical theology is understood to be an effort to defend religious knowledge in a new way, particularly after it had been challenged by a turn of events in European thought. Take empiricism back to its modern origins, back to Englishman FRANCIS BACON (1561–1628), who was the first major Western thinker to propose an empirical method for learning about the world. Bacon was impatient with thinkers who seemed to spin ideas out of their thought or who followed what he called the "idols" of biased perception, private predilection, commercial metaphor, and philosophical dogma. He admired the new scientists, such as Copernicus and Galileo, who looked to physical evidence in the world that stood before them.

JOHN LOCKE (1632–1704) also revolted against those who believed that good ideas could be gained by thought alone. For Locke, the mind possessed no ideas innate to itself, but began as "a blank slate," an "empty cabinet" ready to be filled with clear and distinct ideas delivered by the five senses as they regarded the external world. The store of ideas contributed by the five senses was increased, Locke said, by additional ideas contributed by a kind of "internal sense," whereby one reflects on the ideas gained through sensation and relates those ideas to each other through acts of reason, believing, doubting, or willing.

Locke was followed by other empiricists, principal among them the Scottish philosopher DAVID HUME (1711–1776). Hume went beyond Locke by asserting that if we have only our own impressions ("matters of fact") and only our own ways of relating those impressions ("relations of ideas"), then we have no reason to claim that our beliefs apply to the external world. We merely have head-realities—impressions and ways of relating impressions. Accordingly, such external realities as space, time, and causality are merely *our* habits of speech, only customs of talking about *our* impressions and their logical relations.

But Hume went still further. For him, religion, AESTHETICS, and ETHICS failed to refer even to matters of fact and relations of ideas. Religion, aesthetics, and ethics cannot show how they are based on facts or on the relations of ideas, so that if they are theories, then they are theories without even the weak empirical plausibility that Hume had accorded to sense experience.

Before Hume, an implicit empiricism had been Western religion's best friend. Scriptural JUDAISM, Christianity, and Islam had all used historical evidence to justify their beliefs. God had been encountered not behind closed eyelids and not behind closed doors in dark, silent chambers, but rather in the open spaces of the desert, in the clouds on mountaintops, in the outcomes of military battles, in green pastures and beside still waters, in outdoor sermons before hungry crowds, and at a bloody execution on the outskirts of Jerusalem.

Modern philosophical empiricism could have refined sense knowledge and lent new plausibility to the implicit empiricism of the scriptures and traditions of the ancient Middle East. But Hume prevented that; even if religious language had been empirical, empirical knowledge referred to the self rather than to the world external to the self. In effect, he bent the hook of Western religious thought, so that it caught only the garments of the believer and let the fish in the sea of history swim away. He turned history's time, space, and causality into arid customs of thought and made the mighty acts of God ghostly constructions imaginatively entertained in the private interiors of isolated individuals.

But it was not as though Hume—an elite, European, male—had single-handedly dissolved empiricism and with it the hard, time-tested reality of the masses. Hume's argument was simply an emblem of the emerging, secular, commercial, and scientific practices and beliefs of ordinary Europeans. He and they treasured information, whatever it referred to, and began to have doubts about the supposedly factual religious stories of the ancient Middle East. They created a new, self-critical empiricism that broke the religious bed in which, for millennia, religious claims had been sleeping and exposed religious beliefs to drafts of hostile analysis. No one, certainly not the European masses, had wanted to expose religion to hostile analysis, but this happened anyway.

The well-meaning German philosopher IMMANUEL KANT (1724–1804) tried to save the West from empirical skepticism, but he only made matters worse. He first turned his attention to empirical knowledge, primarily to save SCIENCE, which had long assumed that its empirical knowledge had referred to something real. Agreeing with Hume that science's knowledge might not refer directly to the external world, Kant argued that it was nevertheless true, because it was based on universal structures of the human mind. Space and time, quantity and quality, and substance and causality were universal aspects of thought, Kant said, and it was the human mind that, with these structures, made knowledge of the external world possible, not the other way around. Using mental structures, science synthesized phenomena and thereby arrived at real truth. However, although he may have cast aside Hume's bent hook, Kant seemed also to place the fish of the sea of history in the aquarium of the human mind.

For Kant, science kept one foot in the known world of phenomena, but morality and religion were entirely removed from that world. Morality and religion depended on one's own private will to do what is good, but this will derived neither from sense experience nor from pure and universal reasons of the mind. Nevertheless, Kant argued that the moral will was thoroughly real, so that people should examine it and uncover and affirm what it presupposed. Among those presuppositions was a God who would reward moral efforts in HEAVEN as they were not rewarded on Earth. However, this God was derived from reasoning about one's internal, spiritual life and had no empirical basis.

Kant's efforts were about as helpful to religious empiricism as ocean water is to a thirsty person. Kant may have saved science's indirect access to phenomena of physical history, but at the same time he removed God from physical history. For Kant, religious meaning was derived from reasoning about the subjective human spirit, not from the social and incarnational histories so important to the ancient Israelites and Christians.

The solution offered by Kant and other nineteenth-century philosophical idealists caused the great majority of theologians of the nineteenth and twentieth centuries to locate religious knowledge more in the private and spiritual events of a person's heart and mind than in the public and material events of a society's history. For these theologians, people might sit in the train of spatial-temporal history, but their religious dreams were about a world outside spatial-temporal history. These theologians were more attuned to Plato and Aristotle, whose sublime ideas existed somehow apart from historical contingency, and less attuned to the biblical worlds in which material and spiritual history were united and made up all the world there was.

Anticipations of Empirical Theology

Empirical theology was primarily an American effort to return to the world of Locke and to begin again to interrogate carefully the external world in search of concrete evidence on which to base religious experience and knowledge. Reverting to where Locke had left off, empirical theologians were blessed—some say cursed—with the naiveté of those who assumed that they perceived a world external to themselves.

This recovery began with American theologian JONATHAN EDWARDS, whom historian Perry Miller has called "the first and most radical, even though the most tragically misunderstood, of American empiricists" (Miller 1948:137). Admittedly, Miller's interpretation stands against what may be the more accepted interpretation: that Edwards was a philosophical idealist, more influenced by the CAMBRIDGE PLATONISTS than by Locke's empiricism. According to Miller, the youthful Edwards obtained a copy of Locke's *Essay Concerning Human Understanding* and understood in a flash why Locke had replaced understanding based on ideas innate to the human mind with ideas derived from the five senses. But Edwards became the protege who carried the master's doctrine further than had the master; he bridled at Locke's restriction of perception to the five senses and asserted that there were other forms of perception, specifically what he called "the sense of the heart." The sense of the heart was not only an affection, but also a form of perception—one that, for example, went beyond the idea that God was holy or displeased and actually perceived God's holiness or displeasure, just as the actual taste of the sweetness of honey went beyond the idea that honey is sweet. With this fuller empiricism, Edwards argued, for example, that religious words can be restored through renewing the perception on which they are based; that when SIN alienates the inclinations, one's perception can be newly opened to God's spirit as it is perceived in God's works; and that sensational PREACHING (for example, revivalist preaching about damnation) can enliven the sense of the heart.

Although America had to wait more than 100 years for the next great theorist of religious empiricism, WILLIAM JAMES (1842–1910), this is not to say that empirical theology in various popular forms was absent in America from Edwards's death in 1758 until the 1870s, when James came into his own. Pietistic evangelicals made religious affections key to religious identity, thereby centering theological truth on a religious experience that might be called "religious perception of religious evidence." This PIETISM began at least with the first Great Awakening (1740–1742) (see AWAKENINGS); was sustained by various Congregationalist, Methodist, Baptist, Disciples, Presbyterian, and independent groups; was boosted by a series of large REVIVALS lasting until at least 1875; and grew stronger through the twentieth century and into the twenty-first century. However, connections between pietistic evangelicals and empirical theologians were seldom appreciated, because each group regarded the other suspiciously across a canyon of cultural differences.

Meanwhile, like Edwards, James carried the empiricism of Locke to a deeper level, calling it "radical empiricism." James began as a materialistic empiricist, first as a medical student and then as the psychologist who set up America's first laboratory for psychological research. However, his investigations led him to believe that clear and conscious sensations of medical facts were less important than the relations among the facts—the "near, next, like, from, towards, against, because, for, through"—none of which could be sensed. These relations convey the desire underlying a sensed activity, the goal that it seeks, and the dangerousness, beauty, and utility that it conveys. For James, these are "affective phenomena" or "appreciative attributes," missed entirely by Locke (and, later, by the twentieth-century positivists, who would confine perception to reports of the five senses). Perceiving these relations, we do not just invent, guess at, or think about the feelings and values in the external world, but actually feel them.

In *Varieties of Religious Experience* and *A Pluralistic Universe,* James argued that religious experience itself could be a form of nonsensuous perception. Religion is a person's "total reaction upon life," and

religious perception is "that curious sense of the whole residual cosmos as an everlasting presence, intimate or alien, terrible or amusing" (James 1985:36–37). Within that cosmos, the divine is perceived as "a wider self," "a more," escaping our exact knowledge much as human language escapes the knowledge of the cat dozing at our feet as we converse in a library. James became the first scientist to reconcile and make singular what had been two separate worlds, one religious and spiritual, the other irreligious and physical. Admittedly, James did not reach this point single-handedly, but rather with the guidance of many Europeans—perhaps most obviously the French philosopher Henri Bergson (1859–1941).

James's radical empiricism was extended by the English-American mathematician and philosopher of science Alfred North Whitehead (1861–1947) and by fellow pragmatist John Dewey (1859–1952). When Whitehead, already a famed mathematician and philosopher of science, came to the UNITED STATES at age 63, he published in rapid succession at least seven books, each of which gave abstract knowledge a basis in vague physical experience. For Whitehead, primitive perception became less like a pipeline for clear and distinct impressions and more a means of registering the emotional impact of surrounding circumstances. For example, he pointed to the incomprehensible sense of attraction or repulsion felt as one enters a room, making one feel like an iron filing entering a magnet's field of force. Because of this, and often against their will, people find themselves making spontaneous, half-conscious judgments that are colored in ways they cannot understand. For Whitehead, conscious, clear sense experience and thought were only the unreliable abstractions from this rich soup of feeling. Impishly, Whitehead had stood Plato, René Descartes, Locke, and Hume on their heads; for him, vague, barely conscious, physical feeling was no longer the contaminated effluvia of reliable knowledge, but rather the solid rock on which all knowledge is built.

Whitehead believed that the religious response began as a feeling, not as an idea but rather as a vague intuition of the sacred. It was a perception of the one reality that stood beyond the chaos of the mundane world—the one reality that organizes and evaluates what otherwise is "a mass of pain and mystery" and that lures the perceiver to more intense satisfactions. Calling this reality "God," Whitehead contended that it incites us to embrace, integrate, and enjoy as much of the world's diversity as we can endure, to evolve rather than to devolve or to settle for the flat plane of monotonous repetition. God is best known directly, through mostly unconscious perception rather than through any text, ritual, or institution.

Just as Whitehead, in classic empirical fashion, moved beyond the abstraction of mathematics, John Dewey moved beyond the abstractions of German idealist GEORG WILHELM FRIEDRICH HEGEL and began to think like a Darwinian and to talk of an "immediate empiricism" (see DARWINIANISM). Organisms lived in environments, and organisms and environments changed so regularly that they would continually lose life-sustaining connections with each other. To save themselves from destruction and to attain a new synchronicity with their environments, human organisms envisioned new forms of "the whole." They imagined a new and wider universe, one capacious enough to bring changing environments and organisms back into a working relation with each other. Finally, this whole not only was imagined, but also was perceived with what Dewey called a "sense of totality," "the sense of an extensive and underlying whole," an apprehension of an "imaginative totality"—or, most simply, "a sense of the whole." Perceived aesthetically, Dewey said in *Art as Experience*, this wholeness is an art object; perceived religiously, Dewey said in *A Common Faith*, this wholeness to the universe can be called "God," for it accomplishes what God is said to accomplish.

Four Empirical Theologians

Here was an American intellectual heritage, philosophically rich, theologically original, and religiously suggestive; but, except for Edwards, its authors were philosophers of religion rather than theologians. Four Americans who were modern theologians took up the task of theologically enlarging this prototype for empirical theology, connecting it with biblical and traditional questions of theology as well as with the cosmologies and methods of the sciences. Their writing, as well as writings of those who have echoed and extended their work, can be grasped quickly if it is seen in the light cast by the Edwards and the new philosophers of religion.

In 1919, Douglas Clyde Macintosh's *Theology as an Empirical Science* argued that theology should adopt some of the empirical methods of the natural sciences, and Macintosh proposed a genre of "new theology." A Canadian who taught at Yale University, Macintosh (1877–1948) argued that theologians must first discern what God seems to have accomplished in the world. Only then can they arrive at concepts of God, inferring what God must be if God is to do what God has done. Subsequently, when theologians have more fully formed their concepts of God, they must apply them to the world's evidence and test them for their truth. For Macintosh, theology was based on perception of the world, but was not radical in James's

sense or immediate in Dewey's sense, nor did it rely on the elemental forms of physical apprehension to which Whitehead would turn. Instead, it relied on the reports of the senses to discover God's overt effects in a world of everyday events. Nevertheless, Macintosh's work stood squarely in the line of British ENLIGHTENMENT empiricism and of the basic American turn to empirical evidence advocated by Edwards, James, Dewey, and Whitehead. Macintosh's concept of God also was, however, classically orthodox in making God absolute and unambiguously good.

In *Religious Experience and Scientific Method*, Henry Nelson Wieman (1884–1975) acknowledged that God can be more or less perceived in vague and noncognitive experiences. This meant that what we sensuously perceive is mere oil on the surface of a deep religious ocean of experience. However, because this nonsensuous experience was so ephemeral, Wieman concentrated on what was empirically more obvious: the difference between what we by ourselves are able to create and what in fact we do create. In short, we know that we are given opportunities for creativity that we have not given ourselves. Wieman called the giver of those opportunities "God" and enjoined his readers to admit that they are utterly dependent on this God. In *The Source of Human Good*, Wieman argued that the reality of this source of human good was so palpably obvious that atheism was absurd, so that our principal responsibility was to find ways to collaborate with it. Humans would best collaborate by doing all they could to open themselves to what is strange to them, absorb it, synthesize it, and allow it to change their lives, particularly to advance the creativity of their communities. All of this was possible, however, only because a source of creativity stood behind the process; the experience of this source of creativity was the experience of God.

Bernard Eugene Meland (1899–1993) was Wieman's student and colleague, but, as an empiricist, he was the first major theological voice for the nonsensuous empiricism of James, Dewey, and Whitehead. Meland sought evidence for the divine in the subtle subsurface of the experienced world. Much as James held out for an experience of a "More," Dewey for a sense of the "whole," and Whitehead for an intuition of the sacred, Meland held out for an appreciative awareness of the "Creative Passage" experienced at the vague and indefinite margins of conscious experience. Toward the end of his career, especially in *Fallible Forms and Symbols*, Meland would thunder against fellow theologians, even fellow empirical theologians, who would crudely, he thought, demand precision in human thought about what was deeper than human thought. Meland's corrective was not to invoke a judging God that would correct finite and sinful efforts to describe God, not to invoke the mystics of the East or West who would dismiss the world, but rather to call for more deft and sensitive ways of religiously discerning the concrete world. Meland aspired to lay hold of that which lay behind the surface of cultural, political, and scientific phenomena, without distorting it.

Bernard M. Loomer (1911–1985), like Wieman and Meland, was a professor at the Divinity School of the University of Chicago, but became less rationalistic and more empirical only in the last decade of his life, after he had moved to The Graduate Theological Union in Berkeley, CA. As a disciple of Whitehead, Loomer was a nonsensuous empiricist, concentrating on the aesthetic character of specifically religious experience. He took Wieman's lead and focused on the need to internalize and reconcile within ourselves those things that diverge most from our expectations. But he went beyond Wieman in suggesting that, in their appreciation for ambiguity, people could perceive God nonsensuously, as "the organic restlessness of the whole body of creation," which promoted the creative diversity of the universe. In its concentration on contrast within identity, this perception was more aesthetic than moral or spiritual. Loomer wrote no books, but his essay "The Size of God," written shortly before his death, became unexpectedly influential. There, unlike Wieman, Loomer acknowledged that God was morally ambiguous, promoting both the good and the evil that creativity makes possible.

For all their independent theological genius, the works of these most important empirical theologians (with the possible exception of Macintosh) are best understood as extensions of the breakthroughs achieved by James, Dewey, and Whitehead. None of them seriously attempted to revise biblical interpretation, historic traditions of religious thought, or ecclesiastical symbols. Although their theological writings opened new doors and spawned an empirical style in theology, their full theological promise is yet to be realized.

The Future of Empirical Theology

At first, the wisdom of empirical theology seemed to be demonstrated by the disciples it inspired, and the realization of its full theological promise seemed imminent. But the story of the students and followers of the empirical theologians grew unexpectedly complicated, for empirical theology was made problematic in the 1980s by the new postmodernists' distrust of metaphysics and empiricism, as well as by their fondness for pluralism and relativism (see POSTMODERNITY). The postmodernists challenged empiricism's assumption that evidence could be known objectively and that

religious truth could be justified by reference to its sources. Empirical theology's line of argument split into three forks, none of which simply extended the original trajectory.

Those who most closely followed that trajectory of empirical theology attempted to revise empirical theology for a new age. Some (e.g., Jerome Stone, Tyron Inbody) reconceived empirical theology. Others elaborated the empirical implications of Whitehead's philosophy of religion and formed one branch of what came to be called "PROCESS THEOLOGY." These Whiteheadians focused on naturalism and ECOLOGY (e.g., Donald Crosby, Jay McDaniel), on social justice and economic development (e.g., Marjorie Suchocki, John Cobb), and on the examination of parapsychology and scientific empiricism (e.g., David Griffin).

A second group, more deeply shocked by postmodern attitudes, veered away from the trajectory of empirical theology without abandoning it altogether. They found in postmodern thought new and unexpected grounds for a modest empirical theology. They acknowledged that the naturalistic metaphysics of empirical theology had been undermined. However, they found possibilities for revising empirical theology in philosophical deconstructionism, neopragmatism, and a new historicism. They focused the empirical meanings of history (e.g., William Dean), TRADITION (e.g., Delwin Brown), and pragmatism (e.g., Sheila Davaney). Others called for less explicitly Christian and more pluralistic revisions of empirical theology (e.g., Nancy Frankenberry, Marvin Shaw).

Later, a third group of students and friends of empirical theology (e.g., Frankenberry, Creighton Peden) took shape. They accepted the theological damage caused by the new turn away from metaphysics and toward pluralism and relativism, abandoned efforts at the revision of empirical theology, retained their affection for their former heroes, but called for the decent and complete burial of their theology.

Empirical theology had carried tantalizingly far the latent empiricism of the BIBLE and the explicit empiricism of Francis Bacon. At the beginning of the twenty-first century, a critical reaction to postmodern skepticism is setting in. If this permits the restoration of empirical theology, then its task will be, at last, to return the favor that it long ago received, changing secular CULTURE as it had once been changed by that culture.

References and Further Reading

Dean, William. *American Religious Empiricism*. New York: State University of New York Press, 1986.
Dean, William, and Larry Axel, eds. *The Size of God: The Theology of Bernard Loomer in Context*. Macon, GA: Mercer University Press, 1987.

Dewey, John. *A Common Faith.* New Haven, CT: Yale University Press, 1934.

Frankenberry, Nancy. *Religion and Radical Empiricism.* New York: State University of New York Press, 1987.

Inbody, Tyron. *The Constructive Theology of Bernard Meland.* Atlanta, GA: Scholars Press, 1995.

James, William. *The Varieties of Religious Experience.* Cambridge, MA: Harvard University Press, 1985.

Macintosh, Douglas Clyde. *Theology as an Empirical Science.* New York: Arno Press, 1980.

Meland, Bernard E. *Faith and Culture.* New York: Oxford University Press, 1953.

Miller, Perry, "Jonathan Edwards on the Sense of the Heart." *Harvard Theological Review* 41 (1948): 123–145.

Miller, Randolph Crump, ed. *Empirical Theology: A Handbook.* Birmingham, AL: Religious Education Press, 1992.

Stone, Jerome. *The Minimalist Vision of Transcendence.* Albany, NY: The State University of New York Press, 1992.

Whitehead, Alfred North. *Process and Reality: Corrected Edition.* New York: The Free Press, 1987.

Wieman, Henry Nelson. *The Source of Human Good.* Atlanta, GA: The Scholars Press, 1995.

Winslow, Ola Elizabeth, ed. *Jonathan Edwards: Basic Writings.* New York: New American Library, 1966.

WILLIAM DEAN

ENGLAND

Protestant beliefs first began to make an impact in England during the fifteenth century, and their residual impact was a significant factor in the English Reformation and the creation of a Protestant CHURCH OF ENGLAND by 1558. Tensions between English Protestants in the late sixteenth and early seventeenth centuries resulted in the creation of a number of Protestant churches outside the established Church of England after 1660, and there were further secessions from the established church after the evangelical revival of the eighteenth century. By the mid-nineteenth century, there were many different Protestant churches in England, but Protestantism remained the dominant religion. Although Protestantism was still the religion of two-thirds of English Christians in the late twentieth century, it had been greatly weakened by the growth of Roman Catholicism in England, the growth in the number of people following non-Christian faiths, and the overall decline of religious observance since 1850.

The Origins of Protestantism in England

The origins of English Protestantism are to be found in the teachings of John Wycliffe (c. 1330–1384) and his followers, the Lollards. Wycliffe attacked papal AUTHORITY, advocated a literal interpretation of scripture, and rejected the doctrine of TRANSUBSTANTIATION. The Lollards promoted these ideas in highly populist language. Though Lollardy was driven underground by persecution, its beliefs survived until the 1520s, when

they began to be fused with the doctrines of LUTHERANISM, imported to England as a result of trade with the Dutch and North German ports. Lutheran ideas also began to be adopted by a number of university-based English theologians.

The Reformation in England

Protestant doctrines were not, however, a major element in the first phase of the English Reformation in the reign of HENRY VIII. This involved only a breach with Rome, and Catholic DOCTRINE was strictly enforced, though some leading churchmen, such as THOMAS CRANMER, clearly wished to move the English church in a more Protestant direction. This was only achieved, briefly, in the reign of Edward VI (1548–1553) and, finally, after the succession of ELIZABETH I in 1558. English Protestantism of the late sixteenth century was Calvinist rather than Lutheran in doctrine, both in the BOOK OF COMMON PRAYER and the THIRTY-NINE ARTICLES, but the English church retained both episcopacy (see BISHOP and EPISCOPACY) and the administrative structure of the pre-Reformation church, as well as some modest elements of Catholic ceremonial in its public WORSHIP. Starting in the 1560s, an extreme Protestant lobby within the English church pressed for the abolition of bishops, of special VESTMENTS used by the CLERGY, and of the limited ceremonial permitted by the *Book of Common Prayer.* The late twentieth century brought a major reassessment of the impact of PURITANISM within the English church in the late sixteenth century, and it has been shown that the moderate form of CALVINISM adopted by the church leadership enjoyed widespread support throughout England.

Puritans versus Arminians

Further conflict between Puritans and non-Puritans in England took place in the early seventeenth century as a result of the deliberate rejection of Calvinism and the adoption of ARMINIANISM by many English bishops and clergy. This was combined with the introduction of more ceremony into the church services and relocation of the ALTAR from the body of the church to the east end of the chancel, where it was railed in and covered with an elaborate carpet to emphasize its sacramental nature. Puritan opposition to Arminian bishops, such as LANCELOT ANDREWES and WILLIAM LAUD, was a major factor in the English CIVIL WARS of the 1640s, which resulted in the temporary abolition of episcopacy in 1645 and of the monarchy in 1649. During the 1650s both CONGREGATIONALISM and PRESBYTERIANISM were widely adopted in England. A number of congregations of BAPTISTS had also been formed in the early seventeenth century, and these were also tolerated. More extremist Protestant groups, such as the LEVELLERS and SOCIETY OF FRIENDS, were not.

Episcopacy was re-established with the restoration of the monarchy in 1660. Although efforts were made to accommodate the different groups of Puritans, these were not wholly successful, and a number of Puritan clergy were ejected. These clergy and their followers set up their own Congregational or Presbyterian churches, all of which, together with those of the Baptists, were granted limited TOLERATION in the 1680s. Protestant dissenters from the established church, however, remained relatively few during the first half of the eighteenth century and were excluded from political and public office (see DISSENT). After the withdrawal of the more extreme Puritans, the Church of England reverted to the high church doctrines and practices favored by the Arminian bishops of the early seventeenth century, and this outlook dominated Anglican theology until the mid-nineteenth century. This THEOLOGY included a strong belief in the divine nature of monarchy and the importance of the close links between CHURCH AND STATE.

The Evangelical Revival

During the eighteenth century, both PIETISM and rationalism had a major impact on the Protestant churches in England. Pietism resulted in the Evangelical Revival, which began with JOHN WESLEY, CHARLES WESLEY, and GEORGE WHITEFIELD in the Church of England in the 1730s. Whereas the Wesleys were Arminian in doctrine, Whitefield was a Calvinist. Both groups, however, were anxious to remain within the established Church of England but gradually withdrew, in the case of the Wesleyans not until the 1790s, as a result of Episcopal and clerical opposition. METHODISM, as it was generally termed, was opposed by the bishops on the grounds that it encouraged religious enthusiasm and might lead to political radicalism and a breach in the close relationship between church and state, and also because they believed (wrongly in many cases) that Methodists were seeking to reintroduce within the Church of England the Calvinist doctrines that ANGLICANISM had rejected in the early seventeenth century. In fact, it was the Calvinist minority within Methodism that, with relatively few exceptions, remained within the Church of England and provided the core membership of Anglican EVANGELICALISM in the nineteenth century.

Rationalist influences within the Protestant churches in England had their greatest impact on NONCONFORMITY, because determined action by the bishops ensured that they made little headway in the Church of England. As a result, most English Presbyterian congregations, together with some Baptist and Congregational ones, adopted what was variously described as ARIANISM, SOCINIANISM, or Unitarianism during the second half of the eighteenth century (see UNITARIAN; UNIVERSALIST ASSOCIATION). However, traditional, non-Unitarian, Protestant nonconformity was stimulated by the secessions of the Methodists and some Calvinist evangelicals from the Church of England, with the result that by the religious census of 1851, the numbers of Protestant nonconformists almost equaled the number of those who attended the services of the Church of England, and in some parts of the country (e.g., Cornwall and many midland and northern towns) they greatly exceeded them.

Religious Tensions in the Early Nineteenth Century

Until the second half of the twentieth century, there was general agreement among historians that the growth of Protestant nonconformity in England had been the result of spiritual and theological stagnation in the Church of England in the eighteenth and early nineteenth centuries. This view has now been challenged, and it is clear that, although the Church of England may not have been responding to demands for a more evangelical type of Protestantism, it was far from decadent. From about 1780, there was a major movement of ecclesiastical reform led by the bishops that anticipated parts of the reform program resulting from Parliamentary legislation in the 1830s. Nevertheless, the growth in the numbers of those who had been excluded, or who excluded themselves, from the Church of England resulted in a series of parliamentary measures in the 1820s in which many of the remaining, largely political restrictions on non-Anglicans, both Protestant nonconformists and Roman Catholics, were removed. Pressure from non-Anglicans and anticlericalists also resulted in the administrative reforms sponsored by Parliament in the 1830s, which allowed the Church of England to respond more satisfactorily to the demographic and social changes brought about by INDUSTRIALIZATION.

These same pressures also brought about a Catholic revival in the Church of England, the OXFORD MOVEMENT, determined to reassert the independence of the Church of England from state control and the authority of its bishops and clergy. This movement began with the redefinition of Anglican theology, but through its association with ROMANTICISM and its eventual desire to return to a somewhat ill-defined pre-Reformation "golden age," by the 1840s it had resulted in significant changes to the design of Anglican churches and the presentation of Anglican worship that were widely seen as bringing the Church of England closer to the Roman Catholic Church. These changes were strongly opposed, not just by Protestant nonconformists, but also by evangelicals within the Church of England (see CATHOLICISM, PROTESTANT REACTIONS). It was also opposed by a growing number of liberal or broad church theologians and their supporters, who had generally approved the parliamentary reform program of the 1830s and who wanted the Church of England to adopt both a progressive political outlook and a theology sympathetic to the less literal interpretation of scripture on which both Anglican high churchmen and Evangelicals were agreed. It is a matter of debate among historians as to whether this division of the Church of England into more clearly identified church parties was a strength, in that it promoted comprehensiveness, or a weakness, in that it shattered the broad theological consensus that had existed within the Church of England before the 1830s.

Protestantism in England Since 1850

In due course, both the Catholic and the liberal movements within the Church of England had their impact on Protestant nonconformity, and many of the divisions that existed within the established church were replicated (although usually in a less extreme form) within the various nonconformist churches. The nonconformist churches themselves became almost part of a new, more pluralist, religious establishment. During the second half of the nineteenth century, a number of new Protestant organizations, including the SALVATION ARMY, emerged to offer less structured forms of ministry and worship that had more appeal to the lower social classes, many of whom had, even by the 1851 religious census, ceased to attend services in the more traditional churches. This shift continued in the twentieth century with the establishment of and rapid growth in PENTECOSTALISM, especially among immigrant Afro-Caribbean communities in the major cities. By the early years of the twentieth century, all of the more traditional Protestant churches in England were in severe decline, as was Protestantism as a whole. Along with the growth of new Protestant churches was a significant increase in the Roman Catholic population. This increase had begun in the 1840s with conversions from the Church of England, resulting from the Oxford Movement, and immigration from IRELAND after the potato famine of the 1840s. By the 1990s, even Roman Catholicism was in decline in England, and it was generally estimated that the 10 percent of the population who were regular churchgoers were more or less evenly divided (one-third each) among the Church of England, the Roman

Catholic Church, and the non-Anglican Protestant churches.

Protestantism and the English Nation

Over the four and a half centuries of its existence, Protestantism in England has closely identified itself with a strong sense of English nationalism and has seen its fortunes as being closely bound up with that of the nation as a whole. Despite the long record of religious toleration in England compared with many other European countries, a clear manifestation of militant anti-Catholicism in England was sustained until well into the twentieth century. The vestiges of this remain in the legislation that prevents the monarch from being, or marrying, a Roman Catholic. This alliance between Englishness and Protestantism is deep-rooted and frequently subconscious in a nation that has largely ceased to practice formal religion. However, during the eighteenth and nineteenth centuries, the defense of the Protestant constitution was a matter on which all English Protestants, whether in the established Church of England or in one of the nonconformist churches, could agree. The result was that, despite some pressure from nonconformists for disestablishment in the late nineteenth century, disestablishment never really became a major nonconformist demand in England in the way that it did in WALES, where it was linked with issues of language and nationality. That Protestant bond in England, and the strength of anti-Catholicism, also led to occasions in both the late nineteenth and early twentieth centuries in which evangelicals within the established church and Protestant nonconformists outside it formed alliances against movements in the Church of England that critics felt were moving it closer to Roman Catholicism. As the Church of England began to recognize that religious pluralism was a reality, it became more willing to recognize Protestant nonconformity as almost a part of the Protestant establishment, and ecumenical dialogue between the mainstream Protestant churches in England took place much earlier than that between the Church of England and the Roman Catholic Church (see ECUMENISM, DIALOGUE, INTERCONFESSIONAL).

Although there have been good relations between the long-established Protestant churches in England (which has not always been extended to some of the newer Protestant churches), for much of the last century this led to few examples of organic reunion. Although the different branches of Methodism came together in a formal union in 1932, and a later union between Congregational and Presbyterian churches created the United Reformed Church, attempts to unite the Anglican and Methodist churches failed in the 1960s and 1970s. However, since 1970, a growing number of Protestant churches, including the Church of England, have agreed to share a building, particularly in areas of new housing, and a few of these shared churches have included Roman Catholic participation. There have also been a number of joint initiatives between the mainstream Protestant churches in England in the field of ministerial and theological training.

References and Further Reading

Aston, M. *Lollards and Reformers: Images and Literacy in Late Medieval England.* London: Hambledon Press, 1984.

Bebbington, D. W. *Evangelicalism in Modern Britain: A History from the 1730s to the 1980s.* London and New York: Routledge, 1989.

Chadwick, W. O. *The Victorian Church,* 2 vols. London: Adam and Charles Black, 1966 and 1970.

Clark, J. C. D. *English Society 1688–1932: Ideology, Social Structure and Political Practice During the Ancien Régime,* Cambridge: Cambridge University Press, 1985.

Collinson, P. *The Religion of Protestants: The Church in English Society 1559–1625,* Oxford, UK: Clarendon Press, 1982.

Davies, H. *Worship and Theology in England,* 6 vols. Grand Rapids, MI: Eerdmans, 1996.

Hastings, A. *A History of English Christianity 1920–1990.* London: SCM Press, 1991.

Rupp, E. G. *Religion in England 1688–1791.* Oxford, UK: Clarendon Press, 1986.

Spurr, J. *English Puritanism 1603–1689.* Basingstoke, UK: Macmillan, 1998.

Tyacke, N. *Anti-Calvinists: The Rise of English Arminianism c.1590–1640.* Oxford, UK: Clarendon Press, 1987.

Ward, W. R. *Religion and Society in England 1790–1850.* London: Batsford, 1972.

Watts, M. R. *The Dissenters,* 2 vols. Oxford, UK: Clarendon Press, 1978 and 1995.

NIGEL YATES

ENLIGHTENMENT

The term "Enlightenment" refers to the vast and various trends in thought that marked the European eighteenth century and had a great sociopolitical and cultural impact in Europe and beyond. Supported by the intellectual elites of the time, the movement took on different names—*Lumières, Aufklärung, Enlightenment, Illuminismo, Illustración*—and shapes depending on the different modalities brought on by the cultural and religious context of each country. Enlightenment thought questioned the legitimacy of the powers in place; examined the foundations of social, political, and religious order; developed a criticism of political as well as religious matters; and encouraged tolerance as well as free and encyclopedic knowledge. Fully confident in the powers of reason and the virtues of knowledge, advocates of the Enlightenment dreamed of a better world and chose to be optimistic.

The fight was against obscurantism, ignorance, religious fanaticism, and superstitions in favor of education, separation of politics from religion, freedom of conscience, and human rights. One of the main roots of Western modernity (see MODERNISM) unquestionably grows out of the Enlightenment of the eighteenth century, even though the genealogy of this modernity may require going further back in time than this age, appropriately called "Age of Enlightenment." To take a sociohistorical approach to the Enlightenment is to break out of the simplistic schema that opposes modernity to religion as two antagonistic and external worlds where the progress of modernity would ineluctably cause the decline of religion. The sociohistorical research shows the plurality of historical figures of the Enlightenment and its complex relationship with religion.

The Enlightenment may have been furthered by some great leaders in the fields of philosophy, science, and politics, but it also manifested itself through varied means that contributed to the social spread of ideas. The many societies of the eighteenth century (e.g., learned societies, reading societies, economic societies), the sociability of the salons, the use of French as the language of the intelligentsia at the time, the magazines and books, the relation between thinkers and politicians—all helped create an international network of influence and emulation. Thus the Royal Academy of Berlin, founded in 1701 with the participation of GOTTFRIED LEIBNIZ, became an important center of intellectual life under Frederic II from 1740 to 1770. With the establishment of the Great Lodge of England in 1717, FREEMASONRY championed the Enlightenment by relativizing the differences in faiths and by promoting tolerance and free debate. The spirit of the Enlightenment appeared in FRANCE particularly through the endeavor of the *Encyclopédie ou Dictionnaire Raisonné des Sciences, des Arts, et des Métiers,* which, under Diderot's leadership, gathered a great number of philosophers and scientists, the best known being Montesquieu, Voltaire, JEAN-JACQUES ROUSSEAU, d'Alembert, Buffon, the Baron of Holbach, and Turgot. After many mishaps and in spite of the royal opposition (as soon as Volume II was published in 1752, a warrant from the king's counsel banned the work), the venture was successfully completed. It showed a will to further scientific knowledge, supported by a belief in progress, which had to confront all political and religious barriers that were raised against free investigation. The Jesuits saw in it "Satan's Bible."

What is the Enlightenment? IMMANUEL KANT, in his famous essay, *Was ist Aufklärung?* Explains: "What is the Enlightenment? It is man leaving his self-caused minority. Minority, that is inability to use his own intelligence without another's guidance. A self-caused minority since its cause resides not in a lack of intelligence, but in a lack of determination and courage to use it without another's guidance. *Sapere aude!* Have the courage to use your *own* intelligence! That is the motto of the Enlightenment" (Bahr 1974: 9). Through the demand for a free use of reason the AUTHORITY principle in politics as well as religion is questioned. This questioning rests on the assertion that any human can and must exercise his or her liberty of thought on all things, together with the insistence on the universality of criticism and the affirmation of the rights of the individual (see INDIVIDUALISM). A vital moment in the emergence of the idea of tolerance, the Enlightenment combines universalism and cosmopolitism. Thus the philosopher PIERRE BAYLE (1647–1706), author of the famous *Dictionnaire Critique et Historique* (1696–1697) that aimed to review in a critical fashion all positions, declared in 1700, "I am a citizen of the world, I am neither in the Emperor's service, nor in the King of France's service, but in the truth's service." It is on this universalistic base that the Age of Enlightenment would dream of a better world and generate several emancipation utopias.

This Age was more anticlerical than antireligious. Religions were to be founded rationally, with an insistence on individual conscience and the full acknowledgment of the social purpose of religion. Within this frame of thought some enlightened Christians would seek to join the philosophes by extolling a Christianity stripped of superstitions and taking its inspiration from the early centuries. The spirit of Enlightenment sought an internal transformation, an interiorization of FAITH. This Age is not only that of Reason, it is also that of feeling and subjectivity: *Aufklärung* and PIETISM in Protestantism (with Kant, for example), *Haskala* (Jewish Enlightenment) and Hasidism in JUDAISM, Enlightened Catholicism, and Jansenism kept close ties. Still the acceptance of the Enlightenment was varied and one should not sway too much in the opposite direction by emphasizing unilaterally the symbiosis between Enlightenment and religion. Not only did some religions radically oppose the Enlightenment, but the Enlightenment itself became radical in some instances and countries, which fostered conflicts with religions. This was especially the case in France, where the subsequent history would tend to accredit a fundamental opposition between Enlightenment and religion, religion and progress. By the end of the eighteenth century the French philosopher Condorcet (1743–1794) declared himself openly atheist and led an extremist fight against the Catholic CLERGY. Overall the Enlightenment's relations with Catholicism were more difficult and conflictive than they were with Protestantism (this

in spite of the existence of many Enlightened Catholics).

Protestantism and Enlightenment

"Protestant churches themselves were quite receptive to adopting the ideals of the Enlightenment. The reading of the BIBLE had promoted a rational education, the use of philological means to interpret texts was usual, and the LAITY benefited from it. The plurality of faiths could be positively conceived as a plurality of means to attain SALVATION. The collegial structure of the church—especially with regards to Reformed churches—allowed for peer debate" (Im Hof 1993: 175). Unlike Latin countries of Catholic culture, in Anglo-Saxon countries religion and Enlightenment closely blended rather than being opposed. The quest for a rational version of religion provided, aside from the Evangelical awakening, a stimulus for change. In Great Britain and the UNITED STATES freemasonry was a para-Protestant organization among other religious alternatives rather than a fierce opposition to the church. George Washington himself was a freemason and an Episcopalian. ENGLAND, which simultaneously was the most counterrevolutionary and the most modern country, engendered an Enlightenment that was magisterial and Christian, supported by the towns' moderate clergy. In England social and intellectual change did not encounter a unified resistance that was politico-religious or lead to antagonistic definitions of religious Enlightenment and secular Enlightenment. In English DISSENT there is both a religious form of Enlightenment and an enlightened form of religion. In Protestant countries, such as Great Britain, Lutheran and Calvinist GERMANY, the Swiss reformed Cantons, or Geneva, the Enlightenment had less anticlerical notes than in Catholic Europe. Religious criticism aimed mainly at historical Christianity only rarely led to openly atheist statements, taking instead the shape of a DEISM advocating the return to a natural religion, bereft of mystery and revelation (in England), or of a cultural and social reformulation that would integrate the religious dimension (German *Aufklärung*). Protestant theologians, sensitive to the demands of the Enlightenment, developed a THEOLOGY subjected to rational control, characterized by content more ethical than dogmatic, careful to eliminate all contradiction between FAITH and reason. Within this perspective CHRISTOLOGY was to lose its central position and Christ, more and more deposed of his divine attributes, would acquire a value more exemplary than redemptory.

Numerous Protestant thinkers made key contributions to the Enlightenment. First are the theorists of NATURAL LAW, the Dutch Calvinist Hugo Grotius

(1583–1645) and the German Lutheran SAMUEL PUFENDORF (1632–1694). Their influence was great in an age, the eighteenth century, that sought new bases to international law and was developing HUMAN RIGHTS; Natural Law inspired the cosmopolitan thought of the Age of Enlightenment. Within the realm of SCIENCE the leader was ISAAC NEWTON, who discovered gravitation (he developed some heterodox positions on religion, notably by calculating the date of the Apocalypse). It is mostly in the field of philosophy, however, that the contributions of Protestant thinkers were important. First of all the English JOHN LOCKE (1632–1704), celebrated by Voltaire in his *Lettres Philosophiques* (1734), was a master of the Enlightenment who advocated tolerance based on the differentiation between civil and religious society (*Epistola de Tolerantia*, 1695). In *The Reasonableness of Christianity* (1695) he outlined a religion promoting the harmony between reason and biblical revelation and whose main dogma was the messianism of Christ. His *Essay concerning Human Understanding* (1690), translated in French by the Huguenot refugee Pierre Coste, would become one of the breviaries of the eighteenth century (see HUGUENOTS). Then the French Bayle reminds us that the *Internationale du Refuge Huguenot* represents the first generation of the Enlightenment (Huguenot refugees would contribute to the spreading of Enlightenment thought by translating key works by Pufendorf and Locke into French). Bayle vigorously championed freedom of conscience and tolerance by preaching in favor of the rights of the "wandering consciousness" (*Commentaire philosophique sur ces paroles de Jésus-Christ, Contrain-les d'entrer* 1686). The portrait of Bayle as a nonbeliever drawn by Voltaire does not fit the truth.

Aside from Kant, German Lutheran philosophers were key contributors to the Enlightenment, among whom were Leibniz (1646–1716), GOTTHOLD EPHRAÏM LESSING (1729–1781), and CHRISTIAN WOLFF (1679–1754). Positing that CHURCH and politics were not strictly opposed while being distinctive, Leibniz, as an enlightened man, reestablishes the relationship between politics and religion. He laicized political and social exteriority while consecrating interiority, each needing to remain in its place: the church by not imposing any external obligation on the faithful, politics by not imposing any internal obligations. Through an exchange of letters with the Catholic bishop Bossuet (1627–1704), Leibniz also became the precursor of ecumenical dialogue (see ECUMENISM; DIALOGUE, INTERCONFESSIONAL). Wolff, a disciple of Leibniz, distinguished himself not only by his rational thoughts on God, the world, and man (*Métaphysique Allemande* 1719), but most of all by his defense of Natural Law and the political influence it gave him

over different schools of thoughts. He also produced school textbooks in German and Latin that presented the philosophy of the *Aufklärung*. As for Lessing and his investigation of a wisdom based on religious principles as well as his taste for parables (he used to call himself a "lover of theology"), he sought to further the *Aufklärung* within the realm of religion.

The French philosopher Rousseau (1712–1778), despite a temporary conversion to Catholicism, would remain a philosopher of the Enlightenment strongly affected by Protestantism. Against the materialistic and rationalist atheists of his time, he would become in his "Profession de foi du Vicaire savoyard" (Book IV of the *Emile ou de l'Education*, 1762), the apologist of a religion of the heart where sentiment allows one to apprehend God without objectifying Him. His educational ideas developed in *Emile ou de L'Education*, which were influenced by John Locke's ideas, would inspire several Protestant pedagogues, including the German Johannes Bernhardt Basedow (1723–1790), the Swiss Johann Heinrich Pestalozzi (1746–1827), and the French Jean-Frédéric (or JOHANN FRIEDRICH) OBERLIN (1740–1826). Rousseau, who had returned to Protestantism, would answer the archbishop of Paris who along with many others—in particular the Synod and the Petit Conseil of Geneva—condemned the *Emile*, "I follow Writing and reason as the only rules of my belief; I deny the authority of men and will submit to their formulas inasmuch as I perceive the truth." It was an opportunity for Rousseau to state his Christian identity, "I am Christian, not as a disciple of Priests, but as a disciple of Jesus-Christ" (*Lettre à Christophe de Beaumont* from 1763).

"In America, it is religion that leads to Enlightenment; it is the observance of the divine laws that leads man to freedom," ALEXIS DE TOCQUEVILLE noted in *De la Démocratie en Amérique* (1835). The Founding Fathers of what would become the United States, starting with THOMAS JEFFERSON (1743–1826), the main author of the Declaration of Independence, were influenced by the thoughts of the Enlightenment, and most particularly by Locke. With a thought that links, as Tocqueville had noted, the spirit of religion and the spirit of freedom, "We hold these truths to be self-evident, that all men are created equal, that they are endowed by their Creator with certain unalienable Rights, that among these are Life, Liberty and the pursuit of Happiness.—That to secure these rights, Governments are instituted among Men, deriving their just powers from the consent of the governed" (Declaration of Independence of July 4, 1776).

Faith and Enlightenment do not oppose as reason does to superstition or intelligence to obscurantism. If the eighteenth century sanctioned the failure of an ultraconservative, authoritarian, and unitarian view of religion, it did not sanction the failure of religion in general. The eighteenth century also represented a religious mutation, an in-depth evolution that saw religion turn toward the intimacy of consciences while looking to express itself "reasonably." The autonomy of the secular realms (politics, morality, society, etc.) became one of the greatest passions of the Age of Enlightenment, and Kant would devote himself to ensure a status of autonomy for reason. Were human autonomy set against religion as if belonging to a religious faith implied the negation of human autonomy, theologians would answer that the dependency to God is the condition of true human freedom. By speaking of theonomy, a Protestant theologian such as PAUL TILLICH (1886–1965) would place human and world autonomy within a frame that would situate and transcend it.

References and Further Reading

Bahr, Ehrhard, ed. *Was ist Aufklärung? Thesen und Definitionen* (Kant, Erhard, Hamann, Herder, Lessing, Mendelssohn, Riem, Schiller, Wieland). Stuttgart, Germany: Philipp Reclam Jr., 1974.

Brown, Stewart J. and Timothy Tackett (eds.). *Enlightenment, Revolution and Reawakening.* Cambridge: Cambridge University Press, 2003.

Chaunu, Pierre. *La civilisation de l'Europe des Lumières.* Paris: Arthaud, 1971.

Gusdorf, Georges. *Dieu, la nature, l'homme au siècle des lumières.* Paris: Payot, 1972.

Harrison, Peter. *Religion and the Religions in the English Enlightenment.* Cambridge: Cambridge University Press, 2002.

Im Hof, Ulrich. *Das Europa der Aufklärung.* Munich, Germany: C. H. Beck, 1993 (in English, Oxford: Basil Blackwell).

"Les Lumières et les religions (The Enlightenment and Religion)." *Social Compass* 44 no. 2 (June 1997).

McDermott, Gerald R. *Jonathan Edwards Confronts the Gods: Christian Theology, Enlightenment Religion, and Non-Christian Faiths.* Oxford: Oxford University Press, 2000.

May, Henry F. *The Divided Heart: Essays on Protestantism and the Enlightenment in America.* Oxford: Oxford University Press, 1991.

Paul, Jean-Marie. *Dieu est mort en Allemagne. Des Lumières à Nietzsche.* Paris: Payot, 1994.

Plongeron, Bernard. *Théologie et politique au siècle des Lumières (1770–1820).* Geneva, Switzerland: Droz, 1973.

Stanley, Brian ed. *Christian Missions and the Enlightenment (Studies in the History of Christian Missions).* Grand Rapids, MI: Wm. B. Eerdmans Publishing Co., 2001.

JEAN-PAUL WILLAIME

EPHRATA

See Brethren, Church of the

EPISCOPAL CHURCH, SCOTLAND

The CHURCH OF SCOTLAND, established in 1560 at the time of the REFORMATION, alternated for nearly 130 years between Episcopal and Presbyterian forms but maintained its unity during this period. It was the inability of the Scottish bishops to renounce their loyalty to the exiled King James VII, when William of Orange was proclaimed King of Scots in 1689, that led to the disestablishment of episcopacy and the breaking into two what had hitherto existed as a single Protestant church (see BISHOP AND EPISCOPACY). While almost all Episcopal priests in the south of SCOTLAND were immediately thrust out of their livings, many Episcopal priests in the northern half of the country held on to the parish churches until their deaths despite attempts by the Presbyterian authorities to remove them (see PRESBYTERIANISM). The Toleration Act of 1712 made Episcopal ministry legal provided that they prayed for Queen Anne. This split the Episcopali community into jurors, who prayed for Queen Anne and her Hanoverian successors, and nonjurors, who continued to pray for the exiled Stuart monarchy. The failure of the 1715 Rising, however, was followed by the first of a succession of repressive Penal Laws against episcopacy and the final removal of all Episcopal clergy from the parish churches.

It was during the period from 1720 to 1745 that the main features of the Scottish Episcopal Church were consolidated. The system of college bishops, set up as a temporary measure in 1704 to maintain the Episcopal succession, was replaced by diocesan bishops under the Concordate of 1731. From 1724, the Scottish Prayer Book began to develop along a very distinct line, drawing inspiration from the 1549 BOOK OF COMMON PRAYER, the failed 1637 Scottish Prayer Book, and the studies of Bishop Rattray on the Eastern Liturgies. The emerging high sacramental DOCTRINE of the Scottish LITURGY resulted in disputes during the 1740s over the Usages, disputes that were rendered academic by the 1745 Rising.

The aftermath of the 1745 Rising saw a fresh set of penal legislation enacted against episcopacy in Scotland, resulting in imprisonment and exile for several Episcopal priests. Some Episcopal congregation members from the landed and merchant classes decided they could no longer continue to be considered nonjurors and established Qualified chapels with English or Irish clergymen. Although outright attacks on Episcopalians largely ceased after 1760, the strong downward social pressures led to a steady decline in the church over most of the country. Against this background, Bishops William Falconer and Robert Forbes brought out a new Scottish *Prayer Book* in 1764.

By 1784, half of the church's priests were found in the Diocese of Aberdeen alone, as were three of its four bishops. Those three bishops laid the foundations of the worldwide Anglican Communion in Aberdeen by consecrating SAMUEL SEABURY as the first American bishop in 1784, bequeathing the Scottish Liturgy to the American Episcopal Church in the process. The American Episcopal Church also adopted the Scottish pattern of having a primus—a presiding bishop—rather than an archbishop.

The death of Prince Charles in 1788 paved the way for Scottish Episcopal Church to finally abandon its support for the exiled Stuarts and begin to pray for the Hanoverian monarchy. The primus, Bishop John Skinner, was the principal architect of the church's rejuvenation, and his efforts led to the repeal of the Penal Laws in 1792. The Scottish Episcopal Church was obliged to adopt the THIRTY-NINE ARTICLES, but Scottish Episcopal CLERGY were barred from ministering in the CHURCH OF ENGLAND (a bar that applied equally to American Episcopal clergy). Skinner also started the process of reuniting the Qualified churches with the Scottish Episcopal Church.

The nineteenth century brought the regeneration of the Scottish Episcopal Church. A beginning was made with the erection of new church buildings for the ancient congregations. Edinburgh Theological College was founded in 1810, the oldest such college in the Anglican Communion (followed by General Theological Seminary, New York in 1817, then Chichester Theological College, ENGLAND in 1839). During the middle of the nineteenth century, the present arrangement of seven dioceses was settled and new cathedrals were erected in Perth, Inverness, and Edinburgh. By the end of the century, almost every town in Scotland had an Episcopal congregation. Along with mission work at home, the church began to undertake foreign mission work in Chanda, INDIA and Kaffraria (St. John's) in southern AFRICA (see MISSIONS).

In 1840 an Act of Parliament was passed that allowed Scottish Episcopal clergy to minister for one or two Sundays in any church in England. The Scottish bishops succeeded in having this Act extended to include the clergy of the American Episcopal Church. Not until 1864 did the Church of England allow full communion and interchangeability of clergy with the Scottish and American Episcopal Churches.

The OXFORD MOVEMENT reached Scotland in the 1840s, where it found a measure of ready acceptance, owing to the high sacramental doctrine of the Scottish Liturgy. At the same time, there was an increasing number of Oxbridge-educated bishops, mostly with low-church tendencies, who were deeply suspicious of any deviation from the *Book of Common Prayer*. Bishop Forbes was subjected to an ecclesiastical trial in 1860 by his fellow bishops for his high sacramental views, and several other priests were censured or suspended for their support of the Oxford Movement. In 1863 the Scottish Liturgy was relegated to a secondary place in the life of the Scottish Episcopal Church and the *Book of Common Prayer* assumed dominance.

The low-church/high-church tensions within the Scottish Episcopal Church reached a rupture point in Edinburgh in 1842. What initially seemed like a local dispute between Reverend D. T. K. Drummond, who wished to hold evangelical services, and Bishop Terrot, who insisted on strict liturgical services, caused a number of congregations and clergy to withdraw from the Scottish Episcopal Church and attempt to place themselves directly under the authority of the Church of England. Within a few years, more than 20 of these "English Episcopal" chapels were in existence. They received no official support from the Church of England, and by the end of the nineteenth century most of these congregations had either died out or had united with the Scottish Episcopal Church.

In common with most denominations, the Scottish Episcopal Church reached its maximum size at about the beginning of the twentieth century. After World War I, the main mission effort was concentrated in Scotland's four cities. In 1929 a new Scottish Prayer Book reestablished the primacy of the distinctive Scottish Liturgy. Since World War II, rural depopulation and inner-city slum clearance both have led to the closure of churches. Some expansion occurred in the second half of the twentieth century in Scotland's new towns and in the suburban growth areas of the great cities, while new missions were established in the thinly populated far north and west, making use of itinerant priests. Extension of the ministry beyond full-time stipendiary priests took place in two developments: nonstipendiary clergy were appointed from 1973, while WOMEN were admitted as deacons in 1985 and to the priesthood in 1994 (see WOMEN CLERGY). After some years of experimentation, a modern language version of the Scottish Liturgy was produced in 1982. The nature of foreign mission work changed, as the Scottish Episcopal Church ceased direct involvement in Chanda, India in 1958 and the diocese of St. John's in SOUTH AFRICA became more self-reliant.

In the year 2000, the Scottish Episcopal Church had about 51,500 members (about 5 percent of all Scottish church attenders), and 320 churches and places of worship. Recent ecumenical developments have seen a move to sharing some church buildings, particularly with the Church of Scotland and the Roman Catholic Church.

References and Further Reading

Bertie, David M. *Scottish Episcopal Clergy 1689–2000*. Edinburgh: T. & T. Clark, 2000.

Goldie, Frederick. *A Short History of the Episcopal Church in Scotland*. Edinburgh: St. Andrew Press, 1951.

Luscombe, L. Edward. *The Scottish Episcopal Church in the Twentieth Century*. Edinburgh: Scottish Episcopal Church, 1996.

Strong, Rowan. *Episcopalianism in Nineteenth-Century Scotland*. Oxford: Oxford University Press, 2002.

DAVID M. BERTIE

EPISCOPAL CHURCH, UNITED STATES

Colonial Period

The Episcopal Church in the United States began as the American branch of the CHURCH OF ENGLAND. After the Revolutionary War, the church dropped all identification by name with ENGLAND. Organizing itself independently in 1789, it named itself "the Protestant Episcopal Church in the United States of America." The name "episcopal" (Greek *overseer*, corrupted in Anglo-Saxon to *bishop*) stems from the contentious Commonwealth period in English history when CLERGY and LAITY who wanted the Church of England ruled by bishops used the title for themselves (see BISHOP AND EPISCOPACY). In later centuries, the term *Anglican* (from the Latin for "English") came into common use to describe any church that held the faith and practice of the Church of England.

The Anglican faith first appeared in North America in the sixteenth century, when Anglican chaplains accompanying English expeditions conducted services in what became California and North Carolina. With the establishment of Virginia in 1607, the Anglican faith came permanently to America. During the colonial period, the Church of England became the established church (or official state church, supported by legislation and taxes) in six colonies. Its greatest influence was in Virginia, with 250 Anglican churches by 1775. One of the two Anglican institutions of higher learning in the colonies, the College of William and Mary (which had a divinity school to train Anglican clergy), was founded in 1693 in Virginia's colonial capital of Williamsburg.

In South Carolina Anglicanism was strong in the tidewater "low country" but was almost nonexistent in the religionless "back country." In New York, the church's establishment was limited to the more densely populated lower counties. The second Anglican college in the colonies (King's College, now Columbia University) was established in Manhattan in 1754. Like the College of William and Mary, it has since become secular. Two of the three other Anglican-established churches in North Carolina and Georgia (where JOHN WESLEY and CHARLES WESLEY were the first two clergy) existed largely only on paper. With high clergy salaries and prosperous parishes, Maryland provided an exception. The church was also influential in some colonies where it was not established, particularly in Pennsylvania and Connecticut.

The principal organization that attempted to make the colonies Anglican was the London-based SOCIETY FOR THE PROPAGATION OF THE GOSPEL IN FOREIGN PARTS (SPG). From 1701 through the end of the Revolutionary War, the "Venerable Society" dispatched more than 300 missionaries to America and provided funds for their support and for the construction of Anglican churches. Colonial Anglicans existed without resident bishops. Nominal supervision came from the bishop of London, who appointed clerical representatives called "commissaries." Colonists who desired ordination took an expensive and dangerous journey to England to receive deacon's and priest's orders (see DEACONESS, DEACON). By the start of the Revolution, the Church of England was the second-largest denomination in America (after CONGREGATIONALISM) and the most widely diffused. Although its congregations included large numbers of the lower economic classes, its adherents came disproportionately from the economically comfortable or wealthy.

Reorganization

The American Revolution placed Anglican clergy in a unique situation, for on ordination they swore oaths to support the English monarch. Nevertheless, almost half of the colonial Anglican clergy decided to support the Revolution. Emotionally and financially dependent on England, SPG clergy generally became Loyalists; clergy paid directly by parishes typically became Patriots. The vast majority of Anglican lay people supported the Revolutionary cause. More than half of the signers of the Declaration of Independence and many of the American military leaders were Anglicans.

During or immediately after the Revolution, the Church of England was disestablished (or deprived of state support) in all colonies in which it had been established. In several meetings held in Philadelphia in the 1780s, lay and clerical delegates from Anglican parishes in most states established a constitution, drafted an American version of the BOOK OF COMMON PRAYER, and arranged for the American church to secure the consecration of its own bishops in England. The delegates adopted a unitary form of government headed by a General Convention (normally meeting every three years) presided over by a presiding bishop. The Convention consists of a House of Bishops in which all bishops have seats, and a House of Deputies composed of an equal number of clerical and lay delegates. Dioceses (geographical areas administered by a bishop, divided into self-supporting units called parishes) elect the delegates. Elected bodies of lay-people called vestries govern the parishes and also hire the chief minister, or rector.

The first bishops consecrated—all Patriots—came from Pennsylvania, New York, and Virginia. Preceding them was Samuel Seabury the bishop of Connecticut, a Loyalist whose consecration in 1785 at the hands of Scottish bishops was controversial. Following the consecration in 1790 of the president of the College of William and Mary, the "Protestant Episcopal Church" fulfilled its parent church's mandate that it must have three bishops commissioned in England before it could consecrate its own bishops. These Episcopal bishops immediately began to ordain clergy and to consecrate additional bishops. But many states lacked bishops for years, and from the Revolutionary War until late in the twentieth century, the Episcopal Church suffered from a shortage of clergy.

The reorganized church confronted numerous difficulties. To many Patriots it was, in the memorable words of one Episcopalian, "a piece of baggage left on the shores by the retreating British troops." In addition, the post-Revolutionary period was a time of decline in American religion, when many denominations—and the Episcopal Church above all—lost members to DEISM. Simultaneously, the church lost many members from its lower economic classes to the more egalitarian and emotional BAPTISTS and Methodists (see METHODISM, NORTH AMERICA). Once intended as an evangelical leaven for Anglicanism, Methodism broke away from the Episcopal Church in 1784.

Nineteenth Century

From the second decade of the nineteenth century on, however, the Episcopal Church revived, generally (but not entirely) as a result of the Second Great Awakening (see AWAKENINGS). Bishops in New York, Massachusetts, and Virginia led the revival. Founded in 1835, the Domestic and Foreign Missionary Society sent Episcopal missionaries into the new states of the expanding Union, into NATIVE AMERICAN reservations, and into such countries as JAPAN, CHINA, and LIBERIA. Two parties contended for control of the church. The evangelical party emphasized PREACHING, simple WORSHIP, and personal CONVERSION. The high-church party emphasized the SACRAMENTS, the episcopate, the priesthood, and the visible CHURCH as God's appointed channels for GRACE.

The spread of the OXFORD MOVEMENT to America widened the divisions. Its adherents (called "tractar-ians") asserted doctrinal and historical claims that the traditional high-church party did not. High churchmen, for example, accepted the title "Protestant," while most tractarians emphasized the pre-Reformation heritage and viewed the Church of England as a national Catholic church. From the 1840s on, Episcopal Church life was marked by tensions over whether the church was a form of Catholicism or Protestantism.

The Episcopal Church avoided taking an official stand on SLAVERY, but, like several other denominations, divided into northern and southern branches. By 1866, the southern and northern dioceses had reunited. Before the CIVIL WAR, the church's record of work with African Americans was inadequate. Most Anglican planters in the South resisted the efforts of clergy to baptize and evangelize their slaves, though the Great Awakening of the eighteenth century caused some improvement (see SLAVERY; SLAVERY, ABOLITION OF). By the time of the American Revolution, most slaves had still not become Christians.

The subsequent Second Great Awakening increased Episcopal work with African Americans, often under the auspices of the evangelical party. In the South, however, most converted blacks joined either Baptist or Methodist churches, where they could experience not only emotional worship, but also black leadership. Only a minority—perhaps 35,000, most of whom also departed after the war—became Episcopalians. Those southern African Americans who remained in the Episcopal Church found themselves second-class citizens. Not until the 1950s did black members receive voting representation at General Convention in all dioceses of the Episcopal Church.

The situation was better in the North. There large congregations of African-American Episcopalians developed in major cities and often had black pastors. De facto segregation marked church life, however. Although few black leaders of the CIVIL RIGHTS MOVEMENT were Episcopalians, the civil rights legislation passed in the 1960s allowed African Americans to be elected bishops of leading Episcopal dioceses and to play important roles in the life of the church.

In the later nineteenth century, ANGLO-CATHOLICISM emerged as a new and influential party in the church. Distinct from the high-church party but building on its beliefs, it advocated frequent "eucharists" or "masses," monastic orders (see MONASTICISM), voluntary private CONFESSION, the use of the title "father" for clergy, and prayers for the dead. To the formal but relatively plain ceremonial of the Episcopal Church it added candles, incense, crucifixes, ALTAR-centered churches, processions, a greater use of color, and more elaborate VESTMENTS. It also added such medieval body language as genuflecting and the sign of the cross. In church ARCHITECTURE, it revived such medieval styles as gothic and romanesque. To adherents, Anglo-Catholicism represented the forgotten Catholic heritage of the Episcopal Church, but to its Protestant-minded opponents it was mere "ritualism." Although a minority movement, Anglo-Catholicism significantly affected Episcopal teachings, practices, and church architecture.

A second church party, called the BROAD CHURCH, also emerged. This party sought truth from all sources to confront the new intellectual challenges to Christianity. It took the lead not only in introducing the HIGHER CRITICISM to Episcopalians, but also in demonstrating that the new discoveries of biblical scholars could be reconciled with Christian beliefs. The Broad Churchmen played the same role in reconciling Episcopalians to the controversial teachings of DARWINISM. Although many Episcopalians initially resisted Broad Church views, the movement was so successful that controversies over FUNDAMENTALISM and evolution quieted more quickly in the Episcopal Church than in other mainline denominations. Largely due to the work of the Broad Churchmen, the Episcopal Church became the first denomination in America to advocate the SOCIAL GOSPEL.

The Episcopal Church had long been interested in uniting divided Christianity. Shortly after the Revolution, it absorbed the remaining Swedish Lutheran churches in Pennsylvania and Delaware. Ultimately rejected by the General Convention, the Muhlenberg Memorial of 1853 advocated that bishops ordain Protestant clergy who accepted the essence of Episcopal teachings, yet allow those clergy to continue to minister in their denominations. In 1886 the General Convention did pass the Chicago Quadrilateral, which called for church union on the basis of BAPTISM, the LORD'S SUPPER, governance by bishops, and the AUTHORITY not only of Scripture, but also of the Apostles' and Nicene Creeds. Subsequently the church played a leading role in the Faith and Order Movement and in the WORLD COUNCIL OF CHURCHES. It also joined the Federal Council of Churches and later the NATIONAL COUNCIL OF CHURCHES.

Although the southern dioceses struggled economically for many decades, the massive immigration from Europe that poured into the industrialized United States after the CIVIL WAR caused the northern dioceses to grow both in membership and ethnic diversity (see ETHNICITY). Episcopal parishes benefited the most from the "invisible immigration" from England, but the church also sponsored small missions to other immigrant groups.

Twentieth Century

Because Protestant services of worship at U.S. military academies had long been conducted according to the *Book of Common Prayer*, a disproportionate number of American military officers were Episcopalians. In World War I, the commander-in-chief of the American Expeditionary Force, Episcopalian John J. Pershing, appointed Bishop CHARLES BRENT as chief of the thousands of military chaplains (see CHAPLAINCY). With the exception of its evangelical wing, the Episcopal Church was little involved in the controversies over TEMPERANCE and prohibition following the war. Unlike most Protestant denominations, it continued to use fermented wine in its services of Holy Communion.

Like other denominations, the church experienced serious losses of members, staff, and buildings during the Depression. President Franklin Delano Roosevelt and his wife Eleanor were Episcopalians, as were two of his three Republican opponents and one of his vice presidents. Beginning in the 1930s, NEO-ORTHODOXY began to influence Episcopal clergy, and it continued to do so for several decades.

More than 500 Episcopal chaplains and a substantial number of laity served in the American military forces during World War II. After the war, as new Episcopal churches were constructed throughout the nation, the church's traditional shortage of clergy increased. In 1946 the General Convention abruptly ended 17 years of negotiations for unity with the Presbyterian Church in the United States of America. The rupture displayed the continued tensions between Anglo-Catholics and more Protestant-minded Episcopalians.

The 1960s and 1970s were tumultuous decades. The Second Vatican Council (Vatican II, 1962–1965) fostered increased cooperation and ecumenical dialogue between Episcopalians and Roman Catholics. In addition, it caused the Episcopal Church to make changes in its LITURGY parallel to those made in the Roman Catholic mass. Shaped by contemporary liturgical scholarship and substituting modern language for the Elizabethan original, the 1979 *Book of Common Prayer* was initially controversial among Episcopalians. By inspiring a new spirit of self-examination and openness toward Protestants, Vatican II had the additional effect of reducing the differences and tensions between Anglo-Catholics and other Episcopalians. When some of the ideals of Vatican II failed to be realized in succeeding decades, an increasing number of Roman Catholics not only became Episcopalians, but also rose to leading positions in the church.

The same impetus that had caused Episcopalians to be active in the Social Gospel movement prompted them to play a significant role in the civil rights movement. Led by the Episcopal Society for Cultural and Racial Unity (ESCRU, organized 1959), numerous Episcopalians marched with MARTIN LUTHER KING, JR. In 1964 the General Convention forbade racial discrimination in Episcopal churches. In 1965 a seminary student and ESCRU member was murdered by a segregationist in Alabama. In 1967 the convention established the highly controversial General Convention Special Program to channel millions of dollars to minority groups in American society. During the same period, the church was embroiled in controversy over the Vietnam War.

Beginning in the 1960s, the Episcopal Church began to seriously consider the role of WOMEN. The church had used the term "women's work" to describe the unpaid volunteer work of Episcopal laywomen in SUNDAY SCHOOLS, altar guilds, and similar organizations. New opportunities for Episcopal women had opened in the mid-nineteenth century with the establishment of communities of celibate nuns. Late in the century the General Convention authorized the office of deaconess. Deaconesses (who had to be widowed or single) could teach or administer, but could lead worship only when male clergy were absent. Though always few in numbers, both the sisterhoods (see SISTERHOODS, ANGLICAN) and the deaconesses played a prominent role in the work of Episcopal orphanages, hospitals, and other institutions. The largest and most autonomous organization of women was the Woman's Auxiliary to the Board of Missions, established in 1871.

Most vestries remained all male until the social and sexual revolution of the Vietnam era. In 1967 women gained the right to serve as lay deputies to General Conventions. In 1976 the General Convention approved their ordination to the priesthood (see WOMEN CLERGY). The first Episcopal woman bishop was consecrated in 1989. Combined with the other changes in church practice, the ordination of women caused many traditionalists to leave the Episcopal Church for "Continuing Anglican" churches or for EASTERN ORTHODOXY or Roman Catholicism. Some traditionalists remained in the Episcopal Church, but formed organizations aimed at restoring the old ORTHODOXY. From the 1960s on, a resurgent evangelical movement (often combined with charismatic elements) became a conservative and growing force in the church (see EVANGELICALISM).

When the bishop of New York ordained a lesbian in the 1970s, the Episcopal Church entered the debate over the place and role of homosexuals in the church (see HOMOSEXUALITY, SEXUALITY). Although the twentieth century ended with the General Convention failing to give explicit approval to the ordinations of practicing homosexuals, individual bishops have continued to ordain candidates in whose character and judgment they possess confidence. Homosexuals also played an increasing role in the lay activities of the Episcopal Church. In 2003, the Diocese of New Hampshire elected an openly gay bishop. The election's subsequent confirmation by both houses of the General Convention marked a turning point, even as it prompted the possibility of schism for the Episcopal Church in the USA as well as for the international Anglican Communion.

Like most mainline denominations, the Episcopal Church began to decline in membership in the later 1960s. At the start of the twenty-first century, its baptized membership approximates 2.3 million; among church bodies in the United States, it ranks somewhere between twelfth and fourteenth in size. Although relatively small, the Episcopal Church has had an effect on American history and culture disproportionate to its size. Eleven American presidents, thirty-three Supreme Court justices, large numbers of U.S. senators, congressmen, and corporate chief executives, as well as a substantial number of influential figures in other fields have been Episcopalian.

Summation

The Episcopal Church has always been a small church in America. The large membership that occurred because of its established status in the colonial period quickly disappeared once membership was no longer obligatory. Its records in EVANGELISM, in domestic MISSIONS (where only the Congregationalists sent fewer missionaries to the new south and west), and in liturgical matters (where Episcopal services can seem daunting to newcomers) may all have contributed.

Throughout its history, the church has tended to appeal to the economically comfortable, the educated, and the cultured and aesthetically inclined. The result has been that Americans who are not economically comfortable, not educated, and not especially cultivated or inclined toward aesthetics have joined other churches. Episcopal institutional churches and inner city and mountain missions have provided major exceptions. With a growing Hispanic membership, active ministries with Native Americans, African Americans, and Asian-Americans, and with the continued involvement of "extra-territorial" dioceses in the Caribbean, Latin America and Taiwan, as well as parishes in Europe, the Episcopal Church at the start of the 21st century finds itself challenged to accommodate a greater ethnic and cultural diversity than ever before. The 73rd General Convention (2000) also launched a "20/20" evangelism and mission initiative designed to double active participation in the church by the year 2020.

The Episcopal Church has also displayed a tendency to eschew extremes and to follow a middle path. Many movements—Methodism, Evangelicalism, Anglo-Catholicism, MODERNISM, traditionalism, liberal Protestantism, the charismatic movement, and others—have tried to move the church to the left or to the right, but such movements have tended to be incorporated under the "broad tent" of the church, rather than become definitive. As a result, throughout most of its history the Episcopal Church has been typified by a moderation that weathers crises well.

Until recent decades, internal Catholic–Protestant tensions have kept the church from being as involved in church unions as many of its members have wished. One significant development was Called to common Mission (2001), which established a "Concordat of Agreement" bringing the Episcopal Church into full communion with the EVANGELICAL LUTHERAN CHURCH IN AMERICA (see ECUMENISM; DIALOGUE, INTERCONFESSIONAL). The Episcopal Church also supports the NATIONAL COUNCIL OF CHURCHES and WORLD COUNCIL OF CHURCHES. Despite its ties to the establishment, for more than 100 years the church has been one of the more progressive churches in terms of social matters. Above all, the Episcopal Church has been the church of liturgy and theater among the Protestant churches of the United States.

See also African Methodist Episcopal Church; African Methodist Episcopal Zion Church; Baptists, United States; Catholicism, Protestant Reactions; Ecumenism; Liberal Protestantism and Liberalism; Methodist Episcopal Church Conference; Polity

References and Further Reading

Anderson, Owanah. *400 Years: The Anglican/Episcopal Mission among American Indians*. Cincinnati, OH: Forward Movement Publications, 1997.

Armentrout, Donald S., and Robert B. Slocum. *Documents of Witness: A History of the Episcopal Church, 1782–1985*. New York: Church Publishing, 1994.

Chorley, Edward C. *Men and Movements in the American Episcopal Church*. New York: Scribner, 1946.

Darling, Pamela W. *New Wine*. Cambridge, UK: Cowley Publications, 1994.

Donovan, Mary Sudman. *A Different Call: Women's Ministries in the Episcopal Church, 1850–1920*. Wilton, CT: Morehouse, 1986.

Hein, David, and Gardiner H. Shattuck, Jr. *The Episcopalians*. Westport, CT: Praeger, 2004.

Holmes, David L. *A Brief History of the Episcopal Church*. Harrisburg, PA: Trinity Press International, 1993.

Mills, Frederick V., Sr. *Bishops by Ballot*. New York: Oxford University Press, 1978.

Prichard, Robert W. *A History of the Episcopal Church* (2d ed.). Harrisburg, PA: Morehouse, 1999.

Shattuck, Gardiner H., Jr. *Episcopalians and Race: Civil War to Civil Rights*. Lexington, KY: University Press of Kentucky, 2000.

Woolverton, John F. *Colonial Anglicanism in North America, 1607–1776*. Detroit, MI: Wayne State University Press, 1984. http://episcopalchurch.org

DAVID L. HOLMES

ERASTIANISM

See Erastus, Thomas

ERASTUS, THOMAS (LÜBER) (1524–1583)

Protestant reformer. Thomas Lüber who latinized his name to Erastus, was born in Baden, SWITZERLAND, September 7, 1524, studied THEOLOGY at Basel and medicine at Bologna and Padua, and became a renowned physician who made his mark by repudiating the medical theories of THEOPHRASTUS PARACELSUS. In 1558 he was appointed personal physician of elector Otto Heinrich of the Palatinate and simultaneously professor of medicine at the University of Heidelberg. Trusted spiritual advisor to the elector, he became increasingly involved in ecclesiastical affairs in the Palatinate. In 1577 he wrote advocating the death penalty for witches. A committed Zwinglian/Calvinist, Erastus opposed the introduction of LUTHERANISM in the Palatinate and lost his position at Heidelberg in 1580. Thus forced to emigrate, he became professor of medicine at the University of Basel, where he also received a professorship in moral philosophy shortly before his death. He died in Basel on December 31, 1583.

Erastus is best known for giving his name to the doctrine of Erastianism, which was thought to be found in his book *Explicatio*. This was the notion that government held all sovereignty within a commonwealth and that, therefore, the political power was superior to ecclesiastical power, which in turn had to be submissive to it. In fact Erastus himself favored the Zurich model of the relationship between the political and ecclesiastical power, as introduced by HULDRYCH ZWINGLI.

See also Calvinism

References and Further Reading

Primary Sources:

Erastus, Thomas. *Explicatio gravissimae questionis utrum excommunicatio quatenus Religionem*. London: 1589.

———. *The Theses of Erastus Touching Excommunication*. London: Simpkin and Marshall 1844.

Secondary Sources:

Figgis, J. Neville. "Erastus and Erastianism." *Journal of Theological Studies* 2 (1901): 66–101.

Wesel-Roth, Ruth. *Thomas Erastus. Ein Beitrag zur Geschichte der reformierten Kirche und zur Lehre von der Staatssouveränität.* Lahr: M. Schauenburg 1954.

HANS J. HILLERBRAND

ESCHATOLOGY

The word *eschatology* is derived from the Greek and refers to discourse about the end times, the last events of human history, and the final destiny of the individual human being. In the Christian tradition, eschatological belief relates to the ultimate fulfillment of God's plan for humanity and the ultimate triumph of Jesus Christ and the establishment of His Kingdom. In the Hebrew scriptures, eschatological hope, found especially in the books of Daniel, Isaiah, and Ezekiel, centers on an age of righteousness associated with the coming of the Messiah. Christian eschatology is closely interwoven with millennialism or CHILIASM, the expectation of Christ's end-time return to Earth and his thousand-year reign of justice, righteousness, and peace foretold in Revelation 20 (see MILLENARIANS AND MILLENNIALISTS). Christian eschatology is also closely linked to APOCALYPTICISM, a literary genre in ancient Jewish and early Christian thought through which hidden truths or spiritual realities, often dealing with the final conflict of good and evil, are apprehended by the author through a vision or divine revelation and transmitted to the reader, often in allegorical form. The Book of Revelation, a Christian apocalypse incorporated into the biblical canon, closes the New Testament.

The rich tradition of Protestant eschatological interpretation, now spanning nearly five centuries, is rooted in a still older tradition of Christian eschatological exegesis and expectation. The earliest Christians anticipated Christ's return in their own lifetime, but as Christianity won TOLERATION and then primacy in the Roman world, church leaders and theologians played down the expectations of an imminent end of history. St. Augustine historicized the Bible's prophetic and apocalytic passages, for example, finding eschatological fulfillment in the gradual unfolding of history, rather than in a final moment of eschatological crisis.

The medieval church, with its quasi-monarchical structure, continued to discourage eschatological speculation, particularly by the LAITY. Eschatology flourished at the grassroots level, however, often implicitly challenging the papacy, as in the visionary work of the twelfth-century monk Joachim of Fiore and the fifteenth-century Hussite movement in Bohemia.

Protestant Eschatology from the Reformation through the Great Awakening

This, then, is the eschatological tradition that passed into the Protestant movement in the early sixteenth century. The early reformers held ambivalent eschatological views. On the one hand, they readily used eschatological imagery, particularly biblical allusions to the ANTICHRIST, the Beast, and the Whore of Babylon, to pursue their campaign against Rome. Numerous engravings and polemical writings identify the papacy with these demonic end-time figures, as do the hyper-Protestant marginal notes of the GENEVA BIBLE of 1560.

In general, however, MARTIN LUTHER, HULDRYCH ZWINGLI, JOHN CALVIN, and other early Reformation leaders were deeply suspicious of what they viewed as a dangerous upsurge of eschatological speculation in a highly volatile religious and social situation. Calvin did not include Revelation in his commentaries. Luther declared Revelation "neither apostolic nor prophetic," and relegated it to an appendix in his German New Testament. The early Anabaptists (see ANABAPTISM) and other Protestant radicals, by contrast, were intensely interested in eschatology and saw history's final drama unfolding in their own time. During the turbulent days of the Peasants War in Germany, THOMAS MÜNTZER inspired his followers with eschatological expectations, up to their catastrophic final stand at Frankenhausen in 1525. Nine years later, in 1534, followers of a charismatic Dutch preacher named JAN MATHIIS took over the Westphalian city of Munster, proclaiming it the New Jerusalem. This eschatological experiment soon degenerated into brutality, chaos, and mass starvation, and was crushed by the authorities in 1535. Such excesses confirmed the Protestant leaders' suspicions of excessively literalist or present-minded eschatological interpretations. Although Christ's Second Coming is affirmed in the creed of all Protestant bodies, it has remained a muted theme in the Lutheran, Reformed, and Anglican confessions.

As in the medieval era, however, eschatological speculations periodically erupted in Protestantism's more fervent and evangelical precincts, particularly in times of religious or social crisis. The wave of reform that followed HENRY VIII's establishment of the CHURCH OF ENGLAND, culminating in the Puritan movement, the English CIVIL WAR, regicide, and the rule of OLIVER CROMWELL, for example, was marked by intense end-time anticipation. Puritan writers found profound eschatological meaning in the movement to purify the English church. JOHN MILTON (1608–1674), the poet of PURITANISM, was only one of many who invested these events with eschatological significance.

The so-called Fifth Monarchy Men sect saw Cromwell's rule foreshadowed in the allegorical image in Daniel 2 of a statue representing five successive world kingdoms, the last of which is an end-time reign of righteousness. The mathematician and natural philosopher Sir ISAAC NEWTON (1642–1727) devoted his final years to eschatology, examining the apocalyptic scriptures synoptically to decipher the end-time system they revealed.

The Puritan settlers of New England brought eschatology to America. Michael Wigglesworth's New England physician and theologian *Day of Doom* (1662) is full of end-time anticipations, as are the writings of COTTON MATHER (1663–1728). In these New World eschatological reflections, American realities figured prominently. Sometimes the Indians and sometimes the French Catholics of CANADA were identified with the Antichrist; others speculated that America might be the site of Christ's millennial kingdom.

Eschatological expectation in America flared brightly during the Great Awakening of the 1740s and the Second Great Awakening of the early nineteenth century. The revivalist and theologian JONATHAN EDWARDS (1703–1758) wrote extensively on apocalyptic themes. Espousing a position later called postmillennialism, Edwards proclaimed that through piety, prayer, and evangelism, Christians could achieve a redeemed social order in the present age, paving the way for the millennium as a prelude to Christ's return.

Trends in Eschatology in the Nineteenth and Twentieth Centuries

In ENGLAND the Reverend EDWARD IRVING, a charismatic London minister of the 1820s, preached Christ's imminent return. Irving's convert HENRY DRUMMOND, a wealthy banker and Tory member of Parliament, held a series of prophecy conferences on his estate in the 1820s and 1830s. In America the United Society of Believers in Christ's Second Coming, popularly called SHAKERS, incorporated a strong eschatological strand in their THEOLOGY. In the *Book of Mormon* (1830), which JOSEPH SMITH offered as a divinely inspired history and revelation of future events, American history is refigured in sacred terms, with the newly founded Church of Jesus Christ of Latter Day Saints (see MORMONISM) playing a central role in God's unfolding plan.

Beginning in the 1830s, WILLIAM MILLER of upstate New York, drawing on calculations involving various events and time sequences in the Hebrew scriptures, proclaimed the second coming of Christ "around 1843 or 1844." Eventually, Millerite leaders pinpointed the final date even more precisely: October 22, 1843 (later revised to October 22, 1844). The movement won thousands of adherents, and attracted thousands more of the curious. When the appointed day came and went, a crisis resulted that some called the Great Disappointment. From the wreckage, however, arose the SEVENTH-DAY ADVENTIST church, a Protestant denomination with millions of members worldwide that remains a bastion of eschatological belief, although modern Adventists carefully avoid date-setting.

Meanwhile, a system of eschatological interpretation known as premillennial DISPENSATIONALISM arose in England and spread rapidly to America. The person who systematized and promulgated this scheme, the Reverend JOHN NELSON DARBY (1800–1882), was a founder of a dissenting sect known as the PLYMOUTH BRETHREN. If rightly understood and arrayed in proper sequence, Darby taught, Bible prophecy reveals a series of divinely ordained epochs, or dispensations, each with its distinct means of SALVATION. The end of the present dispensation, the Church Age, he believed, would be signaled by a series of signs foretold by Christ, sometimes in parables, including wars and wickedness, natural disasters, and the restoration of the Jews to the promised land. Next on the prophetic calendar will come the RAPTURE, when all true believers will join Christ in the air, followed by the Great Tribulation (Matthew 24:21) and the rise of a demonic figure, the Antichrist. Antichrist's reign will end after seven years, however, when he is vanquished at the Battle of Armageddon by a triumphant Christ and the raptured saints. Hailed as Messiah by the Jews who survive Antichrist's persecution, Christ will establish his millennial kingdom in the rebuilt temple in Jerusalem.

An indefatigable writer and preacher, Darby toured widely, winning many adherents in America. One convert to dispensationalism, Cyrus Scofield, published in 1909 an annotated Bible with notes based on Darby's system. Through the popular SCOFIELD REFERENCE BIBLE, prophecy periodicals and conferences, schools like Dallas Theological Seminary, and the preaching of dispensationalist ministers, Darby's eschatological scheme pervaded American EVANGELICALISM. The rise of PENTECOSTALISM in the early twentieth century gave further impetus to end-time anticipations.

Other eschatological perspectives gained support as well, however, including the reformist version underlying the SOCIAL GOSPEL preached in many liberal Protestant churches in the early twentieth century (see LIBERAL PROTESTANTISM AND LIBERALISM). Social-Gospel ministers and theologians offered a version of Edwardian postmillennialism adapted to an urban-industrial age. By promoting slum-housing legislation, labor unions, worker-protection laws, the prohibition of child labor, and similar reforms, they taught, Christians could hasten the prophesied KINGDOM OF GOD. In *Christianity and the Social Crisis* (1907), *A Theology for the Social Gospel* (1917), and other works, theologian WALTER RAUSCHENBUSCH translated postmillennialist eschatology into a mandate for social reform. This reformist outlook profoundly influenced the Methodist and Presbyterian churches and other mainstream Protestant denominations, as well as the ecumenically minded Federal Council of Churches (FCC). "The Social Creed of the Churches," adopted by the FCC in 1912, represents the high water mark of the Social Gospel. The young REINHOLD NIEBUHR (1892–1971) espoused the Social Gospel in his early ministry and writings, although he would later harshly criticize what he saw as its excessive optimism about the human condition.

Although the disillusionment that followed World War I undermined the postmillennialist eschatology of the Social Gospel, premillennial dispensationalism, with its darker, more apocalyptic view of history, remained strong in the evangelical, fundamentalist, and Pentecostal churches, which had continued to stress individual salvation and missionary work rather than the christianization of the social order (see FUNDAMENTALISM; PENTECOSTALISM). As the nineteenth-century evangelist DWIGHT L. MOODY memorably put it, expending one's energies on social reform was like polishing the brass fittings on a sinking ocean liner.

After World War II premillennial dispensationalism gradually emerged as the dominant eschatology of grassroots American Protestantism, taking root as a kind of folk theology promulgated more by paperback popularizers, radio preachers, and televangelists than by established church institutions or mainstream theological seminaries. The atomic bomb; the United Nations; the movement for European unity; the establishment of Israel in 1948; the Israelis' recapture of Jerusalem's Old City in 1967; and later the rise of computers, a global economy, and a worldwide communications systems all struck prophecy writers as portentous signs of the times, making plain that the present dispensation would soon end.

Although twentieth-century Protestant ministers and theologians outside the evangelical and fundamentalist subcultures displayed little interest in combing the biblical prophecies for clues to end-time events, successive generations of scholars, especially in Germany, contributed to a renewed awareness of the importance of eschatology in early Christianity. Johannes Weiss's *Die Predigt Jesu Von Reiche Gottes* (*The Sermon of Jesus on the Kingdom of God*) of 1892, and ALBERT SCHWEITZER's *Von Reimarus zu Wrede* (1906), published in English in 1910 as *The Quest for the Historical Jesus*, insisted on the urgency of the first Christians' eschatological expectations.

Schweitzer contended that Jesus's entire ministry was founded on the belief that the world would end very soon. This theme was reiterated by later German theologians such as Klaus Koch, whose *Ratlos vor der Apocalyptik* (1970) appeared in English two years later as *The Rediscovery of Apocalyptic,* and Ernst Kasemann, who in an influential 1969 article declared the apocalyptic worldview "the mother of all Christian theology."

The well-known Swiss theologian KARL BARTH (1886–1968), as part of his larger reassertion of an orthodox tradition that he believed had been lost in post-ENLIGHTENMENT theology, sought to recover a renewed sense of eschatology as a central element in Christian doctrine and in the Protestant REFORMATION. Fundamental to the Christian life, Barth contended, were moments of decision confronted from an eschatological perspective. (For Barth, such a moment had come in 1935 when, teaching in GERMANY, he had refused an oath of allegiance to Adolf Hitler's Nazi regime.) The German Lutheran theologian PAUL TILLICH (1886–1965), who came to America in 1933, drew on existentialism and depth psychology in defining eschatology as "ultimate concern" in his *Systematic Theology* (1951–1963) and *The Courage to Be* (1952), which won a large readership.

Although Continental scholars reasserted the importance of eschatology in early Christianity, millions of American Protestants embraced present-day end-time speculation ever more fervently. As the nation's liberal, mainstream Protestant denominations lost ground after 1970, evangelical, fundamentalist, and charismatic denominations such as the ASSEMBLIES OF GOD and the SOUTHERN BAPTIST CONVENTION, as well as independent community churches and Bible fellowships with no strong denominational ties, surged in membership. Premillennialist eschatological belief loomed large in these churches. Bible prophecy also figured prominently in countless radio and television ministries by such figures as JERRY FALWELL, PAT ROBERTSON, Jack Van Impe, and James Hagee, a San Antonio pastor with a flock of thousands. Robertson's Christian Broadcasting Network (CBN) and Paul and Jan Crouch's Trinity Broadcasting Network (TBN) frequently showcased eschatological themes (see TELEVANGELISM; PUBLISHING, MEDIA).

Paperback writers spread the end-time message as well. Hal Lindsey's *The Late Great Planet Earth* (1970), a popularization of premillennial dispensationalism, became an all-time bestseller and remained in print thirty years later. Many other eschatological popularizers gained prominence in late twentieth-century America. A multivolume series of novels by Tim LaHaye and Jerry B. Jenkins, launched in 1995 with *Left Behind,* offered a fictionalized version of Darby's system. The *Left Behind* series became a publishing phenomenon, with thirty million copies sold by 2001. Movies such as Donald Thompson's "A Thief in the Night" (1972), Matt Crouch's "The Omega Code" (1999), and Peter LaLonde's "Left Behind: The Movie" (2000), based on the LaHaye and Jenkins series, reached large audiences with their eschatological message. Continuing a long tradition in popular Protestant eschatology, these writers, televangelists, and filmmakers wove current events into their scenarios, from communications satellites and the Trilateral Commission to global warming, radical feminism, and Islamic fundamentalism, as signs of the end times or anticipations of Antichrist's rule.

The terrorist attacks on the Pentagon and the World Trade Center in September 2001 pushed popular interest in eschatology to still higher levels. Within weeks prophecy books appeared on the bookshelves incorporating these events, including James Hagee's *Attack on America: New York, Jerusalem, and the Role of Terrorism in the Last Days*. The global reach of U.S. mass culture, including the prophecy-oriented TV programs and paperbacks, reinforced by thousands of charismatic and evangelical Protestant missionaries, spread premillennialist eschatological belief to Latin America and Africa as well.

As the twenty-first century began, eschatology remained central in the Protestant tradition. In the liberal churches, Christ's Second Coming was interpreted allegorically, residually acknowledged in the recitation of a creed, or simply viewed as a mystery whose details were best left unexplored. In the vibrant and expansive evangelical, fundamentalist, and charismatic sectors of American Protestantism, however, and in parts of the world proselytized by U.S. Protestant missionaries, eschatology was not merely a matter of credal affirmation or historical interest, but a vibrant reality, stirring fervent expectations of the approaching end and encouraging believers to search the scriptures and scan the headlines for signs that history's final climax was drawing ever nearer.

References and Further Reading

Barnes, Robert. "Images of Hope and Despair: Western Apocalypticism, ca. 1500–1800." In *The Encyclopedia of Apocalypticism*, vol. 2, edited by Bernard McGinn, 143–184. New York: Continuum, 1998.

Bouwsma, William J. *John Calvin: A Sixteenth-Century Portrait*. New York: Oxford University Press, 1988.

Boyer, Paul. *When Time Shall Be No More: Prophecy Belief in Modern American Culture*. Cambridge, MA: Harvard University Press, 1992.

Davidson, James W. *The Logic of Millennial Thought: Eighteenth-Century New England*. New Haven, CT: Yale University Press, 1977.

Firth, Katharine. *The Apocalyptic Tradition in Reformation Britain, 1530–1645*. New York: Oxford University Press, 1979.

Hill, Christopher. *Antichrist in Seventeenth-Century England*. London: Oxford University Press, 1971.

Moorhead, James H. *World Without End: Mainstream American Protestant Visions of Last Things, 1880–1925*. Bloomington: Indiana University Press, 1999.

Noll, Mark L. *The Scandal of the Evangelical Mind*. Grand Rapids, MI: Wm. B. Eerdmans, 1994.

Numbers, Ronald L., and Jonathan M. Butler, eds. *The Disappointed: Millerism and Millenarianism in the Nineteenth Century*. Bloomington: Indiana University Press, 1987.

Oberman, Heiko. *Luther: Man Between God and the Devil*. New Haven, CT: Yale University Press, 1989.

Penton, M. James. *Apocalypse Delayed: The Story of Jehovah's Witnesses*. Toronto: University of Toronto Press, 1985.

Sandeen, Ernest R. *The Roots of Fundamentalism: British and American Millenarianism, 1800–1930*. Chicago: University of Chicago Press, 1970.

Toon, Peter, ed. *Puritans, the Millennium, and the Future of Israel: Puritan Eschatology, 1600–1660*. Cambridge, UK: James Clark and Co., 1970.

Tuveson, Ernest Lee. *Millennium and Utopia: A Study in the Background of the Idea of Progress*. Berkeley: University of California Press, 1949.

Wacker, Grant. *Heaven Below: Early Pentecostals and American Culture*. Cambridge, MA: Harvard University Press, 2001.

Weber, Timothy P. *Living in the Shadow of the Second Coming: American Premillennialism, 1975–1925*. New York: Oxford University Press, 1979.

PAUL S. BOYER

ESTONIA

The present territory of the Republic of Estonia does not correspond geographically to the area that made up Estonia at the time of the REFORMATION in the sixteenth century. A large part of what is now Estonia belonged at that time to Livonia. Therefore, it is possible to speak of the history of Protestantism in Estonia only in general terms.

The arrival of Protestantism in Estonia was marked by the religious renewal movements and churches that arrived in northern Estonia and Livonia as a result of the reformation of the church started by MARTIN LUTHER in GERMANY. Protestantism reached Estonia from Wittenberg in 1523, initially attaining a following in the larger towns, where the people tried to make use of the reformation of the church for their own economic benefit and to achieve their own political goals. The reformation movement first reached Tallinn and then spread outward to Narva, Rakvere, and Paide. A year later it reached Tartu, then in Livonia but now part of southern Estonia, and from there it continued to broaden its base to Viljandi, Pärnu, and Valga. Finally, it reached Haapsalu in western Estonia and then the islands.

Although local church leaders objected fiercely to the reforms, they spread rapidly across the country thanks to wandering preachers who taught the Gospel in this new way. The first Protestant preachers in Estonia and Livonia to have come from the center of the Reformist movement in Germany and whose names are known today were Johann Lange and Zacharias Hasse in Tallinn and Hermann Marsow and MELCHIOR HOFMANN in Tartu. The Reformist movement then spread from the towns to the countryside, where the country people (at that time the majority of the population of Estonia and Livonia) hoped that the reformation of the church would bring about an improvement in their way of life and began to actively support the reformers. As a result, the movement spread quickly throughout the whole of Estonia and Livonia. After a change in political power in the region, these developments were halted by a Catholic counterrevolution that was successful in the parts of Livonia that had fallen under Polish influence.

The triumphant march of Protestantism across Estonia and Old Livonia was sealed for good during the second half of the sixteenth century, when the period of Swedish supremacy began. Worthy of particular note during this period was the work of Johannes Rudbeckius, bishop of Västerås in SWEDEN, who led the development of a Lutheran church organization in this region. In 1694, a version of the Swedish Church Law adapted for Estonia and Livonia came into force. This laid out the structure of the CHURCH, set requirements for members of the CLERGY, and defined the basic tasks of the church in its role as proclaimer of the Gospel and educator. The Swedish era and Swedish supremacy in Estonia came to an end during the Great Northern War, when Russian forces occupied Tallinn in 1710. However, Protestantism, in the form of LUTHERANISM, had established a firm foothold in the area and had already taken the leading role in church life. In addition to the reform of the church, the most significant advance of this period was the establishment of an educational system and a network of schools for Estonians with Estonian as the common language. Estonian was beginning to spread as a written language, and this development was not even halted by the extensive Russification policies of the Russian Tsarist regime, which reigned for several centuries. One aspect of these policies was the granting of considerable economic and political advantages to the Orthodox Church and its followers (see ORTHODOXY, EASTERN). Estonia's separation from Tsarist Russia and the establishment of an independent Estonian state in 1918 had a significant impact on the church. The Lutheran Church was no longer under the administration of the Russian Lutheran Church but had become independent. In so doing, it also became the largest Christian confession in Estonia.

The Second World War and the subsequent Soviet occupation after 1945 led to a dramatic slowing, and in many areas a complete halt, of the development of church life. Together with the political leaders, officer corps, and intellectual elite of independent Estonia, large numbers of the clergy were also deported or put to death. State and church-run institutions of theological education, where members of the clergy had also been trained, were closed down. Atheism was declared the official ideology. All church organizations were banned, and the churches themselves were subjected to strict control. The churches were prohibited from being involved in welfare work and from working with young people, WOMEN, and children. Although the churches were separated from the state, the state began to control and limit the activities of the churches (see CHURCH AND STATE OVERVIEW). Freedom of belief was retained in theory, but in practice people were not given the opportunity to exercise it.

In the last decade of the twentieth century, a breakthrough occurred in relations between the state and the churches when Estonia left the Soviet Union and re-established the independent state in 1991. There has been a steady progression from the former sense of opposition between church and state, both public and hidden, to a level of cooperation. The Estonian Constitution guarantees freedom of belief to everyone living in Estonia. There is no such thing as a state church in Estonia. All churches and associations of congregations are deemed equal and to have equal rights. The state's relations with the churches and with other religious associations are regulated by the Churches and Congregations Act, passed in 2002. To coordinate relations between the Christian churches and the state and between the Christian churches themselves, and to promote joint efforts to help advance society and proclaim the Gospel, the Council of Estonian Churches was set up in 1989 on the instigation of the Estonian Evangelical Lutheran Church. All of the large Christian churches operating in Estonia are members of the Council.

Of the traditional Protestant churches, only Lutheranism is represented in Estonia today. The Anglican Church and the Reformed churches do not exist. The oldest Protestant church in Estonia, the Lutheran Church has existed in various institutional forms since the arrival of the Reformation in Estonia. After Estonia's separation from Tsarist Russia and the declaration of an independent Estonian Republic in 1918, an independent church based on the Lutheran confession was created. The Estonian Evangelical Lutheran Church (*Eesti Evangeelne Luterlik Kirik*) is now the largest church in Estonia. In its role as the largest church institution, it has been the carrier of national identity for centuries. This became particularly important during the years of occupation.

The church has an Episcopal-synod structure and comprises 169 congregations, divided into twelve deaneries. This network of congregations covers the whole of Estonia. The Lutheran churches tend to be situated in what were the town centers back in the time of the first Estonian Republic, because during the Soviet period it was not possible to set up new congregations or build churches in newer neighborhoods. According to state statistics, church membership currently stands at about 172,000, and the clergy numbers around 190. The church's spiritual leader is the Archbishop, who is assisted by the Bishop and under whom serve the ministers (pastors), deacons, and others who work for the church in various fields.

The focal point of the everyday life of the Lutheran Church is Sunday WORSHIP. The congregations also have SUNDAY SCHOOLS, youth groups, choirs, diaconal centers, and other organizations promoting church life and cooperation in general. The church cooperates with state institutions in areas where the interests of the state and the church meet. The church is expected to express and promote moral values, but as society develops there is an ever-increasing need for diaconal work. The church has its own university offering higher education and training for members of the clergy and church musicians; for military, hospital, and prison chaplains; and for deacons and youth workers.

The Estonian Evangelical Lutheran Church has been a member of the LUTHERAN WORLD FEDERATION since 1963. It also belongs to the European Conference of Churches (1959) and the WORLD COUNCIL OF CHURCHES (1961).

The second largest Christian grouping in Estonia to have grown out of Protestantism is the Baptist Church (see BAPTISTS). The movement reached Estonia in the 1870s and was initially limited to western Estonia, but later spread across the whole country. A union of Estonian Baptist congregations was set up in 1900. After the Second World War, in the second half of the 1940s, the union was amalgamated with the Evangelical Christians, the Pentecostals, and the free congregations. The Union of Estonian Evangelical Christian and Baptist Congregations currently encompasses some eighty-nine congregations with around 6,100 members. The congregations are served by eighty-one members of the clergy. Since 1989, Estonian Baptists have had their own theological seminary for training the clergy for their work in the congregations.

Although the Anglican Church is not represented in Estonia, another church that grew out of the Anglican Church has been active here since 1910: the Methodist Church (see METHODISM; METHODISM, EUROPE). The Estonian Methodist Church has a Congregationalist structure. The highest decision-making body of the Methodist Church is the General Assembly, which selects a person from among the clergy to be the leader of the church (the Superintendent) for the subsequent three years. The church has 1,800 members split between twenty-four congregations and served by twenty-two members of the clergy. The church set up a theological seminary in 1994 with the aim of providing training for people working for the church.

There have been Pentecostalists in Estonia since 1909, although they were forced to join the Union of Evangelical Christians and Baptists during the period of Soviet occupation (see PENTECOSTALISM). They were not given the opportunity of operating as an independent church. After the restoration of the Republic of Estonia, three "exile Estonian" Pentecostal Ministers founded an association of Estonian Congregationalist congregations that today is known as the Estonian Christian Pentecostal Church. It has 3,500 members, thirty-nine autonomous congregations, and sixty-three clergy. The church has had its own BIBLE school since 1992. Several Pentecostal congregations in Estonia have taken the decision to operate as independent congregations, and some have set up small alternative associations of congregations.

Protestantism in Estonia means the liberal theological movement and grouping of clergy that developed within the Estonian Evangelical Lutheran Church (then operating under its former name of *Eesti Evangeeliumi Luteriusu Kirik*) in the 1920s under the name "New Protestantism." This movement had a significant influence on Estonian THEOLOGY and on the development of church life. Its characteristic feature was the interpretation of the didactic basis of the church in the spirit of nineteenth-century German liberal Cultural Protestantism, and it followed the same theological ideas (see LIBERAL PROTESTANTISM AND LIBERALISM). The most important exponents of the idea were Theodor Tallmeister (1889–1947) and Voldemar Kuljus (1898–1979). From 1923 until 1940, the movement published its own magazine first titled *Protestantline Ilm* and then *Protestanlik Maailm* (*Protestant World*).

References and Further Reading

Arbusow, Leonid Jr. *Die Einführung der Reformation in Liv-, Est- und Kurland. Quellen und Forschungen zur Reformationsgeschichte.* Band III. Leipzig, Germany: M. Heinsius, 1921.

Au, Ilmo, and Ringo Ringvee. *Kirikud ja Kogudused Eestis.* Tallinn, Estonia: AS Kirjastus Ilo, 2000.

Saard, Riho. *Eesti Kirikuajaloo Bibliograafia. Viron Kirkkohistorian Bibliografia. Bibliographie der Estnischen Kirchengeschichte (1918–1997).* Edited by Matti Kotiranta.

Helsinki, Finland: University of Helsinki, Gummerus Kir-
japaino Oy Saarijärvi, 1998.

Sild, Olaf, and Vello Salo. *Lühike Eesti Kirikulugu*. Tartu,
Estonia, Akadeemilise K. Kirjastus 1995.

Võõbus, Arthur. *Studies in the History of the Estonian People*,
vols. I–XI and XIII. Wettern, Belgium: Cultura Press, 1984.

———. *Studies in the History of the Estonian People*, vol.
XIV. Wettern, Belgium: Cultura Press, 1985.

Wittram, Reinhard, ed. *Die Reformation in Livland. Baltische
Kirchengeschichte*. Göttingen, Germany: Vandenhoeck &
Ruprecht, 1956.

TIIT PÄÄDEM

ETHICS

A vital contribution of Protestantism is to preclude the
possibility of ethics as a disparate discipline, as a
conversation apart from the grace that exercises dominion. Unless the Word through which we are saved
perpetually conditions the word of ethics, morality can
become menacingly independent. Whether tempting
toward preening pride, scrupulous secularity, or nihil-
istic despair, ethics without constant reference to
"eternal life through Jesus Christ our Lord" lead us
astray. As Paul put it in Romans 5,

> But law came in, with the result that the trespass multi-
> plied; but where sin increased, grace abounded all the
> more, so that, just as sin exercised dominion in death, so
> grace might also exercise dominion through justification
> leading to eternal life through Jesus Christ our Lord.
> What then are we to say? (Romans 5:20-21, 6:1a)

One approach to Protestant ethics is through the question of soteriology. We may plausibly read Protestant
ethics such that for MARTIN LUTHER, JOHN CALVIN, and
MICHAEL SATTLER, ethics and soteriology are inextricably intertwined. Luther's insistence that the study of
requisite morality not become an enterprise severed
from the answer of our SALVATION in Christ is a claim
with which all subsequent Protestants have had to
reckon. We may responsibly interpret each Protestant
TRADITION to suggest that we cannot give form to an
answer regarding what we are to do apart from the
question of what God has done for us through Christ.

The manner of formulating the question of our
salvation will lead to significantly different ethics.
While some Protestant theologians might argue that
"ultimately, nothing is at stake," the ecclesial descendants of Michael Sattler might well argue that for
Anabaptist ethics, *everything* is at stake. In *The Epistle
to the Romans*, KARL BARTH suggests that through
Christ, "all human duties and virtues and good deeds
are set upon the edge of a knife." We may fruitfully
read these two strongly divergent assertions, along
with the testimonies of other Protestant theologians, as
turning on the knife-edge of soteriology. Here we
examine a seminal text by each of four theologians
key to Protestant thought: Saint Augustine, Martin

Luther, Michael Sattler, and John Calvin. In each of
these strands of Protestant thought, God's radically
prodigal work for us provides the requisite way to
understand our own labors.

"That faith which worketh by love" in Augustine's *On the Spirit and the Letter* (412)

Written in the early fifth century, Saint Augustine's
biblical commentary on II Corinthians and Romans,
On the Spirit and the Letter, became an important
interpretive work for Luther and other Protestant writers. All who followed Augustine in the West sought to
secure their allegiance to his ORTHODOXY. *On the
Spirit and the Letter* was crucial in establishing this
important genealogy for the REFORMATION, perhaps in
part because it is more obviously scriptural than some
of his neo-platonic works. In Augustine's distinction
between a letter that is "inculcating and threatening"
and a spirit that is "assisting and healing," early Protestant writers found a strong emphasis on the necessity of GRACE. Although the Reformation reading of
On the Spirit and the Letter is not uncontested, it
serves to set a tone of humility and gratitude for a
Protestant understanding of ethics. Inasmuch as some
Western Christians had earlier come to see the law as
either a specific task to be duly achieved or a particular failing about which properly to repent, Augustine's words on "the holy law" served to reformulate
the question.

From Chapter 9 of *On the Spirit*, the following
passage well exemplifies the humbling and edifying
use to which the Reformation put Augustine's work:

> For there was need to prove to man how corruptly weak
> he was, so that against his iniquity, the holy law brought
> him no help towards good, but rather increased than
> diminished his iniquity; seeing that the law entered, that
> the offence might abound; that being thus convicted and
> confounded, he might see not only that he needed a
> physician, but also God as his helper so to direct his
> steps that sin should not rule over him, and he might be
> healed by betaking himself to the help of the divine
> mercy; and in this way, where sin abounded grace might
> much more abound—not through the merit of the sin-
> ner, but by the intervention of his Helper.

Augustine breaks from some earlier interpretations of
II Corinthians to read "the law" that heightens "iniquity" not merely as the "old law" of Israel before
Christ, but any law that functions apart from God's
mercy. Reading II Corinthians and Romans together,
Augustine finds a new way to interpret the relation
between precept and mercy. The law, whether spoken
by Christ or through Moses, becomes "the letter that
killeth" if humans seek through the law's guidance to
avoid conviction and confusion and to live by their

687

own will and their own wits. One of Augustine's chief rhetorical aims in the treatise is therefore to create "an ardent desire to cleave to [our] Maker"—to create in us a longing for "the intervention of [our] Helper"—and he judges as fatal a use of holy precepts that allows one to eschew the aid of our maker and physician. Only through the grace of God, written by the Holy Spirit as "the finger of God" in our hearts, are we "repaired" of the effects of SIN and "liberated" to receive the law in doxological joy rather than in fear or pride.

In this way, Augustine reads Paul as striving "with much courage and earnestness against the proud and arrogant. . . in order that he may commend the grace of God." This well characterizes Augustine's own task, as he continually reads Romans, II Corinthians, Galatians, and the Psalms as a commendation of grace, reading each text through a hermeneutic wrought by his own argument with those who encourage holiness without continual reference to and praise of the one who heals, writes, and liberates. In this answer to futile striving, Augustine might have placed the accent on original sin and perpetual depravity. But his stress is slightly different, as he commends, continually, the grace of God. He contrasts Pelagian pride with Christian humility not merely to force his interlocutors to bow, but ultimately to encourage doxology. The various strands of his argument in the text return, again and again, to the refrain of praise for the power of God's grace. For example, in treating a verse like Psalm 36:10—"For He extendeth His mercy to them that know Him, and His righteousness to the upright of heart"—Augustine warns that we avoid a reading whereby we might make ourselves "the chief end of living." Rather, we must continue reading that same Psalm to hear "Let not the foot of pride come against me," a word that beckons us toward "that fountain of life, from the draughts of which alone is imbibed the holiness which is itself the good life." It is to this "fountain of life" that Augustine finally returns the reader, as he considers the possibility of a Christian who lives on earth in accordance with all of God's precepts. In the closing lines of the treatise, Augustine suggests that perhaps God has a reason to not yet grant such a thing as complete compliance, for with perfection, the congregation of believers might be led astray to praise ourselves. We are called to rather open our mouths continually to praise the one by whose mercy and goodness we live.

Augustine endeavors to discredit those who would read and attempt to live the law apart from the Spirit that gives life. The alternative, doxological life to which Augustine calls his readers in *On the Spirit* found one bold adherent who sought to define discipleship as perpetual praise and service.

It is to Martin Luther and *The Freedom of a Christian* (1520) that we now turn.

> Should he grow so foolish, however, as to presume to become righteous, free, saved, and a Christian by means of some good work, he would instantly lose faith and all its benefits, a foolishness aptly illustrated in the fable of the dog who runs along a stream with a piece of meat in his mouth and, deceived by the reflection of the meat in the water, opens his mouth to snap at it and so loses both the meat and the reflection. (Martin Luther, *The Freedom of a Christian*)

In *The Freedom of a Christian*, Luther begins working through I Corinthians 9:19 and Romans 13:8 with the aim of avoiding the dog's foolishness. The statements "For though I am free from all men, I have made myself a slave to all," and "Owe no one anything, except to love one another," intertwine to reveal the liberty and slavery of faithful love. For Luther, the servitude that marks Christian ethics requires a radical freedom, a freedom owing to Christ's payment for humankind's sins. Reading *The Freedom of a Christion* is crucial to understanding Luther's Augustinian emphasis on the centrality of grace and praise in a truly Christian life. In this treatise, Luther considers JUSTIFICATION and ethics as interwoven, indeed almost indistinguishable. What Augustine holds inextricably together—the Christian life and doxology—Luther binds again. The Christian life is distinguished as grateful praise, and all that is worthy of our doing is worthy only inasmuch as it is formed by gratitude.

Luther's rhetorical strategy in the text involves first our recognition that we have nothing, but precisely that we might receive life from another. This dire predicament of nothingness is universal, Luther insists, whether we look to the Old or the New Testament: "As we fare with respect to one commandment, so we fare with all, for it is equally impossible for us to keep any one of them." Luther's primary use of the law, what is at times called his "theological use," brings the reader to the point of sheer need:

> Now when a man has learned through the commandments to recognize his helplessness and is distressed about how he might satisfy the law—since the law must be fulfilled so that not a jot or tittle shall be lost, otherwise man will be condemned without hope—then, being truly humbled and reduced to nothing in his own eyes, he finds in himself nothing whereby he may be justified and saved."

We would misread Luther to discover in his rhetoric merely condemnation without hope, for only through finding ourselves "reduced to nothing" are we prepared to receive the "one thing, and only one thing," that is "necessary for Christian life, righteousness and freedom." Luther preaches the reader into a corner so that he or she might not find a way around the Word: "For if [one] could be justified by anything else, [one] would not need the Word, and consequently [one] would not need faith." To use Luther's own metaphor, we receive all of Christ's benefits only if we run, panting with desperation, to the marital bed, and only if we remain in that bed into our old age, like an eager newlywed. As he puts it in another treatise, *Concerning the Letter and the Spirit*, "Grace is only given to those who long for it."

Only after longing for Christ and all his benefits do individuals receive them.. And for Luther, the benefits are not ephemera. The fable of the foolish dog (quoted earlier) provides a helpful entrée to this aspect of Luther's treatise. Found at the crux of his argument, the story of the lost meat and reflection points to a central concern for Lutheran ethics. The dog loses the steak and the image of the steak, because the image remains only inasmuch as the dog resists the urge to snap hungrily at it. The image of the meat glistening in the water is not an illusion, but neither is it real in and of itself. Works of love for one's neighbor are not illusory, but neither do they exist in and of themselves. Loving works exist as loving works only inasmuch as one perpetually recalls this and avoids the temptation to consider the reflection to be the real meat.

To put this differently, for us truly to be freed for the sake of our neighbor, we must be bound by infinite gratitude for all that Christ is giving us, "unworthy and condemned" as we are. Only as we are bound to Christ, subject to Him in humble receptivity, can we become subject to our neighbor in love. Luther here joins Paul's letter to the Romans, with which he began the treatise, to Paul's letter to the Philippians. By being bound to Christ through our condemnation before the law and through relinquishing of ourselves to Christ, we take on the form of a servant. This "emptying" is crucial if we are truly to love our neighbor as Christ intends. Our graced descent becomes the recurring pattern for our life of discipleship—our reflection, if you will, of the meat of FAITH. For us to love our neighbor, we must come to that neighbor as those who are nothing outside our marriage to Christ. As Luther puts it, we become "Christs to one another," inasmuch as we know ourselves saved only by Christ. By this kind of faith, the Christian "descends" to love the neighbor as he or she is also in need.

The metaphors in this treatise are rhetorically rich, as Luther claims that a faithful soul does not merely "share" in the goodness of Christ, but becomes "saturated and intoxicated" with the promises fulfilled in him. There is a kind of union Luther strains to describe whereby those who wed Christ become truly embodied with Christ's goodness. For Luther, the transformation of the faithful to obedient servants has

the form of *kenosis*, but this emptying results in a joyful abundance that enables "the freest service, cheerfully and lovingly done." Because Christ gives all that a soul needs, the life of a Christian is a "surplus," an act of doxology given unreservedly. Through Christian *kenosis* and receptivity, life itself becomes sheer gift and hardly belonging to one individual to hoard, protect, or navigate with precision. Lutheran "ethics" are, quite literally, gratuitous; the Christian life is a life freely given. If service becomes instead a mapped plan for reward or a strategy to avoid punishment, then it is not Christian service. The Christian, "caught up beyond himself into God," is freed to consider "nothing except the need and advantage of the neighbor."

> The whole problem of ethics is so delicate, so dubious, that the addition of one word too much is far more disastrous than the omission of one word which might have been said.

Luther insists in *Freedom of a Christian* that "ethics" per se is a dangerous concept, a temptation to lose faith and, paradoxically, to lose the self-giving activity reflective of true faith. Luther's recurring emphasis is therefore on soteriology, on the gift of Christ, rather than on the particular nuances of the Christian life. But at least one aspect of his emphasis has abiding implications for Lutheran ethics: All Christians are eligible for this MARRIAGE to Christ. By liberally using the holy wedding imagery previously reserved for the cloistered, Luther both levels and elevates the life of faithful service. The barber, the midwife, and the blacksmith are all as bereft of true Christian virtue as the ordained priest—all are condemned, and all are saved, through the same Christ to whom they may be wed in faith. The previously insignificant lives of the masses are just as open to God's holy use as the lives of those who preside over the Mass. Thus Luther brings about what William Lazareth has called "the emancipation of the common life." The daily toils of the common Christian are sanctified through Christ; whether changing diapers, washing dishes, cutting hair, or baking bread, according to Luther each aspect of the embodied life is potentially crucial to the kingdom.

But by freeing the daily lives of the prince and the pauper for Christian service, Luther also entangles sacred living with the daily minutia of trade, community schooling, care of children, and the execution of criminals. The service for which one is joyfully freed by faith can take forms heretofore considered beneath the calling of a true man or woman of faith. How is such seemingly mundane, or even profane, work transformed by the holy freedom to love one's neighbor? Is the difference merely formal, or does Christ's presence in the sinner also bring a material change? In an attempt to explicate scriptural tensions, as well as tensions pressed by those living in the first generation of the Reformation, Luther tries a complicated and somewhat confusing heuristic: that of the two realms, or kingdoms. In his writings, the knife-edge of ethics rests perilously between these realms: one realm ruled by law and order, and another realm ruled by faith and forgiveness. God institutes both, Luther affirms, but the activity of God is different in each. Through one realm, God preserves the stability of creation; through the other, God saves His people, bringing them to grateful, free service for others.

Luther's writings on the interplay of these two realms in the life of the Christian are sufficiently complex to have troubled his followers since. If the Christian lives in both realms, how does this not lead to a split moral personality? How can forgiveness, grace, and mercy coexist alongside judgement, justice, and punishment? Luther's writings on such questions were occasioned by particular questions in the heat of rebellion, DIVORCE, or ecclesial crisis, and his resolutions are less than systematic. At times, the reader is reminded that Luther's true passion is soteriology, not ethics. Yet there are points of beautiful clarity, such as at the end of *Two Kinds of Righteousness*, where he goes into detail to answer the question: "Is it not proper [for a Christian] to punish sin?" The answer, he says, depends on whether the query comes from a private citizen or from a public servant. The public servant must at times "defend the oppressed" by punishing offenders. But the private citizen may seek the punishment of a wrongdoer only if he is certain that he is not "doing from anger and impatience that which he believes he is doing from love of justice." Luther here and elsewhere presses the faithful to suspect our quests for justice over clemency.

But some who heard Luther's call to a liberated priesthood of holy believers thought his double-edged morality a sham (see PRIESTHOOD OF ALL BELIEVERS). They took offense in particular to his resolution on the question of faithful service and ordered violence. Does not participation in the life of Christ preclude bodily harm of another? It is to Michael Sattler, who sought so to reform the early Reformation, that we now turn.

"Abide in the Lord as God's Obedient Children" through the Schleitheim Confession (1527)

Eliminate from you that which is evil and the Lord will be your God and you will be his sons and daughters. Dear brethren, keep in mind what Paul admonishes Timothy when he says, The grace of God that bringeth salvation hath appeared to all men, teaching us that, denying ungodliness and worldly lusts, we should live soberly, righteously, and godly, in this present world.

This document, attributed to Sattler (d. 1527), is an ecclesial epistle written for and by a group of Christian dissenters for the sake of internal hope, unity, and courage in precarious times. For these besieged reformers, *The Freedom of a Christian* was a call to live in uncompromising obedience to the ways of the one who wrought that freedom. These Christians read the Reformation return to Scripture alone, grace alone, and faith alone as bringing in a new, old way of following Christ: the way of peaceful, nonresistant witness to the truth, even to martyred DEATH. Rejecting what they saw as a duplicitous dualism in Luther's two kingdoms, Sattler and his brethren embraced a new, neo-Johannine dualism. True Christians must "withdraw from Babylon and the earthly Egypt" to remain "free from the slavery of the flesh." They must maintain themselves as "fitted for service" in the "perfection of Christ."

In this concise and clear letter, the early Anabaptists (as they were called by their persecutors) laid out the way of Christ's perfection: (1) baptism is for those who repent and believe; (2) the faithful will practice fraternal admonition, or "the ban"; (3) only those will gather at the Lord's table who are of the "one faith"; (4) because "all creatures are in but two classes, good and bad," there will be a separation from all who are not of that "one faith"; (5) the pastor is to arise from among the faithful to lead among them; (6) believers will neither wield sword against one another, nor wield it against their enemy, nor orchestrate the sword by becoming a magistrate; and (7) there will be no swearing by oaths. By way of these instructions, Sattler and his brethren may "walk according to the simplicity of the divine truth."

The form of the document itself testifies to the different world to which these Christians were called. This is a letter concerning unity, written by the faithful to encourage the faithful; it is not a treatise sent out by a rhetorically or theologically gifted vanguard. The epistle is not so much persuasive as declarative. Finally, the testimony to salvation in Christ is inextricably intertwined with the lived testimony of the faithful life of separation, PACIFISM, and martyrdom. The writers take Luther's separation between two realms and declare themselves to be planted firmly on the only cruciform side of that divide. Because "the sword is ordained of God outside the perfection of Christ," those who embody Christ in the world must eschew the sword for any purpose. The perfection to which Sattler and others were calling one another was not perfection subsequent to salvation, but perfection constitutive of it.

By way of their zeal for Christ's way, the people called Anabaptist become Christ's people (see ANABAPTISM). Ethics and soteriology are again wed in this text, but in a way that mirrors in the reverse Luther's wedding. For Martin Luther, ethics separated from faith alone in Christ alone led to pride or despair and the loss of a union. For Sattler, faith separated from the practices of a holy, nonresistant people is a sham, a parody of the Christian life. Discipleship requires fully embodied cruciformity, as the body of the Christian and the collective body of Christ take on the bloody marks of witness. The consequences are perilous, and the knife-edge of discipleship sharpens. But there is no other way, for, as the letter closes, Christ "gave himself for us, that he might redeem us from all iniquity, and purify unto himself a people of his own, zealous of good works."

We turn next to John Calvin's "Capable of joyful obedience," in INSTITUTES OF THE CHRISTIAN RELIGION (1559).

> For, as soon as Christian freedom is mentioned, either passions boil or wild tumults rise. . . Some, on the pretext of this freedom, shake off all obedience toward God and break out into unbridled license. Others disdain it, thinking that it takes away all moderation, order, and choice of things. What should we do here, hedged about with such perplexities?

Calvin begins Chapter 19 in Book III of his *Institutes* with this question. Is there doctrinal space between the dangers of libertarian ANTINOMIANISM and the pride of works righteousness? From the seeming impasse between Sattler's brethren and the followers of Luther, we are prompted to ask this question with Calvin. Calvin's answer involves a reformulation of Luther's freedom, a reformulation more in line with Luther's ideological brother, PHILIPP MELANCHTHON, than with Luther himself. Under Calvin, the freedom brought by justification in Christ alone issues forth in a new relationship to the law. Through Christ, we are "freed from the law's yoke" and thus enabled "willingly to obey God's will." We receive an "eager readiness to obey God," having received the assurance of righteousness through Christ. In this way, Calvin clears soteriological room for a third use, the "proper," "upbuilding," and "liberating" use of God's commands.

Calvin forges a distinction between two "very different" functions of the law, separating the movement of justification before God and of SANCTIFICATION for the chosen. Disputing ANDREAS OSIANDER's "mixing of forgiveness of sins with rebirth," Calvin sets justification and rebirth as two related but distinct movements of grace. There is "no place" for the law "before

God's judgement seat," as the believer turns only to Christ for the justification that forgives our iniquity. But the law is hardly "superfluous for believers"; it continues "teaching and exhorting and urging them to do good." The "condemnatory" use of the law brings the reprobate to search for God's forgiveness in Christ, but the "pedagogical" use is the proper use for the elect (Book II, Chapter 7). This is the use that enables the daily "progress" of the Christian SAINTS and fulfills the concentric promises of the law and the gospel. This section in Book II is often a commentary on the Psalms, as Calvin explicates the workings of the lamp that lights the paths of the faithful. Using the psalmist to interpret Paul's words on the law, Calvin exclaims, "David especially shows that in the law he apprehended the Mediator, without whom there is no delight or sweetness." Through grace, the otherwise "bitter" law becomes "sweet," and the regenerate pant after righteousness.

The disagreement between Calvin and Luther on the matter of the law's sweetness has roots in their interpretation of Romans 7:24, a passage with which Augustine also struggled. While all three agree that Paul is speaking with the anguish of a "spiritual" or "regenerate" man, Calvin tempers the heat of the verse with a rhetorical reading into the next chapter. There, he reminds us, Paul promises that "there is no more condemnation for those who are in Christ Jesus (Book IV, Chapter 15). For those no longer condemned, for those "sanctified by Christ's spirit," we may "cultivate blamelessness and purity of life." As David Steinmetz has written, for Calvin "Paul's cry. . . is not—and can never be—the last word, not even in this life."

Calvin's vision for purity in this life has a particular setting, the city of Geneva, where the variously appointed councils vigorously pursued the progress of the regenerate. Here Calvin's vision of a regenerate people who live according to God's commandments takes on embodied life. The contours of this community, Calvin lays out in Book II, Chapter 8, where, for instance, the command not to take the Lord's name in vain charges that the faithful speak with "reverence" and "praise" for all that we "recognize as done by him." This deepening of the command is characteristic. Calvin explicates the prohibition against killing thus:

> We are accordingly commanded, if we find anything of use to us in saving our neighbors' lives, faithfully to employ it; if there is anything that makes for their peace, to see to it; if anything harmful, to ward it off; if they are in any danger, to lend a helping hand.

Calvin develops each command with the narrative and teachings of Christ. The one whose death brings about the possibility of righteousness also "restored [the law] to its integrity," and the ten dictates of righteousness become the daily works of justice and mercy. The leaders of Geneva, under Calvin's guidance, sought to foster joyful obedience to these dictates, punishing accordingly those who did not obey. When they discovered, for instance, merchants overcharging their customers, doctors with unfair fees, or someone taking advantage of a sojourner, the councils sought justice. Through a wedding of church and *polis*, Calvin envisioned that the faithful might live a newly rigorous adherence to and joy of the law.

This vision inspired, among others, the life and works of JONATHAN EDWARDS, who sought to bring Calvin's Geneva to bear on life in colonial Massachusetts. Whereas Anabaptists struggled to put their trust only in Christ and Luther's followers recognized that Christ alone could secure a holy city, there remained among Calvin's followers the reasonable hope for a truly holy people on earth.

The question remains whether Calvinist ethics resolves the impasse between Luther's dangerous freedom and Sattler's endangered discipleship by blunting the knife-edge of ethics. As Karl Barth wrote in *The Epistle to the Romans,* "The whole problem of ethics is so delicate, so dubious, that the addition of one word too much is far more disastrous than the omission of one word which might have been said." To paraphrase Barth, has Calvin said one word too many?

Can Ethics Be Christian?

The interim between Calvin's Geneva and Karl Barth's cutting indictment of human striving in *Epistle to the Romans* should be noted. The road to Barth's salvo runs through the ENLIGHTENMENT, and in particular the practical morality of IMMANUEL KANT. With Kant's defense of morality in the *Critique of Practical Reason,* the matter of morality and soteriology is entirely transformed. For Augustine, Luther, Sattler, and Calvin, ethics is a variously complicated dialectic of practice and praise, of discipleship and doxology. In Kant's wake, the "sublime and mighty name that dost embrace nothing charming or insinuating but requirest submission" is not God, but "Duty!" God, as it turns out, is a "postulate of pure practical reason"—the divine becomes a morally necessary assumption. Arguably due in part to the tragically bloody wars following the Reformation, many learned Europeans eagerly accepted a fundamental shift away from the dangerously contested realm of explicit Christianity and toward a moral order within the bounds of universal human reason. Given the flammable alliance of nation-state, warfare, and religious disagreement about the holy kingdom, it is not surprising that Western philosophy took up Kant's summons to a merely human "kingdom of ends."

The results reverberate throughout Protestant thought. James M. Gustafson, a leading Reformed ethicisit of the twentieth century, is able to ask the question "Can Ethics Be Christian," the title of his 1975 book, in large part due to the severing of soteriology and morality. This process spans continents and centuries, and Protestants who sought to retrieve original texts were themselves influenced by the growing separation. For example, a century after the Enlightenment, German theologian ALBRECHT RITSCHL read Luther's de-emphasis of metaphysics through Kant's emphasis on practical reason to depict the Jesus of scripture as a moral figure summoning humanity to a new level of "reciprocal moral action." Ritschl's hope for a civil state that would realize the lived gospel of Jesus found a ready adherent across the Atlantic, as WALTER RAUSCHENBUSCH sought to propel a relatively new nation state toward the justice of Jesus. While neither theologian sought explicitly to banish soteriology from the field of ethics, the question had already become framed in such a way that morality was itself an end humanly pursued. As Western Europe and the UNITED STATES became increasingly secularized, questions of faith, DOCTRINE, and doxology became significantly less important than the separate task of civil, moral discourse. Thus, can ethics be Christian?

Intertwined with this trajectory are thinkers who sought anew to problematize ethics for the sake of soteriology. For Danish philosopher SØREN KIERKEGAARD, Protestant ethics is precisely the irresolvable intersection of faith, fear, and obedience. Both DIETRICH BONHOEFFER and Karl Barth sought to amplify Kierkegaard's crisis in order to summon a new generation to mind the growing gap between Protestant faith and Protestant ethics. While their response is itself ineluctably influenced by the Enlightenment, it may be a promisingly Protestant way to proceed.

See also Capital Punishment; Election; Vocation; War; Schleitheim Confession

References and Further Reading

Althaus, Paul. *The Ethics of Martin Luther.* Translated by Robert C. Schultz. Philadelphia, PA: Fortress Press, 1972.

Augustine. "The Spirit and the Letter." In *Later Works – Volume 8.* Translated by John Burnaby. (Library of Christian Classics). Philadelphia, PA: Westminster Press, 1955.

Barth, Karl. *The Epistle to the Romans.* Translated from the sixth edition by Edwyn C. Hoskyns. Oxford: Oxford University Press, 1968.

Bretzke, James T. *Bibliography on scripture and Christian ethics.* Lewiston, NY: E. Mellen Press, c. 1997.

Calvin, John. *Institutes of the Christian Religion.* Edited by John T. McNeill; translated by Ford Lewis Battles. (Library of Christian Classics). Philadelphia, PA: Westminster Press, 1960.

Chadwick, Owen. *The Reformation.* London: Penguin Books, 1990.

Gustafson, James M. *Ethics from a Theocentric Perspective.* Chicago: University of Chicago Press, 1981.

———. *Protestant and Roman Catholic Ethics: prospects for reapprochement.* Chicago: University of Chicago Press, 1978.

Hauerwas, Stanley. *Character and the Christian life: a study in theological ethics.* San Antonio, TX: Trinity University Press, 1975.

———. *Christians Among the Virtues: theological conversations with ancient and modern ethics.* Notre Dame, IN: University of Notre Dame Press, 1997.

———. *The Peaceable Kingdom: a primer in Christian ethics.* Notre Dame, IN: University of Notre Dame Press, c. 1983.

Hillerbrand, Hans, ed. *The Protestant Reformation.* New York: Harper & Row, 1968.

Luther, Martin. *Two Kinds of Righteousness. The Freedom of a Christian. Temporal Authority: To What Extent It Should Be Obeyed.* All three essays in *Martin Luther's Basic Theological Writings.* Edited by Timothy F. Lull. Minneapolis, MN: Fortress Press, 1989.

Steinmetz, David. *Calvin in Context.* New York: Oxford University Press, 1995.

Yoder, John Howard. *The Legacy of Michael Sattler.* Scottdale, PA: Herald Press, 1973.

AMY LAURA HALL

ETHICS, MEDICAL

"Medical ethics" is one of several terms used to identify a broad set of issues and questions arising from both the practice and the research interests of medicine. The "ethics of health care," for example, considers the principles and policies of medical practice and delivery systems, which permit or prohibit therapeutic interventions. "Biomedical ethics" typically refers to the range of life sciences dealt with under the heading "medicine," whereas "bioethics" usually engages the full range of life sciences as they affect persons. "Pastoral medicine" is sometimes used to describe the ways in which a religion's teachings inform and impinge upon medical practice. "Medical ethics" conventionally signifies the body of conventions and rules that govern professional medical behavior and the mores of physicians.

Early History

Although the present status of medical ethics dates from the mid-twentieth century, its genesis is many centuries older, and the evolutionary process that developed what we now know as medical ethics evolved gradually over many millennia. In primitive cultures the shaman or medicine man was (and continues to be) both priest and physician, whose early ethics embraced both religious virtues and medical techniques deeply rooted in vows, prayers, and codes. In modern times, however, medical ethics has become progressively autonomous and emancipated from religious presuppositions.

In medicine's infancy, whatever comfort or relief a patient hoped for from a physician's ministrations was not derived from a set of timeless ideals or a medical ethics in the modern sense. All the same, ancient physicians were likely aware that both patients and colleagues harbored certain expectations of them, if only in the form of the natural virtues of prudence, justice, temperance, and fortitude. It is reasonable to think that the emerging vocation of medicine was, therefore, not without certain self-conscious moral commitments.

As a general rule, from their inception and through evolving stages, what we now know as the "professions" were not without some inchoate sense of purpose, however dimly perceived in antiquity. That purpose contained an incipient ethics that became articulate over time, and typically took the form of principles of right and wrong that defined the character and governed the conduct of members of the profession. Whereas earlier interests in medicine as a vocation focused on its social and cultural role, modern medical ethics is largely driven by emerging innovative issues in research and practice.

There is no evidence that ancient Western physicians were required to swear an oath or accept even an informal code of professional conduct. The Hippocratic corpus, variously dated as from the sixth century B.C. to the first century A.D., is our earliest documentary expression of "medical ethics." Although it mandated both behavior and noble aphorisms for physicians, it was not widely accepted or practiced until the advent of Christianity, whose ideals and virtues were consistent with the major features of the Hippocratic template. In the modern period, medical schools have employed solemn pledges for their graduates using either a version of the Hippocratic oath or incorporating concepts from it. While there is nothing comparable to the Hippocratic corpus in the earlier literature of classical Greece and Rome, there is a Chinese code of medical ethics developed in Sun Ssu-maiao's *The Thousand Golden Remedies,* which dates from the sixth century A.D.

Several moral maxims, the origins of which cannot always be identified in Western medicine, emerged from this period. The most familiar of them is the Hippocratic precept, *primum non nocere* (do no harm)—do not make matters worse by your intervention. Another Hippocratic dictum holds that it is the duty of physicians to preserve (or prolong) life and to relieve pain (or suffering). The precept also requires that the physician's duty is to his primary patient, and that medical decisions are to be made for the benefit of the primary patient without concern for spinoff benefits that might accrue to dependent populations. Yet another hoary maxim from this period is that a physician is under no obligation to offer, nor a patient under any duty to receive, treatments that are not beneficial to the patient being treated. The wisdom of these and other ancient moral maxims has been tested by twentieth-century advances in medical and biomedical technologies, by the advent of sophisticated mechanisms (like double-blind clinical studies) for assessing treatment efficacy, by systems theory and family medicine (which challenge the exclusivity of the primary patient), and by therapies for which the preservation of life and the relief of pain are sometimes not complementary.

Religion

In the ancient world, and prior to the Christian era, primary Jewish commentary on medical topics was contained in the Mishnah and the Palestinian and Babylonian Talmuds. Further rabbinic responsa to questions concerning medical matters are found in various collections of Midrash. Already the ground was being prepared for an anecdotal, case-oriented medical ethics; but the full implementation of this approach was delayed for several centuries by remarkable innovations in medical technology. Meanwhile, the need for summary statements of Jewish law took the form of codes, one of which was written in the twelfth century by Moses Maimonides, who was himself a rabbi and a physician. In the centuries following, five identifiable principles important for Jewish medical ethics have emerged: human life has intrinsic value; the highest moral imperative is the preservation of human life; all human lives are equal; our lives belong to God; the sanctity of human life inheres in the human being as a whole. Over time the work of Maimonides, together with that of Christian scholastics, became the prototype for modern secular codes of medical ethics.

In the first fifteen centuries of the Christian era, the expectations and commitments within the guild of medicine were both deepened and made more explicit as Christian theologians directed interest to the etiology of diseases and the moral merits of medical interventions. In their efforts to take account of the attributes ascribed to God, they widely believed God to be both the origin of, and the remedy for, human suffering and disease: "See now that I, I am He, and besides me there is no god: I put to death and I keep alive, I inflict wounds and I heal; there is no rescue from my grasp." (Deuteronomy 32:39) It may there-

fore be unsurprising that philosophies of medicine in the early Christian era variously held that medicine was an instrument of divine grace to provide relief and, conversely, that medicine demonstrated an absence of faith in its diabolic human attempt to alter the divine purpose.

Evolution of Codes

From the seventeenth century onward, the history of medical ethics took on a distinctively different look. With the advent of the rational ENLIGHTENMENT, monarchial forms of government, frequent revolutions, and a diminished role for religion in social and political life, metaphysical traditions were abandoned in favor of an experimental empirical scientific orientation that increasingly claimed both cultural ascendancy and medicine's allegiance.

Among other notable changes, the notion was developed in GERMANY that physicians are not only agents for the sick but are also the overseers and managers of a country's health; in FRANCE the revolutionary ideology of a right to health care took shape; and medical philosophers in Great Britain and the young UNITED STATES applied common-sense intuition in their efforts to articulate a moral philosophy for medicine that was universal in both scope and application.

Early medical ethics essays in colonial America appropriated the common-sense appeal to moral principles which claimed that each individual is endowed with an innate moral sense which, if properly maintained, could serve as an internalized moral gyroscope. The first of these essays, Samuel Bard's (1742–1821) *Discourse on the Duties of a Physician* (1769), agreed with the eighteenth-century Scottish moral philosopher Francis Hutcheson (1694–1746) that duty and benevolence were the governing moral principles. In 1789 Benjamin Rush addressed some doctor–patient issues in his speech, "Observations on the Duties of a Physician and the Methods for Improving Medicine," in which he focused on the knowledge and skills that identified the physician as a professional. Meanwhile, John Gregory of Edinburgh published his *Lectures upon the Duties and Qualifications of a Physician* (1817), an ambitious essay in which the author spoke to the moral qualities and temperament required of a physician, together with the kind of education suitable to qualify a physician for practice.

Although preceded by several physician-authored essays on the duties of physicians, as well as a code of ethics promulgated by the Medical Society of New Jersey in 1766, the publication of Thomas Percival's (1740–1804) *Medical Ethics* (1803) is generally acknowledged as the beginning of modern Western medical ethics. Percival's book actually has more to do with medical etiquette than with medical ethics. His principal claim was that a physician should be a Christian gentleman—prudent, charitable, honest, trustworthy. Percival's treatise remained the presiding reference for medical ethics into the third decade of the twentieth century, when Chauncey Leake's 1927 edition of his book was published. In sum, these early attempts at formulating a medical ethics proffered a series of benevolent duties: cure the sick; comfort the dying; serve the poor; observe confidentiality and honesty; and do all this unselfishly out of regard for others and not for self.

In 1808 an association of Boston physicians adopted a code of medical ethics that closely followed Percival's model; in 1823 the New York State Medical Society followed suit. In rapid succession codes were ratified by The Medico-Chirurgical Society of Baltimore (1832) and by the College of Physicians of Philadelphia (1843). The newly formed American Medical Association, meeting in Philadelphia and drawing largely from Percival's *Medical Ethics,* promulgated the first national code of ethics in 1847.

The AMA code has been revised several times, most recently as the "Principles of Medical Ethics" (1980), a document bearing little resemblance to Percival's. The seven principles perpetuate the tradition: a physician is to contribute to the community, but as a private citizen; patient care is advocated, but physicians are guaranteed the freedom to choose whom they will serve; and there is no hint that physicians, or the profession as a whole, are obligated to influence the distribution of medical resources to serve the underserved. The principles express prerogatives for self-regulation, stress the individual practitioner's autonomy, and make no affirmation of the equality of patients as persons. There is no lively sense of the common good except as this might spin off from the good one does oneself. The overall cast of this document is of a union or guild document, a statement made by craftsmen to protect themselves in which their prerogatives and rights form the central motif. In the larger cultural tradition of medical ethics, the 1980 AMA "Principles" appear to be the *creatio ex nihilo* (creation out of nothing) of modern doctors. To be sure, there are exceptions to this stance; the code of the American College of Physicians, together with many of the other medical specialty codes, displays a different temperament that tends to reflect an older and more traditional model of covenantal, rather than contractual, physician–patient relationship.

International concern for, and interest in, medical ethics escalated following World War II, and several global codes were adopted. In 1947 the Nuremberg War Crimes Tribunal propounded 10 standards, called "The Nuremberg Code," to guide physicians in all future experiments on human subjects; in 1948 the General Assembly of the World Medical Association adopted a modified form of the Hippocratic oath known as the "Declaration of Geneva"; in 1964 the World Medical Association expanded the ethics of human experimentation and ratified the "Declaration of Helsinki," which was promptly endorsed by nine medical organizations in the United States active in clinical investigations; and, continuing this concern, the "AMA Guidelines for Clinical Investigation" were promulgated in 1966.

The Modern Period

Meanwhile, medical ethics was receiving the attention of scholars outside the medical profession as increasing numbers of theologians, philosophers, lawyers, social scientists, and others began to address the broad range of issues arising from the practice of medicine. Roman Catholic moral theologians and some papal encyclicals have been attentive to medico-moral issues for several centuries. In addition, Judaism lays claim to a lengthy tradition of rabbinic responsa, together with the dicta of religious courts, on these topics. The literature of medical ethics since the REFORMATION contains works, among those already cited, by several Protestant physicians, but deliberate and sustained cognizance of these matters in commentary by Protestant theological ethicists and moral philosophers has been comparatively recent. The tendency of Jewish medical ethics has been case oriented. Roman Catholic theologians, while utilizing carefully wrought natural law principles, have been casuistic as well. In an increasingly secular venue, both of these approaches have been labeled as "legalistic" and, in much current discussion, rejected or disregarded. The tendency among Protestant commentators, among whom are both intentional and nominal Protestants, has been case oriented as well, but without the resource of ecclesial canon or dicta.

There may be several reasons for the recent increase in serious and sustained scholarly attention to medicine and ethics: (1) increased governmental supervision of medical funding and practice following decrees by the Nuremberg Tribunal on human experimentation and other medical activities; (2) exponential advances in technologies of various sorts, but especially biomedical technologies; (3) the role of mass media in disseminating information on medical breakthroughs both large and small; (4) a decline in colonialism together with escalating competition among nations for technical achievement; and (5) increasing attention by government, the general public, and nonmedical academic specialists to the full range of issues in medical education, practice, and research. These and doubtless other developments in the last half of the twentieth century appear to have encouraged what has come to be an eruption of commentary, both verbal and written.

In the twentieth century, the first significant book by a Protestant theologian to address itself to ethical issues arising out of the practice of medicine was Joseph Fletcher's *Morals and Medicine* (1954). Two other scholarly monographs appeared sixteen years later: Paul Ramsey's (1913–1988) *The Patient as Person* and Harmon Smith's (1930–) *Ethics and the New Medicine* (both 1970). In the decades after 1970, a deluge of articles, monographs, symposia, bibliographies, and dictionaries followed. Most prominent among the authors of these texts were religious ethicists, but there were increasingly others—philosophers, physicians, nurses, lawyers, political scientists, historians, and economists—who addressed themselves to burgeoning biomedical technology and changing medical practice. Today one must be acquainted with this wide range of commentary in order to be well-informed.

Some of these works were of general interest, treated many issues, and were frequently adopted as texts for emerging college and university courses. Among them are Edmund D. Pellegrino and David C. Thomasma, *A Philosophical Basis of Medical Practice* (1981); Robert M. Veatch, *A Theory of Medical Ethics* (1981); William F. May, *The Physician's Covenant: Images of the Healer in Medical Ethics* (1983); Thomas Beauchamp and James Childress, *Principles of Bio-Medical Ethics* (1983); *Health and Human Values: A Guide to Making Your Own Decision* (1983), edited by Frank Hanon, John Burnside, and Thomas Beauchamp; the multivolume report of the President's Commission for the Study of Ethical Problems in Medicine and Biomedical and Behavioral Research (1983); and Leon Kass, *Toward a More Natural Science* (1985).

A number of essays and monographs appeared challenging traditional and conventional ways of dealing with medical ethics. Among these were Ivan Illich, *Medical Nemesis: The Expropriation of Health* (1976); H. T. Engelhardt, *The Foundations of Bioethics* (1986); Stanley Hauerwas, *Suffering Presence: Theological Reflections on Medicine, the Church and the Mentally Handicapped* (1986); and Harmon L. Smith and Larry R. Churchill, *Professional Ethics and Primary Care Medicine: Beyond Dilemmas and Decorum* (1986).

Other publications addressed particular topics and problem areas. Illustrative of these works are Robert F. Weir, *Selective Nontreatment of Handicapped Newborns* (1984); Karen Lebacqz, *Genetics, Ethics and Parenthood* (1983); Joel Feinberg, *The Problem of Abortion* (1984); Brian Clark's play, *Whose Life Is It, Anyway* (1980); Paul Starr, *The Social Transformation of American Medicine* (1982); and Larry Churchill, *Rationing Health Care in America: Perceptions and Principles of Justice* (1987).

Writings on medical ethics currently address every aspect of the practice of medicine, together with a broad range of commentary on ancillary matters related to the profession. The *Encyclopedia of Bioethics* (1982) is a standard reference. The *Hastings Center Report* (published by the Institute of Society, Ethics, and the Life Sciences), the *Journal of Medical Ethics* (published by the Society for the Study of Medical Ethics), *Second Opinion* (published by the Park Ridge Center for the Study of Health, Faith, and Ethics), the *Journal of Medicine and Philosophy,* and the *Linacre Quarterly* are among the best-known periodicals of this genre. In addition, The Kennedy Institute of Ethics at Georgetown University annually publishes a *Bibliography of Bioethics,* and the Hastings Center biannually produces a *Bibliography of Ethics, Biomedicine and Professional Responsibility.* These bibliographics list not only entries on clinical topics from womb to tomb, but also inventories of a growing miscellany of monographs and symposia on issues extending from genetics and molecular biology to managed care to after death, out-of-body phenomena. There is, further, a growing list of publications addressing the infrastructure of the practice of medicine. These and other writings comprise a literature that appears in both the popular and professional press, and in other media as well, leaving no important issue unexamined.

Attempts to attribute the genesis of these diverse commentaries to either a single technical *tour de force,* such as cardiac homografts, or to a cluster of insistent events such as the allocation of a scarce, lifesaving resources, have been unconvincing. Very like its ancient history, medical ethics in the modern period has evolved from a constellation of events, some of which have to do with remarkable technical advances in medical and biomedical applications, and some of which have to do with the economic and political milieu within which modern medicine is practiced. The formative years appear to have been the two and one-half decades between the mid-1940s and the early 1980s.

In 1967 Colorado was the first state to revise its abortion statute to legalize abortions for the so-called maternal, fetal, and social indications. Several states followed suit before the U.S. Supreme Court, in its 1973 *Roe v. Wade* decision, provided abortion on request in the first and second trimesters and, with some state-imposed restrictions, in the third trimester.

Artificial insemination issues arose in the late 1960s with several celebrated cases that challenged traditional notions about paternity, whether AID constituted adultery, and provoked child support litigation. In 1978 the first *in vitro* fertilization/embryo implantation baby was born. Systematic genetic screening for ethnic-specific populations, particularly for sickle-cell anemia among African Americans and Tay-Sachs disease among Ashkenazy Jews, was begun in the 1960s. After centuries of pronouncing death on the basis of cardiorespiratory criteria, the French Academy of Medicine proposed brain-function criteria in the late 1950s; the Beecher Committee refined those criteria in 1968, and in 1981 a presidential commission proposed a Uniform Definition of Death Act, which was endorsed by the American Bar Association, the American Medical Association, and the National Conference of Commissioners on Uniform State Laws. The new criteria provided that irreversible cessation of circulatory and respiratory functions, or irreversible cessation of all functions of the entire brain, were sufficient to pronounce a patient dead. In the mid-1970s the case of Karen Ann Quinlan was among the first to test the new brain death criteria. These were halcyon years.

Resident in distinct but related events are some of the controversial claims and counterclaims that gave rise to medical ethics. It became known in 1962, for example, that owing to an insufficient number of dialysis machines, candidates for chronic hemodialysis at Seattle's Artificial Kidney Center at Swedish Hospital were being selected on the basis of criteria that included social utility and were considerably broader than immediate and urgent patient need. Both professional and public response ranged from outrage to admiration. In retrospect, some have said that the committee, appointed by the county medical society and euphemistically known as the "God squad," was making life and death decisions for patients that they had no moral right to make. Others have maintained that, in view of many claims upon only a few machines, the committee was performing a responsible and unavoidable, however onerous, civic duty to both the individual candidates for dialysis and the larger society. Because Belden Scriber's invention in the 1960s of the arteriovenous shunt made chronic dialysis for renal failure a much less hazardous and far more patient-friendly clinical option, this event is seen by some to have triggered, for both the public and the professions, the increased interest in medical ethics.

Willem Kolff reported development of the first successful renal dialysis machine in 1944, but the broad moral issues regarding its availability and the clinical need for it did not arise until the 1960s, when it became clear that renal dialysis was a scarce, life-saving resource and that more patients required dialysis than there were machines to serve them. Ultimately, the United States Congress was willing to allocate sufficient funding to guarantee dialysis to every citizen who qualified for it.

These developments laid the groundwork for the dramatic first successful renal homograft between identical twins performed by Joseph Murray and his team at Boston's Peter Bent Brigham Hospital in 1954. This surgical transplant was not only a breakthrough in biomedical technology, but a harbinger of serious moral issues: in this instance, whether it is ever right or proper to take a normal organ from a healthy person for replacement of a diseased organ in a sick person. Many believed that this procedure violated the ancient maxim that authorized intervention is only for the benefit of the primary patient.

There were, in fact, many noteworthy and morally provocative events preceding the Seattle quandary. In the early 1940s, treating World War II burn victims and building on the earlier work of Emile Holman, which showed that an immune process of some sort was at work in rejecting skin grafts, Peter Medawar confirmed Holman's hypothesis and demonstrated that the process could be inverted by injecting foreign cells into very young animals who then acquired tolerance for "foreign" grafts without rejecting them. Theoretically, human embryos could also become histocompatible with the donors of injected cells; and cyclosporine and other immunosuppressive drugs used in later tissue and organ transplantation would thus have been unneeded had donor and recipient exchanged histocompatible tissue or organs. Such a move was morally repulsive to Medawar, but there is no evidence that his decision *not* to demonstrate this hypothesis in human subjects generated much public or professional attention. Unlike later decisions by some hospitals *not* to admit and treat indigent patients, Medawar's choice clearly did not create an ethical *cause célèbre*.

Methodologies of Medical Ethics

Contemporary writings on medical ethics range from descriptive studies to ideologic advocacy, and the case study method is overwhelmingly popular. Narrative and literature studies have recently provided an innovative tool for both teaching and problem solving. Overall, contemporary medical ethics prefers an ethics of duty and obligation, which is called *deontology*, to an ethics of goals and ends, or *teleology*; indeed both the practice and research interests of medicine are sometimes criticized for not having a discrete and robust goal. Moreover, rejecting the older medical paternalism and reflecting increasingly popular consumer advocacy, utilitarian principles frequently claim the center of attention in current monographs, with little or no attention given to an exposition of the character requisite to being a good physician. The stress on decision procedures and utilitarian principles tends to eschew and avoid the complexity of physician self-perceptions, professional loyalties, and the subtle influences of habits of practice that have been historically at the core of medical ethics. Fear of malpractice litigation has further contributed to increasing substitution of computer and other electronic and mechanical analyses for clinical judgment. The hospital, not the bedside in a home, has come to be the principal site of care.

Whether medical ethics is a species of ethics or a genus unto itself remains an unresolved question. The greater weight of the evidence suggests that what is unique about the moral deliberations that occur within the context of medicine are data, not agreed-upon ethical principles and virtues. Ethics derives from the Greek ηϑος and morals from the Latin *mores,* both of which signified expected, routine, and conventional behavior. In late medieval universities, ethics came to be the study of character and virtue, of the theory of good behavior, while morals came to be the study of proper conduct, of the practice of behavior. That distinction, between an accurate description of behavior and a rational account of why it was appropriate behavior, was initiated in order to bring rationality to conduct, but rationality in modernity is elusive owing to emphasis on individual autonomy and the absence of shared intellectual and moral commitments.

Because the topics associated with medical ethics were foreign to most academic departments—philosophy departments, for example, were largely preoccupied with existentialism and formal criticism of language—most of the earlier twentieth-century commentary on medical ethics was provided by theologians and theological ethicists. It became quickly apparent, however, that for medical ethics (or bioethics or biomedical ethics) to survive and succeed in a pluralistic and increasingly secularized culture, religious/theological language would need to be superceded and replaced by a cultural speech independent of religion, and that the cherished American virtues of autonomy and private conscience could not be violated, even under the rubric of "the common good." Attention turned, quite naturally therefore, from preoccupation with a virtuous character to concerns for public policy and law, with the result that medical ethics, as practiced, has tended more and more to locate its *raison d'être* in regulations and regulatory agencies like institutional review boards and ethics advisory committees.

Among all the species, it was believed that the human species has the unique capacity to give an intelligible account of its behavior. The task of ethics was therefore to assess the congruence or incongruence, the coherence or incoherence, of behavior when measured by belief, or of belief when gauged by behavior. So ethics as ethics is not concerned with codifying behavior, or defining right and wrong conduct; its task instead is to articulate what William Temple called "basic commitments," the beliefs and virtues that describe the character of persons. This method has been largely abandoned in contemporary discussions of medical ethics, and appeal to regulations of various sorts has taken its place.

Herein lie the grounds for an internal debate among medical ethicists: has the shift from decorum and internal conversation to publicly examined decision making been serviceable to either physicians or their patients? Should the subject matter of their consultations be entirely rule governed? Are our choices always principled? Is decision making the *sine qua non* of ethics? Is the democratization of medical decision making as common public property a good thing? Is there a place between physician and patient in medical ethics for character and relationship? Has the fiduciary relationship been sacrificed to a business model?

References and Further Reading

"BioethicsLine," the National Library of Medicine Data Base.

Duncan, A. S. *Dictionary of Ethics.* New York: Crossroads, 1981.

Numbers, R. L., and D. W. Amundsen, eds. *Caring and Curing: Health and Medicine in the Western Religious Traditions.* New York: Macmillan, 1986.

President's Commission for the Study of Ethical Problems in Medicine and Biomedical and Behavioral Research. Five reports with appendices. Washington, D.C., 1981–1983.

Social Science and Medicine. Pergamon Journals Ltd.

Update. Loma Linda University Center for Christian Bioethics. 1985ff.

Trends in Health Care, Law and Ethics (previously *Info Trends: Medicine, Law & Ethics*). UMDNJ-Robert Wood Johnson Medical School.

HARMON L. SMITH

ETHNICITY

Protestant churches are often rooted in ethnic communities but confess faith in the oneness of Christ's CHURCH, which transcends all divisions.

Definition

The Greek roots *ethnikos* and *ethnos* refer to a people or a nation. However, although ethnicity is closely related to national identity, the two are not synonymous. Some modern nation states have a high degree of ethnic homogeneity, but others contain a large number of ethnic groups. These are sometimes distinguished by language, but a sense of shared CULTURE and history can be sufficient to form a strong sense of ethnic identity. Religious profession is often one of the unifying features of an ethnic community. Through their ethnicity, people celebrate the particularity and diversity of human life. However, ethnic identity can also be evoked ideologically to mobilize a community for political or military action. Its dark side can be seen, for example, in racism and ethnic cleansing.

Protestant Churches and Ethnic Identity

Since the day of Pentecost, the Christian church has been called to transcend all barriers of language, nationality, and ethnicity. The Latin Mass of the medieval church was a powerful symbol of unity throughout Western Europe. The sixteenth-century REFORMATION appeared to disrupt this unity, first by promoting WORSHIP in the vernacular and second by organizing the church on a national basis. The principle of *cuius regio eius religio* ("whose region his the religion") ensured that the Protestant faith came to be identified with particular territories and peoples. To its critics, the Reformation had fragmented the church into a miscellany of ethnic religious movements. Its defenders were at pains to stress that shared DOCTRINE and common practice expressed the unity of the church even when it was organized on national lines. Nevertheless the danger remained that the Protestant churches might be compromised by their close identification with particular nations and/or ethnic communities. As Christianity developed in North America, most immigrants adhered to the church that most closely corresponded to their ethnic origins in Europe. When the Protestant faith was taken to other parts of the world through missionary work (see MISSIONS), it tended to replicate the ethnically based divisions of the North Atlantic. These were reinforced by comity agreements, which divided territory geographically among the various missions. The result was often a series of ethnically homogeneous Protestant churches, a pattern favorable to church growth. "Indigenous principles," wrote Donald McGavran, "lead Christians to go to their own folk, to their kith and kin, and thus to grow among their own kind of people. . . . Men like to become Christians without crossing racial, linguistic or class barriers." (McGavran 1970: 350)

Ethnicity and the One Church of Jesus Christ

The church's mission constantly drives it to become fully local, rooted in the native soil of each particular community. The dynamic of the incarnation means that the church grows as Christ comes to be at home in each culture. Yet this process carries the danger that Christian FAITH becomes so bound up with the interests of an ethnic group that it is easily compromised. The church can lose all critical distance from the culture in which it is set. It can put up barriers that divide it from sister churches even in the same locality. When this happens, the church needs to recover its catholic or universal character. Protestant faith requires the dialectic of affirming national and ethnic identity as the sphere within which Christ becomes known and enfleshed, while always relativizing ethnicity by pointing to its destiny in the wider purpose of God that embraces all peoples in and through Jesus Christ.

A definitive moment in the clarification of this issue came in GERMANY in the 1930s. The GERMAN CHRISTIANS argued that their ethnic and national identity was an order of creation granted by God and gave their support to Adolf Hitler's National Socialism. The minority CONFESSING CHURCH argued that the church is constituted by hearing the Word of God—Jesus Christ—and found therein a basis for questioning Hitler's program. Through the BARMEN DECLARATION of 1934, they affirmed the finality of the unity of the church in Jesus Christ.

SOUTH AFRICA'S apartheid system was decisively challenged in 1982 at Ottowa when the General Council of the WORLD ALLIANCE OF REFORMED CHURCHES affirmed that "the Gospel of Jesus Christ demands. . . a community of believers which transcends all barriers of race—a community in which the love for Christ and for one another has overcome the divisions of race and colour." Apartheid in South Africa was declared to be a HERESY. It was made clear that ethnic identity, however its richness may be cherished, can never be accorded a place of ultimacy in the life of the church.

In the post-Cold War age of ethnically based conflict, the church has an urgent obligation to demonstrate the reconciliation brought by Jesus Christ. Protestant churches need to be on guard lest they be coopted by an ethnic group and reduced to functioning as a tribal religion. The migration of people groups into urban melting pots brings anew the question of whether their faith is primarily an expression of ethnic identity or whether they belong primarily to a global community of faith. Protestant faith affirms the integrity of national and ethnic identities but always deabsolutizes them and makes clear that belonging together in Christ transcends all ethnic differences among people.

References and Further Reading

Appleby, R. Scott. *The Ambivalence of the Sacred: Religion, Violence and Reconciliation*. Lanham and Oxford, UK: Rowman and Littlefield, 2000.

Cochrane, Arthur C. *The Church's Confession Under Hitler*, Pittsburgh, PA: The Pickwick Press, 1976.

De Gruchy, John W., and Charles Villa-Vicencio. *Apartheid is a Heresy*. Grand Rapids, MI: Eerdmans, 1983.

Gonzales, Justo L. *Out of Every Tribe and Nation: Christian Theology at the Ethnic Roundtable*. Nashville, TN: Abingdon, 1992.

McGavran, Donald A. *Understanding Church Growth*, Grand Rapids, MI: Eerdmans, 1970.

Volf, Miroslav. *Exclusion and Embrace: A Theological Exploration of Identity, Otherness and Reconciliation*. Nashville, TN: Abingdon, 1996.

Walls, Andrew F. *The Missionary Movement in Christian History: Studies in the Transmission of Faith*. Maryknoll, NY: Orbis Books, 1996.

KENNETH R. ROSS

EUCHARIST

See Lord's Supper

EUTHANASIA

The term *euthanasia* (literally "good" or "gentle" death or "dying well") covers a wide range of issues, depending on whether the patient is conscious/competent and/or whether the physician's conduct is active or passive. Many people distinguish simply between voluntary euthanasia (where a competent, informed person asks another to end his or her life and is not coerced into doing so) and involuntary euthanasia (where a terminally ill person, who does not have the capacity for informed choice, is killed). Because many believe that the person taking the life should be a trained physician, voluntary euthanasia is increasingly termed "physician-assisted suicide."

However, there are other acts or omissions that may also be seen as forms of euthanasia. A physician may withdraw treatment or medical intervention knowing that this will shorten a comatose patient's life. Or a conscious patient may refuse life-sustaining treatment even though the physician is willing to continue treatment. Or, again, a patient might leave a Living Will to the effect that he or she does not wish to be treated in the event of serious illness. Given this wide range of possibilities very few people remain wholly for or against every form of euthanasia. Even among advocates of "direct" or "active" euthanasia few recommend that the lives of *all* of those who are permanently comatose or have severe learning disabilities should be actively terminated.

Among Christians there is no unanimity on euthanasia. On this ethical issue, as on many others, there is a range of beliefs across denominations and within denominations. Even when a particular church takes a firm line against, say, physician-assisted suicide, some of its regular churchgoers will conclude otherwise.

This can be illustrated from opinion poll data. For example, data from *British Social Attitudes* surveys suggested that most people, including many churchgoers, increasingly support changes in the law that would allow physician-assisted suicide for the terminally ill. Seventy-six percent of the whole sample in the 1980s were in favor of this being allowed for the terminally ill and in the 1990s this rose to 82 percent. Support among monthly churchgoers across denominations during these two decades differed little from the sample as a whole—it was 72 and 84 percent, respectively. It was only among weekly churchgoers that a statistically significant difference emerged, with support at 48 and 45 percent, respectively. Among Anglican weekly churchgoers in the 1980s support rose to 66 percent. Clearest opposition to this form of euthanasia was among Roman Catholic weekly churchgoers: here only 39 percent supported it, although among monthly attenders this rose to 75 percent. Age was not a strong predictor of different attitudes. Even a 1990s question about allowing for euthanasia for those who are simply tired of living showed that 6 percent of weekly churchgoers, as distinct from 12 percent of the sample as a whole, agreed to this.

From a theological perspective it might once have been sufficient simply to argue that human life is God-given and should never be taken by human beings outside a context of a just war or just punishment. However, the dilemmas created by modern medicine seem to make such a clear-cut position increasingly difficult to hold. Is withdrawing life-sustaining medical treatment or intensive nursing care from a patient whose cortex is destroyed tantamount to euthanasia or not? Is withholding life-prolonging treatment with the agreement of conscious but terminally ill patients tantamount to assisted suicide or not? Modern medicine makes such questions unavoidable.

It is often argued by theologians in this context that human life is a gift, a gift from a loving God made known in Jesus Christ. The analogy of the gift relationship finds its foundation in God's gift of the Logos and continues in the Logos's gift of life to us. We in turn should respond to this gift with gratitude, thanksgiving, and deep responsibility. In contrast, those who lack this faith may see human life, not as a gracious gift, but as a chance by-product of a world that has meaning only if we choose to give it meaning. In theory at least, this second position allows human beings to shape human life as they will. If people decide to opt for euthanasia then that is their autonomous choice: life can be shaped as they will. Conversely, for Christians life is God-given and is not simply to be shaped by humans as they will, but to be approached gratefully and responsibly.

Yet in the context of modern medicine the contrast between these two positions is not nearly so clear-cut. Christian doctors, committed to the belief that life is God-given, still face the same dilemmas about prolonging the lives of the terminally ill or permanently comatose. Gift relationships are by no means all gracious—some can be highly manipulative, especially the required gifts of submission. Gracious gifts should be treated with gratitude and responsibility, but they may not bind the one to whom they are given—it is manipulative gifts that do that. Gracious gifts can be enjoyed for a while and then shared with, or even returned with gratitude to, the giver. Gracious gifts leave both giver and receiver free. Indeed when God-given life becomes nothing but a burden, it might seem appropriate to return that life prayerfully and humbly to the giver.

The 1998 LAMBETH CONFERENCE of Anglican Bishops identified five "bedrock principles" that are crucial to these issues from a Christian perspective:

> Life is God-given and therefore has intrinsic sanctity, significance, and worth.
>
> Human beings are in relationship with the created order and that relationship is characterized by such words as respect, enjoyment, and responsibility.
>
> Human beings, although flawed by sin, nevertheless have the capacity to make free and responsible moral choices.
>
> Human meaning and purpose are found in our relationship with God, in the exercise of freedom, critical self-knowledge, and in our relationship with one another and the wider community.
>
> This life is not the sum total of human existence; we find our ultimate fulfillment in eternity with God through Christ.

The bishops argued that a combination of the first, second, and fourth principles precludes either voluntary euthanasia or involuntary euthanasia. They also worried about the consequential dangers of legalizing such forms of euthanasia—especially the danger of abuse, the danger of diminution of respect for human life, and the danger of damaging the doctor/patient relationship. They summarized the dangers as follows:

- the virtual impossibility of framing and implementing legislation that would prevent abuse by the unscrupulous
- a diminution of respect for all human life, especially of the marginalized and those who may be regarded as "unproductive" members of society
- the potential devaluing of worth, in their own eyes, of the elderly, the sick, and of those who are dependent on others for their well-being
- the potential destruction of the important and delicate trust of the doctor/patient relationship

However, they argued that the following *are* consonant with their Christian principles:

- To withhold or withdraw excessive medical treatment or intervention (e.g., life support) may be appropriate where there is no reasonable prospect of recovery.
- When the primary intent is to relieve suffering and not to bring about death, to provide supportive care for the alleviation of intolerable pain and suffering may be appropriate even if the side effect of that care is to hasten the dying process (i.e., the doctrine of double effect).
- To refuse or terminate medical treatment (such as declining to undertake a course of chemotherapy for cancer) is a legitimate individual moral choice.
- When the person is in a permanent vegetative state to sustain him or her with artificial nutrition and hydration may indeed be seen as constituting medical intervention.

See also Ethics; Ethics, Medical

References and Further Reading

"Euthanasia." *Studies in Christian Ethics* 11 no. 1 (1998): Special edition.

Gill, Robin, ed. *Euthanasia and the Churches*. London: Cassell, 1998.

The Lambeth Conference 1998: The Reports, Resolutions and Pastoral Letters from the Bishops. London: The Anglican Consultative Council, 1998.

ROBIN GILL

EVANGELICAL (EVANGELISCH)

The term is derived from the Greek euangelium ("good news", i.e. the "good news" of the gospel) and came into widespread usage in the German Reformation. The German equivalent, "evangelisch" used both as noun and adjective became quickly the self-designation for the supporters of the MARTIN LUTHER, HULDRYCH ZWINGLI, and the other reformers. The usage of the term thus preceded the introduction of the terms "Lutheran," "Calvinist," or "Mennonite", which came into usage from the middle of the sixteenth century onward when ecclesiastical boundaries needed to be defined more sharply. "Evangelisch" was, from the beginning, an umbrella term, denoting all those who were partisans of the Reformation. In that sense, the Calvinist churches could be labeled "evangelisch" (evangelical).

In German language usage, the term continues to be used into the present. In popular usage it is considered a synonym for both "Lutheran" and "Protestant", a practice which is understandable in light of the fact that the overwhelming majority of German Protestants are Lutheran. Ther term is not to be understood in a theological, but an ecclesiastical sense. Accordingly, German usage speaks of the "evangelische" church and what is meant thereby is not what in American usage would be an "evangelical church", i.e. a theologically conservative church but rather a "Protestant", and generally Lutheran church. More precisely, the term "evangelisch" denotes the churches of the PRUSSIAN UNION, while the explicitly Lutheran churches in Germany have the designation "evangelisch-lutherisch" (evangelical-Lutheran) churches.

References and Further Reading

Schuch, Martin. *Evangelisch-Katholisch*. Gütersloh: Gütersloher Verlagshaus Gerd Mohn, 2001.

HANS J. HILLERBRAND

EVANGELICAL ALLIANCE

This English movement had its origin in the middle of the nineteenth century, when a number of clergy became concerned about the increasing influenced and impact of the Oxford Movement effort to define the Anglican Church as catholic. A gathering in London in 1846, attended by hundreds of clergy from several countries, marked the official establishment of the Evangelical Alliance. Its goals were the "advancement of evangelical Protestantism," which entailed the objective of affirming traditional, conservative theology in the Protestant mode. The objectives of the Alliance also spelled out the opposition to "infidelity, popery, and other forms of superstition, error, and profanes, especially the desecration of the Lord's Day."

The movement quickly took root in several European countries and the United States as it became clear that the goals of the movement were to affirm the common belief of Protestant Christians, while understanding and deploring the divisions within Christendom. In a way, the Alliance may be considered the forerunner of the various ecumenical efforts of the twentieth century in that its underlying premise was the notion that the challenges of modernity, such as the disregard of the Lord's Day, could be best dealt with in concord among the varous Protestant groupings.

References and Further Reading

Church Unity and Intercession. London: Evangelical Alliance, 1912.

Jordan, Philip D. *The Evangelical Alliance for the United States of America, 1847–1900: Ecumenism, Identity, and the Religion of the Republic.* New York: E. Mellen Press, c1982.

Railton, Nicholas M. *No North Sea: the Anglo-German Evangelical Network in the Middle of the Nineteenth Century.* Leiden: Brill, 2000.

HANS J. HILLERBRAND

EVANGELICAL AND REFORMED CHURCH

The Evangelical and Reformed Church (E & R Church), although in existence for only twenty-three years, exemplified the church union and ecumenical discourse (see ECUMENISM) prevalent in early twentieth-century Protestantism. The church came into existence when union discussions between several denominations resulted in the uniting of two of those denominations, the Reformed Church in the United States and the Evangelical Synod of North America. It ceased to exist as a DENOMINATION because of another church union agreement, uniting the Evangelical and Reformed Church with the Congregational Christian Churches to form the UNITED CHURCH OF CHRIST. The union process that created the E & R Church was distinctive among the many church mergers and unions that occurred worldwide during the first part of the twentieth century because that union was based on the assumption of a common faith and belief within the merging churches. Institutional form and procedure were deemed secondary issues to be addressed once the union was enacted. They would be discerned according to God's leading and to fit the context of the church at the time.

Union Creates Evangelical and Reformed Church

Church union was facilitated by the fact that both the Evangelical and the Reformed churches had roots in German Protestantism. As immigrants from GERMANY and SWITZERLAND came to America they founded congregations where they settled, the Reformed immigrants largely in the Central Atlantic region and those who would create the Evangelical church in the Midwest. Eventually, the congregations within each of these traditions joined together and new denominations were founded. The SYNOD of the German Reformed Church in the United States of America was created in 1793, nearly a century after the first German Reformed congregations were gathered. Mirroring the union of the Lutheran and Reformed churches in Prussia (see PRUSSIAN UNION), pastors of Lutheran and Reformed traditions in the UNITED STATES met in St. Louis, Missouri in 1840 to found the German Evangelical Church Society of the West, the first united church in U.S. history.

Both churches grew in number and expanded geographically, although they remained largely regional institutions. As they grew, each church changed its name to reflect its broader membership. Thus, by the beginning of the twentieth century, it was the Evangelical Synod of North America and the Reformed

Church in the United States that began to discuss church union. By 1918 the Reformed Church had developed a plan for uniting all churches in the Reformed tradition. In 1925 the Evangelical church began official negotiations with other denominations toward organic union. Although other Reformed denominations, such as the PRESBYTERIAN CHURCH IN THE UNITED STATES OF AMERICA and the REFORMED CHURCH IN AMERICA, were a part of initial discussions, the final parties in the negotiations were the Evangelical Synod of North America and the Reformed Church in the United States. After six years of negotiating, a Plan of Union was approved by the Reformed church in 1932–1933 and the Evangelical church in 1933. On June 26, 1934, a union celebration was held and the Evangelical and Reformed Church officially came into existence.

The Plan of Union, the document in church mergers that usually spells out both the ideological terms of the agreement and the mechanics of the process, was unique. It emphasized faith and common belief as the basis for union. The institutional nature of the church was left to be worked out after the union. Protestantism had been created upon and distinguished by concern for doctrinal points and church governance. In the Evangelical and Reformed merger, however, a common faith and belief were assumed. No single statement of faith or creed was designated as authoritative in E & R churches, although all of the historic creeds of both churches were recognized as important, such as the AUGSBURG CONFESSION and HEIDELBERG CATECHISM. Emphasis was placed on looking to the Scriptures first to define Christian faith and life, and to the creeds secondarily. In both it was acknowledged that individual interpretation was appropriate and would create a range of understandings.

Once the union was enacted a committee was created to write a constitution for the new church, including a definition of its form of government. Because the polities, the governmental forms, of the two merging churches were quite different (the Evangelical church being more centralized and the Reformed church based more on congregational autonomy), it was not an easy process. After four years a hybrid polity combining some presbyterian traits and some congregational traits was agreed upon. The Constitution and bylaws were adopted in 1938 and took effect in 1940.

Union Dissolves the E & R Church

In spite of its short existence the Evangelical and Reformed church contributed in several other ways to American Protestantism. It provided several prominent twentieth-century theologians including H. RICHARD NIEBUHR, REINHOLD NIEBUHR, and PAUL TILLICH.

The church cooperated ecumenically with other denominations in mission work, PUBLISHING, and further church union discussions. Even before the Constitution for the E & R Church was approved, church leaders began union discussions with leaders of the Congregational Christian Churches. In 1942 a public announcement of the discussions was made and a proposal for union was approved by both church bodies. Between 1943 and 1949 the Basis for Union underwent ten revisions. Union was initially planned for 1950, but lingering concerns within some of the Congregational Christian Churches delayed the union celebration until 1957. In June of 1957, twenty-three years after the Evangelical and Reformed Church came into existence, it ceased to exist when, in following the prayer of Jesus "that they may all be one" (John 17:22), the E & R Church merged with the Congregational Christian Churches to form the United Church of Christ.

See also Congregationalism; Lutheranism; Mercersburg Theology; Polity; Presbyterianism; Schaff, Philip

References and Further Reading

Dunn, David, ed. *A History of the Evangelical and Reformed Church.* New York: The Pilgrim Press, 1990.

Gunnemann, Louis H. *The Shaping of the United Church of Christ.* Cleveland, OH: United Church Press, 1977.

Hilke, Elisabeth Slaughter, ed. *Growing Toward Unity.* Cleveland, OH: Pilgrim Press, 2001.

Keiling, Hanns Peter, and Ford L. Battles, eds. *The Formation of the United Church of Christ (U.S.A.).* Pittsburgh, PA: Pittsburgh Theological Seminary, 1970.

"Short History Course." May be accessed at http://www.ucc.org/aboutus/shortcourse/index.html

DEBRA L. DUKE

EVANGELICAL FREE CHURCH OF AMERICA

The Evangelical Free Church of America (EFCA) was the result of the merger of two FREE CHURCH organizations in 1950. Born out of the nineteenth-century "evangelical" REVIVALS in northwest Europe, which resulted in organizations separate from the Lutheran church, immigrants to the UNITED STATES from these groups established a number of independent congregations. In 1884 one group of Swedish congregations formed a loose association in Iowa, named the Swedish Evangelical Free Church. A second group of Danish and Norwegian congregations formally organized into the Norwegian–Danish Evangelical Free Church in 1909. In June 1950 these two groups, representing 275 local congregations, formally merged at the Medicine Lake Conference Grounds near Minneapolis, Minnesota, becoming the Evangelical Free Church of

America. The EFCA international headquarters have remained in Minneapolis since then.

The denomination's governing structure is congregational, where each local congregation largely governs its own affairs independently. National and international organization, however, was created to manage certain cooperative endeavors, such as Missions. There is an annual meeting where representatives from each congregation are sent to supervise these endeavors. The Denomination of approximately 1,250 congregations, two universities, and a seminary is divided into twenty-two districts, each managed by a district superintendent and district leadership team. From the Clergy membership, a president is elected to serve the denomination's national activities, preserve its values, and create stronger unity.

Although every congregation is largely independent in its business and ministry, a change that occurred with the 1950 merger was the introduction of a twelve-point doctrinal statement that is now incorporated into each local congregation's constitution. Evidence of the influence of the post-fundamentalist evangelical movement is witnessed in the EFCA statement of beliefs, including clear Trinitarian affirmations, belief in Atonement through the sacrifice of Jesus Christ, assertion of the Bible being authoritative and inerrant (see Biblical Inerrancy), original Sin, the second coming of Christ and human resurrection.

The EFCA has influence greater than its size in American Evangelicalism. First, it supports more than 500 missionaries in Asia, Europe, and Latin America. Second, it holds membership in the World Evangelical Alliance and the International Federation of Free Evangelical Churches, two organizations that provide leadership to millions of evangelicals worldwide. Third, and most important, the EFCA maintains a seminary and two interdenominational universities in North America: Trinity Evangelical Divinity School and Trinity International University in Illinois, along with Trinity Western University in British Columbia, Canada. Graduates from these schools have populated leadership positions in every evangelical-oriented denomination in North America.

References and Further Reading

"About Us–History." Evangelical Free Church of America. 2000. http://www.efca.org/history.html (April 6, 2003).

Melton, J. Gordon, and Martin Baumann, eds. "Evangelical Free Church of America." In *Religions of the World*. vol. 2, 469. Santa Barbara, CA: ABC-CLIO, 2002.

Norton, W. Wilbert, et al. *The Diamond Jubilee Story of the Evangelical Free Church of America*. Minneapolis, MN: Free Church Publications, 1959.

Olson, Arnold Theodore. *Believers Only*. Minneapolis, MN: Free Church Publications, 1964.

———. *Stumbling toward Maturity*. Minneapolis, MN: Free Church Publications, 1981.

H. Chad Hillier

THE EVANGELICAL LUTHERAN CHURCH IN AMERICA

Originating in a 1988 merger of three previous church bodies, at the turn of the twenty-first century the Evangelical Lutheran Church in America (ELCA) included some 5.1 million baptized members, making it the largest Lutheran Denomination in the United States. Slightly less than half of these numbers participate in the sacrament of Holy Communion (see Lord's Supper) or contribute financially, considered marks of active membership. About 30 percent, something more than 1.5 million people, attend weekly worship services.

Approximately 10,800 congregations served by some 17,500 pastors, almost 2,000 of whom are Women, provide Worship as well as a range of other services. There are also somewhat more than 1,000 associates in ministry working at various levels of assistance. The congregations in turn support sixty-five geographical synods, the largest of them in Northeastern Pennsylvania and in Minneapolis, reflecting regional concentrations in the Northeast and the Midwest. A church-wide assembly meets every other year. The national offices are located in Chicago.

Historically, the Lutherans who formed the ELCA have put particular emphasis on four areas. One of these areas is world mission (see Missions). Although the numbers have declined significantly since the merger, in 2000 there were still some 300 missionaries serving in forty-five countries around the world, with concentrations in sub-Saharan Africa and New Guinea. Another area of emphasis has been Higher Education. Eight Seminaries prepare pastors for the Church; in addition, there are twenty-eight affiliated colleges and universities distributed across the country. The best known include Gettysburg College, Wittenberg University, and St. Olaf's College. A third area of emphasis is Chaplaincy, with more than 850 chaplains in the armed forces, another 125 and additional staff serving more than 200 state and private colleges and universities, and roughly 800 providing special ministries in counseling, prisons, and the like.

A fourth area of special emphasis in the ELCA has been social service. Earlier generations of Lutherans were among the leaders in providing for orphans and the elderly; in the 1970s, they owned more than one-third of the nation's nursing home beds, along with some notable hospitals. Lutheran Social Services, organized by state, usually but not always under that name, is one of the largest nongovernmental agencies in the nation. It continues the work with children and the aging, but also provides a broad range of counseling help and related assistance.

Lutheran World Relief (LWR), jointly funded by the ELCA and the LUTHERAN CHURCH-MISSOURI SYNOD (LC-MS), provides for international services such as development and disaster assistance. It has been noted for its effectiveness around the world, generally being among the first church agencies contacted in crises. ELCA funds for LWR are contributed out of the World Hunger Appeal, a long-standing enterprise with some $16 million worth of contributions in 2000.

Since the breakthroughs of the l960s, the Lutherans who eventually formed the ELCA have been active in ecumenical relations both nationally and internationally. Lutheranism's sixteenth-century origins in Roman Catholicism have given a strong priority to improved relations in this connection. The Lutheran–Catholic Dialogues were particularly noteworthy. They included representatives from the churches that merged to form the ELCA with those of the LC-MS in conversation with American Roman Catholic theologians. More recently, the Joint Declaration on the Doctrine of Justification approved by the ELCA, other European Lutherans, and (in a qualified way) the Vatican is said to have achieved new levels of reconciliation. The ELCA has also entered into substantial ecumenical agreements with Episcopalians, Reformed, Moravians, and others. It has solidified relations in its own tradition through the LUTHERAN WORLD FEDERATION.

Governance

A generation ago, Sidney Earl Meade pointed to an axiomatic difference in American Christianity. In Europe, the church has been able to rely on the coercive power of the state to maintain itself financially and otherwise; in the United States, the disestablishment clause of the Constitution has limited the church's power to persuasion. This has inevitably tipped American church governance in the direction of congregationalism, in which the membership holds the last word.

Unlike other sixteenth-century reformers, MARTIN LUTHER and the others associated with the beginnings of LUTHERANISM did not propose an ideal church structure. Some of the original Lutheran documents are explicitly congregational; some are at least tacitly hierarchical. Traditionally, governance has been an issue in which Lutherans have agreed to disagree. The churches uniting in the ELCA had their own traditions; concerns about a looming hierarchicalism delayed the merger and occasioned the first major conflict.

As in other American churches, the congregations provide the basic unit of governance. Some are small, struggling to maintain membership in the aftermath of population shifts that have isolated them in inner cities, small towns, and open countryside. Other congregations are extraordinarily large, particularly in metropolitan areas, with memberships of 5,000 to 7,000. Small or large, maintaining their communities, the congregations call pastors and provide the church's funding, a total of more than $2.3 billion in 2000 (a contribution of something over $500 per communing member).

Thus dependent on the congregations, the ELCA was designed to provide some independence for other layers of authority. This has been difficult for the CLERGY. Pastors, whose responsibilities are defined by PREACHING and administering the SACRAMENTS, learn quickly the importance of responsiveness. The bishops have some constitutional authority in the calling and discipline of parish pastors, but soon learn the perils of acting without congregational support (see BISHOPS AND EPISCOPACY).

There has been relatively more success in efforts to protect other layers of structure, with provisions to give some independence to the SYNODS and the national church. The synods are the next governmental step after the congregations. They provide assistance to the local parishes through the bishops, who are elected to six-year terms, and synodical staff. They in turn pass along a portion of the funding that they receive from the congregations to the national church, termed the "churchwide." The churchwide is responsible for providing leadership in matters such as world mission, outreach, theological education and ministry (see EDUCATION, THEOLOGY: UNITED STATES), social statements, relations with the colleges and universities, and gender- and age-specific ministries. Churchwide assemblies and the church council, which represents the assemblies between meetings, establish policies for the national church. The presiding bishop is chief executive officer of the churchwide offices, and represents the ELCA nationally and internationally. The Conference of Bishops meets twice yearly, providing advice and support.

The traditional American Lutheran ambivalence on AUTHORITY is most evident in the office of bishop. The bishops are the first source of assistance when congregations are seeking pastors or experiencing conflict. (An estimated 40 percent of the parishes were in contention at the turn of the century.) But with this, the bishops' authority has been limited to basically that of advice and consent.

Called to Common Mission (CCM), an agreement with the Episcopal Church, USA, brought the ambivalence about church governance in the ELCA to a head. Traditionally, Lutherans have asserted their connection to the apostolic church of the New Testament through the confession of that Word preached in the New Testament and by the Lutheran reformers. In the Denver Assembly of the ELCA, the church voted to accept apostolic succession through the historic episcopate, which claims connection to the church of the apostles through the office of bishop. Approximately one-third of the ELCA's membership objected to the CCM and similar efforts, seeing evidence of a growing hierarchicalism. The result was the largest conflict since the merger.

History

Lutheranism came to North America with waves of immigrants from GERMANY and the Scandinavian counties. Consequently, it reflects its European origins even as it has become an American DENOMINATION, showing evidence of the power of the "melting pot." Lutherans began arriving in North America well before the founding of the American republic; there are seventeenth- and early eighteenth-century congregations in New York, Pennsylvania, Georgia, and the Virgin Islands. The heaviest immigrations began in the early nineteenth century with Germans who settled in Pennsylvania and other Eastern and Southeastern states, and ended with the Scandinavians, who continued to arrive primarily in the Midwest until the 1920s. In Minnesota, the Dakotas, and some other regions, Lutheran grandchildren of the most recent immigrants—German Russians, Norwegians, Swedes, and Finns—still identify with their ethnic origins.

Like others, Lutheran immigrants generally sought to perpetuate forms familiar from their native lands. Initially, the linguistic groups divided along lines that reflected matters of contention at home. The farmers and laborers who made up the bulk of the immigrants had been strongly affected by the PIETISM of Lutheran revival movements that had swept the state churches (see REVIVALS). Middle- and upper-class immigrants, generally sent by the European churches or immigrating themselves with traditions of leadership, usually reflected more self-consciously Lutheran forms of THEOLOGY and practice. The obstacles to unity posed by these divisions were largely overcome by the later nineteenth and early twentieth centuries, when the linguistic groups merged to form ethnic churches (see ETHNICITY).

Lutheran immigrants brought their heritage to America in the Scriptures, the Lutheran Confessions, and their hymnals (see CONFESSION; HYMNS AND HYMNALS). The confessions, a collection of documents that include Luther's CATECHISMS and the AUGSBURG CONFESSION, have been considered definitive of Lutheranism. Centered around the doctrine of JUSTIFICATION by FAITH alone, they provided a framework for interpreting the new situation in America.

Immersing a European confessional tradition in the American melting pot proved a corrosive process for each wave of immigrants, eating away at already present conflicts, opening up issues with those who had arrived earlier and were already adapting. INDIVIDUALISM, a pervasive Protestantism shaped by revivalism, along with the progressivism of the American people, were some of the major challenges. Some Lutherans, notably the LC-MS and related groups, sought to protect against the confessional tradition by enclosing theologically. The ELCA brought together Lutherans who had, to varying degrees, sought to hold their Lutheranism in a critical conversation with American CULTURE, taking on its challenges.

World War II brought decisive changes for American Lutherans. Within a few years, ethnic Lutherans completed their linguistic transitions. The postwar economy along with the MASS MEDIA broke through Lutheran isolation. Traditional barriers broken, the first multi-ethnic mergers of Lutherans occurred with the AMERICAN LUTHERAN CHURCH (ALC) in 1960 and the LUTHERAN CHURCH IN AMERICA (LCA) in 1962. Cooperative work between the ALC and the LCA and, to a lesser extent, with the LC-MS, raised some hopes during the 1960s that Lutherans in America would finally be able to unite in one church. In the late 1960s and early 1970s, citing matters of biblical and confessional authority, the LC-MS began to pull back within itself. A split-off group, eventually calling itself the Association of Evangelical Lutheran Churches in America, broke away from the LC-MS in 1976, and took a lead in merger talks between the ALC and the LCA.

In 1982, conventions of the three church bodies, listening to one another by phone hookups, voted simultaneously to form a new church. Further enriching the alphabet soup, the Commission on the New Lutheran Church (CNLC) was formed. It negotiated terms of the merger, among other things establishing a system of GENDER and racial quotas for leadership positions in hopes of opening the ELCA to the wider culture. On January 1, 1988, the new church legally succeeded its predecessor bodies.

A number of key people contributed to the mergers leading to and including the ELCA. Frederick Axel Shoitz and Franklin Clark Fry, once dubbed "Mr. Lutheran" by *Time* magazine, exerted shaping influences in the formation of the ALC and LCA. Successors of theirs, Kent Knutson and Robert Marshall, whose friendship was cut short by Knutson's untimely death, set the two churches on an irreversible course toward a merger. David Preus of the ALC, James

Crumley of the LCA, and Will Hertzfeld from the AELC were all critically important in the merger process. Yet to name such individuals is to ignore the collective character of efforts stretching back over generations, as well as that of those who worked more anonymously to effect the change.

In the late 1950s, surveying the massive acculturation of Protestantism in the United States, Winthrop Hudson expressed the hope that the confessional Lutheranism then emerging out of its isolation would lead the way in the recovery of a more specifically Christian identity. The 1988 merger was completed in a somewhat similar hope, that united Lutherans would have a greater impact in American public life. The distance of time has a way of sorting out hope and illusion. At the turn of the century, the ELCA continued to be divided by issues that have historically perplexed American Lutherans—authority, both theological and church-political, and the church's position in relation to public culture. The presenting issues were the office of the bishop and sexual ethics (see SEXUALITY; HOMOSEXUALITY).

Character

Offensive as it may be in some circles, Lutherans have thrived on religious humor in which they have been the butt of the joke. They are portrayed as stolid, taciturn, family oriented, work driven, and inclined to regard potluck suppers and tuna casserole as sacramental. With some allowance for exaggeration, the joke may not be far off.

Wags in the NATIONAL COUNCIL OF CHURCHES once said, "Lutherans provide the foremen and the superintendents for the plants the Episcopalians own." In fact, by origin and by immigration, Lutherans have historically been blue-collar people, the biggest percentage having small-town origins with another larger group growing up in the rust-belt cities of New York, Pennsylvania, and the Great Lakes region. The farm crisis, carrying through the later twentieth century into the twenty-first century, along with technological replacement of labor, has hit Lutherans hard.

The strong educational emphasis of Lutheranism, combined with work habits learned on farms or in skilled labor, have served Lutheran families well, however. If older Lutherans are likely to show signs of an ethnic past, shaking hands revealing years of labor, where the younger Lutherans remain, they are likely to have accredited themselves educationally for work acquiring and distributing information. The two generations have not always come together easily.

Published demographics indicate that in 2000, ELCA Lutherans were some 98 percent white, though committed to welcoming other races. Informed spec-ulation suggested that the church had lost two generations of its young and was on the way to losing a third. The average Lutheran assembly, whether congregational, synodical, or churchwide, looked older and ready for work, as long as there was some humor on the side, but anxious about its future.

References and Further Reading

Hudson, Winthrop S. *Religion in America: An Historical Account of the Development of American Religion Life*. New York: Charles Scribner's Sons, 1965.

Mead, Sidney Earl. *The Lively Experiment: The Shaping of Christianity in America*. New York: Harper and Row, 1973.

Nelson, E. Clifford. *The Lutherans in North America*. Philadelphia, PA: Fortress Press, 1975.

Trexler, Edgar R. *Anatomy of a Merger: People, Dynamics and Decisions that Shaped the ELCA*. Minneapolis, MN: Augsburg Publishing, 1991.

http://www.elca.org. (website of the Evangelical Lutheran Church in America)

JAMES ARNE NESTINGEN

EVANGELICAL REVIVAL

See Evangelicalism

EVANGELICAL UNITED BRETHREN CHURCH

This denomination was the result of the union in 1946 of two church bodies formed among German Americans in the early nineteenth century, the Church of the United Brethren in Christ and the Evangelical Church (see EVANGELICALISM). The former body traces its origin to the evangelistic work of Philip William Otterbein (1726–1813), an immigrant missionary-pastor of the German Reformed Church, who established a partnership in ministry with the "converted" Mennonite, Martin Boehm (1725–1812). Otterbein was educated at the Herborn Academy in Germany, a Pietist-oriented school (see PIETISM). It was Otterbein's embrace of Boehm, following the latter's testimony to the new birth in Christ at a barn revival meeting in Pennsylvania on Pentecost, around 1767, that launched their common mission (see REVIVALS). It represented an eschatologically driven enterprise to form a higher unity among German Americans, based on a shared experience of personal new birth in Christ, that would transcend the barriers of adversarial church bodies of their day (see ESCHATOLOGY). Using that date as their point of origin, the United Brethren declared itself to be the first "American-born" DENOMINATION.

In actuality, Otterbein's intent was not to found a new church, but rather to nurture a revival among German Americans that would transcend existing church structures of all sorts. However, a new denomination it would become. Despite Otterbein's personal friendship with Methodist bishop FRANCIS ASBURY, the United Brethren would eschew the episcopally grounded Methodist ecclesial structures in favor of a more democratic, "nonpartisan" brotherhood in Christ. Their bishops were elected to quadrennial terms from among the "brothers" in conference. In Pietist fashion, the early United Brethren hoped to manifest a "more glorious state of the church on earth" (Otterbein), as an end-time community of the reborn. This brotherhood would extend conference voting privileges in church conferences to lay preachers, recognize the diverse sacramental practices of persons coming from a variety of ecclesial backgrounds, and (by 1851) begin extending preaching licenses to WOMEN. By 1889, the General Conference approved the ordination of women (see WOMEN CLERGY).

The United Brethren adopted a CONFESSION of faith and a discipline at their first General Conference in 1815 (see CHURCH DISCIPLINE). Both were based on documents prepared by Otterbein for use in his Reformed congregation at Baltimore (1774–1813). Their early missionaries, led by Bishop Christian Newcomer, received ordination at the hand of the aged Otterbein, after Newcomer and others had advanced into the Ohio Valley (c. 1810). Their itinerant successors reached to the Pacific Northwest by 1853 (see ITINERANCY). On peace and justice issues, the United Brethren Discipline of 1821 committed members to renounce SLAVERY and slaveholding, making them one of the earliest denominations to adopt an official antislavery position (see SLAVERY, ABOLITION OF). A missionary presence was established in the British colony of SIERRA LEONE in West Africa that began in the 1850s and eventually flourished with the help of an African-American couple, the Joseph Gomers. This mission grew to become the largest Protestant church in that nation. The leaders of the newly independent Sierra Leone in 1960 were graduates of the United Brethren Albert Academy in Freetown. In other overseas fields, beginning with South CHINA (1889) and then JAPAN, the PHILIPPINES, and LATIN AMERICA, United Brethren missionaries were pioneers in establishing indigenous-led united churches, in cooperation with other American mission boards (see MISSIONS; MISSIONARY ORGANIZATIONS). Home mission centers were launched among Spanish-Americans in New Mexico and Florida.

Alongside this work, Jacob Albright (1759–1808), a Pennsylvania-born farmer of Lutheran background, underwent a profound experience of the new birth and then launched an evangelistic mission among his neighbors that resulted in the formation, after his death, of the Evangelical Association (1816). Unlike the United Brethren, this body patterned itself more closely after Methodist DOCTRINE and POLITY. In fact, one of its early names, in addition to the "Albright People," was "The Newly Formed Methodist Conference." However, Albright's ordination had been conferred by his lay associates, rather than by established church authorities. After their humble origin, Evangelicals prized church order and an efficient itinerancy plan. They were the first denomination in America to include in their Book of Discipline an extended essay on the doctrine of entire SANCTIFICATION. Evangelicals also labored among the succeeding generations of German immigrants to the UNITED STATES, and so retained a longer use of that language than did the United Brethren.

By the mid-nineteenth century, both Evangelicals and United Brethren also began founding colleges and then SEMINARIES for the training of Christian workers, although neither church required seminary education for ordination (see HIGHER EDUCATION). Whereas the United Brethren followed the single-track ordination plan of the Reformed Church (elders only), Evangelicals followed METHODISM in adhering to two orders (deacons and elders). Led by their missionary bishop, John Seybert (1791–1860), their expansion beyond their Eastern Pennsylvania base was centered in the upper Midwest and Canada, whereas United Brethren missionaries favored a line of expansion in the lower Midwest.

Fittingly, Evangelicals launched their major overseas mission effort in GERMANY (1850), from where they established a strong "free church" presence throughout German-speaking Europe, including hospitals and benevolent homes operated by a deaconess society, a seminary, and numerous congregations, including locations in all major German cities. Other overseas fields included Japan (where their missionaries first translated the Old Testament into Japanese), central China, and NIGERIA, plus "home" missions in Appalachia, and among urban ethnic minorities (see ETHNICITY).

Both denominations experienced division in the nineteenth century, for which leading causes included controversies over FREEMASONRY and the revision of the original church constitution (the United Brethren in 1889), as well as disagreements over language, polity, and the interpretation of the doctrine of sanctification (the Evangelicals in 1891). The leader of the "Old Constitution" minority among the United Brethren was Bishop Milton Wright, father of the Wright brothers of aviation fame. The schism among Evangelicals was healed in 1922, resulting in the formation of the Evangelical Church. Evangelicals contributed one president of the Federal Council of Churches (Bishop John Stamm) and one president of the NATIONAL COUNCIL OF CHURCHES (Bishop Reuben Mueller). Their church united in 1946 with the Church of the United Brethren in Christ, forming a church comprising more than 700,000 members and almost 5,000 congregations in North America that would be known as The Evangelical United Brethren Church. Its overseas constituency was found in five annual conferences in Europe and West Africa, and was also distributed throughout a variety of indigenous united churches on five continents. Its strong ecumenical commitment resulted in the union of their church with Methodism in 1968, resulting in the formation of the UNITED METHODIST CHURCH, which for a time was the largest Protestant denomination in North America.

References and Further Reading

Behney, Bruce, and Paul Eller. *The History of the Evangelical United Brethren Church.* Nashville, TN: Abingdon, 1979.

Naumann, William. "Theology and German-American Evangelicalism." Ph.D. dissertation, Yale University, 1966.

O'Malley, J. Steven. *Pilgrimage of Faith: The Legacy of the Otterbeins.* Metuchen, NJ: Scarecrow, 1973.

———. *On The Journey Home: The Central Role of Missions in the Evangelical United Brethren Church.* New York: Friendship Press, 2001.

J. STEVEN O'MALLEY

EVANGELICALISM

Words such as *mosaic* and *kaleidoscope* have been used to describe the bewildering diversity of groups that are associated with evangelicalism. Growing out of currents dating back to the Protestant REFORMATION, evangelicalism originated during the eighteenth century as a phenomenon within Protestantism in North America and Britain. By the end of the twentieth century it had become one of the most vibrant, global expressions of Protestantism. Often identified as "conservative" because of its consistent concern for defending certain theological doctrines, it has also been remarkably responsive and adaptable to different cultures and times, creating a dynamic, not static, movement.

The word *evangelical* is derived from the New Testament Greek word *euangelion,* referring to the "good news" of the Christian gospel. Its contemporary usage carries numerous connotations derived from its association with certain groups throughout the history of Protestantism. During the sixteenth century the word was first applied generally to Protestant reformers because of their doctrinal emphasis on JUSTIFICATION by FAITH, the priesthood of all believers, and the AUTHORITY of the BIBLE. It became, particularly in reference to LUTHERANISM in GERMANY, a synonym for Protestantism.

Second, the influence of earlier Puritans and Pietists (see PURITANISM, PIETISM) set the stage for religious REVIVALS in Britain and North America during the eighteenth century. Central figures in igniting these revivals in Britain were GEORGE WHITEFIELD, an eloquent evangelist who effectively used open-air preaching; JOHN WESLEY, an evangelist whose organizational genius led to the creation of METHODISM; and Howell Harris, an aggressive evangelist in Wales. The label "evangelical" was adopted by Protestants who wished to distinguish themselves from coreligionists who did not share the same emphasis on the necessity of a CONVERSION experience, participation in EVANGELISM, and a rigorous approach toward personal holiness. The term was also used to identify a particular party within the CHURCH OF ENGLAND that was sympathetic with the emphases of the Methodist revival. In North America the extraordinary revivals of JONATHAN EDWARDS during the 1730s, and the itinerant preaching of George Whitefield several decades later, set in motion the Great Awakening (see AWAKENINGS). The movement spread to Nova Scotia in CANADA through the efforts of HENRY ALLINE. Known as "New Lights," eighteenth-century evangelicals significantly shaped American culture during the Revolutionary era.

The third historical context to give meaning to the term "evangelicalism" grew out of revival fires during the nineteenth century called the Second Great Awakening. In North America the CAMP MEETINGS organized by Methodist circuit-riding preachers, the new methods of evangelism introduced by CHARLES GRANDISON FINNEY, and the evangelistic activity of BAPTISTS in the southern states resulted in spectacular displays of religious enthusiasm. Common evangelical concerns often transcended denominational differences, giving rise to hundreds of cooperative initiatives in the form of VOLUNTARY SOCIETIES that furthered causes such as TEMPERANCE, SABBATARIANISM, prison reform, and the abolition of slavery (see SLAVERY; SLAVERY, ABOLITION OF). By the mid-nineteenth century evangelicalism had become the prevailing orientation among Protestants in North America, prompting some to designate the era as the evangelical century.

Divisions among Protestants in the United States over slavery during the CIVIL WAR were followed by a flurry of new disputes involving DARWINISM and higher criticism of the Bible. Social and economic changes created by industrialization and urbanization further fragmented the evangelical hegemony of earlier decades. A group of evangelicals particularly concerned about defending orthodox Christianity against the influence of theological Liberalism (see LIBERAL PROTESTANTISM AND LIBERALISM) became known as fundamentalists after the publication of *The Fundamentals* and their involvement in the infamous Scopes "Monkey Trial" in 1925 (see FUNDAMENTALISM). These fundamentalists distinguished themselves from what they perceived as dangerous compromises among more accommodating Protestants by retaining their emphasis on personal Conversion, but adding a more rigorous stress on the inspiration of the Bible, the imminent return of Christ, and separation from "the world." A growing sense of alienation prompted fundamentalist evangelicals to establish a network of hundreds of independent agencies promoting evangelism, global MISSIONS, Bible knowledge, publishing, youth work, radio broadcasting, Bible Schools and colleges (see BIBLE COLLEGES AND INSTITUTIONS), summer conferences, and other activities. This organizational infrastructure provided the foundation for an evangelical resurgence during the 1970s.

The influx of new immigrant groups added still more diversity to evangelicalism in North America during the twentieth century. In addition, a powerful new strand of evangelicalism emerged out of the HOLINESS MOVEMENT that had left Methodism during the 1890s. Pentecostalism, with its emphasis on the supernatural gifts of the Holy Spirit such as speaking in tongues and divine healing, reshaped evangelical demographics and became one of the most significant religious influences in the world during the twentieth century.

During the 1930s and 1940s those directly associated with, or influenced by, the fundamentalist network gradually emerged from their cultural isolation. Strengthened by the growing popularity of evangelist BILLY GRAHAM and the intellectual leadership of CARL F. H. HENRY, founding editor of Christianity Today, the "neo-evangelicals" formed in 1942 the NATIONAL ASSOCIATION OF EVANGELICALS, which became the center of a wider coalition of more ecumenically minded and cooperative evangelical organizations. The aggressive expansion of evangelical churches and organizations, the skillful use of broadcast media by radio preachers during the 1920s and TELEVANGELISTS during the 1970s (see PUBLISHING MEDIA), and the involvement of evangelicals in areas of public life such as education, professional sports, politics, and media, gave "born again" Christians more visibility and attractiveness. By the end of the twentieth century, evangelicalism was once again the largest and most robust force within Protestantism in both North America and Britain.

The multitude of branches associated with evangelicalism has prompted contemporary historians and pollsters to search for a more precise definition that accurately identifies its distinctive features, thus making it possible to measure the extent of evangelicalism. A commonly used approach is illustrated by the descriptive quadrilateral developed by David W. Bebbington. Despite the considerable diversity among evangelicals, he argues there are at least four continu-

ities or qualities that create a kind of conceptual unity if not always an actual unity, and that define the essence of evangelicalism. None of the four characteristics is unique to evangelicals, but the emphasis placed on the combination of these particular characteristics sets them apart from other Christians. Evangelicals are *conversionists,* meaning that people become Christians by repenting and personally experiencing what the Protestant reformers called "justification by grace through faith." Second, they are *crucicentric;* that is, at the center of their theological scheme is the understanding that ATONEMENT was made to God for human sin by the death of Jesus Christ on the cross. Third, they are *biblicist,* that is, they have a particularly high regard for the Bible, considering it to be inspired by God and the final authority in matters of faith and Christian practice. Fourth, evangelicals are known as *activists,* meaning that genuine conversion will be accompanied by a new motivation for doing good and for holy living. This explains the time and energy evangelicals devote to personal piety, to missionary efforts, and to philanthropic projects of all kinds.

According to David Barrett's *World Christian Encyclopedia* (2001), approximately 34 percent of the world's population was Christian at the end of the twentieth century. Although estimates vary depending on the definition being used, it is likely that more than one third of the world's Christians could be considered evangelical. The massive missionary efforts during the past two centuries, and especially the rapid expansion of Pentecostal and charismatic expressions of evangelicalism in the non-Western world, have contributed toward making evangelicalism a global phenomenon.

See also Alline, Henry; Atonement; Awakenings; Baptists; Bible Schools; Camp Meetings; Christianity Today; Civil War; Conversion; Darwinism; Edwards, Jonathan; Finney, Charles Grandison; Fundamentalism; Germany; Graham, Billy; Henry, Carl F. H.; Liberalism; Lutheranism; Mass Media; Methodism; National Association of Evangelicals; Pentecostalism; Revivals; Sabbatarianism; Slavery, Abolition of; Televangelism; Temperance; Voluntary Societies; Wesley, John; Whitefield, George

References and Further Reading

Balmer, Randall. *Blessed Assurance: A History of Evangelicalism in America.* Boston: Beacon Press, 2000.

Bebbington, D. W. *Evangelicalism in Modern Britain: A History from the 1730s to the 1980s.* London: Unwin Hyman, 1989.

Noll, Mark A. *American Evangelical Christianity: An Introduction.* Oxford: Blackwell Publishers, 2001.

———, David W. Bebbington, and George A, Rawlyk, eds. *Evangelicalism: Comparative Studies of Popular Protestantism in North America, the British Isles, and Beyond, 1770–1990.* New York: Oxford University Press, 1994.

Rawlyk, George A., ed. *The Canadian Protestant Experience, 1760–1990.* Burlington, ON: Welch Publishing Company, 1990.

BRUCE L. GUENTHER

EVANGELICALISM, THEOLOGY

"Evangelical" is a word with many meanings. In some contexts it is synonymous with "Protestant," whereas in others it indicates religious enthusiasm or fanaticism. Etymologically, it means "of the Gospel." An evangelical is one who promotes the Gospel of Jesus Christ. The early Protestants (especially Lutherans in Northern Europe) chose the term to designate their movement because of its emphasis on JUSTIFICATION by GRACE through FAITH alone. That SALVATION does not have to be earned was considered "good news" (gospel). In seventeenth- and eighteenth-century Great Britain, evangelicals were a party within the CHURCH OF ENGLAND; they emphasized the Protestant side of the Elizabethan Settlement that created ANGLICANISM. Many of them were Puritan in sympathy and theology. In eighteenth- and nineteenth-century Great Britain and North America, the label came to be used of those affiliated with the Great Awakenings (see AWAKENINGS) and other REVIVALS. In the later nineteenth and early twentieth centuries, evangelicals were those Protestants who promoted and attended revivals and embraced a relatively conservative theology during the rise of liberal theology in mainline Protestant denominations (see LIBERAL PROTESTANTISM AND LIBERALISM). The fundamentalist movement arose in the early twentieth century out of evangelicalism in Great Britain and North America (see FUNDAMENTALISM). It sought militantly to expose and marginalize liberal theology and higher criticism of the BIBLE in Protestant seminaries and denominations. In the 1940s, several fundamentalist leaders, including Harold John Ockenga in New England, began to use the term "evangelical" to describe a new type of conservative Protestantism that is postfundamentalist. Agreeing with much of fundamentalist THEOLOGY (e.g., inspiration of Scripture, deity of Jesus Christ, salvation through the cross of Jesus Christ alone), these newer evangelicals eschewed fundamentalist separatism and anti-intellectualism. They forged a coalition of nonfundamentalist conservative Protestants that included revivalists, Calvinists, Wesleyans, Pentecostals, Pietists (see PIETISM), and BAPTISTS. The NATIONAL ASSOCIATION OF EVANGELICALS was formed in 1941 and came to include fifty denominations and thousands of churches, parachurch organizations, and individuals. Out of this new postfundamentalist movement arose evangelical theology with diverse Protestant roots.

All evangelicals (in the postfundamentalist sense) share four common features. They are intensely *biblicist* in that they believe the Bible to be God's supernaturally inspired, written Word uniquely authoritative for Christian faith and practice. Their biblicism extends to a devotional use as well as a theological use of the Bible. Evangelicals emphasize Bible reading and promote love for the Bible. Evangelicals do not all agree about secondary matters related to a DOCTRINE of Scripture, such as whether it contains incidental errors. Many evangelicals believe that it is inerrant in all matters on which it touches, including history and cosmology (see BIBLICAL INERRANCY); other evangelicals believe that it is infallible for all matters related to salvation, but not inerrant. The second common feature is *conversionism*. Evangelical Protestants believe that every person needs to have a personal encounter with Jesus Christ in a CONVERSION experience involving repentance and faith. Some practice infant baptism, but no evangelical believes that BAPTISM is a guarantee of salvation or sufficient for full reception of salvation. Third, evangelical faith is marked by *crucicentrism*. The cross of Jesus Christ is the focus of evangelical piety, PREACHING, and practice. Evangelicals believe that Jesus Christ's death on the cross is the sole basis for a right relationship between persons and God, because there Christ made ATONEMENT for the sins of the world. They may disagree on the exact nature and scope of the atonement. Finally, part and parcel of being evangelical is *activism* in MISSIONS and "outreach" to people outside the evangelical church. All evangelicals value "witnessing" and proclamation; some add the dimension of social ministry to their activism.

Organs of Evangelical Theology and Evangelical Theologians

Evangelical theology arises out of the evangelical movement. It takes for granted the basic contours of Protestant Christian theology such as *sola scriptura* and justification by grace through faith alone. It also takes for granted basic Christian ORTHODOXY as expressed in the earliest Christian creeds and in the consensus of the church fathers. It is worked out by evangelical theologians in such publications as *Christianity Today* and *The Journal of the Evangelical Theological Society*, which is published by the 3,000-member Evangelical Theological Society, which requires members to have advanced theology degrees and to affirm biblical inerrancy and the Trinity. The leading postfundamentalist evangelical theologian of the second half of the twentieth century was CARL

F. H. HENRY (b. 1913), who served as president of Fuller Theological Seminary and was a founding editor of *Christianity Today* magazine. He produced a massive, multivolume evangelical work of theology titled *God, Revelation and Authority* (1976–1983), and is generally regarded as the "dean of evangelical theologians." Henry is conservative in theology in that he closely follows Protestant orthodoxy; he championed the cause of biblical inerrancy while at the same time criticizing fundamentalism's naive biblicism and harsh separatism. He believes that all serious problems in modern theology arise from defection from commitment to the sole supreme authority of the Bible, which serves as the foundational presupposition of all Christian thought.

Other leading evangelical theologians include EDWARD JOHN CARNELL, Bernard Ramm, Donald G. Bloesch, Millard Erickson, Stanley J. Grenz, Miroslav Volf, and Clark Pinnock. Much evangelical theological reflection focuses on issues of religious authority, proper theological method, the nature of Scripture, God's attributes and relationship to creation, and salvation. Basic evangelical theological mental habits come from the Old Princeton School of theology led by Archibald Alexander, Charles Hodge, Archibald Alexander Hodge, and Benjamin Breckenridge Warfield in the nineteenth and early twentieth centuries. These Presbyterian scholars stood on the shoulders of earlier Reformed scholastic theologians, such as Francis Turretin. Twentieth-century evangelical theology borrowed from them an emphasis on the priority of special, propositional revelation over natural theology and personal experience, as well as commitment to the unique authority of the Bible as God's verbally inspired and inerrant written Word. Not all evangelical theologians are equally influenced by the Old Princeton School theology, however. Some, such as Bloesch, draw on ancient Christian sources, first-generation Reformers, PIETISM, and mediating theologians, such as PETER TAYLOR FORSYTH. Progressive evangelical thinkers, such as Ramm, have been influenced by KARL BARTH and moderate NEO-ORTHODOXY; postconservative evangelical theologians, such as Grenz and Pinnock, have attempted to update evangelical theology with help from postmodern thought and German eschatological theologians WOLFHART PANNENBERG and Jurgen Moltmann (see POSTMODERNITY). Despite this diversity of resources, all evangelical theologians are confessing Protestants who affirm the authoritative sources and norms of Christian thought and resist liberal accommodation to modern CULTURE.

Evangelical theologians may be divided into two broad camps: *traditionalists* and *reformists*. These camps agree about fundamental matters, such as the sole supreme authority of Scripture for Christian faith and practice and the necessity of personal repentance and faith for appropriation of the benefits of Christ's death in conversion (regeneration and justification). They are all heavily influenced by the Protestant reformers MARTIN LUTHER and JOHN CALVIN and by the movers and shakers of the Great Awakening of the 1730s and 1740s, JONATHAN EDWARDS and JOHN WESLEY. However, some evangelical thinkers follow Henry as defenders of orthodoxy, whereas others follow Bernard Ramm in constructive theology. The former are traditionalists, because they appeal to a "received evangelical tradition" including the ancient Christian consensus and the consensus of the first-generation reformers as authoritative, and guard the borders of evangelical thought against doctrinal drift, HERESY, and liberal accommodation. These theologians are not far from their fundamentalist roots in temperament and conservative outlook. They regard theology's primary tasks as critical and ignore or downplay the constructive tasks of theology. The other camp of evangelical theologians comprises reformists or progressives who view theology's constructive task as forever unfinished. For them, evangelical theology is constantly in revision as it is guided by Scripture, TRADITION, reason, and experience (the so-called "Wesleyan quadrilateral"). These two parties of evangelical thinkers often fall into conflict with each other. The former group tends to draw heavy and somewhat narrow boundaries around authentic Christianity, whereas the latter group views authentic Christianity as broad and indefinite.

Issues and Controversies in Evangelical Theology

The basic ethos of evangelical theology is Protestant, and all four major branches of the sixteenth-century Protestant REFORMATION are represented among evangelical theologians. Some are Lutheran or belong to offshoots of the European Lutheran churches, such as the EVANGELICAL FREE CHURCH of America and the Evangelical Covenant Church of America. Many are Reformed and belong to Presbyterian and other churches stemming from the reforming works of HULDRYCH ZWINGLI, John Calvin, and JOHN KNOX. More than a few are Anglican or Episcopalian or members of one of the many offshoots of the Church of England and the EPISCOPAL CHURCH IN THE U.S.A., including METHODISM and the many Holiness and Pentecostal churches (see HOLINESS MOVEMENT; PENTECOSTALISM). Quite a few are Anabaptists (see ANABAPTISM) or Baptists. All share a common Protestant theological ethos that is strongly rooted in Luther's principles of *sola gratia et fides*, *sola scriptura* and the PRIESTHOOD OF

ALL BELIEVERS. Some, however, embrace a sacramental spirituality, whereas others promote a pietist-revivalist spirituality. Some are deeply indebted to the Puritan heritage, whereas others are rooted in the Arminian and Wesleyan tradition (see ARMINIANISM). Many emphasize total divine sovereignty, including meticulous providence and unconditional PREDESTINATION, whereas many others prefer a more synergistic theology of the God–human relationship. All of these and other diversities among evangelical theologians give rise to tensions within evangelical theology. Such tensions are especially exacerbated by the fundamentalist heritage of evangelical theology in the late twentieth century and into the twenty-first century.

Perhaps the most enduring and divisive issue debated by evangelical theologians is the nature of Scripture's inspiration and accuracy. This is the so-called "inerrancy controversy" that waxes and wanes among evangelicals. Evangelicals look back to two theologians of Protestant orthodoxy in the late nineteenth and early twentieth centuries who debated the extent and nature of Scripture's inspiration and accuracy. Benjamin Breckinridge Warfield of Princeton Theological Seminary followed Charles Hodge and Francis Tuerretin in arguing for the "plenary verbal inspiration" of the Bible and derived its strict, detailed inerrancy from that. According to Warfield and those conservative evangelicals who follow his thinking, Scripture can be fully authoritative only if it is a supernaturally inspired (not dictated) message from God that is fully accurate in all matters, including history and cosmology. In contrast, Scottish evangelical theologian James Orr affirmed Scripture's authority and inspiration but denied strict, detailed inerrancy. For Warfield and those who follow his thinking about Scripture, it is adequate to its purpose (salvation) and therefore "infallible" even if it is not inerrant in matters not pertaining to salvation. At its founding, the Evangelical Theological Society required members to confess Scripture's inerrancy, but in the 1960s, Fuller Theological Seminary—the flagship educational institution of North American evangelicalism—dropped its inerrancy statement. In 1976, conservative evangelical theologian and editor of *Christianity Today* Harold Lindsell published *The Battle for the Bible*, which took noninerrantist evangelicals to task for undermining Scripture's authority. A furor ensued among evangelicals that continues into the twenty-first century. Traditionalist, conservative evangelical theologians insist that inerrancy is the only guard against doctrinal drift and cultural accommodation; reformist, postconservative evangelical theologians argue that every reasonable account of inerrancy kills it with the death of a thousand qualifications and that inerrancy tends to elevate Scripture to an idol or "paper pope"

(EMIL BRUNNER). Inerrancy has become a fault line, if not a continental divide, within the community of evangelical theologians.

A second significant controversial issue among evangelical theologians has to do with the doctrine of God. Traditionalists tend to assume an Augustinian perspective on God as by definition and by revelation the all-determining reality. God's primary attribute is majesty or glory. Divine power is exalted and any limitation resisted. These theologians are impressed by Jonathan Edwards's account of God's power and glory. Reformist evangelical thinkers draw more heavily on an Eastern Orthodox (see ORTHODOXY, EASTERN) and Wesleyan (see WESLEYANISM) account of God as primarily love; they regard God as self-limiting in relation to creation and affirm human free will as a limitation on God's power (because of God's voluntary self-restriction). These two doctrines of God constantly give rise to tensions within the evangelical theological community. These underlying tensions came to the surface in open disruption in the late 1990s and early twenty-first century in a controversy over "open theism." Open theism is the belief held by some reformist evangelical theologians that due to a voluntary self-restriction in relation to creation, God does not know the future exhaustively and infallibly. Open theists, such as Clark Pinnock, argue that divine foreknowledge is logically incompatible with creaturely free will and that Scripture portrays God as changing his mind and as learning in history. A number of evangelical theologians rallied around this new view, which was in turn vilified by traditionalists as incompatible with Scripture and God's glory. In 2001, the Evangelical Theological Society passed a resolution affirming God's absolute foreknowledge, and in 2002, it voted to investigate whether open theists may be members. A number of evangelical educational institutions decided not to hire open theists. In response, a group of 110 reformist evangelical scholars signed a manifesto titled "The Word Made Fresh: A Call for a Renewal of the Evangelical Spirit" (2002) that called for greater openness within evangelical theology.

The Future of Evangelical Theology

Evangelical theology is increasingly being accepted as a major school of theology separate from fundamentalism among the theologians of Protestantism. Nevertheless, its future is uncertain. Rifts and controversies continue to create strife among evangelical theologians in North America. At the same time, EVANGELICALISM as a popular movement is spreading throughout the world and becoming indigenous in non-Western cultures and countries. Major conventions of evangelical leaders and thinkers from around the world have taken place in SWITZERLAND (Lausanne 1 and 2) and the PHILIPPINES. These were attended by non-Western evangelicals, who played significant roles in shaping the theologies of these evangelical gatherings, especially as they related to missions and evangelistic endeavors. The future of evangelical theology may rest with the non-Western evangelical communities and their theologians, who tend not to be captivated by categories of Protestant orthodoxy and scholastic methods of doing theology. Many of them are charismatic or "third-wave" Christians, who emphasize the supernatural gifts of the Holy Spirit and "power encounters" between Christians and demonic forces. These theologies of spiritual warfare will no doubt challenge the status quo of traditional Western evangelical thought, which tends to focus on revealed propositions and coherent systems of doctrine.

References and Further Reading

Bebbington, David, and Mark Noll. *Evangelicalism: Comparative Studies of Popular Protestantism in North America, the British Isles, and Beyond.* New York: Oxford University Press, 1994.

Dorrien, Gary. *The Remaking of Evangelical Theology.* Louisville, KY: Westminster John Knox, 1998.

McGrath, Alister. *Evangelicalism and the Future of Christianity.* Downers Grove, IL: InterVarsity Press, 1995.

Marsden, George. *Understanding Fundamentalism and Evangelicalism.* Grand Rapids, MI: Eerdmans, 1991.

Noll, Mark. *American Evangelical Christianity: An Introduction.* Oxford, UK: Blackwell, 2000.

ROGER E. OLSON

EVANGELICALS, GERMANY

The English word *evangelical* was originally used to translate the German word *evangelisch*, a practice that continues to this day. Thus the *Oxford Dictionary of the Christian Church* (1974) renders Evangelische Kirche in Deutschland as "Evangelical Church in Germany." Since the mid-1960s the new word *evangelikal* was introduced into the German language. The main source and advocate of such usage is the German religious news service *IAllianz* (IDEA). It popularized the term *evangelikal* as a transdenominational identifier within German Protestantism.

Most movements and church organizations that are referred to as *evangelikal* had their beginnings well before the mid-1960s. Before that date German evangelicals would speak of themselves as "pietists," implying that they were legitimate heirs of eighteenth century PIETISM and claiming that there was a continuity of experience and THEOLOGY. The link between then and now is to be found in the "awakening movement," or *Erweckungsbewegung,* of the nineteenth

century that eventually emerged as the "Fellowship Movement," or *Gemeinschaftsbewegung,* during the latter part of the nineteenth century. The Fellowship Movement, with its many organizations and suborganizations, often denoted as "*Gnadauer Verband*," has always been part of the established regional territorial evangelical Lutheran churches, or *Landeskirchen.* In its effort to evangelize the country and to bring people together for prayer and fellowship beyond denominational boundaries, the movement has more or less cooperated with the commonly named "free churches," notably the Baptists, the Methodists (see METHODISM), and the Federation of Free Evangelical Congregations, through the Evangelical Alliance (*Evangelische Allianz*). Therefore, the Evangelical Alliance is the loose, transdenominational umbrella organization of German evangelicals and represents the theologically as well as politically conservative wing of German Protestantism. Because of the conservative nature of evangelicalism, the free churches have sometimes voiced their opposition to being classified as *evangelikal.* It is nevertheless true that evangelicals are represented within the "free churches" just as they are a part of the regional churches. Some free churches, notably the Federation of Free Evangelical Congregations, are closer to the evangelical center, whereas others, particularly the United Methodist Church (Evangelisch-methodistische Kirche), are more removed.

EVANGELICALISM emphasizes the experiential nature of the Christian faith. Through evangelistic efforts on the local level, mass media, and national or Europe-wide rallies, people are invited to make a personal commitment to Christ. Soteriology (SALVATION) is, therefore, the center of evangelicalism. Evangelism and missionary work, but also diaconical engagement ("mother houses," hospitals, counseling centers, student work, etc.) are seen as indispensable elements of the Christian faith. Despite differences in ecclesiology among various evangelicals, a common week of prayer is organized annually in early January and a common effort is made in EVANGELISM. The BIBLE is seen as the inspired word of God, but German evangelicals have not clearly distinguished between a fundamentalist ("inerrancy") and an evangelical approach to the Bible and in biblical scholarship (see FUNDAMENTALISM). In politics German evangelicals vehemently opposed laws on ABORTION and, as the "quiet of the land," are generally taking a conservative or rather "disinterested" position.

References and Further Reading

Jung, Friedhelm. "Die deutsche Evangelikale Bewegung—Grundlinien ihrer Geschichte und Theologie." Ph.D. dissertation, University of Marburg, 1990. Bonn: Jahrbuch für Evangelikale Theologie, 2001.

ERICH GELDBACH

EVANGELISM, OVERVIEW

Evangelism is the organized propagation of Christian belief and practice, the "good news" described in the New Testament. Evangelism can be quantified into 45 major components, for each of which most Protestant churches, Missions, and agencies keep detailed records including elaborate annual statistics. These statistics can demonstrate how individuals and thus countries, peoples, languages, and cities and their populations receive Christian evangelism.

Protestants have long specialized in every variety of organized evangelism listed and described in this article, on all continents, in all 238 countries of the world, and in most of its 12,000 languages. In addition, Protestant evangelists have often cooperated with Anglican, Orthodox, Roman Catholic, and independent clergy, workers, and laypersons. Likewise, the recipients of all of the major forms of evangelism are in most places composed of hearers, listeners, viewers, and readers of many backgrounds, ethnicities, ages, religions, nationalities, denominations, and so on. What this means is that evangelism in practice usually operates cooperatively by all churches and Christians of any confession working together.

Origins of Evangelism

Although the theme of God's favor arises at a number of points in the Old Testament, Christian evangelism begins with Jesus's life, death, and resurrection. The mandate for evangelism is encapsulated first in the six New Testament accounts of Christ's Great Commission, and then in the multiple occurrences of the Greek verb *euangelizo* and its vast number of synonyms.

Investigating Evangelism

Christians regard Jesus not only as the good news (*euangelion*), but also as the master evangelizer and evangelist bringing that same good news to the human race. Column 7 of Table 1 analyzes how Jesus converted believers in Palestine and how Christian evangelists attempt to do this today. The words Jesus used form a typology of seven distinct types of words corresponding to seven modes of evangelism. Jesus used five main modes or points of contact with people through words: (1) *hidden words* (his private hopes and prayers), (2) *visual words* (what people saw of his person, his life, his lifestyle, his deeds, and his actions), (3) *personal words* (face-to-face meetings with

an individual or a group), (4) *proclaimed words* (Jesus' preaching and teaching to groups or crowds), and (5) *written words* (Jesus' use of scrolls of the Old Testament as the written Word of God). After his resurrection, Jesus delivered two further mandates: *baptize* and *train*. After his ascension, Jesus then expanded these last two mandates. First, he founded his church, with its church-planting imperative. Second, he launched a leadership training program, selecting, calling out, setting apart, and training a whole new age of sevenfold leadership in ministry: disciples, apostles, prophets, evangelists, healers, pastors, and teachers. He thus expanded the understanding of his Great Commission, which his disciples later expanded into two further categories: (6) *printed words* (literature, tracts, periodicals, books) and (7) *electronic words* (broadcasting, radio/TV, cassettes, computers, etc.).

Quantifying 45 Dimensions of Evangelism

Evangelism is the activity, individual or collective and usually organized, by which Christians set forth and spread their beliefs and practices. The quantification of evangelism boils down to measuring the various modes of contact that persons or populations have had with evangelizers. In short, it means enumerating the duration, quality, and intensity of all conversations and awareness resulting from this contact with Christians, Christianity, Jesus Christ, and the Gospel.

With the foregoing definitions and methodology in mind, we can reduce evangelism to 45 major areas or components, which are listed in Table 2. Here, we label them for shorthand purposes as "ministries." This article provides a brief description of each of these ministries, with relevant statistics for each placed separately in the Appendix as Table 5, giving the total number of evangelism-hours per annum that each type of ministry worldwide generates, the factor by which the media multiples these hours, and the number of persons that each type of evangelism thus reaches. These are given there as each ministry's description, as follows:

- Evangelism-hours originated per year. This is the actual number of hours put in by evangelizers of all Protestant and associated confessions, in each type of ministry each year. For example, a part-time evangelist who preaches for one hour twice a week, each week throughout the year, originates 104 evangelism-hours per annum.
- Media factor. This is a multiplying factor representing the audience exposed to one hour of each variety of ministry.

Table 1. The origins and present ministries of evangelism in (a) Christ's Great Commission, and (b) the richest biblical word Evangelize!

MANDATE IMPERATIVE English	NT Greek	Usages	DOMINANT CHARACTERISTIC	HUMAN ROLE	SUB-TYPES OF EVANGELISM	RESULTING WORDS	OUTREACH MINISTRIES	OVERVIEW	OTHER KEYWORDS (related nouns) Greek, Latin (L)	Usages	DIMENSIONS of "evangelize" Total	Key dimensions	FACETS English
1	2	3	4	5	6	7	8	9	10	11	12	13	14
OVERALL IMPERATIVE													
Evangelize!	euangelizo	133	Authoritative	7-P Evangelism	Pluriform evangelism Evangelistic work	EVANGELIZING WORDS	45	7-P Evangelization	euangelion semeia kai terata evangelizatio (L)	76/133 77/84 41	400	Evangelize with signs following	700
MINICOMMISSION I: EVANGELIZE! CONSTITUENT MANDATES:													
1. Receive!	labete verb: lambano	263	Spirit-dominated	Prayer evangelism	Baptism in the Spirit Spirit evangelism Pneumatization Renewal in the Spirit Intercession Power evangelism	HIDDEN WORDS	2	Pneumatic evangelization	parakletos dynamis pneumatikos exousia	5/34 120/331 28/413 103/107	10	Accompany, Be filled, Breathe, Cooperate, Follow, Participate, Pneumatize, Pray, Receive power, Stay, Wait	33
2. Go!	poreuthentes verb: poreuomai	154	Person-implemented	Pre-evangelism	Apostolate Mission Extension Outreach Primary evangelism Visitation evangelism Visual evangelism Audiovisual evangelism	VISUAL WORDS	11	Preparatory evangelism	apostole missio (L)	4/255 900	45	Act, Contact, Develop, Encounter, Engage, Extend, Go, Help, Impact, Influence, Itinerate, Liberate, Love, Make aware, Occupy, Permeate, Prepare, Reach, Seek, Send, Show, Target, Touch, Transmit, Visit	101
3. Witness!	martyres verb: martyreo	173	Unorganized, private	Personal evangelism	Person-to-person witness Personal work Individual evangelism Conversational talk Dialogue evangelism Gossiping the gospel Seed-sowing Prophetic evangelism	PERSONAL WORDS	2	Presence evangelization	martyria praesencia (L) justitia (L) pax (L) dialogismos	57/173 120 220 200 14/43	60	Be martyred, Be present, Bring, Carry, Confess, Dialogue, Expose, Gossip, Inform, Propagate, Radiate, Report, Say, Share, Shine, Sow, Spread, Talk, Tell, Testify, Witness	132
4. Proclaim!	keryxate verb: kerysso	72	Ordered, public	Preaching evangelism	Public evangelism Mass evangelism Demonstration evangelism Deliverance evangelism Incarnational evangelism Saturation evangelism	PROCLAIMED WORDS	6	Proclamation evangelization	kerygma apologia (L)	8/72 8/18	48	Advertise, Announce, Declare, Demonstrate, Do miracles, Exorcise, Explain, Expound, Give a message, Give opportunity, Herald, Make listen, Preach, Present, Proclaim, Prove, Publish, Read, Reason, Refute, Saturate, Translate	85

MINICOMMISSION II: DISCIPLE!

	1	2	3	4	5	6	7	8	9	10	11	12	13	14
5.	Disciple!	matheteusate verb: matheteuo	266	Convert-oriented	Persuasion evangelism	Paracletic evangelism, Harvest evangelism, Discipling evangelism, Verdict evangelism, Decision evangelism, Lordship evangelism, Healing evangelism, Power healing	WRITTEN WORDS	9	Pressure evangelization	paraklesis, therismos, mathetes, therapeia	29/34, 13/36, 261/266, 3/47	63	Appeal, Catch, Compel, Confront, Conquer, Convert, Convince, Denounce, Disciple, Exhort, Forgive, Give, Harvest, Heal, Impart, Implore, Invite, Offer, Persuade, Press, Reap, Retain, Urge, Warn, Win	128
6.	Baptize!	baptizontes verb: baptizo	111	Church-oriented	Pastoral evangelism	Baptism, Baptizing evangelism, Evangelism that results in churches, Church planting, Incorporation, Shepherding, Celebration evangelism	PRINTED WORDS	9	Planting evangelization	baptismos, koinonia, ekklesia, leitourgeia, eucharistia, katechumenos	23/111, 19/59, 115, 6/15, 15/54, 8	35	Affiliate, Baptize, Bless, Build, Catechize, Confirm, Enroll, Feed, Grow, Incorporate, Initiate, Minister, Multiply, Plant, Praise, Sacramentalize, Serve, Tend, Worship	70
7.	Train!	didaskontes verb: didasko	212	Ministry-oriented	Programmed evangelism	Teaching evangelism, Electronic evangelism, Broadcasting, Radio/TV evangelism	ELECTRONIC WORDS	6	Pedagogical evangelization	didache, diakonia, oikodome	30/212, 34/101, 18/59	21	Broadcast, Celebrate, Cultivate, Edify, Educate, Follow-up, Instruct, Mobilize, Nurture, Program, Teach, Train	43

This table portrays meanings and usages of terms. The columns are as follows:

1. The seven mandates of the Great Commission, as imperatives
2. The Greek New Testament verbs involved
3. Number of usages in Greek OT and NT
4. Dominant feature of each
5. Human role, in English usage
6. Other varieties of evangelistic terminology
7. Typology of resulting types of words
8. Number of related major outreach ministries
9. Theological overview terms
10. Other Greek or Latin key words
11. NT usages of these key words
12. Total dimensions of "evangelize"
13. Key dimensions
14. Total dimensions, synonyms, and facets in English usage

Table 2. Evangelism described under 7 modes of evangelizing words and 45 distinct outreach ministries.

Imperative *1*	Human role *2*	EVANGELIZING WORDS Outreach ministries *3*	Description of "words" (lines in capitals) and ministries (lines in lowercase) (**bold type** = major keywords in each ministry under one of the 7 Imperatives/Mandates) *4*
Receive!	Prayer evangelism	HIDDEN WORDS 1. Intercession 2. Inner renewal/spirituality	WORDS **HIDDEN** IN PRIVATE **PRAYER**, CHARISMATA **RECEIVED**. Continuing earnestly in **prayer**, **interceding** for persons and peoples. Being filled with the Holy Spirit, **waiting**, then **following** Jesus.
Go!	Pre-evangelism	VISUAL WORDS (audiovisual) 3. Christians' lifestyle 4. Audiovisual ministries 5. Plays/concerts/operas/shows 6. "Jesus" Film shows 7. Audio scriptures 8. Scripture leaflets/selections 9. Every-home campaign visits 10. New Reader Scriptures 11. Braille scriptures 12. Signed/deaf scriptures 13. Christian suffering	CHRISTIANS **GO**, HELP, SHOW **VISIBLE SIGNS PREPARING** HEARERS. **Going**, **meeting**, **bringing** the **love** of God by Christian **loving** and **lives**. **Sending out**, **speaking out**, **displaying**, **showing** words and pictures. Shows illustrating Christian doctrine, history, ethics. Portraying the **incarnation**, person, **work**, and **ministry** of Jesus. Making Scripture **available** to nonliterates, reading aloud, **corresponding**. Impacting whole populations with mass **illustrated** leaflets. **Going**, **seeking**, **visiting**, **contacting**, **touching**, **encountering**, **giving**. Providing pictorial literacy primers, **supplying** gospels for new literates. Doing miracles, **giving** sight to the blind. **Reaching** deaf persons with the gospel. **Showing** how Christians live through sickness, **suffering**, even death.
Witness!	Personal evangelism	PERSONAL WORDS 14. Personal evangelism 15. Martyrdoms	CHRISTIANS **WITNESS PERSONALLY** BY **PRESENCE**, WORD, **DEED**, DYING. **Telling** others about Jesus, **speaking**, **gossiping** the gospel, **introducing**, **informing**. The **witness** of those who lose their lives for Christ and are **martyred**.
Proclaim!	Preaching evangelism	PROCLAIMED WORDS 16. Full-time home church workers 17. Foreign missionaries 18. Evangelists 19. Short-term missionaries 20. Part-time evangelizers 21. Mission agencies	WORDS **PREACHED**, **PROCLAIMING** THE GOSPEL IN STRUCTURED SITUATIONS. **Preaching**, **stating**, **reading**. **Translating**, **interpreting**, **expounding**, **saturating**. **Proclaiming**, **announcing**, **declaring**, **heralding**, **presenting**. **Demonstrating**, **saturating**. **Giving opportunity** to many others. **Advertising**, enabling workers to **promulgate** the gospel.

Disciple! Persuasion evangelism	WRITTEN WORDS (Scriptures) 22. Portions/gospels 23. Near-gospels 24. New Testaments 25. Near-New Testaments 26. Bibles 27. Near-Bibles 28. Lingua franca gospels 29. Lingua franca NTs 30. Lingua franca Bibles	**WRITTEN SCRIPTURES PERSUADING, PRESSING DISCIPLE**-OPPORTUNITIES. **Imparting, forgiving, offering, explaining.** Circulating gospels among related languages with no scriptures. **Persuading, discipling, reaping.** **Distributing** the whole story of Jesus to related languages with no scriptures. **Convincing, winning, converting, healing.** **Offering** the Bible's riches to related languages without it. **Catching, confronting** scripture-less languages through lingua francas. Harvesting scripture-less languages through wider-communication languages. **Making** the Bible's riches **understandable** to all through trade and similar languages.
Baptize! Pastoral evangelism	PRINTED WORDS (literature) 31. Denominational materials 32. Local church output 33. Outside Christian literature 34. Church-planting output 35. Institutional ministries/records 36. Christian books 37. Christian periodicals 38. Tracts 39. Other documentation	**BAPTISM,** CHURCH-**PLANTING,** PASTORAL LIFE, **PRINTED WORDS.** **Catechizing, baptizing, confirming, incorporating** new believers, **pastoring.** **Enrolling, affiliating, worshiping, blessing.** **Helping, supporting.** **Planting** new churches, **building,** church **growth.** **Serving, ministering.** **Feeding, growing.** **Tending, shepherding.** **Multiplying** individual ministries. **Praising, singing.**
Train! Programmed evangelism	ELECTRONIC WORDS 40. Programmed training 41. Christian radio programs 42. Christian TV programs 43. Urban media (cable TV, &c) 44. Christian-owned computers 45. Internet/networks/e-mail	**TRAINED BY ELECTRONIC**-MEDIA PROGRAMMED WORDS. **Instructing, teaching, educating, making** people **learn.** **Broadcasting, following-up.** **Telecasting teaching** materials, **cultivating, edifying.** **Working among** all varieties of peoples, especially urban populations, **uniting.** Programming the church's many activities, e-mailing, **faxing.** **Mobilizing** the vast area of Christian resources worldwide; surfing, **training.**

This table portrays meanings and usages of terms and components of evangelism and its related ministries and terminologies.

- Total offers received per year. The end product is this total, which is the number of offers of conversion that actually reach hearers, being the product of the preceding 2 lines. Note that "received" says nothing about the recipients' acceptance or rejection of the message.

Hidden Words

This first mode of evangelism has as its mandate and imperative "Receive!" This mode refers to evangelizing words not visible to the outside world, and especially to words hidden in prayer. Thus these ministries are generally not subject to exact enumeration or precise statistics. Here we label them ministries 1 and 2.

1. Intercession. This first variety of outreach ministry is one that Christians exercise by praying for specific, named causes, situations, populations, and persons. In particular, we refer here to prayer directly related to evangelism. There are currently 30 distinct Protestant global prayer networks for world evangelization, 10 million prayer groups, 20 million Christians in full-time prayer ministry, and some 100 million laypersons who have become daily intercessors. In the 1990s, evangelicals organized a campaign known as "Praying through the 10/40 Window," in which some 20 million evangelicals undertook six months of daily intercession for the evangelizing of the world's 1.6 billion unevangelized persons. Many of the larger networks actually collect and publish annual statistics relevant to, if not directly enumerating, this hidden ministry. Thus Every Home for Christ (EHC) International (formerly World Literature Crusade, or Every Home Crusade) enumerates its prayer materials sent out regularly to its committed intercessors. By 1991, the EHC was distributing 2,640,449 prayer bulletins each year in 28 languages for its work in 169 countries.

2. Inner renewal/spirituality. This refers to that eventual state in which a formerly inactive, lethargic, or dormant church or denomination moves rapidly to being vibrant, enthusiastic, and active. The phrase also covers other major areas of Christian activity and impact, including spirituality, mysticism, spiritual gifts, charismata, and spiritual warfare. In the year 2000, this renewal's active adult church members were estimated at 375 million.

Visual Words

This second mode of evangelism has as its mandate and imperative "Go!" This mode refers to evangelizing words directly visible or audible to all. They are visible signs preparing hearers for the gospel. This covers ministries 3 to 13.

3. Christian lifestyle. This form of evangelism seeks to commend Christian belief and practice by the day-to-day fruits and rewards it may offer. There is a direct parallel here with Jesus' own ministry on Earth. People saw him, heard him, and observed his deeds and his lifestyle. For Jesus, the verb *euangelizo* meant to spread good news with signs following. Contemporary Christian lifestyle consists of myriads of phenomena of these kinds across the world. They engender vast varieties of evangelism and evangelistic ministries. Christians demonstrating a genuinely Christ-like lifestyle today probably number at least 100 million.

4. Audiovisual ministries. Although this descriptive terminology is only a couple of centuries old, it encompasses the vast range of Christian art (paintings, sculpture, tapestry, et alia). MARTIN LUTHER was firmly of the opinion that artistic representation could aid the proclamation of the Gospel. Christian art in vast profusion has appeared throughout Christian history. One ministry centers on one individual Christian whose work has resulted in a billion images of Christ. In 1940, artist Warner Sallman (1892-1968) painted the *Head of Christ.* It has become one of the most enduring images of Jesus in both American and global Christianity. Sallman's version of Christ has appeared in many different media of devotional life, including Bibles, Sunday-school literature, calendars, posters, church bulletins, clocks, lamps, wallet-sized photos, pins, and stickers.

In addition to thousands of works of visual art illustrating the Gospel, there is yet another type: ARCHITECTURE. In England, Canterbury Cathedral has since the Middle Ages depicted the entire BIBLE story in its stained glass windows (originally to evangelize a nonliterate population). Today more tourists and others—more than four million—visit it each year than the total inhabitants in fourteenth-century England.

There are literally hundreds of other audiovisual ministries under this heading.

5. Plays/concerts/operas/shows. This variety of evangelism refers to a whole range of theatrical, cinematic, radio, and television epics, narratives or productions that can be described as clearly evangelistic. The range includes Christian theatre, plays, shows, opera, ballet, musicals, music performances, concerts, and motion pictures of other Bible or Christian subjects in addition to the depiction of the life of Christ. Possibly the most popular and successful evangelistic presentation of all time has been GEORGE FRIDERIC

HANDEL's oratorio "Messiah," an artistic masterpiece written in 1741. Its fifty-three sections of biblical texts are a skillfully crafted statement of Christian DOCTRINE describing the mighty drama of human redemption. "Messiah" is the most-performed major choral work in history, and most likely the single most-performed musical work around the world today. It is also a powerful evangelistic tool—professional, popular, participatory, universally acclaimed, and yet all the time biblical, Bible-quoting, Christ-centered, eschatological. Although not deliberately evangelistic, its phenomenal success in Britain is linked with the evangelical revival in the CHURCH OF ENGLAND, and with JOHN WESLEY's robust doctrine of assurance of SALVATION. Its evangelistic effect is heightened by the absence of the name "Jesus" (used only once, in section 51, from I Corinthians 15:57) and the cautious low-key use of the name "Christ."

Over the last 250 years, performances of "Messiah" have taken place at least once a year, usually at Christmas, in some 3,000 metropolises in some 20,000 churches, cathedrals, choirs, clubs, societies, festivals, colleges, and other venues across the English-speaking world. Performances have average attendances of 200 persons each and vary in length from two to four hours. Performers vary from fifty to over 5,000 at one time. Altogether, these attract four million attendees in person every year.

There are numerous other musical compositions based on the Gospel story. A widely known one is JOHANN SEBASTIAN BACH's "Saint Matthew Passion" (1729), based on the life of Christ. Going beyond this worldwide English-language coverage, there is also a vast coverage of similar musical works composed and presented in nearly sixty other global languages. Many have been hugely successful as dramas, theatre plays, musicals, and radio plays (e.g., "The Man Born to be King" in 1945).

6. Jesus films. There has been a long history of movies portraying the life of Jesus. These include *Intolerance* (1916), *The King of Kings* (1927), *Ben Hur* (1959), *King of Kings* (1961), *The Greatest Story Ever Told* (1965), *The Gospel According to St Matthew* (1966), *Godspell* (1973), *Jesus Christ Superstar* (1973), *Jesus of Nazareth* (1977), *The Last Temptation of Christ* (1988), and *Jesus*, the classic spread in 700 languages worldwide by Campus Crusade for Christ.

7. Audio scriptures. Another audiovisual variety that has blossomed in the twentieth century hinges on recordings (CDs, records, tapes) of the full texts of Christian Scriptures—gospels, New Testaments, Bi-

bles—in several thousand languages. These can then be circulated, bought, sold, copied, reproduced, translated, and—a most important development—broadcast over radio, either at talking speed (for listeners to record) or at dictation speed (for listeners to write down). By 1997, audio scriptures had been prepared and were widely circulating, through the United Bible Societies, Forum of Bible Agencies, Audio Scriptures International, and other specialist agencies, in some 4,600 languages.

8. Scripture leaflets/selections. Jesus sprinkled his teachings with visually evocative quotations from the Hebrew Scriptures varying in length from short texts to well-known narratives and exegesis of longer passages. A similar ministry is performed today through the widespread and continuous scattering, in every walk of life, of short Scripture verses or texts in leaflet form. BIBLE SOCIETIES have formalized these with their category "Selections," defined as 4- or 8-page colorful visually appealing booklets with a number of selected Scripture passages. Scores of agencies publish large ranges and quantities of similar selections.

9. Every-home campaign visits. In his itinerations, Jesus frequently visited people's homes and there delivered major teaching, healing miracles, or other definitive ministry. House-to-house visiting has always been an important initial stage in evangelistic strategy. Massive programs of nationwide campaigns now make this a leading form of evangelism. The first attempt by a mission organization to reach systematically every home in an entire nation took place from 1912–1917 in JAPAN, where the Oriental Missionary Society visited 10,300,000 homes. So successful was this program that it was extended to other countries, and then finally throughout the world. More recently, the major example is Every Home for Christ International (EHC). This organization was begun in CANADA in 1946 as the World Literature Crusade for radio outreach. It then expanded to systematic tract distribution through the EHC, with more than 1.85 billion booklet distributions and more than 22 million written responses for Christ over the succeeding 43 years. Since 1953, EHC has specialized in house-to-house visitation to entire populations of countries. By 1996, the total of all such visits had risen to more than 10 million per year. In addition, there are thousands of small local church or parish visitation campaigns each year.

10. New Reader Scriptures. Jesus was literate himself, accustomed to public reading and exposition of the written Scriptures. He constantly drew attention to them. He challenged skeptics: "Have you never read in the Scriptures. . . " (Matthew 21:42). In 1967 the United Bible Societies inaugurated a new variety of scriptures, designed especially for the newly literate or potential literates, called NRS (New Reader Scriptures). Easy to read, illustrated, attractively printed, the NRS have proven very popular.

11. Braille Scripture.   In the year 1830, a teacher at a school for the blind named Louis Braille developed a raised-dot system that became standard for the English-speaking world. In 1932, Standard English Braille was adopted in the United States. Nonsighted or totally blind persons numbered some 19.3 million worldwide in 2000. In addition, another 30 million persons are legally blind. Of these 49 million, 10 million have access to a Braille Scripture in their own language.

12. Signed/deaf Scriptures.   Sign languages were developed in Europe more than four centuries ago. In Britain, schools for the deaf were begun in the mid-nineteenth century. In 2000, the world contained 365 million deaf (hearing-impaired) persons, of whom 150 million are severely impaired and 23 million are totally deaf. Of these, about 15 percent use or understand a sign language. Sign languages include American Sign Language (ASL), as well as quite different systems used in more than 60 other languages. Of all deaf persons, about 30 million have access to signed Scriptures in their own sign language.

13. Christian suffering.   Jesus promised his disciples that theirs would not be a life of ease but a life of hardship, persecution, and suffering. Jesus taught his disciples to redeem suffering and use it for the glory of God.

Personal Words

The third of the seven modes of evangelism has as its mandate and imperative "Witness!" This refers to evangelizing words at the grassroots—the day-to-day evangelism of ordinary Christians as they go about their work, home life, and social activities. These are words through which individual Christians evangelize others. This results in ministries 14 and 15.

14. Personal evangelism.   Sometimes called "personal work," this is the usually private endeavor of an active Christian to interest or enroll other persons for the faith, usually by means of one-on-one conversation. Personal evangelism is regularly monitored in public-opinion polls. In a survey dated December 1982, the Gallup Organization asked a nationwide representative random sample of Americans the carefully phrased question: "Have you ever tried to encourage someone to believe in Jesus Christ or to accept Him as his or her Savior?" Some 51 percent of all Americans answered "Yes," 41 percent answered "No," and 8 percent answered "No opinion/Don't know."

15. Martyrdoms.   Jesus often warned that a disciple's commitment could result in death. This has subsequently been the case throughout church history. In the twentieth century, martyrdoms have become well known as a result of regular and persistent reports in the media. In the light of twenty centuries of Christian history with its 70 million martyrs, it is safe to say that martyrdom has been the single most significant factor leading to the evangelization and Christianization of a people or nation. The total of all Christian martyrs since World War II has averaged 300,000 a year. This toll fell dramatically to 160,000 a year with the collapse of Communist regimes in Eastern Europe and the USSR during 1989–1992.

Proclaimed Words

This fourth of the seven modes of evangelism has as its mandate and imperative "Proclaim!" These are words preached by professional workers proclaiming and expounding the gospel in structured situations. This covers ministries 16 to 21. They center on the public announcement of Christian belief and practice.

16. Full-time home church workers.   Full-time Christian workers are found virtually everywhere. In this analysis we divide them into home workers (dealt with here as no. 16) and foreign workers (no. 17). The term covers all employees of churches, denominations, agencies, and institutions. These workers may even be self-employed. The category usually covers ongoing employment lasting more than one year, usually long term, and excluding short-term workers (less than one year). The range of vocations covered is vast, from theologians, bishops, and clergy at one end to administrators, accountants, secretaries, and manual laborers at the other. But all may be considered part of the church's proclamation of the Christian faith, by word of mouth, by writing, or by their service and their quality of life. In the year 2000, full-time Protestant home workers, of all confessions, were estimated at 2,100,000 worldwide.

17. Foreign missionaries.   A foreign missionary is defined here as a full-time Christian worker of any age, race, or occupation, who works in a country in which he or she is not a citizen (or national) but is a foreigner (or alien). The estimated total of Protestant foreign missionaries of all confessions was 220,000 in the year 2000.

18. Evangelists. Evangelists are defined here as part-time or full-time Christian workers who specialize in the public or private proclamation of the Gospel, either structured or unstructured. The two titles "evangelist" and "catechist," are almost interchangeable. The following list classifies them by the size of their operations into seven levels:

- *Nonprofessional, part-time evangelists* form the vast bulk of the category. Many denominations in developing countries use a rank or category called "evangelists." Often no salaries are paid.
- *Part-time catechists* are located mainly in Asia and in sub-Saharan AFRICA.
- *Full-time professional evangelists* have mushroomed since 1950, each with an independent evangelistic association.
- *Full-time professional missionary catechists* often have graduated from SEMINARIES, BIBLE COLLEGES, or other training establishments.
- *Macro-evangelists* is the term that best fits those whose evangelistic organizations have grown large enough to support teams of associate evangelists undertaking multiple campaigns, crusades, and macro-crusades. There are at least 500 such macro-evangelists worldwide.
- *Mega-evangelists* are defined here as those evangelists who from time to time actually preach live to crowds of over one million (including both face-to face and over radio/TV). Some 30 well-known evangelists in a variety of cultures across the world fall into this category in the year 2000. German mega-evangelist Reinhard Bonnke preached in 1994 to 1.67 million people who attended six evening meetings in Kaduna, Nigeria, with 500,000 people at the culminating Saturday meeting held in Muhamed Murtala Square. More than 200,000 decision cards were signed by Kaduna citizens declaring that they had received Jesus as Savior. By 1996, Bonnke had preached face-to-face to 28,545,000 persons, of whom 6,053,190 registered decisions for Christ (see TELEVANGELISM).
- *Global evangelists.* This term is reserved here for any evangelist who in practice has addressed, and still can address, the entire globe at once, or who reaches live an audience of around one billion hearers at once (mostly via radio/TV). In the year 2003, only two such persons were attaining this category. The first is BILLY GRAHAM, who preached face-to-face to 180 million from 1940–2003, and over radio/TV to over a billion during Global Mission 1995. The second is John Paul II, who, although not a professional evangelist, has fulfilled this function from 1978 to the present by regularly expounding Christianity, Christ, and the Gospel to multi-million-hearer audiences. In the year 2003, the total number of evangelists worldwide was estimated at some 710,000, and catechists at 520,000.

19. Short-term missionaries. These short-term workers are usually defined as those who work abroad full-time, or in full-time church or other Christian jobs, for a period of more than one month but less than one year in length. The total of short-term Protestant workers serving abroad in the year 2000 was estimated at 400,000 at any one time.

20. Part-time evangelizers. This category is defined here as persons who have secular employment but who nevertheless put in a substantial amount of work each week as part-time or volunteer Christian workers, specializing in spreading the Gospel. This includes Methodist lay preachers, Anglican lay readers, Catholic parish assistants (when not full-time), parish visitors, and a whole variety of roles in almost all denominations. They number 20 million part-time workers.

21. Mission agencies. These are 4,000 agencies that exist specifically to implement the evangelical world mission. They undertake foreign missions and outreach and other cross-cultural mission activity.

Written Words (Scriptures)

This fifth of the seven modes of evangelism has as its mandate and imperative "Disciple!" This refers to evangelizing words taken from the Bible, which has been translated into 3,500 languages, and covers ministries 22 to 30. "Script" means "handwriting; written words, letters, or figures." Jesus constantly quoted the Hebrew and Greek Scriptures, saying "It is written. . . ," or "Have you not read. . . ." To this must be added the whole ministry of writing out Scripture verses by hand, especially in person-to-person correspondence, authoring manuscripts, periodicals, and even in BIBLE TRANSLATION.

Faced today with some 7,000 distinct languages with no Scripture translations yet done, translators have long recognized that a people's access to the Scriptures may be provided, temporarily or even permanently, if translations exist in either of two indirect forms. The first form is *near-scriptures*, which are defined as scriptures in any closely-related language, itself defined here as one within the same language cluster; the three varieties of near-scriptures are here enumerated under ministries 23, 25, and 27. The second form is *lingua franca scriptures*, which are scriptures in any language in wide use among the people, especially a trade language, a lingua franca, even a national language. Using these criteria, the number of peoples with access to Scripture rises dramatically.

22. Portions/Gospels. A portion is a single book of the Bible published separately as a booklet by itself. Portions most frequently appearing vary in length from forty pages long (the Gospel of Luke) to only a page or two (Philemon, John 2, Jude). Most, however, are Gospels. Average length is twenty-five pages. The major distributors of these portions are the world's 180 Bible societies and agencies. Thousands of other organizations, especially local churches, also engage in scripture distribution.

23. Near-Gospels. For a language into which no Scripture has yet been translated, a "near-Gospel" is a copy of a Gospel in a closely-related language within the same language cluster.

24. New Testaments (300 pages). Translation and publication of the New Testament in a new language is not simply a temporary resting-point on the journey to production of the whole Bible. For many agencies, especially the Summer Institute of Linguistics (SIL, also termed Wycliffe Bible Translators [WBT]), the New Testament alone is a sensible end goal. Having completed the New Testament, WBT's translators then move on to other languages that as yet have nothing at all translated. They leave local translators supported by local churches to continue by translating the Old Testament. Total New Testaments distributed by all agencies—free, or subsidized, or commercial—amount to 121 million a year.

25. Near-New Testaments. This term relates to languages in which no Scripture has yet been translated. A "near-NT" is a copy in a closely-related language within the same language cluster.

26. Bibles (1,300 pages). Translation and publication of the whole Bible is so complex a process that such translation has been achieved, so far, in only 450 languages—barely 3 percent of the world's total. Total distribution from all sources by the year 2000 was 54 million a year.

27. Near-Bibles. Among a people with a mother tongue into which at present no scriptures have been translated or produced, a 'near-Bible' is a translation of the complete Bible into a closely-related language within the same language cluster. This may not be entirely satisfactory to the people concerned but since same-cluster languages share more than 80 percent of common vocabulary, it is certainly better than nothing.

28. Lingua franca Gospels. This category refers to any people who have a published Gospel available in a language distant or different from their mother tongue and which is understood by more than 50 percent of the population. Usually this is a language of wider communication (international language, lingua franca, trade language, market language, church language), but sometimes it is simply a neighboring or geographically nearby language.

29. Lingua franca New Testaments. The category refers to a people with a New Testament available in a language of wider communication understood by more than 50 percent of the population.

30. Lingua franca Bibles. This mode of evangelism is particularly powerful in that national and international languages multiply its influence far and wide.

Printed Words (Literature)

The sixth of the seven modes of evangelism has as its mandate and imperative "Baptize!" This encompasses the church's duty to engage in pastoral evangelism, to initiate new believers, to catechize new converts, to plant churches, to train, worship, minister, and multiply. That Christian evangelists are obeying this mandate is evident from the current global total of newly baptized persons per year: 40 million. This results in an enormous volume of documentation. Baptism, church-planting, and pastoral life are surrounded daily by millions of printed Christian words. In all of these, the vast expansion of printed literature plays a central role. They are enumerated here under nine main varieties of evangelism, here termed ministries 31 to 39.

31. Denominational materials. There are at present some 34,000 Christian denominations in the world. The central offices of at least 10,000 of them produce specialized literature to directly assist their local churches in evangelism and outreach. These cover teaching, catechism, baptism classes, Sunday schools, and the like. Baptism candidates are particularly well served.

32. Local church output. Some 3.5 million local churches exist—parish churches, congregations, or other places of worship. All of them in open countries produce large quantities of printed materials directly supporting the church's evangelism and outreach.

33. Outside Christian literature. A quite different form of printed material is experienced through outside languages and influences—through alien or foreign or other-culture Christians who live on the people's territory often with their own alien congregations. But most outside literature comes in, incidentally or accidentally, via the major lingua francas.

34. Church-planting output. A vast amount of printed literature is produced and circulated concerning a whole new ecclesiastical industry—church planting. Around 2,000 denominations and 3,000 mission agencies now incorporate church growth methodology and have organized departments to promote church planting, both in their home countries and on their mission fields abroad. As one result, by the year 2000, newly planted churches each year had risen to some 60,000.

35. Institutional ministries/records. Major Christian institutions number 105,000; minor church-related or Christian-related institutions number another 376,000. Every one of these 481,000 institutions is—or is supposed to be—a center of Christian outreach, evangelism, apologetics, and training. Each produces a voluminous annual output of literature and documentation.

36. Christian books (100 pages). A printed book is defined by UNESCO as one having 48 or more pages. In 1995 the total number of all new titles produced on any subject, secular or religious, reached the astronomical figure of 900,000, and by 2000 it had risen to over 1 million per year. With reprints of older titles, this results in the printing of 30 billion copies a year. Of these, Christian titles and books account for 3 percent per year.

37. Christian periodicals (30 pages). A most important role is played in outreach, evangelism, and apologetics by the 34,500 Christian periodicals, serials, magazines, journals, newspapers and the like, with circulation of some 50 million, and in 3,000 languages.

38. Tracts (2 pages). A tract is a short, concise, self-contained, stand-alone presentation of the gospel averaging a couple of sides of a small piece of paper. There has been a long history of Christian outreach through tract distribution, which was estimated in the year 2000 to total 5 billion tracts per year. A typical example of the evangelistic creativity tracts make

possible comes from Ujjain in north India. At the 1992 Kumbh Mela (Nectar Festival) with 10 million Hindus bathing in a river Ganges confluence, 225 Indian missionary workers distributed 1 million copies of the Gospel of John and 3 million gospel tracts in 33 days. At the 2001 Kumbh Mela, there were 70 million Hindu pilgrims, and similar vast increases in tract distribution.

39. Other documentation. This variety of ministry covers a vast range of activities. One of the most effective of these is placing Christian articles or stories in secular newspapers and magazines. A striking example comes from the former Soviet Union. Since 1990, Christian Agency Good News (ABC) has published evangelistic articles in more than 1.2 billion copies of Russian and Ukrainian newspapers and magazines.

Electronic Words

The seventh and last of the seven modes of evangelism has as its mandate and imperative "Train!" covering ministries 40 to 45.

40. Programmed training. Systematized Christian teaching on evangelism has followed development of secular communications. Bible correspondence courses followed the Penny Post in Britain, and radiophonic "schools of the air" came after the invention of broadcasting. After the invention and rapid expansion of distance education from 1945 in Britain and the United States, theological education by extension (TEE) and TEE and evangelism (TEEE) followed soon after. The TEE movement originated at a Presbyterian seminary in Guatemala in 1963; by 1980, there were over 200 major TEE organizations worldwide with 400 programs and 60,000 extension students in 90 countries. By 2000, virtually everything depended on electronics. Meanwhile, by 1966, Bible correspondence courses were mushrooming worldwide. Responses from individuals by then ranged from 110,000 enrolments in Morocco to 4 million a year in the United States (Catholic as well as Protestant courses). One of the largest denominational programs was that of the 12-million-member SEVENTH-DAY ADVENTIST CHURCH. In 1986, they had 180 Bible correspondence schools in 77 languages with 520,167 annual enrollments and 281,345 graduating. By 2000, some 60 million persons were receiving some kind of electronic programmed instruction and training in some aspects of evangelism and mission.

41. Christian radio programs. Christian broadcasting has since its origin in 1921 reached more people for every hour of evangelism than any other variety. In LATIN AMERICA, the most-heard radio evangelist for a time was Maria Miranda, heard by 100 million per day over 537 stations in 22 countries in 1990. Hundreds of other locally produced Protestant broadcasts are heard daily, even in non-Christian countries: for example, 10 percent of the population of Yemen listens to Christian radio. One of the most influential and long-lasting evangelistic ministries has been 'The Lutheran Hour' over radio station KFUO operated by THE LUTHERAN CHURCH-MISSOURI SYNOD since 1925. By 1931, 5 million heard its preaching each week; by 1987, there were 40 million regular listeners in 31 languages around the world.

42. Christian TV programs. TV activity has been going on in some 180 nations for many years. As an example, in October 1990, three shows were aired on Argentinian TV by CBN (Christian Broadcasting Network); more than eight million people saw the programs, and three million repeated the salvation prayer.

43. Urban media (cable TV, etc.). Urban areas and their 2.6 billion inhabitants have high exposure to the newest forms of electronic evangelism. Of 7,000 metropolises, every year some 1,400 hold citywide evangelistic campaigns featuring radio, TV, relays, satellites, video instruction, computer networks, the Internet, and other media. Results of recent campaigns are even more striking then those of 20 or 30 years earlier. The Rev. Y. Jeyaraj, general superintendent of the ASSEMBLIES OF GOD of INDIA, summed up a recent evangelistic campaign in Madras: "Conservatively, there were more than 250,000 converted." Another new medium of communication is cable television. Urban media programs featuring evangelism are under way in some 3,000 metropolises and cities worldwide.

44. Christian-owned computers. Under this head are included internal or in-house word-processing, databasing, donor lists, accounting, desktop publishing, and other computer-related activities. Around 3 percent of all this relates to evangelism, outreach, and mission.

45. Internet/networks/e-mail. The latest mega-activity to be added to types of evangelism comes from the enormous expansion of electronic mail and online network activity, particularly over the internet with its 400 million users (150 million of whom are Protestants). Thousands of Christian organizations advertise and evangelize via their own home pages on the world wide web.

See also Colonialism; Jehovah's Witnesses; Mass Media; Mormonism; Post-Colonialism; Publishing, Media; Statistics

References and Further Reading

Arias, M., and Johnson, A. *The Great Commission: Biblical Models for Evangelism.* Nashville, TN: Abingdon Press, 1992.

Barrett, D. B. *Selective Bibliography on Evangelism and Evangelization.* Nairobi, Kenya: World Evangelization Research Centre, 1980.

Barrett, D. B., and T. M. Johnson. *World Christian Trends.* Parts 22–25. Pasadena, CA: William Carey Library, 2001.

Castro, E., ed. *Mission and Evangelism: An Ecumenical Affirmation.* Geneva, Switzerland: CWME, 1982.

Coleman, R. E. *The Master Plan of Evangelism.* Old Tappan, NJ: Revell, 1963. (Published in India as *The Lord's Plan to Spread the Good News.* Madras, India: Evangelical Literature Service, 1963.)

Dallimore, A. A. *George Whitefield: Evangelist of the 18th–Century Revival.* London: Wakeman Trust, 1990.

Friedrich, G. "Euangelizomai." In *Theologisches Worterbuch zum Nueun Testament.* vol II, 707–737. Edited by G. Kittel. Stuttgart, Germany: Kolhammer, 1932.

Gumbel, N. *Telling Others: The Alpha Initiative.* Eastbourne, UK: Kingsway, 1994.

Hurd, A. E., and P. D. Peterson, eds. *Missions and Evangelism: A Bibliography Selected From the ATLA Religion Database, January, 1985.* rev. ed. Chicago, IL: American Theological Library Association, Religion Indexes, 1985.

Pollock, J. C. *D. L. Moody (Born 1837) and His Place in Modern Evangelism.* The Evangelical Library Annual lecture, 1987. London: The Evangelical Library, 1987–1989.

Samuel, V. K., and C. Sugden. *Evangelism and the Poor.* Bangalore, India: Partnership in Mission-Asia, 1983.

Senyoni, J. M. M. "Bishop Festo Kivengere's Philosophy of Evangelism." Master's thesis, Trinity Evangelical Divinity School, Deerfield, IL, 1992.

Towns, E. L., ed. *Evangelism and Church Growth: A Practical Encyclopedia.* Ventura, CA: Regal Books, 1995.

DAVID B. BARRETT

EVANGELISTIC ORGANIZATIONS

Cooperative evangelistic associations have been a feature of Protestantism at least since seventeenth- and eighteenth-century Pietists summoned Protestants to show their FAITH by their works and to share their faith with the world around them (see PIETISM). Denominations and state churches have their own associations dedicated to evangelistic outreach, but cooperative efforts have claimed the energies of Protestants who regard cross-denominational task-oriented agencies as effective means to specific ends. Such agencies first appeared in Europe in part as an expression of the Pietist conviction that true Christianity was a matter of the heart rather than of religious affiliation. For 200 years, cooperative efforts have been a particularly vibrant feature of American Protestantism, and—despite their Protestant roots and their early anti-Catholic tenor—in the twentieth century, some have gained substantial Catholic support as well. Often interrelated, claiming support from overlapping constituencies if not institutional connection, evangelistic associations have been a prominent feature of the Protestant moral crusade to save the world. This emanated first from the West, but by the twentieth century it radiated from most places where evangelical Christianity thrived. It is impossible to catalogue all of the evangelistic associations that carry forward Christian cooperative evangelistic efforts. The most enduring tend to cluster around three tasks with evangelistic intent: PUBLISHING, educating, and proclamation.

Bible Societies

Since the Pietist impulse loomed large among those who urged cross-denominational cooperation on behalf of specific tasks, it is not surprising that BIBLE publication was one of the first tasks to which North Atlantic Protestants turned. Carl Hildebrandt von Canstein founded the world's first Bible society in HALLE, Germany's Pietist center, in 1710. In addition to his interest in Bible distribution, Hildebrand devoted himself to developing a new printing method that allowed production at unusually low cost. By 1722, he had added Bohemian and Polish editions to his German stock.

Britons established their first Bible society in 1719, though the SOCIETY FOR THE PROPAGATION OF CHRISTIAN KNOWLEDGE (founded in 1698) also undertook the translation and publication of scripture as part of its mission, as did the Society in Scotland for Propagating Christian Knowledge (founded in 1709 and famous in the American colonies as the supporter of DAVID BRAINERD's evangelism among Native Americans). The best known and most ambitious of the British BIBLE SOCIETIES, the BRITISH AND FOREIGN BIBLE SOCIETY (BFBS), was established in London in 1804 with the enthusiastic support of WILLIAM WILBERFORCE. From the beginning, BFBS leadership united Anglicans and Non-Conformists around their common emphasis on scripture (see ANGLICANISM; NON-CONFORMITY). During the nineteenth century, the BFBS established offices in continental European cities, for example, opening a Bible depot in Vienna in 1850. By 1811, BFBS distributors were at work in Egypt. By mid-century, the BFBS had undertaken the task of providing Bibles in all of the languages of the British Empire. It worked alongside the growing number of British missionaries, supporting their evangelistic outreach by helping translate and by printing scripture (see BIBLE TRANSLATION). By the end of the nineteenth century, the BFBS had more than 7,500 auxiliaries under its umbrella. Until 1901, English law

limited the BFBS's circulation of English-language Bibles to the King James Version (see BIBLE, KING JAMES VERSION). The twentieth century brought the end of that restriction and saw the cooperative production of new Bible translations.

Cooperative efforts in SCOTLAND took a somewhat different course. The two most important local Bible societies, the Edinburgh Bible Society (1809) and the Glasgow Bible Society (1812), disassociated themselves from the BFBS after 1826 and in 1861 incorporated the National Bible Society of Scotland. The emergence of the National Bible Society of Scotland highlights some of the tensions that quickly beset cooperative Bible production. Disagreements over the inclusion of the Apocrypha contributed to the formation of a separate National Scottish Society. The National Bible Society of Scotland enabled evangelistic efforts of Scottish missionaries around the world. In IRELAND, the Dublin Bible Society, founded in 1806, participated in a loose federation of local Bible societies that adopted the name Hibernian Bible Society. Other British tensions surfaced over the refusal of the BFBS to exclude non-Trinitarians; this led to the emergence of a Trinitarian Bible Society.

The creation of European Bible societies was not confined to Britain. The same impulse surfaced in Scandinavia and on the Continent, where several societes enjoyed the patronage of royalty. An incomplete list suggests the extent of this movement, which stood at the evangelistic core of Western Protestantism: Basel Bible Society (1804), Berlin (later Prussian) Bible Society (1805), Russian Bible Society (1812), Swedish Bible Society (1814), Netherlands Bible Society (1814), Icelandic Bible Society (1815), Norwegian Bible Society (1816), and Protestant Biblical Society of Paris (1818). Cantonal Bible societies dotted SWITZERLAND. The Napoleonic Wars notwithstanding, Bible societies grew apace. Perhaps most remarkable was the Russian Bible Society, sanctioned by Czar Alexander I, one of the few that had an ecumenical Protestant base. Thanks to political pressure, representatives of Russia's many churches—Orthodox, Roman Catholic, Uniat, Armenian, and Lutheran—sat on its board, and by 1823 it had 289 auxiliaries. Nicholas I succeeded to the throne in 1825 and closed the Russian Bible Society the next year. Elsewhere as well, these societies sometimes found themselves curtailed by Catholic opposition or by political change.

In the UNITED STATES, the first evangelistic associations with national reach arose out of the Second Great Awakening in the Northeast (see AWAKENINGS). This early nineteenth-century burst of religious energy fueled determination to evangelize and civilize the west. Convinced that biblical morality assured divine favor, the supporters of these societies regarded the publication and distribution of inexpensive uplifting literature as crucial to the planting of the gospel in every western settlement. They supported missionaries to promote SUNDAY SCHOOLS and hired colporteurs to travel the countryside and sell mass-produced religious reading material. Protestants believed that the Bible was the single most important civilizing and Christianizing text. Like their European counterparts, Americans cooperated in Bible publishing and distribution, a task too large and too urgent to be left to any single DENOMINATION.

Protestants in the Northeast established the AMERICAN BIBLE SOCIETY (ABS) in May 1816, when representatives of thirty-five local and state Bible societies met in New York City, drafted a constitution, and vowed to work for the circulation of "the Holy Scripture without note or comment." As in Europe, Americans called for a united Christian (read Protestant) front, deploring the "local feelings, party prejudices, and sectarian jealousies" that fractured Protestantism. On the first ABS board of 36 managers were some of the most distinguished American Protestants of the day, including the Revolutionary War statesman ELIAS BOUDINOT, the first president of the ABS. With headquarters at Bible House in Manhattan, the ABS had for its model the already prosperous BFBS. By 1820, some 100,000 Bibles had poured from ABS presses.

By the twentieth century, Western Bible societies were at work in around the world. As the century progressed, their relationships to national Christian movements changed. More than 125 new national Bible societies emerged to take ownership of the work. Australians established a Bible Union in 1937; the Hong Kong Bible Society was organized in 1950; a Bible Society was established in Cambodia in 1968, ceased operation with the Khmer Rouges takeover in 1975, and reopened in 1993; and an Austrian Bible Society began functioning in 1970 after 23 years of planning by the country's small Protestant minority. Bible societies were active in Chile from 1820, but Chilean Protestants organized their own Bible Society in 1972.

The proliferation of Bible societies in all continents led in 1946 to the founding of the United Bible Societies, an alliance for consultation among the 137 national Bible societies working in more than 200 countries. The ongoing work of Bible societies has been critical to the evangelistic efforts of Protestants (and, more recently, Catholics) around the world. Especially since Vatican II, Bible societies in some countries have drawn support and leadership from Roman Catholics as well as from Protestants. Bible societies offer the biblical message in many translations, forms, and sizes and, in recent decades, in nonprint formats as well.

Related to the conviction that access to the Bible was crucial for Christian evangelism was the creation of WYCLIFFE BIBLE TRANSLATORS. Founded in 1942, Wycliffe Bible Translators represented the vision of William Cameron Townsend, whose commitment to Bible translation was piqued during his visit to native peoples in Guatemala in the World War I era. Committed to providing the Bible to the thousands of language groups that had no Scripture, Townsend instituted the Summer Institute of Linguistics, a linguistics training program that began modestly in an Arkansas farm in 1934. By 1951, courses had spread to Australia and Britain, and a few years later, Wycliffe began enlisting the cooperation of German evangelicals. By the end of the twentieth century, Wycliffe was offering linguistic training courses on every continent, preparing people to work in partnership with native speakers of lesser-known languages. Wycliffe translators have completed at least 450 translations of the New Testament and portions of scripture in many more languages.

A flurry of other publishing agencies accompanied the determination to flood the world with Bibles, as evangelicals saw the usefulness of tracts, pamphlets, and inexpensive books for disseminating their message. In Britain, the Religious Tract Society, founded in 1799, offered cheaply produced moral and evangelistic literature by Anglicans and Non-Conformists. By 1825, the American Tract Society gave national scope to the production of texts ranging from tracts to a magazine to children's storybooks. Tract Society colporteurs soon peddled these printed wares in the remotest reaches of the United States. Such societies were managed by interdenominational boards and supported by the donations of those who shared a commitment to their goals. Noting the overlap of supporters and board members, some suggested that these earliest United States voluntary associations constituted a "benevolent empire."

Supports for Sunday Schools

An enterprise that relied on publishing to enable educational goals was the Sunday School. The growing number of Sunday schools in Britain led in 1795 to the creation of a Society for the Support and Encouragement of Sunday Schools. The London Sunday School Union, formed in 1803, was followed quickly by Sunday School associations in Ireland and Scotland. In 1862, at a meeting in London of representatives of British Sunday school unions, British Sunday school enthusiasts decided to extend their work to the Continent.

Meanwhile, in 1824 the American Sunday School Union (ASU) took shape to facilitate the onward march of the Sunday School movement in the United States and to meet the need of local Sunday School associations for adequate literature and other supplies. The ASU offered lessons, hymnals and, in time, Sunday school novels urging Christian values on the young. These were inexpensive and widely distributed, sometimes constituting the core of a community's first public library. The ASU also raised support for missionaries to establish Sunday schools in the west and in other places where children's religious instruction was neglected. Nondenominational Sunday schools sometimes became the nuclei of regular congregations.

In 1872, the British Sunday School Union and the American Sunday School Union agreed on a uniform lessons series. This marked an important step in making the movement's content, as well as its form, truly international. A World Sunday School Convention met in London in 1889. In 1907, the international Sunday school movement adopted the name World's Sunday School Association. In 1947, this became the World Council on Christian Education. This agency had units in many countries, and became affiliated with the WORLD COUNCIL OF CHURCHES in 1971, after the Sunday school movement had abandoned much of its early evangelistic impetus.

Bible Institutes

Another educational format with explicit evangelistic intent is the Bible institute (see BIBLE COLLEGES AND INSTITUTES). Nineteenth-century innovations, Bible institutes ranged from small enterprises without structured curricula to well-organized, on-the-road-to-accreditation schools. Chicago's MOODY BIBLE INSTITUTE enjoys an international reputation and offers an example of the institutes' objectives. Built on the premise that traditional schools educated would-be Christian workers away from the masses, evangelist DWIGHT L. MOODY opted to train evangelists, missionaries, and other types of Christian workers in the effective use of the English Bible and congregational singing. The school that bears his name (first called the Chicago Training Institute) combined classroom instruction with hands-on experience, and faculty impressed on students the urgency of the evangelistic task. Moody Bible Institute became a powerhouse of nondenominational conservative Protestantism in the United States, and over the past century has sent thousands of graduates to other parts of the world. Students also come to Moody from many countries. The Bible institute model adapts readily to other cultures, and throughout the twentieth century, Bible institutes proved their effectiveness in training an army of energetic evangelists on every continent. For those who cannot attend a Bible institute, correspondence work has long been available, and web-based instruction further expands possibilities. Bible institutes may be denominationally connected, but those that are not function like voluntary associations, depending directly on the contributions of those who share their vision for equipping workers for Christian outreach and nurturing a congeries of related evangelistic activities, including broadcasting, publishing, conferencing, and equipping seminars.

While Moody Bible Institute served both domestic and overseas EVANGELISM, the story of another Bible institute offers a glimpse of an even more direct connection between Bible institutes and foreign MISSIONS. In 1815, a small group of Reformed and Lutheran Pietists from Basel, Switzerland and nearby Wurttemberg, GERMANY applied for permission to open a missionary training institute. The first class of seven students entered in 1816 under the auspices of an interdenominational group, the Evangelische Missionsgesselschaft Basel. The school trained English and Dutch as well as German missionaries, and by 1821 recruited its own missionaries to serve in RUSSIA and AFRICA's Gold Coast. In 1834 the first three missionaries of the BASEL MISSION arrived in INDIA with a commission to establish both schools and churches. The Basel Mission's formative years coincided with the rapid spread of Bible societies throughout Europe, as well as with the parallel founding of numerous foreign missions agencies. In Britain, the Baptist Missionary Society organized in 1792; the nondenominational London Missionary Society, in 1795; and the CHURCH MISSIONARY SOCIETY, the Wesleyan Missionary Society, and the Scottish Presbyterian Society, in 1799. The Basel Mission's training institute was open to all with a Pietist inclination, and its student body included Europeans from most northern European nations. This evangelistic association influenced many missions agencies by the training it offered, and its own missionaries played important roles in providing education and opposing SLAVERY (see SLAVERY, ABOLITION OF).

At about the same time, the Second Great Awakening stirred the west as well as the northeastern United States. Growing numbers of converts and large population shifts pressured denominations to provide pastors and evangelists to serve far-flung constituencies. The founding of SEMINARIES and the need for scholarships resulted in 1826 in the founding of the American Education Association, an enterprise that at first supplemental traditional evangelistic outreach to improve educational opportunities for clergy.

Youth Work

In the twentieth century, several evangelical voluntary associations directly targeted youth. Those associations with the widest reach continue to be active on university campuses worldwide. Bill and Vonnette Bright established Campus Crusade for Christ as an American outreach in 1953. With headquarters in Orlando, Florida, this agency, long since international in scope, has expanded beyond its original student focus. Some 65 percent of its 25,000 workers are outside of North America, in 191 countries, where more than 500,000 registered volunteers assist their efforts. In addition to its evangelistic work on university campuses, Campus Crusade has two widely known evangelistic tools: the *Four Spiritual Laws* (which presents the basic evangelistic message), and the *Jesus Film,* a movie presenting the life of Christ. Translated into 80 languages, the film has been viewed by some 850 million people worldwide.

The second influential student-oriented outreach is INTERVARSITY CHRISTIAN FELLOWSHIP. With roots at Cambridge University in ENGLAND, the movement began in Britain in 1877, shaped by student interest in global evangelism. In 1928, British InterVarsity helped organize a Canadian affiliate. Canadian InterVarsity director Stacey Woods met with University of Michigan students in 1938, and the first United States chapter resulted. In 1941, InterVarsity Christian Fellowship/USA officially organized. InterVarsity USA has more than 1,000 staff members and produces training materials used by hundreds of campus outreaches to students and faculty. Every three years it sponsors a huge missions gathering that uses the facilities of the University of Illinois-Urbana to enlist college students from across the United States in global missions outreach. Outside the west, InterVarsity groups at major university campuses mobilize and nurture Christian students and support broadly based evangelistic programs. InterVarsity Press has become a major supplier of resources that challenge and support Christian thought on contemporary issues.

Missionary Outreach

Evangelistic associations targeting university students are sustained by a broad evangelical impulse to share faith in every possible way. In the early national period in the United States, for example, the determination to be aggressive about planting the Gospel in the vast new territories of the Louisiana Purchase captured the imaginations of Congregationalists in New England, Presbyterians in the mid-Atlantic region, Episcopalians, Baptists, and Methodists as well as of newer groups like the Disciples of Christ. The

era saw expanded foreign trade and the growth of the British Empire, and some Americans also felt the urge to convert the world. As in the colonial era, the first targets were the "heathen" of North America. The Connecticut Missionary Association, established in 1798, produced the *Connecticut Evangelical Magazine* to interest people in this work. A Congregational-Presbyterian Plan of Union in 1801 had as part of its purpose the efficient preaching of the gospel in the West. The Union accelerated efforts and contributed to the founding in New York City in 1826 of the American Home Missionary Association.

Meanwhile, a few students at Williams College in western Massachusetts expressed their interest in foreign missions. During their years at Andover Seminary in Boston, these and other students pursued this interest and gained the support of the General Association of Massachusetts. The same year (1810), Connecticut and Massachusetts Congregationalists cooperated to form the AMERICAN BOARD OF COMMISSIONERS FOR FOREIGN MISSIONS. This society sent its first party of missionaries to India in 1812. Aboard ship, however, Adoniram Judson and Luther Rice changed their minds about Congregationalism and embraced Baptist views (see JUDSON FAMILY). This led in 1814 to the creation of the General Convention of the Baptist Denomination in the United States of America for Foreign Mission. Both societies recruited workers and expanded their global reach. Their contact with other cultures gave them influence over the American perception of other peoples, religions, and cultures and sometimes translated into influence in American foreign policy.

These early missionary societies—like the European Protestant missionary societies that preceded them—were denominational in intent (see MISSIONARY ORGANIZATIONS). By the mid-nineteenth century, nondenominational evangelistic associations took on specific tasks and invited a cooperative approach to missionary outreach. Representative of these groups is the Women's Union Missionary Society of America for Heathen Lands (WUMS), established in November 1860 in New York by Sarah Doremus and women from six denominations. The first North American agency to send single female missionaries, the WUMS drew inspiration from a similar British endeavor and worked especially among WOMEN and children, and it soon had placed missionaries around the world. Part of the era's growing interest in "women's work for women," the WUMS sent women to the secluded women to whom traditional missionaries seldom had access. By the end of the century, a long list of such nondenominational mission agencies recruited workers for worldwide evangelism. Between 1900 and 1920, for example, societies promoting village evangelism originated in India under the auspices of the Ramabai Mukti Mission, an agency led by Indians, and in England as The Fellowship for Evangelising Britain's Villages. Such local agencies worked side-by-side with others that had national constituencies in view.

Faith Missions

None of these groups was better known than the CHINA INLAND MISSION (CIM). Established by the Englishman JAMES HUDSON TAYLOR in 1865, the CIM had no established support structure. Taylor expected his recruits to "live by faith" and pray for answers to their needs. This approach necessitated a network of supporters—often at home, but sometimes elsewhere—who would faithfully remember the needs of their ambassadors abroad. The CIM was an early example of a growing cluster of "faith missions" that veered sharply from the customary practices of the more familiar denominational, or "board," missions. At the turn of the twentieth century, large numbers of conservative evangelicals found faith missions like the CIM or the Africa Inland Mission (founded in 1895 by Scotsman Peter Cameron Scott) satisfactory alternatives to traditional evangelistic organizations that were mired in disputes about the goals of missionary task and the implications of new THEOLOGY for world evangelization. Faith missions required little startup capital and promoted a direct sense of teamwork and cooperation in accomplishing evangelism. More flexible than denominational board missions, they appealed to people who hoped to get a job done quickly.

In the twentieth century, evangelistic associations of all kinds proliferated. New missions agencies represented both new approaches and new technology, and some older agencies adapted or merged to keep up with the times. With the closing of mainland China to Western missionaries, for example, the CIM regrouped and became the Overseas Missionary Fellowship. As missionaries pressed into ever more remote regions, the Missionary Aviation Fellowship arose to provide transportation, and the Moody Bible Institute developed a highly regarded pilot training program. Evangelicals have historically exploited opportunities and been responsive to change, and evangelistic associations that seize particular opportunities offer rapid adaptation to changing times. Evangelistic associations that enlist retirees, sports teams, students, blue-collar workers, health professionals, and other professionals for short-term missionary involvement have become more numerous. Evangelistic associations promote undercover work in closed countries; so-called "tentmakers" (a reference to St. Paul, who supported himself by tentmaking while sharing the

gospel) teach English in China, distribute humanitarian aid in the Middle East, or coach basketball in Indonesia, quietly building relationships that they hope will blossom in conversions.

In the twentieth century, the professionalization and coming of age of revivalism combined with advances in technology to facilitate the formation of yet another cluster of evangelistic associations, these dedicated to fulfilling the goals of individuals or ministry teams. Since the 1950s, the best-known of these has been the Billy Graham Evangelistic Association (BGEA). With roots in another evangelistic association, YOUTH FOR CHRIST, the BGEA incorporated early in the 1950s. Based for many years in Minneapolis, Minnesota (now in Charlotte, North Carolina as well), the BGEA has offices in cities around the world—Sydney, Buenos Aires, Winnipeg, London, Paris, Frankfurt, Hong Kong, Mexico City—and firm ties to native Christian leaders. Although the BGEA engages in evangelism through multiple media—World Wide Pictures, *Decision* magazine (in six languages and Braille), radio broadcasts, and books—the heart of its work is the traditional evangelistic crusades conducted by BILLY GRAHAM and his coworkers. Satellite television has multiplied the visibility of Billy Graham and a host of lesser-known evangelists. Graham's access to the leadership of nations around the world is unprecedented. The international scope of his influence has not been fully assessed. His son, Franklin Graham, has assumed the leadership of the organization.

Thousands of evangelistic associations like Graham's rely on gifts from supporters to enable outreaches around the world. Many originate in the West, but increasing numbers mobilize people in other parts of the world. The Luis Palau Evangelistic Association, for example, based in North America, conducts extensive work in LATIN AMERICA. An Argentinian by birth, Palau uses the media as well as traditional crusades to do evangelism. Headed by Ravi Zacharias, a native of India, the Ravi Zacharias International Ministries focuses its efforts on reaching those who shape the ideas of contemporary CULTURE. Some evangelistic associations outside the West now target Western populations.

Coordinating Efforts

The proliferation of cooperative societies dedicated either directly or indirectly to evangelistic outreach led early to concern in the West about duplication and inefficiency. The EVANGELICAL ALLIANCE—established in a burst of evangelical optimism in 1846 in London by 800 representatives from 10 countries—languished until the 1880s, when a dynamic American Congregationalist, Josiah Strong, took it in hand.

Strong's enthusiasm for most things American and British smacked to some of racism, and his confidence in America's destiny shone through his agenda, but he breathed life into a dying entity. Large Evangelical Alliance congresses he organized in 1886 in London and in 1893 at the Chicago World's Fair built momentum, and by the time his social agenda forced him from the Alliance, Strong had given the organization a new lease on life. In Britain, its offices in London remain a hub for evangelicals of all denominations and none.

The nineteenth-century hope for evangelical cooperation gained global currency in 1951 with the formation of the World Evangelical Alliance (WEA). The WEA is an alliance of alliances. Its members include seven regional organizations: Association of Evangelicals of Africa, European Evangelical Alliance, Evangelical Fellowship of Asia, Evangelical Association of the Caribbean, Evangelical Fellowship of the South Pacific, and Latin American Evangelical Fellowship. Each of these, in turn, comprises evangelical alliances or associations in particular countries, for a total of 113 national evangelical alliances. In addition to these full members, the WEA welcomes as associate members evangelical agencies with significant international commitments. This list includes entities like the Chinese Coordinating Centre of World Evangelization, Food for the Hungry, JEWS FOR JESUS, and many Western-based missionary organizations.

Evangelicals also provide significant support and leadership for the humanitarian work of WORLD VISION INTERNATIONAL. Established in 1950, this partnership of Christians offers health care, education, and humanitarian aid in an effort to assist people to help themselves and pursue justice. While it is not directly evangelistic, World Vision attracts the support of evangelicals who believe that humanitarian aid may create the climate conducive to Gospel witness. Leprosy missions, orphanages, hospitals, adoption agencies, schools, and many other entities play vital roles in enabling and expanding the work of evangelistic associations.

Evangelistic associations channel Christian energies into proclaiming the Christian message. Their proponents exploit all available media, including print media and radio, with startling success. HCJB, the world's first missionary radio station, went on the air in Ecuador on Christmas 1931. Seventy years later, it was one of the world's largest short-wave broadcasters, sending evangelistic programming from Quito in twelve languages and twenty-two dialects and also airing programming from such far-flung places as Seychelles, Swaziland, and the United Kingdom. Another evangelistic association dedicated to radio is Trans World Radio, begun under the direction of American Paul Freed in 1952. It beamed its first broadcast to Spain from a small transmitter in Tangier, Morocco. Fifty years later, it boasted 1,800 hours of programming each week from thirteen powerful transmitters and 2,300 local stations. Its Christian programming reached 160 countries in 180 languages. Served by missionaries and local staff, such broadcast evangelistic associations are the best known of many that flourished in the twentieth century.

Evangelistic associations come and go. Some change significantly over time and modify their early evangelistic goals. The YMCA (see YMCA/YWCA) and, to some extent, the older Bible societies have shed their evangelistic edge. Other agencies disappeared because they could not sustain support, or they merged, or they adapted to altered conditions by changing name or focus. Since World War II, an enormous number of new evangelistic associations jostle with established associations for money and recruits. The communications and transportation revolutions promote global awareness and make possible evangelistic interactions unimagined by earlier generations. Evangelistic associations will certainly adapt their strategies, but they will not go away. They are deeply embedded in the core of what twenty-first-century Christians assume it means to be evangelical. And EVANGELICALISM's entrepreneurial instincts find in the voluntary association model a flexible and efficient means to an all-consuming end.

References and Further Reading

Bays, Daniel, and Grant Wacker, eds. *The Foreign Missionary Enterprise at Home.* Tuscaloosa, AL: University of Alabama Press, 2003.

Bebbington, David. *Evangelicalism in Modern Britain.* London: Unwin Hyman, 1989.

Carpenter, Joel, and Wilbert Shenk, eds. *Erthen Vessels: American Evangelicals and Foreign Missions, 1880–1980.* Grand Rapids, MI: Eerdmans, 1990.

Hall, Peter Dobkin. *Religion and the Origin of Voluntary Associations in the United States.* New Haven, CT: Yale University Press, 1994.

Mott, Jon R. *The Young Men's Christian Association and the Evangelical Churches.* New York: Association Press, 1921.

Weisenfeld, Judith. *African American Women and Christian Activism.* Cambridge, MA: Harvard University Press, 1997.

Wosh, Peter. *Spreading the Word: The Bible Business in the Nineteenth Century.* Ithaca, NY: Cornell University Press, 1994.

Wuthnow, Robert. *The Restructuring of American Religion: Society and Faith Since World War II.* Princeton, NJ: Princeton University Press, 1988.

EDITH L. BLUMHOFER

F

FAITH

The most controversial aspect of Protestantism that emerged during the REFORMATION centered on the Protestant understanding of faith. Scholastic theology heavily influenced the prevailing Roman Catholic view on faith, creating a series of functional dualisms vastly removed from the original biblical understanding. These dualisms focused on the distinction between content of faith (in Latin *fides quae*) and subjective actions of faith (*fides qua*): the distinction between faith of laypersons in assenting to ORTHODOXY without understanding it (*fides implicita*) and faith of clergy in assenting to the same universal truths (*fides explicita*), between faith appropriated through natural means (*fides acquisita*) and faith incorporated into the soul alongside other virtues by supernatural means (*fides infusa*). The dualism drawing the Reformer's most ardent ire involved the distinction between "unformed faith" (*fides informis*), a faith unrelated to love and able to exist alongside mortal sin; and "formed faith" (*fides caritate formata*), a faith formed by and continually active in love. These aspects of faith required meritorious works by the believer to achieve JUSTIFICATION.

MARTIN LUTHER reacted to this formulation through the notion popularly known as justification by faith alone. Luther argued against the priority of love for perfecting faith by emphasizing the free gift of GRACE from God. Luther understood the "righteousness of God" in Romans 1:17 as justifying, not punishing, the sinner. In Hebrews 11:1 he understood faith as trust in God's promises rather than faith achieved through good works. Saving faith focused on the sufficiency of Christ's work divinely imputed to the sinner. This understanding of faith was refined by Luther's contemporaries. HULDRYCH ZWINGLI heavily focused on the certainty of faith through a clear knowledge of ELECTION. For Zwingli, faith was both a pledge of the Holy Spirit that seals the believer's heart, and a trust that God will protect and guide the believer. Faith enables the believer to reconcile contradictory passages and bring understanding to Scriptural meaning. To support his assertion, Zwingli affirmed that faith and Scripture are inseparable, citing Christ's own appeal to Scripture to further demonstrate the certainty of God's guidance. Faith is a sense that God assures us inwardly with the Holy Spirit while acknowledging that external matters contribute nothing to justification. As such, Zwingli understood the LORD'S SUPPER to be little more than a liturgy of "signs." Luther and JOHN CALVIN continued to affirm the divine efficacy of the Lord's Supper and vigorously rejected this radical reappraisal of the sacrament. Unlike Zwingli, Calvin was aware that the believer's faith is always weak and requires regular strengthening through the ministries of the church and the administration of the sacraments.

While all the reformers unanimously described faith as a gift from God, relating it to the workings of the Holy Spirit and Scripture, Calvin provided the clearest exposition on the role of the Holy Spirit in matters of faith. Calvin described faith as the principal work of the Holy Spirit. Believers do not initiate faith, but faith is founded upon the "might of the Spirit." Consequently, the Spirit is the "inner teacher" by whose effort the promise of SALVATION penetrates the believer's mind. Like Zwingli, Calvin affirmed the inseparable relationship between faith and the Word of God and that these "can no more be disconnected from each other than rays of light from the sun" (*Institutes III:2:6*). And while faith is both a matter of heart and mind, Calvin stressed that "the knowledge of faith consist more of certainty than discernment" (*Institutes III:2:14*). For Calvin, certainty is dependent on the activity of the Holy Spirit and the restoration of right worship of God through the genuine teaching and PREACHING of Scripture by the church.

The Roman Catholic reaction to this Protestant formulation was ratified in the Council of Trent (1547), which condemned the "vain confidence of [these] heretics" (see CATHOLIC REACTIONS TO PROTESTANTISM). Other reactions came from Radical Reformers such as Anabaptists and Inspirationists, or Pietists (see ANABAPTISM PIETISM). Many Anabaptists emphasized the importance of good works as testimony to the presence of faith. Pietists, like THOMAS MÜNTZER, emphasized the primacy of experiential revelatory faith as opposed to faith informed by biblical revelation.

The Post-Reformation understandings of faith took on numerous expressions. In reaction to the development of orthodox CALVINISM, JACOBUS ARMINIS began an unpretentious revival of the role of meritorious works in faith. Introducing the notion of faith as a human work upon which the pardon of SIN is suspended, Arminius reacted strongly to the claim that God damns individuals for eternity (see ARMINIANISM). Arminius linked the concept of PREDESTINATION with faith by reducing the decision of faith to a simple human possibility. While agreeing with Calvinists that there was no salvation apart from faith, Arminius accepted that faith was the basis of predestination, rather than the orthodox Calvinist's view that predestination was the basis of faith.

PURITANISM also developed away from mainstream Reformation thought by demanding that certitude be confirmed only through the experience of holy living. The Puritan emphasis on holy living eventually influenced other expressions of Protestantism such as METHODISM and the HOLINESS MOVEMENT. These Protestant expressions accepted that faith and religious knowledge were not derived from objective theological formulation but rather blossom from the experiences of the believer's heart.

The eighteenth-century ENLIGHTENMENT bore witness to a sustained attack on traditional categories of faith and religious dogma through the emergence of Rationalism. Popularly represented as DEISM and Protestant Scholasticism, some Protestant theologians such as Jean Aphonse Turretin sought to reduce Christianity to a core of moral principles and universally held beliefs. Faith was subsumed into an objectified natural religion. The climax of Enlightenment philosophies arrived with IMMANUEL KANT, who redirected contemporary thought by defining the limits of knowledge. Kant drew a sharp distinction between "phenomena" (knowledge which we derive from experience of the world) and "noumena" (a priori transcendental knowledge). This eventually led to the claim that knowledge of the world could not lead to knowledge of God. While Kant intended to eliminate speculative knowledge in order to "make room for faith," he unwittingly reset the course of THEOLOGY, allowing the development of liberalism into diverse expressions (see LIBERAL PROTESTANTISM AND LIBERALISM). In the case of FRIEDRICH SCHLEIERMACHER, certainty of faith was grounded in psychological and emotional experience rather than in natural theology or biblical revelation. Here faith is grounded in a feeling of absolute dependence. Late nineteenth century liberalism tended to view institutionalized religion, traditional creeds, and metaphysics with uncertainty, although this skepticism was offset by a confidence in human progress and the unhindered quest for a unified vision of truth. ADOLF VON HARNACK clearly stated these themes in his 1901 book *What Is Christianity?* Harnack's approach was to define true Christianity by "stripping off the husks and lay[ing] bare the kernel [of truth]." Harnack proposed that the core of Christianity is the personality and teachings of Jesus, which could be summed up through the commandment to love. This ethic of love grounded faith into a praxis of social engagement and framework of evolutionary progress. However, the rising confidence in human progress was shattered by World War I with the theological vacuum appropriated by NEO-ORTHODOXY and FUNDAMENTALISM.

Reacting to liberalism, fundamentalism affirmed previous Protestant faith expressions and theologies within a rationalistic framework by affirming the AUTHORITY, inspiration, and inerrancy of Scripture (see BIBLICAL INERRANCY). Appropriating a form of seventeenth-century Calvinistic scholasticism, fundamentalism was committed to resisting social change in order to preserve what were considered to be the correct articles of faith. Faith was characterized as propositional assent in order to preserve certainty, an approach that has continued on into contemporary forms of conservative EVANGELICALISM.

On the other hand, liberalism heavily influenced neo-orthodoxy, which tended to emphasize the divine origin and nature of faith. Neo-orthodox faith was characterized as active assent to the elusive, mysterious and non-propositional divine prompting. Its most popular exponent was KARL BARTH, and while his views evolved over time, he nevertheless understood faith within the framework of divine immanence. This framework took the form of the "Word of God," which was not a proposition or object but God actually speaking. The real object of inquiry was Jesus Christ, the true foundation of faith. For Barth, certainty was the result of the triumph of God's grace rather than the results of natural theologies or human expression.

In turn, Barth significantly influenced Dietrich Bonhoeffer who formulated the challenging question "Who is Christ for us today?" Bonhoeffer's faith engagement between certainty and uncertainty is clearly seen in his understanding of mystery as the root of everyting comprehensible. And while faith is part of mystery that cannot be transformed into knowledge, Bonhoeffer paradoxically states that "mystery does not mean merely that one does not know something . . . the deepest mystery is not the person farthest away but preciesely the one closest to us" (Feil 1985: 6). This mystery is located at the center of the distinction between faith and theologies, thus influencing Bonhoeffer to urgently define the relation between theory and praxis. As a result, Bonhoeffer placed theology and faith in the service of Christian praxis, and is remembered for such expressions as "a world come of age" and "Religionless Christianity." Bonhoeffer's theology eventually influenced radical theologians of the 1960s, who introduced such expressions as the Death of God and the Ground of Being (see Robinson, John Arthur Thomas) to explain the failure of anthropomorphic religious language in addressing contemporary religious concerns.

Today contemporary theology weaves between radicalism and new conservatism. Faith expressed in Postmodernity is subject to a new openness brought out by the challenges of pluralism, poststructuralism, and Ecumenism. While this openness to inquire into all aspects of faith may create great tension, the engagement of certainty and uncertainty within the ongoing process of redemption will continue to shape the future of Protestant expressions of faith.

References and Further Reading

Primary Sources:

Calvin, John. *Institutes of the Christian Religion.* 2 vols. Edited by J. T. McNeill, Translated by F. L. Battles. Philadelphia, PA: Library of Christian Classics Vols. 20–21, 1960.
Luther, Martin. *Luther's Works. Vol 26, Lectures on Galatians, 1535, Chapters 1–4.* Edited by J. Pelikan. St. Louis, MO: Concordia, 1963.

Secondary Sources:

Berkouwer, G. C. *The Triumph of Grace in the Theology of Karl Barth.* London: Paternoster, 1956.
Dillenberger, John, and Claude Welch. *Protestant Christianity—Interpreted Through Its Development.* New York: Macmillan, 1988.
Feil, E. *The Theology of Dietrich Bonhoeffer.* Translated by M. Rumscheidt. Philadelphia, PA: Fortress, 1985.
Stephens, W. P. *The Theology of Huldrych Zwingli.* Oxford, UK: Clarendon Press, 1986.

Jason C. Harley

FAITH HEALING

Diverse types of faith, or religious, healing are practiced within Protestant churches. The practices vary according to the theological accounts given of the process of healing, the sense of the miraculous, the perception of process, and the place of skills in the performance of the minister. The relationship between religious healing and conventional medicine is often one of tension. In some religious traditions there is a rejection of the world that implies a refusal to use its medical science. Elsewhere, the relationship is complementary, and there is recent evidence of a reformulated healing ministry within the pastoral role of clergy.

Definitions

Religious intervention in matters of human health takes a variety of forms, and we may distinguish a number of categories: those that are attributed exclusively to divine power, those centered on the religious healer, and those dependent on a measure of trust on the part of the individual to be healed.

Miraculous healing excludes those forms of religious healing that may be attributed to the skill of the minister or the process of therapy, including counseling or Prayer. Within the Christian faith the archetypes of this category are the healing miracles of Jesus of Nazareth, which included the raising to life of those reported to be dead as well as relief from less terminal conditions. The notion of miraculous healing is problematic in that some would regard the effect of prayer to be a miracle, whereas others might see it as a kind of therapy. Some skeptics or demythologists might venture to explain the conditions cured by Jesus as psychosomatic and notice that they did not include, for example, the repair of broken limbs. Within the category of the miraculous, *divine healing* is the term applied to beneficial effects on the condition of a sufferer that are attributed to a supernatural power acting independently of the faith of the subject and of the skills of the human agent or healer. The concept of *divine healing* prevails among traditional Pentecostals (see Pentecostalism). *Faith healing,* by contrast, refers to those forms in which an improvement or cure relies on the trust or confidence of the subject. This trust is typically developed in a religious context and invested in an almighty power, but in a secular sense faith can equally be a belief in the self or in the minister of healing or in a set of procedures.

Within the category of religious healing there is a much noticed and distinctive type in the form of *shamanism.* This is the term given to procedures that center on the skills or spiritual endowments of a healer or shaman: its classical forms have been observed in tribal communities in northern Siberia and places remote from Western Protestantism, but shamanic practices have also been recognized in the West, notably by M. B. McGuire.

Although this typology may be useful in identifying approaches to religious healing—and is indeed grounded in the perceptions of practitioners—there is an ambivalence about some cases. Those whose names and reputations are used to attract large audiences to healing meetings may insist that they have no power of their own but that God has chosen to work through them: in this way they define their practice as *divine healing* but the mediated construction of their practice may celebrate the person of the healer.

The Rejection of Worldly Medicine

Tensions between secular medicine and the ministrations of religious professionals have characterized the postures of a number of world-rejecting sects in the nineteenth and twentieth centuries. They are, however, rooted in biblical precedents. It is reported that "the king Asa in the thirty and ninth year of his reign was diseased in his feet, until his disease was exceeding great; yet in his disease he sought not to the Lord but to the physicians. And Asa slept with his fathers, and died in the one and fortieth year of his reign" (II Chronicles 16:12–13).

The inference is that Asa might have recovered from his gout had he turned to prayer. Such is the lesson drawn from the demise of Asa by many of the faithful who distance the religious community from the wisdom of the world. In 1899 a member of a fundamentalist Christian sect in London, the Plumstead Peculiars, declined to call a doctor to his ailing newborn child and, when the child died, faced conviction for manslaughter. "I have an honest belief in the power of prayer," said the father. "When the King was the Prince of Wales and had typhoid, prayers were offered up throughout the land, and he recovered."

The Judge observed: "My recollection is that Sir William Gill [the royal physician] had something to do with the recovery. . . . It is wicked that these people should let their children die, when by taking ordinary precautions which God has placed in their power they could save them."

These examples evidence not an explicit taboo on secular means of healing, but a conviction in the adequacy of prayer and a sense that recourse to a doctor is a sign of weakening FAITH. The reluctance to abandon religious faith for secular science is particularly pronounced in respect of the condition JOHN BUNYAN terms "the Slough of Desspond," more popularly diagnosed as depression. In respect to such conditions, there is a sense that the individual, the religious organizations, and their God ought to be sufficient to restore health. The sense of betrayal of Christian faith and its ministers when seeking help from a doctor or psychologist is prompted partly by the concept of "wholeness" and the equation of SIN and suffering in the teaching of Jesus. He cures with the significant words, "Thy faith has made thee whole" and asks whether it is easier to say "Thy sins be forgiven thee" or "Arise and walk" (Matthew 9:5).

The notion that right belief is the key to good health is in modern times associated particularly with CHRISTIAN SCIENCE. This movement owes to earlier currents the principle of *mental healing* that perceives illness as a condition of the mind. Such a diagnosis may be traced in Christian practice to the theology of a Swedish scientist EMANUEL SWEDENBORG (1688–1772), founder of the religious sect that bears his name. The Swedenborgian principle was that healing could be effected by harmonizing physical and spiritual realities, adjusting the body to the mind, the mind to the soul, and the soul to the angelic order. This idea of mental adjustment was prevalent in the movement called mesmerism, which was fashionable in America in the mid-nineteenth century. It was propagated in the teachings of the mesmerist Charles Poyen, of Phineas Parkhurst Quimby, and subsequently in the writings of MARY BAKER EDDY, the founder of Christian Science. In 1875 she published her *Science and Health with Key to the Scriptures,* citing Matthew 9:2–8 to demonstrate the central tenet that sickness and pain were delusions curable by the correction of mental error:

> It is plain that God does not employ drugs or hygiene, nor provide them for human use; else Jesus would have recommended them in his healing. The sick are more deplorably lost than the sinning if the sick cannot rely on God for help and the sinning can.

JEHOVAH'S WITNESSES, by contrast, are happy to seek healing through hospitals, albeit upon certain conscientious conditions. For Witnesses, secular medicine does not contradict faith in the power of prayer. It is rather that they read in Genesis 9:4 and Acts 15:29 a taboo on consuming bloods and therefore upon blood transfusion. They have in recent years been active in exploring and documenting alternatives to blood transfusion, but there have been cases in Australia and the United States where the children of Witnesses have been made wards of the court to authorize certain treatment.

Although abstention from secular medicine per se or from particular practices has in many cases often been a dimension of a more general rejection of the world, it has not necessarily been so. In the case of the AMISH, for example, taboos on the use of motor transport and electricity are not applied against resort to medical treatment. Resistance is based on a preference for time-honored remedies, not on religious dogma. Curiously, those religious organizations within the Christian faith that have studiously refrained from secular medicine have not been those that used high profile healing events in their outreach or featured in a sensational way the cases of those who have been cured against the expectations of their doctors. Rather, their disposition has been a defensive one.

Healing in the Context of Faith

The historic relationships of religion and health may be regarded within two traditions, both attended by tensions. On one hand, there is an approval for conventional medicine, a willing resort to it, and material and moral support for its practitioners. This accord, in which clergy would deploy medical science in the fulfillment of their pastoral role, was memorably described by the Reverend COTTON MATHER (1663–1728) as the "angelical conjunction." In the late eighteenth century, the founder of Methodism, JOHN WESLEY, published and republished a book called *Primitive Physick,* demonstrating and commending a knowledge of herbal remedies alongside a belief in the power of faith. In England the established church took responsibility for the provision of a number of hospitals: St. Bartholomew's was founded in 1123 and St. Thomas's was started in a parish church by that name in Southwark, where the original operating theater survives. The angelical conjunction was to suffer a fall and enjoy a subsequent rise. In time the differentiation of professions would relieve the clergy of many of the skills they had assumed as obligations of their Christian vocation, including architecture and finance as well as pastoral activities. In the late nineteenth and early twentieth centuries the functions of care passed largely to the state in the name of welfare. The "conjunction" revived as the welfare state faltered. Clergy and lay persons of the mainstream Christian churches sought the skills and practiced in the role of counselors. The notion of healing was broadened to apply to the recovery not merely of a physical but of a mental or emotional condition and of satisfactory relationships. Perhaps as a response to the standard Marxist critique that the hope of a life hereafter enables the faithful to endure the discomforts of the present world, the burgeoning Pentecostal churches of Central America have kept physical dimensions of the human condition in sharp focus. R. A. Chesnut found rather less evidence in Brazil of a conviction in remote consolation than in the hope of immediate relief from the illnesses that attend poverty.

On the other hand, there is a disposition among some religious organizations to direct medical practice according to their own principles. The private hospitals in the United States belonging to, for example, the SEVENTH-DAY ADVENTIST CHURCH are administered according to the divine revelations about health received in the 1860s by its prophetess ELLEN GOULD WHITE (1827–1915).

The practice of miraculous healing in meetings of the revivalist type has recently enjoyed a resurgence through television and modern methods of communication (see TELEVANGELISTS; PUBLISHING, MEDIA). Its effects are visible and its challenge to conventional medicine is derisive. The book that records the miracles God has worked through the healing evangelist Melvin Banks shows on the front cover the picture of a woman holding aloft her walking stick in defiance of the doctors who said she would always need it. Miraculous healing in Catholicism focuses on certain shrines such as Lourdes, whereas the Protestant counterpart is focused on individuals with charismatic gifts.

The presentation of a sick or disabled person at a healing crusade may, if recovery does not follow, result in disappointment if not cognitive dissonance, although nothing else is lost unless the dependency on faith excludes the recourse to conventional therapy. Those affirming a divine plan may recognize a place within it for the secular professions, for example, "It is wonderful how God can use doctors and nurses." However, there are implications of a legal kind when conventional medicine is refused. In the last twenty years there have been a number of cases in which parents have been brought before American courts after the deaths of children whom they had entrusted to Christian Science practitioners. When prayer has not been effective, both parents and practitioners have been variously charged with child abuse, negligence, and manslaughter.

New Directions in Christian Ministry

Until recent years the practice of hands-on healing and therapy has been found rather more in the marginal sects than in the mainstream churches. However, in a much-noticed work, McGuire (1988) has documented the prevalence of healing rituals in the religious life of suburban America. In "the metaphysical movement," Maguire detects elements that derive from various nominally Christian traditions, from New Thought, mesmerism, the mind-cure groups of the 1880s, Spiritualism, Christian Science, and an experimental interest in currents of spirituality that are or were native American, Latin American, Caribbean, and Polynesian. Metaphysical healing is a syncretic movement that is open to alternative pathology and Eastern philosophy and redefines received notions of illness and dysfunction. This is a world of house-groups rather than of rallies and conventions; it is about processes rather than persons, and ritual practices are devolved rather than centralized.

The variety of life and death concerns that are addressed by hands-on therapy rituals in the religious life of the American suburb similarly occupies the ministry of healing in the CHURCH OF ENGLAND. It is a pastoral movement in which healing is recognized as an easing of some problem or discomfort rather than the absolute elimination of an adverse condition. It is not spectacular; it does not celebrate its results; it is not advertised as a crowd-puller, although it is a legitimating principle in the church's mission. The ministry operates, for example, in the rehabilitation of counseling and psychotherapy within the sacred domain, in the hospice movement pioneered in Britain by Dr. Cicely Saunders, and in the provision of healing services within the regular ministrations of the mainstream churches. The purpose of ministry to the dying is to enable them to die well, not to recover to full health. Typically, a parish may designate one service a month as a healing service when those desiring healing may have hands laid on them by ministers who may be available for counsel. There is no expectation of instant cure, the congregation is not invited to behold the effect, and photographers do not stand by. Conventional medicine and the prayerful ministry of the church are perceived to be complementary, whereas in some sects conventional medicine forms are respected, if at all, as agents of the divine will. The church-type ministry looks to the Gospel for its motivation, whereas the tradition of miraculous healing looks to Pauline teachings, notably I Corinthians 12, for its authority.

If ritualized healing is directed by a literal interpretation of a biblical imperative to "Lay hands on the sick and they shall be healed" (Mark 16:18), the church's ministry of pastoral care is, in the spirit of the angelical conjunction, an endeavor to discern the meaning of the Gospel and to convey it to points of need.

References and Further Reading

Chesnut, R. A. *Born Again in Brazil.* New Brunswick, NJ: Rutgers University Press, 1997.

Eddy, Mary Baker. *Science and Health: with Key to the Scriptures.* Boston: Trustees of Mary Baker Eddy, 1906.

Eliade, M. *Shamanism: Archaic Techniques of Ecstasy.* Translated by W. R. Trask. New York: Bollingen Foundation, 1964.

Maddocks, M. *The Christian Healing Ministry.* London: SPCK, 1995.

McGuire, M. B. *Ritual Healing in Suburban America.* New Brunswick, NJ: Rutgers University Press, 1988.

Martin, D. *Tongues of Fire.* Oxford, UK: Blackwell, 1990.

Pullar, P. *Spiritual and Lay Healing.* London: Penguin, 1988.

Trotter, R. T., and J. A. Chavira. *Curanderismo: Mexican American Folk Healing,* 2nd ed. Athens: University of Georgia Press, 1997.

ROGER HOMAN

FALWELL, JERRY (1933–)

American preacher and televangelist. Falwell was born on August 11, 1933 in Lynchburg, Virginia. He is best known as a television evangelist, or "televangelist" and founder of the Moral Majority. His significance lies in his critical leadership in shifting large numbers of fundamentalist Christians away from their historic separation of religion and politics and resulting political inactivism, to an active engagement in politics, which they previously considered to be secular. Falwell's political organization, Moral Majority, which he formed in 1979, played a key role in mobilizing the "Religious Right," beginning with registering new voters.

In defense of FUNDAMENTALISM, Falwell sought to restore the nation's "Christian" underpinnings by attempting to legislate through Congress a Bible-based morality, which he claimed had been eroded by proponents of equal rights for women and homosexuals (see HOMOSEXUALITY), abortion rights, and "secular humanism." His television program, the "Old-Time Gospel Hour," one of the most watched religious broadcasts during the 1980s, offered a platform to the new political movement, the rise of which coincided with that of TELEVANGELISM. The National Association of Religious Broadcasters inducted Falwell into its Broadcasting Hall of Fame in 1985.

The attention he received by the media, most of it negative, while lobbying Congress and President Ronald Reagan and acting as a cultural critic made Falwell a household name through the 1980s. Unsuccessful in implementing the Moral Majority's conservative social agenda, even with the support of the conservative Reagan, whose election the religious right had supported, and unable to raise funds needed to continue, Falwell disbanded the organization in 1989.

Pastor of one of the nation's largest Protestant churches, Thomas Road Baptist Church in Lynchburg, Falwell is also founder and chancellor of Liberty University.

References and Further Reading

Primary Source:

Falwell, Jerry. *Strength for the Journey: An Autobiography of Jerry Falwell.* New York: Simon and Schuster, 1987.

Secondary Source:

Harding, Susan Friend. *The Book of Jerry Falwell: Fundamentalist Language and Politics*. Princeton: Princeton University Press, 2000.

BOBBY C. ALEXANDER

FAMILY

Behind the Protestant understanding of family lies a complex history of devotion and debate. From the REFORMATION on, believers from many different times and places have idealized the human family as a school of godly character, a perfect metaphor of divine love, and a model of Christian unity. Even as the meaning and structure of family life have changed over time, the idealized visions persist—a testimony to its powerful and enduring grasp on the Protestant imagination.

Yet family has also been a potent instrument of controversy. On one level, this is not surprising, given the fact that domestic life encompasses a range of deeply sensitive human issues: SEXUALITY, childrearing, the promise of birth, and the finality of DEATH. In the five centuries since the Reformation, Protestant thinkers have produced an enormous body of work articulating church teaching on such matters, yet Protestant churches have exercised an uncertain jurisdiction over the private lives of their parishioners, often caught in the competing pressures of secular life. Just as the reformers sought to persuade their parishioners against the practice of clandestine marriage in the sixteenth century, modern evangelical leaders have struggled to enforce biblical standards of DIVORCE and remarriage within their broad and often fractious constituencies.

In an even larger sense, however, Protestant discourse about family life has played a major role in matters of religious identity. The periodic need to delineate key beliefs and practices around MARRIAGE, childrearing, and sexuality has often corresponded with some fundamental shifts in Protestant thought. The structure of this essay in fact lifts up three significant examples of this parallel process. The first section deals with the role of family in the Reformation and its importance as a means of articulating important differences between Protestants and Catholics, and as a site for instructing the faithful. The second section discusses the importance of family at another crucial juncture, the post-ENLIGHTENMENT retooling of Christian faith to meet the demands of an industrializing, urbanizing world. The third and final section describes the central role of family in the contemporary encounter between religion and the modern global world, most dramatically encapsulated in the fundamentalist response.

The Reformation

The reformers' rejection of priestly CELIBACY placed family at the center of the Protestant polemic against Catholicism. Whereas MARTIN LUTHER and his followers did not believe that an unmarried priesthood was categorically wrong, they were not willing to make it a requirement for all CLERGY, for they believed that this would lead only to hypocrisy and abuse. Celibacy, they argued, was the gift of a particular few, and marriage was the higher calling required of all believers. Thus Luther urged his fellow Protestant clergy to marry and establish households, following suit himself when he wed Katherine von Bora, a former nun, in 1525.

Although the Protestant Reformers denied that marriage was a sacrament or in any sense a direct means of sanctifying GRACE, they were convinced that marriage was ordained by God for the spiritual benefit of all Christians. For one thing, the married state saved individuals from the temptations of lust, which Luther in particular believed were a serious threat to a godly life. But even the daily give and take of domestic affairs could lead one closer to God; Luther declared that God and all his angels smiled at the sight of a father washing his baby's diapers, for even as menial and dirty a task as this might be undertaken "in Christian faith." Luther's remarkable statement adds weight to historian Steven Ozment's view that the Reformers' emphasis on family life was one of their most enduring legacies, a protest against Catholic ecclesiastical practice that over time became one of the most visible and successful of all Protestant reforms.

In some ways, however, the Protestant Reformation introduced a more secular approach to marriage as an institution regulated primarily by the state, not the church (see CHURCH AND STATE OVERVIEW). The point at issue was the problem of clandestine marriage, in which couples wed by mutual consent without the knowledge or approval of parents or church. The reformers, who wanted entry into marriage to be as easy as possible, blamed the custom on confusion generated by the complexities of canon law. Their solution was to give the state primary legal responsibility for regulating marriage. Thus secular law publicly legitimized a couple's decision to wed while the church provided moral oversight, especially in cases of infidelity or abuse. This series of reforms did not immediately amount to drastic changes in practice, because a great deal of canon law was simply transferred into state statutes, but, as historian John Witte has argued, it did lay a foundation for a more secular, contract-oriented model of marriage in the future.

Family was also an important social context for teaching and establishing the Protestant faith among new believers. It is important to remember that the reformers' assumptions about family life grew out of their sixteenth-century northern European context, in which families were considerably larger and more complex than their modern counterparts. Generalizations about sixteenth-century families are difficult, for the historical evidence has proven frustratingly elusive or incomplete, and their exact composition has been a matter of heated debate among scholars. Yet in broad terms, it is proper to speak of the Reformation era family as a household, a group of related individuals living together under one roof, but often as not including various kin and servants. A married couple formed the center of this arrangement, but the number and configuration of family members could change considerably over time as children came and went, parents aged, and various relatives took up residence, sometimes as servants to the rest of the household.

The Protestant reformers emphasized the father's role as the spiritual head of his household. Although in some ways the reformers' emphasis on the spiritual dimensions of married life elevated the role of WOMEN, Reformation teachings left Western-style patriarchy very much intact. In a voluminous list of sermons on marriage and housekeeping handbooks, Protestant leaders explicitly directed fathers to lead their households in regular times of PRAYER and in attendance at public WORSHIP. The Reformers also provided CATECHISMS for fathers to use for the doctrinal instruction of their children, as well as handbooks detailing the proper means of achieving a unified, Christian household.

Like most sixteenth-century Europeans, the Reformers did not sentimentalize CHILDHOOD, nor did they skimp on applying doctrines of original sin. Not surprisingly, their recommendations for disciplining children often sound harsh to modern ears. This did not mean, however, that sixteenth-century Protestants did not find pleasure in raising children. Most historians no longer accept the thesis developed by French scholar Philippe Aries, that in an age of high infant mortality rates, premodern families did not especially mourn the loss of a child; to be sure, sixteenth-century parents did not romanticize their children's moral capacities, but the very sinfulness of the young made careful parenting all the more critical. Most of the Reformers adopted infant rather than adult BAPTISM, and understood it as a preliminary framework for the development of an adult saving FAITH in Christ. Baptism was not in any sense a guarantee of SALVATION, and each child required a regimen of firm parental discipline, didactic instruction, and constant prayer for his or her eventual salvation.

The English Reformation added another dimension to Protestant understanding, specifically the idea of family as a church within the CHURCH. This metaphor reflected the assumption of Anglican thinkers, as representatives of England's state church, that religion was key to maintaining social order. Thus, family became a microcosm of the secular state, a little commonwealth bound together by respect for properly ordained AUTHORITY residing in the father as head of the household. The English Puritans took the metaphor in a more spiritual direction (see PURITANISM). In their view, the various members of a family constituted a church in miniature, bonded together by the mutual obligations of COVENANT. Thus, although the wife was considered both physically and spiritually the "weaker vessel" of the marriage relationship, her husband could not take advantage of his superior status. He was obliged to provide for her well-being and to live in spiritual partnership with her. Similarly, Puritan parents had covenantal duties toward their children, to provide them with daily necessities and firm discipline, but also regular opportunities for family worship, catechetical instruction, and godly example.

Family relationships provided some of the most elevated spiritual metaphors in Puritan devotional writing. Poet Edward Taylor wrote of the "ravishment" of his soul by Christ the yearning bridegroom; he likened God's work in the heart of a Christian to a woman's patient attention to her household tasks, spinning and weaving thread into a finished cloth garment. Puritan writers were also fond of comparing the believer to a baby feeding contentedly from a mother's breast.

Historian Steven Ozment has suggested that the centrality of family in Puritan life signaled a "domestication" of Protestant belief, as the otherworldly asceticism of the celibate priest gave way to the conviction that God was most clearly manifest in the happy, well-regulated home of the believer. More than just a school of godly character or a guardian against lust, the Puritan household was itself a unique conduit of divine grace. Although perhaps few individual families measured up to this spiritual ideal, in centuries to follow, the model of the Christian family would take an even deeper hold in the culture of Western Protestantism.

Protestants and the Bourgeois Family

From the sixteenth century onward through the nineteenth, families in the West became smaller and more nuclear, that is, centered around a single married couple and their children. Although historians have vigorously debated the meaning, causes, and extent of this change—which did not, of course, affect all families equally—at least part of the force behind it was practical: declining child mortality rates, increased urbanization, and INDUSTRIALIZATION meant that large, extended households were not necessarily an economic advantage. The emerging bourgeois family depended on a single wage earned by the father, who left his domicile each morning to labor in the public world of business and commerce, while mother and children lived more quietly within the private sphere of the home.

The new model identified family as central to the developing world of private life, characterized by an ordered intimacy between spouses, parents, and children. To be sure, access to a private life was certainly economically determined; few working class or rural families could demarcate their lives into separate spheres of home and work. Yet, as it developed in the nineteenth century, the domestic ideal had widespread currency. As market-driven economies made ever-increasing demands on those striving for success, home became the place where morality and religion lodged most deeply.

Although historians have debated the effect of bourgeois domesticity on the status of women, it certainly marked a departure from the traditional patriarchal household of centuries past. In some ways, the bourgeois pattern increased the subordinate status of women, assuming that they would be economically dependent on a male provider and fill a submissive role in the marriage relationship as well. Moreover, in most Western legal systems, women had no independent standing before the law; the legal principle of "femme couvert" meant that a man always took responsibility for his wife's or daughter's property and wages and represented her in the political arena. Yet in other ways, the emerging bourgeois family undercut the old assumptions of patriarchal society by emphasizing the necessity of mutual love and intimacy in marriage. By the late nineteenth century, falling birth rates among middle-class women suggest a shift in the balance of power in the bedroom as well. Indeed, in the long run, women's ownership of the domestic sphere allowed them to assume increasingly direct responsibility for upholding social morality. The social networks that they created on behalf of TEMPERANCE and other moral causes eventually became a platform for voicing a common complaint against their legal and social disadvantages. By the late nineteenth and early twentieth centuries, the legal barriers against women were beginning to fall, marked by the passage of married women's property acts and suffrage amendments in most of the Western industrialized nations.

The intimacy of middle-class family life also centered increasingly on children. By the eighteenth century, and especially in the rising democratic ethos of

the UNITED STATES, the feudal assumption that all children would simply inherit their parents' station in life did not reflect reality. To a degree, the "discovery of childhood" in the early modern West drew from the democratic ethos of the ENLIGHTENMENT and the optimism of Romantic thought. Emile, JEAN-JACQUES ROUSSEAU's archtypical child of nature, was not a stubborn sinner, but rather a young innocent with an innate potential for rational thought and an infinite capacity for good. Falling child mortality rates, paired with declining family size, also contributed to this trend, allowing parents in the urbanized middle classes to devote more specific attention to the moral and intellectual growth of each individual child.

This new ideal of family intimacy did not mesh easily with some forms of Protestant belief. On the most fundamental level, the celebration of childhood innocence came into conflict with the Augustinian doctrine of original sin. In a strictly logical sense, this teaching held that all children came into the world under its stain and were thus liable for eternal punishment, even if death came within minutes of birth. Yet from Augustine's time on, Christian thinkers had struggled against the apparent injustice; Thomas Aquinas in fact posited a "limbo" for the souls of unbaptized children. Even the Puritan divines recognized the difference between the logical implications of a DOCTRINE and the emotional needs of parents grieving the loss of a child.

The emphasis on adult CONVERSION in the evangelical REVIVALS of the eighteenth and nineteenth centuries also posed a quandary for parents. To what extent were they responsible for the spiritual fate of a child not yet at the moral "age of accountability"? Moreover, to what degree could parents expect genuine faith in children who were not old enough to experience a full-fledged conversion experience? In some cases, anxiety about the unchecked sins of childhood led to the conviction that parents had a duty to "break the will" of the young rebels in their care, sometimes through sustained physical punishment. By forcefully repressing a child's sinful tendencies, parents might not save him or her from punishment, but they could limit the pull of temptation to SIN in the years before a full adult conversion was possible.

In many ways, nineteenth-century liberal Protestant thought marked a response to these parental concerns (see LIBERAL PROTESTANTISM AND LIBERALISM). Instead of a transcendent God of judgment, liberals emphasized God's immanence, that is, God's embodiedness in the created world. Rejecting the idea of a depraved human nature, they saw great possibilities for progress and development in each individual person. Reflecting the optimistic spirit of their age, liberal theologians proclaimed the KINGDOM OF GOD, not as a future heavenly state, but rather as the promise of their own age, here on earth.

Two leading theologians, the American Congregationalist HORACE BUSHNELL and the German Reformed thinker FRIEDRICH SCHLEIERMACHER, played a major role in developing a Protestant understanding of Christian nurture. Both men rejected the traditional evangelical view of children as desperate rebels unable to accept or understand divine love. Instead, they affirmed the authenticity of childhood faith at every stage of its development, for although a very young child might not intellectually understand Christian doctrine, he or she still had the capacity for a true faith in God. Although neither theologian romanticized childhood innocence, both emphasized the naturalness and purity of youth and saw childhood as a time of unique openness to the divine. Parents therefore played a crucial role in the child's moral outcome. Thoughtless, cruel, or dissolute treatment could harden the child's spirit toward eventual rebellion against God; in a parallel fashion, firm and gentle childrearing would implant a positive awareness of God's care for creation, and open the way for genuine faith even in a preliterate infant. To Bushnell, even the atmosphere of a Christian home was subtly salvific. A child reared in a calm, loving, peaceful environment, he believed, would have no difficulty eventually accepting God as heavenly father.

The nineteenth century thus saw the gradual identification of the Western bourgeois family as a fundamentally "Christian" institution. Family was not just a place for catechizing and disciplining the young, but itself a means of grace in the lives of parents and children. Regular household devotions were an important sign of godliness, but hardly the only one. Even more telling was the home's peaceful, controlled atmosphere—a true sign of its essentially Christian character.

The Christian home also became an important means of evangelistic outreach for European and American Protestants. In foreign missionary efforts, especially those organized and led by women, Western-style domesticity became a key means of introducing Christianity to non-Western people. By the late nineteenth century, most Western missionaries recognized that reaching native women in their homes could be far more effective in proclaiming the Gospel than simply PREACHING sermons in the public square. But the missionary emphasis on family was far more than a pragmatic strategy: for Victorian Protestants, home was so closely identified with the essence of Christianity that it was all but impossible to separate the two.

The use of family as an evangelistic tool meant, in many cases, a headlong confrontation between Western assumptions and indigenous traditions. When, for example, the Anglican LAMBETH CONFERENCE inter-

dicted polygamy (plural marriage) in 1888, African Christians faced some difficult choices. In African society, polygamy was a sign of economic success and a means of cementing political alliances; some observant converts pointed out the multiple wives of the Old Testament patriarchs. In embracing monogamy, converts sacrificed social power and in many cases treasured personal relationships. For some, the cost was simply too high. In 1917, an act of church discipline against the polygamous marriages of several Nigerian laymen led to a mass exodus of members and, in protest, the formation of the United African Methodist Church.

Fundamentalism and Families

In recent years, family has become central to a new religious polemic, this time embodied in a wave of popular fundamentalist movements. Defining FUNDAMENTALISM is a difficult and often contentious task, a scholarly problem that reflects the rapid, complex growth of antimodern movements around the world today. In their public rhetoric, fundamentalist adherents proclaim a deep antipathy toward modern secularism in all its social, political, and intellectual manifestations. Yet in a larger sense, fundamentalism and modernity exist in a symbiotic relationship (see MODERNISM). Hardly a movement of the rural or unlettered, fundamentalism is most compelling where people feel the most powerless to combat its corrosive effects.

The term "fundamentalist" originally referred to a conservative wing within late nineteenth- and early twentieth-century American Protestantism. Although the movement was not initially successful in halting the spread of liberal theology, by the mid-twentieth century it exercised a broad influence within American Protestant evangelical culture (see EVANGELICALISM), and, by dint of energetic evangelistic work, on the larger world as well.

Family is an important symbolic battleground in the modern "culture wars" (see CULTURE). Although historians have disagreed, oftentimes fiercely, about the extent of a modern-day family crisis, there is no doubt that over the course of the twentieth century, domestic life in the modern West—and, increasingly, the rest of the world as well—has vastly changed. Although fundamentalist adherents often point to ideological movements like feminism as reason for a family "breakdown," the sources of change are in fact much broader, reflecting some deeper shifts in modern social arrangements. Thus, rising educational and income opportunities for younger women have reduced the demands of "the family claim" on their lives. Increasing access to birth control has shortened the average couple's child-bearing years and liberated their sexual expression both within and outside of marriage. Longer years of schooling for young children have decreased the family's educational role and opened up a new range of possibilities for economic and geographic mobility. The transformation has not been as dramatic (nor perhaps as overwhelmingly negative) as some of the more insistent voices have claimed; yet it is clear that modernity has allowed individuals to make life decisions with far greater independence from their families than their grandparents would have ever thought possible.

The conservative emphasis on family has also arisen against a backdrop of reluctance among more liberal Protestant bodies to make binding rules about sexuality. As social scientists have argued, this development reflects broader individualizing trends in North America and Europe and the increasing privatization of marriage and childrearing relationships. Protestant denominations, no less than secular governing bodies, have become averse to regulating the intimate personal relationships of their constituents, perhaps also because they have recognized the futility of even attempting to do so.

The "pro-family" agenda, centered on the conviction that the home is the true bedrock of a moral society, has both a negative and a positive expression. On the one hand is an effort to control sexuality through opposition to ABORTION and HOMOSEXUALITY, and to situate women more emphatically in the home as wives and mothers. On the other hand, pro-family advocates have also sought to address the problem of father absence, a crisis at least as old as the industrial revolution itself. Though the language of groups like Promise Keepers is often unabashedly patriarchal, their purpose is generally much broader. By affirming the father's spiritual responsibilities to his wife and children, they hope to reinvigorate family life and, by extension, Christianity among some of its historically weakest supporters.

The sense of social and spiritual crisis in the now post-Christian West has often obscured the vitality of the faith in other parts of the world. By the late twentieth century, religious demographers were reporting that Christianity's center of gravity had shifted to the southern hemisphere, centered in vigorous Pentecostal and indigenous movements in developing African and Latin American nations (see PENTECOSTALISM; LATIN AMERICA, AFRICA). By 1980, the "average" Christian was not a white, middle-class American, but more likely young, poor, and experiencing all of the hardships of life in a third-world country.

The new global face of Protestantism has posed unprecedented challenges to traditional Western beliefs and practices about family. Discussions on the subject have had to take into account the poverty and exploitation brought on by a rapidly globalizing economy, the sexual victimization of women and children in a world-wide market for pornography, and the ravages of the AIDS virus in Africa and Asia. Long a matter of ethical and theological debate among Western Protestants, family has become a key social concern for the faith's rising generations.

References and Further Reading

Aries, Philippe. *Centuries of Childhood: A Social History of Family Life.* Translated by Robert Baldick. New York: Vintage Books, 1962.

Bunge, Marcia, ed. *The Child in Christian Thought.* Grand Rapids, MI: Eerdmans, 2001.

Demos, John. *A Little Commonwealth: Family Life in Plymouth Colony.* New York: Oxford University Press, 1970.

Hardacre, Helen. "The Impact of Fundamentalisms on Women, the Family, and Interpersonal Relations." In *Fundamentalisms and Society: Reclaiming the Sciences, the Family, and Education,* edited by Martin E. Marty and R. Scott Appleby. Chicago: University of Chicago Press, 1993.

McDanell, Colleen. *The Christian Home in Victorian America, 1840–1900.* Bloomington, IN: Indiana University Press, 1986.

Ozment, Steven. *When Fathers Ruled: Family Life in Reformation Europe.* Cambridge, MA: Harvard University Press, 1983.

Perrot, Michelle, ed. *A History of Private Life, Vol. IV: From the Fires of Revolution to the Great War.* Translated by Arthur Goldhammer. Cambridge, MA: Belknap Press of Harvard University Press, 1990.

Prost, Antoine, and Gerard Vincent, eds. *A History of Private Life, Vol. V: Riddles of Identity in Modern Times.* Translated by Arthur Goldhammer. Cambridge, MA: Belknap Press of Harvard University Press, 1991.

Riesebrodt, Martin. *Pious Passion: The Emergence of Modern Fundamentalism in the United States and Iran.* Translated by Don Reneau. Berkeley, CA: University of California Press, 1993.

Witte, John Jr. *From Sacrament to Contract: Marriage, Religion, and Law in the Western Tradition.* Louisville, KY: Westminster/John Knox Press, 1997.

MARGARET L. BENDROTH

FARADAY, MICHAEL (1791–1867)

English scientist and theologian. Faraday was born at Newington, Surrey, on September 22, 1791, to a former blacksmith and his wife who had recently moved to London from his native Westmorland. After little formal education and apprenticeship to a bookbinder, Faraday became assistant to Humphry Davy at the Royal Institution (R.I.). Here he remained for the rest of his working life, learning from Davy and eventually becoming professor of chemistry and director of the R.I.

Faraday undertook fundamental research at the R.I., working first in chemistry, where he discovered benzene and (with Davy) invented the miners' safety lamp. He soon moved into a lifelong study of electricity, discovering many basic laws in, for example, electromagnetism and electrochemistry and making possible the invention of the dynamo. John Tyndall, the British physicist and Faraday's colleague, described him as "the greatest experimental philosopher the world has ever seen." He also pioneered popular lectures at the R.I. and emerged as one of Britain's best communicators of science. His *Chemical History of a Candle* is still in print and cited as a model of chemical education.

Faraday was a committed member of a small Protestant denomination, the Sandemanian Church. It remained an inspiration and a consolation for the whole of his life. The church's evangelical theology assured him of the divine origin of NATURE and may even have suggested details of his unified field theory of electricity (see EVANGELICAL; EVANGELICALISM, THEOLOGY OF). Certainly it denied him the possibility of using science as an alternative way to God, and at times of crisis and approaching death it brought him "no doubtful hope." The other-worldly values of Sandemanianism were reflected in Faraday's contentment with its simple rituals, a deeply enriching though childless marriage, and his lack of financial ambition. His own extensively marked Bibles testify to the depth of his faith. Faraday died at his house at Hampton Court, which was provided by Queen Victoria for his final years, on August 25, 1867.

References and Further Reading

Primary Source:

James, F. A. J. L., ed. *The Correspondence of Michael Faraday*. London: Institution of Electrical Engineers, 1991 (continuing).

Secondary Sources:

Cantor, Geoffrey. *Michael Faraday: Sandemanian and Scientist. A Study of Science and Religion in the Nineteenth Century*. Basingstoke: Macmillan, 1991.

Russell, C. A. *Michael Faraday, Physics and Faith*. New York: Oxford University Press, 2000.

Williams, L. Pearce. *Michael Faraday, a Biography*. London: Chapman & Hall, 1965.

COLIN A. RUSSELL

FAREL, GUILLAUME (1489–1565)

French reformer. Farel, an early French reformer who was later overshadowed by JOHN CALVIN, was born in Gap in southeastern FRANCE. The son of a notary, Farel studied in Paris with the humanist J. Lefèvre d'Étaples, and taught at the Collège Cardinal Lemoine. A passionate preacher, although not a priest, Farel preached in the diocese of Meaux, under the reform-

ing bishop Guillaume Briçonnet (1521–1523) and later moved to Basel. Friendly with JOHANNES OECO-LAMPADIUS, he fell out with Desiderius Erasmus. Chased out, he went to Montbéliard (1524–1525) where, without formal ordination, Farel celebrated Communion (see LORD'S SUPPER). He moved on to Metz (1525) and Strasbourg.

Farel evangelized French-speaking SWITZERLAND as a teacher in Aigle (1527), then under Berne. With his encouragement Neuchâtel accepted the REFORMATION (1530), and Pierre Viret from Orbe became a pastor (1531). Farel again fled from Geneva in 1532. Over a year later he returned, having brought the Waldensians fully into the Reformation. Farel helped accomplish the suspension of the Mass (August 1535) in Geneva, the destruction of images, and acceptance of the Reformation (May 21, 1536). That year he persuaded Calvin to stay (July) and led the deputation to the Dispute of Lausanne (1536), resulting in the acceptance of the Reformation there and in the region of Vaud.

In Geneva Farel and Calvin drafted *Ecclesiastical Ordinances* and a *Confession of Faith* (1537) but refused Bernese liturgical practices. Geneva expelled them in 1538, and Farel became pastor in Neuchâtel until his death in 1565, journeying often to other Reformed cities. He corresponded with Calvin, and despite his disapproval, married (1558) a young girl staying with her mother in his home. Their son, John (b. 1564), died (1568).

Farel's publications include *Pater noster et le credo en français* (1524), the Lord's Prayer and Apostles' Creed with commentary; *Sommaire et briefve declaration . . .* (c. 1529); and *Maniere et fasson . . .* (1528?), considered the first French Reformed LITURGY. His doctrines were close to those of HULDRYCH ZWINGLI, but later moved closer to those of Calvin on the spiritual communication of Christ's body and blood in Communion.

References and Further Reading

Primary Sources:

Barthel, Pierre, Rémy Scheurer, and Richard Stauffer, eds. *Actes du colloque Guillaume Farel: Neuchâtel, 29 septembre–1er octobre 1980*. 2 vols. Cahiers de la Revue de Théologie et de Philosophie no. 9. Lausanne, Switzerland: Imprimerie La Concorde, 1983.

Farel, Guillaume. *Le Pater noster et le credo en françoys*. Edited by Francis Higman. Textes littéraires français. Geneva, Switzerland: Librairie Droz, 1982. (First published 1524.)

———. *Sommaire et brève déclaration, 1525*. Edited by Arthur-L. Hofer. Neuchâtel, Switzerland: Éditions Belle Rivière, 1980.

Guillaume Farel, 1489–1565: Biographie nouvelle écrite d'après les documents originaux par un groupe d'historiens, professeurs et pasteurs de Suisse, de France et d'Italie. Ornée d'un portrait en couleurs et de vingt-cinq planches hors texte. Neuchâtel, Switzerland: Éditions Delachaux & Niestlé, 1930.

JEANNINE E. OLSON

FOOTWASHING

Both a liturgical act, after the example of Jesus at the Last Supper (John 13), and also a specific example and paradigm of humble service (I Timothy 6:10), foot-washing was part of the baptismal LITURGY in some areas of the early church, and became a stable part of the Maundy Thursday Mass of the Last Supper, in the ritual reenactment of that event, in the medieval Roman rite. It was also more frequently used in medieval monasteries as an expression and intensification of mutual humility and service.

Most REFORMATION churches abandoned this custom, as part of the simplification of WORSHIP. Some early Anabaptists (see ANABAPTISM), however, retained it—or, rather, reinstated it—as a New Testament ordinance that had been misused. BALTHASAR HUBMAIER (1481–1528) washed the feet of the newly baptized after they received Communion, and MENNO SIMONS (c. 1496–1561) commended foot-washing as a rite of welcome to visitors from afar. The Dutch Anabaptist Dietrich Philips (1504–1568) explicitly listed foot-washing as a divinely commanded regular rite of cleansing and humility, and as a distinguishing mark of a true church. At least some MENNONITES followed Dietrich's counsel, and under their influence English BAPTISTS followed suit for some time. The usage provoked sharp mutual insult among churches.

Mennonites have tended, especially since the nineteenth century, to relinquish the practice, partly at least because in the prosperous Western world this degree of intimacy is embarrassing, and because this service is less natural as a hygienic measure where hot water is available all the time in every home. Also, the custom has, according to some observers, shifted its meaning, and become opaque to succeeding generations.

German Baptists, led by Alexander Mack, introduced the usage as part of their celebration of the Eucharist, or LORD'S SUPPER. For the BRETHREN tradition, in its several branches (Old German Baptists, Brethren Church, Church of the Brethren, Grace Brethren, Old Order River Brethren), the celebration has three components: the Love-Feast, the Washing of Feet, and the Lord's Supper. In Brethren understanding all three parts have the same AUTHORITY as commanded by Christ.

Some Protestant traditions (Anglican particularly), moved in part by the Roman Catholic reordering of Holy Week (1955), have revived the rite of footwashing as part of the Maundy Thursday evening Eucharist. Ecumenical contacts have made the Brethren manner of celebration more familiar to other denominations, and the difference of custom began to be seen as a complementarity of New Testament interpretation rather than an issue of conflict. In ecumenical groups the imagery of foot-washing as humble and gentle service has promoted experiments with simple rites of mutual hand-washing, such as a parent might do for a small child. Both giver and receiver are called on to act in simplicity, patience, and humble CHARITY.

The usage and the changing ecumenical relationships have drawn attention to the New Testament data, and the literature is large and growing. The shared Protestant insistence on the normative role of Scripture naturally points to shared exploration of the biblical data. Protestant scholars have felt obliged to question the historicity of John 13, but also to suggest that Luke 22:27 indicates that something like John 13 lies behind the Synoptic tradition. The foot-washing by Jesus is in John presented as an example of humble service to be followed, a revelation of the divine humility, a symbol of the believer's need humbly to accept the sacrificial love of the Savior; it may also be seen as a self-dedicatory act by Jesus himself, an act directing his own will to the sacrificial act that will be given its meaning in a few minutes in the Supper and in a few hours before Pilate and on Calvary.

References and Further Reading

Bender, Harold S. "Footwashing." In *The Mennonite Encyclopedia*, vol. II, 347–351. Scottdale, PA: Mennonite Publishing House, 1956.

Dunn, James D. G. "The Washing of the Disciples' Feet in John 13:1–20." *Zeitschrift für die neutestamentliche Wissenschaft* 61 no. 3–4 (1970): 247–252.

Edgington, Allen. "Footwashing as an Ordinance." *Grace Theological Journal* 6 no. 2 (Fall 1985): 425–434.

Edwards, Ruth B. "The Christological Basis of the Johannine Footwashing." In *Jesus of Nazareth: Lord and Christ: Essays on the Historical Jesus and New Testament Christology,* edited by Joel B. Green and Max Turner, 367–383. Grand Rapids, MI: Wm. B. Eerdman; Carlisle, UK: Paternoster Press 1994.

Graber-Miller, Keith. "Mennonite Footwashing: Identity Reflections and Altered Meanings." *Worship* 66 (March 1992): 148–170.

Hultgren, Arland J. "The Johannine Footwashing (Jn 13:1–12) as Symbol of Eschatological Hospitality." *New Testament Studies* 29 (October 1982): 539–546.

Lawless, George P., O.S.A. "The Footwashing as a Model of Ministry." *Augustinian Heritage* 32 (1986): 135–164.

Thomas, John Christopher. *Footwashing in John 13 and the Johannine Community.* Sheffield, UK: Journal for the Study of the Old Testament Press, 1991.

DAVID H. TRIPP

FELGENHAUER, PAUL
(1593–c.1677)

Protestant mystic. Son of a Lutheran pastor, Felgenhauer was born in Putschwitz, Bohemia on November 16, 1593, and studied at Wittenberg, where he became deacon at the Castle Church. Soon, however, he was forced to leave the town and returned to Bohemia, where he began a prolific writing career. In his *Chronologie* of 1620 he argued that the end of the world was imminent. In this work Felgenhauer echoed the notion, widespread at the time, that the duration of the world was confined to 6,000 years, of which less than 200 years remained. In a second work of the same year Felgenhauer launched a bitter attack on the Lutheran churches and their CLERGY.

Forced to leave Bohemia because of the vicissitudes of the Thirty Years' War and the concomitant dynamic Catholic COUNTER-REFORMATION, he moved to Amsterdam where he continued to publish his mystical writings. After 1638 he appears to have practiced medicine, while at the same time seeking followers for his cause. Expulsions and imprisonment overshadowed the last phase of his life, about which—including the exact date and place of death—nothing is known.

Felgenhauer stood in the tradition of the chiliastic and spiritualist tradition of Protestantism. Importantly, he expressed considerable warmth and empathy toward Jews because he understood religions to express at their core the same truths.

See also Apocalypticism; Chiliasm; Judaism; Lutheranism; Millenarians and Millenialists; Philo-Semitism

References and Further Reading

Schoeps, Hans Joachim, Barocke Juden, Christen, Judenchristen. Bern: Francke, 1965.

HANS J. HILLERBRAND

FELLOWSHIP OF RECONCILIATION

See Peace Organizations

FELLOWSHIP OF SOUTHERN CHURCHMEN

Founded in 1934 and existing as Fellowship of Southern Churchmen (FSC) from 1936 to 1963, this group of radical Protestants, both lay and clergy, men and women, black and white, sought to transform southern culture and society by fighting for justice in labor and in racial relations. Along the way it had to overcome the prejudices and lethargy of the churches themselves in bridging the gap between social justice and the Christian Gospel, as well as face the hostility of a society unwilling to change. Under the inspiration of REINHOLD NIEBUHR'S NEO-ORTHODOXY and CHRISTIAN SOCIALISM, its actions, both by individual members and as a group, ranged from meetings, conferences, investigations on lynching, racially integrated work camps and bus rides, labor organization, pamphleteering, founding of cooperatives, and rallies. Eventually, however, the larger and more aggressive wave of the CIVIL RIGHTS MOVEMENT took the historic stage, and the FSC dispersed as its members found other fields to plow.

Background and Early History

The impetus for the FSC may be seen at the intersection of the southern church and society of the period. The economy of the South from the 1920s through the 1950s was dominated by tenant farming, on the one hand, and textile and mining industries, on the other. In both sectors the holders of capital relied on the region's cheap labor. In both, employers tended to wield almost total control over the lives of the poorly paid workers who lacked recourse to air grievances or to bargain collectively. In the face of these exigencies, the Protestant establishment wavered. Officially many denominations recognized the right of workers to unionize. Because company towns and even churches were often in the dole of these employers, however, there was not only little resistance but also anti-union rhetoric from the pulpit. As to racial justice, Protestants fared no better. Jim Crow was the law of the land, and any deviation was hunted down not only by the authorities, but by the likes of the KU KLUX KLAN. Although Protestant churches at the denominational level usually denounced lynching, explicit opposition to racial violence was by no means common at the local level, even when it occurred on church property. On segregation there was so little DISSENT from the church as to make complicity the norm.

In this state of affairs, about eighty Southern Protestants from both sides of the clerical, racial, and GENDER divide gathered in May 1934 in Monteagle, Tennessee to hear Reinhold Niebuhr speak on pressing questions of the day. Under the initiator James Dombrowski they emerged as the Fellowship of Younger Churchmen, and included many ministers and teachers from the Methodist and Presbyterian folds as well as other professionals from churches high and low. North Carolina, then as later, was the best represented state. The members were influenced by the analyses of Marxism, several with a background in PACIFISM and YMCA work (see YMCA/YWCA), but as Niebuhrian Neo-orthodox they rejected the optimistic progressivism of the SOCIAL

GOSPEL and instead stared human evil in the face as they worked.

Howard Anderson Kester was elected executive secretary. Kester, a Congregationalist who also worked for Niebuhr's Committee on Economic and Racial Justice (eventually merged with the FSC), made his home in Black Mountain, North Carolina, the headquarters of the organization until he resigned in 1943. Under Kester's leadership the FSC and its members worked mainly on questions of land and labor. They investigated labor disputes; propagated a liturgy of the Holy Earth, designed to promote Christian stewardship of land; probed and denounced lynching; and spoke out for the inclusion of black people in the welfare of the nation. In many ways the FSC not only extended the legacy of nineteenth-century Quakers (see FRIENDS, SOCIETY OF), but also anticipated the praxis of LIBERATION THEOLOGY of the following generation.

Transformation and Peak

In 1944 Nelle Morton, a vigorous educator and champion of women's rights, took over at the helm of the FSC, and with this change the group came into its maturity and highest efficacy. First, Morton moved the headquarters to Chapel Hill, where it garnered further support from both liberal church people of the area and students of the University of North Carolina. Moreover, the Fellowship enjoyed the sympathetic patronage of Frank Graham, then head of the university and later senator. Morton also sought to promote teamwork and a stronger collegial fabric among FSC members, whose number exceeded 500 by the end of the decade. She appointed two secretaries, one black and one white.

Although involvement in labor affairs continued, the Fellowship turned increasingly to racial problems, believing them to underlie social and economic injustice in the region. In 1946 an interracial bus ride was organized to test new laws on interstate travel, but this first "Freedom Ride" ran aground when participants boarded an "intrastate" bus to Greensboro. Other efforts at racial integration included work camps in rural areas bringing the races together in cooperative work and life. These projects, however, often faced hostile opposition from white people of the surrounding communities who even coerced the force of law to break up the bold experiments. In response a donation of land in 1948 was slated for a Fellowship Center where work camps could be safely conducted, but funding and support eventually proved insufficient for full execution of the plans.

Decline, Dispersion

In 1949 Morton resigned because of ill health, and, following the short term of Charles M. Jones, distinguished for his own pastoral promotion of desegregation, Howard Kester returned in late 1951 as executive secretary. Although renewed in his enthusiasm, Kester's move of the headquarters back to remote Black Mountain had the effect of canceling the advantages of the Chapel Hill years. In this last period Neale Hughley became the Fellowship's first black president.

By 1957, however, the FSC as an organization was listing. Although its annual conference in Nashville, boldly billed as a Southwide Rally, featured as speaker the young Dr. MARTIN LUTHER KING JR., the event fell short of engendering the wide response expected. In the meantime the more confrontational civil disobedience of other groups, particularly of black membership, gained ascendancy in the struggle for civil rights. The minority of black members in the FSC was not strong enough to give the group leadership in that transformation. After several more meetings and some work camps the FSC voted in 1963 to cease as such and to merge into the new Committee of Southern Churchmen, headed by William Campbell of the NATIONAL COUNCIL OF CHURCHES. With that formal end the members of the FSC turned fully elsewhere to continue their Christian action in the South and beyond. In the three decades of its existence, the FSC went from a vanguard Protestant movement for social witness to being submerged in newer and wider currents of protest and advocacy. If its original views and aims now seemed common, it was partly because of its very agency in making them so.

See also Liberal Protestantism and Liberalism

References and Further Reading

Burgess, David S. *Fighting for Justice: The Life Story of David Burgess.* Detroit, MI: Wayne State University Press, 2000.

Donahue, Don. "Prophets of a New Social Order: Presbyterians and the Fellowship of Southern Churchmen, 1934–1963." *American Presbyterians* 74 (1996): 209–221.

Martin, Robert F. "A Prophet's Pilgrimage: The Religious Radicalism of Howard Anderson Kester, 1921–1941." *The Journal of Southern History* 48 (1982): 511–530.

———. "Critique of Southern Society and Vision of a New Order: The Fellowship of Southern Churchmen, 1934–1957." *Church History* 52 (1983): 66–80.

Salmond, John A. "The Fellowship of Southern Churchmen and Interracial Change in the South." *The North Carolina Historical Review* 69 (1992): 179–199

DAVID U. LIU

FEUERBACH, LUDWIG (1804–1872)

Protestant theologian, philosopher. Feuerbach was one of the most influential critics of Christianity in the nineteenth century. Although he began his career as a idealist, he became the advocate for a new atheistic humanism. He is best known for his view that the concept of God is an involuntary and unconscious projection of human attributes and, hence, that religion is humanity's earliest and indirect form of self-knowledge. He believed that Protestantism was the practical turning point toward this atheistic humanism in the history of the West because of MARTIN LUTHER'S (1483–1546) emphasis on the humanity of God as revealed in Christ. Throughout his life he was concerned with a theory of religion because he was convinced that only when human beings were free of this illusion could they take responsibility for their own welfare.

Early Life and Thought: 1804–1839

Ludwig Feuerbach, the fourth of eight children, was born in 1804 into an old and distinguished German family. His father, Paul Anselm, was a famous professor of jurisprudence and reformer of the Bavarian legal code. He was also a powerful advocate of liberal political reform in an repressive era; consequently, the family lived under a cloud of political suspicion. Deeply religious as a youth, Feuerbach entered the University of Heidelberg in 1823 to study theology. There he came under the influence of the Hegelian theologian Karl Daub (1765–1836) and was captured by the intellectual grandeur of Hegelian philosophy in contrast to the narrower concerns of theology. Against his father's wishes, he transferred to the University of Berlin, ostensibly to study theology but, in actuality, to study philosophy with G. W. F. HEGEL (1770–1831), whom he regarded as the originator of a "new epoch" in philosophy and culture.

For financial reasons, Feuerbach transferred to Erlangen in 1826. After graduation he became a private-dozent lecturing on the history of modern philosophy. Against his father's advice he anonymously published a book entitled *Thoughts on Death and Immortality* (1830), arguing that the Christian doctrine of personal immortality is hostile to true religion. To add offense to conservative injury, he appended aphorisms to the text that were insulting to conservative pietists. The book was met with hostility by his colleagues and banned by censorship. When Feuerbach refused to disclaim its authorship, he was dismissed from his post. In 1833, however, he met the daughter of a wealthy porcelain manufacturer, and married her four years later. Unable to obtain a professorship, he retired to a remote hamlet near Ansbach, where the porcelain factory was located, and devoted himself to writing.

Through the Thirties, Feuerbach's intellectual trajectory moved from an enthusiastic appropriation of Hegel's philosophical project to an outright rejection, with some vacillation in between. His dissertation (1828) argued that the divine ground and unity of the world is reason and, hence, that the logos is the essence of the human. In his *Thoughts on Death and Immortality,* his philosophical idealism took the form of a pantheism in which God is the all-encompassing ground of both personhood and nature. Feuerbach argued that this idealism is incompatible both with Christian theism and the doctrine of immortality, both of which had emerged only in the modern period as crucial elements of Protestant doctrine. Because God is the all-consuming love out of which multiple things appear, true religion is to surrender to this all-encompassing ground and to recognize death as total dissolution. In his repudiation of Hegel in 1838, he rejected the notion of an absolute philosophy and especially the claim that Absolute Spirit constituted the unity of both nature and spirit. He was especially critical of Hegel's identification of thought and being, and argued that the all-encompassing reality was not spirit but nature.

In the middle 1830s, a split developed among the followers of Hegel that had both religious and political implications. On the conservative side were those who argued that Hegelian philosophy was in harmony with Christian theism and justified the support of a Christian state. On the radical side were those who believed that Hegel's Absolute was incompatible with Christian doctrine and who were critical of the existing state. Feuerbach increasingly found himself allied with those like BRUNO BAUER (1809–1882), D. F. STRAUSS (1808–1874), Karl Marx (1818–1883), and Karl Ruge who held a latter view, but when these young (left-wing) Hegelians engaged in either theological or political criticism, they were censored and denied the academic positions for which they had been trained.

Middle Period: 1840–1848

Feuerbach's *The Essence of Christianity* (1841) made him immediately famous in Europe, and he found himself recognized, along with Bruno Bauer, as the intellectual leader of the small group of radical Young Hegelians bent on separating church and state and creating an egalitarian democracy. To do this, they believed it crucial to establish the philosophical principles of a new humanism. In 1842 and 1843 Feuerbach attempted to do this with his *Voläufige Thesen zur Philosophic* [Preliminary Theses Toward the Reformation of Philosophy] and his *Principles of the Philosophy of the Future,* both published in Switzerland because they were forbidden in Germany.

Feuerbach believed that his new philosophy was the inevitable outcome of the Protestant Reformation. Christianity, he argued, had in modern times suffered both a practical and a theoretical dissolution. On the practical side, Luther had dissolved theology into anthropology by arguing that "God in and for himself" should be of no interest to the believer but only the human "God for us" in the man Jesus. And on the theoretical side, theological speculation had moved from theism to Hegel's pantheism, albeit a pantheism that paradoxically claimed to justify Christianity. Feuerbach argued that Hegel's attempt to restore Christianity by identifying the finite with the infinite was only a piece of logical legerdemain in which matter had been made only a "moment" in the life of God. He also argued that the clue to understanding Hegel's philosophy is the way in which Hegel characteristically transformed abstract predicates into subjects; for example, the abstraction "thinking" was turned into a subject "reason." Consequently, the philosophy of the future would simply invert Hegel's logic. Instead of construing the predicate as a subject, it would show that thinking is the activity of existing individuals. Thought comes out of being, not being out of thought.

So far as Feuerbach was concerned, Hegel had confused logic with existence. The philosophy of the future, by contrast, would be based on the insight that to be there (*Da-sein*) in space and time is the primary determination of being. The human being is not merely a bearer of reason but is constituted by its own unique constellation of senses that mediate the world to consciousness. The body is constituted in its mode of being as feeling, and each sense organ has its own unique need for satisfaction. Sensuousness is the link between the body and the consciousness, but because humans are also conscious they are "universal" and free, and this freedom and universality extend themselves over the entire human being. Moreover, the person, the "I," only exists in concrete relations to another person, a "Thou." We are social beings through and through. Hence, the highest and last principle of philosophy is the unity of person with person.

The radical Young Hegelian movement of which Feuerbach was a spokesman did not last long. By the summer of 1843 its two influential journals had been suppressed by the censors and their editors, Karl Ruge and Karl Marx, forced to emigrate to Paris. Moreover, important strategic disagreements had arisen. Marx argued that revolutionary praxis was the only way to bring about social change, while Feuerbach and Ruge insisted one must first change consciousness.

When the revolutions of 1848 swept over Europe, Feuerbach was tempted to leave his solitary life and attended the Frankfurt Assembly as an observer.

While there, he received an invitation from the students of Heidelberg to give a series of public lectures on religion. Denied the use of the university, he delivered the lectures in the Heidelberg city hall.

Feuerbach was most productive between 1841 and 1848, during which he published six major works, of which the best known is *The Essence of Christianity* (1841). The thesis of the book is simple, although the supporting arguments are complex: The concept of God is the involuntary projection by the human mind of its own best attributes, and this projection is then made an object of worship. Just as Hegel argued that the Absolute Spirit objectifies itself in creation and then comes to self-consciousness by reconciling itself to this objectification, Feuerbach argued that humankind objectifies itself in the idea of God and then comes to self-consciousness by reconciling itself to this objectification.

The book is divided into two parts. The first attempts to show that the idea of God is simply the abstracted attributes of human nature—reason, will, and love—conceived as a single being. The argument goes something like this. Human nature is distinguished by virtue of self-consciousness. Self-consciousness is the capacity to envision oneself as a member of a species, but the attributes of this species are necessarily regarded as perfections. The imagination, under the pressure of feeling, seizes on these perfections and unifies them in the idea of a divine separate being. Human beings then fall under the sway of this projection because they desire recognition by another "Thou" and are frightened by the limits of nature and, above all, death. The idea of God promises them both loving recognition and the overcoming of death. Consequently, one can say that although religion is false, it is also the vehicle by which the human race becomes aware of its own real nature. Theology is anthropology.

The predicate of love is the most important of these attributes, and as an analysis of the Christian doctrine of the Incarnation reveals, this love is so great that God is willing to relinquish his own nature for the welfare of humankind. Feuerbach takes this to mean that in Christianity humankind has unconsciously expressed the idea that love is more important than God, that love is itself divine. It also means that insofar as God is believed to be a transcendent being with perfect love, humankind is alienated from its own loving nature. So long as God is regarded as the repository of all goodness and perfection, humankind will be regarded as imperfect and sick.

If Feuerbach considered the first part of the book to be positive because it points out the truth contained in religion, the second part is negative because it demonstrates the bad effects of theology. Feuerbach argues that Christian theology is riddled with contradictions; for example, the concept of God contains both impersonal (metaphysical) and anthropomorphic attributes. But the deepest contradiction, he argues, is between the Christian virtues of faith and love, because faith separates and distinguishes between believers and unbelievers, while love embraces all.

The first edition of *The Essence of Christianity* (1841) was primarily directed at the Catholic understanding of Christianity, but in 1843 Feuerbach made an extensive study of Luther and published a revised edition. Feuerbach argued that Luther differed from Catholicism by virtue of his radical idea that God is a deity "for us." Faith insists that God is by definition "for us" and does not have some mysterious purposes that transcend our welfare. To say "God is good" means "good for us." Luther also saw that the certitude of Christian belief is founded on the Incarnation because there the humanity of God becomes an object for the senses. Only a sensuous being can be a certain being. Here there can be no basis for mistrust. Moreover, the resurrection confirms this love for us because in this event God reveals that all the conditions of our finitude, especially death, have been set aside. We will become gods. In short, to believe is to make God a man and man a god.

Feuerbach came to believe that his projection theory of religion did not adequately explain how the religious folk came to feel they were in touch with a "divine other," and in 1845 he wrote still another book, *Das Wesen der Religion* [The Essence of Religion], in which he argued that the enduring ground and object of religion is nature, upon which we feel ourselves to be absolutely dependent. By nature, Feuerbach means the "not-I"; that is, all those forces from within and without that impinge on the "I." Human beings, he argued, are driven by the urge to happiness, and the realization of this happiness is both dependent on nature's beneficence and limited by its apparent indifference to individual well-being, especially by the fact of death. Human beings want, above all, to live, and impelled by the a urge to live they instinctively transform this desire into a being capable of granting it, a being that recognizes them, hears their complaints, and grants their desires. Religion, in short, arises out of the opposition of the urge to happiness and the limits of nature and death. This is why the belief in miracles and immortality are so often associated with religion. The tomb is the birthplace of the gods.

Final Period: 1848–1872

After the brief exciting hopes and possibilities raised by the revolutions of 1848 were dashed by the failure of the Frankfurt Assembly, Feuerbach retreated once again to his isolated existence. He worked on numerous writing projects, especially in the field of ethics,

where he attempted to construct an ethic based on the urge to happiness. The only book he published during this time was another interpretation of religion, *Theogony* (1860). The basic argument depends once again on the notion that the gods are "for us." The gods are the reified wishes of humankind. Conscious beings are bent on their own happiness but are aware that their needs and desires can be thwarted. Hence, every wish is accompanied by a sense of the nothingness that clings to all life. Religion arises when the person grasps the notion that there are many links between a wish and its realization, and conceives of a being that is not subject to limitation and failure. The gods represent the unity of willing and the ability to succeed. A god is simply a being who can annul the difference between the wish and its realization. Where there are no wishes there are no gods.

In 1859, when the porcelain factory of his wife's family went bankrupt, Feuerbach, dispirited and without money, was forced to move to a small town near Nürnberg, where he lived out his life in ill health, supported only with the financial aid of friends.

References and Further Reading

Primary Sources:

Feurbach, Ludwig. *The Essence of Christianity.* Translated by George Eliot, with an introductory essay by Karl Barth and foreword by H. Richard Niebuhr. New York: Harper & Row, 1957.

———. *Principles of the Philosophy of the Future.* Translated with an introduction by Manfred H. Vogel, Library of Liberal Arts. Indianapolis, IN: Bobbs-Merrill, 1966.

———. *The Essence of Faith According to Luther.* Translated with an introduction by Melvin Cherno. New York: Harper & Row, 1967.

———. *Lectures on the Essence of Religion.* Translated by Ralph Manheim. New York: Harper & Row, 1967.

———. *Thoughts on Death and Immortality from the Papers of a Thinker, Along with an Appendix of Theological-Satirical Epigrams, Edited by One of his Friends.* Translated with introduction and notes by James A. Massey. Berkeley: University of California Press, 1980.

Secondary Sources:

Harvey, Van A. *Feuerbach and the Interpretation of Religion.* Cambridge: Cambridge University Press, 1996.

Toews, John Edward. *Hegelianism: The Path Toward Dialectical Humanism, 1805–1841.* Cambridge: Cambridge University Press, 1985.

Wartofsky, Marx. *Feuerbach.* Cambridge: Cambridge University Press, 1977.

VAN A. HARVEY

FINLAND

The Middle Ages

The first Christian influences came to Finland from both east and west. Because some essential terms like priest (Finnish pappi), cross (risti), and Bible (Raamattu) entered the Finnish language through Slavic languages, the early eastern influence is obvious, although it was later overcome by the western. A large part of medieval ecclesiastical terminology came into Finnish through Swedish.

In the eleventh century both Novgorod and SWEDEN extended their influences into Finland. After more than 200 years of fighting, Sweden and Novgorod signed an everlasting peace treaty in 1323. Most of Finland was to remain under Swedish rule and in the Catholic Church, whereas the easternmost part was left under the domain of Novgorod. As an example of Swedish influence, the English-born bishop Henry of Uppsala in Sweden visited Finland and was killed by a Finnish peasant in 1158, becoming patron Saint of Finland. Inhabitants of the Åland Islands have always spoken Swedish. During the thirteenth century Swedish settlers inhabited large areas around the coasts of the Gulf of Finland and the Gulf of Bothnia.

The cathedral of Turku (Latin Aboa; Swedish Åbo) was consecrated on June 17, 1300. The celebrations were continued on the following day, when the relics of Saint Henry were transferred to the cathedral. Finland was no more a mission field, but an organized diocese, led by the first Finnish-born bishop. The majority of the clergy was educated in the cathedral school of Turku. At this time the first Finns are found in the records of the University of Paris.

The medieval bishops of Turku were, with a few exceptions, members of the Finnish aristocracy and had studied in foreign universities. Most of them were masters of arts from the University of Paris. The bishop had a castle and an armed retinue. He represented the Finns in the Royal Council of Sweden and was assisted by the Cathedral Chapter, which by the end of the Middle Ages contained twelve canons. They elected the bishop, usually one of themselves; took care of the services in the cathedral; and governed the diocese. Most canons had studied abroad. The names of 164 Finns have been found in the records of medieval universities. The Chapter of Turku in most cases covered the costs.

The medieval Church took care of everything that had to do with high culture. The Cathedral school in Turku was not the leading one in Europe, but its curriculum was the same as elsewhere. A young man having learned his Latin there adapted himself without difficulty to the company of masters and students in Paris, Prague, and Leipzig. Nearly all literature used in Finland belonged to the clergy. Most of the extant medieval manuscripts were philosophical, juridical, and theological texts brought back to Finland by the students. The first book for Finland, *Missale Aboense,* was printed by the order of the Bishop of Turku in Lübeck in 1488.

By the end of the Middle Ages, eighty stone churches had been erected, many of them decorated with frescoes. The Dominicans founded a convent in Turku in 1249 and in Viborg in 1398. The Franciscans did not arrive until the fifteenth century. The monastery of St. Bridget of Sweden, founded in Naantali (Swedish Nådendal) near Turku in 1462, became an important center of spiritual life.

The basic Christian texts were no doubt already translated into Finnish during the mission period. In the late Middle Ages priests were obliged to read the Lord's Prayer, Ten Commandments, Ave Maria, and Apostles' Creed in Finnish from the pulpit every Sunday. They had to have these texts written, although none of them have been preserved.

At the end of the Middle Ages there were some one hundred parishes in Finland. Near Turku the distance between the churches could be only a couple of kilometers. In northern and eastern Finland children were baptized only when they were able to ski to the church.

The Finns during this period were brought up to live with the Church and its sacraments. Donations and wills speak for a devout religiosity. Pilgrimages were made to Vadstena to the grave of St. Bridget, to Santiago de Compostella, to Rome, and to the Holy Land.

The Reformation

The REFORMATION in Sweden was a typical *Fürstenreformation,* or Reformation by the Princes, initiated and led by the new king, the powerful and unscrupulous Gustavu Vasa (reigned 1523–1560). He was not very interested in theological issues but saw clearly the political advantages of the new Lutheran teaching, even though it had been declared a heresy. The religious turbulence in GERMANY gave him a pretext to confiscate the property of the church and to crush its political power. The ties to the Holy See were broken by 1523; after that the highest ecclesiastical authority was the king. He wanted to avoid abrupt changes in church ceremonies, which might give cause for opposition and rebellion. This is why the transformation of doctrine, liturgy, church life, and organization was smooth and slow. Importantly, the episcopal structure of the church was left intact.

The king had no interest in culture, which suffered along with the financial position of the church. The young University of Uppsala was closed and the schools fell into decay. On the other hand, the Reformation brought the translation of the New Testament (1526) and the entire BIBLE (1541), as well as several liturgical books, into Swedish. Because most Finns could not understand Swedish, important texts had to be translated into Finnish. Thus the Reformation gave Finns their written language. The Finnish reformer MICHAEL AGRICOLA is also the father of Finnish literature and the Finnish written language.

Lutheran Orthodoxy

Sweden accepted the AUGSBURG CONFESSION in 1593. The Lutheran Church was the state church. During the age of confessionalism, Sweden was one of the great powers in Europe. During the Thirty Years War the Finns joined the Protestant cause.

In the seventeenth century Sweden expanded its territory to the south and east. In the area conquered from RUSSIA, Ingermanland and Kexholms län, Lutheran ministers tried to convert the Finnish-speaking Greek Orthodox population to Lutheranism, although the religion proved to be stronger than the common language; thousands of Greek Orthodox fled over the border to Russia.

Finland got her own university in 1640. The first hundred years of Academia Aboensis left no mark on the history of learning and science, although the university offered better opportunities for the education of the clergy. The bishop of Turku was the vice-chancellor of the university, and the three professors of theology were members of the Cathedral Chapter. A printing press was founded in Turku in 1642.

During the period of Lutheran Orthodoxy, the church had a cultural monopoly similar to that of the Middle Ages. The church preached loyalty to the sovereign, instilled a strong sense of Christian morality in the people, and taught the Finns to read. To know the main articles of the CATECHISM by heart was a precondition for confirmation and thus also for marriage. In western parts of the country most people had that kind of literacy at the end of seventeenth century. Devotional literature (e.g., JOHANN ARNDT) was translated into Finnish and printed.

The Age of Pietism and the Enlightenment

During the eighteenth century the Finnish Church was known for Lutheran Orthodoxy, PIETISM, and ENLIGHTENMENT. Johannes Gezelius the Younger, who became bishop of Turku in 1690, visited as a student the eminent pietist PHILIPP JACOB SPENER in Frankfurt and translated his *Pia Desideria* into Swedish. The manuscript was, however, left unprinted. Pietism made its appearance in Sweden and in Turku first in radical form, prompting the bishops to oppose it. In 1726 the Diet of Estates issued the so-called Conventicle Placard, which prohibited devotional meetings led by laymen, a hallmark of Pietism. It remained in force in Finland until 1870.

Measures against Pietism were of no use. A popular ecstatic REVIVAL broke out in the Turku region. At first the revival manifested itself in ecstatic physical phenomena, including shaking and crying. The pastors, however, managed to keep the revival movement within the old and staple church Christianity.

The eighteenth century in Sweden was the age of the Nordic Enlightenment, a golden era of learning in the natural sciences and economics. In fact, most of the bishops of Turku at that time were natural scientists, two of them having been students of Carl von Linné. Practical church life centered on the vicar as a paternal leader in his parish; people went to him for advice in secular matters as well. His duty was to seek the welfare of the people. Useful unknown plants, above all the potato, first appeared in the vegetable gardens of parsonages. New cultivation techniques, such as ditching marshlands, also began to spread from parsonages.

In the Russian Empire

In 1809 Finland became a Grand Duchy in the Russian Empire. Czar Alexander I promised to respect the constitution and the laws of the previous Swedish rule—the constitution secured the supreme power of the monarch. The czar was the head of the Greek Orthodox Church of Russia, but he pledged to maintain the Lutheran faith in Finland. The union of throne and altar continued in force, even though the throne had moved from Stockholm to St. Petersburg. The bishop of Turku, who had proved his loyalty to the new ruler, was rewarded with a title of archbishop at the time of the Reformation celebrations in 1817.

The church was loyal to the czar. The bishops (a third diocese for northern Finland was established in 1850) kept the Pietist revival movements under close surveillance. These movements emerged at the beginning of the nineteenth century and remained typical for the religious life in Finland. At first they were opposed by both the state and the leading clergy who feared that they would cause political unrest.

Czar Alexander II succeeded to the imperial throne in 1855 and agreed to liberal reforms in Finland. A new Ecclesiastical Law of 1869 was drafted by Frans Ludwig Schauman, professor of practical theology. This law applied not to all citizens but only to the members of the Lutheran Church. The principle of the confessional (Lutheran) character of the state was dropped. Because it was politically impossible to grant religious freedom to the Greek Orthodox, who belonged to the Church of Russia, religious freedom was not established. In 1889 Lutherans were allowed to leave their church and to join other Protestant churches, which in practice meant BAPTISTS and METHODISTS.

The Ecclesiastical Law established a SYNOD as a legislative body. It consisted of clergy and laymen, the latter being in the majority. The synod was given the power to enact and change the Ecclesiastical Law. Bills needed the approval of the Diet and the sovereign, but they did not have the right to change the proposals; so the Finnish Church reached greater independence from the state than its sister churches in Denmark, Sweden, and Norway.

The Church in Independent Finland

Finland became independent in 1917. In the following year a civil war broke out between "the reds" and "the whites," and it ended with the victory of the "white" Finland. It was also a war of classes, and the clergy had taken sides with the whites. This guaranteed a strong position for the church in the 1920s and 1930s, but the connection with the working class remained cold. Information on the position of the church in the Soviet Union made the clergy even more suspicious.

A law dealing with religious freedom was promulgated in 1923, although it never caused the much feared mass exodus from the church; in 1923 less than 20,000 people left the church. Afterward the figure sank to a couple of thousand annually. Religious freedom thus secured the position of the church; it remained a people's church, even though membership was voluntary.

The ecumenical movement reached Finland at the end of the nineteenth century through Christian student and youth movements. Finns were represented in the Life and Work Conference in Stockholm in 1925, but unofficially. Gustaf Johansson, the conservative archbishop of Turku until 1930, did not endorse the "worldly" movement, but after his retirement the situation changed. The Evangelical Lutheran Church of Finland was one of the founding members of the LUTHERAN WORLD FEDERATION and the WORLD COUNCIL OF CHURCHES and has carried on doctrinal dialogues with other churches, such as the Russian Orthodox Church. The dialogue with the Anglican Church was initiated in the 1930s, and the Porvoo Communion was agreed upon between 1989 and 1992.

The Winter War (1939–1940) against the Soviet Union united the Finnish people and healed the wounds of the civil war. The war—felt to be fought for "home, religion and fatherland"—strengthened the position of the church. Military chaplains saw that the soldiers were more religious than they had thought. On the other hand, the service activity of the church in a crisis removed old prejudices.

In the insecure post–World War II atmosphere the church came to be seen as protector of the national identity. In 1946 the Social Democratic party removed from its program the traditional goal of separating state and church and ending religious education in school. The church assumed new tasks such as family counseling. Social work expanded rapidly, as did youth work.

In the 1960s the Finnish church was branded undemocratic and conservative, but since the collapse of COMMUNISM at the end of the twentieth century a new interest in religion has been apparent. The old revival movements have become stronger. The interest of MASS MEDIA in religious life has increased. Churches still have their say in Finnish society. For example, when issues such as human dignity and HUMAN RIGHTS, the moral values of the nation, or development of the environment are discussed, the churches of Finland do participate vigorously with their own contributions and solutions.

At the beginning of the new millennium Finland was still de facto a country of one confession. Eighty-five percent of the population belongs to the Evangelical Lutheran Church. It is a state church, although the remaining bonds between state and church are very loose and the church would like to be called a people's church rather than a state church. Church attendance is low as in other Scandinavian countries. Approximately 10 percent of church members attend a church service at least once a month. Ninety percent of babies are baptized, and 92 percent of the fifteen-year-old age group attend confirmation classes. Both numbers are higher than the membership figures of the church.

In the aftermath of the Russian Revolution and Finnish Independence (1917) the ties of the Finnish Orthodox Church with the patriarchate of Moscow were cut, and in 1923 the Finnish Orthodox Church received autonomous status under the patriarchate of Constantinople. During the Second World War some 70 percent of its members had to leave their homes. The period after the war was a period of vigorous rebuilding, with the state building churches, vicarages, and cemeteries. The Finnish Orthodox Church has about fifty thousand members.

The Roman Catholic diocese of Helsinki was established in 1955. It consists of seven parishes, with about eight thousand members, the majority of them living in Helsinki and the other major cities of southern Finland. The majority of priests and nuns come from the NETHERLANDS and POLAND.

Anglo-American Christianity spread to Finland during the nineteenth century, and Baptists, Methodists, the SALVATION ARMY, and SEVENTH-DAY ADVENTIST churches were established in the country. Their membership remains less than 1 percent of the total population. Pentecostal communities have approximately fifty thousand members.

References and Further Reading

Heininen, Simo, and Markku Heikkiä. *Kirchengeschichte Finnlands.* Göttingen: Vandenhoeck & Ruprecht, 2002.
Heino, Harri. "Religion and Churches in Finland." *Finfo* 10 (1998). [Published by the Ministry for Foreign Affairs, Helsinki.]
The Churches in Finland. Helsinki: The Office for Foreign Relations, The Evangelical Church of Finland, 1996. http://www.evl.fi

SIMO HEININEN

FINLEY, ROBERT (1772–1817)

American clergy. Finley was born in 1772, graduated from the College of New Jersey in 1787, and began a teaching career. Five years later he decided to enter the ministry and returned to his alma mater to study theology under JOHN WITHERSPOON. Finley pastored a New Jersey congregation for almost twenty-two years while also fostering his interests in pedagogy. He ran a school for boys and influenced school curricula to include biblical instruction. Finley also saw SLAVERY as a problem of educational methodology. Subsequently he became involved in issues of race.

In 1816 Finley traveled to Washington, D.C. to promote his plan: *Thoughts on the Colonization of Free Blacks.* He proposed to address the status of free blacks by forming an organization that would transport them to an African colony. Colonization as an idea had been considered for more than thirty years before and others participated alongside Finley for the cause. Finley's activities, however, led public opinion on the matter and attracted the attention of influential government leaders.

After the AMERICAN COLONIZATION SOCIETY was approved with Finley as a coordinator, he returned to New Jersey and endured ridicule for his cause. Returning to his interest in education, Finley resigned from his pastorate in 1817 and accepted a position as the president of the University of Georgia. Falling ill of a fever, he died the same year.

References and Further Reading

Primary Source:

Finley, Robert. *Thoughts on the Colonization of Free Blacks.* Washington, D.C.: 1816.

Secondary Sources:

Brown, Isaac V. *Memoir of the Reverend Robert Finley.* New Brunswick, NJ: Terhune and Leston, 1819.
Egerton, Douglas R. " 'Its Origin is not a little Curious': A New Look at the American Colonization Society." *Journal of the Early Republic* 5 no. 4 (1985): 463–480.

HOWELL WILLIAMS

FINNEY, CHARLES GRANDISON (1792–1875)

American revivalist. Finney was a prominent figure of the Second Great Awakening who scholars consider to be the "father of modern revivalism." Born in Warren, Connecticut, in 1792, Finney's family migrated westward to upstate New York and settled first in Oneida and later in Jefferson County. After a brief law career, he experienced CONVERSION in 1821 and soon dedicated his time to studying theology with Presbyterian minister George W. Gale in Adams, NY. The Presbytery of St. Lawrence licensed him in 1823.

Finney brought the atmosphere of the rural CAMP MEETING revivals to the growing urban population. He delivered his message using a PREACHING style called "new measures" that blended his theological and legal training. He sparked REVIVALS throughout western New York in the 1820s. Abandoning conventional Sunday sermons, Finney preached on consecutive nights in a community for several weeks. His insistence on the human agency of conversions eventually led him away from PRESBYTERIANISM to CONGREGATIONALISM.

Finney settled in New York City in 1832, where he preached at the Second Free Presbyterian Church, and later the Congregationalist Broadway Tabernacle from 1834 to 1837. He accepted a position on the faculty at Oberlin College, Ohio in 1835, where he moved permanently in 1837. Finney served as President of Oberlin from 1851 to 1866. He died in Oberlin on August 16, 1875.

Finney's urban EVANGELISM profoundly shaped the Protestant experience in the UNITED STATES. His theology is outlined in his *Lectures on Revivals* (1835) and *Lectures on Systematic Theology* (1847). Several books of his sermons were published posthumously.

References and Further Reading

Cross, Whitney R. *The Burned-Over District: The Social and Intellectual History of Enthusiastic Religion in Western New York, 1800–1850.* New York: Harper and Row, 1965.
Hambrick-Stowe, Charles. *Charles G. Finney and the Spirit of American Evangelicalism.* Grand Rapids, MI: Eerdmans, 1996.
Weddle, David L. *The Law as Gospel: Revival and Reform in the Theology of Charles G. Finney.* Metuchen, NJ: Scarecrow Press, 1985.

LEE L. WILLIS, III

FIRST AMENDMENT

See Bill of Rights

FISHER, GEOFFREY FRANCIS (1887–1972)

Archbishop of Canterbury. Fisher was born in Nuneaton in the county of Warwickshire, ENGLAND, in 1887. Educated at Oxford, he was ordained as a priest in 1913. He was a headmaster at Repton School in Derby County from 1914 to 1932. Upon retirement from that post, he was named bishop of Chester. He became bishop of London in 1939, a position he maintained through World War II.

Fisher was appointed the CHURCH OF ENGLAND's ninety-ninth archbishop of Canterbury in 1945, a position he was to hold until his retirement in 1961. A strong advocate of ECUMENISM, Fisher was the chairperson of the WORLD COUNCIL OF CHURCHES founding assembly in Amsterdam in 1948. He served as that organization's first president from 1948 to 1954.

In 1959, during a five week tour of INDIA, JAPAN, and KOREA, Fisher conducted the first official visit ever paid by an archbishop of Canterbury to Asian dioceses of the Anglican Communion. The following year, he traveled to the Vatican to meet with Pope John XXIII, becoming the first archbishop of Canterbury to visit the Pope since 1397. That same year he visited the Orthodox patriarchs of Jerusalem and Constantinople (see ORTHODOXY, EASTERN).

In 1961 Fisher was made baron of Lambeth, and he retired to the seaside county of Dorset. He died in 1972.

References and Further Reading

Primary Sources:

Fisher, Geoffrey Francis. *The Archbishop Speaks: Addresses and Speeches by the Archbishop of Canterbury, the Most Reverend Geoffrey Francis Fisher.* London: Evans Brothers, 1958.
———. *Touching on Christian Truth: The Kingdom of God, the Christian Church and the World.* Oxford, UK: A. R. Mowbray, 1971.

Secondary Source:

Carpenter, Edward. *Archbishop Fisher: His Life and Times.* Norwich, UK: Canterbury Press, 1991.

HELEN FARLEY

FISK, WILBUR (1792–1839)

American Methodist minister and educator. Born in Vermont August 31, 1792, the son of a farmer, Fisk was educated at the University of Vermont and Brown University, graduating in 1815. After attending a CAMP MEETING and having a spiritual experience that led him to a PREACHING ministry, he was ordained in the Methodist Episcopal Church in 1822, serving in circuits in Vermont and Massachusetts. However, ill health affected his ministry and he declined offers of election as bishop. In 1826 he was appointed principal of Wilbraham Wesleyan Academy, one of a growing number of Methodist schools whose cause he championed. His ministry thereafter was dedicated to the support of education and tract societies in the work of mission.

In 1831 Fisk became the first president of a chartered Methodist (Wesleyan) University at Middletown, Connecticut where he served until his death in 1839. He viewed his institution as a place where "morality and religion" were to be taught, not through proselytism but by Christian example in teaching through a broad liberal education. He was, through his pattern of life and conversation, the means of the CONVERSION of many students. He initiated a wave of development of theological education in METHODISM, with his dictum that "a cultivated church will have a cultivated ministry." His dying words were: "Education must go hand in hand with religion or the world will never be converted."

As one of American Methodism's first theologians he was a keen controversialist, writing *Calvinistic Controversy* in defense of ARMINIANISM in 1835. He was a fierce advocate of TEMPERANCE. In the SLAVERY debate he upset fellow Methodists by not aligning with abolitionists, favoring colonization instead, and was subject to much criticism in the North East Conference. His work became more widely known after a visit to Europe in 1835. He died February 22, 1839 after a short illness.

References and Further Reading

Prentice, George. *Wilbur Fisk.* Boston: Houghton, Mifflin and Co., 1890.

TIM MACQUIBAN

FLACIUS, MATTHIAS ILLYRICUS (1520–1575)

Lutheran theologian. Born to an Istrian Italo-Croatian family, drawn into evangelical-humanistic circles in Venice as a youth, Flacius's spiritual crisis brought him to study at Basel, Tübingen, and Wittenberg. MARTIN LUTHER's counsel gave him peace. Recognition of his theological aptitude won him Wittenberg's professorship of Hebrew (1544). When colleagues, led by PHILIPP MELANCHTHON, supported the compromising position of the so-called Leipzig Interim in 1549, Flacius resigned in protest against what he considered a betrayal of the gospel and Luther. He quickly became the intellectual leader of the "GNESIO-LUTHER-ANS" gathered in Magdeburg, the center of resistance to imperial, electoral Saxon church policy and "Philippist" theology, particularly on issues of public confession of faith in relation to ADIAPHORA, good works in the Christian life, and the freedom of the will.

Called to the University of Jena (1557), he fell into controversy with his colleague Viktorin Strigel on freedom of the will and with Duke Johann Friedrich the Middler on princely power in church affairs. Dismissed from his professorship, he joined NIKOLAUS GALLUS in Regensburg (1562–1566), aided Lutherans in Antwerp (1566–1567), and lived as a private scholar in Strasbourg and Frankfurt/Main. His oft-reprinted *Clavis sacrae scriptura* (1567) laid the foundations for Protestant hermeutics; his New Testament *Glossa* (1570) incorporated Lutheran insights into the form of medieval biblical commentary. His *Catalogus testium veritatis* (1556) gathered patristic evidence against the papacy, modeling use of historical materials for polemical purposes. His leadership shaped the *Magdeburg Centuries,* the church history composed by Johannes Wigand and Matthaeus Judex (1559–1574). His radical interpretation of Luther's THEOLOGY, especially his definition of original SIN as the essence or substance of sinners, alienated him from most, even in his own circle.

See also Gallus, Nikolaus; Gnesio-Lutherans; Luther, Martin; Melanchthon, Philipp

References and Further Reading

Olson, Oliver K. *Matthias Flacius and the Survival of Luther's Reform.* Wiesbaden, Germany: Harrassowitz, 2002.
Preger, Wilhelm. *Matthias Flacius Illyricus und seine Zeit.* 2 vols. Munich, Germany: Blaesing, 1859, 1861.

ROBERT KOLB

FONTAINEBLEAU, EDICT OF

Issued by French King Louis XIV on October 17, 1685, the Edict of Fontainebleau revoked the Edict of Nantes. It declared CALVINISM illegal in FRANCE and led to the HUGUENOT exodus from France.

In 1598, King Henry IV issued the Edict of Nantes out of political necessity. It brought an end to nearly three decades of religiously motivated civil and political strife, when it became obvious that Calvinism was not strong enough to become the authorized religion in France. The Edict of Nantes created an uneasy truce; it did not, however, settle any major issues. By the mid-seventeenth century (largely because of the Revolution and CIVIL WAR in ENGLAND), Calvinism had become identified with Republicanism. For Louis XIV, the Calvinists represented a religious and political threat to his absolutist ideals and a religious threat to his Catholic Church.

The Edict of Fontainebleau is comprised of only twelve articles. Article 1 formally revoked the Edict of Nantes and ordered the destruction of all R.P.R. (*Religion prétendue réformée*—"The Allegedly Reformed," as they were called by Catholics) churches. Articles 2 and 3 forbade Reformed worship either in private or in public by commoners or the nobility. Articles 4, 5, and 6 dealt with Reformed CLERGY. Those not accepting the Catholic faith were given fifteen days to leave the country. To make CONVERSION to Catholicism more appealing, clergy were granted generous benefits, and the transition from pastor to attorney was made easier. Articles 7 and 8 dealt with children and required Catholic BAPTISM and the closing of Protestant schools. Article 9 allowed for the repatriation of R.P.R. émigrés during a four-month clemency. After that, their property was to be confiscated. Article 10 provided for severe punishment for Calvinists attempting to leave France. Article 11 concerned relapsed Catholics. Article 12, finally, allowed Calvinists "freedom of conscience." The king seemed unwilling to force Calvinists to practice Catholicism.

Despite the threat of punishment, Huguenots fled France by the tens of thousands. They migrated to the United Provinces, GERMANY (notably Prussia), Great Britain, SWITZERLAND, and the American Colonies.

References and Further Reading

Golden, R., ed. The Huguenot Connection: the Edict of Nantes, its Revocation, and Early French Migration to South Carolina. Dordrecht: M. Nijhoff, 1988.
Labrousse, Elisabeth. *Une Foi, Une Loi, Un Roi?* Geneva, Switzerland: Labor et Fides, 1985.

DAVID WHITFORD

FORSYTH, PETER TAYLOR (1848–1921)

British theologian. Forsyth was one of the most influential British Protestant theologians of the early twentieth century. A gifted pastor and educator, he was also a prodigious theological scholar who published some twenty-five books, several hundred articles, and a number of other lesser works (although he resisted the temptation to write a formal, systematic theology), which contributed to the religious debates of his own time. It was only after his death, however, especially after two World Wars had wreaked devastation in Europe, that his THEOLOGY achieved both popular and critical acclaim.

Theological Foundations

Of Scottish birth and ancestry, Forsyth studied classical literature and moral philosophy in his native country before traveling to GERMANY to sit at the feet of the great Protestant theologian ALBRECHT RITSCHL. Although raised within the liberal tradition of Ritschl and GEORG W. F. HEGEL, Forsyth's theology came into its own only as he began to distance himself imperceptibly from the LIBERAL PROTESTANTISM of his youth, then very much in the ascendancy. The catalyst that initiated this important transformation in his religious thinking was never made entirely clear, although it appears to have centered on two primary convictions. First, Forsyth came to believe that his own sinfulness had rendered futile any effort to know God and to advance God's kingdom on earth. Second, he concluded that the serious business of "real life" had not been well served by the principal tenets of liberal Protestantism: liberalism, he remarked, was "too sentimental"; it "interpreted the heavenly Fatherhood by the earthly," instead of the other way around; its "ethic was more altruistic than evangelical, more of effort than of faith"; and it "canonized freedom instead of an authority that makes free." Liberalism was, he concluded, "a spent movement" (*The Examiner,* November 5, 1905:462). In its place, Forsyth embraced an early form of NEO-ORTHODOXY. Although this new theological position has proved difficult to pin down, it could be described as being biblical, positive, and evangelical in nature, although it did not entirely abandon an emphasis on the rational and relational.

The consequence of this spiritual transformation was significant. At a time when evangelical theology had become unfashionable, Forsyth encouraged the church to recover the good news of God's grace, forgiveness, and new life. God offers the world this free gift, Forsyth contended, and it is here—not in the despair of liberalism—that the heart of the Christian life, and of all reality, is found. In advancing these doctrines, Forsyth (as has often been observed) anticipated much of what later emerged in the important work of scholars such as KARL BARTH and C. H. Dodd.

Writings

Forsyth's theology was advanced in numerous books, articles, and lectures. These concentrated principally on three areas: the work and person of Christ, the church and SACRAMENTS, PRAYER and mission. His most influential writings included *Positive Preaching and the Modern Mind* (1907), in which he commends PREACHING as an act of WORSHIP—a divine/human encounter—that is shared by both preacher and congregation; *The Person and Place of Jesus Christ* (1909), a stirring account of the mystery of the Incarnation and perhaps Forsyth's most influential publication; *The Work of Christ* (1910), a confident proclamation of the place of the Cross at the center of all human reality; *The Principle of Authority* (1913), a major work outlining Forsyth's philosophy of religion and his epistemology; *The Justification of God* (1916), an attempt to advance a credible theodicy in the midst of the horrors of the First World War; and *The Church and the Sacraments* (1917), an illustration of the author's growing appreciation for the efficacy of the sacraments of BAPTISM and holy communion.

Biographical

Forsyth was born of modest means at Aberdeen, SCOTLAND on May 12, 1848, the eldest of five children. After graduating from the University of Aberdeen (M.A., 1869) he pursued further studies in theology at the University of Göttingen and at New College, London. In 1876 he was ordained into the Congregational ministry, serving as pastor to five English churches in succession: Shipley, Yorkshire (1876–1880); St. Thomas' Square, Hackney, London (1880–1885); Cheetam Hill, Manchester (1885–1889); Clarendon Park, Leicester (1888–1894); and Emmanuel Church, Cambridge (1894–1901). In 1877 he married Minna Magness (d. 1894), by whom he had one daughter, Jessie; in 1898 he married Bertha Ison. In 1901 he was appointed principal of New College. Four years later he was elected chair of the Congregational Union of ENGLAND and WALES. He made two voyages to the UNITED STATES, in 1899 to address the Congregational assembly being held in Boston, and in 1907 to deliver the LYMAN BEECHER lectures at Yale. In 1910 he became dean of the faculty of theology of the University of London.

By nature Forsyth was practical, compassionate, and energetic, although his health was never robust. He was quick witted, a gifted conversationalist, and (not surprising, given his Celtic origins) deeply passionate and poetic. In many ways he remained something of a populist, disinclined to become involved in the more speculative forms of theology. This may help to explain why he never attained the level of academic fame achieved by less able colleagues. Exhausted by the demands of office, as well as by the moral failure associated with the First World War, Forsyth died on November 11, 1921—Armistice Day.

References and Further Reading

Bradley, W. L. *P. T. Forsyth, The Man and His Work.* London: Independent Press, 1952.
Brown, Robert McAfee. *P. T. Forsyth: Prophet for Today.* Philadelphia, PA: Westminster Press, 1952.

Hart, Trevor, ed. *Justice The True and Only Mercy: Essays on the Life and Theology of Peter Taylor Forsyth.* Edinburgh: T&T Clark, 1995.

Hunter, A. M. *P. T. Forsyth.* London: Westminster Press, 1974.

McCurdy, Leslie. *Attributes and Atonement: The Holy Love of God in the Theology of P. T. Forsyth.* Carlisle, Cumbria, UK: Paternoster, 1999.

Miller, Donald G., Brown Barr, and Robert S. Paul. *P. T. Forsyth: The Man, The Preachers' Theologian, Prophet for the 20th Century.* Pittsburgh, PA: Pickwick Press, 1981.

Pitt, Clifford S. *Church, Ministry and Sacraments.* Washington, D.C.: University Press of America, 1983.

Rogers, John H. *The Theology of P. T. Forsyth.* London: Independent Press, 1965.

GRAYSON CARTER

FOSDICK, HARRY EMERSON (1878–1969)

American preacher. Fosdick was born in Buffalo, New York, on May 24, 1878 and raised in a pious Baptist family. He had a CONVERSION experience at age seven and decided on a life of Christian service. An excellent student, Fosdick graduated at the top of his class in both high school and college. During his years at Colgate University, he experienced his first serious illness, a depression that challenged his FAITH. The illness returned in his first year at Union Theological Seminary in New York City. He left school, turning first to his fiancee and then to his family. He tried to take his own life, but his father interrupted him, and then found him help. Fosdick entered a sanitarium and then took a trip to ENGLAND. He returned to Union in the fall of 1902, recovered, and with a renewed enthusiasm for the ministry, graduated *summa cum laude* in 1904. The dark night of his soul led him to a lifelong commitment to pastoral counseling for others facing similar circumstances. The year that he graduated from seminary he married Florence Allen Whitney, who became his lifelong partner and support in ministry.

Fosdick's first pastorate, First Baptist Church in Montclair, New Jersey, set the pattern for his life. He worked hard at his PREACHING, preparing and honing his sermons, and the church grew under his leadership. He believed that preaching and pastoral counseling were closely related and said on occasion that preaching was pastoral counseling on a group scale. He found time to accept a part-time appointment at Union Theological Seminary as a lecturer, to preach at colleges around the nation, to become involved in civic affairs, and to teach in a variety of BIBLE conferences. He published several books, including *The Manhood of the Master* (1913) and *The Meaning of Prayer* (1915). The sermons and books were very popular and fixed him in the minds of many in his generation as a leading apologist for the Christian faith.

In 1915 Fosdick left his Montclair pulpit to become the Morris Jesup Professor of Practical Theology at Union Theological Seminary. He was an early advocate of America's entry into World War I and wrote a book in support of the war, titled *The Challenge of the Present Crisis.* When the UNITED STATES entered the war, he took a leave from Union and went to Europe for a six-month tour of duty as preacher and chaplain under the auspices of the YMCA (see YMCA/YWCA). His experiences on the front lines and the disillusionment of the postwar era turned him away from war and toward PACIFISM. He later said that his book on the war was the only one he regretted writing. He remained a firm pacifist, even after Pearl Harbor and throughout World War II.

Fosdick made a very important decision in 1918, when he agreed to become the Preaching Minister at First Presbyterian Church in New York City. The placement of a liberal Baptist in one of the most prominent Presbyterian pulpits in the nation brought serious objections from conservative Presbyterians across the land. He became involved in the growing fundamentalist–modernist debate in Protestant life, a debate that raged most vigorously in the two major denominations in his life, the BAPTISTS and the Presbyterians (see PRESBYTERIANISM). In 1922 he preached what became his most famous sermon, "Shall the Fundamentalists Win?" This sermon became a national benchmark of the theological debate, in part because John D. Rockefeller, Jr., arranged to mail a copy to every ordained Protestant minister in America. Two books he wrote in this period added fuel to the theological fire: *Christianity and Progress* (1922) and *The Modern Use of the Bible* (1924). As the debate heated up, the leadership of "Old First" refused to ask him to resign. His status eventually became an issue for the General Assembly of the PRESBYTERIAN CHURCH IN THE U.S.A. which invited him to join the Presbyterian Church on condition that he adhere to the WESTMINISTER CONFESSION OF FAITH.

Faced with many conflicting choices, Fosdick decided to resign from First Presbyterian Church and accept a call to be pastor of Park Avenue Baptist Church in New York City. The congregation, with the support of John D. Rockefeller, Jr., soon moved to a new site on Morningside Heights. The grand gothic-style Riverside Church opened in 1931, and with Fosdick in the pulpit became one of the major centers of Protestant worship. He preached at Riverside and taught at nearby Union Theological Seminary until his retirement from both places in 1946.

At Park Avenue and Riverside, Fosdick assumed a wide variety of leadership roles in Protestant life. Crowds lined up waiting to get into church to hear him preach, typically filling the cavernous sanctuary of

Riverside. In 1927 he launched the "National Vespers Hour," a radio ministry, and quickly became the leading radio preacher in the nation. He continued to write extensively, including *A Guide to Understanding the Bible* (1938). His hymns include the popular "God of Grace and God of Glory" (see HYMNS AND HYMNALS). His work in pastoral counseling led him to the study and use of psychological insights in his work and to the publication of *On Being a Real Person* (1943). A SOCIAL GOSPEL advocate throughout his ministry, he sustained his interest in racial and economic justice issues during his Riverside years and supported the birth-control movement. His voice on these issues was an important one even though he rarely took prophetic positions. He was alert to winds of theological change in the 1930s and announced in an important sermon in 1935 that "The Church Must Go Beyond Modernism." He led an active life in retirement, during which he published his autobiography, *The Living of These Days* (1956).

Fosdick died on October 5, 1969. He is known as one of the most prominent leaders of liberal Protestantism in America in the first half of the twentieth century and arguably the best-known American preacher and pastor of his generation.

See also Fundamentalism; Liberal Protestantism and Liberalism; Modernism

References and Further Reading

Primary Sources:

Archival collections are: The Fosdick Collection at Union Theological Seminary, New York; Fosdick papers at the Riverside Church, New York; and substantial Fosdick materials in the Rockefeller Family and Associates Archives.

Fosdick, Harry Emerson. *The Meaning of Prayer*. New York; London: Association Press, 1915.

———. *Riverside Sermons*. New York: Harper, 1958.

———. *Dear Dr. Brown: Letters to a Person Perplexed About Religion*. New York: Harper, 1961.

Secondary Source:

Miller, Robert Moats. *Harry Emerson Fosdick: Preacher, Pastor, Prophet*. New York: Oxford Univ. Press, 1985.

JOHN PIPER

FOX, GEORGE (1624–1691)

Founder of the quaker movement. Englishman George Fox was born in Fenny Drayton in Leicestershire in July 1624 into a religious family, the son of a successful weaver, Christopher Fox, and his wife Mary, née Lago. A serious and taciturn youth, Fox was intended for the ministry but was instead apprenticed to a shoemaker. When he was about nineteen years old, the hypocritical heavy drinking of his puritan associates initiated in him a protracted spiritual crisis. In September 1643, seemingly unaware of the turmoil of CIVIL WAR that had broken out in the previous August, he began an extended journey in the Midlands and south of England in pursuit of spiritual illumination, but instead experienced acute despair. He sought, in vain, guidance from various ministers of religion, spent time in London in the midst of the English capital's intense religious ferment of the 1640s, and paid two visits to his family in Leicestershire (where an unsuccessful attempt was made to recruit him for military service in the civil war).

Fox continued to look, to no avail, for rescue out of his spiritual dilemmas at the hands of leading godly ministers, but from 1646 on, underwent a set of revelations that slowly began to set him on the road to recovery, although he remained, at that stage, still prone to acute dejection. Included in these insights was a perception that true ministry was not restricted to university-educated clerics and that God did not dwell in churches but in the hearts of the faithful. What he called the "openings" of scripture helped to rescue him from what he termed his condition as a "man of sorrows." Still essentially solitary, from early in 1647 he began a further tour in the Midlands in search of peace of mind, and his depressions began to alternate with exaltations. In the end he found the relief he sought, not in guidance from religious experts, but from a personal encounter with Christ as his savior and guide. Thus Fox acquired what he called a "pure fire" and sense of discernment of truth, giving him deep insights into the creation and the perfectability of humanity. He next felt called to share with others his own newly found son-ship with God and to draw them away from what he saw as the human-centered artifices of the religion of his day.

Early in 1649 his challenge to existing religious systems became overt when, in Nottingham, he vehemently denounced parish worship and faced the first in a series of arrests and imprisonments that punctuated the rest of his career. After a brief incarceration in Nottingham, Fox underwent a year-long jail sentence in Derby until his release in autumn 1651. His missionary range was now about to be extended into the north, into Yorkshire and, eventually, in 1652, to the Westmorland hills, where his encounters with spiritual aspirants known as Seekers brought Fox together with men and women who probably formed incipient Quakerism as much as Fox did. Also in 1652, Fox stopped at the godly gentry home at Swarthmoor in north Lancashire, west of the Westmorland hills, and made a large-scale conversion amidst this religious family, including the wife of the squire, Margaret Fell, whom, after her husband's death, Fox was to marry in 1669.

In 1653 he faced his third major imprisonment, in Carlisle in Cumberland. In the following years the Quaker movement grew at a rapid rate, though Fox was faced with a challenge to his leadership of the movement from the charismatic James Nayler (1617–1660). A further challenge, to the survival of the Quaker movement as a whole, came with the restoration in 1660 of the monarchy and the CHURCH OF ENGLAND, accompanied by repressive legislation against dissidents such as the Quakers. A sufferer along with his movement, Fox underwent imprisonment from 1663 to 1666, but also in the 1660s, with Margaret Fell, built the Quaker organization into a resilient defensive structure of pyramidal regional and national meetings. Fox also played a vital role in the missionary spread of the Quaker movement, conducting an extended itinerancy throughout ENGLAND, but also launched out to IRELAND, the West Indies, America, and the NETHERLANDS. George Fox died in Gracechurch Street, London on January 13, 1691. While recognition must be accorded to Fox's originality and rejection of the religious conventions of his age, particular interpretative emphasis in this article is on his place within the Protestant tradition.

Fox and English Protestantism

In the first place we should recognize the classic English Protestant features of Fox's antecedents and background. His Protestant credentials were, indeed, impeccable. As he proudly tells us in his *Autobiography,* his mother was "an upright woman . . . and of the stock of the martyrs." The latter phrase indicates that Fox could lay claim to descent either from England's Protestants executed by Queen Mary in the mid-1550s or that he was descended from England's pre-Reformation Lollards (their founder, John Wyclif [c. 1329–1384], lived in Fox's native Leicestershire). However, his mother's devout Protestant influence on Fox was more than merely a matter of ancestry. As Fox's Quaker eulogist, WILLIAM PENN (1644–1718), recalled, she fostered his religious development, bringing to bear Stuart PURITANISM's sensitivity to the state of individuals' psyches: she, Penn recalled, "taking notice of his singular temper and the gravity, wisdom, and piety that very early shined through him, refusing childish and vain sports and company when very young, was tender and indulgent over him . . . ."

Thus the ardent Protestant Mary Fox played the kind of religious influencing role toward her son that the pious Susanna Wesley performed toward her sons, the founders of METHODISM, JOHN (1703–1791) and CHARLES (1707–1788) WESLEY. However, young Fox was also exposed to the pious Protestant mentoring of his godly father Christopher Fox, known to his neighbors, sardonically or not, as "Righteous Christer." If the influence of a godly, indeed explicitly puritan, home background were not enough to expose the growing George Fox to the moral, spiritual, and doctrinal strains of English Protestantism, then the teaching he heard as an adolescent in his Fenny Drayton parish church was indubitably of the Reformation. In the late 1630s and early 1640s Fenny Drayton parish was in the safe Protestant hands of Nathaniel Stephens (1606/7–1678), a Calvinist minister with whom young Fox was wont to discuss theology. Though Fox was later to reject Stephens and his teaching, this minister's markedly Protestant outlook provided one of the several forms of Protestantism's impress upon him.

It was the coalescence of such impressions that induced Fox to face, in an anguished, experiential way, those issues of salvation and damnation that also haunted MARTIN LUTHER (1483–1546), JOHN BUNYAN (1628–1688), and John Wesley. Like his predecessor, Luther, and his contemporary, Bunyan, Fox knew despair, the key word for his condition, which he used three times in one short paragraph of his *Journal,* a work that rings with the anguished authenticity of the other great English Protestant spiritual classics of the seventeenth century. In 1646 Fox was beginning to find his way out of the maze of his despondency with a variant of the central Protestant doctrine of justification by faith: " . . . if all were believers, then they . . . passed from death to life . . . ." However, the focus of this formula was the christocentricity of the Protestant Reformation, "relying," as Fox wrote, "wholly on the lord Jesus Christ." Indeed, Fox's Protestant interpretation of Christ's sole saving role was summed up in his realization that all men and women "are concluded under sin and shut up in unbelief, as I had been—that Jesus Christ might have the pre-eminence—who enlightens and gives grace and faith and power. . . . by Jesus, the opener of the door with his heavenly key, the entrance was given. . . . all was done, and to be done, in and by Christ . . . all was done by Christ the life, and my belief was in him." Thus Fox echoed Luther's evangelical centering on Christ crucified as the sole medium of our redemption: as Luther wrote in his commentary on the Epistle to the Galatians, " . . . I openly teach and confess, that no man can obtain the favour of God, righteousness and salvation, but by Christ alone. . . . "

Fox and the Reformation

Fox's christology was, like Luther's, concentrated on the redeeming work of Jesus Christ on the Cross. Fox derived a theology of the cross from the Reformation, whose influences were so pervasive in the England in which Fox grew to maturity. Calvin's impress was even heavier in that profoundly Protestant religious culture, so it should in no way surprise us to hear Fox echoing, and also building on, the thinking of the Genevan reformer. This is particularly the case in the way that Calvin, in the *Institutes,* unfolded Christ's roles as prophet, priest, and king. Christ's all-sufficiency in these "offices"—for example, as prophet where "Outside Christ there is nothing worth knowing"—could be taken to mean that either a teaching authority, or papal or episcopal rule, or sacerdotal ministry or sacrificial rite (the Mass) claimed by a church such as that of Rome were negated by Christ's prophetic, kingly, and priestly offices. When Fox took up analysis of these functions of Christ, he both accepted them and added to them, providing no fewer than eleven such offices, including that of bishop, but in such a way as to follow and build on Calvin in the latter's affirming of Christ as the sole and sufficient ruler of, and provider for, His church.

If Calvin drew attention to Christ's priesthood, Luther is forever associated with insight into the universal priesthood of faith. The concept was set out in his 1520 work, *The Address to the Christian Nobility of the German Nation Concerning the Amelioration of the Christian Estate:* " . . . our baptism consecrates us all without exception, and makes us all priests. . . . All [Christians] have spiritual status, and are truly priests . . . ." In his *Commentary on St. Paul's Epistle to the Galations* (a work better known in England than some of Luther's other writings, thanks to a translated edition of 1575), Luther extended the inclusive, or universalist, implications of the priesthood of all believers to take in the equal status of all under and in Christ: " . . . in Christ . . . there is no difference of persons . . . but all are one. For there is but one body, one spirit, one hope of vocation for all . . . ." The difference between Luther and Fox in this regard is that while Luther tended to pass over the implications for women of this egalitarian doctrine of the church, Fox lovingly expatiated on a church order like that of his SOCIETY OF FRIENDS in which women shared equality of status. Indeed, he drew on a string of holy women of the New Testament, and especially on Mary Magdalene, who announced the Lord's resurrection, to establish that "If male and female have received the testimony of Jesus, they have received the spirit of prophecy." Fox thereby extended the Reformation principle of the priesthood of all believers along a line of logical sequence to female equality fully and explicitly articulate.

This, though, was less a derivation from Luther himself than the working out of the source common to both Luther and Fox, Paul. Luther, who grounded his Reformation theology in Paul, and above all in a doctrine of redemption he found in the Epistle to the Romans, was, predictably, generous in his acknowledgments of his indebtedness to "the apostle." Because the commentary on Galatians is an exegesis of a Pauline epistle, it is not surprising that Luther's reliance on Paul is evident in his citation of him in favor of the elimination, in Christ, of status distinctions. However, in the *Address to the Christian Nobility,* Luther also adduced Paul in favor of the abrogation of differentiations of race, rank, and gender, using such phrases as "This is St. Paul's meaning. . . . This is supported by Romans 12 and I Corinthians 12 . . . ." The only remaining piece that needs to be put in place is Fox's Luther-like dependence on Paul's authority. In *The Woman Learning in Silence,* for example, first published in 1656 and forming the classic statement of Quaker gender egalitarianism in the church, Fox freely cites "the apostle" in favor of his views.

Fox's reliance on Paul should be seen as placing him quite firmly within a broad Protestant tradition, but ought also to be viewed as part of a strongly Protestant appreciation of the authority of Scripture as a whole. Luther's reverence for the Bible is well known; he was, as he said, "captive to the word of God" and in 1519, for example, he wrote, "We must let Scripture have the chief place and be its own truest, simplest and clearest interpreter . . . ." What, though, might surprise those who believe that Fox and the Quakers put scripture on a par with other, and more immediate, forms of revelation is that Fox also recognized the uniqueness and inerrancy of the Bible, as he wrote in *The True Christians Distinguished* (1689):

> The holy scriptures of truth are the truest history that is on the earth of the creation of God; of what God has done himself; and what God has done by his prophets and holy men and women; what God has done by Christ his son. . . . . So the scripture of truth is the best book of truth upon the earth to be read, believed, fulfilled and practised.

There are other senses in which Fox can be identified with the Protestant traditions of the European and English Reformations: for example, as his *Journal* records, he was conventionally and narrowly anti-Catholic. It may well be, though, that Fox, born in the reign that gave the English the Authorized Version of the scripture, was at his most Protestant in his deference to the Bible—as his recent biographer Larry Ingle writes, "a true heir of the Protestant Reformation" (Ingle 1994: p. XX).

References and Further Reading

Barbour, Hugh. *The Quakers in Puritan England.* New Haven and London: Yale University Press, 1964.

Braithwaite, William Charles. *The Beginnings of Quakerism.* Second, Revised (Henry J. Cadbury) Edition. Cambridge: Cambridge University Press, 1970.

Davies, Horton. *Worship and Theology in England from Andrewes to Baxter and Fox, 1603–1690.* Princeton, NJ: Princeton University Press, 1975.

Ingle, H. Larry. *First Among Friends: George Fox and the Creation of Quakerism.* New York, Oxford: Oxford University Press, 1994.

Mullett, Michael, ed. *New Light on George Fox 1624–1691.* York: The Ebor Press, n.d. (1993).

Ross, Hugh McGregor, ed. *George Fox Speaks for Himself.* York: The Ebor Press, 1991.

MICHAEL A. MULLETT

FOXE, JOHN (1517–1587)

English preacher and writer. John Foxe compiled the *Acts and Monuments of These Latter and Perilous Times,* an extraordinarily influential ecclesiastical history that has been known from the beginning as *The Book of Martyrs.* Martyrologies in this encyclopedic collection identify medieval heretics such as Jan Hus and John Wyclif and sixteenth-century Protestants with the "true" church of Christ under attack by the ANTICHRIST, whom Foxe identifies with the pope and the Church of Rome.

Foxe was born in Boston, Lincolnshire, in 1517. Little is known concerning his parentage. As a student at Oxford University, he received B.A. and M.A. degrees. He resigned his fellowship at Magdalen College in line with Protestant rejection of the vow of CELIBACY required of permanent fellows, who entered into religious orders. In 1547 he married Agnes Randall, who bore his many children. After moving to London during the same year, Foxe entered into service of the Duchess of Richmond and tutored the children of her late brother, Henry Howard, Earl of Surrey. During the zealously Protestant regime of Edward VI (1547–1553), Foxe published Latin treatises on religious and social issues, and translated tracts by MARTIN LUTHER and other German Protestants.

Foxe's ordination as DEACON in 1550 initiated his career as a Protestant preacher. At about this time, he began the historical research that occupied the rest of his life. At the accession of Queen Mary I (1553–1558), a militant Catholic, Foxe emigrated from ENGLAND to Strasbourg, FRANCE, where he published the first installment of his history of the martyrs, *Commentarii Rerum in Ecclesia Gestarum* (1554). It focused on late medieval figures, notably John Wyclif, the Lollard martyrs, and Jan Hus, whom Foxe regarded as proto-Protestants. He soon moved to Frankfurt, GERMANY, where he participated in liturgical controversy, and then to Basel, SWITZERLAND, where he worked as a proofreader employed by the printer Joannes Oporinus.

Persecution during the reign of Mary I resulted in the death of more than 300 Protestants. Foxe collected gruesome manuscript records concerning HERESY interrogations, torture, and eyewitness accounts concerning the comportment and last words spoken by Martyrs as they were burnt alive (see MARTYRS AND MARTYROLOGIES). Edmund Grindal, an English exile who later became archbishop of Canterbury, helped gather these martyrologic documents and urged Foxe to compile them in chronicle form. As the martyrologist engaged in this research, he completed *Christus Triumphans* (1556), an "apocalyptic comedy" that embeds persecution and suffering within the transcendent framework of providential history that Foxe derived from the Book of Revelation.

The death of Mary I and accession of Elizabeth I (1558–1603) enabled Foxe to return to England. Before leaving Basel, he published *Rerum in Ecclesia Gestarum* (1559), a sequel to his *Commentarii* that extends his account of religious persecution from late medieval times through the reign of Mary I. After Edmund Grindal ordained Foxe as a priest in 1560, Foxe received patronage from the bishops of Salisbury and Norwich, JOHN JEWEL and John Parkhurst. His failure to rise high in the church hierarchy may be due to his adherence to the first wave of Puritan protest during the 1560s.

In 1563, John Day, the Protestant master printer, published the first edition of THE ACTS AND MONUMENTS. Foxe compiled it as a Protestant alternative to medieval legends of SAINTS, whose accounts of miracles, cures, and magical feats occupied an important place in Roman Catholic devotion. Basing the text on his two previous Latin chronicles in addition to a great variety of manuscript and printed sources, Foxe collaborated with Day in the production of the best-illustrated English book of its age. It is notable for woodcut portrayals of the "true" sainthood of scores of Protestant martyrs.

In collaboration with Day, Foxe oversaw expansion of this massive ecclesiastical history to more than three million words in three revised editions published between 1570 and 1583. This collection of fervid stories supported re-establishment of Protestant theological DOCTRINE under Queen Elizabeth and stirred up intense hostility against the regime of Mary I, the papacy, and the Church of Rome. The book became widely known when chained copies of the 1570 edition were placed in English cathedrals under order from the Convocation. Five more unabridged editions were published by the end of the seventeenth century. These editions contained an extraordinary array of genres (e.g., martyrologies, poems, letters, and tracts).

These folio editions constitute the most physically imposing and complex English books of their time.

Foxe engaged in other projects, including collaboration with Day on an edition of writings by three renowned reformers: *The Whole Works of William Tyndale, John Frith, and Doctor Robert Barnes* (1573). Until his death in London, he labored on a commentary on Revelation that was published posthumously as *Eicasmi seu Meditationes in Sacram Apocalypsin* (1587).

Roman Catholic readers attacked the truthfulness of *The Book of Martyrs* soon after its initial appearance. Although Foxe's handling of documents is generally accurate, he altered sources and selected partisan narratives to which he attached inflammatory comments. Controversy concerning Foxe's trustworthiness underwent renewal during preparation of a nineteenth-century edition of Foxe's text. During the late twentieth century, William Haller's influential thesis that this book praises England as an "elect nation" has undergone qualification by Richard Bauckham and others, who have demonstrated that Haller suppressed the broadly European scope of Foxe's history of Christianity.

References and Further Reading

Primary Source:

Foxe, John. *Facsimile of John Foxe's "Book of Martyrs," 1583: Actes and Monuments of Matters Most Special and Memorable*. Edited by David G. Newcombe with Michael Pidd. Oxford, UK: Oxford University Press for the British Academy, 2000.

Secondary Sources:

Bauckham, Richard. *Tudor Apocalypse*. Appleford, UK: Sutton Courtenay Press, 1978.

Haller, William. *The Elect Nation: The Meaning and Relevance of Foxe's "Book of Martyrs."* New York: Harper & Row, 1963.

Highley, Christopher, and John N. King, eds. *John Foxe and His World*. St. Aldershot, Hants, UK: Ashgate, 2002.

King, John. *Tudor Royal Iconography: Literature and Art in an Age of Religious Crisis*. Princeton, NJ: Princeton University Press, 1989.

Loades, David, ed. *John Foxe and the English Reformation*. Aldershot, Hants, UK: Scolar Press, 1997.

———, ed. *John Foxe: An Historical Perspective*. Aldershot, Hants, UK: Ashgate, 1999.

JOHN N. KING

FRANCE

The French Protestant community is small but disproportionately influential in national life. This has been true for the greater part of its history. Largely a Calvinist constituency, France's Protestant population includes a Lutheran element (especially in eastern France) and a number of minority churches. Questions of liberty and toleration are of considerable importance to all these groups—unsurprisingly, given the centuries of persecution endured by French Protestants in the early modern period. Indirectly, if not directly, these experiences still resonate at the turn of the millennium.

Facts and Figures

Accurate estimates of the total Protestant population in France are difficult in that they necessarily depend on a clear definition of the term "Protestant." Most commentators agree on a figure of one million or approximately 2 percent of the French population. Looser definitions of the term or differently worded questions in a public opinion survey will sometimes attract a larger response. In 1980 for example, 4.5 percent of French people declared themselves to be "close to Protestantism"; clearly this group included many who rarely, if ever, set foot in a Protestant place of worship and some who continued to be members of the Catholic Church.

Protestants in France are split into three groups. The largest (460,000) constitutes the Reformed community—a group lying squarely in the Calvinist tradition (JOHN CALVIN, 1509–1564, was born and educated in France). A smaller but still sizeable group (280,000) is composed of Lutherans, a community found largely in eastern France. The final section (210,000) is made up of a variety of smaller, mostly evangelical groups, many of which owe their existence to waves of evangelism that took place in the nineteenth and twentieth centuries. The great majority of French Protestants are affiliated with the *Fédération Protestante de France*—the exceptions can be found among the smaller congregations that resist membership for both doctrinal and ecclesiological reasons.

A second organizational divide reflects the particular status of all churches (not only Protestant ones) in the Alsace-Moselle region. These *départements* found themselves in Germany rather than France at the time of the separation of church and state (1905). For this reason, the Napoleonic concordat rather than Republican legislation provides the framework for ecclesiastical administration. Protestant pastors (like their Catholic counterparts) are paid by the state, and courses of religious education (Catholic, Protestant, and Jewish) continue in the school system. The University of Strasbourg incorporates both a Catholic and a Protestant theology faculty; the possibility of a Muslim equivalent is currently under review. None of these features are present in metropolitan France.

The geographical distribution of Protestants in France is uneven. Apart from the community in Paris, the majority of the Reformed constituency can be found in a semicircle south of the Massif central, with concentrations in the Ardèche, the Gard and up to a point in the *départements* of the southwest. As the rural exodus continues, the principal centers of Reformed Protestantism (outside Paris) can be found in Marseilles, Nimes, and Montpellier, though important traces of the rural community in the Gard can still be seen, epitomized in the Musée du Désert area. The Lutheran community is found in eastern France, where the links with their German counterparts have been and still are most easily effected.

The economic and social composition of the French Protestant community is equally skewed. It contains disproportionate numbers of professionals, from both the business and the service sector, notably teachers. The rural population (from the Cévennes, for example) is rapidly diminishing given the movement of the population as a whole away from rural areas. There has never been a sizeable urban working class among French Protestants, except in pockets in the east.

Historical Perspective

Long years of persecution provide the dominant theme in the history of French Protestantism. From 1523 (the date of the first burning in this history of martyrdom and reprisal), the Protestants of France were in a position of self-defense. It is important to remember, in this respect, the considerable threat they posed to a unitary state; at the end of the sixteenth century, approximately one-third of the French population were Huguenots. Had the balance of history moved in a slightly different direction, the religious map of Europe would look very different indeed, but this did not happen. France remained a Catholic country that eventually came to terms with the Protestant minority within its boundaries. The struggle, however, continued for centuries.

The persecution was not always equally intense. The first wave came to an end in 1598 with the passing of the Edict of Nantes. This edict was well ahead of its time in accepting the principle of two religions within one state, but contained basic contradictions that became increasingly evident. It was essentially a pragmatic solution to particular circumstance and despite all its claims to be perpetual and irrevocable, it was unlikely to endure in the changing circumstance of the seventeenth century. It is true that French Protestantism enjoyed one of its brief periods of respite under Louis XIII and in the first part of Louis XIV's reign, but this did not last. Through the second part of the seventeenth century, Louis took an increasingly harsh

view of those of his realm who were not of the Catholic faith. The revocation of the Edict of Nantes (1685) was but the culmination of a series of measures, the passing of which implied, with increasing clarity, that a Protestant, by his or her very being, was in contradiction with the king. In 1685 all pretenses were dropped; the Edict of Revocation had the intention of destroying the supposedly reformed church (*Eglise Prétendue Réformée*) and of liquidating those who professed its faith.

Those who could do so, fled, dramatically reducing the size of the Protestant community in France; those who remained simply endured. How they did so (there are countless examples of courage and heroism) constitutes the most significant feature in the collective memory of French Protestantism. It continues to resonate some three hundred years later.

The situation gradually eased in the course of the eighteenth century, leading eventually to the Edict of Toleration in 1787. It was, however, the FRENCH REVOLUTION and the Napoleonic legislation of 1802 that gave the Protestant community its legal existence in a definitive sense. With this in mind, it is hardly surprising that the Protestants became increasingly, if not unanimously, committed to the Republican ideal through the course of the nineteenth century. This should not be seen as a simple or automatic endorsement; rather it came about as each reminder of a conservative alliance between throne and altar (and there were several in the nineteenth century) led to uncomfortable circumstances for the Protestants. The exception in this respect was the Orleanist monarchy (1830–1848); the death of the Duc d'Orléans in an accident in 1842 was as much a disaster for the Protestant community as it was for anyone in France.

The Third Republic offered Protestants a unique opportunity. Not only were they tolerated, they found themselves in a position to contribute positively to the Republican legislation on (a) church and state, and (b) the creation of a Republican school system. The latter, in fact, precedes the former. All three of French politician Jules Ferry's (1832–1893) advisers at this crucial moment in the history of French education were Protestant pastors (Ferdinand Buisson, Félix Pécaut, and Jules Steeg). Such people represented a midway position in the public debates of the period: neither clerical nor anticlerical, they were well placed to make a lasting contribution to the new school system. Their influence far outweighed the numerical significance of the Protestant population at the time. One result of this situation is the commitment of the vast majority of French Protestants not only to the state school system (disproportionate numbers of Protestants become teachers), but to the principle of *laïcité* (the absence of religion in the public sphere) itself.

A final defining moment can be found in World War II. Protestants fought alongside other French people to defend the honor of their country. In this sense, old antagonisms began to diminish (those, for example, between Catholic and Protestant or between clerical and anticlerical), but for some Protestants, not least those in the Cévennes, far more deep-seated reflexes were activated as they resisted the threat from outside. *Résistez* had become the rallying cry of the persecuted HUGUENOTS in the early eighteenth century, and the Cévennes terrain, which once protected the Camisards (so-called because of their distinctive clothing) in their struggles against Louis XIV, now protected the Maquisards in their resistance to the Germans.

Postwar Debates

Jean Baubérot and Jean-Paul Willaime, two distinguished commentators on French Protestantism, describe the Protestant community in three ways: as a Christian denomination, as a religious minority, and as a *religion laïque*. In this sense Protestantism continues to situate itself as the "crossroads" of both political and philosophical life in France. The debates that follow—ecumenism, tolerance, and *laïcité*—pick up the nuances of each of the three descriptions.

Relationships with other Christians, and more especially with the Catholic Church, have evolved in the postwar period. Cemented in a very practical way as a result of the war, they gradually acquired institutional embodiment. Initially this took the form of movements such as the Week of Prayer for Christian Unity and a range of common endeavors in the field of social responsibility. In the 1960s a huge step forward occurred following the Second Vatican Council which, among a whole range of revolutionary decisions, legitimated ecumenical contacts from the Catholic side. The papacy of John XXIV was clearly pivotal in this process.

There is, however, another side to this debate—the very marked mismatch in France in the size of the two constituencies. In a very real sense a total commitment to ecumenism on the part of the Protestant minority is a risky business in that they, rather than the Catholics, are likely to lose their identity if things are pushed to their logical conclusion. The issue of intermarriage illustrates this perfectly. Three-quarters of young Protestants marry out of their faith, raising real issues for the future. A rather different question is raised by more recent ecclesiastical events (a notably more conservative pope on the one hand and both the ordination of women and the relative growth of the evangelical churches on the other). Clearly the progress toward ecumenism can never be taken for granted; the movement ebbs and flows depending considerably on particular and changing circumstances.

The second description—that of a religious minority—raises wider issues than ecumenism, for it involves a new set of circumstances in postwar France. Questions of religious liberty now concern entirely different religious constituencies, notably the growing Muslim population (considerably larger than the Protestant community) and a whole series of sects and new religious movements. The question of Judaism has also acquired new resonance in view of the postwar influx of Sephardic Jews from North Africa, with the result that France now houses the largest Jewish community in western Europe.

What is the attitude of the French Protestant population to this changing situation? Unsurprisingly, given their past, Protestants are vigilant with regard to religious liberty, defending the right of the religious minority to exist within a society shaped not only by a Catholic past, but more recently by a strongly secular state. Both church and state in France run the risk of monopolistic tendencies, and both have some difficulty in coming to terms with a multifaith society in which religious communities aspire to a public as well as private existence. The *affaire du foulard* illustrates this point dramatically: should Muslim girls be allowed to wear their *foulard* (or Muslim scarf) in a state school or does the *foulard* count as a religious symbol, proscribed by law from the school system? The debate divided French society through the 1990s and beyond. It is a debate in which the Protestant community is torn between its desire to defend the liberty of religion while upholding the principles of *laïcité*. An inevitable question follows: Are the two aspirations compatible?

The answer becomes clearer in a more developed understanding of *laïcité* and its applications to the political sphere, the third theme introduced by Baubérot and Willaime. We have already seen that historical circumstance drove French Protestants toward the Republican ideal and to the philosophy that supported it. It seems, however, that *laïcité* does not work as well in an increasingly multifaith society, which is obliged to accommodate religious minorities with very different aspirations. Here there are two schools of thought. The first defends a traditional view of *laïcité*, notable for its anti-Catholicism, but turning very readily into antireligion per se. Such a view is vehemently opposed to the wearing of the *foulard* in the state school and sees the Muslim scarf as a threat to the system. The second approach takes a rather different view, suggesting that the notion of the state or the school as a neutral space should evolve as circumstances alter, permitting a genuine dialogue between those of different faiths. In this situation, the wearing of the *foulard* is rather differently constructed and is no longer a threat to the system. It is interesting that Jean Baubérot, a distinguished spokesman for the Protestant community in France, should be at the forefront of the debates about *laïcité*.

The Future

Recent commemorations of the Revocation of the Edict of Nantes in 1985 and of the edict itself in 1998 have permitted both the Protestant community and France as a whole to reflect on the contribution that Protestantism has made to French society, notably in the field of religious liberty. This is readily acknowledged, almost to the point of admitting that France a whole has, to some extent, been Protestantized—the core values of Protestantism have in many ways become that of the French. But if this is the case, how is it possible for French Protestants to maintain a distinct identity? The question is crucial though not specific to Protestantism; it concerns the fate of minorities more generally. It can be summarized as follows: if assimilation is as complete as possible, what then does it mean to be a Protestant (or indeed a Jew) in France at the turn of the millennium? The answer is unclear.

See also Calvin; Calvinist; Lutheran.

References and Further Reading

Baubérot, Jean. *Le Retour des Huguenots La vitalité protestante XIXe–XXe siècle.* Paris-Genève: Cerf-Labor et Fides, 1985.
———. *Le Protestantisme doit-il mourir? La différence protestante dans une France pluriculturelle.* Paris: Seuil, 1988.
———. "La Laïcité française et ses mutations." *Social Compass* 45 (1998): 175–187.
Baubérot, Jean, and Jean-Paul Willaime. *Le Protestantisme.* Paris: MA Editions, 1987.
Encrevé, André. *Les protestants en France de 1800 à nos jours.* Paris: Stock, 1985.
———. *Histoire des Protestants en France.* Toulouse: Privat, 1977.

GRACE DAVIE

FRANCK, SEBASTIAN (1499–1542)

Spiritualist theologian. A radical spiritualist Protestant, Franck joined the Protestant movement in 1525 and became a minister in a village near Nuremberg. He left his post in 1529 because he found that the REFORMATION brought no visible moral improvement. Both Strasbourg (1532) and Ulm (1539) expelled him at the insistence of their CLERGY. He finally settled in Basel, where he died.

In the face of dogmatic claims by all the churches and sects, Franck disavowed all DOCTRINE, and emphasized the experience of the Inner Word. Franck was one of the most consistent defenders of religious TOLERATION in the Reformation. He felt that the orthodox churches had proven themselves unchristian persecutors, whereas heretics had often been the true followers of Christ (see ORTHODOXY; HERESY). In his letter to Johannes Campanus (1531), Franck dismissed the church and the SACRAMENTS as toys that had been given to immature Christians in the early centuries, but that were no longer needed. In his *Paradoxa* (1534) he argued that God had made the BIBLE obscure so that believers would turn inward to the divine spark found in all men. Although he respected the Anabaptists (see ANABAPTISM) and his fellow spiritualist CASPAR SCHWENCKFELD, who had also lived at Strasbourg and Ulm, he rejected the exclusivity of the Anabaptists, and the "dogmatism" of Schwenckfeld. He gathered no following, although his works influenced later thinkers (e.g., Dirk Volcksherts Coornhert and VALENTIN WEIGEL), and many of his teachings would become staples in the modern world.

See also Spiritualism

References and Further Reading

Primary Source:

Müller, Jan-Dirk, ed. *Sebastian Franck (1499–1542).* Wiesbaden, Germany: Harrassowitz, 1993.

Secondary Sources:

Ozment, Steven E. *Mysticism and Dissent: Religious Ideology and Social Protest in the Sixteenth Century.* New Haven, CT: Yale University Press, 1973.
Weigelt, Horst. *Sebastian Franck und die lutherische Reformation.* Gütersloh, Germany: G. Mohn, 1972.
Williams, George H. *Spiritual and Anabaptist Writers.* Philadelphia, PA: Westminster Press, 1957.

R. EMMET MCLAUGHLIN

FRANCKE, AUGUST HERMANN (1663–1727)

German Pietist. Francke was born in Lübeck on March 22, 1663, son of a distinguished jurist. The early death of his father placed the responsibility for the large family into the hands of his mother. Francke received his early education from tutors and attended the universities of Erfurt and Kiel. In 1684 he moved to Leipzig, where he was the tutor of a student of THEOLOGY and received, in 1685, the degree of magister artium, which authorized him to teach at the university. The following year he founded together with a friend what they called the *collegium philobiblicum,* the "society of the friends of the Bible," which had the purpose of studying the BIBLE. In March of 1687 he moved to Lüneburg. There, while meditating on John 20:31, he experienced a CONVERSION, which he saw as a new life.

In the spring of 1689 he resumed his teaching at Leipzig. His classes, together with his *collegium philobiblicum*, gained attention and a circle of likeminded souls. At the same time the faculty was aghast and prohibited further teaching in August of 1689. In March of the following year Francke received a call to be DEACON at the Augustinian Church in Erfurt. Although he had strong supporters, his Pietist disposition still raised questions about his Lutheran ORTHODOXY, and he had to undergo a public scrutiny of his belief (see PIETISM). Even though his appointment was confirmed, in the end his antagonists carried the day. Erfurt, although a Lutheran town, was legally under the jurisdiction of the (Catholic) archbishop of Mainz, who was solicited by Francke's opponents to move against him. Toward the end of September 1691 he was expelled from Erfurt. The Brandenburg Elector Fredrick III appointed him in December of 1691 professor of Hebrew and Greek at the new university at HALLE, and seven years later, professor of theology there.

At Easter time 1695 Francke had founded a school for the poor with hardly any means at his disposal. He found a theology student as teacher. Similarly Francke began an orphanage without adequate funds. Additional institutions followed, including a high school for the sons of the nobility. The financial needs of these institutions—soon to be called the "Franckian Foundations"—were met both by a steady flow of gifts but also by some revenue-producing activities, such as a bookstore and pharmacy, not to mention governmental privileges. When Francke died in 1727, over 2,000 pupils were receiving instruction, together with 250 students and a teaching corps of some 167 teachers, including eight female teachers. Francke also called attention to the missionary mandate of Christianity, sending missionaries to INDIA and North America, such as HENRY MELCHIOR MÜHLENBERG.

Francke pointedly noted that it was not the goal of education to further lives of prominence or affluence. The goal was to train the young in the love and fear of God. Religion thus occupied an important role in the curriculum, generally some three hours each day, with the average length of instruction initially ten hours daily. Pedagogically, the pupils were disciplined with the notion that they were commanded to follow the pious men and women in the Bible and make the study of CATECHISM and Bible central in their lives.

Francke's significance, in addition to the impressive institutions in Halle, which still exist today, was to have demonstrated that the Pietist orientation was not to be confused with ecstatic and irresponsible religion. Rather, the religion of the heart, which the Pietists embraced, was also socially responsible.

See also Spener, Philip Jakob

References and Further Reading

Primary Sources:

Francke, August Hermann. *Schriften und Predigten.* Berlin/New York: W. de Gruyter, 1981ff.

Raabe, Paul. *August Hermann Francke 1663–1727: Bibliographie seiner Schriften.* Tübingen, Germany: Verlag der Franckeschen Stiftungen Halle im Max Niemeyer Verlag, 2001.

Secondary Sources:

Brown, Dale W. *The Problem of Subjectivism in Pietism: A Redefinition with Special Reference to the Theology of Philipp Jakob Spener and August Hermann Francke.* Evanston, IL: 1962. Ph.D. dissertation, Northwestern Univ., 1962.

Sattler, Gary R. *God's Glory, Neighbor's Good: a Brief Introduction to the Life and Writings of August Hermann Francke.* Chicago, IL: Covenant Press, 1982.

HANS J. HILLERBRAND

FREE CHURCH

"Free Church" is a generic term (originally British) for Christian denominations that rejected the control of the established national church (i.e., CHURCH OF ENGLAND, CHURCH OF SCOTLAND) in regulatory structures, DOCTRINE, WORSHIP, discipline, and ministry. The concept was later extended to North European lands and to North American churches with traditions derived from or sympathetic with those European Free Churches.

The earlier term in England was "Separatists," (partly as a term of disapproval of persons detached from the majority community, partly as a positive assertion of the right of each congregation to separate existence), later "Protestant Dissenters" (i.e., dissenting from the English Act of Uniformity, 1662). This term was replaced by "Nonconformists." In the nineteenth century, a more positive term and ethos were chosen. The original groups denoted were Congregationalists, Baptists, and Presbyterians; the Methodist denominations were added as their separation from the Church of England widened and they made common cause with the existing Dissenters in campaigns for TOLERATION, educational freedom, and representation in other areas of public life (e.g., hospital and prison CHAPLAINCY, government advisory boards). Quakers and Unitarians were, for many political purposes, accepted as allies. By the beginning of the twentieth century, the generic term "Free Church" became current and representation on the political front (e.g., education, hospital and military chaplaincy) was carried out through the Free Church Federal Council. This Council also collaborated with the Church of England in addressing or responding to the British Government on MARRIAGE law reform and similar issues. The range of British Free Churches was extended by the emergence of the PLYMOUTH BRETHREN (or "Christian Brethren"), the SALVATION ARMY, and the Pentecostal denominations (see PENTECOSTALISM).

On the European continent, dissenting minority groups had emerged in the Middle Ages. Hussites survived in some areas, for example, as the Czech Brethren and the (Socinian) Polish Brethren. During the REFORMATION, Anabaptist (see ANABAPTISM) and specifically MENNONITE and, later, German Baptist (Alexander Mack) congregations were established. MENNONITES helped to mentor and encourage the first English BAPTISTS in exile in the Low Countries. The nineteenth century saw "Free" versions of the established national Protestant churches (and of the larger nonestablished churches in America) come into existence, largely in protest against the established churches' perceived compromise with secular trends in society, ETHICS, CULTURE, and philosophy. Included in this tradition were the Free Church of Scotland, Free Church of England, Old Lutherans, Free Lutherans, Free Methodists, and *Gereformeerde Kerk*/Christian Reformed Church). These denominations, together with Continental branches of the British and American Protestant churches, have come to be classified first as "sects" (the concept made popular by ERNST TROELTSCH in his study of the social doctrines of the various Christian groupings) and later as "Free Churches" (*Freikirchen*), especially by Roman Catholic ecumenists, both as a matter of courtesy and also on ecclesiological grounds, because the Second Vatican Council had committed the Roman Church to admitting that Protestant churches are "ecclesial" in character (see CATHOLIC REACTIONS TO PROTESTANTISM).

In the UNITED STATES, the First Amendment to the Constitution makes all churches, Protestant or otherwise, free churches in the sense that none of them is governed by civic legislation in its constitution, doctrine, membership, or manner of worship. The ideal of "a free church in a free state" is in principle realized for all. The "Free Church" category has come to designate the churches of Anabaptist or "radical Reformation" derivation and of other traditions generated in America that place emphasis on the local congregation as self-existent and autonomous, on freedom from imposed creeds or liturgies, and on discipleship as personal choice. These include the Christian Church (DISCIPLES OF CHRIST) and the EVANGELICAL

FREE CHURCH. Polity centers on voluntary association of congregations at various levels.

The classic Free Church concern is for the purity of the church as Christ's bride. Being a Christian is an issue of individual responsibility, even if heritage-baptism is accepted, but belonging to the church is not an option, because Christ's disciples are essentially mutually responsible and interdependent.

The belief among the Free Churches is that the church is not created by the secular realm, nor can it be governed by it. The church is distinct from society in general, and must, if necessary, "come out" and be separate. The Old Testament principles of Israel's holiness are the basis for this. In Britain, however, social witness became significant. In the United States, the public perception is that the older Free Churches (e.g., the AMISH) will abstain from such public debate, except for a consistent lived witness to PACIFISM and studied avoidance of confrontation with groups such as the KU KLUX KLAN. More modern independent and fundamentalist groups will take an overtly right-wing political stance on such matters as war and peace and public welfare (see FUNDAMENTALISM).

Free Churches, as Free Churches in the American sense, cannot be assumed to have a common THEOLOGY. Some are Trinitarian, some are Unitarian, and others avoid insistence on choice in the issue. Some have a particular concern for ESCHATOLOGY, with DISPENSATIONALISM and RESTORATIONISM held as important tenets.

See also Congregationalism; Dissent; Friends, Society of; Lutheranism; Methodism; Nonconformity; Presbyterianism; Unitarian-Universalist Association

References and Further Reading

Dale, R. W. *Manual of Congregational Principles* (1884), 11th ed. London: Congregational Union of England and Wales, 1920.

Jordan, Edward Kenneth Henry. *Free Church Unity. History of the Free Church Council Movement 1876–1946.* London: Lutterworth Press, 1956.

Klingberg, Frank J. *A Free Church in a Free State: America's Unique Contribution.* Indianapolis, IN: National Foundation Press, 1947.

Littell, Franklin Hamlin. *The Free Church.* Boston, MA: Starr King Press, 1957.

Micklem, Nathaniel. *Congregationalism and the Church Catholic.* London: Independent Press, 1943.

Payne, Ernest A. *The Free Church Tradition in the Life of England.* London: SCM Press, 1944.

Redeker, Calvin Wall. *The Free Church and Seductive Culture.* Scottdale, PA: Herald Press, 1970.

Rouner, A. *The Free Church Today: New Life for the Whole Church.* New York; Association Press, 1968.

Torbet, Robert G. *Ecumenism: Free Church Dilemma.* Valley Forge, PA: Judson Press, 1968.

Westin, Gunnar. *The Free Church Through the Ages.* Translated from the Swedish by Virgil A. Olson. Nashville, TN: Broadman Press, 1954.

Williams, D. H., ed. *The Free Church and the Early Church: Bridging the Historical and Theological Divide.* Grand Rapids, MI: Eerdmans, 2002.

DAVID H. TRIPP

FREE CHURCH FEDERAL COUNCIL

The Free Church Federal Council became the Free Churches' Council in 2002. More recently it voted itself out of existence to enter a "collaborative partnership" with Churches Together in England. The Free Church Council of Wales has partnered with Cytun, Churches Together in Wales.

These developments are the culmination of over a century of church unity efforts in ENGLAND and WALES by the free churches. The FREE CHURCH movement is worldwide and traces its roots to the New Testament. It resisted organizational form beyond denominations until the nineteenth century. In the established church context of England these churches and their members were known as dissenters or nonconformists. The form of this unity has been the federation of a variety of independent churches and religious groups for work of mutual interest, including EVANGELISM and social reform efforts.

The initial meeting of representatives of several of the free churches took place in Manchester in 1892, and formally organized as the National Free Church Council in 1896. The first key leaders were Hugh Price Hughes, Charles Berry, and Alexander Mackennal. The Organizing Secretary from 1895 to 1910 was Thomas Law. The initial goals of the organization included affirming Jesus Christ as the sole AUTHORITY in the associated churches and taking the Gospel to the people in the large towns. Individuals involved came from many of the free churches, and initially represented themselves and not their denominations. These included BAPTISTS, Wesleyans, Free Methodists, Primitive Methodists, Calvinistic Methodists, Congregationalists, Presbyterians, and members of the Free Church of England. Persons from other free groups soon joined. The National Council consisted of individuals and representatives of the local Church Councils and Federations. In 1899 The National Council published the Free Church Catechism. In 1919 another federal union emerged called the Federal Council of Evangelical Free Churches. This brought together official representatives of the various denominations. The leader of this effort was J. H. Shakespeare of the Baptist Union.

These two church unity groups ran on more or less parallel lines espousing unity in action among free churches until they united in 1940 to become the Free Church Federal Council. The Council had a moderator, chosen for one year, and an annual congress. The Council worked through local church councils in cities and towns scattered over England and Wales, and through the several denominational members. It worked to do things together that no one group could do alone. It followed the form and function of the similar group in the United States, the Federal Council of the Churches of Christ in the United States of America.

See also Congregationalism; Denomination; Dissent; Nonconformity; Presbyterianism; Primitive Methodist Church; Wesleyan Church

References and Further Reading

Jordan, E. K. H. *Free Church Unity: History of the Free Church Council Movement, 1896–1941.* London: Lutterworth Press, 1956.

Munson, James. *The Nonconformists: In Search of a Lost Culture.* London: SPCK, 1991.

Westin, Gunner. *The Free Church Through the Ages.* Nashville, TN: Broadman Press, 1958.

JOHN PIPER

FREE METHODIST CHURCH OF AMERICA

The Free Methodist Church of America was organized in 1860 after a number of clergy, foremost among them Benjamin Titus Roberts (1823–1893), were defrocked by the Western New York Methodist Episcopal Church. These clergy and sympathetic laypersons joined with a similar group of disenfranchised Methodists from Missouri and Illinois led by John Wesley Redfield (1810–1863). They elected Roberts as their leader at Pekin, New York, in August 1860. Sensitive to populist issues, equal representation was given to CLERGY and LAITY in denominational governance.

Free Methodists sought to live and teach primitive Methodist values and THEOLOGY. The key term was "freedom." The Free Methodists promoted freedom from SIN (SANCTIFICATION), freedom from SLAVERY, freedom from pew rents, and freedom from what they saw as the manipulation of secret societies (lodges, etc.). Roberts promoted the right of WOMEN to preach, a right removed by the church over Roberts' protests in 1896 and not restored until the 1970s. Roberts was also involved in labor organization efforts, maintained a farm and founded Chili Seminary, which eventually became Roberts Wesleyan University. He was an ardent abolitionist and promoted civil rights for African-Americans (see SLAVERY, ABOLITION OF). The Free Methodist Church has never managed to develop strength in the Old South.

An aggressive mission program developed. Extensive efforts were made in SOUTH AFRICA, Central Africa, JAPAN, BRAZIL (especially by Japanese immigrants) and CHINA, with fewer resources committed to other places. In Burundi, Mozambique, and Japan, the missions were soon depending on local leadership and funds. In other areas, especially AFRICA, growth was hampered because of firm mission control. The greatest growth in Africa came with the merger with the churches created by the Congo Evangelistic Society (British Pentecostal) in the 1970s. From 1960, some Free Methodist mission leaders attempted to encourage independence of mission areas by establishing a series of national conferences, each with its own ecclesiastical structure.

The contemporary Free Methodist Church has about 74,000 members in the UNITED STATES and about 360,000 outside of the United States. The denomination has been active in education and supports Central Christian College (McPherson, Kansas), Greeneville College (Greenville, Illinois), Roberts Wesleyan University (Rochester, New York), Seattle Pacific University (Seattle, Washington), and Spring Arbor University (Spring Arbor, Michigan).

See also Methodism; Missions; Primitive Methodist Church

References and Further Reading

Hogue, William T. *A History of the Free Methodist Church.* 2 vols. Chicago, IL: Free Methodist Publishing House, 1918.

Marston, Leslie R. *From Age to Age A Living Witness.* Winona Lake, IN: Light and Life Press, 1960.

McKenna, David L. *A Future with a History: The Wesleyan Witness of the Free Methodist Church 1860–1995.* Indianapolis, IN: Light and Life Communications, 1997.

DAVID BUNDY

FREE WILL BAPTISTS

Free Will Baptist denominations have about 300,000 members in several different organizations. The term "free will" reflects the explicitly Arminian heritage of this tradition, as opposed to the modified CALVINISM or the mixed Calvinist-Arminian heritage of other larger Baptist bodies in America and Europe. The modern Free Will Baptist movement, today centered in the American South but not located exclusively there, is the product of two streams of Baptist life that flowed together in the twentieth century. These two streams had independent, unrelated origins: one northern and one southern, both with roots in the 1700s. Over the next two centuries, both movements faced a series of schisms, crises, and ecumenical mergers that defined and shaped them, while at the same time lowering overall membership.

Both the northern and southern wings of the Free Will Baptist movement stand in the tradition of the GENERAL BAPTISTS, the first group of modern BAPTISTS to emerge, when JOHN SMYTH and Thomas Helwys in 1609 led a group of English Separatist exiles in Holland. Smyth's interest in creating a congregation whose visible membership was identical to the invisible and universal church of true SAINTS ultimately led him to reject the ancient practice of infant BAPTISM and replace it with adult baptism. This view on baptism, however, was just one of several distinctive views held by these English exiles. Others included a commitment to religious liberty, the elimination of state intrusion into private religious matters, a radical understanding of the priesthood of the believer that emphasized individual conscience, and the use of the BIBLE as the final standard for DOCTRINE and practice. Eventually, by the middle of the 1600s, these Baptists moved beyond discussion of the proper candidate for baptism to discussion of the proper mode of baptism. As a result, Baptists embraced baptism by immersion, a practice used by some Christians in the first few centuries, but long abandoned by the 1600s.

Two years after Smyth and Helwys formed their Baptist congregation in Holland, Smyth applied for membership in a Mennonite congregation, taking the majority of his Baptists with him (see MENNONITES). Helwys led a minority group back to ENGLAND, forming a congregation that then spread the new movement throughout the country. These Baptists were firmly Arminian in their theology, which set them off from the mainstream of Puritan thought (see ARMINIANISM; PURITANISM). Eventually, they became known as General Baptists because of their belief that Jesus died for all humanity, not merely the elect. General Baptists believed that ATONEMENT was general rather than particular in its scope.

About a generation later, in the 1630s, a second type of Baptist movement emerged, with no connection to the General Baptists formed by Smyth and Helwys. Calvinistic in THEOLOGY, these Baptists became known as Particular Baptists. The groups were similar in their explicitly Baptist beliefs. Both emphasized the priesthood of the believer in a radical and exaggerated sense, the sole and final AUTHORITY of the Bible in matters of doctrine, and adult baptism. The Particular Baptists differed from General Baptists in their understanding of Calvinist theology. Particular Baptists represented a separate group with separate origins, not a schism from the slightly older Arminian movement. The two groups continued in England over the next 200 years with little conflict or contact. By the end of the 1800s, Calvinism and Arminianism had ceased to be relevant points of discussion for most British Baptists, and the two groups merged.

Both Particular and General Baptists settled in North America beginning in the 1600s and founded churches in New England, the Middle Colonies, and the South. Many of these congregations were mixed, with members from both General and Particular backgrounds. Other congregations were exclusively General or Particular, but the Particular movement proved dominant. Mixed congregations eventually became Particular Baptists in identity, and Particular Baptists and their ideological descendents formed the regional and national organizations that represented most Baptists in the UNITED STATES. However, General Baptists did plant some congregations in the South, especially in North Carolina. Modern Free Will Baptists stand in the tradition of these General Baptists, although there may be more of a nexus than a direct, historical link.

The New England Branch of Free Will Baptists

New England Free Will Baptists grew out of the leadership of Benjamin Randall (1749-1808). Born in New Hampshire, Randall was reared in a pious Congregationalist home. From an early age, he had an interest in religion and the cultivation of personal piety. The conversionist zeal of the Great Awakening, however, proved distasteful to him, at least initially (see AWAKENINGS). He was especially critical of GEORGE WHITEFIELD's dramatic and emotional form of PREACHING, a new direction in homiletics. Despite his ridicule of Whitefield, Randall started to have the classic doubts about the state of his soul that formed the content of colonial CONVERSION narratives. When he heard that Whitefield had died shortly after leaving New Hampshire, Randall became despondent and had his own dramatic conversion experience.

Randall first identified with the CONGREGATIONAL-ISM of his youth, but his church's disinterest in applying discipline to other members disappointed him (see CHURCH DISCIPLINE). He formed a prayer group of like-minded church members who hoped to bring revivalist zeal into the congregation. Instead, he brought reproach from the pastor, and Randall left the congregation. Randall's criticism of the church coincided with another development, his interest in the subject of baptism. It was during this same time that Randall, with no clear external influence, came to the conclusion that the only proper baptism was the immersion of adult converts. After some thought and conversation, Randall was baptized by immersion and joined a Calvinistic Baptist church in Maine.

Over the next several years, Randall preached in Baptist churches in New Hampshire and Maine. Although he was firmly Arminian in his theology from the time of his conversion, he had no clashes with the dominant Calvinism of the area's Baptist Churches. He simply preached on other themes, such as conversion and the importance of morally upstanding behavior. However, some leaders in the churches eventually pressed Randall about his failure to preach on the theme of ELECTION. Randall admitted that he never preached on the issue because he did not believe in it, and, as a result, his ordination ceased to be recognized by the area's Baptists. In turn, a group of Randall's supporters ordained him and started a new congregation on April 5, 1780, based on exclusively Arminian principles. This congregation marks the beginning of the Free Will Baptist movement in New England.

Randall and his supporters started numerous Free Will Baptist churches and recruited many new clergymen throughout New England. As the movement grew at the local level, the need for organizational life above the local congregation grew. Randall worked to create a series of local organizations called monthly meetings, as well as a regional quarterly meeting. Eventually, an organization called the yearly meeting was formed that could rightfully be called the Free Will Baptist Church. Like many denominational titles, though, Free Will Baptist came to be the title of the group only after it had been in existence for about twenty years.

Randall and his Free Will associates had a connectional understanding of Baptist identity, rather than a hyperlocal understanding. The yearly meeting, also known as the Free Will Baptist Connexion, was the church, and the local congregations were extensions. For these early Free Will Baptists, the local congregation derived its authority from its membership in the parent body. By the time Randall died in 1808, the Free Will Baptist movement had spread throughout New England and was strong both at the local level and at the institutional level. The movement continued to flourish after his death, benefiting both from strong internal leadership and the external influences of the Second Great Awakening. The denomination-building spirit of the first half of the 1800s was not lost on the Free Will Baptists of New England. This group formed home and foreign mission societies, created a publication society, and founded an education society, as well as numerous colleges, including Hillsdale, Bates, and Colby.

ECUMENISM shaped much of Baptist identity in the twentieth century, including that of the Free Wills. Just as British Particular and General Baptists no longer found Calvinism and Arminianism strong enough points of identity to prevent merger, many Free Will Baptists and leaders in the larger, historically Calvinist Northern Baptist movement worked for a merger. In 1911, the Free Will Baptist Connexion of New England merged into the larger Northern Baptist

Convention. About half of the congregations declined to participate in the merger, choosing to retain an explicitly Free Will identity. These Free Will Baptists developed stronger relations with the Free Will Baptists of the South, creating the National Association of Free Will Baptists in 1935.

Southern Free Will Baptists

While the northern branch of the Free Will Baptist movement developed largely through the work of one man without any strong connections to any other Baptist movement, the southern branch has a more complex origin that remains the subject of some debate among historians. The debate centers on the connections of the southern Free Will denomination, which formed in a mature institutional sense around 1829, to the earlier General Baptist movement. Free Will Baptist historians understand their movement to be the direct heir of General Baptist life in America. General Baptists, after a period of decline due to the proselytizing of Particular Baptists, emerged with renewed energy under the name Free Will.

Other historians contend that the two movements have no direct links. While the two groups have a similar Arminian theology, these historians contend that the similarity is one of correlation, not causation. The General Baptist movement totally died out. The Free Will Baptists of the 1820s constitute a totally separate movement with no connection to the Generals. Free Will Baptists, however, contend that after a massive numbers of General Baptists affiliated with the more dominant Calvinistic Baptists, a small remnant of churches and leaders worked to rebuild the Arminian Baptist movement. The movement never died out, according to their narrative. Instead, General Baptists survived, but survived very lean years in the late 1700s, which accounts for the paucity of documentary evidence left by the group. Eventually, General Baptists once again became vital and took the name Free Will.

A leading founder of North Carolina General Baptist life was Paul Palmer. Palmer was born in Maryland, baptized in Delaware, and ordained a minister in Connecticut. Around 1720, he arrived in North Carolina, finding General Baptists already there, but without a church. Palmer gathered these Baptists together and organized the first Baptist Church in that state. An itinerant rather than a pastor, Palmer's preaching resulted in the formation of other General Baptist Churches in the state (see ITINERANCY). Palmer was firmly Arminian in doctrine, and he found eager listeners among the English immigrants to the coastal regions of North Carolina. There is no clear date for his birth or death, but the absence of his name from records at a certain point indicates that he died no later than 1750.

One of the converts of Paul Palmer was Joseph Parker. Parker formed a General Baptist Church at Meherrin, North Carolina, that quickly became an important center of Arminian expansion. Parker also saw the population of North Carolina increase, and with that increase, he saw Calvinistic Baptists start to grow in the area. Beginning in the 1750s, Calvinistic and revivalist Separate Baptists not only started new congregations in North Carolina, they worked to convert General Baptists to their views. These efforts to gain new adherents to the Separate movement from among the Generals succeeded from the vantage point of the Calvinists. By the end of the 1700s, most General Baptist congregations had either totally identified with the Calvinist Baptist movement or they had atrophied. This targeting of the General Baptists was directed by leaders associated with the Philadelphia Baptist Association, the dominant Baptist organization of that period and the closest to a national organization that Baptists had. After the departure of large numbers of Generals for the ranks of the Calvinist Baptists, a small group of leaders such as Parker worked to keep the General movement alive.

The Free Will Baptist movement in the South grew out of the disarray among General Baptists in the second half of the eighteenth century. The debate centers on the nature of that growth. It may be that the General Baptist movement totally died. In that case, the Free Will Baptist movement is the ideological heir to the General Baptists, and it emerged to fill the vacuum left by the demise of these earlier Arminians. On the other hand, it may be that the Free Will Baptist movement in North Carolina represents an institutional development that occurred after General Baptists recovered from the decimation of their ranks. The documentary evidence is slim for making a firm conclusion either way. It is certain that there is no clear documentary link between the Generals and the Free Wills. It is also certain that Free Will Baptist is not a term used widely by General Baptists. However, there are scattered references to some General Baptists as Free Will Baptists in the late 1700s. The fact that the Free Will Baptist movement emerges at the time the General Baptist movement may have been "dying out" suggests that Free Will Baptist was simply a new term for an old movement.

Free Will Baptist churches grew strong in North Carolina from the 1830s through the rest of the century. This growth came despite numerous threats to the movement's vitality. Free Will Baptists had their ranks challenged in the antebellum years by the Restorationist movements of both Thomas and Alexander Campbell (see CAMPBELL FAMILY) and the Disciples movement (see DISCIPLES OF CHRIST). Large numbers of Free Will Baptists left for traditions associated with RESTORATIONISM. However, the Free Will Baptists regrouped and gained a clearer sense of their identity. As North Carolina Free Will Baptists migrated to other parts of the South, they carried their Arminian Baptist identity with them, forming a counter-narrative of Baptist identity that challenged the total hegemony of the more Calvinist SOUTHERN BAPTIST CONVENTION. In 1845, the year that the Southern Baptist Convention was formed, the North Carolina General Conference of Original Free Will Baptists was formed. This organization served as the parent body of Free Will Baptist life in the South. The Conference was divided into associations that supervised subregions.

A National Denomination and a Schism

Northern and Southern Free Will Baptists made some attempts to connect their fellowships, although nothing permanent occurred until 1935. The impetus behind uniting the groups came in the merger of Northern Free Will Baptists into the Northern Baptist Convention in 1911. Many Free Will Baptists felt that their movement would be totally eliminated without a strong national DENOMINATION to nurture their Arminian heritage. Southern-heritage Free Will Baptists began working with those Northern Free Will Baptists who remained outside the Northern Baptist Convention. After a series of mergers and cooperative ventures between the two groups, the National Association of Free Will Baptists (NAFWB) was formed in 1935. For the first time, Free Will Baptists had a national denominational infrastructure that paralleled the organizations of other denominations.

As has been the case with other Baptist organizations, the local churches and regional movements created the national denomination rather than vice versa. Free Will Baptists had been present in America since the 1700s. The formation of the NAFWB brought together numerous different streams of Free Will Baptist life, united in their common Arminianism and in their desire to preserve the Free Will Baptist name. However, the national denomination had identity and POLITY issues that would eventually result in the departure of the historically significant North Carolina Conference.

The leadership of the NAFWB was heavily influenced by the twentieth-century FUNDAMENTALISM Movement, especially the separatist brand associated with Bob Jones University in Greenville, South Carolina. The young denomination opened the Free Will Baptist Bible College in 1938, largely modeled after Bob Jones University. Seven years later, North Caro-

lina Free Will Baptists founded Mount Olive College, basing it on the classic liberal arts model of other small denominational colleges. Although not deliberately in competition with the Free Will Baptist Bible College, the two institutions symbolize two different approaches to Free Will identity, one separatist and one ecumenical.

With North Carolina Free Will Baptists moving in a different direction regarding HIGHER EDUCATION, it should come as no surprise that North Carolina would have other conflicts with the national body. These conflicts centered on the autonomy of the local congregation. Many classic Free Will Baptist bodies de-emphasized the total autonomy of the local congregation. Local congregations were accountable in some sense to the parent denomination, a characteristic that Free Will Baptists shared with the General Baptists of an earlier era. In 1960, several members of a North Carolina congregation raised questions about the doctrinal ideas of their pastor and apparently the majority of the church members. The pastor stressed the concept of eternal security of the believer, an idea alien to historic Free Will thought. Those members with concerns brought their issues to the North Carolina Conference. The Conference ruled in favor of the minority, claiming that local congregations are subordinate to the parent denomination. The issue was eventually taken before the civil courts, which sided with the North Carolina Conference. However, the national denomination sided with the local congregation and stressed the issue of absolute congregational autonomy. The tension between NAFWB and North Carolina became permanent and North Carolina leaders withdrew from the national organization in 1962. Their North Carolina-based denomination, with its own college and publishing house, remains a strong, although small, representative of the Free Will Baptist identity.

Today, there are three main denominational bodies in the Free Will Baptist tradition. The NAFWB, based in Nashville, Tennessee, has more than 200,000 members and approximately 2,500 congregations. This group has a standard Free Will Arminian Baptist theology. Wedded to their Arminianism is an embrace of some Reformed developments of the late 1800s, namely BIBLICAL inerrancy. The General Conference of Original Freewill Baptists, based in North Carolina, has a much smaller membership, although the denomination is strong and growing. This group connects its Arminian Baptist identity with mainline Protestantism, seeing itself as one branch or denomination of the larger Church. Finally, there is a smaller Pentecostal Free Will Baptist Church. This movement grew out of the Holiness and then Pentecostal work of G. B. Cashwell, who brought Pentecostal theology to the

Free Will Baptists in the vicinity of Dunn, North Carolina.

See also Baptists, United States

References and Further Reading

Davidson, William F. *The Free Will Baptists in America, 1727–1984.* Nashville, TN: Randall House, 1985.

Dodd, Damon C. *The Free Will Baptist Story.* Nashville, TN: Executive Department of the National Association of Free Will Baptists, 1956.

Million, G. W. *A History of Free Will Baptists.* Nashville, TN: Board of Publication and Literature, National Association of Free Will Baptists, 1958.

Pelt, Michael R. *A History of Original Free Will Baptists.* Mount Olive, NC: Mount Olive College Press, 1996.

MERRILL M. HAWKINS, JR.

FREEDOM, LIBERTY

See Bill of Rights; Dissent; Toleration

FREEDOM OF RELIGION

See Bill of Rights; Toleration

FREEMAN, THOMAS BIRCH (1809–1890)

Methodist missionary. The son of an African father and English mother, Freeman was born December 8, 1809 in Winchester, ENGLAND. He was accepted as a missionary by the Wesleyan Methodists in 1837 and ordained for work in West Africa. Before he left, he married for the first time. His wife died within two months of his arrival at Cape Coast, but he remained in West Africa for fifty-two years, with only two periods on furlough.

Adapting his PREACHING to local customs and practices he exercised a pioneering role in the development of METHODISM on the Gold Coast, appealing to Europeans and Africans alike. He recruited native Africans to ministries as well as attracting successive waves of European missionaries through the publication of his journals *Of various visits to the Kingdoms of Ashanti, Yoruiba and Dahomi to promote the objects of the Wesleyan Missionary Society* (1843), although half of them died within a year of arrival. His mission to the Ashanti captured the imagination of monarch and people in Britain who sent gifts and raised money to support his work. His opposition to the slave trade made the task of mission difficult, as did tribal wars and colonial policies.

Despite Freeman's success in raising funds for the mission, the Committee in London questioned his financial competence, leading to his resignation as general superintendent. After a number of years working for the colonial government as an administrator in the Accra district, he spent the last fifteen years of his life as a circuit minister, during which time the jubilee of the Gold Coast Mission was celebrated (1885). He died in August 1890, revered as the Father of West African Methodism.

See also Africa; Methodism; Missionary Organizations; Missions; Slavery; Slavery, Abolition of; Wesleyanism

References and Further Reading

Birtwistle, Allen. *Thomas Birch Freeman: West African Pioneer.* London: Cargate Press, 1950.

TIM MACQUIBAN

FREEMASONRY

Freemasonry is a worldwide fraternal order of men encouraging morality, charity, and fellowship through secret rituals and meetings open only to members. Although it has undergone many changes since its founding in the early eighteenth century, including a substantial decline in the late twentieth century, the fraternity still boasts some six million "brothers." Masonry's religious connections have been an important part of its appeal, but these ties have also aroused persistent opposition.

The Founding of the Fraternity

The origins of Freemasonry are unclear. Medieval stone masons sometimes met in "lodges" attached to specific building sites and sponsored legendary histories tracing the craft to the creation of Solomon's Temple and before, a lineage appropriated by the later fraternal order. Seventeenth-century craft groups in London and Scotland accepted non-builders into their ranks, but the modern fraternity (what early brothers called "speculative" Masonry to distinguish it from "operative" builders) began in London during the years surrounding 1717. By the end of the 1720s, the new order had developed most of its distinctive forms: a three-degree system of rituals performed within local lodges supervised by national (or regional) grand lodges; charitable aid to Masons and others; the metaphorical use of building tools to represent moral truths; and a membership policy that accepted men of good character regardless of occupation, political loyalties, and even, within certain limits (most notably belief in a supreme Creator), religious belief. Intellectually, Masonry joined together hopes of secret wisdom (seen in boasts about the fraternity's ancient origins) with early ENLIGHTENMENT ideals of order, balance, and mathematical regularity (symbolized by geometry and building), and a stress on unity among men of different backgrounds and beliefs. This ideal of brotherhood drew upon the contemporary critique of sectarian divisions by LATITUDINARIAN theologians.

The new fraternity spread quickly. By 1738, continental lodges had become so popular that a papal encyclical condemned the fraternity as a threat to social unity and true religion. Despite this religious opposition (and continuing official distrust), French Freemasonry continued to attract substantial support among the upper reaches of society. Mid-century French women even created their own Masonic organizations (the fraternity elsewhere still remains almost universally restricted to males). In both FRANCE and Germanic countries, Freemasonry also became identified with the Enlightenment, attracting such brothers as French jurist Charles Montesquieu (1689–1755), French poet Voltaire (1694–1778), Austrian composer Wolfgang Mozart (1756–1791), and JOHANN WOLFGANG GOETHE (1749–1832). When the FRENCH REVOLUTION broke out near the end of the century, a popular theory attributed it to lodges that had been corrupted by the Illuminati, an anti-Jesuit order that had briefly flourished in Bavaria (and that has continued to attract speculation from conspiracy theorists).

European sailors and merchants also spread Masonry into other parts of the world. A lodge met in Calcutta by 1729, although Indian lodges did not accept Hindus or Sikhs until the middle of the nineteenth century. English-speaking Masonry still uses the Bible within its rituals as "the volume of the sacred law" (as well as a key source of language and ritual stories), but the fraternity allows use of other sacred scriptures in non-Christian areas.

Lodges also spread into America, with the first Masonic groups meeting there in the 1730s. Masonic brothers divided on the American Revolution, but a number of the most important leaders were members, including Benjamin Franklin (1706–1790) and George Washington (1732–1799). Post-Revolutionary Masonry gained extraordinary popularity, spreading into nearly every American locality in the years after 1790. Brothers were often called upon to dedicate public buildings (including the United States Capitol, whose cornerstone was laid by President Washington himself in 1792). Post-Revolutionary brothers also increasingly identified their order with Christianity. In the "higher degree" bodies developed in this period to expand on the original three degrees, Masons developed rituals that were often based upon Biblical stories and themes. Some enthusiastic brothers began to claim that the fraternity not only served divine purposes, but even had divine origin.

This broad enthusiasm, however, did not last. The 1826 kidnapping (and possibly murder) of William Morgan, an upstate New York brother who threatened to publish the fraternity's rituals, by zealous brothers set off a substantial movement against Masonry. Drawing upon the emerging ideals of EVANGELICALISM and democracy, opponents argued that Masonry's social exclusivity, broad religious inclusiveness, and use of Biblical material threatened Christianity and republican government. Helping to develop organizational methods of agitation and organization later used by abolitionism and other antebellum reform movements (see SLAVERY, ABOLITION OF), the anti-Masonic movement sponsored newspapers and even a political party that fielded a presidential candidate in 1832 and 1836. The attack was largely successful, virtually destroying Masonry in the northern United States. The fraternity began to revive only in the 1840s.

The Age of Fraternalism and After

Masonry in America and elsewhere became even more popular in the late nineteenth and early twentieth centuries. Masonic forms and ideas inspired and provided models for a host of new fraternal societies, including labor unions, mutual insurance companies, college fraternities, and ethnic organizations. Even American Catholics, attempting to blunt the appeal of Masonry and similar institutions crossing religious lines, established their own fraternal organization, the Knights of Columbus (1882). The language of brotherhood popularized by Freemasonry and its imitators became a key tenet of liberal Protestantism. Despite this growing competition, Masonry remained the largest and most prestigious of all fraternal orders. A variety of associated Masonic organizations took root in these years, including the newly popular Scottish Rite, Knights Templar, and Royal Arch bodies established before the CIVIL WAR (all initiating third-degree brothers into "higher degrees"), the new Order of the Eastern Star, Rainbow Girls, and DeMolay (for, respectively, women, girls, and boys related to Masons), and the Shrine (stressing organized charity and social enjoyment).

The twentieth century posed a variety of significant challenges to the fraternity. The Great Depression slowed Masonic growth. In both GERMANY and France, Nazis persecuted Masons as representatives of cosmopolitan universalism. More problematic for the fraternity in the long run was a substantial decline in membership during the last half of the twentieth century. Although American Masonry grew in the 1940s and 1950s, it thereafter fell from a high point of 4 million members to around 2.5 million. Only the relatively small African American "Prince Hall" branch of the fraternity, established before white Masonry began to accept African Americans in the 1960s, continues to thrive (members have included musician Duke Ellington [1899–1974], Supreme Court justice Thurgood Marshall [1908–1993], and civil rights leader Jesse Jackson [1941–]).

Even during its years of growth and expansion, Masonry continued to be dogged by opposition. The British fraternity has periodically aroused public fears that loyalty to the brotherhood subverts loyalty to the larger society. The Roman Catholic Church remains officially opposed to its members joining the fraternity, although local clergy have often been more accepting. American Fundamentalists (see FUNDAMENTALISM) often reject the fraternity as well. Most religious attacks, besides rather implausible complaints that Masonic rituals encourage Satanic worship, center on the dangers and compromises presumed necessary within an organization that professes religious purposes yet encourages a strong sense of brotherhood among men of different religious beliefs. Masons have usually countered by noting the fraternity's encouragement of charity, morality, and friendship.

See also Fundamentalism; Slavery, Abolition of.

References and Further Reading

Bullock, Steven C. *Revolutionary Brotherhood: Freemasonry and the Transformation of the American Social Order.* Chapel Hill, NC: University of North Carolina Press, 1996.

Clawson, Mary Ann. *Constructing Brotherhood: Class, Gender, and Fraternalism.* Princeton, NJ: Princeton University Press, 1989.

DeHoyos, Art, and S. Brent Morris. *Is It True What They Say About Freemasonry? The Methods of Anti-Masons.* 2nd ed., rev. Washington, D.C.: Masonic Information Center, 1997. members.aol.com/adehoyos/chap1.htm (October 2000).

Dumenil, Lynn. *Freemasonry and American Culture, 1880–1930.* Princeton, NJ: Princeton University Press, 1984.

Gould, Robert Freke. *Gould's History of Freemasonry Throughout the World.* Edited by Dudley Wright. New York: Charles Scribner's Sons, 1936.

Hamill, John. *The Craft: A History of English Freemasonry.* Leighton Buzzard, Bedfordshire: Crucible, 1986.

Jacob, Margaret C. *Living the Enlightenment: Freemasonry and Politics in Eighteenth-Century Europe.* New York: Oxford University Press, 1991.

STEVEN C. BULLOCK

FRENCH REVOLUTION

French Protestants in the late eighteenth century numbered approximately 700,000, or about 2 percent of the French population. The Calvinists lived mainly in the Midi, and the 200,000 Lutherans were centered on the Rhine frontier in Alsace. Before 1787, only the latter were legally protected thanks to the 1648 Treaty of Westphalia, leaving members of the *religion prétendu réformée* (to use the derogatory official designation) vulnerable to sporadic persecution into the 1760s. Spurred on by a *cause célèbre* like the Calas case, enlightened opinion was, by that date, ready to end the related fictions that France was a uniconfessional state and that the HUGUENOTS were disloyal opponents of the Bourbon monarchy. Careful lobbying of Louis XVI's ministers like Malesherbes, Necker, and Breteuil by able pastors like Rabaut de Saint-Etienne eventually elicited the "Edict Concerning Those Who Do Not Profess the Catholic Religion" in November 1787. Members of the Reformed Churches could marry before a royal judge or a *curé* (acting only as a civil officer), register the births of their children, and die knowing they could bequeath their estates to fellow Protestants. It was a limited measure that affirmed the monopoly of the Catholic Church in public WORSHIP and left Protestants still ineligible to hold public office. Notwithstanding its limitations, the Edict inspired most Protestant congregations to heighten their local profiles.

As FRANCE prepared for the meeting of the Estates General in 1789, Protestant laymen made the case for further concessions in the *Cahiers* or list of proposals for constitutional change that they, like other communities, were required to produce. Fifteen Protestant deputies were elected to the Estates General, determined to achieve full citizenship. The Declaration of the Rights of Man and of the Citizen (August 1789) established the general principle of religious liberty, and then a decree of Christmas Eve 1789 abolished the last legal inequalities between Protestants and Catholics. These concessions made Huguenots across France initially most sympathetic to the Revolution, as now they were no longer "foreigners in their own homeland." Protestants took up offices, joined the revolutionary clubs, bought Catholic Church land when it came on the market, and worshiped freely.

Interconfessional tensions increased in the winter of 1789–1790, especially so in Nîmes, a center of the silk industry second only to Lyon and home to a prosperous and ambitious Protestant community. Protestants dominated the officer corps of the town's National Guard and used it as an instrument to achieve post-Revolutionary supremacy in local politics. Worried Catholics in the new *département* of the Gard began to see the whole Revolution as a Protestant plot, and riots erupted in both Montauban and Nîmes in the spring of 1790. The so-called *bagarre,* or brawl, of Nîmes left about 20 Protestants and 300 Catholics dead in four days of street fighting. It was one of the worst outbreaks of violence in the first part of the French Revolution. Protestants in the Gard tended to be pro-Revolutionary because of the political and social benefits that the Revolution had conferred on them, and sectarian violence only began to diminish once members of the Reformed faith felt that their new legal status was beyond doubt. Lutherans were less enthusiastic than their Reformed brethren; the Revolution had brought them little and threatened to deprive them of much.

Protestants tended to support the Republic established in 1792 and became associated with the Girondin faction in the National Convention (to which nine Protestants were elected). When the latter were proscribed after the Jacobin coup of June 1793, the Reformed Church once again faced an uncertain future. Forty-seven of its leaders were executed for their part in the Federalist revolt in the Gard, while ordinary members faced the closure of their *temples* (or their conversion into "Temples of Reason") as part of the state's policy of de-Christianization. These constraints were not always unacceptable. Thus at La Rochelle there is evidence of bourgeois Protestant involvement in the drive against all public expressions of Christian practice. Pastors came under the same pressure as Catholic priests to make public renunciation of their ministry and their faith, and a majority did so. It has been calculated that of some 106 pastors in the synods of Languedoc (about 69 percent) abandoned their pastoral functions during the de-Christianization movement of 1793–1794, with at most one in five pastors attempting to keep some form of ministry going. Ex-pastors often enlisted in the service of the Republic, most famously Jeanbon Saint-André, who was given responsibility on the Committee of Public Safety for the Navy. Those who stayed in their posts had to resume old habits by going back underground, knowing that they risked imprisonment if discovered. With the collapse of the synodal and consistorial structures of the Reformed Church, the LAITY were left to their own devices. Most were not prepared to give up their faith. They may have paid lip-service to the Republican cults but, as at La Rochelle, went on clandestinely with their worship and conducted MARRIAGES and BAPTISMS.

Freedom of worship was not officially restored until the law of 3 *ventôse* Year III (February 21, 1795), when CHURCH AND STATE were formally separated. It was a mixed blessing for the leaderless Protestants when politicians tried to stand back from religious contestation. The way was effectively cleared for a fresh surge of sectarian killings, as Catholic murder gangs hunted down hundreds of Calvinists in the Gard and Lozère during the "white terror." The recovery of a religious life after 1795 was difficult. In Alsace, pastors were able to restart church life quite promptly in 1795, but in Montbéliard, Uzès, the Vivarais, and the Agennais, organization required much attention; worship resumed in 1798 in La Rochelle, in 1801 in Marseille, and not before 1805 in Toulouse.

Services often had to be conducted without a pastor, for, excluding Alsace, there were only 120 pastors active in 1799, at least one-third fewer than in 1789. Another consequence of the Revolution was a diminution of middle-class supporters, traditionally the fundraisers and willing members of the consistories, and the loss of revenue that resulted. After the Revolution, the two-thirds of the Protestant population who lived in the countryside kept the faith of their forefathers alive.

Relations between French Protestants and the state were finally and favorably regularized under the Napoleonic Concordat. Under that agreement and separate Organic Articles of April 1802, the 480,000 Calvinists and 200,000 Lutherans received better terms than those granted to the Catholics. The agreements gave them an unprecedented degree of official recognition, with Protestant churches established on a parallel basis to the Catholics, including provision for regularizing the formation of consistories (intended to ensure dominance by the social elite) and salaried pastors from 1804. But there was also continuing watchfulness by the new prefects in the provinces; Protestant synods could gather only with the express permission of the government. The new arrangement enabled Protestant groups to take up their worshipping and communal life again, and relations with the Catholic majority were seldom a problem thereafter, except in one or two areas like the Gard, the scene of renewed bloodletting during the Restoration of 1814–1815 in a second wave of the white terror.

See also Calvinism; Consistory; Lutheranism

References and Further Reading

Adams, Geoffrey. *The Huguenots and French Opinion 1685–1787. The Enlightenment Debate on Toleration.* Waterloo, Ontario, Canada: Published for the Canadian Corp. for Studies in Religion by Wilfrid Lauride, University Press, 1991.

Bien, David D. *The Calas Affair. Persecution, Toleration, and Heresy in Eighteenth-Century Toulouse.* Princeton, NJ: Princeton University Press, 1960.

Dedieu, Joseph. *Histoire Politique des Protestants Français (1715–1794).* 2 vols. Paris: J. Gabalda, 1925.

Hood, James N. "Revival and Mutation of Old Rivalries in Revolutionary France." *Past and Present* 82 (1979): 82–115.

———. "Protestant-Catholic Relations and the Roots of the First Popular Counterrevolutionary Movement in France." *Journal of Modern History* 43 (1971): 245–75.

Lewis, G. *The Second Vendée: The Continuity of Counter-Revolution in the Department of the Gard 1789–1815.* New York: Oxford University Press, 1978.

Ligou, Daniel. "Les Protestants Français à la veille de la Révolution." In *La France Pré-Révolutionnaire.* Edited by Pierre Léon Féral. Paris: Publisud, 1991, 125–135.

Mours, Samuel, and Daniel Robert. *Le Protestantisme en France du XVIIIe siècle à nos jours (1685–1970)*. Paris: Librairie Protestante, 1972.

Poland, Burdette C. *French Protestantism and the French Revolution. A Study in Church and State, Thought and Religion, 1685–1815*. Princeton, NJ: Princeton University Press, 1957.

Woodbridge, J. D. "The Reformed Pastors of Languedoc Face the Movement of Dechristianization (1793–1794)." *Sécularisation: Problèmes d'Histoire du Christianisme* 13 (1984): 77–89.

NIGEL ASTON

FRIENDS GENERAL CONFERENCE

The largest organization in North America of liberal Quakers belonging to the Religious Society of Friends (Quakers), the Friends General Conference (FGC) was founded in 1900 at Chautauqua, New York. The Conference was a merger of the First-Day School Conference, Friends Union for Philanthropic Labor, Friends Religious Conference, Friends Educational Conference, and Young Friends Associations. Seven Quaker yearly meetings with a combined membership of about 17,000—Philadelphia, New York, Baltimore, Genesee, Ohio, Indiana, and Illinois—participated in the FGC from its beginning.

In accordance with long-standing liberal Quaker traditions, volunteers ran the FGC until 1904, when Henry Morse Wilbur was hired as secretary of the Advancement Committee, dedicated to encouraging the spread of Quaker beliefs and principles. In 1914, J. Barnard Walton became the new advancement secretary, serving until 1951. Walton's indefatigable travels helped to build the FGC and halt the decline of liberal Quaker membership. Jane Rushmore, hired in 1907, built up the FGC's religious education program.

The FGC's best-known program was its week-long summer gatherings, held annually or biennially, with an attendance of 1,500 to 3,000 people. From 1916 to 1968, these conferences were held almost exclusively in Cape May, New Jersey, in even-numbered years. They were held mostly for purposes of education and spiritual renewal. In the mid- to late-twentieth century, the FGC expanded as liberal Quakers from Baltimore to New York healed old schisms with Orthodox Quakers and as many new yearly meetings, often with most members in college towns, joined up, extending the geographical range from Maine and Eastern Canada to Minnesota and from Florida to Texas (but not the West Coast, except Alaska and Western Canada). In 2000, FGC yearly meetings had approximately 32,945 members.

See also Friends, Society of; Society of Friends in North America

References and Further Reading

Birchard, Bruce. "Nurturing Vital Quaker Meetings and Spirit-Filled Friends." *Friends Journal* 46 no. 5 (2000): 6–10.

Haines, Deborah. "Friends General Conference: A Brief Historical Overview." *Quaker History* 89 no. 2 (2000): 1–16.

STEPHEN W. ANGELL

FRIENDS WORLD COMMITTEE FOR CONSULTATION

The Friends World Committee for Consultation (FWCC) is the most broadly representative organization of the Religious Society of Friends (Quakers) worldwide, embracing all branches of Friends. Arising from a proposal at a 1937 conference in Swarthmore, Pennsylvania, it was founded in 1938 at Doorn, the NETHERLANDS. Its first chairman was Carl Heath, an English peace activist. Before World War II, the FWCC's membership was limited mainly to European and American Quakers, but in the postwar era membership expanded to include churches from AFRICA, Asia, AUSTRALIA, and LATIN AMERICA.

The FWCC's most valuable contribution has been the facilitation of Quaker intervisitation. Douglas Steere, philosopher and writer on spirituality from Haverford College, traveled extensively on behalf of the FWCC, especially during the 1960s. Steere was a Quaker observer at the Vatican II Council and a speaker at a Christian–Buddhist dialogue in JAPAN, one among many ecumenical activities in which the FWCC has participated. The FWCC is a chief sponsor of Quaker United Nations Offices in New York and Geneva, SWITZERLAND.

A variety of peacemaking and civil liberties efforts in the UNITED STATES and worldwide have been held under FWCC auspices. In 1967, in response to an FWCC Conference calling for "an all-out attack on want," the FWCC formed the "Right Sharing of the World's Resources" (RSWR), which called for the gift of 1 percent of all Quakers' income to the poor. The RSWR has since become independent of the FWCC. The FWCC's major gatherings are triennial; it has met every three years since 1952. As of 2002, yearly meetings with a membership of 255,246, about three-quarters of the worldwide total Quaker membership of 338,219, were affiliated with the FWCC.

See also American Friends Service Committee; Friends, Society of; Society of Friends in North America

References and Further Reading

Hadley, Herbert. *Quakers World Wide*. London: Friends World Committee for Consultation, 1991.

STEPHEN W. ANGELL

FRIENDS, SOCIETY OF

There is a certain polarization in the identity of the Society of Friends, or Quakers, founded by GEORGE FOX (1626–1691) and others in the middle of the seventeenth century. On the one hand, Quakerism was formed by the Protestant legacy of the REFORMATION; there was, in Fox and also in such a major articulator of Quaker thought as Robert Barclay (1648–1690), a strong proclivity toward Protestant doctrines—of humanity's sinfulness and the certainty of human damnation were it not for the supreme efficacy of Christ's saving DEATH, and of the AUTHORITY of Scripture as God's revelation supplying divine truth in place of what in human beings would otherwise be immutable ignorance. In that kind of formulation, humankind's sole help lay in agencies outside humanity itself; the redemption won by Christ in an action in time past entirely free of positive human involvement, with the Scripture standing apart from men and women as an outside light. To set against that line of thought, an anthropologically more optimistic Quaker approach stressed a capacity for goodness within the human person and an access to the revelation of truth from wellsprings deep within the minds and spirits of women and men: the "inner light." In this article attention will be given to the Quaker ambivalence over what may be simplified as "externalist" and "internalist" tendencies in Quaker religious thought. Here the focus is on the influences of Protestantism, emphasizing the elements of Quaker religious thought that belong within the camp of the Protestant Reformation.

Indeed, the Protestant features of the Society of Friends have sometimes been obscured in a traditional Quaker historiography that saw it as representing a radical breakaway from the conventional English Protestantism of the seventeenth century. Especially in a school of Quaker historical writing that emerged in the nineteenth century, the Quaker founder George Fox and the early Friends were seen as having mounted a sharp reaction away from, and a repudiation of, the most pronounced forms of Calvinist Protestantism in mid–seventeenth-century England, those of PRESBYTERIANISM, Independents, and BAPTISTS, the principal Puritan groupings of the age of the English CIVIL WARS and revolution. Thus in his pioneering survey of mid–seventeenth-century English religious radicalism, *The Inner Life of the Religious Societies of the Commonwealth* (1876), the Quaker historian Robert Barclay quoted the Victorian religious thinker C. H. SPURGEON to the effect that "the Puritans, who had been like the spring buds and blossoms, were getting into the sere and yellow leaf, and the Independents, and Baptists, and other sects, who were at times

thoroughly and even remarkably spiritual, were growing worldly, political and vain glorious" (Barclay 1876:191). The truth was, Barclay himself argued, that Fox and the first Quakers undertook nothing less than the reformation of the English Reformation, whereas the early Quakers' own historiography of their origins used the kind of vocabulary that had earlier been used by writers such as JOHN FOXE to contrast the corruptions of pre-Reformation Catholicism with the light of the gospel shed by godly change under HENRY VIII, Edward VI, and ELIZABETH I. As a contemporaneous account of the hostility that the Friends faced from the mainstream churches in the national establishment of religion in ENGLAND in the Puritan ascendancy of the 1650s put it, "the Baptists sued us for the very tythe eggs. It can hardly be declared the cruel havoc and spoyle the Presbyterians made. Their priests made poor people come up two hundred miles . . . "—to be exploited. The early Friends, then, in their own self-perception, stood not for a linear continuity with Reformation Protestantism, but rather for a rejection of Protestantism's own corruptions and represented the authentic reformation.

George Fox

Fox himself drew the clearest line between the new reformation he claimed to represent and the existing Protestant TRADITION forged in Tudor and Stuart England. In the first place, Fox depicted the self-acclaimed "godly" religion established in the post–Civil War England (into which he erupted as an evangelist from about 1652 onward) as a system of feather-bedding clerical self-interest and self-indulgence. The CLERGY of the mainstream branches of established PURITANISM were "hireling teachers" or "priests," dismissively labeled as such to ensure that they were firmly counted in with the old Catholic clerical estate whose supremacy, Fox implied, had hardly been lessened in a post-Reformation England, where the very parish churches still used for worship had been erected "in ye darke time of popery." However, beyond the moral criticism of an ecclesiastical reformist denouncing the practical shortcoming of an established church, Fox took issue on a more fundamental level with what he portrayed as the false doctrines of England's supposedly Protestant establishment of religion in the 1650s. In particular, he attacked what he saw as contemporaneous Protestantism's obsession with humanity's sinfulness: Fox told Protestant ministers that they "preach up sin . . . Itt was all their workes to plead for itt . . . they came to plead for sin & imperfections. . . ." And indeed it was true that the Protestant preachers of Fox's day, such as JOHN BUNYAN (1628–1688), did make much of SIN, and linked it to their equal stress on the necessity and indispensability of redemption from its effects by Christ's sole saving power, a "Protestant" insistence that Fox fully shared. For Fox lacked the sense of intrinsic human sinlessness per se commonly attributed to English ultra-radical groups, such as the Ranters of the 1650s. Instead, he manifested a strongly Protestant conviction that "Hee hath Taken away my sinne (viz: Christ my saviour). . . " (Fox 1911:56,2).

No doubt, aspects of early Quaker spirituality, including the conviction of identity with Christ as expressed in the Quaker James Nayler's (1617–1660) ride into Bristol in 1656 in imitation of Jesus's Palm Sunday entry into Jerusalem, fostered the contemporaneous perception on the part of more orthodox Protestants that the Quakers' CHRISTOLOGY was only interiorist, replacing the historic and salvific Jesus with an elusive spiritual and internal Christ-spirit present in the devout man or woman. Fox determinedly repulsed such an attitude, in a strong affirmation of the actuality of the saving Jesus who died and rose in historical time. Thus the Reformation's, and above all, MARTIN LUTHER's understanding of the ATONEMENT as a defined and redemptive historical event—in the terms of the BOOK OF COMMON PRAYER, on whose LITURGY Fox was reared, "one oblation once offered," "a full, perfect, and sufficient sacrifice. . ."—was strongly reaffirmed in 1650 when Fox declared his faith that Christ "did suffer without ye gates at Jerusalem . . . there outwardely. . . . " What is particularly interesting is that Fox chose to use a language of externality—"*without* ye gates," "there *outwardely*"—that was designed to emphasize the once-accomplished action of the crucified Christ, who came "to purchase & sanctifie & redeeme" "with his bloode," a vocabulary almost uncannily similar to that used by the self-appointed defender of Protestantism Bunyan in an encounter he conducted in 1656 with the Quaker spokesman Edward Burroughs. On that occasion, Bunyan tried to fault Burroughs as a traitor to the Reformation pillars of Christ's historically achieved redemption once won for us, outside of us. Yet at the beginning of that same decade of the 1650s, Fox himself nailed the nascent Quaker movement firmly to the Protestant mast of acceptance of Christ's primary role as savior of mankind.

In that singularly disputatious decade of the 1650s, a debate that Fox held with a Jesuit in 1658 offered further proof of his embrasure within the English Protestant mainstream, with its vivid current of anti-popery. Fox's debating articles for this encounter began with the motion "whether or noe ye church of Rome was not degenerated from ye Churh [*sic*] in ye primitive times from there life & doctrine & ye power & spiritt that they was in . . . . " He went on to demand

"what scriptures Catholics had for settimg uppe cloysters for Nunns & Monasteryes & Abbeys for men: and for all there severall orders. And what scripture had they for prayinge by beades & to Images: & for makeing Crosses & forbiddinge of meates & marriages & for putting people to death for religion."

The features of Catholicism to which Fox there took issue—MONASTICISM, religious orders, the use of the rosary and veneration of images, compulsory fasting and CELIBACY, religious persecution—informed the common agenda of well-established English Protestant objections to popery, which was habitually depicted as a system both of superstition (as in, e.g., Andrew Marvell's 1677 *An Account of the Growth of Popery and Arbitrary Government in England*) and of unwarranted affronts to Christian liberty. Fox's hapless Jesuit antagonist went on to try to defend the practices of his church with reference to the DOCTRINE of its extra-Scriptural traditions, a source of authority whose authenticity was affirmed by the sixteenth-century Catholic Council of Trent. Fox, though, like any staunch Protestant in the lineage of Luther, riposted by taking his stand on the authority of Scripture alone; when the Jesuit father claimed, in defense of the customs of the Catholic Church, support from allusions in 2 Thessalonians: 3 to what Paul had vouchsafed to that church in the form of "the tradition that we passed on to you," Fox "bid him reade yt scripture againe: & there hee might see howe hee perverted ye Apostles words. . . . "

The more general controversy over Scripture next focused on its proof texts for opposed understandings of the Eucharist. Here Fox insisted on an outright rejection of the Catholic Church's Eucharistic doctrine of TRANSUBSTANTIATION, according to which the elements of bread and wine in holy communion (LORD'S SUPPER) were totally transformed into the very essence of the body and blood of Christ. Fox, adopting a somewhat coarse-grained and materialistically minded skepticism concerning the Catholic formula, proceeded to a rather far-fetched offer of a wager with the "pope & some of his cardinalls & Jesuites" according to which, if the bread and wine of the Eucharist underwent no decay, Fox and his people would promptly become Catholic converts—with a vice-versa clause built into the bet. The tone of the caustic little satire is unmistakably Anglo-Protestant, articulating an evolved national CULTURE of contempt for Catholicism—displayed in, for example, the elaborate anti-popish displays conducted during the campaign in 1679–1681 for the exclusion from the throne of the Catholic James Duke of York. Thus the Quaker founder Fox showed himself to be both formed by and powerfully expressive of his country's entrenched Protestant anti-Catholic culture.

William Penn and Robert Barclay

The strongly etched Protestantism of the early Quaker mainstream was affirmed by one of the movement's best-known early leaders, WILLIAM PENN (1644–1718). It is true that in 1668 Penn, in his *Sandy Foundations Shaken* undermined some of the chief buttresses of Protestantism, including PREDESTINATION and the traditional "forensic" understanding of the Atonement according to which Christ was cast to become man so that, human and divine, he alone could redeem humanity. Even so, it was also Penn who stated, twenty years after that seemingly un-Protestant work of 1668, that he "loved the protestant religion above his life." In the intervening years between 1668 and 1688, English and Welsh Quakerism, sharing in the fullest measure the persecution heaped on the dissenting Protestant groups after the Restoration of Anglican monarchy in 1660, in fact itself underwent a continuing alignment of its doctrines to the Protestant center.

The chief architect of this process was the Scot Robert Barclay (1648–1690), the author of a series of works on Quaker dogmatics, the best known of which is *An Apology for the True Christian Divinity* (1676), described as "one of the most impressive theological writings of the seventeenth century." Before his CONVERSION to Quakerism, Barclay received his early education at Scots College, Paris, a Catholic seminary of which his uncle was principal. Indeed, he later recalled that in his schooling he had been "defiled by the pollutions of popery," but was thereby perhaps led more positively into appreciative approaches to writings of the great medieval Catholic writers, Tauler, St. Bernard, Bonaventure, and Thomas a Kempis. However, in his *Apology,* Barclay was at pains to reveal the distinctiveness of the Quaker way and its pursuit of truths central to the Christian message from which both Catholicism *and* Protestantism were aberrant. His most dramatic severance of his Quakerism from the Protestant core undoubtedly lay in his description of the Reformation doctrine of reprobation—the predestined consigning of sinners to their damnation—as "horrible and blasphemous." Even so, in his attempt to steer a midway course between the churches of the Reformation and of the Counter-Reformation, we find Barclay leaning his tiller closer to Wittenberg and Geneva than to Rome and Paris.

A focal issue—the pillar, indeed, in the midst of the doctrinal battlefield between Reformation and anti-Reformation—on which we might test that last statement is that of JUSTIFICATION, the process by which men and women are accounted acceptable in God's sight. For Barclay, the Catholic understanding of justification was *fundamentally* erroneous ("vitiated"), so

that "Luther did not without great Ground oppose himself to them in this Matter." This was because, in Barclay's view, the Catholic sense of the works by which sinners were justified amounted in fact to a parcel of financial deals, bulls, pardons, and indulgences, the accoutrements of "the Pope's *Doctrine of Merits,* the most beneficial of all his Revenue." As Barclay in his great work progressively distanced himself from Catholicism as an apparatus of delusive external works that did not in fact justify sinners, he proceeded to repudiate with considerable force the centerpiece of Catholic worship, the Mass, in which "they pretend to offer Christ daily to the Father. . . so that a Man for Money can procure Christ thus to be offered for him when he pleases. . . " (Barclay 1765: 165, 167).

If the Catholics trusted too much for their justification in bogus meritorious routines, then the Protestants, Barclay continued, invested too much confidence in FAITH alone to justify. But it was at just this point that, instead a holding a balancing line between the theories of SALVATION (soteriology) of the Catholic and Protestant Churches, Barclay showed his own real affinity with the apprehension of justification that descended down from Luther and JOHN CALVIN to the evolving Protestantism of the later seventeenth century. We can appreciate the full extent of the Protestantism of one of Quakerism's greatest doctrinal formulators in phrases of his that could be taken as textbook layouts of what Reformation soteriology amounts to: "Justification springs of, and from the Love of God:

> Neither can we procure Remission of Sins or Justification by any Act of our own, so as to merit it, or draw it as a Debt from God due unto us; but we acknowledge all to be *of* and *from* his *Love,* which is the original and fundamental Cause of our Acceptance. . . . God manifested this *Love* towards us, in the sending of his beloved Son the Lord *Jesus Christ* into the World, who gave himself for us an *Offering* and a Sacrifice to God. . . . Neither do we think that Remission of Sins is to be expected, sought, or obtained any other Way, or by any Works or Sacrifice whatsoever. . . . So then Christ by his Death and Sufferings hath reconciled us to God, even while we are Enemies. . . .

We can readily trace the lines of those formulas back to Calvin, for although the phrases may be in different order and variant language, the same meaning is unmistakable: Christ's sole and sufficient redeeming action as commissioned by the Father out of God's own love, bringing reconciliation where there had been enmity, and our own lack both of need and capacity to strive to achieve our own justification. As Calvin wrote:

All that we have hitherto said of Christ leads to this one result, that condemned, dead, and lost in ourselves, we must in him seek righteousness, deliverance, life, and salvation . . . . The office of Redeemer was assigned him in order that he might be our Saviour. . . . God. . . as our enemy until he was reconciled to us by Christ. . . . [Therefore], we must fix our eyes and minds on Christ alone, as it is to him alone that our sins, which necessarily provoked the wrath of God, are not imputed to us. Hence that imputation of righteousness without works. . . , the righteousness found in Christ alone being accepted as if it were ours. (Calvin 1875:I, 434–436, 457).

A point of difference might appear to have arisen over Barclay's authentically Quaker appreciation of opportunities for SANCTIFICATION in what has been termed the "transforming power of the Cross." Seen in that light, the Atonement was more than a forensic process of apportioning to sinful men and women, who remained no more than "justified sinner," the imputed fruits of Christ's redeeming action. The second stage, as it were, of redemptive action saw the operation of "this pure and perfect Redemption *in ourselves,* purifying, cleansing, and redeeming us from the Power of Corruption, and bringing us into Unity, Favour, and Friendship with God." Could Calvin's soteriological analysis accommodate such a sense of progress and transformation? Indeed it could—for in his devotional classic, originally part of the INSTITUTES OF THE CHRISTIAN RELIGION and known as the *Golden Booklet of the True Christian Life,* Calvin traced the route of perfection:

The Lord has adopted us to be his children on this condition that we reveal an imitation of Christ who is the mediator of our adoption. . . . Perfection must be the final mark at which we aim, and the goal for which we strive. . . . Let us steadily exert ourselves to reach a higher degree of holiness till we shall finally arrive at a perfection of goodness which we seek and pursue as long as we live. . . . (Calvin 1981:15, 18–19).

Barclay's Quaker-Protestant understanding of a justification that led on to sanctification was, to say the least, to be accommodated within a Protestant schema that led back to Calvin and that ran through a line that led via the greatest expositor of Reformed doctrine in England, WILLIAM PERKINS (1558–1602), who devised a graph that included the stages of effectual calling, justification, sanctification, glorification, and life eternal. The Quaker Robert Barclay ought to be viewed within that English Protestant lineage.

Quietism

A subsequent Quaker spiritual development, quietism, was viewed by the great historian of the Friends, RUFUS M. JONES, as having been bequeathed to the movement as a legacy of mystical and contemplative devotion by Barclay. The eighteenth-century quietist phase of Quaker history, marked as it was by tendencies toward "habit and custom" rather than the pristine "freshness and surprise. . . creative insight and discovery. . . fluidity and mobility" of the first Friends, arose, Jones wrote, especially from Barclay's sense of the essential oppositeness of divine and human illumination. In other words, quietism sprang out of "the absolute despair of human nature which Protestant theology. . . had greatly intensified." Quietist thought, then, insisted on the negation of all that was indigenously human in the makeup of men and women and its replacement by divine inspirations. On the basis of those divine leadings, however, people might be set free for lives not of contemplative inaction, but rather of intense activity.

Indeed, the eighteenth and early nineteenth centuries—Jones's classic "quietist" period—also formed a golden age of Quaker activism in the world, especially the world of social reform and ameliorism. The great prison reformer ELIZABETH FRY (1780–1845) typified those urges, and Quaker radical statesman John Bright (1811—1889) was born and raised within the period of the ascendancy of quietist spirituality among Friends. Whereas English Quakers of that period focused on attempts to create a kind of Christian humanitarianism, their American co-religionists were exercised by the moral stigma of SLAVERY in their own country. JOHN WOOLMAN (c. 1720–1772) was the eighteenth-century American patron saint of the Quaker witness against slavery's inhumanity, although we seem at first hearing to listen to the voice of the ENLIGHTENMENT when we read Woolman's announcement that "all nations are of one blood" and "of a general brotherhood." But the real inspiration for Woolman's humane UNIVERSALISM was not so much secular enlightened liberalism as the Scriptures, and specifically the witness of Genesis 3:20 to the common ancestry of humankind. Indeed, in his Quaker-Protestant voice, Woolman used Scripture as the chief seal of his authority ("Holy Writ"), with citations from Paul and, liberally, from the Old Testament. Woolman, too, was no less "Protestant" in his doctrine of the Fall and of redemption won "thro the wonderful love of God, in Christ Jesus our Lord," a redemptive action that had the capacity to restore humanity to the "primitive harmony" that prevailed before sin sowed discord on earth (Woolman 1776:256, 270).

Even so, the Quaker-quietist preoccupation with personal holiness produced in the eighteenth century a revulsion away from the central doctrines of the Protestant Reformation of salvation won for humankind vicariously through the merits of Christ crucified, benefits transferred to the credit of the justified sinner. Jones calls this traditional Protestant approach, which took its rise directly from Luther and Calvin, "forensic," meaning that it envisaged a legal transaction in which the Father, taking note of the penalty paid by Christ on the cross to take away sins, attributed the fruits of that expiating action to the account of (selected) human sinners, clearing their accounts of sin and guilt and requiring no investment from them into the salvific process, because the Son's work was in itself all-sufficient for atonement. In Woolman himself we encounter an appreciation, which Barclay himself had pioneered, of the participation of suffering saints in the entirety of the work of redemption. Woolman's fellow American Quaker Job Scott was a powerful spokesman of a reaction away from the forensic schema that formed the bedrock of Reformation soteriology. Indeed, we seem to hear in Scott's teaching an echo of pre-Reformation emphases, found above all in Thomas a Kempis's (1379–1471) *The Imitation of Christ,* which portrays Christ as an exemplar and model quintessentially to be followed as the template of our own strenuous achievement of holiness. Of course, as discussed earlier, the second pillar of the Reformation, Calvin, stressed sanctification in the persons of the elect, but Luther had challenged and reversed the Kempian concern with merit and the pursuit of perfection when he declared, in his lectures on St. Paul's Epistle to the Galatians, that:

> Wherefore Paul saith. . . that Christ first began and not we. 'He, even he (saith Paul) loved me and gave himself for me.' As if he said: He found in me no good will nor right understanding; but this good Lord had mercy upon me. He saw me to be nothing else but wicked, going astray, contemning God and flying from him more and more; yea, rebelling against God, taken, led, and carried away captive to the devil (Luther 1956:176).

But Scott was closer to Kempis than he was to Luther when he postulated, not as with Luther, the sinner, that were it not for Christ, moving in inexorable alienation away from God, but instead a movement, in Kempis's pattern, of discipleship, of imitation, and of following within Christ's footsteps to a personal cross of suffering on which sainthood was to be achieved:

> And do not the obedience, suffering and death of Christ, as plainly point out to us the necessity of a life of obedience, self-denial, and death unto sin, as even outward circumcision pointed out the circumcision of the heart? And is it not on the very ground of this necessity of a real self-denial, and death to sin, that Christ insists upon it, that whoever will be his disciple, must first deny himself, take up his daily (mark daily) cross and follow him? Follow him! What is that? Why it is to take his Holy Spirit for our leader and guide into all truth; to take him

for our pattern and example; and to follow him, wheresoever he leadeth us, in the way of regeneration, self-denial, the loss of our life, and death unto all sin (Jones 1921:78).

Thus the Lutheran soteriologic scheme, according to which sinners, on the account of Christ's saving death, are quite passively considered just in God's audit, seems in Scott to be supplanted by a sharp sense of the would-be saint's actively following in a route of seeking perfection by active, earnest, and self-denying endeavor, Christ being the exemplar and stencil-plate. Even so, Scott's rooting in quietism induced in him an appreciation, which returns us to an essentially Protestant outlook, that nothing good in humanity could subsist and activate without being, as Scott put it, "moved" and "initiated" divinely, for works and even prayers arising from the natural "creature" would not "get the blessing," and to "utter a request to God rightly always requires His divine, living, immediate assistance."

Evangelicalism

If the authentic legacy of the Reformation and Protestantism's insistence that anything that is of worth in human hearts and souls is of God is so far advanced in the Quaker quietist Scott, his DENOMINATION was about to undergo a fundamental realignment to the reawakening of Protestantism and its doctrines, especially those of salvation, known as the Evangelical revival and taking its rise from the missionary work of the Methodist founder, JOHN WESLEY (1703–1791). Partly as a result of personal contacts with Methodists, the Quaker minister Mary Dudley (1750–1823) brought into her PREACHING and writing a firm and vibrant emotional reaffirmation of the principles of the Reformation that Wesley himself had imparted to the widespread Evangelical movement that fed new currents of spirituality both inside and apart from the CHURCH OF ENGLAND between the eighteenth and nineteenth centuries (see EVANGELICALISM). Dudley's watchwords were absolutely resonant of the whole Evangelical movement within the Protestant churches in that period: "the original fall and degeneracy of man" rectified by God's "stupendous plan of redemption." Dudley also saw herself as entrusted with the correction of errors in the Quakerism of her day—rationalism on the one hand and confidence in the efficacy of good works to save—which had obscured the message of the scriptures:

> Preach Christ crucified. . . be not afraid to preach the cross of Christ and to proclaim not only what he would do within us by His Spirit, but also what he hath done without [outside of] us, the all-atoning sacrifice which should never be lost sight of.

In such words, Mary Dudley restated Protestant-Quaker principles that can be traced back to Fox and his insistence that Christ "did suffer without ye gates at Jerusalem there outwardely." The central affirmation—whatever the importance in Quaker spirituality of an appreciation of a light and, indeed, of a spirit, of Christ within the believer—was of an objective historical saving action taking place in history and external to our more individual experiences. The difference in the Evangelical period was to an extent one of tone, for whereas Reformation and post-Reformation thought on the issues of salvation and GRACE revolved around the legal and forensic issues with which Luther had to grapple, by the late eighteenth century it may have been the emotional and individualist emphases of the Romantic movement that found their way as influences into Evangelical Quaker discourse, such as that of the Quaker preacher Thomas Shillitoe (1754—1836):

> I feel I have nothing to depend upon, but the mercies of God in Christ Jesus. I do not rely for salvation upon any merits of my own; all my own works are as filthy rags. . . my faith is in the merits of Jesus Christ and in the offering he made for us. I trust my past sins are all forgiven me. . . that they have been washed away by the blood of Christ, who died for my sins.

At the height of the Evangelical ascendancy within Quakerism, in works such as the *Principles of Religion* (1805), Henry Tuke (1755–1814) summarized its positions on such topics as the infallibility of Scripture, the degeneracy of humankind after the Fall, and the absolute indispensability of the Atonement to rectify the terrible consequences of the sin of Adam and Eve. Even so, Evangelical voices did not command the entire Quaker repertoire in the nineteenth century. The American Quaker preacher Elias Hicks (1748–1830) took his stand on the distinctive and venerable Quaker tradition of the inner light and proclaimed an interiorist view that accepted Christ as redeemer—as was the case, of course, in the classic Reformation Christian formulation—but in the shape rather of an inner force: ". . . no other Saviour but such an one who takes His residence in the very centre of the soul of man can possibly bring salvation to man." Hicks's interiority traced the dividing line between his in many ways traditional or conservative Quakerism and the neo-Protestant teachings of the Evangelicals. His insistence on "a portion of God," or even an "inward God," "the uncreated Word," "Christ," within the believer removed the necessity of a salvation that came from any force apart from the self. Scripture, too, that Evangelical and Protestant touchstone and inerrant reservoir of objective revealed truth, was sidelined in Hicks's scheme as being an external source, an "out-ward instrumental help" "to lead the minds of the children of men home to this divine inward principle manifested in their own hearts and minds." The formal "Great Separation" of 1827–1828 between Evangelical and "Hicksite" Friends in North America, a Quaker schism unhealed to the present day, dramatically exposed the tension between the two strands, Protestant and Evangelical versus interiorist and spiritual, that have formed the Quaker identity since the inception of the Society of Friends.

See also American Friends Service Committee; Calvinism; Individualism; Liberal Protestantism and Liberalism; Romanticism; Society of Friends in North America

References and Further Reading

Barclay, Robert (the elder). *An Apology for the True Christian Divinity, being an Explanantion and Vindication of the Principles and Doctrines of the people called Quakers.* 8th ed. Birmingham, UK: John Baskerville, 1765.

Barclay, Robert (the younger). *The Inner Life of the Religious Societies of the Commonwealth.* London: Hodder and Stoughton, 1876.

Calvin, John. *Institutes of the Christian Religion.* Translated by Henry Beveridge. 2 vols. Edinburgh, UK: T & T. Clark, 1875.

———. *Golden Booklet of the True Christian Life.* Translated by Henry J. van Andel. Grand Rapids, MI: Baker Book House, 1952.

Fox, George. *The Journal of George Fox.* Edited by Norman Penney. 2 vols. Cambridge, Cambridge University Press, 1911.

Ingle, H. Larry. *First Among Friends: George Fox and the Creation of Quakerism.* Oxford, Oxford University Press, 1994.

Ingle, H. Larry. *Quakers in Conflict: The Hicksite Reformation.* Knoxville, TN: University of Tennessee Press, 1986.

Jones, Rufus M. *The Later Periods of Quakerism.* 2 vols. London: Macmillan, 1921.

Luther, Martin. *A Commentary on St. Paul's Epistle to the Galatians.* Translated by anonymous, 1575. London: James Clarke, 1953.

MICHAEL A. A. MULLETT

FRONTIER RELIGION

The perception of a religion distinctive to the North American frontier originated in the early twentieth century with the application of Frederick Jackson Turner's "Frontier Thesis" to camp meeting revivalism. These outdoor evangelical events were often huge, spanning several days, with participants camping on site. One result was the appearance of chaos and pandemonium. The most notorious characteristic of CAMP MEETINGS was the seemingly inexplicable bodily expressions of spiritual feeling, particularly the "jerks," which appeared to fit well into Turner's contention that the wilderness environment produced a unique American CULTURE. Camp meeting revivalism, which first appeared in Kentucky in 1800, lent credence to this interpretation. The primitive environment seemed to produce wild expressions of religious feeling. As recent historians have demonstrated, however, the camp meeting format descended from main streams of American Protestant THEOLOGY. The idea of environmental causes has also been abandoned. Despite camp meeting revivalism's origins in the new nation's western region, most appeared in more densely populated neighborhoods, under the direction of ordained ministers, where religious congregations had existed for several years. Moreover, the format quickly spread to urban areas of the east because of its evangelical power. Although the impression of a religiously starved, unrestrained, and ignorant pioneer population persists, it is outdated by more than two decades of scholarship.

Large outdoor evangelical events were not new anywhere in America, but the Kentucky innovation of camping on the meeting grounds greatly intensified religious appeals for spiritual rebirth. Participants coexisted, for a few days at least, in a total environment marked by interdenominational cooperation and New Testament principles, removed from normal daily cares and social distinctions. The Methodists, led by FRANCIS ASBURY, were more comfortable than most other American denominations with emotionally charged spiritual expressions and immediately embraced the new evangelical format. Camp meeting revivalism quickly spread and fueled the new denomination's growth.

The impact in frontier regions was compounded by the decentralized structure of early American METHODISM. Bishop Asbury immediately perceived the camp meeting's potential. He also responded promptly to the expansion of western settlement through a system of itinerant ministers assigned to preaching circuits. The itinerant CIRCUIT RIDERS were able to bring group WORSHIP to the farthest reaches of settlement, where local populations were not yet able to support a permanent ministry. Nearly all white Americans were at least nominally Christian, and although the pious could read Scripture and engage in private PRAYER in the absence of institutionalized religion, the Methodist circuit riders often offered the first opportunity for group worship. Many westerners descended from other denominations, but group worship, however infrequent the circuit rider's visits, and the BAPTISM of children as Christians, lured many families away from their former denominations.

Those denominations that required an educated ministry, such as the Presbyterians, struggled to keep up with the rapid settlement expansion. One response was the formation of a missionary corps of young men. For example, the Connecticut Missionary Society, organized in 1798, sent a regular stream of Congregational ministers to the New Englanders who settled Ohio's Western Reserve. In frontier regions settled by adherents of multiple denominations, the result was often a confusing, although not to say un-Christianlike, interdenominational rivalry. An unattractive aspect of American Christianity, interdenominational competition has yet to be studied in detail. It was no doubt strongest in frontier regions where the availability of affordable land brought believers from different denominations into closer geographical proximity than was usually the case in the seaboard states.

The other target of "home missionary" work on the frontier was the Native American population. Efforts to convert Native Americans to Christianity originated with the beginnings of European settlement. The most significant missionary work during the eighteenth century was by German missionaries John Heckewelder of the MORAVIAN CHURCH and David Zeisberger of the United Brethren in western Pennsylvania and the Ohio Valley. However, CONVERSION to Christianity proceeded slowly and offered little protection from attack. In particular, the infamous massacre of nearly 100 Delaware believers (mostly women and children) at the Moravian settlement known as Gnaddenhutten in 1782 deterred efforts of similar scale. After several wars of conquest in the early years of the republic, religious outreach to the scattered groups of Indian survivors received fresh attention. But the efforts to Christianize Indians met with general resentment or indifference, not only because missionaries demanded a rejection of native religious beliefs, but also because they nearly always required also the adoption of European cultural practices. Christian Indians were expected to abandon traditional GENDER roles, folkways, and systems of justice. A few Americans, such as Methodist James B. Finley and Baptist Isaac McCoy, made Indian MISSIONS a central part of their ministerial career, but many others participated in short evangelical tours. Most found the work arduous and unrewarding, and accepted the first acceptable pulpit offered by Euro-American pioneers.

The ample and affordable land on the frontier also provided a rare opportunity for the members of small denominations and communal societies to settle in close geographical proximity with one another. The most prominent example is that of the Latter Day Saints (Mormons), not only in Utah, but also earlier in Missouri and Illinois. The lower price of frontier land also facilitated the survival of other communal groups, for example, the AMANA COLONY in Iowa and the Swedish Bishop Hill colony in Illinois. In a similar fashion, the availability of frontier land enabled numerous ethnic minorities, such as German Lutherans, to establish geographic enclaves strong enough to support independent congregations and schools, significantly reducing pressure to adopt the English language and assimilate.

Thus, the tendency of the twentieth century was to frame the concept of frontier religion within the narrow confines of extremely chaotic and emotional camp meetings. Scholars have shown that such meetings were not limited to newly settled areas, yet the frontier did exert an effect on American religion, aspects of which remain evident today.

See also Ethnicity; Evangelical United Brethren Church; Evangelicalism; Methodism; Mormonism; Presbyterianism; Revivals

References and Further Reading

Boles, John. *The Great Revival, 1797–1805: The Origins of the Southern Evangelical Mind.* Lexington, KY: University Press of Kentucky, 1972.

Hansen, Klaus J. *Mormonism and the American Experience.* Chicago, IL: University of Chicago Press, 1981.

Johnson, Charles. *The Frontier Camp Meeting.* Dallas, TX: Southern Methodist University Press, 1955.

Olmstead, Earl P. *Blackcoats Among the Delaware: David Zeisberger on the Ohio Frontier.* Kent, OH: Kent State University Press, 1991.

Sweet, William Warren. *Religion on the American Frontier.* 4 vols. Chicago, IL: University of Chicago Press, 1936–1946.

ELLEN ESLINGER

FRY, ELIZABETH GURNEY
(1780–1845)

English Quaker. Although born into a wealthy family, Fry devoted her life to working on behalf of those whom society considered as outcasts—especially prisoners. After her marriage she began to visit London's Newgate prison. Her particular focus was female prisoners, whom the authorities considered incorrigible and who were treated accordingly. In contrast she saw the possibility of rehabilitation and consequently formed an association of Quaker volunteers who ministered to them in a variety of ways, religious and otherwise. These included beginning a school for the women's children who were confined with their mothers, as well as for the WOMEN themselves, most of whom were illiterate. Encountering many prisoners—both male and female—condemned to death, Fry also became a vocal opponent of the death penalty, which could be mandated for offenses as minor as shoplifting. In addition she worked to reduce the suffering of women sentenced to be transported as indentured servants to AUSTRALIA, providing for their needs during the journey. With her brother, Joseph John Gurney, she traveled to the north of

ENGLAND to view jails there and in SCOTLAND, establishing women's associations in each of the towns for the visiting of prisoners. He subsequently described their trip in "Notes on a Visit made to some of the Prisons in the North of England, in company with Elizabeth Fry" (1819).

Before the age of forty, Fry's reputation as a reformer—not only on behalf of prisoners, but also of the mentally ill—had spread even to RUSSIA. Hearing of her work, an Englishman in charge of the new asylum in St. Petersburg wrote to her for advice. She responded with various recommendations, the core of which focused on treating the patients with kindness and a degree of humanity not hitherto shown them. Again, it was the dignity of the individual that concerned her, whether prisoner or mental patient. The two daughters who edited her *Memoirs* point out that for her, "justice and humanity claim conjointly to be heard." She demonstrated this twin focus in her life as an advocate.

See also Capital Punishment; Friends, Society of

References and Further Reading

Primary Source:

Fry, Katherine, and Rachel Elizabeth Cresswell, eds. *Memoir of the Life of Elizabeth Fry With Extracts From Her Journal and Letters.* Montclair, NJ: Patterson Smith, 1974.

Secondary Source:

Rose, June. *Elizabeth Fry.* New York: St. Martin's Press, 1980.

GEORGE ANDERSON

FULL GOSPEL BUSINESS MEN'S FELLOWSHIP

The Full Gospel Business Men's Fellowship International (FGBMFI) is a Christian laymen's organization founded in 1951 in Los Angeles by Demos Shakarian, an Armenian-American, millionaire dairy farmer, and Pentecostal. The Fellowship began as a Pentecostal parachurch organization (see PENTECOSTALISM), with membership open to all Christian men regardless of ecclesiastical and theological background. To protect its identity as a lay organization, the FGBMFI denies official leadership roles to CLERGY and other full-time Gospel workers. "Full Gospel" reflects the Fellowship's adherence to orthodox Christianity and Pentecostal doctrine and refers to the belief that the entire New Testament should be accepted as valid for contemporary Christians, including references to (orthodox Christianity plus Pentecostal doctrine) refers to the preaching of the entire New Testament, including

FAITH HEALING, speaking in tongues, and deliverance from demonic forces. "Business Men" include chief executive officers, entrepreneurs, professionals, politically connected men, military officers, farmers, white-collar employees, and some laborers. The Fellowship encourages men to get back into church life, in order to address what is seen as the predominance of females (or feminization) in many churches. WOMEN are not allowed to join the organization. FGBMFI meetings, usually held in the nonecclesiastical atmosphere of restaurants or hotels, consist of nonsectarian gatherings in which men share the powerful and positive way God works in their lives. Meetings include time for personal testimonies as well as an invitation to men to turn their lives over to Christ.

By adopting modern business techniques of organization and communication, the FGBMFI spread its activities throughout the world, opening approximately 6,000 chapters in over 132 countries by the end of the twentieth century. After the death of Demos Shakarian in 1993, Richard Shakarian, his son, became the new international president. Aligning with the CHRISTIAN RIGHT, the FGBMFI membership promotes conservative economics and politics. The Fellowship uses the Internet to propagate its message and to advertise local, national, and international activities. The FGBMFI seeks to transcend denominational, racial, and cultural barriers. According to the Fellowship's official website, the FGBMFI represents a "vast global movement of laymen being used mightily by God to bring in this last great harvest [untold masses of men filled with the Holy Spirit] through the outpouring of God's Holy Spirit before the return of our Lord Jesus Christ" (www.fgbmfi.org). This sense of prophetic mission provides the Fellowship with a strong foundation to reach men throughout the world.

History

The Shakarian story and FGBMFI development are rooted in prophecy. As told by Demos Shakarian (1913–1993), in the nineteenth century the Shakarian family lived in the Armenian city of Kara Kala when they and other Armenians were directed by prophecy to relocate to the western United States to escape terrible danger from Turkish foes. In the new land, the Shakarians would prosper under God's blessing and God would cause their "seed to be a blessing to the nations." In 1905 the Shakarian family arrived in Los Angeles, where they maintained connections to Armenian Pentecostal church life. Isaac Shakarian, the son, married Zarouhi Yessayian and they named their first child Demos, born in 1913. At age thirteen Demos spoke in tongues at a church service when he was "baptized in the Holy Spirit." In 1932 Demos married

Rose Gabrielian, and their first child, Richard, was born two years later. The Shakarian business became the largest dairy in California and, by the 1940s, the largest private dairy in the world, according to Shakarian. In 1937 Demos received a personal prophecy from his friend Milton Hansen that God had chosen him to "speak of holy matters with heads of state around the world."

Shakarian met and became close friends with British healing evangelist Dr. Charles Price, who preached the "Full Gospel." Price's preaching, healing efforts, and prophecy influenced Shakarian and his vision of a layman's revival. In the early 1940s Shakarian was president of a chapter of the Christian Business Men's Committee (CBMC), an organization of Evangelical laymen (see EVANGLICALISM). It struck Shakarian that during religious meetings women often far outnumbered men. Accustomed to Armenian men being the prime movers in the church, he found it confusing that American men had given up the highest calling of all. Shakarian also realized that many of the businessmen he came in contact with never spoke about God. He organized religious tent meetings that reached beyond the inward-looking Armenian community. One notable event was a major Pentecostal youth rally, in 1948, that overflowed the Hollywood Bowl with over 21,000 in attendance.

In the wake of the Los Angeles Pentecostal evangelistic meetings (see REVIVALS) held by ORAL GRANVILLE ROBERTS, in 1951, Shakarian launched the first meeting of the Full Gospel Business Men's Fellowship, a Pentecostal version of the CBMC. Held at Clifton's Cafeteria, in Los Angeles, the event attracted only eighteen men along with Roberts, Shakarian, and Shakarian's wife Rose. The Full Gospel Business Men's Fellowship of America elected Shakarian as president and named key officers, including a banker, an automobile salesman, a building contractor, and an accountant. The Fellowship ministry challenged the stereotype that Pentecostalism was largely confined to the working class and the economically deprived. Vice President Lee Braxton, for example, piloted his own plane throughout the nation to promote Fellowship growth. Shakarian and the other Fellowship officers worked without salaries. Meetings took place in luxury hotels and ballrooms. "International" replaced "of America" in the official charter recognized by the State of California in January 1953. The FGBMFI doctrinal statement required members to believe in the Trinity, an infallible BIBLE, SANCTIFICATION by the blood of Christ, divine healing, and "the baptism in the Holy Ghost accompanied by the initial physical sign of speaking in other tongues as the Spirit gives utterances."

Development

At the first meeting, Roberts spoke of the expected emergence of 1,000 chapters, but there were still no additional chapters one year later. A disappointed Shakarian persisted in promoting the Fellowship, traveling and spending thousands of dollars of his own money. With the creation of the magazine the *Full Gospel Business Men's Voice* (Thomas R. Nickel offered his print shop and editorial services) and the radio program Breakfast-Broadcast, from Clifton's Cafeteria, the growth of the FGBMFI improved. By the summer of 1953 there were nine chapters throughout the United States. A typical chapter meeting consisted of choruses, prayers, and announcements, followed by testimonies, prayers for the sick, presentation of prophecies, glossolalia, calls for salvation, and an evening banquet. Although a Los Angeles office coordinated Fellowship activities, Shakarian opposed too much focus on centralization. Since 1953, annual international conventions (larger-scale replicas of chapter meetings) take place in major American cities. Throughout the 1950s the crusades of healing evangelists Tommy Hicks, Oral Roberts, and William Branham resulted in the creation of many of the early Fellowship chapters. Each chapter seeks to encourage laymen to be personal witnesses for Jesus, bring healing to those in need, and promote fellowship and unity among Christian churches.

FGBMFI leaders maintain that the driving force of the movement is the Holy Spirit. In 1955, Johannesburg, SOUTH AFRICA was the site of the first overseas chapter. A Fellowship chapter in Toronto, CANADA developed the following year. Healing evangelists, such as Tommy Hicks, promoted the FGBMFI at crusades outside the United States. Accepting an invitation from President François Duvalier to hold meetings in Haiti, the Fellowship demonstrated its willingness to reach out to any part of the world, even nations ruled by dictators. By 1961 eighteen nations were represented at the first European convention in Zurich, SWITZERLAND. To spread its influence, the Fellowship began organizing "airlifts," in which FGBMFI members personally finance a visit to a country for the purpose of sharing the Gospel. The Fellowship's 1965 London "airlift" and convention led to the establishment of chapters in many parts of the country. Airlifts occurred even in war-torn destinations such as Vietnam. Such Fellowship endeavors helped spread Pentecostalism into many nations.

The Charismatic Movement of the 1960s extended to mainline Protestant churches and other denominations throughout the world. Beginning in 1963, a series of Fellowship booklets promoted neo-Pentecostal renewal (mainly with testimonies from *Voice* magazine) in Baptist, Episcopalian, and Methodist denominations. By the late 1960s the Fellowship was one of the few Protestant-dominated organizations attracting Catholic members. The Vatican awarded Demos Shakarian a special award in 1974 for the role the FGBMFI played in the Catholic Charismatic Movement.

In 1975 Shakarian reported that after twenty-four years in existence the Fellowship had a total number of 1,650 chapters in fifty-two countries and that the monthly circulation of *Voice* magazine was 800,000. The magazine was translated into seven languages. He also claimed that 4,000,000 people viewed the "Good News," a weekly half-hour television series in its fourth year, carried by 150 television stations, including outlets in Canada, Bermuda, AUSTRALIA, and JAPAN. The Fellowship's radio program operated in twenty-one languages throughout Europe, South America, and Asia. Corresponding to its impressive growth, the Fellowship completed new international headquarters in Costa Mesa in 1980, at a cost of $5,000,000. Oral Roberts gave the keynote speech, demonstrating his continual and influential role in the development of the Fellowship. The mixture of emphases on faith and prosperity continued at Fellowship activities. Leaders included executives who made the Fortune 500 list of American corporate business giants. The FGBMFI has been characterized as "a society of Spirit-filled capitalists trying to make good in the business world." Faith teachers such as Kenneth Copeland and Kenneth Hagin received support from the FGBMFI, which welcomed their focus on teaching "positive confession" in Christian's right to expect for healing and prosperity, even in the midst of criticism of the "name it and claim it" Gospel.

The Fellowship encountered division among the leadership after Demos Shakarian experienced a massive stroke in 1984. Several leaders requested that Shakarian retire and become Chairman of the Board, but he refused. The charge surfaced that Shakarian was guilty of "irregularities" in reporting travel expenses, and, as a result of the power struggle, U.S. membership dropped significantly. In 1987 the Fellowship voted seven "rebellious" members of the board of directors out of office and Shakarian regained complete control. Outside the United States, the FGBMFI continued to grow and in the late 1980s there were 2,646 chapters worldwide. When Demos Shakarian died in 1993, his son Richard assumed the role of president. Utilizing the Internet, the FGBMFI provides potential members with an abundance of local and global information. Issues of the *Voice* magazine, for example, can be downloaded.

Prospects for the Future

The early FGBMFI leaders came from several churches: the ASSEMBLIES OF GOD, the Pentecostal Holiness Church, the CHURCH OF GOD, the INTERNATIONAL CHURCH OF THE FOURSQUARE GOSPEL, and the PENTECOSTAL CHURCH OF GOD. In the early stage, many Pentecostal clergy leaders distrusted the FGBMFI. Traditional Pentecostal ministers opposed the open ecumenical fellowship and they feared that Shakarian sought the creation of a new denomination or organization that diverted money from churches. From its beginning, however, the Fellowship represented a ministry that was not dependent on clergy leaders. The FGBMFI adopted interdenominationalism, preferring that people remain in their own churches. When it became clear that the Fellowship viewed itself as a service rather than a substitute to churches, Pentecostal church opposition diminished.

Animosity between mainstream Evangelicalism and Pentecostalism was intense. Non-Pentecostal believers took exception to the term Full Gospel, which implied that many denominations failed to preach the Gospel in its fullness. For Evangelicals, glossolalia (speaking in tongues) and healing could not be central and indispensable facets of the Christian experience. Still, the Fellowship offered a bridge between classical Pentecostals and Christians from the historic denominations who had received the baptism of the Spirit. The FGBMFI continues to play an important role in the growth of the charismatic movement and the breaking down of barriers between Pentecostal and non-Pentecostal Christians. The FGBMFI did not claim to seek theological precision; simple testimonies of men facing and overcoming the trials and tribulations of life remain a major component of Fellowship success. Attractive to many Christians is a strong experiential theme that a living God carries out biblical promises to those seeking reassurance.

From its origins, the FGBMFI has also sought to attract men of color and of varied ethnicity. In the 1950s the FGBMFI moved the site of its Atlanta convention to Denver when the selected hotel made arrangements to segregate black businessmen into nearby accommodations. Shakarian's position broke down barriers among African Americans who viewed the Fellowship as the exclusive domain of white men (African Americans, however, still participate in small numbers). The Fellowship's global impact suggests a praiseworthy record on the issue of race relations.

The outreach of the Fellowship continues to be dynamic and varied, including a prison ministry initiated by Andrew Kaminski, an American businessman sent to prison for tax evasion. On the eve of the 2000 Olympics in Sydney, the Australian FGBMFI started an athletic club that would allow them access to the Olympic village to witness to the athletes. Small groups called "fire teams" present testimony of God's love and minister in the power of the Holy Spirit. In recognition of the supportive role that women provide FGBMFI members, Vangie Shakarian (wife of President Richard Sharkarian) organized ways for women to become better involved within the Fellowship. Women hold prayer meetings and speak at many FGBMFI conventions and meetings.

As the Fellowship pursues a greater global impact, it appears to pay scant attention to globalization issues relating to the unequal distribution of wealth. Members share the dream that prosperity will come to those who follow the Lord in the fullness of the Holy Spirit. Successful Fellowship members see themselves as spiritual and social models for the world's poor people. A persistent notion is that by serving the Lord in the power of the Holy Spirit, working hard, and living honestly, anyone can realize the American dream of prosperity. The Fellowship is also unapologetic about its alliances with conservative politicians, such as Richard Nixon, Ronald Reagan, Pat Robertson, and other American and world leaders. Throughout the world, conservative politicians and wealthy men continue to champion the growth of the Fellowship. By means of its strong economic and organizational base and its fervor to share the good news of the Gospel, the FGBMFI shows signs of continuing success as a worldwide recruiting arm for charismatic renewal.

References and Further Reading

Fotherby, Val. *The Awakening Giant: The Miraculous Story of the Full Gospel Business Men's Fellowship International.* London: Marshall Pickering, 2000.

Harrell, David Edwin, Jr. *All Things are Possible: The Healing and Charismatic Revivals in Modern America.* Bloomington: Indiana University Press, 1975.

Poloma, Margaret. *The Charismatic Movement: Is There a New Pentecost?* Boston: Twayne Publishers, 1982.

Quebedeaux, Richard. *The New Charismatics II.* San Francisco: Harper & Row Publishers, 1983.

Sharkarian, Demos. *The Happiest People on Earth: The Long-awaited Personal Story of Demos Shakarian as told to John and Elizabeth Sherrill.* Old Tappan, NJ: Chosen Books, 1975.

Synan, Vinson. *Under His Banner.* Costa Mesa, CA: Gift Productions, 1992.

ERIC R. CROUSE

FULLER, MARGARET (1810–1850)

American spiritual writer. Fuller was born in Cambridgeport, Massachusetts on May 23, 1810. She grew up in an intellectual household of Puritan ancestry, and at age twenty-one began to have mystical visions that led her to a new form of spirituality. Her visions challenged the masculinity of God and the gendered boundaries of religion.

Fuller questioned how the public sphere became "masculine" and why WOMEN were relegated to the private, spiritual sphere. She believed that separation into gendered spheres was a separation of God's true essence, which challenged prevailing GENDER norms. Her spirituality proposed that each gender could transcend its divided self and supported divine intuition. Her *Woman in the Nineteenth Century* focused on liberation from gendered categories for both men and women. In this work, Fuller also identified two elements that live within women: "Minerva," the seat of intellect, and the "Muse," the feminine side representing intuition and religious activity.

Fuller equated women with religion and domesticity, but she did achieve her purpose of not limiting the choice of other roles within religious traditions or in society. As an editor, a literary critic, a Transcendentalist, a journalist, and a foreign correspondent during the Roman Revolution (1848) in ITALY, she demonstrated her beliefs. Unfortunately, Fuller died prematurely in 1850 in a shipwreck while returning from Italy to New York.

See also Emerson, Ralph Waldo; Puritanism; Transcendentalism

References and Further Reading

Primary Source:

Fuller, S. Margaret. *Woman in the Nineteenth Century: An Authoritative Text, Backgrounds, and Criticism.* Edited by Larry J. Reynolds. New York: W. W. Norton, 1997.

Secondary Sources:

Fleischmann, Fritz, ed. *Margaret Fuller's Cultural Critique: Her Age and Legacy.* New York: Peter Lange, 2000.
Von Mehren, Joan. *Minerva and the Muse: The Life of Margaret Fuller.* Amherst, MA: University of Massachusetts Press, 1994.

KELLY J. BAKER

FUNDAMENTALISM

Fundamentalism emerged as a recognizable movement in American Protestantism in the World War I era. It shares some features of other twentieth-century fundamentalisms around the globe, but it arose in response to circumstances within Western Christianity and American culture. Fundamentalists construct their identity and worldview around a sacred text—the BIBLE. They regard the Bible as divinely inspired and thus beyond the reach of human criticism. Their insistence that the Bible provides a detailed map for all

of life means that American fundamentalists see particular social and cultural patterns as part of the created order. God intended men, women, and children to stand in particular relationships to one another and to God, and the state has no right to interfere, especially in the interaction between parent and child. Fundamentalists root their strict moral code in their reading of Scripture.

Fundamentalism arose within American Protestantism as a response to profound social and intellectual changes that became widely evident after the CIVIL WAR. For several generations before Charles Darwin, scientists (especially geologists) had challenged the Genesis creation account, but Darwin's *Origin of Species* (1859) and *Descent of Man* (1871) became the symbols of the mounting conviction that modern SCIENCE was incompatible with traditional Christianity (see DARWINISM). Darwin's evolutionary theory challenged his generation to reformulate basic assumptions of Western culture. His observations and conclusions challenged deeply embedded beliefs and implied a developmental spiral with profound implications for ways of understanding society.

Among Darwin's respondents was Princeton's outspoken Charles Hodge. While some ridiculed Darwin or sought a mediating position, Hodge insisted that Darwin's work was incompatible with ORTHODOXY. In *What Is Darwinism?* (1874), Hodge stated bluntly that evolutionary theory could not coexist with the orthodox view of God as omnipotent Creator. Pulpiteers and popular orators and authors took sides and enlisted the public in the controversy. For decades, debates about creationism between people with local name recognition filled auditoriums around the country.

Modern science did not present the only contemporary challenge to traditional Christianity. At about the same time, the work of German and British biblical scholars, animated by a modern view of history, recast the way in which they approached the sacred text from which American evangelicals took their cues. Some of this new biblical scholarship predated the Civil War, but its impact on American Christianity was felt most urgently in the second half of the nineteenth century. The work of such German scholars as Wilhelm Vatke, DAVID STRAUSS, and FERDINAND CHRISTIAN BAUR reflected on the history of Israel, the life of Jesus, and the rise of Christianity using the same interpretive devices for the sacred that historians used for the secular. Such scholarship excluded the miraculous and providential motifs that had long dominated the Christian view of history. Vatke argued that the Pentateuch was written late in Israel's history; Strauss believed that early Christian Messianic expectations had unintentionally constructed the Christ of the Gospels; Baur applied rigorous historical criteria to the study of the origins of Christianity and to the dating of New Testament writings. Each challenged cherished convictions, but their particular challenges were less important in the long run than the method that they embraced.

German biblical scholars submitted the biblical text to the same rigorous scrutiny they applied to other ancient documents. In 1878, Julius Wellhausen challenged Mosaic authorship of the Books of the Law, and soon a torrent of criticism questioned other long-cherished Protestant assumptions. For devotees of the new method, the Bible yielded its place as the inerrant Word of God to a developmental view of history. Furthermore, historical theology gained respect as a discipline in its own right. Its emphasis on the scientific study of DOCTRINE within the context of Christian history seemed to some to erode the AUTHORITY OF Scripture.

The scholarship produced by advocates of the new method agitated in American SEMINARIES, where it resulted in the well-publicized HERESY trials of several esteemed faculty and CLERGY. The intellectual challenge to orthodoxy was enormous, and a variety of responses followed. Many Congregationalists and the institutions they controlled—like Andover Seminary—embraced the implications of the new scholarship. The historic Methodist preoccupation with religious experience rather than with dogma made it easy for many of them, especially in the North, to do the same (see METHODISM; METHODISM IN NORTH AMERICA). Liberals, as advocates of the new scholarship were known, counted in their ranks significant numbers of Episcopal clergy as well as some BAPTISTS, Presbyterians (see PRESBYTERIANISM) and DISCIPLES OF CHRIST. Seminary graduates from schools affiliated with all of these denominations, especially in the Northeast, soon brought the practical implications of the new theology to America's pews. The University of Chicago Divinity School, invigorated by John D. Rockefeller's money, gathered a faculty of influential advocates of the modern approach to theology. Religious liberalism manifested different qualities in different places (see LIBERAL PROTESTANTISM AND LIBERALISM). Those who fearlessly advocated the accommodation of faith to CULTURE came to be known as modernists (see MODERNISM). The University of Chicago's SHAILER MATHEWS articulated their convictions. Others emphasized social concerns similar to those that motivated the famous Baptist Social Gospeler WALTER RAUSCHENBUSCH. William Newton Clarke's Christ-entered emphasis in the *Outline of Christian Theology* (1898), perhaps the era's most influential systematic theology, represented yet another "take" on liberalism. The movement's popular voice was

CHARLES CLAYTON MORRISON's magazine *The Christian Century*. Novelist Harold Frederic's *The Damnation of Theron Ware* (1896) explored the implications of progressive theology in the life of a young minister.

EVANGELICALISM, still largely based in America's traditional denominations, faced the implications of this intellectual challenge at a moment also defined by rapid INDUSTRIALIZATION and urbanization. Immigration patterns also shifted with the arrival of large numbers of southern and eastern European Jews and Catholics, exacerbating other bewildering social changes. These influences combined to encourage evangelicals to strike out in new directions to confront new conditions. They worked within and around denominations to accomplish this. Many Baptists and Presbyterians resisted progressive ideas. Some Methodists did, too, especially those who understood the Wesleyan tradition through the lens of the HOLINESS MOVEMENT.

Besides writing and preaching about the "old-time religion," such people cooperated in a wide range of voluntary associations (see VOLUNTARY SOCIETIES), publications, and new institutions designed to enable them to reach the urban masses with their message. Nondenominational urban congregations with free pews were a favored venue for urging conversionist Bible-centered Christianity. Evangelist DWIGHT L. MOODY sponsored such a congregation in Chicago; one-time Presbyterian Albert B. Simpson opened a Gospel Tabernacle in Manhattan; and the Church of the Open Door served inner-city Los Angeles. To provide rudimentary training for would-be preachers, missionaries, and lay workers, prominent men and women helped facilitate Bible institutes. Moody explained that institutes existed to train "gap men" to bridge the gap between an educated clergy and the urban masses (see BIBLE COLLEGES AND INSTITUTES). They offered classes in the English Bible and the use of music in evangelism and sent their students out for daily practice on urban streets.

With his reliance on the evangelical message in its most basic form, Moody rallied many who were deeply concerned by the contemporary erosion of traditional Christian faith. Although Moody, a layman with little formal education, did not directly confront the new ideas himself, he convened and made flourish clusters of people who did. They gathered at Moody's Chicago Training Institute (later MOODY BIBLE INSTITUTE) or, most often, during the summer conference season in Moody's boyhood hometown of Northfield, Massachusetts. During the 1890s, Cyrus Ingersoll Scofield, a lawyer turned Congregationalist minister, occasionally joined the group. Scofield brought to Northfield study notes that addressed biblical themes in unusual detail. He developed them for personal use as well as for a correspondence Bible course that he offered out of his Dallas church. Moody and others encouraged their publication, and in 1909 the first SCOFIELD REFERENCE BIBLE appeared. Keyed to the Authorized Version, the notes set out a view of history marked by seven successive dispensations that corresponded roughly with the succession of divine covenants (see DISPENSATIONALISM). Scofield assumed the unity of the biblical text as well as its inerrancy (see BIBLICAL INERRANCY).

Scofield's Bible became a best seller. Its copious notes with their explanations of how God interacted with humanity in each dispensation governed fundamentalist views of the modern world for decades. People carried the Scofield Bible to CAMP MEETINGS, prophecy conferences, REVIVALS, youth meetings, and SUNDAY SCHOOLS, and it became an indispensable fundamentalist handbook. Its notes presented the novel view that the church was a parenthesis in God's plan and might be withdrawn ("raptured") at any time (see RAPTURE). Christ's physical return was always imminent. Moody and his most influential cohorts had claimed that their apprehension of the imminence of the second coming had transformed their lives, spurring them to personal preparedness (a disciplined spirituality) and aggressive EVANGELISM. Scofield now collected, systematized and popularized ideas that British PLYMOUTH BRETHREN and American evangelicals had bandied about for years. For Moody, the "blessed hope" of New Testament promise was the instantaneous surprising departure of the church from the earth, setting the stage for a period of divine judgment known as the Tribulation (see TRIBULATIONISM). (In the 1990s, Tim La Haye and Tim Jenkins built their successful "Left Behind" series around this bit of Scofield's teaching.) Scofield's views promptly became the "stuff" of fundamentalist novels, a genre that modeled fundamentalist THEOLOGY paired with a wholesome lifestyle. The most successful of these came from the pen of Grace Livingston Hill. The author of more that 100 books that sold hundreds of thousands of copies, the Presbyterian Hill used fiction to insist on the practical benefits of careful attention to the Bible read through Scofield's notes. She also urged the traditional American evangelical moral code and insisted on the centrality of CONVERSION.

While not all American evangelicals agreed that the church was a parenthesis, masses of the faithful nurtured the "blessed hope." Their popular literature affirmed it, their Bible institutes typically taught Dispensationalism and their prophecy conferences attracted ever-increasing numbers to hear some of the era's most adept preachers urge them to read the signs of the times in current events and to be ready for the rapture.

As a core of American evangelicals rallied to what they regarded as the essentials of Christian faith, they worked through churches and agencies dedicated to upholding the verbal inspiration of Scripture, the exclusivity of the Gospel message, EVANGELISM, and an empowered LAITY. They cooperated in faith Missions as an alternative to denominational mission boards. Faith missions, targeting specific needs or areas, depended on the direct prayers and support of the faithful to accomplish evangelism. The most famous of the early faith missions was undoubtedly the CHINA INLAND MISSION (CIM), brainchild of the Englishman J. HUDSON TAYLOR. With offices in CANADA and the UNITED STATES, the CIM, under the direction of its long-time North American leader, Henry Frost, enlisted hundreds of young American men and women to go to inland China without salary to spread the gospel.

Tract societies and publishing houses bent the latest technologies to the conservative evangelical cause. At about the same time that the Scofield Bible first appeared, a group of evangelicals concerned about the drift of Protestantism from its moorings pulled together twelve small volumes of essays making the case for the points that conservatives held dear. Edited by people such as Southern Baptist pastor Amzi Clarence Dixon (brother of Thomas Dixon of "Birth of a Nation" fame); educator, pastor, and evangelist REUBEN A. TORREY; and the prominent Jewish convert Louis Meyer, the books were funded by a generous grant from Los Angeles laymen Lyman and Milton Stewart. The Stewarts envisioned a series that addressed current critical issues, and they intended their funds to ensure that the religious leadership of the English-speaking world received copies. The series, known as *The Fundamentals*, appeared between 1910 and 1913. An estimated three million copies circulated before the outbreak of World War I.

The series helped give the mounting movement its enduring name. Other declarations offered lists of basic beliefs. The most famous of these, the "Five Points of Fundamentalism," were part of a formulation developed by the Northern Presbyterian Church during the 1890s and decreed formally in 1910. In that year, the denomination identified Five Points as "essential and necessary" doctrines of the church: (1) the original autograph of Scripture as inspired and without error, (2) the virgin birth, (3) the "satisfaction" theory of the ATONEMENT, (4) the physical resurrection, and (5) the miracles of Jesus. The Presbyterian Church demanded that its seminary professors use inerrancy as a starting point for biblical and theological scholarship. During the 1890s, Charles Briggs of Union

Seminary (New York) and Preserved Smith of Lane Seminary (Cincinnati) were dismissed for heresy, and Union Seminary's church historian, A. C. McGiffert, resigned from the Presbyterian ministry, each in part a victim of the clash between modern scholarly method and affirmations that attempted to capture the historic essence of evangelicalism. (Presbyterians were quick to point out that these were "extra-creedal.")

The most famous public moment in the history of American fundamentalism occurred in July 1925 in Dayton, Tennessee when WILLIAM JENNINGS BRYAN and Clarence Darrow faced each other in a courtroom showdown on evolution. Tennessee law—like that of several other southern states—forbade the teaching of evolution. In both the North and the South, influential pastors and members of such groups as statewide anti-evolution leagues, the Bible Crusaders of America, the Defenders of the Christian Faith, and the World's Christian Fundamentals Association (established in 1919 to promote cooperative national strategies to combat threats like the teaching of evolution) bent their efforts toward keeping creationism in school textbooks. A three-time Democratic presidential candidate and former Secretary of State, Bryan had earned a reputation as an orator. Darrow was the country's most visible attorney, famous for his reasoning, his oratory, and the cases he had defended. The nation hung on newspaper reports of the spectacle that the Scopes trial became. Darrow seemed to handily make a fool of Bryan, though Bryan technically won the case. Reporters, none more ably than the *Baltimore Sun*'s H. L. Mencken, ridiculed fundamentalism as narrow obscurantism. A long list of national spectacles lingers in the collective American memory of the 1920s, but none was more damaging to the public image of fundamentalism than the Scopes trial.

If the public turned to other spectacles, members of American Protestant denominations did not. The struggle for control seemed ever more intense. Polity and the extent of early liberal inroads spared Congregationalists (see CONGREGATIONALISM) and Northern Methodists the bitter infighting that beset Presbyterians and Baptists. Conservatives held the upper hand in the Northern Presbyterian Church, but the Auburn Affirmation of 1924, with more than 1,200 signatures, condemned the famous Five Points of 1910 as well as the biblical literalism that undergirded them. During the 1920s, controversy swirled around HARRY EMERSON FOSDICK, a professor at New York's liberal Union Theological Seminary and regular guest preacher at New York City's First Presbyterian Church. One of the country's best-known preachers, in 1922 the Baptist Fosdick preached a plea for reconciliation that publicist Ivy Lee retitled and transformed into a liberal battle cry: "Shall the Fundamentalists Win?" Fosdick

ultimately resigned the Presbyterian pulpit and moved to the new Riverside Church. Built by John D. Rockefeller specifically for Fosdick, Riverside stood along the Hudson River across Broadway from Columbia University and Union Theological Seminary, where Fosdick intended to influence the best minds of the next generation. Meanwhile, Southern Baptist John Roach Straton also held forth in New York at Calvary Baptist Church, attacking Fosdick and making his sanctuary an influential center in the national struggle for the soul of American Protestantism.

Denominational controversies inevitably involved seminaries. Perhaps the most famous case unfolded at the Presbyterians' Princeton Theological Seminary. In *Christianity and Liberalism* (1923), Princeton New Testament professor JOHN GRESHAM MACHEN insisted that liberalism was not Christianity. Rumblings of dissent troubled the seminary through the 1920s and led in 1929 to the withdrawal of conservatives and the founding of Westminster Seminary in Philadelphia. Author Pearl Buck became a focus of conservative discontent with Presbyterian foreign MISSIONS, and conservatives established an independent foreign missions board. When the denomination barred the Independent Board of Missions, conservatives formed a new Presbyterian denomination (that itself divided in 1937 over premillennialism), known after 1939 as the Orthodox Presbyterian Church.

In 1920 many Baptist fundamentalists in the northeast associated in the National Federation of Fundamentalists of the Northern Baptists. William Bell Riley, Minneapolis Baptist pastor and Bible institute founder, and Texas Baptists J. Frank Norris and T. T. Shields led a BAPTIST BIBLE UNION that assaulted liberalism and evolution. Their inability to agree led in a few years to the disintegration of the Union. In 1928 Norris created the World Fundamentalist Baptist Missionary Fellowship, complete with Bible institute, mission board, and periodical, *The Fundamentalist*. A split in 1950 gave rise to the Baptist Bible Fellowship International. Meanwhile, conservative secessions from the Northern Baptist Convention led to the founding of new denominations, including the General Association of Regular Baptists (1932) (see GENERAL BAPTISTS) and the CONSERVATIVE BAPTIST ASSOCIATION (1947).

As important as the emergence of new denominations were the clusters of independent congregations—Gospel tabernacles, Bible churches, freestanding Congregationalist or Baptist churches—that served a constituency disenchanted with liberalism in the pulpit. Their support for such congregations and for publications, Bible institutes, radio broadcasts, and mission agencies helped organize fundamentalists into a web of overlapping networks that made them a powerful grassroots influence. Even denominations that did not endure splits were not immune to powerful fundamentalist voices. For example, Southern Methodists like L. W. Munhall and Los Angeles's fiery "fighting Bob" Shuler rallied the fundamentalist faithful from many settings.

Such popular voices encouraged the faithful to hold fast to the truths at stake in denominational battles. Since the death of D. L. Moody in 1899, a long list of evangelists had taken up his mantle. Nationally, the most famous was BILLY SUNDAY, a converted professional baseball player whose vigorous PREACHING style captivated audiences across the land. His evangelistic party included several who greatly enhanced his influence—his wife, Helen, Bible teacher Virginia Asher, and songster Homer Rodeheaver. When Sunday died in 1935, *The Christian Century* declared the end of an era and opined that the fundamentalist movement he represented would disappear as well. The liberal Protestant elite failed to notice what was happening on the ground.

Evangelicals had seized on the possibilities of radio and were using it to build a popular constituency unimaginable only a few years earlier. Evangelist Paul Rader used hs Chicago Tabernacle as the base for all-day broadcasting over the city's powerful WBJT (Where Jesus Blesses Thousands)/WBBM. Charles and Grace Fuller's "Old-Fashioned Revival," with its upbeat music, stirring homey sermons, and Grace "Honey" Fuller's motherly reading of listeners' letters, emanated from the Long Beach (California) Auditorium, and became a fixture among conservatives of many denominations. Missouri Synod Lutherans offered "The Lutheran Hour" with the popular Walter Meier, a program that drew a wide non-Lutheran audience (see LUTHERAN CHURCH-MISSOURI SYNOD).

If national and local radio broadcasting revealed growing fundamentalist strength, the increasing number of Bible institutes training laity and clergy refuted liberal hopes of fundamentalist retreat. Nearly 100 new Bible institutes were organized between 1930 and 1950, and their graduates became a fundamentalist army of sorts, working at home and abroad. If they did not directly engage theological issues in ways that demanded national attention, they manifested the enduring appeal of their message.

Fundamentalism was never monolithic, and during the 1940s, some basic rifts became apparent. Three representative clusters of issues reveal some of the inner tensions: (1) engaging the academy, (2) separatism, and (3) PENTECOSTALISM.

During the 1940s, a new generation of conservatives determined to reform fundamentalism by reappropriating the evangelical label and reengaging the academy. Protestantism in general had clearly lost its dominance in defining America's moral life, but men like CARL F. H. HENRY and Harold John Ockenga believed that they had something positive to offer. The fundamentalist label seemed worn and linked to old controversies. A group of young evangelicals eschewed it in favor of a focus on the positive affirmations the tradition held for contemporary concerns. They pursued advanced education, gaining credentials that prepared them to teach and write in dialogue with the scholarly issues of the day. Known as neoevangelicals, in the World War II era these men assumed evangelical leadership roles as teachers, pastors, editors (especially of *Christianity Today*), and theologians. Their determination led to the creation of Fuller Seminary in Pasadena, California. Named for radio evangelist Charles E. Fuller, Fuller Seminary came to represent the promise of serious new evangelical scholarship and the intentions of these reformist fundamentalists.

From the 1930s, separation loomed as a potentially divisive issue for fundamentalists. In the absence of a single cohesive organizing mechanism, interrelated fundamentalist networks often centered in charismatic personalities. A few of these became powerful voices for separation not only from worldliness, but also from churches and agencies affiliated with liberal denominations. Among the most outspoken were Carl MacIntyre, John R. Rice, and Bob Jones. When neoevangelicals reclaimed the evangelical name and sponsored a NATIONAL ASSOCIATION OF EVANGELICALS (NAE), the separatist agenda became a national issue. The NAE welcomed denominations, independent congregations, and congregations affiliated with denominations that held membership in such ecumenical agencies as the Federal Council of the Churches of Christ. Separatists objected to such mixing of fundamentalist truth and liberal Protestant error. The debate in the NAE's *United Evangelical Action* was long and bitter. In the end, the separatists abandoned the NAE's efforts to keep their networks free from the taint of association with error.

While separatism was perhaps the primary dividing point between these neo-evangelicals and old-line fundamentalists, the same people split along similar lines over accepting Pentecostals as evangelicals. Although some Pentecostals had long indicated their affinities for fundamentalism, fundamentalist associations had not warmed to cooperation with Pentecostals. For one thing, the notes to the Scofield Bible held that spiritual gifts had ceased with the apostles, and dispensationalists tended to frown on any who advocated the contemporary centrality of spiritual gifts. The organizers of the NAE indicated their willingness to see the larger picture. On the Five Points or the topics of *The Fundamentals*, Pentecostals and evangelicals found themselves in essential agreement. On their part, separatists tended to be as wary of perceived errors among conservatives as of liberal heresies. Pentecostals became partners in the NAE, but they never won acknowledgment as fundamentalists.

After World War II, differentiating fundamentalists from evangelicals became a thorny task. Some self-professed new evangelicals manifested decidedly fundamentalist predilections, while others abandoned dispensationalism, moved from the legalism and prescription long central to fundamentalism, and advocated responsible Christian freedom. Historian George Marsden once quipped that a fundamentalist might be described as "an evangelical who is angry about something." A generation later, some suggest that the differences within this family of conservative Protestants are as much sociological as theological: Fundamentalist networks offer specific do's and don'ts for all of life, whereas evangelicals exercise choice in a context framed by scriptural injunctions. Another way of sorting might be to regard all fundamentalists as evangelicals, but not all evangelicals as fundamentalists. Bible institutes, colleges, broadcasts, camps, and periodicals still nurture the networks that make fundamentalism a vigorous grassroots movement, and its political voice in the New CHRISTIAN RIGHT renews its public prominence. Social issues—especially those dealing with sexual ethics (see SEXUALITY) and public education—rally the faithful to invoke noisily the movement's highly selective rendering of American history as well as the claims of Scripture.

The case of BILLY GRAHAM offers an example of the differentiation between evangelicals and fundamentalists. By most renderings, Graham, the product of a Southern Baptist home, a fundamentalist Bible college, and Wheaton College, a conservative, undergraduate institution, drew his early support from a mix of fundamentalists and new evangelicals. He used YOUTH FOR CHRIST, a fundamentalist youth movement, as his base for building a team and gaining experience as an evangelist. For eight years, his crusades heartened conservative Christians to hope for a national revival. Then in 1957 Graham launched a crusade at Madison Square Garden. He welcomed ministers of many denominations, liberal and conservative, to the platform and commended his converts to their pastoral care. Livid fundamentalist separatists accused Graham of betraying the Gospel, while many neo-evangelicals supported his stance. The quarrel was not about the Five Points or the doctrines of *The Fundamentals*; rather, it centered on notions of separation and purity that fundamentalists had added to the doctrinal views that first animated their movement.

Fundamentalism retains strong grassroots appeal. In some of its power bases, the Scofield Bible and dispensationalism have yielded to other views of history and other readings of Scripture. In others, the Authorized Version amplified with Scofield's notes remains the only accepted text. The Bible Colleges and institutes serve large constituencies of fundamentalist youth who eschew a liberal arts education in favor of hands-on training for evangelistic outreach. One of the first remains the best known of the institutes, Chicago's Moody Bible Institute. Dallas Theological Seminary, long a bastion of fundamentalist education, JERRY FALWELL's Liberty University in Lynchburg, Virginia, and Bob Jones University in Greenville, South Carolina are among the best known of hundreds of schools that serve the constituency and mobilize tens of thousands of alumni to faithfulness to the cause. Radio preachers, publications, denominations, churches, camps, missions agencies, and political organizations—many with offices in Colorado Springs—channel fundamentalist outreach, and some, like Focus on the Family or Campus Crusade for Christ, straddle the hazy borderline with evangelicalism and appeal to all but the most vehement fundamentalists. Best-selling authors like Hal Lindsay (*The Late Great Planet Earth*) and Tim LaHaye and Jerry Jenkins (the *Left Behind* series) demonstrate continued broad cultural fascination with the vivid fundamentalist picture of the end-times. The perceived lack of moral compass in American life raises the movement's appeal among those who yearn for absolute standards of right and wrong.

See also Creation Science

References and Further Reading

Balmer, Randall. *Mine Eyes Have Seen the Glory: A Journey Into the Evangelical Subculture in America*. New York: Oxford University Press, 1989.

Bendroth, Margaret. *Fundamentalism and Gender*. New Haven, CT: Yale University Press, 1993.

Brereton, Virginia. *Training God's Army: The American Bible School, 1880–1940*. Bloomington, IN: Indiana University Press, 1990.

Carpenter, Joel A. *Revive Us Again: The Reawakening of American Fundamentalism*. New York: Oxford University Press, 1997.

Marsden, George M. *Fundamentalism and American Culture*. New York: Oxford University Press, 1980.

———. *Reforming Fundamentalism: Fuller Seminary and the New Evangelicalism*. Grand Rapids, MI: Eerdmans, 1987.

———. *Understanding Evangelicalism and Fundamentalism*. Grand Rapids, MI: Eerdmans, 1991.

Sandeen, Ernest R. *The Roots of Fundamentalism*. Chicago, IL: University of Chicago Press, 1970.

EDITH L. BLUMHOFER

FUNERARY RITES

As is the case for much of Protestant worship, REF-ORMATION era funerary rites were formed in reaction to what the reformers considered to be serious defects and abuses in the WORSHIP of the medieval church. Protestant responses to the burial practices of the Roman church ranged from attempts to purify and simplify these rites to an outright rejection of all burial ceremony altogether. It would be many generations before Protestant churches created their own distinctive and full funerary rites, but by the mid-twentieth century, most Protestant groups had produced fully developed funeral rites that were well grounded theologically, as witnesses to the resurrection, and expressions of pastoral care to the bereaved. Most recently, the Protestant tendencies toward freedom from institutional constraint and the importance of the individual have combined with certain trends in CULTURE to result in the increase of highly personalized, improvised, free-form memorial services instead of the set official burial liturgies of the churches.

Medieval Roman Burial Rites

To assess the depth and character of early Protestant reactions to medieval practices, it is important to understand how the Roman church actually ritualized the burial of the dead. Unfortunately, most of our knowledge of these rites comes from monastic sources, and, although it is assumed that the burials of ordinary Christians were somewhat similar, there were surely many local variations and departures from the monastic norms.

The typical pattern appears to be as follows: When someone died, bells were rung to notify the community that a death had occurred. At the home of the deceased, the body was washed and shrouded in preparation for burial, sometimes accompanied by the chanting of psalms. The body, covered by a pall, was then carried in procession to the church, where the Office of the Dead, consisting of prayers, psalms, and scripture, was said. After this, the requiem, or funeral, mass proper was observed, followed by prayers and chants for absolution. The body was incensed and sprinkled with holy water and then taken in solemn procession to the grave (either in the churchyard or under the church), where the sign of the cross was administered and the body buried. On the eve of the Reformation, the overall mood of these rites was somber, focusing greatly on SIN, judgment, purgatory, and interceding on behalf of the soul after death.

Martin Luther and Early Lutheran Rites

Although MARTIN LUTHER produced manuals for BAP-TISM and MARRIAGE, he did not do the same for funerals, but he did make his theological objections to the Roman burial practices clear. He saw the death of a Christian not in fearful ways but as "a deep, strong, and sweet sleep" and the coffin as "nothing but paradise." Therefore, he composed a number of confident and hopeful burial Hymns to replace the "dirges and doleful songs" of the Roman ritual (see HYMNS AND HYMNALS). Luther spoke out against such "popish abominations" as vigils, requiem masses, purgatory, the desperate prayers begging for the deceased to be spared the judgment, and "all other hocus-pocus on behalf of the dead."

Because Luther himself created no authoritative burial rite, a number of funeral orders sprang up in the various areas of Lutheran influence (see LUTHERAN-ISM). However, all of these reflect in their own way Luther's desire for simplicity and hopefulness, and express his conviction that funerals should be conducted "with proper decorum in order to honor and praise that joyous article of our faith, namely, the resurrection of the dead." A typical early Lutheran burial order began with a procession, sometimes led by a cross-bearer, from the home of the deceased directly to the grave. Along the way, the worshipers would sing psalms (Psalms 90 and 130 were often included) and hymns, including the "Media Vita" ("In the midst of life we are in death," an eleventh-century text that was well-known in GERMANY and formed the basis of Luther's hymn *Mitten wir im Leben sind*). The burial itself probably took place in silence and was often followed by a brief service at the grave, in the church, or at the home of the deceased consisting of Scripture, hymns, prayers, and sometimes a sermon.

Early Reformed Practices

The early Reformed tradition stands on the more extreme end of the reaction to the medieval Roman burial rites, even to the point that many of its adherents were buried with no ceremony whatsoever. JOHN CALVIN himself seems to have allowed at least the minimum ceremony of a fitting sermon preached at graveside, but the laws of sixteenth-century Geneva were completely indifferent to any ordered funeral practice, being content essentially to warn against unbiblical superstition and to leave the rest to family discretion.

In the early decades after the Reformation, a sparse pattern of burial without ceremony, sometimes followed by a brief sermon on the resurrection, seems to have established itself as the norm among the Reformed churches. As time went on, however, this minimalist approach became more and more difficult to maintain in the face of pastoral needs at the time of death. Gradually here and there among the Reformed communities, some ritual was added to the unadorned act of placing the body in the ground, such as the minister saying words of committal, and the sermons began to display more comfort for the bereaved. These accommodations were never without controversy, however, and the command of the Puritan-influenced *Westminster Directory of Public Worship* (1645) to "let the dead body, upon the day of burial, be. . . immediately interred, without any ceremony" reflects the tendency of the Reformed groups to avoid what they regarded as the pomp and superstition of funeral rituals altogether. It was not until the nineteenth century that anything like complete funeral orders were followed in the Reformed churches.

Early Anglicans, Wesley, and the Methodist Movement

If the Reformed tradition expresses the most drastic rejection of the medieval funerary rites, the most conserving Protestant response to those ceremonies can be seen in the Anglican tradition. Archbishop THOMAS CRANMER, whose liturgical genius lay behind the 1549 BOOK OF COMMON PRAYER, simplified the Roman rites and made them more hopeful, but left much of the Catholic pattern in place, including an optional office of the dead and a eucharistic service observed either before or after burial. Although there were still prayers of petition for the departed (a practice condemned by the Lutheran and Reformed traditions), the theological center of gravity had clearly shifted from fear to hope, from pleading for the soul of the departed to the idea of eternal rest in Christ.

The 1549 *Book of Common Prayer* came under criticism from continental reformers, however. MARTIN BUCER, for example, had complained, "since scripture nowhere teaches us by word or example to pray for the departed. . . I wish that this commendation of the dead and prayer for them be omitted." The 1552 revision of the *Book of Common Prayer* showed the effects of these and other criticisms and included a burial service that is much-abbreviated, eliminates the observance of the Eucharist (see LORD'S SUPPER), and omits the prayers and commendations on behalf of the departed. Subsequent editions of the *Book of Common Prayer* move back and forth between the conservatism of the 1549 version and the more austere tendencies of the 1552 revision.

Among the Methodists, JOHN WESLEY'S 1784 *The Sunday Service of the Methodists in North America With Other Occasional Services* included a burial service that closely followed the then-current (1662) Anglican *Book of Common Prayer*. But perhaps what most set the early Methodists apart was the unofficial but widespread practice of singing, as the body was carried to the grave, joyful hymns with confident evangelical expressions, such as "Rejoice for a brother deceased, our loss is his infinite gain."

As for the service itself, Wesley shortened the *Book of Common Prayer* ritual, and he omitted both the service of committal and the prayer specifically giving thanks to God that "it hath pleased Thee to deliver this our brother out of the miseries of this sinful world." These changes were mainly in keeping with Puritan objections to the *Book of Common Prayer,* but they were also in accord with Wesley's own desire for an emphasis on the gospel and for simplicity. Wesley's own last will and testament called for his body to be carried to the grave by "six poor men" (who would be paid for the service from his estate) and stated that "I particularly desire there may be no herse, no coach, no escutcheon, no pomp, except the tears of them that loved me. . . ." In the nineteenth century, some of the passages Wesley omitted from the *Book of Common Prayer* were restored to the Methodist burial service, including the committal. But the language of the committal was altered to provide an emphasis on the general hope of resurrection rather than on any knowledge of the fate of the deceased (see METHODISM).

Free Church and Anabaptist Churches

The churches of the left wing of the Reformation shared with other Protestants a general suspicion of Roman burial ceremonies and doctrines. With no official liturgies in place, the free churches generally developed funeral practices along the lines of local custom, basically preferring simple observances involving scripture and prayer, at graveside or in the church. CLERGY were sometimes present, but often free church burials were conducted by family members, friends, or other lay persons. Beginning in the nineteenth century, service manuals and other published funeral resources for FREE CHURCH and independent clergy use were developed, such as Gould and Shakespeare's *A Manual for Free Church Ministers* (1905), but these had, of course, no authoritative status.

Contemporary Developments and Issues

Because the first Protestant burial liturgies were reactions to what the reformers considered to be Roman abuses, these services tended to be theological and ritual overcorrections. Many of the initial Protestant services showed little tolerance for any positive reference to the life of the deceased, for any expression of deep grief or any theological emphasis but cheerful hope, and for any local custom that might hint at superstition. What was gained in theological purity, however, was often lost in pastoral compassion. Thus the subsequent development of Protestant funeral liturgies has generally been marked by more rounded services that are increasingly open to the human aspects of grief and loss, more supportive of the need to remember the life of the person who has died, and more adaptable to a wide range of local customs and conventions.

In the mid-twentieth century, most Protestant groups, influenced both by a THEOLOGY of divine compassion and an increasing awareness of the psychology of grief, produced funeral liturgies that were similar enough in form and substance to constitute something of a consensus. These services were generally two-part ceremonies: the funeral proper, with an emphasis on the proclamation of the resurrection, followed by a graveside committal service, in which the deceased was bid farewell and entrusted to God. These services were characterized by brevity, by an emphasis on the hope and thanksgiving for the life of the deceased, by the encouragement to include a funeral sermon, and by sufficient choices in prayers and Scripture readings to make these rites adaptable to various situations (such as the death of a child) and many levels of grief. Most of these twentieth-century revisions attempted to reclaim, at least as an option for the service, the early church custom of observing the Eucharist on the occasion of death, but this practice did not receive wide acceptance.

In the late twentieth century, however, several factors and forces converged to place these consensus Protestant funeral rites under stress. First, the bonds connecting people to the institutional church were loosened, and the kind of innovation and personalization frequently at work in marriage ceremonies began to take hold in death rituals as well. Many Protestants feel quite free to depart from the set liturgies and to create highly individualized and customized funerary rites.

Second, psychological and therapeutic ideas about grief, which earlier had enhanced traditional Christian views of death and loss by adding pastoral care themes to the funeral liturgy, now began gradually to rival those theological views. Thus, the purpose of funerals tended to shift away from an emphasis on hope for the deceased toward a concentration on the "grief work" of the mourner, away from a clear emphasis on the larger theological meanings of death toward more focus on the biography of the deceased and the meaning of loss for the living.

Moreover, a strong consumerist critique of the cost of funerals, a sharp worldwide rise in the rate of cremation, a desire for less melancholy and more celebrative ceremonies, a decreased interest in the symbolism of the physical body of the deceased, and, to some extent, an attempt to turn the focus away from death and toward the hope of the resurrection have combined to encourage the practice of memorial services instead of funerals. Memorial services, in which the body of the deceased is absent, typically are held some days or weeks after the death and feature some elements of the older funeral pattern (e.g., Scripture, prayers, and hymns), but they also often include several eulogies or remembrances of the deceased.

Because of the mobility and fragmentation of contemporary society, the village structure implied in older funeral liturgies no longer pervades. Thus, attendance at funerals and memorial services today is declining (except in the case of the death of a celebrity or someone of unusual recognition), and, consequently, they tend to be smaller gatherings of family and friends rather than community-wide events.

See also Death and Dying

References and Further Reading

Enright, D. J., ed. *The Oxford Book of Death*. Oxford, UK: Oxford University Press, 1983.

Rowell, Geoffrey. *The Liturgy of Christian Burial: An Introductory Survey of the Historical Development of Christian Burial Rites*. London: SPCK, 1977.

Rutherford, Richard. *The Death of a Christian: The Order of Christian Funerals*. Collegeville, MN: Liturgical Press, 1990.

Tucker, Karen Westerfield. *"Till Death Us Do Part": The Rites of Marriage and Burial Prepared by John Wesley and Their Development in the Methodist Episcopal Church, 1784–1939*. Ann Arbor, MI: University Microfilms, 1993.

White, James F. *Introduction to Christian Worship* Nashville, TN: Abingdon, 2000.

THOMAS G. LONG

G

GALLICAN CONFESSION

The Gallican Confession is the earliest comprehensive statement of belief for the Reformed Churches of FRANCE. Delegates to the first National Synod, meeting secretly at Paris, adopted the text in May 1559. The seventh National Synod, held at La Rochelle in 1571, meticulously reexamined and confirmed the various articles. Accordingly, the declaration is also known as the Confession of Faith of La Rochelle. Subsequent gatherings of the national SYNOD reviewed and made minor modifications into the seventeenth century. Although the CONFESSION appears to have fallen into disuse after the 1650s, it was not officially superseded until 1872.

The Gallican Confession's forty articles, preceded by an eloquent preamble, were likely based on a Genevan model or a confession drawn up in 1557 for presentation to King Henry II. The structure, at once simple and elegant, follows a classic pattern. The first eight articles outline the Reformed understanding of God and enumerate the canonical books of Scripture from which this knowledge flows. Three subsequent articles discuss human nature and original SIN. Articles 12–19 treat SALVATION through Christ. The next five take up the divine gift of FAITH and the promise of regeneration. A series of fifteen articles then discusses in turn the DOCTRINE of the CHURCH, ecclesiastical organization, and the SACRAMENTS. The final two articles touch on the temporal magistrates, civil laws, and their relationship to divine AUTHORITY.

References and Further Reading

Primary Source:

Calvin, John. "The French Confession of Faith" (French text with English translation). In *The Creeds of Christendom*, 6th ed., edited by Philip Schaff, vol. 3, 356–382. Grand Rapids, MI: Baker, 1990.

Secondary Sources:

Pannier, Jacques. *Les origines de la Confession de foi et de la Discipline des Églises réformées de France*. Paris: F. Alcan, 1936.
Stauffer, Richard. "Brève histoire de la Confession de La Rochelle," *Bulletin de la Société de l'Histoire du Protestantisme Français* 117 (1971): 355–366.

RAYMOND A. MENTZER

GALLUS, NIKOLAUS (1516–1570)

German lutheran theologian. Gallus, born Nikolaus Hahn, was the eldest son of the mayor of Köthen. Like many affected by Humanism, he Latinized his name to Gallus. In 1530 he enrolled at the University of Wittenberg. There he studied under Justus Jonas, Jacob Schenck, MARTIN LUTHER, and PHILIPP MELANCHTHON. He earned his master's degree in THEOLOGY in 1537. After a brief leave he returned to Wittenberg and in 1540 earned his Studium. He then assumed a teaching position in Mansfeld. In 1543, with the help of Luther and Melanchthon, he received a ministerial appointment in Regensburg. After the defeat of Protestant forces in the Schmalkaldic War in 1548 and the implementation of the AUGSBURG INTERIM, Gallus left Regensburg over his unwillingness to accept the Interim. He first traveled to Wittenberg, but quickly moved on to Magdeburg.

Magdeburg was a well-fortified city that did not fall in the War of Schmalkald and thus became a Mecca for those who still hoped to fight against the Interim. The Interim reinstituted many of the liturgical practices abandoned by the Protestants. To make this acceptable, Melanchthon put forward an interpretation of DOCTRINE where such practices were considered adiaphoristic; that is, they were considered "(theologically) indifferent things." (see ADIAPHORA) From Magdeburg Gallus and such reformers as NIKOLAUS VON AMSDORF, MATTHIAS FLACIUS, and others issued a large number of pamphlets against the Interim. These pamphlets can be grouped in three major categories: (1) those that attacked the Interim, (2) those that defended the AUGSBURG CONFESSION, and (3) those that called for armed resistance to the Interim. Of those pamphlets, broadsheets, and apologies, the most complete and most influential was the *Confession, Instruction, and Warning of the Pastors and Preachers of the Christian Church in Magdeburg*, published in April of 1550 and written by Gallus.

The *Confession* is divided into seven chapters, grouped into three sections. The first section (chapters 1–7) recapitulates the main doctrinal *loci* of the Augsburg Confession. Section two discusses resistance theory, and section three warns of judgment against those who oppose Magdeburg. Over half of the document is devoted to the discussion of armed resistance to tyranny. The Confession is important because of its synthesis of earlier theories of resistance, its innovative interpretation of Romans 13, and its influence on later resistance theories. The *Confession* synthesized early sixteenth-century theories of NATURAL LAW and positive law theories into a unified theory of resistance by lesser magistrates. Gallus's unique reading of Paul's admonition to obey AUTHORITY in Romans 13 argued that only those authorities that are a terror to evildoers are in fact ordained by God. If authorities terrorize the good they betray themselves as agents of the DEVIL. Finally the *Confession* had international fame and influence. Its influence can be seen in the theories of resistance developed by Calvinists (such as THEODORE BEZA and JOHN KNOX) later in the sixteenth century.

In 1553 Gallus returned to Regensburg. During the 1550s and 1560s he was involved in every major intra-Lutheran controversy, including the Adiaphorist Controversy mentioned above, but also the controversies concerning free will, the Council of Trent, ANDREAS OSIANDER, CASPAR SCHWENCKFELD, and Georg Major. Gallus died in 1570.

References and Further Reading

Primary Sources:

Gallus, Nikolaus. *Bekentnis Unterricht und Vermanung der Pfarrherrn und Prediger der Christlichen Kirchen zu Magdeburgk.* Magdeburg: 1550.
———. *Ein Disputation uber Mitteldingen.* Magdeburg: 1550.
———. *Das Regensburger Bekenntnis.* Regensburg: 1560.
———. *Protestation concionaturvm aliqvot Avgvstanae Confessionis, aduersus conuentum Tridentinum . . .* n.p., 1563.

Secondary Sources:

Kolb, Robert. "The German Lutheran Reaction to the Third Period of the Council of Trent." *Lutherjahrbuch* 51 (1984): 63–95.
Olson, Oliver. "Theology of Revolution: Magdeburg, 1550–1551." *Sixteenth Century Journal* 3 (1972): 66–79.
Voit, Hartmut. *Nikolaus Gallus. Ein Beitrag zur Reformationsgeschichte der nachlutherischen Zeit.* Einzelarbeiten zur Kirchengeschichte Bayerns 54. Neustadt a. d. Aisch, 1977.
Whitford, David. *Tyranny and Resistance.* St. Louis, MO: Concordia, 2001.

DAVID WHITFORD

GARRISON, WINFRED (1874–1969)

American church historian and educator. Garrison was born in St. Louis, Missouri, in 1874 and died in Houston, Texas, in 1969. An active member of the Christian Church/DISCIPLES OF CHRIST, he was a prominent historian, receiving his Ph.D. in church history from the University of Chicago in 1897. His publications include over twenty books, most on Christianity in the UNITED STATES.

In 1898 Garrison became an instructor at the Disciples Divinity School, University of Chicago. From 1899 to 1906, Garrison was the president of Butler College. Moving to New Mexico for health reasons, he became president of New Mexico State University. In 1921 Garrison returned to the Disciples Divinity School to become associate professor, from which he retired in 1943. At the age of 81, Garrison helped establish the department of philosophy and religion at the University of Houston.

Multitalented, Garrison was an accomplished violinist, sculptor, linguist, educational administrator, and author. A founding member of the Disciples of Christ Historical Society, Garrison served on that board in various capacities for twenty-eight years. He was also on the editorial board of *The Christian Century* for over thirty years.

Garrison's particular interests were Protestantism, Christian unity, and the development of Christianity in the United States. He noted that Christianity in early America often took on the frontier characteristics of equality, independence, and INDIVIDUALISM (see FRONTIER RELIGION). He maintained that the unity that American Christianity and Protestant denominationalism sought in the new world would be found only by allowing for differences of opinion while uniting on a singular belief in Christ.

See also American Society of Church History; Higher Education; Seminaries

References and Further Reading

Primary Sources:

Garrison, Winfred E. *The March of Faith: The Story of Religion in America Since 1865.* New York: Harper & Brothers, 1933.

———. *Heritage and Destiny: An American Religious Movement Looks Ahead*. St. Louis, MO: Bethany Press, 1961.

Secondary Source:

Disciples of Christ Historical Society. "Garrison Memorial Issue." *Discipliana* 29 no. 3 (1969).

DAVID L. LITTLE

GENDER

Cultural and theological assumptions about gender have played an important role in shaping Protestant thought and practice. Although Protestantism has no single body of teaching or rule of practice about gender roles, changing attitudes about masculinity and femininity have significantly affected Protestant conceptions of church leadership and norms of marriage and family life. Many scholars also find gender identity central to the often unstated dynamics of religious "feminization" within church bodies. The gendered nature of religious experience has also shaped Protestant spirituality, particularly within sectarian movements, where nontraditional gender usages may help symbolize a group's divergence from the Protestant mainstream.

Gender as a Category of Analysis

Gender refers to the many possible social meanings attached to male and female sexual difference. Though these biological givens do not change much over time, ideas about their larger meaning may vary widely, for as scholars argue, gender is a cultural product constructed from the texts, rules, or traditions of a particular time and place. Gender constructions pose ideals of masculine and feminine behavior and appearance, and they influence practices around marriage, sexuality, and child-rearing.

Gender is also a "useful category of historical analysis" (Scott 1988) because, as postmodernist scholars argue, it provides important clues about power relationships within a given society. Conflicts over gender roles, and the use of gendered language, may often point toward larger anxieties about the social order, particularly during times of rapid change. Scholars disagree over the degree to which gender categories are imposed upon or created by persons and groups, though most would agree that such constructions are not rigidly deterministic, but allow room for various forms of individual "negotiation."

Analysis of gender in Protestant history, and in a wide variety of other subject areas, owes much to women's history, but the two are not the same. Gender studies built on women's studies, an area of study that emerged in the 1960s and 1970s, itself an outgrowth of second-wave feminism. The initial purpose of women's studies was compensatory, as a way of making up for the dearth of historical, scientific, and psychological information about women, but the explosion of scholarship on women led to more interpretive questions about gender roles, including new ones about men and masculinity. Attention to gender as an interpretive category has opened new forms of cultural analysis and invited attention to various meanings attached to marriage, sexuality, and parenthood. Gender studies also, of course, raised a host of unanswered questions about masculinity as a specific realm of experience that has changed over time and across cultures.

Sources of Protestant Tradition

In the absence of any received tradition, Protestant assumptions about gender have arisen within the boundaries of certain scriptural norms, and they have both reflected and reinforced prevailing cultural ideas about male and female differences. One influential model of gender in Western thought, for example, is based in Aristotelian biology and on an interpretation of Genesis 1:26–27, that "man" was created in God's image. According to this view, humanity is primarily male and women are derivative, defective beings, forever imperfect because they do not possess the original imprint of the divine. A corollary of this androcentric monism or single-sex model, influenced by Greek psychology and the writings of Augustine, located the divine image in human rationality. Thus masculinity became identified with the capacity for rational thought, and femininity with the realm of emotion and intuition. The view of women as fundamentally flawed and subrational has contributed to the recurring identification within Christian thought of the woman Eve as the primary sinner, and her feminine weakness the means by which humanity was inflicted with original sin.

Another influential set of assumptions about gender, most often associated with nineteenth-century romanticism, viewed men and women as entirely different beings, neither in any sense derivative of the other. Although both sexes were said to reflect different aspects of the divine—men were still identified with objective rationality and women with emotional expressiveness—this model built on a strong identity between femininity and religion. Men were less adept in spiritual matters, it was assumed, because they lacked the requisite feeling, while women were seen as inherently, intuitively suited for religious work.

Protestant assumptions about gender have also been influenced by an array of feminist critiques. In the west, the eighteenth-century ENLIGHTENMENT introduced the principle (though not necessarily the practice) of gender neutrality before the law. This egalitarian model of feminism has greatly affected debates about women's ordination and ecclesiastical representation, especially since the rise of second-wave feminism in the 1960s. As Christianity's center of balance has shifted over the course of the twentieth century from the West to AFRICA, Asia, and LATIN AMERICA, Protestant theologizing about gender has also been challenged by new generations of feminist thinkers, including Latina *mujerista* and African American womanist writers.

Conceptions of Leadership

Protestant assumptions about gender have often formed within the context of debates about women's ecclesiastical roles, arguments in which the range of Protestant theological and social diversity are clearly evident. The common argument against female priests, that they cannot represent Christ because they do not share his male embodiedness, primarily applies to Protestant denominations with a more episcopal structure, where leadership draws from a direct line of succession from Christ and his apostles. However, most other Protestant bodies, especially those with a more congregational basis of government, have struggled to articulate the meaning of gender as a basis for ecclesiastical practice. The issue has forced them to weigh the relative importance of two Protestant principles, biblical warrant and individual freedom—a difficult theological maneuver at best.

On the one hand, Protestant groups are constrained by their understanding of biblical norms. The New Testament, and the Pauline letters in particular, contain scattered but directed passages about feminine submission to masculine authority, including some strictures against women assuming positions of religious leadership. For some Protestants, including many conservative evangelicals, the discussion has ended here: an individual's gender determines eligibility for church office.

This approach has come up against the biblical principle of spiritual equality (Galatians 3:28), however, as well as the historic Protestant emphasis on lay participation. Among pentecostal groups especially, the central importance of the Holy Spirit in calling and equipping individuals for various tasks has, at times, facilitated more equal access to church leadership. Not surprisingly perhaps, women have often been some of the earliest leaders of new spiritual movements, for example, the prophetic church movement in Africa.

As a result of these often countervailing pressures, Protestant practice has assumed an often confusing variety of forms, but the categories are durable. In fact, many of the deliberations among Protestant bodies about the ordination of homosexual persons have resembled previous debates about women in church office. The debate also raises difficult questions about the nature of gender itself and the degree to which an individual's identity is biologically determined or socially constructed. Queries about the origins of gender identity draw on a raft of scientific knowledge—embryological, genetic, and psychological research; yet the even larger question, whether an individual's sexual identity should disqualify him or her for church office, remains an open question within the broadening scope of Protestant belief and practice.

Religion and Domesticity

The REFORMATION, particularly its affirmation of Christian family life, played a major role in shaping modern Western Protestant understandings of gender. The emerging view of marriage as a covenanted relationship built on a principle of spiritual equality, continued to require female submission, but within a framework of responsible male leadership and sexual continence.

To be sure, the Reformers' critique of medieval Catholicism eradicated a pantheon of female saints and mystics, and removed Mary from her intercessory role. The closing of monastic orders also eliminated one major source of women's institutional power within the church; Protestant women would have few formal roles consonant with those of nuns or abbesses, or many powerful, positive models of female spirituality. Religious leadership in the Protestant Reformation was routinely denied to women, as the spiritually "weaker vessel."

Yet the Reformers also introduced some significant new requirements for men as husbands and fathers. Although MARTIN LUTHER (1483–1546) and JOHN CALVIN (1509–1564) did not regard marriage as a sacrament, they held a high regard for the family as a school of religious formation and as a foundation of community life. Fathers especially had a responsibility to catechize their wives and children, and to rule responsibly. The rejection of clerical celibacy affirmed sexuality within marriage and led to increasing appreciation of its spiritual dimensions. Thus, in contrast to medieval acceptance of male incontinence as a necessity of nature, Luther taught that men had the power and the responsibility to control their sexual impulses because fatherhood required the ability to moderate one's personal desires.

The emphasis on the spiritual dimensions of marriage, evident most clearly among English Puritans, also introduced the possibility of a more egalitarian understanding of gender differences. Although the assumption of women's inferiority prevailed, the Puritan stress on inward piety could allow women and men to see each other as Christian companions within the bounds of a divinely sanctioned relationship. The result was an often paradoxical Protestant view of men and women as spiritual equals within a strict social hierarchy.

In the nineteenth century Christian domesticity was a central part of the message of Western missionaries. Women missionaries especially argued that to be Christian was, at least in part, to adopt Western domestic norms. Many missionaries thus challenged a variety of other cultural practices—polygamy, child marriages, and female circumcision—as fundamentally "unchristian," arguing (a bit ahistorically) that only Western-style Protestantism could elevate women to a position of true dignity and power. But in Africa, for example, the subsequent drive to eliminate polygamy introduced new economic and social hardships on the wives and children suddenly ejected from plural marriages.

Still, for women in patriarchal societies, religion can provide a hedge against male power. Church allegiance, especially for example, in Latin American pentecostal groups that forbid alcohol, tobacco, and sexual license, may bring about what one study has called a "reform of machismo" (Brusco 1995), restraining mostly male behaviors and authorizing women to enforce Christian standards of morality.

Feminization and Masculinization

Protestant beliefs and behaviors surrounding gender have often reflected the numerical reality that church membership has been predominantly female. Where churches follow a more open, voluntary structure, women have supported them in strong numbers, at least in part because this openness has allowed significant opportunities for leadership and personal expression, often unavailable elsewhere in society. In the nineteenth century, gender ideology encouraged women to identify with the cause of organized religion on the basis of their presumed spiritual affinity for such work.

Some critics have viewed feminization in a negative light. The tendency to identify religion as "women's work," they suggest, has contributed to its cultural irrelevance in the modern era. Religious feminization has been associated with the rise of sentimental piety, as well as the emergence of a more humanitarian liberal theology out of a presumably "masculine" rationalistic Calvinism. Pressures around feminization have also contributed to resistance against women in church leadership roles, based on the worry that female predominance there would re-move any remaining incentives for men to support organized religion.

Churches have perceived feminization as problematic most often during times of anxiety about low levels of male membership. The problem has increased with the growing social bifurcation, especially in the secularizing West, between what has been perceived as the public (masculine) sphere of business and government, and the private (feminine) sphere of home and church. Movements within Protestantism, such as the "muscular Christianity" of the Victorians, and interdenominational "men's movements" like the Promise Keepers in the late twentieth century, have attempted to redress the imbalance by promoting forms of worship and exhortation aimed directly at men.

Many scholars have also analyzed the role of gender in the emergence of fundamentalist movements, for these often include an aggressively masculine and/or antifeminist message. One of the similarities between Protestant fundamentalism and other non-Western forms is the common conviction that modern religious decline is related to family breakdown and, in particular, female independence from domestic constraints. Religious conservatives often emphasize the necessity of shoring up the traditional family, and restraining women's public role, as a key to moral and spiritual revival.

Gender and Religious Experience

Evidence from Protestant history suggests that men and women may experience religion differently, and often in ways that subvert culturally accepted norms of gender. Nineteenth-century women's evangelical conversion narratives, for example, emphasize sin and unworthiness more than men's do, but they also show women finding new assertiveness as the result of the spiritual encounter. Puritan men who invoked feminine biblical images—like the church as the "bride of Christ"—could access a realm of religious feeling otherwise denied them.

Not surprisingly perhaps, variant or radical forms of Protestantism have often experimented with gender roles. The radical Anabaptists in sixteenth-century Münster, for example, declared a new age of liberation and introduced polygamy—at least partly to deal with an overabundance of women and a relatively small number of men in their millennial society. The Latter-Day Saints have made church-sanctioned marriage a central part of their eschatology, emphasizing its eternally binding, redemptive power.

Many leaders of new sects have been women who challenged prevailing gender ideologies. Mother ANN LEE (1736–1784) founder of the SHAKERS, a radical eighteenth-century sect, envisioned God as both male and female. Many Shakers believed that just as the male Christ had inaugurated one Christian era, a female redeemer (Mother Ann) would begin the next one. Christian Science, a movement founded by a woman, Mary Baker Eddy (1821–1910), and overwhelmingly female in membership, rejected the assumption that the god of the Bible was male, and posited instead a nonmaterial "mother/father" god.

It is fitting then that so much fundamental debate in churches has involved gender issues. Protestantism has been shaped by a range of passionate arguments about the gender of God, maleness and eligibility for church office, and the use of gendered language in worship and in biblical translations. All of these point to the deep resonance of these elusive human categories within the history of Protestantism and in its future.

References and Further Reading

Brusco, Elizabeth. *The Reformation of Machismo: Evangelical Conversion and Gender in Colombia.* Austin, TX: University of Texas Press, 1995.

Fabella, Virginia, and Son Ai Lee Park, eds. *We Dare to Dream: Doing Theology as Asian Women.* Maryknoll, NY: Orbis, 1990.

Hawley, John S., ed. *Fundamentalism and Gender.* New York: Oxford, 1994.

Oduyoye, Mercy, and Msimbi R. A. Kanyoro, eds. *The Will to Arise: Women, Tradition and the Church in Africa.* Maryknoll, NY: Orbis, 1992.

Ozment, Steven. *When Fathers Ruled: Family Life in Reformation Europe.* Cambridge, MA: Harvard University Press, 1983.

Scott, Joan. *Gender and the Politics of History.* New York: Columbia University Press, 1988.

Swanson, R. N., ed. *Gender and Christian Religion.* Woodbridge, Suffolk, U.K.: Boydell Press, 1998.

Tavard, George. *Women in Christian Tradition.* Notre Dame, IN: University of Notre Dame Press, 1973.

MARGARET BENDROTH

GENERAL ASSOCIATION OF REGULAR BAPTIST CHURCHES

The General Association of Regular Baptist Churches (GARBC) is a fundamentalist group of churches that broke from the Northern Baptist Convention (see AMERICAN BAPTIST CHURCHES) in 1932 to form its own Association. It continues today as a Baptist denomination with more than 1,500 churches with a combined membership of 220,000-plus persons with various affiliated mission agencies, educational institutions, and other programs (see BAPTISTS).

Background

Beginning about 1919, when the Fundamentalist–Modernist (see MODERNISM) controversy was raging,

Baptist leaders J. C. Massee and W. B. Riley called fundamentalists within the Northern Baptist Convention to meet each year before the Convention's annual meeting to press their cause. In 1920 Massee was elected president of the newly founded Fundamentalist Fellowship (in Buffalo, New York). Among other things, the Fellowship hoped to get the Northern Baptist Convention to adopt a confessional statement (similar to the New Hampshire Confession). In 1922 this effort failed, with the Convention voting instead that the New Testament was its only rule of faith. This led to the formation in 1923 (in Kansas City, Missouri) of the BAPTIST BIBLE UNION, a group comprising Northern Baptists (led by W. B. Riley), southern fundamentalists (led by J. F. Norris), and Canadian fundamentalists (led by T. T. Shields). In 1932, at the Union's last annual meeting (at the Belden Avenue Baptist Church in Chicago), the GARBC was formed by a group of thirty-four men from eight states.

Early History

At the May 1932 meeting in Chicago, Howard C. Fulton, pastor of the Belden Avenue Baptist Church, addressed the group on "What Regular Old Fashioned Baptists Stand For." Twenty-two churches were represented and elected Harry G. Hamilton, from Buffalo, president of the new GARBC. The aim was to have an association (not a convention) of churches that would be separate from the Northern Baptist Convention. The GARBC adopted the New Hampshire Confession of Faith (1833) with a premillennial revision to the statement in 1934 in Gary, Indiana (see CONFESSION).

By 1933, the GARBC had begun publishing *The Bulletin* (which became *The Baptist Bulletin* in 1934). In 1933 Robert T. Ketcham (1889–1978; born in Nelson, Pennsylvania) was elected vice president of the GARBC in 1933 and president in 1934, a post that he held until 1938. Ketcham was the single most influential person in the GARBC's development. He served as the organization's national representative (1948–1960), editor of *The Baptist Bulletin* (1948–1955), and national consultant (1960–1966). In 1934 the Council of Fourteen was established to carry out the directives of the annual meetings; this became the Council of Eighteen in 1972. The Council meets twice a year; its members are elected by delegates from GARBC churches at the annual meetings.

Developments

Early in its history the GARBC developed relationships with various mission agencies and educational institutions. By design, these agencies and institutions are not organizationally connected with the GARBC, but rather are approved (and listed) by the GARBC. Among the earliest approved mission agencies was the General Council of Cooperating Baptist Missions of North America (founded in 1920, with the name changed to Baptist Mid-Missions in 1953). The first schools approved were the Los Angeles Baptist Theological Seminary, founded in 1927, and the Baptist Bible Seminary in Johnson City, New York.

Currently, the GARBC has twelve approved mission agencies, among which the two best-known for international work are the Association of Baptists for World Evangelism (founded in 1927 as the Association of Baptists for Evangelism in the Orient; the current name was adopted in 1939; headquartered in Harrisburg, Pennsylvania) and the Baptist Mid-Missions (founded in 1920, headquartered in Cleveland, Ohio). There are nine educational institutions approved by the GARBC: Baptist Bible College and Seminary (Clarks Summit, Pennsylvania); Cedarville University (Cedarville, Ohio), Faith Baptist Bible College and Theological Seminary (Ankeny, Iowa), Northwest Baptist Seminary (Tacoma, Washington), Shasta Bible College (Redding, California), Spurgeon Baptist Bible College (Mulberry, Florida), Temple Baptist Seminary and Tennessee Temple University (Chattanooga, Tennessee), and Western Baptist College (Salem, Oregon). Five compassion ministries (most of which are related to work with children) are approved by the GARBC. In 1950 the Regular Baptist Press was established to meet the GARBC's publication needs. Its offices are located in Schaumburg, Illinois.

The national offices of the GARBC were originally located in Chicago. In 1965 the GARBC moved to Des Plaines, Illinois in 1965 and to Schaumburg, Illinois (the current location) in 1976. A new International Ministry Resource Center for the GARBC and the Regular Baptist Press was under construction in 2003. The highest position in the GARBC national office is called the National Representative. The first National Representative was appointed in 1944 (Heber O. Van Gilder, 1944–1948). Robert T. Ketcham was the National Representative from 1948 to 1960. Since then some of the National Representatives have been Paul R. Jackson (1903–1969), Joseph M. Stowell (born 1911) and Paul N. Tassell. In 2003 the National Representative was John Greening.

The GARBC reached 100 churches by 1938, 500 by 1949, and 1,000 by 1962, and has more than 1,500 churches today. The churches are located primarily in the North from New York westward and throughout the Midwest, and in Washington, California, and Florida. The churches also group themselves in various state and regional associations for local work and fellowship purposes.

Distinctives

The GARBC's primary distinctives are their Baptist, fundamentalist, separatist, and premillennialist identities. The church stresses Baptist distinctives in ways similar to all Baptist groups and is strongly committed to the proclamation of the Gospel. The GARBC emphasizes separation from worldliness and ecclesiastical apostasy, defined in part as theological liberalism and compromising accommodation (see LIBERAL PROTESTANTISM AND LIBERALISM). They understand the BIBLE to be inerrant (see BIBLICAL INERRANCY). The creation accounts are understood as literal and historical, and any form of theistic evolution is rejected. As an aspect of their premillennialism, they believe that at the second advent of Christ the SALVATION of Israel as a nation will occur in the Holy Land.

See also Baptist Family of Churches; Baptist Missions; Baptists, United States; Fundamentalism; Millenarians and Millennialism

References and Further Reading

Delnay, R. "A History of the Baptist Bible Union." Ph.D. dissertation, Dallas Theological Seminary, 1963.

Dollar, George W. *A History of Fundamentalism in America.* Greenville, SC: Bob Jones University Press, 1973.

Hopewell, William J. *The Missionary Emphasis of the General Association of Regular Baptist Churches.* Chicago, IL: Regular Baptist Press, 1963.

Hull, Merle H. *What a Fellowship! The First Fifty Years of the General Association of Regular Baptist Churches.* Schaumburg, IL: Regular Baptist Press, 1981.

Murdoch, J. Murray. *Portrait of Obedience: The Biography of Robert T. Ketcham.* Schaumburg, IL: Regular Baptist Press, 1979.

Odell, Calvin. *The General Association of Regular Baptist Churches and Its Attendant Movement.* Salem, OR: Western Baptist Bible College Press, 1975.

Stowell, Joseph M. *Background and History of the General Association of Regular Baptist Churches.* 3rd ed. Hayward, CA: J. F. May, 1949.

DAVID M. SCHOLER

GENERAL BAPTISTS

General Baptists emerged as the earliest group of the new Baptist faith in ENGLAND in the 1610s, and in the UNITED STATES beginning in the 1650s. They were marked by their more expansive, less Calvinistic views (in comparison with other BAPTISTS) on ATONEMENT and ELECTION. As they expressed it in their CONFESSION of 1678, "God's love is manifest to all mankind, in that he is not willing, as himself hath sworn, and abundantly declared in his work, that mankind should perish eternally, but would have all to be saved, and come to the knowledge of the truth. And Christ died for all men, and there is a sufficiency in his death and merits for the sins of the whole world. . . so that if any do perish, it's not for want of the means of grace manifested by Christ to them" (Baker 1974:18). General Baptists believed that God's offer of SALVATION was open to all, not just to a predestined elect (see PREDESTINATION; ELECTION). This stood in contrast to the insistence on "particular" atonement espoused by the Particular (and later the Separate) Baptists. But nearly all early Baptists agreed on other fundamental doctrines and practices, including BAPTISM of adult believers by immersion, religious liberty, the primacy of Scripture over all other religious AUTHORITY, and CONGREGATIONALISM in church government.

Early English General Baptists

Baptists in England and the United States emerged as a separatist movement within seventeenth-century English Protestantism. The early Baptists were divided into two groups, each with its own separate origin and history: the Particular Baptists and the General Baptists. As separatists from the CHURCH OF ENGLAND, the early General Baptists argued that true Christians must break completely from the Church of England and all forms of Christianity that partook at all of popery, and organize themselves into small bands of believers (congregations) led by elders and DEACONS (see CLERGY). A Cambridge graduate named JOHN SMYTH, who had sought asylum in Holland because of persecution, rebaptized himself in 1609, signifying his belief that baptism should be restricted to believers only. Smyth and a group of thirty-six others formed what is generally thought of as the first Baptist church after the publication of Smyth's views on baptism in 1609. One of those members, Thomas Helwys, then split with Smyth, returned to London in the early 1610s, and established a Baptist church there. In 1612, Helwys published (and was jailed for) a short, controversial pamphlet on religious liberty, arguing that "The King hath no power over the immortal soul of his subjects" (Brackney 1988:191).

Despite persecution, the General Baptists grew from five churches and 150 members in 1626 to about forty congregations in 1644. They created the General Assembly of General Baptists in 1654 and subscribed to a confession of faith in 1678. Their church government was relatively centralized in comparison to other groups, because they gave considerable authority to their general assemblies to act so as to "preserve unity" and "prevent heresy," and with "lawful power to hear, and determine, as also to excommunicate" individuals and congregations that were not in accor-

dance with the confession (Baker 1974:19). In the eighteenth century, the English General Baptists fell into disarray and largely died out. Most members joined up with other Protestant dissenters (such as the Quakers, or Friends), evolved into Unitarians or began attending congregations of other more successful Baptist groups (see FRIENDS, SOCIETY OF; DISSENT; NONCONFORMITY).

General Baptists in the United States

General Baptists appeared in Rhode Island in the 1650s. In the United States the General Baptists retained their greatest strength in Rhode Island and other nearby regions through the eighteenth century, although some appeared in the South in the late seventeenth century. Over time, most General Baptist churches eventually merged into other Baptist groups, such as the Particular and then the Separate Baptists.

Under the influence of the Great Awakening "New Light" preaching (see AWAKENINGS), many General Baptist members began to accept more Calvinistic doctrines of limited atonement, whereas others moved in an opposite direction and merged with the growing movement of "FREE WILL BAPTISTS." As a result, the General Baptists exercised relatively little influence in England or the United States after the mid-eighteenth century. In the United States, the Separates and Regular Baptists merged to form the dominant mainstream of Baptist life by the late eighteenth century.

Later Developments Among General Baptists

Small pockets of General Baptist sentiment survived, attracting those who believed in more general views on humankind atonement than the largely Calvinistic limited atonement, mainstream Baptist tradition. Later generations of General Baptists split over a number of issues. Some joined the Free Will Baptists. Others began describing themselves as the "Six-Principle" Baptists, adding to the normal run of Baptist beliefs the idea that the laying on of hands was one of the gospel ordinances that Christians were commanded to obey. They took their principles from Hebrews 6:1–3, verses that outlined their six principles: repentance from sins, faith toward God, baptism by immersion, laying on of hands, resurrection of the dead, and eternal judgment.

In 1824, Benoni Stinson, a young Regular Baptist minister in Kentucky, grew dissatisfied with the harsh CALVINISM that he encountered among Baptist associations in his state. Failing to change its THEOLOGY, Stinson formed a new congregation that came to be called General Baptists. It held to the historic General Baptist view on the universal offer of salvation, and insisted on three ordinances: baptism, the LORD'S SUP-PER, and WASHING OF FEET. Eventually, many of the "Stinsonites" merged with the Free Will Baptists, but a remnant of General Baptists originated by Stinson survives today and supports a small denominational establishment.

See also Americans United for the Separation of Church and State; Feet, Washing of; Unitarian-Universalist Association

References and Further Reading

Baker, Robert. *The Southern Baptist Convention and Its People, 1607–1972.* Nashville, TN: Broadman Press, 1974.

Brackney, William. *The Baptists.* Westport, CT: Greenwood Press, 1988.

Laslie, T. A. H. *History of the General Baptists.* Cedar Bluffs, IA, 1938.

Knight, Richard. *History of the General or Six Principle Baptists, in Europe and America.* Providence, RI: Smith and Parmenter, 1827. Reprint, New York: Arno Press, 1980.

PAUL HARVEY

GENEVA BIBLE

The Geneva Bible was a translation made by exiles to Geneva during the reign of the Catholic queen of England, Mary Tudor (r. 1553–1558). Set in Roman type, with twenty-six engravings and five maps, each book was introduced by a preface and divided into verses. It became the most popular English Bible among Protestants in the British Isles and the New World because of comments in the margins, common in Renaissance books. These served as an interpretive device that placed it squarely in the Protestant camp, identifying the pope as ANTICHRIST. Read in Scottish churches, it also came to the New World with Pilgrims on the Mayflower (1620).

In 1555 JOHN CALVIN had welcomed Marian exiles to Geneva during an intense period of BIBLE publication in this Protestant printing center. Although the exact identity of William Whittingham's team of translators is uncertain, Anthony Gilby and Christopher Goodman participated. After the accession of ELIZABETH I (r. 1558–1603) to the English throne, Whittingham stayed in Geneva until May 1560, seeing the Bible through the press of Rowland Hall.

Frequently reprinted, after 1576, some editions substituted marginal notes revised by Laurence Tomson, based on notes by THEODORE BEZA (1519–1605) and Camerarius. From the late 1590s some Geneva Bibles substituted anti-Catholic notes by Franciscus Junius (1545–1602) on the Book of Revelation.

In 1604 James I (r. 1603–1625) claimed the Geneva Bible's notes allowed disobedience to kings. He ordered a new translation without marginal notes (1611). In 1616 printing the Geneva Bible in ENGLAND was forbidden, and it was imported from Amsterdam. This barrier was lifted after 1640. New marginal notes proved too expensive for the printing industry. A separate volume of annotations and commentary was published instead, enabling the King James Version of the Bible, itself influenced by the Geneva Bible (whose last known edition was 1644), to supersede it in popularity. Modern facsimile editions have allowed work on the enormous impact of the Bible and its marginalia.

See also Bible, King James Version; Bible Translation; Pilgrim Fathers

References and Further Reading

Betteridge, Maurice. "The Bitter Notes: The Geneva Bible and Its Annotations." *Sixteenth Century Journal* 14 (1983): 41–62.

The Geneva Bible: A Facsimile of the 1560 Edition with an Introduction by Lloyd E. Berry. Madison: University of Wisconsin Press, 1969.

Lampros, Dean George. "A New Set of Spectacles: The *Assembly's Annotations*, 1645–1657." *Renaissance and Reformation.* New Series 19 (1995): 33–46.

Sheppard, Gerald T., ed. *The Geneva Bible* (*The Annotated New Testament, 1602 Edition*). Pilgrim Classic Commentaries, vol. 1: The Geneva Bible. New York: The Pilgrim Press, 1989. [A clear facsimile of the Geneva Bible with marginal notes by Laurence Tomson and Franciscus Junius.]

JEANNINE E. OLSON

GENEVA CATECHISM

The 1542 *Catechism of the Church of Geneva* was JOHN CALVIN's second original contribution to sixteenth-century catechetical literature. His first CATECHISM, published in 1537 during his first stay in Geneva, was a short summary of his THEOLOGY with many similarities to the developing INSTITUTES OF THE CHRISTIAN RELIGION. Like the first catechetical efforts of other Reformers (MARTIN LUTHER, JOHANNES BRENZ, MARTIN BUCER), this work proved too complex for catechetical use, and furthermore its author was forced out of Geneva in the following year. When invited to return in 1541, therefore, Calvin demanded thorough religious and moral reforms as a condition. One aspect of these reforms was intensive religious instruction. For this purpose Calvin wrote the Geneva Catechism in November of 1541. It was published in French the next year, and in Latin in 1545.

The sixteenth century saw intense catechetical activity among both Catholics and Protestants. This literature drew on fifteenth-century precedents and embodied a renewed concern for well-informed lay piety. Also influential was Desiderius Erasmus's 1533 *Explanation of the Creed.* Among evangelical catechisms, Luther's *German Catechism* of 1529 and his subsequent (and more effective) *Shorter Catechism* were particularly important. In southern GERMANY the free imperial city of Strasbourg produced a large number of catechisms throughout the 1520s and 1530s, two of them written by Bucer, the most important Strasbourg theologian, in 1534 and 1537, respectively. Calvin lived in Strasbourg during his exile from Geneva, 1537–1541. While there he translated into French the section of Bucer's 1537 catechism intended for young children, demonstrating his respect for Bucer as a catechist, although his 1542 catechism shows more debt to Bucer's 1534 *Short Scriptural Explanation.*

Sixteenth-century catechisms, like their medieval predecessors, consisted of an explanation of the Creed, the Ten Commandments, the Lord's Prayer, and the SACRAMENTS. Luther deviated from his predecessors by placing the Commandments before the Creed. This expressed his belief that the Law functioned primarily to convict us of our sinfulness and drive us to faith in Christ (the "second use" of the Law). This order was followed by many evangelical catechisms, including Calvin's 1537 attempt. The earlier editions of the *Institutes* (up to 1559) also began with the Law as a means of self-knowledge leading to faith in Christ. In southern Germany, however, it was more common to follow the medieval order, and Bucer's 1534 catechism did so. The 1542 Geneva Catechism, written after Calvin's stay in Strasbourg, also began with the Creed. Theologically, placing the summary of the Law after the Creed expressed a focus on the Law as a guide to the Christian life (the so-called third use), which would become typical of "Reformed" Protestantism. However, Calvin's continued use of the "Lutheran" order in the 1539 and 1543 versions of the Institutes should make us cautious about reading too much into this.

Calvin's second catechism, unlike his first, adopted the question-and-answer format typical of the genre. Calvin expands this format into a dialogue, in which the minister might pose objections or make follow-up comments. Pedagogically this method may have made children feel as if they were taking a more active part in the learning process. Even though they were in fact reciting rote responses, the minister's questions would encourage them to think more carefully about exactly why they were giving those particular answers.

The minister's objections also led to the condemnation of erroneous positions. Calvin's catechism is free from direct polemic, but occasionally the minister makes what appears to be a logical inference from what the child has just said, only to be corrected. For instance, after the child asserts that works done in faith are pleasing to God, the minister suggests that it follows that such works merit God's love. This meets with a categorical "No." The minister then objects, "You are not intending to say however that the good works of the faithful are useless?" And later, "But can we believe in order to be justified, without doing good works?" After the child has answered these questions correctly, the minister finally confirms the orthodox position: "Faith then . . . is the root from which [good works] are produced." To which the child responds, "It is so." This rigorous interrogation matches objections made by Catholics and would have been good preparation for the defense of Protestant beliefs in real debate. It also allows Calvin to address controversial issues without directly attacking his opponents.

The catechism is a summary of the Christian faith intended for pastoral purposes. It lacks the polemic of the *Institutes* and also does not engage in detailed exegetical or historical discussion. It focuses on issues of direct pastoral importance—the minister repeatedly asks such questions as, "Do you derive any benefit from this?" (Qu. 41, CR 34:21) Thus, PREDESTINATION is affirmed but not discussed in detail, and more theoretical questions such as the role of the natural knowledge of God are omitted entirely. On the other hand, Calvin's discussion of the sacraments here is arguably clearer and more convincing than the rather involved treatment in the 1559 *Institutes.* Calvin seems much more comfortable explaining how the believer is to regard the sacraments as means of grace (his primary focus here) than attempting to clarify his position among the swirling sixteenth-century controversies on the subject.

Other noteworthy points include Calvin's explicit affirmation of the Trinity in traditional language, in contrast to the 1537 catechism's attempt to avoid non-biblical terminology. Christ's saving work is presented primarily as a victory over death and a liberation from Satan's tyranny, although it is also a satisfaction of God's justice. Calvin defines the church primarily as "the company of those whom God has chosen to save" (Qu. 100, CR 34:41), but he links the forgiveness of sins to membership in the church as "the community of the faithful" (Qu. 105, CR 34:42) explicitly threatening schismatics with damnation.

Although much briefer and to the point than the *Institutes,* the catechism is a remarkably detailed presentation of Christian DOCTRINE (especially when compared to its chief counterpart among the Lutherans, the *Shorter Catechism*). Calvin's stylistic virtues of clarity and confidence are particularly in evidence. The Latin version differs little from the French, although it occasionally adds additional comments and is not a slavishly literal translation.

The 1542 Catechism was supreme among Reformed catechetical literature until the composition of the HEIDELBERG CATECHISM in 1563, which borrowed a good deal from it (including its creative use of the question-and-answer format). It continued, however, to be among the three principal catechisms of the Reformed tradition, and is regarded to this day as one of the major Reformed confessional statements.

References and Further Reading

Primary Sources:

Calvin, John. "The Geneva Catechism." *Corpus Reformatorum* 34 (*Calvini Opera* 6): 1–160. Halle: C.A. Schwetschke, 1834ff.

Thomas, Torrance, ed. *John Calvin, Tracts and Treatises,* vol. 2. Translated by Henry Beveridge. Grand Rapids, MI: Wm. B. Eerdmans, 1958.

———, ed. *The School of Faith: The Catechisms of the Reformed Church.* New York: Harper & Brothers, 1959.

A translation of the Latin text can also be found at the following website: http://www.reformed.org/documents/calvin/geneva_catachism/geneva_catachism.html

A translation of the French text is available on several websites, including http://www.kinder-kreations.com/calvin's_catechism.htm

The 1537 Catechism is found in *Ioannis Calvini Opera Omnia,* Series 3, *Scripta Ecclesiastica,* vol. 2, *Instruction et confession de foi dont on use en l'Église de Genève/Catechismus seu christianae religionis institutio ecclesiae genevensis,* edited by Annette Zillenbiller. Geneva: Droz, 2002. English translation (from 1538 Latin text) by Ford Lewis Battles, in John Hesselink, ed., *Calvin's First Catechism: A Commentary.* Louisville, KY: Westminster John Knox, 1997.

Secondary Source:

Barth, Karl. *The Faith of the Church: A Commentary on the Apostles' Creed According to Calvin's Catechism.* London: Fontana Books, 1965.

EDWIN TAIT

GEORGE, DAVID (1742–1810)

African American churchman. Founder of pioneering black Baptist churches in the American South, Nova Scotia, and West Africa, George was born into SLAVERY in Virginia in 1742. He later fled to South Carolina, where he founded the first black Baptist church at Silver Bluff in 1773. The congregation grew to more than thirty slaves and free blacks under George's direction and was visited by notable black itinerants such as George Liele.

After siding with British Loyalists during the American War of Independence, George was evacuated to Nova Scotia in 1783 along with three thousand other African Americans. At Shelburne he founded one of the first Baptist churches in Nova Scotia; he also itinerated, baptized, and organized seven other Baptist churches in black and white communities throughout the province. Well known for his passionate preaching, George became a target of mob vio-

lence in 1784 when disbanded white soldiers rioted against free blacks. In 1792 he helped organize the emigration of 1,200 blacks to SIERRA LEONE, where he continued his work as a Baptist preacher, church organizer, and political advocate. George delivered his life narrative to the Baptist ministers John Rippon and Samuel Pearce during a visit to ENGLAND in 1793; Rippon published this account in the 1793 edition of *The Annual Baptist Register*. George died in Sierra Leone in 1810.

See also Africa; African American Protestantism; American Baptist Churches; Baptists, United States; Sierra Leone

References and Further Reading

"An Account of the Life of Mr. David George, from Sierra Leone in Africa" (1793). In *Face Zion Forward: First Writers of the Black Atlantic, 1785–1798,* edited by Joanna Brooks and John Saillant. Boston: Northeastern University Press, 2002.

Gordon, Grant. *From Slavery to Freedom: The Life of David George, Pioneer Black Baptist Minister.* Hantsport, Nova Scotia: Lancelot, 1992.

JOANNA BROOKS

GERHARDT, PAUL (1607–1676)

Lutheran hymn writer. Gerhardt was born near Wittenberg on March 12, 1607. Orphaned early in his youth, he attended boarding schools and in 1628 began the study of THEOLOGY at the University of Wittenberg, then the citadel of Lutheran ORTHODOXY. The next years of Gerhardt's life are enigmatic. In 1643 he was in Berlin and eight years later, he was appointed Pastor in the small town of Mittenwalde near Berlin. In 1655 he married Anna Maria Berthold, the youngest daughter of a legal counsel in Berlin in whose house he had stayed as a guest for some time. In 1657 he was appointed DEACON at the parish of St. Nikolaus in Berlin.

Gerhardt's mature years fell into the time of the intense controversy between Lutheran and Reformed (Calvinist) theologians especially in Prussia. The Prussian elector sought to stem the vehement controversy by ordering the omission of the Formula of Concord, with its decided anti-Reformed orientation, in the ordination vows of candidates for the ministry, and furthermore prohibited Prussian theology students from attending the University of Wittenberg. Gerhardt, who sided with the Lutherans, served as theological expert at an important colloquy between Lutherans and Reformed in 1662–1663, indicating his desire to resolve the disagreements. By the same token he refused to subscribe to a government-imposed statement that would have demanded complete silence in all controversial theological issues. Accordingly he was removed from his office in February 1666.

A flood of petitions to the Prussian elector effected his reinstatement, without giving him, however, the authorization to preach. The Berlin city council addressed a new petition to the elector, asking that Gerhardt be allowed to preach. The elector's failure to respond to this new petition prompted Gerhardt to resign his position in February 1667. In October of the following year he was elected archdeacon of Luebben in the Niederlausitz, where he died on May 27, 1676.

Gerhardt's significance in that turbulent age lay in his voluminous contribution to German Lutheran hymnody. The 1653 Lutheran hymnal, published in Berlin (*Praxis Pietatis Melica*), included some eighty of his hymns, a significant number of which are still found in the current German Lutheran hymnal, an indication, surely, of his abiding significance. Although his popularity has been mainly in the German language culture, a number of his hymns, such as O, Sacred Head Now Wounded, have been translated into English.

See also Hymns and Hymnals

References and Further Reading

Primary Sources:

Cranach-Sichart, Eberhard von, ed. Paul Gerhardt. Dichtungen und Schriften. Zug: Verlag der Obelisk, 1957.
Ebeling, Johann Georg. Pauli Gerhardi geistlche Andachten (1667). Selections Instrumentalstimmen zu den Geistlichen Andachten. Bern: Francke Verlag, 1975.
Hewitt, Theodore B. Paul Gerhardt as a hymn writer and his influence on English hymnody. St. Louis: Concordia Pub. House, 1976.

Secondary Sources:

Axmacher, Elke. Johann Arndt und Paul Gerhardt: Studien zur Theologie, Frömmigkeit und geistlichen Dichtung des 17. Jahrhunderts. Tübingen: Francke, 2001.
Grosse, Sven. Gott und das Leid in den Liedern Paul Gerhardts. Forschungen zur Kirchen-und Dogmengeschichte; Bd. 83. Göttingen: Vandenhoeck & Ruprecht, 2001.

HANS J. HILLERBRAND

GERMAN CHRISTIANS

The German Christians (*Deutsche Christen*) were a group of clergy and laypeople in GERMANY in the 1930s and 1940s who sought to synthesize National Socialism (Nazism) and Christianity. They aimed to purge Christianity of everything they deemed Jewish and to transform the German Protestant church into an association based on "blood." Most of the approximately 600,000 members were Protestant, although a few Catholics were involved. By mid-1933, six months after Hitler became chancellor, German Christians had acquired key posts in the Protestant establishment—in national church governing bodies and university faculties of theology, as regional bishops, and on local church councils. Many kept those positions until 1945 and beyond.

Birth of the German Christians

Three impulses converged to form the German Christian movement. In 1932, a group of politicians and pastors met to discuss how to win the Protestant churches of Germany to the Nazi cause. They initially named themselves Protestant National Socialists but decided on German Christians instead. Meanwhile, in Thuringia, Siegfried Leffler and Julius Leutheuser, two young pastors and war veterans, had been preaching religious renewal along Nazi lines since the 1920s. They also called themselves German Christians. The two groups began to cooperate. A third initiative came from the Protestant, folkish associations that emerged after World War I. Dedicated to reviving church life through emphasizing German culture, ANTI-SEMITISM, and nationalism, some of those organizations merged with the German Christian movement.

Instead of breaking with the established Protestant churches, the German Christians tried to take over from within. Their efforts sparked a fight for control known as the Church Struggle. The German Christians's main rival was the CONFESSING CHURCH, another movement within official Protestantism. Most Protestants remained neutral. The German Christians also had opposition outside the church from neopagans who considered even nazified Christianity "too Jewish." Although clergymen were their main spokesmen, the German Christians represented a cross-section of German society: women and men, old and young, teachers, dentists, railroad workers, housewives, and farmers.

Ideology

The German Christians aimed to create a "people's church" that would embrace all "true" Germans and provide a spiritual homeland for the Aryans of the Third Reich. Calling themselves "Stormtroopers of Christ," they attacked every aspect of Christianity that was related to JUDAISM. They rejected the Old Testament, revised the New Testament, expunged words like "Hallelujah" and "Hosanna" from hymns, and denied that Jesus was a Jew. Because the German Christians considered Jewishness racial, they refused to accept conversions from Judaism to Christianity as valid.

Certain ideas about gender helped the German Christians reconcile Nazism and Christianity. According to German Christians, only a hard, manly church devoid of qualities they considered feminine—like compassion—could fight racial impurity. Moreover, they argued, just as Christian faith did not eradicate physical differences between male and female, it did not negate the supposedly biological fact of race.

Growth and Expansion Tactics

The German Christians promoted their views through mass rallies; in newspapers, flyers, and scholarly works; and from the pulpit. Lay members spread the word in schools and at local pubs. The German Christians did more than talk: they disrupted meetings of the Confessing Church, barricaded church buildings, and assaulted and harassed non-Aryans, that is, converts from Judaism to Christianity and their families.

German Christian ideas remained fairly constant, but the movement changed over time. During the first year (1932 to late 1933) the German Christians enjoyed open Nazi support. They swept the Protestant church elections in 1933 and dominated the process that unified Germany's regional Protestant churches into a national Protestant Church. A German Christian, the naval chaplain Ludwig Müller, became Protestant Reich bishop.

Fall of the German Christians

Success was short-lived. Worried that the German Christians caused dissension, Nazi leaders withdrew their support. Tensions surrounding the movement exploded at a rally in November 1933. Before an audience of 20,000 in the Berlin Sports Palace, the speaker, a high school religion teacher named Reinhold Krause, attacked the Old Testament, the concept of sin, and the symbol of the cross as unacceptable signs of Jewish influence. Krause's speech sparked a wave of departures from German Christian ranks by members who wanted to retain traditional Christianity.

For the next two years the movement was in shambles. The national group splintered, but the names of the new factions—Reich Movement of German Christians; The Church Movement of German Christians; The German Christians, National Church Union—indicate that core ideas persisted. By late 1935 the German Christians were reorganizing, and by September 1939, when German troops invaded Poland, almost all the camps had reestablished ties.

War fulfilled many of the German Christians' aims. They had demanded an aggressive Christianity; now they had the nation at arms. They demanded exclusion of non-Aryans and Jewish influences from German religious life; that goal was realized by default through the deportation and murder of people defined as Jews. But the war also brought setbacks. Even the German Christians experienced hostility from Nazi authorities who resented Christianity in any form.

When Hitler's regime collapsed in 1945, the German Christian movement lost all credibility. Former members now had to justify their involvement to Allied occupation authorities, denazification boards, and even themselves. Many pointed to their ideal of the "people's church" to try to prove they had only wanted religious renewal. They rarely mentioned the anti-Semitism that had pervaded their program. In response to Allied pressure, some German Christian pastors were ousted, but within a few years almost all were back in the pulpit. Lay members easily reentered the Protestant mainstream. Some scholars dismiss the German Christians because they constituted a small part of the population—around 1 percent. In the context of the Nazi system, however, the movement was significant. Through their quest for a "racially pure," anti-Jewish church, the German Christians echoed and endorsed the crimes of Nazi Germany.

References and Further Reading

Bergen, Doris L. *Twisted Cross: The German Christian Movement in the Third Reich.* Chapel Hill, NC: University of North Carolina Press, 1996.

Conway, John S. *The Nazi Persecution of the Churches, 1933–45.* New York: Basic Books, 1968.

Ericksen, Robert P. *Theologians Under Hitler: Gerhard Kittel, Paul Althaus and Emanuel Hirsch.* New Haven, CT: Yale University Press, 1985.

———, and Susannah Heschel, eds. *Betrayal: German Churches and the Holocaust.* Minneapolis, MN: Augsburg Fortress, 1999.

Scholder, Klaus. *The Churches and the Third Reich.* Vol. 1: *Preliminary History and the Time of Illusions, 1918–1934.* Vol. 2: *The Year of Disillusionment: 1934.* Translated by John Bowden. Philadelphia, PA: Fortress, 1987–1988.

DORIS L. BERGEN

GERMAN GROUPS IN AMERICA

The appearance of German groups in America had a modest beginning in 1683, with the arrival of a small Mennonite congregation in Germantown, Pennsylvania. Soon others arrived in that colony, drawn by the "Holy Experiment" of the Quaker colonial proprietor, William Penn (1644–1718). The early immigrants included a preponderance of religious mystics (like Johann Kelpius, 1673–1708) and sectarians (including the German Baptist Brethren or Dunkers; Schwenkfelders; the "Community of True Inspiration," whose members later formed the Amana colonies in Iowa; and others), who were characterized by radical Pietist beliefs. In the eighteenth and early nineteenth centuries, German radical Pietists like Conrad Beissel (1691–1768) and George Rapp (1757–1847) founded perfectionistic communities driven by eschatological fervor, such as the Ephrata Cloister (Pennsylvania) and New Harmony (Indiana), respectively. Moravians also migrated to colonial North Carolina and Pennsylvania, where their leader, Count NIKOLAUS LUDWIG VON ZINZENDORF (1700–1760) unsuccessfully attempted to form a unitive movement of Pennsylvania German sects called "The Congregation of God in the Spirit" (1742). In addition, numerous Hessian mercenary soldiers employed by the British during the Revolutionary War remained in this land and contributed to the cultural life of the new nation.

German immigration to the American middle colonies in the eighteenth century was surpassed in the period from 1820 to 1925, when almost six million Germans arrived in the United States, representing the largest nationality group among all American immigrants of that era. Religious freedom linked with a quest for new economic opportunity was a major factor for earlier German immigrants, who coalesced in three kinds of religious groups, the "plain Dutch," the "church Dutch," and the "bush meeting Dutch." (In this usage, "Dutch" is an American colloquialism for "Deutsch," as distinct from immigrants from Holland.)

The Plain Dutch

The "plain Dutch," noted for their conservative garb, included those who identified with the believers' church, or historic peace church tradition. They include some twenty organized Anabaptist church bodies, which take their name from their opponents' reference to their practice of "rebaptizing" their converts in denunciation of infant baptism. They are concerned with restoring a primitive New Testament pattern of church life, based on discipleship and the separation of church and state. They are chiefly represented in America by a variety of MENNONITE church bodies, derived from the name of their Dutch Anabaptist leader, MENNO SIMONS (c. 1496–1561). Those Mennonites who moved to colonial Pennsylvania, as well as Maryland and the Shenandoah Valley of Virginia, were of Swiss and South German Anabaptist orientation. Mennonites who migrated to the American Plains states and southern Manitoba in the late nineteenth century were of Russian-German origin. Groups that emerged from the former immigration include the "Old" Mennonites and the Old Order Amish, who based their beliefs on the decision (c. 1693) of a Swiss Mennonite named Jacob Ammann to reject the new spirit of PIETISM by adopting a tradi-

tionalist view of dress and economic and social life for his adherents. By contrast, the River Brethren (1788), later known as the BRETHREN IN CHRIST, integrated Pietist themes of personal rebirth with an Anabaptist form of church life. Mennonites of Russian-German origin largely became concentrated in the Mennonite Brethren and General Conference Mennonite Churches. Like Quakers, Mennonites have initiated valuable humanitarian service projects as part of their nonviolent witness to the world. Total membership in North American Mennonite bodies was 340,000 in 1984.

The Church Dutch

The "church Dutch" represent the adherents of the official state churches, including Lutherans, German Reformed, and Roman Catholics. Persons of German descent represent the majority of the two largest Lutheran church bodies in America, the Evangelical Lutheran Church in America (5.5 million members at its formation in 1988) and the LUTHERAN CHURCH, MISSOURI SYNOD (2.7 million members). The lineage of the former body reaches back to the organizational work of HENRY M. MUHLENBERG (1711–1787) a product of the Halle (GERMANY) center of Lutheran Pietism, who arrived in Pennsylvania in 1742. In the nineteenth century, German Lutherans polarized between supporters of SAMUEL S. SCHMUCKER (1799–1873) of Gettysburg Seminary (Pennsylvania), who led the effort to "Americanize" Lutherans, and CARL F. W. WALTHER (1811–1887), an immigrant who reacted against German Lutheran rationalism and shaped a distinctly confessional "church" consciousness among Saxons in Missouri. His work soon spread to other states. SYNODS that grew from Schmucker's work were fully involved in the National and WORLD COUNCIL OF CHURCHES. The Missouri Synod, becoming the largest German Protestant denomination in America, maintained German-language services through the era of the First World War, and has continued to provide the most extensive parochial school system in America outside Catholicism. Prior to the twentieth century, German Lutherans tended to maintain an identity distinct from Lutherans of Scandinavian and Baltic origin.

Also numbered among the "church Dutch" were the German Reformed, who arrived in the middle colonies in the colonial era and were initially organized by John Philip Boehm (1683–1749) and then by Michael Schlatter (1718–1790). The latter organized a "coetus" under the jurisdiction of the Synod of Amsterdam. German Reformed had their home in the German Palatinate, and were devoted to an irenic statement of Reformed theology, the HEIDELBERG CAT-

ECHISM (1563). Given this irenic bent, German Reformed in America joined with "unionist" Prussian immigrants, known as the Evangelical Synod of North America, to form the Evangelical and Reformed Church in 1934. The latter body became a part of the UNITED CHURCH OF CHRIST in 1957. Finally, there were the German Catholics, who, along with Irish immigrants, formed the majority of the ten million Roman Catholic immigrants who arrived from Europe in the century following 1820. German Catholic dioceses, especially in the Great Lakes and the Ohio and Mississippi Valleys, formed another bulwark of German cultural heritage, and often resisted the pace of their church's Americanization.

The Bush-Meeting Dutch

A third religious grouping of German Americans has been called the "bush-meeting Dutch," which describes their propensity for open-air revival or camp meeting services and emotional, Pietistic religious expression centered on the centrality of the experience of the "new birth" (*der Wiedergeburt*). Their early leadership was provided by the unionist efforts of a Pietist missionary of the German Reformed Church, Philip William Otterbein (1726–1813) and a "converted" Mennonite leader. Martin Boehm (1725–1813), who laid the foundations for the Church of the United Brethren in Christ (1800). The latter, as well as the Evangelical Association that was founded by a Lutheran lay preacher, Jacob Albright (1759–1808), grew rapidly in the nineteenth century by adapting revivalistic preaching and Methodist patterns of organization to reach German immigrants, among others. The Evangelicals also conducted extensive mission work to their German "Fatherland," establishing a major free church group there in the mid-nineteenth century. These two German-American revival denominations united to form the EVANGELICAL UNITED BRETHREN CHURCH (1946), which was later joined with the Methodist Church to form the UNITED METHODIST CHURCH (1968).

After the abortive liberal revolutions in Germany in 1830 and 1848, significant numbers of intellectual and political activist Germans immigrated to the UNITED STATES. Many were of Jewish heritage. Large numbers of Yiddish-speaking German Jews settled in New York City. The scores of learned editors of German-language newspapers in North America increasingly molded German-Americans into a self-conscious political block that was against slavery and Republican in sentiment. German cultural centers, called *Turnverein*, were established in cities and towns across mid-America. Another wave of German intelligentsia arrived during the oppression of the Hitler era in the 1930s and 1940s, including such notables as scientists Albert Einstein and Wernher von Braun.

The broad mix of religious and ideological groups that has comprised German-American culture reached its height of national influence in the era before the First World War, when (in 1910) 27.5 percent of all American citizens were of German birth or had at least one German-born parent.

References and Further Reading

Ahlstrom, S. E. *A Religious History of the American People.* New Haven, CT: Yale University Press, 1973.

Behney, J. B., and P. Eller. *History of the Evangelical United Brethren Church.* Nashville, TN: Abingdon Press, 1979.

Dolan, J. P. *The American Catholic Experience.* South Bend, IN: University of Notre Dame Press, 1985.

Fackre, Gabriel, and Michael Root. *Affirmations and Admonitions: Lutheran Decisions and Dialogue with Reformed, Episcopal, and Roman Catholic Churches.* Grand Rapids, MI: Eerdmans, 1998.

MacMaster, R. K. *Land, Piety, Peoplehood, The Establishment of Mennonite Communities in America, 1683–1790.* Scottdale, PA: Herald Press, 1985.

Ripley, Lavern. *Of German Ways.* Minneapolis, MN: Dillon, 1970; reprint ed. New York: Barnes & Noble, 1980.

Stoeffler, J. E. *Continental Pietism and Early American Christianity.* Grand Rapids, MI: Eerdmans, 1976.

J. STEVEN O'MALLEY

GERMANY

The Federal Republic of Germany has 356,945 square kilometers and 80 million people. Formally, roughly 42 percent are registered as Catholics, 40 percent as Protestants, and about 8 percent are Muslims. Protestant, in this context, means overwhelmingly Lutheran, for which the German word "evangelisch" is customarily a synonym. A distinctive feature of Protestantism is its territorial delimitation and the influence of particular doctrinal traditions. This goes back to the time of the REFORMATION when the Protestant princes reformed the church in their territories. Protestantism has had a deep impact on cultural, economic, and political developments in society, leading German Christians to reflect on subjects such as guilt and confession, forgiveness and reconciliation, and the church's commitment to the ongoing challenges of our time.

Development of Protestantism

In 1517, Martin Luther's Ninety-five Theses, at first written in Latin and meant for discussion in the faculty of Wittenberg, voiced the demand for a radical renewal of the Catholic Church and became the spark that set the fire. This document, although merely theological, spread like a freedom charter. MARTIN LUTHER

(1483–1546) together with highly gifted scholars such as PHILIPP MELANCHTHON, JOHANNES BUGENHAGEN, JOHANNES BRENZ, and MARTIN BUCER inspired the movement of church renewal. The Swiss reformers HULDRYCH ZWINGLI (1484–1531) and JOHN CALVIN (1509–1564) of Geneva worked somewhat independently from the developments in Germany. The biblical message of JUSTIFICATION by GRACE alone brought these men into conflict with the pope and his curia. In 1521 Luther was excommunicated but stood courageously in front of the emperor Charles V at the Diet of Worms and appealed to his conscience's commitment to the Word of God alone. The religious controversy was resolved in German lands with the Peace of Augsburg (1555), which provided for religious peace on a territorial basis: the territorial rulers had the authority to decide the religious orientation of their territories.

This formally separated Germany into Catholic and Lutheran territories. CALVINISM was not recognized in the Peace of Augsburg but nonetheless demonstrated striking vitality toward the end of the century, with a number of territorial rulers converting to Calvinism. This ecclesiastical bifurcation began to entail cultural ramifications so that North Germany (mainly Lutheran and Calvinist) developed differently from the South.

Theologically the churches undertook to demonstrate their particular theological emphases in almost scholastic fashion. All churches took correct DOCTRINE to be the essence of the Christian religion, leading to the label of ORTHODOXY for that period.

In the late seventeenth century, following confessional orthodoxy, a new movement of personal piety arose. The Reformation stress on personal SALVATION was restated in terms of the personal experience of faith. PHILIPP JAKOB SPENER, JOHANN ALBRECHT BENGEL, and many others emphasized the practical side of piety. The term "Pietists," initially a term of mockery, soon became the universally used label.

Extensive BIBLE study and gatherings with PRAYER, hymns, and an individual way of life became characteristic of PIETISM. After 1700 AUGUST HERMANN FRANCKE in HALLE and later count NIKOLAUS LUDWIG VON ZINZENDORF in HERRNHUT with his community of Moravians began sending missionaries overseas. Pietism was a movement similar to that of JOHN WESLEY'S in ENGLAND, but unlike Wesley's METHODISM it did not result in a separate church. In the nineteenth century the notion of mission to people overseas was stimulated by the establishment of several missionary societies, but only after the German acquisition of overseas colonies in 1885 did the issue of MISSIONS receive general attention. In the early nineteenth century several attempts were made to overcome the fatal divisions of the Reformation era. Effectively a third

Protestant church came into being in addition to the Reformed and Lutheran: the Church of the PRUSSIAN UNION.

The Germany of roughly its current boundaries came into being in 1871. Before that it was divided into more than thirty larger and smaller states, virtually autonomous so that they even waged war against each other. The sovereign determined the confession of his subjects, so that quite often some villages were Protestant whereas over the border of the small state the villagers were Catholic. This confessional "mosaic" is recognizable in the confessional map of Germany until today. In 1918, with the end of World War I, a 400-year-old relationship of "throne and altar" ended, and the churches plunged into a severe crisis. In a time of poverty they had to establish synods and councils and organize their finances. Twenty-eight territorial churches formed a federation in 1922. It lasted eleven years until the Nazis dissolved it and, as they claimed, established a National Church (Reichskirche). During the period of oppression during the "Third Reich" (1933–1945), a renewed understanding of Christian service and mandate developed in the so-called CONFESSING CHURCH.

After the defeat in World War II Germany was divided into two separate states. Under the subjection of the Soviet Union, Eastern Germany, including East Berlin, became the German Democratic Republic (GDR). West Germany constituted the Federal Republic of Germany (FDG). When Protestant church leaders met in Stuttgart in 1945, they adopted a declaration of guilt for the Nazi regime, asking the neighboring Christians and churches for forgiveness. In 1948, a time of growing tension between the two political systems of East and West, the federation of churches known as the Evangelical Church in Germany (EKD) was founded, consisting of the regional churches of both East and West. The churches in both states retained a special bilateral relationship across the inner German border. However, so as not to be relegated to a religious ghetto or to be confined to WORSHIP and private religious needs, the churches in the GDR accepted the permanence of the GDR and its social system and attempted to add their own contributions to society. In 1969 they ended their membership in the EKD and established the Federation of the Evangelical Churches—Bund Evangelischer Kirchen (BEK)—in the German Democratic Republic. The special relationship between the church federation in the East and the EKD in the West, however, continued in joint statements of both churches and took shape in a wide-reaching network of partner relationships between parishes in East and West.

The autonomy of the BEK resulted in a new definition of the goals of church politics, reducing confrontation and seeking cooperation where it appeared possible to both CHURCH AND STATE. However, the fundamental conflict to which committed Christian students and workers were subjected in the educational system of the GDR was never settled. The GDR Ministry of State Security (Stasi), in its effort to control the population, penetrated every organization to gain collaborators and the church was not excluded. After German unification, discerning between cooperation and resistance was difficult. With the extraordinary events set in motion by the rise to power of Mikhail Gorbachev in the Soviet Union, the influence of the Soviet Union on East Germany waned, and the East German people overthrew the Communist government in late 1989 in a peaceful revolution.

When the GDR was established in 1949, under the leadership of the Socialist Unity Party (SED), more than 90 percent of the population were members of the Protestant (Lutheran and Prussian Union) Church. In the 1980s, after half a century of the socialist reorganization of society, only 30 to 40 percent of the population belonged to a Christian church, even fewer in the cities.

Cultural, Economic, and Political Impacts

According to Luther's principle of the PRIESTHOOD OF ALL BELIEVERS, all Christians should be able to read the Bible. Endowed with the ability to find the adequate language, after twelve years' work Luther completed the translation of the entire Bible in 1534 (see BIBLE TRANSLATION). Through this translation he contributed significantly to the emergence of a unified written German language. The disposition of Protestantism to cultivate literacy and to spread regard for the vernacular served to remove the linguistic dominance of Latin of medieval Christendom and to encourage the rise of national boundaries based on languages. It is therefore possible to speak of Protestantism's contribution to the rise of present German society.

All reformers were extremely busy writing essays, counseling letters, and comments on theological and public issues of the day. Neither Luther nor his associates were organizers but rather scholars and educators. The publication of the Bible in German, however, was a signal to many Christians to rely directly on the message of the Word of God and to take responsibility for the life of the church. The real reform of the church, its service, and structure was implemented by town councils or rulers, not by bishops (see BISHOP AND EPISCOPACY). Thus, the responsibility of the LAITY in Protestantism was recognized early. In addition the dialogue with the spirit of the age, particularly in social and scholarly fields, was taken seriously from the beginnings of Protestantism. PAUL TILLICH, for one, argued that "the Protestant principle" of prophetic criticism is to be included in any authentic expression of church life and that it is a genuine value in the secular world.

Sociologist MAX WEBER held that the Protestant ethic—that is, the value attached to hard work, thrift, and efficiency—was an important factor in the economic success of Protestant groups not only in the Reformed parts of Germany but also in the early stages of European capitalism. Worldly success came to be interpreted as a sign of an individual's ELECTION or eternal SALVATION and was therefore vigorously pursued. The emphasis of Calvinism on the religious duty to make fruitful use of the God-given resources at each individual's disposal, and its orderliness and systemization of ways of life were also regarded by Weber as economically significant aspects of the Protestant ethic. Although Weber's thesis was widely accepted, it has been subject to criticism for its monocausal explanation of the rise of capitalism. It has been expanded in favor of multicausal explanations, the argument being that political and social pressures, together with the spirit of INDIVIDUALISM with its ethic of self-help and frugality, were more significant factors (Tawney 1926).

The break from Rome during the period of the Reformation brought a new alliance of "throne and altar" in Protestant territories, a close relation of church and state: the sovereigns assumed leadership, appointed the administrators of the church of their territories, and controlled all important issues. This alliance proved to be a great hindrance when democratic ideas began to spread in the nineteenth century and Protestant pastors condemned this movement as dangerous and atheistic.

In the Federal Republic of Germany, according to its constitution, the relationship between church and state is governed by the principle that there are certain limits on the powers of the state. The constitution does not, therefore, seek to secure all-inclusive authority for the state, but limits its purpose to the maintenance of the common good, of which freedom and social justice are the main aspects. The churches are by their very nature independent of the state and do not derive any authority from it. The state recognizes them as institutions with the right of self-determination. They therefore claim autonomy in carrying out their spiritual and religious mission. State and church are obliged to strive for meaningful cooperation. Schools of theology are integral parts of state universities; schools give religious instruction on behalf of the church; and in the social services area the churches play a large role, shared alike by Catholics and Protestants.

The churches are authorized to collect a "church tax." The legal foundation for the church tax system is found in Article 140 of the German constitution. The church tax is levied as a surcharge on the income tax and amounts to 8 or 9 percent of income tax paid, depending on the state. This church tax is administered and collected by the revenue office and transferred to the churches.

Contemporary Organizational Structures

After decades of separation, the regional Protestant churches in East and West Germany were reunited organizationally in 1991. The eight churches of the Federation of Evangelical Churches (BEK) in the territory of the former German Democratic Republic again became part of the Evangelical Church in Germany (EKD). The synods of the EKD of the West created the legal conditions for restoring the organizational unity, and then the synods of the BEK of the East agreed to the unification of all regional churches under the umbrella of the EKD some weeks later. This procedure made it possible for a new EKD Synod to constitute itself in Coburg on June 28–30, 1991, as the representative body of the twenty-four regional churches, which have a total membership of some thirty million in over 18,100 congregations. The churches of East Germany brought what they endured and experienced during forty years of socialist rule and the twenty years of the Federation of Evangelical Churches. Member churches retain their own character, which applies even more to local congregations.

It is the Council of Christian Churches—Arbeitsgemeinschaft Christlicher Kirchen (ACK)—that aims to promote the unity of the churches in national, regional, and local alliances in Germany. In 1948, before the founding of the Federal Republic of Germany, the Protestant churches and the Old Catholic Church joined together to form the Council of Christian Churches. In 1974 the Roman Catholic Church, through association of the German dioceses and the Greek Orthodox Metropolitan of Germany, joined the ACK. Because of the division of Germany beginning in 1963, the representatives from the eastern part of Germany met separately and founded an organization of Christian churches in the GDR. In 1991 both areas in Germany united in ACK under a new revised constitution. The constitution was also signed by the following churches: Baptist Union, United Methodist Church, Association of Mennonite congregations in Germany, European Continental Province of the Moravian Church, the Syrian Orthodox Church of Antioch in Germany, the Christian Reformed Church in Germany, the Salvation Army in Germany, and Russian Orthodox Church in Germany. Other churches take part with guest status or as observers. Among other things ACK strives for the promotion of theological dialogue, counseling and arbitration, safeguarding of ecumenical responsibilities, and the representation of common concerns on political issues.

Continuing Challenges

Diaconal Work

The Diakonisches Werk of the EKD is an umbrella organization of a great number of initiatives undertaken in the field of church social services. The members represent some 29,000 independent institutions of different size and legal status with about 300,000 full- and part-time employees. Integrated in social legislation, the Diakonisches Werk coordinates and represents, for example, activities in preschools, care of the sick and disabled, immigrants, care of the homeless, former prisoners, and the poor. The main office coordinates and represents the planning and funding for many different tasks that also include aid in disasters and assistance known as "Brot für die Welt" (Bread for the World). In a time of challenge through outbursts of hatred, the German churches have taken a stand on behalf of thousands of refugees from African and Asian countries. Synodical meetings have expressed their concern and have called for Christian love and hospitality for those who have come applying for asylum.

Mission

In the early 1970s German Protestant churches structurally involved themselves in mission work by founding regional associations of mission ("Missionswerke"). The "Missionswerke" accepted the challenge presented by the WORLD COUNCIL OF CHURCHES (WCC) to act against social injustices such as racism and economic exploitation, and to work for justice, peace, and the preservation of creation. To promote mutual ecumenical encounters, German churches invite ecumenical workers to assume pastoral work in traditional parishes or to join those who inform congregations about new developments in the field of mission and ECUMENISM. An increasing number of congregations or church districts have set up direct links with overseas partners. The regional associations of mission have established new international structures where different churches share their multiple needs and possibilities. This means no more "one-way traffic" and not only "two-way traffic" but a multilaterally committed Christian community.

Church Membership

Undoubtedly many formal church members have become discouraged in their faith, and the young generation's indifference toward Christianity is on the increase. Secularization and the attractions of modern life have contributed to a measurable decrease in personal belief and church membership. On the other hand, the German Evangelical "KIRCHENTAG (Church Rally)," founded in 1949 as a lay movement and held every second year, attracts more than one hundred thousand people and is particularly fascinating to the younger generation.

New Spirituality

Particularly in the western part of Germany people are expecting less and less from the church, and a free market of vague spirituality and esoteric counseling is flourishing. Reincarnation therapists, astrologers, religious healers, and other representatives of esoteric religion offer their services. More and more people feel the need of some kind of religious experience. Pentecostal and charismatic groups find it easier than the established churches to meet the challenge (see PENTECOSTALISM). Experts of the regional churches and the Protestant Center on Questions of Weltanschauung—Evangelisches Zentrum fur Weltaunschauung (EZW)—offer orientation and warning, where necessary. However, it seems that the desire for more spirituality also indicates shortcomings of the churches. The questions about dealing with one's own soul, healing the sick (see FAITH HEALING), looking after the dying (see DEATH AND DYING), meditation, and spiritual experience are not dealt with often enough and sometimes disappear behind social and political involvement. There is, however, a growing readiness within the churches to search for new forms of Christian spirituality and to revive forgotten resources of the Christian faith.

Ecology

After pastors and congregations in the 1960s had already given attention to certain environmental problems, the 1970s brought the ecological question to the agenda of many church synods. Initially, it was the discussion about the use of nuclear energy for the production of electricity that led to a passionate debate on the chances of survival of a lifestyle based on a permanent rise of electrical demand. But how to reduce the consumption of energy and to manage the regeneration of power sources? How to avoid enormous mountains of garbage, and how to develop a healthier relationship with nature and the environment? Projects of ecological analysis were initiated and the awareness increased that belief in God as Creator of the World leads Christians to adopt a responsible attitude toward the gifts of creation.

Women

The long tradition of Protestant women's religious orders, the mother-houses of DEACONESSES and sisterhoods, goes back to the middle of the nineteenth century, when Christian unmarried women used the chance of being trained to do social work in the communities. However, because social change does not stop at church portals, the number of those seeking admittance to such orders has become very small. However, WOMEN are still the foundation of the church as active believers and volunteers. In every regional church the Women's Service is autonomous and the umbrella organization on EKD-level covers a wide scope of activities of more than forty women's unions and associations. Women were very much engaged in the Peace and Antiapartheid Movements and through the World Day of Prayer ecumenical contacts and personal relationships develop beyond geographical, social, and cultural boundaries. Although women were allowed to study theology in the 1920s—and it was not until the end of the 1960s that the first women were ordained and called to serve as pastors—today 40 percent of theological students are women and their numbers increase steadily in congregations. Women no longer allow themselves to be put off with subordinate functions, but assume leadership roles in the church. In 1992 Maria Jepsen from Hamburg became the first Lutheran woman bishop. The discussion about equality of women gained momentum with the women's movements in the 1970s and found a strong backing at the Women's Forum of the "Kirchentag." FEMINIST THEOLOGY—quite often a stumbling block and a cause of offense—has become an important source of renewal from within the church.

Interreligious Encounter

To live side by side with people of different faiths is still a new experience for many Germans. Although there have been smaller communities of Buddhists, Hindus, or Bahais for many years, it was in particular the recruitment of hundreds of thousands of foreign workers since the 1960s, mainly from Turkey, Morocco, Tunisia, and Yugoslavia, that made Germans feel the need of interreligious encounter. Today about 80 percent of the six million Muslims in Germany are of Turkish origin. This has confronted Germans forcefully with another religion, although prejudices and ignorance can be overcome by conversation and familiarity. From time to time congregations hold interreligious prayer services for justice and peace, sometimes as a prelude to an intercultural week. Jews, Hindus, Buddhists, Muslims, Alevis, and others gather with Christians to read from their Holy Scriptures and pray in their own languages. It is a cause for hope that in Germany, too, people of different faiths overcome existing prejudices and barriers and join together.

See also Barmen Declaration; German Christians; Lutheranism; Lutheranism, Germany; Missions, German; Worms, Diet of

References and Further Reading

Moltmann, J., ed. *Religion der Freiheit. Protestantismus in der Moderne.* Munich: Christian Kaiser, 1990.

Nowak, Kurt. *Geschichte des Christentums in Deutschland* (History of Christianity in Germany). Munich: C. H. Beck, 1995.

Tawney, R. H. *Religion and the Rise of Capitalism.* New York: Harcourt Brace, 1926.

Tillich, Paul. "Der Protestantismus als Kritik und Gestaltung." In *Gesammelte Werke* vol. 7. Stuttgart: 1962.

Troeltsch, Ernst. *Protestantism and Progress: A Historical Study of the Relation of Protestantism to the Modern World.* Eugene, OR: Wipf & Stock Publishers, 1999.

Weber, Max. *The Protestant Ethic and the "Spirit" of Capitalism and Other Writings.* Translated by Peter Baehr and Gordon C. Wells. New York: Penguin Twentieth-Century Classics, 2002.

DIETER BECKER

GHANA

The first of the modern African states, achieving independence in 1957, Ghana's boundaries are those of the former British territory of the Gold Coast. The latter grew incrementally from a small coastal area at the beginning of the nineteenth century to a considerable enclave early in the twentieth century, the last significant accession being part of the former German colony of Togo after World War I. There are many ethnic groups and many languages, with the Akan (in several subdivisions) in the central and southern part of the country being the most numerous.

Christianity first appeared with the Portuguese, who built a trading post and sought the conversion of local rulers. When the Dutch superseded the Portuguese in the seventeenth century, the Protestant presence began. Although the Dutch trading company declared the extension of the Reformed faith to be one of its aims, both the will and the means were often lacking. Other European powers—Denmark, Britain, Brandenburg-Prussia—set up their trading stations. Most of these "forts" or "factories" had a chaplain, and sometimes this post was held by a local. Thus the Dutch fort had the Africans J. C. Protten and Jacobus Capitein (the latter with a doctorate from Leiden) and the English Philip Quaque (1741–1816), taken to England for education as a boy, and returning to Africa ordained. Long afterward a memorial tablet commemorating Quaque's long ministry at Cape Coast impressed and inspired SAMUEL ADJAI CROWTHER.

Regular mission work began with the arrival of the BASEL MISSION, first to the Danish and later to the British sphere, which gradually absorbed the other powers. Missionary mortality was high, and the missionary Andreas Riis moved to the state of Akuapem, on a mountain ridge where health risks were less but where the king was insistent that God had given different ways of life to black people and white. The Basel Mission accepted the challenge to show that there were black people who followed the Christian way by bringing in Jamaican Christians who long remained pillars of the evangelistic, pastoral, and agricultural work of the mission. Akropong, the Akuapem capital, was the base for a particularly fine translation of the Scriptures into Twi, later revised by C. A. Akrofi.

Meanwhile, British Wesleyans arrived, following the discovery by a Methodist ship captain of a Bible reading and prayer group meeting among Africans in the British sector. The Methodists suffered numerous fatalities, until the arrival of the enterprising THOMAS BIRCH FREEMAN, himself of mixed blood. Freeman extended the mission and made the long journey to Kumasi to open negotiations with the powerful ruler of Ashanti. For a long time the Anglican presence was restricted to colonial locations, whereas the North German (or Bremen) Mission began work among the Ewe in the eastern sector. It was to lead to the emergence of the Evangelical Presbyterian Church.

The period of World War I brought several charismatic figures. Prophet WILLIAM WADÉ HARRIS himself came to Western Ghana. A mulatto clerk called John Swatson established a whole chain of churches and presented them to an astonished Anglican bishop. Above all the illiterate independent preacher KWAME SAMPSON OPPONG brought many thousands into the Methodist pastoral care in long-resistant Ashanti. The other main development of the World War I years was the deportation or internment of the Basel missionaries as enemy aliens and their replacement by a far smaller group from the United Free Church of Scotland. Although institutional work suffered, the development probably hastened the formation of an autonomous Presbyterian Church of Ghana. AFRICAN INSTITUTED CHURCHES, such as the Musama Disco Cristo Church, arose with new readings of scripture on issues such as healing. Another major church that came into being was the Church of Pentecost, which combined features of a Western Pentecostal church with those of an African prophet-healing church. It numbered among its members the remarkable poet-singer Afua Kuma, a traditional midwife who adapted the idiom of traditional praise songs to the praise of Christ. Like other West African countries, Ghana has been deeply influenced in recent years by the charismatic movement, which has both affected the main Protestant (and Roman Catholic) churches as well as produced countless new churches and deliverance ministries. Ghana provided the forum for the first church–state clashes among the new African states.

See also: Methodism, Global; Missions; Pentecostalism; Presbyterianism; Wesleyanism

References and Further Reading

Baeta, C. G. *Prophetism in Ghana.* London: SCM, 1964.

Bartels, F. L. *The Roots of Ghana Methodism.* Cambridge: Cambridge University Press, 1965.

Bediako, Kwame. *Christianity in Africa: The Renewal of a Non-Western Religion.* Edinburgh: Edinburgh University Press, 1995.

Debrunner, Hans. *History of Christianity in Ghana.* Accra: Waterville Press, 1967.

Pobee, John. *Kwame Nkrumah and the Church in Ghana.* Accra: Asempa Press, 1982.

Smith, Noel. *History of the Presbyterian Church in Ghana.* Accra: Ghana Universities Press, 1965.

ANDREW F. WALLS

GIDEONS INTERNATIONAL

A voluntary organization known for placing copies of the BIBLE in hotels, hospitals, prisons, and senior citizen homes among other institutions, the Gideons is also the oldest Christian business and professional men's association in the United States. The idea of the organization was first formed in a meeting in the Central Hotel in Boscobel, Wisconsin, in September of 1898. Traveling businessmen John Nicholson and Samuel Hill were strangers who found themselves sharing a room because the hotel was completely booked. Nicholson (1859–1956), a native of Buffalo, New York, worked for papermakers Bradner Smith & Co. in Chicago. Hill (1867–1936) was born in Hardwick, Vermont, and worked for H. M. Hooker Co. of Chicago, in wholesale paint and glass. They discovered they shared a common Christian faith (both were converted in their teens). They talked to early in the morning about forming an association that would help Christian businessmen remain faithful to Christ during their travels and encourage them to share their faith with other businessmen.

The idea took no concrete shape until the following year, when in July 1899 Nicholson and Hill formed the Gideons with W. J. Knights (1853–1940)—a native of New York who represented wholesale grocer John S. Gould & Co. of Chicago. The group's name was taken from the Old Testament story in Judges 7, in which Gideon led a band of Israelites to victory over the Midianites. Surrounding the Midian camp from cliffs above in the middle of the night, they blew trumpets, broke pitchers, waved torches, and shouted

"The sword of the Lord and of Gideon!" whereupon the frightened Midianites fled. The three men likewise wanted to do whatever it was that God wanted them to do, to hold up their torches just where they stood (wherever their business took them) and speak up for God.

The little group elected Hill as president, Knights as vice-president, and Nicholson as secretary-treasurer, and soon a logo was created that incorporated a two-handed pitcher with a flame protruding from the top, placed in a circle, which represented a trumpet. This became a lapel pin that Gideon members wore on the road to identify one another. It is also the logo found on Gideon Bibles.

By the Gideons' first annual convention in 1900, 600 members had been enrolled, and local "camps" (or chapters) began to be formed, the first in Chicago, in September 1900. The organization grew rapidly (over 1,600 members by 1901, and double that two years later), a magazine was started (*The Gideon*), and by 1905 the first full-time staff member was hired at the national headquarters (in Chicago, now in Nashville, Tennessee).

According to the 1901 bylaws, "The object of the Gideons shall be to recognize the Christian traveling men of the world with cordial fellowship; to encourage one another in the Master's work; to improve every opportunity for the betterment of the lives of our fellow travelers, business men and others, with whom we may come in contact; scattering seeds all along the pathway for Christ." This says nothing about distributing Bibles. Instead, early on there was a strong emphasis on personal EVANGELISM and an expectation that members would speak in public forums on behalf of their FAITH. Some new members balked at this and left when some leaders insisted such practices were part of being a "real Christian."

Bible distribution was first conceived in 1903 when Gideon Fred Woodcock, treasurer of the Chicago camp, visited the British Isles. There he discovered that a Christian Association for Christian Travelers, which had existed for some thirty years, placed books "for wholesome reading" (including the Bible) in the hotels their members frequented. Woodcock took the idea back to the UNITED STATES. Because of financial difficulties the organization was not able to act on the idea until 1908, where at the annual convention the Gideons pledged themselves to placing Bibles in every hotel in the country. The first shipment of twenty-five hotel Bibles was sent to Superior Hotel in Iron Mountain (now Superior), Montana, in November of that year.

At first the Gideon's contracted with the AMERICAN BIBLE SOCIETY to furnish Bibles, but when the demand became too great, the organization switched to the publishing house of Thomas Nelson and Sons of New York. Since 1936 the National Bible Press has been the major printer of Gideon Bibles. In the early years there was some debate over the translation to be distributed: the American Standard Version was preferred at first, but slowly the King James Version took precedence (see BIBLE, KING JAMES VERSION). In 1974 the New International Version was also approved for use in Gideon Bibles, although today the New King James Version is the alternate to the King James.

Gideons expanded their Bible distribution program to hospitals (1916) and to public schools in 1941 ("except where forbidden by law"), to members of the armed services in 1941 (distributing only New Testaments and Psalms editions), and to prisons in 1957.

Independent Gideons organizations were founded in CANADA in 1911 and SWEDEN in 1919 (both eventually amalgamated with what has become Gideons International). With the formation of the Gideon International Extension Committee in 1947 the work expanded rapidly overseas, beginning in 1949 with the establishment of Gideons in the British Isles, with dozens more international ministries added during the following decade.

Gideon literature is replete with stories of individuals who come across a Gideon Bible and whose lives are subsequently changed. One example: An executive in radio explained how his excessive drinking had destroyed his family and led him to the edge of a nervous breakdown; "the future held no promise," he wrote. When he entered his hotel room he spotted a Gideon Bible: "In a distracted way, I picked it up and started to read. Old familiar words I had learned as a child, when I knelt before an altar covered by the checkered gingham apron of her whom we called Mother, words of life, quick and powerful, leaped out from those pages, and found their way into my troubled heart." Other testimonies speak of the mere sight of a Gideon Bible bringing attacks of conscience upon men about to commit adultery, forgery, and so on.

Today Gideons has 150,000 members in 176 countries and distributes more than 59 million Bibles annually. It is financed by contributions from churches and individuals, conceiving of itself "as an extended missionary arm of the church" whose "sole purpose is to win men, women, boys and girls to a saving knowledge of the Lord Jesus Christ through association, personal testimony, and distributing the Bible in the human traffic lanes and streams of everyday life."

See also American Bible Society; Bible Translation

References and Further Reading

Moore, A. B. T. *A Brand from the Burning*. Minneapolis, MN: Lund Press, Inc.

Palmer, Kenyon A. *Kenyon Palmer's Scrapbook: Compilation of Christian Experiences in His Work with the Gideons*. Chicago, IL: Gideons International, 1952.

Thompson, Phyllis. *The Gideons: The Story of the Gideons International in the British Isles*. London: Hodder and Stoughton, 1984.

Westburg, Paul A. *They Stood Every Man in His Place: A 60-Year History of Gideons Internation, 1899–1959*. Chicago, IL: Gideons International, 1959. http://www.gideons.org

MARK GALLI

GLADDEN, WASHINGTON (1836–1918)

American theologian. Washington Gladden was one of the leading preachers in American CONGREGATIONALISM, serving the First Congregational Church of Columbus, Ohio, from 1882 to 1918. He published more than 50 books, many of them sermon collections. Although he is best known today as a pioneer of the Protestant SOCIAL GOSPEL, he was just as important in his own time as a popularizer of LIBERAL PROTESTANTISM, helping a generation of evangelically minded Protestants deal with the challenges of modern biblical criticism and the reconciliation of SCIENCE and FAITH.

Career

Born February 11, 1836, in Pottsgrove, Pennsylvania, Gladden was raised by an uncle in Owego, New York, after his father died in 1841. He attended Williams College from 1856 to 1859. His career reflected his belief in the twin power of pulpit and pen. Brief service to Congregational parishes in Brooklyn and the Bronx, New York, preceded important Congregational pulpits at North Adams, Massachusetts (1866–1871), Springfield, Massachusetts (1875–1882), and Columbus, Ohio (1882–1918). His desire to discern the social forces at work in society also produced an interest in journalism, and he wrote significant articles for the *Springfield Republican*, the *Independent* (a national religious weekly), and the *Century* (an important periodical).

Gladden helped organize American Congregationalism, serving as moderator of the Congregational Association of Ohio and as moderator of the National Council of Congregational Churches (1904–1907). He supported ECUMENISM and the formation of the Federal Council of Churches, serving on its Commission on the Church and Social Service. In 1905, he created a national stir in the churches by calling on the AMERICAN BOARD OF COMMISSIONERS FOR FOREIGN MISSIONS, in which he had been active, to repudiate a $1,000,000 gift from John D. Rockefeller as "tainted money."

In addition, Gladden was a cofounder with Richard Ely and others of the American Economic Association in 1885, an organization dedicated to overturning the dominant laissez-faire philosophy of economics and government in America. He also helped create the American Institute of Christian Sociology at Chautauqua, New York, in 1893.

During World War I, Gladden condemned the militarism and uncritical patriotism that led to war and the failure of the churches to promote a culture of peace, but he eventually supported Wilson's decision to enter the war and entertained hopes for a new social order that would follow. Gladden died in Columbus, Ohio, on July 2, 1918.

Gladden's Social Gospel Theology

Washington Gladden believed that Christians were obliged to make religion "a regenerating force in human society," by which he meant a spiritual force transforming human relationships and social institutions in accord with the "law of love." His social gospel was rooted in his liberal THEOLOGY. As a seriously minded religious youth, the fatherless Gladden failed to achieve the sort of personal CONVERSION experience that was believed necessary for reconciliation with God. Failing to find such solace, he eventually concluded that simply trusting in God's enduring presence, love, and "friendship"—or "fatherhood," as he later termed it—was the true essence of the Christian life. Inspired by the antislavery movement (see SLAVERY, ABOLITION OF) sweeping through New York State, young Gladden quickly equated friendship with God with solidarity, or "brotherhood," with all human beings suffering degradation. The goal of a Christian life is not primarily to win personal happiness in heaven, he wrote, but "to realize the KINGDOM OF GOD in this world."

His viewpoint became embedded in American Protestant spirituality through his famous hymn "O Master, Let Me Walk with Thee." Here it is Jesus who walks the "lowly paths of service" ahead of his disciples, summoning them to sweeten and strengthen their faith in work "that triumphs over wrong." For Gladden, Christ is a creative and liberating spiritual force working out his will in history and society. The churches should aim not at promoting themselves or the nation, but rather at inspiring disciples who can discern the reconciling ministry of Jesus and participate in its actualization, what the social gospel as a whole called the Kingdom of God. He articulated a new model for the Christian pastor and LAITY in which they became a "working church," embracing service to all areas of human life and culture (see PRIESTHOOD OF ALL BELIEVERS). Although he came from rural America, Gladden embraced the modern city as a place of human potential and a sacred laboratory for an emerging Christian social order.

Gladden was particularly important in helping to change Protestant attitudes toward the labor movement and industrial democracy. By 1886, he was moving away from simple "good will" as a solution to industrial strife and calling for labor to organize in response to the increasing concentration of power by employers. By 1911 he was advocating industrial democracy and active government intervention to protect the rights of labor. He supported the cooperative movement and municipal ownership of key public utilities, even serving a term on the Columbus city council.

Gladden's Liberal Theology

Like some other famous preachers of the time, such as Henry Ward Beecher and Phillips Brooks, Gladden was important for popularizing the liberal theology being developed by theologians and biblical scholars at major Protestant SEMINARIES. He openly rejected the traditional doctrines of original sin and substitutionary ATONEMENT of Christ. Profoundly influenced by the thinking of HORACE BUSHNELL and FREDERICK WILLIAM ROBERTSON, he regarded all language as necessarily metaphorical, thus rejecting doctrinal orthodoxies and BIBLICAL INERRANCY. Adopting the notion of "progressive revelation," he believed that biblical history only gradually reveals the divine nature, displaying it most paradigmatically in Jesus' ministry of service to the world rather than in a set of doctrinal assertions (see MODERNISM).

During the last two decades of his life, Gladden sought to help ordinary Christians harmonize their religious beliefs with advances in scientific knowledge. In a series of sermons and books, he suggested that the evolutionary model of science and the work on religious experience by such scholars as WILLIAM JAMES provide new grounds for faith. Human religious awareness may have evolved in response to real divine forces at work in the universe. The work of creation is not finished; at the heart of the universe is a Christlike moral pull (or divine *Logos*) drawing the world toward a loving and reconciling end. In his autobiography, Gladden concluded that

> . . . the work of creation is not yet finished, and never will be. The work of creation is a continuous process. . . . And the Spirit in whose image our spirits are fashioned, and with whom we are made for fellowship, is here, all the while. . . . He is near us, in the pulsations of our hearts, in the movements of our minds, living and working in us and manifesting Himself in every natural force, in every law of life. (*Recollections* 1909:426–427).

See also Christology; Cultural Protestantism; Higher Criticism; Hymns and Hymnals; Kingsley, Charles; Maurice, Frederick Denison; Revivals; Sheldon, Charles; Socialism, Christian

References and Further Reading

Primary Sources:

Gladden, Washington. *Applied Christianity: Moral Aspects of Social Questions*. Boston, MA: Houghton, Mifflin, 1886.
———. *Who Wrote the Bible? A Book for the People*. Boston, MA: Houghton, Mifflin, 1891.
———. *The Christian Pastor and the Working Church*. Edinburgh, UK: T. & T. Clark, 1898.
———. *Social Salvation*. Boston, MA: Houghton, Mifflin, 1902.
———. *Recollections*. Boston, MA: Houghton, Mifflin, 1909.
———. *Present Day Theology*. Columbus, OH: McClelland & Co., 1913.

Secondary Sources:

Dorn, Jacob H. *Washington Gladden: Prophet of the Social Gospel*. Columbus: Ohio State University Press, 1967.
Knudten, Richard D. *The Systematic Thought of Washington Gladden*. New York: Humanities Press, 1968.

WILLIAM M. KING

GLADSTONE, WILLIAM EWART (1809–1898)

English politician. Gladstone was born in Liverpool, England, on December 29, 1809, the son of John Gladstone, a city merchant of Scottish Presbyterian ancestry. He was educated at Eton and Christ Church Oxford and elected to Parliament in 1832, serving for more than 60 years, with four terms as Liberal Prime Minister (1868–1874, 1880–1885, 1886, and 1892–1894). His was "a political outlook that was conditioned by the Christian Faith" (Bebbington 1993:xii). He died at Hawarden on May 19, 1898.

Gladstone became a High Churchman devoted to the defense of the CHURCH OF ENGLAND, resisting the movement from ANGLICANISM to Roman Catholicism. In 1838 he wrote *The State in Its Relations with the Church*, stressing his desire for a national church that encouraged religious unity. He combined a Protestant emphasis on the open BIBLE and a Catholic emphasis on the doctrine of the CHURCH and the AUTHORITY of bishops (see BISHOP AND EPISCOPACY). His anti-Catholicism led him to resign from the government in 1845 over the Maynooth Grant. He later disowned his friend Henry Manning, who became a cardinal. In 1874 he wrote *The Vatican Decrees* against infallibility and other Roman Catholic doctrines, yet he opposed the Public Worship Regulation Bill in defense of the rights of Anglo-Catholic Ritualists (see ANGLO-

CATHOLICISM) and self-regulation by the church. His adherence to his church did not prevent dialogue with dissenters, who became a significant support for the Liberal Party (see DISSENT, NONCONFORMITY). His attendance at the Metropolitan Tabernacle in 1882 to hear CHARLES SPURGEON preach brought much criticism.

Gladstone regularly partook of communion and observed the fasts of the church. His view of religion and society was molded by his belief that "community is the very essence of the Church of Christ," a repudiation of earlier EVANGELICALISM that stressed the more individualistic social ethics.

References and Further Reading

Bebbington, David W. *William Ewart Gladstone: Faith and Politics in Victorian Britain*. Grand Rapids, MI: Eerdmanns, 1993.

TIM MACQUIBAN

GLORIOUS REVOLUTION

The Glorious Revolution is the name commonly given to the 1688–1689 displacement of the Catholic king of ENGLAND and SCOTLAND, James II (1633–1701), by his Protestant son-in-law, William III (1650–1702).

Events

The revolution was sparked by James's desire to remove legal impediments on English Catholics. Initially he hoped to do this through parliament, but the legislature he called in 1685 refused to repeal laws banning Catholic worship or the test acts that prevented anyone but CHURCH OF ENGLAND communicants from holding public office. This left James having to use his prerogative to pursue his objectives. Between 1686 and 1688 he claimed a royal power to evade the test legislation and to issue "declarations of indulgence" permitting a wide freedom of conscience (see TOLERATION).

Early reaction among the Protestant English was muted. Although most saw the king as advancing an authoritarian view of kingship and an objectionable religion, many comforted themselves that he was aging. His daughter and heir, Mary (married to William, prince of Orange and stadtholder of most of the United Provinces of the NETHERLANDS), was a staunch Protestant, who most thought would reverse James's policies. In the summer of 1688, however, James's wife, Mary, gave birth to a son. Faced with the prospect of a perpetual Catholic dynasty, leading figures began to plot with William to help him invade. William, who wished to control England and bring it to war against his archenemy, Louis XIV of FRANCE, set sail from

Holland in October. A widely circulated manifesto asked for English support.

William landed at Torbay on November 5. Over the next month, preplanned risings took place in support in the north of England, and leading conspirators in James's army defected. All this destroyed the king's morale. His army advanced to Salisbury Plain to oppose William, but James then ordered it to retreat, and amid every sign of nervous breakdown, he fled London on the night of December 11. Although apprehended in his first escape, he reached the safety of France by Christmas.

William's path to the throne was now clear. A provisional government, consisting of all peers in London, invited the prince to assume temporary executive power. In response he organized a "convention" (a body to be constituted in the same way as a parliament but without a king) to decide the future of the realm. When this group met (January 22, 1689), many of its members objected to replacing James with a foreign Dutchman, but it soon became clear that other solutions would not work. James had become generally unacceptable; a proposal for a regency was defeated; and suggestions that William's wife become queen became untenable when the prince threatened to leave England rather than accept this arrangement. Everybody knew William's withdrawal would produce political chaos, so the convention offered him the throne on February 13. The only two restraints on William were a novel joint monarchy in which Mary joined her husband as reigning monarch and a "Declaration of Rights," which negated James's claims about the prerogative.

In Scotland the pattern of events was similar. Order broke down when James fled; William called a convention that offered him and his wife the throne. In IRELAND William's authority was at first frustrated by the majority Catholic population who rose in support of James. However, victories at Derry (1689), the Boyne (1690), and Aughrim (1691) secured the western realm for the new regime and placed the minority Irish Protestants in an ascendancy that would complicate Irish history henceforth.

The Revolution and Protestantism

At first glance, the Glorious Revolution looks like an assertion of the antipopish Protestantism, which had dominated seventeenth-century Britain. It certainly was that. A Catholic king had been removed, and acceptance of William meant joining his crusade against Louis XIV. This was not a purely religious war, given that William had Catholic allies in Spain and Austria, but it was nevertheless a fight against the leading enemy of Protestantism, and arguably pre-

served the reformed faith in Europe. Beyond this basic interpretation, however, the relation between revolution and faith was complex. The events of 1688 saw a weakening, because some arguments against James came to rest on appeals for greater tolerance of Catholics, but also a final realization of British Protestantism.

As William and his British supporters opposed the old king, they stressed the difference between his intransigent faith and the nonpersecuting religion of the Protestants. Thus the Orange manifesto took its stand on James's violation of English and Scots law, not his religion. Spokesmen such as the prince's chaplain, Gilbert Burnet, warned that lynching Romanists would make Protestants worse than their rivals. This rhetoric tempered anti-Catholic excess, and, when combined with the new king's highly tolerant attitudes to all confessions, eased religious tensions.

Against this, the revolution strengthened links between Britishness and Protestantism by defining the nation's faith in the clearest manner yet. First, the English convention resolved that kingship "of this protestant realm" was incompatible with Catholicism. When incorporated into the later BILL OF RIGHTS (1689), this resolution barred Catholics from the throne and declared that any monarch who converted once crowned would be treated as if naturally dead. Although often overlooked, this provision was one of the revolution's most radical acts, reversing the relationship between sovereignty and national religion. Hitherto, England, WALES, and Ireland had been Protestant because their kings had made them so. Now kings must be reformed Christians because their nations were.

A second strengthening of British Protestantism came through the toleration act of April 1689. Passed through the Westminster parliament to ease the political divisions of Protestantism, this did not repeal the test acts, but it did grant freedom to worship outside the establishment under certain conditions (see DISSENT; NONCONFORMITY). Its effect was to define England as a Protestant nation still more clearly. The prime condition for religious freedom was agreement with the established church's *doctrinal,* as opposed to ecclesiological, articles. Because these mapped out the main tenets of orthodox trinitarian Protestantism, it widened the boundaries of acceptable worship from the established denomination to a broader reformed Christianity. When coupled with the fact that Scotland had abolished its English-style church at the revolution, and replaced it with a presbyterian kirk (see PRESBYTERIANISM), the toleration act ensured that the Britain born in the 1707 union would become a Protestant, not simply an Anglican, entity (see ANGLICANISM).

References and Further Reading

Claydon, Tony. *William III*. Harlow: Longman, 2002.
Israel, Jonathan, ed. *The Anglo-Dutch Moment*. Cambridge: Cambridge University Press, 1991.
Jones, J. R. *The Revolution of 1688 in England*. London: Weidenfeld and Nicolson, 1984.
Pincus, Steven. "To Protect English Liberties." In *Protestantism and National Identity*, edited by Tony Claydon and Ian McBride. Cambridge: Cambridge University Press, 1998.

TONY CLAYDON

GNESIO-LUTHERANS

Although the term "Gnesio-Lutherans" may be comparatively recent, it refers to a party within the later Lutheran REFORMATION emerging in the aftermath of the Schmalkald War. Originally called "Flacians" by their opponents, the Gnesio-Lutherans became a loosely affiliated, colorful band of controversialists led by NICKOLAUS VON AMSDORF and MATTHIAS FLACIUS (Illyricus). In a series of conflicts that erupted along a theological fault line in the Lutheran reform opened by PHILIPP MELANCHTHON, they developed an influential theory of political resistance and set the stage for a restoration of MARTIN LUTHER's influence in the Lutheran Formula of Concord.

Origins

Finally making good on a threat first leveled in the DIET OF WORMS in 1521, the Holy Roman Emperor Charles V went to war against the political–military alliance supporting the Lutheran Reformation in 1547. Assembled in the Schmalkald League, the Lutherans had had the superior forces but had been weakened by several factors, among them the death of Luther in 1546. Charles made quick work of the League's divided armies, but his own alliance was not stable enough to impose an end to the Lutheran reform. Temporizing, Charles sought compromise in the AUGSBURG INTERIM of 1548. When that failed, Duke Moritz of Saxony, who gained the reunification of Ducal and Electoral Saxony as a reward for his military support of the emperor, proposed a further compromise. Although never officially adopted by the empire, it has been termed the "Leipzig Interim." Eventually, Charles was forced to withdraw entirely, conceding terms initially in the Peace of Passau of 1552 and, finally, the Peace of Augsburg of 1555.

In late medieval–early modern European life, liturgics—the rituals of the Western mass and associated practices—were a fundamental expression of religious and therefore also political unity. Recognizing its religious importance, in 1526 Luther published his German Mass, using traditional Catholic forms but revising them on the basis of his understanding of the biblical doctrine of JUSTIFICATION by FAITH alone. The critical turn was from sacrifice to sacrament, from the mass as a meritorious act of the CHURCH for God to the LORD'S SUPPER as God's act distributing the gifts of Christ's death and resurrection to the faithful. On this basis, Luther was particularly critical of such standard medieval practices as the canon of the mass or eucharistic prayer; the reservation of the host, in which the bread used in the mass was reserved on the altar; Corpus Christi processions, in which the bread was carried through the community in a sacred vessel; and communion in one kind only, in which the priests alone received the wine of the mass.

Understanding his vocation as a call to preserve the religious as well as the political unity of the empire in its place in Europe, Charles V was particularly concerned about the Lutheran revisions. In preparation for the Diet of Augsburg in 1530, originally called to restore unity, the emperor demanded an account of the liturgical variances and accompanying practices. In the negotiations that followed the diet, such matters of religious practice became the fundamental issues. Thus, after the Schmalkald War, Charles immediately sought to roll back the Lutheran revisions. In the Augsburg Interim, he allowed two concessions that had been on the table at Augsburg: the marriage of CLERGY (see CLERGY, MARRIAGE OF) and communion in both kinds.

Philipp Melanchthon, who had agreed to such terms at Augsburg, had in the meantime come under considerable criticism for his conciliatory efforts. But with Luther's death, he had taken religious leadership in the Lutheran reform and urged support for Charles V's policies. His yielding appears to have been more principled than opportunistic—Melanchthon had his own particular concerns for religious and political unity. His critics, however, rejected the distinction. In his own defense, Melanchthon appealed to the liturgical concept of ADIAPHORA. An adiaphoron is a practice of the church not mandated biblically that thus might be treated as a matter of choice. Supporting Charles's imposed liturgical renewal and working with Duke Moritz, Melanchthon argued that he was conceding only in adiaphora, sometimes erroneously termed "matters of indifference."

In fact, however, there were some other issues involved. One was a matter of leadership. Throughout the Reformation, Melanchthon had had difficulties maintaining authority. He was alternatively yielding and harsh, a combination that raised questions about his predictability and trustworthiness. Another issue was theological. In the later 1520s, Melanchthon began a series of revisions of the teachings he had shared with Luther. In the years following 1536 and 1541, these modifications manifested themselves in substantial variations on such critical theological matters as the nature of Christ's presence in the sacrament, the bondage of the will, the nature of CONVERSION, and related issues. In the view of critics, the Leipzig Interim, though it never gained legal status, appeared to consolidate Melanchthon's experimentation.

Matthias Flacius, a Croatian drawn to the Lutheran Reformation, arrived in Wittenberg in 1547. He was to become known as a biblical scholar and church historian, author of the *Clavis Scriptorum* and the *Magdeburg Centuries*. But in his days in Wittenberg, he was Melanchthon's secretary, working with him in the faculty. That service ended when Flacius published some compromising letters in which Melanchthon privately deplored the conciliations that he had been publicly supporting.

Forced out of Wittenberg in the ensuing controversy, Flacius fled to temporary safety in Magdeburg, a city still successfully resisting Charles V. There he joined forces with Nickolaus von Amsdorf, a longtime friend of Luther's who had become the reforming bishop in that city, and Nikolaus Gallus, a pastor. Together, with Flacius in the lead, they attacked Melanchthon and his arguments. The defining issue, as summarized in the Formula of Concord that officially settled the matter, concerned "ceremonies of ecclesiastical practices that are neither commanded nor forbidden in God's Word but that were introduced in the churches for the sake of good order or decorum" (BOOK OF CONCORD). Mounting a range of objections to Melanchthon's appeal, Flacius argued that in a time of persecution, when political and military force are used to mandate adiaphora, such practices lose their optional character and so must be resisted.

Eventually, in the mid-1550s, Melanchthon and Flacius settled that issue. But in the intervening years, controversy had erupted around a whole series of other issues, exacerbating hostilities. Altogether, although there were also side matters, six controversies were engaged: after the adiaphorist, the synergistic, concerning the role of the will in conversion; the majoristic, on the relationship of faith and good works; the antinomian, another round on a perennial debate in the Lutheran reform concerning the role of the law in the life of faith; the crypto-Calvinist, on the nature of Christ's presence in the sacrament; and the Osiandrian, named for ANDREAS OSIANDER of Nuremberg, who proposed an alternative to Melanchthon's understanding of justification by faith.

The various theologians involved in these conflicts, which generally featured generous use of invective and caricature, fell into two parties. The Philippists, so called polemically by their opponents, included Melanchthon's more loyal students, associated with him at the University of Wittenberg. The "Flacians," "Gnesio-," or "true Lutherans," equally polemical labels, were dispersed from Magdeburg by a military reversal in 1551. But they were never as concentrated geographically. Some of the more notable theologians included in the party were Johann Wigand, who returned to Magdeburg briefly before setting off for other points; Tileman Hesshus, who served for a time in Heidelberg; Joachim Westphal of Hamburg; Anton Otto from Nordhausen; and Andreas Poach of Erfurt. The Gnesio-Lutheran theologians had strong support from pastors in Braunschweig, Hamburg, Lubeck, and Luneberg. Like some of his companions, Flacius became an itinerant, finding it difficult to hold a position because of his own polemical excesses, particularly in the synergist controversy, and his outspoken views of political AUTHORITY. He also won the enmity of some of the other Gnesio-Lutherans, such as Otto and Poach.

Contributions

One of the factors in the inflammatory rhetoric of the conflict between the Gnesio-Lutherans and their Philippist opponents may be their very closeness theologically. Generally, the issues that divided them were as much cultural as they were matters of faith: The Gnesio-Lutherans sought to reclaim Luther's apocalyptically driven, relationally oriented conclusions in matters of SIN and GRACE; the Philippists were more cautious, stressing the continuity of biblical faith with other ancient literature, the unity of CHURCH AND STATE, and the integrity of personal striving in the achievement of new life in Christ. Where they differed in emphasis, however, the two parties generally shared a common theological method that they had both learned from Melanchthon. There were exceptions, however, such as von Amsdorf, Otto, and Poach, who reflected more direct appropriation of Luther's way of thinking.

For all of their contentiousness, the Gnesio-Lutherans left a significant legacy. The doctrine of political resistance that they developed in Magdeburg completed a process of development in Luther's own thought. It left its impression in Article X of the Formula of Concord and, as a more developed doctrine, in CALVINISM. The Gnesio-Lutherans also played a significant part in the Formula of Concord's attempts to restore the LUTHERANISM of the earlier Reformation.

References and Further Reading

Primary Sources:

Confessio et Apologia Pastorum & reliquorum ministrorum Ecclesiae Magdeburgenesis. Magdeburg, 1550.

Flacius Illyricus, Matthias. *Catalogus testium veritatis: Qui ante nostram aetatem reclamorunt Papae.* Basel, 1556.

Secondary Sources:

Brecht, Martin, and Reinhard Schwarz, eds. *Bekenntnis und Einheit der Kirche: Studien zum Konkordienbuch.* Stuttgart, Germany: Calwer Verlag, 1980.

Haikola, Lauri. *Gesetz und Evangelium bei Matthias Flacius Illyricus: Eine Untersuchung zur Lutherischen Theologie vor der Konkordienformel.* Lund: C.W.K. Gleerup, 1952.

Kolb, Robert. *Nikolaus von Amsdorf (1483–1565): Popular Polemics in the Preservation of Luther's Legacy.* Nieuwkoop, Netherlands: B. de Graaf, 1978.

Olson, Oliver. *Matthias Flacius Illyricus and the Survival of Luther's Reform.* Wiesbaden, Germany: Harrassowitz, 2002.

Preus, Robert D. *The Theology of Post-Reformation Lutheranism: A Study of Theological Prolegommena. Vol. 2, God and His Creation.* Saint Louis, MO: Concordia, 1972.

Schoenberger, Cynthia Grant. "The Confession of Magdeburg and the Lutheran Doctrine of Resistance." Ph.D. dissertation, Columbia University, 1972.

JAMES ARNE NESTINGEN

GOETHE, JOHANN WOLFGANG VON (1749–1832)

German writer. Goethe was born on August 28, 1749, in Frankfurt am Main, GERMANY, and died on March 3, 1832, in Weimar. He was brought up with tutors under the supervision of his father, Johann Caspar Goethe (1710–1782). In 1765 he began studying law in Leipzig but in 1768 broke off his studies and returned to Frankfurt because of illness. He spent time with Susanna Katharina von Klettenberg (1723–1774) and frequented her Pietist circle.

In 1771 he finished his studies in Strasbourg; there he met JOHANN GOTTFRIED VON HERDER. From 1771 to 1775 he prepared for a law career in Frankfurt and in 1772 did practical training at the supreme court in Wetzlar. From April to October 1775 he was engaged to Anna Elisabeth (Lili) Schönemann (1758–1817). At the invitation of Duke (later, in 1814, Grand Duke) Karl August (1757–1828), Goethe resettled in Weimar, Saxony. His career as a civil servant in Weimar included being privy councilor for legation, royal tutor, counsel of state, minister, true privy councilor, and minister of state. Between 1786 and 1788 he made his first tour of ITALY. After 1788 he enjoyed the lifelong companionship of Christiane Vulpius (1765–1816), whom he married in 1806. In 1788 he was freed from official duties. In 1789 his son August von Goethe was born (died 1830). From 1791 to 1817 he was director of the royal theater of Weimar. In 1792–1793 he took part in a military campaign against FRANCE. In 1794 his friendship with JOHANN CHRISTOPH FRIEDRICH VON SCHILLER began. In 1801 he made the acquaintance of GEORG WILHELM FRIEDRICH HEGEL (1770–1831) and in 1808 met with Napoleon (1769–1821) in Erfurt. In 1812 he visited Ludwig van Beethoven (1770–1827).

Career

Goethe is considered the most important poet in the German language. His literary career spans six decades, from 1770 to 1830, during which time the world was transformed forever by events such as the American and FRENCH REVOLUTIONS. By 1770 his early works had already changed the concept of poetry, creating an autonomous art form that served no longer to illustrate something beyond itself, such as a philosophical or theological idea—as did the literature of the ENLIGHTENMENT—but based what truth it contained in personal experiences and perceptions. His most important works include the countless poems now referred to as poems of personal experience, inspired by love—first for Friederike Brion (1752–1813) and later for other women—and also by nature's beauty; the dramas *Die Mitschuldigen* (1768–1769), *Götz von Berlichingen mit der eisernen Hand* (1773), *Clavigo* (1774), *Stella* (1776/1816), *Iphigenie auf Tauris* (1779/1781), *Egmont* (1788), *Faust* (1808/1832), *Torquato Tasso* (1790), *Die Natürliche Tochter* (1803); the narratives *Die Leiden des jungen Werthers* (1774), *Reineke Fuchs* (1794), *Unterhaltungen deutscher Ausgewanderten* (1795), *Wilhelm Meisters Lehrjahre* (1795–1796), *Herrmann und Dorothea* (1797), *Die Wahlverwandtschaften* (1809), *Wilhelm Meisters Wanderjahre oder die Entsagenden* (1821/1829), *Novelle* (1828); the biographical writings *Aus meinem Leben: Dichtung und Wahrheit* (1811/1833), *Sankt Rochus-Fest zu Bingen* (1817), *Belagerung von Maynz* (1822), *Campagne in Frankreich 1792* (1822), *Italiänische Reise* (1829); many works on natural sciences, including *Die Metamorphose der Pflanzen: Elegie* (1799–1800) and *Zur Farbenlehre* (1810); and reviews, theoretical writings on art, and more than twenty thousand letters.

Religion and Philosophy

Goethe grew up within the orthodox Lutheran environment of Frankfurt am Main (see ORTHODOXY), was spiritually very close to his mother, Katharina Elisabeth (née Textor, 1731–1808), and was schooled early in life in the ancient languages in order to study THEOLOGY. However, in Strasbourg he grew estranged from the Pietist circle (see PIETISM) he had been frequenting on recommendations made to him in Frankfurt. The only contact that lasted was with JOHANN HEINRICH JUNG-STILLING. His last known taking of the

Sacrament took place on August 26, 1770. In an anonymously published letter, *Brief des Pastors zu an den Pastor zu* (Letter of the Pastor of to the Pastor of), he confesses a belief in a religion of loving understanding that assumes an individual's unmediated relationship to God in a Protestant sense but seeks this outside of all sacrament and churchly ritual. He also opposed any dogmatic or orthodox definition of belief and championed enlightened tolerance, because "God and love are synonymous" (WA, I, 37, p. 156). Over the years his fundamental rejection of all abstract systematizing would grow ever more pronounced.

In *Leiden des jungen Werthers* (Sorrows of Young Werther) he goes a step further toward secularization by suggestively placing his protagonist in the role of Christ. Werther sacrifices himself for the happiness of his friends and takes as his final meal bread and wine, the food of the Last Supper. In *Faust*, Goethe uses biblical figures and motifs to enrich and enliven his poetry but not to demonstrate theological or religious truths. Fixed and certain convictions meant nothing to him, only the continual renewal of thought. In *West-Östlichen Divan* (1819/1827) he wrote: "Und solang du das nicht hast,/Dieses: Stirb und werde!/Bist du nur ein trüber Gast/Auf der dunklen Erde" (WA I, 6, p. 28)—a secularized version of Matthew 10:39 (also Mark 8:34, Luke 17:33, John 12:25, and I Corinthians 15:36).

The popular belief that Goethe was a pantheist requires some clarification. Indeed an explanation of his religious beliefs must be based in part on his writings in the natural sciences. There he repeatedly states that only in the observation of nature can one perceive the divine. In, for example, a letter to Friedrich Heinrich Jacobi (1743–1819) dated January 6, 1813, he also qualifies his pantheism:

> I cannot, with the manifold directions of my being, have enough with only a single way of thinking; as poet and artist I am a polytheist; a pantheist, however, as a scientist, and none more crucial than the other. If I need a god for my person, as a moral being, so it is provided. The heavenly and the earthly things are a realm of such expanse that only the organs of all creatures taken together are able to comprehend it. (WA IV, 23, p. 226)

This passage reveals Goethe's great tolerance and even sympathy for Roman Catholicism—in 1814 he dedicates a holy picture to the Saint Rochus chapel in Bingen, Germany. This tolerant stance becomes the pedagogical landscape depicted in his late work *Wilhelm Meisters Wanderjahre*, where his teachings of deep respect and reverence are explained and qualified. There is reverence "for that which is above us," "for that which is below us," and "for that which is

equal to us," and from these comes the greatest of all, reverence for oneself.

See also Literature, German

References and Further Reading

Primary Source:

Goethes Werke. Weimar: Hermann Böhlaus Nachfolger, 1887–1912. (Weimar edition, abbreviated WA.)

Secondary Sources:

Boyle, Nicholas. *Goethe: The Poet and the Age.* Oxford: Oxford University Press, 1991–.

Williams, John R. *The Life of Goethe: A Critical Biography.* Oxford: Oxford University Press, 1998.

ULRICH KARTHAUS

GOGARTEN, FRIEDRICH (1887–1967)

German theologian. Gogarten was born in Dortmund, GERMANY, January 13, 1887, and died October 16, 1967, in Göttingen. He studied art history, German literature, and psychology in Munich and theology in Jena, Berlin, and Heidelberg. He was pastor in Stelzendorf, Thuringia (1917–1925), and Dorndorf near Jena (1925–1931) while serving as lecturer in theology at the university of Jena. He was awarded an honorary doctorate in THEOLOGY by the University of Giessen in 1924. From 1931 to 1935 he was professor of theology at Breslau from 1931 to 1935, and from then until his retirement in 1955 professor at Göttingen.

In 1922 he founded, together with KARL BARTH and Eduard Thurneysen, the journal *Zwischen den Zeiten.* Hitler's Third Reich and the ascendancy of the German Christian movement caused the founders to part company over Gogarten's seeming acceptance of the GERMAN CHRISTIANS' identification of God's law with the people's law. Gogarten himself was not part of the German Christian movement.

His work manifests influences of ERNST TROELTSCH, Johann Gottlieb Fichte, and Martin Heidegger as well as the personalism of Martin Buber, Ferdinand Ebner (1882–1931), and Eberhard Grisebach (1880–1945). The strongest influence, nonetheless, was MARTIN LUTHER and his understanding of the nature of the gospel. Neo-Lutherans, especially the church historian KARL HOLL, were significant interlocutors in his reflections on the relation between faith and history. For Gogarten history is the encounter of the "I and Thou" even as revelation is the personal calling of the "I" by the "Thou." The subject of revelation, and of FAITH, is Jesus Christ, the historical event of the personal unity of God and humanity. Christ is the "Thou" of God calling the "I" into responsibility toward the "Thou" of other humans and of the world. This conceptualization allowed Gogarten to develop his understanding of true worldliness: it alone enables authentic responsibility to God and humans and the natural world. That such worldliness, or secularization, is the gift of the gospel is Gogarten's enduring contribution to Protestant theology.

References and Further Reading

Primary Sources:

Gogarten, Friedrich. *Demythologizing and History.* New York: Charles Scribner's Sons, 1955.
———. *The Reality of Faith. The Problem of Subjectivism in Theology.* Philadelphia, PA: Westminster Press, 1959.
———. *Christ the Crisis.* Richmond, VA: John Knox Press, 1970.
———. *Despair and Hope for Our Time.* Philadelphia, PA: Pilgrim Press, 1970.

Secondary Source:

Shiner, Larry E. *Secularization of History: An Introduction to the Theology of Friedrich Gogarten.* Nashville, TN: Abingdon Press, 1966.

MARTIN RUMSCHEIDT

GOMAR, FRANZ (1563–1641)

Dutch theologian. Gomar was born January 30, 1563, in Bruges, Flanders, and died January 11, 1641, in Groningen, Friesland. He studied in Strasbourg under Johannes Sturm; in Neustadt, Rheinpfalz, under Zacharius Ursinus, Franz Junius, and Girolamo Zanchi; and in Oxford, Cambridge (Master of Arts in philosophy, 1584), and Heidelberg, where he obtained a Ph.D. in theology in 1594. After serving as minister of the Flemish community in Frankfurt am Main from 1586 to 1593, he was appointed professor of theology in Leiden in 1594.

In 1604 Gomar became involved in increasingly acrimonious disputes with his colleague JACOBUS ARMINIUS on the issue of PREDESTINATION, a conflict that intensified as Gomar disputed with the followers of Arminius after the latter died in 1609. Unsolved dogmatic issues, the problem of church discipline, and the question of the role of the Church in the State all led to conflict within the Reformed Churches of the Netherlands. Gomar taught strict supralapsarian predestination and also vehemently defended the authority of Presbyterians and SYNODS. He was a strong opponent of Arminius, whom he accused of Pelagian and Jesuit tendencies. As the Gomarians demanded that the conflict be settled by a national synod, the heads of state were drawn into the debate. Several conferences between followers of Arminius and supporters of Gomar (known since 1611 as REMONSTRANTS and counter-Remonstrants) came to nothing. After the appointment of Conrad Vorstius as Arminius's successor, Gomar resigned from his position as professor in Leiden in 1611, and in the same year himself became a minister and professor in Middelburg, Zeeland. In 1615 he took up a position in Saumur in France, and in 1618 became professor in Groningen. From 1618 to 1619 he was an influential figure in the Dordrecht Synod, where he was responsible for the condemnation of the Remonstrants, without, however, being able to impose strict supralapsarianism. Gomar edited a translation of the Old Testament ("Statenvertaling") and established a center of Reformed orthodoxy in Groningen, where he expounded New Testament and dogmatics. He was also known as "the hammer of the Arminians." A pugnacious, controversial, and yet peace-loving teacher, Gomar was a seminal influence on many students over several decades and an important thinker in an Europe seared by the Thirty Years' War.

See also Arminianism; Presbyterianism

References and Further Reading

Primary Source:

Opera theologia omnia. 3 vols. Amsterdam: Iansonius, 1644 (Second edition, 1664).

Secondary Sources:

Belzen, J. V. *Vroom, Vurig en Vreedzaam: Het leven van Franciscus Gomarus.* Houten: Den Hertog, 1996.
Itterzon, G. P. A. *Franciscus Gomarus.* The Hague: 1930 (reprinted Groningen, 1979).
Sell, A. P. F. *The Great Debate: Calvinism, Arminianism and Salvation.* Eugene, OR: Wipf and Stock, 1982.

ANDREAS MÜHLING

GOMARIANS

In the seventeenth century, Reformed orthodox theology experienced its peak in the NETHERLANDS. The resolutions of the Synod of Dort of 1618–1619, in which almost all larger Reformed churches with the exception of the HUGUENOTS took part, condemned ARMINIANISM and adopted the Calvinist teaching of PREDESTINATION defended by FRANZ GOMAR (Franciscus Gomarus), without, however, adopting the supralapsarianism—the teaching that God's PREDESTINATION had occurred *before* the Fall—which he defended. After the defeat of the followers of Arminius, Gomar became one of the greatest theological authorities in the Netherlands, and his work was fundamental for Dutch ORTHODOXY. In their *Synopsius purioris Theologiae* (1625) Johannes Polyander, Andreas Rivetus, Antonius Thysius, and Antonius Walaeus, theologians of Leiden, sought to summarize all the orthodox material influenced by Gomar on the basis of the CANONS OF DORT. However, the structuring of federal theology, inter alia by JOHANNES COCCEJUS, meant that the teaching of predestination defended by the followers of Gomar began to be replaced by the concept of "Heilsgeschichte," an interpretation of history stressing God's saving GRACE. The orthodoxy influenced by Gomar was already on its way out during his lifetime. Gisbert Voetius, Gomar's most influential student, had an impact in that he integrated puritanical influences into the THEOLOGY of Gomar and called—analogously to puritanical demands—for further reformation (see PURITANISM).

Leading this *"Nadere Reformatie,"* Voetius's theology, decisively influenced by Gomar, formed an at once critical and controversial counterpoint within the church and society of the Netherlands. On the basis of the resolutions of the Synod of Dort, the reform movement led by Voetius entered into fierce debates not only with state authorities about the autonomy of the church, as in the so-called five-chapter dispute of the 1650s and 1660s in Utrecht; the criticism was also directed against theological adversaries: in the so-called Sabbath dispute equally sharp attacks were lodged against Coccejus and his "federal theology" based on "heilsgeschichte" as against the "new" philosophy of René Descartes or the chiliastic sermons of Jean de Labadie with his insistence on the separation of the devout from the world (see CHILASM). Finally the Voetius reform movement inveighed, in the end without success, against the traditional customs and celebrations with their alleged tendency to "profane" Sundays.

References and Further Reading

Asselt, Wilhelm J. v. *De scholastieke Voetius: een luisteroefening aan de hand van Voetius' Disputationes selectae.* Zoetermeer, The Netherlands: Boekencentrum, 1995.

Berg, Johannes v.d. "Die Frömmigkeitsbestrebungen in den Niederlanden." In *Geschichte des Pietismus: Der Pietismus vom siebzehnten bis zum frühen achtzehnten Jahrhundert, Göttingen,* edited by Martin Brecht, vol. 1, 57–112 [particularly 78–88]. Leiden, The Netherlands: E. J. Brill, 1993.

Duker, Arnoldus C. *Gisbertus Voetius,* vols. 1–3 and index. Leiden, The Netherlands: E. J. Brill, 1897–1915.

Lieburg, Frederik A. v. "De Nadere Reformatie in Utrecht ten tijde van Voetius, Rotterdam 1989." In *Protestantische Theologie der Neuzeit,* edited by Jan Rohls, vol. 1, 78–88. Tübingen, Germany: Mohr, 1997.

Ruler, Johannes A. v. *The Crisis of Causality. Voetius and Descartes on God, Nature and Change.* Leiden, The Netherlands: E. J. Brill, 1995.

Sell, A. P. F. *The Great Debate: Calvinism, Arminianism and Salvation.* Worthing, UK: HE Walter Ltd., 1982.

ANDREAS MÜHLING

GOODSPEED, EDGAR JOHNSON (1871–1962)

New Testament scholar. Goodspeed, eminent Greek scholar, specialist in New Testament and early Christian literature, and America's leading translator of the Scriptures, was a tireless proponent for the use of modern language versions of the BIBLE in public worship. As a graduate student at the University of Chicago (Ph.D., 1898), Goodspeed developed a keen interest in manuscript study and the collection and deciphering of Greek papyri. His familiarity with them enabled him to refute current theories of the Aramaic origins of the New Testament and demonstrate that it was written in colloquial Greek. The New Testament, he believed, should therefore be translated into everyday English.

Other Americans since Andrews Norton (1855) had published translations of the New Testament in contemporary idiom, and three modern language versions (Moffatt, Weymouth, and the Twentieth Century) enjoyed wide circulation, but these were intended for private reading. Goodspeed intended his for public use. He thus challenged the entrenched position of the King James Version in American Protestant churches.

The New Testament: An American Translation (1923) offered a novel presentation. Goodspeed, an accomplished essayist, used modern paragraphing and kept verse numbers unobtrusive to facilitate narrative flow.

An unfortunate press release of a sample translation of the Lord's Prayer (taken from Luke instead of the familiar Matthean version) aroused a torrent of protest on editorial pages across the nation. Goodspeed became the target of critics with little knowledge of the history of the English Bible, who challenged his scholarly credentials and accused him of "monkeying with the Bible." These attacks cemented Goodspeed's commitment to Bible education among the general public. He became a popular platform speaker and produced numerous books for nonspecialists, including *The Story of the Bible* (1936), *How Came the Bible?* (1940), and *How to Read the Bible* (1946).

Goodspeed taught at the University of Chicago (1902–1937) and published more than sixty books. He is best known for his theory that the publication of Acts provided the stimulus for gathering the Pauline letters and the writing of Ephesians (by Onesimus) as an encyclical to head this collection.

See also Bible Translation; Bible, King James Version

References and Further Reading

Primary Source:

Goodspeed, Edgar Johnson. *As I Remember*. New York: Harper & Brothers, 1953.

Secondary Sources:

Cook, James. I. *Edgar Johnson Goodspeed: Articulate Scholar*. Chico, CA: Scholar's Press, 1981.
Orlinsky, Harry, and Robert G. Bratcher. *A History of Bible Translation and the North American Contribution*. Atlanta, GA: Scholars Press, 1991.

ROBERT LEE CARTER

GORDON, ADONIRAM JUDSON (1836–1895)

American theologian. Gordon was born on April 19, 1836, in New Hampton, New Hampshire. As a Baptist minister, he embraced historic premillennialism early in his pastoral ministry. Four different influences, like four separate tributaries, flowed into his concern with the doctrine of premillennialism: moderate CALVINISM, the phenomenon of revivalism and MISSIONS, the development of personal piety, and the Higher Life ministry of the Holy Spirit. Eventually these influences merged to make the picture more complete, showing the dominance of premillennialism in his life. Every aspect of his ministry—missionary endeavors; defense of WOMEN's ministry; his relationship with his wife, Maria Hale Gordon; his broad associations with other evangelical leaders; social ministry; the founding of the Boston Missionary Training School in 1889 (now two separate institutions, Gordon College and Gordon-Conwell Theological Seminary); and the publication of a monthly journal, *The Watchword*—were subsumed under this theme.

Gordon was educated from 1853 to 1856 at the New London Literary and Scientific Institution (now Colby-Sawyer College, New London, New Hampshire). From 1856 to 1860 he attended Brown University (Providence, Rhode Island). He received his theological training at Newton Theological Institution (Newton, Massachusetts), graduating in 1863. He then served as pastor of the Baptist Church in Jamaica Plain, Massachusetts (from 1863 to 1869), and for 25 years (1869–1895) at Clarendon Street Baptist Church, Boston.

Gordon's ministry was expansive. Among those with whom he worked were evangelist DWIGHT LYMAN MOODY and Presbyterian missions advocate and fellow premillennialist, ARTHUR TAPPAN PIERSON. Gordon led a prosperous congregation, served on his denomination's mission board, edited hymn books, authored hymns, and wrote several books, in addition to editing a monthly premillenarian journal, *The Watchword*, for

seventeen years. His most widely recognized hymn is the tune to "My Jesus, I Love Thee."

Gordon died from complications of pneumonia on February 2, 1895, in Boston at the age of 58.

See also Higher Life Movement; Millenarians and Millennialism; Hymns and Hymnals

References and Further Reading

Primary Sources:

Gordon, A. J. *In Christ*. 1872.
———. *Congregational Worship*. 1874. Boston, MA: Young & Bartlett.
———. *The Watchword*. 1878–1895. Boston, MA: Gould.
———. *Two-Fold Life*. 1882. New York, NY: Fleming H. Revell.
———. *The Ministry of Healing*. New York: Revell, 1883.
———. *Ecce Venit*. New York: Revell, 1889.
———. *The Holy Spirit in Missions*. 1893. New York, NY: Fleming H. Revell.
———. *The Ministry of the Spirit*. Philadelphia, PA: American Baptist Publication Society, 1894.

Secondary Source:

Gibson, Scott M. *A. J. Gordon: American Premillennialist*. Lanham, MD: University Press of America, 2001.

SCOTT M. GIBSON

GRACE

"Amazing grace, how sweet the sound, That saved a wretch like me! I once was lost, but now am found, Was blind, but now I see. / 'Twas grace that taught my heart to fear, And grace my fears relieved; How precious did that grace appear The hour I first believed!"

This hymn, written by the British theologian John Newton in 1779, continues to be popular in the English-speaking Protestant world. It illustrates two characteristic features of the Christian understanding of grace, especially in Protestantism. Grace marks God's saving and—in a certain sense—also God's judging action on the human being who is blinded because he or she is helplessly self-centered and lost in an obsession with self-interest. God's grace absolves and endows the sinner with the perception of God's passionate will and God's faithfulness. The abundance of life that is created and promised by God is surprising, because no one who is blind can expect an unseen reality. It amazes because God's grace is overwhelming: it liberates in such a way that any resistance would be absurd. Through grace, human beings encounter the living God. Grace teaches the due fear of God's judgment and at the same time relieves one from the fear of God's wrath. God establishes an asymmetrical relationship with human beings through grace. Grace arises from the inexhaustible justice of God—no human being deserves it and can claim it. It is the unmerited favor of God and divine inspiring, regenerating strength. God's free grace corresponds to the surprised and incessant joy of those who are showered with this incomprehensible gift. It precedes all that we can expect from ourselves, for us, for others, and for the world.

Grace is derived from the Latin *gratia*. Its theological meaning had been developed especially by the Apostle Paul based on the Greek *charis*. In Hebrew, it corresponds to "goodness," "kindness," and "steadfast love," often in conjunction with "faithfulness" (e.g., Genesis 24:27). It is prominent in the narratives, in wisdom literature, and above all in prayers. God's benevolence surpasses God's wrath; it surpasses the time-space of human alienation from God's will: "For his anger is but for a moment; his favor is for a lifetime" (Psalms 30:5). Wrath passes, grace stands. It is as if the sun breaks through the clouds after it had been concealed temporarily. This can be misunderstood. One might think grace was the inmost nature of God, which was intermittently interrupted by other expressions and impulses. Yet God's grace is not an emotion, not even a basic mood that might be interrupted by others' feelings. God's grace emanates from God's unchanging purposes; it acts determinedly and is not a temporary cheerful state of mind or a good temper. God's "steadfast love endures forever" (Psalms 100:5). The pious can rely on it, and the unfaithful will never escape it. The appropriate answer to God's grace is human obedience toward God's commandments, which are signs of God's faithfulness.

Paul argued that God's grace realizes its abundance in the weakness of afflicted people who experience that they have nothing to offer to God nor to summon up against God (II Corinthians 12:8). Jews and Gentiles perceive God's grace by JUSTIFICATION, "by his grace as a gift, through the redemption that is in Christ Jesus" (Romans 3:24), "by faith apart from works prescribed by the law" (Romans 3:28). Grace constitutes a space of living in communion with Jesus Christ. To cut oneself off from Christ means to fall away from grace (Galatians 5:4). Grace (*charis*) embodies itself in particular gifts (*charismata*), such as prophecy, ministry, and exhortation (I Corinthians 12:4–11). Paul explained that the only appropriate answer to God's grace is faith, trust in God's promises, and consent to God's will. FAITH is an indication of God's gift. It points to God and God's SALVATION as we find it in Jesus Christ. It refers us to God's sovereign initiative in reconciling the world with God (II Corinthians 5:18). God never purely reacts. God's action reveals his steadfast love and enduring faithfulness.

The early fathers emphasized that human beings can only be receptive for God's grace, yet grace inspires and forms the human being as a whole. Augustine stressed the notion of prevenient Grace (*gratia praeveniens*): God's mercy is prior to all human expectation and understanding. Experienced in PRAYER, it is irresistible. Thomas Aquinas stated that grace does not contradict NATURE. According to Aquinas, God's creation cannot be totally corrupted by human SIN; grace heals the incomplete natural notion of God: "Grace does not destroy nature, but perfects it" (*Summa theologiae*, I, q. 1, a. 8, ad 2). MARTIN LUTHER rediscovered the biblical usage: Grace is not an attribute or a mood of God, but God's action out of loving-kindness. In this way Luther not only corrected the traditional doctrine of grace, but also radically revised it by establishing it as the primary rule of all theological understanding. God's grace is His saving action, realized as the justification of the sinner who remains dependent on God's grace all the time. Human beings are saved through grace alone (*sola gratia*) only by faith (*sola fide*); both correspond to God's presence in Jesus Christ (*solus Christus*). The reformer opposed an understanding of grace that had been and to some extent still is popular in the Roman Catholic praxis of penitence: God's grace is God's aid for the appropriate life; it is like a drive belt that actuates human conduct of life according to God's intention. In the twentieth century, DIETRICH BONHOEFFER criticized "cheap grace" as the mere acceptance of God's reconciling work that avoids true discipleship obedient to God's will communicated by Jesus Christ. KARL BARTH argued against the teachings of EMIL BRUNNER that grace is revelation that alone makes possible every true notion of God, of God's will and of God's action. Therefore, there can be no "natural" recognition of God.

North American Protestantism has been marked by two contrasting perceptions of grace in relation to sin, God's healing and encouraging power, and the task of sanctification. On the one hand is the continuing, if diminished, influence of JONATHAN EDWARDS, with the Calvinist notion of irresistible divine grace toward the elect and the picture of "sinners in the hands of an angry God." On the other hand, METHODISM has mediated JOHN WESLEY's view of the universal availability of prevenient grace, and his notion of the "cooperation" of the believer toward "perfection": "God works, therefore you can work; God works, therefore you must work" (sermon "On Working Out Our Own Salvation"). All this demonstrates that grace remains a very complex and multifaceted topic of Christian theology and piety.

See also Theology

References and Further Reading

Bonhoeffer, Dietrich. *Discipleship*. Dietrich Bonhoeffer Works, vol. 4. Minneapolis, MN: Fortress, 2000.

Bradshaw, Timothy, ed. *Grace and Truth in the Secular Age*. Grand Rapids, MI: Eerdmans, 1998.

Brunner, Emil, Karl Barth. *Natural Theology: Comprising "Nature and Grace" by Emil Brunner and the Reply "No!" by Karl Barth*. London: Centenary Press, 1946.

Cobb, John B. *Grace and Responsibility: A Wesleyan Theology for Today*. Nashville, TN: Abingdon, 1995.

Gerrish, Brian A. *Grace and Gratitude: The Eucharistic Theology of John Calvin*. Minneapolis, MN: Fortress, 1993.

Hanson, Bradley. *A Graceful Life: Lutheran Spirituality for Today*. Minneapolis, MN: Augsburg, 1999.

McGrath, Gavin J. *Grace and Duty in Puritan Spirituality*. Bramcote, UK: Grove Books, 1991.

Sproul, Robert C. *Grace Unknown: The Heart of Reformed Theology*. Grand Rapids, MI: Baker, 1997.

GERHARD SAUTER

GRAHAM, BILLY (1918–)

American evangelist. Born William Franklin Graham Jr. on November 7, 1918, on a farm outside Charlotte, North Carolina, to William Franklin and Morrow Coffey Graham, Billy Graham became the most famous and successful evangelist of the twentieth century. He preached in person to more than eighty million people in more than eighty countries and reached countless other millions via radio, television, films, books, magazines, and newspaper columns.

Life

Graham attended Bob Jones College for one semester; the Florida Bible Institute, where he began PREACHING and changed his denominational affiliation from Associate Reformed Presbyterian to Southern Baptist; and Wheaton College, where he met and married Ruth Bell, the daughter of a medical missionary to CHINA, and undertook his first and only stint as a local pastor. In 1945 he became the field representative of a dynamic evangelistic movement known as YOUTH FOR CHRIST International. In this role, he toured the UNITED STATES and much of Great Britain and Europe, teaching local church leaders how to organize youth rallies and forging friendships with scores of Christian leaders who would later join his organization or provide critical assistance to his crusades when he visited their cities throughout the world.

The New Evangelicalism

The exposure and stature Graham gained through Youth for Christ and nationally publicized early crusades in Los Angeles, Boston, Washington, and other major cities between 1949 and 1952 enabled him to become a key leader in a young movement that called itself "the New Evangelicalism." The term signified a form of conservative Christianity that consciously separated itself from traditional FUNDAMENTALISM by its tendency to be tolerant of minor theological differences among essentially like-minded believers, a conviction that evangelical faith could and should be set forth and defended in an intellectually rigorous manner rather than simply asserted dogmatically, and a more positive attitude toward social reform than Fundamentalists had held since the end of World War I. Stunningly successful months-long revivals in London (1954) and New York (1957); triumphant tours of the Continent (1954, 1955), the Far East (1956), AUSTRALIA (1959), and AFRICA (1960); the founding of the magazine, *Christianity Today* (1956); the launching of nationwide television broadcasts on ABC (1957), and a public friendship with President Dwight Eisenhower and Vice President Richard Nixon firmly established Billy Graham as the acknowledged standard-bearer for evangelical Christianity.

As Graham came to recognize the extent of his influence, he determined not only to help EVANGELICALISM become more dynamic and self-confident, but also to shape the fundamental direction of contemporary Christianity. That determination manifested itself significantly in several major international conferences sponsored or largely underwritten by the Billy Graham Evangelistic Association (BGEA). In particular, the 1966 World Congress on Evangelism in Berlin, attended by 1,200 evangelical leaders from 104 nations, and the 1974 the International Congress on World Evangelization in Lausanne, Switzerland, attended by 2,400 delegates from 150 countries, helped evangelicals see themselves as a worldwide Christian force, alongside Vatican II and the WORLD COUNCIL OF CHURCHES.

Subsequently, BGEA-sponsored conferences in Amsterdam in 1983, 1986, and 2000 provided more than 22,000 on-the-job itinerant evangelists from 185 countries with encouragement and instruction, not only in theology and spiritual development, but also in such mundane matters as sermon preparation, advertising and fund-raising, and effective use of films and videotapes. Smaller gatherings throughout the world afforded similar training to additional thousands of evangelists.

Graham and Politics

Graham's preaching during the early years of his ministry was filled with political themes, and he eagerly sought ties with political leaders, who often reciprocated, viewing him as a valuable political ally. When Lyndon Johnson became president after John F. Kennedy's assassination in 1963, Graham provided valuable support and legitimation for Johnson's causes—the War on Poverty, the Civil Rights Act, the war in Vietnam—and drew sharp disapproval from those who felt he had compromised his ability to speak with a prophetic voice. This line of criticism intensified after Nixon won the White House in 1968. An openly enthusiastic supporter, Graham remained staunchly loyal to the beleaguered president until the revelations surrounding Watergate finally forced some recognition of his old friend's darker side. Deeply stung, Graham drew back from overt political involvement, rarely visiting the White House during the Ford and Carter administrations. When the movement known as the Religious Right surfaced in the late 1970s, Graham declined to participate in it, warning his brethren to "be wary of exercising political influence" lest they lose their spiritual impact. He returned to Washington more frequently and more publicly during the presidencies of Ronald Reagan and George Bush, with whom he had been friends since the 1950s, but his contribution appears to have involved symbolic legitimation rather than strategic counsel, a course continued by his appearance and prayer at Bill Clinton's two inaugurations.

Because of the staunch anticommunism of his early preaching, few developments in Graham's ministry proved more surprising than his success in penetrating the Iron Curtain. Beginning in 1978, virtually every Soviet-controlled country progressively gave him privileges that no other churchman, including the most prominent and politically docile native religious leaders, had ever received. These efforts culminated in state-broadcast services in packed stadiums in Budapest (1989) and Moscow (1992). Graham used these visits to preach, to encourage Christian believers, and to explain to Communist leaders that their restriction of religious freedom was counterproductive, hampering diplomatic relations with America.

World Impact

Graham's hundreds of crusades have had an immense, if ultimately immeasurable, impact on local churches, on American and world Christianity, and on millions of individual lives. To extend the reach of the crusades, the BGEA has used radio, television, film, and other mass media more efficiently and effectively than any other evangelistic ministry. Crusade services have long been transmitted live to numerous other venues, beginning with landline telephone relays in the 1954 London Crusade and culminating in the 1995 "Global Mission," when the famed evangelist's distinctive voice and familiar message soared upward from his pulpit in Puerto Rico to a network of thirty satellites that broadcast to receiving dishes in more than 165 countries.

In recognition of his achievements, Graham has received, among many accolades and prizes, both the Presidential Medal of Freedom (1983) and the Congressional Gold Medal (1996) the highest honors these two branches of government can bestow upon a civilian.

References and Further Reading

Primary Sources:

Billy Graham Evangelical Association, BillyGraham.org. http://billygraham.org (2002).
Graham, Billy. *Just As I Am: The Autobiography of Billy Graham.* San Francisco, CA: Harper-Collins, 1997.

Secondary Sources:

Frady, Marshall. *Billy Graham: Parable of American Righteousness.* Boston: Little, Brown, 1979.
Martin, William. *A Prophet with Honor: The Billy Graham Story.* New York: William Morrow, 1991.
———. "Fifty Years with Billy." *Christianity Today.* (November 13, 1995):20–29.

WILLIAM MARTIN

GREAT AWAKENINGS

See Awakenings

GREBEL, CONRAD (c. 1498–1526)

Anabaptist leader. Grebel was born in Zurich c. 1498. His father, Jacob von Grebel, was a prominent member of the Zurich city council and a prosperous entrepreneur. Grebel's student years in Vienna and Basel, beset by lack of direction and family conflict, ended without a degree. His marriage to a woman below his station caused a rupture with his family. There were two sons and a daughter.

Early in 1522, Grebel experienced a religious CONVERSION under the impact of the evangelical preaching of the reformer HULDRYCH ZWINGLI. Grebel's passionate paean to Zwingli's preaching of the gospel was appended to Zwingli's *Apologeticus Archeteles* that year. Grebel's fervent partisanship made him into a ringleader of a group of young lay supporters.

Grebel was in every respect a Zwinglian. His commitment to Zwingli's *sola scriptura* and to the competence of the Christian congregation to decide questions of faith drove him and several others to agitate for the BAPTISM of adult believers as the scriptural way of safeguarding the competence of the Christian congregation. This presupposed the abandonment of baptizing infants, which Zwingli, for socioreligious reasons, would not do. In the resulting conflict neither Zwingli nor his disciples could yield, and on January 21, 1525, a parting occurred when Grebel and his companions baptized one another. They did not perceive this act as schismatic nor as abandoning Zwingli's reform program for Zurich.

ANDREAS KARLSTADT may have influenced their view of baptism, whereas THOMAS MÜNTZER certainly influenced them on the importance of personal FAITH. Because of their defiant act of baptizing, which Zwingli and the Zurich city council saw as "rebaptism," they were decried as schismatics, arrested, and imprisoned. Grebel bitterly complained about his mentor's betrayal of thorough reform. Escaping from prison, he worked as a fugitive to gain support for his vision but died, perhaps from the plague, in May 1526. He is now considered to be the proto-Anabaptist. The Anabaptist movement, of which he is a progenitor, has survived to the present in the MENNONITE Churches.

See also Anabaptism

References and Further Reading

Primary Source:

Harder, L., ed. *The Sources of Swiss Anabaptism.* Scottdale, PA: Herald Press, 1985.

Secondary Sources:

Bender, Harold S. *Conrad Grebel.* Scottdale, PA: Herald Press, 1950.
Goertz, Hans-J. *Konrad Grebel.* Hamburg, Germany: Mennonitscher Geschichtsverein, 1998.

WALTER KLAASSEN

GRUNDTVIG, NICOLAJ FREDERICK SEVERIN (1783–1872)

Danish church reformer. Son of a pastor, Nicolaj Grundtvig was born in Udby, DENMARK, on September 8, 1783. After studying in Copenhagen he served as a private tutor and then as history teacher. From the beginning of his career, Grundtvig was embroiled in controversy. His trial sermon in Copenhagen in 1810 had the rather provocative title "Why Has the Word of God Disappeared from His House?" and, not surprisingly, it prompted the Copenhagen clergy to file a complaint against him. A year later Grundtvig experienced a CONVERSION, which entailed his commitment to affirm the traditional Lutheran THEOLOGY against ENLIGHTENMENT change. Between 1811, the year of his ordination, and 1826 he served various parishes. The publication of his polemic *Kirkens Genmäle* (The Church's Reply) in 1826, directed against an eminent liberal theologian, led to a civil suit against him and prompted his resignation from the ministry, the imposition of a fine, and censorship of his publications.

In 1832 Grundtvig began to preach weekly in Christianshavn and it was there that his concern for reform and renewal triggered an increasing number of devotees and followers. The acceptance of the position of chaplain in a Copenhagen hospital gave him the authorization to preside over the LORD'S SUPPER. Here Grundtvig's reform movement had its beginnings. It significantly influenced the Danish Lutheran church in a variety of ways for decades. Grundtvig's some 1,400 hymns enriched Danish and even Anglophone hymnody. His movement advocated freedom for the CLERGY from liturgical and theological restrictions. His understanding of the Christian faith was that it was joyous. Grundtvig also focused his attention on education, establishing folk schools, a kind of continuing education venture, which focused on practical subjects.

Late in his life his contributions to both the Danish church and to the country—Grundtvig was a firm believer in the harmony of church and society—were recognized by his appointment, in 1861, as bishop of the (entire) Danish church. Grundtvig died in Copenhagen on September 2, 1872.

See also Hymns and Hymnals

References and Further Reading

Primary Sources:

Christensen, Georg, and Hal Koch, eds. *Vaerker I Undvalig.* 10 vols. Copenhagen: 1940–1949.
Grundtvig, N. F. S. *Selected Writings.* Philadelphia, PA: Fortress Press, 1976.
———. *A Grundtvig Anthology: Selections from the Writings of Nicolai Frederik Severin Grundtvig, 1783–1872.* Cambridge, UK: J. Clarke; Viby, Denmark: Centrum, 1984.
———. *What Constitutes Authentic Christianity?* Philadelphia, PA: Fortress Press, ca. 1985.
———. *Tradition and Renewal: Grundtvig's Vision of Man and People, Education and the Church, in Relation to World Issues Today.* Copenhagen, Denmark: Det Danske Selskab, 1983.

Secondary Sources:

Allchin, A. M. *N.F.S. Grundtvig: An Introduction to His Life and Work.* Aarhus, Denmark: Aarhus University Press, 1997.
———, ed. *Heritage and Prophecy: Grundtvig and the English-speaking World.* Aarhus, Denmark: Aarhus University Press, 1993.
Knudsen, Johannes. "One Hundred Years Later. The Grundtvigian Heritage." *Lutheran Quarterly* 25 (1973): 71ff.
Lindhardt, Poul Georg. *Grundtvig.* London: SPCK, 1964.
Skarsten, Trygve R. "Rise and Fall of Grundtvigianism in Norway." *Lutheran Quarterly* 17 (1965): 122ff.

HANS J. HILLERBRAND

GUSTAVUS ADOLPHUS (1594–1632)

Swedish monarch. The king of SWEDEN from 1611 until his death in 1632, Gustavus Adolphus was known as the "Lion of the North: Savior of Protestants" during the Thirty Years' War because he checked the power of Hapsburgs and ensured the survival of Protestantism in Europe. He died at the Battle of Lützen, although his army won the battle.

Born on December 9, 1594, in Stockholm, Sweden, Gustavus Adolphus was the son of Charles IX of the Vasa dynasty, and Kristina of Holstein-Gottorp. He was married to the daughter of the elector of Brandenburg-Prussia, Maria Eleanora. He was also known as Gustav II Adolf in Swedish. A deeply religious Lutheran, Gustavus Adolphus received a classical education in law and history as well as THEOLOGY. During his reign he founded the city of Gothenburg and was the founder of the University of Dorpat in Tartu, Estonia, which then belonged to the kingdom of Sweden.

War in Northern Europe

From his father Charles IX, Gustavus Adolphus inherited a war with DENMARK, which controlled both sides of the entrance to the Baltic Sea. Sweden and Denmark signed the peace treaty of Knäred in 1613, whereby Denmark gained Elvsborg in pledge for a large sum of Swedish silver coins to be paid within six years. Denmark's King Christian IV did not expect to lose the pledged territory, underestimating the determination of Gustavus Adolphus, who ensured that Sweden paid what was due within two years.

Sweden was also involved in a conflict with RUSSIA. A peace treaty signed at Stolbova in 1617 ensured Sweden gained Ingermanland and the province of Kexholm, depriving Russia of its coast towards the Baltic Sea. Though these engagements were strategically vital for the security of Sweden, Gustavus Adolphus was anxious to come to the aid of Protestant forces in Europe. Sweden's resources were tied up in a long-standing war with neighboring, Catholic POLAND, effectively preventing them from joining the Protestant cause. With the help of diplomats from Catholic FRANCE, ENGLAND, and Brandenburg, Adolphus freed himself from the war against Poland with the Treaty of Altmark signed in September 1629. By the end of this year, Gustavus Adolphus controlled much of the east Baltic coast, effectively dominating Baltic trade.

The Thirty Years' War

Gustavus Adolphus is most remembered for his defense of the Protestant lands in GERMANY. As long as the Protestants of northern Germany were secure, Adolphus felt that Sweden was safe from the onslaught of Papism: "As one wave follows another in the sea, so the Papal deluge is approaching our shores." To this end, he proposed the creation of two Protestant leagues in Germany, one charged with military affairs and the other with civil administration, to keep the Catholic powers, particularly Ferdinand II of Spain, at bay.

French cardinal and statesman Duc de Richelieu desired an alliance with Gustavus Adolphus to form an effective foil to the Hapsburg power in Europe. Further, he sought to bolster his strength with the help of Maximillian of Bavaria and the Catholic league. Both Gustavus Adolphus and Richelieu were pragmatists. Although they held opposite views on religion, they both recognized their mutual need to form a realistic opposition to Ferdinand II. Richelieu surmised that Ferdinand's army would be more intent on limiting the damage inflicted by the forces of Adolphus than on posing a threat at the French border. Sweden also pledged to protect the trade interests of France, while not interfering with Saxony and Bavaria.

Gustavus Adolphus landed with an army of 13,000 men in Peenemünde in Pomerania in 1630. With the aid of the Protestant Saxon army, he engaged the Catholic field marshal Tserclaes Tilly in the battle of Breitenfeld, defeating his forces in 1631. The Swedes triumphed because of the superior flexibility of their army formations. Further, because Sweden was a relatively poor country that could not afford all the metal for heavy artillery, the cannons of the Swedes were smaller and very mobile. Gustavus Adolphus turned a potential weakness into an advantage. An astute scholar of military tactics, he also had stressed attack above defense, and considered mobility to be of paramount importance.

In 1632, Adolphus signed a treaty of alliance with Richelieu at Bärwalde, which provided a subsidy to the Swedes of 400,000 riksdaler per year until 1636, and again engaged the forces of Tilly at the Battle of Lech. The Swedish army was victorious, and Tilly sustained a fatal wound. Gustavus Adolphus and the Swedish army advanced as far south as Munich in Bavaria. The Bavarians, most of whom were Catholics, feared that Gustavus Adolphus would compel them to become Protestants, but the king believed that faith should be a matter of conscience.

Ferdinand II feared that Gustavus Adolphus would invade Vienna and appealed to Albrecht Wallenstein,

Duke of Friedland, to defeat the Swedes. Wallenstein moved north to interrupt the supply routes of the Swedish army. Gustavus Adolphus followed Wallenstein, and on November 6, 1632, the armies met at Lützen. Though the Swedes won, Gustavus Adolphus was killed in the battle, misled by poor eyesight and dense fog to charge into an enemy formation. His achievements had limited the Hapsburg power and ensured the survival of Protestantism in Europe.

After the death of Gustavus Adolphus, the Swedish Riksdag of the Estates decided that he would be known as Gustavus Adolphus the Great (*Gustav Adolf den Store*).

See also Lutheranism, Scandinavia

References and Further Reading

Ahnlund, Nils. *Gustav Adolf the Great*. Westport, CT: Greenport Press, 1983.

Fletcher, C. R. L. *Gustavus Adolphus and the Thirty Years' War*. New York: Capricorn Books, 1963.

Garstein, Oskar. *Rome and the Counter-Reformation in Scandinavia*, Vol. 4, *The Age of Gustavus Adolphus and Queen Christina, 1622–1654*. Leiden, The Netherlands: E. J. Brill, 1992.

Roberts, Michael. *Gustavus Adolphus: A History of Sweden*, Vol. 2, *1626–1632*. London: Longmans, Green, 1953.

Trueman, C. "Gustavus Adolphus and Sweden." The Thirty Years War. http://www.historylearningsite.co.uk/gustavus_adolphus.htm (May 21, 2003).

HELEN FARLEY

HALLE

Located on the Saale river in Sachsen-Anhalt, GER-MANY, Halle achieved prominence in European Protestantism through the establishment of a progressive university and August Hermann Francke's Pietist orphanage in the 1690s, making Halle a center of both the ENLIGHTENMENT and PIETISM in early eighteenth-century Prussia. After 1740, Pietist influences waned, and the university became the leading voice of theological rationalism under SIEGMUND JAKOB BAUMGARTEN and JOHANN SALOMO SEMLER.

Lutheran Links

With the rise of the Protestant movement in the early 1520s, both MARTIN LUTHER and THOMAS MÜNTZER quickly won adherents in Halle. Although the city had become a favorite residence of Albrecht, the archbishop of Magdeburg, it also had a Hanseatic tradition of independence from episcopal authority. Albrecht aggressively countered the new movement in the city by reinvigorating Catholic piety and expelling Protestant dissenters, although over the next two decades he was unable to stem the support for the new reforms among the townspeople (see DISSENT). He withdrew from the city in 1541 and opened the way for the establishment of the REFORMATION. Justus Jonas, one of Luther's closest associates, came from Wittenberg to lead the institutional reforms. After the Interim in 1548, the archbishop sought to reimpose Catholicism, but the Peace of Augsburg (1555) secured the establishment of Protestantism in Halle.

After 1555 Lutherans consolidated their gains in Halle, although, as in many other Lutheran cities, conflicts over Philippism (see PHILIPP MELANCHTHON) and crypto-CALVINISM marked the second-half of the sixteenth century. The Thirty Years' War left Halle and its economy in shambles, and Halle's influence on Protestantism in Germany was minimal for much of the seventeenth century. After the death of the last administrator of the archbishopric in 1680, the territory fell to the elector of Brandenburg. Under control of the Reformed Hohenzollerns, Halle's fortunes would change considerably and the city would play an important role in the confessional politics of an expansionist Brandenburg–Prussia and shape eighteenth-century German Protestantism.

Elector Friedrich III established a new university in Halle in the early 1690s. The jurist CHRISTIAN THOMASIUS, who had been driven from the University of Leipzig for his support of the Pietist cause, became the first professor at the new academy in 1690. Many of Thomasius's students followed him from Leipzig to Halle. Under Thomasius and his colleagues the law faculty at Halle would became the leading representative of Enlightenment jurisprudence in Germany. Friedrich also wanted to establish a theology faculty in Halle that could provide candidates for clerical office in his territories. He became a protector of Pietist interests, and his appointments to the new theology faculty were all ardent Pietists. Joachim Justus Breithaupt became first professor of theology in 1691. The next year, his friend and former colleague in Erfurt, A. H. Francke, was appointed pastor in nearby Glaucha and professor in the philosophical faculty. The university received its official charter in 1694 and quickly became a center of both Pietism and the early Enlightenment in Germany.

Closely related to the university was the orphanage founded by Francke in 1695. Unlike older models Francke's orphanage was organized as an educational institution devoted to the cultivation of piety and ability. It drew students far beyond the city of Halle. By the time of Francke's death in 1727 the schools of the Francke Foundations, as the orphanage and its institutions were known, had more than 2,200 students and employed more than 160 teachers. Francke had further established a pedagogical institute for training teachers, the first of its kind in central Europe, and he made the Foundations a center for missionary activity. Although Francke initially funded the operations through donations, he was increasingly able to support his work through the profits of a printing house and the production of pharmaceuticals. The successes of the foundations—shrewdly publicized by Francke—established an international and much emulated reputation for the institutions' work.

Alliance Against Traditionalism

In the early decades, the Pietist and Enlightenment parties in Halle saw themselves as allies against the forces of traditionalism—whether legal or theological—and advocates of a new model of education that was practically oriented, emphasized instruction in German and Latin, and was opposed to the older disputational paradigm. There were, however, underlying conflicts between Pietist biblicism and the enlightened rationalism in Halle. The alliance faltered in 1723 when Francke orchestrated the expulsion of the rationalist CHRISTIAN WOLFF from the university. The death of Friedrich Wilhelm I in 1740, however, marked the end of the Pietist phase in Halle. That same year Wolff triumphantly returned to Halle. The Foundations continued under Francke's son, Gottfried August, but the university, including the faculty of theology, moved toward rationalism.

The career of Baumgarten (1706–1757) marks an important transition in the period between Pietism and Rationalism in the theology faculty at Halle. A product of Halle Pietism, Baumgarten nevertheless integrated elements of Wolffian rationalism into his theology and aimed to provide a scientific (*wissenschaftlich*) basis for theology. Semler built on Baumgarten's work and became a pioneer in the use of the historical critical method. Semler rejected Francke's emphasis on the simultaneous cultivation of piety and learning and instead encouraged the inclusion of secular disciplines into theological training. Under Semler, Halle became the leading university of theological rationalism and NEOLOGY in Germany.

The establishment of the University of Berlin in 1810 severely weakened Halle's central position in Prussian higher education. The influence of rationalism continued, but FRIEDRICH AUGUST GOTTREU THOLUCK took the theological faculty in a more conservative direction after his arrival in 1826. During his long tenure as professor of theology, Tholuck sought to combine his revival-oriented piety with academic

theological inquiry, and under his influence Halle became a center of biblical theology, a tradition carried on by his student Martin Kähler (1835–1912).

During the 1930s conflicts over National Socialism and the CONFESSING CHURCH divided the theological faculty at Halle. In 1946 the Francke Foundations were dissolved and its schools secularized. After the reunification of Germany, the Foundations were revived in 1992. With its rich libraries and archives, Halle is today a major center for the study of Pietism and the Enlightenment.

References and Further Reading

Berg, Gunnar, and Hans-Hermann Hartwich, eds. *Martin-Luther-Universität: von der Gründung bis zur Neugestaltung nach zwei Diktaturen.* Opladen, Germany: Leske & Budrich, 1994.
Francke, August Hermann. *Pietas Hallensis: or, an Abstract of the Marvellous Footsteps of Divine Providence.* London, 1707.
Holloran, John Robert. "Professors of Enlightenment at the University of Halle 1690–1730." Ph.D. dissertation, University of Virginia, 2000.
Schmitt, Hanno. "On the Importance of Halle in the Eighteenth Century for the History of Education." *Paedogica historica* 32 (1996): 85–100.

JONATHAN N. STROM

HAMANN, JOHANN GEORG (1730–1788)

German theologian. Hamann was born in Königsberg (now Kaliningrad) (East-Prussia) on August 27, 1730, and worked there as a translator and customs officer. The decisive turning point in his life came in 1758 in London through an intense study of and meditation on the BIBLE. He died June 21, 1788, in Münster, Westphalia.

The task of being a witness to the Gospel, to which Hamann was called in London, did not lead him, a life-long stutterer, into a public church office. Instead, he was a servant of the divine word as a publicist and writer, with his reviews in the "Königsbergsche Gelehrte und Politische Zeitungen" and with his succinct small leaflets ("Fliegende Blätter"). These were meant to disseminate the Gospel, as it was summarized by MARTIN LUTHER in his small catechism, throughout society, and in doing this Hamann caused offense. Hamann was aware of his mixed dialectic relationship to his readers; his writings were full of both riddles and candor. He was a writer in a dialectic of concealment and publicity, determined by the mystery of the Messiah and his parables, as told in Mark (Mark 4:11ff.), as well as in Pauline and Johannine theology.

Hamann's aim was to be "Philologus crucis," a philologist of the cross. The cross was the source of strength for his critical philology, with which he criticized the philosophers HERMANN REIMARUS (1694–

1768) and G. E. Lessing (1729–1781), Moses Mendelssohn, Frederick the Great, and last but not least, by his "Metakritik über den Purismus der Vernunft," IMMANUEL KANT (1724–1804). In particular contradiction to his contemporaries, Hamann wrote about the responsible perception of one's fellow creatures (especially in the "Aesthetica in nuce"; 1762). He also wrote concerning reason and language, time and history, sexuality and marriage, as well as politics.

Hamann's importance for literary studies, philosophy, and theology cannot be overstated. This becomes especially clear in the doctrine of God of this extraordinarily informal "Father of the Church": For Hamann, God is, in his speaking work and working speaking, "author" and "poet"—"God a writer!" As such, God writes the book of nature and history, and in doing so God also writes each individual's life history. Through its "ride to hell of self-knowledge," each individual human is understood and interpreted by God; God himself is the best interpreter of God's words and their last critic, their judge.

Hamann, no irrationalist, but a radical Enlightenment thinker, sees God as the one who addresses him, together with all creatures, through fellow creatures. Therefore, thinking and reason constitute language. With the help of the theology and philosophy that are inherent in the translation of such language effective in the act of translation, Hamann attempts to answer the problem of Being. With respect to his ontological hermeneutics, Hamann is superior to Kant and G. W. F. Hegel (1770–1831). Hamann sees God, in contrast to Kant, not as a limited concept, and not, as Hegel does, as a smooth and unhindered mediation.

Hamann turns away sharply from the dogmatism of reason proposed by the representatives of natural religion and their speculative theology. Instead he welcomes the scepticism of Hume's *Dialogues Concerning Natural Religion* (1779), and shares Kant's "sceptical tactic." However, he does not follow him on his critical way, which itself becomes dogmatic in its assertion of the "purity" of reason because Kant fears skepticism (by the assertion of the "purity" of reason). Kant, in Hamann's view, does not put an end to the affair of interplay between dogmatism and scepticism, but perpetuates it.

Whereas the puristic tendency of Kant's transcendental question, which abstracts from all particulars, leads to the idea of a limit, Hamann's metacritique resists this limit with a center having its core situated in the events of the crucifixion and resurrection of Jesus Christ. This center, laid down in the title of Hamann's leaflet "Golgatha und Scheblimini!," determines Hamann's life, to the last detail of his reading and writing. The mutual participation of the specific features of the divine and human nature in the person

of Jesus Christ ("communicatio idiomatum") is the "main key to all human knowledge." God shows humanity and humiliation not only in the cross, but also as creator. God shows it also as the Holy Spirit, who "is the writer of stupid and humanly silly, yes even sinful human stories." With this theology of condescension, Hamann succeeds in thinking God, in leaving behind the alternative of Idealism and Materialism, by integrating the true elements of both in the medium of the word, and following Luther in a very impressive way.

See also Kant, Immanuel; Luther, Martin; Reimarus, Hermann

References and Further Reading

Primary Sources:

Bayer, Oswald, and Bernd Weißenborn, eds. *Johann Georg Hamann, Londoner Schriften. Hist.-krit.* Munich: Verlag C. H. Beck, 1993.

Nadler, Josef, ed. *Johann Georg Hamann, Sämtliche Werke.* 6 vols. Vienna: Herder Verlag, 1949–1957.

Seils, Martin, ed. *Johann Georg Hamann, Eine Auswahl aus seinen Schriften.* Wuppertal: R. Brockhaus-Verlag, 1987.

Ziesemer, Walter, and Arthur Henkel, eds. *Johann Georg Hamann, Briefwechsel.* 7 vols. Wiesbaden and Frankfurt am Main: Insel-Verlag, 1955–1979.

Secondary Sources:

Bayer, Oswald. *Vernunft ist Sprache. Hamanns Metakritik Kants.* Stuttgart-Bad Cannstadt: Frommann-Holzboog, 2002.
———. "Johann Georg Hamann als radikaler Aufklärer." *Zeitgenosse im Widerspruch.* Munich: Aufklarer, 1988.
Jørgensen, Sven-Aage. *Johann Georg Hamann.* Stuttgart: Metzlersche Verlagsbuchhandlung, 1976.

OSWALD BAYER

HANDEL, GEORGE FRIDERIC (1685–1759)

Composer. Born in HALLE, Germany, February 23, 1685, Handel visited leading German musical centers, including Berlin and Leipzig, at an early age. In 1702 he enrolled at Halle University and was quickly appointed organist of the Halle Domkirche (cathedral). The following year he joined the Hamburg opera orchestra, soon becoming harpsichordist-conductor and composing four operas. For most of 1706 to 1710 he lived in Italy, staying in Rome, Florence, Naples, and Venice. On returning to GERMANY he accepted the post of Kapellmeister (conductor) to the Elector of Hanover, assured that he could take immediate leave to visit Düsseldorf and ENGLAND. After a year in England he returned to Hanover, but by October 1712 he was once more in England. Aside from travel to the continent to see his family, restore his health, or recruit singers, he spent the rest of his life there, leasing a house in Brook Street, Mayfair, from 1723 and taking British citizenship in 1727. His only extended sojourn outside England was a season in Dublin (1741–1742) when he first performed *Messiah*. His other major works were first performed in London. Handel died April 14, 1759, in London and was buried in Westminster Abbey.

Career

The trajectory of Handel's career from Halle to England shows a progression through contemporary opportunities to learn, practice, and gain prestige. He could have become an esteemed German provincial church organist and composer like JOHANN SEBASTIAN BACH, but he had a strong ambition to be free to compose and direct—especially opera—as he wanted, with first-rate performers, on a world stage. He diplomatically declined most offers of contractual obligations and salaried posts, while showing (in his early career especially) a remarkable flair for gaining rapid access to influential figures and attracting patronage without ties. He spoke and wrote four languages, composed settings in six, rapidly assimilated local styles, and accommodated local tastes. He composed in every genre of his time, pushed out the boundaries of existing genres, and introduced new ones, notably English oratorio, English unacted secular drama, and the organ concerto.

Religion and politics, inextricably connected in Handel's time, coincided throughout his own life, and later in his work. His father had served as a field surgeon in the Thirty Years' War, during which Halle was twice besieged and the Domkirche organist's free lodging was badly damaged. During Handel's childhood Huguenot and Calvinist refugees were allowed to settle in Halle (see HUGUENOTS; CALVINISM), and Jews were readmitted in 1692 (see JUDAISM). On his mother's side Handel came from a family of Lutheran pastors (see LUTHERANISM), but the Domkirche had a predominantly Calvinist congregation, which affected the terms of his employment there. Visiting Italy entailed moving between supporters of different sides in the War of Spanish Succession, as well as working in a Catholic society, but as the world center of large-scale, high-quality music it was the obvious next move after the staging post of the free City of Hamburg.

Nothing surviving from his earlier years anticipates the reach of Handel's sacred compositions for Rome, notably the scintillating *Dixit Dominus* for soloists, chorus, and orchestra. In Italy he wrote liturgical settings and sacred motets and cantatas, and his first oratorios: *Il trionfo del Tempo e del Disinganno,* a moral allegory to a text by his admirer Cardinal Pamphili (reworked in 1737 and 1757); and, for Marquis Ruspoli, the intensely dramatic *La Resurrezione,* one of his three works concerning the life of Christ. He was fêted for his virtuoso keyboard playing, richly housed in the palazzi of cardinals, and immediately accepted as a composer for the Roman Catholic church. However, he chose not to develop a career as such, or to stay in Rome, and left Italy after achieving international operatic success. According to John Mainwaring, offers of employment were made to him, along with persuasions to convert, both of which he declined, being "resolved to die a member of that communion in which he was born and bred." According to John Hawkins he found the level of religious toleration available in Britain personally attractive and "would frequently declare the pleasure he felt in setting the Scriptures." In later life Handel was a devout attender of his local church, St. George's Hanover Square (naturalization required Anglican conformity). In his music he expressed a sense of his Lutheran origins most clearly in his Funeral Anthem for Queen Caroline (1737), formerly the Hanoverian Electoral Princess: it draws on two chorales and the work of several composers from their shared tradition.

Political circumstances complicated Handel's career in England. His celebration of Queen Anne as peacemaker, and his Te Deum and Jubilate for British celebrations of the Peace of Utrecht, resulted in the termination of his employment with the Elector of Hanover, to whom the peace was anathema, but who was the future King of England. The Jacobite Rebellion of 1715, besides interrupting musical life, was a reminder of the threat to the Hanoverian regime and the Protestant succession in Britain, and may have prompted Handel's otherwise unexplained setting of the Passion text by B. H. Brockes (a work partly copied out by J. S. Bach) for performance in Germany. He was often identified by the London nobility and gentry—on whose favor the furtherance of his career depended—as the servant of the widely resented foreign monarchy. The unprecedentedly grand music he wrote for state ceremonials, notably the Coronation Anthems (1727), conspicuously allied him with the crown, from which he received three pensions. His almost cult status was attested by the erection of his statue in Vauxhall pleasure gardens in 1738, an unheard of tribute for any musician, let alone a living one. Such dominance of the cultural scene was resented as social presumption by the upper classes, and his public performances were periodically snubbed.

From the moment of his arrival, efforts by English authors to make Handel the fountainhead of a secure tradition of English opera failed. He chose to make his name in Italian opera, but in-fighting between generations of the royal family, who were major patrons, made an always financially risky enterprise even less sustainable. The Royal Academy (Italian) opera company began ambitiously in 1719 with Handel as one of its principal composers, but dissolved in 1728; thereafter he mounted productions increasingly as his own manager. The Opera of the Nobility, begun in 1733 by the opposition party around Frederick Prince of Wales, took away most of his leading singers, but itself ran aground. Handel wrote his last opera in 1740. His subsequent refusal to write for the Earl of Middlesex's opera company again damaged his popularity. The outbreak of the 1745 Jacobite Rebellion, however, unified national feeling behind the Hanoverians in defense of Protestantism and liberty against Catholic FRANCE, and the enthusiastic response to Handel's religious-nationalist oratorios of the late 1740s set a pattern of esteem that lasted the rest of his life. He died an affluent and honored citizen of his adopted country.

Works

Despite Handel's prominence as a composer of forty-two Italian operas, his London public was probably more familiar with his music—both his compositions and his dazzling improvisations on the organ—for the Anglican church (see ANGLICANISM). Early in his English career he accepted the hospitality of James Brydges (Earl of Carnarvon, later Duke of Chandos), who was building a princely mansion at Cannons, near London, and for whom he wrote a grand Te Deum and the eleven anthems that became known as the Chandos Anthems. His works for state religious occasions, besides those already mentioned, include the Dettingen Anthem and Te Deum, the Anthem for the Peace of Aix la Chapelle, and royal wedding anthems. He provided an anthem for the Foundling Hospital, a newly established charity for abandoned children, of which he became a governor. He also wrote five anthems for the Chapel Royal. Many of his church compositions were frequently heard on festive and charitable occasions. As poems in their praise testify, their scale and impact satisfied the contemporary appetite for the religious sublime, and Handel reused some of them in his oratorios.

Cannons was the only private house in Britain with a substantial musical establishment, and there Handelian oratorio began. At the home of his previous English host, the Earl of Burlington, Handel had encountered leading poets of the day—John Gay, Alexander Pope, and John Arbuthnot—and from that "club of composers" emerged his enchanting masque *Acis and Galatea,* probably first performed at Cannons in

1718. During the same period, also for Cannons, and with some of the same collaborators, he wrote his first biblical oratorio, *Esther.* "Unauthorized" public performances of both works in 1732 prompted Handel to mount his own newly enlarged versions, and so, unpremeditatedly, he introduced oratorio in English to the British public. For most of the next decade his seasons combined English oratorio and Italian opera, until in 1741 he turned to oratorio alone. "Oratorio" is now loosely used to describe all the English works that he originally performed in the theater, and to include secular works ranging from quasi-operas and masques on mythological stories (e.g., *Semele; The Choice of Hercules*) to odes (*Alexander's Feast; L'Allegro, il Penseroso ed il Moderato*). Handel's seventeen religious oratorios are mostly based on the Old Testament or Apocrypha; only *Messiah* draws on the New Testament and liturgical texts outside the psalms, and only *Theodora* has a story set in Christian times.

The 1718 *Esther* set the pattern in being a newly written text dramatizing the biblical and apocryphal narratives, employing the recitative-and-aria style of Italian opera, and making full use of a chorus. The dramatization involved embroidering or inventing incidents—usually suggested by the source material—and selecting and paraphrasing Scripture. Sometimes there was an intermediary source between the BIBLE and the libretto, usually a work of literary distinction; in the case of *Esther,* it was Racine's neoclassical choric drama. The anthems inserted into the 1732 *Esther* represent the other and less frequent strain of libretto composition, using actual scriptural text. Only *Messiah* and *Israel in Egypt* consist entirely of texts taken from the Bible with only minor verbal adjustment, but here too the librettist shaped the works, by selection, juxtaposition, and sequencing of the biblical verses.

Italian opera (and Italian oratorio) lacked a chorus, and the chorus of English oratorio gave Handel the opportunity to write grand, varied, and dramatic music, and afforded his audience the awe-inspiring sensations that signaled the highest art. Handel did not, so far as we know, write or choose the subjects of any of his English librettos. Their authors were able and cultivated people. Several were deliberately contributing to the making of high art, and two at least were writing in the cause of the Protestant religion: Charles Jennens (*Saul, Messiah, Belshazzar,* and possibly *Israel in Egypt*) and the Rev. Thomas Morell (*Judas Maccabaeus, Alexander Balus, Theodora, Jephtha*).

Of the librettists of the religious oratorios whose identities are known, two—James Miller (*Joseph and his Brethren*) and Morell—were CHURCH OF ENGLAND ministers; one, Jennens, was a devout nonjuring Anglican; and one, Samuel Humphreys (the 1732 *Esther, Deborah,* and *Athalia*), compiled a massive biblical commentary from standard Anglican exegeses. The oratorios are further rooted in Anglicanism through their "cathedral" musical style (which made them anathema to the Methodist JOHN WESLEY), their assertion of the church–state bond reinforced by the reuse of anthems for state occasions, and their textual analogy of national Protestant defiance of European Catholic autocracies. Yet they also appealed to nonconformists (see NON-CONFORMITY), on account of their lack of doctrinal insistence and their depiction of an elect, embattled, minority religious community succeeding over corrupt, hedonistic apostates and heathens. Their celebration of hard-won freedom of religion and nationhood was congenial to Englishmen— and later Americans—of any persuasion. They also incorporate the views of England's leading ENLIGHTENMENT philosopher, the third earl of Shaftesbury, through their criticism and improvement of Old Testament ethics and personalities, and their dramatization of the principles of "sensibility." The conflict between enlightenment and religious fervor would have been familiar to Handel from his youth. It reached a head at Halle University during his year there (1702–1703) in the clash between the philosopher Christian Thomasius and the Pietist August Hermann Francke (see PIETISM). Handel's oratorios are remarkable in accommodating both views.

During the nineteenth century the oratorios were regarded principally as sacred works. In the twentieth century they were celebrated as dramas of individuals and nations, and as showing a pantheist and humanist Handel overriding the sectarianism of his librettists and his times. More recently, exploration has focused on the richness of their response to the ideas of their day. Besides making copious reference to current political life and theory—both government and opposition—they reflect diverse, but connected, religious and aesthetic concerns.

Handelian oratorio responded to the artistic reform movement calling for uplifting, instructive, national art, and (in music) English word settings; to the taste for sentimental drama; to the desire for a national-religious epic and the use of Greek tragedy as a model for music dramas; to the enthusiasm for the Bible as literature, for the religious sublime, and for biblical paraphrase; and, above all, to the rallying of ORTHODOXY against freethinking. The period of Handel's oratorio composition (1732–1752) was also the period of the major English defense against DEISM, and the oratorios, with their insistence on providentialism, on the truth of prophecy and miracles, on the integrity of Scripture, and the dependency of the New Testament on the Old, and prominently utilizing the common

antideist armory of evidence, were major—and uniquely lasting—contributions to that defense. The outstanding instance, an oratorio unlike any of his others but firmly rooted in antideist literature, is *Messiah,* a deliberate affirmation by Jennens of the Christian creed and its universal authority, and a paean to the propagation of the gospel.

More generally, through the accessibility and emotive power of Handel's music, and through their LATITUDINARIANISM and avoidance of dogmatism (even in *Messiah*), the oratorios fulfilled the widespread contemporary call to make the truths of religion movingly convincing and thus revitalize religious feeling and reform behavior. In this respect English oratorio was a Protestant annexation of its Catholic original, and can be seen as a form of "counter-COUNTER-REFORMATION." Through oratorio the Roman church used music as an inducement to worship and conversion. Handel's English oratorios lay claim to the oratorians' form of religious expressiveness and stamp it with Protestantism by taking as their sources not the New Testament or hagiography, but the Old Testament and Apocrypha, invoking and capitalizing on the time-honored parallel between the religious-political dispensation of the ancient Israelites and that of Protestant Britain (see CATHOLIC REACTIONS TO PROTESTANTISM; CATHOLICISM, PROTESTANT REACTIONS). The rebuttal of Catholicism is clearest in the one Christian drama, *Theodora,* which reflects contemporary English admiration for the purity of the early church (not, as is sometimes anachronistically supposed, the influence of METHODISM). It presents a voluntary religious community whose elite is defined by spiritual excellence, instead of a religious structure heavy with doctrines, hierarchy, and priesthood; it identifies Christianity with freedom of thought and belief, rather than prescribed belief and practice; it celebrates religious observance that is private and spontaneous, not public and ritualized; and it opposes fresh, pure, individual belief to tradition, authority, and world domination.

References and Further Reading

Primary Source:

[Mainwaring, John.] *Memoirs of the Life of the Late George Frederic Handel.* London, 1760. Facsimile Buren: Frits Knupf, 1975.

Secondary Sources:

Burrows, Donald. *Handel.* Oxford: Oxford University Press, 1994.
Burrows, Donald, ed. *The Cambridge Companion to Handel.* Cambridge: Cambridge University Press, 1997.

Dean, Winton. *Handel's Dramatic Oratorios and Masques.* London: Oxford University Press, 1959.

Hawkins, John. *A General History of the Science and Practice of Music*, 2 vols. London, 1776. Repr. London: J. Alfred Novello, 1853.

Hicks, Anthony. "Handel, George Frideric." In *The New Grove Dictionary of Music and Musicians, 2nd ed*, edited by Stanley Sadie and John Tyrrell. London: Macmillan, 2001.

Smith, Ruth. *Handel's Oratorios and Eighteenth-Century Thought.* Cambridge: Cambridge University Press, 1995.

———. "The Meaning of the Libretto of Handel's *Judas Maccabaeus*." *Music & Letters* (1998): 50–71.

RUTH SMITH

HARKNESS, GEORGIA (1891–1974)

American theologian. Harkness was the first professional woman theologian in the UNITED STATES and the first female theologian to teach in Protestant seminaries in the United States. Born April 21, 1891, and raised in the tiny upstate New York village of Harkness, named after her grandfather, she was the second daughter and youngest of four children of J. Warren and Lillie (Merrill) Harkness. Her parents took her in their arms to the Harkness Methodist Episcopal Church when she was three weeks old, beginning her lifelong commitment to the church as a loyal critic from within.

After attending the one-room elementary school, which served as the family's church on Sundays, Harkness graduated from nearby Keeseville High School and received her A.B. from Cornell University in 1912. She was deeply influenced by the Student Volunteer Movement in college and took its pledge to become a foreign missionary. Feeling needed at home, she instead taught for a short time at high schools in Schuylersville and Scotia, New York. Unsatisfied with this career direction, Harkness entered the newly formed Boston University School of Religious Education to pursue an alternative calling to be a director of religious education. By the time she received her two master's degrees (and A.M.) in 1920, she decided that her calling was to teach in higher education and she remained at Boston University to gain a doctorate in philosophy.

Harkness began her teaching career as assistant professor of religious education in 1922 at Elmira College, one of the country's earliest women's colleges, teaching philosophy there until 1937. She moved to Mt. Holyoke College in Holyoke, Massachusetts, for two years. In 1939 Harkness accepted the invitation from Garrett Biblical Institute in Evanston, Illinois to become one of the first professors of applied theology in a United States seminary, although she had hoped to be named to the professorship in systematic theology. After eleven years Harkness moved to the Pacific School of Religion in 1960, remaining there until retirement in 1961.

Professor of applied theology rightly described Georgia Harkness, a social prophet within the Methodist and Protestant churches beginning with her early years at Elmira College. She became a pacifist in 1924 after visiting war-torn Europe following World War I and spoke out against any use of nuclear weaponry throughout her lifetime (see PACIFISM). She gained international attention at the Oxford Conference of the WORLD COUNCIL OF CHURCHES in 1938 when she described the churches as one of the main bastions of male dominance in society. Having received local ordination in the Methodist Episcopal Church in 1938 Harkness was credited with doing more than anyone else to bring full ordination and conference membership to women in her denomination in 1956. In 1948 she called on the Methodist Church to eliminate the Central Jurisdiction, made up of black congregations, before joining with the Evangelical United Brethren to form the United Methodist Church in that year. The Central Jurisdiction was abolished the following year, and the United Methodist Church became an integrated denomination.

One hour before his death in 1937, her father told his daughter that he hoped she would write more about Jesus Christ. This led her to rethink her own spiritual and professional commitments. Harkness moved from an early emphasis and rather arid writings on philosophical idealism to become an evangelical liberal, combining the personal evangelical emphasis of her childhood with her liberal commitment to social justice as an adult. She gained scholarly distinction as a theologian of the laity, interpreting theological issues in understandable language. Over her lifetime she preached and lectured through the world. Her thirty-eight books and countless articles on THEOLOGY, spiritual life, ministry of the LAITY, and ETHICS, drawn from Biblical interpretation, are written in both narrative and poetic form. She also wrote over 200 hymns, including "Hope of the World," which opened the second assembly of the World Council of Churches in 1954 in Evanston, Illinois.

Throughout her lifetime, Harkness used pen, pulpit, and platform to hold the churches responsible for the social implications of Christianity. A prefeminist and lone female voice, she challenged and worked together with such giants among male theologians of her day as KARL BARTH, REINHOLD NIEBUHR, and PAUL TILLICH. Her words to the church sound more like the liberation theologians of the twenty-first century than of a woman scholar of the mid-twentieth century.

The United Library at Garrett Evangelical Theological Seminary holds the Georgia Harkness major manuscript collection, consisting of her autobiographical essay, written for the Pacific Coast Theological Group in the 1950s, letters to and from Harkness, manuscript and printed copies of sermons, essays, speeches, poems, and hymns, as well as published clippings and course syllabi. A further invaluable source is over two hundred letters exchanged between Harkness and Edgar Sheffield Brightman over a twenty-five-year period in the Department of Special Collections at the Library at Boston University.

Of the thirty-eight books that she wrote, *Understanding the Christian Faith* (1947), *Gospel and Our World* (1949), *The Faith by Which the Church Lives* (1940), *Toward Understanding the Bible* (1954), and *Women in Church and Society* (1971) are representative of her mature emphasis on applied theology, the ministry of the laity, and social ethics. *The Dark Night of the Soul* (1945) is a pastoral care approach growing out of her recovery from depression. Her books on spiritual growth include *Prayer and the Common Life* (1948) and *Mysticism* (1973), and representative of her devotional books, some written in poetry, are *Grace Abounding* (1969), *Through Christ Our Lord* (1950), *Be Still and Know* (1953), and *Holy Flame* (1935). Characteristic of her earlier books, written from the prospect of philosophical idealism, are *Conflicts in Religious Thought* (1929) and *The Recovery of Ideals* (1937). Harkness contributed countless articles for *The Christian Century,* including the only one by a woman in the series on "How My Mind Has Changed" (March 15, 1939), *Zion's Herald,* and *The Christian Advocate.*

Harkness died in retirement in Claremont, California, survived by her companion of many years, the musician Verna Miller. She was buried in Harkness, New York. Garrett Evangelical Theological Seminary honored her pioneering role by establishing the Georgia Harkness Chair to be held by a woman in theological studies.

See also Ethics; Feminist Theology; Liberation Theology; Methodist Episcopal Church Conference; Theology, Twentieth-Century, North American

References and Further Reading

Carpenter, Dianne Evelyn. "Georgia Harkness's Distinctive Personalistic Synthesis." Ph.D. dissertation, Boston University, 1988.

Gilbert, Paula. "Choice of the Greater Good: The Christian Witness of Georgia Harkness Arising from the Interplay of Spiritual Life and Theological Perspective." Ph.D. dissertation, Duke University, 1984.

Keller, Rosemary. *For Such a Time as This: The Life, Work, and Thought of Georgia Harkness.* Nashville, TN: Abingdon Press, 1992.

Keller, Rosemary, ed. "Georgia Harkness Theologian of the People." In *Spirituality and Social Responsibility: Voca-*
tional Vision of Women in the United Methodist Tradition. Nashville, TN: Abingdon Press, 1993.

Scott, Martha. "Georgia Harkness: Social Activist and/or Mystic." In *Women in New Worlds,* vol. I. Edited by Rosemary and Thomas Keller. Nashville, TN: Abingdon Press, 1981.

———. "The Theology and Social Thought of Georgia Harkness." Ph.D. dissertation, Northwestern University, 1984.

ROSEMARY KELLER

HARNACK, ADOLF VON (1851–1930)

German theologian and historian. Harnack was born a Baltic German in Dorpat (Livonia) on May 7, 1851, son of the professor of theology, Theodosius Harnack, who was considered one of the leading Lutheran scholars of his time. Through his active participation in the Church of Livonia, Theodosius Harnack moved away from PIETISM and developed into a consciously Lutheran churchman.

Having grown up in conservative confessional surroundings, Adolf began studying evangelical theology in Dorpat in 1869. However, serious tensions quickly arose between him and his father as Adolf was influenced by the church historian Moritz von Engelhard and sought to apply the historical-critical method rigorously to the history of dogma. Beginning with the winter semester of 1872 Harnack studied at the University of Leipzig, a bastion of conservative confessional LUTHERANISM at the time, obtaining his doctorate in 1873 with a dissertation entitled *Zur Quellenkritik der Geschichte des Gnosticismus* and qualifying as a university lecturer in 1874 with his postdoctoral thesis *De Apellis monarchica.* Both works examined the problems of gnosticism and its sources. At the young age of twenty-three Harnack became a lecturer in Leipzig and already at twenty-five associate professor at the Leipzig faculty. During the period in Leipzig Harnack broke his ties to conservative confessional Lutheranism. His reading of the works of ALBRECHT RITSCHL caused him to distance himself still further from traditional Lutheran theology.

An extremely popular academic teacher with the students in Leipzig, Harnack soon gathered around him a group of talented scholars who were to gain a significant influence in the fields of theology and church policy. Among them were MARTIN RADE, Friedrich Loofs, William Wrede, and Emil Schürer. Together with Schürer he established the *Theologische Literaturzeitung (Theological Literary Journal),* which still exists today. Within a few years this became one of the most influential theological review journals. Because of denominational reservations, he declined the offer of a position in Breslau, but in 1879 Harnack accepted a professorship at Giessen in Hesse, which appeared unproblematic because it was not dominated by conservative New Lutheran thinking. In

Giessen he began working on his three-volume *Lehrbuch der Dogmengeschichte* (*Handbook of the History of Dogma*), the first volume of which was published in 1886 and earned him a name in the theological world.

In this study Harnack remained true to his rigorous historical-critical approach: he rejected the idea that dogma existed in the early church as historically comprehensible. Rather, it was the hellenization of the original Gospel, a disastrous turn from the point of view of the development of piety. Harnack used the original Gospel of Jesus as a criterion for the assessment and portrayal of the history of dogma, which he maintained had been used by conservative historical study as an instrument to strengthen its own position and objectives. Harnack opposed this diagnosed misuse of the history of dogma by the conservatives with his own historical message. He maintained that the historiography of dogma amounted to more than either the description of a cultural history or the history of the development of dogmas. Its objective could be correctly established only if the history of dogma were interpreted as a history of institutions. Striving in this way to demonstrate the historical relativity of dogmas, he sought to open up new paths to faith beyond theological arbitrariness. Historical-critical historiography of dogma seeks in this way to provide clear orientation and thus to strengthen human faith beyond manipulated dogmas by seeking to capture the deep inner substance of Christianity.

In 1866, the year of publication of the first volume of his *History of Dogma,* Harnack was appointed to a professorship in Marburg, and in 1888 moved to Berlin. By then his *History of Dogma* was widely read, but met with hefty criticism from conservative circles. Conservative theological and church circles sought to prevent his Berlin appointment. However, a public and at times polemical controversy, in the course of which the governing council of the Prussian Evangelical Church denied its consent to Harnack's appointment, did not prevent his being called to Berlin. Nevertheless, from then on Harnack's relationship to the official church authorities remained strained. He was not appointed to church examination committees, nor elected a member of a church synod. The advocates of "positive," that is, traditional Christianity saw in Harnack an influential opponent who was weakening the fundamental confessional principles and making space for a theological subjectivism. Harnack found himself the target of attacks, which intensified into the so-called Apostolicum dispute, a controversy over the continued viability of the Apostles Creed. A direct consequence of this controversy was the establishment of a "positive" professorship at Berlin for the correction of Harnack. It was occupied by Adolf Schlatter (1852–1938), and it allowed Harnack's pursuit of scholarly, organizational, and political tasks unencumbered by ecclesiastical concerns.

Harnack rapidly became one of the most controversial, but at the same time one of the most influential, Berlin professors. He was supported and encouraged by the Prussian minister of education and cultural affairs Friedrich Althoff and by the liberal historian Theodor Mommsen. In 1890, Harnack was appointed to the *Preußische Akademie der Wissenschaften*. After assuming numerous responsibilities in the academy and the university, he took up the position of director of the Prussian State Library in 1905. In 1911 he became the first president of the *Kaiser-Wilhelm-Gesellschaft zur Förderung der Wissenschaften,* now the Max Planck Society. Additionally, Harnack grew to be a close advisor of Emperor Wilhelm II on aspects of church policy. Harnack cofounded the *Evangelisch-Sozialen Kongress,* which saw its task in dealing with the social question from the perspective of Protestantism, and from 1903 to 1912 was its president.

Thus before the outbreak of World War I Harnack was highly regarded as a theologian and scientific organizer not only in GERMANY but also abroad. At the beginning of the war, Harnack supported the political objectives of Germany. Like the majority of German intellectuals he was initially convinced that the war had been forced on the Empire and constituted a legitimate form of self-defense. Harnack therefore supported the emperor in an advisory capacity and brought his excellent reputation to bear journalistically for the German war aims. However, as the war continued, he began as early as 1915 to join the pacifists in calling for rapprochement and peace as well as campaigning for wide-reaching democratic reforms within German politics. In addition Harnack made intensive use of his foreign contacts to bring about if not a pro-German, at least a neutral, friendly attitude among the American public. Harnack considered the all-out submarine warfare initiated by the German command to be political stupidity, and saw the resulting entry of the United States into the war as a personal failure.

After the German defeat and the revolution in 1918–1919 Harnack supported the new democratic parliamentary republic. Unlike many of his colleagues, however, he did not join any particular party but rather continued to see his task in serving science by acting, in his capacity as a scholar, as advisor to the political institutions and creating scientific political committees. He played an active role in establishing the *Notgemeinschaft der Deutschen Wissenschaft* (Emergency Association of German Science) after the war.

The political and theological development of the Weimar Republic was a source of great concern for Harnack. His declaration of belief in the republic met with hefty criticism within conservative church circles. In the elections for German president in 1925 Harnack openly supported the Catholic Wilhelm Marx from the Catholic-influenced Center party, who was competing against the war hero Otto von Hindenburg for the position of president. Harnack's analysis of the general political situation in the Weimar Republic and the situation in terms of church policy led him to pessimistic conclusions in the latter years of his life. Harnack saw German Protestantism to be in danger of being taken over by politically reactionary forces. He saw the new theological generation, which had been shaped to a great extent by experiences of war, as characterized by an ahistorical, anticultural basic position. Harnack reproached KARL BARTH in a 1923 correspondence with him, arguing that if detached from cultural points of reference Barth's theological writings on revelation could lead only to a fatal self-isolation. According to Harnack the ahistorical views propagated by Barth formed the core of an irrational critique of culture, which threatened the basic values of a Christian humanist culture.

The liberal cultural theologian also regarded the theological program of the "New Lutherans" such as Emanuel Hirsch and FRIEDRICH GOGARTEN as a matter for great concern. In his opinion their concepts could lead only to a confessionalism, which had long been outgrown. Harnack was equally skeptical of the close interlinking of the historical theological approaches of young conservative theologians with political rights. He saw this as sowing a seed from which nothing good could grow for church policy.

Harnack died on June 10, 1930, in Heidelberg while on a business trip as president of the *Kaiser-Wilhelm-Gesellschaft*. His ashes were buried in Berlin. The last speaker who, on behalf of the students, addressed those gathered on the occasion of the funeral service was DIETRICH BONHOEFFER. Bonhoeffer's words on the responsibilities of men and women in the modern world are linked not least to the work of Harnack.

Harnack was the last German-speaking theologian who exercised great authority from a theological point of view and at the same time was socially influential, politically significant, and important as a scientific organizer. Despite this, during his lifetime as a theologian Harnack remained a church historian whose name is still associated with a progressive understanding of the history of dogma. Harnack's basic theory was that a method of interpretation consisting of unprejudiced historical criticism should be used to determine the original Gospel of Jesus, undistorted by church dogma. He believed that, despite the insights of the "Religionsgeschichtliche Schule" ("History of Religions School"), no research could be carried out into the life of Jesus—the message of Jesus could be extracted by means of careful historical study. However, any critical work on dogmas was conditional on having an accurate edition of the relevant source texts. Thus in 1891 the *Kirchenväterkommision* (Committee on the Church Fathers) was formed at the proposal of Harnack and Theodor Mommsen (1817–1903), which assumed the task of editing old church literature from before 325 and publishing this in fifty volumes. By 1924 *Texte und Untersuchungen* published by Harnack already ran to forty-five volumes and thus had provided essential working materials for "Patristicism."

The Gospel of Jesus, the contents of which Harnack summarized using the key terms "faith in God," "love of humans," and "trust in the Kingdom of God" in his most well-known work *Das Wesen des Christentums* (*What is Christianity*) published in 1900, was, he maintained, the most pure form of human religiousness. Harnack believed these three concepts to be mutually dependent, together forming the *"Wesen des Christentums"* (this translates literally as the "essence of Christianity") and therefore to be of the utmost cultural significance. Harnack allowed that Protestantism was the most mature form of Christianity because by resorting to the biblical fundamentals this had relaxed the connection to old confessional statements. He maintained that Protestantism recognized the individuality of Christians and made this a principle of church institutions.

The reception of Harnack's work has basically never been interrupted. However, his theology is of questionable relevance within the theological debate today. Although his studies had a decisive influence in the content-related disputes into the 1930s, this influence was broken by "dialectic theology." However, to understand the marked break in the reception of Harnack's work we need to look at more than the theological level alone. The political lack of clarity of so-called cultural Protestantism that Harnack personified with regard to German National Socialism discredited cultural Protestantism as a whole and at the same time had a serious impact on the reception of Harnack's work after 1945.

After 1945 discussions on Harnack within Protestantism were restricted to small circles of specialists. In Germany, but also in the UNITED STATES and ENGLAND, it was Harnack's *Wesen des Christentums* in particular that was discussed (Niebuhr, Glick, Sykes). In the United States Harnack's approach was usually assessed negatively despite his influence in the first half of the twentieth century having been considerable, because of his promotion of patristic thinking.

In German-speaking research Harnack's work became a focus of greater attention on the occasion of his 150th birthday jubilee in May 2001. In this context the question raised again of the relationship between "Protestantism and culture" is motivated by the basic position of apologetics of scientific theology in relation to a society that seems to have an ever-decreasing requirement for this theology. The existential crisis of institutions that through this are also threatened with the loss of their link to society is a further reason for the fresh interest in Harnack and his work. Whether there will really be a heightened new reception of the work of Adolf von Harnack remains to be seen.

References and Further Reading

Primary Sources:

Harnack, Adolf. *Lehrbuch der Dogmengeschichte.* Tübingen, Germany: J. C. B. Mohr, 1931.
———. *Entstehung und Entwicklung der Kirchenverfassung und des Kirchenrechts.* Leipzig: 1910; reprint Darmstadt: 1980.
———. *Die Mission und die Ausbreitung des Christentums in den ersten drei Jahrhunderten.* Wiesbaden, Germany: VMA-Verlag, 1924.
———. *Geschichte der altchristlichen Literatur bis Eusebius.* Leipzig: J. C. Hinrichs, 1893–1904.
———. *Marcion. Das Evangelium vom fremden Gott.* Leipzig: J. C. Hinrichs, 1924; reprint Darmstadt, Germany, 1960.
———. *Das Wesen des Christentums.* [Lecture, 1900]. Gütersloh, Germany: Gütersloher Verlagshaus, 1977.
———. *Protokollbuch der Kirchenväter-Kommission der Preußischen Akademie der Wissenschaften 1897–1928.* Edited by Christoph Markschies. Berlin/New York: Walter de Gruyter, 2000.
———. *Reden und Aufsätze.* Edited by Ulrich Volp. Mandelbachtal-Cambride: Edition Cicero, 2001.
Harnack, Adolf von. *The Apostles' Creed.* London, A. and C. Black, 1901.
———. *Essays on the Social Gospel.* London, Williams & Norgate; New York, G. P. Putnam's, 1907.
———. *History of Dogma,* 7 vols. London, Williams & Norgate, 1896–99.
———. *History of Dogma.* New York, Dover Publications, 1961.
———. *The Mission and Expansion of Christianity in the First Three Centuries,* London, Williams and Norgate; New York, G. P. Putnam's sons, 1908.
———. *What is Christianity?* Lectures delivered in the University of Berlin during the winter-term 1899–1900, New York, G. P. Putnam's sons; London, Williams and Norgate, 1901.
———. *Thoughts on the Present Position of Protestantism,* London, A. & C. Black, 1899.

Secondary Sources:

Glick, G. Wayne. *The Reality of Christianity.* New York: Harper & Row, 1967.
Hübner, Thomas. *Adolf von Harnacks Vorlesungen über das Wesen des Christentums.* Frankfurt: Peter Lang, 1994.
Kantzenbach, Friedrich Wilhelm. "Adolf von Harnack." In *Theologische Realenzyklopädie (TRE),* edited by Gerhard Krause, vol. 33, 450–458. Berlin: Walter de Gruyter, 1985.
———. "Adolf von Harnack—Das Wesen des Christentums." In *Programme der Theologie.* Munich, 1978.
Kinzig, Wolfram. "Harnack heute. Neuere Forschungen zu seiner Biographie und dem 'Wesen des Christentums.'" *Theologische Literaturzeitung* 126 (2001): 473–500.
Niebuhr, H. Richard. *Christ and Culture.* New York: Harper & Row, 1951.
Pauck, Wilhelm. *Two Historical Theologians.* New York: Oxford University Press, 1968.
Sykes, Stephen. *The Identity of Christianity. Theologians and the Essence of Christianity from Schleiermacher to Barth.* London: SPCK, 1984.

ANDREAS MÜHLING

HARRIS, WILLIAM WADÉ
(c. 1860–1929)

African churchman. Harris was born at Half Graway, Liberia, circa 1860, and died at Harper, Liberia on June 23, 1929. He belonged to the Grebo people of LIBERIA. Brought up by a Methodist uncle, Harris became a catechist and teacher for the Episcopal Church. In 1910, while in prison for sedition, he had a vision in which Gabriel called him to fulfill all the commands of Matthew 28:19. On his release, he preached and baptized in his home area. In 1913, following the death of his wife, he set off "into all the world."

With two female companions, Harris walked the whole breadth of the Ivory Coast (then a French colony) where missions, almost all Catholic, were new, and then into the western Gold Coast. The women sang praises to God, drawing a crowd; Harris, after explaining his mission to the chief, preached, and baptized those who responded. His message centered on repentance, turning to God, complete abandonment of other divinities and all traditional cult objects or fetishes, and on SALVATION through Christ, who was returning as judge. The PREACHING was reinforced by healings (see FAITH HEALING), demonstrations of spiritual power, and triumphant confrontations with traditional priests (and occasionally with colonial officials and Catholic priests, if these tried to obstruct his work). A huge movement to Christianity resulted. In the 18 months before the French deported him to Liberia, Harris baptized an estimated 100,000 people in the Ivory Coast, and perhaps 10,000 (including JOSEPH CASELEY-HAYFORD) in the Gold Coast. He formed worshiping congregations, appointed leaders, offered rudimentary teaching based on the Ten Commandments, left Bibles, and urged his hearers to accept teaching from missions as this became available.

In the 1920s Harris agreed that the British Methodist mission should assume care of the Ivory Coast congregations, but he seems to have regretted this later, being increasingly disillusioned with mission teaching and practice on MARRIAGE and on money. He consecrated John Ahui as his representative. Independent *eglises Harristes* still flourish.

Harris died in Harper, Liberia on June 23, 1929, but he is the seminal figure for all forms of Ivory Coast Christianity. He was also the first and most remarkable of the African charismatic figures who, independently of the missions, led mass movements toward Christianity in the period from about 1913 to 1935.

See also Africa; African Instituted Churches; Colonialism; Missionary Organizations; Missions

References and Further Reading

Haliburton, G. M. *The Prophet Harris*. London: Longman, 1971.
Shank, David A. *Prophet Harris, the "Black Elijah" of West Africa*. Leiden, The Netherlands: Brill, 1994.
Walker, Sheila S. *The Religious Revolution in the Ivory Coast*. Chapel Hill, NC: University of North Carolina Press, 1983.

ANDREW F. WALLS

HARTSHORNE, CHARLES (1897–2000)

American philosopher and theologian. Hartshorne was born on June 5, 1897 in Kittanning, Pennsylvania, the son of an Episcopalian minister. He attended Haverford College between 1915 and 1917 before serving as a medical orderly in the United States military. Returning to academia to complete his A.B., A.M., and Ph.D. at Harvard University by 1923, Hartshorne went on to accept a Sheldon Travelling Fellowship to Germany, where he attended lectures by Martin Heidegger and Edmund Husserl. He returned to Harvard between 1925 and 1928, as an instructor and Research Fellow, assisting Alfred North Whitehead for one semester and also, with Paul Weiss, editing the collected papers of Charles Sanders Pierce. The works of Whitehead and Pierce were to have far-reaching influences on Hartshorne's own philosophical thought, leading to his consequential conception of God as subject to the processes of time and change. In 1928, Hartshorne accepted a post at the Department of Philosophy of the University of Chicago where, in due time, he received a joint position in the Divinity School. He remained teaching at Chicago until 1955, then moved to professorships at Emory University (1955–1962) and the University of Texas at Austin (1962–1976). He died on October 9, 2000.

Hartshorne was a prominent advocate for what came to be known as process philosophy. His written works include: *Man's Vision of God and the Logic of Theism* (1941), *The Divine Relativity: A Social Conception of God* (1948), and *Aquinas to Whitehead: Seven Centuries of Metaphysics of Religion* (1976). Identifying his own thought as principally philosophy rather than theology, Hartshorne argued against the classical theistic understanding of God as omnipotent, omniscient, and immutable. Instead, he maintained that God's perfection consists precisely in the ability to respond to change. A defender of Anselm's famous ontological argument, in a period when the rationality of theism had become vilified within the academy, Hartshorne sought to demonstrate that the so-called philosophical "proofs" for the existence of God—the ontological, teleological, and cosmological arguments—jointly reinforce the claims of one another.

References and Further Reading

Primary Sources:

Aquinas to Whitehead: Seven Centuries of Metaphysics of Religion. The Aquinas Lecture, 1976. Milwaukee: Marquette University Publications, 1976.
The Divine Relativity: A Social Conception of God. The Terry Lectures, 1947. New Haven: Yale University Press, 1948.
Man's Vision of God and the Logic of Theism. Chicago: Willett, Clark & Company, 1941. Reprint, Hamden, CT: Archon Books, 1964.

Secondary Sources:

Cobb, John and Franklin Gamwell, eds. *Existence and Actuality: Conversations with Charles Hartshorne*. Chicago: University of Chicago Press, 1984.
Hahn, Lewis, ed. *The Philosophy of Charles Hartshorne*. LaSalle, IL: Open Court, 1991.

KATHRYN BEVIS

HASTINGS, LADY SELINA (1707–1791)

English evangelical leader. Born August 24, 1707, the second daughter of Earl Ferres, she married Theophilus Hastings, ninth earl of Huntingdon in 1728 and bore him four children. Through the influence of her sisters Betty and Margaret she became acquainted with the work of the Methodists in the first wave of religious revival in England and was converted in 1739. By 1748 she had transferred her attention to GEORGE WHITEFIELD's Calvinistic variety of METHODISM rather than the ARMINIANISM of JOHN and CHARLES WESLEY, although she retained their friendship. She helped a number of men receive ordination and employed them as her chaplains until the church authorities refused to allow this spirit of independence. She had particular links with Thomas Haweis and her cousin, Walter Shirley, notable evangelical clergymen, and was a friend of Toplady and Dodderidge.

She built some chapels and acquired others in what became known as the "Lady Huntingdon's Connexion," by 1791 in an association numbering twenty-three districts and over sixty chapels, located in fashionable spa towns and cathedral cities such as Brighton, Bath, Chichester, and Worcester.

The doctrinal basis of the association was the *Fifteen Articles,* a selection of the THIRTY-NINE ARTICLES of the CHURCH OF ENGLAND. In 1768, after the expulsion of evangelical students from Oxford, she opened a College at Trefeca, WALES, as an academy for preachers. John Fletcher was its first president, but he resigned in 1771 over the renewed debate between Calvinists and Arminians, as did Joseph Benson. On the death of George Whitefield she took over responsibility for the Bethesda Orphan House in Georgia but this burnt down. Lady Selina died June 17, 1791 at her home in Spa Fields, London and was buried at Donington Park.

See also Calvinism; Evangelicalism

References and Further Reading

Welch, Edwin. *Spiritual Pilgrim.* Cardiff: University of Wales Press, 1995.

TIM MACQUIBAN

HAUGE, HANS NIELSEN (1771–1824)

Norwegian lay preacher. Hauge was born into a farmer family in the agrarian community of Rolvsøy in what was then the kingdom of DENMARK and NORWAY. In 1796, as he walked in the fields, he experienced a special calling from God to preach and to urge his fellow countrymen to conversion and a different lifestyle. This sparked the first thorough revival movement in Norway, called Haugianism, which dominated religious life of the country during the first half of the nineteenth century. Hauge, firmly rooted in the country's Lutheran tradition, emphasized a personally experienced salvation and a puritan way of life stressing the importance of inner-worldly vocational work. His followers were, to a great extent, industrious people who took part in the modernization of the Norwegian economy. Hauge himself was arrested in 1804 as preaching gatherings were prohibited by law for those who were not ordained. In 1809 he was temporarily released in order to assist in alleviating the country's serious economic problems following the Napoleonic wars. In 1813 he was finally sentenced to pay a fine of 1,000 *riksdaler* for ignoring the prohibition on lay preaching. Hauge continued to urge people to remain within the Lutheran state church and to pay respect to the clergy. His own activity, however, gradually changed into maintaining his religious network and caring for his economic activities.

Haugianism came to lay a foundation for Norwegian religious life both in Norway and among Norwegian emigrants in North America, its importance being of both a religious and an economic nature. A Lutheran-formed and serious-minded religious outlook combined with a puritan lifestyle characterized his followers. Toward the second half of the century, Haugianism was increasingly contested by more evangelically oriented revival movements, but Hauge's influence is still the most important single contribution to Norwegian religious life after the REFORMATION.

References and Further Reading:

Kullerud, Dag. *Hans Nielsen Hauge: Mannen som vekket Norge.* Oslo: Forum Aschehoug. 1996.
Shaw, Joseph M. *Pulpit Under the Sky: A Life of Hans Nielsen Hauge.* Reprint, Minneapolis: Greenwood Press, 1955.

JON P. KNUDSEN

HAYFORD, JOSEPH EPHRAIM CASELY (1866–1930)

African writer. Born to the family of a Ghanaian Methodist minister on September 28, 1866, Casely Hayford became a successful writer, journalist, politician, and lawyer. His greatest contribution to Protestantism was his positive appraisal of the life and ministry of the West African prophet WILLIAM WADÉ HARRIS, one of the leaders in the AFRICAN INSTITUTED CHURCHES movement.

As a lawyer Casely Hayford worked with Aborigines Rights Protection Society against the Lands Bill of 1897, to preserve the African land tenure system. As a politician Casely Hayford served as a member of the Legislative Council from 1916 until 1930. He was the moving force behind the founding of the National Congress of British West Africa, and the Gold Coast Youth Conference, precursors to Ghana's political parties.

As a journalist he wrote articles arguing racial equality and the need for representation of Africans at the highest levels of administration of their affairs. His novel *Ethiopia Unbound* (1911) was one of the first texts of modern fiction produced in English in West Africa. A vigorous defense of black people, the work was also critical of Christianity as a mainly white religion.

As an educational reformer, he helped establish Achimota College in 1927, which was a precursor to the establishment of the University College of the Gold Coast in 1961.

With his interest in the life of Wadé Harris, Casely Hayford was a pioneer scholar in African Independency. His controversial portrayal of Harris as a legitimate prophet was one of the earliest triumphs of the African Christian Independency movement.

Casely Hayford died August 11, 1930.

See also Africa

References and Further Reading

Primary Sources:

Hayford Casely, J. E. *Ethiopia Unbound.* London: Cass Library of African Studies, 1974.
———. *West African Leadership: Public Speeches Delivered by J. E. Casely Hayford.* London: Arthur Stockwell, 1949.
———. *William Waddy Harris: The West African Reformer, the Man and His Message.* United West Africa, 1915; London, C. M. Phillips, 1915.

Secondary Sources:

Kimble, David. *A Political History of Ghana, 1850–1928.* London: Oxford University Press, 1963.
Sampson, Magnus J. *Gold Coast Men of Affairs.* London: Dawsons of Pall Mall, 1937.

CASELY B. ESSAMUAH

HEAVEN AND HELL

At the outset of the Protestant REFORMATION, the AUGSBURG CONFESSION (1530) affirmed biblical and traditional views of heaven and hell; since then views have varied dramatically among denominations, congregations, and even individuals. Views now range in a spectrum from a physical, "literal heaven" to no heaven at all. As for hell, beliefs are even more spongy, with a definite tendency, except among evangelicals, to ignore it.

Overview

The Bible affirms the reality of both heaven and hell. The Lord's Prayer itself addresses a "Father in heaven" and prays that his will be done "on earth as it is in heaven." The New Testament can scarcely be understood without reference to the kingdom of God as a radical change from our present lives. The range of interpretations of biblical passages is vast. At one extreme they are taken as physical statements about physical reality; at the other they are dismissed as superstitious errors on the part of Jesus and the biblical writers; in between, a huge variety of metaphorical interpretations exist. In Protestantism in the West during the past three centuries the tendency has been in the direction of the extremes; many non-Western societies, however, offer a rich and vivid sense of heaven. This article can mention only some of the deepest questions and a few alternatives.

What Are Heaven and Hell?

Are heaven and hell the "afterlife" or "eternal life"? That is, do we live on in time after the end of our earthly lives, or are our whole lives subsumed in God's eternity? What is it in us that lives eternally? Do we become one with God as a raindrop does with the sea, or does our essence live on, or our personality, or our body? Usually it is believed that the soul or character lives on, but the Bible and tradition give no precise idea of what the Greek *pneuma*, soul or spirit means, and Paul speaks of a *soma pneumatikon* (soul-body or spiritual body). Two quite different strands run through Protestantism: the immortality of the soul (which derives from Greek philosophy) and the biblical idea of bodily resurrection. The apostle Paul declared that there was no point in a Christianity that did not affirm the physical resurrection.

The kingdom of God (*basileia tou theou*) is a main theme of the New Testament. It is clear that Christ is our ruler: a *basileus,* emperor had connotations of majesty and power almost inconceivable in the twenty-first century. Sometimes the kingdom seems to be among us now or "in our hands"; sometimes on this earth now or at the end of time, sometimes in some more divine state of existence such as "heaven." The New Testament envisions a radical change that will soon occur at the end of time or last days (*ta eschata*) and will radically transform the world. Christ's first coming was incarnate as Jesus born of Mary, and Christ will come a second time to complete the transformation of the cosmos. The world may come to an end with the last judgment and the final destruction of evil at that time; after the judgment, time may disappear, or Christ may reign a thousand years before finally eliminating all space and time. The Last Judgment is often contrasted with the personal judgment that each person faces at the end of life, but almost all Protestants believe that the last merely confirms the personal judgment: God does not change his mind in the meantime. But then where is the soul between the time of our personal death and the general resurrection at the end of time? Protestants have all eschewed the Catholic idea of purgatory, so that opinion varies from the soul's being in some sort of interim state before rejoining its body to a view that at our death we are lifted from time into eternity, the moment of our death being also the moment of our resurrection. Some, particularly nineteenth-century pietists, believed that the souls are with us as our companions.

Both time and space are problematic: where are heaven and hell? Early Protestant views were in line with previous Christian ones that the earth was a sphere at the center of the cosmos, with hell inside of it, and heaven beyond all the spheres of moon, sun, and stars. Such views became untenable and unnecessary with the discoveries of modern astronomy, since which most educated Protestants believe that heaven (and hell) are not "out there" anywhere in the physical cosmos but in another mode of being entirely, sometimes within us, sometimes in another spiritual dimension.

What does heaven mean? Is it a radical change and transformation to something far beyond our experience? Are we made perfect by union with God, by our fulfillment as individuals, or as the perfection of community? Does it mean that we are absorbed into God, or that we encounter him intensely face to face, or that we are fulfilled to our utmost perfection as individuals? If it is the last, how old will we be, and in what state of mind or body? Will we feel ourselves "individuals" at all, recognizing our families and friends as our own? Will we be so bound to one another in love that heaven is more a realization of community than of self? If the point of life is to love God and neighbor, is heaven the fulfillment of that love to the point that differences dissolve in a more perfect union? If heaven is a community, on what level do we feel that community—our families and friends, our congregation, our geographical community, the whole earth, or the whole cosmos? Is everyone equal in heaven or are some closer to God, some deeper in love, than others? John Calvin made it clear that whatever differences in earthly station and authority exist between us, they will not exist in heaven, where the only ruler is Christ.

Does perfection in heaven mean stasis or a dynamic motion to ever more perfect perfection? Will we be in an eternal state of unchanging glory or will we continue to know more, feel more, love more, even serve more? Sixteenth-century reformers tended to see heaven as an eternal moment of praise and adoration of God; many nineteenth-century pietists believed that if salvation was achieved through good works, then surely good works (service to God and others) must continue in the other life.

Going to Heaven or Hell

How does one go to heaven or hell? Better put, how does one come to be in the state of soul and character that is heaven or hell? Does this occur by complete predestination, where God eternally determines which persons are in which state, by human free will to choose, or by God's foreknowledge that our free choice sometimes chooses hell? In complete predestination, God damns to eternal hell those whom he does not choose to save; in other views, damnation is our own free choice to live in an evil state. Is divine grace the source of our salvation, as the original reformers insisted, or are works the source, as nineteenth- and

twentieth-century pietists believed? The pietists placed an unusually strong emphasis on the reward and punishment aspect of the afterlife: if you choose to do good works, you will be saved. A quite different position among sixteenth-century radicals, and recently gaining great popularity among liberal Protestants, is universalism, the theology that everyone is saved and everything is purified and redeemed at the end. Very rare, however, has been any view that you can change your mind after you die; rather, this is the life that God gives us and in this life we eternally form our character.

Biblical descriptions of heaven are lavish with music, gems, gold, light, brilliance; descriptions of hell describe fire, sulfur, torture, and darkness. Some Protestants, perhaps not realizing that in thinking about heaven and hell we are limited by human imagination and words in trying to understand what is beyond all our capacities to know, take these descriptions as physical truth. From the beginning of Christianity, all sorts of details (woods, fountains, dancing, and so on) have been added, particularly by groups such as the Latter-Day Saints, whose heaven is extremely physical. The physicality of heaven derives not only from the specific biblical descriptions but also from the biblical doctrine of resurrection. We rise in our bodies (however transcended); that concept has continually raised questions of food and sex, as well as other bodily functions. More abstractly inclined Protestants are content with the idea that heaven is essentially the full presence of everyone and everything transfused by God and without defect, while hell is the state of absence of all these qualities. In most views, heaven is a place that is dynamic rather than static, so that it must have some sort of real metaphorical time, for metaphor does not mean distance from reality.

References and Further Reading:

Bernstein, Alan. *The Formation of Hell.* Ithaca, NY: Cornell University Press, 1993.
McDannell, Colleen, and Bernhard Lang. *Heaven: A History.* New Haven, CT: Yale University Press, 1988.
Russell, Jeffrey Burton. *A History of Heaven.* Princeton, NJ: Princeton University Press, 1997.
Zaleski, Carol, and Philip Zaleski, *The Book of Heaven.* Oxford: Oxford University Press, 2000.

JEFFREY BURTON RUSSELL

HEGEL, GEORG WILHELM FRIEDRICH (1770–1831)

German philosopher. Georg Wilhelm Friedrich Hegel was born on August 27, 1770, in Stuttgart, Germany. His father was an administrative official in the Württemberg ducal bureaucracy. Hegel attended the Prot-

851

estant seminary (*Stift*) at Tübingen for five years beginning in 1788, most likely with plans to enter either the clergy or the civil service. On graduation from Tübingen he worked as a private tutor in Bern (1793–1796) and Frankfurt (1797–1800). His father died in 1799, leaving Hegel an inheritance that allowed him to pursue what had in the meantime become his chief interest, philosophy. In 1801 he secured a teaching position at Jena and taught there until 1806. FRIEDRICH W. J. VON SCHELLING (1775–1854) was teaching there as well and the two collaborated on the *Kritisches Journal der Philosophie* (*Critical Journal of Philosophy*) until Schelling departed Jena in 1803. In 1801 Hegel published a book on the difference between Johann G. Fichte and Schelling. As a result of their collaboration on the *Critical Journal* and the 1801 book Hegel was publicly regarded as a disciple of Schelling; however, in 1807 Hegel published *Phänomenologie des Geistes* (*Phenomenology of Spirit*), which marked an intellectual and personal break with Schelling and set Hegel on the path of becoming one of the premier philosophers of Germany.

In late 1806 Hegel lost his position at Jena when the university was shut down in the wake of the Battle of Jena. From 1807 until 1808 he supported himself by editing a newspaper in Bamberg. From 1808 until 1816 he was rector of and professor at a gymnasium (i.e., school) in Nuremberg. While at Nuremberg he published the *Science of Logic* (volume one in 1811–1812; volume two in 1816). He married in 1811. From 1816 until 1818 he was a professor at Heidelberg. There he published, in 1817, *Enzyklopädie der Philosophischen Wissenschaften* (*Encyclopedia of the Philosophical Sciences in Outline*), his "system." From 1818 until his death, on November 14, 1831 (from cholera), he was a professor in the philosophical faculty in Berlin. During his Berlin years Hegel published only one new book, *Grundlinien der Philosophie des Rechts* (*Outlines of the Philosophy of Right* 1821). However, he also prepared second and third editions of the *Encyclopedia* (1827 and 1830) and at the time of his death was nearly finished with a second edition of the *Wissenschaft der Logik* (*Science of Logic*). After his death, his lectures on the philosophy of history, history of philosophy, philosophy of religion, and philosophy of art were published by his followers.

Hegel in Context

To grasp Hegel's relation to and importance for Protestant thought, it is necessary to see him in his intellectual and political context. Hegel's era was a time of heightened theological tension. In the previous generation Christian theology had been shaken to its roots by the combination of historical criticism of the BIBLE and creeds and by rationalism. In addition the 1780s witnessed the so-called pantheism controversy, when Friedrich H. Jacobi published his account of conversations he had had with GOTTHOLD E. LESSING. In this account he revealed Lessing's sympathies with Benedict Spinoza, who was commonly thought to have been a pantheist. Lessing's declaration seemed to be an endorsement of this pantheism. A decade later Johann Fichte was forced to resign his professorship at Jena because of accusations that his philosophy supported atheism. In Hegel's day most theological responses to these issues took one of three forms. First, there was a resurgence of confessional ORTHODOXY, buttressed by the support of a militant and doctrinally conservative PIETISM and emphasizing a traditional conception of the supernatual. Leading representatives included FRIEDRICH A. G. THOLUCK and Ernst W. Hengstenberg. Second, there was an accommodation to the deistic critique of Christianity (see DEISM). This resulted in a rationalistic and reductionistic form of theology in which the supernatural was largely if not totally eliminated. Julius A. L. Wegscheider and Karl G. Bretschneider represented this option. Third, there was an attempt to rethink theology in the light of romantic impulses. In practice this meant reinterpreting doctrines as verbal expressions of a noncognitive intuition of God. FRIEDRICH SCHLEIERMACHER was the outstanding representative of this tendency. The theological tensions were exacerbated by related political issues. Hegel's adult life spanned a revolutionary era, from the beginnings of the French revolution in 1789 to the European-wide uprisings in 1830. For the most part, these revolutionary movements aimed at introducing liberal-democratic reforms, which Hegel supported. Between these revolutions stood the reactionary Congress of Vienna (1815) that, upon the final defeat of Napoleon, restored to power the feudal aristocracies that had been dethroned as a result of Napoleonic reforms. The result of this political ferment in the Germany of Hegel's day was an increasingly conservative political climate that sought to return to the union of CHURCH AND STATE that characterized the prerevolutionary era. The effect was a renewed emphasis on orthodox theology and on the suppression of politically dangerous ideas. These trends meant trouble for Hegel in particular because he supported and was supported by the liberal reformers of politics, church, and education who increasingly found themselves out of step with the aristocratic power structure (see LIBERAL PROTESTANTISM AND LIBERALISM).

Although Hegel proposed a philosophical resolution to the theological problems of the day, he believed that his philosophy was nonetheless grounded in the central tenets of Lutheran theology. This conviction is illustrated by an event in 1826. In the course of a lecture, Hegel made some disparaging remarks about the Roman Catholic doctrine of the Eucharist (see LORD'S SUPPER). Called to account by the educational authorities Hegel responded in a letter that justified his views on the basis of their faithfulness to Lutheran theology. Further, he declared his pride in having been baptized and raised a Lutheran and professed his intent to remain one. That Hegel's remarks were not merely defensive posturing to avoid trouble can be seen from his affirmative remarks about LUTHERANISM and, more generally, Protestantism in his lectures on the philosophy of history and the history of philosophy.

However, in spite of his professed loyalty to and admiration of the Lutheran tradition, Hegel did not present his philosophy as simply a restatement of that tradition's theology. On the contrary, the relation between theology and Hegel's philosophy is complex and subtle. On the one hand he believed that Christian DOCTRINE is based on revelation and contains the truth about God. The content of theology and philosophy is the same, that is, the truth. On the other hand, he held that there are grave problems with the usual exposition of these doctrines, which conveys the true content of religion in a highly unsuitable and misleading form. The key to grasping Hegel's view is to understand the distinction he made between conceptual thinking (*begreifen*) and imaginative thinking (*vorstellen*) in theology.

Imaginative thinking is the typical form in which theological doctrine presents its subject matter. Although it is a genuine form of thought, in it we think by means of images drawn from sensation. For example, the doctrine of the Trinity employs the familial relation between father and son. In this case, the eternal divine life is portrayed with images drawn from daily experience. However, these images are wholly inadequate to the task of knowing the truth. The only possibility for obtaining knowledge, he believed, was to give doctrine a scientific form attained through pure conceptual thinking, that is, through philosophy.

Hegelian Dialectics

To understand why only conceptual thinking provides the adequate form for truth, it is necessary to come terms with Hegel's view of dialectics. Hegel was convinced that actuality is marked by movement that embraces unity and diversity. Organic life, for instance, is a process whereby a seed becomes a plant. There is a dialectical relation between the seed and the plant because although they are in an important sense

distinct, there is also an important sense in which they are one. The oneness consists in the fact that seed and plant are two steps in a movement that encompasses them both. In our ordinary thinking we distinguish the seed from the plant as two things; that is, we focus on the distinction between the two. However, we miss the underlying movement (seed to plant) that is their unity and, if we think dialectically (i.e., conceptually), then we grasp the unity as well as the distinctions (seed, plant as well as the movement of seed to plant). Conceptual thinking is therefore itself a dialectical movement. In conceptual thinking we think according to the pattern of actuality. In it, the form of our thinking is identical with the form of actual being. In ordinary understanding and imaginative thinking, however, the form of our thinking does not match the form of actuality and therefore is inadequate to the truth.

What is true of organic life is true of all actualities, including God. (Hegel typically wrote of absolute spirit and not God. God is not identical to absolute spirit in Hegel's philosophy; however, for the sake of exposition, "God" will be used.) The eternal divine life is a dialectical movement. The doctrine of the Trinity, with its affirmation of relations of origin among Father, Son, and Spirit, is a theological statement of that dialectical movement. Accordingly, the doctrine of the Trinity possesses the truth about God. Unfortunately theologians employ imaginative thinking and not conceptual thinking when they expound the doctrine. Just as, in the case of seed and plant, ordinary understanding puts the emphasis on distinctions and misses the movement that is the unity, so in the case of the Trinity theologians normally emphasize the distinctions of the Trinitarian persons (insofar as they regard them as individually existent personal beings) and miss the dialectical and unifying movement that encompasses the persons. So, although the doctrine of the Trinity contains the truth about God, its theological exposition has always been wholly inadequate. An adequate form for this doctrine requires conceptual thinking. Only this form of thinking is identical with the dialectical character of the divine life and can be said to state the truth in a scientific form.

Hegel's views about conceptual thinking help explain his irritation with the theological tendencies of his day. Although sympathetic with the rational approach of the ENLIGHTENMENT, Hegel scorned the proclivity of rationalistic theologians to reject doctrines such as the Trinity because of their supposedly irrational character. In doing so, Hegel charged, they were emptying religion of all content and thus forsaking the truth. They could do so only because the reasoning they employed was not conceptual thinking but instead merely ordinary understanding. Hegel was likewise dismayed by Schleiermacher (who lectured in the theological faculty at Berlin and with whom Hegel carried on a running public controversy) and the pietistic theologians. By emphasizing feeling and intuition and making them the source of theology, they too had emptied religion of content. In addition they gave the cause of science a bad name by deprecating human reason. Not surprisingly Hegel believed that he was rescuing the truth of religion from the depredations of contemporary theologians. As he once stated, not only was philosophy in his day orthodox—*only* philosophy (i.e., his philosophy) was orthodox.

Responses to Hegel

Hegel's estimate of his own orthodoxy was not universally shared. In particular his tenure in Berlin was marked by charges of pantheism and atheism. The basis of these charges was Hegel's understanding of God's relation to the universe. Hegel understood this relation dialectically. Just as seed and plant are best thought of, not as distinct things, but instead as two aspects of a larger movement, so God and the universe are not distinct entities but are dialectically related. The universe is, in some sense, an aspect of the divine life. God attains actuality through the world-process. Although Hegel was clear that God is not simply identical with the world, the qualified and dialectical identity he affirmed was still too much for conservative theologians.

However, not all theologians were opposed to Hegel. There were two influential theologians in particular who converted to Hegel's views and formed an important part of the Hegelian school of the 1820s and 1830s: PHILIPP MARHEINEKE (1780–1846, professor in Berlin) and Carl Daub (1765–1836, professor in Heidelberg). It was Marheineke who, after Hegel's death, produced the first edition of Hegel's lectures on the philosophy of religion in an attempt to fix Hegel's meaning and settle differences in interpretation. Unfortunately, in the judgment of his peers Marheineke's editorial procedures were deficient; however, a revised edition by BRUNO BAUER also did not settle the disputes. Daub, Marheineke, and, initially, Bauer emphasized the side of Hegel's philosophy that affirmed the identity of content between theology and philosophy. In other words, they were, within the confines of Hegel's school, conservative. A radical application of Hegel's thought to theology emerged after Hegel's death when DAVID F. STRAUSS (1808–1874), LUDWIG FEUERBACH (1804–1872), and others began emphasizing the inadequacy of theology's imaginative thinking. It was the atheistic conclusions of this group that induced the Prussian government to call Schelling to Berlin in 1841 to combat the pernicious effects of Hegel's philosophy. At length it was not Schelling's lectures that diminished the influence of Hegel's philosophy but rather shifting philosophical tendencies as in the next generation Germany experienced the rise of scientific materialism and a revival of interest in IMMANUEL KANT's philosophy. Nonetheless vestiges of Hegel's philosophy can be seen in the work of such contemporary Protestant theologians as JÜRGEN MOLTMANN and WOLFHART PANNENBERG.

References and Further Reading

Primary Sources:

Hegel, Georg Wilhelm Friedrich. *The Difference between Fichte's and Schelling's System of Philosophy.* Translated by H. S. Harris and Walter Cerf. Albany: State University of New York Press, 1977.

———. *Encyclopedia of the Philosophical Sciences in Outline, and Critical Writings.* Edited by Ernst Behler. New York: Continuum, 1990

———. *Lectures on the Philosophy of Religion. Introduction and The Concept of Religion,* vol. 1; *Determinate Religion,* vol. 2; *The Consummate Religion,* vol. 3. Edited by Peter C. Hodgson and translated by R. F. Brown, et al. Berkeley: University of California Press, 1984.

———. *Phenomenology of Spirit.* Translated by A. V. Miller. Oxford, UK: Clarendon Press, 1977.

———. *Philosophy of History.* New York: Dover, 1956.

———. *Hegel, the Letters.* Translated by Clark Butler and Christiane Seiler. Bloomington: Indiana University Press, 1984.

———. *Hegel's Philosophy of Right.* Translated by T. M. Knox. London: Oxford University Press, 1977.

———. *Hegel's Science of Logic.* Translated by W. H. Johnston and L. G. Struthers. London: G. Allen & Unwin Ltd., 1951.

Secondary Sources:

Dickey, Laurence. "Hegel on Religion and Philosophy." In *The Cambridge Companion to Hegel.* Edited by Frederick C. Beiser. Cambridge, UK: Cambridge University Press, 1993.

Hodgson, Peter C. "Hegel's Christology: Shifting Nuances in the Berlin Lectures." *Journal of the American Academy of Religion* 53 no. 1 (1985): 23–40.

Jaeschke, Walter. *Reason in Religion: The Foundations of Hegel's Philosophy of Religion.* Translated by Michael Steward and Peter C. Hodgson. Berkeley: University of California Press, 1990.

Merklinger, Philip M. *Philosophy, Theology, and Hegel's Berlin Philosophy of Religion, 1821–1827.* Albany: State University of New York Press, 1993.

Stepelevich, Lawrence S. "Hegel and Roman Catholicism." *Journal of the American Academy of Religion* 60 (1992): 673–691.

SAMUEL M. POWELL

HEIDELBERG CATECHISM OF 1563

Efforts to introduce the REFORMATION into the Palatinate began late, and their success depended on the cogency of a catechetical document that could avoid the controversies that had embroiled various parties in the early decades of the Reformation. In a region in which Lutheran and Reformed claimed a sympathetic presence, a CATECHISM appealing to both loyalties promised to be the most effective. For a number of reasons, there were far fewer catechisms than confessions in the sixteenth century (see CONFESSION). They were meant for the LAITY and their rudimentary question-and-answer style provided little room for detailed discussion of semantic or doctrinal points. At the same time the simplicity and clarity demanded by the genre guaranteed that the successful catechism would gain broad acceptance indeed.

The Heidelberg Catechism was the work of a committee that included the Wittenberg graduate Zacharius Ursinus (1534–1583), JOHN CALVIN's protégé Caspar Olevian (1536–1587), and members of the THEOLOGY faculty at Heidelberg. They sought to combine the best parts of a number of current catechetical texts, including Calvin's own 1545 GENEVA CATECHISM, a possible model despite the desire of the Palatine prince Frederick III for an instructional manual on biblical foundations that was visibly independent of Genevan influence. The Catechism accomplished several goals: in its simplicity it made the essentials of evangelical faith accessible to all, and it did this with a collage of biblical terms that instilled much of the sacred text into the youthful mind of the reader.

In 129 questions spread out over a cycle of a year of Sundays, divided into three sections on human misery, redemption, and thankfulness, the Catechism offers a succinct summary of evangelical FAITH. Intended for the theologically unsophisticated layperson, it presupposes little knowledge of the BIBLE or of the dogmatic TRADITION. Instead it appeals to the believer's awareness of original SIN; a sense of hopelessness before a righteous deity; and a divinely granted zeal to live a life of holiness, here termed thankfulness. Hence from the first question onward, Jesus Christ is termed a savior and redeemer of a radically sinful humanity, an agent of the Father's redemptive will, whose ATONEMENT for humanity is made certain for the regenerate by the work of the Holy Spirit.

The first part of the Catechism, "On human misery," identifies revealed law as the means to recognize one's sinfulness; the command to love God and neighbor reveals the total extent of original sin. The rudimentary level of discussion called for a simplicity that suggests a more radical stance on many of the positions being articulated than one finds in contemporary confessions. The answers to questions about human sinfulness, for example, state with unequivocal clarity that humanity fell into a state of "hating" God and neighbor (q. 5), not simply being disinclined or impeded in loving them, as lengthier or subtler expositions of faith during these years tended to hold.

The second section, concerning human redemption, similarly presents its affirmations phrased with a sometimes disarming simplicity. Continuity between the faith of the Old Covenant or Testament and the New is underscored in a number of ways. The promise of redemption that constitutes the gospel, for example, is described as having been revealed in Eden and preserved by the patriarchs and prophets, then finally and fully revealed in Jesus Christ.

In addition to filtering a great deal of scriptural language, the Catechism also adopts the terminology of classic creedal statements, ensuring the catechumen's familiarity with part of the ancient tradition. The Nicene Creed in fact provides many of the questions of the second part of the Catechism; many of the questions ask for explanations of individual clauses of the Creed. In keeping with its intention of inclusiveness, the Catechism underscores the communion in Christ of the members of the church. It is Christ who gathers and preserves the members of the true church (q. 54), those who are justified solely by their faith in him (q. 60).

Under the third rubric, thankfulness, the Catechism provides precepts for the life of the regenerate Christian. In keeping with the Reformed doctrine of the role of Law in a life of SANCTIFICATION—that the justified Christian returns to the Law as a guide for a life—this final section is organized around the Decalogue, or Ten Commandments, and the Lord's Prayer, the answers serving as a running commentary to those texts.

The rhetorical simplicity of the Catechism leaves unexplained certain points of DOCTRINE. Regarding the Eucharist (see LORD'S SUPPER), for example, the bread and wine are not said to be transformed into the body and blood of Christ, although they are called that in the customary use of sacramental language (q. 78). Given the intensity of controversies over the Eucharist during these years, such a facile explanation was sure to arouse, rather than quell, discord over the meaning of the terms "body" and "blood." Several departures from contemporary Reformed symbolic documents are notable indications of the Catechism's eclecticism, inclusiveness, or both. The doctrine of PREDESTINATION, also already a topic of intense dispute, is absent; in its place is an affirmation of God's providential care for all creatures (q. 27).

Regardless of its conciliatory intentions, publication of the Catechism brought a flurry of controversy, especially from theologians like the Lutherans Tilemann Heshusius (1527–1559) and MATTHIAS FLACIUS (1520–1575) who saw "ungodliness" and "idolatry" in the use of ALTARS, baptismal fonts, crucifixes, and the like. They urged superintendents to monitor devotional life at the parish level to prevent the restoration of such deviations. It was partially in defense of his work that Ursinus composed a massive *Commentary* to the Catechism, which explained in great detail the positions stated succinctly in the original document. The clarifications of Reformed doctrine in the *Commentary* defined some of the enduring divisions between the Lutheran and Reformed confessions.

See also Calvinism; Lutheranism

References and Further Reading

Cochrane, Arthur C., ed. *Reformed Confessions of the 16th Century.* Philadelphia, PA: Westminster Press, 1966.
Ursinus, Zacharias. *The Commentary on the Heidelberg Catechism.* Translated by G. W. Willard. Grand Rapids, MI: Wm. B. Eerdmans, 1956.
Visser, Derk. *Zacharias Ursinus.* New York: United Church Press, 1983.

RALPH KEEN

HELVETIC CONFESSION

The Second Helvetic Confession (1562) was in one sense the successor to the 1536 document, known as the First Helvetic Confession (sometimes also called the Second Confession of Basel), prepared at Basel under the aegis of HEINRICH BULLINGER (1504–1575) and others. In more important ways, however, it stands with the Reformed confessional enterprise of the 1560s as another effort to consolidate doctrines in dispute and protect the church from internal strife and political threat. The dangers were all too real in the wake of religious wars, the proceedings of the still-sitting Council of Trent, and divisions within LUTHERANISM that threatened to undermine a branch of the REFORMATION that many Swiss Evangelicals still looked to as a model.

Anticipating the end of his active career as a Reformer in Zurich, Bullinger in 1561 began to prepare a "brief exposition" of the faith as a theological last will. The resulting CONFESSION was anything but brief, but it was clear and comprehensive, the mature work of an influential theologian's studies and pastoral experience. It would in time be embraced by churches in the Swiss cantons and beyond; and it earned endorsement in SCOTLAND, Holland, POLAND, Bohemia, and HUNGARY.

Affirming the necessity and sufficiency of scripture as DOCTRINE, and stating that the word of God is the preached word, the Confession acknowledges the guidance of the ancient Fathers in biblical interpretation, while dismissing from the church any purely human traditions, such as the use of images and the hierarchical ordering of clerical ranks. Thus the four christological creeds of the fourth and fifth centuries are accepted as valid confessions of faith, as are "all similar" symbolic documents, their truth being in their faith rather than the AUTHORITY of the assemblies that promulgated them. Ministers are called to the common service, as equals, to the work of PREACHING the word of God, administering the SACRAMENTS, and ensuring order within the church by means of suitable discipline (see CHURCH DISCIPLINE).

The Confession's doctrine of God preserves traces of Bullinger's predecessor, HULDRYCH ZWINGLI, whose Platonist affinities are found, for example, in the definition of God. Without abandoning the more anthropomorphic definitions grounded in biblical depictions of divine activity, the deity of the Second Helvetic Confession is a self-sufficient, eternal and infinite, necessarily (but inexplicably) existing highest good, manifested in three eternally distinct Persons, differentiated by their properties. Predictably, however, the THEOLOGY of the Confession is predominantly shaped by the exegetical tradition and centered on the doctrines of SIN and GRACE. The human condition being one of sin, in which persons freely choose evil, reconciliation through Christ is the only path to God.

As with evangelical confessions generally, the doctrine of JUSTIFICATION is the core teaching here. In chapter 15 of the Confession, faith in Christ is the sole source of righteousness; it is given rather than earned; and it does not imply any sharing in Christ's own righteousness. The believer experiences CONVERSION, and in so doing understands that both conversion and absolution are divine gifts (ch. 14). The regenerate believer remains in a state of sin, but the freedom and temptation to do evil have been weakened, and the experience of grace replaces the condemnation of the law. Despite the insistence on righteousness being only imputed or reckoned, rather than granted or actually bestowed, the regenerate Christian's FAITH is an active one, and the believer is driven to works of piety and charity. Since the beginning of the Reformation opponents had read "faith alone" to mean that mere assent was sufficient for SALVATION. Bullinger takes pains to correct that impression.

The CHURCH, in the words of the Confession, is a truly catholic (or universal) communion of the faithful, although there may be members of a given congregation who are not part of this invisible church. Condemning the claim to "catholicity" of the Roman church, the Confession holds that the universality of the true church is not measured in tangible extent and numbers. Rather the body of true believers may at times be so marginal as to escape notice, and judgment, by the larger population of the unregenerate who may falsely imagine themselves the true church. In the light of continuing controversies and condemnations, identifying the Reformed churches as a minority threatened with persecution helped to brand their opponents as among the reprobate.

Few doctrines were more intractable to mediating efforts than that of the Eucharist (see LORD'S SUPPER), but here Bullinger's conciliatory stance is most evident. Holding, in common with other evangelical confessions, that sacraments consist of a divine word of promise and an outward sign intended to seal and strengthen it, the Confession recognizes only the dominically instituted rites of BAPTISM and Eucharist as sacraments, and denies that they can be made holy by a priestly consecration or are able to communicate holiness to the recipient. Steering a course between the Real Presence of the Roman Catholic and Lutheran churches and the sacramentarianism of Zwingli and others, the Confession holds that the body and blood of Christ are consumed in the Eucharist, but in a spiritual rather than a physical manner. The eating of the bread and drinking of the wine are necessary parts of the rite, but the material elements are mere signs of the spiritual realities that make the Eucharist a sacrament.

The language of COVENANT plays a significant role in the Confession, in part to link the church to the people of the Old Testament. Although two peoples are acknowledged, they are described as being united within a single Messianic fellowship (ch. 17). Likewise, the Confession holds that the sacraments were given to both peoples, insofar as both received a word of promise and external signs to seal the promise, but that the signs of the ancient sacraments were replaced by baptism and the Eucharist. In emphasizing the continuity of the covenantal relationship with God, the Confession contributed to the federal theology of later decades and centuries.

See also Counter-Reformation

References and Further Reading

Cochrane, Arthur C., ed. *Reformed Confessions of the 16th Century.* Philadelphia, PA: Westminster Press, 1966.
Koch, Ernst. *Die Theologie der Confessio Helvetica Posterior.* Neukirchen, Germany: Neu-Kirchener Verlag, 1968.

RALPH KEEN

HENRY VIII (1491–1547)

English king. The second son of Henry VII (1457–1509) and Elizabeth of York, Henry ascended the English throne on his father's death in 1509, his elder brother Arthur having predeceased them in 1502. Physically imposing and intellectually gifted, Henry devoted his early years as king to war, hunting, and the life of the court. He read and spoke several languages, including Latin, and was an able singer and dancer. Although he left the minutiae of government to his ministers (especially Cardinal Wolsey [1475–1530] in the 1510s and 1520s; and THOMAS CROMWELL [1599–1658] in the 1530s), he was always in control. He was initially devoted to his first wife, Catherine of Aragon (1485–1536), but her sad sequence of ill-fated pregnancies (which left only one surviving child, a daughter, Mary Tudor, born in 1516), took its toll on his affections, though for a king he was but moderately unfaithful. Fiscal exhaustion after a decade of intermittent and largely fruitless war with FRANCE (1512–1524), combined with concern for the security of the dynasty in the absence of a male heir, put the succession and domestic policy at the head of his agenda from 1527 until 1540. With the succession secured by the birth of a son, Edward, to his third wife, Jane Seymour (1509–1537), in 1537, he was able to relive his youthful pursuit of glory in the 1540s with invasions of both SCOTLAND and France. There were no further children from his subsequent marriages, in which he experienced disappointment with Anne of Cleves (1515–1557) and betrayal with Catherine Howard (1520–1542), before finding contentment in old age with Catherine Parr (1512–1548).

Henry VIII and Protestantism

Henry VIII was no Protestant—a word that was barely entering the English language when he died in 1547, and was, in any case, hardly applicable to him. Zealous, if conventional, in his piety (he often heard several masses a day, especially when not hunting), he always took an educated interest in theology. Preachers of the highest caliber were summoned to his court, and throughout his life he enjoyed theological discussion with scholars such as John Colet (1466–1519), Thomas More (1478–1535), and HUGH LATIMER (1485–1555). His theological awareness led him to challenge MARTIN LUTHER'S (1483–1546) *Babylonian Captivity of the Church* with a refutation, the *Assertio Septem Sacramentorum* (Assertion of the Seven Sacraments) published in 1521. Henry was thus one of Luther's earliest opponents, and he mobilized the scholars of England in the same cause, with John Fisher (1469–1535) and Thomas More the best known of those who wrote against the early Protestants at his behest. Henry's book (not entirely his unaided work, with Thomas More generally mentioned) was stylishly written, but held few surprises. It barely even touched on justification by faith alone, concentrating instead on the eucharist and the sacrifice of the mass, which always remained close to his heart. Luther's vitriolic reply left Henry with an abiding hatred of the German Reformer.

Although REFORMATION doctrines made some headway in ENGLAND in the early 1520s, mostly through the circulation of Latin works in educated circles, it was not until William Tyndale (1495–1536) published an English New Testament in 1525 that combating Protestantism at home became a pressing concern for Henry's government. Concern was heightened by the discovery of a suspected Protestant, Robert Barnes, at Cambridge University, and Henry appointed John Fisher to preach at his recantation in February 1526. Tyndale's first edition was mostly intercepted and burned (only two copies survive), but aided by sympathizers among the wealthy London merchants, he went on publishing and distributing his New Testament and began producing pamphlets advocating Protestant ideas. Henry's bishops began to find Protestants in their dioceses (scholars and clerics at first, but from about 1530 layfolk also), and Thomas More famously wrote against the new doctrines in English. When Henry appointed him Lord Chancellor in 1529, government action against Protestants intensified. Thomas More was personally involved in prosecutions, and in 1530 helped Henry and his bishops draft proclamations banning a growing list of dissident publications. Tudor justice was harsh, and the first of many Protestants to be executed in England under Henry was Thomas Hitton, burned at Maidstone in 1530 (the penalty of burning was already in force for the native heresy of Lollardy).

The fortunes of English Protestantism changed in the 1530s because of the king's need to separate from his first wife and remarry in the hope of begetting a male heir. Because ITALY was dominated by Emperor Charles V, Catherine of Aragon's nephew, it was impossible for Pope Clement VII (1478–1534) to grant the annulment of the marriage sought by Henry. In the early 1530s Henry began to consider unilateral action. He bullied the English clergy into supporting him, forcing them first to recognize him as their supreme head (which they grudgingly admitted in 1531 "as far as the law of Christ allows") and then to concede him a veto over ecclesiastical legislation (1532). This move led to the resignation of Thomas More, which took some of the edge off the English persecution of Protestants (although the bishop of London, John Stokesley, carried on the fight). What gradually improved conditions for Protestantism in England was the influence on the king of three people at the heart of "the king's great matter": Anne Boleyn (1504–1536), whom he married around January 1533; Thomas Cromwell, who emerged as the king's leading adviser in these years and masterminded the separation; and THOMAS CRANMER (1489–1556), who in 1532 was recalled from Nuremberg (where he had been ambassador to Charles V) to be the new arch-

bishop of Canterbury, and who actually granted the "divorce" in April 1533. All three were, to varying degrees, interested in what at the time was often called the "new learning."

The break with Rome, which sealed Henry's separation from Catherine and remarriage, was enacted in a series of laws, most importantly the Act of Supremacy (1534), which recognized Henry in unqualified terms as the "Supreme Head on Earth under Christ of the Church of England." This change was implemented through an unprecedented program, of preaching and propaganda, which opened the door to Protestant influence. Even during the campaign for the divorce, Henry's government had canvassed support from English Protestant scholars who had fled abroad, such as Tyndale and Barnes. Now, the most enthusiastic preachers and writers against the papacy were precisely those who were attracted to evangelical doctrine: men such as Hugh Latimer and Nicholas Shaxton (chaplains to Anne Boleyn), Thomas Swynnerton, and Thomas Garrett. Shaxton and Latimer soon became bishops, and it is noteworthy that during Anne's three years as queen, all but one of the nine men made bishops were identifiably evangelical in their sympathies. Despite Anne's fall in 1536, Cromwell and Cranmer continued to nudge Henry in a Protestant direction. Cromwell certainly saw the potential of the Protestant Reformation for consolidating the royal supremacy. Lutheran themes of political obedience, first introduced to an English public by William Tyndale, were taken over wholesale by the CHURCH OF ENGLAND. In 1535 and 1536 there was talk of PHILIPP MELANCHTHON (1497–1560) coming to England, and from then until 1538 the English government carried on negotiations for a political and theological alliance with the Schmalkaldic League.

Although Henry's hatred for Luther was undiminished, conditions for evangelicals improved. The stringent heresy laws were relaxed in 1534, and for some years no moderate evangelical Protestants were burned in England. Most importantly, official policy against permitting the Bible in English was gradually reversed. Cranmer was lobbying Henry VIII for this as early as 1534. Miles Coverdale's (1487–1569) first complete English Bible, printed abroad in 1535, was dedicated to Henry in real hope. In 1536 the first royal injunctions for the Church of England instructed parishes to obtain an English Bible, a message endorsed by the second injunctions of 1538. By this time an officially sanctioned version was in print, and 1539 saw the publication of Henry VIII's "Great Bible," with a programmatic Holbein woodcut on the title-page depicting the king handing down God's word to his grateful people. Cromwell was given a monopoly license to enable him to control the Bible business, and during his ascendancy Protestant books were, for the first time, printed in England. Indeed, the AUGSBURG CONFESSION was translated and printed in 1536 with a dedication to Cromwell himself. The translator, Richard Taverner, made his way in royal service under Cromwell's patronage and a few years later dedicated to Henry a translation of the strongly evangelical *Commonplaces* of Erasmus Sarcerius. Cromwell and Cranmer protected and promoted evangelical preachers, and evangelical notes were even sounded in official statements on doctrine such as the Ten Articles of 1536 and the Bishops' Book of 1537.

While the boundaries of heresy had been shifted, they had not been torn down. Henry's deep devotion to the Blessed Sacrament meant that native Lollardy and the more radical teaching of the Sacramentarians (disciples of HULDRUCH ZWINGLI [1484–1531] and later JOHN CALVIN [1509–1564] who denied the real presence of the body and blood of Christ in the eucharistic host) remained anathema. Even more disturbing were the teachings of the Anabaptists, who began to appear in England after the collapse of the kingdom of Munster in 1534. A dozen Dutch men and women were burned in various towns in 1535. In 1538, action against Anabaptists was intensified. Henry issued a proclamation ordering them to leave the country on pain of death, and set up a commission including both conservatives and evangelicals to search them out. At much the same time he became more concerned with the Sacramentarians. His proclamation against the Anabaptists was promulgated on the very day he presided at the show-trial of John Lambert. Lambert robustly defended his denial of the real presence (which broadly followed the teachings of Zwingli and John Frith), although under the circumstances he was doomed before he started. Henry himself argued against Lambert and, having urged him in vain to recant, personally pronounced the death sentence.

The Lambert case heralded a chill in the climate for English Protestants. Theological negotiations with the Schmalkaldic League, despite hopeful early signs, had foundered on Henry VIII's intransigence over, for example, the sacrifice of the mass and clerical celibacy. As a potential Catholic crusade seemed to loom in 1538, Henry responded by emphasizing the more conservative aspects of his religious settlement. These moves culminated in the Act of Six Articles (1539), which enshrined specific aspects of Catholicism in English law and laid down death by burning for those who denied TRANSUBSTANTIATION. As a result, although persecution was aimed chiefly against Sacramentarians and Anabaptists, moderate evangelicals had less room for maneuvering in the 1540s than in the 1530s. Many fled the country, and Protestant books once more had to be printed abroad. The King's Book of 1543 was more conservative in tone than its predecessor, the Bishops' Book; restrictions were placed on the reading of the English Bible; and censorship of Protestant literature was renewed.

Henry's personal religious beliefs after 1535 are somewhat enigmatic. Both Catholics and Protestants felt it worth dedicating books to him, and Cranmer tells us how the king dealt with these gifts. He rarely read them himself, but passed them to scholarly clerics around the court for comment, carefully soliciting views from representatives of both the (traditional) "old learning" and the (evangelical) "new learning." This self-conscious balancing of old and new in theology was typical of Henry's later years. It can be seen, for example, in his establishment of the six preachers in Canterbury Cathedral, where he chose three men of the old learning to balance three of the new; and more grimly in 1540 when, in a gesture of ecumenical intolerance, he despatched three Protestants to the stake for heresy, literally, side-by-side with three Catholics to the scaffold for treason. This idiosyncratic aspect of Henry's mature religious views and practices is best summed up in his will. Notoriously, this requested the intercession of the Blessed Virgin Mary and all the saints, and provided for thousands of masses for his soul. It is less well known that its preamble was rich in the themes of evangelical theology.

Although the last years of Henry's reign are often described as a period of conservative reaction, not all Protestants found conditions intolerable. Sacramentarians and Anabaptists remained vulnerable to burning, but few evangelicals met this fate. There was a conservative attempt to turn the king against Cranmer by revealing how far he was promoting Protestantism in Kent, but it backfired. Meanwhile, Henry's last marriage, to Catherine Parr, brought him once more under the influence of a moderate evangelical, and he entrusted the education of Edward and Elizabeth to Cambridge scholars (such as John Cheke [1514–1557]) who stood at the evangelical end of the spectrum of permitted beliefs. Evangelicals were ensconced at Henry's court and held office in his church. If the religious temper of the country as a whole was far from Protestant, the damage he had inflicted upon traditional Catholicism had at least opened a door to further change. Henry VIII was no Protestant himself, but his reign was the reason that Protestantism was in other people.

References and Further Reading

Fraenkal, P., ed. *Henry VIII*, Assertio Septem Sacramentorum. Münster: Aschendorff, 1992.

MacCulloch, D., ed. *The Reign of Henry VIII: Politics, Policy and Piety.* Basingstoke: Macmillan, 1995.

———. *Thomas Cranmer: A Life,* New Haven: Yale University Press, 1996.

Rex, Richard. *Henry VIII and the English Reformation.* Basingstoke: Macmillan, 1993.

———. "The English Campaign Against Luther in the 1520s," *Transactions of the Royal Historical Society,* 5th series, 39 (1989): 85–106.

Scarisbrick, J. J. *Henry VIII.* London: Ayre and Spottiswoode, 1968.

RICHARD REX

HENRY, CARL F. H. (1913–)

Theologian, professor, editor, and writer. Henry is widely recognized as one of the outstanding leaders and intellectual spokesman for American evangelical Christianity of the twentieth century (see EVANGELICALISM). Born of German immigrant parents in New York City on January 22, 1913, and raised in Central Islip, Long Island, Henry overcame the religious indifference of his upbringing with an experience of a personal CONVERSION in 1933. This event led to his affiliation with a Baptist congregation (see BAPTISTS), the end of his brief newspaper career, and his decision to attend Wheaton College in Illinois. Earning two degrees (A.B. and M.A.) from that institution, he continued his studies at Northern Baptist Theological Seminary (B.D. and Th.D.) and Boston University (Ph.D.). His published dissertation, *Personal Idealism and Strong's Theology* (1951), showed him to be an astute critic of the turn-of-the-century Baptist theologian, Augustus Hopkins Strong.

Henry's academic career began with a teaching stint (1942–1947) at his alma mater, Northern Baptist Theological Seminary, before being invited to be part of the founding faculty at Fuller Theological Seminary in Pasadena, California. As professor of theology and philosophy at Fuller from 1947 to 1956, Henry was a pivotal part of an institution intended to engage critical modern theological scholarship while also reforming the fundamentalist aberrations of conservative Protestantism. To those ends, a flurry of writings from Henry streamed forth: *The Uneasy Conscience of Modern Fundamentalism* (1947), *Remaking the Modern Mind* (1948), *Giving a Reason for Our Hope* (1949), *The Protestant Dilemma* (1949), *Fifty Years of Protestant Theology* (1950), *The Drift of Western Thought* (1951), and *Glimpses of a Sacred Land* (1953). In these varied works, Henry's concern for the rational articulation and defense of the Christian faith became evident, but also apparent (especially in *The Uneasy Conscience*) was his clarion call to awaken evangelical social consciences and overcome their separatist tendencies.

Having established himself in the evangelical world, Henry was invited by BILLY GRAHAM and Nelson Bell to give editorial leadership to the newly founded *Christianity Today*, intended to be something of an evangelical counterpart to the more mainline Protestant *Christian Century*. Consistent with his vision for an evangelical faith that was intellectually credible and in touch with the national pulse, Henry moved to Washington, D.C. to launch the new periodical. During his twelve-year tenure (1956–1968) at the magazine, Henry succeeded in making *Christianity Today* a major voice of American evangelicalism and, in the process, also surpassed the *Christian Century* in paid subscriptions.

Henry resigned as editor of *Christianity Today* in 1968—as he later put it in his own autobiography, *Confessions of a Theologian* (1986), "an involuntary termination after twelve years of sacrificial labor"—after disagreements with the executive committee of the magazine and especially its politically conservative benefactor, J. Howard Pew. After a year of research and study at Cambridge University, Henry became professor-at-large at Eastern Baptist Theological Seminary in Philadelphia, where he taught from 1969 to 1974. In 1974 he became lecturer-at-large for WORLD VISION, an evangelical social agency that helped provide an international speaking ministry. At that time Henry also began to serve as visiting professor of theology at Trinity Evangelical Divinity School in Deerfield, Illinois, and the World Journalism Institute.

Assenting Christian Truth

Henry's early interest in ETHICS as demonstrated in *The Uneasy Conscience* was continued in additional publications in this field. *Christian Personal Ethics* (1957), *Aspects of Christian Social Ethics* (1964), and serving as editor-in-chief of *Baker's Dictionary of Christian Ethics* all testify to his passion for evangelicals to make their social witness consistent with their piety.

Preeminently, though, these years were devoted to the writing of his six-volume magnum opus, *God, Revelation and Authority* (1976–1983). Convinced that "in every church epoch it is the fate of the Bible that decides the fate of Christianity," Henry's labor of love is single-minded in its defense of biblical authority and its response to all would-be detractors. For Henry, Scripture is no mere witness to divine revelation, it is itself God's epistemic Word, a divine self-disclosure of truth given in propositional form, secured by the plenary verbal inspiration of the original (inerrant) texts, and entirely fitting for a God who "speaks" as well as "shows." Thus, Henry contends that anything less than a full biblical inerrancy—that the superintendence of the Spirit in inspiring the original texts protected the human authors from error in all that they teach, be it theology and ethics or science and history—severely jeopardizes the foundations of the church's faith and leaves it precariously poised above the slippery slopes of a relativistic quagmire.

Both Henry's defenders and his critics acknowledge that his best work lies primarily in the areas of philosophy of religion and theological method. In following his mentor Gordon Clark in asserting that truth applies only to propositions, Henry's work presents the case for revelational theism or evangelical rationalism as a cognitive disclosure of God's will and purposes. Postmodern thinkers question, however, whether cognitive truth is the only or even primary kind of truth that Scripture intends to convey (see POSTMODERNITY). Thus, from their vantage point Henry's theological methodology betrays an indebtedness to ENLIGHTENMENT thinking that is yet to be acknowledged.

Nonetheless, Henry's influence in contemporary theological debates across the spectrum of Protestant camps remains formidable. His insistence on propositional revelation and the universal truth claims of Christianity in opposition to tendencies to reduce FAITH to language of subjective experience command a hearing. Although all evangelical Protestants do not march to his beat, it is indisputable that Henry was a creative force in shaping the "new evangelicalism" that emerged from northern fundamentalism after World War II and that his spirit still broods over the movement today.

References and Further Reading

Cerillo, Augustus, Jr. and Murray W. Dempster. "Carl F. H. Henry's Early Apologetic for an Evangelical Social Ethic, 1942–1956." *Journal of the Evangelical Theological Society* 34 (1991): 365–379.
Hunsinger, George. "What Can Evangelicals and Postliberals Learn from Each Other? The Carl Henry/Hans Frei Exchange Reconsidered." *Pro Ecclesia* 5 (1996): 161–182.
Patterson, Bob E. "Carl F. H. Henry." In *Makers of the Modern Theological Mind.* Waco, TX: Word, 1983.

STEVEN R. POINTER

HERBERT, GEORGE (1593–1633)

English cleric, poet, and younger brother of free thinker EDWARD LORD HERBERT of Cherbury. George Herbert was born April 3, 1593, in Montgomeryshire, ENGLAND. He died March 1, 1633, at Bemerton, Wiltshire, England, and was buried in the parish church in which he served as rector. Herbert was educated at Westminster School and Trinity College, Cambridge, receiving B.A. (1613) and M.A. (1616) degrees. Drawn to the study of theology and service to the church after completing his university studies, he held several posts at Cambridge, including University Orator after 1620, and served in Parliament (1624), before finally receiving ordination as deacon in 1624. While still a DEACON, he was appointed a canon of Lincoln Cathedral and prebend of Leighton Bromswold, Huntingdonshire in 1626. Herbert was finally ordained to the priesthood in 1630, after which he received an appointment as rector of the parish churches at Fugglestone and Bemerton in Wiltshire, serving there until his death three years later. Herbert is best known for two posthumously published works, a collection of religious poetry, *The Temple* (1633), and a study of pastoral care, *A Priest to the Temple, or the Country Parson* (1652). Both works give evidence of Herbert's concern for maintaining high standards of Christian conduct and for grounding the Christian experience in the corporate life of the CHURCH. In the *Christian Parson,* Herbert laid out the rules that guided his ministry at Bemerton and Fugglestone in an idealized portrait of pastoral life. For Herbert, the priest's primary calling was to be a teacher, whose goal, whether through PREACHING, catechizing, or personal example, was to form parishioners into a community defined by obedience to God's will.

See also Literature

References and Further Reading

Primary Sources:

Herbert, George. *The English Works of George Herbert, Newly arranged and annotated and considered in relation to his life.* Boston & New York: Houghton, Mifflin and Co., 1905.
———. *The Works of George Herbert.* Oxford, UK: Clarendon Press, 1945.
———. *Select Hymns Taken out of Mr. Herbert's Temple, 1967.* Los Angeles: William Andrews Clark Memorial Library, University of California, 1962.

Secondary Sources:

Charles, Amy M. *A Life of George Herbert.* Ithaca, NY: Cornell University Press, 1977.
Wall, John N. Jr., ed. *George Herbert: The Country Parson, The Temple.* (Preface by A. M. Allchin.) New York: Paulist Press, 1981.

R. D. CORNWALL

HERDER, JOHANN GOTTFRIED (1744–1803)

German philosopher. Born August 25, 1744, at Mohrungen (Morąg, Poland), Herder is one of the most prominent and prolific German theologians, philosophers, and literary critics of the ENLIGHTENMENT. His major contributions to the history of Protestant thought lie in the fields of biblical interpretation, philosophy of religion, and universal history. Herder's theology centers on the diversity of human responses to the world as divinely created, and on processes of education through which human beings move toward their destiny, that is, true humanity. Herder understood the notion of humanity as a dynamic equivalent to the biblical notion of the image of God. Herder died December 18, 1803, in Weimar, Germany.

For Herder the Old Testament provides prime examples of poetic expressions of religious insight and inspires a concept of an original revelation that resounded in particular religious and philosophical traditions ever since the primeval age. The essential significance of the New Testament is seen in its presentation of Jesus as an authoritative teacher and a unique model of true humanity, and Herder is critical of any more sophisticated CHRISTOLOGY. As an exegete Herder advocates an approach to individual biblical texts irrespective of later innerbiblical or—Jewish or Christian—doctrinal developments. Following Robert Lowth, he shows considerable originality as a reader of the BIBLE who aims at a theological appreciation of the texts as religious documents from a specific culture in antiquity. Despite his emphasis on the diachronic as well as synchronic plurality of human ways of speaking about God, Herder does not take a relativist view but makes Genesis 1–3 and the figure of Jesus the standard of faith.

Herder's work is of little interest for a theology in which the notion of humanity is dismissed in favor of a doctrine of SIN and JUSTIFICATION, but it retains its value for a theology that engages with the concept of natural religion.

In the Lutheran church in GERMANY, Herder was a senior clergyman serving as the court preacher at Bückeburg (1771–1776) and at Weimar (1776–1803). As a student at the university of Königsberg (1762–1764) he had met with traditional doctrine and apologetics, represented by T. C. Lilienthal at the theological faculty, as well as with the challenge of contemporary critical philosophy, based on the work of writers like ISAAC NEWTON, Shaftesbury, DAVID HUME, and JEAN-JACQUES ROUSSEAU, and represented by IMMANUEL KANT at the philosophical faculty. In his writings of 1770–1774 he distanced himself from an orthodox notion of revelation (On the Origin of Language), but also from a moralist strand of Enlightenment theology as represented in the work of Johann Joachimspalding in Berlin (To Preachers: Fifteen Provincial Letters). Encouraged by JOHANN GEORG HAMANN, he concentrated on an exegetical study of Genesis 1–3, which he wrote in an intriguing style at the peak of the German Storm and Stress (Sturm und Drang) movement (Oldest Document of the Human Race). Building on these seminal works he published a series of influential books during his Weimar years (Letters concerning the Study of Theology, 1780–1781; The Spirit of Hebrew Poetry, 1782–1783 [English translation 1833]; Ideas for the philosophy of the history of humankind, 1784–1791 [English translation 1801]; Christian Writings [mainly on New Testament interpretation], 1794–1798).

References and Further Reading

Primary Sources:

Adler, H., and E. A. Menze, eds. Johann Gottfried Herder: On World History: An Anthology. Armonk, NY and London: M. E. Sharpe, 1997.

Bunge, M., ed. "Johann Gottfried Herder: Against Pure Reason." In Writings on Religion, Language, and History. Minneapolis, MN: Fortress Press, 1993.

Gaier, U., et al., eds. Werke. vol. 10 (in 11 vols.) with commentary. Frankfurt: Deutscher Klassiker Verlag, 1985–2000.

Menze, E. A., and K. Menges, eds. Johann Gottfried Herder: Selected Early Works 1764–1767. University Park: Pennsylvania State University Press, 1992.

Suphan, B., et al., eds. Sämmtliche Werke. 33 vols. 1877–1913; reprinted Hildesheim, Germany: Georg Olms Verlag, 1967/68.

Secondary Sources:

Baird, W. History of New Testament Research I: From Deism to Tübingen. Minneapolis: Fortress Press, 1992.

Berlin, I. "Herder and the Enlightenment." In Vico and Herder: Two Studies in the History of Ideas. New York: Viking, 1976.

Byrne, P. Natural Religion and the Nature of Religion: The Legacy of Deism. London and New York: Routledge, 1989.

Clark, R. T. Herder: His Life and Thought. Berkeley: University of California Press, 1955.

Frei, H. The Eclipse of Biblical Narrative: A Study in Eighteenth and Nineteenth Century Hermeneutics. New Haven: Yale University Press, 1974.

Koepke, W. Johann Gottfried Herder. New York: Twayne Publishers, 1987.

Menges, Karl, et al. Herder Yearbook. Publications of the International Herder Society. Columbia, SC: Camden House, 1992.

Mueller-Vollmer, K., ed. Herder Today. Berlin and New York: Walter de Gruyter, 1990.

CHRISTOPH BULTMANN

HERESY

The word derives from the Greek hairesis, meaning choice, and was in the Jewish context initially used to denote those who departed from the Rabbinic tradition. It was used by Jews for the Christians, who in turn promptly used the term (see I. Cor. 11:18–19;

Gal. 5:20; 2 Pet. 2:1) for those who deviated from the true (Christian) religion.

During the first two centuries of the Christian experience there was tremendous pluralism (much like the modern and postmodern periods) among Christians in their dynamic search for an appropriate response to the God revealed in Jesus the Christ. Heresy often preceded ORTHODOXY. In the fourth and fifth centuries, trinitarian, christological, and anthropological discussions in the ecumenical councils resulted in orthodoxy as an established formula (as seen in the Nicene and Chalcedonian creeds, for example). However, these adopted creedal standards required interpretation by someone or some entity to determine when they had been violated. Catholic Canon Law defined heresy as the "pertinacious" denial or calling into doubt of one of the truths necessary to Christian belief. Majority vote, power politics, and authoritarianism then became key ingredients in the definition of heresy and heretics.

From Arianism to Catharism and Waldensianism, the ancient and medieval countryside was dotted with renewal, dissenting, schismatic, and heretical movements as judged by the long arm of Roman Catholic orthodoxy. The "search and destroy" history of the medieval inquisition is seen repeatedly. The pages of Western religious history are stained with the blood of the heretics within these "heretical" movements.

Sixteenth-century western Europe was ripe in a number of ways for a major challenge to this kind of "closed orthodoxy" and abusive papal authority. Probably the greatest heretic in western religious history was MARTIN LUTHER (1483–1546) himself, the father of the Protestant movement. This observation raises another important point—the contextuality of heresy—for Luther considered himself to be far more orthodox in relation to the essence of the Christian faith than the church authorities who condemned him. Even in this most graphic of heretical movements, however, the inherent law of the institution again acted as a powerful braking element, and did not part with certain sociological forms such as retaining a formal state relationship. All the "magisterial" reformers believed in one church in one state. Luther, however, had opened Pandora's pluralistic box with the principles of the priesthood of every believer and *sola scriptura* (scripture is the sole authority). Christians could now interpret scripture for themselves rather than always relying on authority figures.

Luther dramatically blazed the trail for the modern and postmodern periods in his openness to the judging and renewing activity of the living God in regard to the pilgrimage of the church. Although he affirmed: "It is not the end, but the way. It is not all glistening and shining, but it is all being swept," Luther did not

anticipate the kind of "sweepers" who would emerge. Just as the *free church* tradition (free from the state) would later be renewed by its own individual heretics, its own tradition was a heretical form of renewal for the established church tradition. Magisterial reformers were challenged by "radical" reformers who, for the most part, agreed upon the necessity of separating the reformed church from the authority of the temporal realm. They were more concerned with a people in covenant rather than a *corpus christianum,* and at times were more interested in the restoration of ancient Christianity than the reformation of medieval Christianity. They were opposed, as heretical movements, by both Roman Catholics and magisterial reformers. This heresy was often labeled as "sedition" and a crime against the state. Authority and majority vote continued to spell out their own definitions of heresy as creeds and scripture were interpreted.

The pluralism that Protestantism brought to the religious scene blurred the meaning of heresy. Hundreds of creeds and confessions were written in numerous Protestant circles and always interpreted within a particular context by authority figures. There was even variety within denominational families, especially in the United States, where principles of the *separation of church and state* and religious liberty nurtured even more pluralism. For example, by the twentieth century BAPTISTS alone expressed themselves in over fifty different groups. Even the ecumenical age with its briefer confessions and emphasis on unity did not solve the complexity of the meaning of heresy in Protestant circles. An accused heretic and his or her heresy in one denomination might only be considered a conservative and orthodox church-person in another. False simplifications of heresy by some evangelicals, especially fundamentalists, blurred the issue even more. The last decade of the twentieth century witnessed an active interest in heresy and heretics on both doctrinal and moral grounds. Heresy issues emerged in numerous denominational circles (for example, the militant fundamentalists and their political takeover of the Southern Baptist Convention resulted in a plethora of informal heresy trials), and a climate of hyperintoleration in doctrinal and moral issues resulted. Politics, jealousies, power struggles, antiintellectualism, limits of knowing, grudges, personal animosities, and confusion of ethics with doctrine have all played roles in the decisions made concerning heresy in contemporary Protestant circles.

There is no universally accepted definition of heresy in the modern Protestant world, for there exists multifaceted pluralism and sometimes narrow contextualism. Austrian theologian Karl Rahner (1904–1984) suggested that hardening "the form in which the truth of the gospel is expressed is then itself nothing but the dangerous symptom of an indifference to this truth." If he is correct, perhaps we have returned to the first two centuries of Christian history when there were no doctrinal parameters as Christians struggled to express themselves on matters of ultimate concern. The British Congregationalist P. T. FORSYTH (1848–1921) once said that a "live heresy is better than a dead orthodoxy." Put another way, there is no heresy in a dead religion. In this case, once again, heresy precedes orthodoxy as the wheel continues to turn.

References and Further Reading

Christie-Murray, David. *A History of Heresy.* New York: Oxford University Press, 1989.

Hultgren, Arland J., and Steven A. Haggmark, eds. *The Earliest Christian Heretics.* Minneapolis: Fortress Press, 1996.

Lambert, Malcolm. *Medieval Heresy.* New York: Holmes and Meier, 1977.

Nigg, Walter. *The Heretics.* New York: Alfred A. Knopf, 1962.

Rahner, Karl. *On Heresy.* New York: Herder and Herder, 1964.

Shriver, George H., ed. *American Religious Heretics.* Nashville: Abingdon Press, 1966.

———, ed. *Dictionary of Heresy Trials in American Christianity.* Westport, CT: Greenwood Press, 1997.

Wakefield, Walter L., and Austin P. Evans, eds. *Heresies of the High Middle Ages.* New York: Columbia University Press, 1969.

GEORGE H. SHRIVER

HERRNHUT

Herrnhut, near Dresden in Saxony (central GERMANY), was one of the most important religious communities in Europe in the eighteenth and nineteenth centuries. A center of German PIETISM, Herrnhut developed a distinctive social and religious life that was almost monastic in its discipline. Members of the community voluntarily gave up much of their autonomy in order to pursue the religious goals of the community. The cultivation of a relationship to their Savior led to an elaborate and joyful liturgical life that focused on the atonement. This Moravian piety was spread through the publication of hymnals and liturgy books.

Herrnhut also established numerous boarding schools, such as the one attended by FRIEDRICH SCHLEIERMACHER (1768–1843), and sent out hundreds of tutors, teachers, and lay religious leaders who established Pietist cell groups throughout the Baltic, NETHERLANDS, and Scandinavia. Herrnhut remained the headquarters of the MORAVIAN CHURCH's Unity Board and Board of World Missions until the disruptions of two world wars. The Moravians were so closely associated with Herrnhut that they were commonly called Herrnhuters.

Herrnhut was founded on the estate of Count NIKOLAUS VON ZINZENDORF in Saxony in 1722 by a Czech émigré named Christian David (1690–1722). David had been converted during a Pietist revival, and he urged several Czech Protestant families to leave Catholic Moravia and Bohemia and seek refuge under Zinzendorf's protection. They named their new village Herrnhut, "under the Lord's protection." The refugees hoped to restore the old Hussite church known as the *Unitas Fratrum,* which had been virtually destroyed during the Thirty Years War. Zinzendorf already had plans to develop a Pietist complex similar to HALLE on his estate. As Herrnhut developed, both goals were pursued in a creative synthesis. Soon Herrnhut was attracting not only Moravians but also mystics, seekers, and various separatists. By 1727 there were about 300 residents, most of whom were members of the Lutheran and Reformed churches.

Dissent quickly developed because of diverse church traditions and theological perspectives. In order to establish principles for their life together, Zinzendorf drew up a covenant, called the Brotherly Agreement, which firmly established Herrnhut as an exclusive religious community within the Lutheran parish of Berthlesdorf. This agreement, among diverse Protestant factions, marks a milestone in the history of ECUMENISM. The Brotherly Agreement also allowed the Moravians to revive vestiges of the *Unitas Fratrum* without violating the Treaty of Westphalia. Soon after the signing of the Brotherly Agreement, Herrnhut began training and sending out missionaries to non-Christian peoples (see Moravian Church).

Philipp Jakob Spener's (1635–1705) idea of the *ecclesiola in ecclesia* (little churches in the church) took a distinctive form in Herrnhut as the residents built a new Christian social order. The basic unit of their society was not the private family but the "choir" or religious group. By 1740 virtually every person in Herrnhut was a member of a particular choir (e.g., boys, girls, single men, single women, married men, married women, widowers, and widows). The choirs worshiped together, usually ate together, and provided mutual support and admonition. The single men and single women also established communal housekeeping and lived in large choir houses.

Theologically, the choirs were based on the conviction that the incarnation of Christ had already blessed all stages of human life. Devotions in the choirs related Jesus's experience as a child, adolescent, and adult to the life of the believer. The choirs also provided a way for the church to subordinate individual desires for the common mission. Young persons were raised in the awareness that at any time they might be asked to go into the mission fields or accept a teaching or preaching post. Even earthly marriage was brought under the control of the church at Herrnhut. Marriages were arranged according to the needs of the community, and for many years the final decision was submitted to the lot. The choir system and arranging of marriages continued until early in the nineteenth century.

In addition to the choir system, Herrnhut created an efficient social service system. Diaconal ministers were responsible for the care of orphans, the sick, and elderly. Zinzendorf and other nobles established institutions such as an apothecary, orphanage, and publishing house. Economic life was included in the overall Herrnhut system as the community took charge of apprentice training, the regulation of trade, and creation of new industries. Competition was discouraged in favor of cooperative enterprises, and labor was seen as an integral part of spiritual development. This intentional approach to economics was applied in all Moravian communities and furthered the mission enterprise. Moravians preferred to send artisans and craftsmen to the mission field rather than pastors because they could follow Paul's model of being a "tent-maker" evangelist. Herrnhut's products were prized throughout Europe, particularly after Abraham Düringer took charge of the economy and established his industries in the 1750s.

In 1736 the Saxon government examined Herrnhut in order to decide whether to disband the community on the grounds of religious and social irregularities. Because of its hardworking, law-abiding, and quiet lifestyle, Herrnhut was allowed to continue to exist under its own religious and social laws; however, Zinzendorf himself was exiled. This threat of expulsion encouraged the Moravians to found other religious centers in Europe and America. The most famous were Herrnhaag, near Frankfort, Lamb's Hill in ENGLAND, New Herrnhut in St. Thomas, and Bethlehem in Pennsylvania. All of the Moravian communities were modeled on Herrnhut. Herrnhut's fame attracted many visitors, the most famous of whom was JOHN WESLEY (1703–1791), who was favorably impressed in 1738.

Several Moravian practices and observances were begun in Herrnhut during its early years. Among them were the love feast (or agape meal), the unbroken prayer watch, the singing service, the easter sunrise service, and the Daily Texts (losungen). The Daily Texts continue to be chosen in Herrnhut and remain one of the most widely used devotional guides in the world, especially in Germany.

After Zinzendorf's death in 1760, the governing board of the church resided in Herrnhut, but in the mid-nineteenth century the American and British provinces were granted a measure of independence from German control. Herrnhut continues to serve as the headquarters for the Moravians in Europe and houses the extensive archives of the worldwide Moravian Church.

References and Further Reading

Gollin, Gillian Lindt. *Between Two Worlds: A Study of Changing Communities.* New York: Columbia University Press, 1967.
Nelson, James. "Herrnhut: Friedrich Schleiermacher's Spiritual Home." Ph.D. dissertation, University of Chicago, 1963.
Sommer, Elisabeth. *Serving Two Masters.* Lexington: University of Kentucky Press, 2000.
Uttendorfer, Otto. *Alt-Herrnhut.* 2 vols. Herrnhut: Missionsbuchhandlung Verlag, 1925.

CRAIG D. ATWOOD

HICKS, EDWARD (1780–1849)

American "Primitive" painter. Hicks was born April 4, 1780, in Attleborough, Pennsylvania, and died August 23, 1849, in Newtown, Pennsylvania. By profession Hicks was a decorative painter. By commitment and avocation he was a passionate Quaker, widely known for his preaching. He was deeply, often contentiously, involved in Quaker politics, admonished on occasion for the intensity of his public statements. He was widely admired for his presentation of Quaker principles, particularly that of obedience to the Inner Light rather than external authority.

Hicks came reluctantly to easel painting, reconciling himself to it only as an instrument of ministry. The charm of the "primitive" conceals a strong and original intelligence. He painted landscapes with Quaker farms, illustrating in their orderliness, simplicity of forms, and purity of tone, the Quaker way of life. The fruitful, serene, and orderly landscape exemplified the peace of God.

He is best known for his paintings of *The Peaceable Kingdom* (Isaiah 11:6–9). The landscapes are more natural but equally peaceful. Most contain in the background a scene of WILLIAM PENN concluding a peace treaty with the Indians, a human act fulfilling the intent of the pictures. The surface is taken up with the animals and the child or children. These deserve to be studied together because they are exegeses of the text. The distinctive personalities of the animals exemplify types of people, according to the doctrine of the humors. Inside the overarching peace there are various tensions in the presentation of the animals; God's peace is not a simple thing, being the reconciliation of powerful psychic and dramatic forces.

See also Friends, Society of

References and Further Reading

Mather, Eleanor Price, and Dorothy Canning Miller. *Edward Hicks: His Peaceable Kingdoms and Other Paintings.* New Brunswick, NJ: Associated University Presses, 1983.

Weekley, Carolyn J. *The Kingdoms of Edward Hicks.* Williamsburg, VA: The Rockefeller Folk Art Foundation, 1999.
JOHN W. DIXON JR.

HIGHER CRITICISM

The term Higher Criticism was first used by pupils of Christian Gottlob Heyne (1729–1812; professor and librarian at Göttingen, 1763–1812) to distinguish two branches of the philological criticism of ancient texts (mainly Greek and Latin but also biblical). Johann Gottfried Eichhorn (1752–1827), who studied under Heyne and succeeded Johann David Michaelis (1717–1791) as professor of philosophy in Göttingen from 1788 to his death, asserted in the preface to the second edition of his *Einleitung in das Alte Testament* (1790) that Higher Criticism was not a new term to any pure humanist.

The distinction between Higher and Lower Criticism was based on the ancient classical distinction between Great Philology and Little Philology as reported by Dionysius the Thracian, whose grammar remained influential into the eighteenth century. Eichhorn used the terms Great and Little Criticism in the paragraph on the Higher Criticism and its little sister, Lower Criticism, in volume 5 of his *Repertorium* (1779). The term "Higher" was meant to indicate that this criticism was nobler and more important than textual criticism. Friedrich August Wolf in his Göttingen lectures on philology of the winter semester of 1798–1799 referred to the term as current but repudiated the assumption that Lower Criticism was any less demanding. Eichhorn in his article of 1779 on Moses' reports of the Flood argued that Higher Criticism showed that Moses either used or himself combined two ancient sources that sometimes intertwined and sometimes ran parallel. Eichhorn argued that Lower Criticism could work better when able to assume the results of Higher Criticism. Eichhorn later extended his source criticism of the Pentateuch and discovered that Jean Astruc (1684–1766), son of a Protestant pastor who converted to Catholicism on the revocation of the EDICT OF NANTES and devoted himself to the education of his sons, had in 1753 anticipated his original analysis. Eichhorn argued that Isaiah 40ff. was later than Isaiah 1–39.

Although FRIEDRICH SCHLEIERMACHER used the terms in his *Kurze Darstellung des theologischen Studiums,* he said that higher and lower so intermingled that they could not be separated. The term was used in Germany to characterize rationalistic criticism. Eichhorn was a rationalist, although the leading British and American higher critics argued that their criticism advanced true religion.

British and American Higher Criticism

From about 1857 onward, and particularly in the 1880s and 1890s, Higher Criticism was more talked about in the United Kingdom and America than it had ever been in continental Europe because Higher Criticism was the bone of contention in four famous actions for HERESY.

Samuel Davidson (1806–1898), an Irish Presbyterian who taught biblical interpretation at Belfast College (1834–1841), before leaving the Presbyterian ministry and being appointed professor at Lancashire Independent College, Manchester, in 1842, was compelled to resign in 1857 on denying the Mosaic authorship of the Pentateuch. He became a Unitarian. In 1862 he published *An Introduction to the Old Testament: Critical, Historical, and Theological* to supersede the earlier book that had forced his resignation. He reminded any who thought he had been occasionally too free "that there is a time to utter the conclusions of the higher criticism; that superstition should not enslave the mind for ever."

JOHN WILLIAM COLENSO (1814–1883), bishop of Natal in South Africa, was deposed by the bishop of Cape Town in 1863 for challenging the traditional authorship and accuracy of the books from Genesis to II Kings. He argued that they were edited by a Deuteronomistic editor. The Privy Council upheld his appeal on the grounds that Cape Town had no jurisdiction. He was excommunicated in 1866, but retained the cathedral and endowments of the see. All this brought Higher Criticism to public notice.

WILLIAM ROBERTSON SMITH (1846–1894), professor at the Free Church College in Aberdeen, was eventually dismissed from his post in 1881 over articles on the BIBLE (1875) and Hebrew language and literature (1880) in the ninth edition of the *Encyclopaedia Britannica*. He had argued in the *British Quarterly Review* (April 1870) that "the fundamental principle of the higher criticism lies in the conception of the organic unity of all history . . . an ancient writing which is no frigid product of the school, but is instinct with true life, must be the product of the age which contained the conditions of life it unconsciously reflects." Deuteronomy put into the mouth of Moses "the highest and most spiritual view of the law . . . to expound and develop Mosaic principles in relation to new needs."

Charles Augustus Briggs (1841–1913), professor at Union Theological Seminary, New York, was condemned by the General Assembly of the Presbyterian Church in 1891 for denying that Moses wrote the Pentateuch and that Isaiah wrote Isaiah 40ff. He was ordained an Episcopal priest in 1899. He wrote *The Higher Criticism of the Hexateuch* (1893).

The term Higher Criticism was little used after World War I. Robert M. Price revived it by founding *The Journal of Higher Criticism* (1994) with an effigy of FERDINAND CHRISTIAN BAUR on the cover (justly, although Baur himself spoke of historical criticism). Less controversy has surrounded the higher criticism of the New Testament. Eichhorn's solution of the Synoptic Problem has been largely accepted, except for his view that the original documents were in Aramaic. W. Robertson Smith's statement that John's Gospel was "an unhistorical product of abstract reflection" was already current. Paul's epistles have largely escaped analysis into sources, the only question being which were genuine and which not. E. Earle Ellis (1927–) has argued that Paul and his assistants used five types of preformed traditions in compiling the letters. Higher Criticism as traditionally understood is not dead.

See also Baur, Ferdinand Christian; Bible; Colenso, John William; Heresy; Nantes, Edict of; Schleiermacher, Friedrich; Smith, W. Robertson

References and Further Reading

Osgood, Howard. "The History and Definition of Higher Criticism." *The Bibliotheca Sacra* 49 no. 196 (1892): 529–545.
Reid, George J. "Biblical Criticism (Higher)." The Catholic Encyclopedia. 1908. http://www.newadvent.org/cathen/04491c.htm
Zenos, Andrew C. *Elements of the Higher Criticism.* New York: Funk and Wagnalls, 1895.

J. C. O'NEILL

HIGHER EDUCATION

Protestantism brought changes to higher education both by what it accomplished in itself, and by what it accomplished through those who reacted against it. Realizing there are many nuances and definitions of Protestantism—or indeed, Protestantisms—this article uses Protestantism in a broad definition, encompassing the later developments from the original Protestant and Reformed usage. As such, this article addresses higher education, particularly university education, as it was influenced by early and later developments of Protestantism. It looks at the introduction of Protestant universities in Europe, Asia, the UNITED STATES, and AFRICA and notes some of the effects these universities have had within their respective countries.

Universities are of medieval origin. Some of the first universities, defined as institutions with organized faculty and community of students, were found in Bologna, Cambridge, Oxford, and Paris in the twelfth and thirteenth centuries. These began as gatherings around well known teachers. Often developing from cathedral schools, the universities were tied to the Catholic Church of the time. Only universities could bestow degrees, and their charter to do so had to be granted by a universal ruler, either the pope or emperor.

Universities became important centers of learning and culture with a common worldview, which reflected the current ideas of Christendom. The privilege of a doctor was to teach without further examination at any university in which his services should be rendered. Degree holders had their educational attainments recognized equally throughout the Christian Empire. In this way the education received at universities both reflected and perpetuated a common unity of knowledge throughout an extended Christendom.

Protestantism and Higher Education in Europe

The first Protestant leaders were often university educated, and many of them were university professors and educators as well. MARTIN LUTHER (1483–1546) was professor of biblical literature at the University of Wittenburg in Saxony when he posted his ninety-five theses on the Wittenburg church door. PHILIPP MELANCHTHON (1497–1560) also taught at the University of Wittenburg and helped make it one of the most influential centers of Protestant theology in GERMANY. Protestant THEOLOGY sought to give precedence to biblical languages and the original text of the BIBLE over and against Catholic philosophically oriented scholasticism and Thomism.

Most German universities were Lutheran in theology. The first Protestant university to be established in Germany was the University of Marburg (f. 1527). It was also the first German university to have a charter granted by a princely ruler (PHILIP OF HESSE) rather than by papal authority. Other Protestant universities founded during this time were Königsberg (now Kaliningrad, f. 1544), Jena (f. 1558), and Helmstedt (f. 1575).

JOHN CALVIN (1509–1564) moved to Geneva in 1536 and among other activities established the Geneva Academy in 1559 to train reformed ministers. Initially focused on the preparation of church leaders, the academy attracted students from throughout Europe. The GENEVA BIBLE was prepared and published by this institution, further enhancing its reputation. The academy would later become the nucleus of the University of Geneva. Calvin had a great interest in higher education, and as a result Protestant Calvinist universities were established internationally afterward in many cities including Leiden (1575), Edinburgh (1582), Amsterdam (1632), and Utrech (1636).

In ENGLAND the universities of Oxford and Cambridge became centers for Protestant teaching. Because of this, many Catholic educators and students left, finding a more congenial atmosphere elsewhere. Yet Oxford and Cambridge vacillated between Protestantism and Catholicism in the early years according to the religion of the reigning monarch. Whatever the prevailing views, Protestant or Catholic, religious conformity was expected and enforced. Professors and students alike were made to swear their allegiance to confessional statements of ORTHODOXY subscribed to by each institution. Occasionally opposition brought death. In 1555 and 1556 three Cambridge University–educated Protestant leaders, THOMAS CRANMER (1489–1556), HUGH LATIMER (1485–1555), and NICOLAS RIDLEY (c. 1500–1555), were burned at Oxford during the brief reign of the Catholic queen, Mary Tudor (1516–1558). The result of this action was a strong development of REFORMATION Doctrine over and against Catholicism with the ascension of the Protestant queen ELIZABETH I (r. 1558–1603). In this way Catholicism left its mark on the Protestant theology of Oxford as it defined itself for the future.

CAMBRIDGE UNIVERSITY played an important part in English Protestant politics. THOMAS CROMWELL (c. 1485–1540), chief minister to HENRY VIII, was also the chancellor of Cambridge for five years and emphasized the study of Greek, Hebrew, and biblical divinity there. Politics and Protestant theology were firmly entwined at Cambridge. William Cecil (1520–1598) also attended Cambridge and was Elizabeth's first minister from 1559 to 1598. The archbishops of Canterbury during this time, MATTHEW PARKER (1504–1575), Edmund Grindal (1519–1583), and JOHN WHITGIFT (1530–1604), were all from Cambridge as was Thomas Cranmer years before.

The effect of Protestantism on higher education was to immediately alter the relationship of the university to the Catholic Church. The nature of theology often became polemic toward Catholicism and Thomism, or at least oriented toward a self-sufficient biblical authority removed from TRADITION and a human representative of deity. Catholic monks and scholars who taught at universities or were students there left for safer haven. By removing the universal authority of the pope, Protestantism may have paved the way for, or contributed to, an existential INDIVIDUALISM centuries later that acknowledged no central defining authority. Ultimately this individualism often led to a separation from the deeply religious identity that initiated the original institution.

Protestantism and Higher Education in Asia

The influence of Protestantism, although centuries later than in Europe, inspired many efforts of higher education in Asia. From a religious point of view important aspects of this education were CONVERSION and to prepare leaders for local ministries. An important aspect of many of these universities was the introduction of the education of WOMEN.

In China, Yenching University, later to develop into Beijing University, was founded in 1919 under Methodist influence. This university was a conglomeration of other educational institutions and afterward continued to expand into the arts and sciences. Yet much of the origins for the present-day Beijing University had their foundations in Protestantism. Other Protestant institutions of higher education include Fukien Christian University (1915); Ginling College, a Christian women's college (1915); Shantung Christian University (1902); University of Nanking (1910); and St. John's University (1879). These are only a few of the universities that began under Protestant influence.

In KOREA, once known as the Hermit Kingdom, higher education flourished under Protestant influence. Atypical in Asia, Korea has over 40 percent of the population claiming Christianity as their religion. Yonsei University, Korea's oldest Protestant university, was founded in 1885 under Presbyterian influence. It has grown to a student population of 30,000 and is influential as a multidisciplinary university. Ewha Women's University, which attained university status in 1945 but traces its roots to Ewha Girls' School that began in 1866, started under Methodist influence. Other institutions of higher education have proliferated as well, with many being started by Protestant groups.

In INDIA, Serampore College was founded in 1818 with WILLIAM CAREY as one of the leaders in beginning this institution. Although begun by those involved in the English Baptist Missionary Society (see BAPTIST MISSIONS), this institution was open to all persons regardless of their caste or creed. As either faculty or students, the college had Anglicans, Baptists, Congregationalists, Disciples, Lutherans, Methodists, Presbyterians, and members of other denominations as well. Eventually this college became a part of the University of Calcutta. Protestantism founded other colleges, and by 1910 there were forty-six Protestant Christian colleges in the Indian territory of India, Burma, and Ceylon. Many of these institutions also had a significant positive influence on the role of women in the Indian society.

Protestantism and Higher Education in the United States

The first universities established in the United States began under Protestant auspices, although by this time Protestantism had developed well beyond Lutheran and Calvinistic beginnings. Harvard (1636) is the oldest university and was initiated under Congregationalist influence. William and Mary (1693) began under the influence of the Episcopal church. Yale (1701) was also established to serve the Congregationalists. The College of New Jersey (1746), which became Princeton, was America's fourth oldest university, established by the Presbyterian and Reformed churches. Rhode Island (1764), which later became Brown University, was established by the Baptists. The Charity School (1740), which became the University of Pennsylvania, and King's (1754), which later became Columbia University, were established by the Episcopalians. Queens (1766), which later became Rutgers, was established by the Presbyterian and Reformed churches. These early universities along with many others had strong ties to their respective founding churches. At the same time these institutions were neither ministerial training institutions nor exclusively for students from the founding Protestant denomination.

Protestant higher education had a favorable beginning in the United States. Denominations could start their college the way they believed best, without centuries of tradition to throw off. In this setting every major Protestant religious group sought to begin its own college or university. These institutions, although initially small, helped further galvanize religious sentiment. Each institution can claim educated national and international leaders. Yet as colleges grew and expanded their courses over time, they tended to lose contact with their initial affiliated religious heritage. Eventually little trace could be discerned of the distinctive founding heritage for the majority of the early American Protestant educational institutions. There has been renewed scholarly interest in this consistent cycle.

Protestantism and Higher Education in Africa

Protestant higher education was late in coming to Africa. Education was initially through mission schools. These schools served to teach literacy and serve as agents for conversion, and were the first Protestant educational institutions. As well, they prepared future leaders for serving in administrative and governmental capacities in the individual African countries. In 1827 the CHURCH MISSIONARY SOCIETY, an Anglican missionary group founded with the original purpose of returning and advancing the cause of freed slaves, established Fourah Bay College to train Africans as educators, church leaders, and leaders in society. Located near Freetown in SIERRA LEONE, Fourah Bay is the oldest institution of higher education in West Africa. SAMUEL A. CROWTHER (ca. 1806–1891), a freed African slave who became an Anglican bishop and later did extensive and successful mission work in Nigeria, was in the first class of this new institution. Fourah Bay College exerted widespread influence in the areas of MISSIONS, leadership, and higher education throughout West Africa and was affiliated with the University of Durham in England in 1876. With this move, African students could earn British degrees without leaving Africa. Eventually Fourah Bay College became a part of the University of Sierra Leone.

There are numerous reasons for the late appearance of Protestant institutions of higher education in Africa. Protestantism came with the trading companies and colonizing powers, which were not influential until the nineteenth century. Although missionaries came before and without the oversight of these capital and colonizing ventures, eventually the two often advanced in close relationship to one another. Because of this, many Africans saw Protestantism and education as a tool of control. Also for the colonizers, higher education was sometimes seen as a hindrance to their rule. Britain ruled by a policy of indirect rule, working through already established local leaders. Higher education had the potential to upset this arrangement by placing power in the hands of younger, though more educated, individuals. As well, both FRANCE and Britain as colonizing powers deliberately excluded Christian missionary efforts and therefore Protestant higher education from Muslim controlled areas. Recognition and utilization of Muslim traditional leaders in positions of colonial government and military leadership by colonizing powers enhanced the reputation of Islam and served to further the Muslim cause. Education was seen by these local Islamic leaders as tools of Western domination, and therefore avoided.

Conclusion

Higher education was influential in the spread of Protestantism internationally as well as locally. Because universities were an established institution throughout Europe, they developed and facilitated the Protestant message throughout Western civilization first. As the influence of the Western world eventually expanded into Asia and Africa it took along these institutions of universal knowledge.

As time went on, Protestant forces found and often centered in colleges and universities became more tolerant. Initially holders of both Catholicism and variations on the theme of Protestantism were often forced to flee universities that were Protestant strongholds and find a more congenial home elsewhere. Eventually antagonism faded and it was not unusual to find Catholics at Protestant universities and vice versa. Tolerance further developed until it became the norm to find believers of any religion enrolled in Protestant higher education (see TOLERATION).

One of the oft-repeated patterns of Protestant higher education has been a drift in educational purpose away from the originating ideal and religious motif. As decades or centuries pass by, the religious dimension in particular is separated from the university and pushed into the background. Eventually religious roots are ignored or denied. The continuing challenges for the relationship of Protestantism to higher education are to uphold a distinctive identity while sustaining a broad spirit of tolerance, to encourage independent thought and inquiry while preserving an effective reliance on Protestant religious roots, and to maintain a vigorous academic debate regarding Protestant spirituality and the central place of the Bible in Protestantism.

See also Colonialism

References and Further Reading

Bays, Daniel H., ed. *Christianity in China: From the Eighteenth Century to the Present.* Stanford, CA: Stanford University Press, 1996.

Bediako, Kwame. *Christianity in Africa: The Renewal of a Non-Western Religion.* Edinburgh: Edinburgh University Press, 1995.

Benne, Robert. *Quality with Soul: How Six Premier Colleges and Universities Keep Faith with Their Religious Traditions.* Grand Rapids, MI: Wm. B. Eerdmans, 2001.

Burtchaell, James Tunstead. *The Dying of the Light: The Disengagement of Colleges and Universities from Their Christian Churches.* Grand Rapids, MI: Wm. B. Eerdmans, 1998.

Cherry, Conrad. *Hurrying toward Zion: Universities, Divinity Schools, and American Protestantism.* Bloomington: Indiana University Press, 1995.

Flynt, Wayne, and Gerald W. Berkley. *Taking Christianity to China.* Tuscaloosa: The University of Alabama Press, 1997.

Hughes, Richard, and William B. Andrian, eds. *Models of Christian Higher Education: Strategies for Survival in the Twenty-first Century.* Grand Rapids, MI: Wm. B. Eerdmans, 1997.

Marsden, George. *The Soul of the American University: From Protestant Establishment to Established Unbelief.* New York: Oxford University Press, 1994.

———, and Bradley J. Longfield, eds. *The Secularization of the Academy.* New York: Oxford University Press, 1992.

Schaff, Philip. *Germany: Its Universities, Theology, and Religion.* New York: Sheldon, Blakeman and Company, 1857.

Sloan, Douglas. *Faith and Knowledge: Mainline Protestantism and American Higher Education.* Louisville, KY: Westminster/John Knox Press, 1994.

Sundkler, Bengt, and Christopher Steed. *A History of the Church in Africa.* Cambridge: Cambridge University Press, 2000.

DAVID L. LITTLE

HIGHER LIFE MOVEMENT

Higher Christian Life was the name of a mid-nineteenth-century movement in Anglo-American Protestantism that stressed the possibility of a "higher" (or sometimes "deeper") Christian experience than most enjoyed. Considering most Christians complacent about their spiritual state, "higher life" advocates insisted on the availability of a quality of piety, embraced in an act of faith, that brought one into constant, conscious fellowship with Christ and enabled the believer to live in a state of holiness and consecration. Those who identified with this movement often manifested more enthusiasm for religious experience than for theology. A principal text that helped shape their identity came from the pen of William Boardman, a peripatetic Presbyterian who published *The Higher Christian Life* in 1858. Boardman's views had affinities for Methodist holiness teaching, and he moved in nondenominational circles that brought him into contact with prominent holiness leaders.

The principal features of the higher Christian life—rest, joy, peace, spiritual power—resembled those of holiness piety, but Boardman articulated a path to these blessings in this life that avoided much holiness jargon. He hoped to appeal more broadly to Christians whose social standing or religious predilections made them wary of Methodism. Influenced as well by evangelist CHARLES GRANDISON FINNEY's teaching on a second crisis experience as normative for the converted, advocates of the higher Christian life penetrated denominational boundaries with their message. Although the practical differences among holiness and higher life advocates were often minor, their distinct approaches and methods had enormous importance for their self-understanding. The ideal of knowing Christ in a personal, intimate, growing relationship that envisioned Christ as king of the believer's life suggested a perspective that valued otherworldliness over engagement in this world's concerns. It turned piety inward and judged harshly the alleged carnality of contemporary Christianity.

The higher Christian life was "higher" only in the sense that its advocates deemed the contemporary church deficient. They insisted that this higher Christian life was, in God's scheme, the blueprint for ordinary Christian living. In the 1870s Boardman teamed with a Quaker couple, Robert Pearsall and HANNAH WHITALL SMITH, who shared his interests in this spirituality. Their efforts in England gave rise to the KESWICK MOVEMENT. From Smith's pen came *The Christian's Secret of the Happy Life,* the classic, enduring statement of the simple piety that was the goal of the higher Christian life.

See also Holiness Movement

References and Further Reading

Primary Sources:

Boardman, W. E. *The Higher Christian Life*. Boston: H. Hoyt, 1858.
Smith, Hannah W. *The Christian's Secret of a Happy Life*. Chicago: F. H. Revell, 1875.

Secondary Source:

Blumhofer, Edith L. *Restoring the Faith*. Chicago: University of Illinois Press, 1993.

EDITH L. BLUMHOFER

HOBBES, THOMAS (1588–1679)

English philosopher. Hobbes was born just outside of Malmesbury, Wiltshire, England on April 5, 1588, prematurely and "a twin with fear," as he said, both because of the impending invasion of the Spanish Armada and his lifelong timidity. His book *Leviathan* is widely considered the greatest work of political philosophy in English. He died at Hardwick Hall in Derbyshire on December 3, 1679. Reputed by many to be an atheist, Hobbes's long and prosperous life caused his enemies consternation. According to another view, Hobbes was, as he represented himself as being, a loyal member of the CHURCH OF ENGLAND. The opposition to him was attributed in large part to a variety of factors including his demythologizing attitude toward the BIBLE, his unsuccessful attempt to reconcile Christianity with modern science, and his defense after the English CIVIL WAR of absolute sovereignty and of the civil sovereign's authority over the Church. This is not to mention his acerbic wit.

Hobbes attended Magdalen Hall, Oxford, from about 1602 until 1608, when he received his B.A. He then entered the service of William Cavendish as tutor to his son William, the future second earl of Devonshire. He served one or another branch of the Cavendish family for more than a half century. He toured the Continent with William in 1614. One result may have been his authorship of the essays that appeared in the anonymous *Horae Subsecivae*. The essay "Of Rome" reports the viewing of numerous Roman Catholic relics, including a piece of the Cross, a vial of Jesus's blood, and "one of the thorns, which was in derision set upon our Savior's head." Although not accepting all the miraculous stories, the author implies that he thinks that some of them are true. He ends his essay with advice for members of the Church of England visiting Rome. Except for his translation of Thucydides *History of the Peloponnesian War* (1629), Hobbes's intellectual life was undistinguished until the 1630s.

Science and Christianity

Most of Hobbes's time in the 1630s was devoted to the study of modern science, especially with a group associated with William Cavendish, later the duke of Newcastle. However, he probably visited the circle of Protestant intellectuals at Great Tew, Oxfordshire, where the main topics of conversation were the Bible and the foundations of Christianity, topics that Hobbes later wrote about extensively. One of Great Tew's leading members, WILLIAM CHILLINGWORTH, wrote in *The Religion of Protestants,* "The Bible is the only true religion of Protestants," and Hobbes represented himself as sympathetic with that view.

Hobbes's political views dramatically altered his life in the 1640s. A decidedly nonstalwart royalist, he anticipated the Civil War and fled to FRANCE in late 1640. He feared for his life because of the views he expressed in *The Elements of Law, Natural and Politic,* which circulated around the end of the Short Parliament (1640). In Paris he became a member of Marin Mersenne's circle, whose members focused on mathematics, science, and the problem of reconciling modern science and Christianity. One of them, his friend Pierre Gassendi, tried to hitch Epicurus to Roman Catholicism, and another, Thomas White, tried the same thing with a refurbished Aristotle. Hobbes's answer to the problem, which was made explicit in *Leviathan,* was to expound on a point made by Chillingworth, JOHN DONNE, and others. Christianity contains doctrines above reason but nothing contrary to reason. Hobbes separated faith and reason, and the realm of religion from the realm of science. Faith is trust in a person and yields belief. Reason is the calculation of consequences from propositions and yields science. When people become citizens of a state, they put their faith in their sovereign. Hobbes is content to let the sovereign define the content of faith; hence his easy acceptance of the THIRTY-NINE ARTICLES.

In 1642 his book *De Cive* was published in France. Its last part, "Of Religion," defends views that were broadly acceptable to English royalists. He argued that God rules over humans by nature and over the Israelites by the old covenant. At the Second Coming, Christ will rule over all people by the new covenant. The only belief needed to attain heaven is that Jesus is the Christ or Messiah. All the other Christian truths follow from that one. Most of his critics, Catholic and Protestant alike, wanted a stronger statement about dogma. Nevertheless, *De Cive* made Hobbes's reputation as a Christian political theorist. A second, expanded edition of *De Cive* was published in 1647, and a translation of it, *Philosophical Rudiments Concern-*

ing Government and Society, was published in London in 1651.

Free Will

In 1645, Hobbes debated fellow exile bishop John Bramhall on the topics of free will and PREDESTINATION in front of William Cavendish, then marquis of Newcastle. At Newcastle's request, Hobbes wrote out his view in *Of Liberty and Necessity*; Bramhall wrote his *A True Defence of Liberty* in reply. Neither work was intended for publication. However, Hobbes's work was published in 1654 without his knowledge. Bramhall's book was published the next year, and Hobbes replied to Bramhall in *The Questions Concerning Liberty, Necessity and Chance* (1656).

The will, according to Hobbes, is the last desire a person has before acting. Because that desire is itself caused by some preceding event either inside or outside the person, according to natural laws, there is no such thing as a free will. Indeed, according to Hobbes, the phrase "free will" is incoherent, because only substances can be free or not. So a person is free when the cause of the person's action comes from within, in contrast with having the action caused by a violent external cause like a wind blowing a person across a field.

Bramhall, like other defenders of free will, thought that Hobbes's view undermined a necessary condition for responsibility. There can be no praise or blame, and hence no justified assignment of people to heaven or hell (see HEAVEN AND HELL), unless their actions are truly their own. So free will must exist. Bramhall in effect was defending ARMINIANISM. In contrast, Hobbes aligned himself with MARTIN LUTHER's view. More generally, Hobbes's view is Calvinistic (see CALVINISM). Because God is the cause of all things, God is the ultimate cause of all human actions also, including the sinful ones. However, God is not culpable because a person is culpable only when he or she breaks a law. Because God by his sovereignty is subject to no law, God breaks no law. As for praise or blame, praise belongs to those who keep the law, blame belongs to those who break the law.

Leviathan and Religion

After the institution of the Commonwealth in 1649, Hobbes decided to return to England. His magnum opus *Leviathan* was published in 1651, to a stormy reception. Many objected to views presented in the first two parts of the book: his argument that the natural condition of human life was "solitary, poor, nasty, brutish and short," his claim that what is naturally good is whatever a person desires, and his belief that SALVATION in this world comes from the establishment of an absolute sovereign. Even more objectionable were the third and fourth parts of the book, "Of a Christian Commonwealth" and "Of the Kingdom of Darkness." He was the first major author to argue in print that Moses was not the author of the entire Pentateuch. Also, he implied that God was material and that spirits are nothing but the imaginings of a fevered or demented brain. He undercut belief in revelation by saying that the sentence, "God appeared to me in a dream" means the same as "I dreamed that God appeared to me." He undercut belief in prophets by adducing biblical evidence that showed that prophets are often wrong, sometimes deceived by other prophets, and sometimes lie, as God asserts in the book of Jeremiah. At best, true prophets can be identified only after their predictions come true, that is, after it is too late for people to derive any benefit from them. He undercut belief in miracles by observing that only people ignorant of natural science can witness them, and held, as many members of the Church of England did, that miracles were no longer important because they ended with the death of the last apostle. Not even his attack on Roman Catholicism, which described the papacy as "nothing other than the ghost of the Roman empire, sitting crowned upon the grave thereof," pleased most Protestants because his criticisms could be understood as applying also to presbyterian and episcopal CLERGY (see CATHOLICISM, PROTESTANT REACTIONS).

Although Hobbes's positions are arguably consistent with Christianity, his contemporaries, like most current scholars, thought that they proved he was intent on surreptitiously undermining Christianity. However, there is no consensus about whether Hobbes himself was an atheist, an agnostic, or a deist (see DEISM).

Some of Hobbes's views are Calvinist. He professes that God predestines humans for reward or punishment, that Jesus died only for the elect, and, as indicated above, that God, being the cause of all things, is the cause of sin. Like negative theologians Hobbes asserted that God is so great as to be incomprehensible. The proof is straightforward. Everything that humans know begins with sensation and is finite. God cannot be sensed and is infinite. The apparently descriptive language that Christians use about God is not literally true, but honorific. God is said to be simple, motionless, merciful, and all-seeing because to say such things honors God. God should be honored, not described, because God should be an object of worship, not science.

Hobbes did endorse a form of the First Cause argument for the existence of God. Every event in the world has a cause that is itself caused by something earlier, although it would be impossible for this chain of causes to extend infinitely because then the movement of nothing would be explained. Therefore, there must be a first cause, whom people call God. (The weak point in this argument is that by Hobbes's philosophy, every cause has a cause and hence God himself should need a cause.)

During the 1650s and 1660s Hobbes devoted most of his time to advancing his scientific and mathematical views, including various unsuccessful proofs that a circle can be squared. However, he defended his religious views in several notable works, especially *Mr Hobbes Considered in his Loyalty, Religion, Reputation and Manners* (1662) and *An Historical Narration Concerning Heresy and the Punishment Thereof* (1680). (The latter may have been a response to a failed attempt in 1666 to have him tried for HERESY.) Hobbes deflated heresy by describing the word's early use: any opinion. Christianity itself was originally a heresy, and it was only when it acquired political power that the church used the word as a term of abuse. English monarchs rarely used the charge of heresy to physically punish laypersons, the Catholic Queen Mary I being the notable or notorious exception. ELIZABETH I reversed Mary's policies. Heresy is also discussed in similar terms in an appendix to the Latin version of *Leviathan* (1668).

Hobbes continued fighting for his views into the 1670s when he was well into his eighties. In the 1670s he produced notable, if flawed, translations of Homer's *Iliad* and *Odyssey*. He died in late 1679 at the age of 91; he is buried inside the church of St. John the Baptist, Hault Hucknall, Derbyshire.

References and Further Reading

Primary Sources:

Hobbes, Thomas. *Leviathan.* Edited by A. P. Martinich. Peterborough, Ontario: Broadview Press, 2002.
———. "The Questions Concerning Liberty, Necessity, and Change." In *The English Works of Thomas Hobbes,* edited by William Molesworth, vol. 5. London: John Bohn, 1840.

Secondary Sources:

Curley, Edwin. "Calvin and Hobbes, or, Hobbes as an Orthodox Theologian." *Journal of the History of Philosophy* 34 no. 2 (1996): 257–271.
Manenschijn, Gerrit. " 'Jesus is the Christ': The Political Theology of *Leviathan.*" *Journal of Religious Ethics* 25 no. 1 (1997): 35–64.
Martinich, A. P. *The Two Gods of Leviathan.* Cambridge: Cambridge University Press, 1992.
———. *Hobbes: A Biography.* Cambridge, UK: Cambridge University Press, 1999.
Tuck, Richard. "The Christian Atheism of Thomas Hobbes." In *Atheism from the Reformation to the Enlightenment,* edited

by Michael Hunter and David Wootton. Oxford, UK: Oxford University Press, 1992.
Wright, George. "Hobbes' 1668 Latin Appendix to Leviathan." *Interpretation* 35 (1991): 323–413.

P. MARTINIC

HOFMANN, MELCHIOR (1495?–1543)

Anabaptist leader. Melchior Hofmann was an Anabaptist leader noted for visionary and eschatological ideas. A Swabian, in the 1520s he preached Lutheran reform in the Baltics, Sweden, and Schleswig-Holstein, but this opposition to MARTIN LUTHER's (1483–1546) view of the Eucharist, his radical ideas, and his claim of direct revelations from God created conflict with the authorities and Lutheran preachers. His 1526 *Exposition of the Twelfth Chapter of Daniel* predicted the end of the world in 1533. He moved to Strassburg in 1529, where he linked up with other visionaries and joined the Anabaptists. Some said he was the prophet Elijah. His *Exposition of the Secret Revelation of John* predicted the appointment of 144,000 apostolic messengers and named Strassburg as the site of Jesus's return and the expected spiritual Jerusalem. Arrested in 1530, he escaped and moved to East Frisia with some 300 followers, where he organized an Anabaptist congregation in Emden. Alternating between Holland and Strassburg, he continued his apocalyptic preaching but was rearrested in 1533. The Strassburg authorities, suspecting him of sedition, put him in prison, where he died in 1543. Hofmann published over twenty-five writings, including his important book on BAPTISM, *The Ordinance of God* (1530), and a book on Romans. Melchiorite ideas contributed to revolutionary Anabaptism at Münster, even though Hofmann would probably have opposed that undertaking.

References and Further Reading

Primary Source:

Hofmann, Melchior, "The Ordinance of God." Translated by George Huntston Williams. In *Spiritual and Anabaptist Writers: Documents Illustrative of the Radical Reformation.* Edited by George Huntston Williams and Angel M. Mergal. Philadelphia: The Westminster Press, 1957. 182–203.

Secondary Source:

Deppermann, Klaus, *Melchior Hoffman [sic]: Social Unrest and Apocalyptic Visions in the Age of Reformation.* Translated by Malcolm Wren. Edited by Benjamin Drewery. Edinburgh: T. & T. Clark, 1987.

ROLLIN S. ARMOUR SR.

HOGG, JAMES (1770–1835)

Scottish romantic poet and novelist. A shepherd born near Selkirk, SCOTLAND, Hogg received little formal education, but taught himself and displayed considerable skill at versifying the pastoral scenes and stories of Lowland Scotland. Discovered early in his career by Sir Walter Scott, the "Ettrick Shepherd" moved to Edinburgh, where he interacted with the major figures of British ROMANTICISM. After five years, he returned to a dual career in rural Scotland, supporting himself financially through writing while unsuccessfully farming until his death.

Hogg's most famous work, a psychological thriller, *The Private Memoirs and Confessions of a Justified Sinner* (1824), adeptly combined murder mystery with theological critique, using typically Romantic literary devices to produce a sardonic portrait of Calvinistic ANTINOMIANISM prevalent in rural Scotland. The novel depicts the ill-fated joining of Robert Wringhim Colwan with the DEVIL, who uses his protégé's theological views to drive him to murder and insanity. His namesake and guardian, the Rev. Robert Wringhim, raises him to believe that Robert's eternal SALVATION is irrevocably secure, while simultaneously asserting the reprobation of his older brother and father. Rapt in this knowledge, the young man meets with a mysterious BIBLE-toting (but never-praying) stranger, who agrees perfectly with all his views of PREDESTINATION and ultimately convinces him to smite the nonelect (see ELECTION). Caught between the theological rationale of the devil and purported devotion to God, Robert descends into madness and suffers the judgment that he so readily pronounces on others. Although some have read the novel as a blanket condemnation of religious dedication, Hogg remained a sincere Christian, whose writings criticized religious hypocrisy while championing the devotional piety and theological discernment of the common layperson.

See also Calvinism; Literature

References and Further Reading

Jinkins, Michael. "The Devil's Theology: Theological Reflections on James Hogg's The Private Memoirs and Confessions of a Justified Sinner." *Evangelical Quarterly* 62 no. 2 (1990): 157–174.
Smith, Nelson C. *James Hogg*. Boston, MA: Twayne Publishers, 1980.

STEPHEN R. BERRY

HOLIDAYS AND FESTIVALS

Early Protestants took great pains to differentiate *holy day* from *holiday,* typically by insisting on the sacred nature (hallowed by God) of the former and the profanity (hallowed by men) of the latter. This distinction was not salient before the sixteenth century. Indicating a day or period when ordinary occupations are suspended, often but not always for festive purposes,

holiday as a concept is a product of the Protestant REFORMATION. Over the course of several centuries, Protestant holidays took shape such that they partially resembled the festivals that had accompanied the many holy days of the Catholic Church (see CATHOLICISM, PROTESTANT REACTIONS). Closely associated with holiday, but distinct in meaning and function, festival has a long history in the Western world; the word is derived from the Latin *festum* ("public joy, merriment, revelry") and *feria* ("abstinence from work in honor of the gods"). Although continuing to be a forceful concept for Catholic peoples, festival barely registers as a religious concept in regions dominated by Protestantism.

Early Protestant reformers succeeded in their attempts to rationalize holidays and festivals: both the numbers and duration of holidays have severely attenuated between the sixteenth and twentieth centuries. However, indulgence, wastefulness, and materialism reemerged with a vengeance, threatening to crowd out the liturgical and religious messages of Christmas and Easter, essentially the only holidays that survived the reformation of the calendar. On the other hand, Protestantism suffuses civic holidays that commemorate the nation-state and its people's sacrifices. Theological debates within Protestantism over holidays and festivals have received little scholarly attention; the study of the history of holidays themselves, however, is a cottage industry. This essay focuses on three moments in that history that intersect with major developments in Protestantism. It first addresses calendar reform between the sixteenth and eighteenth centuries; then turns to the ascent of the modern Christmas and Easter in the nineteenth century; and closes with the prominent place of civic holidays as keystones to the civil religions of modern nation-states in the twentieth century.

The Reform of the Calendar

In the wake of the Protestant Reformation, the same theological and moral objections to popular CULTURE that animated a range of Europeans also fed efforts to reform and reshape the religious calendars of Protestant countries. The numerous saints' days bequeathed by Roman Catholicism and the christological structure of the liturgical year (layered as it was over pre-Christian rites and festivals) each contained numerous pagan elements. Furthermore, the intermingling of profane practices with sacred observances was anathema to many Protestants. From a moral perspective, the popular culture to which the reigning calendar gave shape allowed for far too much debauchery, idleness, and neglect of work. As MARTIN LUTHER observed, "With our present abuses of drinking, gambling, idling, and all manner of sin, we vex God more on holy days than on others." He further decried the many days of work lost and the excessive spending engendered by a calendar rich with holy days, festivals, and feasts. Whereas Luther was far more moderate than many other Protestant reformers, his theological and moral critique of holy days became standard within the varieties of Protestant justifications for the reform of the calendar.

It was in sixteenth- and seventeenth-century ENGLAND that an enduring divide within Protestantism concerning the calendar, and holidays, emerged. This divide can easily be summed up in the shorthand juxtaposition of Anglican against Puritan (see ANGLICANISM, PURITANISM). In 1536 Henry VIII limited the number of holy days, largely in the attempt to introduce a regular rhythm of work. Some feasts were kept as high holy days, including those of the Apostles, the Blessed Virgin, the Nativity, and Easter day; others were demoted to days to be kept holy; and others were banished altogether. The Parliament of Edward VI in 1552 restored some of the holy days that had been eliminated, such that twenty-seven holy days, in addition to fifty-two Sundays, were set aside from work for PRAYER and WORSHIP. Several years later the BOOK OF COMMON PRAYER featured the holy days in red letters, thus the term "red letter day" came to connote holiday. Because Protestant theology insisted that SAINTS could not intercede on behalf of supplicants, the few saints' days that remained in the calendar, such as the feasts of St. George, St. John the Baptist, and St. Michael the Archangel, were occasions to honor the saints, rather than to pray to them.

Still, for Puritans and other reform-minded Protestants these Anglican alterations to the calendar were hardly sufficient because they perpetuated both Roman and pagan beliefs and rituals. In the 1570s successful attacks on the observance of Christmas and other holy days in SCOTLAND fed the zeal of reformers. They maintained that scriptural sanction for the observance of holy days was limited solely to Sabbaths. In 1640 nonconformists (including Puritans) who gained the upper hand in England abolished observance of Christmas and all the saints' days (see NONCONFORMITY). At the same time, across the Atlantic Protestant reformers of various stripes (Puritans, BAPTISTS, Presbyterians, and Quakers) succeeded in establishing a calendar devoid of all holy days but the Sabbath (see PRESBYTERIANISM; FRIENDS, SOCIETY OF). With the Restoration in 1660, Charles II revived the Anglican ecclesiastical calendar with its moderate round of holy days.

Although more research needs to be done, it seems clear that it was during the last quarter of the seventeenth century that theologians differentiated holy days from holidays, with some proclaiming the necessity, and indeed the beauty, of each, and others declaiming holidays as perversions and blasphemy. The Edwardian calendar, with slight alterations under ELIZABETH I, stayed in place through the eighteenth century. Over the decades the popular observance of saints' days and holidays (which had continued despite official injunctions) diminished in frequency and intensity, although ministers like COTTON MATHER could still be found decrying the "Mad Mirth, long Eating, hard Drinking, lewd Gaming, rude Reveling" of the Christmas season. By the nineteenth century, middle-class Protestants rarely celebrated holidays; deeply religious though they were, it was the Sabbath that provided the rhythm for their year. As one contemporary observed: "The *red-letter days*, now become, to all intents and purposes, *dead-letter days*."

Modern Holidays: Festivals of Consumption

Consumer capitalism, which began to take shape in the eighteenth century and was ascendant by the nineteenth, played the most significant role in reviving the two holidays—Christmas and Easter—that now demarcate the Protestant calendar. Although the wild and wanton celebration of the nativity waned in Protestant circles during the seventeenth and eighteenth centuries, the public festivities (above all, wassailing) and private customs (e.g., gift-giving) that accompanied New Year's did not. In seeking to transform the celebration of New Year's into a religious occasion for the renewal of Christian commitment, evangelical Protestants unwittingly rediscovered Christmas during the first half of the nineteenth century (see EVANGELICALISM). Christmas suited their purposes far better than did New Year's eve, in that it more easily fit into a Christian, domestic, and commercial framework. In terms of Christianity, Christmas provided the opportunity to revisit the birth of Christ, which was becoming more and more important in Protestant circles because of the rise of a liberal theology that in stressing the goodness of mankind was highly Christocentric (see LIBERAL PROTESTANTISM AND LIBERALISM). In the nineteenth century, a period when private domesticity gained powerful ideological force, Christmas became the preeminent moment for enshrining the FAMILY, and thereby constricting unruly public behavior. Above all, as a network for retailing and marketing spread, whetting the desires and appetites of Anglo-American, British, and Continental Protestants, Christmas became a sanctioned moment for indulgence, primarily in the form of gift-giving and feasting. At first it was the domestic and commercial aspects of Christmas that took hold of the LAITY's imagination; in the late decades of the nineteenth century Protestant clergy introduced Christmas sermons, decorations, pageants, and HYMNS, which met the laity's expectations for consecration of the nativity of Christ.

With the exception of Anglicans and Lutherans (see LUTHERANISM), most Protestants did not celebrate Easter until the last quarter of the nineteenth century. Here again, consumer capitalism was responsible for transforming an austere and somber moment in the Christian cycle into an exuberant rite of spring. As creating beautiful church interiors assumed more and more importance among a range of Protestant denominations, holiday decorations were granted special importance in that they glorified God and uplifted Christians. One proponent of floral decorations at Easter explained: "The joy of our hearts at the Resurrection of our Saviour—the seal of the completion of His work on earth—must surely be even greater than on the festival of His birth. The festival, coming as it does in early spring, is best commemorated by the use of as many flowers as possible." The emphasis on church décor inevitably led to the "Easter parade" of hats and dresses, obtained in the marketplace along with confections, novelties, and cards made specifically for Easter. The Easter egg, an ancient symbol of fecundity, returned as a commodity, as did rabbits and chicks. Although Easter has never taken on the massive commercial powers of Christmas, it was again the admixture of domesticity, Christianity, and commerce that recast the liturgical moment as a holiday for Protestants in the late nineteenth century.

Although it is clear in hindsight that the commercialization of Christmas and Easter resuscitated the holidays for Protestants, theological and social critiques of the market-orientation of each celebration have been standard fare for more than a century. However, as the leading religious historian of American holidays, Leigh Eric Schmidt, has explained "a common feature of festivity is to overindulge, to eat, drink, or spend to excess, lavishly to use up resources otherwise diligently saved. The surfeit of gifts and spending associated especially with Christmas, but also with other holidays, gives expression to a kind of festal excess that is often fundamental to celebrations." It is then the admixture of commerce and Christianity that has allowed Christmas and Easter to flourish in a calendar that Protestants have otherwise purged of festivity.

National Holidays and Civil Religion

Just as the modern Christmas and Easter resulted from the interweaving of Christian and capitalist imperatives, a potent mix of Protestantism and patriotism has given shape to civic holidays that celebrate the modern nation-state. As the historian David Cressy has shown, the calendar of early modern England was "an important tool for declaring and disseminating a distinctively Protestant national culture." To the Protestant calendar were added national, secular holidays, such as royal accession day and Gunpowder Plot day: on these days the convening of religious services, the ringing of church bells, and the offering of prayers marked the festivities. Similar nationalist rites and cycles characterize the calendars of most nation states, regardless of their religious orientation. Nevertheless, Protestantism has energized the emergence of what sociologist Robert Bellah identified in 1967 as Civil Religion, that is a distinct set of religious symbols and practices that serves to solidify the political legitimacy of nation-states.

Nowhere has civil religion flourished more vigorously than in the United States. The Declaration of Independence, the Constitution, and the BILL OF RIGHTS are scripture for the civil religion of the United States; by the same token, the Fourth of July and Thanksgiving are the high holy days for this religion, with Memorial and Veterans Days playing minor, though important, roles. Founding Father John Adams predicted that Independence Day "will be celebrated by succeeding generations as the great anniversary festival. It ought to be commemorated as the day of deliverance, by solemn acts of devotion to God Almighty. It ought to be solemnized with pomp and parade, with shows, games and sports, guns, bells, bonfires and illuminations, from one end of this continent to the other." Throughout the nineteenth and into the twentieth century, religious and political oratory on the Fourth of July has focused on the nation and its people's divine mission and blessings. Thanksgiving Day, originating in the American CIVIL WAR, was according to one chronicler "originally regarded with almost the same reverence as was shown for Sunday. Religious services were held in the churches and after the services the families gathered around the table." Today spectator sports join religious services, political oratory, and festive dinners. Although CHURCH AND STATE are separate in the United States, the material and rhetorical symbols constituting its civic holidays make it clear that it is a Protestant God's country. Were it not for the reform of the calendar accomplished by a variety of Protestants animated by a variety of theological convictions, there would be no room for the civil religion, let alone the civic holidays, which with Christmas and Easter provide contemporary rhythms of work, rest, consumption, festivity, and thanksgiving.

See also Sabbatarianism

References and Further Reading

Bellah, Robert, and Phillip E. Hammond. *Varieties of Civil Religion.* New York: Harper & Row, 1980.

Burke, Peter. *Popular Culture in Early Modern Europe.* New York: Harper & Row, 1978.

Cox, Harvey. *The Feast of Fools: A Theological Essay on Festivity and Fantasy.* Cambridge, MA: Harvard University Press, 1969.

Cressy, David. *Bonfires and Bells: National Memory and the Protestant Calendar in Elizabethan and Stuart England.* Berkeley: University of California Press, 1989.

Dennis, Matthew. *Red, White, and Blue Letter Days: An American Calendar.* Ithaca, NY: Cornell University Press, 2002.

Hall, David D. *Worlds of Wonder, Days of Judgement: Popular Religious Belief in Early New England.* Cambridge, MA: Harvard University Press, 1989.

Hill, Christopher. *Society and Puritanism in Pre-Revolutionary England.* New York: Schocken Books, 1964.

McCrossen, Alexis. *Holy Day, Holiday: The American Sunday.* Ithaca, NY: Cornell University Press, 2000.

Pleck, Elizabeth. *Celebrating the Family: Ethnicity, Consumer Culture, and Family Rituals.* Cambridge, MA: Harvard University Press, 2000.

Schmidt, Leigh Eric. *Consumer Rites: The Buying and Selling of American Holidays.* Princeton, NJ: Princeton University Press, 1995.

ALEXIS McCROSSEN

HOLINESS CHURCHES

See Holiness Movement

HOLINESS MOVEMENT

The Holiness Movement is a predominantly North American Protestant religious movement arising in the nineteenth century. It was characterized by an emphasis on the Wesleyan doctrine of SANCTIFICATION and focused on the postconversion experience of "entire sanctification." The Holiness Movement was centered in a deeply emotional and experiential FAITH, with the result that quasi-Methodist sects were formed.

History

In the mid-nineteenth century, members of the Methodist Church, then the largest church body in the United States, became dissatisfied with the declining moral standards of their church. The Methodists' DOCTRINE of "Christian perfection" was believed to have been abandoned for spiritual and moral complacency. A distinct movement came into being, which sought to address these issues.

The Holiness Movement was officially founded in the "National Camp Meeting Association for the Promotion of Christian Holiness," which met in Vineland, New Jersey, in July of 1867 (see CAMP MEETINGS). Large crowds attended the meetings, where thousands claimed to have received the "second blessing" of sanctification. The "first blessing" was CONVERSION itself. The Association, which later became known as the National Holiness Association, reported to have over 200 full-time "holiness evangelists."

The Methodist lay preacher and advocate of women's ordination, PHOEBE PALMER, was a catalyst for the Holiness Movement (see WOMEN; WOMEN CLERGY). Palmer, later known as "the Mother of the Holiness Movement," taught that perfection in love eliminated all sinful desires. She held "Tuesday Meetings for the Promotion of Holiness." These were prayer meetings, beginning in 1839, that were influential in the spreading of the Holiness Movement. The Movement spread through house meetings similar to Palmer's, sparking a larger revival. Characteristic of the Holiness Movement was its support as one of the first churches to accept women to ministry.

The revivalist CHARLES GRANDISON FINNEY subscribed to the Holiness Movement's teachings. He and his colleagues at Oberlin College, Ohio, formed the Oberlin Perfectionism branch of the Movement. Advocates of the Holiness Movement included William Boardman, author of *Higher Christian Life* (1858); James Caughey, author of *Methodism in Earnest* (1850); and Asa Mahan, author of *Guide to Christian Perfection* (1839) and second president of Oberlin College. In America the journal *Guide to Christian Perfection* (1839–1845), later the *Guide to Holiness* (1846–1901), was founded by Timothy Merritt and edited by Phoebe Palmer. The journal's distinctive devotion to Holiness doctrine had the effect of bringing this doctrine to other denominations in North America and across the Atlantic to ENGLAND.

The Holiness Movement found an audience in Europe in the 1870s where the HIGHER LIFE movement held conventions during the time of the Second Great Awakening. *The Christian's Secret of a Happy Life* (1875), by HANNAH WHITALL SMITH, was inspired by her personal experience with the holiness camp meetings. Her book increased the popularity of the Movement especially in England. There the KESWICK MOVEMENT originated from the Holiness Movement's teaching on sanctification, although taking a more expansive view of divine GRACE.

Theology and Issues

The Holiness Movement taught a modified form of JOHN WESLEY's Arminian doctrine of grace, which emphasized a cooperation of the human and divine will in the granting of Christian perfection. The postconversion event of "entire sanctification" incorporated several aspects. Foremost, the experience resulted in a divine cleansing from the tendency to commit willful SIN. This became an unreserved consecration and surrender to the will of God. A divine enablement was given to the believer, which was an unconditional love for God and neighbor. This experience is commonly referred to as "entire sanctification," "holiness," the "second blessing," "the blessing," the "baptism with (or of) the Holy Spirit," "Christian perfection," or "full salvation." The divine enablement often coincided with the experience of avoiding worldly behavior, such as immodest dress, card playing, gambling, drinking, and association with secret societies.

Sectarian tensions had begun to form between supporters of the Holiness Movement and the Methodist bishops in the last decades of the nineteenth century (see BISHOP AND EPISCOPACY). The "stay-inners" and the "come-outers" typified two divisions of the Methodist Church. Some, such as H. C. Morrison, later president of Asbury College and Theological Seminary in Kentucky, was a "stay-inner" who remained with the Southern Methodist Church. However, others left the Methodist church as early as 1843. The once exuberant and revivalistic Holiness Movement was waning by 1900, with the newly forming Pentecostal Movement on the rise (see REVIVALS; PENTECOSTALISM).

The Holiness Movement was reported to have several doctrinal eccentricities. *The Divine Church* (1883), written by John P. Brook, represented the radical ECCLESIOLOGY of the Movement. Brook was one of the more theologically astute of the "come outers," who argued that all human organizations of Christianity were "The Church of Sect." Instead of his Methodist Episcopal Church being governed by episcopal oversight, Brook believed that Christ was to be the sole Ruler of the church.

Many within the Holiness Movement sought after the phenomenon of the "baptism of fire." This sect of the Movement was led by Benjamin Irwin and originated in Iowa, in 1895. Irwin's followers were characterized by their receiving a miraculous visitation of the Spirit after the "second blessing." Those who received "the baptism of fire" would scream, shout, or fall into trances. The conservative teachers of the Holiness Movement rejected this splinter group, regarding the "second blessing" and the "baptism of fire" as one and the same.

Some twenty-three Holiness denominations arose between 1893 and 1900. Current denominations, formed in the period of the Holiness Movement, are the CHURCH OF GOD (1881), the CHURCH OF THE NAZARENE (1908), and other denominations using "Holiness" as part of their names. The Church of the Nazarene is the largest of the Holiness churches, which has a strong presence in North America and the United Kingdom.

See also Arminianism; Awakenings; Methodism, England; Methodism, North America; Orthodoxy; Sectarianism; Wesley, John; Wesleyan Holiness Movement

References and Further Reading

Dieter, Melvin Easterday. *The 19th-Century Holiness Movement*. Kansas City, MO: Beacon Hill Press, 1998.
Harper, Albert F., gen. ed. *Great Holiness Classics*. 6 vols. Kansas City, MO: Beacon Hill Press, 1984–1994.
Jones, Charles Edwin. *A Guide to the Study of the Holiness Movement*. Metuchen, NJ: Scarecrow Press, 1974.
———. *Perfectionist Persuasion: The Holiness Movement and American Methodism, 1867–1936*. Metuchen, NJ: Scarecrow Press, 2002.
Kostlevy, William C., and Gari-Anne Patzwald, eds. *Historical Dictionary of the Holiness Movement*. Lanham, MD: Scarecrow Press, 2001.
Smith, Hannah Whitall. *The Christian's Secret of a Happy Life*. Ulrichsville, OH: Barbour Publishing, 2002.

CHRISTOPHER M. COOK

HOLL, KARL (1866–1926)

German church historian. An influential church historian and a founding figure of modern studies on MARTIN LUTHER, Karl Holl was born on June 15, 1866, in Tübingen and died on June 23, 1926, in Berlin. He grew up in a religiously and politically liberal family. After studying THEOLOGY and philosophy in Tübingen (1884–1888), where he and many of his contemporaries were influenced by the theology of ALBRECHT RITSCHL, Holl experienced a religious crisis. From his study of original sources, he came to acknowledge that the truth of biblical revelation presumed by Ritschl was not unambiguously clear. A solution came in 1894 when ADOLF VON HARNACK secured him a position in Berlin as a scholarly collaborator with the commission of church fathers for the Prussian Academy of Sciences. Holl qualified to teach at a university in 1896, and in 1900 received a position in Tübingen as professor of church history. In 1906 he returned to Berlin as a professor. His scholarly work stood for years in the shadow of his famous colleague Harnack.

Faculty members praised Holl as an extraordinary scholar of the church fathers. In his countless works on the early church and on other periods of church history through his day, he brilliantly combined subtle philological criticism, sharp-minded analysis, and crucial philosophical-theological research of original sources. Holl made a broad impact on church history with the publication of his book on Luther in 1921. It appeared at the same time as the second edition of KARL BARTH's commentary on the letter to the Romans and supported the turn away from liberal theology in German Protestantism. With the systematic examination of Luther's early works, Holl produced a new understanding of the reformer's theology that was far more extensive than previous versions. The nine essays in this volume focused on Luther's doctrine of JUSTIFICATION as well as his hermeneutics, ECCLESIOLOGY, ETHICS, and theory of the state.

Although Holl argued in strict historical terms, he was convinced that Luther's thought held direct relevance to the present. Thus he felt obliged to address contemporary issues, especially during World War I and the period after 1918. Unlike his colleagues, Holl did not distort Luther as a nationalist figure. He also valued JOHN CALVIN, although he considered Luther's theology superior. During World War I, Holl joined the right-wing German Fatherland Party, which militated against the peace accord ratified by the German parliament and for a continuation of the war. Holl had a very reserved relationship to the Weimar Republic. He hoped that Luther's religiously realized moral idealism would lead to Germany's spiritual renewal. In 1933, many of Holl's students, among them Erich Vogelsang, Hermann Wolfgang Beyer, Hanns Rückert, Heinrich Bornkamm, Helmuth Kittel, and especially Emanuel Hirsch—thought that they could interpret and find this notion of renewal in the emergence of German nationalism. Such political-theological definitions sharpened the contrast between advocates of dialectical theology and advocates of the "Luther Renaissance."

See also Neo-orthodoxy

References and Further Reading

Primary Source:

Holl, Karl. *Gesammelte Aufsätze zur Kirchengeschichte,* vols. 13. Tübingen, Germany: 1921 and 1928.

Secondary Source:

"Johannes Wallmann, Karl Holl, und seine Schule." *Zeitschrift für Theologie und Kirche* 4 (1978): 1–33.

MARTIN GRESCHAT

HOLOCAUST

The term "Holocaust," from the Greek for "a burned offering," has been used since the 1960s to refer to the murder of approximately 6,000,000 European Jews by Nazi Germans and their collaborators during World War II (1939–1945). Since the 1970s, the Hebrew word "Shoah" (catastrophe) has entered common usage as a synonym.

Hatred of Jews was the center of Nazi ideology. Hitler and his associates preached what the scholar Saul Friedländer calls "redemptive anti-Semitism": the belief that Jews were the root of all evil, and

Germany could be saved from collapse only by destruction of Jews and Jewish influence. Religious prejudices were just one element in Nazi ANTI-SEMITISM, with its pseudoscientific notions of "blood" and "race" and its paranoia about international conspiracies, but for many Christians in GERMANY and throughout Europe, old habits of Christian anti-Judaism helped normalize the new strain of hatred.

Debate continues over whether the label "Holocaust" includes persecuted groups other than Jews. Jews were the main target of Nazi genocide; against the Jews National Socialist Germany mobilized all of its resources: bureaucratic, military, legal, scientific, intellectual, and religious. But the Nazi German state also initiated systematic mass killing of people deemed handicapped and European Gypsies (Roma). These programs shared with the genocide of the Jews personnel, methods of killing, and goals of so-called racial purification. In these cases—Jews, Gypsies, and the handicapped—the perpetrators sought out children for killing, an indication that the intention was total annihilation.

National Socialist Germany also persecuted, incarcerated, and killed Communists, homosexual men, Jehovah's Witnesses, and African-Germans, as well as many Polish gentiles and Soviet prisoners of war. Often members of these groups shared the torments heaped on Jews, Gypsies, and the handicapped. These cases are not usually included under the term "Holocaust," however; they were either less massive in scope and less total in intention than the Jewish genocide—for example, Jehovah's Witnesses, of whom about an estimated 2,000 were killed in German camps—or, as with the three million Soviet POWs killed or left to die of hunger and disease, those targeted did not include children.

It is difficult to determine when the Holocaust began, because a series of steps culminated in the slaughters Nazi jargon labeled the "final solution" to the "Jewish problem." In January 1933, Adolf Hitler was appointed chancellor of Germany. Within months his regime introduced measures to crush Communists, exclude Jews from public life, and sterilize supposed bearers of hereditary diseases. Hitler also began preparing for war in search of *Lebensraum*—living space in eastern Europe for the allegedly superior "Aryan race."

Only 37 percent of Germans ever voted for Hitler's National Socialist German Workers' Party, and in 1933 many Germans had misgivings. However, Hitler proved masterful at engineering foreign policy successes and organizing shows of public support that generated enthusiasm. Moreover, key elites—Protestant church leaders and many top Catholics, conservatives, university professors, and civil servants—

welcomed the new regime. They applauded its hard line against "godless Bolshevism" and praised its pledge to honor "blood and soil" and break the supposed stranglehold on cultural life of Jews, "degenerates," homosexuals, and liberals. Many Protestants hoped that the Nazi revolution would spark a revival of public Christianity and restore their church to what they believed was its rightful place at the center of German life. In March 1933, the Nazi government opened the first concentration camp at Dachau, near Munich.

By 1935, Nazi legislation defined "Jews," and by contrast "Aryans," a necessary step toward isolating, expropriating, and murdering Jews in the German Reich and the areas that it controlled. Although Nazi ideologues insisted that Jewishness was racial, their legal definition relied on religious distinctions. Germans with three or four grandparents of the Jewish faith counted as "non-Aryans," that is, "Jews," regardless of their own or their parents' affiliations and beliefs. The laws also created categories for *mischlinge*, Germans of "mixed blood." Both Christian German churches, Roman Catholic and Protestant (*Evangelisch*), cooperated by providing the baptismal certificates on which proof of "Aryan blood" depended.

The November 1938 pogrom, which came to be known as *Kristallnacht*, was the first widespread, violent public attack on Jews and Jewish property in the Third Reich, which by late 1938 included Austria and part of Czechoslovakia. Groups of Nazi thugs—stormtroopers, Hitler Youth, party elites—torched synagogues, smashed windows of Jewish shops, plundered Jewish homes, and assaulted Jewish women and men. Other Germans joined in the looting; some looked on or grumbled about disruption of public order. Some 20,000 Jewish men were incarcerated in concentration camps. In the wake of the pogrom, many Jews fled Germany. Between 1933 and 1939, the Jewish population of Germany dropped from around 500,000 (about 1 percent of the population), to between 200,000 and 300,000. Many sought refuge elsewhere in Europe—FRANCE, POLAND, the NETHERLANDS—where they fell into German hands again during the war.

It was not Jews, but rather people deemed handicapped who became targets of the first program of mass killing. Beginning in 1939 with an initiative to murder children, the euphemistically named "euthanasia" or T-4 Program involved doctors, nurses, bureaucrats, and social workers, as well as administrators of mental hospitals, many of them church-run, in the slaughter of 70,000 to 80,000 Germans considered "lives unworthy of living." Despite efforts at secrecy, information leaked out. Public protest peaked in 1941 when private citizens and prominent churchmen—

Protestants as well as Catholics—denounced the murders. Although Hitler announced a halt, killings continued under cover.

In September 1939, Germany invaded Poland. The Holocaust was inextricably linked to the war. National Socialist goals of racial purification and spatial expansion made WAR not only necessary but desirable in the minds of Hitler and Nazi "true believers." War delivered into German hands the large Jewish populations of eastern Europe—Poland, Ukraine, ROMANIA, HUNGARY, and elsewhere—as well as the Jews of the west: France, Belgium, and the Netherlands. War hardened the perpetrators and numbed onlookers.

With the war, Nazi persecution expanded and accelerated. Ghettoization of Jews in Poland began in 1939; by June 1941, with Germany's invasion of the Soviet Union, Nazi perpetrators began implementing total annihilation. Mobile killing squads, the *Einsatzgruppen*, accompanied regular German military into Soviet territory with orders to shoot high-ranking Communists and Jews. In killing fields and death pits, from southern Ukraine to Lithuania, the Einsatzgruppen shot more than one million Jews. They also murdered Gypsies and patients from mental hospitals. By late 1941, the killers sought more efficient methods and had begun experimenting with poison gases used in the T-4 Program. By 1942, the Nazi killing centers of Belzec, Chelmno, Treblinka, Sobibor, Majdanek, and Auschwitz-Birkenau were in full operation. The Nazis did not restrict attacks to religious Jews; they also targeted secular Jews and Christians who had converted from JUDAISM, as well as children and in some cases grandchildren of converts.

In 1944 and 1945, as Allied forces closed in, SS leader Heinrich Himmler ordered the killing centers evacuated and the remaining inmates killed or relocated to German-held territories. Death tolls on the resulting "death marches" were high; "liberation" came too late for many. Those Jews who survived found themselves without homes, families, or communities. As they struggled to begin new lives—in the displaced-person camps of Germany, in Palestine and later Israel, in the UNITED STATES, CANADA, AUSTRALIA, SOUTH AFRICA, and LATIN AMERICA—some tried to put the past behind them. Others vowed to remember.

The decentralized nature of Protestantism makes it almost impossible to draw comprehensive conclusions about its relationship to the Holocaust. On the one hand, examples of institutional failure are easy to find. Inside Germany, the pro-Nazi GERMAN CHRISTIAN movement (*Glaubensbewegung "Deutsche Christen"*) openly endorsed anti-Jewish measures. Its members controlled the governing bodies of most of Germany's regional Protestant churches and used their positions to attack Jews, Judaism, and so-called "non-Aryan

Christians." They also promoted efforts to purge all aspects of Judaism from Christianity. Even the CONFESSING CHURCH did little to protect the few "non-Aryan" pastors in its midst. Some North American Protestant Churches, particularly those with organizational or ethnic ties to Germany, propagated a positive view of National Socialism, at least until the United States entered the war.

On the other hand, however, institutional Protestantism also fostered heroism. Some Protestant groups in North America worked hard to learn about conditions in Europe and to lobby their governments to accept refugees. French HUGUENOTS in the villages surrounding Le Chambon-sur-Lignon, led by their pastor Andre Trocme and his wife Magda, saved the lives of many Jews. They were inspired at least in part by their Protestant faith and love of Scripture. In occupied DENMARK, an overwhelmingly Protestant country, church leaders publicly decried Nazi anti-Semitism and encouraged participation in rescues. Danes mobilized to protect their 8,000 Jewish fellow citizens, and almost every Danish Jew survived.

How have Protestants dealt with the complex legacy of the Holocaust? The answer depends on which Protestants and where. In North America, many Protestants, although fascinated with the hero DIETRICH BONHOEFFER, tend to think of the Holocaust as irrelevant to their faith. In Germany, in contrast, the relationship between the Protestant Churches, their adherents, and Nazi crimes has been the subject of intense debates since late 1945, when German Protestant leaders, under pressure from the world ecumenical community, issued the Stuttgart Declaration of Guilt. The declaration never explicitly mentions Jews or any specific crimes of Nazi Germany or the Protestant churches, but it does ask forgiveness "for not witnessing more courageously, for not praying more faithfully, for not believing more joyously, and for not loving more ardently."

In the half-century since World War II, Jewish–Christian dialogue has moved beyond the tentative contrition of the Stuttgart Declaration. For example, the 1997 Apology of the French Catholic bishops begged forgiveness from the Jews of France for teaching contempt for Jews. Protestants and Catholics alike have benefited from Jewish thinkers who articulated some of the burning issues connected with the Shoah. Does the Holocaust demand that humanity adopt a relentless position of questioning toward God? Does it call for rejection of ideas of "covenant" and "chosen people?" Is the Holocaust a challenge to affirm Judaism so as not to hand Hitler a "posthumous victory," as Emil Fackenheim argues? Is it, as Emmanuel Levinas writes, about "loving the Torah more than God," experiencing the

force of a God who hides his face through the intermediary of a teaching, the Torah? Protestant theologians, such as Franklin Littell, have posed these and other questions, although most of the discussion they generate—like that among their Catholic counterparts—still focuses on Christians as bystanders rather than perpetrators in the Holocaust.

References and Further Reading

Berenbaum, Michael, and Abraham J. Peck, eds. *The Holocaust and History: The Known, the Unknown, the Disputed and the Reexamined.* Bloomington, IN: Indiana University Press, 1998.
Bergen, Doris L. *War and Genocide: A Concise History of the Holocaust.* Lanham, MD: Rowman & Littlefield, 2003.
Ericksen, Robert P., and Susannah Heschel, eds. *Betrayal: German Churches and the Holocaust.* Minneapolis, MN: Augsburg Fortress, 1999.
Friedländer, Saul. *Nazi Germany and the Jews, Vol. 1, The Years of Persecution.* New York: Harper Collins, 1997.
Hilberg, Raul. *The Destruction of the European Jews.* 3 vols. Chicago: Quadrangle Books, 1961; rev. ed., New York: Holmes and Meier, 1985.
Wistrich, Robert. *Hitler and the Holocaust.* New York: Modern Library, 2001.
Yahil, Leni. *The Holocaust: The Fate of European Jewry.* Translated by Ina Friedman and Haya Galai. New York: Oxford University Press, 1990.

DORIS L. BERGEN

HOLY COMMUNION

See Lord's Supper

HOMESCHOOLING

Homeschooling represents an increasingly viable option for educating children in a family context, reflecting traditional and contemporary ideals about child development, parental responsibility, and social identity. For the greater part of human history, most children were educated at home, by relatives, in the subjects deemed most important by their families: subsistence skills and crafts, household accounting, and faith. Since the industrial revolution, most governments have taken charge of childhood education.

In the late nineteenth century in the UNITED STATES, many Roman Catholic families turned to parochial schools for the educational and faithful formation of their children, whereas most Protestants found public schools matched their denominational and ideological identity. As the twenty-first century progresses, however, a number of Protestants are finding that public education does not meet their parenting and pedagogical priorities. Homeschooling allows Protestant families to combine an appreciation of INDIVIDUALISM with a reconstruction of community; homeschooling can accommodate particular learning aptitudes and personalized instruction, while providing the time and opportunity for socializing and combining resources with other like-minded families. Homeschooling represents an alternative to institutionalized educational practices and a return to more particularized formation.

Protestant homeschooling families tailor their home education to fit their identity and their priorities. Many use homeschooling to counter the popular secularization and evolutionism (see DARWINISM) with curricula that feature CREATION SCIENCE, EVANGELICALISM, and FUNDAMENTALISM. Others highlight ties between CHURCH AND STATE (through curricula that emphasize God's work through democracy and capitalism) or resist such ties (by underscoring Christian identity over nation-state citizenship). Still others specialize in performing arts, academics, sports, or BIBLE, depending on their talents, interests, and convictions, while distancing themselves from unwanted indoctrination. In these ways, Protestant homeschooling enables families to reclaim the primary responsibility for childhood education, restore Christian formation to a prominent role in their children's lives, and reconstruct the social settings for learning and growing.

Homeschooling allows Protestant families to determine the context, content, and style of their children's education. Approaches range from the radically unstructured unschooling to the reproduction of a particular school setting in the home, and everything in between. Some families designate one stay-at-home parent as primary educator; some split the educational activities more evenly; some single parents juggle work and education responsibilities, with or without the help of extended families and other community members. Families may assemble learning materials on their own or select from an extensive market of curricula designed for homeschooling. Homeschooling support groups all over the world offer families chances to team teach, share expertises, and exchange ideas.

Laws about government supervision of homeschooling families vary among countries, states, and provinces. In general, homeschooling families are responsible for providing their children with an education comparable to that provided by the government. The evaluation of homeschooled children's learning process ranges from standardized testing to certified individualized assessment to parental discernment. Most colleges and universities welcome applications from students who have been homeschooled through elementary and high school; homeschoolers generally adapt well to college settings.

See also Education, Overview

References and Further Reading

Holt, John Caldwell. *Learning All the Time: How Small Children Begin to Read, Write, Count, and Investigate the World Without Being Taught.* Cambridge, MA: Perseus Books, 1990.

Saba, Laura, and Julie Gattis. *The McGraw-Hill Homeschooling Companion.* New York: McGraw-Hill Trade, 2002.

Zeise, Ann. *Regional and World Wide Homeschooling: A–Z.* http://www.gomilpitas.com/homeschooling/regional/Region.htm (April 15, 2003).

MARGARET B. ADAM

HOMILETICS

See Preaching

HOMOSEXUALITY

Homosexuality was barely a topic of discussion within any Christian tradition between the origins of Protestantism in the sixteenth century and the middle of the twentieth century. The presumption of nearly all churches was that homosexuality was a perversion of God's created order. By the end of the twentieth century, however, the debate over homosexuality had become (and remains) one of the most divisive and disputed issues confronting most Protestant denominations. Debates over homosexuality have become a touchstone for fundamental disagreements over the interpretation and application of Scripture, the roles and functions of TRADITION, reason, and experience, and very different understandings of Christian identity and GENDER formation. Traditional presumptions about homosexuality have been challenged on all of these fronts, and although nearly all Protestant denominations remain officially opposed to homosexual expression, there has been significant movement by many in the Protestant traditions toward acceptance of gay and lesbian Christians in the church. This acceptance reflects developments in larger European and American society at the end of the twentieth century.

Debate over Scripture

The BIBLE serves as the springboard for virtually all discussion about homosexuality. Traditional interpretations of scripture have appealed to the creation story in Genesis 1–2, the story of Sodom and Gomorrah in Genesis 19:1–9 (see also parallel stories in Judges 19 and Ezekiel 16:46–56), the prohibitions in Leviticus 18:22 and 20:13, and the Pauline statements in Romans 1:26–27, I Corinthians 6:9, and I Timothy 1:10 as all pointing to divine condemnation of homosexual expression. From this perspective of biblical interpretation Protestant churches have viewed homosexuality as a sinful violation of God's created natural order. With a growing emphasis, however, on both ancient and modern contextual readings of the biblical accounts, these traditional interpretations have been increasingly challenged. Those advocating full inclusion of gay and lesbian people in the church have argued, for example, that the story of Sodom and Gomorrah has to do with sexual violence and rape rather than homosexuality. Similarly, the prohibitions from Leviticus must be seen within the literary and historical context of the whole Holiness Code (Leviticus 17–26), which contains a number of other prohibitions that have traditionally not been followed. Many interpreters of Paul's letters have called attention to Paul's Greco-Roman cultural context, in which pederasty and slave prostitution appear to have been the primary models of homoerotic expression in view.

Matters get more complicated by debates over the appropriate translation of biblical terms from the original Hebrew and Greek languages. In I Corinthians 6:9, for example, the Greek term *arsenokoitai* (literally "men who go to bed") has been variously translated as "sexual perverts" (RSV), "homosexual offenders" (NIV), and "sodomites" (NRSV). Given that the term "homosexual" was not coined until the nineteenth century, scholars have increasingly agreed on the need to avoid anachronistic translations and interpretations of the Bible that read contemporary terms and conceptions back into the biblical texts. Beyond debates over biblical texts directly addressing same-sex relations, advocates of more traditional biblical interpretations have contended that scripture endorses heterosexual MARRIAGE as normative, whereas others have questioned whether this is a norm that necessarily excludes gay and lesbian unions.

Debate over Tradition, Reason, and Experience

Taking its lead from the plain sense of scripture, Protestant tradition in the late twentieth century was extremely cautious in changing its approach toward homosexuality. Conscious of the task of being a church *semper reformans* (always reforming), the leadership of most Protestant denominations took seriously the call by many to reconsider its traditional teachings on homosexuality. In the UNITED STATES, for example, the UNITED METHODIST CHURCH, the PRESBYTERIAN CHURCH U.S.A., the UNITED CHURCH OF CHRIST, the EVANGELICAL LUTHERAN CHURCH in America, and the EPISCOPAL CHURCH all engaged in multiyear studies of how to respond to the presence of gay and lesbian Christians in their congregations and in their church leadership. Such deliberations led to deep divisions in

each of these denominations, as year after year some church leaders called for the church to change with the times and be more inclusive of gay and lesbian Christians, whereas others called just as strongly for the church to take a firm stand against endorsing any form of homosexual expression, especially by ordained clergy.

Those seeking inclusion of gay and lesbian Christians in the church have emphasized sexual *orientation* as a natural God-given predisposition that individuals discover as they mature. Those seeking to uphold traditional sanctions against homosexuality have emphasized centuries of church teachings against same-sex *practices* and, although not seeing homosexual orientation itself as a matter of personal SIN, have argued that such an orientation is a distortion of God's creative purposes. From this perspective homosexual persons can be welcomed into the church but are called to abstain from same-sex relations. Most Protestant churches in recent years have issued official pronouncements ruling against the ordination of noncelibate homosexual Christians, as well as against the blessing or recognition of same-sex unions. Still, significant and vocal movements within the various Protestant denominations have continued to call for full acceptance of openly gay and lesbian clergy and for recognition of gay/lesbian unions and committed relationships. The United Church of Christ and the UNITED CHURCH OF CANADA have not prohibited the ordination of gay/lesbian clergy. In 2003, the Episcopal Diocese of New Hampshire elected as its bishop a priest who was in a long-term homosexual relationship. The national General Convention of the Episcopal Church subsequently confirmed the election.

Protestant churches have also sought to incorporate into their reasoning about homosexuality some of the more significant findings from the psychological and biological sciences, although these findings continue to be the subject of tremendous debate. In particular, churches have paid attention to the 1973 decision of the American Psychiatric Association to stop treating homosexuality as a pathology or disordered condition in need of treatment. Some controversial biological research has also suggested various genetic factors contributing to homosexual orientation. These developments have encouraged many to rethink the NATURAL LAW tradition and the degrees to which the formation of gender identity is a function of essential sexual identity and/or of changing social constructions. The significant debate that has ensued in the church has basically been between two camps. On the one hand the majority position advocates that heterosexual marriage has always been God's intended and exclusive norm for the expression of human sexuality (emphasizing the unitive and procreative functions of sex in marriage). On the other hand the minority position advocates that changing notions of gender roles are crucial in shaping all sexual identities, ancient and modern, and that there have always been various notions of sexual identity attributed to divine sanction: olygamy, CELIBACY, eunuchs, levirate, and monogamous marriages, for instance. Although homosexuality has been increasingly accepted as a normal and natural way to live in American and European societies at large, more traditional Protestant churches have called into question both the psychological and physical health of homosexual expression. A number of parachurch and controversial change ministries have arisen that seek to heal people of their homosexuality.

Perhaps the most important and difficult component to factor into Protestant attitudes toward homosexuality involves the ways people have experienced the presence of gay and lesbian Christians in the various denominations. The "coming out" of many prominent Protestant church leaders as gay/lesbian/ bisexual persons has forced churches to respond to the tension created by their effective ministries in light of traditional church teaching against homosexuality. The personal witness of successful and capable gay/ lesbian Christian leaders has been a powerful presence that has convinced many to push churches to be more accepting of these leaders in particular and to encourage the larger society to be more accepting of homosexual persons in general. At the same time the traditional Protestant rejection of homosexuality has led many gay and lesbian Christians to leave the church completely or to find local congregations that have publicly embraced an inclusive attitude toward homosexual persons. The rejection of gay/lesbian Christians in several Protestant denominations also led to the formation of the Universal Fellowship of Metropolitan Community Churches, a denomination dedicated to the full inclusion of gay/lesbian/bisexual/transgendered Christians. In sum Protestant churches have often been of two minds in their approach to homosexuality. On the one hand many denominations have passed binding resolutions ruling against the ordination of noncelibate gay/lesbian Christians and against same-sex unions. On the other hand most denominations have also passed resolutions calling on elected government officials to pass legislation that makes discrimination against homosexual people illegal.

Changing Views of Homosexuality

A significant factor in twentieth century debates over homosexuality in Protestant (and Catholic) churches can be traced in changing views about homosexuality in the larger society. Three general overlapping stages can be seen in popular attitudes toward homosexuality. At the beginning of the twentieth century homosexuality was viewed as a perversion of God's natural order and was punishable as a crime against God and society. As the century progressed and as general attitudes toward appropriate sexual behavior became more relaxed, a more accepting attitude began to develop toward homosexuality. The language associating homosexuality with "perversion" started to be seen as harsh and judgmental. In the latter half of the twentieth century the language of "sexual preference" began to be employed. This term still suggested personal choice in the realm of sexual activity, but same-sex "sexual preference" increasingly came to be seen as a relatively benign departure from societal norms. Toward the end of the twentieth century, in addition to the language of "sexual preference," the term "sexual orientation" gained prominence, which suggested that an individual had no real choice about gender identity and sexual attraction, and that such identity was more of a given. Because homosexuals were not personally responsible for choosing their sexuality, a movement developed that encouraged healthy and self-affirming homosexuals not to be ashamed of their identity, but to accept their homosexuality as a natural predisposition and orientation. This acceptance led, in the last decades of the twentieth century, to "gay pride" and to a sense of belonging to a gay community seeking and gaining acceptance from the larger society. Such acceptance has led to the tacit nonenforcement of most laws against homosexuality, to the decriminalization of many older laws against homosexual behavior, to the recognition of same-sex domestic partners by many businesses and some states, and to the wide depiction of gay and lesbian people as normal individuals through the vehicle of popular entertainment. These developments and changes in societal attitudes toward homosexuality have had a significant effect on most Protestant traditions, with the result that at the beginning of the twenty-first century many churches are more open than ever toward gay and lesbian Christians, while at the same time most official denominational pronouncements have ruled against the full inclusion of noncelibate gay and lesbian couples. This tension has led to serious debate in the churches about whether Protestant churches are behind the times and failing to follow the lead of God's reforming Spirit by including gay/lesbian Christians, or whether churches are most faithful in holding firm against recognizing any homosexual relationship as legitimate.

The Roman Catholic Church has also faced significant debate and discussion about homosexuality, although on somewhat different terms than those of the Protestant tradition. First, whereas Protestant churches have spent a great deal of energy addressing the issue of whether to allow the *ordination* of noncelibate gays/lesbians, this has not really been an issue for the Roman Catholic church because all priests are by definition celibate, be they homosexual or heterosexual. In the Protestant tradition clergy are typically married, and this automatically raises the question of how gay or lesbian couples serve as models for Christian marriage, which has traditionally been envisioned in heterosexual terms. Second, in the Roman Catholic tradition the role of *procreation* in marriage has been central, although the unitive function of sexuality has also gained in importance. This has meant that, because homosexual unions cannot by themselves procreate children, homosexual unions cannot receive the blessing of the church. By contrast in the Protestant tradition the *unitive* function of sexuality has typically held slightly greater importance than procreation (hence the common use of birth control in the Protestant tradition and not in official Roman Catholic teaching). Thus critics of homosexual relationships have raised questions about the biological complementarity of same-sex couples. Those advocating the appropriateness of blessing same-sex relationships in the church argue that it is wrong to define sexual complementarity in exclusively heterosexual terms.

See also Sexuality

References and Further Reading

Abelove, H., M. A. Barale, and D. Halperin, eds. *The Lesbian and Gay Studies Reader*. New York: Routledge, 1993.

Brawley, Robert L., ed. *Biblical Ethics and Homosexuality: Listening to Scripture*. Louisville, KY: Westminster/John Knox Press, 1996.

Comstock, Gary D., and Susan E. Henking, eds. *Que(e)rying Religion: A Critical Anthology*. New York: Continuum, 1997.

Hartman, Keith. *Congregations in Conflict: The Battle over Homosexuality*. New Brunswick, NJ: Rutgers University Press, 1996.

Melton, J. G., ed. *The Churches Speak on Homosexuality: Official Statements from Religious Bodies and Ecumenical Organizations*. Detroit, MI: Gale Research Inc., 1991.

Nelson, James B., and Sandra P. Longfellow, eds. *Sexuality and the Sacred: Sources for Theological Reflection*. Louisville, KY: Westminster/John Knox Press, 1994.

Schmidt, Thomas E. *Straight and Narrow? Compassion and Clarity in the Homosexuality Debate*. Downers Grove, IL: Intervarsity Press, 1995.

Siker, Jeffrey S., ed. *Homosexuality in the Church: Both Sides of the Debate*. Louisville, KY: Westminster/John Knox Press, 1994.

JEFFREY S. SIKER

HOOKER, RICHARD (1554–1600)

Church of England theologian. Richard Hooker is considered a theorist of the Elizabethan settlement and a major contributor to the theology of the early Church of England. Hooker took his B.A. and M.A. at Oxford in 1574 and 1577, respectively, before becoming a fellow of Corpus Christi College in 1579. His first sermon came at St. Paul's Cross in London in 1581 on the topic of soteriology (SALVATION). Hooker argued that, although God wished all humans to be saved, the process depended on the correct response from believers. Meant as an anti-Calvinist statement (see CALVINISM), Hooker delayed drawing the conclusions this view demanded until near the end of his life, just before the Arminians put forward views almost identical to Hooker's (see ARMINIANISM). In 1585 Hooker became master of the Temple Church in London, the church attended by members of the Inns of Court, the training institutions for common lawyers. At nearly the same time and with the backing of Archbishop of Canterbury JOHN WHITGIFT (?–1604), he engaged in a major polemic with the Presbyterian Walter Travers. His marriage in 1588 to Joan Churchman brought him a large dowry from her merchant tailor father, a fortuitous event in that Hooker displayed little ambition for higher office and spent the rest of his life on his writing and his priestly duties.

Building on the earlier work of JOHN JEWEL (1522–1571), his first patron, and Whitgift, Hooker's eight volumes *Of the Lawes of Ecclesiastical Politie* (published between 1593 and 1662) took the new Protestant establishment back to first principles of divine and NATURAL LAW. The first four books of this work supported that establishment almost as soon as they appeared and provided a compelling argument for conformity. Gradually Hooker's work acquired more and more authority, until by the nineteenth century it was almost considered the foundational text of the Anglican church (see ANGLICANISM), and a comprehensive and coherent explication of it. In the last quarter of the twentieth century, scholars pointed out inconsistencies and contradictions in Hooker's writing, but these criticisms were largely overturned in favor of the coherence and unity of all eight books, although it has been generally admitted that Hooker wrote originally as a polemicist. (For just one of many references to current events, see VII.18.7.) This realization has led to the further rejection as anachronistic of the notion that Hooker's work could have theorized an Anglican middle way. Historians of the late twentieth century agree that there was already a very broad theological consensus in an English national church and that it overlapped to a marked degree with the magisterial reformers on the continent, as did Hooker's work.

In 1593 John Windet, Hooker's cousin, published the first four books of the *Lawes,* perhaps because no other publisher was interested. The work had little commercial appeal, earning Hooker only £30. Until his death at his church of Bishopsbourne in 1600,

Hooker worked on the rest of his volumes, but lived to see only the publication of book V by Windet in 1597. The remaining three books presented numerous textual and publication problems, but Hooker's friend John Spenser saved what now remains of them, although not in Hooker's autograph. James Ussher saw to the publication of books VI and VIII in 1648, but VII did not appear until 1662.

A Lawful Universe

Hooker made his purpose and his audience explicit in the preface to the *Lawes,* lending support to the interpretation that he designed the entire work as a unit and wrote it sequentially. He named Calvinists, Familists, and ANABAPTISTS as his target (later adding all separatists), but not Catholics. Claiming that he wanted ecumenical understanding, Hooker tried to reduce controversial points to first principles that could be broadly accepted. Hooker set out from an Aristotelian framework to argue that the universe was entirely governed by law according to a system of causes ordained by God. All law was therefore divine. Despite the weakness of human reason by comparison with the divine, humans could nonetheless attempt to discern these causes and thus know the universe's structure. They could be assured that God never broke God's own law. They could also be assured that the universe was strictly hierarchical, as was its mirror in civil society. Hooker used these basic principles to ground both civil and ecclesiastical governments.

How to resolve disputes and prevent them from destroying civil order was Hooker's initial problem. Instead of relying on coercion, Hooker turned to divine providence. Humans, who began as an almost Lockean "book, wherein nothing is," could gain virtue through education. The key point was learning how to deal with things in different, morally neutral actions that became good or evil through the combined force of knowledge and will. The will was free, but its right action depended on reason, which in turn depended on law. Humans had discovered law by natural reason and decided together to be eternally bound by its precepts. Positive law was made by the community and only by it, but once such law existed, the members of the community had to obey. The best manner of life was "to study which way our willing obedience both unto God and man may be yielded even to the utmost of that which is due" [III.9.3].

Like his humanist predecessors, with whom Hooker had much in common, his view of civil society was heavily indebted to Cicero and to Roman law. Unlike some of the humanists, Hooker also had a thorough familiarity with medieval canon law and sacramental practice, which he often put to good use,

as for example when he adapted the doctrine of circumstances to his idea of church polity. Like most medieval thinkers and many of the humanists, Hooker borrowed most from Aristotle, especially the principle that any legitimate government demanded the consent of the governed. The way Hooker applied that principle, however, left the governed with very little recourse. The fact that "corporations are immortal," for example, meant that laws made hundreds of years earlier remained in force. Although insisting that kings required consent to their rule, Hooker gave subjects no protections against tyranny. The basis of Hooker's notion of political obligation was St. Paul's commonly cited letter to the Romans 13:1–5, which stated that subjects were obligated in conscience to obey civil AUTHORITY. Because Hooker also said almost at the outset that "my whole endeavor is to resolve the conscience" [Preface], making of his book an enormous manual of casuistry, it becomes clear that believers had little room for legitimate resistance to the established order. This led to a nearly complete "chiefty" or "principality" of church government inherent in the English crown. Although Hooker regularly criticized bishops for failing to take advice from their clergy and opined that the prince also needed counsel, he laid down no institutional machinery for providing it. The limits of his notion of consent emerge from his attacks on the presbyterians for playing to the crowd. In practice, consent meant little.

Curiously, despite his deemphasis of law's coercive power, Hooker stoutly maintained that it needed "a constraining power," to be supplied by human officeholders, above all the bishops. Ultimately, Hooker appealed to what became an almost distinctively "Anglican" concept of the mean, which he argued was "prelacy, the temperature of excesses" [VII.18.12]. Hooker strongly supported the bishops, including their dignity and their economic power, labeling them "receivers of God's rents" and bitterly criticizing expropriation of ecclesiastical property. Bishops deserved "a state of wealth proportionable" to the "great jurisdiction" they exercised, at least at the present when power demanded wealth [VII.24.18].

A Liberal Conservative

Hooker combined liberal-sounding views in the abstract with their use in much more coercive fashion. Similarly, he swayed back and forth between institutionalized forms of power and vaguer, almost transcendent, notions of who exercised it. Both these oscillations arose from his primary concern with the community, not with humans nor their institutions. Such distinctions were of no importance, provided only that a proper Christian church had correct belief.

As long as it did, there was no difference between the body politic and the mystical body of the church, both of which coalesced, after all, in the church's external political form. Hooker's emphasis on collectivity led him to reject PREDESTINATION and the gathered church Calvinists often deduced from it, and to offer in their place a strongly sacramental way of salvation, embracing all members of the visible church. Against the "Puritans" Hooker argued that no human society, not even the church as a political body, could lose its right to legislate, as it would if a permanent model of church government were really to be found in the New Testament (see PURITANISM). (He further criticized them by claiming that scripture provided only one kind of law, not the only source through which humans learned God's intentions.) Hooker put some of his own most cherished principles under pressure in defense of the community: TRADITION, for example, was not immune to its will and reason. Hooker's stress on finding the most comprehensive form of Christianity, the largest possible community, led him to invoke the authority of general councils through which all Christian nations could be united. As he put it in book I, humans would find it easier to put into effect Christ's "heavenly precepts . . . concerning peace and unity, if we did all concur in desire to have the use of ancient councils again renewed" [I.10.15].

No doubt one reason that Hooker's work proved so appealing was its eclecticism of both substance and approach. Thus, although Hooker drew heavily on the medieval Schoolmen for content, he used his humanist education when constructing arguments based on them. Instead of deploying the favored medieval device of the syllogism, he used the more rhetorically appealing enthymeme, a syllogism with one premise (usually the minor) left out. Hooker's work, despite its solid philosophical grounding, is at least as important for its rhetoric. Like some of his Henrician predecessors, perhaps especially Thomas Starkey (whose work Hooker could not have known), Hooker played with language, especially at critical moments, above all when discussing key terms for political society. Book VIII's treatment of sovereignty and related ideas brusquely turned its back on the kind of precision that Jean Bodin and other contemporaries had taken much care over. It may not be an accident that many critics have thought this the most "constitutional" part of Hooker's work, just as Starkey was for long regarded as the first modern liberal (see LIBERAL PROTESTANTISM AND LIBERALISM). In fact, both were confronted with the same problem—how to resolve the competing claims of community and ruler—and both solutions were distinctively time-bound. Hooker, whatever his long-term appeal, was also very much a man of his century in his selection of sources, stretching from the

recently rediscovered Cyprian (a third-century father with a markedly ecumenical appeal in the sixteenth century, largely because of his notion of the papal office) to Hermes Trismegistus, then thought to be the source of a theology more ancient than Moses's and the patron of magicians, but really a mythical figure.

References and Further Reading

Primary Sources:

Hill, W. Speed, gen. ed. *The Folger Library Edition of the Works of Richard Hooker.* 7 vols. Cambridge, MA and Tempe, AZ: Harvard University Press and Medieval and Renaissance Texts and Studies, 1977–1998.

———, ed. *Studies in Richard Hooker: Essays Preliminary to an Edition of his Works.* Cleveland: Case Western Reserve University Press, 1972.

Secondary Sources:

Allen, J. W. *A History of Political Thought in the Sixteenth Century.* London: Unwin, 1928.

Archer, Stanley. *Richard Hooker.* Boston: Twayne, 1983.

Kirby, W. J. Torrance. *Richard Hooker's Doctrine of the Royal Supremacy.* Leiden: Brill, 1990.

Lake, Peter. *Anglicans and Puritans? Presbyterianism and English Conformist Thought from Whitgift to Hooker.* London: Allen and Unwin, 1988.

McGrade, A. S. "The Coherence of Hooker's Polity: The Books on Power." *Journal of the History of Ideas* 24 (1963): 163–182.

Walton, Izaak. *The Life of Mr. Richard Hooker.* In *The Works of that Learned and Judicious Divine Mr. Richard Hooker,* edited by John Keble. Oxford: Clarendon Press, 1888.

THOMAS F. MAYER

HOOKER, THOMAS (1586–1647)

English-American Puritan. Hooker was born in Markworth, Leicestershire, England, in July 1586. He matriculated at Queens College, Cambridge, in 1604 but soon transferred to Emmanuel College, a hotbed of PURITANISM, where he first took baccalaureate and masters degrees, then served as fellow and catechist. He was silenced for NONCONFORMITY in 1629, and fled to the NETHERLANDS two years later, returning secretly in 1633 to ship out for the recently settled American colony of Massachusetts Bay, where he became first pastor of the congregation at Newtown (later Cambridge). Following a series of territorial, theological, and personal disputes, he led a migration to Connecticut in 1636, founding the church at Hartford, where he died on July 7, 1647.

Hooker gained transatlantic renown as an analyst of the CONVERSION experience, particularly the "preparatory" stages before GRACE, anatomized most thoroughly in his work *The Application of Redemption* (1656). Valued for his political advice and skills, he influenced Connecticut's legal and constitutional structure, urging its founders to dissociate freemanship from church membership (unlike Massachusetts), and he twice moderated intercolonial synods, most notably the 1637 meeting that facilitated ANNE HUTCHINSON's banishment. One of three New Englanddivines invited to attend the WESTMINSTER ASSEMBLY, he declined to serve, but attempted to influence its deliberations literarily in such works as *A Survey of the Summe of Church Discipline* (1648), which advocated a congregational over presbyterian polity, and *The Covenant of Grace Opened* (1649), which defended infant BAPTISM. Preacher, polemicist, civic leader, and, most of all, an acute pastoral psychologist, Hooker contributed as much as any firstgeneration American Puritan to constructing the culture of Reformed Protestantism that became known as "the New England Way."

See also Conversion; Hutchinson, Anne; Nonconformity

References and Further Reading

Bush, Sargent, Jr. *Thomas Hooker: Spiritual Adventure in Two Worlds*. Madison: University of Wisconsin Press, 1980.
Shuffelton, Frank. *Thomas Hooker, 1586–1647*. Princeton: Princeton University Press, 1977.

CHARLES L. COHEN

HOPKINS, SAMUEL (1721–1803)

Congregational misister, theologian, and abolitionist. Hopkins was born in 1721 in Waterbury, Connecticut, graduated from Yale College in 1741, and then studied at JONATHAN EDWARDS's (1703–1758) "school for the prophets" in Northampton, Massachusetts. He pastored in Housatonic (later named Great Barrington), Massachusetts from 1743 to 1769, and at the First Congregational Church of Newport, Rhode Island from 1770 until the year of his death, 1803.

Hopkins was arguably the greatest student of Jonathan Edwards and the most significant theologian of late eighteenth-century New England. Along with Joseph Bellamy (1718–1760), he was a leading expositor of the New Divinity, the first indigenous school of American CALVINISM, and the initial and most significant stage of the New England Theology—the most enduring intellectual tradition in United States history. The term "new divinity" was originally a label of scorn devised by Old Calvinist ministers who complained that Hopkin's theology represented a radical departure from traditional Reformed doctrine. The movement was also variously called Hopkinsianism or Hopkintonianism, although proponents of it preferred the names Consistent Calvinism or Edwardseanism. It attracted many of the most talented thinkers of Yale College and became a powerful force in New England CONGREGATIONALISM well into the nineteenth century.

Theology

Drawing upon the religious thought of Edwards—especially his *Freedom of the Will* (1754), *Original Sin* (1758), and *True Virtue* (1765)—Hopkins reshaped Reformed theology to address the challenges of ENLIGHTENMENT thinking, to demonstrate the rationality and moral accountability of Calvinist doctrine, and to combat the dual threats of ARMINIANISM and *antinomianism*. In so doing he creatively appropriated key Enlightenment concepts to make Calvinism more responsive to the intellectual and social changes of eighteenth-century culture. This is most notably seen in his effort to construct an apologetic that demonstrated the consistency of Reformed dogma with divine benevolence and to explore the meaning and implications of benevolence for Christian living.

Hopkins rejected those principles that compromised traditional Reformed tenets of divine sovereignty, original sin, irresistible grace, human depravity, eternal punishment, and the necessity of supernatural revelation. His forceful and provocative restatement of Calvinist concepts—pushing them to their logical limits—gave his theology the distinctive qualities for which it is known. First, in order to reconcile divine providence and benevolence with a Reformed understanding of sin, he argued that God willfully permitted and superintended sin to produce the best possible universe. Second, in combating Arminian tendencies surrounding the practice of preparation for grace, Hopkins alleged that unrepentant "awakened" sinners who used the means of grace (i.e., church attendance, Bible study, prayer) committed greater evil than "unawakened" sinners who neglected those means. Such awakened sinners aggravated their guilt by resisting the gospel message. Third, in an attempt to eliminate selfish motives for seeking salvation, he developed the extreme, hypothetical position that the truly regenerate would so submit to God's will that they would be willing to be damned if God's glory required it. Finally, in advancing his theory of holiness as "disinterested benevolence" to being in general, he was so intent on curtailing the influence of British benevolist moral philosophy in New England—and its sanctioning of natural self-love as a basis for virtue—that he seemingly left little room for a genuinely Christian self-love. He typically used self-love as a synonym for selfishness—a condition that inflicts all unregenerate love—in order to set it apart from a proper regard for self that is consistent with regenerate or true virtue.

Hopkins's lifelong theological work was summarized in his eleven hundred page *System of Doctrines* (1793), the most significant eighteenth-century American systematic theology. The *System* codified New Divinity teachings and became the basis for the theological training of future Edwardsean clergy. Written at a time when *deism* in America was reaching its heyday, and when doctrinal system building was being discredited by Enlightenment empiricists, Hopkins defended the place of scriptural, systematic divinity among the sciences. Here he articulated two doctrines that were hallmarks of the New Divinity: a governmental theory of ATONEMENT and a constitutional view of original sin that connected human sin to Adam not by means of a theory of imputation but by means of a divine constitution.

Slavery and Social Reform

Hopkins's doctrine of disinterested benevolence, with its call to radical, self-denying Christian service, provided a morally rigorous basis for social reform and evangelism that inspired evangelical social activists, religious reformers, and missionaries of the early nineteenth century. In his own life, the implications of his teaching were most clearly seen in his opposition to SLAVERY. From the slave-trading port of Newport, Hopkins became one of New England's earliest and most outspoken abolitionists (see SLAVERY, ABOLITION OF). Convinced that slavery and the slave trade were America's greatest sins, opposition to them was for him a litmus test of the ethical purity of the American Revolution. He was one of the few colonial leaders who consistently applied the libertarian rhetoric of the revolution to all of America's inhabitants. He also attempted to establish a mission colony of ex-slaves back in AFRICA in order to spread Christianity and promote the coming millennium (see MILLENARIANS AND MILLENNIALISM)—hoping that some greater good might arise out of the injustice of slavery.

See also Slavery, Abolition of; Millenarians and Millennialism

References and Further Reading

Primary Sources

Hopkins, Samuel. *The Works of Samuel Hopkins, D.D.* 3 vols. Boston: Doctrinal Tract and Book Society, 1852.

Secondary Sources

Breitenbach, William. "The Consistent Calvinism of the New Divinity Movement." *William and Mary Quarterly* 41 (1984): 241–264.

————. "Unregenerate Doings: Selflessness in New Divinity Theology." *American Quarterly* 34 (winter): 479–502.
Conforti, Joseph A. *Samuel Hopkins and the New Divinity Movement: Calvinism, the Congregational Ministry, and Reform in New England Between the Great Awakenings.* Grand Rapids, MI: Christian University Press, 1981.
Guelzo, Allen C. *Edwards on the Will: A Century of American Theological Debate.* Middletown, CT: Wesleyan University Press, 1989.
Jauhiainen, Peter D. "An Enlightenment Calvinist: Samuel Hopkins and the Pursuit of Benevolence." Ph.D. dissertation, University of Iowa, 1997.
West, Stephen, ed. *Sketches of the Life of the Late, Rev. Samuel Hopkins, D.D.* Hartford, 1805.

PETER D. JAUHIAINEN

HOUSE CHURCHES, BRITISH

During the late 1960s and 1970s in Britain, groups of evangelical Protestants began abandoning their churches to gather in houses; the term "house church" derives from this.

Their theological roots lie in the nineteenth-century Brethren movement and Catholic Apostolic Church, and in twentieth-century classical PENTECOSTALISM. Like earlier Pentecostalists, adherents saw being "born again" as essential for entering the Christian community, and practiced believers' baptism in water and "of the Holy Spirit," this latter experience issuing in *charismata* ("spiritual gifts") such as speaking in TONGUES, a feature they share with the charismatic movement, with which they are often linked.

Three distinctives set them apart from their Pentecostal forerunners. First, they believed denominations should not exist and must be replaced by the church or "kingdom." The second distinctive is ECCLESIOLOGY. They aimed to "restore the church" to what they perceived as the New Testament pattern for church life, leading Andrew Walker (1985) to name them "Restorationists." Their emphasis on and literal interpretation of the BIBLE share similarities with FUNDAMENTALISM. In their leadership structure men known as apostles, around whom church groups gathered, had responsibility for overseeing networks of churches, which were in turn led by elders. Third is the (often criticized) doctrine of discipleship or "shepherding," in which Christians submitted themselves to leaders' guidance and AUTHORITY.

From the mid-1970s two principal groupings emerged. Walker (1985) calls these R1 (the more conservative group including leaders Bryn Jones, Tony Morton, and Terry Virgo) and R2 (the more liberal group including the leader Gerald Coates). About a dozen networks developed during a period of rapid growth through the 1970s and early 1980s. From the late 1980s growth slowed and fragmentation increased. "R2" churches became more open and ecumenical, adopting the title "new churches," whereas

"R1" churches kept their original emphases. "New church" quickly also became an umbrella term for the whole house church movement. Most congregations now worship in public buildings rather than houses, but their emphasis on the local church as an extended family remains.

British "new church" membership stands at 120,000–140,000; attendance is double this. The largest network is Terry Virgo's New Frontiers International, with 300 congregations worldwide, the majority in Britain.

See also House Churches, Asia; Restorationism

References and Further Reading

Walker, Andrew. *Restoring the Kingdom: The Radical Christianity of the House Church Movement.* London: Hodder and Stoughton, 1985.
———. "Crossing the Restorationist Rubicon: From House Church to New Church." In *Fundamentalism, Church and Society*, edited by Martyn Percy and Ian Jones. London: SPCK, 2002.

KRISTIN J. AUNE

HOUSE CHURCHES, INTERNATIONAL

For three centuries after Christ, Christians met for fellowship and worship in private homes. The earliest known church building was found in Dura-Europos, dated to the mid-third century. It was apparently a typical house that was renovated for the meeting of Christians. At some point it ceased being used as a home and was dedicated entirely to church functions. After the introduction of the basilica in Constantinople, the church building became the primary meeting place for Christians. Nonetheless homes were often used for meetings such the Cluny "cells" in Viking-dominated Gaul or JOHN WESLEY's mid-week class meetings in eighteenth-century Anglican ENGLAND. These were exceptions to the rule; church ARCHITECTURE has been a central feature of Christianity since late antiquity.

An unexpected development for Christianity came in the mid-twentieth century with the meteoric rise of the house church movement to over 100 million participants worldwide by 2000. This was caused indirectly by massive religious oppression, especially under Communist authorities, and, most significantly, in CHINA. Although prayer and worship meetings were common long before 1949, the Communist authority's attempts to curb or control religious practice made houses the only viable meeting place for many Chinese Christians. Nonetheless house meetings were highly dangerous and groups had to remain very small to avoid detection. Independent churches from the beginning met in homes, emphasizing personal EVAN-GELISM. Witness Lee's Local Church, which typified these churches, would find its congregations shouting in unison "Denominationalism is a sin."

These churches were better prepared for the brutality of the Cultural Revolution and remained quietly active from 1950 to 1980. After 1980, often in opposition to government-approved churches, the house churches, most led by poor farmers from Henan, began to grow rapidly and organize themselves. One unique feature of these churches is a pyramid structure where house churches at the grass roots level are unaware of similar churches in the same network. Western observers have consistently underestimated their numerical strength because their contact is limited to the lower levels of the pyramid. By the year 2000 the dozen largest of these movements, together with 300 smaller networks, numbered in excess of one million house churches. The leaders of the larger networks have met in recent years for fellowship and strategy. Paradoxically, rapprochement between these movements and government-related churches, in Protestant, Independent, and Catholic contexts, has been steadily growing.

Another significant house church movement is found among African churches, whether they are Protestant, Anglican, Catholic, or Independent. In these cases either church buildings were never built or the locus of weekly fellowship is found primarily in homes.

Partly because of the success of house churches in China and AFRICA, Christians on all continents have adopted and adapted many of its features into traditional models. The cell church model, a parallel development, is one of the more successful. In many cases there are few discernible differences between these two movements. Other countries with significant house or cell churches include BRAZIL, Cambodia, INDIA, INDONESIA, the PHILIPPINES, Singapore, South KOREA, and more modestly the UNITED STATES. The future of the house church movement in Asia and around the world appears to be bright as new movements continue to spring up and existing ones grow and mature.

See also House Churches; Wesley, John

References and Further Reading

Castillo, M. Q. *The Church in Thy House.* Manila, The Philippines: Alliance Publishing, 1982.
Simson, W. *Houses That Change the World: the Return of the House Churches.* Carlisle, UK: OM Publishing, 2001.
White, L. M. "House Church." In Ferguson, Everett. *Encyclopedia of Early Christianity,* 439–440. New York: Garland. 1990.

Yun, Brother, with P. Hattaway. *The Heavenly Man: the Remarkable True Story of Chinese Christian Brother Yun.* London: Monarch Books, 2002.

TODD M. JOHNSON

HROMÁDKA, JOSEF LUKL (1889–1969)

Czech theologian. The most influential representative of Czech Protestantism in the twentieth century, Hromádka was born in Hodslavice, northern Moravia on June 8, 1889. As a Lutheran, he studied THEOLOGY in Vienna, Basel, Heidelberg, and Aberdeen. Affected by the tragedy of World War I, he gave up his original allegiance to the study of CULTURAL PROTESTANTISM and rediscovered the biblical message as the source of his theological orientation. As a pastor and professor of the United Church of Czech Brethren (since 1918), he struggled for a new orientation of Czech Protestantism in the newly founded Czechoslovak republic.

Hromádka identified himself with the new state and tried to enrich its democratic climate by making a genuine Protestant contribution. Philosophically, he was close to the democratic vision of T. G. Masaryk. Socially, he endorsed the socialist ideas in the tradition of the Czech Reformation (Hussites and Czech Brethren) as well as those of Swiss religious socialism (LEONHARD RAGAZ). Theologically, he moved in the direction of the dialectical theology of KARL BARTH, who became his personal friend. Thus in many respects, Hromádka was recognized as the "voice" of Czech Protestantism both in his country and ecumenically. Without compromising, he mobilized the resistance of his church and his state to the threats of fascist ideology.

After the German occupation of Czechoslovakia in 1939, Hromádka had to leave his country. He found refuge in the UNITED STATES, where he became an influential teacher at the Princeton Theological Seminary. After World War II, he returned to his home country, which in 1948 had become a communist nation. Hromádka tried to find place for his church under difficult conditions, avoiding the false alternative of an opportunistic cooperation with, or a rigid opposition against, the new system. Although often disappointed, he kept hoping that the oppressive totalitarian structure might be eventually changed in the spirit of true socialism. Thus he became one of the protagonists of a Christian-Marxist dialogue. The sovereign "yes" of the Gospel is valid even in the Christian approach to atheists. In this sense, Hromádka worked at home and in the international ecumenical movement. He was one of the "founding fathers" of the WORLD COUNCIL OF CHURCHES and served as vice-president of the WORLD ALLIANCE OF THE REFORMED CHURCHES. Because of his socialist positions, he was often attacked. But even a justified criticism of some of his one-sided theses should not overlook his basic theological integrity and his prophetic call for the churches to search for an unbiased witness even in adverse conditions.

Hromádka died on December 26, 1969 in Prague.

See also Neo-orthodoxy; Socialism, Christian

References and Further Reading

Primary Sources:

Hromádka, Josef L. *Doom and Resurrection.* Richmond, VA: Madrus Louse, 1944.
———. *Gospel for Atheists.* Geneva, Switzerland: 1965.
———. *Thoughts of a Czech Pastor.* London: SCM Press, 1970.
———. *Looking History in The Face.* Madras, India: 1982.
Hromádka, Josef Lukl. *The Church and Theology in Today's Troubled Times.* Prague: Ecumenical Council of Churches in Czechoslovakia, 1956.
———. *Theology Between Yesterday and Tomorrow.* Philadelphia, PA: Westminster Press, 1957.
———. *Challenges of Remembering.* Prague, Czechoslovakia: Christian Peace Conference (International), 1998.
Luknic, Arnold. *Ecumenical Theology of Josef Lukl Hromádka, 1911–1939.* Diss. Aquinas Institute of Theology, 1983.
Opocenský, Milan. *From the Reformation to Tomorrow.* Geneva, Switzerland: World Alliance of Reformed Churches, 1999.

JAN MILIC LOCHMAN

HUBMAIER, BALTHASAR (1480–1528)

Anabaptist reformer. Hubmaier, a student of John Eck, received a doctorate in THEOLOGY at the University of Ingolstadt. An effective administrator and preacher, he became prorector of the University of Ingolstadt in 1515 and then pastor and chaplain at the Regensburg cathedral. In 1521 he was appointed priest in the town of Waldshut, which although on the Swiss border was in Austrian-Habsburg territory.

By 1522 Hubmaier began to study MARTIN LUTHER's writings and, with a group of friends, the Pauline epistles. In the midst of these studies, he received—and accepted—a call to return to the Regensburg cathedral. Within a year, however, he was back in Waldshut where he came increasingly under the influence of the reformer HULDRYCH ZWINGLI at a time when the latter and his close followers were beginning to grapple with the issue of BAPTISM. Probably through the Zurich group Hubmaier was led to Erasmus's paraphrases on Matthew and Acts where the prince of humanists presented his unique interpretation of Christ's Great Commission (Matthew 28:19–20), an interpretation with powerful implications for the interpretation of baptism. It was a time, Hubmaier asserted, in which even Zwingli agreed that "children should not be baptized before they [were] instructed in the faith."

Hubmaier attended the Second Zurich Disputation on October 26–28, 1523, where the Catholic Mass and images were discussed. When, at the close of the disputation, Zwingli turned the implementation of reforms over to "my lords" of the town council, Hubmaier, along with other more radical followers of Zwingli, began to criticize the reformer.

Upon his return to Waldshut in the fall of 1523 Hubmaier began to implement his own reforms. He delivered his *Eighteeen Articles* on the Christian faith, abolished the laws on fasting and CELIBACY, and married—all with the tacit approval of the town council. However, Waldshut was not autonomous, as were the Free Imperial Cities; its overlord was Charles V's brother, Ferdinand Archduke of Austria, an ardent Catholic. Therefore, some time between the end of October and December 11, 1523, the Austrian government in Innsbruck wrote a letter to the Waldshut authorities demanding, on the basis of the Nuremberg Imperial Edict of March 6, 1523, that Hubmaier reverse his reforms.

Nuremberg Edict

This Nuremberg Edict was the product of the "public policy" of Frederick the Wise vis-à-vis Luther's reformation. It crystallized around ANDREAS RUDOLF KARLSTADT's celebration of an evangelical mass on Christmas day 1521. Frederick, although he had gone to great lengths to protect Luther's right to preach the "holy Gospel," was adamantly opposed to introducing any innovations into the Catholic Church service until they were approved by Christendom. He therefore opposed Karlstadt's innovations. When the Imperial Governing Council, on January 20, 1522, mandated the undoing of those innovations, Frederick prevailed on Luther himself to rescind the reforms. This policy eventually came to be embedded in the Nuremberg Imperial Edict, and like Frederick's policy, the edict essentially mandated two seemingly contradictory things. First, no innovations were to be introduced into the Church's liturgy, ritual, and so forth until a Christian Council could have resolved the problem of Luther's teachings, given that the latter could lead to unrest or revolt in the realm. Second, only the "holy Gospel" should be preached, although it should be preached according to the "interpretation of those teachers approved by the Christian Church." Who were the teachers approved by the Christian Church? The Church Fathers or the Scholastics? Humanists and Protestants chose the former; Catholics, the latter. There was, therefore, an immediate division of opinion on this matter, although it was the first stipulation that caused the real problem: if one began to preach "only the holy Gospel," might one—in the process—discover the Mass to be "an abomination in the sight of God"? Moreover, if one did, would one have to continue to celebrate it Sunday after Sunday? Protestants used the edict to justify preaching of the "holy Gospel" whereas Catholics used it to attack Protestant "innovations."

The Innsbruck government, therefore, in its late 1523 letter to the Waldshut authorities argued that Hubmaier was preaching a "heretical" version of the holy Gospel and introducing innovations clearly condemned by the Nuremberg Edict of 1523. The Waldshut town council, in its response of December 11, 1523 to this letter, referred specifically to the Nuremberg Edict, saying it had been read from the pulpits of their churches by two priests from Constance. They thus knew what it said and argued that they, as well as Hubmaier, were being obedient to it. The council defended Hubmaier's preaching, saying that it was Hubmaier's intention, as he had said from the pulpit after the promulgation of the edict, to preach the "pure and clear Gospel from here on out, which he has done according to our understanding. We even invited the dean and priests to see if he preached anything but the clear and pure Word of God." If the Austrian authorities wished, the mayor and council continued, they could act in compliance with the edict and send several of the bishop of Constance's theologians to check on Hubmaier's ORTHODOXY. If these authorities could prove Hubmaier's interpretation of the Scriptures wrong, Hubmaier would surely change his interpretation. To do this on the basis of Scripture alone was difficult, as Catholics had learned by this time, and so the Innsbruck government did nothing. In virtually every debate in the Reformation between the contending parties, if it was based on the BIBLE, the Catholics lost. Clearly, the two conflicting interpretations of the edict confronted one another in Waldshut. In the end, however, it was military might that carried the day, not biblical scholarship.

Issues of Baptism

By September 1, 1524, Austrian pressure forced Hubmaier out of Waldshut, so he went to Schaffhausen. There he wrote his pamphlet *On the Burning of Heretics,* a ringing defense of religious liberty. His presence in the city caused problems, however, so he returned to Waldshut. Officially, Hubmaier still belonged to Zwingli's party, but on January 17, 1525, Zwingli and his followers met in a last attempt to resolve their dispute over baptism. Although the Zurich council declared Zwingli the official winner of the debate, the radicals refused to acknowledge either the decision or the persuasiveness of the reformer's arguments. On January 21 these followers proceeded to baptize one another upon their confession of faith, introducing "adult" or "believer's baptism" to the world of the sixteenth century.

At this point Hubmaier began to discourage parents from having their infant children baptized; but he still baptized children of parents who were weak in their new faith and wished their children baptized. On February 2, 1525, he published his *Public Declaration,* offering to prove—in public disputation—that infant baptism was without biblical foundation. With broad popular support, he also began to abolish the Mass, and on Easter 1525 was himself baptized upon his faith by Wilhelm Reublin.

Zwingli responded to these events in two ways. First, he enlisted the Zurich town council in his fight against the radicals; and, second, he began to write against them publicly. His first attack was entitled *Concerning Baptism, Rebaptism and Infant Baptism.* Hubmaier, now his most articulate opponent, replied with his *Concerning the Christian Baptism of Believers,* the best defense of believer's baptism written in the sixteenth century.

In Waldshut Hubmaier baptized large numbers of believers, so large some scholars have spoken of ANABAPTISM in WALDSHUT as a mass movement. However, with the defeat of the peasants in the great Peasant War of 1524–1525, in the summer of 1525—an event that Hubmaier was involved in, although as yet that involvement was not public—the Innsbruch government could impose its "Catholic interpretation" of the Nuremberg Edict of the German chief (1524) on Waldshut. On December 5, 1525, Hubmaier fled the city and sought sanctuary in Zurich; but Zwingli was now his enemy. Although the Zurich authorities refused to turn Hubmaier over to the Austrian government, they had him imprisoned after he "lost" a debate with Zwingli and forced him to recant his views. He did so on April 15, but under great qualms of conscience. The recantation did him no good with either Zwingli or the town council, however.

Hubmaier managed to escape Zurich, wandered about for a time, spent some time in Augsburg where he baptized Hans Denck, and, in the summer of 1526 arrived in Nikolsburg in Moravia. Here, under Leonhard von Liechtenstein, Hubmaier and the Anabaptists found sanctuary for a time. The Anabaptist congregation in Nikolsburg grew rapidly under Liechtenstein's protection, and with the arrival of the printer Froschauer, originally from Zurich, Hubmaier could publish his increasingly prolific writings. In late 1526, however, after the Battle of Mohacz, Moravia came into the hands of Ferdinand of Austria, Hubmaier's old nemesis. Because Nikolsburg was becoming such an Anabaptist sanctuary and Hubmaier such a powerfully attractive personality, it was only a matter of time before the Catholic Austrian government would seek to capture Hubmaier and destroy the movement. In August 1527 Ferdinand cited the counts of Liechtenstein to appear before him and demanded the capture of Hubmaier. Four weeks later Hubmaier was in custody and taken to Vienna.

At the heart of the accusations against Hubmaier was his activity in Waldshut; thus, the Nuremberg Edict formed the legal basis for Ferdinand's execution of Hubmaier. Before that happened, however, Hubmaier was allowed to meet and discuss his plight with an old classmate, Johann Fabri, now a high official of the bishop of Constance. The meeting took place in late 1527 and lasted three days. The first day they discussed the Bible and infant baptism; the second day, they discussed the SACRAMENTS in general—the MASS, intercession of the SAINTS, and purgatory. On the last day, they discussed FAITH, good works, Christian liberty, free will, the worship of Mary, and a few other matters. At the close, Hubmaier presented a confession of his faith, called *An Account of* [*His*] *Faith,* which dealt with twenty-seven articles so worded that any Christian could subscribe to them. In matters of baptism and the Mass, the "two most important articles," Hubmaier was willing to await the decision of the future church council mandated by the Nuremberg Edict. However, the Austrian authorities wanted more, and they wanted it now, demanding an unconditional recantation. This Hubmaier could not give them; and so on March 10, 1528 he was burned at the stake.

Significance

Balthasar Hubmaier was one of the most important literary spokespersons for Anabaptism. His tracts on believer's baptism have never been surpassed. At the same time, he saw the reformation of the church from a context much larger than that of most of his Anabaptist brothers. He read widely, quoted Erasmus's interpretation of the Great Commission from his paraphrases, discussed the issue with him, and knew the arguments of all the contending parties. He was also the person who originated the argument that Anabaptists should not be persecuted by the Catholic Church because the latter itself regarded initiation into a monastery as a second baptism. As Luther himself observed, it was the Catholic Church that was the real "rebaptizer."

In 1527 Hubmaier addressed the issue of the church ban, arguing that nothing would ever be right in the church until proper church discipline would be exercised. The tract was a frontal attack on the emerging Protestant state churches. In the same year he wrote a tract defending "the freedom of the will." Borrowing arguments from Erasmus, Hubmaier insisted that man's spirit had remained good in spite of the fall, but that it was—at the moment—under the control of the flesh. Since Adam's fall, he argued, the flesh was useless although the spirit was willing to do good. The human soul was therefore caught between the warring factions. Once the soul had been healed by Christ, it could be freed and could once again obey the Spirit.

Hubmaier also wrote on communion (see Lord's Supper), stressing that the bread and the cup were a memorial of Christ's broken body and shed blood. However, unlike most of the early Swiss Brethren, or Anabaptists, he was not a *Staebler* (nonresistant) and was not totally opposed to the use of the sword (see Pacifism). He saw a legitimate role for the use of the sword by the government, and he argued that the authorities had the right to demand obedience from their subjects in this regard. This more positive approach to government and its use of the sword has won him the approval of Baptist historians who nearly universally regard Hubmaier as the ideal Anabaptist. Although a powerful spokesperson, Hubmaier is therefore not entirely typical of early Swiss Anabaptism. At the same time, his attempts at theological compromise in Zurich and later in Vienna during his captivities have detracted from his legacy. However, he strongly opposed some of the influences coming from Saxony and Thuringia, especially the eschatological violence of Hans Hut.

The case of Hubmaier and Waldshut, and later Hubmaier and Nikolsburg, raise some interesting issues for early South German/Swiss Anabaptism because both centers present us with instances in which Anabaptists cooperated with the local political authorities. Are these cases of "Magisterial Anabaptism"? Indeed, for a brief period of time Hubmaier's movement constituted the "official" church in both regions. Could Anabaptism, even while practicing believer's baptism, become a "territorial church"? The argument has been made that even the Swiss Brethren, before their final break with Zwingli, sought to convince the latter that their form of Christianity would find great support among the people of Zurich. To what extent, then, did the fact that Zwingli and the Zurich authorities refused to go along with them, and forced them into an oppositional minority group determine their view of the church? It is clear that Luther as well as Zwingli—before they gained the support of the political authorities in their regions—defined the true church in terms of the "congregation of believers." Yet when they gained political favor and support, they accommodated themselves to the inherited territorial church structure. Could Anabaptism do the same, as the case of Hubmaier seems to indicate? Whatever the case, Hubmaier's Anabaptist experiment in Waldshut and Liechtenstein does raise some intriguing questions.

References and Further Reading

Primary Source:

Westin, Gunnar, and Torsten Bergsten, eds. *Balthasar Hubmaier: Schriften.* Gütersloh, Germany: G. Mohn, 1962.

Secondary Sources:

Bergsten, Torsten. *Balthasar Hubmaier: Seine Stellung zu Reformation und Täufertum 1521–1528.* Kassel, Germany: Oncken, 1961.

Estep, W. R. Jr., and Torsten Bergsten. *Balthasar Hubmaier: Anabaptist Theologian and Martyr.* Valley Forge, PA: Judson Press, 1978.

Loserth, Joseph. *Balthasar Hubmaier und die Anfänge der Wiedertäufer in Mähren.* Brünn, 1893.

———. *Die Stadt Waldshut und die vorderösterreichische Regierung 1523–1526.* Vienna, 1891.

Sachsse, C. D. *Balthasar Hubmaier als Theologe.* Aalen, Germany: Scientia Verlag, 1914.

Schreiber, J. H. *Balthasar Hubmaier. Stifter der Wiedertäufer auf dem Schwarzwalde.* (vol. 1). *Taschenbuch für Geschichte und Altertum in Süddeutschland.* (vol. 2), 1838 and 1839.

Vedder, Henry C. *Balthasar Hubmaier, the Leader of the Anabaptists.* New York: AMS Press, 1971.

Windhorst, Christoph. *Täuferisches Taufverständnis: Balthasar Hubmaiers Lehre zwischen traditioneller und reformatorischer Theologie.* Leiden, The Netherlands: Brill, 1976.

Abraham Friesen

HUDDLESTON, TREVOR (1913–1998)

English bishop. Huddleston was born in Bedford, England, on June 15, 1913. Educated at Oxford, he participated in the Christian Socialist Movement and the Ecclesiology of the Oxford Movement. It was from these beginnings that a pattern was formed whereby fresh exposures in his life would intertwine with, and build on, his verbal and written output; onto the Catholic brick would be placed a socialist brick, an antiracial brick, an anticlass brick, a multifaith brick, and so on. His work was his life.

Huddleston was ordained in 1941 and, attracted by their active missionary focus, became a monk at the Anglican Community of the Resurrection, Mirfield, Yorkshire. He was appointed to the township of Sophiatown, near Johannesburg, South Africa, with a people he loved, and he became involved in setting up community cultural projects. In his work, Huddleston influenced many future political leaders of South Africa. Archbishop DESMOND TUTU tells of being inspired to his religious vocation when Huddleston doffed his hat on meeting Tutu's mother, an unheard of action by a white man to a black lady.

After witnessing government abuses in the detainment and relocation of townsfolk and the threatened takeover of the local school through the Bantu Education Act, Huddleston became one of the leading figures in the campaign to end apartheid, arguing that such a system could be neither reformed nor collaborated with. In recognition of his work for oppressed South Africans, Huddleston was awarded the title "Isitwalandwe" by the Congress of the People.

In 1956 Huddleston was controversially withdrawn from South Africa just as his book *Naught for Your Comfort,* an international best-seller highlighting the abuses of apartheid on the black populous, was published. Back in England, he helped found the Anti-Apartheid Movement and was among the first to advocate economic sanctions and a sports and cultural boycott of South Africa.

In 1960 Huddleston returned to Africa as bishop of Masasi, Tanzania, and worked closely with President Julius Nyerere on the development of national independence. He was later appointed to a bishopric in London, then Mauritius, and finally as archbishop of the Indian Ocean. On retirement, he worked tirelessly as president of the Anti-Apartheid Movement.

Although acknowledged by many who did not share his Anglo-Catholic churchmanship for attempting to create an effective Christian witness in the face of injustice and oppression, Huddleston was criticized for expounding a political gospel message that distracted from the evangelical mission to proclaim a message of saving souls. He was also criticized for his advocacy of socially focused interfaith acts of worship.

Huddleston responded by saying that SIN is never just a personal matter, but has social consequences, and the CHURCH, as salt to the earth, has a responsibility to address these. This came out of an incarnational THEOLOGY, recognizing the image of God in each person as being the basis for fellowship. Alongside this was a conviction that God is concerned not with SALVATION of the soul, but rather with reaching the whole person and in breaking the oppressive bondage of social sin. The Gospel must be culturally relevant, and salvation is a social process shown both through BAPTISM as a point of incorporation into a community and through sharing communion as a sacrament of fraternity.

Huddleston died in Oxford, England, on April 20, 1998. A leading figure in the Anti-Apartheid Movement throughout the second half of the twentieth century, he is best known as a prophetic missionary bishop who highlighted social and racial injustices and as an advocate for a multifaith dialogue.

See also Dialogue, Interconfessional; Ecumenism; Socialism, Christian

References and Further Reading

Primary Sources:

Huddleston, Trevor. *Naught for Your Comfort.* London: Collins, 1956.
———. *God's World.* London: Fount, 1988.

Secondary Source:

Denniston, Robin. *Trevor Huddleston: A Life.* London: Pan/Macmillan, 2000.

JAMES CHAPMAN

HUGUENOTS

Although the origins and meaning of the word remain obscure and the subject of continuing debate, Huguenot was the designation frequently attached to members of the French Reformed Church from the mid-sixteenth century through the end of the eighteenth. During the initial decades of the REFORMATION in FRANCE, the term tended to be used in connection with Protestant political and military efforts—the Huguenot party or the Huguenot military forces, for instance. Eventually, the expression enjoyed extensive application, a practice that was reinforced with the proscription of Protestantism in France toward the end of the seventeenth century. The immense Huguenot diaspora after the revocation of the EDICT OF NANTES in 1685 meant the spread of French Protestant refugees throughout Europe and the wider Atlantic world. These immigrants jealously guarded their Huguenot identity and, even today, their descendants maintain Huguenot societies from Europe and the British Isles to North America and South Africa.

Initial Persecution and Warfare

Protestant ideas circulated in France soon after MARTIN LUTHER issued his stirring call for the reform of Latin Christianity in the late-1510s. By the 1540s and 1550s the Calvinist or Reformed tradition (see CALVINISM) had come to dominate French Protestantism. At the same time harsh persecution by the crown and Catholic Church prompted many early followers to seek refuge in Geneva, whose reform the Frenchman JOHN CALVIN had guided. The city and its church served, in turn, as a springboard for the spread of Calvin's theological views and ecclesiastical polity.

Significantly, a number of these French Protestant émigrés trained for the ministry at Geneva. They and others eventually returned to their native France and organized Reformed churches. Beginning in the mid-1550s, Calvinist churches took root at Paris and other important cities, and by 1559 Reformed pastors and elders secretly gathered at Paris in the first national SYNOD.

The growth of the Huguenot churches provoked strong Catholic and monarchial reaction, and in 1562 religious warfare erupted. The strife shattered France for nearly four decades and subsided only with King Henry IV's proclamation of the Edict of Nantes in 1598. Organized and reasonably well-financed armies vied on the battlefield in a series of eight civil-religious wars. Even after 1598, fierce if less widespread conflict erupted on several occasions during the second and third decades of the seventeenth century. Cardinal Richelieu's siege and destruction of La Rochelle in 1628 and the Peace of Alès the following year finally broke Huguenot military power and effectively ended the movement's political influence.

Beyond the clash of rival confessional armies, the assassination of individual political leaders and less premeditated, more spontaneous outbreaks of collective violence—murderous riots and brutal massacres—accentuated the bitterness of these religious wars. A series of clashes during the spring and summer of 1562 was the prelude to wider conflict. In March soldiers loyal to the ultra-Catholic duc de Guise massacred Huguenot worshipers at the eastern French town of Vassy. Over the next several months, Protestants and Catholics fought acrimonious street battles for control of urban areas everywhere in the realm. Thereafter, the disturbances only worsened. The Protestants of Nîmes in southern France massacred some one hundred Catholics, mostly priests and prominent laymen, in September 1567. The most famous and horrifying episode was the Saint Bartholomew's Day massacre of August 1572. When Huguenot nobles gathered at Paris to celebrate the marriage of their young leader Henry of Navarre to the king's sister, the king and queen mother seized the opportunity to eliminate their political rivals. Fanatical Parisian Catholics quickly transformed the affair into a religious bloodbath. Over the course of three days they shot, stabbed, and drowned thousands of Huguenots. Eventually, the carnage spread to other major French cities.

The deadly violence finally came to an end with the Edict of Nantes of 1598. It created an intelligible and logical structure in which Catholics and Protestants could live together without violence and bloodshed. The arrangement permitted the exercise of the Reformed religion, but under restricted circumstances.

Huguenots received guarantees of their civil and political rights, including the ability to defend many cities in which they lived and worshiped. The Reformed faithful were assured access to public and royal offices as well as admission to educational institutions. Protestants also feared religiously prejudiced Catholic judges, and in those regions where the Huguenots were especially numerous, the Edict created special bipartisan law courts, the so-called *chambres de l'Édit*. Equal numbers of Protestant and Catholic judges staffed the tribunals, which were competent to adjudicate any civil or criminal case in which at least one of the litigants was Protestant.

In the decades after the Edict of Nantes, a significant cultural flowering occurred within the Huguenot community. French Protestants established a series of institutions for higher learning; they offered seminary and to some extent university training. Other members of the Huguenot elite gathered regularly in provincial literary and scientific academies to debate political and religious questions, evaluate their own attempts at history and literature, and review the latest discoveries in science. At Paris they participated in salon society and wrote elegant poetry. Huguenot architects even designed important public buildings, including the Luxembourg Palace.

Demographic Realities and Organizational Structures

Despite these substantial, sustained efforts and encouraging initial successes in the religious sphere and wider cultural domain, the Protestant movement in France never advanced beyond the status of a permanent if vigorous religious minority. The Reformation clearly attracted a sizable following among the nobility and urban bourgeoisie. Many artisans and even persons from the rural agricultural world were drawn to Protestantism as well. Yet the protracted strife over the second half of the sixteenth century took its toll. Estimates of the Huguenot population vary widely. The ranks of French Protestants initially swelled to ten percent of the population, roughly 1.8 million in the decade between 1560 and 1570. During the same period there were perhaps 1,400 Reformed churches in France. More important, among the politically influential nobles, Huguenot strength may have been close to fifty percent. This early, rapid growth likely peaked on the eve of the Saint Bartholomew's Massacre of 1572. Thereafter, the numbers declined precipitously. By the end of the sixteenth century Huguenots were roughly seven to eight percent of the total population, accounting for about 1.2 million persons. Over the course of the seventeenth century, the Huguenot numerical strength waned further. The situation likely stemmed from gradual absorption into the Catholic majority through intermarriage and the monarchy's relentless pressure for conversion. When Louis XIV finally revoked the Edict of Nantes in October 1685, French Reformed society totaled 800,000 to one million persons.

The Huguenot presence was heavily concentrated in the western and southern portions of the kingdom. Protestants lived on the Atlantic coast at La Rochelle and were spread across the provinces of Normandy and Poitou. To the south, Reformed communities at towns such as Castres and Montauban, Montpellier and Nîmes became legendary. In addition, a dense network of Protestant villages permeated the rural mountainous region of the Cévennes. In many ways the Cévennes were and continue to be the southern backbone of French Protestantism. Roughly four-fifths of all Huguenots lived in the west and south. Here they established the churches and consistories, which, in turn, formed the basis for an extensive and uniform national ecclesiastical system.

Everywhere in France, the Huguenots organized their churches according to an energetic ecclesiastical POLITY developed by Calvin and his associates. The structure centered on the local church and its CONSISTORY, all the while maintaining an elaborate system of colloquies and synods from the regional to the national level. The consistory was a supervisory body whose members—pastors, lay elders, and lay deacons in the French Reformed churches—met regularly, usually once a week, to plan and direct the religious life of the entire congregation. These officials had primary responsibility for ecclesiastical administration, poor relief, and morals control.

The profound religious changes associated with the Reformation meant a reform of both belief and of behavior. The centerpiece in the latter effort—a reform of lifestyle—was a profound moral and social disciplining of the community (see CHURCH DISCIPLINE). The Huguenots created elaborate mechanisms for the maintenance of moral order and supervision of the faithful. The pastors and elders energetically sought to encourage virtue and suppress vice. They offered guidance and religious edification with frequent sermon services and CATECHISM lessons. At the same time these church authorities seated in the consistory worked arduously to identify SIN and impose penitential discipline through a graduated system of shaming techniques that included censure and admonition, private and public repentance ceremonies, and excommunication. In short, the church and its officials sought to mold proper Christian behavior and cement confessional identity.

In the political sphere, the Huguenots never enjoyed sustained support from the French monarchy or its governing officials. At best, they aspired to harmonious alliances with local secular authorities in the towns and regions, which they dominated. Accordingly, the Protestant faithful, their churches and the associated ecclesiastical institutions had a strained and ambivalent relationship with the political powers. They were, at best, grudgingly tolerated and, more often than not, actively oppressed. The continual strain and strife inevitably shaped, restricted, and blunted the ambitious Reformed effort to revive the pristine splendor of early Christianity.

The Great Struggle

The choices that Huguenots faced in 1685 when the crown abrogated the Edict of Nantes were few and unpleasant: they could abandon their Protestant faith, pretend to convert, go into exile, or actively resist. Some Protestants were, of course, celebrated in their defiance. They took refuge in the mountains and forests, or the anonymity of large cities; many among them were eventually arrested and punished. For most people, however, overt resistance and the prospect of prison, the galleys, or execution held little appeal. The vast majority of Huguenots had been coerced into abjuring already on the eve of the Revocation. Hence, Louis XIV and his advisors could offer the fiction that the Edict of Nantes was no longer needed. Yet these conversions were hardly sincere. At the same time, a fifth or more—150,000 to 200,000—of all French Protestants went into exile to the Swiss cantons, various German principalities, the NETHERLANDS, the British Isles, and eventually to North America, SOUTH AFRICA, Scandinavia, and RUSSIA. They, of course, carried their religion and culture with them. At the same time the departure of so many members of the social and intellectual elite, people who had traditionally led the Huguenot community, had a stunning effect on the faithful who remained in France. French Protestantism became less structured, and those who rose to positions of leadership tended to be less educated, as well as rustic, proletarian, and feminine.

Soon after the Revocation, Huguenots began to assemble clandestinely and illicitly in the *désert* or wilderness, a strong biblical image that underscored their determination. Rural artisans and others of lesser social and economic status dominated the earliest assemblies. Women also assumed a stronger, more conspicuous presence than they had previously enjoyed. They conducted religious services in secluded woods and private homes, directing the assembled faithful as they prayed, reading passages from Holy Writ, and singing psalms. Many women suffered long and painful incarceration. Those caught attending illegal religious assemblies or engaging in other dissenting and insubordinate acts were placed in Catholic hospitals and nunneries. Women whose offenses royal authorities judged particularly egregious went to prison. Some remained there half-forgotten for years. The most celebrated among these courageous female resisters were the several dozen who were imprisoned for decades in the Tour de Constance at Aigues-Mortes. Marie Durand, for example, was confined at the age of fifteen and passed thirty-eight years in the tower prison before her release. Others died without the slightest expectation of discharge. Finally a number of young women and eventually young men became prophetesses and prophets. They protested the oppression of Protestants in a less confrontational yet unconventional and highly effective manner.

Prophesying was likely the most startling development associated with the Revocation and the disappearance of an educated pastorate and established ecclesiastical structures. The movement began in February 1688 when an illiterate teenage shepherdess from the rural Dauphiné began to sing psalms and preach in her sleep. Although previously unable to converse in anything other than the local dialect, she offered sermons in "perfect French" during her trance-like state. Other young women and men soon followed suit, giving voice to their apocalyptic inspiration and spiritual visions. In a series of illicit prophesying assemblies, they shook violently, wept, and cried out for repentance. Although explanations vary, these prophetesses and prophets appear to have taken psychological refuge in acting out biblical texts, thereby expressing their anguish over the disaster that had befallen their religious community.

The prophesying movement spread across southern France and eventually turned violent as the more zealous adherents sought to wreak God's retribution on their Catholic oppressors. The murderous, protracted revolt of the Camisards—so designated for the white shirts that the insurgents often wore—began with the assassination of the abbé du Chaila, a much detested Catholic clergyman and royal agent in the Cévennes. When, in July 1702, he arrested a group of seven adolescent Protestants, three girls and four boys, who were fleeing to Switzerland, reaction was swift and furious. The prophet Abraham Mazel gathered fifty or more followers and liberated the young prisoners. In the melee, the abbé and three of his companions were killed. The act touched raw, exposed nerves on both sides of the bitter confessional struggle. Some Protestants turned to similar acts of vengeance, such as murdering priests and burning churches. Others waged better-organized, more lasting, and initially successful guerrilla warfare. Royal troops responded predictably with further repression and reprisals. The war dragged on for eight years and led to the death of numerous Protestants as well as Catholics.

Although the active persecution of Huguenots slowly eased, the restoration of civil status occurred only with the Edict of the Toleration in 1787 and the beginnings of the French Revolution two years later. Not surprisingly, the long ordeal of the *désert* has become the heroic age, eclipsing even the violent struggle of the sixteenth century. For modern descendants within and outside of France, the anguish of the eighteenth century, together with the great diaspora, defines the meaning of Huguenot, emphasizing religious perseverance and communal solidarity.

References and Further Reading

Benedict, Philip. *The Huguenot Population of France, 1600–1685: The Demographic Fate and Customs of a Religious Minority.* Philadelphia: American Philosophical Society, 1991.

Garrisson, Janine. *Protestants du Midi, 1559–1598.* Toulouse, France: Privat, 1980.

Holt, Mack P. *The French Wars of Religion, 1562–1629.* Cambridge, UK: Cambridge University Press, 1995.

Mentzer, Raymond. *Blood and Belief: Family Survival and Confessional Identity among the Provincial Huguenot Nobility.* West Lafayette, IN: Purdue University Press, 1994.

———, and Andrew Spicer, eds. *Society and Culture in the Huguenot World, 1559–1685.* Cambridge, UK: Cambridge University Press, 2002.

Prestwich, Menna, ed. *International Calvinism, 1541–1715.* Oxford, UK: Clarendon Press, 1985.

Van Ruymbeke, Bertrand, and Randy Sparks, eds. *Memory and Identity: Minority Survival among the Huguenots in France and the Atlantic Diaspora.* Columbia, SC: University of South Carolina Press, 2003.

RAYMOND A. MENTZER

HUMAN RIGHTS

The contemporary concern with human rights did not originate, as commonly supposed, with the emerging secular modernity of nineteenth-century Western society. Rather, the issue of rights and the wider consideration of the advancement of democratic institutions can be said to have largely been assisted by the REFORMATION or at least certain forms of Protestantism. This was most apparent with LUTHERANISM and English PURITANISM, which both pulled in the same direction with respect to the rights of the lay individual that was enshrined in the notion of the PRIESTHOOD OF ALL BELIEVERS. Here, much was typified by the work of eminent seventeenth-century Protestant theologians such as PHILIPP JAKOB SPENER and AUGUST HERMANN FRANCKE who taught that the Christian LAITY not only possessed the right to offer God the unmediated petition of PRAYER but should enjoy the liberty of interpreting scriptures as seen fit. However, the concern of the early Protestants with individual rights was not one that advocated a stringent moral or legalistic framework. Indeed, in the seventeenth century, largely as a reaction to Roman Catholicism, there was a broad refusal of ANTINOMIANISM—the rejection of an abstract moral law.

Structurally the developing correlation between Protestantism and human rights came, paradoxically, with the emergence of the secular society that it indirectly engendered. The key was the differentiation of religious and civic institutions. At a broad comparative level the advancement of issues relating to rudimentary human rights was historically observable in the developing Protestant countries (or at least those with sizable Protestant majorities). Religious pluralism and TOLERATION were strongly associated both with the stability of pluralistic democratic regimes and the struggle against religious monopoly. Protestantism, through its increasing fragmentation, added to the growing acceptance of pluralism, albeit fostering a tolerance in a narrow religious sense. In Catholic and Orthodox nations, by way of comparison, the characteristic symbiosis appears to have been absent and was, to a large degree, connected with the enduring relationship between church and state and the continuing ecclesiastical monopoly of the former (see ORTHODOXY, EASTERN; CATHOLIC REACTIONS TO PROTESTANTISM).

The link between early Protestantism and the concern with rights marked the congruency of political and religious revolutions. Evidence of this was the enactment of the Bill of Rights in ENGLAND (1689) and the ascendancy of Parliament over the monarch as a result of the so-called Revolution of the Saints. In the case of northwest Europe, the issue of human rights was also in the context of nation-building shortly after the Reformation. This was even more the case in the UNITED STATES in the eighteenth century where the Puritan communities were also driven by the cause of religious freedoms—a call for liberty that ultimately became intertwined with the advocacy of political liberties and the Rights of Man as espoused by Thomas Paine and others. Indeed, it was in the United States where the religious culture of DISSENT became universalized and eulogized. Although the American constitution has the built-in guarantee of religious expression, and civil liberties generally, the constitution itself is discernibly in the form of a COVENANT comparable to those of God with man in biblical times.

The subsequent development of the relationship between Protestantism and human rights over the last two centuries, however, has not proved to be a straightforward one. Indeed, what has become a controversial area has frequently divided the Protestant constituency. Certainly, it has been the case that Protestant contingents developed their own sectional interests, which proved to have ramifications for how rights were interpreted. Frequently the issue of rights became linked to political moralizing at best or, at the worst, personal or collective expediency. This was certainly evident during the American CIVIL WAR. For Protestants in the North, the antislavery cause was accompanied by the conviction that victory would usher in a reign of religious righteousness. In contrast the matter of rights in the South was to some extent directly or indirectly related to the issue of slaveholding within Protestant churches (see SLAVERY; SLAVERY, ABOLITION OF).

Sectional interests apart, Protestant attitudes over the last two centuries have largely been determined by theological persuasion, where liberal and conservative impulses and biblical interpretation have proved to have significant influence on orientations toward the secular world and broader civil issues. The area of rights was contested in England during the eighteenth century by conservative Protestant bishops who denounced the liberal politician's stress on the "natural rights" philosophy as a SIN because it suggested rebellion and undermined the security of CHURCH AND STATE. From the middle of the nineteenth century the emphasis on rights was perceived by conservative Protestants as reflecting the despicable development of modernity (see MODERNISM). This was part of a wider critique of INDIVIDUALISM and of the spirit of Arminian theology, which was held as placing too much emphasis on the private interpretation of scripture (see ARMINIANISM). For many conservative Protestants, the prevailing view at the beginning of the twentieth century was that democracy and all that it entailed, like SCIENCE and technology, was an evil of the modern world. An extension of rights, alongside the SOCIAL GOSPEL, came to be understood as part of the increasing influence of liberal theology (see LIBERAL PROTESTANTISM AND LIBERALISM). Progressive reform was judged as Satan's way of lulling the world from God's impending wrath. Evident here was the influence of a prevailing gloomy premillenarianism that, at its extremist dispensationist pole, brought a cultural pessimism that bordered on world-rejection.

In contrast to these developments, there was also a sense in which Protestant EVANGELICALISM endorsed a human rights agenda on its own account. This can be traced back to the eighteenth-century Calvinist vision of an all-embracing Christian CULTURE. Typified by CHARLES FINNEY, the idea was for reform through political institutions and social action. This vision was later to be commonly proclaimed by Arminian Protestantism in conjunction with social reform and reformist parties. An example of this was the link between nineteenth-century METHODISM and the emergence of the Labour Party in Britain. The emphasis here, however, was primarily on social and political rights, given that Protestant reformism did not breed a militant secularism or extreme Left-wing ideology.

Since the 1960s liberal Protestants have advanced the cause of human rights, which have continued to be extended and transformed. Many liberals allied themselves to the CIVIL RIGHTS MOVEMENT and translated the concern with rights into pressure-group politics. Some Baptist churches, for example, advanced the cause of black people in the United States. Moreover, since the second half of the twentieth century the gradual revival of human rights issues can also be seen as a response to the weakening position of Christianity in Western culture. The key concern has been in being relevant to the modern world and to sharing in its spirit of progress. This has proved to also be a vision within liberal churches with the distinct agenda of rights including the call for WOMEN and gay clergy (see WOMEN CLERGY; HOMOSEXUALITY). Although conservative Protestants may lament such developments, their forays into such social issues as ABORTION and religious education reverberate with the discourse of "human rights" so perceived. In turn this indicates the cultural preoccupation with the ever-extending field of rights in Western societies and the need for Protestants of different theological persuasions to engage with the secular world on its terms.

See also Clergy; Dispensationalism; Ethics; Millenarians and Millennialism; Secularization

STEPHEN HUNT

HUME, DAVID (1711–1776)

Scottish philospher. Hume is widely regarded as the founder of the modern philosophy of religion. A religious skeptic and an astute critic of both natural and revealed religion, he attacked the cosmological and design arguments for the existence of God, undermined the force of miracles as evidence for revelation, and sought to uncover natural causes of religious belief. Deeply concerned about the negative ethical and social effects of religious belief, he held that morality could be detached from religion and understood in purely naturalistic terms.

Biography

Hume was born in Edinburgh, Scotland, into a family with links to the staunchly Calvinist Evangelical faction within the CHURCH OF SCOTLAND. As a youth, Hume examined himself according to the catalog of vices provided by *The Whole Duty of Man,* a popular devotional work, but became a religious skeptic after reading the rationalist works of JOHN LOCKE (1632–1704) and Samuel Clarke. After an unremarkable career at the University of Edinburgh, followed by a stint as a clerk, Hume turned to philosophy, publishing his first work in 1739. In 1744 he pursued a chair in moral philosophy at Edinburgh, but when both that chair and a chair at Glasgow went to others he recognized that his religious views precluded any academic appointment. Hume did succeed in winning a post in 1752 as librarian to the Faculty of Advocates in Edinburgh, but he was dogged by controversy, and the General Assembly initiated excommunication proceedings against him in 1756. Although liberal clergy derailed these proceedings, Hume felt unwelcome in Scotland and spent several years abroad. Paris received Hume with open arms in 1763, but Hume considered the atheism of Holbach and his associates yet another form of unwarranted dogmatism. Dying of cancer in his native Edinburgh, Hume impressed the Scottish biographer James Boswell (1740–1795) with his cheerful equanimity in the face of death.

The Treatise

Hume's *Treatise of Human Nature* (1739–40) revealed the metaphysical skepticism implicit in Locke's empiricism, while suggesting that the common affairs of life could continue undisturbed. The *Treatise* did not overtly discuss theological matters, but in reducing the soul to a bundle of perceptions and thus questioning its unity, Hume challenged philosophical arguments for the immortality of the soul. Further, in arguing that statements about causality are simply statements of observed regularities, Hume undermined the cosmological argument to God as First Cause. In suggesting that moral arguments, which derive prescriptive ought-statements from descriptive is-statements, involve an unwarranted logical leap, Hume discredited natural law theory, which drew normative conclusions about God's will for humanity from observations of the salient features of human nature. Hume's discussion of the virtues and vices in Book III of the *Treatise* made no appeals to divine laws or to divine design of human nature. In Hume's naturalistic ethics, a virtue is a character trait that is pleasurable or useful to the virtuous person or those affected by him or her. Our capacity to care about the welfare of others is explained by sympathy, and requires no reference to God's benevolent design of human nature.

The essay "Of Miracles" is thought to have been withheld from the *Treatise* in order to avoid offending Bishop JOSEPH BUTLER (1692–1752), whose approval Hume courted, but Hume included it in his next work, the more popular *Enquiry Concerning Human Understanding* (1748). Hume argued that evidence for a miracle could never outweigh our accumulated experience of the regularities of nature, and thus it would always be more reasonable to deny than to accept the occurrence of a miracle.

The Dialogues

Hume's *Dialogues Concerning Natural Religion,* which he began writing in 1751 but published only posthumously, is modeled after Cicero's dialogue *De Natura Deorum.* In this work, the skeptic Philo, who is generally recognized as Hume's spokesman, undermines the centerpiece of natural theology by showing that the design argument can lead at most to the conclusion that "the cause or causes of order in the universe probably bear some remote analogy to human intelligence" (Hume 1993:129). Those, like the character Cleanthes, who champion this argument as justifying a robust theism, have failed to proportion the inferred cause to the observed effect, and have illegitimately extended the ideas of cause and effect to the origin of the universe, beyond the realm of experience. When the orthodox Demea argues that we are led to God not by speculative reason, but by our sense of misery and dependence on God, Philo argues that the evil and suffering in the world imply rather that the deity lacks any recognizable moral attributes and is indifferent to human affairs.

The Natural History

Hume was not content solely to reveal weaknesses in arguments for religious belief; he also sought, notably in *The Natural History of Religion* (1757), to show that religious belief has purely natural causes. Far from emerging out of careful reasoning, as deists argued, or revelation, as the orthodox claimed, Hume suggested that religion had its origins in the fear of unknown causes. Polytheism, not philosophical theism, was the first form of religious belief. Theism emerged naturally out of polytheism, because believers hoped by flattery to achieve greater control over the gods, and thus elevated one god to absolute power. Theists are incapable of sustaining a conception of God that is adequate to their claims of divine infinity and perfection; in fact, they entertain contradictory conceptions of God as loving benefactor and as arbitrary tyrant, as utterly simple yet possessing changing thoughts and passions. Self-deception and zeal emerge to protect beliefs that cannot be defended by rational means, and theism is thus typified by intolerance.

See also Calvinism; Deism

References and Further Reading:

Primary Sources:

Hume, David. *Principal Writings on Religion.* Edited by J. C. A. Gaskin. Oxford: Oxford University Press, 1993.

Secondary Sources:

Gaskin, J. C. A. *Hume's Philosophy of Religion.* 2nd ed. London: Macmillan, 1988.
Herdt, Jennifer A. *Religion and Faction in Hume's Moral Philosophy.* Cambridge: Cambridge University Press, 1997.
Yandell, Keith. E. *Hume's "Inexplicable Mystery": His Views on Religion.* Philadelphia: Temple University Press, 1990.
JENNIFER A. HERDT

HUNGARY

At the turn of the sixteenth century, Protestantism dominated Hungarian society, but then gradually lost ground in the face of the Catholic COUNTER-REFORMATION. Hungarian Protestantism was profoundly affected by the politics of central Europe, but the region's largest Protestant community survived the impact of Catholic persecution, revolts, and revolutions, the breakup of the Hungarian state, and a period of Communist rule.

The Hungarian Reformation

REFORMATION ideas spread to Hungary in the middle decades of the sixteenth century, during a period of profound political instability in central Europe. In 1526 the Ottoman army under Sultan Suleiman I "the magnificent" (approximately 1494–1566) had won a crushing victory at Mohács over the Hungarian king, Louis II. The Ottomans were later able to push even further north, and by the 1540s had established control over much of central and southern Hungary. The remaining areas of the Hungarian kingdom were divided into two. Royal Hungary, ruled by Habsburg kings, stretched from the Adriatic coast up to the mountains of modern Slovakia. The eastern part of the Hungarian kingdom, including Transylvania, was ruled by elected princes.

This catastrophic collapse of the Hungarian kingdom discredited the spiritual power of the Catholic Church and disrupted existing church structures. As ideas about reforming religion spread from the west, they were quickly accepted by many nobles and in towns. The Habsburg court encouraged the diet to pass antireform laws, but these had little impact. From the 1540s Lutheran ideas received support in the German-speaking towns of Transylvania and Upper Hungary, where a version of the AUGSBURG CONFESSION was adopted in 1544. The influence of Swiss reformers then gained ground among Hungarian speakers from the late 1550s. Although a sense of linguistic and ethnic community may have made some contribution to the outcome of the Hungarian Reformation, the role of the socially privileged elite of nobles and urban magistrates was generally decisive in the reception or rejection of different forms of Protestantism. In eastern Hungary the Reformed or Calvinist Church (see CALVINISM) dominated the confessional landscape toward the end of the sixteenth century. The magnates, gentry, and market towns of counties beyond the river Tisza mostly adhered to a Calvinist confession drawn up by Péter Méliusz Juhász at Debrecen in 1567, and Reformed clergy also recognized the Second HELVETIC CONFESSION.

In the Transylvanian principality the Lutheran, Reformed, and Antitrinitarian (see ANTITRINITARIANISM) churches were all granted legal status in the 1560s (see also ROMANIA). The remarkably tolerant resolutions of the 1568 Transylvanian diet at Turda (Torda) devolved to clergy the task of preaching the word of God "according to their understanding of it." On the whole the German-speaking community in Transylvania remained in the Lutheran Church (see LUTHERANISM). The Reformed Church in Transylvania was dominated by Hungarian speakers, as was the anti-Trinitarian or Unitarian Church, which emerged after debates in the 1560s between Hungarian clergy about the doctrine of the Trinity.

Although Protestants in the Transylvanian principality gained constitutional recognition, Protestant clergy in Royal Hungary remained entirely reliant on powerful noble families to protect them. Freedom for Protestants to worship was granted only to the small number of royal free towns. Despite this, around three-quarters of people living in Hungary and Transylvania were attending services in Lutheran or Reformed churches by the 1570s. The Habsburg court and Catholic hierarchy attempted to undermine this growth of Protestantism (see CATHOLIC REACTIONS TO PROTESTANTISM). Attempts by Rudolf II to close down the Lutheran church in Košice (Kassa) in 1604 provided one of the sparks of Protestant rebellion against the progress of Counter-Reformation. A Reformed noble, István Bocskai, led his forces to victory over Habsburg armies in eastern Hungary, and was elected as Transylvanian prince. The terms of the 1606 Peace of Vienna, confirmed by the diet in 1608, extended freedom of religion to nobles, towns, and military garrisons in Royal Hungary, and the rights of the Lutheran and Reformed churches were guaranteed.

However, Habsburg kings continued to work together with the Catholic hierarchy and the Jesuits during the early decades of the seventeenth century to reconvert prominent Hungarian nobles and to curtail Protestant freedoms. The Habsburgs' ability to promote Catholicism was checked by the need to retain the support of the nobles for defense against the Ottomans, and by the interventions of a series of Reformed Transylvanian princes. Prince György I Rákóczi's entry into the Thirty Years War against the Habsburgs led to compromise between Ferdinand III and the decreasing number of Protestant nobles at the diet of 1646–1647. Some Protestant church buildings that had been taken over by Catholics were returned, and the religious freedoms agreed in 1608 were confirmed. However, Protestants in Royal Hungary soon faced new persecution as churches were again seized by Catholics and Protestant ministers were expelled from their parishes. Protestants living in Ottoman Hungary were in some ways in a more favorable position than those in Royal Hungary by the late 1650s. Although there were restrictions against renovating church buildings in Ottoman Hungary, there were many Protestant congregations and some active schools.

The Protestant Churches

The Lutheran and Reformed churches adopted a hierarchical form of government, with superintendents charged to lead church provinces and archdeacons in charge of regions within each province. The key issue that brought division between those in Hungary who favored church reform was understanding of the sacraments, and especially the Eucharist (see LORD'S SUPPER). Reformed clergy could not agree with Lutherans that Christ was "really present" in the sacrament, and their confession argued that the Eucharist was merely a sign and pledge of salvation by faith. Protestant churches in western Hungary remained united until the beginning of the seventeenth century, but then this issue also saw them divide into distinct Reformed and Lutheran churches. Despite Calvinist opposition to religious imagery, there were almost no incidences of ICONOCLASM in Hungary during the Reformation.

Protestant ideas spread through preaching and printed literature. Protestants recognized the importance of improving the standards of the clergy, and made efforts to develop their education in local colleges. Because Hungary did not have a university, many Protestant student ministers were sent abroad to foreign universities from the late sixteenth century, particularly to Wittenberg and Heidelberg. Hundreds of Reformed students later traveled to study in the Dutch Republic and ENGLAND from the early seventeenth century. Protestants also developed printing presses in many towns. The first complete translation of the BIBLE into Hungarian was available from 1590 thanks to the work of Gáspár Károlyi, minister at Vizsoly in northeastern Hungary. Other printed books were produced by Protestants from the late sixteenth century, including CATECHISMS, creeds, statements of DOCTRINE, sermons, schoolbooks, and HYMNALS. The HEIDELBERG CATECHISM was translated into Hungarian by Dávid Huszár in 1577, and in 1607 Albert Szenczi Molnár rendered the psalms into Hungarian verses to the settings of the Genevan Psalter.

In the early seventeenth century Reformed clergy were inspired by contact with western Calvinist centers to produce practical theological literature for their congregations. Prominent figures such as János Tolnai Dali and Pál Medgyesi returned home from the Dutch Republic and England to attempt to improve popular piety and moral discipline. These so-called Puritans (see PURITANISM) also supported the development of Presbyteries (see PRESBYTERIANISM) to enforce higher standards of morality. Although the formation of presbyteries received some support in western and northeastern Hungary, the traditional form of church government by a clergy hierarchy was upheld by a national synod at Satu Mare (Szatmár) in 1646. At the beginning of the eighteenth century PIETISM gained support among Lutheran clergy, also aiming to encourage moral discipline and spiritual renewal.

From Counter-Reformation to Toleration

In Royal Hungary, Protestants faced growing Catholic persecution, which culminated in the 1670s when Protestant clergy faced trial on charges of treason. Some clergy converted, others resigned from the ministry, and those who stood firm were imprisoned and then forced to march to Italy, where they were sold as galley slaves to the Spanish. This incident became well known in the western Protestant world, and the Dutch admiral Michael de Ruyter eventually liberated twenty-three Protestant ministers off Naples in 1676.

Toward the end of the seventeenth century, Habsburg success in battle against the Ottomans extended their control over more territory, and by the early eighteenth century most Protestants in western and southern Hungary lacked access to a place of worship or a minister to conduct services. Contact with western Protestants was also hindered by the state authorities. Commissions were appointed to look into Protestant grievances, but the restrictions continued. Some relief for Protestants came with the decree of TOLERATION issued by Joseph II in 1781. The Catholic Church retained its privileged status, but all Protestant communities of at least 100 families were permitted to build a church, even if the law at first prevented these buildings from having a tower, bell, or entrance onto a main street. Protestants were also allowed access to public offices, could become members of guilds, and were no longer compelled to attend Catholic services. However, in mixed marriages, marriage law required that if the father was Catholic then all children must be brought up as Catholics; if the father was Protestant then only his sons could become Protestants.

Protestantism in the Nineteenth Century

Lutherans and Calvinists were granted basic freedoms of religious practice at the end of the eighteenth century, but the continuing inequalities that Protestants faced formed part of the agenda of Hungarian national reform in the nineteenth century. Indeed, Protestant communities, which had always been among those least supportive of Habsburg rule in Hungary, became central to Hungarian Nationalist movements (see NATIONALISM). During the 1848 revolution, legal equality was declared between four accepted churches: Catholic, Lutheran, Calvinist, and Unitarian. Protestant support for the revolution was enthusiastic, and the Transdanubian Reformed Church province even called on its ministers to take part in the fighting. In April 1849 Hungarian independence was declared at the Reformed college chapel in Debrecen, announced by the Lutheran Lajos Kossuth.

After the 1848 revolution was crushed, the Protestant churches faced renewed persecution. Religious freedoms were established again only after the 1867 Compromise with Austria. In 1881 the Reformed Church could hold its first national synod at Debrecen, the Hungarian Calvinist "Rome." This synod was able to lay down the foundations of a national church, with a synod to meet every tenth year to decide on church laws and a council that represented the church between these synods. The late nineteenth century saw increased educational activity from all the Protestant churches, and concern for domestic mission from the 1880s in the face of declining church membership.

In 1895 a law accepting the free practice of religion was passed by the Hungarian parliament. This law declared that the practice of civil and political rights was entirely independent from religious faith. The full benefit of these laws was offered to the traditional religious groups: Catholic, Calvinist, Lutheran, Unitarian, Jewish, and Orthodox (see JUDAISM; ORTHODOXY, EASTERN). These churches, synagogues, and their schools could receive state subsidies, their clergy were offered a minimum salary, and their religious teachers were given a state salary. A second category of religions, which included a Baptist Church that had emerged in the nineteenth century, was recognized. BAPTISTS also enjoyed full legal freedoms, but could not claim state subsidies. Finally, smaller tolerated denominations were allowed to function under rights of free association. These laws remained in place up to the end of the SECOND WORLD WAR.

Protestantism in the Twentieth Century

By 1910 the Reformed Church had recovered in numbers, thanks to considerable efforts at home mission and the relaxation of laws against Protestant churches. There were over two and a half million Reformed Church members before the FIRST WORLD WAR, served by over 2,000 clergy and over 3,000 teachers. The Protestant churches, and the rest of Hungarian society, faced the trauma of defeat in the FIRST WORLD WAR and then the reduction of Hungarian territory by over two-thirds in the 1920 Trianon peace treaty. One-third of ethnic Hungarians found themselves outside the borders of Hungary. The states that gained Hungarian territory, especially Romania, Yugoslavia, and Czechoslovakia, all had many new Protestant subjects.

Within the territory of the new Hungarian state, a 1920 census revealed that 21 percent of the population were Reformed (approximately 900,000), with a further 6 percent Lutheran. The desire to recover territory lost under the Trianon treaty bred an intolerant nationalism in the interwar period. None of the Christian churches had a distinguished record in challenging the rise of fascism and ANTI-SEMITISM in Hungarian society. Reformed superintendent László Ravasz even supported a 1938 law that legalized the expropriation of Jewish property.

After defeat as Germany's ally in the SECOND WORLD WAR, the postwar Communist regime limited the role of all churches in public life. In 1947 the privileges offered by the state to the churches were revoked. In 1948 the Protestant churches agreed to a formal separation from the state. The last census to measure religious affiliation in 1949 found that 70 percent of the population were Catholic, 22 percent Calvinist, and 5 percent Lutheran. Among the smaller religious groups, Baptists were measured at 0.2 percent (approximately 20,000), and Unitarians at 0.1 percent. In 1951 the Church Affairs Office was established to organize policy toward all Christian churches, and the churches from that point became increasingly subordinated to the state (see CHURCH AND STATE, OVERVIEW). The 1956 revolution brought religious instruction back into schools for several months, but this effort to break free from the Communist bloc was quickly overwhelmed by Soviet intervention.

By the time Communist rule softened in the years of "goulash-communism," the numbers of active Protestants had decreased considerably, especially in Budapest and in other large towns. Only 18 percent of the population were Calvinist by this time, with 4 percent Lutheran, and almost 10 percent declared themselves outside any denomination. From the downfall of the Communists in 1989, laws have been passed establishing freedom of conscience and religious activity. The state surrendered its monopoly on education, the Church Affairs Office was closed, and some appropriated church property was returned by the state. The Reformed Church has developed its seminaries in Budapest, Debrecen, and Sárospatak, and all the Protestant churches have produced new religious books and undertaken some missionary work, especially among students. The historic Protestant churches face many challenges to establish their role in a post-Communist society, including competition from some new Christian movements.

References and Further Reading

Bucsay, Mihály. *Der Protestantismus in Ungarn, 1521–1978. Ungarns Reformationskirchen in Geschichte und Gegenwart. 1. Im Zeitalter der Reformation, Gegenreformation und katholischen Reform.* Vienna: Böhlau, 1977.

Evans, Robert. "Calvinism in East Central Europe: Hungary and Her Neighbours." In *International Calvinism, 1541–1715.* Edited by Menna Prestwich. Oxford: Clarendon, 1985.

Makkai, László. "The Hungarian Puritans and the English Revolution." *Acta Historica* 5 (1958): 13–45.

Murdock, Graeme. *Calvinism on the Frontier, 1600–1660. International Calvinism and the Reformed Church in Hungary and Transylvania.* Oxford: Clarendon Press, 2000.

Révész, Imre, ed. *History of the Hungarian Reformed Church.* Translated by George Knight. Washington, DC: Hungarian Federation of America, 1956.

Unghváry, Alexander. *The Hungarian Protestant Reformation in the Sixteenth Century under the Ottoman Impact.* Lewiston, NY: Edwin Mellen Press, 1989.

GRAEME MURDOCK

HUTCHINSON, ANNE (1591–1643)

American lay theologian. Called the "American Jesabel" by JOHN WINTHROP (1638–1707), governor of the Massachusetts Bay colony, Anne Hutchinson is one of the most notorious heretics in the history of American Protestantism (Hall 1968:310). Immigrating to Boston in 1634 with her large family, Hutchinson quickly assumed a position of religious authority within the community. The meetings that she held at her house to review the previous week's sermon grew to an unprecedented size and attracted both women and men. When she began at these meetings to denounce all the colony's ministers, except JOHN COTTON (1585–1652), for preaching a covenant of works, the ensuing controversy divided the colony into two opposing factions. In November 1637, after a very bold and articulate defense of her theological positions, the general court banished Hutchinson from the colony; in March 1638 she was excommunicated by the Boston Church. Moving first to Rhode Island and then to the New York frontier, she and several family members were killed in 1643 in an Indian raid.

Because the Massachusetts Bay ministers preached that sanctification, or good works, was evidence of JUSTIFICATION, Hutchinson accused them of legalism. Because she denied the necessity of works and maintained that assurance of salvation came through an immediate witness of the Spirit, they accused her of ANTINOMIANISM. In addition to this theological disagreement, historians have perceived in the controversy a class conflict, for the supporters of Hutchinson were disproportionately drawn from Boston's rising merchant class. Historians have also explored the role of gender in the controversy. Acting to suppress not only a rival interpretation of the relation between faith and works but also the possibility of women's religious leadership, the bay ministers established a link between heresy and female power that would persist in the religious imagination of Protestant America for generations.

References and Further Reading

Battis, Emery. *Saints and Sectaries: Anne Hutchinson and the Antinomian Controversy in the Massachusetts Bay Colony.* Chapel Hill: University of North Carolina Press, 1962.

Hall, David D., ed. *The Antinomian Controversy, 1636–1638: A Documentary History.* Middletown, CT: Wesleyan University Press, 1968.

Lang, Amy Schrager. *Prophetic Woman: Anne Hutchinson and the Problem of Dissent in the Literature of New England.* Berkeley: University of California Press, 1987.

AVA CHAMBERLAIN

HUTTERITES

The Hutterites (also known as the Hutterian Brethren) were a group of Germanic religious dissenters that coalesced around the charismatic leadership of JAKOB HUTTER (after whom they were named), developing into a distinctive church around 1530 in Moravia (Slovakia). Committed to basic Anabaptist Practice and faith (see ANABAPTISM), they developed a unique attachment to a communitarian life (*Gütergemeinschaft*) in which all personal and family possessions were shared. Today the Hutterites number around 30,000, scattered among some 300 colonies (farming communities) mainly in western Canada and the midwest and western United States. They have substantially maintained the faith and practice of their fore-

bears, making them the longest lived family-oriented communitarian movement in history.

History

During much of the sixteenth century, nobles in and around the region of Moravia were independent enough to allow a measure of religious freedom in their territories. The promise of religious tolerance drew thousands of dissenters to the area, most of whom were Anabaptists. Austrian Tirol (homeland of Jakob Hutter) also provided hundreds of pilgrims who made their way to what they often described as the "Promised Land" in Moravia.

Backed by a large contingent of Tirolian Anabaptists, Hutter was able to forge from various groups a united movement that became the Hutterites. Although Hutter was captured on a return visit to Tirol and executed at Innsbruck in 1536, the Hutterite church maintained its cohesion and commitment to their faith and practice. During the first half of the sixteenth century, the church endured periods of severe persecution at the hands of the Hapsburg Kings of Austria, at times being forced to take refuge in caves. However, by the mid-1550s the nobles again were able to resist the king's repeated order to rid the land of dissenters (see DISSENT). In exchange for the economic benefits brought to their land by the industrious dissenters, the nobles allowed them to practice religion as they chose. The Hutterites referred to this time (1550s–1620) as the "Golden Years."

Numbering as many as 20,000 scattered among some 100 colonies, they prospered enormously. Although they did not mix with the national population, living largely in their separated communitarian colonies, their numbers consistently increased because of an active mission outreach to Germanic lands in central Europe. In small and large groups, Anabaptists emigrated to Moravia, often bringing with them orphaned children whom local authorities had abandoned. They were organized under a single bishop over the entire church, with both a spiritual leader (*Diener des Wortes,* Servant of the Word or Preacher) and a leader responsible for temporal affairs (*Diener der Notdurft,* Servant of Temporal Concerns or Colony Manager) for each colony. Agriculture was an integral part of the Hutterite economy, although their main economic contribution was small industry. A broad range of crafts, including iron and copper works, carpentry, mill works, wagon building, leather works, wine production, farm management, and, perhaps the most important, their highly sought after ceramic works, made them almost indispensable for the local economy and its tax base. (Religious freedom included for a time allowance for the Hutterites to pay taxes and/or provide public service in lieu of military service and to exclude taxes directly related to military causes.) The communitarian economy allowed them to underprice competition, which often incited considerable resentment among the populace, which along with the religious dissent created a continually volatile existence. Nonetheless, under the direction of gifted and capable leaders, such as Peter Walpot and Peter Riedemann, both their economic stability and spiritual commitment were effectively maintained during this period.

At the outbreak of the Thirty Years War (1618–1638), circumstances changed abruptly. The Hapsburg dynasty again achieved the upper hand over the nobles and were able finally to rid their lands of the "Anabaptist menace." The expulsion from Moravia was catastrophic for the Hutterites. Not only did they lose about half their number, but they were forced to leave their well-established economic base for the much less politically stable and economically depressed Hungarian lands. They also entered a no-man's-land situation in which they were caught between the rival claimants of the Hapsburgs, local nobles, and Ottoman Turks, each of whom periodically sent troops into the area to support their respective claims. This, along with renegade marauding bands, wreaked havoc among the Hutterite settlements. At times entire colonies were exterminated. The end of the Thirty Years War brought no reprieve; in fact, the sociopolitical instability increased throughout the remainder of the seventeenth century.

In spite of the dire circumstances, the Hutterites experienced one of their greatest leaders, Andreas Ehrenpreis, often referred to as the movement's second founder. Many within the church began to feel that the stringent organizational structures required by community of goods were no longer tenable under such difficult economic circumstances, and many began to leave the church to live as independent families in the nearby communities. Under his direction monumental efforts were undertaken to stem the tide of spiritual and temporal disintegration. Although the church had over the years produced numerous ordinances defining and directing the various crafts and requirements of craft foremen, as well as those for the spiritual leaders, they began to proliferate during the Ehrenpreis era. New and revised ordinances were written to enforce a greater allegiance to the concept and practice of community of goods, which under Ehrenpreis received an even greater emphasis than it had in the past. For him, it became the ultimate expression of Christian faith and practice.

Ehrenpreis's efforts were heroic but abortive. Soon after his death in 1662, the church decided to temporarily abandon community of goods, and soon thereafter most began to assimilate into the local culture. A remnant of nineteen people, however, remained loyal to the faith in Transylvania (central, northwestern Romania) and were later (1756) joined by a few Lutherans who were converted to their faith. A small group of sixty-seven faithful fled the Hapsburg suppression in this area and emigrated to Walachia (southern Romania) in 1767 and later to Russia in 1770 because of the promise of religious freedom. For the next century the Hutterites settled in Ukraine, where community of goods was sporadically practiced, although most families continued to maintain the spiritual and historical heritage of the movement. In 1870 the Czar declared universal military conscription, undermining the initial invitation of nobles for the Hutterites to live on their lands as pacifists (see PACIFISM). With a few exceptions, the church as a whole decided to emigrate to the United States, which they began to do in 1874. They settled in South Dakota because it reminded them so much of the Russian Steppes that had been their home for over a century.

In spite of their historical heritage and theological homogeneity, soon after the immigration long-standing differences resulted in a division into three distinct groups, *Lehrer-Leut, Darius-Leut,* and *Schmiede-Leut.* All three groups practiced community of goods, but carefully maintained differences that would not be easily discernible to outsiders. As a result of a very high birth rate, the church grew phenomenally from some 400 in the 1870s to nearly 30,000 in 100 years. Their economic prosperity was equally remarkable.

However, during WORLD WAR I a number of their young men submitted to the draft but nevertheless refused to bear arms, for which many suffered considerable hardships. In fact, two of their young men were so severely mistreated in a military camp that they died. Because of this, with the exception of one colony, the entire church moved to Canada, where they were granted exemption from military service. Since that time, the U.S. government has granted them conscientious objector status (see CONSCIENTIOUS OBJECTION) and many have returned and have spread throughout the north-central and western United States, where they continue to prosper.

Doctrine and Writings

Of all Anabaptist groups, the Hutterites were by far the most prolific in producing literature, including theological treatises, letters, HYMNS, and sermons. Their literature reflects a literalist interpretation of the

BIBLE with an understanding that both FAITH and behavior contribute to SALVATION, in which the individual Christian is intimately bound to the life of the church. Their primary objective was to restore the New Testament church, which they felt the Roman Catholic Church had distorted through its traditions and the Protestant churches had not fully reformed. One of their first major works was the "Great Article Book" (*Die Fünf Artikel des Grössten Streites Zwischen Uns und der Welt,* "Five Articles Concerning the Great Struggle Between Us and the World"), which contained the five primary principles of the Hutterite faith: a rejection of infant BAPTISM for adult baptism, a rejection of the Catholic view of the reality of the elements of the LORD'S SUPPER in favor of a symbolic understanding, the necessity of community of goods as an expression of true Christian devotion (*Gelassenheit*), pacifism, and allowance for the DIVORCE of a nonbelieving spouse (although remarriage after such a divorce was not allowed). One copy included, as a fifth point, the rejection of oath-taking. It is most likely that Peter Walpot composed the book around 1547.

Another work of great significance was the Great History Book (*Geschichts-Buch und kurzer Durchgang vom Anfang der Welt,* "History Book and brief Overview from the Beginning of the World") now translated as the *Chronicle I* (*Chronicle II* is a translation of the *Klein-Gechichtsbuch,* "Short History Book," in process). As was common to history books of the era, it began with creation but quickly came to the account of the rise of Anabaptism, and then concentrated on Hutterite history from 1528 to 1665. It also includes a condensed version of the "Great Article Book" and a number of letters by prominent leaders. *Chronicle II* continues the account of the Hutterite church from 1665 to 1947, including a number of interesting documents, diaries, and treatises.

The major theological work of the early Hutterites was the treatise written by Peter Riedemann called *Confession of Faith (Rechenschaft Unserer Religion, Lehr und Glaubens).* It includes the five principles but elaborates in greater detail many of the other ideas and practices of the Hutterite faith, systematically arranged.

The Hutterite church was a careful collector and preserver of its own literature, which it used extensively to maintain the faith but also put to use in more practical ways. In the larger church colonies boarding schools were set up that provided elementary EDUCATION in reading, writing, and arithmetic for both boys and girls before they were apprenticed to a craft around the age of 12. This was one of the most advanced elementary educational systems in Europe at the time. The numerous missionary letters, treatises, hymns, and later sermons served as the educational material used to teach reading and writing in the schools. There were hundreds of letters to and from missionaries and other church leaders that were shared among the colonies and archived to be made available for various purposes.

As noted, during the Ehrenpreis era both temporal and spiritual ordinances proliferated. In addition, a new genre of literature began to appear: the sermon. There are over 500 sermons from this period that are yet extant. In fact, these very sermons are the source of all preaching among the Hutterites today. Each Sunday, the preacher chooses selections from these sermons to read to the church. Only on the rarest of occasions will a preacher write a new sermon. Ehrenpreis also edited a number of collections of hymns, which together with the sermons make up the contemporary liturgy of the Hutterite church.

References and Further Reading

Primary Sources:

The Chronicle of the Hutterian Brethren, 1525–1665, vol. I. Rifton, NY: Plough Publishing House, 1987.

Riedemann, Peter. *Confession of Faith.* Suffolk, England: Hodder and Stoughton with The Plough Publishing House, 1950.

Zieglschmid, A. J. F., ed. *Das Klein-Geschichtsbuch der Hutterischen Brüdern.* Philadelphia: The Carl Schurz Memorial Foundation, 1947. (Will appear again as *The Chronicle of the Hutterian Brethren, 1665–1947,* vol. II, in process.)

Secondary Sources:

Dyck, C. J., et al., eds. *The Mennonite Encyclopedia.* 5 vols. Scottdale, PA: Herald Press, 1990.

Gross, Leonard. *The Golden Years of the Hutterites.* Scottdale, PA: Herald Press, 1980.

Harrison, Wes. *Andreas Ehrenpreis and Hutterite Faith and Practice.* Kitchener, ON: Pandora Press, 1997.

Hostetler, John A. *Hutterite Society.* Baltimore: The Johns Hopkins University Press, 1974.

WES HARRISON

HUTTER, JAKOB (c. 1500–1536)

Anabaptist leader, founder of Hutterites (Hutterian Brethren). Born around 1500 in Moos, a hamlet in South Tyrol, Hutter became a hatmaker by trade and received a rudimentary education. As early as 1527 Anabaptist teachings began to infiltrate Tyrol, an area already given to ideas of religious and social reform. Around 1528 or 1529 Hutter converted to ANABAPTISM and quickly became a recognized leader in the region. In 1529 he made the first of several trips to Moravia to investigate reports that "God had gathered a people in his name to live as one heart, mind, and soul, each caring faithfully for the other" (*Chronicle* 1987:84). Throughout the sixteenth century a few Moravian nobles were occasionally able to maintain religious freedom on their lands. These circumstances drew thousands of religious dissidents from all over Europe, most of whom were Anabaptists. Hutter united with a group in Austerlitz, being particularly attracted to their practice of community of goods (sharing all possessions as community property). This tenet of faith would become the cornerstone of the movement to which Hutter emphatically dedicated himself and his teaching. From 1531 to 1533 the church was severely plagued with controversies over leadership. Although Hutter was active during this time as a missionary in Tyrol, he was also indirectly involved with the leadership question. In 1533 he returned to Moravia for the fourth time and soon established himself as the sole leader of the group, called HUTTERITES or Hutterian Brethren, which now numbered about 1,000, including some 300 children. Hutter proved to be an indefatigable and resourceful leader, providing the practical and inspirational direction necessary to keep together such a large group.

The determination of the Hapsburg King Ferdinand I to rid all his lands of the Anabaptist "heresy" eventually caused Hutter to return to Tyrol. Having recently married, Hutter and his wife Katherine continued the same mission activity he had participated in before. Unfortunately, by this time his practices were too well known by the authorities, and he and his wife were soon arrested. Hutter was interrogated incessantly, tortured severely, and finally burned at the stake in Innsbruck in late February or early March 1536. His wife gave birth to a child while in prison, but later escaped. However, she was recaptured two years later and executed. Nothing further is known about the child.

Only eight letters from Hutter are extant. They are filled with pastoral expressions of concern and exhortations to remain faithful despite the ever-present threatening forces of evil. One letter was addressed to a local noble in Moravia as an apology of the movement as harmless people who desired to live their faith in love to all people and as a charge to the nobles themselves to repent and join the true faith.

References and Further Reading

Primary Source:

The Chronicle of the Hutterian Brethren, 1525–1665, vol. I. Rifton, NY: Plough Publishing House, 1987.

Secondary Sources:

Fischer, Hans, G. *Jakob Hutter: Leben, Frömmigkeit, Briefe.* Newton, KS: Mennonite Publication Office, 1956.

Gross, Leonard. "Jakob Hutter: A Christian Communist." In *Profiles of Radical Reformers,* edited by Hans-Jürgen Goertz. Scottdale, PA: Herald Press, 1982. 158–167.

Hutter, Jacob. *Brotherly Faithfulness: Epistles from a Time of Persecution.* Translated by the Hutterian Society of Brothers. Rifton, NY: Plough Publishing House, 1979.

Packull, Werner O. *Hutterite Beginnings.* Baltimore: The Johns Hopkins University Press, 1995.

WES HARRISON

HYMNS AND HYMNALS

Pre-Reformation Traditions

Vernacular religious song was not the invention of the REFORMATION era. There was a long European history of such songs, including English carols, Dutch *geestelijke liederen,* Italian *lauda spirituales,* and German *leisen.* MARTIN LUTHER knew of and utilized the para-liturgical German *leisen* that were closely associated with the LITURGY and the festivals of the church year (see HOLIDAYS AND FESTIVALS). Examples include the fifteenth-century *Wir glauben all an einen Gott,* based on the Nicene Creed, the fourteenth-century *Gelobet seist du, Jesu Christ* (Christmas Day), the twelfth-century *Christ ist erstanden* (Easter Day), textually and musically related to the Easter sequence *Victimæ paschali laudes* and the thirteenth-century *Nun bitten wir den Heiligen Geist* (Feast of Pentecost), all of which, with others, Luther revised and expanded. But whereas previous generations had sung these *leisen* extraliturgically, after mass on the respective festivals, Luther directed that the new evangelical hymns—whether reworkings of older material or newly created—should be sung intraliturgically, that is, within the reformed mass by the congregation at large.

Luther's liturgical use of vernacular hymnody had been anticipated by the Bohemian Brethren, the followers of reformer Jan Hus (c. 1372–1415), who had sung Czech hymns in worship during the final decades of the fifteenth century. German-speaking Brethren translated many of these Czech hymns into their own language, issuing them in a hymnal published in Prague as early as 1501. Other collections of German versions of Czech hymns were *Ein New Gesangbuchlen* (Jungbunzlau, 1531), edited by Michael Weisse, and *Ein Gesangbuch der Brüder inn Behemen und Werherrn* (Nuremberg, 1544), edited by Johann Horn; hymns from both collections were utilized by Lutherans in Wittenberg and elsewhere.

The Latin hymns of the daily office were also influential in the development of Lutheran hymnody. Manuscript and printed *Hymnaria,* although designed for use by CLERGY and choirs, nevertheless provided a model for later Lutheran collections of vernacular congregational hymns, because many of these German hymns, like the earlier Latin office hymns, were intended to be sung during the primary seasons of the church year. But the Latin hymns themselves continued to be sung in Lutheran worship, especially in those churches that maintained a choir made up of pupils from the local Latin school.

Lutheran Tradition

The theological imperative for congregational hymnody came from Luther's understanding of the DOCTRINE of the PRIESTHOOD OF ALL BELIEVERS, which stood in contradistinction to the particular priesthood of Catholicism. Although it took five years after the 1517 debate concerning indulgences for Luther to make the connection between doctrine and practice, once he had linked the two he saw that unison congregational song was a powerful demonstration of the doctrine of universal priesthood, because every member of the congregation was involved in the activity. But Luther was also aware of the practice of the early CHURCH. In the *Formula missae* of 1523, he wrote: "I also wish that we had as many songs as possible in the vernacular which the people could sing during mass, immediately after the gradual and also after the Sanctus and Agnus Dei. For who doubts that originally all the people sang these which now only the choir sings?"

Before the end of 1523, the year that the *Formula missae* was published, Luther and his colleagues began creating a basic corpus of congregational song for Reformation WORSHIP, both ecclesiastical and domestic. They revised and reworked old German *leisen;* translated Latin office hymns into the vernacular, and modified, where necessary, their associated plainsong melodies; created *contrafacta,* either by rewriting preexisting religious folksongs or by supplying folk melodies with new "evangelical" texts; and wrote newly created hymns, both texts and tunes. These "new" hymns were first published on broadsides, but, beginning with the so-called *Achtliederbuch* (a small hymnal of just eight hymns published in Nuremberg in 1524), an extraordinary number of hymnals—at least 500—were published, with and without music, in German-speaking lands over the next quarter of a century.

Even before he and his colleagues had really begun to assemble a basic corpus of vernacular congregational song, Luther saw the primary function of such singing in liturgical terms. In the *Formula missae,*

following the passage cited above, he wrote: "Poets are wanting among us, or not yet known, who could compose evangelical and spiritual songs, as Paul calls them (Col. 3:16), worthy to be used in the church of God (after the Gradual and also after the Sanctus and Agnus Dei, etc.)." Sufficient progress had been made over the ensuing two years so that when Luther drew up his vernacular liturgy in 1525—the *Deutsche Messe,* published in Wittenberg early in 1526—there was a sufficient number of hymns available in Wittenberg for congregational use. Thus Luther was not only able to refer to hymns, but also to include some texts, with tunes, within the document. The traditional structure of the mass was retained, but, as in the *Formula missae,* the content was theologically reinterpreted. The five parts of the traditional ordinary were retained, except that in the *Deutsche Messe* Luther developed the principle that the congregation could sing them in hymnic forms. Over the course of time, a complete sequence of "ordinary" hymns became customary: *Kyrie, Gott Vater in ewigkeit* (Kyrie), *Allein Gott in der Höh sei Ehr* (Gloria), *Wir glauben all an einen Gott* (Credo), *Jesaja dem Propheten das geschah* (Sanctus), *Christe, du Lamm Gottes,* or *O Lamm Gottes, unschuldig* (Agnus Dei).

The new congregational hymns were to be not only liturgical, but also biblical. In the initial months when Luther and his colleagues were writing their earliest hymns, the reformer created a new genre that was to have enormous significance for hymnic congregational participation in Reformation churches: the psalm-hymn, or metrical psalm, that is, the biblical psalm in the vernacular rendered into a strophic and rhymed form. Near the end of 1523, Luther wrote thus to a colleague Georg Spalatin:

> Following the example of the prophets and fathers of the church, I intend to make vernacular psalms for the people, that is, spiritual songs so that the Word of God even by means of song may live among the people. Everywhere we are looking for poets. Now since you are so skillful and eloquent in German, I would like to ask you to work with us in this and to turn a psalm into a hymn as in the enclosed example of my work (Psalm 130: *Aus tiefer Not schrei ich zu dir*). But I would like you to avoid new-fangled, fancied words and to use expressions simple and common enough for the people to understand yet pure and fitting. The meaning should also be clear and as close as possible to the psalm. Irrespective of the exact wording, one must freely render the sense by suitable words.

Luther wrote no less than five metrical psalms during this earliest period of writing (1523–1524): *Ach Gott, vom Himmel sieh darein* (Psalm 12), *Es spricht der Unweisen Mund wohl* (Psalm 14), *Es wollt uns Gott genädig sein* (Psalm 67), *Wär Gott nicht mit uns diese Zeit* (Psalm 124), and *Aus tiefer Not schrei ich zu dir* (Psalm 130)—all in the same meter. He wrote *Wohl dem, der in Gottes Furcht steht* (Psalm 128) and *Ein feste Burg ist unser Gott* (Psalm 46) later, in 1525 and 1528–1529, respectively.

Other Lutherans followed Luther's example and wrote metrical psalms, thus establishing the genre that was to become almost universal in the churches of the Reformation, especially those that were Reformed in their THEOLOGY.

Evangelical Tradition

The Reformation in Strassburg, the leading city of Alsace, situated on the borders between FRANCE and GERMANY, although influenced by Wittenberg Lutheranism, nevertheless charted a somewhat independent course with regard to theological and ecclesiastical reforms. These reforms were certainly "evangelical," but not consistently Lutheran and not yet Reformed, in the sense of later CALVINISM. During the first period of hymn writing by Luther and his colleagues, 1523–1525, these German Lutheran hymns, especially the metrical psalms, were republished in Strassburg soon after their first appearance in Wittenberg. But there were two significant differences. First, the Wittenberg hymns were given new "Strassburg" tunes, composed or edited by Mathias Greiter and Wolfgang Dachstein, cantor and organist, respectively, of Strassburg cathedral. Second, additional congregational songs written by various Strassburgers were added to those of the Wittenbergers. Congregational singing was taken seriously in the city and area of Strassburg. In his 1543 CATECHISM, MARTIN BUCER, the leading reformer of the city and surrounding area, included a whole section on the importance of participation in the *Kirchengesang* (congregational hymnody), which he saw as second in importance only to participation in corporate PRAYER in the worship assembly.

The contents of the Strasbourg hymnals published in the 1520s and 1530s demonstrate a growing marked preference for metrical psalms, a fact that was to have far-reaching consequences not only for the later hymnals and psalters published in Strassburg, but also for the development of Genevan psalters. This later Calvinist psalmody had its genesis in the metrical psalmody of Strassburg. In 1537, JOHN CALVIN was called by Bucer to minister to the relatively small group of French-speaking protestants in Strassburg. It was here that Calvin encountered German metrical psalms and was stimulated to create French metrical psalms to be sung to the same melodies used by the German congregations in Strassburg. These were published as *Aulcuns pseaulmes et cantiques* (Strasbourg, 1539), the first fruit of what was to become the French Genevan Psalter.

Reformed Traditions

The character of the Swiss Reformed churches was shaped in large measure by the two primary languages of the Cantons: German and French. The churches of the German-speaking Cantons were focused on HULDRYCH ZWINGLI (and later HEINRICH BULLINGER) in Zurich; those of the French-speaking Cantons, on Calvin in Geneva. Each language-group developed specific theological emphases, patterns of worship, and different conclusions with regard to the practice of congregational song.

Zwinglian

Probably the most musically gifted of the sixteenth-century reformers, Zwingli paradoxically excluded music from the churches in Zurich. A principal reason for this action was Zwingli's theological understanding of the nature of worship. He saw outward observances as of little value when compared to the inner spiritual life, which he regarded as the essence of Christianity. Outward rites and gestures with ceremonial music, such as in the Roman mass, obscured the essence of true worship. Although he did accept the principle of corporate speech, as opposed to corporate song, for the public worship of the churches of Zurich, introduction of this practice was disallowed by the Zurich magistracy. However, Zwingli's exclusion of corporate song and other music from public worship has been misunderstood as a prohibition of all music from all worship. On the contrary, music was important in his own devotional life, and Zwingli is known to have written both words and music for at least three religious songs: the Pestlied, a metrical version of Psalm 69, and the Kappeler Lied. He also believed that music had important secular functions, especially in EDUCATION, and made provisions for the study of music in his reformed curricula for the schools attached to the Zurich churches. Although he gave a role to music in the secular sphere, and also in the realm of private devotion, he nevertheless excluded the possibility of music in public worship. Hymnody was therefore not generally admitted into the worship of those churches that were among the first to adopt Zwinglian theology and practice. In the churches of Zurich, all music was excluded from worship for the remainder of the century, Zwingli's nonmusical ecclesiastical agenda being continued by his successor, Bullinger. Thus in 1561, when drafting the Second HELVETIC CONFESSION (not published until 1566), Bullinger included the following somewhat defensive statement: "If there are churches which have a true and proper sermon (*orationem* = service of worship) but no singing, they ought not to be condemned. For all the churches do not have the advantage of singing." The reason for his defensiveness on the issue was the growing influence of Genevan psalmody, which caused the churches following the Zurich model to become exceptions rather than the rule in Reformed SWITZERLAND.

Calvinist

Calvin's 1539 Strassburg collection of congregational songs included nineteen metrical psalms, six of which were written by Calvin himself and the remainder of which were written by Clement Marot, poet to the French court, whose psalm versions had not hitherto appeared in print. Calvin returned to Geneva in 1541, and a year later issued his Genevan liturgy, *La Forme des prieres et chantz ecclesiastiques* (Geneva, 1542), which also included an expanded version of his Strassburg psalter containing more metrical psalms by Marot. Calvin's goal was to produce the complete biblical psalter rendered into rhyme and meter, the principle being to render accurately the substance of the biblical text in vernacular verse. Marot continued to work with Calvin on the project; indeed, the French poet not only wrote more metrical psalms, but also produced other versifications that replaced Calvin's earlier examples. After Marot's death in 1544, Calvin turned to THEODORE BEZA to continue the work on a complete French metrical psalter. Within a few years, eighty-three psalms had been completed, and the important and influential edition of the French psalter could be published: *Pseaumes octante trois de David* (Geneva, 1551), for which Louis Bourgeois was the musical editor. The objective of a complete psalter was eventually realized in *Les Pseaumes mis en rime, par Clement Marot, & Theodore Beza* (Geneva, 1562). This contained all 150 psalms, written in 110 different meters, with 125 tunes edited by Claude Goudimel. It is difficult to overestimate the influence of these Genevan psalters, because virtually every European language group emulated them in one way or another by producing other vernacular collections of metrical psalms in the following century. Significant psalters following the French Genevan model were produced in English, Dutch, German, various East European languages, and even Russian in the early eighteenth century.

Anglican

The general European religious environment influenced the rise and development of English metrical psalmody. In ENGLAND, during the reign of HENRY VIII, Lutheran hymns and psalms were translated into English in the mid-1530s by MILES COVERDALE, who published them as *Goostly psalmes and spirituall songes* (London, 1535). Fifteen of the forty-one texts were metrical psalms, a foretaste of what was to come later. Coverdale's collection was ordered to be burnt, because its contents were "too Lutheran." Thus the promising beginning that the *Goostly psalmes* represented never matured, although one of its translations was later used, almost verbatim, by THOMAS CRANMER in drawing up the burial service for the 1549 *Book of Common Prayer,* and at least two of the melodies were later refashioned into English metrical psalm tunes.

Henry VIII's death in 1547 brought a new era of vernacular psalmody. Thomas Sternhold, a personal courtier to both Henry VIII and his successor Edward VI, wrote poetic versions of the psalms that were reported to have circulated in manuscript and at the English Court. Early in the reign of Edward VI, when the Reformation ideals were openly pursued, nineteen of Sternhold's metrical psalms were published as *Certayne Psalmes chosen out of the Psalter of David, and Drawen into Englishe metre by Thomas Sternhold grome of ye Kynges Maiesties Roobes* (London, 1547). Sternhold continued work on writing metrical psalms, with the intention of completing the psalter, but died soon after his psalms first appeared in print. After his death, an expanded edition of his psalms was edited by John Hopkins: *Al such psalmes of David as T. Sternhold didde in his life time draw into English metre, Newly emprinted* (London, 1549). An additional eighteen versions by Sternhold were included, and Hopkins contributed a further seven, making a total of forty-four metrical psalms. This small collection proved to be popular, and at least ten reprints, dated between 1550 and 1554, are extant, implying that they were widely sung, at least in London, during the reign of Edward VI.

During the Marian years, 1553–1558, when the English church reverted to Catholicism and the Roman mass, Sternhold's psalter was expanded in various English Protestant exile congregations in Germany and Switzerland. In Strassburg, the Sternhold and Hopkins metrical psalms were augmented by English translations of Luther's *Vater unser im Himmelreich and Erhalt uns, Herr, bei deinem Wort.* In Wesel, a new edition of Sternhold and Hopkins was printed by Hugh Singleton, *Psalmes of David in Metre* (Wesel, 1555), an expanded edition that, in addition to the basic corpus of forty-four Sternhold and Hopkins metrical psalms, included seven psalm versions by William Whittingham, who had been in Frankfurt before moving to Geneva. The Wesel English psalter also included a number of metrical canticles: five anonymous, one by Whittingham, the Strassburg translation of Luther's "Lord's Prayer" hymn, and five by William Samuel, one of the two assistant ministers of the English exile congregation in Wesel. In Frankfurt, a split occurred within the exile congregation, with one party favoring Prayer Book worship and the other demanding a form more akin to the French liturgy of Calvin in Geneva. Ultimately the Prayer Book party remained in Frankfurt, while the others, including Whittingham and (later) JOHN KNOX, migrated to Geneva. Soon after arriving in the city, Whittingham published (in February 1556) the Calvinistic liturgy that had been drafted in Frankfurt. It included a modified and expanded version of the Sternhold and Hopkins psalter with its own title page: *One and fiftie Psalmes of David In Englishe metre, whereof 37 were made by Thomas Sternholde: and the rest by others. Conferred with the hebrewe, and in certeyn places corrected as the sens of the Prophete required* (Geneva, 1556). The revisions were made in accordance with Calvinist ideals, with the biblical text of the psalm primary and poetry secondary. Rhyme and meter were acceptable, but poetic paraphrase was not. The versions of Sternhold and Hopkins thus had to be "conferred with the Hebrew" and corrected accordingly. At least three later editions of the Anglo-Genevan psalter were issued between 1558 and 1560, with additional psalms by Whittingham, Pullain, and Kethe. The no longer extant 1559 edition was probably the first to include Kethe's version of Psalm 100, "All people that on earth do dwell," the oldest metrical psalm (and also the oldest congregational song) in the English-speaking world that has been sung continuously since its first appearance.

Following the death of Mary in 1558, her half-sister ELIZABETH I succeeded to the English throne, and the Reformation in England began again. English exiles abroad were now free to return. Among other things, they brought with them their experience of continental hymn and psalm singing, as well as the psalters they had used in their exile congregations. Thus a complex pattern of psalter publication was embarked on in London between 1559 and 1562. The basic corpus of metrical psalms of Sternhold and Hopkins, in their revised Genevan versions, were supplemented by more psalms by Sternhold, discovered after his death, and more contributed by Hopkins (who had survived the Marian years), and a number of other Elizabethan writers. Various metrical hymns and canticles that originated in Strassburg, Wesel, Frankfurt, and Geneva were also incorporated at the beginning and the end of the evolving English psalter.

In September 1562, the first complete English metrical psalter was published: *The Whole Book of Psalmes, collected into Englysh metre by T. Starnhold I. Hopkins & others: conferred with the Ebrue, with apt Notes to synge them withal* (London, 1562). Apart from one or two adjustments made over the following year or so, the English metrical psalter was now complete. It then ran through an extremely numerous sequence of editions, being reprinted again and again, in some years several times, throughout the next three centuries. Indeed, the Sternhold and Hopkins psalter, or, as it was later known, the Old Version, remained in print well into the nineteenth century in England. It proved to be the foundation stone on which the English tradition of metrical psalmody and hymnody was built.

Puritan, Presbyterian, and Independent

In SCOTLAND, under the leadership of John Knox, a Marian exile in both Frankfurt and Geneva, the Reformation developed in a Genevan direction. The Anglo-Genevan liturgy of 1556 was reprinted with only minor revisions in Edinburgh in 1564, and the complete metrical psalter issued with it was basically the eighty-seven psalms from the last revision of the Anglo-Genevan psalter of 1560, with the remainder taken from the English psalter of 1562: *The C.L. psalmes of David in English metre* (Edinburgh, 1564). The greater number of psalms from the Anglo-Genevan psalters made the Scottish psalter closer to the Franco-Genevan tradition, especially with regard to tunes, than its English counterpart.

The more extreme Puritans found Elizabethan England too unsympathetic to their views. After the Dutch Calvinist Reformation at the end of the 1570s, many cities of the NETHERLANDS were more amenable, especially Middleburg, Leiden, and Amsterdam. In Middleburg by the end of the sixteenth century, a number of imprints of both the English and Scottish psalters were produced for these exile congregations. In the early seventeenth century, a new metrical psalter was produced for English-speaking Separatists abroad by Henry Ainsworth: *The Book of Psalmes, Englished in both Prose and Metre* (Amsterdam, 1612). Ainsworth's aim was to produce metrical versions that were more faithful to the biblical psalms than *The Whole Book of Psalms* of Sternhold and Hopkins, and written in as many of the meters of Calvin's psalter as possible, so that more of the rugged Genevan psalm tunes could be sung by English Puritans and Separatists. Some of the English Separatists in the Netherlands, together with others from England (later known collectively as "the PILGRIM FATHERS"), sailed to the New World on the Mayflower, arriving in the New World in December 1620. The psalms they took with them were those of the metrical psalter of Henry Ainsworth. Thus congregational song in English-speaking North America at this time was metrical psalmody, either the psalms of Sternhold and Hopkins, preferred by Anglicans and some Puritans (later known as Independents, and later still as Congregationalists), or the psalms of Ainsworth, the psalter of the Separatists.

In the congregations of the Bay Company, the psalms of Sternhold and Hopkins were considered to be inaccurate renderings of the biblical texts, and the psalms of Ainsworth, with their many different meters, too difficult to sing. Thus the so-called "Bay Psalm Book" was created, the first book of any kind to be published in *British North America: The Whole Book of Psalms Faithfully Translated into English Metre* (Cambridge, Massachusetts, 1640). The key words on the title page, "Faithfully Translated," the equivalent of "conferred with the Hebrew" on the title page of Sternhold and Hopkins, expressed the Calvinistic concern for literal accuracy, and was expounded in the final paragraph of the preface to the *Bay Psalm Book*:

> If therefore the verses are not always so smooth and elegant as some may desire or expect; let them consider that God's Altar needs not our polishings: Ex.20. For we have respected rather a plain translation, than to smooth our verses with the sweetness of any paraphrase, and so have attended conscience rather than elegance, fidelity rather than poetry, in translating the Hebrew words into English language, and David's poetry into English metre; that so we may sing in Sion the Lord's songs of praise according to his own will; until he take us from hence, and wipe away all our tears, & bid us enter into our Master's joy to sing eternal Alleluias.

Over the following century, the *Bay Psalm Book* was revised, reprinted, and widely used not only in New England, but also in England and Scotland, where it was reprinted a number of times.

Radical Traditions

The Anabaptists of the sixteenth century (see ANABAPTISM), the representatives of the so-called Radical Reformation, were the forerunners of the later Baptist tradition (see BAPTISTS) and included such groups as MENNONITES, HUTTERITES, and Swiss Brethren. The Anabaptists were persecuted and treated with suspicion by Catholics and Protestants alike. Some of their members were summarily executed in particularly barbarous ways. To honor the memory of these Anabaptist saints, narrative songs recounting their sufferings and faith were written and sung by their coreligionists. The earliest song that Luther is known to have written was in the nature of one of these martyr songs. In July 1523, he received the news that two young friars from the Augustinian monastery in Antwerp had been burnt at the stake in Brussels as "Lutherans." In response and in the narrative style of popular folk songs, Luther wrote a "new song," *Ein neues Lied wir heben an*. In it the martyrdom of the two men is described and their faith and witness commended. There may be a connection between Luther's martyr song and such songs of the Anabaptists, because they postdate Luther's; at the very least, they share many common features with the then-current narrative ballad. A number of Dutch martyr songs were written by David Joris and his followers between 1529 and 1536 to celebrate the lives and deaths of executed Anabaptists. These were later collected together and issued by Joris as *Een Geestelijck Liedt-Boecxken*, perhaps published around 1540 or at some later date. The Swiss Brethren produced a hymnal in 1564, *Etliche schöne Christliche Gesang*, which was later incorporated into the *Aussbund* of 1583, the principal hymnal of the Anabaptist tradition, especially the Mennonites. It is still in use, textually unchanged, in some American Mennonite communities today.

Later Movements and Influences: Metrical Psalmody Renewed

At the end of the seventeenth century, three important factors led to a renewal of the singing of metrical psalms: the metrical psalms of the Poet Laureate Nathan Tate and Nicholas Brady (chaplain to King William III), the change to "regular singing," and the radical psalms of ISAAC WATTS. These developments had far-reaching consequences in Britain and British America.

In England in the latter part of the seventeenth century, there was growing dissatisfaction with the poetic limitations of the metrical psalms of Sternhold and Hopkins. The Stationers Company of London not only held the copyright to the Old Version, they also had an effective veto on any other version of the psalms. To circumvent the Stationers Company, Brady and Tate applied for, and were granted, Royal permission to publish *A New Version of the Psalms of David in English Metre, fitted for Publick Use* (London, 1696). Their choice of "New Version" meant that the psalter of Sternhold and Hopkins would thereafter be referred to as the Old Version. But before the New Version could be established in public worship, its authors withdrew it in response to considerable criticism. Over the next two years, Tate and Brady reworked their psalms, substantially revising some of them, and reissued them in 1698. But even some of these revisions were criticized, so the authors undertook one final revision before the definitive edition was published later that same year, 1698.

The first church at which these new psalms were sung was St. Martin-in-the-Fields, London, in January

1699. Eventually the New Version of Tate and Brady became acceptable to many CHURCH OF ENGLAND congregations, but it never completely displaced the Old Version. By and large, in rural England the psalms of the Old Version continued to be the main form of congregational psalmody in the worship of the churches, in some places until fairly late in the nineteenth century, but in urban England the New Version was generally the preferred psalter. Although Tate and Brady accepted the Calvinist principle of rendering the biblical psalms in strophic verse, they were also concerned with doing so with a greater sense of poetry.

The bishop of London commended the New Version for use in the churches served by his clergy. Because his episcopal oversight extended beyond the boundaries of the diocese of London to include all Anglican churches of the British colonies, this commendation had far-reaching consequences. In particular, it was a major factor in the extensive use of Tate and Brady texts within and beyond ANGLICANISM in British North America throughout the eighteenth and early nineteenth centuries.

Hard on the heels of these poetic concerns came a far-reaching musical revolution. Until this time, the performance practice of psalmody was "lining out," that is, the congregation singing line by line, repeating them after the clerk or cantor. But this kind of call-and-response singing did not make too much sense when every line of every psalm was effectively sung twice, and where members of the congregation had to suspend their understanding while waiting for the next line that was essential to the meaning of the line they had just sung. Thus, at the beginning of the eighteenth century there was a movement to displace "usual singing" (lining-out, singing line by line) by "regular singing" (stanza by stanza). With regular singing came two far-reaching developments. First was the production of new tune books that introduced new tunes, therefore expanding the basic repertoire of the old psalm tunes. Second was the rise of the singing master, who not only sold the new tune books but also created parish singing schools to teach the new way of singing, that is, by reading the notes in the tune book rather than echoing the lining out of the parish clerk. This development was to have far-reaching consequences on hymnic development in the eighteenth century, especially Methodist hymnody.

The singing school tradition had a longer life in America, influencing the emergence of New England composers such as William Billing, Lewis Edson, and many others, in the early national period of the United States of America, and continuing well into the nineteenth century.

ISAAC WATTS was brought up as a Dissenter or Independent, a denominational affiliation that became known as CONGREGATIONALISM, and he later became an ordained minister (see DISSENT; NONCONFORMITY). Early in life he had begun to write metrical psalms and paraphrases in the attempt to improve on what he was called on to sing on Sunday. Eventually these congregational songs were published. The first edition of *Hymns and Spiritual Songs* (London, 1707) included a number of metrical psalms, but these were withdrawn from later editions because by this time Watts was working on a metrical psalter, which was eventually issued as *The Psalms of David Imitated in the Language of the New Testament, And Applied to the Christian State and Worship* (London, 1719). "Imitated in the Language of the New Testament" contrasted with "conferred with the Hebrew" of the title page of the Old Version, and represented a significant hermeneutical and theological shift. The authors of both the Old and New Versions strived to put the substance of the Hebrew psalms as accurately as possible into English verse. In contrast, Watts specifically interpreted these Old Testament songs by incorporating the substance of New Testament teaching into them. In his preface to *The Psalms of David Imitated* he explained his purpose and method:

> I have not been so curious and exact in striving every where to express the antient [sic] Sense and Meaning of David, but have rather exprest myself as I may suppose *David* would have done, had he lived in the days of *Christianity*. And by this means perhaps I have sometimes hit upon the true intent of the Spirit of God in those Verses farther and clearer than *David* himself could ever discover, as St. *Peter* encourages me to hope. 1 *Pet*.1: 11,12. . . . In all places I have kept my grand Design in view, and that is *to teach my Author to speak like a Christian.*

Watts had been anticipated by Luther, who had introduced New Testament teaching into his psalm versions (such as Psalm 46, *Ein feste Burg*), but in the English-speaking world, this new hermeneutic was revolutionary. Although many voices were raised against "Watts Whims," their perceptive poetry made it impossible to ignore them. Over time, they were not only widely accepted, but also frequently imitated.

The revolution that Watts brought about was his insistence that Christian congregational song cannot be confined to the Old Testament psalms, but must embrace the totality of Scripture. In doing so he laid the foundation on which later English hymnody would be built. At the same time he exposed weaknesses in the old metrical psalm tradition. The success of Watts's psalms and hymns eventually brought about the disintegration of the almost monolithic tradition of English metrical psalmody, which, though it continued for a few generations, was almost finally stifled by the increasing volume of hymn and hymnal production of the nineteenth century. Watts' success was in his use of an almost exclusively monosyllabic language to create epigrammatic opening lines and lofty thoughts in connected stanzas. He contributed numerous "classic" hymns to English hymnody, among them "I'll praise my Maker while I've breath," "Jesus shall reign where'er the sun," "Nature with open volume stands," "Our God, our help in ages past," and "When I survey the wondrous cross."

The hymns and psalms of Watts were widely sung by American Congregationalists and Presbyterians, among others, throughout the eighteenth century, a practice that continued after the American Revolution with the texts suitably revised (together with additional psalms and hymns) by Joel Barlow, TIMOTHY DWIGHT, and others.

Pietism and the Evangelical Revival

German PIETISM, which flourished at the end of the seventeenth and the beginning of the eighteenth centuries, grew out of the combined influences of English Puritan devotional writings and the effects of the devastation of the Thirty Years War during the first half of the seventeenth century. *The Practice of Piety* by Lewis Bayly, published in the early 1600s, was widely read not only in English, but also in several other European languages, including German. Its spirituality caught the spirit of the era, especially in Germany, where the effects of warfare, famine, and disease created a subjective religious response, as can be seen in the poetry of Martin Opitz and the hymnody of Martin Rinckart (*Nun danket alle Gott*), Johann Heerman (*Herzliebster Jesu*), Tobias Clausnitzer (*Liebster Jesu, wir sind hier*), and especially Paul Gerhardt (*Befiehl du deine Wege, Nun ruhen alle wälder*, and *O Haupt voll Blut* ["O Sacred Head"]). The new hymns were set to new melodies that were lighter and more expressive than the older chorale tunes, which had become slow and ponderous by this time. Many of the new tunes were written by Johann Crüger and Johann Georg Ebeling, successively organists of the Nikolaikirche, Berlin, where PAUL GERHARDT was the pastor.

These subjective hymn texts and freer hymn tunes became the model for the hymn-writers and composers of later Lutheran Pietism, when its existence was formalized following the publication of PHILIPP SPENER's *Pia Desideria* (1675). Under the leadership of Spener's successor AUGUST HERMANN FRANCKE, the movement called for a continuation of what they saw as Luther's incomplete Reformation. All remnants of Roman Catholic theology and liturgy were to be elim-

inated from public worship, and private worship was to be exemplified by personal devotion built on fervent prayer and intensive BIBLE study. Further, the only music of public worship should be the newer type of hymns, with their subjective texts and livelier tunes, that these Pietists were already singing in their private worship. The Pietist hymnal was Johann Anastasius Freylinghausen's *Neues Geistreiches Gesangbuch,* first published in HALLE in 1704. It was reprinted numerous times, reaching its nineteenth edition by 1759; a second part issued in 1714 went through four editions by 1733; and the two parts, composed of some 1,600 hymns, were issued in one volume in 1741 and reprinted in 1771. This collection not only became the hymnal of German Lutheran Pietism, but also became a primary resource for the MORAVIAN CHURCH as reconstituted by Count NIKOLAUS VON ZINZENDORF in 1722 and for METHODISM under JOHN and CHARLES WESLEY.

John Wesley encountered Moravian hymn-singing on board the ship *Simmonds* on his way to Georgia in October 1735 to February 1736. He translated some of these German hymns sung by the Moravian missionaries, and they were subsequently included in his *Collection of Psalms and Hymns* (Charleston, 1737). After their experiences of CONVERSION (or assurance) in London in May 1738, the two brothers created and directed the continuing intensification of hymn singing in the emerging Methodist movement. Charles began writing what would prove to be an astonishing output of hymn texts in a variety of poetic forms, meters, and images. In common with the embryonic Moravian communities in England, the Methodists in the 1740s are reported to have sung the "swift German" tunes of the Freyinghausen type.

Beginning in 1738, the Wesleys issued many different collections of hymns, composed almost exclusively of texts by Charles, culminating in *A Collection of Hymns for the People Called Methodists* (London, 1780), which provided the basic anthology of hymns for later Methodism. Through these publications, the English-speaking world was introduced to a whole range of hymnody that has become part of the basic corpus of English hymns. Among these hymns are "Christ Whose Glory Fills the Skies," "Hark! The Herald Angels Sing," "Hail the Day That Sees Him Rise," "Love Divine, All Loves Excelling," "O for a Thousand Tongues to Sing," "Rejoice the Lord Is King," and "Ye Servants of God." Such hymns were taken over in many other hymnals of the later eighteenth century, among the most influential being GEORGE WHITEFIELD's *A Collection of Hymns for Social Worship, more particularly design'd for the use of the Tabernacle Congregation in London* (London, 1753); Martin Madan's *A Collection of Psalms and*

Hymns, Extracted from Various Authors (the Lock Hospital hymn book) (London, 1760); Augustus Toplady's *Psalms and Hymns for Public and Private Worship* (London, 1776); and *A Select Collection of Hymns to be universally sung in all the Countess of Huntingdon's Chapels* ("Collected by her Ladyship") (London, 1780). Another influential collection was *Olney Hymns* (London, 1779), which contained only the hymns of John Newton and William Cowper and disseminated such hymns as "Amazing Grace," "How Sweet the Name of Jesus Sounds," "O for a Closer Walk With God," and "God Moves in a Mysterious Way." This remarkable hymnodic output of the Evangelical Revival of the eighteenth century laid the foundation for the developments of the following century, which were equally as remarkable but in different ways.

Nineteenth-Century Movements

At the beginning of the nineteenth century, several different influences and movements contributed to the ongoing development of hymnody in the churches that had their origins in the Reformations of the sixteenth century. First, there was the consolidation of the evangelical movement in CAMP MEETING revivalism that was the outgrowth of the Scottish Presbyterian practice of annual eucharistic celebrations. At these non-eucharistic camp meetings, a new style of hymnody was developed. The evangelical hymns of the eighteenth century, especially those of Watts and Wesley, were extended by repetitive refrains added to the end of each stanza and/or to the end of each line within a stanza. A lighter musical style that could be picked up quickly at first hearing, was created for these expanded hymn-texts. Over time, a significant sequence of camp meeting hymnals was published. Ultimately the camp meeting hymn style would be incorporated into the later SUNDAY SCHOOL hymnals and eventually evolve into the gospel hymn.

Second, particularly in the southern states of America, folk hymns that had hitherto been transmitted orally began to appear in tune books, many of them in shape-notes, in the early decades of the century. Among them was *The Sacred Harp*, first published in 1844, which created a singing tradition that continues today. Although HENRY WARD BEECHER included some of these tunes in his *Plymouth Collection* (New York, 1855), it was not until the twentieth century that these tunes entered into mainline denominational hymnals.

Third, from the second decade of the century, Lowell Mason undertook to reform congregational hymnody in the UNITED STATES. He was concerned that most congregations did not sing very much; the congregation tended to be replaced by the choirs of sing-ing schools who sang fuging tunes in rural churches and by paid quartets of singers in urban churches. Mason saw that a musical reform was necessary if congregations were to be encouraged to sing. They needed simple and straightforward tunes, but not the light and sometimes extravagant tunes that had been generated by the evangelical REVIVALS of the previous century. Hymn tunes had to be "good" music, so he borrowed the philosophy and practice of William Gardiner, who had published *Sacred Melodies from Haydn, Mozart and Beethoven: Adapted to the Best English Poets* (2 vols., London, 1812–1815). Music from the "best" contemporary (or near contemporary) composers was adapted into hymn tunes. Gardiner was not the first to make such adaptations—some eighteenth-century tune books had included adapted versions of arias and choruses from the oratorios of Handel and Haydn—but he was the first to exploit the technique as a matter of principle. Mason, however, out-Gardinered Gardiner by producing an extremely large number of adapted tunes in a dazzling sequence of tune books. Beginning with *The Boston Handel and Haydn Society Collection of Church Music* (Boston, 1822), and ending with *Carmina Sacra Enlarged: The American Tune Book* (Boston, 1869), he issued some forty different collections of church music, mostly devoted to congregational hymnody, that were reprinted and revised numerous times. These tune books encouraged others, notably Thomas Hastings and William Bradbury, to produce other collections. They were also quarried by later hymnal editors, and a significant number of Mason's tunes are still found in contemporary American hymnals.

Fourth, there was the discovery that, contrary to popular belief, hymns, as opposed to metrical psalms, were not illegal in the worship of the Church of England. A famous ecclesiastical court case was brought by the members of St. Paul's Church, Sheffield, against their incumbent, Thomas Cotterill, who had produced an anthology of congregational song in which hymns outnumbered 150 metrical psalms by more than two to one. It was shown that the Church of England had never concluded that metrical psalms were the only legitimate congregational songs for Anglican worship. The aftermath of the court case was that, at the request of the archbishop of York, Cotterill produced a new edition of his hymnal in which the hymns approximately equaled the number of metrical psalms: *A Selection of Psalms and Hymns for the Use of Saint Paul's Church in Sheffield* (London, 1820). Included at the beginning of the small volume was a commendation written by the archbishop of York. The result of the court case, the archbishop's commendation of the collection, and the fact that the publisher also made available editions with a generic title page that omitted reference to St. Paul's Sheffield, ensured a wide dissemination of the *Selection* and encouraged the production of similar volumes. Many such locally produced hymnals appeared over the next generation.

Fifth, there was the OXFORD MOVEMENT, which was to exert an all-pervasive influence on the patterns and content of worship far beyond the boundaries of England or Anglicanism. This was essentially a reform movement with the aim of revitalizing the Church of England by examining its spiritual nature and historical roots, a movement that moved increasingly toward Catholic doctrine and practice. The principal leaders were JOHN HENRY NEWMAN, JOHN KEBLE, R. H. Froude, and EDWARD B. PUSEY, who together, from 1834, edited and wrote *Tracts for the Times;* hence the other name for the movement, Tractarianism. Many of the tracts were liturgical, and some specifically drew attention to Latin hymnody. Thus Newman's Tract 75, *On the Roman Breviary as Embodying the Substance of the Devotional Services of the Church Catholic* (1836), included fourteen Latin hymns in translation. Newman later published an anthology of Latin hymns from the Roman and Paris breviaries as *Hymni ecclesiae* (Oxford, 1838). The ideal of the Tractarians was for the English church to adopt, in translation, the Latin hymns of the liturgy from which the *Book of Common Prayer* was substantially created. Edward Caswall published *Lyra Catholica* (London, 1849), a collection of translations from the Roman missal and breviary, and John Mason Neale, with Thomas Helmore, produced *The Hymnal Noted* (London, 1851–1856), a comprehensive hymnal of translated Latin hymns, with plainsong notation, to be used in conjunction with the English Prayer Book services. Neale also published further translations of Latin hymnody and others from Greek sources, together with a few original hymns. Although the ideal of singing only translated Latin hymns in the English church was never realized, these translations were widely used, and a good many of them remain in current hymnals.

The Tractarian Movement also indirectly led to other translations. There were those who reacted to the Tractarian idealization of late medieval Catholicism and looked to European Protestantism instead. German Protestantism was in the public eye: Queen Victoria was married to Albert of Saxe-Coburg; Mendelssohn, whose music made significant use of the German chorale, was frequently in the United Kingdom; and there was a growing awareness of the music of J. S. Bach, who was seen as the quintessential Protestant composer. For those out of sympathy with the Catholic emphases of the Oxford Movement, the German Protestant chorale became a viable prospect. Thus Frances Elizabeth Cox published translations of German hymns in *Hymns from the German* (London,

1841; revised and enlarged in 1864), and Arthur Tozer Russell's translations appeared in two collections: *Hymns for Public Worship and Private Devotion* (London, 1848), published for the London German Hospital, and *Psalms and Hymns, Partly Original, Partly Selected, for the Use of the Church of England* (London, 1851). But the most significant translator of German hymns was Catherine Winkworth, who, between 1855 and 1869, published almost 400 translations of German hymns. Her first collection was issued as *Lyra Germanica* (London, 1855), and a second series followed in 1858. Five years later she collaborated with two musicians to produce *The Chorale Book for England* (London, 1863), and her last collection containing translations was *The Christian Singers of Germany* (London, 1869). Some of her translations have become classic English hymns in their own right, among them "Comfort, Comfort ye my People," "Praise to the Lord, the Almighty," and "Now Thank We all our God." Catherine Winkworth's translations of German hymns have been used more extensively in American hymnals than in their British counterparts, especially those produced by Lutheran bodies in the final quarter of the nineteenth century, when many congregations were beginning to move from German to English as the language for worship.

The most important hymnological outcome of the Oxford Movement was the creation of *Hymns Ancient & Modern*, the cooperative product of a number of Tractarian clergy. The editorial committee was chaired by Sir Henry W. Baker; John Keble and John Mason Neale were appointed advisers; and William Henry Monk, organist and director of music at King's College, London, oversaw the music. After a number of trial compilations were given restricted circulation in 1859–1860, the words-only edition of *Hymns Ancient & Modern for Use in the Service of the Church* was published in time to be used on Advent Sunday 1860, with the full music edition appearing the following year. Between 1861 and 1868, when a *Supplement* was issued, four and a half million copies of the basic edition were sold. The original edition with its supplement also crossed the Atlantic, being reprinted at least fourteen times in New York and Philadelphia between 1866 and 1888. In 1869, it was decided that a revised and enlarged edition of the hymnal was needed. Theologically and ecclesiastically, the revision was much broader in scope than the original Tractarian hymnal had been, and it incorporated more of contemporary writing, thus proportionately reducing the influence of translated Latin hymnody. Similarly, the presence of John Stainer on the music committee ensured that the predominant style became the somewhat self-indulgent, chromatic four-part harmony, with a propensity for seventh chords, that has come to be recognized as "the Victorian hymn tune." The revised and expanded edition was issued in 1875. A supplement was added in 1889, which further broadened the total content of the hymnal. *Hymns Ancient & Modern* thus quickly became the most important and influential collection of the nineteenth century. It was used extensively by hymnal editors throughout the English-speaking world and was the primary model for the many denominational hymnals published on both sides of the Atlantic in the final quarter of the nineteenth century, and continued to exert a marked influence on twentieth-century hymnals.

Sixth, there was the phenomenon of gospel hymnody. As indicated earlier, gospel hymnody developed from the camp meeting style as it evolved through the Sunday School movement. Between 1840 and 1870, an astonishing sequence of Sunday School hymnals was published. Among the most influential were those of William Bradbury, notably *The Golden Chain* (1861) and *The Golden Shower* (1862), which were frequently reprinted. The gospel hymn finally emerged as an identifiable genre during the final quarter of the century with the evangelistic enterprises of organizations such as the YMCA (see YMCA, YWCA) and of such individuals as DWIGHT L. MOODY. Although primarily an American phenomenon, gospel hymnody nevertheless had an important early British dimension. IRA SANKEY first published his gospel hymns *Sacred Songs and Solos* (London, 1873), a sixteen-page pamphlet, for use during Moody's revivalist meetings in Great Britain. The basic collection was expanded and continued to be available in Britain at the same time as its American counterpart, *Gospel Hymns and Sacred Songs* (New York, 1875), an amalgam of Sankey's pieces in the genre and those of P. P. Bliss that had been published in *Gospel Songs* (Cincinnati, 1874). There were many imitators and numerous collections were published. The genre is probably best epitomized in the gospel hymns of the prolific FANNY CROSBY.

Twentieth-Century Developments

The Reformation churches in the twentieth century have continued the development of inherited hymnodic traditions in many and varied ways—as well as pursuing new directions, such as the notable expansion from the narrow confines of monoculturism into the broader concerns of multiculturalism, the exploration of GENDER, and linguistic issues, and so forth— but space precludes a thorough investigation. Nevertheless, some of the major influences can be charted, at least in outline.

The first half of the century, devastated by two World Wars and disoriented first by the Wall Street crash and then the Great Depression, created a conservative mindset. The hymnody of the period was therefore characterized primarily by a conservation of the familiar. New hymnals were produced, but their orientation was a backward-looking continuation of the major strands of nineteenth-century traditions. That is not to say that new hymns were not being written and published, but these "twentieth-century" hymns were generally written in the older styles. There were exceptions, such as HARRY EMERSON FOSDICK's "God of grace and God of glory," but few gained entry into the regular hymnals until after the 1950s and 1960s. The themes of the hymns that were written during the first half of the century reflected various concerns of the age. In the aftermath of World War I, peace themes were prominent; the deprivations of the post-Depression years fostered the SOCIAL GOSPEL of LIBERAL PROTESTANTISM reflected in many of the hymns of the period; the beginnings of the ecumenical movement that would eventually lead to the formation of the WORLD COUNCIL OF CHURCHES gave rise to hymns that expressed the fundamental unity of faith of worldwide Christianity (see ECUMENISM); and after the testing of the hydrogen bomb in the late 1940s, it became painfully clear that humanity had the expertise to destroy itself. Hymn writers such as Albert Bayly expressed a new perspective on the need for the human race to depend on the providence of God.

The iconoclastic 1960s proved to be a watershed with regard to the creation of new hymnody. The last three decades of the twentieth century saw an unprecedented period of hymn writing in a variety of textual and musical styles, and an almost bewildering sequence of hymnal publication. On the one hand, there has been the British hymn explosion, whose leading writers and composers have been Fred Pratt Green, Fred Kaan, Brian Wren, Erik Routley, and Peter Cutts, among many others, and the American hymnal explosion, in which every major denominational grouping has already produced its own hymnals or has plans to do so. The former has already been described and analyzed, but the latter has yet to receive the attention it deserves.

One of the most (some would say *the most*) significant ecumenical developments of the twentieth century has been the liturgical movement. The Catholic Church played a leading role in this movement, which proved to be of catalytic importance with regard to its own reformation of worship initiated by the Second Vatican Council. But these reforms have had an impact on the older Reformation churches as well. For example, the introduction of the three-year lectionary outside Catholicism has materially effected a greater

918

biblicism among those traditions that prided themselves on their biblicity! That is because the wider spread of the lectionary revealed whole areas that had not been covered hitherto in "Protestant" hymnody, especially in the English-speaking world, and this has stimulated hymn writing on these neglected biblical themes. But not only has much of contemporary hymnody become more biblical, it has also become more "liturgical" in its usage. Thus as Catholicism has been embracing the "Protestant" hymn in its worship, many Reformation churches have been singing their hymns within a "Catholic" liturgical structure. The latter part of the twentieth century brought a reinforcement of the insights of Tractarian Anglicans, Genevan Calvinists, and Wittenberg Lutherans, who all, one way or another, saw congregational song not as incidental to worship but rather as part of its liturgical substance.

See also Anglican Chant; Music

References and Further Reading

Baker, Frank, ed. *Representative Verse of Charles Wesley.* London: Epworth, 1962.

Barr, Cyrilla. *The Monophonic Lauda and the Lay Religious Confraternities of Tuscany and Umbria in the Late Middle Ages.* Kalamazoo, MI: Medieval Institute, 1988.

The Bay Psalm Book: A Facsimile Reprint of the First Edition 1640. Edited by Zoltán Haraszti. Chicago, IL: University of Chicago Press, 1956.

Benson, Louis F. *The English Hymn: Its Development and Use in Worship* (1915). Richmond, VA: Knox, 1962.

Brumm, James. "The Mysterious American Odyssey of Hymns A & M." *The Hymn Society of Great Britain and Ireland Bulletin* 12 no. 2 (1988): 24–26.

Bucer, Martin. *Martin Bucers Katechismen aus den Jahren 1534, 1537, 1543.* Edited by Robert Stupperich. (*Martin Bucers Deutsche Schriften*, Bd. 6/3). Gütersloh, Germany: Mohn, 1987.

Clarke, W. K. Lowther. *A Hundred Years of Hymns Ancient and Modern.* London: Clowes, 1960.

Diehl, Patrick S. *The Medieval European Religious Lyric: An Ars Poetica.* Berkeley, CA: University of California Press, 1985.

Drain, Susan. *The Anglican Church in Nineteenth Century Britain: Hymns Ancient and Modern (1860–1875).* Lewiston, NY: Mellen, 1989.

Dunstan, Alan. *The Hymn Explosion.* Croydon, UK: Royal School of Church Music, 1981.

Farr, David. "Protestant Hymn-Singing in the United States, 1916–1943: Affirming an Ecumenical Heritage." In *The Hymnal 1982 Companion,* edited by R. F. Glover. New York: The Church Hymnal Corporation, 1991. 505–554.

Fraser, Ian. "Beginnings at Dunblane," *Duty and Delight: Routley Remembered.* Edited by Robin A. Leaver and James H. Litton. Carol Stream, IL: Hope, 1985. 171–190.

Foote, Henry W. *Three Centuries of American Hymnody.* Cambridge, MA: Harvard University Press, 1940; reprint, with additions (n.p.): Archon, 1968.

Fornançon, Siegrfried. "Johann Crüger und der Genfer Psalter." *Jahrbuch für Liturgik und Hymnologie* 1 (1955): 115–120.

Garside, Charles. *Zwingli and the Arts.* New Haven, CT: Yale University Press, 1966; reprint, New York: Da Capo, 1981.

Greene, Richard. *Early English Carols*, rev. ed. Oxford, UK: Clarendon Press, 1977.

Honders, A. Casper. "The Reformers on Church Music." In *Pulpit, Table, and Song: Essays in Celebration of Howard G. Hageman.* Edited by Heather Elkins and Edward C. Zaragoza, Lanham, MD: Scarecrow, 1996. 46–52.

Jenny, Markus. *Zwinglis Stellung zur Musik im Gottesdienst.* Zurich, Switzerland: Zwingli Verlag, 1966.

———. "The Hymns of Zwingli and Luther: A Comparison." In *Cantors at the Crossroads: Essays on Church Music in Honor of Walter E. Buszin.* Edited by Johannes Riedel, 45–63. St. Louis, MO: Concordia, 1967.

———. *Luther, Zwingli, Calvin in ihren Liedern.* Zurich, Switzerland: Theologischer Verlag, 1983.

Keyte, Hugh, and Andrew Parrott. *The New Oxford Book of Carols.* Oxford: Oxford University Press, 1992.

Knuttel, J. A. N. *Het Geestelijk Lied in de Nederlanden voor de Kerkhervorming.* Rotterdam, The Netherlands: Brusse, 1906; reprint, Groningen, The Netherlands: Bouma, 1974.

Leaver, Robin A. "Isaac Watts's Hermeneutical Principles and the Decline of Metrical Psalmody." *Churchman* 92 (1978): 56–60.

———. *Catherine Winkworth: the Influence of Her Translations on English Hymnody.* St. Louis, MO: Concordia, 1978.

———. "British Hymnody, 1900–1950." In *The Hymnal 1982 Companion.* Edited by R. F. Glover. New York: Church Hymnal Corp., 1991. 474–504.

———. "British Hymnody Since 1950." In *The Hymnal 1982 Companion.* Edited by R. F. Glover. New York: Church Hymnal Corp., 1991. 555–599.

———. "Renewal in Hymnody." *Lutheran Quarterly* 6 (1992): 359–383.

———. "Charles Wesley and Anglicanism." In *Charles Wesley: Poet and Theologian.* Edited by S. T. Kimbrough. Nashville, TN: Kingswood, 1992. 157–175, 241–243.

———. "Are Hymns Theological by Design or Default?" *New Mercersburg Review* 18 (Autumn 1995): 12–33.

———. "Lampe's Tunes." *Hymns on the Great Festivals and Other Occasions: Hymn Texts by Charles Wesley and Samuel Wesley, Jr., Music by John Frederick Lampe,* facsimile (1746) with introduction by Carleton R. Young, Frank Baker, Robin A. Leaver, and S. T. Kimbrough, Jr. Madison, NJ: Charles Wesley Society, 1996. 31–44.

Luff, Alan. "The Hymn Explosion after 25 Years." *The Hymn* 46 (April 1995): 6–15.

Luther, Martin. *Luther's Works: American Edition.* Edited by Jaroslav Pelikan and Helmut T. Lehmann. St. Louis, MO: Concordia, 1955; reprint, Philadelphia, PA: Fortress, 1986.

———. *Martin Luther Deutsche Messe 1526* (Facsimile). Edited by Johannes Wolf. Kassel, Germany: Bärenreiter, 1934.

McCart, Thomas K. *The Matter and Manner of Praise: The Controversial Evolution of Hymnody in the Church of England, 1760–1840.* Lanham, MD: Scarecrow, 1998.

McMullen, Dianne Marie. "The Geistreiches Gesangbuch of Johann Anastasius Freylinghausen (1670–1739): A German Pietist Hymnal." Ph.D. dissertation, University of Michigan, 1987.

Patrick, Miller. *Four Centuries of Scottish Psalmody.* London: Oxford University Press, 1949.

Pemberton, Carol A. *Lowell Mason: His Life and Work.* Ann Arbor, MI: UMI Research Press, 1985.

Pidoux, Pierre. *Le Psautier Huguenot du XVIe Siècle.* 2 vols. Basel, Switzerland: Bärenreiter, 1962.

Pratt, Waldo Seldon. *The Music of the French Psalter of 1562: A Historical Survey and Analysis.* New York: Columbia University Press, 1939; reprint, New York: AMS Press, 1966.

Rattenbury, J. Ernest. *The Eucharistic Hymns of John and Charles Wesley.* London: Epworth, 1948.

Reimann, Hannes. *Die Einführung des Kirchengesangs in der Zürcher Kirche nach der Reformation.* Zurich, Switzerland: Zwingli Verlag, 1959.

Riedel, Johannes. "Leisen Formulae: Their Polyphonic Settings in the Renaissance and Reformation." Ph.D. dissertation, University of Southern California, 1953.

Schmidt, Leigh Eric. *Holy Fairs: Scotland and the Making of American Revivalism.* 2nd ed. Grand Rapids, MI: Eerdmans, 2001.

Schulz-Widmer, Russell. "Hymnody in the United States Since 1950." In *The Hymnal 1982 Companion.* Edited by R. F. Glover. New York: Church Hymnal Corp., 1991. 600–630.

Stackhouse, Rochelle A. *The Language of the Psalms in Worship: American Revisions of Watts' Psalter.* Lanham, MD: Scarecrow, 1997.

Stevens, John. *Words and Music in the Middle Ages: Song, Narrative, Dance, and Drama, 1050–1350.* Cambridge: Cambridge University Press, 1986.

Temperley, Nicholas. "Middleburg Psalms." *Studies in Bibliography: Papers of the Bibliographical Society of the University of Virginia,* 30 (1977): 162–170.

———. *The Music of the English Parish Church,* 2 vols. Cambridge: Cambridge University Press, 1979–1983.

———, ed. *The Hymn Tune Index: A Census of English-Language Hymn Tunes in Printed Sources from 1535 to 1820.* 4 vols. Oxford, UK: Clarendon, 1998.

Thompson, Bard, ed. *Liturgies of the Western Church.* Cleveland, OH: World Books, 1961; reprint, Philadelphia, PA: Fortress, 1981.

Wasson, D. Dewitt. *Hymntune Index and Related Hymn Materials.* 3 vols. Lanham, MD: Scarecrow, 1998.

Watson, J. R. *The English Hymn: A Critical and Historical Study.* Oxford, UK: Clarendon Press, 1997.

Wolkan, Rudolf. *Die Lieder der Wiedertäufer: Ein Beitrag zur Deutschen und Niederländischen Literatur- und Kirchengeschichte.* Berlin, Germany: Behr, 1903; reprint, Nieuwkoop: de Graaf, 1965.

Woolf, Rosemary. *English Religious Lyric in the Middle Ages.* Oxford, UK: Clarendon Press, 1968.

ROBIN A. LEAVER

I

ICELAND

Iceland is a partly ice-covered (e.g., Vatnajökull, 8,400 square kilometers) volcanic island—astride the Mid-Atlantic Ridge, with over fifty active vents—of 102,973 square kilometers (or 39,699 square miles, compared to the state of Pennsylvania at 46,058 square miles, and Ireland, 32,589 square miles) between NORWAY and Greenland, just south of the Arctic Circle. Less than one tenth of the island is habitable. Until recently agriculture was largely pastoral (with some fishing) and sensitive to weather, so that famine was not uncommon.

Iceland was settled by the Norse—with some Celts—after 870. The Alþing, the parliament of an aristocratic republic without an executive branch, was established in 930. In 1000 (or 999) the Alþing adopted Christianity as the national religion. In the early period, churches were proprietary: political leaders often functioned also as priests. Increasing disorder among very powerful families led to the acceptance of the rule of the king of Norway from 1262 to 1264. In the thirteenth century Icelanders produced one of the major bodies of medieval European vernacular literature, the Icelandic sagas. The Gregorian Reform, struggling for "libertas ecclesiæ," and canon law were also introduced, by St. Þorlákr, thus breaking the identity of political and spiritual leadership. There were two dioceses until 1796: the southern, at Skálholt, and the northern, at Hólar. Both sees, some monasteries, and some important farms (such as Oddi) had schools. A deteriorating climate ("the little Ice Age"), the virtual end of Icelandic shipping, and the transfer of power to Copenhagen contributed significantly to the isolation of Iceland in the fifteenth century. In that age Iceland was vulnerable to pirate raids, British fishing vessels, volcanoes, and pack ice.

The REFORMATION arrived in DENMARK, after a tentative generation, by right of Christian III's victory in the civil war concluded in 1536. The new ways were introduced to Norway and Iceland by decree, the two countries redefined as provinces of Denmark. The Reformation in Iceland was therefore a "revolution from above" (Vilborg Auður Ísleifsdóttir). Until the end of the eighteenth century people lived in small groups on thousands of farms. The usual means of disseminating reformed ideas—towns, literate merchant classes, book fairs—did not exist. Nor did the usual audience: there was no pre-Reformation preparation, movement, or agitation; there were no heretics in the later Middle Ages, no active disenchantment with the church. Some visiting merchants may have brought ideas (in German), but among Icelanders only a small group of clerks in the offices of the bishop of Skálholt (some of whom had studied abroad) including Gizurr Einarsson and Oddr Gotthálksson seemed interested in the Reformation. When the king sent his Church Ordinance to Iceland (probably 1538) it was ignored or rejected by the bishops and CLERGY (see BISHOP AND EPISCOPACY). In 1539 local authorities seized and dismantled the monastery of Viðey. Attempts to suppress more monasteries and to interfere at Skálholt led to the killing of the entire Danish administration—in fact only a few people. Skálholt's bishop Ögmundr Pálsson retired in 1540. He and the king sponsored as his successor his evangelical clerk Gizurr Einarsson, a choice Ögmundr came to regret and attempted to reverse. Gizurr appealed to the military authorities who restored Danish power in 1541. The Reformation was then installed in the southern diocese, which accepted the Ordinance. Gizurr worked hard to implement the new THEOLOGY and LITURGY, but without radical revolution. He encouraged the translation, printing, and use by priests of the

Scriptures and evangelical books (see BIBLE TRANSLATION).

Jón Arason, bishop of Hólar, rejected the Ordinance in 1540. The government left him alone for some years. After Gizurr's death in 1548, however, Jón moved to reverse events at Skálholt, securing his own appointment as administrator of the see and the election of a candidate with good papal credentials. Supporters of Gizurr elected their own candidate, approved by the Crown, whom Ján kidnapped and held prisoner at Hólar. In 1549 he secured control of Skálholt, although he overreached himself and was taken prisoner. He and his two sons were beheaded at Skálholt on November 7, 1550. Revenge killings followed, by Jón's family and supporters, but the dispatch of two warships and troops ended all resistance to the Crown. The northern diocese accepted the Ordinance in 1552.

Monasteries were suppressed, the land taken by the Crown (see MONASTICISM). The bishops kept much of the land and part of the tithes, but lost other power (such as fines). The ecclesiastical transformation was complete in only fifteen years, yet many usages from pre-Reformation days continued, so that building a community of faith as the reformers understood it remained a challenge. The Scandinavian languages were passing through the same sort of revolution as that which created modern English; Icelandic did not. Danish books—such as were used in Norway—did not serve an evangelical church in Iceland. The first press in Iceland was not set up until mid-century; it later came into the possession of Guðbrandr Þorláksson, bishop of Hólar from 1571 to 1627. Therefore the first Icelandic translation of the New Testament, that of Oddr Gottshálksson, was published in Denmark in 1540. Later, however, bishop Guðbrandr oversaw the printing of the complete translation of the BIBLE in 1584, and many pamphlets, translations of Hymn books, and other pious works (see HYMNS AND HYMNALS). The Bible helped stabilize the Icelandic language. The two sees continued their schools, now the only ones in the country. They also continued the tradition of scholarship, the study not only of Scripture but also of the history of Iceland, of the church, and of early Norse literature. Scholars such as Angrímr Jónsson, bishop Finnur Jónsson, Árni Magnússon, and bishop Brynjólfr Sveinsson (who saved *Codex regius*) worked in the schools or were commissioned to write by the bishops. The church also undertook the task of extending literacy, so that all Icelanders could read Scripture.

The witchcraft hysteria came slowly to Iceland and was inspired from abroad. In the years between 1625 and 1685 at least 120 were tried and twenty-five executed, including two women.

A most moving voice of Lutheran Iceland is that of the poet Hallgrímr Pétursson (for whom the new and very large church in Reykjavík, Hallgrímskirka, is named), whose *Passíusálmar* (*Hymns of the Passion*) are still deeply cherished and widely read.

In 1796 the two sees and their schools were combined in a new see in Reykjavík. Their property was absorbed by the Crown, which undertook to pay the costs. In 1874 a new constitution was established by Christian IX. Following from that came autonomy of local congregations in many important matters, freedom of association and religious freedom for non-members of the state church. In the nineteenth and twentieth centuries there has been a growth of such groups as the Lutheran Free Church and spiritualists.

Iceland became independent in 1944. The population continues, at least formally, to be over 90 percent Evangelical Lutheran.

See also Lutheranism

References and Further Reading

Einarsson, Stefán. *A History of Icelandic Literature.* New York: Johns Hopkins Press for the American-Scandinavian Foundation 1957.

Hood, John C. F. *The Icelandic Church Saga.* London: SPCK, 1946.

Hugason, Hjalti, ed. *Kristni á Íslandi.* Reykjavík: Albing: 2000.

Karlsson, Gunnar. *The History of Iceland.* Minneapolis, MN: University of Minnesota Press 2000.

RICHARD LUMAN

ICONOCLASM

Protestant Christianity is iconoclastic in two senses, the abstract and the concrete. An "iconoclast" [Gk. *eikon* = image + *klastes* = breaker] is someone who destroys images, especially those that carry special meaning to a specific culture. An iconoclast, in the widest sense of the term, is someone who identifies certain objects, institutions, or ideas as "false" and calls for their removal. Iconoclasts do not actually need to destroy images; someone who attacks images verbally can be called iconoclastic. This type of abstract iconoclasm that challenges cherished beliefs and institutions verbally is always broadly understood, and applied beyond religion. An iconoclast can also be someone who actually attacks physical images and sacred objects. Literal iconoclasm is understood less broadly, as religiously motivated, but is usually taken to mean the destruction of all holy objects, not just images. In the case of REFORMATION iconoclasm, altars, relics, chalices, consecrated hosts, holy water fonts, vestments, missals, lamps, windows, and organs could also be attacked as idolatrous.

Since the sixteenth century, all Protestants have been iconoclasts in the abstract sense, insofar as they reject many of the truth claims of the Roman Catholic Church, along with many of its rituals and symbols. However, not all Protestants have been iconoclasts in the literal sense. On the contrary, the question of whether the symbols of Catholicism should be destroyed became one of the most divisive issues separating the various major traditions of the Protestant Reformation.

From the very start of the Reformation, Protestants disagreed about iconoclasm. Although there are no hard and fast lines that can be drawn among the different Protestant traditions that emerged in the sixteenth century, and there are always plenty of exceptions to be found to any rule, the Lutherans normally objected to the wholesale destruction of images, and even allowed biblically focused art in their churches. The Anglicans also adopted an ambivalent attitude toward images and their place in the life and worship of the Church of England. The Reformed, for the most part, became the most vehement iconoclasts, and much of this article focuses on them. The Radicals tended to oppose religious imagery on biblical grounds, but they varied in their attitude toward iconoclasm. At one end of the Radical spectrum, pacifists such as the Swiss Brethren and the MENNONITES shied away from all violent acts, including the breaking of images. At the other end of the spectrum, militant revolutionaries, such as those who took over Münster in 1534, destroyed images along with anything else they deemed ungodly.

Perceptions of the significance of iconoclasm for the history of Protestantism vary widely. For some in the Reformed tradition, the iconoclastic heritage of the Reformation is very significant; for others in the Protestant tradition, it is just a blip on the screen, or worse, an embarrassment. For Catholics the subject has always been significant, although not always well understood. It is important to keep in mind that, although Protestants were at odds with one another when it came to their attitudes toward religious imagery and iconoclasm, Catholics in the sixteenth and seventeenth centuries tended to think that iconoclasm was one of the chief distinguishing features of Protestantism. In fact, for many early modern Catholics, iconoclasm and Protestantism were inseparable.

History

Protestant iconoclasm began in earnest with ANDREAS BODENSTEIN VON KARLSTADT (c. 1480–1541), a colleague of MARTIN LUTHER (1484–1546) at the University of Wittenberg. Karlstadt agreed with Luther on many theological issues, but differed with him on the interpretation of the two key biblical passages that prohibit the use of religious imagery in worship (Exodus 20:4–6; Leviticus 5:8–10). Karlstadt was the first of the Protestant Reformers to argue that the prohibition of images was one of the Ten Commandments, and could not be ignored: "I say to you that God has forbidden images with no less diligence than killing, stealing, adultery, and the like" (*Abthung*, p. 22).

Luther never agreed with this position. To him, the command against images was no more valid for Christians than circumcision and the dietary laws of the Covenant of Moses. In March 1522 Luther forced Karlstadt to leave Wittenberg, largely because of their disagreement over this issue. This difference of opinion points clearly to a hermeneutical rift within the Protestant tradition, one that would evolve into a major watershed between Lutherans and most other Protestants. Although Luther and Karlstadt both agreed on the primacy of the BIBLE as the ultimate authority, and pressed for reforms in accordance with it, neither man could accept the other's interpretation of the meaning of the commandment against images. This was no small disagreement. Although Karlstadt would vanish into relative obscurity, his position would be championed by HULDRYCH ZWINGLI, JOHN CALVIN, and other Reformed Protestants, and the rift among the opponents of Roman Catholicism on this issue would become deep and long. In the *Small Catechism* Luther does not mention the prohibition of images at all in his listing of the Ten Commandments. In the *Catechism of the Church of Geneva,* however, the Second Commandment reads: "you shall have no graven images . . . nor bow down, nor serve them."

Reformed Protestants would make the rejection of images one of their central principles, along with a highly spiritualized interpretation of all symbols and sacraments. Consequently, the destruction of images and sacred objects became one of the earmarks of this tradition, as it spread throughout Switzerland at first, in the 1520s, and later, throughout Europe. In France, the Netherlands, Germany, and the British Isles, the iconoclastic legacy of the Reformed tradition would cause widespread damage and, in some places, erase much of the artistic heritage of medieval Catholicism.

Discerning the relation between the ideology of iconoclasm and other factors that might have led to it—social, political, and economic—remains a difficult task, and a challenge for historians. It is always tempting to try to isolate grievances that might have led to iconoclasm, and also to distinguish some of these as a leading cause for the destruction of an entire symbolic code, but in the long run, it is unwise to avoid complexity when dealing with this subject. As the Protestant Reformation gained ground in the sixteenth and seventeenth centuries, there were perhaps as many reasons for iconoclasm as there were iconoclasts, and as many different types of iconoclasm as there were communities affected by it. Because symbols function on multiple levels of meaning, so do the actions taken against them.

Generally, Reformation iconoclasm can be divided into two major types, legal and illegal. Throughout Catholic Europe, the destruction of sacred objects was prohibited by law, and was punishable as blasphemy or sacrilege. Destroying images and holy objects, therefore, required challenging the law. Iconoclasm could be effected lawfully, after a local or national government had withdrawn its protection from sacred objects. Sometimes this destruction was orderly, such as in Zurich, in 1524; but it could also be disorderly, as in Bern in 1528; or it could be a combination of order and disorder, as in Scotland in 1559 and France in 1561–1562. Iconoclasm could also be an illegal act and a form of rebellion. Unlawful iconoclasm aimed not only to destroy specific objects, but also to call into question the legality of these objects. In many ways iconoclasm was a revolutionary tactic, employed at the local and national levels, as Reformed Protestantism made inroads into Catholic communities.

Theology

"Idolatry" is a relative, highly charged term that presupposes a definition of what is true and false in religion because idols are never universally recognized as such: rather, they are often identified as the deities of "the other." Protestant iconoclasm was firmly rooted in the ancient condemnation of heathen idolatry found in the Hebrew Bible. In the sixteenth century, however, the definition of idolatry was applied to Christian rather than pagan worship, and extended beyond the veneration of images, or the worship of any physical object, to any form of devotion that was judged to be incorrect.

The way in which "idolatry" was defined by the leaders of the Protestant Reformation, therefore, depended on their exegesis of the Bible and on the theology of worship they developed from their interpretation of the sacred text. All in all, the Reformation critique of "idolatry," and the iconoclasm produced by it, depended on four interrelated principles.

1. *Biblicism.* First of all, iconoclastic theology was firmly rooted in the principle of *sola scriptura*. A literal interpretation of the biblical texts that prohibit images can lead directly to an iconoclastic theology. However, iconoclasm was not derived so simply and purely from biblical injunctions. Protestant biblicism was also strengthened by a sense of primitivism, or the notion that the early Christian past provided a true model for the reformation of Church and society. It was not just the prohibition of visual symbols in *Exodus* and *Leviticus* that convinced iconoclastic reformers of the need to wipe out Catholic symbols and rituals, but also the fact that, as they saw it, there was no evidence for the existence of much of medieval worship in the early Apostolic Church.

Of course, agreeing on *sola scriptura* did not necessarily lead to any agreement on how to interpret sacred texts. The biblical injunctions against images are a prime example of this hermeneutical rift among the Reformers. An interpretative framework had to be in place first for Reformed Protestants to arrive at the conclusion that the Bible prohibited images to Christians as well as Jews.

2. *Metaphysics.* The prohibition of images was interpreted as valid and reasonable by the Reformed because of certain key assumptions they accepted about the relationship between the natural and supernatural realms. The guiding principle of iconoclastic metaphysics—and therefore also of iconoclastic hermeneutics—is the incompatibility of spirit and matter. The iconoclastic theology of the Reformed was summarized in the adage *finitum non est capax infiniti*: the finite cannot convey (or contain) the infinite. This was a principle that Reformed Protestants applied to all ritual and symbols, and it was the very marrow of iconoclastic theology. This principle, in turn, was derived from three interrelated components.

- *God as radically transcendent.* The Reformed tradition assumed that the supernatural realm was radically "other." All things divine, therefore, were above and beyond the natural and created order. Zwingli argued that the things of earth were "carnal," and that they were "enmity against God." He also argued that matter and spirit were as incapable of mixing as fire and water. John Calvin would expand on these arguments, and press further for an understanding of the spiritual and the material as antithetical poles. In Calvin's words: "whatever holds down and confines the senses to the earth is contrary to the covenant of God; in which, inviting us to himself, he permits us to think of nothing but what is spiritual" (*CO,* vol. 24, p. 387).

- *Matter as inferior to spirit.* Reformed metaphysics proposed that since matter is incapable of bringing humans to the divine realm, there can be no physical relation between image and prototype, symbol and reality. Even worse, as the Reformed saw it, worship offered to any material object has a negative value. This notion of an inversion was turned into a practical equation by

Zwingli, who went as far as to say: "the more you give to the material, the more you take away from the spiritual." (*ZW*, vol. 8, pp. 194–195.) For these reasons, the Reformed denied the validity of the distinction between "veneration" (*dulia*) and "worship" (*latria*) made by Catholics—the very distinction upon which much of the symbolic structure of Catholicism rested.

- *Teleology.* For iconoclasts, the commandment against images needed to be obeyed not only because it was the will of God, but also because it was reasonable. As the iconoclastic theology of the Reformed saw it, the very meaning of human existence was perverted by the "falsehood" of Roman Catholic rituals and symbols. This understanding of the nature and purpose of human existence rested on the assumption that the proper end of human life is to know God and to glorify him by worship and obedience. Idolatry, therefore, not only subverts the meaning of human existence by making it impossible for individuals to reach their proper end; it also threatens the well-being of society as a whole.

3. *Anthropology.* Reformed iconoclastic theology was based also on the central Protestant belief in the total corruption of human nature. In Reformed theology, the cause for idolatry is not found in the material world itself, but in human beings. John Calvin would argue: "Every one of us is, even from his mother's womb, a master craftsman of idols" (*CO*, vol. 24, p. 423). This understanding of the nature of idolatry is what made it impossible for the Reformed to regard any religious image as harmless: as they saw it, if given the opportunity, every human being will be naturally compelled to worship idolatrously.

4. *The social dimension.* Iconoclastic theology also had a social component. In the first place, images and symbols were attacked as dangerous because idolatry was believed to incite the wrath of God. Reformed theology tended to view the presence of idolatry in any community as pollution, and spoke of iconoclasm as cleansing. The GENEVA CATECHISM of 1545, for instance, devotes extensive attention to the divine punishments attached to the second commandment, particularly to the threat of having God's punishments extend to the third and fourth generations in an idolatrous, polluted society. Second, iconoclastic theology also argued that the material resources "wasted" on idols were an affront to Christian charity. As the Reformed iconoclasts saw it, the wealth poured into the creation of Catholic symbols should be redistributed to the poor and needy. Third, opposition to Catholic "idolatry" was also based on animosity toward the

educational system they represented. The medieval church had long argued that images were the *libri pauperum,* or books of the poor and illiterate. Protestant iconoclasts rejected this argument because it rested on the unscriptural assumption that images could teach anything. They also rejected it because, as they saw it, images served to promote and sustain a spiritual caste system: images were another way in which the Catholic clergy kept the laity under their thumb.

The Meaning of Iconoclasm

No single factor can fully explain the development of iconoclasm in the Protestant Reformation of the sixteenth century. Iconoclastic theology is very complex, and so are the reasons for its appearance and acceptance. Moreover, iconoclasm itself is ultimately an act, or event, not just an idea. Although derived from ideology, iconoclasm does not necessarily depend on it totally. Protestant iconoclasm aimed not only to destroy the physical "idols" of Catholicism, but to abolish a complex symbolic system, and to remove the clerics who upheld it. Reformation iconoclasm was thus revolutionary on two fronts. First, it was a theological upheaval and a redefinition of the sacred. Reformation iconoclasts denied certain relations between body and soul, or heaven and earth, and redefined the meaning of symbol and ritual. Reformation iconoclasm was also revolutionary in a functional sense because it was an act of violence against the symbolic code of medieval Christianity and its guardians, the Roman Catholic clergy. The young men who led the iconoclastic riot that turned Geneva into a Reformed city knew this, for they referred to the images they destroyed as "the gods of the priests."

Iconoclasm is always an expression of discontent. In the case of the Protestant Reformation, iconoclasm was a forceful protest against the medieval past. It was a means of proving the "falsehood" of Roman Catholicism, and of desacralizing its symbolic structure. In a positive sense, iconoclasm was also a means of affirming change and of calling for a thorough reform of religion and society.

See also Bible; Calvin, John; Geneva Catechism; Karlstadt, Andreas Bodenstein von; Luther, Martin; Mennonites; Reformation; Zwingli, Huldrych

References and Further Reading

Primary Sources:

Baum, W., E. Cunitz, and E. Reuss, eds. [*CO*]: *Johannes Calvini Opera Quae Supersunt Omnia, Corpus Reformatorum.* Brunswick, 1863–1880.

Egli, E., and G. Finsler, eds. [ZW]: *Huldreich Zwinglis Sämtliche Werke, Corpus Reformatorum*. Berlin: C. A. Schwetschke und Sohn, 1905–1990.

Lietzmann, Hans, ed. [*Abthung*]: *Karlstadt, Andreas Bodenstein von, Von Abthung der Bylder und das Keyn Bedtler unter Christen Seyn Sollen* (1522). Bonn: A. Marcus and E. Weber, 1911.

Secondary Sources:

Aston, Margaret. *England's Iconoclasts*. Oxford: Clarendon Press, 1988.

Christensen, Carl. *Art and the Reformation in Germany*. Athens: Ohio University Press, 1980.

Crew, Phyllis Mack. *Calvinist Preaching and Iconoclasm in the Netherlands, 1544–1569*. New York: Cambridge University Press, 1978.

Davis, Natalie Zemon. "The Rites of Violence: Religious Riot in Sixteenth Century France." *Past and Present* 59 (1973): 51–91.

Eire, Carlos M. N. *War Against the Idols: The Reformation of Worship from Erasmus to Calvin*. New York: Cambridge University Press, 1986.

Freedberg, David. *Iconoclasm and Painting in the Revolt of the Netherlands*. New York: Garland, 1988.

Garside, Charles. *Zwingli and the Arts*. New Haven: Yale University Press, 1966.

Michalski, Sergiuz. *The Reformation and the Visual Arts*. New York/London: Routledge, 1993.

Philips, John. *The Reformation of Images: Destruction of Art in England 1535–1660*. Berkeley: University of California Press, 1973.

Wandel, Lee Palmer. *Voracious Idols, Violent Hands: Iconoclasm in Reformation Zurich, Strasbourg and Basel*. New York: Cambridge University Press, 1994.

CARLOS M. N. EIRE

ICONOGRAPHY

Two dominant meanings lay claim to the term "iconography." Among ART historians, the word designates a method of deciphering the meaning of an image by identifying patterns in the use of subject matter. Like the nomenclature designating many fields of inquiry, iconography refers both to a particular subject and to the method of studying that subject. Thus, just as "philosophy" is the study of ideas or thought as well as the particular set of ideas of one school of philosophical investigation, so iconography can refer both to the procedure for analyzing subject matter as well as the motifs of a particular image. Scholars will, therefore, examine a given image's iconography by using the iconographical method to determine what the image's subject matter may signify.

The other widely recognized significance of "iconography" is the ancient practice of painting Byzantine icons, or, more literally, of "icon writing." Byzantine icons exhibit highly organized patterns or visual formulae that have been passed down over the centuries and carefully observed by icon painters.

Accordingly, both senses of iconography apply to the study and creation of icons. This essay, however, focuses on the art historical use of the term because it is of greatest significance in the history of Protestantism. Part I examines the significance of iconography as an element in visual communication and the study of images. Part II considers prevalent examples of iconography in the history of European and American Protestantism.

I. Iconography as Art Historical Method

As a form of communication, images rely on patterns or visual formulae whose meanings are conventional, which means that they draw their meaning in large part from what amounts to a visual lexicon. In many instances, these lexicons actually exist in the form of emblem and pattern books. More commonly, however, iconographical traditions consist of conventional subjects handed down over time. According to one textbook definition,

> Iconography is that branch of the study of art, which investigates works of art according to their conceptual contents. It seeks to examine ideas brought to expression in artistic products according to their subject matter, origin, and gradual evolution, and therefore to lead to the accurate comprehension of the language of images. [Künstle 1928:5]

Iconographical analysis proceeds by comparing a given image with its precedents to determine by virtue of consistency and variation what the image means. Meaning, by this procedure, is a function of adherence to or deviation from a tradition of signification. For example, beginning with the REFORMATION, Protestants in Northern Europe found the portrayal of Jesus blessing the children (Mark 10:16) a very appealing subject, and probably invented the iconographical theme (Christensen; Hofmann, 241). During the nineteenth century in the UNITED STATES the motif continued to enjoy wide appeal in popular prints. This appeal was likely attributable to the rise of a THEOLOGY and practice of domestic nurture, according to which mother shaped the formation of the child's soul while the absent pater familias worked outside the home. Mother and Jesus were often likened to one another in the illustrations of Christian instructional books and tracts. In the biblical text and in previous iconography the disciples were frequently shown attempting to free Christ from the attention of the children, only to suffer his rebuke. During the nineteenth century in the United States, however, portrayals of Christ blessing the children sometimes eliminated the disciples altogether, thereby paralleling the absence of the father from domestic scenes of maternal nature. The home was the sovereign sphere of the Christian mother, an ideal visualized in the popular iconography of Christian nurture.

The study of iconography has taken two directions among scholars since the eighteenth century: the classifiers and the contextualists. The first are those who assemble vast catalogues of visual motifs in the attempt to facilitate the identification of images. Such scholarship tends toward a scientific taxonomy, stressing description, rigorous classification, and exhaustive attempts at a comprehensive collection of variations. The knowledge produced by this method is indispensable in determining the significance of an image. However, historians interested in examining the broader relations of images to their historical epochs may prefer to use iconographical knowledge as a basis for further study, which consists of the contextualization of a motif in its historical moment. In addition to a taxonomy of the image, then, these scholars wish to understand the participation of images in the intellectual and imaginative life of an age.

In an enormously influential essay of 1939, art historian Erwin Panofsky distinguished these two analyses of images as different, but interdependent forms of study: iconography and iconology (Panofsky). Whereas iconography compares a motif with its predecessors and carefully describes its variation from as well as its continuity with this tradition, iconology seeks to explain why the differences and continuity occurred when and where they did. If iconography asks where a visual motif came from and what it shares with motifs that came before it, iconology seeks to discern the world of ideas and cultural values manifest in images. Iconology considers the relationship between an image and its cultural and intellectual milieu; iconography attends to the connection between an image and images similar to it in the past and at present. W. J. T. Mitchell succinctly summarized Panofsky's distinction of iconology and iconography as the difference between interpreting "the total symbolic horizon of an image [and] the cataloguing of particular symbolic motifs" (Mitchell, 2). Whereas iconography *describes* an image by delineating its debt to and difference from a visual tradition, iconology *interprets* an image by discerning its relationship to a cultural repository of ideas. Influenced by his countryman and one-time colleague at the University of Hamburg, German philosopher Ernst Cassirer, Panofsky maintained that art was a symptom of CULTURE, a visual manifestation of underlying principles or "symbolic forms" that are also expressed in LITERATURE, ARCHITECTURE, philosophy, religion, and SCIENCE. The aim of iconology is to discover and interpret cultural artifacts as symbolic expressions of a culture's underlying forms (Holly). The assumption is that art bears the same "mental habits," as Panofsky put it, evident in other cultural expressions. According to Panofsky, the iconologist is one whose final object of explanation is the set of cultural structures that inform an image. Panofsky wished to explain a worldview, what amounted to the mind of a culture as it become apprehensible in individual works of art.

Throughout the twentieth century, iconology focused on the intellectual content and philosophical implications of artistic subject matter. As an art historical practice, therefore, iconology has tended to pursue the interpretation of an image's conceptual signification, relying on the textual determination of an image's meaning. Indeed, images were regarded as a kind of "language" that spoke an intellectual content. Thus, iconology regards art as a form of cultural thought, although some scholars found wanting in this approach the social analysis of art, that is, scrutiny of the ideological and other social functions of imagery. At present, scholars interested in the social nature of seeing have foregrounded the social and political operations of art and non-art imagery. This need not displace iconological study, as some studies have clearly demonstrated (Miller), but consideration of the social function of images attends more to visual practice, popular reception, and popular culture than traditional iconology has undertaken, since the primary assumption of iconology is that works of art are manifestations of thought rather than of social order and identity.

II. Protestant Iconography

To understand Protestant iconography and its interpretive potential for the scholar, it is instructive to reflect on certain conditions and features common to many Protestant uses of the image. Although it has sometimes been assumed that Protestantism led to a decline in the visual arts or even a proscription of imagery, the fact is that Protestant artists in Europe, North America, and around the world have made robust use of images, although often not in the same sacred spaces as Roman Catholic or Orthodox traditions (see ORTHODOXY, EASTERN). Even though the use of images in LITURGY and formal WORSHIP, located in the sanctuaries of church interiors, characterized visual piety in the Eastern and Western rites, Protestants have historically used images in the area of the pulpit and ALTAR rather sparingly. More common is the appearance of images in instructional spaces such as modern SUNDAY SCHOOL rooms, parochial school rooms, and in public halls, where the devout gather for meals, meetings, and fellowship, although the most common location for sacred imagery among Protestants is the home.

A second important aspect of Protestant visual piety is teaching. Protestants have widely affirmed the ability of images to help teach and admonish principles of the faith as prescribed by scripture, creed, or sectarian theology. As a result, Protestant iconography has almost always operated with close ties to texts. Even though JOHN CALVIN objected that images were unable to teach anything about the Gospel, in practice Calvinist Protestants have availed themselves of the moral and instructional value of pictures and buildings (Calvin, 90–103; Finney). One thinks of the rich iconography of seventeenth-century Dutch painting and print culture, in which silent exhortations to pure living seek viewers of still life imagery and genre scenes, and where the compelling moral example of Jesus is visualized by Rembrandt in etchings as well as dramatic paintings.

MARTIN LUTHER explicitly endorsed the didactic role of images, even calling in one sermon on wealthy burgers to cover the sides of their houses with paintings of stories from the Hebrew Bible for the sake of public instruction (Luther, 99). Luther happily included woodcut illustrations in his German editions of the BIBLE (as did many translations produced in ENGLAND from HENRY VIII to James I) and both Catholic and Lutheran parties made avid use of visual propaganda to ridicule their opposition in the attempt to influence public opinion for or against the cause of the Reformation (Scribner; Pettegree). In colonial New England, primers and almanacs were illustrated with religious imagery, inculcating a textual as well as a cultural literacy of Protestantism. Primers were the most important educational text in addition to the Bible during the eighteenth century in North America. In the nineteenth century the mass production of print, including illustrated print, exploded in the UNITED STATES and Europe. Among the leaders in the United States of the new print culture were zealous Protestants who believed that a literate populace was the safeguard of republican government as well as of Protestant hegemony. Illustrated school books, children's newspapers, primers, tracts, almanacs, and Protestant classics such as JOHN BUNYAN'S PILGRIM'S PROGRESS poured from Protestant presses and were widely circulated at very inexpensive prices (Morgan 1999). This print culture relied on an established range of iconography to serve its distinctly Protestant aims (see PUBLISHING MEDIA).

Linking images to texts may have appealed to Protestants because it helped clarify an image's meaning, ensuring its legibility, narrowing the act of signification from such open-ended processes as suggestion and allusion to a neater, more controlled semiotic operation. Images and words can be used to reinforce one another such that the image delivers a message that is primarily textual, preexisting the image and merely using it as a means of conveyance. Protestants have often accompanied illustrations with inscriptions, quotations, names, captions, or even longer passages of text to harness the image and prescribe its meaning-making. Protestant images often are organized in narrative suites, linked to a Bible passage, or are highly allegorical or emblematic, carefully encoded with an antecedent content that is first, and properly, textual. In fact, Protestantism is so far from being aniconic that it must be said that the highly textual nature of Protestant visual piety conforms quite naturally to the textuality of iconography as a system of visual communication. As many scholarly studies have shown, accordingly, there is no dearth of Protestant visual practice and iconography.

This strong reliance on the text derives from the AUTHORITY of the Bible as the revealed Word of God, which Protestants have traditionally regarded as the unrivaled authority in religious life, available to each believer for close study and devotional reflection. The deity, according to Protestants, chose to reveal itself in words. Words are, therefore, the principal, among some Protestants, even unparalleled avenue for coming to know God and receive God's message of SALVATION. Even though in practice words can be as fractious, as unstable, and as tendentious as images, they lend themselves to a religious practice that stresses the acquisition of discursive knowledge as the basis for redemption. The Protestant must know who God is, what the divine message for humankind is, and how one should respond to it to be saved. Protestant salvation consists fundamentally in knowing the right thing.

The stress laid on the proper contents of knowledge among Protestants shaped a highly dogmatic approach to all aspects of teaching in the early Reformation. This is evident in early Protestant art in GERMANY. Lucas Cranach the Elder, his studio, and his son produced several detailed altar paintings, which amount to elaborate visual compendia of Lutheran DOCTRINE. Often called "Law and Gospel," the central principle of Lutheran theology and homiletics, these pictorial programs compile central events in the scriptures that form a history of salvation from Adam to the resurrection of Jesus. If the didactic scenes were not enough, captions often identify the figures and indicate their theological significance (Schiller; Christensen; Hofmann).

CONVERSION or regeneration was not merely a rational process of acquiring the right information. Protestants have always regarded conversion as involving the entire, embodied human being, often summed up metaphorically as the "heart." The heart was the seat of the will, and therefore important in the Augustinian and Pauline anthropologies of both Luther and Calvin. In the Calvinist or Reformed tradition of Protestantism (see CALVINISM), regeneration was understood to be a protracted process of conviction, contrition, and conversion, a gradual operation in which individuals submit themselves to the work of the Spirit of God. Puritan preacher John Flavel (1627–1691) characterized the entire process of call and redemption as "Christ Knocking at the Door of Sinners' Hearts," the title of a set of his sermons published in 1689. According to Flavel, who based his discussion on Revelation 3:20, "Behold, I stand at the door and knock," the soul was "a magnificent structure" with "such stately rooms as thy understanding, will, conscience, and affections" (Flavel, 8). Staunchly affirming the Calvinist notion of human depravity and divine sovereignty, Flavel insisted that the will was unable "by its own power [to] open itself to receive Christ by faith" (Flavel, 55–56). God must convict the conscience, bend the human will to Christ, and remove the many natural barriers barring the soul from GRACE.

In seventeenth-century Germany the image of Christ knocking at the door of the heart was eroticized by a mystical tradition leading toward PIETISM. Lutheran poet and hymn writer Johann Franck (1618–1677) wrote the hymn "Soul, Adorn Thyself with Gladness" in 1649, which urges the soul to prepare itself for the lover who comes calling:

Hasten as a bride to meet Him
And with loving rev'rence greet Him;
For with words of life immortal
Now He knocketh at thy portal.
Haste to ope the gates before Him,
Saying, while thou dost adore Him,
Suffer, Lord, that I receive Thee,
And I never more will leave Thee.
[*Lutheran Hymnal*, 305]

Regarded as a lover, the ravisher of the human heart, Christ knocks to court the soul, which is able to open the door. The relationship is not one of enmity and judgment, but longing and intimacy.

The motif acquired different meanings during the nineteenth century, when it was visualized in paintings, drawings, and prints that circulated throughout Europe, Britain, and the United States. In his vastly popular "The Light of the World" (1851–1853), British painter William Holman Hunt (1827–1910) created what eventually became a Protestant icon of Jesus. His picture, although criticized at first for its departure from precedent (Bennett, 31–34) seems to combine the erotic lover of the soul with the Puritan notion of human resistance to the knocking Savior, at least if one compares the image with what Hunt said about it years afterward. His notes read like a laundry list of carefully encoded symbols that evince the Prot-

estant penchant for fastening images to texts, and recall the Puritan mix of divine goodness and human depravity adumbrated by John Flavel:

> The closed door was the obstinately shut mind, the weeds the cumber of daily neglect, the accumulated hindrances of sloth; the orchard the garden of delectable fruit for the dainty feast of the soul. The music of the still small voice was the summons to the sluggard to awaken and become a zealous labourer under the Divine Master; the bat flitting about only in darkness was a natural symbol of ignorance; the kingly and priestly dress of Christ, the sign of His reign over the body and the soul, to them whom could give their allegiance to Him and acknowledge God's overrule. [quoted in Landow, 34]

The shift toward modern EVANGELICALISM, with its intensely "personal relationship" grounded in an individual calling from Jesus, is evident in the way Hunt turned Christ toward the viewer to create not only a representation of Christ's summons at the heart of a third party, but a direct appeal to those who look upon Hunt's picture. Flavel had taught that the "Behold" of Revelation 3:20 signified a "term of notification or public record, wherein Christ takes witnesses of the most gracious offer," public testament that will be reviewed on the Day of Judgment when each soul stands before God (Flavel, 11). Flavel construed the relationship of the soul to Christ in juridical terms, as part of a larger accounting the soul will have to make one day before the Great Judge. Hunt, by contrast, visualized the "Behold" as the savior's inviting presentation of himself in the quintessential moment of evangelical "witness," as if to endorse the modern practice of colportage and door-to-door EVANGELISM used by British and American evangelicals since the early nineteenth century.

The legacy of Flavel was not lost on nineteenth-century EVANGELICALISM. In 1826 the American Tract Society issued the Rev. John Scudder's hard-edged sermon to youth, "Knocking at the Door," in which the missionary feared that Christ's knocking had not yet affected the heart of the "young friend" to whom he directed his remarks. Scudder used the motif of Revelation 3:10 with the full fury of the revivalist preacher, thrusting the reader toward conversion by means of an unmitigated appeal to terror. "Today! he is knocking, perhaps *for the last time*. If you reject him, I shall not wonder if he abandons you. . . . I shall not wonder if *this day* a seal is put in heaven to your everlasting damnation" (Scudder, 16; emphasis in original).

However, this was not the spirit recognized in Hunt's picture and celebrated by those who admired it. Hunt's image influenced several hymns, including some compiled by IRA SANKEY in his *Sacred Songs and Solos,* and the hymn by HARRIET BEECHER STOWE,

"Knocking, Knocking, Ever Knocking" (1867; Maas, 78). Inspired by an image of Christ knocking at the door of the soul by German Nazarene painter, Philipp Veit, Hunt's image, in turn, compelled numerous imitations (Vaughan, 225), perhaps the most widely reproduced of which during the twentieth century was Warner Sallman's *Christ at Heart's Door*, 1942 (Morgan 1996). A member of the pietistic Swedish Evangelical Covenant Church in Chicago, and someone who experienced a revivalist awakening as a teenager, Sallman intended with his picture to foster evangelical conversion at the personal behest of Jesus. His image, however, endorsed an Arminian view of human agency in conversion (see ARMINIANISM). Notes published with the picture pointed out that the door on which Christ knocked bore no handle or knob whereby the savior might open the door. "The door has no latch for it can be opened only from within, and the soul itself is the key" (*Series of Interpretations*). This had also been DWIGHT L. MOODY's reading of Revelation 3:20. In the margin of his Bible the popular Chicago-based revivalist wrote: "The latch of the door is on the inside" (Moody 1895, 188). Flavel had identified "free-grace" as the "golden key" to the door of the soul (Flavel, 52), but the Arminian disposition of modern Pietism had come to think differently of the soul's agency. Responsibility for the act of free acceptance lay with the soul itself, which possessed both the free will to reject the divine offer and the capacity to cast aside the barrier that Flavel had considered impervious to any but the Holy Spirit.

As if responding to a criticism of Hunt's picture by Moody, who considered the lantern held by Christ in the British picture to be insultingly superfluous in that Christ himself is "the Sun of Righteousness" (Moody 1899, 149), Sallman eliminated the lantern and portrayed an incandescent Jesus projecting a heart-shaped radiance on the door and stone facade of the soul's benighted dwelling. Once again, Moody might have prompted him in the matter (Sallman enrolled as a young man at the MOODY BIBLE INSTITUTE). In a sermon, Moody instructed his listeners: "if you want the love of God in your hearts, all you have to do is open the door and let it shine in. It will shine in as the sun shines in a dark room. Let him have full possession of your hearts" (quoted in Gaustad, 192). The legibility of the motif of Christ at the door of the heart was clearly paramount for both Hunt and Sallman given that Hunt combined (and Sallman preserved) multiple biblical references to anchor the image with semantic redundancy. In addition to Revelation 3:20, Hunt had identified several biblical texts as inspirational for his picture: Romans 13:12, "the night is far gone, the day is near," accounts for the nocturnal lighting; Psalm 119:105 registers in the lantern: "Your word is a lamp to my feet and a light to my path." And the title of the painting comes from John 8:12, "I am the light of the world. Whoever follows me will never walk in darkness but will have the light of life" (Parris, 117). The hortatory, evangelical implication is even clearer in the remainder of Romans 13:12: "Let us then lay aside the works of darkness and put on the armor of light." Among conservative Protestants, hermeneutical ambivalence is no virtue. The most cherished Protestant image is often the most legible one.

Sallman's devout admirers prized his images for their legibility. He retained the nocturnal setting and emblematic details (thistles and thorny vines blocking entrance to the heart) from Hunt's conception, but the soft and luminous Jesus faces the soul he would save. Jesus inclines toward the door as if to whisper tender words through the tiny screen in front of him. The very words might be the intimate exchange cherished between the soul and the lover-savior in the 1912 hymn, "In the Garden:"

> I come to the garden alone
> While the dew is still on the roses;
> And the voice I hear,
> Falling on my ear
> The Son of God discloses.
> And He walks with me,
> And He talks with me,
> And He tells me I am His own,
> And the joy we share as we tarry there
> None other has ever known. [Miles, 187]

The eros of this private union softens the Calvinist theology of depravity, lending humanity a humble, but real part to play in the regeneration of the soul.

Repugnant as it is to orthodox Calvinists, the Arminian claim for free will brought with it a recognition of the potential of the sanctified life, that is, life after conversion. Whereas the classical Reformed tradition situated the devout in an anguished uncertainty about their eternal welfare, which remained hidden behind the cloak of PREDESTINATION, other Protestant traditions stressed both the importance of personal decision in regeneration as well as the work of the Holy Spirit in the role of SANCTIFICATION in everyday life after conversion. The ongoing presence of God in comfort, encouragement, PRAYER, and guidance found important and widespread visual expression in such images by Sallman as *The Lord is My Shepherd* (1943), *Christ in Gethsemane* (1941), and *Christ Our Pilot* (1950), in the work of other artists who produced such images as *Praying Hands* (after a drawing by Albrecht Dürer) or Eric Enstrom's much admired *Grace* of 1918, showing an aged man at prayer over his meal, or in any one of a dozen versions of Guardian Angels or Christ Blessing Children. Mottoes had been a standard part of Christian homes in the nineteenth century, typically familiar Bible verses or gnomic admonitions to live the godly life or preserve domestic bliss. Protestants often speak of these kinds of images and objects as reminding them of their commitments or the moment of their decision to follow Christ. They also regard such iconography as a kind of advertisement to and subtle influence over family members, friends, coworkers, and visitors to their homes.

Until the late nineteenth century in the United States, Protestants eschewed an existential relation with images. Images were forms of information—from the early doctrinal programs of Lutheran altar painting and print illustration to the American nineteenth- and twentieth-century millennialist charts and diagrams inspired by WILLIAM MILLER's 1843 lithograph illustrating in a visual and numerical logic the second return of Jesus enciphered in the prophetic books of Daniel and Revelation (Numbers and Butler; Morgan 1999). Several changes late in the century, however, led to a shift in Protestant thought about images. Modern reproductive technology such as halftone engraving and offset lithography made possible the inexpensive distribution of imagery. Clergy and educators realized that pictures could exert an affective influence on viewers and that the fine arts could contribute effectively to religious instruction and the nurture of children.

In a popular visual culture of celebrity and fame, Jesus emerged as teacher, hero, and contested historical figure whose likeness became a visual register of the needs and theological dispositions of diverse groups. His iconography among Protestants borrowed extensively from traditional Catholic fine art. By the end of the nineteenth century, however, Protestant artists and viewers had settled on a very familiar physiognomy that was corroborated (more or less) both by the history of Christian art since the later Middle Ages and by a fascinating literary document in circulation since the fourteenth century. A letter purporting to be written by a contemporary of Jesus, Publius Lentulus, offers a brief description of the face of Christ in terms that Protestants easily recognized: high forehead, shoulder-length hair parted in the center, large eyes, a beard, and a solemn facial expression (Morgan 1999). The features of the face grew so familiar that they served as iconographical motifs in themselves. The image became a visual portrayal of the text that described the face of Christ. Currier & Ives and other popular lithography firms produced versions of the letter and its visual counterpart. In the twentieth century Warner Sallman produced what was very likely the most widely recognized version of the face. By Sallman's lifetime, Protestants were able to see in this face the very likeness of the historical Jesus,

responding to it in a way that recalls Catholic response to the Veil of Veronica or the Shroud of Turin (Morgan 1996). Among Protestants who embraced what may be called a "CHRISTOLOGY of friendship," a view of Christ as the believer's intimate and closest companion, Sallman's "portrait" amounted to nothing less than a snapshot, a Protestant icon, of the incarnate Lord.

Sallman's image of Jesus appealed not only to evangelical and mainline American Protestants, but, although for different reasons, to groups as various as American Catholics, MENNONITES, Mormons, and Copts. Moreover, this enormously reproduced picture of Christ, put into global circulation by Protestant missionaries, also appealed to Christians around the world. The broad appeal of the same image suggests the inadequacy of iconography as a method for determining the significance of an image, unless we take the unlikely view that this picture meant the same thing to very different groups. In fact, viewers tend to appropriate the image as well as the artist to themselves. Catholics made Sallman a Catholic artist; Protestants regarded him and his picture as manifestly Lutheran, Methodist, or Baptist, as the case may be. Some viewers saw Sallman's Jesus as gentle and comforting; others as a masculine affirmation of their need for a "manly" savior. Consequently, iconographical investigation must be supplemented by the study of reception because the meaning attributed to an image is not limited to whatever may be encoded in the image's motifs. The cultural "text" that one viewer reads in an image is not the same as the text another sees in the same picture. Inasmuch as this extra interpretation helps to discern the world of ideas and values that inform the image, the study of images pursues the iconological knowledge that Erwin Panofsky envisioned as the higher end to which iconography can make a fundamental contribution.

References and Further Reading

Bennett, Mary. *William Holman Hunt*. Exhibition catalogue. Liverpool, UK: Walker Art Gallery, 1969.

Calvin, John. *Institutes of the Christian Religion*. Translated by Henry Beveridge. Grand Rapids, MI: Wm. B. Eerdmans, 1962.

Christensen, Carl C. *Art and the Reformation in Germany*. Athens: Ohio State University Press, 1979.

Finney, Paul Corby, ed. *Seeing Beyond the Word: Visual Arts and the Calvinist Tradition*. Grand Rapids, MI: Wm. B. Eerdmans, 1999.

Flavel, John. *Christ Knocking at the Door of Sinners' Hearts*. Rev. edition. New York: American Tract Society, 188-.

Hofmann, Werner, ed. *Luther und die Folgen für die Kunst*. Exhibition catalogue. Munich, Germany: Prestel-Verlag, 1983.

Holly, Michael Ann. *Panofsky and the Foundations of Art History*. Ithaca, NY: Cornell University Press, 1984.

Künstle, Karl. *Ikonographie der Christlichen Kunst*, vol. 1. Freiburg im Breisgau, Germany: Herder & Co., 1928.

Landow, George P. *William Holman Hunt and Typological Symbolism*. New Haven and London: Yale University Press, 1979.

Luther, Martin. *Against the Heavenly Prophets in the Matter of Images and Sacraments* [1525] In *Luther's Works*, vol. 40. Philadelphia, PA: Muehlenberg Press, 1958.

Maas, Jeremy. *Holman Hunt and The Light of the World*. Aldershot, UK: Wildwood House, 1987.

Miller, David C., ed. *American Iconology: New Approaches to Nineteenth-Century Art and Literature*. New Haven, CT: Yale University Press, 1993.

Mitchell, W. J. T. *Iconology: Image, Text, Ideology*. Chicago: University of Chicago Press, 1986.

Moody, Dwight L. *Fifty Sermons and Evangelistic Talks*. Cleveland and New York: F. M. Barton, 1899.

Morgan, David, ed. *Icons of American Protestantism: The Art of Warner Sallman*. New Haven, CT: Yale University Press, 1996.

———. *Protestants and Pictures: Religion, Visual Culture, and the Age of American Mass Production*. New York: Oxford University Press, 1999.

Numbers, Ronald L., and Jonathan M. Butler, eds. *The Disappointed: Millerism and Millenarianism in the Nineteenth Century*. Bloomington: Indiana University Press, 1987.

Panofsky, Erwin. "Iconography and Iconology: An Introduction to the Study of Renaissance Art." [1939] Revised and reprinted in *Meaning in the Visual Arts*. Garden City, NY: Doubleday Anchor, 1955.

Parris, Leslie, ed. *The Pre-Raphaelites*. Exhibition catalogue. London: Tate Gallery Publications, 1994.

Schiller, Gertrud. *Iconography of Christian Art*. Translated by Janet Seligman. 2 vols. Greenwich, CT: New York Graphic Society, 1971–1972.

Scribner, R. W. *For the Sake of Simple Folk: Popular Propaganda for the German Reformation*. Oxford, UK: Clarendon Press, 1994.

Scudder, Rev. J., "Knocking at the Door: An Appeal to Youth," No. 31 [1826], in *Publications of the American Tract Society*, vol. 1. New York: American Tract Society, 1849.

A Series of Interpretations of the Sallman Religious Masterpieces. Indianapolis, IN: Kriebel & Bates [ca. 1955].

Vaughan, William. *German Romanticism and English Art*. New Haven, CT: Yale University Press, 1979.

DAVID MORGAN

INCULTURATION

Inculturation is a term emerging in (principally) post–Vatican II Catholic theology to denote the process by which local cultures and their values function in the proclamation and reformulation of the Christian message and in its embodiment in life. It presupposes an "incarnational" understanding of the Church in which Christ "takes flesh" in local cultures so that they become as appropriate a vehicle for the manifestation of Christ as was the culture of first-century Jewish Palestine. Inculturation theology was informed by the generally positive value accorded to local cultures in such encyclical documents as *Lumen Gentium*. It superseded terms such as "adaptation" and "indigenization," which emphasized the agency of missionaries.

Inculturation theology responds to the accusation that Christianity in Africa or Asia is a foreign implant, while recognizing that foreignness has too often been a feature of its church life.

Contemporary Protestant mission theology also struggles with problems of the interaction of gospel and culture, without developing any single interpretive concept or agreed terminology. ("Contextualization" has been a popular term in some quarters, again often with reference to missionary method rather than to the church's experience.) Some social scientists have suggested "enculturation" as a neutral, nontheological term to indicate a process of exchange between elements of the Christian tradition and elements of local culture. The debates reflect the modern recognition of culture as constituting a coherent realm, not merely the agglomeration of "customs" recognized in earlier times. It also reflects a general acknowledgment that the positions reached by Western Christianity as a result of its own processes of cultural interaction are not necessarily normative for the rest of the world. The term "inculturation" is already used with a range of meaning, and there are signs that it is coming into general use to denote the Christian interaction with local culture or Christian embodiment within it. Accordingly it seems appropriate to use the term, if perhaps anachronistically, in considering approaches to the issues of cultural interaction in Protestant mission history.

Issues of culture have arisen recurrently in the history of Protestant missions, and indeed in all cross-cultural diffusions of the Christian faith. Protestants were not well placed to learn from Catholic missions, either in LATIN AMERICA, where Christianity in European form was imposed by force, or in CHINA, INDIA, JAPAN, or Vietnam, where circumstances required that missionaries find a niche within an alien society, and where some, notably Jesuits, achieved a deep level of identification with local cultures and churches arose that could not be readily dismissed as foreign institutions. Old controversies over soteriology and popular images such as that of Jesuits as dissembling deceivers long diverted Protestants from weighing the experience of Catholic missions and into denouncing them. Early Protestant MISSIONS were influenced by the Pietist movement in Germany, by English PURITANISM in North America, and by the evangelical revival everywhere. All of these were movements of social criticism, developing a radical Christian lifestyle and rejecting many of the regular lifestyles associated with the nominally Christian societies in which these movements originated. On the one hand, this tended to predispose them to still harsher views of non-Christian societies, as being under the dominion of Satan; on the other, it preserved them from blatantly racial exaltation of their own societies. In common with their contemporaries, they also tended to hold a unitary and somewhat static view of civilization, identified with the intellectual, literary, artistic, and technological inheritance of the West since the Roman Empire, suffused with Christian teaching. Many Protestants believed the spread of this civilization to be a necessary precursor of any successful evangelization of the non-Christian world. Evangelicals and Pietists, although agreeing that Christianity and civilization were inseparable, for the most part saw civilization as a fruit of the Gospel rather than its harbinger.

As a rule, early Protestant missionary views of non-Western cultures tended to be severe. There were exceptions; DAVID LIVINGSTONE, for instance, seems to have been accepting from an early stage of African ways of life, finding their analogues among his own recent ancestors in the Scottish Highlands. It is not uncommon, however, to find missionaries whose first reactions were of dismay or even revulsion, coming to very different assessments as their acquaintance with the society and its people deepened. Without in any way diluting their sense of that society's need of Christ, they found not only admirable features within the culture, but sometimes also evidence of pre-Christian divine activity. These discoveries often emerge with deeper knowledge of language and traditions. This came more readily where there were written scriptures to be studied, and so generally sooner in India and China than in nonliterate societies. Protestant thought was undoubtedly partly shaped by theological and other intellectual currents in the West, and missionary activity helped to shape new social sciences such as anthropology. However, far more important in developing thought about cultural issues was the experience of living in other societies, and especially the experience of the development of churches there. A great variety of issues and approaches might be identified; here it must suffice to refer to five particularly influential models.

1. Civilization Models

The widespread views of civilization mentioned above took on special significance for missions in the light of the SLAVERY question. Until the nineteenth century, the Africans best known to Western Christians were those who had been brought to slavery in the Americas. Most of those in Britain, and many of those in America who supported missions, were strongly opposed to slavery. Slavery raised questions about the constitution of the African race. Evangelicals insisted on the unity of all humanity in nature and in grace. The implication followed that Africans, far from being fit only for menial service, must, as recipients of

God's salvation, be capable of the highest human attainments, those reflected in "civilization"—that is, Western civilization. Early missions among Africans, both in Africa and the Americas, stressed the growth of (Western) civilization as evidence of the power of the Gospel. The communities where this was most obvious—in the CARIBBEAN, in SIERRA LEONE, and among the Khoi (Hottentots) in SOUTH AFRICA—represented broken or uprooted peoples whose immediate connection with their land, their kin, and their past had been broken, and whose new identity was being formed with Christian and Western materials. The success of such civilization models challenged racist assumptions about African inferiority; Africans were clearly capable of all the attainments of the West, but it concealed the issue of the value of African culture in and of itself. In India the Scottish missionary Alexander Duff (1806–1878) set out to provide an entire Christian worldview that would include the whole encyclopedia of scientific knowledge and displace the Hindu system among India's intellectual leaders. He saw a brief period of success, where a number of young Brahmins, already disaffected with the old ways, responded; this movement declined, however, as other ways appeared of combining traditional ideas with Western scientific knowledge and social reform. Civilization models declined as the importance of the slavery issue declined, and evangelical thinking turned away from social to more directly "spiritual" issues; as acquaintance with African communities and their languages developed; and as confidence in the excellence and sufficiency of Western civilization waned.

2. National Church Models

By the middle of the nineteenth century mission leaders such as RUFUS ANDERSON and Henry Venn were urging the establishment of self-governing, self-supporting, and self-propagating churches as the object of missionary endeavor, and recognizing that these were likely to deviate in some respects from the patterns of the churches of America and Europe. Indeed Venn invoked the Reformation doctrine of national churches: there could be national churches in India or Yorubaland that reflected the national peculiarities of their countries as the national Protestant churches of England, Scotland, Germany, and Scandinavia reflected theirs. A corollary was that missionaries should not stay as pastors of churches once they were established. In practice the situation was more complex. Some Anglican missionaries, among them bishop JOHN WILLIAM COLENSO in Natal, worked with the idea of the church influencing the whole organism of society, as notionally in England, rather than, like other missions, seeking to call out a church from its society. Traditional institutions, even (in a strictly delimited form) polygamy might be tolerated if not absolutely incompatible with Christian teaching. A number of German missionaries, inspired by the Volkskirche idea, worked for the conversion of the society as an organic whole. Bruno Guttmann, for instance, immersed himself in the community life of the Chagga of Tanzania, seeking not so much individual conversions as consensual response to the Gospel in clans and age-sets. In this way a national leadership of the church and a Christian leadership of the community developed together. The experiment had started in a German colony; by the time Tanzania was advancing toward independence, there were complaints that this comprehensive but essentially conservative approach to traditional culture had left the community disadvantaged in such matters as secondary schools that other missions retained, often as a remnant of the civilization model. Christian Keysser and Georg Vicedom developed parallel approaches in Papua New Guinea. The French Protestant Maurice Leenhardt (1878–1954) found the structure of a national church already in place in New Caledonia and removed imported features to give it space to develop.

3. Fulfillment and Restorationist Models

These developed in India and China and other areas where ancient civilizations with developed literary traditions were still visible. Missions often took the view that these were now irrelevant to the great mass of the people who were largely unaffected by them; however, there were important elements in Protestant missions that saw them as vital determinants of Christian work. The Scot William Miller (1838–1923) realized that Duff's dream of the displacement of Hinduism was impossible. What Christian education should now attempt was to awaken dormant tendencies already in Hinduism, so that the Christian message, so readily shrugged off as foreign, could be heard by Hindu intellectuals. K. M. Banerjea (see INDIAN THEOLOGY), converted through Duff, found an "Aryan witness" to Christ in the Vedas, the ancient Hindu scriptures that Duff had scorned. J. N. Farquhar (1861–1929), faced with the rising national movement and growing resentment at British rule, threw himself into the study of the religious literature of India, making it readily available, producing comprehensive guides to it that are still in use, and arguing that Christ is the fulfillment of its highest aspirations. In China JAMES LEGGE (1815–1897) devoted his life to the study and translation of the Chinese classics and argued that the ancient religion of China was monotheistic, a sort of primal revelation. Such approaches looked to In-

dian and Chinese appropriations of Christianity that would affirm the best glories of the past and move to a Christian future that would retain continuity with that past.

4. Modernizing Models

These models have been most noticeable in Japan and China. In Japan Protestant missionaries were welcomed for a time as agents of the Western education and technology that were needed for national advance. Groups of young Western-educated young men, often samurai, converted at Sapporo and elsewhere, leading to an expectation, not justified by the event, that Japan would turn to the religion as well as the technology of the West. In fact some Japanese Christians, such as Uchimura Kanzo (1861–1930), set up a critique of the West and its lack of spiritual sensitivity, and propounded a Japanese version of Christianity. In China Timothy Richard (1845–1919), beginning as an evangelistic missionary, found himself deeply involved in famine relief, and from there moved to consider the structural causes of famine in China. These were all removable by the application of modern methods, and use of those methods would derive from a true doctrine of God and creation. Much of his later career was concerned with propagating these ideas through literature and other means, with a view to a converted and regenerated China, although always with deep respect for Chinese culture, history, and societal structures, and with an increasingly sharp critique of Western imperialism and militarism. Other missionaries linked Christian mission in China to modernization, especially in the period after the fall of the empire when Western values seemed to be attractive to rulers of China. Later developments led to the rejection of missions as part of a foreign imperialist enterprise, and thereafter to a major expansion of Christianity through Chinese agency.

5. Hospitality Models

The Norwegian Lutheran missionary K. L. Reichelt (1877–1952) realized that ordinary mission methods in China made no impression on Buddhist monks, although many of these were clearly sincere seekers after truth and often burdened by a sense of sin. He developed a meeting point, later formalized as a brotherhood, where Christians and Buddhists might pray and study the scriptures in an environment that was not threatening but welcoming. Although he remained at heart a pietistic Lutheran, he was accused by some of syncretism and by others of Romanism. His Tao Fong Shan Centre (eventually located, through the exigencies of war, in Hong Kong) is one of many examples of mission endeavors aimed at providing hospitality to people of faith in terms of a local culture.

These and other models adopted by Protestant missions indicate that issues of inculturation were arising, although variously described and very differently addressed, throughout the days of the Protestant missionary movement. The great international missionary conferences, from the WORLD MISSIONARY CONFERENCE at Edinburgh in 1910 to the International Missionary Council meeting at Tambaram in 1938, concentrated on issues raised by other faiths, rather than the cultures shaped by those faiths, which continued to shape the corporate minds of the churches for whose emergence missions had been the catalyst. Culture came to the center of discussion after World War II, following closer consideration of the nature of the church and in the wake of decolonization, the emergence of new nations, and a revival of confidence in the cultures of Africa and Asia.

The inculturation process was by then well established in many newer Protestant churches, and it has been the process in these churches, rather than particular policies of missions, that has determined the present situation. There have been reconstitutive models for the appropriations of Christianity, as in the cases of Sierra Leone and the Caribbean already considered. The sense of Christian identity here, and the adoption of Western cultural models, was always clear; what was less clear was that African elements were also incorporated into the reconstituted identity to all. There were interactive models of appropriation in many parts of Africa, where the central institutions of a community were gradually brought into a mutually accepting relationship with Christian teaching, sometimes with reserved areas of autonomy where the power of ancestral consciousness was particularly strong. There have also been reinterpretive models, seen perhaps most clearly in many AFRICAN INSTITUTED CHURCHES, but not only there, where aspects and institutions of African life are reinterpreted and given new significance in the light of the Bible. The huge presence of the charismatic movement in Africa has given impetus to this process by the relationships it is forging between African worldviews and Biblical teaching. In none of these models of appropriation does it make sense to distinguish between "Christian" and "African" elements—they are fully integrated.

Meanwhile, new Asian theologies of culture are appearing. It is noticeable that, although missionary models of cultural interaction in India concentrated on the Brahminical Hindu tradition, the fact that the great majority of Indian Christians are Dalits, with their history of oppression, or Tribals with a non-Indic identity, is producing quite new interpretations of the relationship between past tradition and Christian identity (see Indian Theology and TRIBAL MOVEMENTS, INDIA). Ultimately most inculturation questions are about a satisfactory definition of the relations between local or national and Christian identity.

See also: Missionary Organizations; Pietism

References and Further Reading

Bediako, Kwame. *Theology and Identity: The Impact of Culture upon Christian Thought.* Oxford: Regnum, 1992.
———. *Christianity in Africa: The Renewal of a Non-Western Religion.* Edinburgh: Edinburgh University Press, 1995.
Bevans, Stephen B. *Models of Contextual Theology.* Maryknoll, NY: Orbis, 1992, 2002.
Walls, Andrew F. *The Cross-Cultural Movement in Christian History.* Maryknoll, NY: Orbis, 2002.

ANDREW F. WALLS

INDEPENDENT FUNDAMENTALIST CHURCHES

This organization is one of the oldest and largest fundamentalist associations in the UNITED STATES that emerged out of the interdenominational BIBLE conferences of the early twentieth century as a protest against the liberalism and MODERNISM in the larger Protestant denominations. Its formal beginnings can be traced to the formation of the American Conference of Undenominational Churches in 1923. This group joined a number of Congregational churches in 1930 to form the Independent Fundamentalist Churches of America (IFCA). While maintaining a strong stance on ecclesial separatism from denominations and religious apostasy, and critical of the neo-evangelical NATIONAL ASSOCIATION OF EVANGELICALS, the IFCA left the American Council of Christian Churches (ACCC) in 1952 because the latter was too extreme in its separatism. The IFCA could not abide by the strict ACCC position on separation from other conservatives, including the more moderate National Association of Evangelicals, who did hold to a strict separatist position.

The association renamed itself IFCA International in 1996 in recognition of its global mission and diverse constituency, and to place less emphasis on FUNDAMENTALISM and its exclusionary position out of concern that "independent" and "fundamental" might be misunderstood. Churches, lay people, and ministers can become members of the association, which has its headquarters in Grandville, Michigan.

Consistent with the fundamentalist movement's insistence on unwavering doctrinal fundamentals and purity, the IFCA International demands adherence to verbal plenary inerrancy of the Bible, total depravity of humans, the virgin birth and full deity of Christ, the sacrificial ATONEMENT, the CHURCH as the local and independent gathering of believers apart from denominational systems, and premillenial dispensational ESCHATOLOGY. The organization affirms the two ordinances of the LORD'S SUPPER and Believer's BAPTISM and is strictly congregational in governance, informal in WORSHIP, and advocates expository PREACHING and the literal interpretation of the Bible.

See also Biblical Inerrancy; Congregationalism; Denomination; Dispensationalism; Liberal Protestantism and Liberalism; Millenarians and Millennialism

References and Further Reading

Melton, J. Gordon. Encyclopedia of American Religions. New York: Triumph Books, 1991.

Van Plew, Wright. "A Time to Stand Firm: A Brief History of the IFCA International." http://www.ifca.org/voice/00May-Jun/vanplew.htm (5 May 2003).

TIMOTHY E. FULOP

INDIA

Before European Colonial Presence in India (until 1498)

The general assumption that the history of Christianity in India is as old as Christianity itself refers to its early beginnings in South India. Among the St. Thomas (or) Syrian Christians in South India, there is strong oral tradition that emphasizes the ministry of the Apostle Thomas, one of the twelve apostles of Jesus Christ (Matthew 10:3, Mark 3:18; John 11:16, 15:5, 20:25, 29), in South India. Accordingly, following the ancient trade route between South India and the Middle East, St. Thomas is believed to have reached Kudungalur (i.e., Cranganore) on the southwest Coast of the modern Kerala State. After an eventful ministry that succeeded in establishing a few local churches with Indian converts, he is said to have moved to Mylapore, currently a suburb of the city of Chennai (Madras). The same tradition points out that Indian religious leaders, who did not like the ministry of St. Thomas, killed him. Early European travelers (e.g., Pantanus in the second century, Marco Polo in 1288), Church Fathers (e.g., Ambrose, fourth century), and the apocryphal book entitled Acts of Thomas (early third century) make several allusions either to the tomb (supposedly) of St. Thomas on St. Thomas Mount in Chennai or to the Christian population in southern India. Historically convincing contemporaneous evidences of the life and ministry of St. Thomas the Apostle, however, are yet to be found.

Other traditions link the beginning of Christianity in India either with the Apostle Bartholomew (Matthew 10:3; Mark 3:8; Luke 6:14) in the region of Thana, near the city of Mumbai (earlier, Bombay), or to immigrations of Syriac-speaking Christians from Persia. According to the Jacobite Mar Thoma IV (1721) there were two migrations of Christians from Persia to Kerala: in 345 a certain Thomas of Cana led about four hundred families; in 823–825 Mar Sabriso brought another group of immigrants; both groups were welcome and were socially integrated into the prevailing culture. In the course of time they attained high social rank and political power. They owned large pieces of land, traded spices with business people from many parts of the world, and led a simple, but dignified life. From the fourth century onward, the Christians in India accepted the ecclesiastical authority of the Persian Church and used the Syriac liturgy. They were oriental Christians in India, belonging to the ecclesiastical jurisdiction of the patriarch of Antioch. Because of this Persian connection, they had Syriac liturgy, theology, and church administration, until the sixteenth century. Their metropolitan, the chief ecclesiastical head, appointed a Persian bishop to take care of the spiritual affairs of the Indian church and an Indian archdeacon to look after the civil life of the Christians. In consultation with the archdeacon, the bishop would ordain Katanars, the local pastors.

All the religious and political tensions, splits, and theologies of the patriarchate in Antioch influenced the Indian church directly or indirectly. The Indian Christians got integrated into the prevailing cultural and social context in India; by faith they were Christian, although by ecclesiastical affiliation they were Syrian. They made use of a flagstaff and a wooden gong. They went on processions, undertook pilgrimages, and observed days of fasting and feasting. They administered Qurbana (i.e., Eucharist) in two elements. Their priests were married. Despite their achievements, this community was inward looking. Lack of pastoral care and dependency on non-Indian bishops were bound to weaken this community.

During European Colonial Presence in India (1498–1947)

The Portuguese naval officer, Vasco da Gama (1469–1524) reached Calicut in 1498 and forced the Indian ruler of Calicut (1502) to sign a trade treaty. This event marked the beginning of a long presence of several European powers in India. With regard to church relations Vasco da Gama's arrival in India had far-reaching consequences: in 1494, Pope Alexander entrusted Portugal with the ecclesiastical jurisdiction over all countries in the Eastern hemisphere. Vasco da Gama's contemporary, Cabral, brought Franciscan missionaries to the city of Cochin in 1500. Franciscan missionaries strengthened their centers and began to expand their influence. In 1514 Pope Leo confirmed the Padroado missionaries the right to select, appoint, and maintain bishops and to build churches. After Goa, the Portuguese capital city in India, was established in 1510 and raised to an archdiocese covering all territories between India and China. By 1534, more European missionaries arrived in India: Dominicans (1503), Jesuits (1542), and Augustinians (1572). When the Portuguese met the St. Thomas Christians and discovered their involvement in the spice trade, they entered into a trade agreement with them. However, they soon found that the faith expressions and practices of St. Thomas Christians differed greatly from the teachings of the Roman Catholic Church, especially after the anti-Protestant Council of Trent (1545–1563). In their efforts to counter Protestants in Europe and to gain new adherents in non-European countries, the Portuguese political authorities and the Padroado missionaries desired to establish the faith and practice of the Roman Catholic Church over that of the St. Thomas Christians in India. With the help of the Jesuit Francis Roz, Dom Alexis de Menezis, the archbishop of Goa, called for a synod at Diamper (i.e., Udayamperur, June 20–27, 1599). While he arranged for subjugating the St. Thomas Christians to Roman Catholicism, he opposed the unhealthy (Brahminical) practice of untouchability and the discrimination against women among the Christians. However, the St. Thomas Christians did not tolerate the imposition of the Latin rite; they wanted to have their Syrian tradition and liturgy in Syriac. On January 3, 1653, most of them gathered at a church in the place of Mattancherry. They touched a rope tied to the cross of the church and vowed (i.e., Coonon Cross Oath) not to continue their relationship with the Roman Catholic Church any longer. This historical event marked the beginning of the major ecclesiastical split in India—those who rejected the Latin rite were known as the New Party, which later became the Jacobite Church. A small number of Christians, known as the Old Party, continued to be Roman Catholics. The representatives of the New Party not only ordained their archdeacon Thomas as Mar Thoma I, but also approached the Syrian Orthodox patriarchate of Antioch for help. Consequently St. Gregorious Abdul'Galeel, the Syrian metropolitan of Jerusalem, came to Kerala in 1665 and revived the Syriac tradition. During the seventeenth century Christians in Kerala had to encounter rival church leaders, traditions, and further splits.

During the years 1542–1773 (until the Suppression) the Jesuit missionaries toiled not only on the coastal regions, but also in the main cities of South India. Some Jesuits from the College of St. Paul's in Goa accepted the invitation of the Mughal Emperor Akbar (1556–1605), the proponent of Din-i-Ilahi, and went to his court (1580–1583) to demonstrate the Christian message in word and deed. Although this type of mission work among the aristocrats lasted almost two centuries, it did not result in many conversions, although it influenced the Mughal art, literature, and history. The Jesuit mission to the common people had more success. The Italian Jesuit Roberto de Nobili (1577–1656), founder of the Madurai Mission, may perhaps be the greatest missionary of this time. From his arrival in the cultural city of Madurai in 1606 he learned the dominant South Indian languages (Tamil, Telugu, and Sanskrit), became well acquainted with the major literature of these languages, and studied the cultural specialties of the South Indians. In his attempt to study the worldviews and behavior patterns of the South Indians he tried to separate religion from social custom. He created many phrases to communicate the Christian message, and he managed to lead people of different caste groups to worship in one church building and to receive the sacraments from his own hand. He removed the derogatory name of Christians as Paranghis (i.e., a synonym for drinking wine, eating beef, and leading a morally loose life). His own contemporary, the Portuguese Jesuit John de Brito (1647–1693), preached the Christian message in and around the city of Madurai and adjacent kingdoms. The works of the Jesuit missionaries and two Dutch East India Company chaplains (Philip Baldaeus and Abraham Roger) in the seventeenth century need to be mentioned. They preached the Christian message and took the thought patterns of Indians seriously. Roman Catholic missionaries belonging to the Propaganda Fide (established in 1622) complicated the missionary work of the Protestant missionaries in India.

In the meantime the traders of East India Companies from ENGLAND (1600–1874), NETHERLANDS (1602–1798), DENMARK (1616–1845), and FRANCE (1664–1769) began to make inroads on the Portuguese sea power. Although in England there was a close link between state and church, the British colonial authorities in India were careful not to allow any Protestant missionary work in their territories in India. Because of the peculiar domestic and national situation, Frederick IV, king of Denmark (1699–1730), established a cross-cultural mission to Tranquebar, a small Danish colony (1619–1845) on the east coast of South India. At the recommendation of his counselors, in 1705, he sent two German Pietists, B. Ziegenbalg (1682–1719) and H. Pluetschau (1677–1746) to Tranquebar. Ziegenbalg learned the Tamil language, studied Tamil literature, and translated the New Testament and a few other works of German Pietists into Tamil, organized a church based on several South Indian social principles, educated less-privileged people to attain economic self-sufficiency, and prepared Indian Christians to shoulder responsibilities for their own church. Among his successors the linguist Benjamin Schultze (1689–1760), the Bible translator Johann Philip Fabricius (1711–1791), and the missionary-diplomat Christian Frederick Schwartz (1726–1798) were some leading figures whose multifaceted contributions to Indian society are remembered gratefully.

In 1758 John Zecharias Kiernander (d. 1799) reached Calcutta and pioneered Protestant mission work. He established schools and founded the Old Church. The Baptist missionary WILLIAM CAREY (1761–1834), who reached Calcutta in 1793, had to first work in an indigo factory for seven years before he was allowed to settle down in Serampore, a Danish colony (1755–1845) near Calcutta. His contributions to Protestant Christianity in India and Indian society are fondly remembered. Because of the change of the British public mind toward Christian missions, the works of C. F. Schwartz, Carey, and Charles Grant, an influential director of the English East India Company, a "pious clause" was inserted in 1813; in the following year the first Anglican bishopric was established in Calcutta. Few chaplains (e.g., Claudius Buchanan, 1766–1815) and residents of the East India Company (Sir Thomas Munro, 1761–1827) and bishops (e.g., Reginold Heber, 1783–1826) showed much interest in missionary work in India. After the reports of Buchanan and Munro on St. Thomas Christians, the CHURCH MISSION SOCIETY sent its missionaries to Kerala in 1815 to start a "Mission of Help." Their efforts to translate the Syriac Bible and liturgy into Malayalam, the local vernacular language, had far-reaching consequences and led to the separation of a reform group (1836) under the leadership of Abraham Malpan from other Syrian Christians. After the charter of the East India Company was revised in 1833 explicit provisions were made to allow Christian mission agencies from Europe, North America, and other countries to work in India (see MISSIONS; MISSION ORGANIZATIONS). Lutheran, Baptist, Anglican, Congregationalists, Methodists, and other denominations established their branches in India. In some places, mostly because of the efforts of Indian Christians, a large number of people came into the Christian church.

This sudden increase demanded new mission approaches. Despite some rivalries (e.g., regarding geographical territories of mission work and the types of missionary works), there were many meetings between different mission agencies (e.g., in Madras in 1900 with preceding conferences in the cities of Allahabad, Bombay, etc.). These meetings emphasized the need for united mission enterprise. V. S. Azariah (1874–1945) played an important role in establishing the Indian Missionary Society (1903) and the National Missionary Society (1905). His address at the Edinburgh Missionary conference of 1910 (see WORLD MISSIONARY CONFERENCE) pointed out the need for Western missionaries to consider non-Western Christian leaders as their friends and partners. Two years later Azariah was ordained as the first Indian bishop. HENDRIK KRAEMER's book, *The Christian Message in a Non-Christian World,* created much controversy at the International Missionary Conference held at Tambaram in 1938. Indian Christian leaders, both clergy and laity, reacted severely to Kraemer's view that the faith of the non-Christian people did not possess (salvific) truth. The members of the Rethinking Group (A. J. Appasamy [1891–1975], V. Chakkarai [1880–1958], and P. Chenciah [1886–1956]) tried to express in Indian categories their understanding of Christian faith. In the context of rising Indian nationalism, Western and non-Western Church leaders in India realized the need for a united Christian witness. The National Christian Council of India was established in 1914 to represent all non–Roman Catholic churches in India. In 1927 all the Lutheran Churches in India established the Federation of Evangelical Lutheran Churches. Anglican, Congregational, and Presbyterian churches found ways of uniting; representatives of these traditions inaugurated the CHURCH OF SOUTH INDIA (CSI) in September 1947 in Madras. The merger of these various traditions is considered to be "the second great miracle after Pentecost."

After European Colonial Presence in India (1947–)

In 1947 India attained political freedom from British imperialism. Indian Christian leaders felt the need for authentic Indian expression of Christian faith, theology, education, pastoral training, and church architecture. The Ashram Movement gained popularity: in 1930 the Sat Tal Christian Ashram was founded in the place of Nainital by Stanley E. Jones. Soon other Christian ashrams (Christkula Ashram in Tiruppattur, Saccidananda Ashram in Santivanam) were established in parts of India. Ashrams became a place for Christians and non-Christians to transform personal and social life, "agree to disagree," but to unite for love, service, and often East–West dialogue. Independent India offered an opportunity for renewed Christian social activity. P. D. Devanandan (1901–1962) and M. M. Thomas (1916–1996) showed how the Christian message could help in building the nation, especially in the context of poverty and religious pluralism. After the publication of the Niyogi Committee Report on Christian Missionary Activities (1956) and the passage of the Freedom of Religion bills by the governments of Madya Pradesh, Orissa, and Arunachal Pradesh (1968–1971), it became increasingly clear that the Indian "secular democracy" would not welcome non-Indian missionaries. Hence, Indian Christian leaders began their own missionary movements.

Today the Friends Missionary Prayer Band (FMPB) and Indian Evangelical Mission are two large indigenous mission agencies sending Indian missionaries from south and northeastern India to other parts of India. It is known that through the holistic work of FMPB, the Maltos, a people group in the State of Bihar and once on the verge of extinction, have now experienced a great transformation. In 1970 the Church of North India (CNI) was founded as a united and uniting church to witness to the words and deeds of Jesus Christ. Currently the CSI and CNI are trying to establish one church in India. Many decades of theological and secular education made available to the marginalized groups of Indian Christians have begun to yield results: at present the Dalits ("those who are broken") claim their rightful share in formulating Indian Christian theology, administering church properties, and undertaking church leadership. Although the caste is addressed as a social and religious evil, effective functional alternatives have yet to be found. The Indian church has also slowly realized the need for the participation of women in the religious and secular life of Christians. However, the Indian church is involved in works for justice, social peace, and preservation of creation. The social, educational, vocational, medical relief, and other humanitarian services rendered by Christians in India have not resulted in large numbers of conversions to Christianity, but function as "salt and light" by providing all interested people an alternative lifestyle. Some Indian Christian leaders have made significant contributions to the worldwide Church, its ecumenical partnership, and discussions on pluralism and dialogue. Indian Christian immigrant workers in the UNITED STATES, AUSTRALIA, and Western Europe significantly influence the life of churches in the West. The long history and experience of the church in India provides much opportunity for mutual learning and enrichment.

See also Indian Theology

References and Further Reading

Downs, Frederick S. *History of Christianity in India: Northeast India in the Nineteenth and Twentieth Centuries,* vol. 5, pt. 5. Bangalore, India: CHAI, 1992.

Grafe, Hugald. *History of Christianity in India: Tamilnadu in the Nineteenth and Twentieth Centuries,* vol. 4, pt. 2. Bangalore, India: CHAI, 1990.

Hamby, E. R. *History of Christianity in India: Eighteenth Century,* vol. 3. Bangalore, India: CHAI, 1997.

Indian Church History Review. *Bulletin of the Church History Association of India.* Bangalore, India: 1967–.

Kuriakose, M. K., compiler. *History of Christianity in India: Source Materials.* Delhi, India: ISPCK, 1982.

Mundadan, Mathias. *History of Christianity in India: From the Beginning up to the Middle of the Sixteenth Century (up to 1542),* vol. 1. Bangalore, India: CHAI, 1984.

Neill, Stephen. *A History of Christianity in India: the Beginnings to AD 1707.* Cambridge, UK: Cambridge University Press, 1984.

———. *A History of Christianity in India, 1707–1858.* Cambridge, UK: Cambridge University Press, 1985.

Thekkedath, Joseph. *History of Christianity in India: From the Middle of the Sixteenth to the End of the Seventeenth Century (1542–1700),* vol. 2. Bangalore, India: CHAI, 1982.

P. DANIEL JEYARAJ

INDIAN THEOLOGY

Protestantism first arrived in INDIA when the Tranquebar mission began work in 1706 among Tamil-speaking people. The considerable literature that survives from the church that resulted from this work is only now beginning to be catalogued and studied.

In the early nineteenth century the Baptist missionaries in Serampore, Bengal provided a spark that lit the fire of Indian Protestant theology. The first flames came from Ram Mohan Roy (1772–1833), although he never became a Christian. Roy came from a Bengali Brahmin family. Study of Persian and Arabic led him to a deep appreciation for Islam and monotheism, and a desire to purge all religions of idolatry and superstition. He devoted his life to the abolition of *sati,* or widow immolation, and other social reforms. Roy's reformation of Hinduism was as much indebted to rationalists and Unitarians in the West as to Muslims and Trinitarian Christians in India (see UNITARIAN-UNIVERSALIST ASSOCIATION. He settled in Calcutta in 1815, publishing Vedantic Hindu texts and agitating for social and religious reform. His view of Hinduism was that the original scriptures, the *Vedas,* had been corrupted by later writings, specifically the *Puranas.*

In 1820 Roy published a collection of extracts from the four gospels, especially Jesus' sermons and parables, *The Precepts of Jesus the Guide to Peace and Happiness.* This quickly led to a literary debate with the Baptist Joshua Marshman, who objected to a piecemeal approach to the New Testament. For Roy, Jesus was a great teacher and "messenger" of God who imparted teachings that were "more conducive to moral principles and more adapted for the use of rational beings" than any other. Claims about Christ's divinity were later additions by the church, as was the idea of Christ's DEATH as atoning sacrifice. The DOCTRINE of the Trinity was not only unnecessary to SALVATION, it was irrational and a reversion to the polytheistic trends in religion that Roy was fighting. The simple plan of salvation was to follow the precepts of Jesus. In 1828 Roy established a religious association of reformed Hinduism. However, Roy also expressed a vision of Christ and of Christianity that made sense within the Hindu world, while at the same time radically challenging that world. His legacy is not merely that of an outsider to the CHURCH; a number of Bengali Christians came to FAITH in Christ through their study of Roy's *Precepts of Jesus*.

Ram Mohan Roy died in ENGLAND in 1833. In terms of Indian Protestant THEOLOGY his most interesting successor was Keshub Chander Sen (1838–1884) who joined the *Brahmo Samaj* at the age of nineteen. Although Roy had been highly rationalistic and regarded mystical spirituality with suspicion, Sen was a man of spiritual fervor and passion, open to *bhakti*, loving, ecstatic devotion to a particular god. Roy had rejected the idea of divine incarnation, believing that it compromised monotheism; Sen embraced the ideas of incarnation and avatar (temporary manifestation of the divine in human form). Sen was never baptized, but from his early years in the *Brahmo Samaj*, was an enthusiast for the life of Christ, and Christ increasingly became the center of his life and the focus of his thinking.

Sen, departing from the rationalistic unitarianism of Roy, also embraced the concept of God as Trinity. The trinity was conceived as *Sat, Cit, Ananda*, or Truth/Being, Wisdom, and Bliss, a classical Hindu description of *Brahman* (God) corresponding in Sen's thought to Father, Son, and Holy Spirit. In a series of lectures, notably *Jesus Christ: Europe and Asia* (1866) and *India Asks, Who is Christ?* (1879), Sen developed his idea of Christ. Christ, who said "I and my Father are one," was divine humanity through *kenosis*: he was a human being who emptied himself, who utterly abandoned his self, so that Divinity filled the void. This union of Christ with the Father was not an ontological but a mystical one, and Jesus sought to extend to others that spiritual oneness with the Father: "As thou, Father, art in me, that they may also be one in us." The self-sacrifice on the cross is also exemplary for all humanity. Christ calls all to be filled with Christ. Later in life Sen moved closer to Christian ORTHODOXY in his understanding of Jesus, seeing his death as an atoning medium that brings God and humanity together, and using the language of sacrifice and substitution to describe Jesus' death.

Sen, although utterly devoted to Jesus Christ, was never attracted to the Christian church in India, which he believed was too Westernized. He led the *Brahmo Samaj* to establish the "Church of the New Dispensation," a new Christ-centered eclectic religion. Jesus corrected and fulfilled Hinduism, and indeed fulfilled the best in each faith. Christ was hidden in the Hindu religion, and was present in all that is good in every philosophy.

Ram Mohan Roy and Keshub Chander Sen were developing understandings of Jesus and the Christian God within the Indian religious context. A critique came from certain Indian Christian thinkers. The works of Krishna Mohan Banerjea (1813–1885), Lal Behari Day (1824–1829), and Nehemiah Goreh (1825–1895) form the core of this Protestant theological response, and the work of Goreh can be taken as illustrative. He was born Nilakantha Shastri Goreh into a Brahmin family from Maharashtra, but grew up in Benares. A missionary introduced him to the BIBLE. Goreh's grappling with the Bible eventually led to his conversion and BAPTISM in the Anglican Church in 1848, at which time he took the name Nehemiah. He had already gained a reputation as a Sanskrit scholar and exponent of traditional Hinduism. He continued in deep study of scriptures and religion, with periods of doubt and conflict. He was ordained into the Anglican priesthood in 1870.

In 1860 Goreh published *A Rational Refutation of the Hindu Philosophical Systems*, an apologetic work in dialogue with Hindu scholars. Goreh undertakes to prove that Hinduism is not coherent within itself. At the same time he puts forward Christian beliefs and doctrines as a rationally acceptable alternative. For example, the theory of creation underlying the *advaita* theological tradition in Hinduism ultimately denies the reality of creation, while at the same time it posits that creation is one with *Brahman*, who is real. In place of this self-contradictory doctrine of Creator and creation Goreh turns to the Christian doctrine of a Creator God who makes creation *ex nihilo*. Goreh goes on to argue the irrationality of Hindu views on SIN, the human condition, and salvation, and the congruence of the Christian views of these matters. Goreh, who lived simply in Indian style, refusing even clerical dress, came to the conclusion that orthodox Hindus were prepared by their religion and philosophy to receive the gospel as no other people save the Jews had been. The Hindu belief in *avatar* was a preparation for the incarnation. Christ is a fulfillment of the longings of Hinduism.

A few Protestant missionaries seriously engaged Hindu thought in theological terms. The Scot, John Nicol Farquhar (1861–1929) arrived in India in 1891 to teach in Calcutta. After a decade he was able to devote himself to personal EVANGELISM and scholarly research and writing, his works including a theology of religion entitled *The Crown of Hinduism* (1913). Here Farquhar worked out a fulfillment theory of religions, first suggested by Keshub Chander Sen. Farquhar built his work on evolutionary assumptions, arguing that all social institutions can be placed on an ascending scale of value and effectiveness. The crown of all religions on this evolutionary scale is Jesus Christ. In him, Farquhar argued, all people can find the answers to all their religious questions, including human and social questions, which are given unsatisfactory or no answers in non-Christian religions. Farquhar's fulfillment theory fell out of favor after a couple of decades, but was picked up by Indian Roman Catholic theologians after the Second Vatican Council (1961–1965).

One of Farquhar's most prominent critics was another Scottish missionary, Alfred George Hogg (1875–1954), teacher and then principal of Madras Christian College from 1902 to 1939. Hogg argued that Christ fulfills, not Hinduism but the need of which India had begun to be conscious. Christ may bring a Hindu to realizations of new needs, which Christ manifestly fulfills. Hogg proposed that rather than being unfulfilled or incomplete, Hinduism presented to the people of India a well-integrated and complete system of belief. Christ made people aware that there were possibilities and potentials beyond their present system of belief, and Christ alone was the hope for fulfilling these. In *Karma and Redemption* (1909), Hogg argues that the doctrine of *karma* fits wonderfully into a system in which there is no other purpose in life than expiation. There is no possibility of true morality in the doctrine of *karma* because every good and every evil act must inexorably be worked out in the life of the soul; *karma* operates within a judicial system but without a judge. Mercy and even love are therefore not possible in this system; everything that happens to a person is a result of previous deeds. Christ and Christianity, on the other hand, propose a moral universe, governed by a moral God, where forgiveness, mercy, and love are not only possible, but demanded. Christ offers to the Hindu a new point of reference. Hogg was the outstanding missionary theologian in India during the first half of the twentieth century, who in his efforts to relate Christianity to Hinduism left behind a generation of students and admirers, both Hindu and Christian.

The missionary who had built up Madras Christian College, where Hogg served, was another Scot, William Miller (1838–1923). His influence underlay the work of a trio of outstanding South Indian Protestant theologians of the early twentieth century. Vengal Chakkarai (1880–1958), a lawyer, evangelist, and ardent nationalist, converted to Christianity in his twenties, and in 1927 published *Jesus the Avatar*. For Chakkarai, Jesus, who through *kenosis* became the Christ, is still today the *avatar*. However, unlike Hindu *avatars*, the incarnation of Jesus is not temporary and static but permanent and dynamic. Moreover, the Spirit is identified with the risen, living Christ at work in the world today. Chakkarai also insisted that knowledge of God begins with a personal experience of Christ, and he formulated a doctrine of the "Christhood of God." Because an experience of Christ was crucial for a true knowledge of God, the immanence of Christ (and God) was important in Chakkarai's thought.

Chakkarai's brother-in-law, Pandipeddi Chenchiah (1886–1959), another lawyer and the chief judge of Pudukkottai State, converted as a small boy from Hinduism along with his father, but retained his Hindu cultural heritage. He wanted Indian Christianity to shed its foreignness and focus on "the raw fact of Christ," who is the "True Man," the "New Man." Becoming one with Christ makes believers "new creatures" and the beginning of the "new creation." Chenchiah stressed the need to experience Christ, but a Christ who was permanently human, not an incarnation of God that has returned to God—in fact, not an *avatar* as Chakkarai argued. Christ as the New Man is the bridge between humanity and divinity, something absolutely novel. Believers are to become "Christs" themselves, as Sen had said. Chenchiah thus emphasized the resurrection and Pentecost: the Christian life is a "*yoga* [way of achieving union with God] of the Spirit," the Holy Spirit being *mahasakti* (new cosmic energy), which abides on earth. Chenchiah argued that the Hindu *sastras* (scriptures) held an equivalent place in preparing India for the Gospel to that of the Old Testament for the early Christians.

Bishop Aiyadurai Jesudasen Appasamy (1891–1975) was brought up in a Christian home. As a bishop his attitude toward the church as institution was more positive than that of many Indian theologians, who saw it as inherently Western. Appasaamy was immersed in the *bhakti* tradition, which seeks union with a personal God through intense personal devotion. In 1928 he published *Christianity as Bhakti Marga,* and in 1931 *What is Moksa?* These works expound John's gospel in conjunction with Hindu Tamil *bhakti* poets.

Appasamy envisioned the Christian life as one of intense devotion to Christ, with the goal of *moksa* (salvation—in Hindu theology, salvation from the cycle of *karma* and *samsara*) and union with God, not absorption into the divine but loving personal union with Christ who said, "Abide in me." The union of the believer with Christ models the union of Christ with God, which Appasamy interpreted as one where the Son perfectly conforms to the Father's will. He argued (against the Chalcedonian formula as well as against Hindu *advaita* philosophy) that the union between Father, Son, and believer is not metaphysical but moral. Christian *bhakti*—which includes an ethical dimension of love toward neighbor—is the way to Christian *moksa*. A life devoted to the deep love of

God, conforming to the will of Jesus, leads to eternal life. Appasamy conceived of the Logos as present or immanent in the world, both in creation and in humanity; the Logos is *antaryamin* (indweller). Jesus is Logos and also *avatar*; he is *avatar* not as theophany (as in the classical Hindu understanding) but as incarnation. Jesus breaks the bondage of the fear of *karma* for those who believe in him. In developing his Christ-centered and God-centered theology of *bhakti,* Appasamy interpreted Christian dogma in the light of John's gospel and the philosophy of Ramanuja.

The year 1947 was pivotal for India: the country gained its independence from the British Empire. Paul David Devanandan (1901–1962) saw that Christianity in postindependence India had to deal with a new factor, the secular state. Devanandan was born in Madras, the son of an ordained minister. Returning to India after study at Yale, he taught at United Theological College in Bangalore before becoming director of the Christian Institute for the Study of Religion and Society. Devanandan's pioneering work consisted in showing his Hindu friends how they could reform Hinduism from within to adapt to the new context produced by the secular state, and how some of their religious and philosophical struggles could be resolved only by Christ. For Devanandan, Christian theology was a product of dialogue with Hindus, and its evangelistic purpose was to change Hindu thinking about religion as it had been traditionally understood.

Devanandan sought to redefine some Hindu understandings according to Christian thinking. One was the understanding of the personality of God. In the most profound Hindu teachings, God is devoid of personality—*Brahman* is ultimately *nirguna* or without qualities. Yet Christianity believes in a personal God, and Devanandan proposed that the ancient Hindu concept of *purusa* (person) be used to rethink how God, for the Hindu, may be both personal and yet Ultimate Truth. Hindu understanding about creation might also be transformed. In classical *advaita* thought, creation is one with the Creator. Devanandan, in dialogue with Hindus and borrowing from Chenchiah, stressed that the Creator is not only differentiated from creation, but God is purposively moving to new creation because humanity's sin has marred the old creation. Talk of a new creation would help Hindus to participate in the difficult but exciting task of building a new India as a secular state. Other areas where Devanandan sought transformation through dialogue with Hindus were history, *maya,* and human community. He sought to redefine not only the Hindu worldview but also the terms in which Christian doctrine is expressed.

P. D. Devanandan's successor as director of the Christian Institute was Madathiparampil Mammen

(M. M.) Thomas (1916–1996). M. M. Thomas, like so many Indian Protestant theologians, was a layman. He continued and developed Devanandan's emphasis on dialogue, which he believed should take place on three levels: how each religion can contribute to the general welfare of society and humanity; dialogue that grapples with the central theological issues of each faith; and dialogue between persons about their personal faith commitments. Thomas's interest was in the first type of dialogue. In *The Acknowledged Christ of the Indian Renaissance* (1969) Thomas shows how the Christian faith, since the time of Ram Mohan Roy, has introduced new elements in India that have resulted in fundamental changes in the core of Hindu society and thought. This insight of Thomas's signals his interest in a theology that, like that of Devanandan, would inspire people to positive action in the building up of the new India.

Thomas admires Hindu reformers such as Ram Mohan Roy and Mahatma Gandhi, but finds their refusal to embrace Christian beliefs a hindrance to providing the proper answers to modern India's most pressing problems. The church, he argued, needs to participate in secular history for the purpose of increasing human dignity and developing human personality. These goals are not devoid of theological content because the secret of true humanism is found in the divine humanity of Jesus Christ: "the Gospel of Jesus Christ and his New Creation," as Thomas says, echoing Chenchiah. Thomas called for Christians to engage in nation building without in any way abandoning their distinctive Christian witness.

The work of interreligious dialogue was brought to a more global stage by Stanley Samartha (1920–2001) of Karnataka. Samartha was a pastor and educator before becoming the first director (1970–1981) of the WORLD COUNCIL OF CHURCHES Subunit on Dialogue with People of Living Faiths and Ideologies. His theological contributions were related to the task of interreligious dialogue.

In the mid-1980s nothing less than a theological revolution began in Indian Protestant theology when Dalit Theology pushed aside two centuries of Christian thought expressed by means of the philosophy and religion of classical brahminical Hinduism. The term *dalit,* meaning "oppressed" or "crushed," refers to the large numbers of Indians known as "outcaste" or "untouchable" or "harijan." Because the majority of Indian Protestants come from *dalit* groups, Dalit Theology is first of all theological reflection based on the experience of most Indian Christians, and because *dalits* have been, and continue to be, oppressed by members of Hindu castes who draw on classical brahminical Hinduism for their self-understanding and their understanding of the socioreligious order, Dalit

Theology is a challenge to the legitimacy of doing theology in terms of brahminical religion and philosophy. Dalit Theology has looked mostly to LIBERATION THEOLOGY to provide the hermeneutical lenses through which to undertake a theology of the oppressed in India. Thus the immediate future direction of Indian Protestant theology is far from settled. It is certainly not outside the realm of possibility that Dalit Theology and traditional Indian Christian theology will engage in fruitful future dialogue. Indeed it is difficult to see how Protestant theology in India can neglect either the experience of the majority of its church members or the religious and cultural milieu in which it finds itself, because the two are inextricably linked in India and the Indian church.

See also Conversion; Dialogue, Interconfessional; Ecumenism; Mass Movements (India); Missions; Tribal Movements (India)

References and Further Reading

Anderson, Gerald H. *Biographical Dictionary of Christian Missions.* New York: Macmillan, 1998.
———, et al. *Mission Legacies.* Maryknoll, NY: Orbis, 1994.
Boyd, Robin H. S. *An Introduction to Indian Christian Theology.* Madras, India: Christian Literature Society, 1975.
Jeyaraj, P. Daniel. "The Influence of the Protestant Reformation on India." *Princeton Seminary Bulletin* XXIII no. 3 (2002): 267–291.
Lossky, Nicholas, et al. *Dictionary of the Ecumenical Movement*, 2d edition. Geneva, Switzerland: WCC, 2002.
Sunquist, Scott W. and Dale Irvin. *A Dictionary of Asian Christianity.* Grand Rapids, MI: Wm. B. Eerdmans, 2001.
Thangaraj, M. Thomas. *The Crucified Guru: An Experiment in Cross-Cultural Christology.* Nashville, TN: Abingdon, 1994.
Thomas, M. M. *The Acknowledged Christ of the Indian Renaissance.* London: SCM, 1969.
Webster, John C. B. *A History of the Dalit Christians in India.* San Francisco: Mellen Research University Press, 1992.

ARUN W. JONES

INDIVIDUALISM

The first religious individuals are the renunciants bred by rejection of the world at the core of every salvation religion, according to MAX WEBER (1946). Renouncing the world represented within the framework of cosmological dualism crystallizes an other-worldly true self in constitutive relationship to God or cosmological equivalents of divinity in nonbiblical traditions such as the Buddhist Dharma. This enables the individual to transcend social membership embodied in kinship and political and economic institutions to live in but not of the world by congregating in distinctly religious communities of worship such as the Jewish synagogue, Christian church, and Buddhist sangha.

The ethos of the Christian Gospel calls for sanctifying the self for God through renouncing everything that disturbs communion with God and exercising everything that binds the self with God's will, as ERNST TROELTSCH (1960:999) summarizes it. It also demands a neighborly love that overcomes in God all the conflict and subordination of human law and social order, while it unites souls in a deep spirit of mutual understanding and self-sacrificing love made in the image of God and proclaimed by Jesus in the message of the KINGDOM OF GOD to come. This is an ideal that requires a new world order to be fully realized. It cannot be realized within this world without compromise, thought Troeltsch, so the history of the Christian ethos and its institutionalization becomes the constantly renewed search for this compromise, and fresh opposition to it.

Ecclesiastical Protestantism collapses the corporatist Catholic hierarchy of an ascent from NATURE to GRACE into the Lutheran ethic of the calling in the world of everyday work and householding God gives each individual. It gives rise to the activist sharpening of Christian calling in the this-worldly ASCETICISM of a Calvinist "Protestant Ethic" to order the holy community rationally and restore it within the life of the world. Ascetic Protestantism draws Christian sects away from radical opposition to the world in their efforts to live out the ideal of the Sermon on the Mount, and it resists the ANTINOMIANISM of modern mysticism in its celebration of individuals as free spirits in a purely inward communion with God and one another.

A peculiarly Protestant individualism stems from this soteriological shift away from a hierarchical structuring of both this world and the next. It revises cosmological dualism by bringing the two worlds into more direct confrontation through making SALVATION more immediate and open to all persons, less mediated by SACRAMENTS, special ascetic and devotional practices, and priestly or monastic roles. Protestant reformers reemphasize the radical separation between divine and human. Yet they proclaim the world as the theater of God's glory and will, in which selves justified by FAITH instead of specifically salvific acts serve God in every walk of life. Conceiving the capacity of faith as a gift already received from God unifies human identity within individuals in relation to God and encourages their autonomous action in the world to do God's will. It also makes it necessary, notes Robert Bellah (1970:37), to "accept the ambiguity of human ethical life and the fact that salvation comes in spite of sin, not in its absolute absence." More autonomous selves more engaged in the world to work out their salvation nonetheless rely on strict doctrinal ORTHODOXY, ethical rigorism, and tightly binding though voluntaristic religious groups to sustain their identity as faithful Protestants. By replacing clergy–laity distinctions between two levels of religious perfection with the division between elect and reprobates, Calvinist Anglo-Protestantism in particular helps fuel the historic movement from hereditary kingship and feudal aristocracy to more democratic forms of self-revising, self-governing political order. These are based on more contractual and voluntary modes of association among persons seen as individuals in their roles as both citizens and church members within a PRIESTHOOD OF ALL BELIEVERS. Because it so centrally shaped the moral character and convictions of Americans as democratic citizens, Alexis de Tocqueville concluded that religion should be considered as "the first of their political institutions." He also defined the danger of an individualism cut loose from its religious moorings, with all persons free to find their beliefs within themselves and to turn their feelings in on themselves. Once democracy breaks the hierarchical chain of reciprocal duties and virtues forged by traditionally fixed social stations and frees each link as an equal, then "Each man is forever thrown back on himself alone, and there is danger that he may be shut up in the solitude of his own heart" (1966:292, 506–508).

At its best, modern religious individualism draws from Protestant THEOLOGY since FRIEDRICH SCHLEIERMACHER an emphasis on the need for all doctrinal beliefs to receive personal reinterpretation, and all religious liberties to lead to both deeper self-understanding and greater social responsibility for the shared fate of humankind. The search for personal meaning and social relevance at the heart of the modern quest for salvation after HEAVEN, especially among the more educated, has led spiritual seekers to explore forms of ritual practice, artistic expression, therapeutic care, and social action well beyond the boundaries of traditional religious institutions. More open and flexible patterns of membership have in turn made for more permeable boundaries and fluid types of organization in most of the major Protestant denominations, and spurred conflicts within them over orthodox belief and faithful discipleship as well as church growth and decline across generations.

Recent works of moral and social inquiry in America probe the dangers of a this-worldly individualism severed from constitutive relationship to God and self-centered in utilitarian or expressive cultural terms. From this standpoint comes radical reconstrual of JAMES MADISON's deist remonstrance (see DEISM), for example, that the sovereignty of individual conscience and conviction requires free exercise of religion precisely to honor its divine Creator and the lawful order of nature and nature's God because "It is the duty of every man to render to the Creator such homage and such only as he believes to be acceptable to him" (1971:299). Freedom of conscience to worship God and follow reason comes to be contested and recast as freedom of choice to pursue one's own interests and express one's own feelings.

Modern forms of utilitarian and expressive individualism, respectively attuned to the institutional arrangement of economic and bureaucratic life today and to lifestyle leisure, have long coexisted with religious and civic ideals of the dignity, indeed the sacredness, of the individual, defined by moral duties, virtues, and practical relationships within the traditions of biblical religion and classical republicanism in American CULTURE. The question posed by *Habits of the Heart* (1985:143, 243) and related cultural critics is whether an individualism centered on the self as a nexus of interests and feelings, and counted as a client-citizen of the welfare state, can actually sustain a public *or* a private life coherently. If not, they ask, can civic and religious forms of individualism be critically reworked through communities of shared moral practice and argument? Can we rebalance the moral ecology of private life and public institutions by renewing genuine individuality in relation to a larger social whole and cultural conversation? This challenge invites the Protestant denominations to pursue their own ongoing reformation in ways that balance the religious individualism inherited from Christian sects as ingathered elects composed of come-outers, and illuminated by the inward communion of modern mystics and spiritual seekers, with the social realism of the church as the Pauline Body of Christ, the fundamental sacrament that precedes and nurtures every faithful individual in redemptive relationship to God.

See also Calvinism; Denomination; Lutheranism; Sectarianism; Secularization

References and Further Reading

Bellah, Robert N. "Religious Evolution." In *Beyond Belief.* New York: Harper & Row, 1970.
———, Richard Madsen, William M. Sullivan, Ann Swidler, and Steven M. Tipton. *Habits of the Heart.* Berkeley: University of California Press, 1985.
Dumont, Louis. "A Modified View of Our Origins: The Christian Beginnings of Modern Individualism." *Religion* 12 (1982):1–27.
Madison, James. "Memorial and Remonstrance." [1785] In *The Papers of James Madison.* Edited by William T. Hutchinson and William M. E. Rachal, vol. 7, 298–304. Chicago: University of Chicago Press, 1971.
Tocqueville, Alexis de. *Democracy in America.* [1835]. Translated by George Lawrence. New York: Harper & Row, 1966.

Troeltsch, Ernst, *The Social Teaching of the Christian Churches.* [1911]. Translated by Olive Wyon. New York: Harper & Row, 1960.

Weber, Max. "Religious Rejections of the World and Their Directions." [1915]. In *From Max Weber,* edited by Hans H. Gerth and C. Wright Mills. New York: Oxford University Press, 1946.

———. *The Protestant Ethic and the Spirit of Capitalism.* [1904–1905]. Translated by Talcott Parsons. New York: Scribners, 1958.

STEVEN M. TIPTON

INDONESIA

History and Politics

Indonesia consists of five main islands and a number of island groups, totaling 800,000 square miles, in southeast Asia. The population of approximately 220 million is unevenly distributed between Western Indonesia, which includes Sumatra, Java, and Bali (85 percent), and the rest of the country. There are about 300 ethnic groups, with about 250 different languages. The Malay language, originally spoken by the coastal people of East Sumatra and Malaya who embraced Islam in an early stage and subsequently *lingua franca* in the whole Archipelago, has been adopted and developed as the official language of Indonesia. There are five religions recognized by the State: Islam, Protestant and Catholic Christianity, Hinduism, and Buddhism, constituting 87 percent, 7 percent, 3 percent, 2 percent, and less than 1 percent, respectively, of the population. Especially in Java, mystical groups (*kebatinan*) rooted in traditional Javanese CULTURE, are influential.

Hinduism and Buddhism came from INDIA in the first centuries B.C. and flourished in a number of kingdoms on Java and Sumatra, producing monuments such as Borobudur and Prambanan. Contacts with CHINA were much more transitory. Islam entered Indonesia about 1300 A.D. from the north and spread to most islands in a gradual process continuing until today. Only Bali and Southeast Indonesia including Irian, and the interior of Sumatra, Kalimantan, and Sulawesi remained outside the sphere of Islam.

While this process was under way, Europeans, opening a direct route to the famous Spice Islands, found their way to Indonesia. In 1511 came the Catholic Portuguese. The Protestant Dutch arrived in 1596 and pushed their Portuguese rivals out of the Archipel. In the next three centuries the whole of Indonesia gradually came under Dutch rule, not without fierce resistance in many regions. In 1942 the country was occupied by the Japanese. After the capitulation of JAPAN independence was proclaimed (August 17, 1945).

The Republic of Indonesia is founded on the *Pancasila,* the Five Principles, which include the belief in God, humanity, national unity, consultative democracy, and social justice. So the Republic claims to be neither a Muslim state nor a secular state. Western INDIVIDUALISM was rejected as well as Marxism. However, the Pancasila state was threatened from two sides. Communists tried to conquer the state, first through an armed insurgency, then through political mass organizations. After a coup in 1965 the Army took over and eliminated COMMUNISM both politically and physically, establishing the military dictatorship of General Soeharto (1967–1998), which claimed to be founded on the Pancasila. On the other side, extreme Muslims attempted to establish a Muslim state in West Java and South Sulawesi, and the Muslim political parties tried to strengthen the influence of Islam in a legal way. In the 1955 elections these parties got 45 percent of the vote. In the first free elections after the downfall of Soeharto (1999), after two decades of intensive Islamization, their share of the vote was still the same.

Until the 1980s, Christians occupied important posts in the successive cabinets, in the bureaucracy and in the armed forces. The Muslims, however, were making up for their disadvantage in the fields of education, economics, and politics, the effects making themselves felt in the 1990s.

Protestant Christianity

Possibly from the seventh century onward, Christian merchants from Persia and India came to Indonesia, but they left only very faint traces. In the sixteenth and seventeenth century, the Portuguese and Spanish brought Roman Catholicism to the Eastern part of the Indonesian archipelago. This effort was hampered by the subordination of the mission to trade interests. After the Dutch took over, Catholic populations were Protestantized. Only in East Timor and Flores could the Portuguese maintain themselves and their religion.

The Dutch East India Company (VOC, 1602–1799) forbade Roman Catholicism in its territories. Missionary activities were restricted to regions where they served its interests, that is, mainly to Eastern Indonesia. Even there, they were concentrated mainly in areas that were vital to the VOC, like Ambon and the surrounding islands. Even though Java was the Company's power base, there was never a mission among the Muslim Javanese and Sundanese inhabiting the island. The church could do little to improve this situation because it depended completely on the Company for the transport and salaries of its personnel. This dependency also prevented it from becoming an indigenous church. The New Testament was available

945

in Malay in 1668, the complete BIBLE only in 1733. The Church was led by Dutch ministers. Indonesians could only serve as unordained teacher-preachers without AUTHORITY to administer the SACRAMENTS. Church life had to conform entirely to patterns prevailing in the NETHERLANDS. In some centers Indonesians could be appointed members of the church council. At the end of the eighteenth century there were 55,000 Protestant Christians and a smaller number of Roman Catholics.

In 1799 the Dutch State took over all assets of the bankrupt VOC. Freedom of religion was proclaimed. As a consequence Catholic priests could again enter the country (1808). The existing Protestant congregations were organized into the Protestant Church in the Netherlands Indies. This church had no mission work of its own because it was financed by the state, which professed to be neutral in religious matters. However, the way was now open to missionaries from the newly formed Protestant missionary bodies (see MISSIONARY ORGANIZATIONS). Between 1811 and 1850, a number of British and American Missionaries worked in Java, Sumatra, and West Kalimantan. In the same decades the Dutch Protestant MISSIONS reached out to the neglected Christians in the outer regions, such as North Sulawesi in the Sangir archipelago, which had never been served by resident ministers or Protestant missionaries. At the same time, by the efforts of a number of lay people, Europeans and Eurasians, the Christian faith first put roots among the Javanese.

In the meantime, as a result of theological conflicts, in Holland a number of new missionary bodies came into being. These started work in New Guinea (Irian, 1855), North Sumatra (1857), the North Moluccas (Halmahera, 1866), Central Sulawesi (1892), and South Sulawesi (1852/1913/1930). Southern Central Java and Sumba became the mission field of the Calvinist Gereformeerde Kerken. In 1836 the German Rheinische Mission (RMG) started mission work among the Dayak in South Borneo, and in 1861 the first RMG missionaries arrived in North Sumatra. After World War I the BASEL MISSION took over work in Kalimantan from the RMG. These missions stressed the use of tribal languages instead of Malay, and (especially after 1890) endeavored to conserve indigenous culture and social structures, to the point of incorporating them into the incipient church. In the twentieth century several Anglo-Saxon missions entered the Netherlands Indies: SALVATION ARMY (1894), SEVENTH-DAY ADVENTISTS (1900), CHRISTIAN AND MISSIONARY ALLIANCE (1930). The Pentecostal movement was brought in from Europe and America about 1920 and first took root among Eurasians (see PENTECOSTALISM). Usually these missions refused to cooperate with the existing missions and churches, and founded churches of their own. In the same period the Protestant Church started missionary work in the South Moluccas and Timor. For these Anglo-Saxon mission bodies and for the Protestant Church, Malay was the vehicle of their mission work; they were not interested in conserving indigenous language and culture.

Among the Protestant pioneers and church founders were Joseph Kam (Ambon 1815–1833), the landowner C. L. Coolen (East Java 1827–1873), L. I. Nommensen (North Sumatra 1862–1918), A. C. Kruyt (Central Sulawesi 1892–1932), and R. A. Jaffray (South Sulawesi 1930–1945).

In colonial times missionary work was accompanied by the conviction that Western civilization and Western models of Christianity, and even Western humans, were superior. As a consequence, the congregations were kept under close supervision and church independence was postponed until a long nurturing process would have resulted in sufficient Christian maturity. Throughout the nineteenth century no Indonesians were ordained minister or priest except by the RMG in North Sumatra (first 1885). In the Protestant missions, and even more so in the Protestant Church, a functional hierarchy existed in which invariably Europeans held the top positions. Almost without exception Indonesian mission personnel worked as local teacher-preachers, with only a basic education. They served as the (essential) link between the "white" church government and the indigenous church members.

This is not to say that Indonesians did just receive the Gospel in a passive way. Those who became Christians did so by their own will, consciously, and for their own reasons, which mostly were not those expected and often assumed by the missionaries. Moreover in all mission fields Indonesians played a decisive role in bringing their fellow-countrymen to the faith. Especially in the first stage of church founding, these native preachers often had no formal tie with the mission. In North Sumatra there were the Batak chief Pontas Lumbantobing (ca. 1830–1900) and Solomon Pakianathan (1881–1961, Methodist); in Java, Paulus Tosari (1813–1882), Tunggul Wulung (ca. 1803–1885), and Sadrach (1840–1924).

In the twentieth century things gradually changed. Between 1878 and 1886 theological seminaries had been founded in North Sumatra, Java, North Sulawesi, and Ambon. In 1934 a theological academy was established in Jakarta. A number of Indonesians were ordained and some of these worked on an equal footing with Europeans. A number of churches in North Sumatra, Java, North Sulawesi, and the Moluccas became independent. The Dutch HENDRICK KRAEMER (1922–1936 in Indonesia) was instrumental in bringing about this development. However, European influence remained very strong even in the independent churches, the general idea being that character, moral soundness, and organizational abilities of the Indonesian Christians still had to be brought up to European levels. In the meantime the number of Christians grew steadily; in 1941 there were about 1.7 million Protestants and 600,000 Catholics in a population of 60 million.

In 1942 Indonesia was occupied by Japan. In the confusion of the transition period there were bouts of persecution by fanatical Muslims in some areas. By the Japanese, Christianity was tolerated and to a certain point protected, even if among the Dutch-oriented Ambonese scores of congregation leaders were killed. However, the Japanese tried consistently to make the churches into channels for their war propaganda and confiscated almost all mission schools and hospitals. The churches were forced to join regional councils of churches (*Kiristokyo Rengokai*), which included mainline Protestants, Catholics, and other Protestant groups. Japanese CLERGY were sent to Indonesia and, within the narrow margins allowed them, succeeded in providing protection and practical assistance to the churches.

Because nearly all foreign missionaries were interned, the war proved that Indonesian Christianity was able to govern itself. Moreover the declaration of national independence in 1945 caused a quick progress in church independence. Most Protestant churches that had not been independent before the war became so between 1946 and 1949. After the war of independence theological education grew quantitatively and qualitatively. Christian universities sprang up in Pematangsiantar, Jakarta, Salatiga, and elsewhere. During the next decades leading Indonesian theologians were J. L. Ch. Abineno, P. D. Latuihamallo, and S. A. E. Nababan. The laymen T. S. G. Mulia and T. B. Simatupang were instrumental in founding and leading the Indonesian Council of Churches. In politics J. Leimena and A. M. Tambunan can be mentioned. The status of the missionaries changed from that of guardians to fraternal workers. The school system founded by the missions before 1942 could in part be maintained; the Protestant daily *Sinar Harapan* became one of the leading newspapers in the country; the Badan Penerbit Kristen was the leading Protestant publishing house.

After World War II the growth of the church accelerated, especially in tribal societies, but, in the aftermath of the 1965 coup d'état, also in Muslim Java. In 1952 the SOUTHERN BAPTIST CONVENTION sent to Indonesia a number of its missionaries expelled from China (1952). At the same time an evangelical movement emerged (see EVANGELICALISM), stimulated from GERMANY and America. Leading figures were

Petrus Octavianus and Chris Marantika. In Batu (Malang, East Java) the Indonesian Missionary Fellowship (IMF) founded the influential Indonesian Bible Institute (1959). The movement spread among the traditional churches, where it often was a divisive element. As a result it gave birth to a number of new churches and Christian organizations.

The percentage of Christians (including Roman Catholics) is highest in thinly populated Eastern Indonesia, especially in the provinces of Irian (85 percent), NTT (75 percent), and North Sulawesi (55 percent). Between 25 and 50 percent is Christian in the Moluccas, North Sumatra, and West Kalimantan; 10 to 25 percent in Central Sulawesi, Central and East Kalimantan, and in the capital city of Jakarta; 5 to 10 percent in the Autonomous Region of Yogyakarta (Central Java) and South Sulawesi; 3 to 5 percent in Central and East Java and Southeast Sulawesi; 1 to 3 percent in Sumatra outside North Sumatra and South Kalimantan; under 1 percent in West Java, Bali, and West Nusatenggara. Of the total of Christians more than 25 percent are living in Java (mostly ethnic Javanese), more than 20 percent in North Sumatra (mostly Batak), less than 10 percent in Kalimantan (mostly Dayak), more than 10 percent in Sulawesi (mostly Minahasans and Torajans), and 30 percent in the rest of Eastern Indonesia.

Present Situation

Originally Christianity was planted by the Dutch Reformed Church. The RMG, which had a mixed Reformed-Lutheran background, brought a Lutheran strain to North Sumatra; the Dutch MENNONITES founded churches in Central Java and the Methodists in Sumatra (see METHODISM). In 1950, churches of these denominations founded the Council of Churches in Indonesia [*Dewan* (since 1984: *Persekutuan*) *Gereja-Gereja di Indonesia*, DGI/PGI]; in 2003 the PGI includes 80 affiliated churches totaling about 13.5 million members, of whom more than 3.5 million are in the BATAK PROTESTANT CHRISTIAN CHURCH, the largest Protestant Church in Southeast Asia.

The Indonesian BAPTISTS (about 150,000 baptized members) are in part affiliated with the Indonesian Baptist Alliance (*Gabungan Gereja Baptis Indonesia*, GGBI). Most churches issuing from Christian and Missionary Alliance (C&MA) mission work have united in the Gereja Kemah Injil Indonesia, whose six member churches total about 500,000 members, more than half of which are in Irian Jaya. In 1979 the Indonesian Pentecostal Council (*Dewan Pentakosta Indonesia*, DPI) was founded. Tentatively the combined membership of the DPI member churches can be put at 1.5–2 million, of whom relatively many are of Chinese descent. Adventists (numbering about 200,000) and a number of independent bodies do not belong to any national church council. It should be noted that the lines between the denominations are not rigid. Among the PGI members now are churches of Baptist, C&MA, and pentecostal stock. The Indonesian Evangelical Fellowship (*Persekutuan Injili Indonesia,* PII), founded in 1971 by churches and organizations sprung from the evangelical movement, also counts many C&MA and pentecostal churches among its members. In 2003 according to a conservative estimate, the total membership of the Protestant churches in Indonesia is 16 million (Catholics 6 million). The extreme fragmentation of Indonesian Protestantism (about 500 church bodies) must be attributed, apart from the vastness of the country and its ethnic variety, to the multitude of Western denominations that have felt compelled to enter the country and proclaim their variety of the Gospel.

After 1970 a theological reorientation in DGI/PGI circles and the increasing influence of American evangelicalism caused a growing antithesis between "evangelicals" and "ecumenicals," which makes itself felt in evangelization, literature work, theological education, even if the Indonesian cultural and religious context does not seem to warrant such an American-style antithesis. Relations between Protestants and Catholics, which were strained until the 1960s, have improved. Generally the churches more or less follow Western liturgical, confessional, and theological patterns. In contrast with AFRICA, there are hardly any churches or groups consciously incorporating pre-Christian religious elements into Christian WORSHIP and practice. Also, there are hardly any theologians using Indonesian religious concepts in formulating an Indonesian Christian THEOLOGY. However, on a personal level a magical-mythical vision of reality may strongly influence the way church members perceive and express the faith.

After 1945 Christians earned their legitimate place as members of the nation by participating in the war of independence against the Dutch (1945–1949). Nevertheless their relation to the state is still determined by their minority position. The churches, of whatever denomination, tend to conform to the government policy of the moment. The Council of Churches in Indonesia even made Soekarno's "revolution" a theological issue in the early 1960s and did the same with Soeharto's "development" in the 1970s. In 1984–1985 all churches (in fact all religious organizations) had to insert a formula recognizing the *Pancasila* as sole foundation for the life of the nation into their church order or statutes. For daily matters the churches communicate with the government through the Ministry of Religion (*Departemen Agama*), which has departments for each of the five recognized religions; the minister is always a Muslim.

After the downfall of the Soeharto regime in 1998 the churches were no longer used as they regained their freedom of movement, but then the relation to Islam, always uneasy, became an acute problem. Islam has long considered Christianity the "religion of the Dutch," and Muslim fears that the process of Westernization would bring Christianization in its trail were fueled by the numbers of Muslim youth in Christian schools converting to Christianity in the 1970s and early 1980s. Christians suspect Muslims of striving for an Islamic state and do not appreciate that they have to take a step back now that Muslims are making good their advantage in education, economics, and politics. In a minority situation Christians have problems in getting permission for church building; where they are a majority, the Muslim presence may be felt to be gratuitous. With the exception of converted Muslim theologians, very few Christians have a good knowledge of Islam and dialogue has hardly been practiced (Th. Sumartana). In its closing years the Soeharto regime tried to woo the Muslim majority: pupils in the state schools were no longer allowed to follow religious education according to the religious affiliation of their parents, and mixed marriages were rendered practically impossible; in this way important channels for Christianization were cut off. From 1996 onward Muslim extremist groups were left a free hand in attacking churches if it suited the regime. In 1999 open war broke out between Christians and Muslims in the Moluccas and in Central Sulawesi; here and in the cities of Java hundreds of church buildings as well as several mosques were destroyed. However, Indonesian Islam is not a homogeneous solid mass. Traditional Islam, organized in the Nahdatul-Ulama (NU) under the leadership of Abdur-rahman Wahid (president of the Republic 1999–2002) accepts the Pancasila State and favors religious tolerance, whereas reformist Islam advocates Islamization of the state. Mixed groups like Dian/Interfidei, Institute for Interreligious Dialogue, are trying to build mutual understanding.

See also Asia; Asian Theology; Batak Protestant Christian Church; Dialogue, Interconfessional; Ecumenism; Education

References and Further Reading

Aritonang, Jan S. *Mission Schools in Batakland (Indonesia) 1861–1940.* Leiden/New York/Cologne: Brill, 1994.

Boland, B. J. *The Struggle of Islam in Modern Indonesia.* The Hague, The Netherlands: Nijhoff, 1971.

Boxer, C. R. *The Dutch Seaborne Empire 1600–1800.* London: Hutchinson, 1977.

Cooley, Frank L. *The Growing Seed. The Christian Church in Indonesia.* Jakarta, Indonesia: BPK Gunung Mulia, 1981.

End, Th. van den. *Ragi Carita. Sejarah Gereja-Gereja di Indonesia* (*A History of the Churches in Indonesia*). 2 vols. Jakarta, Indonisia: Badan Penerbit Kristen, I, ^{7}1999, II, ^{3}2000.

———. "Indonesia." In *The Reformed Family Worldwide: A Survey of Reformed Churches, Theological Schools, and International Organizations*, edited by Jean-Jacques Bauswein and Lukas Vischer, 220–270. Grand Rapids, MI: Wm. B. Eerdmans, 1999.

Hoekema, H. A. *Denken in dynamisch evenwicht. De wordings-geschiedenis van de nationale protestantse theologie in Indonesië (ca. 1860–1960)* [*The Genesis of a National Protestant Theology in Indonesia (ca. 1860–1960)*]. Ph.D. Dissertation, Leiden University, 1994 (bibliography).

Latuihamallo, P. D. "State, Religion and Ideologies in Indonesia." In *Religion, State and Ideologies in East Asia*, edited by M. M. Thomas and M. Abel. Madras, India: Christian Literature Society, 1975.

Makoto, Hara. "Christianity in Indonesia under Japanese Military Rule." *Japanese Religions* 22 no. 2 (1997): 97–106.

Sumartana, Th. *Mission at the Crossroads. Indigenous Churches, European Missionaries, Islamic Association and Socio-Religious Change in Java 1812–1936.* Jakarta, Indonesa: BPK, 1993.

Wawer, Wendelin. *Muslime und Christen in der Republik Indonesia.* Wiesbaden, Germany: Steiner-Verlag, 1974.

TH. VAN DEN END

INDUSTRIALIZATION

The Industrial Revolution began in ENGLAND around 1780 with the mechanization of cotton spinning in Lancashire. From there, mechanization spread to other parts of the British textile industry, then to other British industries, then to other parts of the world—with immense economic, social, political, and religious consequences. In the 1830s Belgium and some regions of France WERE experiencing their own Industrial Revolution. GERMANY and the UNITED STATES followed soon after, and by the late nineteenth century southern and eastern Europe and Scandinavia were also industrializing. Since World War II there has been major industrial growth in Asia and LATIN AMERICA, whereas in Europe and North America the period since the 1970s has seen the decline of manufacturing and a large rise of employment in service-related enterprises.

The patterns of change in nineteenth-century Britain have been repeated in numerous countries since. There was a big shift of population from the countryside to cities and industrial regions, leading eventually to rural depopulation, and a sharp drop in the numbers working on the land. Landed wealth declined, whereas industrial and commercial wealth brought political as well as economic power. Cities like Manchester, Birmingham, and Glasgow grew rapidly under the leadership of a new aristocracy of factory owners and merchants. These cities were socially segregated, and

in the crowded and often unhealthy factory districts there was a concentrated working-class population, with its own organizations, including trade unions and political parties. Industrialization also tended to mean increasing religious pluralism. In the nineteenth century Catholic and Jewish immigrants flooded into Protestant cities like London, New York, or Berlin. Since World War II Muslims, Hindus, and Sikhs, as well as Christians of many unfamiliar kinds, responded to the demand for cheap labor, or sometimes the business opportunities, in industrialized Europe and North America. Classical sociology claimed that this great mixing of populations bred a sophisticated relativism. If this has happened, it has been a very long term process. At least in the short run, the mixing of populations of different backgrounds has more often strengthened ethnic and religious identities (see ETHNICITY). In nineteenth-century cities, Catholics and Protestants, Christians, and Jews, were frequently in conflict, sometimes violent. In the later twentieth century the large migration to European cities of Muslims from Turkey, North Africa, and south Asia led to similar tensions, although hostility to Islam was often justified in secularist or racist, rather than Christian, terms.

In the long term, industrialization revolutionized standards of living, lifestyles, and often mentalities. Britain again offers a model of how this happened. Whereas the first generation of industrial entrepreneurs were often devout and relatively austere, their children and grandchildren wanted to live the lives of gentlemen. The later nineteenth century saw many large employers moving out of the cities to country estates and a life increasingly dominated by leisure. Those who had been brought up as Dissenters (see DISSENT) were moving to the CHURCH OF ENGLAND or sometimes to agnosticism. For the mass of the people the benefits of industrial wealth and the possibilities of increasing leisure came more slowly. Not until the later nineteenth century were the better-off sections of the working class beginning to enjoy cycling, going to professional soccer and cricket matches and music halls, and making day trips to the seaside. In the 1920s and 1930s cinema and radio surpassed all older forms of leisure, although only in the 1950s and 1960s did former luxuries, such as televisions, cars, and foreign holidays become a possibility for the mass of the population. A new age of affluence had dawned, and with growing leisure opportunities a mental revolution was completed that had been developing slowly over several decades. One symbol of this revolution was the demise of the set-apart Sunday, which had been gradually eroded since the 1890s, but which survived into the 1960s before collapsing in the face of growing demands for leisure. Partly at stake was individual freedom and the repudiation of any attempt to regulate the moral standards of the community. Partly it was about the rejection of all forms of puritanism and the embrace of hedonistic values. In the relatively impoverished society of the later nineteenth century, churches offering low-cost facilities were major players in the field of leisure; by the later twentieth century commercial interests predominated.

Religion, like every other area of life, felt the effects of these dramatic changes, and in some countries Protestants played a prominent part in helping to bring them about. The following discussion looks at ways in which Protestants may have contributed to the Industrial Revolution, some of its consequences for them, and some of their responses to its consequences.

In looking at the contribution of Protestantism to industrialization, one must inevitably start with the "Weber Thesis." Max Weber's famous essay, *The Protestant Ethic and the Spirit of Capitalism,* first published in 1904–1905, was prompted by figures showing that in southern Germany, where the majority of the population were Catholics, Protestants were more likely than Catholics to be successful in business. He cited evidence that this was also true in other countries, and that these Protestant businessmen were especially numerous in the Calvinist churches and in various smaller denominations, such as METHODISM and The SOCIETY OF FRIENDS (Quakers). He traced this back partly to the Protestant concept of "calling," according to which every "secular" occupation is a vocation, through which one can serve God; partly to the disciplined lifestyle promoted by these religious groups. He linked the latter to their anxiety as to whether they were saved, and the consequent drive to live in a consistent way that would show that the GRACE of God was working through them. The combined effect of these factors was a tendency to sanctify work. This contributed to the early stages of capitalist development both because of the importance of capital accumulation and because of the need to break with "traditional" working habits. Later, when capitalist industry had become well established, religious motivation was no longer necessary, although inherited wealth usually was, so the majority of successful businessmen were descendants of the successful businessmen of earlier generations, whose religion *did* contribute to their success. The Weber Thesis has been endlessly debated, and there is still no consensus. It seems that he is right in identifying a connection between Protestantism, especially in its sectarian forms, and early industrial entrepreneurship, but that he failed to find a fully convincing explanation. In predominantly Catholic states such as France or Bavaria, Protestants were heavily overrepresented among early industrialists. In mainly Protestant countries, such as England, some Nonconformist denominations, such as the Quakers, were also overrepresented (see NONCONFORMITY). Many other religious and ethnic minorities have distinguished themselves in business. However, some specific aspects of eighteenth- and nineteenth-century Protestantism, especially in sectarian forms, may also be relevant, including high levels of literacy, skills acquired through lay office in the congregation, the ascetic lifestyle mentioned by Weber, and the role of nationwide sectarian networks. There is less evidence that Protestantism contributed directly to industrialization in Latin America or KOREA. The massive growth of PENTECOSTALISM since the 1950s has taken place mainly toward the lower end of the social hierarchy among such groups as small farmers, artisans, and service workers. Protestants have tended to improve their situation in a modest way, but most of them have started so low in the occupational hierarchy that major entrepreneurial success has seldom been possible.

The qualities and skills that favored success in business could also equip sectarian Protestants for leading roles in labor organization. In Britain the period from the 1840s to the 1920s saw a strong sectarian, especially Methodist presence in the trade unions, and when the modern Labour Party emerged in the early twentieth century, it was said to "owe more to Methodism than to Marx." This claim has been almost as hotly debated as the Weber Thesis. However oversimplified it may be, though, it contains an important truth, that Dissenting Protestants of all kinds were heavily overrepresented among the early leaders of the modern British working-class movement. This was especially true of the miners, for long the largest occupational group in Britain, and it is appropriate that the most revered figure in British labor history, Keir Hardie, was both a miner and a member of a small Scottish Dissenting sect, the Evangelical Union. Protestants were also prominent in the American labor movement in the nineteenth century. The popular critique of capitalism drew heavily on the BIBLE, and especially the Prophets.

Early industrialization disrupted existing patterns of life, sometimes with devastating consequences. Migrants to new industrial districts were attracted by the hope of higher wages, but they could also face the loss of family support, harsh factory discipline, and frequent periods of unemployment. They might find it difficult to maintain traditional religious observances, whether because of Sunday work or because of a lack of churches and priests. Established churches, whether Catholic or Protestant, were usually slow to adapt to the rapid movements of population, and many of them never entirely recovered from the losses suffered during early industrialization. Sectarian churches, with their flexible organization, often adapted more readily. In many parts of northern England the Methodists took the place of the Church of England as the main form of organized religion in the later eighteenth and early nineteenth centuries. Lay preachers could take the place of ordained ministers, and small unpretentious chapels, or even private houses, could be used for worship. Baptist, Congregational, and Calvinistic Methodist chapels sprang up all along the mining and iron-working valleys of South Wales. In SWEDEN, too, free churches flourished in new industrial settlements, whereas Lutheran congregations dwindled. Something similar happened when Latin American countries, such as BRAZIL and Chile, began to industrialize in the twentieth century. In mining and factory districts many workers turned away from the Catholic Church, which seemed too much linked with TRADITION and old social hierarchies. For some of them Socialism or COMMUNISM became a secular faith, although others found their SALVATION in pentecostalism. Since the 1960s one of the areas of fastest economic growth in the world has been East Asia. Here too, most notably in South Korea, rapid social change and the consequent weakening of traditional social structures and religious patterns have been conducive to the growth of Protestantism. By 1980 it was estimated that 20 percent of the South Korean population were Protestants, including not only members of the long-established Presbyterian (see PRESBYTERIANISM) and Methodist churches, but also the newer pentecostals.

By no means did all Protestants welcome the growth of mechanized industry. In Europe the CLERGY of the established churches were often rooted in the countryside and accustomed to a regime of rural paternalism. They were especially critical of Sunday labor, although they often presented a more generalized critique of the relentless pursuit of profit and the neglect of the workforce by early factory owners. Political or religious differences might play a role here. For instance, Conservative clergy were especially alert to the failings of Liberal factory owners. However, these early doubts often changed to more favorable evaluations—both in Europe, and especially in the United States. In the "Gilded Age," after the Union victory in the CIVIL WAR, many American preachers presented industrialists in a heroic light. Business success was seen as the logical consequence of faith in God and the practice of Protestant virtues. The famous Brooklyn preacher HENRY WARD BEECHER contrasted Europe and its hereditary elites and massive social inequalities with the free American Republic, and declared that "The general truth will stand that no man in this land suffers from poverty unless it be more than his fault—unless it be his *sin*."

In the early and mid-Victorian years similar ideas were also common in Britain. The years around 1850 saw the emergence of a new breed of industrial paternalists—men who had survived the stormy years of the early 1840s when many of their rivals had suffered shipwreck, and who now felt secure enough to offer a capitalism with a human face. Many of them had close connections with a church, whether Anglican or Dissenting. Some of their wealth was poured into building churches and paying the minister's salary, and the ministers were naturally grateful. The paternalism of these years tended to be two-edged: the churches, schools, houses with gardens, and sports fields went hand in hand with firm discipline and sometimes with the absence of what were seen as less desirable facilities such as pubs. Both in Britain and in the United States successful businessmen rose to positions of prominence within many Protestant denominations. Their business skills were valued, and their gifts of money were essential for the success of many denominational projects. A typical figure was Sir Robert Perks, the railway magnate and Liberal MP, who was one of the most powerful figures in British Methodism at the start of the twentieth century.

By this time, the influence of the "Christian businessman" was beginning to decline, as family firms were being absorbed into large corporations, run by professional managers. In the twentieth century the lay leaders of the British churches were increasingly drawn from the professions, rather than business. Meanwhile, many Protestant preachers had become less sure of the benefits of industrial capitalism. The Christian Socialists, with their schemes for worker cooperatives, appeared in England as early as 1848, although the movement was short-lived (see SOCIALISM, CHRISTIAN). By the 1880s and 1890s unease was much more widespread. Christian Socialism had revived in Britain. The SOCIAL GOSPEL had emerged in the United States. In Germany, the Evangelical Social Congress, founded in 1890, acted as a focal point for a diverse band of Protestant critics of the existing social order, ranging from the Liberal Max Weber to the Social Democrat Paul Göhre to the anti-Semite Adolf Stoecker (see ANTI-SEMITISM). What all had in common was a recognition of the dangers inherent in the unfettered power of many great industrialists and of the need for the state to take a more active role in improving working-class living and working conditions.

These debates continue to the present day. In 1983 the main churches in AUSTRALIA published a report, *Changing Australia,* that criticized current trends toward privatization and deregulation, and that, although less specific about the alternatives, favored a more socialist approach. The Church of England's famous report of 1985, *Faith in the City,* focusing especially on the needs of impoverished "Urban Priority Areas," reached similar conclusions and provoked a furious counterattack by ministers of the free-market Thatcher government, who accused it of "Marxism." Meanwhile the "Prosperity Gospel" preached by many of the pentecostal churches both in the United States and in AFRICA returned to the mid-Victorian view according to which poverty is a SIN and the successful businessman is to be regarded as a model Christian. Indeed, according to this Gospel, economic success is the inevitable result of faithful adherence to biblical principles.

References and Further Reading

Gutman, Herbert. *Work, Culture and Society in Industrializing America.* New York: Vintage Books, 1977.

Jeremy, David. *Christians and Capitalists.* Oxford, UK: Clarendon Press, 1990.

Lehmann, Hartmut, and Guenther Roth, eds. *Weber's Protestant Ethic: Origins, Evidence, Contexts.* Cambridge: Cambridge University Press, 1993.

May, Henry F. *The Protestant Churches and Industrial America.* New York: Harper and Brothers, 1949.

McLeod, Hugh, ed. *European Religion in the Age of Great Cities 1830–1930.* London: Routledge, 1994.

Moore, Robert. *Pit-men, Preachers and Politics.* Cambridge: Cambridge University Press, 1974.

Roberts, Richard H., ed. *Religion and the Transformations of Capitalism: Comparative Approaches.* London: Routledge, 1995.

Rostow, W. W. *The World Economy.* London: Palgrave Macmillan, 1978.

Smith, Mark. *Religion in Industrial Society: Oldham and Saddleworth 1740–1865.* Oxford, UK: Clarendon Press, 1994.

HUGH MCLEOD

INFANT BAPTISM

See Baptism

INSTITUTES OF THE CHRISTIAN RELIGION

The Institutes of the Christian Religion is the classic sixteenth-century exposition of Reformed theology. JOHN CALVIN (1509–1564) built on the work of such REFORMATION pioneers as HULDRYCH ZWINGLI and MARTIN LUTHER, whose work was often topical and polemical. Calvin had a systematic cast of mind, and his *Institutes* presented the theological insights of the Reformation as an organized whole. The work was first published in 1536. The author revised and expanded it until 1559.

Early Editions

The *Institutes* was Calvin's first major theological work. The Latin 1536 edition was essentially an introduction to, and a defense of, the Protestant faith. Its heart was an exposition of traditional catechetical texts: The first three chapters explained the Ten Commandments, the Apostles' Creed, and the Lord's Prayer. The next two sections treated the controversial topic of the sacraments: The fourth chapter dealt with Baptism and the Lord's Supper, the two sacraments Protestants affirmed; the fifth chapter demoted the five remaining Roman Catholic sacraments. The sixth and final chapter dealt with the outworking of the Protestant faith in life, under the headings of Christian freedom, ecclesiastical power, and civil government.

The purpose of the work shifted with Calvin's first revision in 1539: rather than an initial instruction in the faith, it was now presented as a theological textbook. He expressed the intention of writing biblical commentaries, and instructed that the two parts of his work should be read together. The Institutes would present summaries of biblical teachings, allowing him to avoid digression in his commentaries. The number of chapters was expanded to seventeen, and the discussion was amplified by scriptural, Patristic, classical, and contemporary references. Substantial new material was added on such themes as the knowledge of God and the knowledge of humanity, repentance, JUSTIFICATION, the similarities and differences between the Testaments, PREDESTINATION, providence, and the Christian life. In 1543 a third edition with twenty-one chapters was published.

Later Editions

Calvin declared himself satisfied with the restructured edition of 1559, with its eighty chapters divided into four books. This included much new material, especially engagement with his theological opponents.

The first book treats "The Knowledge of God the Creator." This includes discussion of the sin that prevents one from knowing God through creation, our consequent need for the BIBLE to find knowledge of God, the danger of idolatry, the Triune nature of God, the image of God in humanity, and God's providential care for creation.

The second book is on "The Knowledge of God the Redeemer in Christ, First Disclosed to the Fathers Under the Law, and Then to Us in the Gospel." Here he includes discussion of sin and its consequent damage to human free will, the COVENANT of God with humanity in the Old and New Testaments, the person of Christ, and the work of Christ.

Although the second book is specifically on the knowledge of the Redeemer, the third and fourth books considered implications of this knowledge. The third book is "The Way in Which We Receive the Grace of Christ: What Benefits Come to Us from It, and What Effects Follow." This includes the working of the Holy Spirit, the Christian life, justification, PRAYER, and the doctrine of election.

The fourth book is "The External Means or Aids by Which God Invites Us Into the Society of Christ and Holds Us Therein." The focus of this book is primarily the Church in its polity, its powers, its discipline, and its sacraments. He concludes with a chapter on civil government.

Other Latin editions with minor changes were published in 1545, 1550, 1553, and 1554. Translations came quickly, putting the *Institutes* into the hands of the less learned public. In 1541 Calvin published his own translation of the work into French. Further French translations followed the expansion of the Latin text, in 1545 and 1560. Sixteenth-century editions were published in Spanish, Italian, Dutch, German, and English. In the seventeenth century Czech, Hungarian, and possibly Arabic translations were published.

Place in Protestant Belief

There have long been more opinions on Calvin's *Institutes* than readers of it. In theological education it has not always been prominent, even among Reformed Christians. It was early displaced in America by the work of FRANCIS TURRETINI. In the nineteenth and early twentieth century discussion of Calvin's *Institutes* was present in the Princeton Theology and MERCERSBURG THEOLOGY. KARL BARTH and EMIL BRUNNER both drew on Calvin's *Institutes* in their dispute over natural theology. By the late twentieth century the book was again used in introductory theology courses in some seminaries. The *Institutes* remains a subject of significant scholarly work, and its voice is still heard in many theological discussions.

Many nonreaders of Calvin believe that his text is dominated by the doctrine of double predestination. Scholars are aware that the doctrine of the knowledge of God shapes the work more prominently, that he presents predestination as a biblical teaching that provides assurance to troubled believers, and that methodologically his driving concern was to discern and present the clear, consistent teaching of the Bible as a whole.

See also Barth, Karl; Bible; Brunner, Emil; Calvin, John; Covenant; Justification; Luther, Martin; Mer-

cersburg Theology; Prayer; Predestination; Reformation; Turretini, Francis; Zwingli, Huldrych

References for Further Reading

Primary Sources:

Calvin, John. *Calvin: Institutes of the Christian Religion* [*1559*]. The Library of Christian Classics, vols. XX–XXI. Edited by John T. McNeill, translated by Ford Lewis Battles. Philadelphia: Westminster Press, 1960.
———. *Institutes of the Christian Religion, 1536 Edition*. Translated by Ford Lewis Battles. Rev. ed. Grand Rapids, MI: The H. H. Meeter Center for Calvin Studies, and William B. Eerdmans, 1986.

Secondary Sources:

Dowey, Edward A., Jr. *The Knowledge of God in Calvin's Theology*. Expanded Ed. Grand Rapids, MI: William B. Eerdmans, 1994.
Ganoczy, Alexandre. *The Young Calvin*. Translated by David Foxgrover and Wade Provo. Philadelphia: Westminster Press, 1987.
Niesel, Wilhelm. *The Theology of Calvin*. Translated by Harold Knight. Philadelphia: Westminster Press, 1956.
Wendel, François. *Calvin: Origins and Development of His Religious Thought*. Translated by Philip Mairet. New York: Harper and Row, 1963. Reprint, Grand Rapids, MI: Baker Book House, 1997.

GARY NEAL HANSEN

INTERCHURCH WORLD MOVEMENT

The Interchurch World Movement of North America (IWM) was a grandiose but short-lived (1919–1921) attempt by mainline Protestant missionary leaders to create a unified and aggressive interdenominational missionary agency. It hoped to mobilize all of Protestant America in rebuilding the postwar world according to "Christian" social principles. Despite the prominence and ebullience of its organizers, the IWM collapsed in surprising fashion due to financial indebtedness and declining support.

History

Organized in February 1919, the IWM adopted the motto "the giving of the whole gospel to the whole world by the whole church." In fact, it represented about 30 American Protestant denominations and perhaps 25 percent of all Americans. Still, it saw itself as the "unofficial" American religious establishment, strategically allying top Protestant, business, and governmental leaders in "Christianizing" the globe.

A media-driven national fundraising campaign was launched in spring 1920, seeking $176 million for denominational agencies and $40 million for the IWM, which was to come from "friendly citizens," identified as unchurched industrial and financial philanthropists with Protestant sympathies. John D. Rockefeller, Jr., a member of the IWM Executive Committee, pledged $5 million to get the campaign off the ground. A building was rented in New York City for a staff of more than 2,600 employees.

The Collapse and the Steel Strike Report

Initial public enthusiasm and national media attention could not keep the IWM from facing financial failure in summer 1920 and disbanding in April 1921. Although denominational giving went well, pledges from the "friendly citizens"—which the IWM needed to cover its own operational expenses—did not. By the summer of 1920, the IWM leaders faced an $8 million debt and public embarrassment.

Growing postwar isolationism played a role in the IWM's collapse, but vague objectives and reckless financing were probably more fatal factors. A contributing factor may have been conservative distrust of social liberalism within the IWM. In October 1919, the IWM Department of Industrial Relations launched a detailed investigation of the U.S. Steel strike (1919–1920) and labor conditions in the steel industry. Its report, written by Methodist Bishop and SOCIAL GOSPEL advocate Francis J. McConnell, documented unjust working conditions and unfair labor practices, including company use of *agents provocateur* during the strike. The IWM deliberately postponed approving and publishing the controversial report until after the financial campaign, but the investigation itself likely caused potential donors fearful of postwar radicalism to withhold support.

These events revealed the fissures existing in modern American Protestant life and the increasing secularity and pluralism of society. They left the Federal Council of Churches, formed in 1908, as the leading agency of Protestant cooperative efforts in America.

See also Church World Service; Cultural Protestantism; Gladden, Washington; Liberal Protestantism and Liberalism; Missions; Missionary Organizations; Mott, John Raleigh; National Council of Churches; Rauschenbusch, Walter

References and Further Reading

Ernst, Eldon. *Moment of Truth for Protestant America: Interchurch Campaigns Following World War I*. Missoula, MT: Scholars Press, 1974.

Interchurch World Movement. *Report of the Steel Strike of 1919*. New York: Harcourt, Brace and Howe, 1920.

WILLIAM M. KING

INTERNATIONAL CHURCH OF THE FOURSQUARE GOSPEL

This Pentecostal denomination was established by AIMEE SEMPLE MCPHERSON and incorporated in Los Angeles in 1927. Its headquarters church, Angelus Temple, opened as the centerpiece of McPherson's scheme for interdenominational worldwide evangelism on January 1, 1923, and the denomination commemorates this date as its anniversary.

A Canadian Salvationist, McPherson's first husband, Robert Semple, was an Irish immigrant who had recently embraced PENTECOSTALISM. Members of this religious movement thought that the end of the world was imminent. Its members prayed for an experience they called the baptism with the Holy Spirit and believed that this baptism would be manifested by speech in unknown Tongues (see TONGUES, SPEAKING IN). They expected tongues and other New Testament spiritual gifts (I Corinthians 12 and 14) to be part of their corporate worship, and they set out to announce to the world a message that had three primary components: (1) the imminent return of Christ; (2) the urgency of global EVANGELISM; and (3) the presence of Christ to do in the end times what he had done in New Testament days—especially heal the sick, meet every need, empower for service and bestow the Holy Spirit.

These convictions animated the Semples' choice to become missionaries, and in 1910 they left for Hong Kong. Widowed soon after their arrival, Aimee returned to the United States later that year. After a second marriage (to Harold McPherson) in 1912 she again began evangelizing in 1915, traveling up and down the east coast in ever larger tents to accommodate her growing public. In 1918 she moved to Los Angeles, without her husband from whom she had separated amicably. She traveled from there in evangelistic endeavors that filled huge municipal auditoriums, preaching to an adoring public that seemed to begrudge her nothing.

Her desire to have her own place led to the construction of Angelus Temple as well as to the initiation of a number of related efforts that enlisted partners and built her national constituency. In 1924 a radio tower was built atop the Temple, and McPherson began broadcasting on KFSG—Kall Foursquare Gospel. By then she had launched a Bible training school that came to be known as the Lighthouse of Foursquare Evangelism (LIFE), a children's church some 1,000 strong led by her own children, Roberta and Rolf, and the rudiments of a social program that responded to local disasters and pressing social needs. Angelus Temple became famous as well for McPherson's illustrated sermons, lavish dramatic presentations that routinely packed the house. In sensation-crazed Los Angeles, McPherson was indisputably a sensation. She took her cues from the creativity of the SALVATION ARMY and from her neighbors in nearby Hollywood and manifested unfailing resourcefulness in front of crowds, although her business instincts proved less dependable.

As McPherson's endeavors multiplied, it became necessary to organize and incorporate them. She oversaw the formation of an evangelistic association, which she envisioned as an interdenominational agency intent on spreading the gospel around the world. As her efforts grew she did not allow her early Pentecostal associations to alienate her from others intent on Revival (see REVIVALS) and evangelism.

Until her death in 1944 McPherson—with her son and successor, Rolf—dominated the church's small board of directors (rounded out by Aimee's mother and daughter until their separate nasty departures). Her poor health and the church's complicated financial state in the 1930s curtailed her U.S. outreach beyond Los Angeles. With the coming of World War II, she took to the streets to sell war bonds and appeared more often in her pulpit. When she died in September 1944 her son, Rolf, replaced her as the president of the International Church of the Foursquare Gospel. He served until 1988.

With the passing of its founder the ICFG adopted a polity that diminished family control. The denomination is governed by a president (elected to a four-year term), a board of directors, a Foursquare cabinet, and an executive council. The board of directors frames the philosophy of the corporation. The denomination is divided into nine districts (in 2001 it announced aggressive plans to establish a significant number of new districts), and the cabinet includes the district supervisors and representatives chosen by the ministers of each district. The executive council includes the cabinet and other local superintendents, and determines the agenda for the annual spring denominational business meetings.

The denomination has grown significantly since McPherson's death. It includes over 1,800 congregations in the United States where it numbers nearly 270,000 members. The first Foursquare Church abroad opened in the PHILIPPINES in 1927. Others followed quickly. Worldwide, Foursquare churches claim over 3.5 million attendees and estimate a constituency nearing 5 million. The missionary efforts of the Foursquare Church have been particularly successful in parts of LATIN AMERICA and in the Philippines. From small beginnings, missionary outreach has expanded to include 127 countries and nearly 50,000 pastors, teachers, and other workers. The ICFG holds membership in the NATIONAL ASSOCIATION OF EVANGELICALS.

In general the agencies that McPherson established have remained central to the work of the ICFG. Her Bible school became LIFE Pacific College and moved from its longtime home in Echo Park, Los Angeles to suburban San Dimas. The denomination also operates LIFE Bible College East in Christiansburg, Virginia, and Pacific Life Bible College in Surrey, British Columbia. The inner-city building that McPherson constructed for her first training school is now know as Angelus Bible Institute and serves a Hispanic constituency. Thirteen other certified Bible institutes, schools of ministry, and church-run educational efforts supplement the opportunities for practical ministerial training. The best known of these is undoubtedly King's College and Seminary, the schools founded by the best-known ICFG leader, Jack Hayford, long-time pastor of The Church on the Way in Van Nuys, California, and prolific author, conference speaker, and broadcaster.

References and Further Reading

Blumhofer, Edith L. *Aimee Semple McPherson, Everybody's Sister.* Grand Rapids, MI: Eerdmans Publishing Co., 1994.
Cox, Raymond L. *The Foursquare Gospel.* 1969.

EDITH L. BLUMHOFER

INTERNATIONAL PENTECOSTAL HOLINESS CHURCH

The International Pentecostal Holiness Church (IPHC) is one of several denominations that had their origins in the nineteenth-century WESLEYAN/HOLINESS revival who, although retaining the revival's emphasis on Christian Perfection as a second work of grace subsequent to the believer's JUSTIFICATION, also came to expect a third work of grace, a personal BAPTISM with the Holy Ghost evidenced by speaking in other Tongues.

Two groups of churches born of the holiness revival contributed to its organization. The first was a group of congregations associated with the North Carolina Holiness Association founded in 1897 under the leadership of Abner Blackman Crumpler, a Methodist Episcopal Church South minister. Although his conference acquitted him of charges related to his holiness evangelism brought against him in 1899, Crumpler nevertheless left the Methodists. A year later, at Fayetteville, North Carolina, he held the first convention of what generally were called the Pentecostal Holiness Churches (PHC). From 1901 until 1909 the new denomination was known as the Holiness Church. In 1908 the denomination, influenced by the AZUSA STREET PENTECOSTAL REVIVAL of 1906 through the Pentecostal preaching of Gaston B. Cashwell, officially adopted the belief that the baptism of the Holy Ghost and fire accompanied by speaking in other tongues (see TONGUES, SPEAKING IN) as its initial evidence was promised to every "fully cleansed believer" as the third work of grace subsequent to his or her justification and SANCTIFICATION. The church claims to have been the first body to officially adopt such a statement of faith. Consequently, Crumpler left the denomination. The word "Pentecostal" was restored to the name the following year.

Churches organized through the ministry of holiness evangelist Benjamin H. Irwin constituted the second group. It was the older and larger of the two with its origins in the Iowa holiness association. Irwin's movement, teaching that a "baptism of fire" followed the experience of entire sanctification, quickly attracted a significant following in the Carolinas and Georgia. In 1898 Irwin's converts among ministers from the holiness associations of the area joined him to form a national Fire-Baptized Holiness Association at Anderson, South Carolina in 1898. By 1902, after Irwin had left the movement under suspicions of moral turpitude, the association's churches led by Joseph Hillary King became the Fire-Baptized Holiness Church. In 1911 it joined with the Pentecostal Holiness Church, both groups adopting the latter's name for the new Pentecostal denomination.

The Tabernacle Pentecostal Holiness Churches affiliated with Holmes Bible College in Greenville, South Carolina joined the new denomination in 1915. Three years before the union, the Fire-Baptized Holiness church had released twenty-seven black churches with 925 members to form their own Fire-Baptized convention under W. E. Fuller. Shortly after the merger the few black congregations that remained in the merged body were dropped from the conference rolls. After the 1970s the IPHC established agreements of affiliation with several of the continuing black churches that had their roots in the denomination.

The cardinal doctrines of the church include: justification by FAITH, entire sanctification, the Baptism in the Holy Ghost evidenced by speaking in tongues, divine healing, and the imminent premillennial second coming of Christ. Traditionally the church has considered these beliefs to constitute basic Pentecostalism. Subsequently it consistently resisted any efforts within the newly developing Pentecostal revival that it felt threatened the integrity of its Pentecostal confession and experience. This was most evident in its efforts to refute the "finished work" teaching espoused by some early Pentecostals that led to their rejection of the revival's traditional Wesleyan THEOLOGY and the eventual formation of a theologically more Reformed-oriented ASSEMBLIES OF GOD denomination in 1914. In 1921 a dissident group left the church to organize the Congregational Holiness Church. They opposed the

PHC's strong stand against the use of any human means and medicines in conjunction with its reliance on divine healing.

A quadrennial general conference representative of the regional district conferences of local churches is the denomination's highest governing body, establishing the denomination's doctrines and polity. A superintending bishop elected by the general conference serves as the chief executive officer. The IPHC is a member of the NATIONAL ASSOCIATION OF EVANGELICALS and the Pentecostal and Charismatic Fellowship of North America and was an active participant in their formation. Its educational department supports Advantage College (Sacramento, California), Emmanuel College (Franklin Springs, Georgia), Southwestern Christian University (Oklahoma City, Oklahoma), and affiliates with Holmes Bible College (Greenville, South Carolina). Its North American membership is over 200,000 and historically centered in the American south. Since 1960, through its overseas mission stations in seventy nations, it has developed into a world fellowship with almost two million adherents. The current denominational offices are based in Oklahoma City, Oklahoma.

The church has fostered and shaped many ministries that have significantly influenced evangelical Protestantism. The most prominent of these is the healing and educational ministry of ORAL GANVILLE ROBERTS, the founder of Oral Roberts University. Another prominent member, church historian Vincent Synan, is a leading figure in a movement that has sought to encourage dialog between the traditional Pentecostal denominations and contemporary charismatic PENTECOSTALISM as well as between traditional Pentecostalism and traditional Wesleyan/Holiness groups.

See also Holiness Movement

References and Further Reading

Jones, Charles Edward. *Black Holiness: A Guide to the Study of Black Participation in Wesleyan Perfectionist and Glossolalic Pentecostal Movements.* ATLA Bibliography Series, no. 18. Metuchen, NJ and London: The American Theological Library Association and the Scarecrow Press, 1987.
Synan, Harold Vinson. *The Old-Time Power: A Centennial History of the International Pentecostal Church.* Franklin Springs, GA: Advocate Press, 1998.

MELVIN E. DIETER

INTERVARSITY CHRISTIAN FELLOWSHIP

InterVarsity Christian Fellowship (IVCF) is an evangelical Protestant interdenominational campus ministry in North America. Founded in 1928, IVCF advocates a broadly evangelical Protestant theology and emphasizes personal piety, Bible study, apologetics, EVANGELISM, and foreign MISSIONS. Involving an estimated 34,000 students and faculty in 1999–2000, the organization sponsors a variety of ministries, ranging from prayer meetings to foreign missions, on more than 560 college and university campuses in the United States.

History

IVCF traces its roots back to England when the Cambridge Inter-Collegiate Christian Union formed as a result of the merger of several different conservative Protestant student organizations at Cambridge University in 1877. Soon evangelical unions spread to other colleges and universities. In 1919 various college unions in Britain held the first Inter-Varsity Convention. In 1928 Inter-Varsity Fellowship of Evangelical Unions was established as a national organization and launched a ministry in Canada. In 1934 C. Stacey Woods, an Australian and Wheaton College graduate, became the general secretary of IVCF in Canada. Woods helped establish an IVCF chapter at the University of Michigan in 1939, and two years later helped organize an independent American branch of IVCF. In the aftermath of the fundamentalist-modernist controversy of the 1920s–1930s (see FUNDAMENTALISM), theologically conservative students often withdrew from campus ministries, such as the YMCA, because they had taken on a more liberal theological orientation (see LIBERAL PROTESTANTISM). Consequently, IVCF found a natural audience among conservative students. Since the emergence of the neo-evangelical movement in the late 1940s (see EVANGELICALISM), which criticized fundamentalism for its anti-intellectualism, divisiveness, and lack of a social conscience, IVCF has experienced exponential growth. In 1941–1942 IVCF reported chapters on 46 different campuses, ten full-time staff members, and an operating budget of $18,000. In 1970–1971 IVCF had 394 undergraduate chapters, 232 staff members, and a budget of more than two and a half million dollars. In 1999–2000 IVCF reported having more than 700 affiliate chapters, more than 1,000 staff members, and a budget of over 45 million dollars.

Theological Orientation

Attempting to steer a middle course between fundamentalism and liberal Protestantism, IVCF advocates a broadly evangelical Protestant theology (see EVANGELICALISM [theology]), which attempts to attract students from fundamentalist and mainline Protestant church backgrounds. IVCF's Statement of Faith, which every staff member, trustee, and student leader is required to sign, reflects this orientation. The statement affirms five doctrines: the divine inspiration, trustworthiness, and authority of the BIBLE; the deity of Jesus Christ; the necessity and efficacy of the substitutionary ATONEMENT and bodily resurrection of Jesus Christ for the redemption of the world; the presence and power of the Holy Spirit in the lives of Christians; and the expectation of the personal return of Jesus Christ. IVCF is interdenominational in character. IVCF draws financial support from individuals and local churches. IVCF's board of trustees represents a wide range of Protestant traditions, including Assemblies of God, Methodist Church, and PRESBYTERIAN CHURCH (USA). Both men and women have been involved in the leadership of IVCF. In 1948 IVCF's trustees passed a resolution denouncing racial segregation and instituting a nonsegregational basis for all IVCF activities.

Various Campus Ministries

One unique feature of IVCF undergraduate ministry is the fact that it is student-led. Paid staff workers serve as advisors to student leaders. In addition to undergraduate chapters, IVCF sponsors a number of specialized ministries, including groups devoted specifically to nursing students, graduate students, faculty members, fraternity and sorority members, and international students. In 1976 IVCF initiated a ministry to seminary students, the Theological Students Fellowship (TSF). In 1985 TSF folded because of a lack of support.

Urbana Missions Convention

From its inception, InterVarsity has encouraged student involvement in foreign missions. IVCF's first missions conference, held in Toronto in 1946, attracted 576 students from 151 colleges. Since 1948 this missions conference has been held almost triennially at the University of Illinois. The 2000 Urbana Missions Convention attracted more than 19,000 students as well as more than 240 mission agencies. The Urbana conference has attracted some of the most popular evangelical speakers, such as John Stott and BILLY GRAHAM, in the trans-Atlantic Protestant world.

In addition to the Urbana Missions Convention, IVCF sponsors a number of missions enterprises. IVCF coordinates urban mission projects to various American cities in which students work with urban churches during spring break or for an entire summer. In 2001 IVCF organized such projects in nearly 30 major American cities. IVCF also arranges student involvement in summer-long foreign missions projects through a number of different agencies.

Other IVCF Organizations

In 1947 IVCF launched a publishing program from Havertown, Pennsylvania, InterVarsity Press (IVP), to print and distribute Bible study guides and other books. In 1960 IVP moved to Chicago; in 1966 to Downers Grove, Illinois; and in 1995, to Westmont, California. IVP has enjoyed tremendous growth. In 1952 IVP sold an estimated 178,000 books and booklets. In 2000 IVP employed 65 people, offered an estimated 700 titles, and sold over 2 million works, including an increasing number of academic works by conservative theologians and biblical scholars. IVCF began publishing a monthly periodical, *HIS Magazine,* in 1941, which has been succeeded by *Student Leadership Journal.* Both IVP and the Urbana missions conference have served as key conduits in the influence of post–World War II English Evangelicalism's influence on conservative American Protestantism.

InterVarsity also operates four major conference centers where it holds weekend spiritual retreats, week-long student leadership development sessions, and a number of pastor seminars and family camps. In 1970 IVCF launched a multimedia communications division, TWENTYONEHUNDRED Productions. InterVarsity's national offices moved from Chicago to Madison, Wisconsin in 1969.

See also Atonement; Bible; Colleges; Evangelicalism; Evangelical Revival; Evangelism; Fundamentalism; Graham, Billy; Liberal Protestantism; Missionary Organizations; Missions; National Association of Evangelicals; Presbyterian Church; Universities; World Missionary Conferences; Youth for Christ

References and Further Reading

Howard, David M. *Student Power in World Evangelism.* Downers Grove, IL: InterVarsity Press, 1970.

Hunt, Keith, and Gladys Hunt. *For Christ and the University: The Story of InterVarsity Christian Fellowship of the U.S.A., 1940–1990.* Downers Grove, IL: InterVarsity Press, 1991.

Johnson, Douglas. *Contending for the Faith.* Leicester, England: Inter-Varsity Press, 1979.

Shelley, Bruce L. "The Rise of Evangelical Youth Movements." *Fides et Historia* 18 (1986): 47–63.

Woods, C. Stacey. *The Growth of a Work of God.* Downers Grove, IL: InterVarsity Press, 1978.

P. C. KEMENY

IONA COMMUNITY

Founded in 1938 by Sir George F. MacLeod on the island of Iona, Scotland, The Iona Community originally had a two-fold purpose: (1) to unite unemployed workers with pastors in rebuilding the venerable Iona Abbey; and (2) to create an extended community of members committed to a discipline of prayer and social action. Because the rebuilding project was arduous, membership was at first limited to men. It was later expanded to include women and extended also to other Protestant and Roman Catholic and Eastern Orthodox believers. In 2002 there were 240 full members of the community, supported by more than 1,500 associate members and a like number of committed friends.

A small residential staff at the Abbey hosts thousands of retreatants during the year, but most members are scattered in many different locations. Its self-monitored discipline requires stated times of prayer and BIBLE study, work, sharing a percentage of income, social action, frequent local meetings, and three plenary meetings plus one week at Iona each year.

Iona is famed in Christian history as the site where the Celtic monk Columba (521–597), with twelve companions, landed in CE 563 to begin the conversion of Scotland. After the sixteenth-century REFORMATION, the Abbey was abandoned; its reconstruction was completed in 1965.

George F. MacLeod (1895–1991) was noted for his staunch pacifism, eloquent preaching, and engagement in controversial issues. Among his best-known books are *We Shall Rebuild* (1945) and *Only One Way Left* (1956), both often reissued. In 1956 he was appointed a chaplain to the queen, in 1957 elected moderator of the General Assembly of the CHURCH OF SCOTLAND, and in 1989 was awarded the prestigious Templeton Prize in religion.

The Iona Community is a leading example of church renewal in the post–World War II era. Its current activities include *Wild Goose Publications, The Coracle* (a bimonthly periodical), well-attended youth camps, and liturgical reform.

See also Bible; Church of Scotland; Reformation

References and Further Reading

Bloesch, Donald G. *Centers of Christian Renewal.* Philadelphia/Boston: United Church Press, 1964.

Morton, T. Ralph. *The Household of Faith.* Glasgow: Iona Community, 1951.

———. *The Iona Community Story.* Glasgow: Iona Community, 1955.

Website: http://www.ionacommunity.org.uk

DONALD F. DURNBAUGH

IRELAND

The island of Ireland received Protestantism through two routes. From England, in the mid-sixteenth century, came the ANGLICANISM of HENRY VIII. The English settlers of the mid-eastern strip of Ireland (known as the Pale of Dublin) received it through the Irish Parliament's Act of Supremacy (1537), establishing the king as head of both church and state. In 1560 the Church of Ireland was established on the Anglican model, but developed permanently the CALVINIST PROTESTANT features promoted by ELIZABETH I rather than the ANGLO-CATHOLIC ones of her father Henry. Church of Ireland membership never extended much beyond English settlers and their descendants. The native Irish and some English settlers resisted attempts to impose Reformation, sometimes through war (1579–1583, 1595–1603).

From SCOTLAND came Calvinist PRESBYTERIANISM as interpreted by JOHN KNOX and others in the Scottish Confession (1560). In 1603 the Scottish king, James VI, became James I of England and Ireland. Although Anglican himself, he made it possible for Scottish migrants to settle in Ireland's northern province of Ulster, despite bringing with them their Presbyterian tradition.

Shortly after, English Protestant settlers began to arrive (1610) as part of James's plantation scheme. The English moved to the south and west, whereas the Scots stayed in the north and east, near to their Scottish homeland. At first the Scots and their ministers were integrated into the Church of Ireland, developing a strong presence during the Puritan English Republic under OLIVER CROMWELL (1649–1660). In response to a Catholic rebellion he finally crushed (1641–1650), Cromwell secured a more comprehensive Protestant plantation throughout Ireland. At the same time he disestablished the Church of Ireland and banished the bishops. With the collapse of the Republic the monarchy was restored (1660). The bishops then returned to a reestablished church and proceeded to expel Presbyterians from it. Presbyterians, some of whom were already organized into presbyteries, then developed their organization sufficiently to set up the Presbyterian Synod of Ulster (1690).

The forces of King William of Orange extinguished any further Catholic threat to Protestants by crushing the last Catholic rebellion (1689–1691). Ireland's Protestant aristocracy and farmers then prospered. Owning seven-eighths of all farming land, they were the backbone of the Church of Ireland. Beneath them in the social order were Presbyterians, who lived mainly in the north of the country and, below them, the much larger Catholic population. All Protestants together made up twenty percent of Ireland's population, a proportion that has remained relatively constant up to recent times.

The American War of Independence (1776) and the French Revolution (1789) inspired "new light" or liberal Presbyterians to lead and participate in the Republican rebellion of the United Irishmen (1798). However, poor organization saw Irish Republicans pitted against Royalists in some areas and Irish Cath-

olics against Anglo-Irish Protestants in others, and helped lead to the failure of the rising. Its sectarian violence also alienated Protestants from the movement. From here on, Protestants would remain mainly supportive of the English Crown as their protector. The Orange societies, established in the 1790s to defend Church of Ireland interests, would reemerge as a powerful religious political force in the late nineteenth century, dedicated to the Protestant dominance of at least part of Ireland and to the continuance of political union with Britain.

The nineteenth century began with the closure of Ireland's (Protestant) Parliament. Then Anglo-Irish hegemony collapsed altogether with the disestablishment of the Church of Ireland (1869) and the return of land to the mainly Catholic peasantry (1881–1903). The period also saw the rise of Irish nationalism, which nearly all Protestants opposed. The decisive national moment came in 1885, when it became clear that the British Liberals intended to establish a parliament for Ireland that would put the majority Catholic Irish in control. At this point Protestants settled their internal disputes and set up the Unionist Party, dedicated to maintain the union of Ireland with Britain. A compromise was secured in 1920 with the partition of Ireland. Northern Ireland (six of the nine counties of Ulster) remained in the United Kingdom, whereas the rest of Ireland achieved full independence (1922). From then on until the mid-1970s, the southern (Republican) state remained predominantly Catholic, and Northern Ireland a Protestant state for a Protestant people, but with its aggrieved Catholic minority subjected to significant institutionalized discrimination.

In recent times the number of Protestants living in the southern state has declined from ten percent (1911 *Census*) of the population to three percent (1991 *Census*), or to 104,000 out of 3.5 million. In Northern Ireland the number of Protestants has decreased from sixty percent (1951 *Census*) to forty-six percent of its 1.6 million population (1991 *Census*). Compared with the other parts of the United Kingdom, Protestants in Northern Ireland retain high levels of regular church attendance (forty-five to fifty-two percent for the main churches; *Northern Ireland Attitudes Survey* 1992–1993), while at the same time keeping alive the tradition of cross-denominational Gospel Halls.

Protestantism has strong traditional and anti-Catholic features as well as weaker, though significant, ECUMENICAL ones. The Church of Ireland retains its position on the Protestant-Calvinist wing of Anglicanism. The Presbyterian Church in Ireland remains controlled by its more conservative people rather than its more liberal clergy. The leadership of the small METHODIST CHURCH is conservative, yet, like the two larger churches, retains benign relationships with Roman

Catholics. In all three, however, probably a majority still experiences strong anti-Catholic feelings and fundamentalist tendencies. These are even more prominent in the smaller churches and sects that make up twenty percent of all northern Protestants, such as BAPTISTS, Elim Pentecostals (who originated in Northern Ireland), Christian Brethren, the Free Presbyterians of the Rev. Ian Paisley, and some independent congregations. A modified COVENANT politics is still alive, and is arguably a factor in the street politics and marching of the Orange Orders.

Ecumenical features of Protestantism are limited to a minority that often combines their commitment to reconciliation with an equally firm one to evangelicalism. They have played significant roles in the development of the peace process in Northern Ireland from the very beginning of the Troubles (1968–1998), seeking ceasefires between paramilitaries, and setting up or participating in interchurch communities (such as Corrymeela, Columbanus, and Rostrevor), where opponents have met to share experiences and prayer. A number have participated in the Inter-Church Group on Faith and Politics and in the work of ECONI (Evangelical Contribution on Northern Ireland). Integrated Catholic-Protestant schools have also emerged, most of them now supported by the state. Protestants from overseas have also contributed, notably Mennonites from the United States, and an interchurch graduate and adult education school, the Irish School of Ecumenics, has survived and developed mainly on the basis of Protestant donations from abroad as well as from within Ireland.

See also Anglicanism; Anglo-Catholicism; Baptists; Calvinist Protestant; Covenant; Cromwell, Oliver; Elizabeth I; Ecumenicalism; Henry VIII; Knox, John; Methodist Church; Presbyterianism; Scotland

References and Further Reading

Acheson, A. *A History of the Church of Ireland, 1691–1996*. Dublin: Columba Press/APCK, 1997.

Cooke, D. *Persecuting Zeal: A Portrait of Ian Paisley*. Cork: Brandon Press, 1996.

Holmes, F. *The Presbyterian Church in Ireland: A Popular History*. Dublin: Columba Press, 2000.

McCaughey, T. P. *Memory and Redemption: Church, Politics and Prophetic Theology in Ireland*. Dublin: Gill & Macmillan, 1993.

Richardson, N., ed. *A Tapestry of Beliefs: Christian Traditions in Northern Ireland*. Belfast: Blackstaff Press, 1998.

Tanner, M. *Ireland's Holy Wars: The Struggle for a Nation's Soul, 1500–2000*. New Haven, CT: Yale University Press, 2001.

Website: http://cain.ulst.ac.uk/ni/religion.htm

JOHN FULTON

IRVING, EDWARD (1792–1834)

Presbyterian minister and founder of the Catholic Apostolic Church. Born in Annan, SCOTLAND on August 4, 1792 Irving studied mathematics at the University of Edinburgh and taught school at Haddington and briefly at Kirkcaldy before returning to Edinburgh to study theology in 1815. Four years later he accepted a call to assist THOMAS CHALMERS at St. John's in Glasgow. After his ordination in 1822 he was sent to Caledonian chapel in Hatton Garden, a shabby district of London. His magnetic personality and brilliant oratory soon attracted visitors, including George Canning, England's foremost statesman. Canning introduced Irving to members of parliament as "the most eloquent preacher I have ever heard." Thereafter, the 500-seat chapel could not accommodate the crowds. Plans were laid to build a larger church on Regent Square in a more fashionable part of the city.

Irving's fall from grace was as dramatic as his ascendancy. By the time the new church was built in 1827, he was charged with HERESY. He argued that in the Incarnation, Christ had taken on Adam's fallen nature. He was found guilty and expelled from the CHURCH OF SCOTLAND in 1832. Eight hundred members followed him to form what would become the first congregation of the Catholic Apostolic Church, popularly known as the Irvinites.

In the midst of his trial Irving had become interested in ESCHATOLOGY. Convinced of Christ's imminent return, Irving proclaimed that the gift of Tongues was about to be restored to the church (see TONGUES, SPEAKING IN). With it would come the restoration of the apostolic office. Several members of his church soon received this gift, although Irving did not; three who had were named apostles. Irving was recognized as an "angel," an inferior position in the emerging new church, thereby effectively removing him from power. He died two years later on December 7, 1834 in Scotland, a broken man.

References and Further Reading

Primary Source:

Irving, Edward. *Collected Writings of Edward Irving*. 5 vols. London: Alexander Strahan, 1864–1865.

Secondary Sources:

Dallimore, Arnold. *Forerunner of the Charismatic Movement: The Life of Edward Irving*. Chicago: Moody Press, 1983.

Flegg, Columba Graham. *"Gathered Under Apostles": A Study of the Catholic Apostolic Church*. Oxford, UK: Clarendon Press, 1992.

D. WILLIAM FAUPEL

ITALY

Historiography

The assumption that "Italians are Catholic" has deeply affected the way that historians have written about Protestantism in Italy. Ronald Keith Delph, for instance, notes Delio Cantimori's tendency to explain the failure of Italian humanists to "go protestant" in terms of their personal Catholic piety, whereas Salvatore Caponetto notes the tendency of Italian historians to write the Valdesi (Waldensians), and thus a large part of the porous Franco-Italian borderlands, out of Italian history. Defining what "Italian" means and what content was appropriate to "Italian history" thus guided a significant proportion of postwar religious history, in the same way (as Giorgio Spini has shown) that Protestantism elsewhere was entangled in the German and Swiss national myths. This attitude to Italian Protestantism changed slowly through the 1970s and 1980s, with an increasing maturity of the Italian nationalist project leading to the rediscovery of a wider religious history.

Waldensian Origins

Typical was the attitude to the Waldensians. The "Valdesi," fleeing a purge of heretics in FRANCE, entered the high valleys of northwestern Italy in the fourteenth century, and survived a number of attempts at extermination and suppression until after the movement identified itself with Calvinist Protestantism at the "Sinodo d'Angrogna" at Chanforan (1532). This has often been treated by historians as a Piedmontese sideshow, a view that (as Caponetto shows) is retreating in the face of mounting evidence of widespread (if often not very deep) Reformational influence in Italy. The Waldensians were not only important to Italian Protestantism because they were early (and so were to provide a continuing touchstone of identity for Italian Protestants), but because they would provide an important geographical conduit for Protestant ideas coming down from the north, and for admirers of MARTIN LUTHER fleeing the Inquisition toward Geneva. Their determined missionary push (led by Bonello and Pascale, members of John Calvin's Venerable Company) after Chanforan was halted only by the execution of their leaders (1560) and the massacre of thousands of "ultramontane" peasantry in Calabria (1561) and mass assimilation in Puglia seemingly wiped out Waldensian influence in the south. Through the period of effective inquisitorial repression (1542–ca. 1800) the Waldensians created a "second front" for the House of Savoy (so contributing to the survival of Geneva), and in the longer run, provided the inevitable experience of living reluctantly in a multireligious state that the Savoyards would take into the combined Italian monarchy in 1861. Internationally, Waldensian resistance (and experience of events such as the "Holy Massacre" of the Valtellina in 1569) also provided important "martyrological" elements, "the Israel of the Alps," for the identity of anti-Catholic elements of Protestantism. OLIVER CROMWELL intervened to stop Catholic repression in 1655, leading to the "Patents of Grace" restoring the status quo introduced by the Treaty of Cavour (1561). After a gritty, bloody guerrilla war the Valdesi were saved by entry of Vittorio Amedeo II into the (largely Protestant) League of Augsburg formed to restrain Louis XIV's French imperialism. Protestant churches would send support and agitate for international representation of their case until after World War II when the Italian Republic was reestablished as a secular, religiously tolerant state.

Catholic and Counter-Reformation

The "other reformation" in Italy increasingly coming to light relates to the infiltration of Lutheran ideals and international thought into a putative stronghold of the Counter-Reformation that, because of Italy's fractured political, economic, and cultural life, proved almost impossible to isolate from modernizing trends. Renaissance commercial expansion created business and cultural networks for Italians all over Europe, networks that provided for the movement of Protestant ideas back into Italy, and places of refuge for those with the intellectual or financial capital to move their operations out from under the gaze of the Holy Office. The flood of humanist reforming publications into Italy was fostered by the presence of sympathizers in the church (such as the "spirituali" behind the Consilium de emendanda ecclesia, 1537, which included such leaders of the Catholic Reform movement as Reginald Pole, Gasparo Contarini, Gregorio Cortese, Giacopo Sadoleto, and Federigo Fregoso), the court (particularly through the della Rovere connections of the Gonzaga family, the patronage of Vittoria Colonna, and the influence of Juan de Valdes), scholarship (Marcantonio Flaminio, for instance, or the influence of LUTHERANISM in the Florentine Academy, and the cosmopolitan student base at the University of Padua), and the arts (of which Michelangelo's Sistine Chapel conceptualization is perhaps the best documented, but not the only, example—see for instance Jacopo Pontormo). Until their comprehensive defeat at the Council of Trent, following the collapse of discussions at Regensburg, this network of reforming, often Augustinian or Erasmian, and warmly spiritual people, provided an elite readership and protection for "Lutherans" in Italy. As Pole wrote in the 1530s,

"Heretics be not in all things heretics. Wherefore I will not so abhor their heresy that for the hate thereof I will fly from the truth" (Fenlon 1972:37), a sentiment he supported by providing in his see of Viterbo a temporary refuge from the persecution outside. Books and tracts by Luther, PHILIPP MELANCHTHON, and the reformers filtered into the country, hand to hand, under wine bottles, wrapped in deceptive covers or anonymously under pseudonyms. Translations, paraphrases, and the rise of a vernacular press helped in the dissimulation, forcing the church to respond edition by edition and to devote enormous energies in pursuit of authors and readers—just possession of a BIBLE or works promulgating JUSTIFICATION by FAITH alone (such as the widely influential Beneficio di Cristo by Benedetto Fontanini, ca. 1543) was enough to spark prosecution. In this way Protestant THEOLOGY spread among the educated classes—merchants, nobility, and especially higher artisans—particularly where, in places such as Venice or Lucca, traditions of local political independence and suspicion of papal territorial claims blunted inquisition. In other areas, such as Sicily, divisions between (largely Spanish) rulers on the one hand and merchants and professionals on the other, provided cracks through which reforming ideas could work.

The very successes of the REFORMATION in northern Europe, however, mobilized the Habsburg coalition dominating the South, resulting directly in the Council of Trent, and the rise of a rigidly Counter-reformational pope in the Theatine, Pietro Caraffa (Paul IV). He set about cleaning house with a vengeance ("the pope seems to be intending to fill his prisons with cardinals and bishops on behalf of the Inquisition," wrote Pietro Carnesecchi) (Caponetto 1998:308), breaking the resistance of secular authorities and turning the Holy Office into an effective arm of government supervision. This sort of reactionary, communally based oppression would remain a key conditioning element for Italian religious life until the 1960s, uniting church and local magistracy in a culture of suspicion and control, particularly in the poorer south. The ultimate effectiveness of this mechanism of control depended on relationships between state and church on the governmental level, however, and so periods of close control (under the Spanish, in Naples, for instance, or under Austrian control, and later, under the concordat with the Fascist regime) varied with periods of greater liberty of religious expression (in Savoy, for instance, under d'Azeglio, or during the period after unification when the pope became known internationally as the "prisoner in the Vatican"). Book burnings, the Index, and tridentine medievalism contributed to the rising belief (held in large parts of the British Empire, for instance) that Catholicism was unsuited to modernizing, industrial societies marked by religious pluralism, a concept given scholarly respectability in MAX WEBER's work on Protestantism and the Spirit of Capitalism. It was a conception that would make Italian Protestants ever open to international links and influences, and dubious of Catholic intentions.

Italian Protestant internationalism found its first bases in the networks of emigrés and exiles that developed from the commercial cities of Italy, in particular from Lucca and Venice. Through Celio Curione, Pietro Martire Vermigli, and Aonio Paleario, Lucca's infiltration by Erasmian thought through its widespread mercantile interests turned gradually into widespread Protestantism, particularly through the Arnolfini family and among the Augustinians at San Frediano. Having shared Tuscany's turmoil with regard to Savonarola and French invasion, Lucca was unusual in producing a coherent stream of emigrants as repression of CLERGY intensified into a systematic rooting out of nicodemist (those who outwardly conformed to Catholicism) influence. Paleario was arraigned by the Inquisition, which he called "a dagger poised against learning and the freedom of conscience." Vermigli fled in 1542, along with the most famous Italian preacher of the day, Bernardino "Ochino" Tommasini. They were followed by an extraordinary efflux of leading laymen—the Arnolfini, Burlamacchi, Calandrini, Diodati, Micheli, Minutoli, and Turretini families, among others—who followed their commercial ties through France, Germany, Holland, and ENGLAND, before settling in and coming to play a central role in the life of Geneva and Basel. They—particularly those involved in the famed "Gran Bottega"—did well, intermarried, and their children went on to have an extraordinary impact on reformed Protestant theology and life, including defense of the rights of HUGUENOTS (Fabrizio Burlamacchi), BIBLE TRANSLATION and leadership of the Venerable Company (Giovanni Diodati), theology, and formation of the Formula Consensus (Francesco Turretini). Their wealth and "tough faith" played a significant role in allowing the survival of the "perfect school of Christ" that JOHN KNOX found in visiting John Calvin's Geneva. In other places they joined seamlessly with the Huguenot exile, contributing pastors and leaders to such leading congregations as the French church in Threadneedle Street, London.

International Protestantism

This base in Geneva, with longstanding interests in the Waldensians, provided a base for the expansionary religious societies in the nineteenth and twentieth centuries, first from Britain and then from the UNITED

STATES. The BRITISH AND FOREIGN BIBLE SOCIETY, as Spini has noted, saw Italy in strategic terms, and undertook to supply the Valdesi with texts in their native French. A Waldensian Bible Society was founded about 1814, the first fruits of the BFBS's long-term commitment to Italian tract and Bible distribution. Literary EVANGELISM was backed up by the missionary societies, seeing English Methodists working in Italy from 1859, and American Methodists from 1872 (see MISSIONARY ORGANIZATIONS). The two groups joined in 1946 and merged with the Valdesi in 1946 to form the Waldensian Evangelical Church (constituting, at the time of union, some 30,000 members in Italy, and 15,000 in South America). The Methodist stream (which Bouchard estimated at about 6,000 members in thirty-six churches at the beginning of the 1990s), although it produced some dynamic individuals, was thus to be more important in terms of its ecumenical contribution than in numbers of conversions.

As Giorgio Spini has noted there are very few international Protestant movements that have not produced at least marginal offspring in Italy. From 1887 the SALVATION ARMY (about forty officers, and 2,000 adherents) began operations in Rome, although its uniformed presence and British origins attracted more attention than it perhaps wanted, suffering extensively under Catholic and Fascist regimes. English BAPTISTS began MISSIONS in 1863 and were particularly successful in the Central Southern part of Italy, where they are now organized under the UCEBI (Unione cristiana evangelica battista d'Italia). In 1992 Bouchard estimated some 10,000 members and adherents, among whom the largest influence is now their connection to American Baptists, particularly the SOUTHERN BAPTIST CONVENTION. The swing to America is particularly evident from the 1870s, in part because of the rise of circular Italian migration and labor patterns embracing the United States as the prime option. American groups such as the SEVENTH-DAY ADVENTISTS have thus done well in Italy—presenting a total population of some 20,000 in the early 1990s, a phenomenon matched or exceeded by such groups as the Mormons (see MORMONISM) and JEHOVAH'S WITNESSES.

This internationalism, intrinsic to Protestantism from the 1790s, but intensified in Italy by Catholic host culture hostility often expressed through various levels of official repression, regularly made Protestants the object of suspicion. In times of hypernationalism they were considered fifth-columnists, whereas for the Catholic hierarchy they were a dagger poised at the heart of the carefully constructed social compact the popes had been building at least since the thirteenth century, or (as the forgery of the Donation of Constantine indicated) even earlier. From the six-teenth century Protestants were paralleled in Catholic and public sources with illuminism, FREEMASONRY, libertarianism, secularists, indifferentism, and every other enemy that threatened the Catholic compact. This became something of a self-fulfilling prophecy, given that Protestants did indeed pursue their hunger for religious freedom into support of Jacobin, Napoleonic, and later, Risorgimento forces. Spini, for instance, notes the persistent legend among Protestants that immediately behind the Republican bersaglieri as they burst into Rome on September 20, 1870, "came a colporteur, Luigi Ciari, with a Bible wagon pulled by a large dog who answered to the name of Pio Nono [Pius IX]" (Spini 1998:341). Political freedom inside a secular state held out the promise of religious freedom, a fact that Catholic functionaries well knew. As P. Cavalli, S.J. wrote in the review *Civilta Cattolica* (April 3, 1948): "Protestants proceed from the law of liberty, catholics from the law of truth. In the case of conflict between these two principles, truth must have supremacy, as even Protestants cannot deny. . . . Now, the Catholic Church, convicted of her divine prerogatives, of being the One True Church, must retain for herself alone the right of liberty, because this alone falls within the competency of the truth, and never in that of error." The self-referential nature of majority Italian Catholicism made it, locally, and under its concordat with Mussolini's Fascist regime (1929–1945), institutionally, oppressive. The constancy of this element in Italian CULTURE has seen Italian Protestant leaders at the head of campaigns against official and unofficial religious bigotry. For this reason, Italian Protestants of all persuasions have been highly active both politically and socially, in the defense of minority rights, and the construction of orphanages, charitable institutions, schools, and the like. As Bouchard notes, this has meant that the divisions between fundamentalists (see FUNDAMENTALISM) and SOCIAL GOSPEL followers have been more muted in Italy—first, because these Protestant factions are not in contention with one another for control of the public culture, and second, because all protestant denominations need to maintain elements of both tough biblical faith and social presence.

Twentieth-Century Pentecostalism

This has been as true of pentecostals in Italy as it has of other Protestant groups. Although it is true that (as per Stretti) "the origins of Italian Pentecostalism lie in the United States," it is also clear from oral testimony that the same sort of scattered indigenous experience of pentecostal phenomena seen in INDIA, the United States, AUSTRALIA, and AFRICA before 1900 was also seen in Italy. Giuseppe Beretta, for instance, was converted among Baptists in Sicily in 1900, and reported being told to keep quiet about his own experiences lest he be considered demon-possessed. There was greater freedom in the diaspora. In 1890 the Chiesa Evangelica Valdese, for instance, sent Filippo Grill to Chicago to care for Italian Waldensians and the growing number of Italians gathering in Methodist and Presbyterian churches, who were prepared to convert to Protestantism once outside the restraints of their home towns. Leaders of these small groups were swept up into the AZUSA STREET REVIVAL movement from 1907, with the return of William Seymour to Chicago. These rapidly spread the message of the baptism through Italian communities throughout the world, Pietro Ottolini and Giacomo Lombardi returning to Italy to evangelize and establish communities in Liguria, Rome, and the South; Luigi Francescon, on the other hand, went on mission to South America, where he established a movement that today numbers in the millions. They were supported by less-structured returns by people from the diaspora, spreading small holiness pentecostal communities in many small towns, particularly in the South. These survived under considerable pressure, despite prohibition under fascism, and consistent oppression from the local priest or "maresciallo."

After World War II the Christian churches of North America, into which many of the diaspora congregations had gathered, was effectively trumped by the superior international bargaining power of the ASSEMBLIES OF GOD, and so the mainline Italian pentecostal church developed as the "Assemblee di Dio in Italia" (ADI). Although effectively founded in 1928, therefore, the national convention of 1947 is widely seen as a "second founding" of the ADI in Italy. This development reflected the ambivalence that early Italian pentecostals had with regard to formal organization, and their literalistic readings of the Scriptures. Early and regular divisions occurred over issues of organization, the consumption of blood, the wearing of veils, and consumerism, for instance. The EVANGELISM of other pentecostal and Protestant movements such as the British-based Elim churches or American Foursquare (see INTERNATIONAL CHURCH OF THE FOURSQUARE GOSPEL) also provided options for individuals dissatisfied with ADI's organized holiness emphases, as did groups such as Jehovah's Witnesses. The tight local congregationalism of the movement, however, ensured survival and postwar growth inside a fellowship closely linked through interpersonal relationships. This has raised fundamental questions over ADI's relationship to other Protestant works. It did not, for instance, join the Federation of Italian Protestant Churches, formed in 1967, or the Federation of Evangelical Pentecostal Churches, emerging from intercommunal ministerial conferences held since 1983, to ecumenical initiatives and to the charismatic movement. The growth of numerous independent charismatic churches in Italy through the 1980s has relativized ADI's dominance in the field, leaving it with about half the total number of Italian pentecostal adherents. In 1999, symbolic of its institutional position as the largest of the Italian Protestant groupings (with around 950 centers constituting some 150,000 members and adherents), the ADI came to an "agreement" with the Republic "actuating" the religious liberty law of October 1988. With an independent charismatic church movement growing rapidly, the ADI has tended to retreat from engagement, out of the fear that "charismatic" churches represent less biblical, more "Catholic" options. Therefore, it tends to run parallel to rather than in leadership of Italian Protestantism, leaving it with the challenge of cultural isolation and decreasing relevance in an Italian culture that is more dynamic than at any time in the nation's history.

Conclusion

Protestantism continues to grow in Italy, although institutionalization has proceeded rapidly in traditional denominations and in those groups that have been encapsulated by the Catholic presumptions of the culture. There is little evidence of "protestantization" as seen in other cultures (e.g., JAPAN) coming into modernity, although the creation of an "open religious market" is obviously advantageous to Italian Protestant churches. The sort of oppression, economic misery, and mass migration that created the background for Italian Protestantism over the past four centuries has retreated rapidly in the face of economic growth and European Community membership. This leaves new challenges of self-definition for Italian Protestants in the twenty-first century.

References and Further Reading

Bouchard, Giorgio. *I valdesi e l'Italia: prospettive d'una vocazione.* Torino, Italy: Claudiana, 1988.

Cantimori, Delio. *Eretici italiani del Cinquecento: ricerche storiche,* rev. edition. Firenze, Italy: G.C. Sansoni editore nuova, 1978.

Caponetto, Salvatore. *The Protestant Reformation in Sixteenth-century Italy.* Translated by Anne C. Tedeschi and John Tedeschi. Kirksville, MO: Thomas Jefferson University Press, 1998.

Delph, Ronald K. Italian Humanism in the Early Reformation. Agostino Stevco (1497–1548). Ph.D. Diss Michigan, 1987.

Firpo, Luigi. *Scritti sulla Riforma in Italia.* Napoli, Italy: Prismi, 1996.

Menchi, Silvana Seidel. "Le Traduzioni Italiane di Lutero nella Prima Metà Del Cinquecento." *Rinascimento* 2 no. 17-8 (1977/8): 31–109.

Rochat, Giorgio. *Regime fascista e chiese evangeliche: diret-tive e articolazioni del controllo e della repressione.* Torino, Italy: Claudiana, 1990.

Spini, Giorgio. *Risorgimento e protestanti,* rev. edition. Milano, Italy: Il Saggiatore, 1989.

————. *Studi sull'evangelismo italiano tra Otto e Novecento.* Torino, Italy: Claudiana, 1994.

Stretti, Eugenio. *Il Movimento Pentecostale: Le Assemblee di Dio in Italia, Presentazione di Francesco Toppi.* Torino, Italy: Claudiana, 1998.

Tourn, Giorgio. *I valdesi: la singolare vicenda di un popolo-chiesa (1170–1976).* Torino, Italy: Claudiana, 1977.

————. *Italiani e protestantesimo: un incontro impossibile?* Torino, Italy: Claudiana, 1997.

MARK HUTCHINSON

ITINERACY

The term "itineracy" in Methodist usage (in its traditional and unique spelling) denotes the body of traveling preachers that "itinerate" under the supervision of a bishop who appoints them to serve particular places (or "charges") and regulates their movement at various time intervals. If Conference is the body of Methodist preachers related to each other in time and space, itineracy is the skeleton that connects the pastors to church communities and animates the entire Methodist body. Some commentators have employed the image of itineracy as a "wheel moving within a wheel" to depict the machinelike nature of how Methodist preachers are deployed for the maintenance of existing churches, and the missional establishment of new churches.

As with many structures of ministry and POLITY in METHODISM, itineracy is rooted in Methodist origins as a missionary renewal movement within ANGLICANISM. Itineracy began with JOHN WESLEY'S own field PREACHING (from 1738 to 1791), intended to serve the growing desire of common people outside of the boundaries of the Anglican church to hear the Methodist message of assured and total CONVERSION. Moreover Wesley came to believe that other preachers who joined him in responding to this evangelical revival should be willing to itinerate not simply where they wanted to go, or even where there was need—but should rather go where they could do the most good. Over time Wesley gathered around him "traveling preachers," or "helpers," laypersons fully committed to the Methodist mission and Wesley's discipline (see CHURCH DISCIPLINE). These preachers covenanted to submit to Wesley's direction wherever and whenever they were needed, to serve "The United Societies of the People Called Methodist." Over time these appointments took shape in "circuits." Wesley felt that moving preachers frequently through these circuits kept the societies stimulated, and helped match the gifts of preachers to the needs of maturing Christians. Moreover itineracy was especially aimed to promote Methodist preaching deeper into Britian, "to spread scriptural holiness and reform the nation, especially the churches." Wesley recaptured the sense of the wandering preachers in early and medieval church history—indeed calling this wandering essential to find the "wanderers from God."

Historical Developments of the Itineracy in America

From the 1760s Methodist LAITY immigrated to the American colonies, and societies grew informally. Lay preachers converted under Wesley—such as Robert Strawbridge, Thomas Webb, and Philip Embury—began itinerating in America to establish and nurture Methodist societies. Once these societies successfully entreated Wesley to send full-time lay preachers from the British circuits from 1769, Wesley appointed superintendents to extend his AUTHORITY into America. This promoted regular itineration between the various centers of emerging American Methodism in Maryland, New York, and Philadelphia. The itinerant system became crucial to the missionary success of the movement in America, particularly because the continent's immense size required great movements of preachers across frontiers to establish connected Methodist societies.

With the conclusion of the Revolutionary War, Methodism in America became an independent church with a small cadre of ordained pastors, and no longer simply a connection of societies loosely related to Anglicanism as in Britain. FRANCIS ASBURY emerged as an important figure, who through force of his example and exhortation wove together a network of itinerant preachers (ordained and lay) across the entire Eastern seaboard. He was the first Protestant bishop to cross the Alleghenies. Although he made his endless Episcopal rounds, he faithfully met his preachers in conferences to keep order and movement among his largely young, single, and preferably celibate preaching corps. From the time of his arrival in America in 1771, Asbury insisted on stimulating his colleagues to move out from the cities. He led by example, traveling up to 270,000 miles in his ministry of forty-five years. For Asbury and the early Methodists a call to preach was a call to travel, without promise of even shelter for the night, much less a furnished parsonage in a church or "station charge." Yet a promise was made then as now: if accepted by the conference as a member, and if a pastor accepted Episcopal appointments and accountability, then a guarantee of a place to preach was offered. Both bishops Asbury and THOMAS COKE extolled the value of itineracy as reconstituting the primitive and apostolic plan of ministry.

The cost of itineracy was substantial. It successfully connected preachers with people in the far-flung communities and knit together both church and society, although attrition was high. Many preachers left the itineracy or "located," because of fatigued bodies, family stress, and the loss of earning potential during the prime of their lives. The system worked best with single preachers. Asbury regarded MARRIAGE as the prime enemy of the Methodist itinerant mission, and complained often that the DEVIL and Marriage were getting his preachers. After Asbury's death in 1816, and because of the growing wealth of Methodists, cultural and financial support increased for pastors to settle down and serve full time "station" pastorates. During the era of the CAMP MEETING (roughly 1803–1850) and the second Great Awakening (see AWAKENINGS), ever larger groups of Methodists and other evangelical Protestants gathered for large REVIVALS in central geographic areas. The emergence of these camp meetings meant that riding large circuits was no longer as critical to reach new converts. These factors combined so that Methodist itineration shifted in the first half of the nineteenth century toward pastors serving longer appointments in station churches, rather than the continual movement through circuits across a wide geographic area.

Examples of average lengths of itineration are instructive. When Asbury arrived in 1771, the Philadelphia and New York appointments were exchanged quarterly. During the 1770s until 1790s, preachers received new circuits on average of every six months. Asbury preferred no more than one-year appointments while he lived. Yet from 1794 to 1804, many pastors remained up to two years in a circuit, and apparently even Asbury could not prevent it. In 1804 it was stipulated that no preacher was to remain in the same appointment more than two years. This rule of thumb generally prevailed, but in the 1830s, with the growth of wealth among Methodist laity, bishops were often pressed (usually unsuccessfully) for longer appointments. The General Conference of 1844 granted that the bishop should not continue a preacher in the same appointment "more than two years in six, nor in the same city more than four years in succession." Preferences for repeat appointments were apparently forming, and in 1856 these stricter limits were repealed. Once the southern branch (Methodist Episcopal Church South [MECS]) was established in 1845 they carried the two-year limit with them—except for New Orleans where it was felt that two years was a minimum to build up resistance to yellow fever. With an increased number of larger station churches, along with the increase of appointments to the growing national general agencies requiring specialized skills and longer tenures, pressure came to raise the overall limit for appointments in the MEC in 1864 to three years. An experiment with five-year limits was adopted in 1888, only to be repealed in 1900. On the Southern side after the CIVIL WAR, longer tenure was thought necessary for the rebuilding of the church. In 1866 a move was made to abolish limits in the MECS, but a compromise was reached with the adoption of a mandated move at four years. This four-year limit continued in southern appointments until the reunion with the MEC in 1939 formed the Methodist Church. The newly reunited Methodist Church carried no limits on itinerant appointments. Commentators have noted a direct historical relationship between the growing institutional wealth of METHODISM and the lengthening of itinerant appointments.

Disagreements among pastors with their bishops about appointments have occurred from the very beginning of Methodist history. In 1771 Asbury admonished his colleagues Richard Boardman and Joseph Pilmore to leave the comforts of New York and Philadelphia to preach in the country. They complied somewhat reluctantly. Asbury was also at the center over disagreements concerning his absolute authority to make appointments. A schism on the matter developed at the first duly constituted General Conference in 1792, when Thomas O'Kelly and others walked out and formed The Republican Methodist Church. They did so on the view that preachers in a democratic country should have the right of appeal in an appointment, lest the movement smack of "popery." Pressures toward more participation in the appointment process have thus been an important part of the American Methodist story.

The trend toward more participation in appointments has resulted in a type of localization of preachers and the marginalization of episcopal authority (see BISHOP AND EPISCOPACY). Signs of this could be seen as early as 1830 in the major schism forming the Methodist Protestant Church, which abolished bishops and sought democratic accountability in appointment-making through conference-elected superintendents. Larger, richer, and more powerful congregations emerged in the late nineteenth century, which could subvert the itineration process and directly "call" their own pastors. Throughout the twentieth century, Methodist itineration has been slowly modified through increased layers of consultation between district superintendents, congregations, laity, and pastors. Itineracy has thus clearly changed with America.

Present Challenges for Itineracy

As society has become increasingly mobile, and local churches tend to lose their experienced lay leaders more frequently, there is a perceived need for more continuity in pastoral leadership. Moreover, as the administration of larger churches becomes more complex, there is a corresponding requirement for more specialized leadership. In this sense the very success of the itinerant system as an organized missional form has set up tensions within it. Along with increasing numbers of WOMEN and two-clergy couples, bishops are responding to these trends and opting in favor of longer pastoral tenures with more local consultation. Appointments made through this consultation process are indeed often more sensitive to the needs of pastors and local congregations. Yet this has limited episcopal and conference authority in some cases to appoint as Wesley did—to go not where gifts and graces of pastors are needed, but where these gifts are needed most. The consultation process has localized the ministry of Methodist pastors to a degree, and modified the itinerant system away from a missional form toward the maintenance of existing congregations.

Indeed, Methodism in its earliest period was characterized by an itineracy committed to a mission "from center to circumference," with the only reward a new circuit and new work in the frontier. Today itineracy often appears organized to support the consolidation of congregations existing for over a century, while delivering pastors on a career track from the margins to the larger congregations existing in the city centers of America. Although the itinerant system is under stress in an age of INDIVIDUALISM, consumer choice, and employment rights, the matching of preachers to congregations is still critical. Itineracy provides a less invasive and regularized possibility to move preachers when their work is done or gifts no longer match a congregation. For those committed to it, itineracy can create stronger, more flexible, and less insular churches in the long run. However, the system requires a very high level of commitment, coopera-

tion, and trust in the process between preachers, their families, and their churches. Bishops and superintendents must also remain flexible in their approach to appointments and concede some power to local constituencies. For itineracy to continue playing a missional role in American Methodism all parties must continue to communicate in transparent ways concerning what is at stake in their appointment consultation decisions. If mutual accountability and a missional flexibility can be maintained, then the United Methodist itineracy can continue to animate vital congregations connected in this national and international Protestant church.

See also Circuit Rider; Methodism, North America; Women Clergy

References and Further Reading

Dunlap, E. Dale. "The United Methodist System of Itinerant Ministry." In Perspectives on American Methodism. Nashville, TN: Kingswood Books, 415–430.

Heitzenrater, Richard P. "Connectionalism and Itinerancy: Wesleyan Principles and Practice." In *Connectionalism: Ecclesiology, Mission, and Identity, United Methodism and American Culture,* edited by Russell E. Richey, Dennis M. Campbell, and William B. Lawrence. vol. 1. Nashville, TN: Abingdon Press, 1997.

Richey, Russell E. "Itineracy in Early Methodism." In *Send Me? The Itineracy in Crisis,* edited by Donald E. Messer. Nashville, TN: Abingdon Press, 1991.

———, and Kenneth E. Rowe, eds. *Methodist History: A Bicentennial Historical Consultation.* Nashville, TN: Kingswood Books, 1985.

Wigger, John H. "Fighting Bees: Methodist Itinerants and the Dynamics of Methodist Growth, 1770–1820." In *Methodism and the Shaping of American Culture,* edited by Nathan O. Hatch and John H. Wigger. Nashville, TN: Kingswood Books, An Imprint of Abingdon Press, 2001.

W. HARRISON DANIEL

J

JABAVU, DAVIDSON DON TENGO (1895–1959)

South African educator and writer. Davidson D. T. Jabavu was the son of John Tengo Jabavu (1859–1921), one of the most eloquent representatives of the educated African elite in SOUTH AFRICA in his generation. A Mfengu Methodist, John Tengo was South Africa's first black newspaper editor, and his paper *Imva Zabontsundu* reflected the outlook of those seeking African political, educational, and economic advance within a multiracial South Africa. He could irritate white opinion; the paper was closed for a time after it attacked British policy in the Anglo-Boer War in the matters of the concentration camps for Boer families and the treatment of Africans. At that time J. T. Jabavu left the Wesleyan Methodist Church in protest at its acceptance of such wartime excesses, and joined the SOCIETY OF FRIENDS.

Davidson Jabavu was thus born into the African elite, and in Cape Colony in 1895, where, unlike the rest of South Africa, many of the African elite had the right to vote. The theoretical equality of "civilized men of all races" did not, however, translate into equality of opportunity; and Jabavu, after his education at the Lovedale Institution of the Scottish mission, found he could progress no further in South Africa. He therefore attended the Colwyn Bay Institution in WALES, and thereafter the Universities of London and (for teacher training) Birmingham. He also took some time in the UNITED STATES before returning to South Africa as the first African staff member of the Fort Hare Native College. He assisted the academic transformation of the college as it attained its later status as a university college. His own status rose to that of professor of Latin and Bantu languages, and head of the department of African studies.

As mission thinking developed and the missionary movement became more international in outlook, especially after the formation of the International Missionary Council, Jabavu was identified as an articulate spokesman of African Christianity. There had been no such spokesman at the WORLD MISSIONARY CONFERENCE at Edinburgh in 1910; but Jabavu was active at the Le Zoute Conference of 1926, which redefined the Christian mission in AFRICA, with EDUCATION as one of the major aspects of mission policy. He was also present at the meeting of the International Missionary Council itself in Jerusalem in 1928. He also made an impact, notably on the powerful Thomson Samkange, at the Southern Rhodesia Native Missionary Conference in 1931.

By this time Jabavu was a national figure for his defense of African rights. Having formed associations of farmers and teachers and a Cape Voters' Association, all representative bodies of "civilized" Africans, he founded the All African National Convention. This body, established in 1935, arose to counter moves to prevent Africans from owning land (and thus, in the Cape, gaining the vote) or selling their labor freely. For a time the Convention united a broad spectrum in opposition to the erosion of African rights, but with the rise of the Nationalists and their triumph in 1948, it faded and was eventually disbanded. The ideal of "the equality of civilized men of all races" was irrelevant in an age of apartheid. Apartheid left no room in which to exercise Jabavu's brand of multiracial constitutional politics and African advance by means of education on a European pattern. Black opposition was now radicalized, and his form of moderate Social Christianity had little appeal. Jabavu, disillusioned with politics, concentrated thereafter on his academic work at Fort Hare, leaving to a new generation of African leaders—such as Z. K. MATTHEWS and ALBERT

LUTHULI, people nurtured like himself on mission education and imbued like him with Christian social ideas—to cope with the new situation. White domination was now underpinned by an ideology claiming a Christian and Reformed inspiration, and this posed challenges of a new kind.

Jabavu's works on the changing political situation include *The Black Problem* (1921) and *The Segregation Fallacy and Other Papers* (1928). His principal academic treatise was *The Influence of English on Bantu Literature* (1943). He also wrote extensively in Xhosa.

References and Further Reading

Primary Source:

Jabavu, D. D. T. *The Life of John Tengo Jabavu.* Lovedale, South Africa: Lovedale Institution Press, 1933.

Secondary Sources:

Elphick, R., and R. Davenport, eds. *Christianity in South Africa: A Political, Social and Cultural History.* Berkeley: University of California Press, 1997.
Higgs, Catherine. *The Ghosts of Equality: The Public Lives of DDT Jabavu of South Africa.* Athens: University of Ohio Press, 1997.
Smith, E. W. *The Christian Mission in Africa.* London: International Missionary Council, 1926.

ANDREW F. WALLS

JACKSON, SHELDON (1834–1909)

American clergyman. Born on May 18, 1834, in Minaville, New York, Jackson was an itinerant missionary who is said to have traveled more than a million miles.

After graduating from Princeton Theological Seminary in 1858, Jackson taught Native American boys in Oklahoma, served as an army chaplain, and led a church in Minnesota, but he longed for a grander assignment. In 1869 he convinced his denomination to appoint him superintendent over a vast territory stretching from Iowa to Utah. Still restless, in 1877 he seized on a letter from an army private stationed in Alaska, who detailed that territory's degradation and begged for "a shepherd who may reclaim a mighty flock from the error of their ways." Jackson dove in, establishing churches and schools and using his connections to powerful fellow Presbyterians, including President Grover Cleveland, to fight corruption in Alaska's fledgling government.

Jackson attracted criticism for neglecting some areas of his ministry, notably the lower Rockies and work with whites, to focus on native Alaskans. He also found himself in the middle of an emerging church–state debate as disgruntled Alaskan officials questioned his dual role as missionary and, from 1885, educational agent for the federal government. Embattled, Jackson lost influence, but his legacy persists through such edifices as Sheldon Jackson College in Sitka, Alaska. A friend once said of Jackson that he could not resist "running ahead of the crowd, climbing a hill, scaling a mountain, following a valley, opening a schoolhouse. . . constantly searching out the land." Jackson died May 2, 1909, in Asheville, North Carolina.

See also Church and State, Overview; Missions, North American; Native Americans; Chaplaincy

References and Further Reading

Primary Source:

Jackson, Sheldon. *Alaska, and Missions on the North Pacific Coast.* New York: Dodd, Mead, 1880.

Secondary Source:

Bender, Norman J. *Winning the West for Christ.* Albuquerque, NM: University of New Mexico Press, 1996.

ELESHA COFFMAN

JAMES, WILLIAM (1842–1910)

American psychologist and philosopher. James was born January 11, 1842, in New York City, the first child of Mary Robertson Walsh and Henry James, Sr., and elder brother of novelist Henry James and diarist Alice James. James's father, a Presbyterian, studied for two years at Princeton Theological Seminary (1835–1837). Frustrated with orthodox CALVINISM and the church, and funded by his modest inheritance, Henry Sr. embarked on an eclectic career as a writer and lecturer of minor repute on religious and social subjects, influenced by EMANUEL SWEDENBORG and Charles Fourier.

Due to his father's liberal conception of individual development, William received an uncommon education at home and, during adolescence, in various European schools. After exploring a vocation as a painter, he enrolled at the Lawrence Scientific School at Harvard, studying chemistry, then comparative anatomy and physiology, then medicine; his sole earned degree of M.D. was conferred in 1869, though he never practiced. James began lecturing on physiology at Harvard in 1873, and spent his career there. He offered the first course in psychology proper in the United States in 1876, and set up one of the first two experimental psychology laboratories in America. In 1880 he was formally appointed in philosophy. He continued to teach in both fields until his retirement in 1907.

Works and Interests

James's intellectual contributions were manifold, spanning psychology, moral philosophy, religion, epistemology, and metaphysics, in addition to addressing public issues of his day such as anti-imperialism. He also had an enduring, if skeptical, interest in parapsychology. His writings exhibit an exceptional style—enlivened by image and metaphor—that is unparalleled; he is still one of America's leading persons of letters. *The Principles of Psychology* (1890) became an immediate classic for its comprehensive, engaging presentation of the then-new field, as well as its introduction of "the stream of consciousness." *The Will to Believe and Other Essays in Philosophy* (1897) established James in moral and religious philosophy with its title essay, although the book is much wider in scope. *The Varieties of Religious Experience* (1902) was and remains James's most widely read text, focusing on first-person accounts of religion and their fruits, effectively launching (albeit inadvertently) the study of mysticism and contributing to the psychology of religion. James's innovations in metaphysics are forwarded within the posthumously published *Essays in Radical Empiricism* (ed. Perry, 1912), which date from 1904–1905 and delineate his notion of "pure experience." *Pragmatism* (1907) popularized the theories of meaning and truth known by that name, as well as developed James's philosophy of religion, which is further advanced in *A Pluralistic Universe* (1909), a defense of "radical empiricism" against rationalism. *The Meaning of Truth* (1909), James's last completed essay collection, revisits pragmatic epistemology.

Trained as a man of science in a scientific age and committed to empiricism, James nonetheless continuously broached religious topics; indeed he is noteworthy for arguing that philosophies and worldviews must be judged by their ability, among other criteria, to account for and accommodate human beings' religious concerns. Not a member of any particular religious community, James saw himself as developing out of the tradition of liberal New England Protestantism (see LIBERAL PROTESTANTISM AND LIBERALISM). His own perspectives on religion, although routinely unorthodox, resonate with this lineage: he asserts the primacy of the will among other human faculties and emphasizes conduct and action in his psychology; he attends to individual experience, and contends that defensible knowledge comes by attention to fruits, not roots; he presumes the importance of understanding CONVERSION for getting to the bottom of what is distinctively religious; he understands God (or the divine) as sharing personality (the possession of interests) with us; and he justifies holding some beliefs ahead of evidence for them, within certain constraints.

This "will to believe" (or "right to believe") doctrine is one of his most celebrated and enduring ideas. Focusing on cases demanding decision or action in which the stakes are momentous and the opportunity unrepeatable, James defends the value and rationality of logically noncontradictory belief as well as the potential efficacy of such belief in determining future facts. The "faith ladder" of reasoning that James constructs from this becomes crucial in his justifications of religious hypotheses and philosophical viewpoints, and responsive to human needs.

James's views on religion and the divine were not static through his career. His work from the 1880s through 1900 assumes a dualistic theism, specifying God as an independent "deep power" that shares in some intimate sense the better of our interests, and that may make for righteousness. From a moral perspective, the supposition of God enhances the claims we make on ourselves, opening out the infinite perspective and ensuring both the maintenance of our ideals and a maximal appeal to our moral energies. *Varieties* proves transitional for James's theism, interrogating the apparently active effects of the divine on individuals, and moving toward metaphysical questions. Working from empirical evidence, James seeks to assess the value of religious experience for humans and the potential for verifying the content of religious claims. His conclusions are stronger on the former than the latter, although he does suggest that evidence supports the plausibility of basic religious claims concerning the divine. In *Varieties* James extends his earlier assumption of supernaturalism, but specifies it as "piecemeal," meaning that God's power and scope may be finite. This supports James's meliorism, the view that our voluntary efforts may be critical to the making of righteousness in conjunction with those of the divine. James also characterizes the divine as a "wider self through which saving experiences come," rather than the radically transcendent being of traditional theism, opening the door to both a real pluralism with regard to God(s) and a nonreductive psychodynamic account of religious experience through subliminal consciousness. After 1903 James modified his position further in connection with his developing radically empiricist metaphysics, referring to God no longer as a supernatural but rather a "superhuman" power. In his later works he emphasized the sociality and collaborative character of divine–human relations as understood from an empirical perspective, and developed his notion of experience into a panpsychical conception of all reality—natural, human, and divine.

This later position, although not logically coercive for belief, is nonetheless presented as compelling because of its compatibility with commonsense religious belief and its consistency with the plural demands of our theoretical, moral, aesthetic, and practical rationalities.

References and Further Reading

Lamberth, David C. *William James and the Metaphysics of Experience.* Cambridge: Cambridge University Press, 1999.

Levinson, Henry Samuel. *The Religious Investigations of William James.* Chapel Hill: The University of North Carolina Press, 1981.

Perry, Ralph Barton. *The Thought and Character of William James.* 2 vols. Boston: Little, Brown & Co., 1935.

Putnam, Ruth Anna, ed. *The Cambridge Companion to William James.* Cambridge: Cambridge University Press, 1997.

Simon, Linda. *Genuine Reality: A Life of William James.* New York: Harcourt Brace, 1998.

DAVID C. LAMBERTH

JAPAN

Protestant Beginnings

Japan's first experience with Christianity took place during the so-called Christian century that extended from the middle of the sixteenth century to just before the middle of the seventeenth. During these years Portuguese and Spanish Catholic missionaries raised a Christian community of nearly half a million people in a CULTURE that was already technically advanced and literate. However, for political reasons, the Tokugawa shogunate, which ruled Japan from 1603 to 1868, eradicated Christianity. In the late 1630s the shogunate felt so threatened by Christianity that it adopted a policy of national seclusion, which closed Japan to almost all foreign contact. Only a small underground sect, the *Kakure Kirishitan* (hidden Christians) in the Nagasaki region, was able to preserve their religion in secret. During the Tokugawa era, anti-Christian thought became both ingrained and broad based because attacks on Christianity were backed up by the prestige of Japanese TRADITION, by traditional thought that was intimately connected with established religion, and through the use of arguments for the defense of the fatherland and of Japanese religion. Various anti-Christian arguments with strong xenophobic undertones or spy conspiracy theories were put forward to justify its prohibition. These would resurface after 1859 in the face of the new Christian challenge brought by Protestant missionaries.

During the early nineteenth century Protestant missionaries had accompanied Western trade expansion into the Pacific and East Asia. In 1837 missionaries were on board the *Morrison* during its unsuccessful attempt to open American trade relations with Japan. In 1846 Bernard Bettelheim started missionary work at Naha, Okinawa. In 1853 the arrival of the United States squadron under Commodore Matthew C. Perry in Uraga Bay rendered useless the Japanese policy of national seclusion. However, it was not until the 1858 Harris Treaty, which opened commercial relations between the UNITED STATES and Japan and also allowed religious establishments, that the possibility of missionary residence in the treaty ports appeared. In 1859 the first resident American Protestant missionaries landed, including the Episcopalian Channing M. Williams; the Dutch Reformed missionaries, Guido F. Verbeck and R. S. Brown; the Presbyterian medical doctor, James C. Hepburn; and the Baptist Jonathan Goble, all of whom were destined to become famous. Prohibited from propagating the Gospel to the Japanese, these first missionaries devoted their energies to language study, translation of the Gospels (see BIBLE TRANSLATION), and to the teaching of English in government schools, or, in the case of Hepburn, medical work. The opening of the American CIVIL WAR in 1861 retarded the growth of the missionary movement. Indeed before 1870 there were only some fifteen Protestant missionaries in Japan.

Understandably, during the 1860s very few Japanese became Protestant converts. Some like the Japanese Sam Patch, a shipwrecked sailor, or Niijima Jō, the founder of what became Dōshisha University in Kyoto, who had illegally left Japan to study overseas, were introduced to Christianity outside of Japan. In Japan itself converts were mostly Japanese language teachers, missionary servants, or young pupils at schools where missionaries taught. Among missionary achievements, there was the 1867 publication of Hepburn's superlative English–Japanese dictionary, and the opening of the first coeducational school in Japan by Mrs. Clara Hepburn.

Meiji Protestantism 1868–1912

The downfall of the Tokugawa shogunate with the 1868 Meiji Restoration brought no change in policy toward Christianity. The new Meiji government was loath to give ground to the Western powers on the issue of religious TOLERATION. It stood firm during its first major diplomatic crisis with the Western powers over its persecution of the Urakami Christians near Nagasaki in 1868–1869. In 1872 the Yokohama Band, the name given to the first major group of converts, formed the first Protestant church in Japan, the nondenominational Yokohama *Kirisuto Kōkai,* with James Ballagh, a Reformed missionary, as its pastor. Among its members were such famous Christians as Uemura Masahisa, Ibuka Kajinosuke, and Honda Yōichi. The Yokohama Band would play a crucial role in the spread of Protestantism by working as language teachers, evangelists, and helpers to missionaries. Later, many became ordained ministers.

Government attitudes toward religion were important to future Protestant growth. From 1868 onwards the government saw the importance of using autochthonous quasi-religious rituals and ceremonies to reinforce its power and control, and in helping to legitimize the modernization of the Japanese monarchy through linking the present with the mythical past. In 1873, at the instigation of the Iwakura Embassy, then visiting North America and Europe, the proscription edicts against Christianity were removed from public view. This was interpreted by Western missionaries as allowing the open propagation of the Gospel among Japanese, and led to a wide range of European and North American societies sending missionaries to Japan (see MISSIONARY ORGANIZATIONS). Nevertheless, Christianity still remained officially banned, and the government lent support to Buddhist sects to counter its spread. In the late 1870s Christianity faced new evolutionary arguments imported from the West in addition to the traditional ones available to the opponents of Christianity (see DARWINISM). In the late 1880s Buddhist scholars began to attack Christianity on the grounds that Buddhist theology was superior to Christian THEOLOGY. In the 1889 Meiji Constitution religious freedom was constitutionally guaranteed, although its meaning still had to be defined. This was especially true in terms of church–state relations at the governmental and bureaucratic levels, but also applied to issues surrounding the relationship between Japanese NATIONALISM and patriotism and Christian faith at the personal level. To the government, religious freedom came to mean that the role of religion in society was to serve the interests of the state, and it was prepared to act to ensure that religious freedom did not compromise those interests, particularly in education.

During the 1870s the Protestant movement experienced considerable growth. Convert bands coalesced around missionaries or Western lay Christians teaching in new schools of Western Studies in the treaty ports, and also in provincial towns and cities. Protestant bands were formed in Shizuoka, Hirosaki, Niigata, Osaka, Kumamoto, and Sapporo, as well as in the Tokyo area in Tsukiji, Shiba, and Koishikawa. These Christian bands developed along skeins of contact, friendship, family relations, and, in rural areas, family influence and economic power. The Kumamoto Band was particularly important because many future leaders of the *Kumiai Kyōkai* (Congregational Church) were members, including Kozaki Hiromichi, Ebina Danjō, and Yokoi Tokio. Uchimura Kanzō, the founder of the Non-Church Movement (*Mukyōdai*)

was a member of the Sapporo Band, as was Nitobe Inazō, the author and educationalist. A large percentage of the early converts were ex-samurai attracted to Protestantism through the educational work of missionaries and the influence of leading intellectuals and educators like Nakamura Masanao, the translator of John Stuart Mill's *On Liberty,* and Tsuda Sen, an agricultural expert. Personal loyalty to an outstanding leader, Japanese or missionary, provided a common pattern in Christian CONVERSION.

There was an assumption among early Protestants that Christianity was the basis of Western civilization and that Japan must become a Christian nation if it wished to be successful in adopting Western technology. Yamaji Aizan, an early historian of Meiji Protestantism, argued that samurai on the losing side in the Restoration turned to Christianity in an effort to regain lost status. However, conversion was not restricted to ex-Tokugawa samurai, and many converts, particularly in rural areas, were not samurai. Although Christian ideas were introduced into Japan through Chinese-language sources as well as through English-language and Western studies, the desire to acquire new knowledge to equip themselves better to changing times was common to most converts regardless of class.

The student population in the major cities became a prime target of missionary efforts and great emphasis was placed on educational work. During the 1870s and 1880s the mission school forerunners of Dōshisha University (Congregational) in Kyoto, and, in Tokyo, Aoyama Gakuin University (Methodist), Meiji Gakuin University (Presbyterian/Reformed), and Rikkyō University (Anglican) were established as missionaries strove to cater to the great demand for Western knowledge. During the same years schools for girls were founded, including the Ferris Joshi Gakkō (Reformed) in Yokohama and the Tōyō Eiwa Jo Gakkō (Methodist) in Tokyo. Mission schools for girls made a vital contribution to the development of women's education. A vast network of Christian schools grew through the early twentieth century, reaching an important milestone with the postwar foundation of the International Christian University in Tokyo.

During the Meiji period Protestantism also exerted a significant influence on emerging popular movements for social and political change. Protestants were active in the Popular Rights Movement of the 1880s, and a decade later Christians were among the leaders of the first major environmental protest over the pollution caused by the Ashio Copper Mine. Others like Tokutomi Sohō were active in journalism, and Tokutomi Roka and Arishima Takeo were important literary figures. A number of the first leaders of the Japanese socialist and labor movements were Protestants or influenced by Christianity.

Protestant Developments (1912–1931)

The Achilles' heel of Japanese Christians was the doubt that was cast in the minds of non-Christian Japanese about their loyalty to Japan and even their Japaneseness after they became Christians. The desire of Christians to prove themselves as loyal was expressed in broad support for Japanese imperialism and overseas expansion. After the Sino-Japanese War of 1894, Japanese missionary work began in Taiwan, KOREA, Manchuria, Singapore, and North America. By 1912 the desire for an independent Christianity in Japan was developing toward the creation of a Japanese Christianity (*Nipponteki Kirisutokyō*) distinct from that Christianity propagated by Western missionaries. There was also a strong desire among Protestants for Christianity to be recognized along with Shinto and Buddhism as one of the three major religions of Japan.

During the 1910s and early 1920s Protestants, like Suzuki Bunji, played an important role in the embryonic trade union movement. Yoshino Sakuzō, a Tokyo Imperial University professor, was one of the leading opinion makers in the political movement for democracy and universal suffrage. Protestant influence was also evident in the early development of both rural and urban movements, including the initial organization of the tenant-farmer association and also in the *Zenkoku Suiheisha,* an organization for the outcaste class. However, these activities met with considerable hostility from church leaders who did not wish Christianity to be seen as opposing the status quo. As a result, many Christian political and social activists either abandoned their Christian beliefs or moderated their political and social views. Missionaries also made important pioneering contributions to the development of social welfare work in the Tokyo slums, in the care of lepers, in opening schools for the blind and sanatoria for tuberculosis victims, and in prison work.

In 1922 the ecumenical movement in Japan reached a milestone with the formation of the National Christian Council (NCC) (see ECUMENISM). The NCC included most Protestant denominations, Christian schools, and social institutions. Although its actual power over individual denominations was limited to moral persuasion, the NCC did play an important role in coordinating the cooperative endeavors of the Protestant movement, including church union. It did much to help in supervising relief measures for Christian churches after the 1923 Great Kantō Earthquake, and, at the international level, presented reasoned Christian protests against the United States Congress's 1924 Anti-Immigration Bill. Increasingly the NCC also assumed the duty of representing the Protestant movement in its dealings with the government. Furthermore, it was deeply involved in supporting evangelistic initiatives. The most significant was the Kingdom of God movement begun in 1929. During the first half of the 1930s this movement's impact on the direction of the evangelistic efforts of both Japanese Christians and Western missionaries cannot be overestimated. Under the leadership of KAGAWA TOYOHIKO it was the largest interdenominational evangelistic endeavor in Japanese Christian history, and had the support of all the major Protestant groups and the missionary movement. The connection between this united evangelistic effort and the growing movement toward church union in the early 1930s also needs to be stressed. By the early 1930s the Protestant movement had some 300,000 adherents.

The Dark Age (1931–1945)

The years from 1931 to 1945 were a dark age in Japanese religious history, reminiscent of the witch hunts of medieval Europe. Religious groups were callously persecuted, especially new religions like Ōmotokyō, but also some Christian groups including the Holiness Church, PLYMOUTH BRETHREN, the SEVENTH-DAY ADVENTISTS, the SALVATION ARMY, and the *Nihon Seikōkai* (the Japanese Anglican Church) because the authorities thought they held heterodox ideas or were too closely identified with foreign countries. During the early 1930s the Shrine Question—that is, the participation of Christians in state-sponsored Shinto ceremonies—emerged as a major problem for Christians because it touched the sensitive topic of their loyalty, patriotism, and attitude toward the emperor, as well as the issue of freedom of religion and the national Shinto system. To maintain the façade of freedom of religion, the government proclaimed that the ceremonies at state Shino shrines were exercises in civil religion and beyond the control of religious sects. Protestants in Japan accepted this view, but those in Korea or Taiwan did not—with tragic consequences. The impact of the Shrine Question was particularly felt in Christian schools, which were already being forced to get rid of their foreign teachers and connections. During the late 1930s the nature of Japanese Christianity, under pressure from ultranationalism and emperor-centered militarism (*tennōsei*), changed to be a new nationalistic religion not only distinct from Western Christianity but also increasingly devoid of Western influences.

After the opening of the Sino-Japanese War in 1937, the government pressed for the union of religious groups, including Protestant denominations, to enhance its control. The Religious Organizations Law came into effect in early 1940. By late 1940 it was evident that the government intended to combine all Protestant denominations into a single church. During this time virtually all Western missionaries decided to withdraw from Japan. In December 1941 the union Protestant Church, the *Nihon Kirisutokyōdan* (the United Church of Christ in Japan), received government recognition. Among the major Protestant denominations, only a rump of the *Nihon Seikōkai* chose to stay outside the union church, and lost its standing as a religious organization. Although church union took place only because of government pressure, it is also true that the government was able to exploit the genuine desire of many Protestant leaders for Protestant union. Government demands for church union and for Christian participation in the national spiritual mobilization in support of Japan's war effort resonated with long-held Christian hopes not only for church union but also for leadership of the Protestant movement in East Asia. For the most part Christian leaders were both willing, even enthusiastic, to throw their support behind the war effort because they were all sincere nationalists. During the Pacific War all Protestants suffered great hardships, and some were persecuted and imprisoned, but Christianity survived.

Postwar Protestantism

A new era in Japanese Christian history opened with the end of World War II in East Asia in 1945 and the beginning of the Allied occupation of Japan. The surrender of Japan brought about an end to *tennosei* and opened the way for a broader range of beliefs and practices under a new postwar constitution that guaranteed complete religious freedom. The occupation years between 1945 and 1951 saw a Christian boom and rapid growth. Although the *Nihon Kirisutokyōdan* remained the largest Protestant denomination, a number of Protestant groups left the union church to reform their own churches, including the *Nihon Seikōkai* and various Reformed and Presbyterian groups. Despite the plethora of Protestant denominations, the Protestant movement still faced great challenges. Some of these related to the internal character of the church rather than external conditions. During the 1950s and 1960s the question of the church's wartime responsibilities created internal tensions. Likewise the Western image of the Protestant church and its continued reliance on Western Christian help caused the church to be prone to swings in Japanese public opinion about the United States. In the 1970s and 1980s the identification with the Western approach to spirituality meant that the Protestant movement was not in a position to capitalize on the new religiosity among

Japanese seen in the popularity of new religions. Although Japanese Protestants have played an important role in campaigns against the renationalization of the Yasukuni Shrine, against the censorship of textbooks, and for world peace, the church has difficulties in attracting young people. At the millennium, although Christian-founded universities play an important role in Japanese higher education, the number of Christians among their faculties has steadily declined and some denominations suffer from a shortage of candidates for the ministry.

References and Further Reading

Breen, John, and Mark Williams, eds. *Japan and Christianity: Impacts and Responses.* London: Macmillan Press, 1995.

Dohi, Akio. *Nihon Purotesutanto Kirisutokyōshi (A History of Protestant Christianity in Japan).* Tokyo: Shinkyō Shuppansha, 1982.

Dōshisha Daigaku Jinbun Kagaku Kenkyūjo. *Nihon no Purotesutanto shokyōkai no kenkyū (Studies on Various Japanese Protestant Churches).* Tokyo: Kyōbunkan, 1997.

Drummond, Richard Henry. *A History of Christianity in Japan.* Grand Rapids, MI: Wm. B. Eerdmans, 1971.

Ion, A. Hamish. *The Cross and the Rising Sun: The British Protestant Missionary Movement in Japan, Korea, and Taiwan, 1931–1945.* Waterloo, Canada: Wilfrid Laurier University Press, 1993.

———. *The Cross in the Dark Valley: The Canadian Protestant Missionary Movement in the Japanese Empire, 1931–1945.* Waterloo, Canada: Wilfrid Laurier University Press, 1999.

Ohama, Tetsuya. *Meiji Kirisutokyō kyōkaishi no kenkyū (Studies in the History of Meiji Christianity).* Tokyo: Yoshikawa Kōbunkan, 1979.

Powles, Cyril Hamilton. *Victorian Missionaries in Meiji Japan: The Shiba Sect 1873–1900.* Toronto, Canada: University of Toronto/York University Joint Center on Modern East Asia, 1987.

Saba, Wataru, ed. *Uemura Masahisa to sono jidai (The Life and Times of Uemura Masahisa).* 8 vols. Tokyo: Kyōbunkan, 1937–1941.

Sumiya, Mikio. *Nihon no shakai shisō: kindaika to Kirisutokyō (Social Thought in Japan: Modernization and Christianity).* Tokyo: Tokyo Daigaku Shuppankai, 1968.

Yamaji, Aizan. *Essays on the Modern Japanese Church: Christianity in Meiji Japan.* Translated by Graham Squires with introductory essays by Graham Squires and A. Hamish Ion. Ann Arbor: Center for Japanese Studies, University of Michigan, 1999.

A. Hamish Ion

JEFFERSON, THOMAS (1743–1826)

Third president of the United States and eminent figure of the American ENLIGHTENMENT. Jefferson defended "pure" religion, but often attacked the major institutional manifestations of Protestantism in America. He especially targeted those churches that allied themselves with the power of the state, particularly the ANGLICANISM of his homeland of Virginia and the

CONGREGATIONALISM of New England. In the first instance he moved in the earliest days of the American Revolution to disestablish the CHURCH OF ENGLAND and to enlist Virginians in a struggle for complete religious liberty. In the latter instance, he had less direct impact on the New England establishment, though his enmity toward it never weakened. By helping to destroy the Federalist Party, he removed the power base of a politicized Congregationalism.

Jefferson and Religious Liberty

Jefferson is readily and correctly identified as a passionate promoter of religious liberty. With his younger colleague, JAMES MADISON (1749–1812), he did all that he could to see that Virginia cleansed itself of all lingering taints of an alliance between church and state. In fighting a war against ENGLAND, few would defend the notion of continued official support for the Church of England. To some, however, this did not mean an abrupt, and perhaps even brutal, severing of all ties between the civil and the ecclesiastical orders. Patrick Henry, for example, thought it made good sense to establish Christianity in general, while conceding that one could not show any special favoritism to England's national church. To Madison and Jefferson, however, this compromise represented a betrayal of the spirit of liberty for which the patriots had fought from 1776 to 1783. To maintain any kind of religious establishment would, in Madison's words, warn the refugee "to seek some other haven," for America would no longer be an asylum "to the persecuted and oppressed of every nation and religion."

Though Jefferson had composed a bill for establishing religious freedom in Virginia as early as 1777, it took a reluctant legislature almost a decade to declare "that no man shall be compelled to frequent or support any religious worship, place, or ministry whatsoever." On the contrary, "all men shall be free to profess, and by argument to maintain, their opinions in matters of religion." When at last the bill became law in 1786, Jefferson took great satisfaction that his own state housed "the first legislature who has had the courage to declare that the reason of man may be trusted with the formation of his own opinions." In Paris, at the time his bill passed, Jefferson like a proud father saw it translated into French and Italian and "sent to most of the courts of Europe." England in particular, but much of Europe in general, thought that the newly independent states would soon collapse into anarchy, but this Statute for Establishing Religious Freedom was the best evidence, Jefferson asserted, that America was moving steadily toward greater enlightenment, not giving way to lawlessness and chaos.

Jefferson saw Virginia's bold step as a giant one, but insufficient by itself, for the new nation as a whole had to adopt a similar stance. When Madison happily wrote to Jefferson in Paris at the end of 1787 that delegates in Philadelphia had drawn up an impressive constitution, Jefferson replied with compliments, but immediately asked about the guarantees for religious liberty and other civil freedoms. The result of his widely shared concern was, of course, a Bill of Rights: the first ten amendments to the Constitution adopted in 1791. The very first of those specified that "Congress shall make no law respecting an establishment of religion, or prohibiting the free exercise thereof." As president, Jefferson in 1802 put his own powerful spin on those words by declaring in a public letter that Congress had thus erected "a wall of separation between church and state."

In his two terms as president, as well as in the nearly two decades of his retirement, Jefferson continued to worry about any and all religion allied with or seeking to exercise political power. He worried about the Congregational clergy who had gotten a "smell of union between church and state," and when, in 1818, Connecticut finally broke its ties with the church, Jefferson immediately wrote to John Adams of his delight that "this den of the priesthood is at length broken up, and that a protestant popedom is no longer to disgrace the American history and character." When later he founded the first "truly modern" university, the University of Virginia, he set up every safeguard to keep sectarian influences out of his school. By the 1820s it was the Presbyterians, not the Anglicans (now identified as Episcopalians), who sought to frustrate his plans. In so doing, they won Jefferson's harsh condemnation as "the most intolerant of all sects, the most tyrannical, and ambitious." Such strong language could suggest to many that Jefferson was not only against religous power, but that he was against religion itself.

Jefferson and "Pure" Religion

This, however, was clearly not the case. Jefferson condemned dogmatism and what he called scholastic subtleties. He found Platonism or Neoplatonism the enemy of the simple religion of Jesus, and of CALVINISM he wrote that it "has introduced into the Christian religion more new absurdities than its leader had purged it of old ones." Priests and preachers took refuge in mysteries and miracles, avoiding the "weightier matters of the law" such as good works and simple charity. The gospel that Jesus proclaimed, Jefferson argued, was simple enough for any peasant to understand, but professional theologians were determined to make it difficult and obscure, as they spread darkness rather than light. "The metaphysical insanities of Athanasius, of Loyola, and of Calvin," Jefferson concluded, "are to my understanding mere relapses into polytheism, differing from paganism only by being more unintelligible."

But was it not possible to rescue the pure religion of Jesus? Inspired by scientist and educator Joseph Priestley (1733–1804) and others, Jefferson gave much energy and much thought to doing just that. In writing "The Philosophy of Jesus," in providing an outline of a revised "Christian system," and in compiling what came to be called the "Jefferson Bible," the nation's third president saw his time as ripe for completing the Reformation begun in the sixteenth century. Jefferson believed that reason and religion must be allies, not enemies, and that by rejecting mysteries and irrational dogmas it was possible—in the age of Enlightenment—to recapture a purified Chritianity: "the most sublime and benevolent code of morals which has ever been offered to mankind."

See also Church and State, Overview; Deism; Enlightenment; First Amendment; Priestly, Joseph.

References and Further Reading

Primary Sources:

Jefferson, Thomas. *Writings.* Edited by Merrill D. Peterson. New York: Library of America, 1984.

Secondary Sources:

Adams, Dickinson W., ed. *Jefferson's Extracts from the Gospels.* Princeton: Princeton University Press, 1983.

Gaustad, Edwin S. *Sworn on the Altar of God: A Religious Biography of Thomas Jefferson.* Grand Rapids, MI: Eerdmans, 1996.

Peterson, Merrill D., and Robert C. Vaughan. *The Virginia Statute for Religious Freedom: Its Evolution and Consequences in American History.* Cambridge: Cambridge University Press, 1988.

EDWIN S. GAUSTAD

JEHOVAH'S WITNESSES

Jehovah's Witnesses began in the last quarter of the nineteenth century as a small Adventist sect (see SECTARIANISM) of Bible students under the leadership of CHARLES TAZE RUSSELL. They adopted the name "Jehovah's Witnesses" in 1931 to emphasize their distinctive beliefs that the proper translation of the personal name of God in Hebrew Scriptures is "Jehovah" (Exodus 3:15) and that the correct name for believers is "witnesses" (Isaiah 43:10; Acts 1:8). Dedicated to the fervent proclamation of the belief that Jesus Christ will soon return to defeat Satan, the adversary of God's righteous rule, in the battle of Har-magedon

and establish the millennial paradise on earth, Jehovah's Witnesses have grown to an active membership of nearly six million in 234 countries. Like other sectarian movements in American Protestantism, such as the Church of Jesus Christ of Latter-day Saints (MORMONS) and CHRISTIAN SCIENCE, the Jehovah's Witnesses regard their community and its teachings as the restoration of true Christianity from the apostasy of all other churches. Jehovah's Witnesses claim neither a new revelation nor an inspired founder, but insist that they derive their THEOLOGY and practices solely from a literal interpretation of the BIBLE and that they strictly follow the example of the first-century apostles. In imitation of their zeal, Jehovah's Witnesses devote themselves to distributing literature, conducting Bible classes, attending frequent congregational meetings, and closely regulating their personal and family lives by a rigorous moral code. Jehovah's Witnesses acknowledge the theocratic authority of the Governing Body and the administrative offices of the Watchtower Society.

Jehovah's Witnesses have gained adherents across the globe; over eighty percent live outside the United States, with concentrations in LATIN AMERICA and AFRICA. Many people are attracted by the vision of the KINGDOM OF GOD as paradise on earth, harmoniously integrating all ethnic groups in a perfect social order, free from prejudice and injustice, where war is unknown, lost loved ones are reunited with their families, and every individual experiences supreme happiness.

Origins

The nineteenth century in America was marked by religious enthusiasm, including waves of revivalism, proliferation of utopian groups, and the rise of Adventism (see MILLENARIANS AND MILLENNIALISM). Despite the failed prophecy of WILLIAM MILLER (founder of the SEVENTH-DAY ADVENTIST CHURCH) that the world would end in 1844, interpretations of biblical ESCHATOLOGY, especially in the books of Daniel and Revelation, remained popular among American Christians. The detailed chronologies inspired by the DISPENSATIONALISM of JOHN NELSON DARBY (British founder of the PLYMOUTH BRETHREN), and the elaborate calculations of the Adventists, heightened expectations that the study of biblical prophecy would disclose the future by deciphering the code of divine revelation. Among those excited by that prospect was Russell.

Russell was born into the middle-class home of a clothing store owner in Allegheny, Pennsylvania, in 1852 and raised in the tradition of PRESBYTERIANISM. However, as a teenager he became dissatisfied—like others alert to the spiritual possibilities of self-reliance—with the Calvinist doctrines of original sin, eternal hell, and double PREDESTINATION. He happened into the evening service of an Adventist Church and became newly convinced of the divine inspiration of the Bible. Despite the distractions of the family business from his formal education, Russell began his own earnest study of the Scriptures, assisted by several Adventist associates. From George Storrs, editor of *Bible Examiner,* Russell accepted the doctrine that the soul dies with the body and that immortality is a divine gift for faithful believers only. The unrighteous faced not eternal punishment, but annihilation. Russell learned from Nelson H. Barbour, editor of the Adventist periodical *Herald of the Morning,* that the invisible "presence" of Christ had already occurred in 1874, inaugurating a forty-year "harvest" of true Christians. The return of Christ, then, was a spiritual event intended not to destroy the inhabitants of earth but to bless them. Russell defended this interpretation in a pamphlet, entitled *The Object and Manner of Our Lord's Return,* published in 1877. Russell never adopted the SABBATARIANISM of the Adventists, however, and soon broke with Barbour over the latter's rejection of the substitutionary value of Christ's death, a point Russell regarded as central to the vindication of God's justice in the ATONEMENT.

In 1879 Russell began publishing his own monthly journal, *Zion's Watch Tower and Herald of Christ's Presence.* By 1880 Russell felt the need to draw groups of his readers into classes for study and fellowship. He regarded these small congregations as the beginning of the gathering of the true "body of Christ," whose responsibility was to fulfill the role of the "faithful and discreet slave" who supplies spiritual food to the rest of the household of faith, according to Jesus's parable in Matthew 24:45–47. In 1881 he declared that the "faithful and discreet slave" represented the collective ministry of those anointed by God's "holy spirit" to share in messianic authority. In 1884 Russell formed Zion's Watch Tower Tract Society to unify the scattered congregations of Bible students. They held their first convention in Allegheny in 1891.

Russell traveled constantly, wrote voluminously, and lectured with tireless energy. His was a dramatic presence, tall, with flowing beard, and histrionic gestures. His followers admired his dedication and modesty and gave him the honorific title "Pastor." Russell's central passion was "publishing" his ideas in every possible form: itinerant preaching; teaching classes; contributing to newspapers and magazines (in 1913 Russell's sermons reached fifteen million readers); and writing a small library of books, periodicals, and tracts over a period of thirty-seven years. He

encouraged his students to serve as colporteurs, going door to door with literature, at one time even accompanied by phonographs or dioramas. One popular production, "Photo-Drama of Creation," using motion pictures and slides synchronized with sound, had been shown to over nine million viewers in North America, Europe, and Australia by the end of 1914.

In 1886 Russell began an ambitious series of books titled *Millennial Dawn,* with the first volume called *The Divine Plan of the Ages.* He was convinced that he had discerned God's intention in history through the study of prophetic Scriptures. The key was his calculation that the "seven times" of Daniel 4:16 referred to the period of foreign domination over Israel (Luke 21:24), begun in 607 B.C. and destined to end in A.D. 1914 with the coming of the kingdom. When World War I began, some "Russellites" were certain they would be taken immediately into heaven. By the end of 1915, however, Russell explained that the defeat of the Ottoman Empire signaled only the beginning of the end. He taught that the return of Christ would not occur suddenly, but would extend over "a period of presence, as was the first advent." He translated the Greek term *parousia* as "presence," rather than "coming," and explained the arrival of the kingdom as a gradual "dawning." In the meanwhile Christ was calling those chosen to reign with him in heaven, including Russell and the Bible students, as "spiritual Israel."

In 1909 Russell moved the headquarters of his publishing operations to Brooklyn, New York, and named the complex "Bethel," or house of God. Not long after, Maria Ackley Russell served him with divorce papers, ending a long period of contention over her role in the organization. To this day women do not hold governing positions nor serve as elders in local congregations. Russell died in Texas on October 31, 1916, returning from a speaking tour.

Organization

Russell's successor as president of the Watch Tower Tract and Bible Society was Joseph Franklin Rutherford (1869–1942). Born on a farm in Missouri, Rutherford worked his way through college and after serving two years as an apprentice received his license to practice law at age twenty-three. He later served occasionally on the circuit court and was thus known as "Judge." Rutherford had provided legal counsel to Russell in the purchase of land for Bethel and was a member of the board of directors of the Watch Tower Society. Like Russell, Rutherford was physically imposing and a charismatic speaker. His disposition, however, was far less irenic and his style of management highly centralized. Rutherford and seven other directors were imprisoned under the Sedition Act of 1918 for their polemical writing against participation in the war. After nine months they won release on appeal, but many Bible students became targets of persecution, and the organization was in disarray. Rutherford took the opportunity to challenge the election of several directors, whom he replaced by his own supporters. He introduced a monthly "service sheet" to record in detail the evangelistic activities of members, increased the construction of Kingdom Halls, and began publishing a new monthly magazine called *The Golden Age* (later, *Awake!*). In 1919 he introduced the enthusiastic slogan, "Millions Now Living Will Never Die!"

Rutherford wrote extensively, beginning with *Harp of God* in 1921. He abandoned Russell's Zionism, as well as his prophetic speculations based on the Great Pyramid. In his own attempts to interpret prophecy Rutherford identified "Babylon the Great" of Revelation 17 with the League of Nations (abetted by the Vatican), foretold the return of biblical patriarchs (and built a mansion for their residence in San Diego, called Beth Sarim, where he resided in comparative luxury from 1930 until his death), and set the date 1925, and later 1940, for the coming of the kingdom. At the annual convention of 1931 Rutherford declared that henceforth "we desire to be known as and called by the name, to wit, Jehovah's witnesses." Since then, the use of "Jehovah" as the personal name of God has become a major point of DOCTRINE. In 1935 Rutherford declared that most of the growing body of Jehovah's Witnesses belonged to that "great crowd, which no man was able to number, out of all nations and tribes and peoples" (Revelation 7:9), who would not ascend to heaven, but live in the earthly paradise. Between the world wars Rutherford led the Witnesses through a series of court battles over freedom of speech and press, right of assembly, and distribution of literature. His death from colon cancer marked a major transition from charismatic to institutional authority.

Expansion

Nathan Homer Knorr (1905–1977) became the third president of the Watch Tower Society in 1942. Born in Pennsylvania, Knorr joined a congregation of Bible students as a teenager, was baptized at age eighteen, and promptly moved to Brooklyn to work in the Bethel headquarters, where he rose through the ranks to a place on the board of directors. Knorr's long presidency was marked by increased organizational growth, more sophisticated promotional methods, and greater uniformity in the programs of local congregations, including training in public speaking through Theocratic Ministry Schools. Known as "Brother," Knorr was more modest than his predecessors and in 1943 he established a policy of anonymous publications. In 1960 the Watchtower Society published the *New World Translation of the Holy Scriptures*. This version reflects the doctrinal vocabulary of the Watchtower Society and was largely the work of Frederick W. Franz.

In the postwar years Knorr traveled extensively, rebuilding branch organizations in Europe and establishing others in Asia, Latin America, the Middle East, and the Pacific islands. During the social tumult of the 1960s the Watch Tower Society intensified its defense of the divine inspiration of the Bible and tightened its discipline over sexual behavior (see SEXUALITY). As a result many young people were "disfellowshipped," expelled from their congregations, and cut off from all contact with other Jehovah's Witnesses, including members of their own family. This severe punishment was justified by reference to I Corinthians 5:9–11. At the same time, male workers at Bethel were allowed to marry, reversing earlier views of marriage and children as distractions from kingdom work (following I Corinthians 7:32–34). In 1971 the board of directors of the Watch Tower Society reorganized into a Governing Body on the model of the original apostles, composed of eleven men, plus the president, all of whom belonged to the "anointed class." The Governing Body issued binding directives, held all legal authority over the vast holdings of the Watch Tower Society, approved all publications, and was the final arbiter of doctrinal and behavioral questions. The Governing Body delegated many administrative duties to committees whose members it appointed. Knorr extended the apostolic model in 1972 by restoring to local Kingdom Halls the authority to elect their own ruling body of male elders. Near the end of his tenure Knorr, like his predecessors, became involved in controversy over failed prophecy. Beginning in 1966 many Jehovah's Witnesses began to speculate that the 6,000 years of human history (based on biblical genealogies from Adam) would end in 1975. Despite official cautions about the tentativeness of the date, many disappointed members later defected. Knorr died of a brain tumor in 1977.

Consolidation and Reorganization

Frederick W. Franz (1893–1992) became the fourth president of the Watchtower Society at age eighty-three. Born in Kentucky, Franz attended classes in biblical Greek at the University of Cincinnati. After studying Russell's writings, he left school to work as a colporteur and joined the Bethel family in 1920. Under Franz's leadership the Watchtower Society responded to the decline in membership after 1975 with a flurry of publications, including a revised reference edition of the *New World Translation* (1984), a new commentary on the Book of Revelation (1988), and a two-volume Bible encyclopedia (1991). By 1992 the Society had 800 translators rendering the Bible into scores of languages. Franz also strengthened local programs of education and developed the Ministerial Training School to train single male missionaries. The ranks of pioneers nearly tripled and the number of congregations grew to 70,000, many in Kingdom Halls that were constructed in a few days by special teams of builders. However, his tenure was not without controversy. The emphasis on greater dedication required stricter discipline, more weekly meetings for study and training, and more rigorous application of standards for disfellowshipping (resulting in the expulsion of his own nephew). Franz died at the age of ninety-nine.

Milton G. Henschel (1920–) became the fifth president of the Watchtower Society at the end of 1992. He served as secretary to Knorr, accompanying him on his travels, and rose to the presidency after decades of service at Bethel. His administration completed the transition from strong individual authority to corporate bureaucracy. Henschel belongs to the aging cohort of Jehovah's Witnesses who believed that they would not all die until Christ returned to take them to heaven to rule with him over paradise on earth. Ironically it was during his tenure that the Watchtower Society abandoned this belief. In 1995 *The Watchtower* revised its interpretation of Jesus's promise that "this generation will not pass away until all these things have taken place" (Matthew 24:34) to mean that there will always be those who oppose the truth until the kingdom arrives. Claiming a "progressive" understanding of revelation, drawn from Proverbs 4:18, the Watchtower Society declared that Jehovah's Witnesses are no longer to regard the generation of 1914 as "a rule for measuring time."

The institutional effects of this change were momentous. Members of the Governing Body, including the directors of the Watch Tower Society, are chosen exclusively from the "anointed class," whose membership Rutherford announced closed in 1935. (Some younger members had been recognized as "anointed" since then, but only as replacements for unspecified original members who had fallen away from the faith.) Thus the pool of available leaders was dwindling. In October 2000 the Watch Tower Bible and Tract Society of Pennsylvania, the parent corporation of about 100 Watchtower organizations, announced that its president and board of directors would henceforth be totally separate from the Governing Body and that its powers and assets would be divided among several corporations with their own presidents. All the members of the Governing Body resigned from the board. Milton Henschel was replaced as president by Don A. Adams, and all administrative positions were also filled by younger "brothers of the other sheep." The Governing Body no longer has legal authority, nor will it be subject to legal action, but will continue to offer spiritual guidance.

Jehovah's Witnesses worldwide remain organized into over thirty zones, which are in turn divided into branches; branches into districts; and districts into circuits, each composed of twenty congregations. A circuit overseer visits each of his congregations twice a year to guide the local body of male elders. When membership in a Kingdom Hall reaches 200, another congregation is formed. The 1999 *Yearbook* reported 89,985 congregations.

Teachings

Jehovah's Witnesses derive their religious teachings from a literal interpretation of the Bible, except where a figurative meaning is obviously intended (e.g., "four corners of the earth"). Thus, they reject doctrines formulated by the early councils of the Christian church under the influence of Greek philosophy, such as the Trinity. For Jehovah's Witnesses there is only one supreme "God of gods" (Psalm 136:2), who revealed his sacred name YHWH to Moses (Exodus 3:14). Whereas translators have substituted God and Lord for the divine name, Jehovah's Witnesses insist it is properly rendered in English as "Jehovah" (Psalm 83:18, KJV). Jehovah created the entire world in six "days" (each lasting 7,000 years) as recorded in Genesis 1–2, with no process of evolution. God created all things through the agency of Jesus in his preexistent form as the Word of God, called "Logos" in John 1 and "Wisdom" in Proverbs 8. As Jehovah's "master workman," he is chief among the "sons of God" (Job 1:6) and is known in Hebrew Scriptures as Michael the archangel. Although Jesus is not equal to Jehovah, he was "with" God in the beginning and is properly called "a god" (John 1:1, NWT). Jesus is not eternal, but he was the "firstborn of all creation" (Colossians 1:15). Jehovah's Witnesses pray to God in the name of Jesus, but deny that the Bible identifies him as a "person" within a triune Godhead (see ANTI-TRINITARIANISM). They understand "holy spirit" as Jehovah's "active force" in the world.

Among the heavenly beings serving Jehovah was one called Lucifer. But he rebelled against God and became Satan, the "adversary" of divine government. The DEVIL deceived Eve and Adam in the Garden of Eden into also defying God's sovereignty. Jehovah created the first human couple perfect, but through their free act of disobedience they and all their progeny became subject to sin, sickness, and death. Satan continues throughout history to attack God's rule not only by tempting individuals with selfish desires, but also by deceiving humanity through his control of false religions, unjust economic systems, and idolatrous NATIONALISM. Jehovah's Witnesses separate themselves from the "world system" by rejecting all political activities (including voting), influences of popular culture, social associations with non-Witnesses, and alliances with other religious organizations. They are outspoken in criticism of the Roman Catholic Church and the United Nations as precursors of the one-world government controlled by the ANTICHRIST in the last days.

To rescue humans from sin and death, Jehovah transferred the life of Jesus to the womb of the VIRGIN MARY to be born as the perfect human, the "second Adam." At his baptism Jesus was anointed by the holy spirit as Messiah. By remaining sinless throughout his life, Jesus could serve as the perfect sacrifice required to ransom humanity from the power of Satan, thus vindicating the authority of Jehovah's rule over the earth. Christ's obedience bought back what Adam's disobedience had forfeited: the opportunity to live eternally in paradise on earth. According to Watchtower teaching, Jesus was executed on a single piece of timber, a "torture stake," rather than a cross. God raised Jesus from the dead in a "spiritual body" and made him a "life-giving spirit" (I Corinthians 15:44–45; I Peter 3:18) with authority to rule over all other creatures as head of the messianic kingdom (Philippians 2:9–11). An "anointed class" of 144,000 believers, foreseen in Revelation 14, will assist Christ in his rule. They will not be resurrected, but will dwell in heaven as "spirit beings." They are the subjects of the "new covenant" Jesus announced at his last meal on the eve of his death. They are also called the "little flock," the "faithful and discreet slave," the "bride of Christ," and "a royal priesthood." They are called by divine election, confirmed by inner conviction, and since 1918 have ascended to heaven as spirit beings upon death. From there they will administer divine government over the paradise on earth, ruling the "great crowd" of those who joined the faith after 1935. The present role of the "great crowd" is to assist the "anointed remnant" in bearing witness to Jehovah's kingdom.

Although Christ's rule began when he cast Satan out of heaven in 1914, his government will be established on earth only after a catastrophic battle with cosmic forces of evil at Har-magedon in the near future. Then Jesus will separate all people on earth into loyal "sheep" and rebellious "goats" (Matthew 25:31–34). The faithful will enter millennial paradise, a thousand years of peace and harmony in a restored earth. The reprobate will be immediately annihilated. Then the dead who did not have the chance to hear the gospel during their lives will be resurrected to join the "great crowd." At the end of the millennium Satan will be released briefly to test all those on earth. Those who prove loyal to Jehovah will be rewarded with eternal life. Those who succumb to Satan's temptation will suffer "the second death" (Revelation 20:14–15). Jehovah's Witnesses believe that only those who persevere will be saved in the end. They do not teach that one is eternally secure after an initial confession of faith (as do most evangelical Christians), but that one must continue to "exercise faith" through works of service to the kingdom.

Worship

Jehovah's Witnesses meet several times a week in simple buildings with spare furnishings called "Kingdom Halls." Services consist mainly of study of materials produced by the Watchtower Society, and of training in techniques of promoting their teachings in local neighborhoods. Worship also involves singing of hymns, written in a distinctive doctrinal vocabulary. Active members exercise their faith by devoting eight to ten hours a week in door-to-door witnessing. Those who spend considerably more time are designated "pioneers." To supply them with literature the Watchtower Society invests heavily in the most advanced communications technology, from offset presses to phototypesetting computer software. Jehovah's Witnesses distribute annually millions of copies of *The Watchtower,* translated into 130 languages, and of *Awake!* in 80 versions. Although Jehovah's Witnesses have not used television, the Watchtower Society has recently launched an official site on the World Wide Web.

Jehovah's Witnesses observe the two SACRAMENTS recognized by other Protestants: water BAPTISM and the LORD'S SUPPER. They baptize by immersion only those candidates who have completed lengthy preparatory study. Baptisms often occur at large conventions as a public sign of dedication to the work of proclaiming the kingdom. Jehovah's Witnesses observe the "Lord's Evening Meal" once a year, on Passover eve (14 Nisan on the Jewish calendar), in which only members of the "anointed class" partake of the "emblems" of bread and wine. In 1999 only 8,755 of this "heavenly class" survived. As the number of partakers dwindles, however, the Watchtower Society records a growing number of observers. The significance of the ritual today is to identify those who attend but do not participate as those with the "earthly hope" of paradise.

Practices

Jehovah's Witnesses share with Christian FUNDAMEN-TALISM a restrictive sexual morality, condemning as "fornication" any instance of premarital sex, adultery, and HOMOSEXUALITY. ABORTION and some forms of birth control are forbidden. They abstain from tobacco and drugs, but follow the Bible in allowing limited use of alcohol. Gambling is deplored as an expression of greed. Magic, divination, and spiritualism are deceptions of Satan in which demons impersonate the dead and can even possess the living. Jehovah's Witnesses do not celebrate Christmas or Easter because both involve pre-Christian customs. Neither do they acknowledge individual birthdays because the only examples of such celebrations in the Bible are by pagan rulers. Because Jesus died on a "torture stake" Jehovah's Witnesses do not use the cross in their worship; it is a symbol they associate with "ancient false religions."

Jehovah's Witnesses are well known for their refusal to pledge allegiance to national governments, for which dissent they have been imprisoned in many countries, including the United States during both world wars (see CHURCH AND STATE, OVERVIEW). In Nazi GERMANY Jehovah's Witnesses were among the non-Jewish groups consigned to concentration camps. They do not practice PACIFISM, but maintain a neutral stance toward the state. Because all worldly governments are under the power of Satan, they refuse to participate in patriotic demonstrations or military service. In 1943 the Supreme Court, in the case of *Barnette v. West Virginia,* upheld the civil right of Jehovah's Witness children not to salute the flag in schoolroom exercises.

Perhaps the most controversial of Watchtower Society policies is the prohibition of intravenous blood transfusion, first promulgated in 1945. Since then, Jehovah's Witnesses have interpreted the apostolic command to "abstain . . . from blood" (Acts 15:20) as unconditional because any means of taking blood into the body violates the principle that the "life (soul) is in the blood" (Genesis 9:4; Leviticus 17:11). In 1961 *The Watchtower* announced that any member who accepted a blood transfusion would face disfellowshipping. Not even transfusions of one's own blood are allowed because storage would violate biblical directions for disposing of blood (Deuteronomy 12:16). Kidney dialysis is permitted as long as the blood circulates continuously through the filtering apparatus and returns to the patient's body. Since 1978 hemophiliacs have been allowed to choose treatment with blood components.

Future Challenges

Jehovah's Witnesses have entered a new stage of their history by renouncing attempts to set specific dates for the coming kingdom and modifying their theocratic organization. It remains to be seen whether these moves will silence the recurrent criticisms of the Watchtower Society for issuing "false prophecies" and for exerting absolute control over its members. To date, there has been no organized internal feminist dissent from the patriarchal patterns of domestic life and congregational authority. Those who voice disagreement with the Watchtower interpretation of biblical teaching about the role of women find themselves in danger of being "disfellowshipped." The challenge facing contemporary Jehovah's Witnesses is how to retain apocalyptic fervor, moral discipline, and exclusionary group loyalty under the pressures on younger families to accommodate to prevailing cultural standards as the promise of the kingdom is extended into an indeterminate future.

References and Further Reading

Bergman, Jerry. *Jehovah's Witnesses: A Comprehensive and Selectively Annotated Bibliography.* Westport: CT: Greenwood Publishing Group, 1999.

Conkin, Paul K. "Apocalyptic Christianity: Adventists and Jehovah's Witnesses." In *American Originals: Homemade Varieties of Christianity.* Chapel Hill: University of North Carolina Press, 1997.

Curry, Melvin D. *Jehovah's Witnesses: The Millenarianism World of the Watch Tower.* New York: Garland Publishing, 1994.

Franz, Raymond. *Crisis of Conscience: The Struggle Between Loyalty to God and Loyalty to One's Religion.* Atlanta, GA: Commentary Press, 1983.

Harrison, Barbara Grizzuti. *Visions of Glory: A History and a Memory of Jehovah's Witnesses.* New York: Simon and Schuster, 1978.

"Jehovah's Witnesses: Watchtower Society Official Web Site." http://www.watchtower.org (accessed January 15, 2000).

———. *Jehovah's Witnesses: Proclaimers of God's Kingdom.* Brooklyn, NY: Watchtower Bible and Tract Society of New York, 1993.

———. *Knowledge That Leads to Everlasting Life.* Brooklyn, NY: Watchtower Bible and Tract Society of New York, 1995.

———. *Revelation—Its Grand Climax at Hand!* Brooklyn, NY: Watchtower Bible and Tract Society of New York, 1988.

———. *You Can Live Forever in Paradise on Earth.* Brooklyn, NY: Watchtower Bible and Tract Society of New York, 1982.

Penton, M. James. *Apocalypse Delayed: The Story of Jehovah's Witnesses.* Toronto: University of Toronto Press, 1985.

Reed, David A. *Blood on the Altar: Confessions of a Jehovah's Witness Minister.* Buffalo, NY: Prometheus Books, 1996.

Stafford, Greg. *Jehovah's Witnesses Defended: An Answer to Scholars and Critics.* Huntington Beach, CA: Elihu Books, 2000.

DAVID L. WEDDLE

JEREMIAD

Jeremiads are Protestant sermons that generally emphasize the vengeful nature of divine justice, specifically enumerate the local or immediate transgressions warranting the deity's deserved wrath, reprovingly point to present indications of divine disfavor, and direly forecast looming future judgments unless the offenders reform. The term derives from the name of the Old Testament exilic prophet Jeremiah, who grieved over the destruction of Jerusalem and the desolation of Judah.

The related jeremiad themes of divine displeasure and ensuing adversity inform several European Protestant works, including Thomas Vincent's *God's Terrible Voice in the City* (1667). However, as a developed rhetorical form narrowly focused on a single community of believers, the jeremiad prominently emerges in Puritan New England during the 1660s and 1670s (see PURITANISM). Typical is *The Day of Trouble is Near* (1674), INCREASE MATHER'S aptly titled rebuke of his fellow Puritans as idolatrous New Israelites hazardously worshiping material prosperity instead of God. Whether colonial Puritan piety had actually diminished or was only clerically perceived to be declining during the 1670s is open to debate. Also unresolved is the issue of whether the colonial jeremiad pessimistically prophesies doom at the hands of a frowning deity or optimistically reaffirms a Puritan identity that God never abandons. In the former view, jeremiads reflect a static world view in which God either supports or rejects; in the latter view, jeremiads subtly accommodate history by endorsing an ongoing process of divine censure followed by divine favor. Either way, this form of sermon exhibits a clerical desire to affirm TRADITION, including ministerial AUTHORITY, during an uneasy time of social, political, and economic change.

References and Further Reading

Bercovitch, Sacvan. *The American Jeremiad*. Madison, WI: University of Wisconsin Press, 1978.
Miller, Perry. *The New England Mind: From Colony to Province*. Cambridge, MA: Harvard University Press, 1953.

WILLIAM J. SCHEICK

JESUS MOVEMENT

The Jesus Movement (JM) is a term developed by popular media in the 1960s and 1970s to refer to a movement among some relatively well-educated and affluent young people, originally mainly within the UNITED STATES, who were embracing a communal lifestyle based on variants of Christian Protestant THEOLOGY. Sometimes the terms "Jesus People," or the more derogatory "Jesus Freaks," have been employed by those referring to this phenomenon. Considerable attention was paid to early Jesus Movement groups, as debate swirled over whether they were "truly Christian." Their well-publicized lifestyle that included long hair and very casual dress contributed to this debate, as did their exuberant efforts to share their beliefs and values.

The Movement gained considerable momentum and attention for about three decades, and also spread to other countries, becoming worldwide by virtue of actions by a few of the JM groups, particularly the Children of God (COG), which at one time had outposts in close to 200 countries. Some estimates by scholars suggest several hundred thousand participants at one time or another in the JM. However, the Movement lost momentum in the 1990s, and is survived now by a few of the better known Movement groups such as Jesus People USA, centered in Chicago, and The Family (formerly known as the Children of God). Many remnants of Jesus Movement groups also flowed into pentecostal-oriented nontraditional churches, such as Calvary Chapel, from which Shiloh, one of the larger Movement groups in the late 1960s, had come.

One major theological and cultural variation developed within the Movement involved linking experientialism with FUNDAMENTALISM, as young people embraced selected beliefs associated with fundamentalist Protestantism, while also engaging in such activities as glossolalia, or speaking in TONGUES (the COG were an exception; members did not practice glossolalia). Most participants in JM groups had histories of heavy experiential involvement with drugs, alcohol, tobacco, and premarital sex, but participation in the JM groups often led to significant changes in behavior, with "getting high on Jesus" seeming to serve as something of a substitute for previous activities. Thus some scholars have written about the Jesus Movement as serving a "half-way house" function for many participants who had become disaffected from normal society and were involved in experimental lifestyles of one kind or another. Participation in the Movement helped many of these young people return to more conventional society, even if that was not their original intent when joining a specific JM group.

Recruitment and Resocialization

Most Jesus Movement groups gained new members by street proselytizing, seeking converts among young people who were moving around society, having cut their ties with families and left their normal "social locations." When large numbers of young people were adrift, especially during the Vietnam War era, such recruitment methods worked well. Outreach operated out of JM group communal houses located close to major transportation arteries and places where young people congregated, particularly in west coast urban centers in America. Some JM groups grew rapidly, especially if they established communal centers where converts could garner food, shelter, and friendship, along with the Jesus message. Later, as the "target population" of young people lessened, recruitment dropped off and other ways to attract new members were sought. This included holding "Jesus rock" concerts, opening "Christian coffee houses," witnessing on college campuses, and developing promotional activities based on distribution of tape recordings of BIBLE studies or Jesus rock music. None of these methods was particularly successful, although they did on occasion attract considerable attention to a given JM group.

Resocialization took many forms, but tended, especially among communal JM groups, to involve efforts at total immersion of new recruits in the subculture of the group. Other JM groups were more casual at training new members, but often may have typically sent new converts on missions to gain more recruits or to establish an outpost far from friends and family, accompanied only by a group of fellow believers. The resulting isolation had an indirect insulating effect that would encourage the new convert to absorb the group's CULTURE relatively quickly.

Growth and Outreach Activities Lead to Controversy

Most of the early recruits were single young people (indeed, most were males). This basic demographic fact contributed greatly to the early history of most JM groups being characterized by considerable geographic mobility. Members, few of whom were burdened with familial considerations, could be sent by group leaders to far-away places to engage in mission activities or in establishing a new communal outpost. Or an entire group could pick up and move, or decide to "live on the road," as did the COG for a number of years. This much-publicized group drove their caravan of buses across America for a time, camping when they wanted to engage in street proselytizing or shame some traditional churches for being too materialistic. The COG then left America and went to dozens of other countries, eventually establishing a presence in a large number of them. Other JM groups, even if less attention-seeking, were nonetheless also quite mobile, expending considerable effort and resources at "spreading the Word" in America and elsewhere.

Thus literally thousands of energetic young people became involved in missionizing and proselytizing activities around the United States and eventually in

dozens of other countries, leaving the impression of a large and very active movement developing first among America's youth and spreading around the globe. This impression was fostered by major coverage by mass print and electronic media of the time, as America, during a time of considerable turmoil over the Vietnam War and race issues, initially celebrated the apparent "return to that old-time religion" by many young people. It seemed to many that participation of young people in JM groups was preferable to being involved with "sex, drugs, rock and roll" and the antiwar movement.

Later the mass media as well as the general public and policy makers soured on most Jesus Movement groups' efforts at recruitment, as some unsavory actions (such as the COG's "flirty fishing," which for a time used sex as a recruiting tool) were revealed, and as it became clear that most JM groups were "high demand" religions that expected participants to "forsake all" to "follow Jesus" and do the bidding of group leaders intent on converting others or developing the size and influence of their particular groups. Accusations of "brainwashing" and "mind control" were made against some JM groups, as some family members of recruits and others sought to exert control over the groups and to limit their ability to recruit new members. Such accusations were refuted by scholars studying JM groups and related "New Religions," although such claims persisted and led to much difficulty for some JM groups. Indeed, the first "deprogramming" ever recorded (the first of many thousands, in the United States but also in other countries) involved a member of the COG, the most controversial of the JM groups.

Families, Children, and Change

Although the first generation of participants in JM groups was predominantly single males, as time passed more females were attracted, facilitating the eventual establishment of families. This led in turn to the arrival of children, sometimes in very large numbers in JM groups that did not generally practice birth control, such as the COG and Shiloh, the two largest such groups. Recent membership figures on, for instance, The Family (formerly the COG) demonstrate the size of this "problem" that led to changes in JM groups that lasted more than one generation. As of about 2001, The Family had approximately 10,000 members worldwide, with well over half of them being children.

The presence of families, and especially large numbers of children, had a "domesticating" effect on JM groups. The mobility of the groups was stymied, causing them to become much more sedentary, and leading to some consolidation as mission activities in other countries were curtailed somewhat. Divisions of labor were established within the groups that had some members doing missionizing and traveling, whereas others stayed home to care for the children and find ways to support the growing families, as well as other activities of the group. Huge amounts of resources were needed to sustain such large families, and the attention of group members and leaders had to be focused on this matter.

The presence of many children also led to major controversies with public officials over care and schooling of the children. Some JM groups insisted on HOMESCHOOLING their children, claiming that to send them to public schools would have a corrupting influence on them. Also, alternative schools were established in some groups, such as Shiloh, for a time, which became a drain on group resources and also allowed more governmental intervention. Child custody battles erupted in some groups, brought on by one parent deciding to leave the group and wanting to take custody of his or her children. Some JM groups, especially the COG, were accused of child sex abuse, accusations deriving from the rather libertine lifestyle led for a time by adult members of the group. These accusations led in the 1980s and early 1990s to large numbers of children being temporarily removed from Family homes in several different countries, including FRANCE, Spain, Argentina, and AUSTRALIA. In all instances the children were eventually returned; however, and in one major case in Australia, the government had to pay damages for the actions taken to gain control over the children.

In some groups the increase in familial responsibilities led eventually to a major shift of focus from one of outreach and recruitment to one focused internally, as the groups tried to support the new family-oriented culture and lifestyle that had developed. Instead of spending most time and resources sending out recruitment teams, ways had to be found to work for funds, or otherwise gather the resources needed for group sustenance and survival in a situation that involved many more "nonrevenue" members requiring support by those whose activities could generate revenue.

Many different methods of group support were tried, as most JM groups experimented with methods of raising money or engaging in activities that would help furnish needed material goods for the group. Street solicitation for money was one method tried by some groups, but this was by no means the most prevalent. The COG used this method, distributing their voluminous literature (the infamous "Mo Letters") and asking for money in exchange, a method called "litnessing." They also engaged in scavenging activities that sought out discarded fruits and vegetables from local markets, as well as other ways of maintaining the group that depended on the largesse of others. Shiloh used little direct solicitation, but instead relied on work teams in agricultural and construction industries for much of their support, as well as donations from members and their parents, and contributions from governmental agencies (i.e., federal surplus food programs). Shiloh and other groups also sold music tapes and put on concerts occasionally as others experimented with other ways to support themselves.

The Movement Dissipates

The Jesus Movement still exists in one sense because a few of the groups that began as part of the movement continue to function and even thrive, even if changed somewhat by the material concerns just discussed. However, the high point of the Movement occurred in the 1970s and early 1980s when there were JM groups operating in many different cities in America, in rural areas, in a number of other countries. From that point, however, the Movement lost momentum, caused by the lack of availability of ready recruits, shifting societal contexts, and internal problems deriving in large part from the maturing of the membership and the establishment of families by many of the participants. Thus the energy that had developed within the Movement groups was dissipated, and former members went many different directions. Many of them flowed into nontraditional Protestant evangelical and pentecostal groups. Some remained a part of one of the groups that did not die out completely, and many just left the JM groups and reentered a more conventional lifestyle.

References and Further Reading

DeSabatino, David. *The Jesus People Movement: An Annotated Bibliography and General Resource.* Westport, CT: Greenwood Press, 1999.
Ellwood, Robert. *One Way: The Jesus Movement and Its Meaning.* Englewood Cliffs, NJ: Prentice Hall, 1973.
Enroth, Ronald, Edward Ericson, and C. B. Peters. *The Jesus People: Old Time Religion in an Age of Aquarius.* Grand Rapids, MI: Wm. B. Eerdmans, 1972.
Richardson, James T., and Rex Davis. "Experiential Fundamentalism." *Journal of the American Academy of Religion* 51 (1983): 397–425.
———, Mary Harder, and Robert Simmonds. *Organized Miracles: A Study of a Contemporary, Youth, Communal Fundamentalist Organization.* New Brunswick, NJ: Transaction Books, 1979.
Stewart, David T., and James T. Richardson. "Mundane Materialism: How Tax Policies and Other Governmental Regulation Affected Beliefs and Practices of Jesus Movement Organizations." *Journal of the American Academy of Religion* 67 (1999): 825–847.

Taslimi, Cheryl R., Ralph W. Hood, and P. J. Watson. "Assessment of Former Members of Shiloh: The Adjective Check List 17 Years Later." *Journal for the Scientific Study of Religion* 30 (1991): 306–311.

JAMES T. RICHARDSON

JESUS, LIVES OF

Introduction

Understood in their broadest sense, the "lives of Jesus" are narratives constructed from the actions and words of Jesus of Nazareth. From this perspective the "lives" are not new, but date to the canonical gospels produced by early Christian communities. However, close readings of the gospels reveal that they are not objective histories, but documents carefully shaped by theological and confessional concerns. Although the gospels offer a portrait that explicates the meaning of Jesus as the Christ, they do not question that he is the Christ. It is this element that distinguishes modern lives of Jesus from the gospel accounts. That is to say, modern lives seek to understand, on grounds other than belief or theological conviction, what about the teaching, life, or internal makeup of Jesus suggested to his followers that he was indeed the Christ. In their more technical sense they are usually identified with the "Quest for the Historical Jesus," a rubric derived from the English title to ALBERT SCHWEITZER's monumental history of the nineteenth-century lives of Jesus, *The Quest for the Historical Jesus: A Critical Study of its Progress From Reimarus to Wrede* (1910).

Considering the remarkable breadth and forms that "lives of Jesus" have taken and the fact that their authors cover a wide span of religious commitments, one cannot suggest that they are uniquely Protestant in either form or content. Nevertheless, there are certain trajectories that the lives have taken that show the influence of Protestant thought and inclinations. In particular one can note three of these influences. First, the focus on discovering the Jesus hidden among or by creedal statements follows from a fundamental Protestant tenet assigning prominence to scripture in matters of THEOLOGY and FAITH. Second, the lives shift the locus of AUTHORITY from ecclesial structures to personal forms of encounter. That is to say, many of the writers expect that the discovered Jesus confronts the individual directly, either through the power of his recovered teaching (e.g., RUDOLF BULTMANN) or his force as moral exemplar (e.g., Ernst Renan). Finally, the insistence that statements concerning the uniqueness or continuing importance of Jesus be demonstrated rather than simply claimed are an instance of the Protestant commitment to expressing religious claims in forms that are accessible to both ecclesial and secular publics. Thus, although the lives are not specifically Protestant works, they are clearly connected to Protestantism's philosophical foundations and religious commitments.

Distilled to their essence, the lives of Jesus are attempts to answer two questions, "Who was Jesus?" and "Why is he significant?" The two questions are deceptively simple to frame, but, on closer inspection, they are deeply ambiguous and vexing. Behind them lie other difficult questions such as: What did Jesus actually say and do? How did he understand his relationship to God and to his contemporaries? What was the relationship of his self-understanding to that of his followers? These questions are not simple, and how one answers them dictates the shape and sense of the "life" one wishes to compose.

Three characteristics of the "lives" are typical. First, they are written from a historical rather than confessional stance. Second, they presume a distinction between the person of Jesus and the portraits of him found in the canonical gospels. Third, because of this distinction, the lives supply both a portrait of who Jesus of Nazareth was and reasons why he continues to hold significance. In this regard, "lives of Jesus" are simultaneously historical and hermeneutical endeavors, presenting both events of the past and distinctive interpretations of their current meaningfulness.

History of the Lives

The "lives" have their own peculiar history, and in some fashion they are as hard to classify as the object of their inquiry. It is best to differentiate them on the bases by which their authors establish the significance of Jesus. Usually this has been by one of four methods: reconstructing historical evidence, analyzing Jesus' self-consciousness, identifying philosophical or ideological ideals embodied in his life and teaching, or asserting his cultural significance. However, for heuristic purposes they can be divided into four periods: the Initial Quest (1750–1910), the period often referred to as "No Quest" (1910–1953), the New Quest (1953–1979), and what has been termed the "Third Quest," which began around 1980 and continues into the present.

The Initial Quest

The first modern "lives" were products of the ENLIGHTENMENT critique of external authority, the REFORMATION DOCTRINE of *sola scriptura,* and a reexamination of the relationship of human reason to divine revelation that is indebted to Deist philosophy (see DEISM). When these philosophical and cultural shifts were coupled to the already recognized fact that the gospel accounts offered conflicting reports of the time and motivation for Jesus' actions and teaching, the appearance of the "lives" became inevitable.

The initial quest had two goals: to rediscover the actual Jesus hidden under layers of dogmatic belief, and to reinterpret that Jesus for contemporary audiences. The authors of these lives believed that for the power of Jesus' teachings and actions to be unleashed and so transform modern society, they had to be liberated from the shackles of church dogma, particularly the belief that Jesus was both divine and human. HERMANN SAMUEL REIMARUS is often cited as the author of the first critical life of Jesus. Because deist interpreters such as THOMAS CHUBB had already produced critical works on Jesus, this is incorrect. Nevertheless, Reimarus added scholarly precision to the previous efforts and made evident their explosive nature. Reimarus wrote a manifesto "Apology, or Defense for the Reasonableness of Reverence for God" that ranged from the necessity of reason in matters of faith to the impossibility of accepting biblical accounts as historically true. Between 1774 and 1778 Reimarus's son-in-law GOTTHOLD EPHRAIM LESSING published seven portions of the work under the title, the *Wolfenbüttel Fragments*. In the seventh fragment, "The Aims of Jesus and His Disciples," Reimarus argued that Jesus never claimed divine status, never intended to inaugurate a new religion, and did not desire to be worshiped. Rather he sought to bring about deliverance from the Roman occupation of Palestine. Thus, the disciples had corrupted Jesus' teaching, and to understand the true Jesus one must disclaim all doctrines of divinity.

Three important features for future lives were established by Reimarus's work. First, explaining the relationship of Jesus' teaching to later presentations by his disciples becomes a matter of historical and theological significance. Second, Jesus must be understood within the context of JUDAISM, which though itself ambiguous, is critical for an accurate life of Jesus. Third, a proper understanding of the KINGDOM OF GOD is crucial in any life of Jesus.

Reimarus wrote to expose the erroneous beliefs and doctrines of the Christian faith. Not a few scholars sought to refute such notions by employing the same historical means Reimarus used. However, the methods were employed to show that Jesus' initial followers did not corrupt his message, but maintained continuity with his teaching and purpose. The life written by Heinrich Paulus, *The Life of Jesus as the Foundation of a purely Historical Account of Early Christianity* (1828), is a good example. Paulus's life of Jesus typifies rationalist approaches to the life of Jesus. Paulus allowed that God could act within human history or the natural order, but that God's actions must follow the inherent laws of NATURE and human existence. Paulus also argued that the reported "miracles" actually happened, but that the term miracle was a misnomer used by gospel writers, because they did not know or understand the secondary historical or natural causes for the strange things they had witnessed. Hence, healings or nature miracles could be properly comprehended when a rational explanation could be offered. In his life of Jesus, Paulus sought to provide plausible understandings of the miracles and thus distill from them their true meaning.

The core of Paulus's work is devoted to explanations of the miracles, to discern from those stories the truths they sought to communicate about Jesus and his message. An example of his procedure can be seen in his treatment of Jesus' command that the sea become still. Paulus suggests that when Jesus is reported to have calmed the sea (Mark 4:35–41), the boat in which he was traveling was blocked from the wind at exactly the moment when he yelled his command to the sea. The disciples missed the coincidence and attributed to Jesus the power to command the elements of nature. This is repeated for most of the miracle stories in the gospels. Oddly, Paulus does not suggest that Jesus ever attempted to correct these misperceptions or sought to provide explanations for the supposed miracles. Instead he seemed to have encouraged the misunderstandings. Paulus's explanations may have succeeded in saving the veracity of the disciples' accounts, but in doing so, Paulus inadvertently suggested that Jesus was perpetrating fraud and deception. Ironically, the miracles are saved at the expense of their performer.

Paulus's arguments and explanations, along with those of every other rationalist, were refuted completely by the powerful life of Jesus composed by DAVID FRIEDRICH STRAUSS, *The Life of Jesus Critically Examined* (1845). Strauss's life of Jesus is the colossus of nineteenth-century lives, and remains one of the most important ever written. Translated by GEORGE ELIOT, the life is a monumental work of over 1,400 pages, the majority of which are devoted to demonstrating the inadequate and incoherent nature of previous explanations of the gospel materials. With an unrelenting and clear argumentation, Strauss exposes the philosophical difficulties in maintaining traditional dogmatic explanations of the reports. However, the efforts of the rationalists come in for even more criticism. Strauss repeatedly demonstrates that the rationalist explanations strain credulity even more than those of the supernaturalists. By the end of his analysis it is hard to conceive how anyone thought of these explanations as reasonable or rational.

In place of these explanations Strauss maintained that the gospels were mythological reinterpretations of traditions about Jesus derived from the Old Testament stories or actual events in Jesus' life. Following a Hegelian understanding of metaphysics and history, Strauss argued that the goal of the myths was to demonstrate that in Jesus the absolute meeting of the finite and the infinite occurred. Strauss did not believe that this had happened in the individual person of Jesus, but that "Jesus" as an icon represented the fact that all of humanity could participate in such an experience. Thus, Jesus was only unique by the fact that he was the first human to represent the possibility of the final union of Spirit and humanity, not by his actual nature.

Strauss's analysis was met with a firestorm of protest and challenge; to the present day his mythical recasting of the gospel material is continually challenged. Nevertheless his critique of the rationalist and the supernaturalist approaches to the gospels has never been answered adequately, and remains a desideratum for contemporary interpreters of the gospel materials.

Ernest Renan, who used his travels through Palestine and Syria to fill in the gaps of the gospel narratives, produced a countervailing life. His book *The Life of Jesus* was immensely popular throughout Europe. Appearing in 1863, it sold over 66,000 copies in six months. Renan's sketch is only a semblance of history. In fact, it is a romantic novel, with the gentle loving Jesus as its hero. Only after his rejection by religious authorities does Jesus become a revolutionary. Renan's depiction was complete down to the demeanor of the mule that Jesus rode, including the length of his eyebrows. Its popularity attests to the power of LITERATURE, but it has little of historical interest or accuracy.

A significant breakthrough in the "lives" occurs with the work of Johannes Weiss, whose *Preaching of Jesus Concerning the Kingdom of God* appeared in 1892. Although only sixty-seven pages, it sounds a critical note in the production of the lives by demonstrating that the Kingdom of God was not an internal spiritual disposition, a set of ethical demands, or a compendium of universal truths, as suggested by the liberal and romantic lives, but a term used by Jesus to express his belief that the public earthly reign of God was imminent (see APOCALYPTICISM).

Schweitzer's portrait, presented in the last section of his history of the quest, builds on Weiss's understanding, and he too insists that Jesus was committed to an imminent eschatological expectation. Indeed, it is the extreme nature of the ESCHATOLOGY that elevates Jesus to cultural significance beyond his own. Schweitzer does not transform Jesus' eschatological PREACHING into modern-day spirituality or morality, but emphasizes its alien nature. Precisely because of his foreignness, he stands as a challenge to the morality of his own day and continues to stand as an indictment of every moral system since that time. However, it is not the content of Jesus' preaching that commends him, nor his mistaken Messianic self-consciousness. Rather it is the courage and commitment that he displayed in his self-sacrifice. Schweitzer posits that Jesus' initial belief in the coming Messianic trials did not materialize. As a result Jesus concluded that he alone could inaugurate the coming of the kingdom, forcing its inception by his sacrificial death. As Schweitzer describes it, Jesus therefore "lays hold of the wheel of the world to set it moving on that last revolution which is to bring all ordinary history to a close. It refuses to turn, and he throws himself upon it. Then it does turn; and crushes him. Instead of bringing in the eschatological conditions, he has destroyed them. The wheel rolls onward, and the mangled body of the one immeasurably great Man, who was strong enough to think of himself as the spiritual leader of mankind and to bend history to his purpose, is hanging upon it still. That is his victory and his reign" (Schweitzer 1910:370–371).

Repercussions of the Initial Quest

Strauss's investigation showed the futility of the rationalizing approach to the miraculous in the gospel materials while also demonstrating the force of the mythic language. Schweitzer's chronicle of the nineteenth-century lives was devastating, demonstrating that the "lives" were too often transpositions of their author's values onto the person of Jesus. They revealed, therefore, not what was distinctive about Jesus, but what the interpreter and his/her CULTURE understood to be of eminent value. When one coupled it with William Wrede's demonstration that the gospel of Mark could not be used as a historical framework for a portrait of Jesus, the façade of historical neutrality was demolished. Moreover, by following Weiss, Schweitzer had demonstrated that any understanding of the kingdom of God that ignored the kingdom's radically eschatological nature was in error. A historical understanding of the kingdom of God could not be reduced to an ethical ideal or to a set of timeless truths, but was a proclamation that the reign of God was about to occur on earth in a public manner.

As neutral histories, the initial lives must be considered as failures for three reasons. First, their imaginative substitutions for the gospels' integrative frameworks were deeply flawed. Second, the authors impressed upon Jesus a character that was the epitome of nineteenth-century reason and ETHICS, but bore little resemblance to that of an itinerant Palestinian teacher. Third, the writers substituted ethical and philosophical interpretations of the Kingdom of God for

Jesus' eschatological preaching about the imminent in-breaking of God's reign.

The Period of No Quest

The failings of the initial lives and the challenges of Strauss, Weiss, and Wrede brought the lives to a standstill. The difficulties in discerning and arranging the sifted gospel material while avoiding the pitfalls of modernizing Jesus made the task almost impossible. From this point lives of Jesus focused on the nature of Jesus' teaching and on reinterpretations of his eschatological message. In 1926 Rudolf Bultmann published *Jesus* [Eng. trans. *Jesus and The Word* (1934)]. In this work he assembled the core of Jesus' teachings and concluded that Jesus presented his hearers with a radical call to relinquish self-reliance and accept that they were completely dependent on God's benevolence for their existence.

Bultmann sought to explicate the fundamental preaching of the early CHURCH in terms that would communicate with contemporary audiences by exposing the mythic form of this preaching and translating it into a form that would be meaningful in modern settings. His mode of "remything"—called demythologization—expressed the essential nature of the gospel in existential terms.

Bultmann did not actually compose a life of Jesus because he believed neither that one could or should be written. In the introduction to his work he makes this clear:

> This book lacks all the phraseology which speaks of Jesus as great man, genius or hero; he appears neither as inspired nor as inspiring, his sayings are not called profound, nor his faith mighty, nor his nature child-like. There is also no consideration of the eternal values of his message, of his discovery of the infinite depths of the human soul or the like (Bultmann, 1934:8).

Here is a dismissal of every solution proposed by the initial quest, replaced by attention "limited to what he *purposed*, and hence to what in his purpose as a part of history makes a present demand on us" (Bultmann, 8).

Bultmann maintained that his interpretation of Jesus' message demonstrated a link between the preaching of Jesus and the preaching about Jesus because just as Jesus had presented the crisis of God's immediate call, so too, his followers created the same moment of existential crisis in their claim that the crucified Jesus was indeed God's Christ. Bultmann's interpretation also allowed for another conception of Jesus' eschatological message about the end of the world's structures. According to Bultmann, this was actually a mythical expression of Jesus' existential challenge clothed in the conceptual garb of first-century Judaism, that is, the eschatological preaching was a mythic profession of the radical contingency of human existence. Once this was recognized a modern listener could comprehend the nature of Jesus' claims, and being confronted by them, experience the demands of faith.

The New Quest

Bultmann's dicta held sway for approximately three decades. Then, in 1953, a former Bultmann student, Ernst Käsemann, delivered a lecture questioning his claim that significant historical evidence for a life of Jesus could not be found. Käsemann maintained that not only could coherence between Jesus' message and that of the early church be established, but that coherency extended to the behavior of Jesus as well. Käsemann's essay, "The Problem of the Historical Jesus," argued that if the message of Jesus could point to the message of Easter, then one could use the message of Easter to discern elements in Jesus' life that were historically feasible. He thus called for a reexamination of the historical Jesus, initiating a New Quest.

The quest, which includes the work of Gerhard Ebeling and Ernst Fuchs, follows Bultmann in recasting the nature of historical inquiry as existential inquiry, but departs from him in arguing for its theological necessity. It also expands his understanding of valid historical data by delineating three criteria for authenticating sayings and actions of Jesus. A minimum historical base would be created if one accepted only those sayings or actions that were dissimilar to those found in Judaism and were distinct from the desires and needs of the early church. One could add to this base by accepting other teachings that were consistent with the first group and, finally, by considering materials that had multiple attestation.

Only one New Quester, Gunter Bornkamm, wrote a life of Jesus. Bornkamm's *Jesus of Nazareth* (1960) provides a minimalist sketch that follows many of Bultmann's analyses and his understanding of Jesus' primary message. The work expands Bultmann's data by incorporating actions of Jesus that produce the same call to decision that could be experienced in his preaching, such as Jesus' eating with outcasts and his healing of sinners.

Two problems plagued the New Quest. First, the complexity of its philosophical conceptions of language and history led more to debate than historical inquiry. Second, the criteria for discerning authenticity were circular and sometimes in tension with one another. As a result the Quest remained more a form of methodological and theological protest than a source of more "lives."

The Third Quest

In the last twenty years, lives of Jesus have begun to appear with such regularity that this period has been referred to as a Third Quest. Although it shares many traits with its progenitors (and often some of their failings as well), three characteristics distinguish this quest from its predecessors. First, it employs not only historical means of investigation, but methods gathered from sociology, anthropology, archeology, and literary criticism. Second, there is a concerted effort to situate Jesus more accurately in his cultural context, both Hellenic and Jewish. By means of multiple analyses of the social culture in which Jesus lived, writers are attempting to construct better understandings of the social, political, and economic factors that affected his teaching and activity. Third, the recent quest expands the materials considered as reliable sources for information about Jesus. In addition to the archeological and sociological data that are used, many lives also make use of the Gospel of Thomas and apocryphal gospels such as the gospel of Peter, and they place a significant emphasis on "Q" (the hypothetical source for material shared by Matthew and Luke, but not found in Mark).

The newest quest tends to take three paths. One traces lines of consistency between Jesus and the gospel accounts; another suggests that these do not occur; and a third relies on defining moments in Jesus' life and teaching to locate his social significance. The first group is typified by the work of N. T. Wright, A. E. Harvey, E. P. Sanders, and J. Meier. The second group is often identified with the Jesus Seminar, a collection of biblical scholars coordinated by Robert Funk who meet regularly to determine and isolate the authentic sayings of Jesus. Members of the seminar stress the noneschatological nature of Jesus' preaching, focus on his mission, and suggest that Jesus is better understood as an ancient Cynic or sage philosopher than as an itinerant eschatological prophet. Representative works include those of Marcus Borg and John Dominic Crossan.

Members of the third group include third-world interpreters, feminist scholars, and African American critics who maintain that many of the distinctive features of Jesus' preaching and actions, particularly as they reflected preference for the poor and the marginalized of society, were eliminated or diminished as the church became more a part of mainstream culture. The work of authors like Elisabeth Schüssler Fiorenza, Leonardo Boff, and Miguez Bonino are indicative of the approaches taken. Members of this group understand their work as a form of recovering Jesus' true message. In this regard they bear resemblance to the first quest, except for them Jesus must be freed from the confines of social conformity and not dogmatic creedal claims. The incisive nature of these lives attests to their importance in bringing to light significant aspects of Jesus' claims and actions.

It is clear that the lives of the third quest are as varied as those of the first. In fact, it may be misleading to refer to this most recent activity as a coherent or cooperative venture. In many ways there are similarities to the previous quests; both historical and interpretive issues are addressed, the challenge to find the Jesus underneath the traditional epithets is still present, and a recognition that the conceptions of truth that are regnant in the culture require response is also at the forefront.

Conclusion

This history of the lives shows a constant ebb and flow in their production and their significance. Sometimes there appears to be a premium on creating new investigations. At others there is almost complete silence. This oscillation is a function of two factors: one internal to the search itself, the other of the audiences the lives address. The historical data from which lives of Jesus are created is always incomplete. There are simply too many gaps in our knowledge of Jesus, his contemporaries, and his earliest followers to remedy this. Moreover, it is unlikely that this situation will be changed either by recourse to other sources from antiquity or to more appeals to sociological and anthropological studies of Judaism or Roman culture. Further, because they seek to answer both historical and interpretive questions, as the significant values that are dominant in the culture shift, so too will the portraits of Jesus expand or contract to meet them. Finally, as long as Jesus remains a cultural icon as well as the fundamental figure of Christianity, lives of Jesus will continue to appear in the culture's media, be they critical histories, films, novels, plays, or musicals. To the degree that the authors of these new and different lives attend to strengths and weakness of their predecessors, they will succeed as interesting reinterpretations. To the degree that they fail to do this, they will fall prey to the same fate as those they seek to replace.

See also Bible and Literature; Bible Translation; Christology; Theology, Twentieth Century

References and Further Reading

Allen, Charlotte. *The Human Christ: The Search for the Historical Jesus.* New York: Free Press, 1998.

Bornkamm, Gunther. *Jesus of Nazareth.* Translated by Irene McLuskey and Fraser McLuskey with James Robinson. New York: Harper and Bros., 1960.

Bultmann, Rudolf. *Jesus and the Word.* Translated by Louise Pettibone Smith and Erminie Huntress Lantero. New York: Charles Scribner's Sons, 1934.

Crossan, John Dominic. *The Historical Jesus: The Life of a Mediterranean Jewish Peasant.* San Francisco: Harper Collins, 1991.

Fiorenza, Elisabeth Schüssler. *Jesus and the Politics of Interpretation.* New York: Continuum, 2000.

Herzog, William R., II. *Jesus, Justice, and the Reign of God.* Louisville, KY: Westminster/John Knox Press, 2000.

Johnson, Luke Timothy. *The Real Jesus: The Misguided Quest for the Historical Jesus and the Truth of the Traditional Gospels.* San Francisco: Harper Collins, 1996.

Keck, Leander. *Who is Jesus: History in Perfect Tense.* Minneapolis, MN: Fortress Press, 2001.

Meier, John P. *A Marginal Jew: Rethinking the Historical Jesus.* 3 vols. Anchor Bible Reference Library. New York: Doubleday, 1991–2001.

Renan, Ernst. *The Life of Jesus.* Modern Library. New York: Random House, 1927.

Sanders, E. P. *The Historical Figure of Jesus.* London: Allen Lane/Penguin Books, 1993.

Schweitzer, Albert. *The Quest of the Historical Jesus.* Translated by W. Montgomery. New York: Macmillan, 1956.

Strauss, David Friedrich. *The Life of Jesus Critically Examined.* Lives of Jesus Series. Translated by George Eliot. Reprint. Introduction by Peter C. Hodgson. Philadelphia, PA: Fortress Press, 1972.

Telford, William R. "Major Trends and Interpretive Issues in the Study of Jesus." In *Studying the Historical Jesus: Evaluations of the State of Current Research,* edited by B. Chilton and C. A. Evans, 33–74. New Testament Tools and Studies 19. Leiden, The Netherlands: E. J. Brill, 1994.

Wright, N. T. *Jesus and The Victory of God: Christian Origins and the Question of God.* Minneapolis, MN: Fortress Press, 1996.

S. J. KRAFTCHICK

JEWEL, JOHN (1522–1571)

English theologian. John Jewel was born in the parish of Berimber, Devonshire, England, on May 24, 1522, and died at Monkton Farleigh, Wiltshire, on September 23, 1571. He studied at Merton College, Oxford, and received his B.A. from Corpus Christi College in 1540. On the accession of Queen Mary in 1553, he lost his fellowship at Corpus Christi College and was forced to flee from ENGLAND. He was a Marian exile at Frankfurt in March 1555, but then joined Peter Martyr Vermigli at Strasbourg soon thereafter; the next year he followed him to Zurich. When Mary died in 1558, he returned to England. Jewel served as bishop of Salisbury from January 21, 1560, until his death.

Jewel was chosen to lead the literary offensive against the Roman Catholics who met at the Council of Trent (1545–1563), and to define the position of the CHURCH OF ENGLAND against Roman Catholic criticism. The Roman Catholic critics saw in Protestantism the multiplication of sects and gross immorality resulting from the Protestants' lawlessness and irreligion because of their doctrine of JUSTIFICATION of GRACE by FAITH and their repudiation of the DOCTRINE of papal AUTHORITY. Protestants and members of the Church of England were seen as immoral, heretical, divisive, and schismatic. Jewel was commissioned to respond to these accusations, and in 1562 he published his *Apologia pro Ecclesis Anglicana,* which was the first systematic statement of the Church of England against the Church of Rome. It was translated into English as *An Apology of the Church of England.*

The *Apology* had a twofold purpose: to present the truth about and refute the rumors against the Church of England, and to show the errors of the papacy that prevented the English Church from joining the Council of Trent. He defended the Church of England as the true church, and insisted that the English Reformation was the restoration of the true church in England after Roman medieval abuses. He denounced transubstantiation, purgatory, the CELIBACY of CLERGY, and the worship of SAINTS and images as "trifles, follies and baubles." Using scripture and the first four ecumenical councils, Jewel defended the two sacraments of BAPTISM and Eucharist (see LORD'S SUPPER), communion with both the bread and wine, and the threefold orders of bishops, presbyters, and deacons. He insisted that the practices and beliefs of the Church of England were older and thus better than later Roman Catholic innovations.

See also Bishop and Episcopacy; Catholic Reactions to Protestantism; Catholicism, Protestant Reactions; Clergy, Marriage of; Deaconess, Deacon

References and Further Reading

Primary Sources:

Ayre, John, ed. *The Works of John Jewel.* 4 vols. Cambridge, UK: Parker Society, 1845–1850.

Booty, John E., ed. *An Apology of the Church of England by John Jewel.* New York: Church Publishing, 2002.

Secondary Sources:

Booty, John E. *John Jewel as Apologist of the Church of England.* London: SPCK, 1963.

Southgate, Wyndham Mason. *John Jewel and the Problem of Doctrinal Authority.* Cambridge, MA: Harvard University Press, 1962.

DONALD S. ARMENTROUT

JEWS FOR JESUS

The term "Jews for Jesus" has been used since the early 1970s to designate Jewish believers in Jesus, Jews who have embraced the Christian faith yet retained their identity as Jews. The group that has formally carried the name "Jews for Jesus" originated in

1970 in San Francisco under the leadership of Moishe Rosen, a missionary of the American Board of Mission to the Jews. The organization aimed to evangelize Jews who were influenced by the counterculture, adapting its evangelization messages and manners to the style of the new generation. Members of the group wore jeans and T-shirts, grew their hair, and embraced the musical trends of the day. Jews for Jesus also gave expression to the new emphasis in American CULTURE on ETHNICITY and the searching for roots. It advocated the idea that Jews did not have to give up on their identity as Jews, but rather could rediscover themselves as Jews at the same time that they embraced Jesus as their savior. The organization has used Jewish names, symbols, and expressions in its missionary literature. It also has emphasized its support for the State of Israel and has called its musical band "The Liberated Wailing Wall." Starting out as a local group in the San Francisco Bay area, Jews for Jesus has grown to become one of the largest missions in the nation, with branches outside America as well.

In its THEOLOGY and style, Jews for Jesus has become part of a larger movement of Jewish Christians that came about in the 1970s and 1980s. Often calling themselves messianic Jews, or Jewish believers in Jesus, such communities have promoted the idea that Jews who embrace Christianity should not assimilate into the general Christian culture or join regular churches, but instead should create their own communities and retain their Jewish heritage. Jewish-Christian congregations differ as to the amount of Jewish TRADITION they choose to retain. The more "traditionalist" communities have introduced Arks and Torah scrolls into their assemblies, their members wear yarmulkes during services, and they celebrate Jewish holidays such as Chanukah and Purim. All Jewish-Christian congregations celebrate Passover, and most have chosen to conduct their prayer meetings on Friday nights or Saturday mornings. The notion that they have transcended the historical boundaries between JUDAISM and Christianity, overcoming old, seemingly irreconcilable differences and injuries to amalgamate the Christian faith with Jewish ethnicity, has served as a source of energy and a sense of mission for the movement's members. By the early 2000s, there were about 300 congregations in America, as well as dozens more in Israel and throughout the Jewish world, and the movement is growing.

Jews for Jesus, and the movement of Jewish believers in Jesus in general, have advocated the faith and values of the conservative evangelical segment of Christianity. As such, they point to a great adaptability by evangelical Christianity in its relation to the cultural choices of the baby boom generation. They also reflect the growing appreciation of this segment of Christianity for Jews as the object of biblical prophecies and as a nation destined to regain its old status as the Chosen People.

See also Evangelicalism; Evangelism; Jesus Movement; Philo-Semitism

References and Further Reading

Ariel, Yaakov. *Evangelizing the Chosen People: Missions to the Jews in America 1880–2000*. Chapel Hill, NC: University of North Carolina Press, 2000.

Feher, Shoshanah. *Passing Over Easter*. Walnut Creek, CA: Altamira Press, 1998.

Harris-Shapiro, Carol. *Messianic Judaism: A Rabbi's Journey Through Religious Change in America*. Boston, MA: Beacon Press, 1999.

Lipson, Juliene G. *Jews for Jesus: An Anthropological Study*. New York: AMS Press, 1990.

Pruter, Karl. *Jewish Christians in the United States: A Bibliography*. New York: Garland Publishing, 1987.

Rausch, David A. *Messianic Judaism: Its History, Theology and Polity*. New York: Edwin Mellen Press, 1982.

Rosen, Moishe, and William Proctor. *Jews for Jesus*. Old Tappen, NJ: Fleming H. Revell, 1974.

YAAKOV ARIEL

JOHNSON, JAMES (c. 1839–1917)

African missionary. Johnson was born in the SIERRA LEONE colony, a settlement founded in the late eighteenth century as a Christian experiment and a haven for recaptured African slaves. By the time he was old enough to go to school, the colony was largely Christian thanks to the energetic efforts of evangelical missionary agencies like the Church Mission Society (CMS). Educated by the CMS and ordained in the Anglican Church, Johnson's illustrious career spanned the best part of six decades and included extended service in both Sierra Leone and Nigeria.

Throughout his career Johnson combined an effective pastoral ministry with extensive missionary labor. A penchant for crusading piety earned him the sobriquet "Holy Johnson." Remarkably influential in church and society, he had a seat on the Lagos Legislative Council from 1886 to 1894 and was made assistant bishop of Western Equatorial Africa in 1900.

Intrepid, energetic, visionary, and given to dogmatism, Johnson emerged as the prophet of the late nineteenth-century African Church movement. He decried the "foreignness" and foreign control of the emerging African church, and proclaimed the ideal of an autonomous "nondenominational" African church that was accommodated in all respects to the African heritage. Arguably ahead of his time, he remains a complex individual who advocated African names but never changed his own, and who remained unwaveringly loyal to the Anglican church even when his militant advocacy for independent African churches inspired an African independent church movement.

He is best remembered as one of the most significant transitional leaders in late nineteenth-century West Africa who embodied the tensions and dilemmas inherent in the "mission-to-church" process. Ultimately the ideals and ideology that he championed were destined—albeit in modified forms—to shape the future of African Christianity and set the stage for a new epoch in the history of Protestantism.

See also African Theology; Anglicanism; Missions

References and Further Reading

Primary Source:

Johnson, James. *A Brief History of my Life*. London: Unpublished reports, 1908.

Secondary Sources:

Ayandele, E. A. *Holy Johnson: Pioneer of African Nationalism, 1836–1917*. London: Frank Cass & Co. Ltd., 1970.

Hanciles, Jehu J. *Euthanasia of a Mission: African Church Autonomy in the Colonial Context*. Westport, CT: Praeger Publishers, 2002.

Sanneh, L. *West African Christianity: The Religious Impact*. New York: Orbis Books, 1983.

JEHU J. HANCILES

JOHNSON, SAMUEL (1709–1784)

English scholar and literary critic. Born in Lichfield, ENGLAND in 1709, Samuel Johnson was a lay member of the CHURCH OF ENGLAND, writer, poet, literary critic, and theological and ethical commentator on church and society. Johnson's career was desultory and often disappointing. His Oxford education (Pembroke College) was interrupted by ill health, and his M.A. came to him only after the appearance of his best-known work, his *Dictionary of the English Language* (1755). His doctorate was an honorary Doctorate of Laws, conferred first by Trinity College, Dublin, and then by Oxford. He published much about Shakespeare, and on the works of other English poets (*Lives of the English Poets, 1779–1781*). His *Rambler* (1749–1752) and *Idler* (1758–1760) commented sharply on contemporary irreligion and superficiality. He saw a key to the religious state of the nation, in its weakness and possible rejuvenation, in the observance of the Lord's Day.

A staunch Protestant, Johnson insisted that the Roman Church had an underlying piety: ". . . there is no idolatry in the mass; they believe God to be there, and they adore him" (Boswell's *Life*, 1769). He encouraged a high regard for the English church and for its

LITURGY. He persuaded his colleague and biographer James Boswell in *The Journal of a Tour to the Hebrides* that "a form of prayer for publick worship is in general most decent and edifying. *Solennia verba* have a kind of prescriptive sanctity, and make a deeper impression on the mind than extemporaneous effusions, in which, as we know not what they are to be, we cannot readily acquiesce."

Johnson is best understood through his prayers in his *Prayers and Meditations*, published posthumously, as he had wished, in 1785. He fasted in Holy Week, and renewed his baptismal COVENANT at every Easter. He perceived the central issue of religion and all life as redemption (*Rambler*, No. 110): "Where there is no hope, there can be no endeavour. A constant and unfailing obedience is above the reach of terrestrial diligence; and therefore the progress of life could only have been the natural descent of negligent despair from crime to crime, had not the universal persuasion of forgiveness, to be obtained by proper means of reconciliation, recalled those to the paths of virtue whom their passions had solicited aside; and animated to new attempts, and firmer perseverance, those whom difficulty had discouraged, or negligence surprised."

Johnson died in London in 1784.

See also Catholicism, Protestant Reactions

References and Further Reading

Primary Sources:

Johnson, Samuel. *Prayers and Meditations*. Edited by Elton Trueblood as *Doctor Johnson's Prayers*. New York: Harper, 1947.

———. *The Yale Edition of the Works of Samuel Johnson*. New Haven, CT: Yale University Press, 1958.

Secondary Sources:

Boswell, James: *The Journal of a Tour to the Hebrides with Samuel Johnson* (1785). London and New York: Thomas Nelson & Sons, n.d.

———. *The Life of Samuel Johnson, LLD.* (1791). Edited by Edward Malone. London: Griffin, Bohn, 1862.

Strachey, Lytton. "Johnson, Samuel," in *Dictionary of National Biography,* Vol. X, 919–935. London: Oxford University Press, 1921.

DAVID H. TRIPP

JONES, RUFUS MATTHEW (1863–1947)

Quaker philosopher. Rufus Jones was a proponent of the mystical life and the leading voice in Quakerism for the first half of the twentieth century (see FRIENDS, SOCIETY OF). Reared on a farm in South China, Maine, Jones taught philosophy for many years at Harverford College in Pennsylvania. He shared the liberal, progressive, optimistic spirit of his age, but was no mere rationalist. A contemporary of EVELYN UNDERHILL and Dean Inge, he lived in an era of revived interest in mysticism. The ideas of RALPH WALDO EMERSON and WILLIAM JAMES had a powerful influence on his thinking.

Jones was a both a scholar of mysticism and an experienced mystic, and wrote of the spiritual life with a vividness that was contagious. He was especially attracted to the fourteenth-century mystics Eckhart and Tauler, although the mysticism that he promoted for his own day differed. He distinguished negative from affirmative mystics. The former stressed withdrawal from the physical world perceived by sense and studied by reason, searching for God through ASCETICISM, and annihilation of the self, striving for the fleeting moment of ecstasy, the loss of individuality in the endless ocean of divinity. Affirmation mystics, however, valued the natural world as the place where divinity revealed itself. Union with God heightened rather than destroyed personality, driving the mystic back into the world for service. No longer reserved for the few, the mystical life was within the reach of all who could trust their intuition of the nearness of the God who dwelt within them.

Jones himself was a person of service, a founder and longtime chairperson of the AMERICAN FRIENDS SERVICE COMMITTEE, whose relief efforts in Europe after the two major wars of the twentieth century earned the agency the Nobel Peace Prize in 1947. The generation of Rufus Jones brought about a renaissance in Quakerism in study and practice. Jones reinterpreted Quaker history, portraying Quakers as heirs to the medieval continental mystics. Focusing on Quakers' inner experience, rather than on DOCTRINE, he labored to heal the nineteenth-century divisions among the Friends. He yearned to bring more than just Quakers into dialogue and was an active ecumenist. Through his gifts as a much-traveled orator and a writer of more than fifty books, he exerted a greater influence on other Protestants than any previous Friend.

See also Ecumenism; Emerson, Ralph Waldo; James, William; Society of Friends in North America

References and Further Reading

Primary Sources:

Fosdick, Harry Emerson. *Rufus Jones Speaks to Our Time.* New York: Macmillan, 1951.
Walters, Kerry. *Rufus Jones: Essential Writings.* Maryknoll, NY: Orbis, 2001.

Secondary Sources:

Hinshaw, David. *Rufus Jones: Master Quaker.* New York: Putnam, 1951.
Vining, Elizabeth Gray. *Friend of Life: The Biography of Rufus M. Jones.* Philadelphia, PA: Lippincott, 1958.

MICHAEL BIRKEL

JOWETT, BENJAMIN (1817–1893)

Anglican cleric and biblical scholar. Jowett was born April 15, 1817 at Camberwell, ENGLAND and died October 1, 1893 at Balliol College, Oxford. Educated at Balliol he spent the remainder of his career at the college and university, where he served as a tutor and later master of the college, as well as vice-chancellor of the university. Ordained in 1845, Jowett was, by nineteenth-century Anglican standards, a theological liberal with affinities for JOHN LOCKE, GEORG W. F. HEGEL, FRIEDRICH SCHLEIERMACHER, and FERDINAND C. BAUER. A noted Greek scholar, he served as Regius Professor of Greek at Oxford and produced translations of Aristotle and Plato. As a biblical scholar he wrote important commentaries on Paul's letters to the Thessalonians, Galatians, and Romans (1855), basing his commentaries on the German philologist Karl Lachmann's recently published Greek text. This text was based in part on the oldest known Greek texts, instead of the *textus receptus* that provided the basis for the authoritative King James Version of the BIBLE.

His essay "On the Interpretation of Scripture" appeared in the controversial, and by British standards, liberal *Essays and Reviews* (1860). In the essay he argued that readers of Scripture should read it as they would any other book. Yet, in spite of arguing for a scientific approach to Scripture, he made little use of historical critical methodologies. Instead he focused on literary and philological issues, approaching the text more as a classical scholar would approach Aristotle or Plato, seeking to discover the plain sense of the original authors. Still, he helped pave the way for later critical scholars, including B. F. Westcott and F. A. Hort. As a churchman Jowett worked to create a tolerant and comprehensive CHURCH OF ENGLAND, and as an educator he argued for allowance of divergent viewpoints and the admission of Protestant nonconformists to the universities.

See also Bible, King James, Version; Broad Church; Liberal Protestantism and Liberalism; Nonconformity; Toleration

References and Further Reading

Barr, James. "Jowett and the 'Original Meaning' of Scripture." *Religious Studies* (1982): 433–437.
Hinchliff, Peter. *Benjamin Jowett and the Christian Religion.* Oxford: Oxford University Press, 1987.

R. D. CORNWALL

JUDAISM

For centuries the Christian Church joined governmental authority in restricting the legal and social standing of Jews and condemning Judaism. According to church teaching, Jews, since they had rejected Jesus as Messiah, were condemned to God's wrath, even as their suffering and plight since the destruction of the Second Temple were indication of divine rejection. Even though the REFORMATION placed many of the doctrines of the medieval church under scrutiny, this did not include the TRADITION of Christian hostility toward the Jews. Initially a number of Jewish scholars welcomed the Reformation, suggesting that the Reformation heralded the coming of the Messiah: some were encouraged by MARTIN LUTHER's tract "*That Jesus Christ Was Born a Jew.*" Yet the subsequent writings of Luther and the other reformers concerning Jesus and Judaism hardly differed from traditional perspectives.

While the reformers' widespread disavowal of traditional affirmation and tenets might have entailed a new understanding of Judaism and Jews, there were nonetheless some reformers who adopted a more sympathetic attitude, even though they shared their coreligionists' contempt for Judaism and the Jewish nation. Justus Jonas, a companion of Luther, for example, stressed the missionary dimension of Luther's views. In his opinion Christians have a duty to lead Jews to Christ. Another Lutheran, ANDREAS OSIANDER, the reformer of Nuremberg and pastor at the Church of St. Lorenz in Nuremberg, produced a work that refuted the traditional blood-libel charge. In his view it was ludicrous to believe that Jews should murder children and then use their blood for ritual purposes. Jewish law, he pointed out, specifies that Jews are forbidden to kill any human being, and to make the use of blood from animals, much less a human child. No Jew, he noted, had ever made such a claim about other Jews. The origins of this charge were no doubt attributable to the unsubstantiated claims of those whose children had died of neglect or unknown causes.

Other reformers emphasized the total depravity of humankind. In their view gentiles and Jews stood guilty before God. Thus it would be a mistake to insist that the Jews were particularly villainous. JOHN CALVIN, the Genevan reformer, for example, argued that when Scripture spoke of the Jews and their sinfulness, the Jews were seen as a symbol of all humanity. When Jesus spoke of the hypocrisy of Jews in building the sepulchers for the prophets they themselves had killed, Calvin noted that there was a contemporary parallel: "The world, in general, while not daring to scorn God utterly or at least rise up against Him to His face, devises a means of worshipping God's shadow in place of God: just so it plays a game over the prophets." Even though Christians might erect statues of Peter and other SAINTS, their treatment of the faithful in their own day illustrates how they would react if Peter were among them.

Unlike Luther, who believed that God's special covenantal relationship with the Jews had come to an end, Calvin maintained that God often had to judge Israel. However, this does not mean that God's COVENANT with the Jews has been broken. Commenting on Matthew 27:25 ("his blood be on us and on our children"), Calvin stated that even though God had avenged the death of Jesus with fearful means, he had left a remnant so that the covenant would not be destroyed: "God in their very treachery displays the constancy of his faith, and to show that his covenant was not struck with Abraham to no effect. He rescues those he freely elected from the general destruction. Thus his truth ever arises superior to all obstacles of human incredulity."

During this period it was believed among the reformers that there would be a large-scale conversion of the Jewish people. Calvin's successor at Geneva, THEODORE BEZA, revived Luther's view that Christian churches were largely responsible for the current unbelief among the Jews: "Those who today call themselves Christians . . . are very certainly punished and will be in the future, because, solely under the guidance of wickedness and perversity, they have mistreated in every way these people, so holy in their forefathers, actually hardening them further (against Christianity) by settling before their eyes the example of an odious idolatry. As for myself, I gladly pray every day for the Jews."

Beza went on to acknowledge the justice of divine anger against the Jewish people, but he pleaded that Christ would remember his covenants: "Grant that we (gentiles)," he prayed, "may advance in thy grace, so that we may not be for them (Jews) instruments of thy divine wrath, but that we may rather become capable, through the knowledge of thy words and the example of a holy life, of bringing them back into the true way by virtue of thy Holy Spirit, so that all nations and all peoples together may glorify thee for eternity."

The early reformers thus reformulated previous Christian teaching about Jews. The traditional consensus that Jews exerted a pernicious influence on Christian society was restated. Some theologians, such as Osiander, Calvin, and Beza, despaired of the Jews' refusal to accept Christ, yet basing themselves on Scripture they anticipated the eventual conversion of the Jewish people. Despite this shift in attitude among a number of Christian thinkers, anti-Jewish agitation that had inaugurated a series of expulsions from the latter half of the fifteenth century continued in intensity. Senior clergy as well as secular rulers were involved in frequent attacks on the Jewish population, and expulsions continued to the latter part of the sixteenth century.

There were, however, some Protestant figures who adopted a more positive appraisal of Judaism. The Huguenot scholar Joseph Justus Scaliger, who served as professor at the University of Leiden from 1593, for example, argued that it was only possible to establish the true text and meaning of Scripture by gaining an understanding of rabbinic sources. Jews, he maintained, should be permitted to return to western Europe not simply because of their economic importance, but because of their learning. In his view, Christians would be able to bring Jews to Christ if they understood Talmudic and post-biblical literature.

The seventeenth century brought a lively interest in Jewish learning among certain reformed circles. It was believed that the church's future and the imminence of the Second Coming was bound up with the CONVERSION of the Jews. Some suggested that the conversion of the Jews would not be an event toward the end of the age, but rather foreshadowed a time of blessing for the CHURCH on earth. Such a notion arose out of intense BIBLE study, particularly in connection with the Book of Revelation, which was seen as offering a detailed account of church history from Pentecost to the Day of Judgment.

The Cambridge scholar Joseph Mede held that the future millennium would be inaugurated or shortly followed by the return of the Jews to Christ in their ancient land. In his view, the Jews would be converted in a supernatural manner. Other scholars believed that Revelation 13–19 contained a divine promise of the overthrow of the enemies of the Gospel, interpreted as both the papacy and the Turks. This would be preliminary to a period of latter-day glory for the church, which would see the conversion of the Jews as part of the movement of the Spirit of God. Through this process earthly kingdoms would submit to the gospel so that they could be said to have become "the kingdoms of our God and of his Christ."

Even among reformers critical of millenarianism, there was a widespread belief in the conversion of the Jews. Hence Robert Baillie, one of the Scottish commissioners to the Westminster Assembly, contended on the basis of Romans 11 that the Jews would eventually turn to Christ. In the NETHERLANDS Protestant theologians followed a similar line. In the marginal notes on Romans 11 the reformed translators of the 1637 Dutch version of the Bible argued that the "whole of Israel" in this epistle implies the fullness of the people of Israel "according to the flesh." Thus,

they maintained that the Jewish nation would eventually acknowledge Christ as Lord.

By the middle of the seventeenth century, as England was suffering from CIVIL WAR, it was suggested this tragedy was the result of God's judgment for previous cruelty and indifference toward the Jewish people. Those who pleaded for Jewish readmission contended that if Jews were allowed back into Britain, they would hear some of the best gospel preaching on earth. This, they went on, would bring about their conversion to Christ, leading to a golden age for the church. To these religious arguments were added economic and political concerns. As part of this campaign OLIVER CROMWELL invited Menasseh ben Israel, an Amsterdam scholar and rabbi, to ENGLAND to argue the case for the Jews to be readmitted to England. This visit, however, stirred up considerable opposition from numerous critics such as the pamphleteer Willam Prynne and other Puritans who were skeptical about the mass conversion of the Jews (see PURITANISM). In their view the reference to Israel in Romans 11:25f. referred to the whole New Testament church of both gentiles and Jews. Other Puritans adopted a more welcoming attitude. Edward Elton, for example, remarked that Christians ought "not to hate the Jews (as many do) only because they are Jews, which name among many is so odious that they think they cannot call a man worse than to call him a Jew; but, beloved, this ought not to be so, for we are bound to love and to honour the Jews, as being the ancient people of God, to wish them well, and to be in earnest in prayer for their conversion."

Such sentiments were not widely shared; throughout Europe Jews were viewed with contempt and hostility. These attitudes reached a climax with the publication of *Entdecktes Judenthum* (*Judaism Unmasked*) in 1711 by Johann Andreas Eisenmenger who served as professor of oriental languages at Königsberg. In his view, the best way to defend Christianity against the Jewish threat was to rehearse the traditional medieval charges against the Jews. This work illustrated that despite the changing attitudes brought about by the Reformation, deep-seated Judeophobia persisted in the early modern period.

Undeterred by such an attack, the Jewish community believed it could curtail the distribution of Eisenmenger's treatise. Enlisting the support of the court Jew, Samson Wertheimer, as well as various German princes, they gained the support of the emperor Leopold. Although the book was eventually published after Eisenmenger's death by permission of the king of Prussia, the emperors retained their ban on the book because it was perceived as prejudicial to the public and to the Christian religion. The early modern period thus witnessed the continuation of the long tradition of

Christian ANTI-SEMITISM alongside a growing awareness of the need to improve the position of Jewry. Voices were raised on different sides of this debate by leading figures of the Reformation. Yet even those Reformers who encouraged their coreligionists to adopt a more positive attitude toward the Jewish community shared many of the prejudices of previous ages.

The ENLIGHTENMENT, however, brought about a dramatic alteration in the condition of the Jews; nonetheless, a number of Christian writers continued to attack Jewry on rationalist grounds. In FRANCE, Protestants influenced by the Enlightenment sought to ameliorate the condition of the Jews, yet even they were unable to free themselves from Christian assumptions about Jewish guilt for killing Christ. During this period a number of major thinkers of the age sought to encourage Judeophobia. To escape from such denigration, enlightened Jews disassociated from Judaism and a number sought to gain social acceptance by banding together as a new Jewish-Christian sect.

By the end of the eighteenth century, the spirit of the Enlightenment encouraged Christian Europe to improve the condition of Jewish existence. With the establishment of the Napoleonic era, Jewish life dramatically changed. In France the summoning of the Great Sanhedrin heralded Jewish emancipation. In such a climate Jewish reformers attempted to adapt Jewish WORSHIP to modern conditions. Reform temples appeared throughout GERMANY, yet ironically many Jews influenced by the Romantic movement were indifferent to such alterations to Jewish practice. Instead of providing a basis for the improvement of Judaism, the Reform movement undermined traditional Judaism and intensified Christian antipathy to the Jewish faith.

In the nineteenth century a number of Jewish apologists endeavoured to ameliorate the condition of the Jewish population. In England the Tory Prime Minister advocated Jewish emancipation; such activity provoked a hostile response from various critics who denigrated Judaism in terms reminiscent of previous centuries. In France the Dreyfus Affair stimulated anti-Jewish feelings and revived the medieval Christian charge of ritual murder, giving rise to widespread anti-Jewish sentiment. At this time the Christian legend of the Wandering Jew, who was destined to roam the earth for having rejected Christ became a major theme of French literature. French Judeophobia was further intensified by the writings of socialists. Similarly, in Germany advocates of racism as well as philosophers vilified the Jewish people and their traditions.

During the second half of the nineteenth century, the Jewish community suffered further outbreaks of hostility. In Germany various racist publications attacked Jews, and the researches of Christian biblical scholars undermined the traditional belief that the Torah was given by God to Moses on Mount Sinai. Similar attitudes were expressed in France by a variety of Christian writers. At the end of the century the Dreyfus Affair in France raised fundamental questions about the viability of Jewish life in the diaspora. In the years leading up to World War I, Jews were viewed as scapegoats for the problems that beset German society. After World War I, economic problems related to war reparations and widespread unemployment led to the rise of Hitler and Nazism with its government-imposed anti-Semitic policies.

Following World War II, the devastation of Europe in general and the displacement of what remained of the Jewish population increased the desire among Jews to establish the state of Israel, which occurred in 1948. While many Christians favored this development, some evangelical Protestants and fundamentalists have strongly supported Israel owing to their millennialist beliefs in "end time" prophesy, the imminent return of Christ, and the importance of the conversion of the Jews in this view.

In modern times, ways are being sought to transcend the legacy of anti-Semitism. Various Protestant groups have issued decrees denouncing anti-Semitism and encouraging positive Jewish–Christian encounters in a broad ecumenical spirit. Pioneering Christian scholars have attempted to understand the Jewishness of Jesus—modern CHRISTOLOGY, they believe, should be purged of any anti-Jewish bias. God's enduring covenant with the Jewish people has been emphasized, and various theories have been propounded to illustrate that Jesus' death and resurrection do not replace God's revelation on Mt. Sinai. In this context the traditional idea of Christian mission has been replaced by the notion of Christian witness. No longer do most Christians feel compelled to convert the Jewish people; rather, Judaism is affirmed as a valid religious tradition with its own spiritual integrity. These are signs of hope as Jews and Protestants stand together at the beginning of a new millennium.

See also Holocaust; Millenarians & Millennialism; Philo-Semitism

References and Further Reading

Cohn-Sherbok, Dan. *Anti-Semitism: A History.* Stroud: Sutton, 2001.

———. *The Crucified Jew: Twenty Centuries of Christian Anti-Semitism.* London: Harper Collins Religious, 1992.

Flannery, Edward. *The Anguish of the Jews.* New York: Paulist Press, 1985.

Grosser, Paul. *Anti-Semitism: Cause and Effects.* New York: 1983.

Grosser, Paul and Edwin Halperin. *Anti-Semitism: The Causes and Effects of a Prejudice.* Secaucus, NJ: Citadel Press, 1976.

Keith, Graham. *Hatred Without a Cause.* London: Paternoster, 1997.

Lindemann, Albert. *Anti-Semitism before the Holocaust.* New York: Longman, 2000.

Littell, Franklin. *Crucifixion of the Jews.* New York: Harper and Row, 1975.

Litvinoff, B. *The Burning Bush: Antisemitism and World History.* New York: Dutton, 1988.

Nichols, William. *Christian Antisemitism: A History of Hate.* Northvale, NJ: Jason Aronson, 1993.

Parkes, James. *Antisemitism.* London: Vallentine, Mitchell, 1963.

Poliakov, Leon. *History of Anti-Semitism.* Vol. 1. 4 vols. London: Elek Books, 1965–1985.

DAN COHN-SHERBOK

JUDSON FAMILY

Adoniram Judson was one of the first American foreign missionaries and remains one of the most famous in mission, and especially Baptist, history. Judson was born in Malden, Massachusetts, and graduated from Brown University (1807) and from the first class of Andover Seminary (1810). He was one of the founders of the AMERICAN BOARD OF COMMISSIONERS FOR FOREIGN MISSIONS (ABCFM) in 1810, under whose auspices he and others sailed for India on February 19, 1812. He married Ann ("Nancy") Hasseltine (1789–1826) on February 5, 1812, and the two were commissioned on February 6, 1812. En route to INDIA, they became convinced of believer's BAPTISM by immersion and were baptized on September 6, 1812 by WILLIAM CAREY in Calcutta. The Judsons left the ABCFM, had to leave India, and then went to Burma (Myanmar). In 1814 the Baptist General Convention for Foreign Missions was established in the UNITED STATES to support them.

The Judsons won converts to Christianity and engaged in translation work. Adoniram produced a major Burmese dictionary (2nd ed., 1849) and a Burmese translation of the Bible (1834). Ann bore two children who died in infancy; in 1826 Ann died and was buried in Burma. Her heroism expressed through letters and publications made her one of the most famous female missionaries in American history. Both the nineteenth and twentieth centuries saw a veritable flood of hagiographic literature on Ann Judson.

In 1834 Adoniram married Sarah Hall Boardman (1803–1845), the widow of George Dana Boardman, and also a missionary in Burma. Sarah was also a translator. She bore seven children with Adoniram, five of whom outlived both parents (Abby Ann became a Spiritualist in 1890, and Edward did pastoral work in New Jersey and New York City, where he established the Judson Memorial Baptist Church).

When Sarah became ill in Burma, the Judsons sailed back to the United States. Sarah died en route and was buried on St. Helena.

In the United States for less than a year, Adoniram met and married in 1846 Emily Chubbock (1817–1854), who was a popular romance author under the pseudonym Fanny Forester. They returned to Burma. Adoniram became ill in 1850 and went to sea for his health, where he died and was buried. Emily bore two children, one of whom died in infancy; the other (Emily) lived to 1911. Emily returned to the United States in 1851 and prepared the materials for Francis Wayland's (he was president of Brown University) biography of Adoniram (1853). Emily died the next year.

See also American Baptist Church; Baptists; Baptist Missions, Missions; Bible Translation; Spiritualism

References and Further Reading

Anderson, Courtney. *To the Golden Shore: The Life of Adoniram Judson.* Boston: Little, Brown, 1956; reprint, Valley Forge, PA: Judson, 1987.

Brumberg, Joan Jacobs. *Mission for Life: The Story of Adoniram Judson.* New York: Free Press/London: Collier Macmillan, 1980.

James, Sharon. *My Heart in His Hands: Ann Judson of Burma: A Life with Selections from her Memoir and Letters.* Durham, UK: Evangelical Press, 1998.

Robert, Dana. *American Women in Mission: A Social History of Their Thought and Practice.* Macon, GA: Mercer University Press, 1997.

Wayland, Francis. *A Memoir of the Life and Labors of the Rev. Adoniram Judson, D.D.* 2 vols. Boston: Phillips, Sampson, and Company, 1853.

DAVID M. SCHOLER

JUNGIANISM

Jungianism is the term given to theories of the Swiss psychiatrist Carl Gustav Jung and his system of depth psychology, which he called "analytical psychology." It is similar to Freudianism, Sigmund Freud's theory of psychoanalysis. In a pejorative sense, the terms refer to overly zealous followers who subscribe to a set of teachings that have become hypostatized into the equivalent of a religion. In a more benign, sociological sense, such terms can also mean the final stage of a movement that has become a recognized social institution.

It is not surprising that the constructs of depth psychology should have taken on a religious meaning, for analogies between Freud and Jung and the Old and New Testaments abound in the history of depth psychology. While Freud identified with his Jewishness, he maintained that he was an atheist and that psychoanalysis was a science and not a religion. However, his comments on religion, while pejorative, refer almost exclusively to images from the Old Testament. Jung, meanwhile, ranged throughout the Old and New Testament—his *Answer to Job*, for instance—but he was primarily engulfed in the *Imago Christi* of the New Testament, the Virgin Mary, and the aesthetic and moral struggle against evil as it was waged in the Gospels. Jung even embarked on a quest later in his life to analyze and unite the symbolism of the Catholic and Protestant faiths. He was also knowledgeable about the symbolism of different world religions and the iconography of preliterate cultures. Thus, analytical psychology was much more visionary, metaphorical, and cross-cultural than Freud's system.

One reduced the symbolism of other cultures to fit the theory of psychoanalysis. The goal of Freud and his followers was to convert others not to Judaism, but rather to the analytic way of thinking. They did this chiefly by addressing the great problems of modernity—alienation, material attachment and loss, the importance of delayed gratification, and the threat of instantaneous annihilation. Jung's analytical psychology, on the other hand, included the myth of the resurrection of Jesus, but now transmuted into a secularized psychology of transcendence. In this process, individuation was initiated by a confrontation between consciousness and the unconscious, leading to an expansion of consciousness. The end product was the integration of the opposites by means of the transcendent function, a condition that Jung considered a state of spiritual maturity. Jung was more interested in a shift of the center of personality from the ego to the self. For him, the outward details of a life were always preempted by the vicissitudes of inner spiritual transformation.

The religious analogy is made a little more complicated, however, by historical comparisons between theories of depth psychology and certain traditions of religious mysticism. In Jung's personal life, the religious influences appeared to have come from transformative visions experienced at an early age, growing up in a Protestant household where his father had been a minister stationed in an asylum for psychiatric patients, and other influences, such as an early exposure to Asian religions and other family members' involvement with the occult. This was to prove problematic for later interpreters, as we now have a growing corpus of works on Jung and Christianity, Jung and SPIRITUALISM, Jung and Shamanism, and Jung and Asian thought, all trying to understand Jung's connection to religion, organized or not.

The most scathing (and also, unfortunately, now the most well-known) exegesis on Jungianism has been the faulty scholarship of the clinical psychologist Richard Noll. In *The Jung Cult* (1994), Noll asserted that Jung was a Gnostic sun worshipper, his depth psychology was self-consciously launched as a religion, and his followers were the new acolytes of a worldwide spiritual movement whose purpose was to displace Christianity. Noll followed this erroneously conceived academic study with a widely circulated trade book titled *Aryan Christ: The Secret Life of Carl Jung* (1997). In it, he further maintained that Jung was not only a Gnostic sun-worshipper out to destroy the institutions of Christianity, but also a Nazi. Thus, Jung's followers were automatically also Nazi sympathizers.

The Jung historian Sonu Shamdasani was able to correct Noll's distorted and sensationalist interpretation by publishing *Cult Fictions: c.g. Jung and the Founding of Analytical Psychology* (1998). Nevertheless, the damage had been done. Noll's work was widely discussed in the public press, more so in the UNITED STATES than abroad, while Shamdasani's work, even though awarded the prestigious Gradiva Award of the psychoanalysts, had only a small circulation, mainly in ENGLAND.

It is of some historical note that the early Jungians in the United States were primarily women, while most of the key Freudians were men. Beatrice Hinkle, Kristine Mann, Constance Long, and Eleanor Bertine were among the early women physicians who formed the core of the first New York group. Francis Wickes and Christiana Morgan were other well-known early figures. Other Americans who spent long periods with Jung included Carol Baumann and Jane Cabot Reid. Today, according to the Jungians themselves, there are generally considered to be three centers of Jungian thought: the so-called Zurich school, which follows the writings of Jung's students, such as Marie von Franz; the object relations school of Melanie Klein in England, and the Archetypal Psychology of James Hillman in the United States. At the same time, Jung has had an influence in liberal religious circles, particularly in the work of such writers as Arnold Toynbee, Victor White, PAUL TILLICH, and Ann Ulanov.

Finally, Jungians may take some comfort in the fact that even as general interest in psychoanalysis has declined, the spread of Jung's ideas has increased. Jung's ideas have remained alive in the enclaves beyond science, particularly in religious circles, within the psychotherapeutic counter-culture, and also in popular movements such as those associated today with WOMEN'S spirituality. Jung's cross-cultural emphasis on world religions must be counted as part of this influence, as was the tremendous impetus of Joseph Campbell's views on world mythology, originally grounded in Jungian ideas. Campbell suggests that any new depth psychology of the future may look more Jungian than Freudian, even though both the names of Freud and Jung will probably not be associated directly with such developments. Meanwhile, as the secularization of the religious impulse continues, Protestant denominations may either have to assimilate such new depth psychologies or else get left behind as outdated cultural institutions no longer able to speak to the breadth and depth of contemporary experience.

References and Further Reading

Primary Sources:

Jung, C. G. *Erinnerungen, Träume, Gedanken (Memories, Dreams, Reflections)*. Recorded and edited by Aniela Jaffé. Translated from the German by Richard and Clara Winston. New York: Pantheon Books, 1963.
———. *Psychology and Religion*. New Haven, CT: Yale University Press/London: Oxford University Press, 1938.

Secondary Sources:

Clarke, J. J. *Jung and Eastern Thought: A Dialogue With the Orient*. New York: Routledge, 1994.
Charet, F. X. *Spiritualism and the Foundations of C. G. Jung's Psychology*. Albany, NY: State University of New York Press, 1993.
Clift, Wallace B. *Jung and Christianity: The Challenge of Reconciliation*. New York: Crossroad, 1982.
Gunn, R. J. *Journeys into Emptiness: Dogen, Merton, Jung, and the Quest for Transformation*. New York: Paulist Press, 2000.
Miller, David L., ed. *Jung and the Interpretation of the Bible*. New York: Continuum, 1995.
Noel, Daniel C. *The Soul of Shamanism: Western Fantasies, Imaginal Realities*. New York: Continuum, 1997.
Noll, Richard. *The Jung Cult: Origins of a Charismatic Movement*. Princeton, NJ: Princeton University Press, 1994.
———. *The Aryan Christ: The Secret Life of Carl Jung*. New York: Random House, 1997.
Shamdasani, Sonu. *Cult Fictions: C. G. Jung and the Founding of Analytical Psychology*. New York: Routledge, 1998.
Taylor, Eugene. *Shadow Culture Psychology and Spirituality in America*. Washington, DC: Counterpoint, 1999.

EUGENE TAYLOR

JUNG-STILLING, JOHANN HEINRICH (1740–1817)

German author. Jung, called Stilling, one of the "Stillen im Lande" (of Psalm 35: 20), had many occupations, but above all he was a religious author and is seen as the "Patriarch der Erweckung" (patriarch of the awakening movement).

He was born in pietistic family tradition in a small village of Siegerland (Western Germany) and tried many occupations (tailor, teacher, clerk, in various locations) until he studied medicine at Strasbourg (where he befriended JOHANN WOLFGANG VON GOETHE, who was studying law there). Between 1772 and 1778

he was a physician specializing in surgical ophthalmology in Elberfeld, and he continued his medical work for the remainder of his life, successfully treating many thousands of blind people. Between 1778 and 1803 he was a professor of political economy at Kaiserslautern, Heidelberg, and Marburg. He spent the final years of his life (1803–1806 at Heidelberg, 1806–1817 at Karlsruhe, where he died) without professional responsibilities, sponsored by the grand duke of Baden. He wrote religious books, engaged in extensive correspondence (he wrote about 25,000 letters during his life), and served as spiritual advisor to the grand duke.

Jung turned to religious writing in 1794–1795 and became known all over Europe through his religious novel *Das Heimweh* (*Homesickness,* 5 vols., 1794–1796, many translations) and several religious periodicals, especially *Der Graue Mann* (1795–1816, published in German in newspaper installments in North America, probably in Germantown, Pennsylvania). As a result, he became a central figure for nearly all religious groups of his times such as the Deutsche Christentumsgesellschaft with its center in Basel and the Herrnhuter Brüdergemeine/MORAVIAN CHURCH as well as many individuals belonging to the awakened people in GERMANY, SWITZERLAND, and other countries. Indicating and interpreting the signs of the time, he called for a return, in opposition to the ideas of the ENLIGHTENMENT, to the original Christian faith, based on Scripture and on Jesus Christ, and to penitence before the last judgment. His opponents saw him as a mystic dreamer.

References and Further Reading

Primary Sources:

Benrath, G. A., ed. *Johann Heinrich Jung-Stilling: Lebensgeschichte*. Darmstadt, Germany: Wissenschaftliche Buchgesellschaft, 1976, 1984, 1992.
Güthling, W. *Jung-Stilling, Verzeichnis der selbständigen Schriften*. 1962.
Sam, M. M., ed. *Das Heimweh*. Dornach, Switzerland: Verlag am Goetheanum, 1994.
Sämmtliche Schriften. 13 vols. and supplement (without the economic works), 1835–1838. Reprint Hildesheim, Germany, 1979 (in 8 vols.).
Schwinge, G., ed. *Jung stilling Briefs*. Göttingen, Germany, 2002.

Secondary Sources:

Geiger, M. "Aufklärung und Erweckung." Ph.D. dissertation, University of Basel, 1956.
Hahn, O. W. "Jung-Stilling zwischen Pietismus und Aufklärung." Ph.D. dissertation, University of Mainz, 1988.
———. *J. H. Jung-Stilling*. 1990. *Selig sind, die das heimweh haben,* Second edition. Gießen: Brunnen-Verlag, 1998.

Lück, Wolfgang. "Jung-Stilling, Arzt-Kameralist-Schriftsteller zwischen Aufklärung und Erweckung." Marburg, 1992.

Propach, G. "Jung-Stilling als Arzt." Ph.D. dissertation, University of Cologne, 1982.

Schwinge, G. "Jung-Stilling als Erbauungsschriftsteller der Erweckung." Ph.D. dissertation, University of Mainz, 1993.

Stecher, G. "Jung-Stilling als Schriftsteller, 1913." Ph.D. dissertation, University of Berlin, 1911. Reprinted 1967.

Vinke, R. "Jung-Stilling und die Aufklärung." Ph.D. dissertation, University of Mainz, 1986/87.

GERHARD SCHWINGE

JURIEU, PIERRE (1637–1713)

French clergy. Jurieu was born in Mer near Orléans and became a leading French Reformed pastor and publicist during the reign of Louis XIV. He was Pierre du Moulin's grandson, Andre Rivet's great nephew, and was nephew to Pierre and Louis du Moulin. The latter taught him that the church owes its independence from secular AUTHORITY to popular sovereignty. Later Jurieu embraced Grotius's NATURAL LAW philosophy, but whether his writings furthered secularism, republicanism, and constitutional liberalism is a matter of disagreement among twentieth-century scholars. Some view Jurieu as antimodern, opposed to INDIVIDUALISM, only reluctantly relinquishing the strong attachments most HUGUENOTS had to ABSOLUTISM (G. Dodge, Q. Skinner, H. Kretzer). Others see him as a contributor to liberal political thought (F. Baumer, F. Knetsch, D. Spini). Jurieu disapproved of TOLERATION of SOCINIANISM or any secularism harmful to Christian ORTHODOXY.

Educated at Saumur, Jurieu succeeded his father as pastor at Mer. From 1674 he taught Hebrew and THEOLOGY at the Academy of Sedan until its suppression (1681). A refugee in Rotterdam, he taught theology at its Walloon academy (1681), exchanging polemics with Catholic historians (Bossuet, Maimbourg, Fénelon), the Jansenist Arnauld, and moderate Calvinists (Saurin, Bayle, Basnage, Jaquelot).

Admired by many, Jurieu was criticized for confessional rigidity and for prophesying Huguenot repatriation and Catholicism's demise (1689). These failing, he predicted their occurrence in the new century. Despite ridicule Jurieu pursued his political visions, promoting the Brandenburg alliance with the House of Orange. Disillusioned when the Peace of Ryswick (1697) failed to repatriate the Huguenots, he provided a sense of purpose and hope to exiles of the Huguenot diaspora.

See also: Catholicism, Protestant Reactions

References and Further Reading

Dodge, Guy Howard. *The Political Theory of the Huguenots of the Dispersion.* New York: Columbia University Press, 1947.

Kretzer, Hartmut. *Calvinismus und französische Monarchie im 17. Jahrhundert.* Berlin, Germany: Duncker & Humblot, 1975.

Spini, Debora. *Diritti di Dio, Diritti dei Popoli.* Turin, Italy: Claudiana Editrice, 1997.

BARBARA SHER TINSLEY

JUSTIFICATION

The doctrine of justification is one of the hallmark teachings of historic Protestantism. It emerged as one of the principal doctrinal differences between the Roman and REFORMATION churches—although by no means was it the only theological difference. Its significance for Protestantism is evident in MARTIN LUTHER's insistence that this was the *articulus stantis et candentis ecclesiae* (the article by which the church stands or falls) and likewise in JOHN CALVIN's description as the "main hinge on which religion turns." At the most basic level this distinctive Protestant DOCTRINE deals with the fundamental question of how a sinful human being can enter into a right and proper relationship with a God who is absolutely holy and righteous. The term "justification" is derived directly from the BIBLE (Romans 3–5), although the theological understanding of the biblical term has developed considerably over time. "Justification" is one of several terms in the New Testament, such as "salvation" or "redemption," that deal with the soteriological question of how sinners enter into a right relationship with the righteous and holy God. In the course of the sixteenth century, this doctrine came to be one of the defining beliefs of historic Protestantism. Indeed, this question lay at the heart of the theological-pastoral concerns of the Augustinian hermit, Martin Luther.

The Protestant Understanding

If one is to gain an understanding of what Luther and other Protestants meant by justification, then one must consider the theological context of the later Middle Ages. Luther's belief that all humanity possesses a will enslaved by SIN meant (or "led him to conclude") that the sinner was unable to exercise genuine saving FAITH, against which Luther reacted. Like most others, Luther underwent considerable development in his understanding of justification. As a young Augustinian hermit, Luther was initiated into the *via moderna,* a school of thought in which the righteousness of God is manifested in the fact that God rewards the individual who does *facere quod in se est* ("to do what you are able to") and punishes those who do not. The righteous God as expressed in the *via moderna* was an utterly scrupulous and impartial judge. According to this understanding, the individual, not God, must take the initial step (no matter how paltry) in the process of justification by recognizing his/her own spiritual weakness and then turn with humility to God asking for GRACE. In accord with God's COVENANT with humanity, God treats this humility as fulfilling the prerequisite necessary for justification. In response God bestows justifying grace upon the individual, enabling the performance of meritorious works, thus permitting a relationship with the righteous God. In this particular scheme justification had to do with *making* the individual inwardly righteous, thus entitling entrance into a relationship with the righteous and holy God. This understanding derives principally from Augustine, who misunderstood the term *iustificare* to mean "to make righteous." Augustine's misreading of the term became normative for the medieval church.

If Luther did eventually diverge from Augustine's definition of justification, he still drank deeply from Augustine's conception of the priority of grace in SALVATION. As early as 1515, while lecturing on Romans, Luther came to see that the individual, because of sinfulness, could not initiate this process of justification. Furthermore—again under the influence of Augustine—Luther concluded that the whole idea of *facere quod in se est* was in reality a Pelagian HERESY. By rejecting the notion that the individual has the inherent ability to initiate the process of justification, Luther moved inexorably to challenge the soteriological framework of the *via moderna*.

Although Luther's rethinking on justification probably began around 1515, it did not reach its definitive shape until 1518–1519. He came to understand that the righteousness of God (*iustitia Dei*) does not refer to a divine attribute but to a divine act of grace toward the hapless sinner. As he developed his understanding, distinctive features emerged. Perhaps his most distinctive idea was the concept of *iustitia Christi aliena* (the alien righteousness of Christ). Luther argued that justification is not based on one's own righteousness but on a righteousness that is alien or extrinsic to the sinner. He insisted that, because of the Fall, individuals have no righteousness in themselves and therefore, if one is to be justified, it must be based entirely on an external righteousness, by which he meant the perfect righteousness of Christ. This perfect righteousness of Christ belongs to the Christian (in an external not internal sense) because of his/her union with Christ. There is for Luther a "wonderful exchange" that takes place in this union between the Christian and Christ: individual sins are exchanged for the righteousness of Christ. It is notable that Luther does not initially employ the language of imputation, although it is clearly subsumed in the wonderful exchange.

One of the most characteristic features of Luther's view of justification is his understanding of the nature and place of faith. His belief that all humanity possesses a will enslaved by sin meant (or "led him to conclude") that the sinner was unable to exercise genuine saving faith. If there is to be true faith, it must come as a gift from God. Authentic faith is not mere assent (*assensus*) to the historic teaching of Christianity, but a grasping faith (*fides apprehensiva*) that takes hold of Christ and his righteousness. Thus Christ is not only the object of the individual's faith, Christ is also present in true faith. For Luther this grasping faith is not viewed as a human work and as such cannot be considered as the cause of justification; rather, faith is understood as the instrument by which one is justified. Above all, Luther's assertion that justification is by faith *alone* (*sola fide*) and the notion of the alien righteousness of Christ underscore one of the key concerns for Luther—justification has everything to do with God's grace and nothing to do with human merit.

Many fail to appreciate that Luther envisioned justification as both an event and a process. What later Protestants were inclined to separate, Luther kept together, at least initially. He was quite clear that there is a moment when the sinner is actually justified by faith, that is, when the alien righteousness of Christ has been transferred to him, although this is only the beginning of a process in which the Christian makes moral progress until the final resurrection, when he will possess a perfect righteousness created in him by the Holy Spirit. Especially in his early writings, justification is often conceived as a healing process in which God regards the sinner as totally righteous in anticipation of the perfect righteousness to come at the final consummation. At points, the relationship between justification and SANCTIFICATION is so closely drawn that Luther does not hesitate to use the rubric of justification to include the process of sanctification as well as the event of justification.

What is almost certainly the most misunderstood aspect of Luther's doctrine is his concept of *simul iustus et peccator* (simultaneously righteous and a sinner). This concept points to the obvious tension between the imputed alien righteousness of Christ and the present reality of the sinful nature in the Christian life. Because of Luther's belief that the Christian is not *made* righteous in the present life, but only in the final resurrection, he acknowledged an eschatological tension between the present sinful reality and the future promise of righteousness. By this phrase he does not mean that Christians are partly sinful and partly righteous in this life; rather that they are totally sinful in themselves and totally righteous in Christ through the gift of faith. This paradoxical language caused many Catholics and Anabaptists (see ANABAPTISM) to conclude that Luther's conception of justification was bewildering at best and antinomian at worst.

In response to such accusations Luther replied that the justification of sinners in no way permitted a devaluation of good works in the life of the Christian. Good works, Luther insisted, were a necessary consequence but not a cause of justification. Such necessary good works, however, could not in themselves produce assurance for the Christian. The many years of struggle with *Anfechtungen* (spiritual anxiety) proved to Luther that if assurance is grounded in demonstrable human works, then full assurance will always be undermined by the unrelenting quest to determine whether one's good works were adequate and whether they issued from genuinely virtuous intentions. Luther's doctrine of original sin prevented any such assurance of salvation or justification if grounded on one's deeds. True assurance could and should be found only in the faithfulness of God to his promises of mercy.

In the 1530s Luther's close friend and colleague at the University of Wittenberg, PHILIPP MELANCHTHON, made a fundamental refinement to Luther's doctrine (initially in his *Apology,* 1530), which then became normative for both Lutheran and Reformed branches of Protestantism. Instead of viewing justification as "healing" as Luther earlier had maintained, Melanchthon recast justification in a legal or forensic framework. Whereas Augustine and the medieval church taught that the sinner is *made* righteous in justification, Melanchthon taught he is *declared* or *pronounced* righteous on the basis of the imputed righteousness of Christ. Melanchthon drew a sharp distinction between justification (the event of being declared righteous) and sanctification (the process of being made righteous). This refinement of Luther's doctrine represents a further break from the teaching of the church up to this point. This forensic conception of justification was taken up by virtually all subsequent Protestant reformers and came to represent a standard difference between Catholics and Protestants.

The Reformed branch of Protestantism embraced substantially the same doctrine as Luther and Melanchthon, but construed it differently and maintained a different emphasis. Calvin's view, which gained ascendancy in the later sixteenth-century Reformation, was formulated in the 1540s and 1550s. Calvin revived Luther's emphasis on the believer's union with Christ through faith as the means by which that union is achieved. This union has a twofold effect that Calvin called "double grace." The first effect of the believer's union with Christ leads directly to forensic justification. Through the imputed righteousness of Christ, the believer is declared to be righteous in the sight of God. However, there is a second simultaneous

effect of this union with Christ, that is, that on account of the union with Christ—and not on account of his justification—the believer begins the process of being made like Christ through sanctification (or as he sometimes calls it, regeneration). Calvin seems to have undergone some development on this matter early in his Protestant career, but by 1540 the main lines of his distinctive configuration were in place. Instead of giving priority to either sanctification or justification, Calvin turned his attention to their common source, union with Christ, which granted them equal standing, distinct, but not separate. It has not escaped the notice of scholars that Calvin treats sanctification before justification in the 1559 edition of the INSTITUTES OF THE CHRISTIAN RELIGION. This is not significant except to show that Calvin's real interest was the believer's union with Christ, and that justification and sanctification are merely two consequences of that signal event. For Calvin, where there is justification there also will be sanctification.

One of the important historiographical insights garnered from a historical analysis is the fact that the Protestant doctrine of justification was not static, but went through a process of theological development. To be sure, Luther set the course that others would follow, although a proper understanding of this period must recognize that Luther's initial insights provoked decades of Protestant refinement from both Lutheran and Reformed theologians. It also provoked one of the more interesting ecumenical attempts at reconciliation between Protestants and Catholics at the Colloquy of Regensburg in 1541 (see REGENSBURG COLLOQUY). Protestants, led by Melanchthon, and Catholics, led by Gaspero Cardinal Contarini, actually reached agreement on a doctrine of "double justification," affirming two formal causes of justification—the external righteousness of Christ and the internal righteousness of the Christian. In the final analysis both Luther and the pope rejected this theological compromise and from that point on genuine dialogue ceased until the twentieth century. In the later years of the Reformation the theological trend in Lutheranism was to emphasize forensic justification, with the result that sanctification was often neglected. The Lutheran reformer ANDREAS OSIANDER rejected forensic imputation in favor of an "essential" justifying righteousness, which galvanized Lutheran opposition and significantly reinforced the forensic emphasis of the doctrine of justification.

Although the Reformed Church did not give the same prominence to the doctrine as did the Lutherans, the same general trajectory is evident also in the Reformed branch. The earliest Reformed conceptions of justification tended to place great emphasis on the close proximity of sanctification and justification, which for some meant that sanctification was constitutive of justification. HULDRYCH ZWINGLI, MARTIN BUCER, HEINRICH BULLINGER, Peter Martyr Vermigli, and JOHANNES OECOLAMPADIUS all envisaged a close relationship between sanctification and justification. However, the WESTMINSTER CONFESSION did not follow this theological accent. The Westminster divines tended to be more linear in their soteriology, derived no doubt from their understanding of the *ordo salutis* (order of salvation). The effect of these later developments within the Reformed tradition was a tendency to drive a wedge between justification and sanctification to make a clear distinction between imputed and inherent righteousness. The main reason for the trend toward forensic justification lies in the fact that the Council of Trent obliged Protestants to define their own theology more distinctively. Just as Trent defined its doctrine over against Luther and early Protestants, so also later Protestants defined their doctrine over against Trent.

The Council of Trent

The Council of Trent was summoned in 1545 to formulate a comprehensive response to Luther. One of the more vital issues was the doctrine of justification. The sixth session of Trent reached its definitive conclusions regarding justification on January 13, 1547. Against Luther, Trent strongly defended Augustine's view that justification is the process of renewal that brings about a change in both the outer status and the inner nature of the sinner. For the theologians at Trent justification was not only "forgiveness of sins" but also "regeneration and sanctification" through the voluntary reception of grace. They strenuously argued that sinners were justified on the basis of an internal righteousness graciously infused or imparted to the sinner by God. Perhaps the key to understanding the reaction of Trent is their fear that Luther's view of justification would lead inevitably to ANTINOMIANISM. When Luther insisted that justification was by faith alone, Catholics understood him to say that one could be justified without any need for obedience, good works, or spiritual renewal. To these theologians, Luther's concept of justification undermined all morality. By the final session at Trent the doctrinal battle lines had been drawn.

The English Church

During the seventeenth century orthodox Protestants on the continent remained more or less in harmony with their sixteenth-century forebears when it came to the doctrine of justification. The Anglican Church was generally in accord with the Protestants on the continent, although some peculiar developments of its own

were evidenced (see ANGLICANISM). The early English reformers seem to have been somewhat confused in their understanding of Luther's doctrine of justification. There was a decided tendency to embrace an Augustinian understanding of justification as *making* one righteous, but following Luther, insisting this was by faith alone. After the return of the Marian exiles there was a renewed doctrinal conformity with the Reformed theologians on the continent. RICHARD HOOKER, one of the preeminent Anglicans, asserted the imputation of Christ's righteousness, that faith was not a work of man but a gift from God and distinguished (but did not separate) justification and sanctification. Seventeenth-century Puritans for the most part followed this trend, although some Puritans, such as RICHARD BAXTER, diverged from the mainstream by identifying faith as the formal cause of justification instead of the righteousness of Christ. Later Caroline divines departed substantially from Hooker and PURITANISM, favoring a concept of justification that spoke of inherent righteousness as the basis for justification, of faith as a human work, and a blurring of the distinction between justification and sanctification. With the restoration of Charles II, the Puritan view of justification was increasingly neglected.

In the eighteenth century, JOHN WESLEY developed his own brand of ANGLICANISM with distinctive implications for his doctrine of justification. In the early years of his ministry, Wesley adhered to typical late seventeenth-century Anglican theology of justification. At its core was his conviction that God does not declare righteous anyone who is not doing all they can to be righteous. For Wesley it was not faith alone, but faith and works that lead to righteousness. After his dismal missionary adventure in Georgia (1736–1738), however, his conception of justification underwent change. Wesley moved away from the Anglican version of justification, although he did not embrace a typical Lutheran or Reformed view without modification. Within his broad overarching concept of universal ATONEMENT and his self-described Arminian view of salvation (see ARMINIANISM), he recognized that justification was not about being made righteous, but a legal declaration made by God for the sake of Christ. Although he rejected the idea of the imputation of Christ's righteousness to the believer, he maintained that justification concerns forgiveness and acceptance. Some have argued that Wesley identified imputation with antinomianism and thus rejected the idea. Wesley discarded the notion that one must first attain holiness before justification is granted, but he was careful to preserve his understanding of a prevenient grace given to all, thus enabling all to respond to the gospel call if they will.

With regard to the doctrine of justification, Wesley's main distinction centered on his idea of Christian perfection. For Wesley regeneration was especially significant because it endowed the believer with extraordinary spiritual power to love, trust, and hope. In place of the traditional Protestant idea of progressive sanctification *toward* holiness, he substituted growth *in* holiness. Having rejected the imputation of the righteousness of Christ to the believer, he looked to the believer (in the power of the Holy Spirit) to advance in the righteousness already acquired in regeneration. Thus personal righteousness is about realization rather than progression. Full sanctification or Christian perfection, as Wesley termed it, is at the completion of regeneration and constitutes the final condition for salvation and entrance into the presence of God. Christian perfection comes by faith and occurs at some point (usually at the end of life) in the process of sanctification. Of course, with his Arminian convictions, this state of justification and the attainment of Christian perfection could be forfeited through a lack of faith.

Nineteenth-century England saw the emergence of the OXFORD MOVEMENT. In 1837 JOHN HENRY NEWMAN gave a series of lectures in the university church of St. Mary the Virgin, Oxford, on the topic of justification. These lectures were published the following year as *Lectures on Justification* and represented his effort to articulate his understanding of the true Anglican position. In these lectures Newman attempted to steer a middle course between what he judged to be the doctrinal distortions of the classical Protestantism (especially the Lutheran tradition) and Catholicism. Newman argued that the essence of justification, which consisted in the presence of the Triune God within the soul of the believer, invariably brings certain spiritual consequences. These consequences entail both being *declared* righteous and being *made* righteous. For Newman justification and sanctification are bestowed simultaneously with the indwelling of God in the soul of the believer. Justification is therefore notionally distinct but not separate from sanctification, given that both derive from the same indwelling presence of God in the soul of the believer. Based on his understanding of the effectual power of God's word, what God declares about the sinner is necessarily brought into reality. Those who are declared righteous are actually made righteous. In sum, justification involves both a declaration of Christ's righteousness (through imputation) as well as being made righteous. Although Newman was at pains to critique the Protestant view, his understanding of justification appears to bear an uncanny resemblance to the view of Calvin.

Newman's understanding of the role of faith in justification is intriguing. As an Anglican he accepted the official declaration (article 11) that "we are justified by faith only," although he elaborates on the instrumental role of faith in justification. Faith is the sole *internal* instrument of justification, but he adds that the SACRAMENTS also serve as an *external* instrument of justification. In Newman's words, "justification comes *through* the sacraments; is *received* by faith; *consists* in God's inward presence and *lives* in obedience."

The Enlightenment

In the aftermath of the wars of religion in the seventeenth century, the European continent underwent a theological paradigm shift. No longer was the CHURCH or the BIBLE a sufficient guide to truth. Instead, ENLIGHTENMENT thinkers looked beyond scripture and orthodox theology to a new and more rational basis for spiritual direction. As a general rule the Enlightenment of the eighteenth century did not devote a great deal of attention specifically to the doctrine of justification. Yet it did undermine the orthodox understanding inasmuch as it ignored or simply rejected one of the indispensable presuppositions of justification—the doctrine of original sin. Historically, one of the pillars of the Protestant orthodox conception of justification, whether Lutheran or Reformed (or even Catholic), was the fundamental presupposition that every person enters this world alienated from God because of original sin. However, the exaltation of human reason and moral optimism so characteristic of the Enlightenment could not abide any doctrine of justification based on original sin, for such a doctrine violated both their tenets of rationality and morality. English thinkers such as JOHN TOLAND and JOHN LOCKE had little room for an orthodox understanding of original sin and thus little interest in the doctrine of justification. English Deists (see DEISM) preferred a purely moralist conception in which divine pardon depends on an independent act of repentance, undoubtedly inspired by the moral example and teaching of Christ.

In GERMANY the *Aufklärung* (Enlightenment) followed the same general trend as the English Deists. Some early advocates formally retained the forensic notion of justification, but God's legal declaration of pardon, they argued, was based on an inherent righteousness within the individual. Later advocates of the German *Aufklärung* rejected completely any semblance to the orthodox Protestant understanding of justification. Christ's death, far from atoning for sin, serves as the supreme example and inspiration for humanity to emulate the outstanding moral character of Christ. Presupposed in this moralistic view is the autonomy of the individual, who is regarded as possessing all that is needed for justification. By the end of the eighteenth century the orthodox foundations of the Protestant doctrine of justification had been undermined by the rationalism and moralism of the Enlightenment.

Developments in Modernity

FRIEDRICH SCHLEIERMACHER reacted against the rationalistic and moralistic conceptions of justification espoused by the Enlightenment thinkers and moved in an entirely new direction. According to Schleiermacher, all Christian doctrine, including justification, was viewed as nothing more than individual consciousness of Christian religious feelings (*Gefühl*). Indeed, justification was not viewed as the objective pardon of sinners by God, but was instead the subjective consciousness of God (not knowledge of God) that is elevated and stimulated through the mediation by the supreme God-consciousness of Christ. Thus salvation is not an objective rescue from the consequences of sin, but a subjective alignment or attunement with the unknowable God through Christ's personal example of God-consciousness mediated through the Christian community. A number of key elements of the orthodox concept of justification are missing in Schleiermacher. Christ is not necessarily the only or unique mediator, and the orthodox conception of original sin is rejected as illogical. Justification or redemption thus became a radically anthropocentric conception, not only of religion, but of all its doctrines including justification. Schleiermacher's understanding of soteriology, although subjected to serious criticism, fundamentally reoriented the theological landscape.

One of the most significant theological developments in the mid-nineteenth century was the decline of Hegelianism. This prompted ALBRECHT RITSCHL to reformulate the doctrine of justification without the Hegelian interpretative framework and led to the recovery of the objective aspect of justification that had been lost in the *Aufklärung*. In 1870 he published his most famous work, *Christliche Lehre von der Rechtfertigung und Versöhnung* (*The Christian Doctrine of Justification and Reconciliation*). In this pioneering work he sought to break from the moralistic concepts of justification that came to dominate European thought of the early nineteenth century and to restore the objective dimension of the doctrine. In his effort to establish the objectivity of justification he particularly stressed the synthetic judgment of God in justification—that is, he affirmed that justification is a creative act of the divine will in which the declaration of the righteousness of the sinner effects rather than endorses the righteousness of man. He thus eliminated any

claim by the morally renewed man to be justified on that account.

Although restoring the objective dimension of justification, Ritschl nevertheless modified three critical aspects of the historic Protestant view of justification—the forensic nature of justification, the doctrine of original sin, and the function of Christ in justification. First, Ritschl argues that justification should be conceived as extrajudicial; that is, just as the ruler may relax the law for the greater public good, so Ritschl argues that God pardons the sinner for the greater good of the KINGDOM OF GOD. Second, he rejects the Augustinian doctrine of original sin as a rationalistically constructed doctrine that fails to account for the link between Adam and humanity as well as for the different degrees of sin among individuals. Finally the role of Christ seems to be reduced to a symbolic extension of God's grace without any essential connection with that grace. Christ is therefore viewed as the one who reveals the real situation between God and man, rather than the one who by God-self established a new relationship between God and man. Ritschl, despite restoring the objective nature of justification, nevertheless reverted to a subjective understanding of the role of Christ and therefore exhibits a tendency to marginalize his death.

It should be noted that for Ritschl all Christian doctrine is not about facts but about value judgments, that is to say, doctrines are not so much about scientifically verifiable propositions but rather about the impact of God in a person's life and the moral value of that impact for the highest good. The essence of Christianity and the focal point for the doctrine of justification concerns building the kingdom of God in meaningful and practical ways from a motive of love. This kingdom of God is not a metaphysical spiritual entity, but a religion of world transformation through ethical actions. Ritschl's conception of justification, which combined the objective conception of the doctrine with a subjective influence of Christ, is generally representative of theologies of justification in the period from 1880 to the beginning of World War I.

Karl Barth

Generally considered the greatest theologian of the twentieth century, KARL BARTH's view of justification warrants consideration, not because he fully developed a new understanding of the doctrine but because his theological outlook has important implications for this doctrine. In general Barth's theology may be described as an extended reflection on the fact that God has spoken to humanity (*Deus dixit*) in Christ, thus overcoming the epistemological chasm separating them. Christianity therefore is not so much about justification by faith alone as about God revealing himself to the individual. As such, soteriological considerations are secondary to his focus on revelation. Indeed, it has been argued that Barth has placed the divine revelation to sinful humanity at precisely the point where Luther placed the divine justification of sinful humanity.

Second, Barth's conception of *gemina praedestinatio* (double predestination) has significant implications for his doctrine of justification. Instead of grounding predestination in the eternal will of God whereby some are elected to eternal salvation and some to eternal damnation, as the reformers did, Barth made Jesus the ultimate focal point of his understanding of double predestination. Christ, according to Barth, represents the ELECTION of all humanity and at the same time the reprobation of all. That is to say, in Christ all are elect and will share in eternal life, but Christ is also reprobated for all. Although Barth was reluctant to admit a doctrine of *apokatastasis* (universal salvation), this seems to be the logical trajectory of his doctrine of double predestination. Inevitably his doctrine of justification seems to relativize sin and divine judgment, which in turn diminishes any historic understanding of justification.

Ecumenical Theology

One of the most important developments within Protestantism since the Second World War has been the rise of the ecumenical movement, with its willingness to revisit past theological divisions with a view to overcoming them if at all possible. The new openness between Roman Catholic and Protestant churches may be partly explained by the progressive attitudes adopted by the Second Vatican Council (1962–1965) and the early work of the Swiss Catholic theologian Hans Küng. In his major study, *Justification: The Doctrine of Karl Barth and a Catholic Reflection,* he compared the view of the Protestant theologian Karl Barth with the Council of Trent and argued that there was a fundamental theological agreement. There were many dissenting voices, both Catholic and Protestant, centering on Küng's Thomistic interpretation of the theology of Trent and a selective understanding of Barth's ideas. Perhaps the most trenchant criticism to emerge was Küng's failure to take into consideration the historical context of the Council of Trent. Despite such criticisms Küng's book encouraged ecumenical discussions between Catholics and Protestants. It is no exaggeration to say that Küng inaugurated a new era of positive ecumenical discussions of a doctrine that had been viewed as an insuperable obstacle between Catholics and Protestants. In the later third of the twentieth century a significant number of dialogues

took place, of which we will look at just three of the most important: the dialogue between Roman Catholics and their Protestant counterparts, Lutherans, Anglicans, and evangelicals.

In 1972 the Joint Study Commission of the LUTHERAN WORLD FEDERATION and the Vatican Secretariat for Promoting Christian Unity published the document now generally known as the "Malta Report," which laid the foundation for ecumenical discussions. These discussions bore fruit in 1983 with the publication of a document entitled *Justification by Faith.* This document undertook an analysis of the historical development of the doctrine as well as an assessment of the nature and significance of the controverted issues between Roman Catholics and Lutherans. Six areas of "convergence" were recognized in this document: the forensic nature of justification, sinfulness of the justified, sufficiency of faith, concepts of merit and satisfaction, and criteria of authenticity. The framers of this document noted that, despite differing theological perspectives, similar concerns and foundational beliefs could be deciphered. The participants distinguished between misunderstandings and genuine disagreements. The document tried to resolve misunderstandings by identifying the common beliefs regarding original sin, the recognition that final salvation rests entirely in God's free gift of grace, that the ground of justification can only be God's grace, and that those who are justified will necessarily be renewed by the Holy Spirit and enabled to perform good works.

The document also recognized genuine areas of disagreement. Most important, both groups accepted the fact that there is a fundamental difference between a doctrine of justification based on the external righteousness of Christ and the intrinsic righteousness of the individual. The participants, however, explained these genuine disagreements as *complementary* rather than *contradictory*. That is to say, that although they fully recognized the difference between forensic justification and justification based on inherent righteousness, they nevertheless argued that these are essentially different ways of conceptualizing the same theological insight. On the crucial question of the formal cause of justification, the participants asserted that both answers are legitimate but different ways of conceptualizing the ultimate foundation of one's justification. One of the fundamental issues not considered by the participants is how the doctrine of justification was regarded as unacceptable by Trent in the sixteenth century but is now regarded as legitimate.

Further discussions between the Lutheran World Federation and the Pontifical Council for Promoting Christian Unity achieved a "consensus on basic truths of the doctrine of justification." The crucial paragraph of the Joint Declaration on the Doctrine of Justification reads: "Together we confess: By grace alone, in faith in Christ's saving work and not because of any merit on our part, we are accepted by God and receive the Holy Spirit, who renews our hearts while equipping and calling us to good works." Despite extensive protest from Lutheran theologians that the document papered over continuing major differences, it was signed by representatives of the Lutheran World Federation and the Roman Catholic Church at Augsburg on October 31, 1999. Thus the doctrine of justification in itself is no longer a dividing point of theology between Lutherans and Catholics. It will be up to the Lutheran churches in the various countries to accept the statement.

The matter of justification was also discussed between the Church of England and the Roman Catholic theologians, the results of which were published under the title *Salvation and the Church* (1987). This ecumenical discussion stressed the points of agreement between the two communions: the first movements that lead to justification are God's working; that justification is an unmerited gift of God; that justification necessarily leads to good works; and that justification involves the communal life of the church rather than a solitary individual life of faith. Participants conceded the forensic nature of justification, but argued that this image must be complemented by other images. Some critics have argued that this joint commission "marginalized" the underlying disagreements, especially concerning the formal cause of justification, for the sake of ecumenicity.

What is perhaps one of the more surprising developments at the end of the twentieth century is the dialogue between Catholics and evangelicals. In 1997 a distinguished group of high-ranking Roman Catholics and prominent evangelical Protestants issued a statement called *The Gift of Salvation* that focused on the doctrine of justification. Neither the document itself nor any of the participants officially represented their respective communions; rather the document was intended as a "good faith effort" of individual evangelicals and Catholics to speak to the issue of justification. Signatories intended this as a collaborative effort of individuals who speak from, but not for, their ecclesial constituencies. Remarkably the two groups reached agreement on "what the Reformation traditions have meant by justification by faith alone (*sola fide*)." Many other interrelated issues such as the Eucharist (see LORD'S SUPPER), BAPTISM, and Marian devotion were not addressed in this document. Discussions continue into the third millennium. Although many theological disagreements remain between Catholics and Protestants, the centuries have softened the rancor over justification, so that now, Lutherans, Anglicans, and some evangelicals are willing to dialog about the historical doctrine that was for the Protestant reformers the standard by which the church stands or falls.

See also: Catholic Reactions to Protestantism; Catholicism, Protestant Reactions; Dialogue, Inter-Confessional; Ecumenism

References and Further Reading

Anderson, H. George, T. Austin Murphy, and Joseph A. Burgess, eds. *Justification by Faith: Lutherans and Catholics in Dialogue VII*. Minneapolis, MN: Augsburg, 1985.

Balthasar, Hans Urs von. *The Theology of Karl Barth*. New York: Holt, Rinehart and Winston, 1971.

Barth, Karl. *Protestant Thought from Rousseau to Ritschl*. New York: Harper & Brothers, 1959.

Boisset, J. "Justification et sanctification chez Calvin." In *Calvinus Theologus: Die Referate des congrés Européen de recherches Calviniennes*. Edited by W. H. Neuser, 131–148. Neukirchen, Germany: Neukirchen Verlag, 1976.

Greschat, Martin. *Melanchthon neben Luther: Studien zur Gestalt der Rechtfertigungslehre zwischen 1528 und 1537*. Witten, Germany: Luther-Verlag, 1965.

Hefner, Joseph. *Die Entstehungsgeschichte des Trienter Konzils: Ein Beitrag zur Geschichte des Reformationszeitalters*. Paderborn, Germany: Ferdinand Schöningh, 1909.

James, Frank A. "*Dei Iustificatione*: The Evolution of Peter Martyr Vermigli's Doctrine of Justification." Ph.D. dissertation, Westminster Theological Seminary, 2000.

Jedin, Hubert. *A History of the Council of Trent*. 2 vols. Translated by Ernest Graf. St. Louis, MO: Herder Book Company, 1957. 1966.

Knox, D. B. *The Doctrine of Faith in the Reign of Henry VIII*. London: James Clarke, 1961.

Küng, Hans. *Rechtfertigung: Die Lehre Karl Barths und eine katholische Besinnung*. Einsiedeln: Johannes Verlag, 1957.

McGrath, Alister E. *Luther's Theology of the Cross: Martin Luther's Theological Breakthrough*. Reprint. Oxford: Blackwell, 1990.

———. *Iustitia Dei: A History of the Christian Doctrine of Justification*. Cambridge: Cambridge University Press, 1993.

Newman, John Henry. *Lectures on the Doctrine of Justification*. 3rd ed. London: Livingtons, 1874.

Ritschl, Albrecht. *The Christian Doctrine of Justification and Reconciliation*. Edinburgh: T & T Clark, 1871.

Rupp, E. Gordon. *The Righteousness of God: Luther Studies*. London: Hodder & Stoughton, 1953.

Stephens, W. P. *The Theology of Huldrych Zwingli*. Oxford, UK: Clarendon Press, 1986.

Vignaux, Paul. *Justification et prédestination au XIVe siècle: Duns Scot, Pierre d'Auriole, Guillaume d'Occam, Grégoire de Rimini*. Paris, 1934.

Yarnold, Edward, "*Duplex Iustitia*: The Sixteenth Century and the Twentieth." In *Christian Authority*, edited by Gillian R. Evans, 204–223. Oxford: Oxford University Press, 1988.

FRANK A. JAMES III

K

KAGAWA, TOYOHIKO (1888–1960)

Japanese social reformer and evangelist. In the 1930s Toyohiko Kagawa was the most widely recognized Japanese Protestant in the Western world. Hailed by the U.S. press as "Japan's Gandhi," "Japan's Schweitzer," or "the St. Francis of Japan" because of his reputation for PACIFISM and selfless service to JAPAN's poor, translations of his theological and economic writings were brought out by major publishers. He addressed over a million people in the United States and Europe on speaking tours in which he stressed his belief that the gospel demanded social and economic reform. *Brotherhood Economics* is the most concise expression of his vision of a world economy based on cooperative rather than capitalist enterprises. Especially admired by liberal Protestants, Kagawa delivered the Rochester Theological Seminary's Rauschenbusch Lectures in 1936. A biography published in 1932 by the Protestant missionary William Axling was crucial in establishing the reputation that led Kagawa to such venues.

Kagawa was born in 1888 in Kobe, Japan. As a teenager he was introduced to Christianity by Southern Presbyterian missionaries, Drs. Charles Logan and Harry W. Myers. "It is not the Bible alone which has taught me what Christianity means, but the love of these two homes," he later said. This concern with concretely following the gospel was dramatically expressed when, at age twenty-one, he took up residence in the slums of Kobe, preaching in the streets and turning his new quarters into a homeless shelter. Beginning with this intimate work with the poor, he went on to found schools, hospitals, orphanages, and cooperatives. His first major book, *A Study of the Psychology of the Poor* (Hinmin shinri no kenkyu) (1915), drew on his slum experience. He later used the royalties from a best-selling autobiographical novel, *Crossing the Death Line* (Shisen o koete) (1920) and other writings to fund his social programs. Extending his social concerns into the political realm, he also became a union leader and founding member of Japan's socialist party.

On the eve of World War II Kagawa collaborated with the U.S. missionary E. Stanley Jones and other Protestant leaders in efforts to avert war that included international prayer vigils and lobbying government officials. After World War II his efforts centered on cooperatives and world peace. He died in 1960.

See also Liberal Protestants and Liberalism; Rauschenbusch, Walter; Schweitzer, Albert; Social Gospel

References and Further Reading

Axling, William. *Kagawa.* New York: Harper and Brothers, 1932.
Bamba, Nobuya, and John F. Howes. *Pacifism in Japan: The Christian and Socialist Tradition.* Vancouver: University of British Columbia Press, 1978.
Bikle, George B. Jr. *The New Jerusalem: Aspects of Utopianism in the Thought of Kagawa Toyohiko.* Tucson: University of Arizona Press, 1976.
Schildgen, Robert. *Toyohiko Kagawa: Apostle of Love and Social Justice.* Berkeley, CA: Centenary Books, 1988.

ROBERT SCHILDGEN

KANT, IMMANUEL (1724–1804)

German philosopher. One of the major figures in Western philosophy, Immanuel Kant was born into the modest home of a Prussian harness-maker in the Pietist stronghold of Königsberg (now Kaliningrad, RUSSIA). Notoriously, he lived his entire life in and around his hometown. Kant's close relationship with his devout mother served as his introduction to the Pietist emphasis on morality over doctrine and on the sincerity of inner personal conviction over appeals to external religious AUTHORITY, (see PIETISM). He never abandoned the basic features of this religious outlook. After his education at the university in Königsberg and a period as a private tutor, Kant assumed teaching duties at the university and remained there his entire career. A lifelong bachelor, Kant became a central figure in the ENLIGHTENMENT and was well known for the lively conversation and convivial atmosphere associated with mid-day meals he hosted in his home. His popularity and liveliness as a lecturer contrasted sharply with a writing style that Kant himself once characterized as "dry, obscure, opposed to all ordinary notions, and, moreover, long-winded."

For good reason Kant is sometimes referred to as the "philosopher of Protestantism." In a series of three great *Critique*s and associated writings on ETHICS and religion Kant attempted to secure the philosophical foundations of Newtonian SCIENCE while also emphasizing the centrality of human freedom in our understanding of the moral and religious life. His resulting legacy resides in several broad themes that have shaped modern Protestant thought in profound and lasting ways: an embargo against the claims of speculative metaphysics and natural THEOLOGY; an emphasis on the priority of the "inner" meaning of Christian FAITH, which, for Kant himself, meant its "moral" meaning; and a commitment to reconciling the potentially competing demands of biblical faith and the modern scientific outlook. Kant is thus the prototype of the "mediating" or "accommodationist" religious thinker who insists on an underlying fit or compatibility between religious faith and modern secular consciousness. The progressive, intellectually alert believer need not fear that faith will come into conflict with modern standards of intelligibility. Consequently, Kant is perhaps more accurately thought of as the "philosopher of *liberal* Protestantism" because his legacy is clearly evident in the traditionally liberal effort to disclose moments of continuity, compatibility, or overlap between Christian faith and natural states of human consciousness.

For two decades beginning in 1755 Kant wrote on a range of topics characteristic of the era's interest in science, natural theology, and logic, although it was only with the publication of the *Critique of Pure Reason* in 1781 (2d edition, 1787) that the so-called critical standpoint for which Kant is famous fully emerged. Against the background of interminable philosophical debates concerning the basic claims of metaphysics and natural theology, Kant insisted on an examination (or "critique") of reason's own powers as a necessary task before the demonstration of metaphysical claims, including claims about the existence of God. This reorientation of philosophical perspective—which Kant compared to Copernicus's proposal

to shift our perspective on the heavens by 180 degrees—resulted in a much more active conception of the knowing mind. From Kant's new critical standpoint the knowing subject of experience shapes the object known, rather than the other way around. The radical nature of this point of departure is clearly evident in Kant's claim that even space, time, substance, and causality are properties of the knowing mind's rulelike activity, rather than features of the external world. The general lesson here—that what we know is fundamentally shaped by who we are—has deeply influenced subsequent Western thought, even as the details of Kantian philosophy have been called into serious question.

Kant's critical standpoint had austere epistemological implications, given that valid knowledge claims were now limited to experience, or to the conditions of the possibility of experience. Kant eagerly displayed the subversive implications of this position by stigmatizing traditional speculative metaphysics as "dogmatic" rather than "critical," by which he meant that metaphysics manufactured illusory knowledge claims out of the play of mere concepts. Such a result naturally suggests that metaphysics—including that part of it demonstrating the existence of God, freedom, and immortality—is no longer a useful partner for theology. In a famous section of the *Critique,* Kant himself dismantled the traditional proofs for the existence of God, thereby vividly spelling out the negative consequences for natural theology of the critical standpoint.

From the start, however, Kant indicated his intention to deny the pretensions of theoretical knowledge "in order to make room for faith." With the publication of his *Groundwork of the Metaphysics of Morals* in 1785 followed by the *Critique of Practical Reason* in 1788, Kant made it clear that by "faith" he meant *moral* faith, grounded in practical, as opposed to theoretical, reason—that is, reason in its capacity to "prescribe" the world that "ought to be" rather than reason in its capacity simply to "describe" the world that "is." Moral faith is what is necessarily entailed by one's taking seriously an incorrigible sense of moral obligation that is a sheer "fact of reason" for any rational being. Just as Kant had taken for granted the validity of Newtonian physics, he took as given this fundamental sense of moral obligation, or duty. In turn, this sense of duty entails an awareness of freedom, given that (in a rational universe) one must be free to act if obligated to do so. Kant's powerful vision of the *a priori* character of the sense of duty and the associated consciousness of freedom form the foundation of his religious philosophy.

In what is perhaps the key feature of his religious thought Kant demonstrated the necessity of moving from this incorrigible awareness of freedom to the "postulation" of the immortality of the soul and, ultimately, of God's existence. At one point defining a "postulate" as a "necessary hypothesis," Kant insisted that, as a postulate of practical reason, the existence of God enjoys a far greater degree of rational certainty than the older, traditional proofs could ever provide because the postulation process finds its point of departure in an incorrigible awareness of oneself as a free and morally obligated being. The transition from this awareness to the postulates is effected in the *Critique of Practical Reason*'s so-called moral argument, which is subsequently reaffirmed in the *Critique of Judgment* (1790). The argument is sustained by a teleological conception of reason itself, revealing "needs" and "interests" of reason requiring satisfaction. Chief among these interests is Kant's concept of the "highest good," which results when reason reflects on the total product of virtue. Kant defined the highest good as the proportioning of virtue and happiness—indeed, virtue itself is defined as "worthiness to be happy." For Kant, immortality and God follow ineluctably from reflection on the highest good, insofar as reason has an irrepressible "interest" in the perfection of virtue (which clearly does not occur in this life) and in the rewarding of virtue with happiness (which requires a moral judge). In short, immortality and God *must* be postulated, for otherwise the incorrigible experience of moral obligation simply spins free in a metaphysical abyss—with no purchase on reality—suggesting the utter futility of moral earnestness. Precisely by making God's reality as real and "close" to one as one's sense of oneself as a being under moral obligation, Kant thus believed he had secured moral theism from the philosophical quarrels of the day.

Running through this argumentation as a powerful, subterranean current is Kant's deep commitment to the notion that the universe is a reasonable place and that moral striving, however imperfect in this life, is ultimately redeemed. Kant thus deployed a set of arguments designed to rescue moral theism from the cold wasteland of merely theoretical reason. Kant's first *Critique* may have secured Newtonian physics from philosophical doubts raised by DAVID HUME, but it provided no metaphysical comforts. Only with the shift to reason in its practical aspect—the shift, as Kant put it in a famous remark, from the "starry heavens above" to the "moral law within"—does human life regain its stature and intrinsic integrity. This implicitly dualistic perspective was reinforced by a further dualism enabling Kant to accommodate the competing tendencies of a deterministic Newtonian science and his emphasis on freedom. Here, Kant drew on a distinction between the world as it appears to us and the world as it is in itself—the world as "phenomenon" and as "noumenon"—which was a natural outcome of his initial emphasis on the active role played by the knowing mind in the fashioning of our experience of the world. The twin dichotomies of theoretical/practical and phenomenal/noumenal thereby underwrite the characteristically Kantian turn "inward," to the private world of moral experience, as the true locus of the religious life. Faith is consequently freed from any dependency on the outer, public world of historical events in general and of putatively miraculous events in particular. Fatefully, Kant thus fashioned a safe and invulnerable space for faith on the very eve of a century that would witness the full force of historical criticism of scripture as well as the increasing momentum of the natural sciences.

After the completion of his three *Critiques* in 1790, Kant demonstrated that his constructive, creative thinking about the religious life had hardly drawn to a close. In the provocatively titled *Religion within the Limits of Reason Alone* (1793) Kant surprised his followers by proposing an account of "radical evil" that seemed to betray the very spirit of the Enlightenment by locating the source of moral evil in the will rather than in ignorance. Underwritten by an overtly Pauline appeal to a natural—but not necessitated—"bent" or propensity toward evil, Kant's theory of radical evil evidently called into question humanity's ability to save itself from its self-made problem. In short he appeared to be undercutting his own emphasis on freedom by proposing a theory suspiciously reminiscent of the one doctrine against which most of the proponents of "Enlightenment" had firmly positioned themselves: the doctrine of original SIN. In his own effort at a resolution of the problem, Kant offered striking yet ultimately elusive remarks concerning our possible need for "grace" and "supernatural cooperation" in the recovery from radical evil. He emphasized that, at most, we can have only the rational "hope" that such divine aid will be forthcoming—only religious "fanatics" and "enthusiasts" claim to have sure knowledge of God's intentions and acts. However, in his related emphasis on doing our moral best to deserve or merit this potential divine assistance, Kant clearly courted an account of JUSTIFICATION far more Catholic than Protestant in nature.

Also in the *Religion* Kant devised an account of the moral value of the historical side of religion. The historical side—embodied in revelation, scripture, priesthood, and CHURCH—serves as the "vehicle" for pure moral faith. Such visible, tangible features satisfy a natural human demand for something "sensibly tenable" in the religious life, implying—among other things—an emergent Kantian theory of religious symbolism. Throughout, Kant emphasized that the historical aspect is a matter of complete indifference and, indeed, the source of needless stale quarrels if not viewed through the lens of moral concerns. His eagerness to avoid improper emphasis on the historical aspect is immediately evident in his rhetorical question: "I raise the question whether morality should be expounded according to the BIBLE or whether the Bible should not rather be expounded according to morality." With this principle Kant helped to define modern biblical hermeneutics in terms of the principle that what is "written" is different from what is "meant," and that the former should be judged in light of the latter. The text becomes meaningful only in the light of wider canons of intelligibility that are brought *to* the text.

Not surprisingly Kant's moral emphasis would yield a CHRISTOLOGY based on the insight that Jesus is the personification of a moral disposition totally well-pleasing to God. As matters of sheer theoretical interest, the historical details of Jesus's life are of no religious significance. The significance of Jesus resides instead in a moral essence that is, in fact, immediate to all rational beings in the form of an "archetype," that is, the "archetype of the moral disposition in all its purity." In effect Jesus is the embodiment of what all persons might ideally be. Even so, Kant attempted to steer away from the suggestion that we should "imitate" Jesus, given that sheer imitation potentially compromises the full exercise of freedom. Instead we should allow the example of Jesus to animate the moral archetype that dwells in our own reason and assume full responsibility for our moral destiny. Despite a provocative remark suggesting that Jesus breaks the "power" of radical evil to "hold" us against our will, Kant did not associate a traditional doctrine of ATONEMENT with Jesus because such a doctrine would too obviously undercut Kant's prior emphasis on personal autonomy and, therefore, responsibility. Here, Kant's tendencies were clearly Pelagian.

During the nineteenth century, Kant's influence was readily evident in the several varieties of liberal Protestant theology that attempted to satisfy the intellectual and cognitive challenges of the day while also emphasizing the moral core of the Christian message, typically focused in christology. For such influential figures as ALBRECHT RITSCHL in GERMANY or H. T. Mansel in Britain, the Kantian suspicion of metaphysics, combined with a heightened sense of "value" in human experience, provided fresh ways of understanding faith and revelation while simultaneously offering a welcome detour around the cognitive problems posed to Christian faith by an increasingly secular CULTURE. The explicitly moral element in Kant's thinking would be maintained by the liberal Protestant effort to improve the world, based on a progressively immanent understanding of the KINGDOM OF GOD.

Kant's own sketch of an "ethical commonwealth" in the *Religion,* with its suggestion of moral progress based on a deepened sense of community, found strong echoes in the liberal emphasis on the "fatherhood of God and the brotherhood of man" characteristic of ADOLF VON HARNACK and numerous others. One could even argue that the typically Kantian combination of moral earnestness and the priority of "practice" continues even today in numerous varieties of LIBERATION THEOLOGY.

Finally for all Protestant thinkers eager to avoid associating faith with a sacrifice of the intellect, Kantian epistemology offered welcome strategies of compartmentalization. Neither revelation nor faith was based on theoretical claims, on metaphysics, or on appeals to "external" evidence. Instead revelation and faith were themselves viewed as a kind of valuing lodged in a privileged zone of interiority and, thereby, self-validating and not open to external criticism. Consequently the critical fires of historical criticism or Darwinian science could burn freely, without any threat to faith. Indeed the Kantian strategy of compartmentalization, warding off the negative implications of historical criticism, remained implicit even among those who explicitly repudiated the "moral" emphasis of Kant's liberal tradition, such as the generation of neo-orthodox theologians of the post–World War I era. Despite its sustained polemic against Protestant liberalism, NEO-ORTHODOXY relied heavily on Kantian epistemology in such matters as the distinction between the "Jesus of history" and the "Christ of faith," thereby carrying forward the strongly Kantian element in the earlier work of M. Kähler and W. Hermann. It is indeed an open question whether influential conceptions of faith as a kind of "self-understanding" (RUDOLF BULTMANN) or "the state of being ultimately concerned" (PAUL TILLICH) are simply existentialist variations on Kantian moral awareness. Likewise, recent developments associated with "postliberal" theology have raised serious questions about the very idea of "mediation" between faith and natural forms of human consciousness, bringing Kant's legacy back into the theological discussion in fresh ways.

See also Higher Criticism; Jesus, Lives of; Liberal Protestantism and Liberalism

References and Further Reading

Primary Sources:

Kant, Immanuel. *Critique of Judgment.* Translated by James Creed Meredith. Oxford, UK: Clarendon Press, 1952.

———. *Critique of Practical Reason.* Translated by Mary Gregor. Cambridge: Cambridge University Press, 1997.

———. *Critique of Pure Reason.* Translated by Norman Kemp Smith. New York: St. Martin's Press, 1965.

————. *Groundwork of the Metaphysics of Morals.* Translated by Mary Gregor. Cambridge: Cambridge University Press, 1996.

————. *Religion within the Limits of Reason Alone.* Translated by Theodore M. Greene and Hoyt H. Hudson. New York: Harper Torchbooks, 1960.

Secondary Sources:

Barth, Karl. *Protestant Thought from Rousseau to Ritschl.* Translated by Brian Cozens. New York: Simon & Schuster, 1969.

Despland, Michel. *Kant on History and Religion.* Montreal, Canada, and London: McGill-Queen's University Press, 1973.

Fackenheim, Emil L. "Immanuel Kant." In *Nineteenth Century Religious Thought in the West,* edited by Ninian Smart, John Clayton, Patrick Sherry, and Steven T. Katz. vol. I. Cambridge: Cambridge University Press, 1985.

Michalson, Gordon E. Jr. *Kant and the Problem of God.* Oxford, UK: Blackwell Publishers, 1999.

Reardon, Bernard. *Kant as Philosophical Theologian.* London: Macmillan Press, 1988.

Rossi, Philip J., and Michael Wreen, eds. *Kant's Philosophy of Religion Reconsidered.* Bloomington and Indianapolis: Indiana University Press, 1991.

Wood, Allen W. *Kant's Moral Religion.* Ithaca, NY and London: Cornell University Press, 1970.

Yovel, Yirmiahu. *Kant and the Problem of History.* Princeton, NJ: Princeton University Press, 1980.

GORDON E. MICHALSON JR.

KARLSTADT, ANDREAS RUDOLF BODENSTEIN VON (ALSO CARLSTADT) (1486–1541)

German theologian. Karlstadt was one of the important and prolific early German reformers—he had over 85 publications with some 200 reprints—who is difficult to situate wholly into a theological tradition. Trained in scholasticism, but with strong mystical and humanistic interests, Karlstadt sided with MARTIN LUTHER early on, although his later views were more in line with those of HULDRYCH ZWINGLI and HEINRICH BULLINGER. Even though he articulated many of the anticipated traditional theological emphases of the Anabaptist tradition (see ANABAPTISM), he himself cannot be counted an Anabaptist. (Among other reasons, he lacked a strong statement on believers' BAPTISM and never fully developed the notion of a believers' CHURCH.) Probably he is best regarded as a forerunner of PIETISM because his preoccupation with the "inner experience" of the divine in the believer's "yieldedness" (*Gelassenheit*) to Christ was further developed by that tradition, particularly Gottfried Arnold and the HALLE Pietists.

Born in Karlstadt am Main, Andreas Bodenstein attended the University of Erfurt (1499–1503), the University of Cologne (1503–1505), and the new university at Wittenberg where he received his master's degree in 1505 and his doctorate in THEOLOGY in 1510. (Perhaps because Luther received his own doctorate under Karlstadt in 1512, scholars until recently thought he was older than Luther, placing his birth in 1480 or 1481, or even 1477.) While teaching in the arts faculty at Wittenberg before the conferral of his doctorate, Karlstadt advocated a Thomism tempered by Scotism. From 1510 Karlstadt taught at Wittenberg, traveling to ITALY in 1515–1516 where he received a doctorate in civil and canon law, a degree that seemingly guaranteed quick ecclesiastical advancement. However, like Luther, Karlstadt returned to Wittenberg disappointed by the secularization of the city. Soon afterward he adopted Luther's Augustinianism, claiming with Luther that the human will is wholly incapable of willing the good and is therefore completely passive with respect to divine GRACE.

Karlstadt and Luther stood together at the 1519 Leipzig debate against Johann Eck of Ingolstadt, the prominent defender of the Roman church. Karlstadt argued the proper relationship between faith and works, while Luther called into question the absolute authority of the pope and councils of the church. Returning to Wittenberg, Karlstadt devoted himself to the study of the BIBLE and to his writing, producing a number of important tracts, including *De canonicis scripturis* in which he practiced early biblical criticism, arguing for the full canonicity of the Old and New Testaments (including, to Luther's displeasure, the Book of James). Assuming the leadership of the "Wittenberg Movement" during Luther's stay on the Wartburg in 1521–1522, Karlstadt quickly pressed for ecclesiastical reforms: celebration of the Mass in the vernacular, abandonment of VESTMENTS, communion of the LAITY in both kinds (bread and wine), abolition of private masses, elimination of monastic vows, the MARRIAGE of priests (he himself married Anna von Mochau in January of 1522), and the radical purging of worship images. (Karlstadt argued that reliance on such images could harm "weak consciences.") Luther's disagreement with these reforms prompted his return from the Wartburg to Wittenberg, where his *Invocavit Sermons* delineated a slower approach to actual reform.

From Luther's perspective, Karlstadt had erred in his insistence that change of external practices must precede an inner change on the part of the faithful and that WORSHIP should be purely "spiritual," without such external embellishments as clerical vestments. Elector Frederick the Wise supported Luther's stance and curtailed Karlstadt's preaching activities at Wittenberg. Karlstadt resigned his academic post in 1523 and went to minister to the congregation of Orlamünde. There he renounced his academic titles as unbiblical, abandoned the use of the organ and images in worship, rejected infant baptism, argued against the real presence of Christ in the LORD'S SUPPER, and established a nonhierarchical model of Christian community emphasizing the laity. In 1524 he was expelled from Saxony and with his family wandered from place to place, spending time in Rothenburg, Holstein, and Zurich, among other places. He may well have been involved in the revolutionary turbulence of 1524–1525. His widening chasm with Luther, and his uncompromising rejection of infant baptism and Christ's real presence in the Lord's Supper caused Karlstadt considerable difficulties over the next years. Finally, after serving as an archdeacon at Zurich for four years, Karlstadt became a professor of Hebrew at Basel in 1534, gradually modifying some of his earlier radical positions, for example, his opposition to infant baptism and the value of university education. He died from the plague in Basel on Christmas Eve in 1541.

Crucial in Karlstadt's theology is the influence of German mysticism. Karlstadt advocated that the believer must "let go" (Gelassen) of attachments to temporal things, and must "be yielded to" (Gelassen) the promise of God. The believer's Gelassenheit itself becomes the temple of God, for in detaching from the flesh of the world, the believer is filled with the spirit of Christ Himself. In his 1535 inaugural disputation at Basel, Karlstadt identified the mystic's divine spark of the soul with the imago dei. Whereas JUSTIFICATION effects a regeneration of this image, SANCTIFICATION outwardly displays that image through the transformation of the believer in his/her "yieldedness" (Gelassenheit). Karlstadt worked within the medieval understanding of the flesh/spirit distinction, claiming that GRACE empowers a fulfillment of the law. Although Karlstadt was polemicized by Luther and subsequent Lutheran theologians (and although Karlstadt was sometimes too aggressive and less than careful in his own polemics), it is difficult not to be moved by the intensity with which he described the Christian life of faith, mortification, repentance, love, and freedom.

References and Further Reading

Primary Sources:

Karlstadt, Andreas Rudolf Bodenstein von. The Essential Carlstadt: Fifteen Tracts. Edited and translated by Edward J. Furcha. Waterloo, Ontario, Canada: Herald Press, 1995.
———. Karlstadts Schriften aus den Jahren 1523–25. 2 vols. Edited by Erich Hertzsch. Halle, Germany: Niemeyer 1956–1957.

Secondary Sources:

Barge, Hermann. Andreas Bodenstein von Karlstadt. Leipzig, Germany: Friedrich Brandstetter 1905.
Bubenheimer, Ulrich. Gelassenheit und Ablösung: Eine psychohistorische Studie über Andreas Bodenstein von Karlstadt und seinen Konflikt mit Martin Luther. Karlstadt, Germany: Volkshochschule Karlstadt 1981.
Hasse, Hans-Peter. Karlstadt und Tauler: Untersuchungen zur Kreuzestheologie. Gütersloh, Germany: Mohn, 1993.
Pater, Calvin. Karlstadt as the Father of the Baptist Movements: The Emergence of Lay Protestantism. Toronto, Canada: University of Toronto Press, 1984.
Sider, Ronald. Andreas Bodenstein von Karlstadt. The Development of His Thought 1517–1525. Leiden, The Netherlands: E.J. Brill, 1974.
Zorzin, Alejandro. Karlstadt als Flugschriftenautor. Göttingen, Germany: Vandenhoeck & Ruprecht, 1990.

DENNIS BIELFELDT

KEBLE, JOHN (1792–1866)

English theologian. On July 14, 1833, John Keble gave a sermon on "national apostasy" that is generally credited with galvanizing the Tractarian, or OXFORD MOVEMENT in the CHURCH OF ENGLAND. Already a member of a group of like-minded Oxford University fellows, Keble joined their combination of protest against the Church of England's alignment with the state to their conviction that the church's apostolic ministry and WORSHIP must be recovered.

Keble was born April 25, 1792, in Gloucestershire, the son of a Church of England cleric. He was elected a fellow of Oriel College, Oxford in 1811 after receiving honors in undergraduate studies. After ordination in the church he served in various parishes, in the process becoming noted for writing hymns and poetry. He returned to Oxford in 1831 as professor of poetry and soon became associated with JOHN HENRY NEWMAN, Froude, EDWARD PUSEY, and the other Tractarians. Summarized in his pivotal sermon, and in the eight tracts that he authored, his theological view centered on the necessity that the Church of England emphasize its distinctive marks of identity that were threatened by Erastianism, the superiority of the state over the church. For Keble the CHURCH must be led by its bishops and priests, and its pastoral ministry must emphasize the necessity of CONFESSION and absolution, as well as the sacraments of BAPTISM and the Eucharist (see LORD'S SUPPER). To be a true Christian, he emphasized, one must be in communion with the church, and the church must be consistent with its apostolic heritage. Keble did not follow Newman and some of the other leading Tractarians into the Catholic Church. Instead he married Charlotte Clarke in 1835 and in 1836 became a highly regarded parish priest at Hursley, where he served for thirty years while continuing as a spiritual advisor and writer. He edited the words of the sixteenth century theologian RICHARD HOOKER. Over two dozen collections of his sermons were also published. Keble died at Bournemouth on March 29, 1866.

See also Bishop and Episcopacy; Clergy; Hymns and Hymnals

References and Further Reading

Battiscombe, Georgina. *John Keble: A Study in Limitations.* New York: Knopf, 1963.
Chadwick, Owen. *The Spirit of the Oxford Movement.* Cambridge: Cambridge University Press, 1990.
Griffin, John R. *John Keble, Saint of Anglicanism.* Macon, GA: Mercer University Press, 1987.
Henery, Charles R., ed. *A Speaking Life: The Legacy of John Keble.* Harrisburg, PA: Morehouse, 1995.

WILLIAM SACHS

KECKERMANN, BARTHOLOMEW (c.1572–1609)

German philosopher and Calvinist theologian. Keckermann was born in Gdansk to a merchant family, and he attended school there between 1587 and 1590. As a recipient of a grant from the city council of his home town he went to GERMANY. He studied at Wittenberg, Leipzig, and Heidelberg, where he received his master's degree in 1595. In Heidelberg he taught philosophy, rhetoric, and Hebrew. In 1600 he was appointed to the chair of Hebrew at the university. Because of pressures from the Gdansk City Council, he turned down the offer of the chair in philosophy, and in 1602 he returned to Gdansk, where he took the position as co-rector of the Gymnasium (the high school) a position which he resigned after a short period of time. He obtained the chair of philosophy, which he occupied until his early death on July 25, 1609.

Broadly educated, particularly hard working, with international renown as an outstanding teacher, Keckermann had encyclopedic ambitions. His works included the whole range of contemporary knowledge. At the same time he sought to ground knowledge on a solid basis, which he found in Aristotelian logic. This explains why the methodological problems played such a key role in his works (for example, in his *Systema Logicae* of 1600 and his *Praecognita logicae* of 1603).

Keckermann's philosophy represents an attempt to link two traditions: the humanist tradition (PHILIPP MELANCHTHON, Jakob Sturm, Peter Ramus) and the neo-Averroistic tradition found in Padova, in particular the philosopher Giacomo Zabarelli who highly influenced Keckermann. Hence his work has an eclectic character but also a dogmatic flavor, stemming from Keckerman's teaching experience. As teacher he exposed his deep knowledge to his students—fairly but as *ex cathedra* monologue. On the other hand, didactic values accounted for the popularity of Keckermann's works in many European Protestant schools in the first half of the seventeenth century.

References and Further Reading

Facca, Danilo. "Walczaca logika B. Keckermanna" ("Militant" Logic of B. Keckermann). *Archiwum Historii Filozofii i Mysli Spolecznej* 45 (2000): 5–23.
Freedman, Joseph S. "The Career and Writings of Bartholomaeus Keckermann (d. 1609)." *Proceedings of the American Philosophical Society* 143 (1997): 305–364.
Van Zuylen, W. H. *Bartholomaeus Keckermann. Sein Leben und Werk.* Leipzig, Germany: Robert Noske, 1934.
Vasoli, Cesare. "Logica ed 'encyclopedia' nella cultura tedesca del tardo Cinqueecento e del primo Seicento: Bartholomaeus Keckermann." In *Atti del Convegno internazionale di Storia della Logica.* 97–116. Bologna, Italy: 1983.

LECH SZCZUCKI

KENYA

See Africa

KEPLER, JOHANNES (1571–1630)

Astronomer. Kepler was born in the Swabian imperial city of Weil der Stadt. His family moved to the Lutheran duchy of Württemberg, where his scholastic talents won him a ducal scholarship to prepare him for the ministry. In 1589 he began to study at the University of Tübingen. At that time PHILIPP MELANCHTHON's (1497–1560) belief that mathematics and astronomy aided one's knowledge of the divine led to an emphasis on these subjects. Kepler studied them at Tübingen with Michael Maestlin, who taught him to accept the Copernican over the Ptolemaic system.

In 1594 Kepler was sent to Graz to fill a vacancy in mathematics. There he wrote his first book, *The Secret of the Universe.* Its main thesis suggested a relationship between the distances between the six planets in the Copernican system and the five regular solids, but it also set forth many of the issues that were to occupy him throughout his career. The book brought him to the attention of Tycho Brahe, and Kepler joined him in Prague in 1600. This gave Kepler access to the best observational data available, and he used them to come up with his laws of planetary motion, the first two of which—the elliptical orbits of the planets and the relationship between their velocity and distance from the sun—were published in his *New Astronomy* in 1609. While in Prague he also did important work on elucidating the process of vision.

The overthrow of Kepler's patron, Emperor Rudolf II, in 1611 led him to seek a new position. He was refused a post at Tübingen, possibly because he rejected the Lutheran interpretation of the Eucharist in favor of the Reformed, and ended up in Linz, where he was denied communion because of his beliefs. There he formulated his third law, showing the relationship between the mean distance from the sun and the period times of any two planets, which he published in

Harmony of the World. He also published important work on mathematics. His superior planetary tables led to the study of his work in the years after his death in 1630.

References and Further Reading

Primary Sources:

Kepler, Johannes. *Gesammelte Werke.* Edited by Max Caspar, et al. Munich: C. H. Beck, 1937–.

———. *The Secret of the Universe.* Translated by A. M. Duncan. New York: Abaris, 1981.

———. *New Astronomy.* Translated by William H. Donahue. Cambridge and New York: Cambridge University Press, 1993.

———. *The Harmony of the World.* Translated by E. J. Aiton, et al. Philadelphia, PA: American Philosophical Society, 1997.

Secondary Source:

Caspar, Max. *Kepler.* Translated and edited by C. Doris Hellman. Rev. ed. by Owen Gingerich. New York: Dover Books, 1993.

SHEILA J. RABIN

KERK, GEREFORMEERDE

See Dutch Reformed Church

KESWICK MOVEMENT

Animated by a trans-Atlantic Protestant fascination for a "higher" Christian life, the Keswick Movement takes its name from the site of its annual convention in ENGLAND's picturesque Lake District.

The movement traces its beginnings to the determination of two American couples to promulgate abroad a particular conception of the Christian life. William and Mary Boardman, Presbyterians who spent years yearning for spiritual empowerment, believed they found it in what they termed the "higher" Christian life. William's book, *The Higher Christian Life* (1858; republished in London in 1860), outlined his conviction that most Protestants failed to realize the potential of the Christian experience he found described in scripture. In a simple response of FAITH to Christ's words, Boardman believed he had been empowered to live in more intense, conscious, moment-by-moment dependency on Christ. The "higher" Christian life could be reduced to the simple appropriation of Christ as All. Boardman's efforts helped extend so-called full salvation teaching within some Reformed settings. He carried his message to Britain's Mildmay Convention in 1869. Between 1873 and 1875 he worked occasionally in England with Robert and Hannah Smith.

Finding Allies

The Smiths had come to similar conclusions by a different route. Well-to-do members of the Society of Friends from the southern tip of New Jersey, they embraced the systematic BIBLE study method associated with the PLYMOUTH BRETHREN and came into contact with proponents of the HOLINESS MOVEMENT. Both influences set them apart from their Quaker cohorts (see FRIENDS, SOCIETY OF) and inclined them toward a particular spirituality. Gifted speakers and writers, they began in the 1860s giving their testimonies about practical holiness wherever they could gain an audience. Robert Smith took as his theme the phrase "Jesus saves me now," emphasizing the conscious, ever-present, sin-cleansing work of Christ in the soul. As long as one kept "under the blood," one was free from SIN. HANNAH WHITALL SMITH summarized her views as *The Christian's Secret of a Happy Life* (1875), a book that quickly became a Protestant classic. Her secret was essentially the same as Boardman's message: Christian happiness came in letting go, in relying on the perfect moment-by-moment cleansing blood applied to the soul. "The rest of faith" followed abandonment of one's self to God. Stop trying, the Smiths urged, and start trusting Christ for all.

The Boardmans and the Smiths belonged to loose networks of people who pursued practical holiness and who saw in that pursuit the key to churchwide revival. They challenged Christians to experience in the present the spiritual truths they claimed to know and on which they staked their eternal hopes. Discernible progress in the Christian life was available for the asking. One would never be sinless, but one could know freedom from the inward struggle with sin by following clear advice:

> Let in the Overcomer, and He will conquer thee;
> Thy broken spirit taken in sweet captivity
> Shall glory in His triumph and share his victory.

Mission to England

In 1873, the Boardmans and the Smiths arrived in England eager to penetrate the CHURCH OF ENGLAND with their message. They discovered a convergence of indigenous influences that had prepared the way—reinvigorated WESLEYAN HOLINESS MOVEMENT teaching; Quaker piety; Plymouth Brethren emphases on faith and scripture; Anglican EVANGELICALISM, especially as expressed in the spiritual aspirations of the annual Mildmay Conventions. Evangelists DWIGHT MOODY and IRA SANKEY were also in England 1873–1875, benefiting from the same impulses in their proclamation of their revival message. The people they attracted stood in the tradition of ROMANTICISM, with its emphases on love and purity. In his pathbreaking *Evangelicalism in Modern Britain,* historian David

Bebbington notes that this movement found a place in "the most far-reaching cultural shift of the century."

The Smiths found receptive audiences wherever they went. They presided over a large Oxford Convention for the Promotion of Holiness in 1874. Smith then toured the Continent, finding remarkable resonance with his message in Berlin. He returned to a convention at Brighton that drew over 8,000 participants and more than 200 pastors from the Continent. Hannah Smith offered Bible readings that filled the largest venues. She was billed as a "chief speaker." For ten days, one journalist reported, the crowds "waited upon God" for the purpose of discerning "His will as to the possibilities of Christian holiness" for "quickening of spiritual life in the Churches."

Later in 1875 Canon Harford-Battersby welcomed to his parish church in Keswick a much smaller group of people intent on holiness. This became the first Keswick Convention, and it initiated an annual tradition. It also unleashed a storm of opposition from Calvinists (see CALVINISM) troubled by the perceived popularity of instantaneous SANCTIFICATION. Over the next few years, Keswick proponents took heed and clarified their differences with those who urged a crisis experience of holiness. They concluded, rather, that freedom from sin—"the rest of faith"—became reality as the consecrated believer yielded moment by moment to the Holy Spirit who counteracted sin. The Smiths' theme—by now set to music and sung by their followers in several European languages—"Jesus saves me now" meant just that.

Varied Audience

The first generation of Keswick leaders were Anglicans (see ANGLICANISM), although the audience and the convention preachers always represented a broader constituency. Frequent visitors from the Continent and the United States augmented the numbers and gave an international flavor. The Convention released *The Keswick Week,* a record of the activities and addresses of the annual conventions. By the 1890s speakers identified with the movement (known as Keswick missioners) brought Keswick's version of practical holiness to other parts of the world in winter speaking tours. The Convention grew to include missionary appeals and to feature firsthand reports of Christian expansion abroad. Keswick recruited "Holy Ghost" missionaries—men and women convinced of the reality of full salvation here and now. (The first Keswick missionary was the Irishwoman Aimee Carmichael, who went to INDIA in 1893.) Annual conventions in other parts of the world soon worked to bring Keswick's particular emphasis into the movement.

A hymnal, *Hymns of Consecration and Faith,* soon collected songs that nurtured the Convention's particular forms of piety (see HYMNS AND HYMNALS). Frances Ridley Havergal proved particularly adept at giving hymnic form to Keswick yearnings. Compilers found other women's hymns especially appropriate, too—the prolific American FANNY CROSBY, Charlotte Elliott, and Jean Sophia Pigott. They wrote of consecration, submission, and surrender, and contributed to a refashioning of devotional practice. Collections of Keswick addresses and books by popular Keswick speakers such as the South African Andrew Murray, Baptist F. B. Meyer, G. Campbell Morgan, J. Hudson Taylor, and Handley Moule extended the audience.

During the first decade of the twentieth century, both the Welsh Revival and PENTECOSTALISM challenged the Keswick Convention to consider boundaries for its teaching. The emotion that characterized the Welsh Revival of 1904 and 1905 threatened to disrupt the decorum that had become a hallmark of Keswick. For a few years from 1907, devotees of the emerging Pentecostal movement brought their understanding of the baptism with the Holy Spirit to Keswick. Convention regulars embraced the same language with different expectations. Pentecostalism introduced tongues speaking as uniform evidence of Spirit baptism; Keswick proponents found evidence of the Spirit's empowering presence in holiness of heart and life. The convention moved into the 1910s having successfully excluded ecstatic behavior and utterance.

Once established, the Keswick Convention featured well-known interdenominational and international speakers, a popular program of Bible readings, and well-attended missionary rallies. Its roots in the broad trans-Atlantic late nineteenth-century pursuit of holiness meant that the preaching of Frenchman Theodor Monod, Andrew Murray, F. B. Meyer, or Anglican Evan Hopkins was equally well received. The Keswick Convention became the hub of an international interdenominational network bound by an earnest conviction about the centrality of practical holiness in the Christian life. Featuring Christ-centered piety centered in "death to self" by the "counteraction" of the Holy Spirit's reign within the soul (rather than by eradication of sin or struggle with sin), the core Keswick message is perhaps captured best in the lines of favorite Keswick hymns:

The victory has been purchased on Calvary's cross for me;
Sin shall not have dominion: the Son hath made me free!
The temple has been yielded and purified of sin;
Let thy Shekinah glory now flash forth from within
Let all the earth keep silence, the body henceforth be
Thy silent docile servant moved only as by Thee.

Jesus, I am resting, resting in the joy of what Thou art;
I am finding out the greatness of Thy loving heart.
Hidden in the hollow of His blessed hand,
Never foe can follow; never traitor stand.
Not a surge of worry; not a shade of care;
Not a blast of hurry; touch the Spirit there.

Many of the early American supporters of Keswick were protofundamentalists (see FUNDAMENTALISM), and throughout the twentieth century, American conservative Protestants have been featured on Keswick programs. Smaller American Keswicks, meanwhile, feature similar teaching venues. From the formative years when Hannah Smith offered Bible readings that rivaled her husband's PREACHING in popularity, WOMEN have occasionally found public voice at Keswick, although typically featured speakers have been men. The best-known woman speaker early in the twentieth century was Jessie Penn-Lewis, a prolific author, editor, and interpreter of the Welsh Revival.

Keswick teaching appeals across Protestant denominations because its focus is more on the quality of Christian life than on theological precision. It has influenced Protestantism in broad but often unrecognized ways, especially through the books of its proponents (staples on evangelicals' bookshelves) and through its hymns (favorites in many collections). Wheaton College Archives and Special Collections, Wheaton, Illinois owns a substantial research collection of Keswick materials.

See also Higher Life Movement; Methodism Movement

References and Further Reading

Barabas, Steven. *So Great Salvation.* London: Marshall, Morgan & Scott, 1952.
Pollock, John. *The Keswick Story.* London: Hodder & Stoughton, 1964.
Stevenson, Herbert F. *Keswick's Authentic Voice.* Grand Rapids, MI: Zondervan, 1959.
———. *Keswick's Triumphant Voice.* Grand Rapids, MI: Zondervan, 1963.

EDITH BLUMHOFER

KIERKEGAARD, SØREN AABYE (1813–1855)

Danish theologian. Kierkegaard, whose surname in old Danish means "churchyard," with all the familiar connotations of a graveyard, was born in Copenhagen in 1813. He was the youngest of seven children born to Michael Pederson Kierkegaard and his second wife Anne Sørensdatter Lund. Michael Kierkegaard (1756–1838) was born into an impecunious family in rural Jutland. As a young man, an uncle brought him into the dry goods business in Copenhagen. In a short while he owned his own store. He invested in real estate and stocks and soon was so well off that his children would never have to worry about making a living. On one level, Kierkegaard led a very privileged life, but on another it was psychological hardscrabble. His father was a difficult taskmaster who, Kierkegaard said, prepared him well for the life of faith but ruined his chances for worldly happiness.

The Early Years

Before Søren Kierkegaard was twenty-one, his mother, four of his siblings, and a number of in-laws had died. Kierkegaard's father confided that the endless treks to the graveyard were divine punishment for the fact that as a very poor shepherd boy on the heaths of Denmark he had cursed God. Kierkegaard's father told his remaining two sons that as punishment for his boyhood transgression he would live to bury all of his children. In both his melancholy and his peculiar understanding of faith, Kierkegaard's father made a deep impression upon his famous son's life and works.

In 1830 Kierkegaard entered the University of Copenhagen. At the behest of his father he matriculated in theology, but studied widely in the liberal arts. Many scholars regard Kierkegaard as having been in rebellion against his father during his early years at the university; however, in 1837 he reconciled with the patriarch, who died the following year. At the time of his father's death, Kierkegaard had been studying at the university for eight years, but despite his father's goading he had still failed to take his exams. Explaining that he could no longer argue with a dead man, he began to apply himself. In 1840 Kierkegaard finished and defended his dissertation, "On the Concept of Irony: With Constant Reference to Socrates."

At the epicenter of Kierkegaard's life was his forlorn relationship with Regine Olsen. In 1837 Kierkegaard fell in love with Regine. Three years later they became engaged. Almost immediately after the engagement, Kierkegaard began to have second thoughts. A little more than one year later he broke it off. Confiding in his diaries, Kierkegaard offered a number of reasons for this break, which was so brutal as to nearly sap Regine's will to live. For one, he wanted to protect her from the terrible melancholy that afflicted the entire Kierkegaard family. For another, he did not feel that he could answer his calling to be a religious writer and a husband at the same time. Either way, she remained the wife of his soul and like his father, Regine is never far below the surface of Kierkegaard's thought.

Two weeks after ending his engagement Kierkegaard left for Berlin, where, along with Karl Marx (1818–1883), he attended the lectures of the German philosopher Friedrich Schelling. There, in the crucible of the break with Regine, Kierkegaard came into his genius and his muse. In but a few months, in which he was also taking classes, Kierkegaard wrote the lyrical but sprawling *Either/Or* which, stylistically speaking, is one of the most peculiar philosophical tracts ever written. He also wrote his *Two Upbuilding Discourses.* Kierkegaard soon became disenchanted with Schelling, returned to Denmark, and began a period of astounding literary productivity. Over the next three years he penned *Fear and Trembling, The Concept of Anxiety,* the sharply chiseled *Philosophical Fragments,* the immense and somewhat uneven *Stages on Life's Way,* and a shelf of edifying discourses. In 1844 Kierkegaard resolved that after one more book he would lay down his pen and take a pastorate in a rural church. His finale was to be the keystone of his philsophical writings, the *Concluding Unscientific Postscript.* However, soon after the publication of this book Kierkegaard was drawn into a fray with the popular left-leaning Danish weekly the *Corsair.* Nearly everyone read the *Corsair* and many feared turning up in one of its political cartoons. Kierkegaard appeared in many of them and became something of a negative media star in Denmark. The battle with the *Corsair,* which ended in the editors resigning and in Kierkegaard having to resign himself to living a more private life, made it clear to Kierkegaard that he should continue with his authorship.

Published Works

In 1849 Kierkegaard published what may well be the most profound study of Christian psychology ever written, *The Sickness unto Death.* Between 1851 and 1855 came the black hole in Kierkegaard's life. While writing a torrent of journal entries he published nothing, but in 1855 he launched a frontal assault on the Danish State Church. At the funeral of the Danish prelate and Kierkegaard family pastor, Bishop J. P. Mynster, the priest and theologian H. L. Martensen delivered a eulogy in which he described Mynster as "a witness to the Truth." Throughout his authorship, Kierkegaard had argued that the likes of Mynster and Martensen had let the criterion for being a Christian slip so low that people no longer had a useful barometer of what it meant to have faith. Bishop Mynster enjoyed great power and led an opulent lifestyle. For Kierkegaard being a witness to the truth would entail existentially mirroring the truth by imitating the person of Jesus Christ. As far as Kierkegaard was concerned, Mynster did not take a single step along this road and so Kierkegaard found the very idea of one of the leaders of the church calling Mynster "a witness to the Truth" woefully misleading. With Martensen's hyperbolic encomium, Kierkegaard came to the end of his rope. Starting his own journal, *The Instant,* Kierkegaard attacked Martensen and the church establishment of which he was such an integral part. Kierkegaard was so angry that he stopped attending services, commenting that he would no longer participate in a process that "made a fool of God." Throughout the period of the attack, Kierkegaard was fast becoming gravely ill. On September 25, 1855, Kierkegaard delivered his final fusillade in *The Instant.* A week later he fell unconscious on the street. On November 11, at the age of forty-two, he died of causes still uncertain. There was a minor riot at Kierkegaard's internment at Assistance Cemetary in Copenhagen. During the last few months of his life, Kierkegaard not only refused the sacraments, he refused to see members of the clergy as well, including his celebrated brother, Pastor Peter Christian Kierkegaard. After Dean Tryde, a member of the clergy, performed the committal, Kierkegaard's nephew Henrik Lund vigorously protested that having a clergyman at the head of the grave was contrary to all of Kierkegaard's wishes. Lund's lengthy graveyard comments received some applause and there were a few tense moments before the large crowd dispersed.

Kierkegaard wrote the bulk of his most celebrated works and certainly his most philosophical books under pseudonyms. There is much debate among Kierkegaard scholars about his reasons for taking this tack. While the use of pseudonyms was common in Denmark at this time, Kierkegaard offered a variety of explanations for his use of pen names. For one, he claimed that he wanted to present his readers with various life possibilities or perspectives quite different from his own. Once again, Kierkegaard held that he did not live in the same categories as expressed in some of his works, for example, *The Sickness unto Death,* and therefore could not pretend as though the positions taken in such books were his own. For still another reason, Kierkegaard wanted to deflect his reader's interest away from his personality. Whatever the explanation, he took his noms de plume seriously, and in his journals and his non-pseudonymously written *From the Point of View of My Work as an Author,* he insisted that the opinions expressed in the pseudonymous works not be treated as though they were his own.

Conflict with Other Philosophers

Kierkegaard struggled both mightily and brilliantly against the ENLIGHTENMENT notion that faith was subservient to reason. His main antagonists were philosopher GEORG WILHELM FRIEDRICH HEGEL (1770–1831) and the Danish Hegelians who, on Kierkegaard's reading, would have us believe that faith was, in effect, a simplified version of philosophy to be consumed by the simple folk who could not understand the likes of German philosopher Immanuel Kant (1724–1804) and Hegel. While he was not an irrationalist, Kierkegaard argued, for the most part obliquely, that faith is beyond reason in the sense that reason cannot decide the question of faith. More than that, Johannes Climacus (pseudonymous author of *Philosophical Fragments* and *The Concluding Unscientific Postscript*) describes the object of faith as an absolute absurdity. The claim that, relative to his creation, God is an absurdity, has been the source of much debate among interpreters of Kierkegaard. Whereas some maintain that for Kierkegaard the object of faith is a logical contradiction (for instance, the eternal come into time, the immortal to die), others such as Stephen Evans contend that Kierkegaard, who upholds the law of noncontradiction against Hegel, did not believe that faith requires the willingness and ability to believe in self-contradictory propostions or nonsense.

According to Kierkegaard's most philosophical persona, Johannes Climacus, reason must either step aside before the object of faith or take offense. Taking up on Jesus's oft stated, "Do not take offense in me," Kierkegaard believed that the possibilities of faith and offense were inextricably tied to one another, so that when the thorn of the possibility of offense was removed, so was the possibility of faith. On Kierkegaard's reading, the rationalized and so volatilized idea of God peddled by Enlightenment theology removed just this possibility.

In his masterwork *Fear and Trembling,* Kierkegaard tries to restore both the difficulty and the primitivity of faith. He centered this book on the Genesis story of Abraham and Isaac, and in so doing strove to remind his reader that reason and revelation or faith may well conflict. Once more, now as in Kierkegaard's time, many believe that being faithful amounts to nothing more or less than being moral; that is, they believe that faith is somehow reducible to ethics. However, in *Fear and Trembling* Kierkegaard astutely notes that speaking solely from an ethical point of view, Abraham, the father of faith, was guilty of murder. Thus, we have Kierkegaard's strange apology in which he insists, albeit indirectly, that revelation is beyond reason and that the content of faith cannot be reduced to moral duties or a recipe of rules for the good life.

While he does not follow Schleiermacher in reducing faith to a feeling, Kierkegaard places great emphasis on the importance of passion. A critic of the epoch, Kierkegaard chides his age for its excess of reflection and lack of passion and decisiveness. Kierkegaard was nicknamed "Enten/Eller" (Either/Or) and with good reason, as he tried to press people into deciding for or against God, rather than imagining that they could be born into the fold and at the same time act in no markedly different way from atheists. Kierkegaard stressed the significance of the will to the point where some Kierkegaard scholars have charged him with being a volitionalist, that is, someone who holds the untenable psychological thesis that we can will to believe whatever we wish to believe. Other Kierkegaard scholars have countered that far from being a volitionalist, Kierkegaard believed that faith is the result of sheer grace. Still other Kierkegaard scholars, such as Jamie Ferreira and Steven Emmanuel, have developed a compromise position, holding that for Kierkegaard faith involves both the will and grace.

Then what, according to Kierkegaard, is faith? *The Concluding Unscientific Postscript* teaches that faith is a clinging with the highest passion to an objective uncertainty. In Kierkegaard's more direct communiqués, that objective uncertainty is marked as the person of Jesus of Nazareth. As already stated, Kierkegaard was a virulent critic of the Danish State Church and of the notion that one could, as it were, be born into the faith. In his *Fear and Trembling,* Kierkegaard admonished that a fire sale was in progress with regard to faith. That is the criterion, for what it means to believe had been so diminished that many people wrongly believed themselves to be Christians. Kierkegaard looked to Socrates as a kind of secular saint and, like the gadfly of Athens, Kierkegaard wrote as though he were the gadfly of Christendom. While Socrates relieved many of his interlocutors of the idea that they had knowledge, Kierkegaard strove to extricate his readers from a false sense of their own faith. In myriad different ways, Kierkegaard taught that there is no believing in Christ without seeking to imitate his suffering, humiliation, hope, and love.

In his seminal *Works of Love,* Kierkegaard argues that there is only one form of love, love of God. Unless they are grounded in love of God, all other forms of preferential love (friendship and erotic love), are best understood as manifestations of improper self-love. In this book, Kierkegaard unpacks the New Testament, and comes to the conclusion that hard as it may be for the worldly individual to understand, and contrary as it may seem to the Kantian perspective to which Kierkegaard was otherwise sympathetic, love is best understood as an obligation that commands action. And yet, the author of this same book teaches that there is fundamentally only one action that we can perform to help our neighbors and that is to help them love God.

Kierkegaard is often called the father of existentialism. He had enormous impact on the philosophers Jean-Paul Sartre (1905–1980), Miguel Unamuno y Jugo (1864–1936), Martin Heidegger (1889–1976), and Karl Jaspers (1883–1969). Kierkegaard was also much revered by genial analytic philosopher, Ludwig Wittgenstein (1889–1951). Indeed, Wittgenstein's writings on ethics and religion owe much to the Danish philosopher. Kierkegaard also helped shape the thinking of the grand masters of twentieth-century theology, KARL BARTH (1886–1968), RUDOLF BULTMANN (1884–1976), PAUL JOHANNES TILLICH (1886–1965), and REINHOLD NIEBUHR (1892–1971). Finally, due to his views on authorship, concretely manifest in his pseudonymous writings, postmodern thinkers have found an ally in Kierkegaard.

References and Further Reading

Primary Sources:

Kierkegaard, Søren. *Kierkegaard's Writings.* Edited and translated by Howard V. Hong and Edna Hong, Henrik Rosenmeier, Reidar Thomte, Juila Watkin et al. Princeton, NJ: Princeton University Press, 1978.

Secondary Sources:

Emmanuel, Steven. *Kierkegaard and the Concept of Revelation.* Albany: State University of New York Press, 1996.

Evans, C. Stephen. *Passionate Reason: Making Sense of Kierkegaard's* Philosophical Fragments. Bloomington and Indianapolis: Indiana University Press, 1980.

Ferreira, M. Jamie. *Transforming Vision: Imagination and Will in Kierkegaardian Faith.* Oxford: Clarendon Press, 1991.

Ferguson, Harvie. *Melancholy and the Critique of Modernity: Søren Kierkegaard's Religious Psychology.* London and New York: Routledge, 1995.

Green, Ronald. *Kierkegaard and Kant: The Hidden Debt.* Albany: State University of New York Press, 1992.

Gouwens, David. *Kierkegaard as a Religious Thinker.* Cambridge: Cambridge University Press, 1996.

Hannay, Alastair. *Kierkegaard: The Arguments of the Philosophers.* Edited by Ted Honderich. London and New York: Routledge and Kegan Paul, 1982. Rev. ed.: New York: Routledge, 1991.

Hannay, A., and Marino, G. *The Cambridge Companion to Kierkegaard.* Cambridge: Cambridge University Press, 1998.

Kirmmse, Bruce, *Kierkegaard in Golden Age Denmark.* Bloomington and Indianapolis: Indiana University Press, 1990.

Pelikan, Jaroslav. *From Luther to Kierkegaard.* St. Louis, MO: Concordia Publishing House, 1950.

GORDON MARINO

KILHAM, HANNAH (1774–1832)

English educator. Hannah Spurr was born in Sheffield, England, on August 12, 1774, to a family well established in trade although not affluent (her father being a master cutler), which provided her a good education. She became known as an educator, philanthropist, and pioneer of African linguistics. Brought up an Anglican, she joined the Methodists in 1794, and in 1798 married Alexander Kilham, leader of the Methodist New Connexion, the first major division in METHODISM after JOHN WESLEY's death. Kilham died the same year, leaving his wife with an unborn child (who died in infancy) and a stepdaughter (who was to be her biographer).

Disillusioned with Methodism, especially the gap between the professed sentiments of the hymns and the lives of those who sang them, Hannah joined the SOCIETY OF FRIENDS in 1803. She was active in charitable schemes for the poor in ENGLAND and IRELAND, and notably in BIBLE SOCIETIES, the antislavery cause, and EDUCATION among the poor. These interests combined to turn her interests toward AFRICA.

In 1820 she began the study of the Wolof and Mandinka languages, guided by two redeemed slaves from the Gambia area of West Africa. She produced Scripture passages and reading materials in the languages. In 1823, although nearing fifty, she organized and led a party, which included the language informants, on an agricultural and educational mission to Gambia. She also visited SIERRA LEONE, where she found that, although crowds of Africans drawn from many parts of the continent and rescued from slave ships were in school, they were all being taught in English, not in their vernaculars. She revisited Sierra Leone in 1827–1828, and for a longer time from 1830, when she set up a school in the liberated African village of Charlotte and developed her ideas of language study and vernacular teaching. Her assistant for Yoruba study was almost certainly SAMUEL CROWTHER. She was in the process of visiting LIBERIA when she died at sea on March 31, 1832.

Hannah Kilham's activities in Africa were carried out amid her many concerns elsewhere, particularly famine relief in Ireland. Indeed, it is possible that she had too many concerns for any one of them to be brought to completion. She was an advocate and pioneer of MISSIONS, albeit of a clearly defined character, in a denomination that had at the time somewhat distanced itself from the missionary movement—and in a period when female initiatives of the kind were virtually unknown. She was a pioneer in the study of African languages, at a time when this was a field outside the competence of the learned world. She envisaged an institute in London where the main languages of Africa could be studied, with two native speakers of each language operating in a purpose-built (and specially heated) building. In her work for African vernacular education, she was far ahead of her time.

See also Bible Translation; Slavery, Abolition of

References and Further Reading

Biller, Sarah. *Memoir of Hannah Kilham.* London: Darton and Harvey, 1837.
Dickson, Mora. *The Powerful Bond.* London: Dobson, 1980.
Greenwood, J. Ormerod. "Hannah Kilham's Plan." *Sierra Leone Bulletin of Religion* 4 (1962): 9–22, 61–71.
Hair, P. E. H. "Hannah Kilham and African Languages." *Journal of the Friends' Historical Society* 49 (1960): 165–168.

ANDREW F. WALLS

KIMBANGU, SIMON (1889–1951)

African religious leader. Founder of the Church of Jesus Christ on Earth Through the Prophet Simon Kimbangu, Kimbangu was born in 1889 in the village of Nkamba in the lower Congo region of AFRICA. His early life and religious activities are shrouded in much myth and legend. As a young boy, Kimbangu came under the influence of the English Baptist Missionary Society missionaries, was baptized in 1915 along with his wife, Marie-Mivilu, and received his schooling at the Baptist mission school in nearby Wathen (although he was rejected for religious leadership).

When an epidemic broke out in Nkamba in 1918, Kimbangu reputedly received a calling to heal the sick through a voice from Christ, who told him that he, rather than Western missionaries, was chosen to convert his fellow Africans. Frightened, Kimbangu fled to Kinshasa (then Leopoldville) to work at an oil refinery for three years before returning to Nkamba in 1921. Again, Kimbangu received the call to heal, but this time he began a ministry that lasted from March until September and attracted many followers to Nkamba, which became known as the "New Jerusalem." Alarmed that this mass movement might translate into political protest against Belgian colonial rule, the authorities ordered Kimbangu's arrest on June 6, 1921, but he eluded arrest until voluntarily surrendering on September 12. Kimbangu was given the death sentence, which was commuted to life imprisonment by King Albert, and he lived out his life in the prison at Lubumbashi until his death on October 12, 1951.

Under the leadership of his son, Kuntima Diangienda, the Kimbanguist movement, with its emphasis on absolute dependence on God, divine healing and charismatic phenomena, and the rejection of polygamy, traditional magic, and fetishes, evolved into an indigenous church, the Church of Jesus Christ on Earth Through the Prophet Simon Kimbangu. This church was accepted into the WORLD COUNCIL OF CHURCHES in 1969 and today counts upward of 5 million members.

See also African Instituted Churches; Baptist Missions; Faith Healing

References and Further Reading

Martin, Marie-Louise. *Kimbangu: An African Prophet and His Church.* Grand Rapids, MI: Eerdmans, 1976.
MacGaffey, Wyatt. *Modern Kongo Prophets: Religion in a Plural Society.* Bloomington: Indiana University Press, 1983.

TIMOTHY E. FULOP

KING, MARTIN LUTHER, JR. (1929–1968)

American churchman and civil rights leader. Martin Luther King Jr. was born on January 15, 1929, in Atlanta, Georgia, into a middle class black Baptist family with CLERGY on both his father's and mother's side. After skipping two grades in public school King entered Morehouse College in Atlanta at age fifteen. His call to the ministry led him to Crozer Theological Seminary in Chester, Pennsylvania (now Colgate Rochester Crozer Divinity School in Rochester, New York), from which in 1951 he graduated at the head of his class. His graduate education continued at Boston University where he received his Ph.D. in systematic theology in 1955 with a dissertation on the notion of God in the work of PAUL TILLICH and Henry Nelson Weiman.

After receiving several offers from academic institutions, King decided to return to his native South and became pastor of Dexter Avenue Baptist Church in Montgomery, Alabama. Then in 1960 he became co-pastor with his father at Ebenezer Baptist Church in Atlanta. He held this position as well as indispensable leadership in the CIVIL RIGHTS MOVEMENT until his assassination in Memphis, Tennessee, on April 4, 1968. He was buried in Atlanta near Ebenezer Baptist Church, survived by his wife, Coretta Scott King, and four children.

King authored five books and scores of articles and delivered thousands of speeches and sermons in the UNITED STATES and abroad. In 1964 he became the youngest person to receive the Nobel Prize for peace. He is primarily known as a civil rights activist who, through nonviolent means, sought to correct social injustice.

Philosophy of Nonviolence

King's understanding of nonviolence was based on the Christian teaching of love found in the Sermon on the

Mount and on Mahatma Gandhi's method of Ahimsa (noninjury). The spirit and content of nonviolence were from Jesus; the path and method were from Gandhi. This philosophy can be summed up in the following way: nonviolence was always the unvarying principle; noncooperation and civil disobedience were the two main strategies; various tactics would be used from picketing, boycotting, demonstrating, parading without a permit, conducting sit-ins, and refusing to obey certain local discriminatory laws.

An account of King's pilgrimage to nonviolence is found in chapter 6 of his first book, *Stride Toward Freedom*. There, King outlines the bases of nonviolence. (1) Nonviolence is not a method for the weak or for cowards. It is not passive nonresistance to evil, but active nonviolent resistance to evil, often in the face of great odds. (2) Nonviolence does not seek to defeat or humiliate opponents, but to win them over by way of friendship and understanding. This is done to create the Beloved Community. (3) Nonviolence as a method of attack is directed against forces of evil and systemic injustice, rather than against persons doing evil. (4) Nonviolence is predicated on the willingness to accept suffering without retaliation. "Unearned suffering is redemptive." (5) Nonviolence avoids external physical violence but also internal spiritual violence. (6) Nonviolent protest is based on the belief that the universe is on the side of justice. "The moral arc of the universe is long, but it bends toward justice." King's leadership for civil rights in campaigns from Montgomery to Memphis saw the practice of these principles evolve with integrity and effectiveness.

Montgomery, Alabama: Segregated Public Transportation (December 1955–December 1956)

The catalyst for this campaign was Rosa Parks's refusal to stand for a white man who wanted her seat in a bus on December 1, 1955. Soon a bus boycott, under the inspiration of King, was organized with the help of E. D. Nixon, a local black labor leader, and the Woman's Political Council. For a year, black workers carpooled, walked to work, and otherwise avoided the buses. Their success was achieved near the end of 1956. The Montgomery Improvement Association was formed to coordinate the various tactics of the boycott, a form of noncooperation. Soon after the Montgomery campaign, in 1957, King, along with other young black clergy, formed the Southern Christian Leadership Conference to provide a new vision for the South and, in their words, to "save the soul of America." That organization exists today.

Birmingham, Alabama: Public Transportation (1963) Selma, Alabama: Voting Rights (1965)

King faced these issues in Birmingham: (1) the desegregation of lunch counters, rest rooms, fitting rooms, and drinking fountains; (2) hiring and promoting of black workers on a nondiscriminatory basis; (3) the dropping of all charges against jailed demonstrators and (4) the creation of a biracial committee for implementing a timetable to realize these goals. In Birmingham he ratcheted up the strategy of nonviolence from noncooperation to nonviolent direct action by way of several forms of civil disobedience. They ranged from picketing to marching to large-scale voluntary jailing, especially on the part of young people. Here demonstrators also met the most resistance from Eugene "Bull" Conner, the Commissioner of Public Safety, who ordered the use of electric cattle prods, police dogs, billy clubs, and fire hoses against them. In addition, there were bombings and burnings of homes and motels. The televised images of these events tapped the conscience of the United States and sufficient pressure was brought to bear on both houses of Congress by black and white citizens alike that within a year the Civil Rights Act of 1964 was passed. It was also during this campaign that King served an eight-day jail sentence and during his imprisonment on April 16, 1963, wrote his famous *Letter from Birmingham Jail*, one of the significant Christian documents of the twentieth century.

The Selma campaign was waged to ensure voting rights for black citizens, the majority population of Dallas County. In employing the same nonviolent direct action used in Birmingham, local black people and many northern whites met again with physical danger from local white citizens, led by Sheriff Jim Clark and the KU KLUX KLAN (KKK). This was particularly evidenced by events surrounding "Bloody Sunday," March 7, 1965, one of the defining moments in the Civil Rights Movement. About 600 marchers, led by John Lewis, planned the fifty-mile walk from Selma to Montgomery. They had to cross the Edmund Pettus Bridge as they left Selma and were met there with police on horses who beat and trampled the marchers. Several days later King led a successful march to Montgomery. The success of the Selma campaign led to the passage of the Voting Rights Act of 1965.

The March on Washington, D.C. (1963)

Soon after the Birmingham campaign, the March on Washington was organized, culminating at the Lincoln Memorial for August 28, 1963. It was the occasion for King's famous "I Have a Dream" speech in which he clarified his vision of the Beloved Community. The ideals expressed in the speech of human dignity, the worth of human personality, racial integration, and a society ruled by the law of love were based on the Western religious ideals of the Messianic Era and the KINGDOM OF GOD as well as on the political ideals of the nation's founding documents, primarily the Declaration of Independence, which describe the American ideal of a "holy commonwealth."

King's Opposition to the Vietnam War

His public stand against the U.S. policy in Vietnam in the spring of 1967 found King arguing the interconnection of what he called the three basic evils in America—racism, poverty, and WAR. He saw a disproportionate number of black soldiers and national resources being expended in what he perceived to be an unjust war. This was one of King's most controversial statements and he was criticized by black and white leaders alike for "mixing peace and civil rights." King's response was "justice is indivisible" and "I have worked too long and hard now against segregated public accommodations to end up segregating my moral concern."

The Poor Peoples' Campaign, Washington, D.C. (1968)

In his Christmas Eve sermon at Ebenezer Baptist Church in 1967, King revealed sorrowfully that his "dream" had turned into a "nightmare." To illustrate this he cited certain class issues as increased black poverty, white backlash, his rejection in the Chicago suburbs, and the urban riots in northern cities. This new content, centering on economic concerns of housing, education, health, and jobs, including all of America's poor—African American, Latino, Native American, and Appalachian whites—called for new tactics. As a result King's method of nonviolence as an agent for social change moved from noncooperation in Montgomery to nonviolent direct action in Birmingham and Selma (all three campaigns having to do with civil rights) to massive civil disobedience, nonviolent sabotage, and in King's words the need "to dislocate the functioning of a city [Washington, D.C.] without destroying it." The primary concern at this time was democratic socialism or *class*. King felt in 1968 that this tactic was more necessary, effective, and radical than the sit-ins, boycotts, and demonstrations of previous civil rights' days. The success of the Poor Peoples' Campaign was seriously compromised by King's assassination in Memphis, Tennessee, on April 4, 1968, where he was advocating a higher standard of living for garbage workers.

King as a Broker of Twentieth-Century Protestant Thought

Although King was a social activist, he was also a Christian thinker who unified major strands of liberal Protestant theology to undergird, philosophically, his campaigns for social justice. The central themes of liberalism he encountered at Crozer and Boston, such as emphasis on religious experience, the humanity of Jesus, a strong ethical orientation, confidence in human reason and in the goodness of human beings, the dynamism of history, and a respect for other points of view, easily found their place in King's mind and heart because he had heard much of this, in one form or another, from the black church and from President Benjamin Mays and Professor George Kelsey at Morehouse (see LIBERAL PROTESTANTISM AND LIBERALISM). His most influential teacher at Crozer, George Washington Davis, introduced King to evangelical liberals such as William Adams Brown, to the SOCIAL GOSPEL of WALTER RAUSCHENBUSCH, and the Personalist philosophy of Edgar Sheffield Brightman, whose thought he would examine in depth at Boston. Because of his liberal belief in the capacity for human goodness, King was open to nonviolence as a method of social change practiced by Gandhi, who was also introduced to him by Davis. King was receptive as well to the lectures and writings of such pacifists as Mordecai Johnson and A. J. Muste, although the practical significance of these ideas would not be realized by King until the Montgomery bus boycott. King's liberal leaning, especially his interest in nonviolence, were challenged by his reading of the Christian realist, REINHOLD NIEBUHR, rigorously taught by Professor Kenneth Smith at Crozer. It was this liberal theology, validated by the prayers, sermons, spirituals, and devotion to God of the black church, that fueled King's desire to resist injustice.

The Beloved Community

This was a theme in liberal Protestantism from JOSIAH ROYCE (1913) to Walter Rauschenbusch (1917) to Lynn Harold Hough (1941). King began talking about the Beloved Community in his sermons in 1955–1956 and it was mentioned or implied in almost all his major addresses for the rest of his life. This ideal human society was the vision that fundamentally motivated his life and thought.

King's "brokering" of theology was most clearly seen in his understanding of this community. The social gospel provided a theological framework with which to articulate it. Nonviolence provided the means to establish it. Personalism provided the philosophical base for supporting the personal nature of the community, and Niebuhr's realism served to qualify King's optimism about its possible realization in history. King's dream for this community was one where "all barriers that divide and alienate humanity, whether racial, economic, or psychological" would be removed. This ideal was not limited to America. Toward the end of his life King's vision became global; he often spoke of "the world house," a world where "we must transcend our races, our tribe, our class, and our nation."

King showed how the Christian gospel of love could be used to transform a racist and unjust society into one well on the way to racial harmony and social justice.

See also Kingdom of God

References and Further Reading

Primary Sources:

King, Martin Luther, Jr. *Stride Toward Freedom: The Montgomery Story.* New York: Harper and Row, 1958.
———. *Strength to Love.* New York: Harper and Row, 1963.
———. *Why We Can't Wait.* New York: Harper and Row, 1963.
———. *Where Do We Go From Here: Chaos or Community?* New York: Harper and Row, 1967.
———. *The Trumpet of Conscience.* New York: Harper and Row, 1968.

Secondary Sources:

Baldwin, Lewis V. *To Make the Wounded Whole: The Cultural Legacy of Martin Luther King, Jr.* Minneapolis, MN: Fortress Press, 1992.
Erskine, Noel Leo. *King Among the Theologians.* Cleveland, OH: The Pilgrim Press, 1994.
Garrow, David J. *Bearing the Cross: Martin Luther King, Jr. and the Southern Christian Leadership Conference.* New York: William Morrow, 1986.
Smith, Kenneth, L., and Ira G. Zepp, Jr. *Search for the Beloved Community: The Thinking of Martin Luther King, Jr.* Valley Forge, PA: Judson Press, 1974.
Watley, William D. *Roots of Resistance: The Nonviolent Ethic of Martin Luther King, Jr.* Valley Forge, PA: Judson Press, 1985.

IRA G. ZEPP JR.

KINGDOM OF GOD

For much of Protestantism, the Kingdom of God is the central symbol of God's activity in the world. Often depicted in historical terms, the Kingdom represents God's influence on the social and political order. Although some Protestant theologians and leaders describe the Kingdom as present, most combine the emphasis on the present with an eschatological dimension. A few restrict the term to the future. In which case, the Kingdom of God may be identified with the millennial reign (Revelation 20:2). CHILIASM, millennialism, and millenarianism describe theological interpretations of this prediction (see MILLENARIANS and MILLENNIALISM). While these terms are often interchangeable, many contemporary scholars reserve chiliasm and millenarianism for theologies that predict a catastrophic break in history, followed by an earthly golden age. Some reserve the full and final conception of the Kingdom for a "new creation" that will transcend and transfigure current conceptions of time and space.

Biblical Background

Protestants derive their understanding of the Kingdom of God from the BIBLE. For centuries, Protestants read Scripture as a synthetic whole, and therefore their Kingdom doctrine systematized teachings from both the Old and New Testaments. Since about 1800, however, many Protestants have adopted a critically analytic approach that understands biblical concepts in their historical context and then insists on the need to restate ancient truths in modern form.

In the New Testament, the word "Kingdom" appears primarily in Mark, Matthew, and Luke. Mark and Luke use the "kingdom of God," while Matthew uses the "kingdom of heaven." The history of the Kingdom sayings is obscure. The earliest communities reinterpreted the sayings of Jesus in the light of their own situation. Later, unknown editors collected these sayings and between A.D. 65 and 110 the Gospel authors combined them with a narrative of Jesus' life. Nonetheless, a rough outline of the development of the Kingdom tradition is possible. Jesus drew heavily on the various Isaiah traditions. He believed that Isaiah's promise of a God who will comfort the poor and the maimed was fulfilled in God's ministry, but God's rule had not yet reached its full extent. The parables of the wheat and the tares, the mustard seed, and the leaven contrast the Kingdom's humble beginnings with its glorious future. The disciples are, hence, to pray that God's Kingdom will come on earth "as in heaven." At some point, this earlier tradition was reinterpreted apocalyptically. Those with "eyes to see and ears to hear" understand the signs of the times as certainly as sailors see the signs of changing weather. God's act will be soon. It is uncertain how much of the apocalyptic outlook goes back to Jesus himself.

Although the Kingdom figures prominently in the synoptic gospels, the term is almost absent from the Fourth Gospel and Paul's letters. There are only seven references to the Kingdom in the letters attributed to Paul, and five of those passages (I Corinthians 4:20; I

Corinthians 6:9; I Corinthians 15:50 and Galatians 5:21) contrast the righteousness of the Kingdom with the unrighteousness of the church. John's two references (John 3:3 and 3:5) associate the Kingdom with the mysterious movements of the Spirit.

Early Christianity

Many early Christians shared the Revelation hope for a millennium between A.D. 100 and 300. Saint Irenaeus (c.120–c.200) and Tertullian (died c.225) continued the chiliastic tradition, stressing the importance of God's earthly Kingdom. At a time when believers suffered social rejection and occasional martyrdom, the millennial hope helped them to retain their faith. In contrast, many Gnostic Christians interpreted the historical assertions of the Bible, including the millennium, as symbols of heavenly or cosmic realities.

Belief in an earthly millennium faded around the year 200. Many bishops repudiated millennial teachings when they excommunicated the Montanists, a millenarian sect that practiced ecstatic prophecy. Contemporaneously, Clement (died c.215) and Origen (c.185–c.254), two Alexandrine theologians, applied Greek philosophic and scientific methods to Christian teaching. For those who followed their lead, the Kingdom was spiritual: the believer's present obedience to God as the moral ruler. Millennial peace and justice were symbols of the concord of the heavenly realm.

The Imperial Church

The Emperor Constantine (c.288–c.337) and his successors, with the exception of Julian, made the Christian Church first the favored and then the exclusive religion of Rome. This turned matters of faith into matters of state, and tended to identify God's rule with the government. For the church historian Eusebius (c.263–c.340), Constantine's government was the climax of Christian history. In his *Life of Constantine,* Eusebius depicted the emperor as a new David, anointed by God. In effect, Christ exercised his rule on earth through the godly ruler.

In the Eastern Roman Empire, this theology promoted an exaltation of the emperor's person. In the West, the situation was more complicated because rulers often had to share power with ecclesiastical officials. Nonetheless, the royal theology thrived. Bishops crowned kings, anointed them with holy oils, and said prayers for their families at mass. In term, kings represented God's power on earth.

The identification of the earthly kingdom with God's reign has rarely monopolized Christian thinking. Augustine of Hippo (354–430) began his episcopate believing that God was Rome's protector and Christianity, the highest expression of Roman culture. The barbarian invasions of the West and, finally, of his own North Africa, however, led him to rethink this identification. In his *City of God,* Augustine argued that the city of God and the city of man coexisted together. The human city was ruled by pride, avarice, and other vices, and, hence, could never be the Kingdom, although it was necessary for human righteousness. The visible church was not the Kingdom either. Like the earthly city, the church was a mixed multitude of wheat and tares. Only in heaven would God rule directly. John's millennium, Augustine believed, was a symbol of the church and did not refer to an earthly reign of Christ.

Monastic movements represented another approach to the kingdom. Through such practices as prayer, fasting, voluntary poverty, and solitude, the monks attempted to make their communities obedient to Christ. Each monastery was, in effect, an outpost of the Kingdom of Christ.

Abbot Joachim of Fiore (1132–1202) taught that world history passed through three ages or reigns: the Kingdom of the Father, the Kingdom of the Son, and the Kingdom of the Spirit. The advent of this last kingdom, Joachim believed, was near. Later, Joachim's teachings were popular among the followers of Francis of Assisi (c.1182–1226). Francis established his order of brothers around the ideal of absolute poverty: they were to own nothing and to beg their meals. Although the order became less radical as time passed, a minority insisted on the literal fulfillment of Francis's example. These "Spirituals" believed that Francis had inaugurated Joachim's Kingdom of the Spirit and that they were the first fruits of God's millennial reign. Although the Spiritual Franciscans were suppressed, their ideas inspired many medieval millennial movements, some of whom advocated violent revolution.

The Reformation

The fifteenth-century invention of moveable type revolutionized learning by providing readers and professional scholars with uniform, easily readable texts. Printed book production made Europe a common market in ideas, with new works spreading across the continent rapidly. Simultaneously, Europeans launched a program of trade, exploration, and discovery. New routes to India were discovered, and Christopher Columbus accidentally landed in the Americas. Exploration in turn transformed everyday life as new products and foods, such as coffee (Arabia), sugar (India, later Americas), spices (Asia), chocolate (Americas), and tobacco (Americas) were introduced. To many, such changes were signs that God was about to begin the millennium. Spanish missionaries, for instance, gathered NATIVE AMERICANS into self-sustaining communities that they believed were signs of God's New Age.

MARTIN LUTHER (1483–1546) followed Augustine in his doctrine of the Kingdom. In both his Large and Small Catechisms, Luther interpreted the petition "Thy Kingdom (Reich) Come" as the Christian's response to God's will. To pray for the Kingdom is, thus, to become obedient to revelation and its demands. Like Augustine, Luther distinguished between the two kingdoms, using his understanding of law and gospel to interpret the relation of CHURCH AND STATE. Man's Reich must use legislation and the sword to affect its will. In contrast, God's Reich directly rules the hearts of believers. Both kingdoms are, of course, ultimately rooted in God, and Luther speaks of the earthly kingdom as God's left hand and the heavenly kingdom as God's right.

Without intending it, Luther inspired millenarian speculations. Although he questioned Revelation's canonicity, Luther frequently identified papal Rome with the whore who sat on seven hills. Further, editions of Luther's Bible translation often featured woodcuts depicting the pope as Antichrist, being thrown from heaven. Such pictures spoke louder than words. When ordinary people read Luther's Bible, their eyes moved from the image of the pope's damnation to the text's prophecy of a coming millennial reign; the conclusion that the fall of Rome was a step toward the Kingdom was natural, almost inevitable.

By 1524, interest in establishing the millennial Kingdom had become common. The German peasants, who had long suffered injustice, carefully read the Bible and derived from it, as well as from an assessment of traditional law, a list of demands for social change. THOMAS MÜNTZER (1489–1525) and other preachers gave their demands an explicitly millennial interpretation that identified the peasants' cause with the Kingdom. Partially in reaction, Luther supported the opponents of the peasants, claiming that the princes were doing God's will in putting down the rebellion. Luther's extreme royal theology went in a different direction than his more balanced two kingdoms theology.

The South German and Swiss Reformers made the Kingdom a central part of their theology. HULDRYCH ZWINGLI (1484–1531) believed that the Bible contained blueprints for society, and, hence, governments ought to adopt its teaching. At about the same time, the sectarian Anabaptists turned explicitly to the New Testament for their Kingdom teaching (see ANABAPTISM). Although the Anabaptists were not a unified movement, most taught that faith was a voluntary matter, a point reinforced by their insistence on believer's baptism. In addition, they hoped their churches might be holy commonwealths that renounced war, the oath, and economic injustice.

Radical Anabaptists, inspired by MELCHIOR HOFMANN'S (c.1500–1543) millennial speculations, attempted to establish a millennial Kingdom in Münster. Besieged by an imperial army, their commune practiced polygamy and the community of goods. Although the princes defeated the Münster rebels, as they earlier defeated the peasants, the Anabaptist hope for a new Kingdom did not vanish.

Although Geneva's JOHN CALVIN (1509–1564) shared Zwingli's Old Testament passion, Calvin, a humanist and lawyer, understood that laws reflected cultural as well as divine mandates. Calvin knew that biblical injunctions could not replace the civil code, but he believed that disciplined people living in a well-regulated state were a social approximation of the Gospel. Under his leadership, Geneva was characterized by a practical utopianism. MARTIN BUCER (1491–1551), an older contemporary of Calvin, used similar ideas in his De regno christi (1557), the first systematic Protestant study of the Kingdom of God.

Early Modern Protestantism

Although Johann Andreae's (1586–1654) Christianopolis (1619), which depicted an ideal society based on biblical materials, was an important exception, Calvin and Luther's understanding of the Kingdom dominated most Continental theology. In contrast, English Protestantism developed another approach to the Kingdom rooted in that country's history. John Wycliff (1330–1384) taught a simple biblicism that became commonplace, and the English people long believed themselves God's New Israel. Further, the English Reformation made England Protestant, then Catholic, then Protestant again. Whatever the archbishop said at the coronation, religious change fatally wounded the belief that the king was the vice-regent of God. Each reign created martyrs whose deaths witnessed to God's direct power over conscience. In addition, ENGLAND was Europe's trader, and its ships carried books and ideas as well as cargo. Numerous refugees and foreign scholars taught in its universities.

English interest in the Kingdom and in the millennium developed rapidly after the ascension of ELIZABETH I (1533–1603). Elizabeth was a master of the new media of print, and her court writers depicted her as a new Deborah called to save Protestantism. The queen was blessed by shrewdness and luck. The defeat of the Spanish Armada, for instance, resulted from her careful, secretive building of the Royal Navy, Francis

Drake's genius, and a massive storm. Although her ministers harried them, gagged their leaders, and prohibited their gatherings, Elizabeth was unable to silence the Puritans who believed that her church was not sufficiently reformed (see PURITANISM). If anything, persecution whetted their appetite for millenarianism. By 1600, English presses were churning out studies of the Revelation, including Thomas Brightman's *Apocalypsis apocalypseos* (1609, 1611) and Joseph Mede's *Clavis apocalyptica* (1627). Bishop James Ussher's (1581–1656) chronology, the *Annales veritas et novi testamentum* (1650), provided dates valuable to anyone calculating Christ's return.

James I (1566–1625) and Charles I (1600–1649) intensified Elizabeth's anti-Puritan measures. In the 1640s, when open war between Parliament and the Crown erupted, many English people believed that the Kingdom of God was at hand. These popular speculations were particularly strong in OLIVER CROMWELL'S (d. 1658) New Model army where the Fifth Monarchy Men, named after Daniel's prophecy, had a large following. Many Puritan leaders were also millennialists. Cromwell, for example, advocated the readmission of the Jews because he believed that their conversion was a precursor to the Second Coming.

Those Puritans who went to America were fascinated by the Kingdom and the millennium. Both JOHN COTTON (1585–1652) and INCREASE MATHER (1639–1723) studied Revelation carefully, searching for evidence of fulfilled prophecies. The conversion of the heathens, one of the signs, seemed at hand in the Indian missions, and only a few prophecies remained to be fulfilled before the Kingdom arrived. Moving to a new land and establishing their own holy commonwealths reinforced these Puritan hopes.

Although Sir Isaac NEWTON (1642–1727) spent his later years studying the various millennial prophecies, both English and American millennialism receded after the restoration of Charles II. Soured on enthusiasm by the excesses of the Revolution, JOHN LOCKE (1632–1704) and others identified religion with reason and morality. The appropriate eschatology was a belief in rewards and punishments after death and, perhaps, continuing confidence in England's special place in history.

Some late seventeenth-century interpreters offered a more rational view of the millennial tradition. Hugo Grotius (1583–1645), Daniel Whitby (d. 1726), and Moses Lowman (d. 1752) argued that the biblical description of millennium was symbolic. The spread of the Gospel would usher in an indefinite period of peace, justice, and economic plenty. While the millennium's approach could be charted through the usual prophetic signs, such as the fall of the papal Antichrist, the Kingdom would come through human action, not direct divine intervention. Christ's Second Coming would follow on the millennium.

This "postmillennial" theology supported the Christian activism of eighteenth-century pietists (see PIETISM). In Germany, August Hermann Francke (1663–1727), supported by the Prussian ruling family, launched a major assault on Germany's spiritual ills. Francke sought to reform theological education, making it more biblically centered, established an orphanage, began a girls school, created a bible society, and sent the first Protestant missionaries to India. Anglo-American evangelicals lacked such rich fiscal resources. Although evangelist GEORGE WHITEFIELD (1714–1770) dreamed of establishing an American HALLE in Georgia, he was unable to raise the needed funds. His friend, theologian JONATHAN EDWARDS (1703–1758), advocated midweek prayer meetings for missions to hasten the millennium, and JOHN WESLEY (1703–1791) was a dynamo of Kingdom righteousness. He warred with alcoholism and slavery, carried out an active ministry to the poor and imprisoned, collected for charity, and, in doing so, managed to create a new denomination.

After Napoleon's fall, post-millennialism entered its classical age. Protestant missionary activity, secured by the Royal Navy and protected by the British Empire, carried Christianity to Asia and to AFRICA. Other Protestants joined the British in this missionary effort. Many American denominations, such as the Baptists and Congregationalists, formed their national denominations to support the cause. MISSIONS to the homeland also flourished. Johann Hinrich Wichern (1808–1881), a German pastor, established the Inner Mission to coordinate a number of Christian initiatives, and the Deaconess movement established the first school for nurses at Kaiserswerth. Traveling evangelists dotted the American west with churches. On the darker side, postmillennial theology contributed to modern NATIONALISM. Each Protestant nation saw itself as essential to the final triumph of the Redeemer's Kingdom, and often confused its own political goals with the divine plan.

Modern Protestantism

By 1800, many thoughtful observers believed that the modern world posed unique theological and ethical issues. Even those who opposed the newer directions of thought—and many did—found that they had to consider the implications of the new science for theology, but the issues were only primarily intellectual. Science, new techniques of manufacturing and communication, and a rising standard of living offered new economic and social possibilities. At the same time, these developments made such ancient evils as war and poverty more terrible.

Philosopher IMMANUEL KANT (1724–1804) helped to define the modern period by investigating the limits of rational discourse. Although Kant did not accept religion's truth claims, he believed that religion provided symbols that enabled individuals and communities to live moral lives. In effect, "Christ," "forgiveness," and "atonement," reconciled the demands of moral law and actual human behavior. Kant used the phrase "philosophical chiliasm" to refer to his belief that the Kingdom of God symbolized the hope for a world of truth and justice.

Theologian FRIEDRICH SCHLEIERMACHER (1768–1834), a founder of the University of Berlin, resolved to reconcile the thought of the ENLIGHTENMENT and the Christian faith. To do this, he shifted the theological center from God to the historical Jesus. As Schleiermacher understood Jesus, Jesus had a perfect consciousness of God that others might share through him. In so doing, believers became incorporated into God's Kingdom of Righteousness, which Christ's influence created and sustained.

Schleiermacher wrote just as the historical approach to the New Testament was becoming accepted. FERDINAND CHRISTIAN BAUR (1792–1860) of Tübingen was an early representative of these new studies. His developmental approach to the New Testament stressed the ways in which the earliest churches had reinterpreted faith as the church moved from Palestine to Rome. In Baur's view, much of the New Testament was late in its composition, and he doubted the attributed authorship of many New Testament books. DAVID FRIEDRICH STRAUSS (1808–1874), a follower of G. F. W. HEGEL (1770–1831), carried Baur's argument one step further. According to Strauss, the earliest churches gradually replaced Jesus with a mythological portrait that made Christ a divine man. The meaning of the Kingdom thus varied with the location of a particular passage in this longer development.

Theologian ALBRECHT RITSCHL (1822–1889) used the new historical studies in creating his theology. According to Ritschl, the Kingdom of God was the core of the teachings of the historical Jesus, and, hence, should be the heart of present-day faith. By accepting Jesus's proclamation, Ritschl maintained, believers were placed in a new relationship to God that incorporated them into God's Kingdom. Through acts of love and obedience, the Christian brought the world into a new relationship with God, which in turn further advanced God's reign. After 1880, Ritschl's students occupied the important theological chairs in Germany, and representatives of his position were also found in Anglo-American theological schools.

Ritschl's Kingdom theology appealed to Christian activists who wanted to build a new society. In the United States, for instance, the Baptist WALTER RAUSCHENBUSCH (1861–1918) saw the Kingdom as humanity organized according to the will of God. Others joined him in advocating this SOCIAL GOSPEL, including the founders of the Federal Council of Churches. In Europe, LEONHARD RAGAZ (1868–1945), the translator of Rauschenbusch into German, taught a similar doctrine as did the editors of the influential periodical *Christliche Welt*.

The intellectual challenge to Ritschlean theology came from the historical study that helped to make it influential. In 1892 Johannes Weiss published *Die Predigt Jesus vom Reiche Gottes*. The book argued convincingly that Jesus' understanding of the Kingdom of God was typical of Jewish apocalyptic thought. ALBERT SCHWEITZER'S (1875–1965) *Quest for the Historical Jesus* (1906) built on Weiss's insights and argued that Christ died believing that his death would end history.

World War I and the Depression

While intellectual criticism did not destroy Ritschlian theology, human experience made it difficult to affirm. In 1914 a general European war erupted that was followed by a worldwide depression of epic proportions and yet another world war. In this context, the Ritschlian celebration of the Kingdom seemed naïve and irrelevant to social problems.

When the Great War began, many national leaders identified their country's causes with the Kingdom. The most effusive was Woodrow Wilson (1856–1924), a master of Protestant rhetoric. The Great War, he argued, would end with a just peace and the establishment of a League of Nations that would make future wars impossible. Unprecedented carnage, shameless war profiteering, and a draconian peace exposed the hollowness of Wilson's words. In SWITZERLAND, a young Protestant pastor, KARL BARTH (1886–1968), published *The Epistle to the Romans* (1919), a commentary that stressed the discontinuity between God and human activity. Barth's new direction in theology quickly caught the attention of younger European theologians, including FRIEDRICH GOGARTEN (1887–1968), EMIL BRUNNER (1889–1966) and RUDOLF BULTMANN (1884–1976).

Many turned to the existential philosophy of SØREN KIERKEGAARD (1813–1855), FRIEDRICH NIETZSCHE (1844–1900) and Martin Heidegger (1889–1976) to address the post–World War I world. Existentialism was a philosophic stance or orientation that made few objective truth claims. Instead, existentialists recognized that science had made traditional metaphysics unbelievable. Knowledgeable people, after all, knew that atoms, not some ethereal substance, constituted reality, but the existentialists did not want to relinquish metaphysical language altogether because philosophy illuminated the deeper problems of human experience. Many theologians saw traditional Christian doctrine in the same way. Although few believed these teachings literally, they provided a fruitful way to understand human life. Rudolf Bultmann's (1884–1976) essay, "The New Testament and Mythology," suggested that contemporaries might best understand Jesus's eschatological Kingdom as a radical call to decision or commitment.

In Germany the defeat in World War I led to social disillusionment. The 1920 political struggles pitted different secular millenniums against each other. National Socialism, for example, promised to construct a new one-thousand-year Reich on the basis of racial purity. This millennium would come after a titanic struggle between good and evil. The Communists, flush from their victory in Russia, pressed for an ideal workers' state that might restore prosperity and dignity. The German churches, which lost many legal and constitutional privileges after the war, had difficulty addressing these conflicts. However, the new eschatology enabled some church leaders, especially in the CONFESSING CHURCH, to protest against any identification of the secular and divine order (see GERMAN CHRISTIANS). The Kingdom was as powerful in its absence as in its presence.

The world war accelerated the UNITED STATES' loss of innocence. The Social Gospel movement declined. In its place, such American theologians as REINHOLD NIEBUHR (1892–1971) and H. RICHARD NIEBUHR (1894–1962) proposed a realist theology that stressed sin and ambiguity as part of life. American realism, however, was not European neo-orthodoxy, although it drew on similar sources. Much of the older Social Gospel interest in direct Christian action continued, even as the Kingdom language was critiqued.

Theologian H. Richard Niebuhr summarized the American theological tradition in his *Kingdom of God in America* (1937). Niebuhr described American Protestant thinking as moving from a Kingdom that was dependent on sovereignty (the Puritans) through a Kingdom within individuals and movements (EVANGELICALISM) to a more social Kingdom (the Social Gospel). Ever the careful dialectician, Niebuhr refused to privilege any of these positions. Jonathan Edwards (1703–1758) and Walter Rauschenbusch were both part of the American dialogue.

During the 1920s American Protestant conservatives lost the Modernist-Fundamentalist controversy, and many withdrew from their churches to establish their own institutions. Many advocated premillennial DISPENSATIONALISM, an interpretation of prophecy that had been popular in the nineteenth century. Dispensationalism began with the British millenarian, JOHN NELSON DARBY (1800–1882), whose teachings were modified in American prophecy courses, Bible study programs, and Bible schools. To stabilize this theology, Cyrus Scofield (1843–1921) asked a committee to help him edit the *SCOFIELD REFERENCE BIBLE*. Reading Jesus' teachings about the Kingdom in a literal way, Scofield concluded that Jesus believed that the Kingdom would follow shortly after his resurrection. Instead, God inserted a great parenthesis into prophetic history that would end with the Rapture. After Jesus appeared to take his people home, the fulfillment of prophecy would resume and, after a great tribulation, the saints would reign with Christ in the millennium. The Kingdom was, like a Christian America, a hope radically deferred.

Late Modernity

Not surprisingly, the nuclear age has been a period of intense interest in eschatology. In Germany the two most influential postwar theologians were WOLFHART PANNENBERG (1928–) and JÜRGEN MOLTMANN (1926–), who published influential studies of the Kingdom in the 1970s. Although both began with an eschatological understanding of Jesus' teachings, they diverged at significant points. In the *Theology and the Kingdom of God* (1969), Pannenberg stressed the intertwining of the present and future Kingdom of God. Thus, the coming Kingdom effects the present, which already contains the future. In contrast Moltmann, in the *Trinity and the Kingdom* (1980), saw the Kingdom as the work of the Trinity, which keeps the world's future open for the future Kingdom of glory.

In the United States, MARTIN LUTHER KING, JR. (1929–1968), an African American civil rights leader, made important contributions to the discussion of the Kingdom of God. A complex thinker, King combined elements of American religious liberalism, African American religion, and his Baptist tradition. In addition, King believed that Gandhi's nonviolence was the way for an oppressed people to confront their opponents. King assumed leadership of the CIVIL RIGHTS MOVEMENT during the Montgomery Bus Boycott (1955), and his theology was contained in the documents that he prepared for that public task. His 1963 speech at the Washington monument, "I Have a Dream," summed up his vision of the coming Kingdom.

The theology of liberation was a theological response to the grinding poverty of the Third World (see LIBERATION THEOLOGY). Peruvian theologian Gustavo Gutierrez's (1928–) *Teologiá de la liberación* (1971) was an attempt to bring together insights from Marxism, particularly as expressed through such thinkers as Ernst Bloch (1885–1977), the concrete situation in Latin America, and the need for political action. To further their understanding of the Kingdom, liberation theologians established *communidades ecclesiales de base* or base communities. These small lay-led communities provided a place for ordinary people to develop their religious and political concerns.

Among Roman Catholics, liberation theology has become less influential. In 1985, Brazilian theologian Leonardo Boff (1938–) was summoned to Rome to explain his *Igreja: Carisma e poder* (1981). Boff was silenced and the pope's new appointments in Latin America were conservative. In North America, however, liberation theology sparked the development of a number of theologies concerned with human rights, including feminist and gay theology (see FEMINIST THEOLOGY; HOMOSEXUALITY). These new theologies began with the particular group's religious and theological insights as sources of action and reflection. Feminist theologians, although generally supportive of the broader liberation emphasis on the Kingdom, have critiqued that language as gender specific. In their place, they have suggested substitutes, such as the Dominion of God.

Popular religion, particularly in the United States, also saw an expanding interest in apocalyptic theologies. Unlike earlier dispensationalists, such authors as Hal Lindsey, who wrote *The Late Great Planet Earth* (1970), pointed to contemporary events, including the threat of nuclear war, as signs that God was about to act.

Despite its popularity, many conservative theologians questioned dispensationalism. Fuller Seminary's George Elton Ladd, for instance, published a series of thoughtful conservative works, beginning with his *Blessed Hope* (1956), that questioned the doctrine's biblical basis. His colleague, Daniel Fuller, criticized the teaching from a more systematic perspective. Despite extensive controversy in the Evangelical Theological Society, Fuller Seminary and other evangelical schools rejected dispensationalism as an institutional norm, although those faculties continued to include some advocates. At Dallas Theological Seminary, long the dispensational flagship, a younger generation of scholars moved toward a "progressive dispensationalism" that removed many of the harsher elements of the traditional system.

Present

The collapse of the Soviet Union and the end of the Cold War has apparently coincided with the beginnings of another period in theology. Throughout the 1990s, both theology and popular faith moved away from the apocalyptic and social concerns of the late modern period. In their place there is a new interest in the personal apprehension of religion. Interest in mysticism, eastern religions, and nontraditional spiritual disciplines is common. There is increasing concern with how people will manage, not social deprivation, but the considerable economic blessings of current Western and American life. Perhaps this theology will allow the Kingdom to lie fallow for a season until a new band of prophets summons it again to deal with the perpetual crises of society.

References and Further Reading

Frostin, Per. *Luther's Two Kingdom Doctrine: A Critical Study.* Lund, Sweden: Lund University Press, 1994.

Glasson, T. F. *Jesus and the End of the World.* Edinburgh: St Andrew Press, 1980.

Humphries, Michael L. *Christian Origins and the Language of the Kingdom of God.* Carbondale: Southern Illinois University Press, c. 1999.

Kwon, Hyuk Seung. *The Zion Traditions and the Kingdom of God: A Study on the Zion Traditions as Relevant to the Understanding of the Concept of the Kingdom of God in the New Testament.* Jerusalem: Hebrew University, 1998.

Moltmann, Jürgen. *Trinity and the Kingdom of God,* Translated by Margaret Kohl. New York: Harper & Row, c. 1981.

Niebuhr, H. Richard. *The Kingdom of God in America,* Middletown, CT: Wesleyan University Press, 1988.

Oort, Johannes van. *Jerusalem and Babylon: A Study into Augustine's City of God and the Sources of His Doctrine of the Two Cities.* Leiden, New York: E. J. Brill, 1991.

Pannenberg, Wolfhart. *Theologie und Reich Gottes.* Gütersloh, Germany: Gutersloher Verlagshaus G. Mohn, c. 1971.

Perrin, Norman, *The Kingdom of God in the Teaching of Jesus.* London: SCM Press, 1963.

Ragaz, Leonhard, *Signs of the Kingdom: A Ragaz Reader.* Edited and translated by Paul Bock. Grand Rapids, MI Eerdmans 1984.

Schweitzer, Albert. *The Quest for the Historical Jesus: A Critical Study of Its Progress from Reimarus to Wrede.* New York: Macmillan, 1968.

Weber, Timothy, *Living in the Shadow of the Second Coming: American Premillennialism. 1875–1982.* Chicago: University of Chicago Press, 1987.

Weiss, Johannes. *Jesus' Proclamation of the Kingdom of God.* Translated by Richard Hyde Hiers and David Larrimore Holland. Philadelphia, PA: Fortress Press, 1971.

GLENN T. MILLER

KINGSLEY, CHARLES (1819–1875)

Anglican clergyman, Christian Socialist, and Victorian novelist. Son of a Devonshire vicar, Kingsley studied at King's College, London, and Magdalene College, Cambridge. While a student at Cambridge, Kingsley struggled with his own Christian beliefs and read SAMUEL TAYLOR COLERIDGE, F. D. MAURICE, and others. He was not, however, a disciplined student, and he immersed himself in college sports. He graduated and was ordained to the priesthood in 1842, eventually obtaining appointment to a living at Eversley, Hants.

His reaction to the emergent OXFORD MOVEMENT was sharply negative; he dismissed ASCETICISM of any sort and was no admirer of the medieval church. A critical aside about JOHN HENRY NEWMAN led to the latter's *Apologia Pro Vita Sua.* Kingsley became a keen follower of Maurice and called for the church to address the needs of the poorer classes. Indeed, he became a leader of the Christian Socialist Movement for which he was often the target of harsh criticism. Kingsley tended, in fact, to be apolitical, seeking to improve the lot of the disadvantaged through education and cooperative reforms. Kingsley was not a systematic thinker but is considered one of the early leaders of the liberal BROAD CHURCH Movement within ANGLICANISM.

He was also a prolific poet and novelist, his most notable novels being *Yeast* (1850), *Westward Ho!* (1855), and the children's book, *The Water-Babies* (1863). By the time of his death, he had gained a degree of acceptance in the CHURCH OF ENGLAND, serving as canon of Chester (1869–1873) and Westminster (1873–1875) and as one of Queen Victoria's chaplains in ordinary (appointed 1859).

References and Further Reading

Primary Sources:

Kingsley, Charles. *The Works of Charles Kingsley.* 28 vols. London: Macmillan, 1880–1888.
Kingsley, Mrs. Charles. *Charles Kingsley: His Letters and Memories of His Life.* 2 vols. London: Henry S. King, 1877.

Secondary Sources:

Chitty, Susan. *The Beast and the Monk.* London: Hodder & Stoughton, 1974.
Martin, Robert B. *The Dust of Combat: A Life of Charles Kingsley.* London: Faber & Faber, 1959.

GILLIS J. HARP

KINGSLEY, MARY (1862–1900)

English missionary theorist. As a champion of West African CULTURE in the late nineteenth century, Mary Kingsley's contribution to the missionary project in that area is best known for her antipathy toward and criticism of the MISSIONS. Born October 13, 1862, in Islington, London, Kingsley died in SOUTH AFRICA on June 3, 1900, while nursing Boer prisoners. Her uncle was the famous CHARLES KINGSLEY, Christian Socialist and novelist. After the death of her parents Mary Kingsley went on two extended journeys to what are now Angola, Cameroon, Gabon, NIGERIA, and SIERRA LEONE. These journeys lasted respectively from August to December 1893, and December 1894 to November 1895.

Kingsley's travels resulted in three books: *Travels in West Africa* (1897), an ethnographical work; *West African Studies* (1899); and *The Story of West Africa* (1900), a historical overview of the area. However, it is Kingsley's first publication, "The Negro Future," a letter to the *Spectator* in 1895, that announced her sympathy for the West Africans and her hostility toward the missions. In this letter Kingsley refuted beliefs that the Africans were drunken idiots—a portrait she claimed was perpetrated by Protestant missionaries. In "The Development of Dodos," published in *National Review* in March 1896, she asserted that Protestant missionaries failed in West Africa because they tended to regard the African minds as so many jugs to be emptied only to be refilled with Protestant DOCTRINE.

Although Kingsley was opposed to Protestant missions, by which she meant Anglican, she made friends with French and American missionaries in Gabon and became an admirer of MARY SLESSOR, the Scottish Presbyterian who established a mission in the Okoyong region in Nigeria. Kingsley's attitude toward mission culture was unusual for a woman brought up very much with Victorian values, and certainly accounts partially for the originality in her writing.

See also Anglicanism; Christian; Colonialism; Missionary Organizations; Presbyterianism; Socialism

References and Further Reading

Birkett, Dea. *Mary Kingsley: Imperial Adventuress.* Basingstoke, UK: Macmillan, 1992.
Brown, Don. *Uncommon Traveler: Mary Kingsley in Africa.* Boston: Houghton-Mifflin, 2000.
Frank, Katherine. *A Voyager Out: The Life of Mary Kingsley.* Boston: Houghton Mifflin, 1986.
Gikandi, Simon. *Maps of Englishness: Writing Identity in the Culture of Colonialism.* New York: Columbia University Press, 1996.
Howard, Cecil. *Mary Kingsley.* London: Hutchinson, 1957.
Lindquist, Suen. *The Skull Measurer's Mistake: And Other Portraits of Men and Women Who Spoke Out Against Racism.* New York: New Press, distributed by W. W. Norton, 1997.

MARIA NOËLLE NG

KIRCHENTAG

German Protestantism knows of three different movements that are called *Kirchentage.* Between 1848 and 1872 church notables met once a year to discuss questions of church policy or theological problems. In the Weimar Republic the *Kirchentag* was the highest official committee of the *Deutscher Evangelischer Kirchenbund,* which united the individual regional churches in a loose federation. Since 1949 the church conferences are lay meetings and a large public manifestation of Protestantism in Germany.

In view of the revolution of 1848, which threatened the traditional position of the churches and against the background of long-standing issues, the first *Kirchentag* took place in September 1848 in Wittenberg. The aim was to achieve a closer union of the individual regional churches and the splintered Protestantism. As a renewal and unification movement, it integrated large parts of Protestantism with the exception of the confessional Lutherans and die-hard liberals. However, the *Kirchentage* could not achieve its aims, and after the *Reichsgründung* (founding of the German Empire) in 1871 the movement came to an end.

Nonetheless, as a result of some sixteen conferences, important impulses for theological discussion and for the movement of church constitutions went out. The *Kirchentage* are connected with what is called Inner Mission, that is, evangelism and social work and their yearly meetings. The speech of Johann Heinrich Wichern at the *Kirchentag* in Wittenberg 1848 stands as the beginning of this charitable movement.

With the end of the *landesherrlichen Kirchenregiment* (territorial church government) and the beginning of the politics of separation of CHURCH AND STATE, the churches were forced to reorganize their constitutions. The first *Deutscher Evangelischer Kirchentag* in Dresden in September 1919 initiated the process of reconstruction. The *Kirchentag* became an official institution of the *Deutscher Evangelischer Kirchenbund,* which was founded in 1921. Three times (1924, 1927, 1930) the church parliament met. Each time a special topic was the central point of the meetings: 1924 in Bethel (Bielefeld) the social question (*soziale Frage*), 1927 in Königsberg the patriotic or national question (*völkische Frage*), 1930 in Augsburg the denominational question. The adopted statements and the discussions can be regarded as important manifestations of Protestantism in the Weimar Republic.

In 1949 Reinold von Thadden-Trieglaff organized the *Deutsche Evangelische Woche* in Hannover, which originated the *Kirchentags* movement. In spite of the strong resistance of leading persons of the church in the beginning, the *Kirchentag* developed into a public forum where religious, theological, social, and political challenges of the present could be broadly discussed. The topics, such as the relationship to DEMOCRACY, the problem of WAR and peace, the ecological movement, and Jewish–Christian dialogue,

determined German Protestantism and were themes of the meetings.

These lay meetings, taking place every two years, became a sign of German Protestantism during the postwar period. Until 1961, the year of the building of the Berlin wall, the meetings were focused on the Cold War problem and German separation. Up to 650,000 persons have participated in the meetings. After a crisis in the 1960s the *Kirchentage* are today a fixed component of public life, in which young people in particular look for religious experiences and social challenges.

References and Further Reading

Kreft, Werner. *Die Kirchentage von 1848–1872.* Frankfurt/Main: Peter Lang Publishing, 1994.

Nowak, Kurt. *Evangelische Kirche und Weimarer Republik.* Göttingen, Germany: Vandenhoek & Ruprecht, 1981.

Rogge, Joachim. "Kirchentage und Eisenacher Konferenz." In *Die Geschichte der Evangelischen Kirche der Union,* edited by Joachim Rogge and Gerhard Ruhbach, vol. 2, 42–55. Leipzig: Evangelische Verlagsanstalt, 1994.

Schröter, Harald. *Kirchentag als vorläufige Kirche. Der Kirchentag als besondere Gestalt des Christseins zwischen Kirche und Welt.* Stuttgart: Kohlhammer, 1993.

Steinacker, Peter. "Kirchentage." In *Theologische Realenzyklopädie,* edited by Gerhard Müller, vol. 19, 101–110. Berlin and New York: de Gruyter, 1990.

Wright, Jonathan R. C. *"Above Parties": The Political Attitudes of the German Protestant Church Leadership 1918–1933.* London and New York: Oxford University Press, 1974.

NORBERT FRIEDRICH

KNOX, JOHN (C.1514–1572)

Scottish reformer. Born around 1514 in Haddington, near Edinburgh, Scotland, John Knox was probably educated at St. Andrews University before being ordained a Catholic priest in 1536. The date and circumstances of his CONVERSION are unknown, but by 1544 he was associated with George Wishart, whose Protestant ministry in SCOTLAND led David Cardinal Beaton, archbishop of St. Andrews, to have him burned as a heretic in March 1546. Two months later Beaton was himself assassinated, and his murderers were besieged in the Episcopal castle at St. Andrews. There Knox joined them, and, in April 1547, he was persuaded that his vocation lay as a Protestant preacher. His ministry, however, had inauspicious beginnings, for in July 1547 St. Andrews' castle fell to the French, and Knox spent the next nineteen months as a French galley slave.

Released from captivity in March 1549, Knox settled in Edward VI's ENGLAND. It was there that he established his reputation as a leading light of the radical wing of the English church. His dogmatic biblicism, focused initially on the idolatry of the Catholic Mass, led him to oppose the stance of the moderate leadership of the Protestant establishment in England over kneeling at communion. This rift was to become more pronounced after the accession of Catholic Mary Tudor in 1553 and the flight of English Protestants to the Continent. Appointed minister of the English congregation at Frankfurt in 1554, Knox's hard-line stance on liturgical issues caused such bitter disputes that in 1555 he was forced to take refuge in Geneva.

Although Knox found his stay in Geneva a formative experience, it was initially short-lived, for in the winter of 1555–1556 he returned secretly to the north of England and from there embarked on a clandestine PREACHING tour of Scotland. Thereafter, his close identification with the English church and people was diluted by a reawakened concern for the fate of Scottish Protestants. His early writings from exile were addressed exclusively to his former English congregations, but by 1558, notably in his notorious *First Blast of the Trumpet Against the Monstrous Regiment of Women*, his vision was self-consciously British. Hence, when on the accession of ELIZABETH I in 1558 Knox was prevented from returning to England, his disappointment was allayed by the opportunity to effect radical reform in his native land.

On Knox's return to Scotland in May 1559, his iconoclastic preaching triggered a Protestant rebellion against the Catholic French regent, Mary of Guise, whose daughter Mary Queen of Scots had married the French dauphin in April 1558. While the rebellion was poorly supported, a Protestant settlement was eventually secured in 1560 through the intervention of England. However, plans for closer union between the Protestant British kingdoms were dashed by the decision of the Catholic Mary Stuart to return to Scotland in August 1561. Knox's fury with the Protestant nobles who acquiesced in Mary's return, and who defended her right to practice Catholicism privately, proved fruitless. Knox was politically marginalized, and, although he railed against the queen's Mass from the pulpit, he played little role in the events that led to Mary's overthrow in 1567. While he preached at the coronation of the infant James VI in July 1567, and supported the anti-Marian party in the civil war that followed Mary's escape from captivity in 1568, age and ill health increasingly curtailed his activities. He died in Edinburgh on November 24, 1572.

Knox was not a systematic thinker and left no body of theological work. Although he helped shape the defining documents of the Scottish Reformation—the reformed *Confession of Faith* and the *First Book of Discipline*—most of his surviving writings are polemical tracts written in response to specific circumstances. Effectively sermons, distinguished by their pungent and often prophetic rhetoric, they display Knox's close identification with the Old Testament prophets on whom he modeled his public persona. This is particularly apparent during the period of the Marian exile, when Knox wrestled with the problem of finding scriptural AUTHORITY for resistance to Catholic tyranny. For all their prophetic fury, however, Knox's writings are less politically radical than is often assumed. While the *First Blast* was a sweeping indictment of female governance, his other key tracts of 1558—the *Appellation* and the *Letter to the Commonalty*—fall some way short of the revolutionary populism subsequently ascribed to them. Yet Knox did develop the remarkably powerful and enduring idea that, like Old Testament Israel, the peoples of Scotland and England were bound by a COVENANT with God to promote and defend the "true religion."

It was fear and despair in the face of a broken covenant that both fuelled the abusive language of the 1558 tracts and shaped what was to be Knox's most lasting memorial, the *History of the Reformation of Religion in Scotland*. The *History* began life as a record of the events of the Scottish Reformation of 1559–1560, but in the course of Mary Queen of Scots' short reign evolved into an extended sermon on Scotland's covenanted status and the folly of breaching God's law by tolerating a Catholic sovereign. Brilliantly written, and inevitably highlighting Knox's own role in contemporary events, the *History* is an invaluable source for historians of the Scottish Reformation. Above all, however, it provides unique insights into the mind of a self-styled instrument of God whose influence on the course of the British Reformation was profound and long lasting.

See also Calvinism; Presbyterianism

References and Further Reading

Primary Sources:

Knox, John. *The Works of John Knox*. Edited by David Laing. 6 vols. Edinburgh: Wodrow Society, 1846–1864.
———. *John Knox's History of the Reformation in Scotland*. Edited by W. C. Dickinson. 2 vols. London: Thomas Nelson and Sons, 1949.
———. *On Rebellion*. Edited by Roger A. Mason. Cambridge: Cambridge University Press, 1994.

Secondary Sources:

Kyle, Richard G. *The Mind of John Knox*. Lawrence, KS: Coronado Press, 1984.
Mason, Roger A., ed. *John Knox and the British Reformations*. Aldershot, UK: Ashgate Publishing, 1998.
Ridley, Jasper. *John Knox*. Oxford, UK: Clarendon Press, 1968.

ROGER A. MASON

KOELLE, SIGISMUND WILHELM (1823–1902)

Missionary linguist. Koelle was born in Kleebron, Würtemberg, Germany, on July 14, 1823. He was one of many young Würtemberger Pietists recruited by the (Anglican) CHURCH MISSIONARY SOCIETY (CMS) through the Basel Mission Seminary. After study there he entered the CMS College at Islington in 1845 and was ordained DEACON in 1846 and priest in 1847. Having displayed exceptional academic gifts, he was sent to Tübingen to study Semitic languages under J. H. A. Ewald.

Developments in West Africa were opening the possibility of reaching the peoples of the interior, but this was conceivable only with the large-scale involvement of African missionaries, who must therefore be trained and equipped. SIERRA LEONE was the most eligible source of potential African missionaries, and its Fourah Bay Institution was the obvious place to concentrate their training. Koelle was accordingly appointed to the institution in 1847 to teach Hebrew and Arabic (the latter in expectation of encounters with Muslim peoples). He worked there until 1853 and, with the encouragement of the CMS Secretary Henry Venn, laid the foundations of comparative African linguistics. He identified well over a hundred languages, belonging to a vast area of West and Central Africa, that were still being spoken in Sierra Leone, and in his massive *Polyglotta Africana* produced materials for their analysis and comparison, as well as revealing something of their richness. He also produced substantial grammars of two of them, Vai (Liberia) and Kanuri (northeast Nigeria).

In 1853 Koelle returned to Britain to see his works through the press, and married Charlotte Elizabeth Philpot, daughter of a prominent clergyman. In impaired health, instead of returning to West Africa, he served briefly in Cairo, and then, from 1856 to 1859, in Haifa, employing his Arabic, and developing a learned but confrontational approach to Islam. In 1862 he was appointed to Constantinople, where K. G. Pfander (1803–1865), the best-known contemporary Christian apologist to Islam, was already stationed. Here Koelle turned his attention to Turkish and other Turkic languages, producing a large amount of material, much of it never published, both original and translated. Left as the sole missionary, heavily circumscribed by the authorities, he saw minimal response in terms of converts. In 1877 the CMS, in a financial crisis, closed the unviable mission and retired Koelle. However, he refused to leave Constantinople and worked independently on a Turkish translation of the Anglican prayer book. In 1879 he and a Muslim scholar, Ahmed Tewfik, who was assisting him were

the center of a diplomatic incident, where the British government made a robust response to their arrest. Koelle had to leave; Tewfik was banished, escaped, went to ENGLAND, and was eventually baptized there, the prelude to an extraordinary career. Koelle retired to England and continued to write, including the erudite but highly polemical *Mohammed and Mohammedanism* (1889). He died February 18, 1902, in London.

Koelle, prodigiously learned, angular, and somewhat eccentric, remains a pivotal figure in African linguistics, which he always saw in terms of its relevance to the spread of the gospel. The *Polyglotta Africana* and the Vai and Kanuri grammars all appeared in new editions in the 1960s. Earlier they brought Koelle an honorary doctorate from Tübingen and the Volney Prize of the Institut de France. The same missionary dedication marks his later, less illustrious work on Turkish, Turkic languages, and Islam, and his theological and devotional volumes.

See also Africa; Basel Mission; Missions; Missionary Organizations

References and Further Reading

Primary Source:

Koelle, S. W. *Polyglotta Africana.* 2d edition, with biographical introduction by P. E. H. Hair and linguistic commentary by David Dalby. Graz, Austria: Akademische Druk und Verlagsanstalt, 1963.

Secondary Sources:

Church Missionary Society Register of Missionaries. London: CMS, 1904.
Stock, Eugene. *History of the Church Missionary Society.* vols. 2 and 3. London: CMS, 1899.

ANDREW F. WALLS

KOREA

Introduction

Protestantism in Korea, which largely descends from North American Methodist and Presbyterian MISSIONS of the last quarter of the nineteenth century, has been typified since its inception by four characteristics: initial self-evangelism, an association with Korean nationalism and concepts of progress, a strong theological conservatism and pietism coupled with social involvement, and rapid and significant increases in membership. In spite of the presence of denominations, there is such general uniformity in Protestant practice and the structure of the denominations that a uniquely Korean Protestantism may be said to have emerged in which METHODISM and PRESBYTERIANISM have mutually influenced each other. Without question this Korean Protestantism was the most dynamic religious force in twentieth-century Korean society, having a significant impact on the development and growth of Roman Catholicism, Buddhism, and new religious movements in Korea. Its development has also been shaped in key respects by the core values of Korean society and CULTURE. Korea under the Chosùn dynasty (1392–1910) became the most thoroughly Confucianized society of East Asia. Concepts and core values such as filial piety, loyalty, an emphasis on EDUCATION, concepts of AUTHORITY and social hierarchy, and the application of moral values in society and government have all come to shape the life and practical theology of the Korean Protestant community.

The Advent of Protestantism: 1882–1910

From the middle of the nineteenth century, there had been several missionary probes to the "Hermit Kingdom" of Chosùn, which like JAPAN had closed itself to significant outside contact from the late seventeenth century. Early missionary explorations were conducted by the Dutchman Karl Friederich August Gützlaff (1803–1851), who explored the Manchurian and Korean west coasts in 1832, by the Welshman Robert Jermain Thomas (1839–1866), who was aboard the American trading vessel the *General Sherman* in September 1866 when it ventured up the Taedong River to P'yùngyang, and the Scotsman Alexander Williamson (1929–1890), who visited the customs barrier between Manchuria and Korea in 1867. None of these attempts had any long-lasting impact on the religious scene in Korea.

The first Protestant missionary who had an impact on Korea was John Ross (1842–1915) of the United Presbyterian Church of Scotland mission to Manchuria who, with a group of Korean merchants in Manchuria acting as a team of translators, made the first translation of the New Testament into Korean. In 1882 the first portions of this translation were printed and circulated. The entire New Testament was translated, bound, and distributed as a single volume in 1887. The Ross Translation introduced key theological terms that are still in use, such as *Hananim* (Ruler of Heaven) for God, and—because it used exclusively the Korean alphabet *Han'gùl*—was a significant factor in the revival and widespread use of this script.

Koreans who had been converted to Christianity through reading Ross's translation were responsible for the establishment of Christian communities in northwestern Korea, in the capital, and in the communities along the northern bank of the Yalu River, which was nominally Korean territory at that time. The existence of these communities before the arrival of the first foreign missionaries in 1884 and 1885 is an eloquent testimonial to Ross's conviction that Christianity was spread best by convinced converts rather than by foreign missionaries. Korean Protestantism was self-evangelized from the beginning—EVANGELISM through the distribution of Scripture.

From the mid-1880s foreign missionaries began to arrive, including Horace N. Allen (1858–1932) of the Northern Presbyterian Church in 1884, Horace G. Underwood (1859–1916) of the same mission, and Henry G. Appenzeller (1858–1902) of the Northern Methodist mission in 1885, followed almost immediately by several other missionaries. By the end of the ninth decade of the nineteenth century, a foreign-mission enterprise was well under way, building on the foundations that had been laid by Ross's converts. By the end of the 1880s several of modern Korea's major institutions had already been established, such as three Western-style medical institutions including Severance Hospital and Ehwa Woman's University Hospital, and leading schools such as Paejae Boys' High School, and Ewha Girls' High School. At the same time the Religious Tract Society for the distribution of Scriptures and religious materials was created as the Tri-Lingual Press, the first Western-style publishing house (see PUBLISHING MEDIA).

The 1890s saw continual growth in the numbers of converts and the creation of Christian literature, including dictionaries, manuals of the Korean language, and translations of devotional works, such as JOHN BUNYAN'S PILGRIM'S PROGRESS. At the same time the question of how to create independent church institutions was also widely debated. In 1890 John L. Nevius (1829–1893), a Presbyterian missionary in Shantung, China, was invited to come to Korea to explain to the missionaries there his mission methods (now called the Nevius Method) for creating a self-propagating, self-governing, and self-supporting church, which became the universally accepted policy of Protestant missions in Korea. By the beginning of the twentieth century the prospects for Korean Protestantism seemed bright.

The rise of Protestantism in Korea must be set against the drama of the decline in political and economic power of the Chosùn dynasty, the search by progressive young intellectuals for a way to revitalize their nation, and growing Japanese imperial encroachment on the Asian continent. Young, nationalist Christians saw in the model of institutional mission work—particularly education and the creation of schools—a way to restore Korea to its rightful place on the world stage. Today many Korean schools claim a Christian, but not a mission, foundation because of the efforts of these Christians during the first decade of the twentieth century. The success of the Protestant churches in the twenty-five years after the arrival of foreign missionaries was attributed to the association of Christianity with the "progressive" West, and the emphasis that the first generation of missionaries placed on the responsibility of local Christians for the growth and support of their churches. Kenneth Wells in *New God, New Nation: Protestants and Self-reconstruction Nationalism in Korea* stresses the importance of the mixture of religious faith and nationalism at a time when the nation was facing a political crisis.

The numerical growth in the churches' membership in the decade before the annexation of Korea by the Japanese Empire in 1910, is often attributed to the Great Revival of 1907 in P'yùngyang, the effect of which quickly spread throughout the peninsula, and into both the Korean and Chinese communities in Manchuria. Although the event has to be seen against the background of the political uncertainties of the time, it cannot be gainsaid that this revival, which combined a concern for personal purity and potential national demise, unleashed a great spiritual energy among Koreans for the evangelization of the nation. At the time of the annexation in 1910, 1 percent of the population adhered to Protestantism. The Japanese Protestant Church today, which is at least a generation older than the Korean church, has yet to equal this achievement.

By 1910 the institutional church was well established—the first SEMINARIES had been founded, the first seminarians had graduated, and the first Korean ministers had been ordained. In 1908 all Protestant missionaries, except the High Church Anglicans, had accepted a comity agreement that divided the peninsula into mission spheres, which would avoid unnecessary competition by authorizing the presence of only one DENOMINATION in a particular region. A vote taken among the missionaries at the same time to create a United Church of Christ in Korea was rejected by the home churches in North America. Nonetheless the comity agreement, the use of a single translation of the BIBLE, a common hymnal, and other pan-denominational activities have helped to create a sense of a common Protestant Christianity in spite of the contemporary presence of many denominations.

Colonial Subjugation: Korea under Japanese Rule, 1910–1945

Throughout the colonial era there was continual growth in membership, and the extension of social and political engagement. In 1914, in the first decade of Japanese rule, there were 196,000 Korean adherents representing 1.1 percent of the population. By the end of Japanese rule in 1945, Protestant adherence had quadrupled to 740,000 persons, representing over 3 percent of the population. This numerical growth was paralleled by involvement in Korean society, the extent of which may be symbolized by four political events: (1) the Conspiracy Trial of 1912; (2) conflict over "patriotic" schools; (3) involvement in the March First Movement of 1919; and (4) the Shintō Shrine Controversy.

In 1912, 124 persons were accused of attempting to assassinate the governor-general, Terauchi Masatake (1852–1919), of whom ninety-eight were Christians, a sign that the colonial regime perceived Christians to be a section of the population that represented an organized challenge to their domination of Korea. In the end, the cases against all but six of the alleged conspirators were thrown out for lack of evidence. This trial, more than any other event, had the effect of creating a link in the popular imagination between Korean nationalism and Christianity. In Korea, imperialism was Japanese, not Western.

Korean Christians and Christian missions continued to found schools throughout Korea during the second decade of the twentieth century. To secondary-level institutions, the mission bodies added tertiary-level institutions such as Sungsil College (Union Christian College, 1905) in P'yùngyang, and Ewha Woman's College (1910), and Yùnhŭi College (Chosen Christian College, 1915) in Seoul, forming a complete nonstate educational system. Conflict between the Protestant community and the colonial government became acute when the Government-General announced in 1915 that all private schools would be required to use Japanese as the national language, and also that they would be forbidden to provide religious instruction or conduct religious worship. These edicts caused great consternation among both the mission community and the Korean Christian community, and for the latter became one of the principal reasons for their involvement in the Korean Independence Movement in 1919.

The March First Movement, which effectively created the sense of modern Korean nationhood, was largely the work of Korean religious leaders. Thirty-three persons signed the Declaration of Independence from Japan, of whom fifteen signatories were Christians. The principal Christian influence they had on the character of the movement came from their insistence on nonviolent behavior during the demonstration. The Japanese colonial regime harshly suppressed the movement, in which thousands were killed and injured. Christians in particular were persecuted. Churches were burned down by Japanese troops, many Christians were executed, and in one spectacular incident villagers were herded into a local church that was then set alight. In spite of a Japanese news blackout, the suppression of the movement became known because a few missionaries went to CHINA and cabled their mission boards at home, which in turn lobbied Western governments to condemn Japanese brutality. Christian involvement in the organization of the movement, Christian suffering in the suppression of the movement, and foreign Christian condemnation of Japanese brutality strengthened the link made between Protestant Christianity and Korean nationalism in the minds of both Koreans and Japanese.

Two strands of Protestant Christianity emerged in the aftermath of the suppression of the March First Movement—a more theologically liberal and socially active strand, and a more theologically conservative strand concerned largely with "church" affairs. This split took root during the 1920s at a time when the Government-General took a more culturally (but not politically) permissive attitude toward its Korean subjects. Great numerical gains in church membership were made with the theologically more conservative strand coming to dominate the churches. However, during this same period, the government of Japan itself came to be dominated by xenophobic groups supporting a Shintō-based nationalism that required the participation of all of the nation's citizenry in rites conducted at State Shintō shrines.

The erection in 1925 of the principal Shintō shrine for Korea, the Chōsen Jingu, set the stage for a conflict with the church that was to last for twenty years and had ramifications far after independence from Japan had been achieved. Although attendance at Shintō rituals was said to be a "patriotic" rather than a "religious" act, Korean Christians saw participation in them to be both idolatrous and offensive to their own sense of nationality. After 1930 Japanese rule became increasingly harsh as the colonial regime tried to create a forced conformity with Japanese practices. Korean Christian resistance to shrine worship led the colonial regime to take increasingly harsh measures against the churches. In 1938 the colonial regime used force to make the General Assembly of the Presbyterian Church, the General Conference of the Methodist Church, and other Christian bodies pass resolutions stating that shrine worship did not contravene Christian faith. Between 1938 and 1945 about 2,000 Protestants were arrested for noncompliance in shrine worship, of whom at least fifty people died as a result of their incarceration and torture. Missionaries were deported for their refusal to support the shrine edicts. The Presbyterian missions closed their schools rather than permit their students to attend shrine rituals. Methodists, on the other hand, turned their schools over to Korean control, which often meant compliance with government regulations.

The Government-General attempted to "Japanize" the denominations by merging them with their Japanese equivalent denominations, and by controlling the content of WORSHIP. In the dying days of the colonial regime in 1945, all Protestant churches were merged into a single institution that was a branch of the Japanese Protestant church, the *Kyotan*. The Government-General forbade the reading of the Old Testament or the Revelation of St. John the Divine in the New Testament because of the prophetic revelation in these books of God's condemnation of the powers of this world. Churches were closed, their property sold off, and on one occasion a church was made into a Shintō shrine. These actions demonstrated both the fear and scorn with which the authorities held the Christian churches, and further confirmed the link between Korean nationalism and Christianity. Although the Shintō Shrine controversy demonstrated the tenacity of Korean Christians in the face of political oppression, their movement was principally religious and not political.

Divided Nation/Industrial Nation: Korea after Liberation, 1945–

After liberation from Japanese rule at the conclusion of the Pacific War in August 1945, the Protestant churches faced three problems: (1) the different policies regarding religion in the American and Soviet zones of occupation; (2) questions of complicity with Japanese rule by church leaders; and (3) the legacy of the Japanese-imposed church union. In northern Korea, the Soviet zone of influence, Christians formed political parties including the *Kidokkyo sahoe minju-dang* (Christian Social Democratic Party) and the *Kidokkyo chayu-dang* (Christian Liberal Party), which were soon suppressed. Conflict arose in 1946 when Christian leaders wanted to commemorate the uprising of March 1, 1919, which was seen by the regime as bourgeois. There was yet another early clash of Christians with the Communist authorities over the holding of elections for a People's Assembly on a Sunday, which ran counter to the strong Sabbatarian views of many Christians.

Control or suppression of the Christian community in the north was important not only because Christians represented a separate voice on social and political matters, but also because of the size of the Christian community. In the late 1940s the center of Christianity in Korea was in the north, not the south, an irony of history considering the current size of the Christian Church in South Korea. Objections made by the Joint Presbytery of the still-unified Protestant church were countered by the authorities with the formation of the *Kidokkyo kyodo yùnmaeng* (Federation of Christians), which all church officers were required by law to join. All those who refused to join were arrested for belonging to an illegal organization. Churches were confiscated and put to secular uses. Large numbers of Christians fled to the south, whereas many of those who had remained in the north were rounded up shortly before the onset of the Korean War in June 1950 and executed en masse. Little was heard about the state of Protestantism in the north until the mid-1980s when it was announced that a hymnal and a translation of the New Testament had been published in 1983 and a translation of the Old Testament in 1984. In the late 1980s delegations representing North American and European churches reported taking part in worship in the homes of individual Christians. In 1988 the government of North Korea announced that it had built and opened a new Roman Catholic and a new Protestant church for use by their respective religious communities. Subsequently officials designated as leaders of the Christian community in North Korea have met with various Western and South Korean church leaders to discuss national unification. However, the church organizations in North Korea are not freely formed associations but are the creations of the government, their representatives being government-approved personnel.

In southern Korea the laissez-faire policy of the American Military Government (1945–1948) left the church free to handle its own affairs. Two issues emerged: the continuation of the Japanese-created unified church, and the question of complicity by church leaders with the Japanese colonial regime. By late 1945 a bloc of Methodists had bolted from the union church to reform the Methodist Church, which effectively ended the union church. Conflicts over attendance at Shintō rituals, and the perversion of the use of Scripture were more difficult to resolve. In 1947 some Methodists claimed that those who wanted the union to continue in fact were the same people who had collaborated with the Japanese. The Presbyterians similarly were split when a group left the Presbytery to form the Koryù Group. This group, claiming descent from those Christians who had made a COVENANT against shrine worship, took a hard line against any one who had attended a shrine ritual. The split over shrine worship is one of the most significant and long-lived controversies in Korean church history and is indicative of the extent to which THEOLOGY has determined the course of the church's history.

During the Korean War (1950–1953) church institutions, such as the universities, were forced to seek a temporary location in the southeastern part of the peninsula around the port of Pusan. After the conclusion of hostilities in 1953 most of the churches' efforts were spent on the provision of social services to a war-weary population and on repairing the material damage done to churches and church institutions. Housing, transportation for refugees, emergency medical aid, distribution of clothing and food, and the establishment of orphanages were all undertaken in the immediate postwar period. These activities were heavily supported by foreign church mission bodies. Mission support also was provided for the maintenance of Yonsei University, Severance Hospital, and Ehwa Woman's University. By 1957 the church had grown to 844,000 adherents representing 3.7 percent of the national population. Thus, although there had been significant numerical growth in church membership, the percentage of Christians within the national population had remained fairly constant over a twenty-year period.

Following postwar economic stabilization, the decade the 1960s stood at the threshold of the period of Korea's rapid urbanization and INDUSTRIALIZATION, and was also the time when the ideas of "Church Growth" (*kyohoe sùngjang*) became the theme for the evangelization of the nation. In the decade 1957–1968 the Protestant community both doubled in numbers of adherents to 1,900,000 persons, and doubled in percentage representation within the national population from 3 to 6 percent. The 1960s also saw greater social and evangelistic outreach in projects for people within Korea who were considered to be suppressed members of society, such as prostitutes and new industrial laborers, as well as international outreach through overseas missions and the provision of relief supplies to foreign nations. A new national evangelistic tool was created with the establishment of a nationwide radio network, the Christian Broadcasting System.

In the 1970s, after the proclamation of the Yushin (Revitalizing Reforms) Constitution, which entrenched President Pak Chùnghùi (Park Chung Hee, 1917–1979) in power, Christian political movements emerged, pressing for a more democratically based, representative system of government. This phenomenon represented a reemergence of the liberal, politically active strand of Protestantism, which had lain virtually dormant since the 1920s. It is important to note that it was politically liberal laymen and -women, not the leadership of the Protestant churches, who called for the restoration of democracy, for social justice, and for fairness in dealings with the workers of the new industrial state. Many Christians were imprisoned and tortured during this period for their political opinions. For nearly twenty years the political opposition to undemocratic government came largely from the Christian community, including Roman Catholic LAITY and CLERGY. During the same twenty-year period, Christians were also active in a variety of social movements, which may be typified by the movement for women's rights in terms of inheritance and marital relations. Led by Christian laywomen such as the Methodist Yi T'aeyŭng (Lee Tai-young, 1914–1998), the battle was enjoined largely with the *Yudo-hoe* (Confucian Association) and conservative legislators who saw these developments as a threat to the Confucian moral structure of Korean society.

Although criticized for maintaining unnecessary Western cultural characteristics, Korean Protestantism has accommodated itself at certain key points with Korean culture, the most outstanding example of which is the practice of the *ch'udo yebae* (mourning ceremony) rituals. Filial piety (*hyo* in Korean), reverence for ancestors and obedience to parents, is one of the core values of Confucian thought and practice. Visible expression of this moral value was seen in the performance of the Confucian ancestral or *chesa* ceremonies. Korean Christians from the beginning emphasized the teaching of the fifth of the Ten Commandments to honor one's father and mother as a Christian reflection of this Confucian ethic. From at least the first decade of the twentieth century Korean Protestants have performed Christianized ancestral memorial rituals called *ch'udo yebae,* which are now found in the liturgy books of every Protestant denomination. Normally performed for one's immediate relatives such as parents and grandparents, there is no formal prohibition against remembering more distant relatives.

Minjŭng sinhak (Theology of the People), which emerged in the mid-1970s, is a further reflection of the indigenization of Protestantism in Korea. Parallel in some ways with Latin American LIBERATION THEOLOGY, *Minjŭng sinhak* uses two key concepts—the *minjŭng* (the people) and *han* (enmity, grudge). *Minjung* theology says that the *minjung* are the proper subject of history and that to understand history one must understand how God has worked to overcome the *han* of the people. Using the example of the liberation of the Hebrew slaves from Egyptian bondage, these theologians argue that God acts in response to the suffering of the people. From the 1990s this theology, perhaps because it was perceived to be too intellectual, has ceased to be popular in Korea.

Other features of Korean Protestant practice reflect the indigenization and localization of Christianity. *Tongsùng kido,* joint congregational prayer conducted out loud in the middle of a service, is far more fervent than congregational prayers in other national churches such as in Japan or North America. In the post–Korean War period Protestant churches have adopted two American Protestant practices—the revival meeting (*puhùng-hoe*) and the retreat center (*kido wùn,* often mistakenly called a prayer mountain). Frequently the conduct of a revival meeting will move into being a gathering for healing by the evangelist in charge (see REVIVALS; FAITH HEALING). Likewise, the retreat centers often are not places for meditation, but venues for obtaining spiritual healing of physical ailments. Both of these practices reflect the role that Korean shamans played as the principal healer in traditional times.

A considerable degree of mutual influence of the denominations on each other can be shown in the great similarity in ecclesiastical practice. All churches in Korea have small group meetings of ten or so of their members (called *kuyùk-hoe* by the Presbyterians and *sùk-hoe* by the Methodists), which are modeled on Methodist class meetings. Likewise, Methodism, which elsewhere does not have lay elders appointed for life but stewards elected for a fixed term, in Korea has lay elders on the model of the Reformed churches. These features combined with the use of a common hymnal, a common translation of the Bible, and a similar liturgical format have created a common Korean Protestantism in spite of the existence of denominationalism.

Protestant Christianity has been the most dynamic religious factor in Korea during the twentieth century. Protestantism has influenced the development of modern medicine, modern education, concepts of equality between classes and genders, and also has had an impact on post–Korean War new religious movements. Thirty-one Korean universities claim a Christian origin, of which three are considered among the top five universities in the country. Unlike Japan where new religious movements are often a mixture of Buddhism and Shintō, Korean new religious movements are a mixture of Christianity and native traditions.

The 1995 Korean National Population Household Census, the last quinquennial census to ask for information about religious adherence, reveals some interesting characteristics about Korean Protestantism at the end of the twentieth century. First, 19.7 percent of the population claimed to adhere to a Protestant denomination. Second, of those people who self-identified themselves as belonging to an organized religion, 51.8 percent claimed to belong to a Christian denomination (39.1 percent to a Protestant denomination) or 6 percent more than the 45.7 percent of the respondents who claimed adherence to a form of Buddhism. Third, Protestantism shows a slight female predominance in membership because 53.3 percent of Protestants were female compared with 46.7 percent who were male. Fourth, Protestantism is young. Of self-identified Protestants 72.5 percent are between the ages of fifteen and forty-four years. Fifth, the largest single group of self-identified adherents is found among the youngest group, persons aged between fifteen and twenty-four years, accounting for more than a quarter of all self-identified Protestants. Sixth, the census also revealed that nationally where Protestantism is strong, Buddhism tends to be weaker and vice versa. In the region of the nation's capital, Protestantism accounts for a quarter of the population, or 50 percent greater than the size of the Buddhist groups in the same area. That is, Protestantism is typically stronger in those areas that are more highly urbanized and undergoing the greatest social change, whereas Buddhism is strongest in the culturally more traditional regions.

See also Asian Theology; Bible Translation; Communism; Ecumenism; Evangelism; Missionary Organizations; Women Higher Education

References and Further Reading

Baker, Donald L. "Christianity 'Koreanized.' " In *Nationalism and the Construction of Korean Identity,* edited by Hyung Il Pai and Timothy R. Tangherlini. Berkeley: Institute of East Asian Studies, University of California, 1998.

Clark, Allen D. *A History of the Church in Korea.* Seoul: Christian Literature Society of Korea, 1971.

Clark, Donald N. *Christianity in Modern Korea.* Lanham, MD: University Press of America, 1986.

———. "History and Religion in Korea: The Case of Korean Christianity." In *Religion and Society in Contemporary Korea,* edited by Lewis R. Lancaster and Richard K. Payne. Berkeley: Institute of East Asian Studies, University of California, 1997.

Grayson, James Huntley. "Dynamic Complementarity: Korean Confucianism and Christianity." In *Religion and the Transformations of Capitalism: Comparative Approaches,* edited by Richard H. Roberts. London/New York: Routledge, 1995.

———. *Early Buddhism and Christianity in Korea: A Study in the Emplantation of Religion.* Leiden, The Netherlands: E. J. Brill, 1985.

———. *Korea: A Religious History,* rev. edition. Richmond, VA: Routledge Curzon, 2002.

Paik, L. George. *The History of Protestant Missions in Korea, 1832–1910.* (1927 reprint). Seoul: Yonsei University Press, 1971.

Shearer, Roy E. *Wildfire: Church Growth in Korea.* Grand Rapids, MI: Eerdsmans, 1966.

Soltau, T. Stanley. *Korea: the Hermit Nation and its Response to Christianity.* London: World Dominion Press, 1932.

Vos, Frits. *Die Religionen Koreas.* Stuttgart, Germany: W. Kohlhammer, 1977.

Wasson, Alfred W. *Church Growth in Korea.* New York: International Missionary Council, 1934.

Wells, Kenneth M. *New God, New Nation: Protestants and Self-reconstruction Nationalism in Korea, 1896–1937.* Honolulu: University of Hawaii Press, 1990.

JAMES HUNTLEY GRAYSON

KRAEMER, HENDRIK (1888–1965)

Dutch scholar and missiologist. Kraemer was both an excellent scholar in linguistics and religious studies and an outstanding lay theologian and missiologist. In and outside the NETHERLANDS he came to the fore in the tumultuous transition period from colonialism to postcolonialism. In INDONESIA he paved the way for a process that is well described in the title of his book *From Mission Field to Independent Church* (1958). Moreover, he pleaded for the transformation of missionary work done by Western missionary societies into common missionary work done jointly by the churches in the East and West. Christian mission, he argued, is not the duty of Western "free enterprise" organizations but the responsibility of the universal instituted church as the body of Christ.

Kraemer was born May 17, 1888. After his stay in an orphanage in Amsterdam (1900–1905) and his training at the Mission House in Rotterdam (1905–1909), Kraemer studied Indonesian languages at Leiden University (1911–1921). Here the famous Islamologist Christiaan Snouck Hurgronje supervised his Ph.D. study and awarded it cum laude. After a short stay in Egypt (1921) Kraemer served the Netherlands Bible Society in INDONESIA (1922–1937). Next he was appointed professor of the history and phenomenology of religion at Leiden University (1937–1947). Finally he moved from the Netherlands to SWITZERLAND to serve as the first director of the WORLD COUNCIL OF CHURCHES' newly established Ecumenical Institute at Château de Bossey, Céligny, near Geneva (1948–1955). After retirement he returned to the Netherlands. He died November 11, 1965.

In Indonesia Kraemer did Bible translation work, although he engaged himself in other work as well: theological education, visiting various mission fields, leading indigenous churches into independence, and studying Javanese culture, nationalism, Islam, and church growth. In 1928 he attended the Jerusalem meeting of the International Missionary Council and established cooperation with JOHN R. MOTT and other missionary leaders. In 1928–1933 he published two volumes of Islam studies in Indonesian language, which were banned by the government after Indonesia's independence. In 1934 he established the major Indonesian theological seminary, *Sekolah Tinggi Theolo-gia* (*STT*), at Jakarta. Kraemer's book *The Christian Message in a Non-Christian World* (1938), published with a foreword by the archbishop of York and thoroughly influenced by the dialectical theologians KARL BARTH and EMIL BRUNNER, pleaded for "biblical realism" as a tool to understand, approach, and evaluate non-Christian religions. In opposition to William E. Hocking, main compiler of the influential inquiry *Rethinking Missions* (1932), Kraemer emphasized discontinuity between Christian faith and the non-Christian religions. His exclusivistic THEOLOGY OF MISSIONS and religions was strongly opposed by both Western liberals and Indian inclusivists at the 1938

Tambaram (Madras) International Missionary Council meeting and thereafter.

In 1936 Utrecht University celebrated its 300th anniversary: Barth and Brunner as well as Kraemer were awarded honorary doctorates. A year later Kraemer moved to Leiden University. His inaugural address dealt with the problem of syncretism. He lectured on all religions but showed a special interest in Islam. His book *Islam as a Religious and Missionary Problem* (1938) is a good compendium of his view on Islam. It was heavily criticized by other scholars in religious studies because they disliked his connecting religious studies with missions. Before, during, and after World War II Kraemer engaged in the revitalization of his own church, the Netherlands Reformed Church. During the war he opposed the Nazi ideology, supported the Messianic Jews, and was temporarily imprisoned. In 1945 he participated in the establishment of the Socialist Party.

After retirement and return to the Netherlands, Kraemer published several books. The two major works of this period, *Religion and the Christian Faith* (1956) and *World Cultures and World Religions: The Coming Dialogue* (1960), are modifications of his 1938 views: the key issues of his prewar views are indeed maintained but the term "biblical realism" is no longer used and the term "dialogue" is introduced for the first time. His popular work *Why Christianity of All Religions?* (1962) makes it even more evident that his prewar and postwar views cannot be played off against each other. Other influential English books also translated into various languages are *The Communication of the Christian Faith* (1956) and *A Theology of the Laity* (1958).

From Tambaram (1938) to New Delhi (1961) Kraemer thoroughly dominated the missionary and missiological scene. Johannes Verkuyl and other Western and Eastern missiologists continued Kraemer's thinking in one way or another, but Indian theologians such as Stanley J. Samartha pleaded for a "post-Kraemer theology." In 1988 Tambaram was revisited and Kraemer's heritage reviewed again. On that occasion Bishop J. E. Lesslie Newbigin opposed theological pluralists such as W. Cantwell Smith and Samartha, and found himself compelled to stand with Kraemer.

References and Further Reading

Hallencreutz, Carl F. *Kraemer towards Tambaram: A Study in Hendrik Kraemer's Missionary Approach.* Lund: Gleerup, 1966.

Perry, Tim S. *Radical Difference: A Defence of Hendrik Kraemer's Theology of Religions.* Ontario: Wilfrid Laurier University Press, 2001.

Retnowinarti, et al. *Hendrik Kraemer: Bibliografie en Archief.* Leiden-Utrecht, The Netherlands: Interuniversitair Instituut voor Missiologie en Oecumenica, 1988.

"Tambaram Revisited." Special issue of *International Review of Mission* 78, no. 307 (July 1988).

Van Leeuwen, Arend Th. *Hendrik Kraemer: Dienaar der Wereldkerk.* Amsterdam: Ten Have, 1959. German translation: 1962.

Yates, Timothy. *Christian Mission in the Twentieth Century.* Cambridge, UK: Cambridge University Press, 1994.

JAN A. B. JONGENEEL

KRAUTH, CHARLES PORTERFIELD (1823–1883)

American Lutheran theologian. Krauth was born March 17, 1823, in Martinsburg, Virginia, and died January 2, 1883, in Philadelphia, Pennsylvania. The son of a Lutheran pastor, Krauth studied at Gettysburg College and Seminary, and became a licensed missionary and then Lutheran pastor in and around Baltimore, Maryland. He also served in West Virginia, Virginia, the West Indies (for a Reformed congregation without a pastor), in Pittsburgh, Pennsylvania, and finally in Philadelphia. Krauth resigned from his last parish to edit the *Lutheran and Missionary,* opposing the "Americanizing" of LUTHERANISM, a growing trend in his General Synod.

"Americanizing" was epitomized by SAMUEL SIMON SCHMUCKER, whose Definite Platform greatly minimized Lutheran confessional commitment in order to attain common ground with Reformed theology. Once more tolerant and irenic, Krauth's studies of the Lutheran Confessions fostered a more conservative attitude, although he sought to balance firm theological conviction with a generous spirit on a personal level. When the General Synod opened its Philadelphia Seminary in 1864, Krauth became professor of dogmatics. There he helped organize the General Council, a new association reflecting a more traditional and conservative Lutheran stance.

Krauth wrote to address challenges in the increasingly complicated denominational scene in America. His *Fundamental Articles of Faith and Church Polity* formed the basis for the General Council's constitution. Facing church fellowship questions, Krauth wrote fourteen articles for *The Lutheran,* material later recast as *Theses on Pulpit and Altar Fellowship.* For the sake of confessional THEOLOGY Krauth urged Lutherans to avoid unionism and syncretism, terms that especially connoted Reformed Calvinist theology in various forms, a theology that appeared similar to Lutheranism yet in Krauth's eyes had significant differences. While serving on the seminary faculty Krauth also became a philosophy professor at the University of Pennsylvania. In addition to works mentioned, he also wrote *The Conservative Reformation and Its The-*

ology and edited Berkeley's *Principles of Human Knowledge*.

See also Calvinism; Confession; Lutheranism, United States

References and Further Reading

Primary Source:

Krauth, Charles Porterfield. *The Conservative Reformation and Its Theology.* Philadelphia, PA: General Council Publication Board, 1913; reprint, Minneapolis, MN: Augsburg Publishing House, 1963.

Secondary Source:

Spaeth, Adolph. *Charles Porterfield Krauth.* 2 vols. First edition, New York: Christian Literature Company, 1898; Second edition, Philadelphia, PA: General Council Publication House, 1898–1909; reprint (2 vols. in 1), New York: Arno Press, 1969.

ROBERT ROSIN

KRÜDENER, BARBARA (1764–1824)

Latvian mystic. Born in Riga, Latvia, in 1764, Barbara Juliane von Krüdener devoted twenty-two years of her life to PREACHING, traveling, and prophesying throughout central Europe. She married a Russian diplomat at age 18, but separated from him a few years later. After briefly living in Paris, Krüdener published an autobiographical and sentimental romance novel entitled *Valerie* in 1804. Returning to Riga the same year, she was shocked by the DEATH of an acquaintance and sought comfort for her disordered nerves. Confiding in her shoemaker, a Moravian, Krüdener found spiritual peace after she converted to his faith. She once again fell ill upon his death. As remedy, her doctor ordered her to German spas for treatment. During these travels, she met Queen Louise of Prussia and a prophet of CHILIASM, a belief in the millennium. Throughout her journeys, Krüdener's religious development was influenced by the contacts she made on her travels.

After a short visit with the Moravians at HERRNHUT, Krüdener met a pietistic priest who instructed her in the mysteries of the supernatural world. She also sought instruction at the Protestant parsonage of Sainte Marie-aux-Mines, and she traveled throughout GERMANY and SWITZERLAND holding BIBLE classes and warning of the approaching millennium. She had identified Napoleon as the angel in the Book of Revelation (9:11). In 1815 her eccentricity and exuberance attracted the attention of Czar Alexander I of RUSSIA, who attended her meetings. Krüdener relocated to St. Petersburg, from where she was exiled in 1821 for promoting the cause of Greek revolutionaries and the formation of the Holy Alliance. After fleeing St. Petersburg, Krüdener joined a Pietist colony in the Crimea, where she died there in 1824.

See also Millenarians and Millennialism; Moravian Church; Pietism

References and Further Reading

"Krotoschin, R., Barbara Julian, Baroness Von (1764–1824)." *1911 Edition Encyclopedia.* Pagewise Inc. 2002. http://www.39.1911encyclopedia.org/K/KR/KROTOSHIN.htm
Ley, F. "The Baroness Julie de Krüdener in Paris (1802–1804)." *Revue D'Histoire Litteraire De La France* 99 no.1 (Jan–Feb 1999): 99–108.

HOWELL WILLIAMS

KU KLUX KLAN

The Ku Klux Klan (KKK) is a secret, Anglo-Saxon terrorist organization begun after the U.S. CIVIL WAR (1861–1865) and continued into the twenty-first century. The Klan flourished briefly during the postwar Reconstruction period as an attempt by southern whites to undermine the political influence of blacks and Republicans. It resurfaced as a Protestant society in 1915 through the work of William J. Simmons, an ex-Methodist minister. The movement spread throughout southern society as a white, nativist (see NATIVISM) order with Protestant orientation in its many secret rituals. Promoting itself as the defender of American values, white supremacy, and traditional religion, the Klan offered violent opposition to the presence of "outsiders" including African Americans, Jews, and Roman Catholics (see ANTI-SEMITISM; CATHOLICISM, PROTESTANT REACTIONS TO). Its most infamous symbol, the burning cross, probably originated from Thomas Dixon's 1906 book, *The Clansman,* a novel promoting the inferiority of blacks. During the 1920s the order spread throughout the United States with a membership that may well have included one out of ten white Protestant males. The increasing use of violence led to a decline in its membership by the 1930s.

With the rise of the CIVIL RIGHTS MOVEMENT in the 1950s and 1960s, the KKK was revived in perhaps its most virulent forms. Civil rights workers, including MARTIN LUTHER KING, JR., were frequent targets of Klan threats and attacks. The Klan instigated violence against the Freedom Riders in Alabama in 1961, opposing integration and extension of voting rights. The society offered strenuous opposition to integration, the extension of voting rights, and all efforts to abolish "separate but equal" facilities in the South.

Although reduced in membership, the Klan has continued to function into the twenty-first century, promoting white supremacy and associations with the antigovernment "militia" movements.

References and Further Reading

Chalmers, David. *Hooded Americanism: The History of the Ku Klux Klan.* Durham, NC: Duke University Press, 1987.

Encyclopedia of Religion in the South. Macon, GA: Mercer, 1984.

Garrow, David J. *Bearing the Cross: Martin Luther King, Jr. and the Southern Christian Leadership Conference.* New York: William Morrow, 1986.

BILL J. LEONARD

KUTTER, HERMANN (1863–1931)

Swiss theologian. Kutter was born in Bern into a pietistic family. He studied Protestant THEOLOGY and philosophy, especially Plato and German Idealism, in Bern, Basel, and Berlin. After serving as minister of a Reformed congregation in a rural Swiss parish for eleven years, he was elected minister of the important Neumünster Church in Zurich in 1898 and remained there until he retired in 1926. He died in St. Gall, SWITZERLAND, in 1931. Kutter was one of the pioneers of the Religious-Social Movement in Switzerland and a forerunner of dialectical theology.

Incisive for his life and work was the influence of and contact with Christoph Blumhardt after 1889. He argued that the main task of the CHURCH was the proclamation of the KINGDOM OF GOD and the commitment to ameliorate the social situation of the working class. Besides many printed sermons, which often focused on social issues such as *Die soziale Frage* (*The Social Problem*) or *Geld und Geist* (*Money and Spirit*), both published in 1906, and other publications on church history and systematic theology, after 1903 he published several polemical books on the foremost social, political, and religious issues of the time. Most of them appeared in more than one edition and also were translated in other languages (Chicago 1908, England 1910). Kutter's important books were *Sie müssen* (*They Must,* 1903), *Gerechtigkeit* (*Justice,* 1905), *Wir Pfarrer* (*We Clergy,* 1907), *Die Revolution des Christentums* (*The Revolution of Christianity,* 1908).

Kutter helped many young theologians to overcome the difficulties in their ecclesiastical duties. He was in contact with other contemporary representatives of religious socialism, such as LEONHARD RAGAZ, and he influenced younger Swiss theologians such as Eduard Thurneysen and KARL BARTH. Nonetheless he was a loner, as in his relationship with the Social Democratic Party, because of his radical and prophetic message to preach, first and exclusively, the gospel of the unrestricted presence of God in Jesus Christ among humankind.

See also Neo-Orthodoxy

References and Further Reading

Primary Source:

Kutter, Hermann Jr. *Hermann Kutter's Lebenswerk.* Zurich, Switzerland: EVZ, 1965.

Secondary Source:

Nigg, Walter. *Hermann Kutters Vermächtnis.* Bern, Switzerland: 1941.

GERHARD SCHWINGE

KUYPER, ABRAHAM (1837–1920)

Dutch Reformed theologian. Kuyper, a Dutch Reformed theologian, church reformer, journalist, educator, and politician, was the major force behind the rise and development of a modern Dutch pluralist society in the twentieth century. In the mid-nineteenth century NETHERLANDS, the Dutch National Reformed Church and the Dutch state were still closely linked and governed by an elite group that enjoyed the privileges of a restricted franchise based on wealth. By law the affairs of the DUTCH REFORMED CHURCH were regulated by a state bureau of religion. With the state paying ministers' salaries, the government demanded a say in the placement of clergy as well as in appointments to the faculties of theology in the state universities. Consequently Roman Catholics and dissenting Protestants were effectively marginalized, especially in the nation's schools, which were increasingly dominated by a secular and liberal ideology. Although the new Dutch Constitution of 1848 permitted alternative schools, the bureaucratic obstacles placed in the way made it virtually impossible to establish them.

In response to this situation Kuyper led a sizeable group out of the National Reformed Church, founded a new independent Christian University (Free University of Amsterdam), started and led the first modern Dutch political party mobilizing the "common folk" into a politically significant group (the Antirevolutionary Party), formed a coalition government with Roman Catholics, and inspired a renaissance of Calvinist thought eventually known as neo-Calvinism.

Kuyper was born October 29, 1837, into a clerical family in the theologically liberal Dutch National Reformed Church and received his own education at the University of Leiden, completing a doctorate in 1862 with a dissertation on the Polish reformer Jan á Lasco. By his own account Kuyper's theology at this point was moderately liberal, a judgment echoed by his devoutly Calvinist peasant parishioners in the Reformed Church of Beesd, the small village in the southern Dutch province of Gelderland that was Kuyper's first pastoral charge. It was here in fulfilling his minister's duties that Kuyper was "converted" to a more orthodox version of CALVINISM and began to identify with the cause of the Reformed dissenters, particularly their protest against compulsory state-controlled education (see ORTHODOXY, DISSENT).

Kuyper's reform work began with efforts to broaden the franchise in the church by giving greater authority to local church officials who could be selected and elected by the church members themselves. Beyond the formal, procedural challenges to the church authorities, Kuyper also led the protest against doctrinal indifference in the national church, calling for a return of fidelity to the traditional confessions and THEOLOGY as established by the Synod of Dort (1618–1619). The culmination of these efforts led in 1886 to the second major secession from the National Reformed Church in the nineteenth century (the first took place in 1834). Important for the Dutch nation as a whole, the eventual union of these two groups along with their public legitimation played a significant role in establishing the Netherlands as a pluralist nation.

As Kuyper's efforts moved beyond church reform into the area of education he realized that an effective political movement required not only energetic and sophisticated organization but a public voice. From 1872 on, several years before the founding of the Antirevolutionary Party in 1879 or the establishment of the Free University of Amsterdam in 1880, Kuyper started and edited a weekly (*The Herald*) and daily newspaper (*The Standard*) as the voice of this new Calvinist movement. His tireless journalistic efforts and political organizing finally paid off in 1901 when the Antirevolutionary Party together with the Roman Catholic political party acquired a majority of seats in the Dutch parliament. Kuyper became prime minister of the new government, a position he held for four years. This cooperative alliance was the dominant governing party during the twentieth century in the Netherlands until the 1960s.

Kuyper's neo-Calvinist vision began with the conviction of divine sovereignty. This sovereignty begins with the grace of regeneration in individual believers but then extends organically to culture and society. In Kuyper's characteristic language, God is sovereign over all "spheres" of life—politics, business, labor, education, and the arts, as well as church and family. From this primordial principle Kuyper derived four secondary ones: antithesis, common grace, sphere sovereignty, and a distinction between the church as institution and as organism.

For Kuyper Calvinism was more than a churchly, confessional tradition. It was a *Weltanschauung,* a world-and-life-view, a life system antithetically opposed to other life systems such as paganism and, particularly, modernism. The spirit of modernism, captured in the French Revolution's slogan *Ni Dieu, ni maitre,* came to expression especially in the political sphere where an idolatry of the state replaced God's ordinances. Kuyper's political ideology was antirevolutionary as well as antistatist. However, Kuyper did not take his antithetical stance to imply a rejection of all non-Christian culture. Like Augustine's metaphor of Israel plundering the gold of the Egyptians, Kuyper too believed that there was much valuable even in pagan culture. This value was not to be credited to human cleverness or goodness but to the universal or common grace of God whereby God bestows gifts on all people indiscriminately and also actively restrains their evil, sinful impulses.

God was sovereign not only of the church but of the world. Kuyper's most famous saying is: "There is not a square inch of all creation over which Christ the Lord does not say, Mine!"

Kuyper drew important social implications from this doctrine. In his view divine sovereignty was seen to be exercised directly over such sovereign spheres as the school and the family rather than through the mediation of either the church or the state. This conviction led Kuyper to advocate a principled pluralism that honored both structural and religious diversity. One of his major political accomplishments was the eventual legal establishment of a religiously plural education system.

For Kuyper it was important that Christian communion come to expression not only in the institutional church gathered around Word and SACRAMENTS but as a unified organism in public life. His ambition was to inspire conservative Dutch Calvinists to leave behind pietist and sectarian withdrawal from civic, social, and political life and thus to re-Christianize the Dutch nation, not by maintaining institutional, ecclesiastical privilege but through the voluntary activity of Christians in free churches and distinctly Christian organizations. Hence his profound appreciation for the spirit of American voluntarism so eloquently described by ALEXIS DE TOCQUEVILLE in his *Democracy in America.* Kuyper died November 8, 1920.

See also Calvinism; Ecumenism

References and Further Reading

Primary Sources:

Bratt, James D., ed. *Abraham Kuyper: A Centennial Reader.* Grand Rapids, MI: Eerdmans, 1998. (A helpful collection of occasional essays.)

Kuyper, Abraham. *Principles of Sacred Theology.* Translated by John Hendrick De Vries. New York: Scribners, 1898; reprint Grand Rapids, MI: Eerdmans, 1965.

———. *Lectures on Calvinism.* Grand Rapids, MI: Eerdmans, 1931.

————. *The Work of the Holy Spirit.* Translated by J. Hendrick De Vries. New York and London: Funk & Wagnalls Co., 1900.

————. *The Problem of Poverty.* Translated by James W. Skillen. Grand Rapids, MI: Baker, 1991.

Secondary Sources:

Bolt, John. *A Free Church, A Holy Nation: Abraham Kuyper's American Public Theology.* Grand Rapids, MI: Eerdmans, 2001.

Heslam, Peter S. *Creating a Christian Worldview: Abraham Kuyper's Lectures on Calvinism.* Grand Rapids, MI: Eerdmans, 1998.

Langley, McKendree R. *The Practice of Political Spirituality: Episodes in the Public Career of Abraham Kuyper.* Jordan Station, Ontario: Paideia, 1984.

McGoldrick, James E. *Abraham Kuyper: God's Renaissance Man.* Auburn, MA: Evangelical Press, 2000.

Praamsma, Louis. *Let Christ Be King: Reflections on the Life and Times of Abraham Kuyper.* Jordan Station, Ontario: Paideia, 1985.

JOHN BOLT